HANDBOOK OF
AFRICAN AMERICAN PSYCHOLOGY

We dedicate this work to our ancestors for their tireless commitment to the development of the field of African American psychology, including Robert V. Guthrie, Asa G. Hilliard III, and Reginald L. Jones. We also dedicate these words to the legacy of many unsung sheroes who have been assigned to a historical footnote to our field like many women in other disciplines, including Mamie Phipps Clark and Inez Beverly Prosser. A special recognition is given to the memory of A. Toy Caldwell-Colbert, whose mentorship and professional commitment have enhanced so many of us in countless ways.

HANDBOOK OF
AFRICAN AMERICAN
PSYCHOLOGY

editors

HELEN A. NEVILLE
University of Illinois at Urbana-Champaign

BRENDESHA M. TYNES
University of Illinois at Urbana-Champaign

SHAWN O. UTSEY
Virginia Commonwealth University

Los Angeles • London • New Delhi • Singapore • Washington DC

Copyright © 2009 by SAGE Publications, Inc.

All rights reserved. No part of this book may be reproduced or utilized in any form or by any means, electronic or mechanical, including photocopying, recording, or by any information storage and retrieval system, without permission in writing from the publisher.

For information:

SAGE Publications, Inc.
2455 Teller Road
Thousand Oaks, California 91320
E-mail: order@sagepub.com

SAGE Publications Ltd.
1 Oliver's Yard
55 City Road
London EC1Y 1SP
United Kingdom

SAGE Publications India Pvt. Ltd.
B 1/I 1 Mohan Cooperative
 Industrial Area
Mathura Road, New Delhi 110 044
India

SAGE Publications Asia-Pacific
 Pte. Ltd.
33 Pekin Street #02-01
Far East Square
Singapore 048763

Printed in the United States of America.

Library of Congress Cataloging-in-Publication Data

Handbook of African American psychology/edited by Helen A. Neville, Brendesha M. Tynes, Shawn O. Utsey.
  p. cm.
Includes bibliographical references and index.
ISBN 978-1-4129-5687-1 (cloth) — ISBN 978-1-4129-5688-8 (pbk.)

  1. African Americans—Psychology—Handbooks, manuals, etc. I. Neville, Helen A. II. Tynes, Brendesha M. III. Utsey, Shawn O.

E185.625.H35 2009
155.8′496073—dc22   2008022453

This book is printed on acid-free paper.

11 12 10 9 8 7 6 5 4 3 2

Acquisitions Editors:	Erik Evans, Cheri Dellelo
Editorial Assistant:	Lara Grambling
Production Editor:	Tracy Buyan
Copy Editor:	Kathy Anne Savadel
Typesetter:	C&M Digitals (P) Ltd.
Proofreader:	Wendy Jo Dymond
Indexer:	Jean Casalegno
Cover Designer:	Bryan Fishman
Marketing Manager:	Stephanie Adams

CONTENTS

Foreword ix
William E. Cross, Jr.

Introduction xiii
Helen A. Neville, Brendesha M. Tynes, and Shawn O. Utsey

Acknowledgments xxiii

PART I. HISTORICAL FOUNDATION

1. Foundations for an African American Psychology: Extending Roots to an Ancient Kemetic Past 3
   Thomas A. Parham

2. Sankofa: History of and Aspirations for Black Psychology Through the Eyes of Our Elders 19
   M. Nicole Coleman and Adanna J. Johnson

PART II. AFRICAN/BLACK PSYCHOLOGY

3. Theoretical and Conceptual Approaches to African and African American Psychology 35
   Linda James Myers

4. African Psychology, or *Sahku Sheti*: An Application of the Art of Spiritual Liberation and Illumination of African People 47
   Ezemenari M. Obasi and Anthony J. Smith

5. Africentric Theories of African American Personality: Basic Constructs and Assessment 61
   Kobi Kambon and Terra Bowen-Reid

6. Assessing African-Centered (Africentric) Psychological Constructs: A Review of Existing Instrumentation 75
   Shawn O. Utsey, Benita Belvet, and Nicole Fischer

PART III. CONTEXTUALIZING ATTITUDES AND BEHAVIORS

7. Religion and Spirituality 91
   Jacqueline S. Mattis and Carolyn R. Watson

8. Black Families 103
   Harriette Pipes McAdoo and Sinead N. Younge

9. Intimate Relationships of African Americans 117
Anita Jones Thomas, Rabiatu Barrie, and Brendesha M. Tynes

10. Hip-Hop Music and Culture: A Site of Resiliency
    for the Streets of Young Black America 127
    Yasser Arafat Payne and LaMar Rashad Gibson

11. The Role of Media Use and Portrayals in African
    Americans' Psychosocial Development 143
    Brendesha M. Tynes and L. Monique Ward

12. Racism, White Supremacy, and Resistance:
    Contextualizing Black American Experiences 159
    Helen A. Neville and Alex L. Pieterse

PART IV. EDUCATIONAL ISSUES

13. African American Children's Early Learning and Development:
    Examining Parenting, Schools, and Neighborhood 175
    Iheoma U. Iruka and Oscar Barbarin

14. Academic Motivation and Achievement of African American Youth 187
    Cynthia Hudley

15. African American English 199
    Anne Harper Charity Hudley

16. Stereotype Threat: A Review, Critique, and Implications 211
    Claytie Davis III and Crystal Simmons

17. Racial Identity and Peer Pressures Among
    Gifted African American Students: Issues and Recommendations 223
    Donna Y. Ford and Gilman W. Whiting

18. The Talent Quest Model and the Educating of African American Children   237
    A. Wade Boykin and Constance M. Ellison

PART V. GROUP IDENTITY

19. Racial Socialization: Roots, Processes, and Outcomes 255
    Keisha L. Bentley, Valerie N. Adams, and Howard C. Stevenson

20. Racial Identity Development During Childhood 269
    *Dena Phillips Swanson, Michael Cunningham, Joseph Youngblood II,
    and Margaret Beale Spencer*

21. Racial Identity Theory: Adults 283
    Kevin Cokley and Collette Chapman

22. Cultural Mistrust: A Core Component of
    African American Consciousness 299
    Francis Terrell, Jerome Taylor, Jeffery Menzise, and Ronald K. Barrett

23. African American Lesbians and Gay Men:
    Life Between a Rock and a Hard Place 311
    Beverly Greene

PART VI. PSYCHOLOGICAL, PHYSICAL, AND BEHAVIORAL HEALTH

24. Black Americans and Mental Health Status: Complexities and New Developments — 335
    Tara R. Earl and David R. Williams

25. Psychological Health in School-Age Populations — 351
    Frank C. Worrell

26. Conceptualizing Mental Health for African Americans — 363
    Suzette L. Speight, Sha'Kema M. Blackmon, Desmond Odugu, and J. Corey Steele

27. Positive Psychology: African American Strengths, Resilience, and Protective Factors — 375
    A. Toy Caldwell-Colbert, Fayth M. Parks, and Sussie Eshun

28. Behavioral and Emotional Strengths in People of African Heritage: Theory, Research, Methodology, and Intervention — 385
    Michael Canute Lambert and William K. Smith

29. From Anxiety and Depression to Suicide and Self-Harm — 401
    Rheeda L. Walker and Lora Rose Hunter

30. Psychosocial Aspects of Sickle Cell Disease: A Primer for African American Psychologists — 417
    Shawn M. Bediako

PART VII. PRACTICE: PREVENTION AND INTERVENTIONS

31. Counseling and Psychotherapy With African Americans — 431
    Madonna G. Constantine, Rebecca M. Redington, and Sheila V. Graham

32. Therapy With African American Men and Women — 445
    Kumea Shorter-Gooden

33. Social and Cultural Factors in the Cognitive and Clinical Assessment of African American Adults — 459
    Deidre M. Anglin and Naa Oyo A. Kwate

34. Drug Use Among African American Youth: Implications for Prevention — 469
    Faye Z. Belgrave, Trenette Clark, and Aashir Nasim

35. Black Liberation Psychology and Practice — 483
    Chalmer E. Thompson and Dorienna M. Alfred

PART VIII. TRENDS AND FUTURE DIRECTIONS

36. African American Psychology: Trends and Future Directions — 497
    Helen A. Neville, Brendesha M. Tynes, and Shawn O. Utsey

Author Index — 503

Subject Index — 531

About the Editors — 545

About the Contributors — 547

FOREWORD

Black, as in *Black Psychology*, is a fairly modern term hesitantly embraced by Negroes in the aftermath of the assassination of Martin Luther King Jr. Before his death, many Negroes were uncomfortable using any self-referent other than *colored* or *Negro*, and to shout out the phrase "Yo' Black mama" signified the playing of the "dozens" and not an expression of affection. *African*, as in *African Psychology*, is all the more contemporary and seeks to impale the terms *Negro*, *colored*, *Black*, and even *nigger* with an unambiguous cultural underpinning. The discourse on African Psychology is precise, categorical, and razor sharp, with intellectual boundaries that are steely, thick, and unyielding. By comparison, Black/African American Psychology is culturally imprecise and reflective of hybridity and the jumble of cultural, class, and positionality factors that make model building, hypothesis testing, and interpretative findings "messy." Built on a binary that positions Afrocentric in opposition to Eurocentric, African Psychology tends to approach hybridity with considerable skepticism. However, hybridity, culture fusion, and psychological intersectionality dominate the psychology of Africans in the Diaspora. Hybridity is historic and hardly pathological; as cases in point, both the (Black) Russian poet Alexander Pushkin and the (Black) French novelist Alexandre Dumas were iconic "hybrids" who "lived" and interrogated binaries to produce changes in the literary aesthetic of both France and Russia. The current collection gives voice to both "Black" (Black/African American) and "African" Psychologies and the implied as well as explicit tensions between the two perspectives.

HYBRIDITY: VARIATIONS ON BLACK/AFRICAN AMERICAN PSYCHOLOGY

Hybridity, or *diunitalism*, as in the fusion/juxtaposition of the opposite ends of Black–White binary, and *African–American intersectionality*, as in the matrixing of Blackness with multiculturalism, social class, disability, gender and gay/lesbian/bisexual/transgender issues, best describes the psychology of people of African descent throughout the Diaspora and the United States in particular. Consequently, authors for the majority of the chapters in this volume take as the point of departure (Black) hybridity and (Black) intersectionality. Most Blacks in the United States claim the categories African American, bicultural, biracial, Afro-Caribbean, and, to a lesser extent, multiracial or (Black) multicultural, and so on, and a fraction, albeit a growing fraction, professes the categories Afrocentric or Africentric. To turn the spotlight on hybridity is not to make Africanity invisible or without relevance. To the contrary, Africanity *informs* the Black American experience in that slavery did not so much destroy Africanity as transform it into something part Irish, part English, part Native American, and part Spanish.

In the not-too-distant past, being able to say one is part Irish, part Native American, or whatever, was a way some Blacks distanced themselves from their African heritage. However, advocates of a Black (i.e., hybrid) psychology are not side-stepping the issue of Africanity; instead, they make it part of a matrix of concerns as does, for example, A. Wade Boykin in his *triple quandary theory* of everyday Black existence (see Chap. 18, this volume). Likewise, James Jones's (2004) formulation, called *TRIOS*, although grounded in an African sensibility, incorporates other cultural strands known to be intimately associated with the way black people think, act and feel. Margaret Beale Spencer's very elaborate, dynamic, and multidimensional theory of (Black) adolescent development is centered on African as well as Western concepts of social status and stigma, social class, mainstream culture, and traditional African American culture (e.g., Spencer's [1995] Phenomenological Variant of Ecological Systems Theory Model is described in Chap. 20, this volume). Chapter 10, by Yasser Arafat Payne and LaMar Rashad Gibson, shows how the hip-hop movement has attained international stature precisely because it fuses elements of social class, gender, and (Black and White) culture. We need to remember that Black hybridity/intersectionality is only secondarily a "psychological" construct. Black syncopation found in (Black) gospel music, (Black) jazz, and hip-hop expresses hybridity; the blues tradition captured in the writings of Richard Wright, Zora Neal Hurston, Langston Hughes, Audrey Lord, or Robert Reid-Pharr reveals mind sets that cannot be appreciated without resort to models of hybridity and intersectionality.

Black/African American Psychology is often critiqued for being too reactionary and too race based rather than culture driven. Although there is merit to such criticism, a more accurate critique would point out the confusion and ambiguity in how *race*, *Black*, and ethnicity/culture are defined. Many Black scholars have staked their reputation on the ability to differentiate race and culture/ethnicity. There are scales that purport to measure racial identity and others that measure culture and ethnicity. The trouble is that in real-world usage these measures turn out to be highly correlated. Why? Given the limited space available here, I want to stress one line of reasoning that says that the concept of race, even at the point of invention in the minds of 18th-century European racists, defined a biological construct, or a cultural construct, or both. They really were not very precise. Thus, in the racist discourse about Africa, race could mean the (Black) physicality of "Africans," or it could mean African languages, African religions, Africans ways of doing—which is to say *race* meant the physicality of Africans as well as everything associated with African (Black) life (culture). It was either–or and both–and.

Historically, race has taken on cultural meanings even when the intent was to be racial (physical). Thus, at the turn of the 20th century, the Irish were a race separate from the French, German, or British races. In contemporary times, such racialization of ethnicity lies behind the Tutsi and Hutu genocide in Rwanda or the Serbian and Croatian conflict in the Balkans. Nazism was a racial system, but most of its victims were White! Nazis imagined there was a biologic difference between Germans and Jews, Germans and Poles, or Germans and Hungarians, but the horror that was Nazism involved the separation of groups using cultural information and cultural markers. Because race connotes physicality here in the United States, we easily lose sight of the way ethnicity and religion have been racialized in other contexts, a trend with which our Mexican and Middle Eastern brethren are all to familiar.

The plasticity of the concept of race entered the discourse in Black Psychology through the writings of Frantz Fanon and Albert Memmi, among others. In *Black Skins, White Masks*, Fanon (1967) switches back and forth between Black and White as markers of "race" or markers of racial and *cultural* miseducation; and Memmi's (1965/1991) discourse on the stages of liberation is as much cultural as racial. When we, Blacks in America, used Fanonian thinking to construct our Negro-to-Black models, *race* seemed to mean both physicality and culture. Look at the items on scales such as the Racial Attitudes Identity Scale, the Cross Racial Identity Scale, or Multi-dimensional Inventory of Black Identity; these scales make explicit reference to both "race" and "culture" and in point of fact are better understood to measure race as well as culture.

Finally, Black Americans can mark an encounter as *racial* (Black/White), with elements of physicality, discrimination and oppression in the mix, and then in the next breath be perfectly comfortable using phrases like *Black music*, *Black literature*, *Black jazz*, *Black theology*, and *Black language* (Ebonics), where *Black* clearly signifies *culture*. It is simply a mistake to critique Black/African American Psychology as too race bound and lacking in cultural emphasis, because hybridity has always been about a diunital approach to race/culture where the lived experiences make it difficult to make a sharp distinction between the two. The confusion is not so much among Black psychologists themselves, nor can we "blame" the people who participate in our studies. Racists have racialized both our bodies and our culture, and when (Black) researchers come along and ask questions about race, a Black respondent is as likely to provide a culturally loaded response as a "purely" racial reaction.

AFRICAN PSYCHOLOGY

African Psychology, as presented in the *Journal of Black Psychology*, various Black studies journals, and seminal textbooks in Black Psychology published between 1970s to the present, is an invention, a social construction hammered out by Black intellectuals in the Americas—especially the United States. It is a formulation derived from the *imagination* of Blacks living outside Africa—descendents of slaves lacking direct contact with Africa for over 100 years—who are looking "back" to Africa for solutions to predicaments, problems, and dilemmas enveloping Blacks throughout the Diaspora and especially United States. My intent for underscoring the social constructivist aspects of American-based Africentric Psychology is not that of negation or trivialization but to remind readers of the *positionality* of its architects and the historical context shaping their interpretations and translations. It is also important to note that the overwhelming majority of African Psychology theorists are African American men, another positionality factor that must be weighed when approaching the theory for the purposes of deconstruction, constructive critique, and interpretation.

African Psychology is a form of looking back through time and space for the purpose of moving forward and creating hope. It declares a sense of connection between Black Americans and the worldviews, cosmologies, histories, and religions of Black people on the continent of Africa that in point of fact most Black Americans accord only minimal significance. African Psychology seeks not consensus, popularity, or conformity but new ways of thinking grounded in old ways of knowing. Can something lost but now remembered provide new answers to modern problems?

African Psychology pushes risk taking, as it attempts to engage in a conversation with otherwise deracinated Black folks whose only claim to Africanity is nominal, at best. One of the most frustrating dilemmas of advocates of Africanity is the resistance they encounter in Black people whose attitudes are instantly clouded by stereotypes at the mere mention of the word *African*. African Psychology has its critics and internal contradictions. For example, in stressing "natural law," African Psychology has shown itself to be as misguided as many other systems of thought, when the focus is on the hybridity that results from the fusion of Blackness and gay/lesbian/bisexual/transgender issues. The Rwandan Genocide should have been unthinkable and impossible in accordance to African Psychology, and it is only when we combine elements of ethnicity, modernity, colonialism, and social class (i.e., an intersectional analysis) that a reasonable explanation is forthcoming—not that *any* explanation makes us less sorrowful. But to recognize the internal contradictions of a philosophical system is not to trivialize the need to study, practice, or engage it—to make it the centerpiece of praxis. The facts of World War I and World War II, or the Jewish Holocaust, or any other exemplar of Western failure simply does not negate all that is Western. Likewise, the revelation of human exploitation and sacrifice behind the building of the Egyptian Pyramids or the discovery of ethnic conflict within the continent of Africa (Rwanda or Somalia) do not provide a rationale for dismissing the serious study and application of African Psychology.

The test of a psychological framework is not perfection or utopia but its capacity for human coherence, meaning making, and problem solving. The chapters in this volume put African Psychology to the test. Is it a coherent system; can key aspects of the theory be empirically explored through qualitative and quantitative methods; can it revitalize decrepit systems of social services into loving, efficacious, and healing systems; can it unearth identity dynamics that help clients rethink their otherwise–self-handicapping propensities; can it better explain Black-on-Black conflicts; can it help Black couples find greater happiness; does it open up pathways for wayward Black youth on the brink of self-destruction; and does it open the minds of Black researchers to new theorems, overlooked variables, and undertheorized propositions and models? More so than a panacea, the chapters in this volume show that African Psychology is critical to a comprehensive analysis of the Black condition in the United States. It is part of the matrix of theories that should and perhaps must be included in the mapping of Black life, along with conceptualizing based on social class, gender and sexuality, and disability.

Parting Remarks

This volume offers mature, sophisticated, and advanced statements by advocates for African Psychology and Black/African American Psychology, and the advantage goes to the readers, who can feast on the rich intellectual offerings. For me, personally, reading the chapters written by the younger voices from both camps was a special treat because, as I enter the early winter of my career, these thinkers provided me with a peek into the future. On many fronts, our community continues to be forced to shoulder spirit-bending compromises and unspeakable outrages; consequently, it is no small comfort to discover that with the publication of this handbook, the keepers of the psychology of the Black experience are alive; bursting with new ideas, steel edged in their professionalism and competence, eager for constructive debate, and yet full of grace, dignity, and humility. The current volume is a worthy extension–continuation of the seminal compilations of the past, and one can imagine that both Asa Hilliard and Reginald Jones are looking down and tipping their hats to the editors of this outstanding volume to signify *a job well done.*

Harambee and Black Love,
William E. Cross, Jr.

References

Fanon, F. (1967). *Black skin, White masks.* New York: Grove Press.

Jones, J. M. (2004). TRIOS: A model for coping with the universal context of racism. In G. Philogene (Ed.), *Kenneth B. Clark: Essays in honor of a social activist and scholar* (pp. 161–190). Washington, DC: American Psychological Association.

Memmi, A. (1991). *The colonizer and the colonized.* Boston: Beacon Press. (Original work published 1965)

Spencer, M. B. (1995). Old issues and new theorizing about African American youth: A phenomenological variant of ecological systems theory. In R. L. Taylor (Ed.), *Black youth: Perspectives on their status in the United States* (pp. 37–69). Westport, CT: Praeger.

INTRODUCTION

Black Americans have a long, rich presence in the United States and currently constitute about 13% of the population. The intellectual contributions of Black Americans to the core disciplines (e.g., history, sociology, literature) have been well documented, and the emergence of new interdisciplinary fields reflecting African American studies has flourished over the past 4 decades (e.g., African American Psychology). Interestingly, books in African American Psychology are relatively few compared to other fields, such as African American history, African American literature, and African American sociology. The purpose of this handbook is to provide an overview of the development and state of the field since the founding of the modern African American Psychology with the formation of the Association of Black Psychologists exactly 40 years ago and the publication of Joseph White's "Toward a Black Psychology," published in *Ebony* magazine in 1970. Moreover, the handbook is designed to present theoretical, empirical, and practical issues that are foundational to African American psychology. This collection builds on the foundational work of other scholars, most notably Reginald Jones. In his series of edited works, titled *Black Psychology*, Jones (1972–2004) serialized developments in the field. The first of the works appeared shortly after the call for an independent field in 1972, and the fourth and last was published in 2004, a year before his death. In these collections, Jones captured the pulse of the theoretical and empirical trends in the field of African American Psychology.

We intentionally structured this handbook to provide an overview of critical foundational issues (e.g., history, contextual factors influencing behavior, child and adolescent development, applied concerns), in-depth coverage of specific themes unique to the field (e.g., racial identity, African self-consciousness, cultural mistrust), and emerging theoretical areas (e.g., liberation psychology, positive psychology). Thus, this anthology incorporates other issues that are typically not covered in related books (e.g., an extensive examination of educational topics; a separate section on the development of African/Black Psychology; salient issues of the 21st century, such as the Internet, hip-hop, and youth culture; and systematic consideration of within-group difference related to gender, class, age, and sexual orientation). Each contributor synthesizes the debates and research in the field; identifies gaps in the literature; and points to future directions in research, training, and/or practice. The authors of the handbook reflect the scholars who are well established and whose work has appeared in other collections, such as Kobi Kambon and Howard Stevenson (*Black Psychology* [Jones, 1972–2004]), Thomas Parham (*The Psychology of Blacks: An Africentric Perspective* [Parham, White, & Ajamu, 1999]), Faye Z. Belgrave (*African American Psychology: Theory, Research, and Practice* [Belgrave & Allison, 2006]), Linda J. Myers, Harriette Pipes McAdoo, and Jerome Taylor (*African American Psychology: Theory, research, and practice* [Burlew, Banks, McAdoo, & Azibo, 1992]) as well as newer, emerging scholars whose work is gaining increasing attention.

As the field of Black Psychology has developed over the decades, two distinct subdisciplines have emerged that are sometimes in contentious debate with one another. These are African American Psychology and African or African-centered Psychology. The theories and research consistent with the African American approach tend to focus on factors related to Black American experiences within the multiple social and cultural contexts of their lives in the United States; for example, the influence of the majority and mainstream culture and also African Americans' unique cultural experiences. Theoretical underpinnings combine insights in the fields of Black Studies and the broader field of psychology. Research consistent with African or African-centered Psychology draws on historic connections to Africa and tends to focus on common cultural values and experiences of African-descended people. Among the core tensions between the two subfields include beliefs about the existence of an African worldview endorsed by all people of African descent, the degree to which race is viewed as biological or a social construction, the relevance of racism as an analytical construct, and the utility of or relevance of Western psychological constructs. In this handbook, both perspectives are represented. However, because much of this volume highlights research and theories from an African American Psychology perspective, we include a separate part consisting of several chapters on African Psychology. Also, a number of the authors incorporate both African American and African Psychological theories and research; we see this integration and conversation between the two perspectives as a contribution to the literature. This handbook consists of 36 chapters and is organized around eight parts. As a way to contextualize the discussion of current developments and trends in the literature, a brief history of African American Psychology is provided first. The two chapters in the first part complement one another—the first chapter provides a broad overview of historical developments and the second a personal account of living legends. In this part, key concepts, theories, and contributions to the development of Black psychology over the years are unearthed. In Chapter 1, Thomas A. Parham skillfully weaves a master narrative in which the psychohistory of Blacks and their journey to the Americas is placed within context; he outlines the role that this context plays in psychological and behavioral realities of Black Americans. Building on the work of Robert Guthrie's (1976, 1998) *Even the Rat Was White,* Parham outlines key historical issues in the development of African American psychology. He extends this work also by summarizing central themes and concepts associated with the practice of psychology in ancient Kemet, a point in time long preceding the interference of Europeans on the continent.

Using life histories, M. Nicole Coleman and Adanna Johnson uncover the experiences of five psychologists who have contributed to the field in immeasurable ways. In Chapter 2, Coleman and Johnson capture the professional experiences and reflections of Janet Helms, Linda James Myers, Joseph White, Daniel Williams, and Robert Williams as they discuss the emergence of the field of modern African American Psychology and their own professional development. The insights these pathfinders provide help inform future training, practice, and research directions that build on an in-depth understanding of where we have been and a critical analysis of what has worked, as well as areas of growth.

Part II, titled "African/Black Psychology," provides an introduction to and comprehensive review of the theories and applications germane to the discipline of African Psychology. In this part, readers are (re)acquainted with the theories and concepts of African Psychology rooted in the philosophies and deep thought of both ancient Kemet and West Africa. Readers will discover the similarities and differences between classical African Psychology and the various schools of African American and Black Psychology. This part also introduces readers to techniques and clinical applications of African Psychology. Furthermore, the authors of the chapters in this part review and critique the current instrumentation used by African-centered scholars in psychology to assess African-centered psychological constructs. Part II concludes with an examination of one of the subfields of African Psychology: African Personality.

Part II is of particular importance in that it addresses some of the criticisms and limitations that have been leveled against the discipline since it began to emerge (or reemerge) in the early 1970s. One of these criticisms has been the lack of reliable, valid measures to assess the proposed theoretical constructs proffered by the theoreticians of the discipline. Another major limitation cited by critics of African Psychology has been the absence of specific techniques for the clinical application of African Psychology. Not only are these specific issues addressed in this part, but the chapters also collectively review and critique the most recent theoretical and empirical literature in the area, thereby updating readers on recent advancements in the field.

African Psychology aims to liberate Black psychologists and the people they serve from the conceptual encapsulation and hegemony of Western psychology. Furthermore, African Psychology provides a culturally relevant framework for understanding the personality and behavior of persons of African descent from theoretical and conceptual models that are centered in an African worldview. The chapters in this part are especially timely in light of the recent certification credentialing in African/Black Psychology instituted by the Association of Black Psychologists. The licensure certification proficiency program of the Association of Black Psychologists is a mechanism by which to evaluate the preparedness of mental health clinicians, researchers, and other psychologists to provide culturally relevant services to people of African descent. It is anticipated that the chapters in this part will provide a valuable resources for clinicians, researchers, educators, and consumers alike, regarding the theories and techniques of African Psychology.

In Chapter 3, Linda James Myers provides a context for understanding the evolution of African, African American, and Black Psychology. This background is essential for understanding the similarities and differences among the subdisciplines. To provide further clarity, she reviews the various schools of thought in African, African American, and Black Psychology. She concludes the chapter by suggesting some areas of African Psychology that would benefit from additional exploration and development.

In Chapter 4, Ezemenari M. Obasi and Anthony J. Smith introduce a number of concepts grounded in the philosophical and spiritual systems of ancient Kemet and West Africa. These concepts are central to the clinical application of African Psychology and provide readers with a framework for understanding the mechanisms by which individuals achieve optimal psychological and spiritual functioning. This chapter includes a case study in which the methods and techniques of African Psychology are illustrated for purposes of instruction.

In Chapter 5, African Psychology pioneer Kobi Kambon and his coauthor, Terra Bowen-Reid, expand on one of the earliest subfields of African Psychology—African Personality. They provide an overview and update of Kambon's theory of African (Black) Personality. Readers are (re)introduced to the African Self-Consciousness Scale, the most widely used measure of any African-centered psychological construct. This chapter concludes with an update and evaluation of the empirical literature surrounding the use of the African Self-Consciousness Scale.

In Chapter 6, Shawn O. Utsey, Benita Belvet, and Nicole Fischer provide a review and psychometric evaluation of the most commonly used measures of psychological constructs in African Psychology. The purpose of this chapter is to describe and evaluate the reliability and validity of the most commonly used measures of African-centered psychological constructs. This information should be of particular interest to clinicians and researchers alike, providing them with direction in the selection and use of instruments to assess personality and related constructs in African Psychology.

Part III consists of six chapters designed to contextualize African American attitudes and behaviors. These chapters cover potential sources of strength within the African American community, including religion, spirituality, family, and intimate relationships. This coverage builds on the strengths-based mission of African American Psychology, by adopting an approach that highlights protective factors that promote resiliency. Discussions of the influence of larger systems on human behavior are also included, particularly the role and meaning of rap music and hip-hop culture for youth; the influence of media, with an emphasis on new media; and the structure and ideological arms of racism. The chapters outline contextual factors that influence the psychological, cognitive, and behavioral development of African Americans. These socializing forces are discussed first as a way to inform the later theoretical and applied sections. Unlike other fields within psychology, African American psychological research and practice often incorporate a multidisciplinary approach to understand the complexities of attitudes, behaviors, and beliefs. The chapters in Part III build on this approach to offer insights about the influence of contextual factors on psychological and behavioral health.

We begin Part III with an examination of religion and spirituality, often identified as core protective factors in promoting psychological health. Because the concepts religion and spirituality are typically conflated in the field, in Chapter 7 Jacqueline S. Mattis and Carolyn R. Watson unpack the similarities and differences between these concepts. Although the authors identify key readings in African American religious traditions, the crux of the discussion centers on the complex influence of religion and, to a lesser degree, spirituality, on positive mental health outcomes. Seminal studies on the ways in which gender and other within-group factors influence African Americans' understanding and meaning-making around religion and spirituality are also covered.

In the 1950s and 1960s, cultural deficit models gained prominence in the social science literature and within public discourses as a way to counter the fallacious assumptions found within the scientific racism tradition. Within this framework, biological notions of racial inferiority/superiority were supplanted with presuppositions suggesting that differences across a range of social and economic indexes were instead due to cultural deficits as a result of slavery and systematic oppression. The character assassination of the Black family reflects the scholarship emerging during this time; these works portrayed Black families as dysfunctional and "broken." In Chapter 8, Harriette Pipes McAdoo and Sinead N. Younge challenge historical and prevailing notions of the Black family as a tangle of pathology. Moreover, the authors draw on the family studies and related literatures to provide an integrated picture of potential structures and strengths of the Black family. McAdoo and Younge provide alternative frameworks for understanding what constitutes a family and the specific factors within the family that can either promote or hinder positive well-being, including parenting styles and racial and gender socialization.

In Chapter 9, Anita Jones Thomas, Rabiatu Barrie, and Brendesha M. Tynes examine the development and influence of male–female intimate relationships. They begin with a discussion of the role and nature of friendships in African American youth and the relationship between friendships and intimacy on issues of sexuality. Although the authors include a discussion of the issues raised in the popular press around mate availability and mate selection, they also discuss empirical research on other noteworthy issues, including racial and gender socialization. Also consistent with the thrust of Part III, strengths and areas of resilience identified in the theoretical and empirical literature are outlined.

In Chapter 10, Yasser Arafat Payne and LaMar Rashad Gibson provide a fresh and compelling examination of hip-hop music and culture. The contributions of youth to our society are vastly understudied. The authors argue that structural oppression, resilience, and cultural innovations gave rise to the development and popularity of hip-hop among African American youth. In this well-informed, interdisciplinary review, Payne and Gibson situate the historical development of hip-hop culture, now a worldwide phenomenon. They provide a rich lyrical analysis to highlight voices of youth, primarily males from "the streets," to understand, define, and provide insight into the influence of systemic factors on people's lived experiences.

In Chapter 11, Brendesha M. Tynes and L. Monique Ward provide an insightful overview of the role of (new) media on the psychosocial development of African Americans. They highlight the ways in which the media (re)produce systems of hierarchy and specifically address the influence of media (including amount and type of media consumption) on the psychosocial development of African Americans across the life span (e.g., self-concept, body image, violence and aggression). In addition to reviewing the seminal and early works on media, the authors engage new emerging scholarship that theorizes the role of race in interactive media forms. They also identify ways in which media and technology can promote individual and community empowerment.

Helen A. Neville and Alex L. Pieterse propose a new model of racism and White supremacy in Chapter 12. The Psychosocial Model of Racism is designed to synthesize the disparate interdisciplinary literature on the link between racism and psychological and behavioral health. In the proposed model, racism is characterized as consisting of structural and ideological components. The various types of racism are described, as are the multiple ways in which African Americans either buy into or resist racism in everyday life. Seminal research on racism related stress is reviewed.

Building on Part III's ecological analysis, Part IV focuses on child and adolescent development in relation to education. More specifically, the chapters in this part highlight research on the contextual, psychosocial, and cultural factors that may account for both the racial disparities in achievement as well as academic success for African Americans. The chapters engage and critique some of the most widely cited theories (e.g., oppositional identity, the acting-White hypothesis, and stereotype threat) used to explain African American underachievement while also encouraging readers to move beyond group-level explanations to consider within-group variation and individual differences. Traditional notions of what has been known to promote successful outcomes for European American children, such as authoritative parenting, are challenged, and many of the unique barriers African American children face are brought to light. Also among the chapters is a consideration of understudied, or less widely cited, but important literature for psychologists, educators, and clinicians to consider. These include how to meet the psychological needs of the gifted and how teacher attitudes about African American English may impact their judgments about student competence. Taken together, the chapters provide greater understanding of the complex interactions within and between proximal and distal processes involved in educating African American children.

In a climate of high-stakes testing under No Child Left Behind and one-curriculum-fits-all schooling, little room is left to address the developmental and cultural needs of students. These and other factors have led to a steady stream of African American students dropping out of schools. Recently, the America's Promise Alliance released a report that suggests the largest cities in the United States are experiencing an educational crisis, with as few as 25% graduating in some cities, such as Detroit. These statistics make a fundamental shift in educational practices imperative. The chapters in Part IV provide culturally specific recommendations to teachers, parents, and communities for improving African Americans' schooling experiences and ultimately addressing the crisis. In addition, evidence of the success of interventions that draw on students' assets or cultural resources is provided.

In Chapter 13, Iheoma U. Iruka and Oscar Barbarin draw on Bronfenbrenner's ecological theory to describe the family, school, and neighborhood factors that may shape early schooling experiences of African American children. In addition to synthesizing previous research, the authors present findings from the Early Childhood Longitudinal Study—Kindergarten Cohort to describe the role such factors as parent and school participation in literacy-based activities play in children's early learning and development.

Cynthia Hudley, in Chapter 14, moves beyond structural explanations for group-level educational disparities between African Americans and their counterparts to describe a construct that may account for individual differences in performance: academic motivation. She notes the motivation-related attitudes, beliefs, and behaviors that may influence achievement.

In Chapter 15, Anne Harper Charity Hudley discusses the phonological, grammatical, prosodic, and pragmatic features of African American English. Charity Hudley also notes that language is a central aspect of African American children's identity and discusses the ways in which misunderstandings and devaluations of African American English speakers may impact performance. Other constructs influencing academic performance, including stereotype threat, are covered in this part of the book. Claytie Davis III and Crystal Simmons provide in Chapter 16 an overview of the seminal studies on stereotype threat and the subsequent criticisms that have been levied since the publication of this original work. They also discuss interventions to reduce the impact of stereotype threat as well as potential mediators and moderators.

In Chapter 17, Donna Y. Ford and Gilman W. Whiting discuss the underrepresentation of African Americans in gifted education and the role played by teacher perceptions and testing issues. The affective and psychological needs of African American gifted students are also recounted, with a focus on fostering the development of a positive racial identity among this population.

Although not focusing on gifted students specifically, A. Wade Boykin and Constance M. Ellison present in Chapter 18 basic principles and research associated with the Talent Quest Comprehensive School Reform Model. The Talent Quest model is an intervention that advocates reforming core educational practices by enhancing school leadership, attending to the developmental and cultural needs of the "whole child," and a focus on more meaningful learning and interactions between students and school personnel.

Among the numerous contributions of African American Psychology to the larger fields of psychology and Black Studies are theorizing and measuring individual-level racial processes. In Part V, researchers provide a critical overview of the development of core racial processes, including racial socialization, racial identity, and cultural mistrust. They also review and critique the extant literature. The research in these areas has deepened our understanding of how individuals make sense of race and racism and the influence of this understanding on behaviors. The individual-level processes covered in this part consistently have been found to be related to psychological and educational outcomes.

In addition, in the emerging group identity scholarship there is increased attention given to the ways in which race intersects with other social identities and how this intersection in turn influences psychological, cognitive, and behavioral functioning. Throughout this handbook, the authors review the literature on the intersection of race and gender (or race–gender) on psychological outcomes. There is a dearth of research considering the way in which sexual identity may intersect with race as well. This part includes a chapter on the influence of race, gender, and sexual identity (and their interface) on African American lesbian and gay men.

In Chapter 19, Keisha L. Bentley, Valerie N. Adams, and Howard C. Stevenson critically review the racial socialization literature, covering the seminal research of the 1980s and 1990s as well as the more current research trends and debates. The authors summarize and evaluate current measures of racial socialization and propose a model of understanding the transmission of racial/ethnic/cultural experiences, knowledge, beliefs, and styles.

Because of the centrality of racial identity to the field, two pertinent chapters are included in this collection, one focusing on children and the other on adults. In Chapter 20, Dena Phillips Swanson and her colleagues describe the development of racial identity in children from a cognitive–developmental, life span, and ecological perspective. The Phenomenological Variant of Ecological Systems Theory, a model of racial identity development that integrates both an individual's context and perceptions, also is highlighted.

Kevin Cokley and Collette Chapman provide a hard-hitting analysis in Chapter 21 of the historical development and current advancements in racial identity theory and research with adults. Tracing the examination of Black racial identity to W. E. B. Du Bois's (1903) classic work, *Souls of Black Folk,* the authors chart out the development of the field, including an overview of the seminal theories. A review of the empirical literature documenting a link between racial identity attitudes and mental health, educational, and social attitudes is also provided.

In Chapter 22, Francis Terrell and his colleagues provide a comprehensive review of the literature on cultural mistrust that includes an integration and analysis of more than 125 articles on the topic. The authors discuss the adaptive nature of developing a healthy distrust of White individuals and institutions as a way to survive a realistically threatening environment. Empirical findings suggest that the mistrust that Blacks have of Whites influences a range of psychological, educational, and behavioral processes, including help-seeking behaviors, interpersonal relationships, and academic performance.

In Chapter 23, Beverly Greene provides a sweeping overview of the risk and protective factors related to a range of developmental issues among lesbian and gay men. In her analysis, she skillfully integrates the way in which structures of oppression and multiple identities work to shape experiences related to relationships, family, parenting, and identity formation. Her review weaves a rich and textured consideration of clinical applications.

A popular image of Blacks in the public imagination is that of a group of people who are downtrodden and pathological, a people who because of slavery and racial oppression have been irreparably damaged. The sets of chapters presented in Part VI provide a different, competing image of Blacks—an image in which Black Americans have at their disposal a wide range of protective factors promoting positive well-being and optimal functioning. The authors of the chapters in Part VI do not skirt issues related to the negative influence of racism and other forms of discrimination on life changes as exemplified by racial disparities in physical health, wealth, educational attainment, and so on. The chapters thus contextualize mental and physical health, paying close attention to differential experiences and outcomes among youth and adults.

In Chapter 24, Tara R. Earl and David R. Williams outline research on the prevalence and severity of mental health disorders among Blacks, paying special attention to within-group differences. They also discuss factors that contribute to disparities in access, service utilization, and quality of care. In addition, risk and resilience factors that may explain mental health status are enumerated.

Similarly, Frank C. Worrell examines psychological health among school-age youth in Chapter 25. His review echoes many of the conclusions drawn in the previous chapter, most notably that Blacks and Whites for the most part experience comparable rates of psychological disorders. Both chapters highlight the ways in which Black Americans are resilient in light of the multiple risk factors they encounter (e.g., overrepresentation among the poor and high-crime neighborhoods, racial discrimination), and both identify the specific ways in which racism operates in the creation of racial disparities in terms of access to quality, culturally sensitive health and educational services.

Part VI also includes three chapters that outline positive psychological functioning. In Chapter 26, Suzette L. Speight and her colleagues review several key definitions of mental health within traditional psychology and within the fields of African American and African Psychology. A strength of this work is the inclusion of an integrated review of three approaches (i.e., racism/stress, Africentric, and combination) as a way of understanding the theoretical tensions, research conclusions, and future directions for work on the mental health of African Americans.

Building on the theme of psychological well-being, in Chapter 27, A. Toy Caldwell-Colbert, Fayth M. Parks, and Sussie Eshun situate positive psychology within the African American Psychology tradition. The formation of modern African American Psychology is built on the principles of a strength-based approach, and scholars for years have focused on issues related to positive well-being and optimal functioning. The crux of positive psychology centers on uncovering healthy normal developmental processes that encourage optimal functioning, including, hope, resilience, optimism, survival, and so on. Caldwell-Colbert and her colleagues provide an overview of the key components of positive psychology, multicultural perspectives to this approach, and theoretical and research applications of positive psychological trends within the field of African American Psychology. We are especially honored that this chapter is included in the book. True to the spirit of Toy and her commitment, she diligently worked on the chapter, even while she was very ill. We received the final version of the chapter 2 weeks prior to her passing. We think it only fitting that her last professional writing focuses on optimism, hope, compassion, and resilience, which beautifully exemplify her professional contributions and approach to life.

In Chapter 28, Michael Canute Lambert and William K. Smith continue the exploration of strengths; however, with an emphasis on children and adolescents. After contextualizing the area of study, they provide a nuanced discussion of theoretical concerns and tensions. They also provide an insightful and detailed discussion of methodological limitations of the extant literature, and they discuss in detail the Behavioral Assessment of Children of African Heritage as a model for developing strength-based model for Blacks.

Part VI concludes with two chapters that address specific health issues: mental health and physical health. Rheeda L. Walker and Lora Rose Hunter provide an in-depth analysis of anxiety, depression, and suicide among Black Americans in Chapter 29. Patterns, symptoms, differential diagnoses across these psychological conditions and behaviors, as well as the challenges in diagnoses and measurement, are outlined. The authors identify the culturally relevant patterns and characteristics of and the sociocultural factors influencing these phenomenon across the life span. Because of the significant negative consequences of depression and suicide-related behaviors, the authors incorporate a discussion of specific culturally sensitive prevention and intervention strategies.

In Chapter 30, Shawn M. Bediako examines the psychosocial aspects of sickle cell disease in African Americans. Specifically, he discusses the psychological consequences of sickle cell disease, issues related to coping and adjustment, and the cultural implications of the disease. The therapeutic implications are discussed in terms of pain management, coping and adjustment, and African-centered clinical intervention strategies. Overall, this chapter provides psychologists with a deeper understanding of the psychosocial aspects of a very significant health disparity affecting the African American community.

In Part VII, many of the psychological theories, concepts, and processes presented in preceding chapters are brought to life through a discussion of a range of real-world applications. Topics include individual psychotherapy, assessment, prevention, and system-level interventions. Thus, these works tackle multiple paths to improving the mental health of African Americans as individuals and as a community.

In Chapter 31, Madonna G. Constantine, Rebecca M. Redington, and Sheila V. Graham review the theoretical and empirical research related to mental health practice, with an emphasis on within-group differences. Coverage of critical issues, such as the way in which expectations about race and racism reveal themselves in the therapy process, is included. The authors outline core Africentric values and discuss strategies to incorporate the influence of and promotion of these values on mental health and treatment.

In Chapter 32, Kumea Shorter-Gooden builds on Constantine and colleagues' discussion of gender issues in therapy. After defining *gender*, she scrutinizes the literature examining core psychological issues associated with African American women and men, separately. Both race–gender challenges (e.g., gender role strain, invisibility syndrome, sexual devaluation, and Superwoman phenomena) to mental health outcomes and resiliency factors (e.g., reliance on spirituality and religion, social support) are incorporated. Race–gender therapeutic considerations when working with African American men and women are discussed, including strategies influenced by Africentric principles.

Deidre M. Anglin and Naa Oyo A. Kwate address social and cultural factors in the psychological assessment of African American adults in Chapter 33. The authors begin this chapter by providing a cultural context for questioning the contemporary assessment practices used with African American populations. The legacy of scientific racism and European cultural hegemony has created an environment in which traditional assessment techniques are viewed with suspicion. The two broad areas covered in this chapter include neuropsychological assessment and clinical psychiatric assessment. The authors stress the importance of considering cultural factors in the assessment process.

In Chapter 34, Faye Z. Belgrave, Trenette Clark, and Aashir Nasim document the prevalence of alcohol and drug use and abuse among African Americans. Similar to the mental health chapters, they note the racial group comparability in the substance usage across developmental stages, with Whites reporting significantly higher rates than Blacks in some instances. The authors identify risk and protective factors related to substance use. In addition to outlining the general prevention intervention approaches, Belgrave and her colleagues review the literature on culturally relevant substance use prevention.

Psychologists have the ability and moral obligation to intervene on multiple levels to promote the mental health of Black Americans. In Chapter 35, Chalmer E. Thompson and Dorienna M. Alfred provide a nuanced discussion of theory and practice issues related to Liberation Psychology. In their analysis, they unpack the theoretically dense literature on oppressed groups' self-activity to liberate themselves mentally, physically, and structurally from the confines of systematic discrimination and White supremacy. In doing so, they review the seminal works of Black scholars in the United States and around the globe. Patterns of Black oppression (e.g., political and economic exploitation) and praxis to challenge and disrupt White supremacy for the purpose of liberation are discussed.

The eighth and final part consists of just one chapter. In it we as the editors reflect on the collection and identify trends outlined in the works. We also propose future directions to further grow the fields of African American Psychology.

The chapters in this handbook outline what African American and African psychological perspectives can bring to bear on psychological and educational research and practice. It is our hope that readers gain a solid grounding in the field through the extensive coverage of the theories and empirical literature. We also hope this work will be used to train future practitioners who serve African American populations. We envision this handbook facilitating the development of a critical lens with which to examine/conduct future research on African Americans. In addition, this work is designed to be a tool for current and future researchers who will ensure the continued viability of the field of African American Psychology for the next 40 years and beyond.

Helen A. Neville, Brendesha M. Tynes,
and Shawn O. Utsey

REFERENCES

Belgrave, F. Z., & Allison, K. W. (2006). *African American Psychology: From Africa to America*. Thousand Oaks, CA: Sage.

Burlew, A. K. H., Banks, W. C., McAdoo, H. P., & Azibo, D. A. (Eds.). (1992). *African American Psychology: Theory, research, and practice*. Newbury Park, CA: Sage.

Du Bois, W. E. B. (1903). *The souls of Black folks*. New York: Signet Classic.

Guthrie, R. V. (1976). *Even the rat was white: A historical view of psychology*. New York: Harper & Row.

Guthrie, R. V. (1998). *Even the rat was white: A historical view of psychology* (2nd ed.). Needham Heights, MA: Allyn & Bacon.

Jones, R. L. (1972–2004). *Black Psychology*. Berkeley, CA: Cobb & Henry.

Parham, T. A., White, J. L., & Ajamu, A. (1999). *The psychology of Blacks: An African centered perspective*. Englewood Cliffs, NJ: Prentice Hall.

White, J. (1970, August). Toward a Black Psychology. *Ebony, 24,* 44–45, 48–50.

ACKNOWLEDGMENTS

To see the culmination of this work come to fruition is a dream come true, and I sincerely thank all of those involved in making this collective vision a reality. This journey was made possible by the commitment and patience of our contributing authors; the publisher and our editorial assistant (Lara Grambling) our production editor (Tracy Buyan) and copy editor (Kathy Anne Savadel), and the willingness of my coeditors to engage, raise critical questions, and trust the process. I appreciate the ways that I have grown through my interactions with my coeditors as we hammered out the details of the book; some of these conversations were difficult, but always enjoyable. I thank Jioni Lewis for her assistance early on in helping us get organized and to my current and future students who motivate me to seek new explanations to understand our current realities. Most important, I wish to express my deepest gratitude to my family and friends who provided me with unconditional love and support, most notably my mother, Lillian Neville; my stepdaughters and their families (Jamila Cha-Jua-Lee, Leila Alexander, and Montenia Bickerstaff); and my life partner, Sundiata Cha-Jua.

Helen A. Neville

To see this project develop from an idea Helen had as we were teaching African American Psychology to what it has today has been nothing short of amazing. The conversations along the way and the extraordinary contributions of our authors have made me think more critically about the research in the field and the materials I use to teach. It has been an incredible honor to go through the process with such giants in the field as my coeditors. I am especially grateful to them for their invaluable insight, hard work, and dedication to this work. Many thanks also go to Saroj Hardit and LaNeisha Waller for their research assistance. Cheri Dellelo also deserves special thanks for her faith in the volume early on. I also appreciate everyone working behind the scenes, from the editorial assistant Lara Grambling and the production and copy editors, Tracy Buyan and Kathy Savadel, respectively, to the artist who created the book cover. Most important, I would like to thank my grandmother Nancy Moody, who passed away during the completion of this work, for her love of education, her sacrifice, and her prayers for me. I am also grateful for my mother, Beverly Tynes, and the rest of my family and friends for their love, support, and encouragement.

Brendesha M. Tynes

My efforts on this project are dedicated to those Africans who died so I could live, who ran so I could walk, and who survived so I could thrive. It is on their shoulders that all of us stand, and I hope that this work will be worthy as a small offering for their sacrifice. I would also like to acknowledge those African healers (psychologists) who did not complete their graduate studies or never received tenure because they refused to compromise the liberation of their people. It is through their efforts and sacrifice that I was able to complete my graduate training and find a space in the academy that allowed me to be part of this effort. Finally, it was Betsy Watson, an enslaved African woman who begot Martha Graham, who herself was enslaved, who begot another enslaved woman named Caroline Graham, who begot Ana Graham, who begot Carrie Utsey, who gave birth to me. To all of them, I give thanks for both my life and my spirit for liberation.

Shawn O. Utsey

Sage Publications would like to thank the following reviewers for their valuable input:

    Asa G. Hilliard III–Baffour Amankwatia II, Georgia State University

Carlotta M. Arthur, Smith College

Dashiel Geyen, Texas Southern University

Ladonna Lewis, Glendale Community College

Thaddeus P. Mathis, Temple University

G. Susan Mosley-Howard, Miami University

Valjean McNeill Whitlow, Georgia State University

PART I

Historical Foundation

1

FOUNDATIONS FOR AN AFRICAN AMERICAN PSYCHOLOGY

Extending Roots to an Ancient Kemetic Past

THOMAS A. PARHAM

There is something wrong with a psychology and psychological analysis that leaves African descent people strangers to themselves, aliens to their culture, oblivious to their condition, and inhuman to their oppressors. (Hilliard, 1997, p. xii)

To the uninitiated scholar, or the less than critical student, the discipline of Black or African Psychology may appear to be an ethnic branch extending from a tree that has European and American roots. After all, the study of psychology's roots, as taught in most undergraduate and graduate psychology departments, extends as far back as the laboratories of Wilhelm Wundt in 1879. There, scholars who had certainly been influenced by the three movements of empiricism in philosophy, Darwinian theory in biology, and experimental physics and physiology, hailed the advances of the science of psychology as a vehicle through which they could study human behavior (Fernald & Fernald, 1978). Even the Americanization of the discipline, with its focus shifting from structural to functional aspects, was no better at engaging the true science or art of psychology in studying the more authentic connections to psychology's ancient African roots.

Within the context of a 2008 academy, scholars can no longer afford to embrace the same ideology that relegated African Psychology's past to a status that was more latent than visible. Thus, I argue that it was from African roots and a tree colored with the worldview ideology of Black people that Western psychology sprung, and it is Western psychologists' own sense of conceptual incarceration, fortified with a distorted value system, that keeps traditional psychology locked in a chamber of intellectual distortion. That chamber of distortion has eliminated the spiritual core of the discipline by refusing to recognize or acknowledge anything (i.e., any variable) that cannot be measured. That distortion has taken the core concept of the soul or spirit and redefined it as "the study of human behavior," with a specific focus on measuring and classifying the cognitive, affective, and behavioral dimensions of an individual's personality. That chamber of distortion continues to embrace an epistemological system of knowing that determines significance only at or beyond the .05 level.

Among the limitations of this approach is the recognition that traditional psychology, in its attempts to understand the lifestyle, thought, feelings, and behaviors of people of African descent, fails to capture their *ethos*, or "emotional tone." In introducing the concept of ethos here, I mean to suggest, as Ani (1980) did before me, that it is related to the emotional substance of a cultural group solidified by a set of common experiences, common heritage, and common culture. That emotional tone creates a shared synthesis of energy or spirit, which helps to symbolize and even define our uniqueness as a people. Thus, if a discipline were truly interested in understanding "the psychology" of a people, concepts such as spirit, ethos, and cultural uniqueness could not be so easily ignored and/or dismissed. It is interesting, though, that it is not, in my opinion, traditional psychology's task to reclaim the discipline's African roots. That task rightly belongs to generations of African American scholars who have and must continue to seize the power to define and frame the discourse for ourselves and our people.

Therefore, the purpose of this chapter is to introduce the reader to the psychohistory and culture of people of African descent and to discuss the roots of Black Psychology's real past.

A Broken Compass

Much of the history of persons of African descent is told from the context of slavery. There are numerous accounts of the horrific conditions that African people endured on their journey from an African homeland to varying parts of the Diaspora (Bennett, 1966; J. H. Franklin, 1974; Van Sertima, 1976; among others). J. H. Franklin (1974), for example, in his pioneering work *From Slavery to Freedom*, documented both the ways in which primarily West African countries and states functioned before European invasion, and the harsh, brutal treatment African-descent people endured throughout slavery, the Civil War, emancipation, Reconstruction, and up to the Black revolution of the 1960s and 1970s. Bennett (1966), in his groundbreaking and now-classic text *Before the Mayflower*, sought to describe the contributions of Africans and Ancient Egyptians. Not only did Bennett call for a reevaluation of history as a way to dispel the myths of Africa as a "dark continent," but he also carefully documented the deprivation, brutality, and chronic dehumanization that Africans in the New World were made to endure. In a similar way, Van Sertima (1976), in his text *They Came Before Columbus*, wrote about the civilizations that existed and the magnificent contributions African people gave to the world before they were forced to confront the realities of a life of oppression and brutality in colonial and post-colonial America. Although these authors and their historical accounts of the African people's struggle through the Middle Passage and beyond represent some of our best recording of a horrendous past, they do not disagree with—and, in fact, argue in favor of—the notion that slavery and the African Maafa[1] represents only a snapshot in time, rather than the beginning of the African presence on this planet.

In a similar way, the history of people of African descent within the discipline of psychology is no less skewed in that much of it has centered its analysis in the context of a racist worldview that saw African people as genetically, intellectually, and emotionally inferior, as well as culturally deprived when compared with their European and American counterparts (Belgrave & Allison, 2006; Guthrie, 1976, 1998; Jenkins, 1982). Traditional psychology's so-called science somehow lost its objectivity when is came to persons of African descent—in part, I suspect, because historical contributors to the literature were themselves contaminated with the social *zeitgeist* of America's obsession with race. Here, reliance on such principles as Darwin's survival of the fittest, Galton's notion of eugenics (the science of heredity), McDougall's theory of instincts, and Mendel's theory of genetic differences (which were later used to highlight differences between Caucasians and Africans), influences behavioral scientists' observations and inferences about persons of African descent.

Although scholars such as White (1972), Khatib (1980), and White, Parham, and Parham (1980) have all spoken to this dilemma, Robert Guthrie's (1976, 1998) work *Even the Rat Was*

White is perhaps best positioned to provide readers with a comprehensive overview and documentation of how traditional psychology applied its theories and techniques in ways that contributed to the dehumanization of persons of African descent. My emphasis here on "applied" is not accidental, for even if one could argue for the legitimacy and integrity of a particular theory or construct in Eurocentric psychology, the ways in which these ideas and materials were utilized by White psychologists to reinforce and validate notions of a White supremacist denigration of people of African descent is unquestionable. Guthrie's work, on behalf of African American Psychology, both helps us to understand these proverbial skeletons in the closet of European American psychology and documents for all to see how shameful these practices were.

Particularly poignant are Guthrie's (1976, 1988) discussions regarding "the psychology of race," "psychometric scientism," and "the psychology of eugenics." Not only is the historical documentation that Guthrie provides astounding, but so is the knowledge that European and American psychologists would stoop to such depths to create a case for the supposed intellectual and genetic superiority of the White race over Black people and would use this new "science" to help further their racist agenda challenges one's sensibilities.

Guthrie's (1976, 1998) work is itself reinforced by scholars such as A. Thomas and Sillen (1972), whose text *Racism and Psychiatry* should also be considered a classic. Whereas Guthrie focused more on the scientific aspects of psychology, Thomas and Sillen concentrated on the more applied aspects of psychology and psychiatry. Their work discusses how racist ideology contaminated the diagnostic nosologies used to classify mental disorders and disease in persons of African descent and elaborates on how terms such as *drapetomania* (flight-from-home madness) were invented to characterize attempts by Black people to escape their bondage as "crazy." Imagine for a moment the disciplines of psychiatry and psychology saying to African-descent people that to run away from your enslavement and oppression at the hands of White Europeans and Americans is an act of madness. That, in and of itself, is interesting, if not depressing. Thomas and Sillen also advanced the notion, as Sue (1978) would later do, that it was impossible to appreciate the status of Black folks in the psychiatry/psychology literature without reference to three general themes: (1) inferiority, (2) cultural deprivation, and (3) multicultural issues. Their work, and that of others (Parham, White, & Ajamu, 1999), includes an extensive discussion of these themes and the studies that helped to characterize them.

As a consequence of this myopically focused research and scholarship, much of African people's psychosocial history, even that which is produced by scholars of African descent, is told from a context of hard-core racism and a people's reaction to the severity and trauma of social oppression (Akbar, 1992; Fanon, 1967; C. Williams, 1974). Even the earliest texts—*Black Psychology* by R. L. Jones (1972, 1980), *Psychology of the Afro-American* by Jenkins (1982), *The Psychology of the Black Experience* by Pugh (1972), and others—appear to assume a reactionary posture (and necessarily so) in responding to traditional psychology's assault on Black people's sense of self (Banks & Grambs, 1972); the African American family (Billingsley, 1968; McAdoo, 1981); the African American community (F. Jones, 1972; C. Thomas, 1972); and the testing and labeling of African American children in America's primary, middle, and secondary schools (R. L. Williams, 1972; R. L. Williams & Mitchell, 1980).

The limitation—and, dare I say, challenge—of such a narrowly focused perspective is at least threefold. First, it anchors the study of African-descent people's psychology in an inaccurate space and time, with historical references to a people's psychological-mindedness being centered in slavery and beyond. Second, the analysis, however good, measures only and reveals how we have reacted and adapted to social oppression and says little about "who" we were and "how" we were before the imposition of the Maafa experience. Third, it has our identity studies (Carter & Helms, 1987; Cross, 1971, 1980; Parham & Helms, 1981, 1985), which would emerge sometime later, focused on racial identity rather than cultural identity. This last point is a significant one, because it is a cultural rather than a racial analysis that best illuminates the psychology of a people. It is important here to be crystal clear on this point.

Race is not a biological construction but rather a social construction, used not only to categorize people by degrees of melanin content in their skin but also to stratify groups in some artificial social hierarchy that assigns worth, and access to opportunity and privilege, on the basis of skin color. Culture, on the other hand, is at the center of any group's analysis, and I argue, as Ani (1980, 1994) has before me, that it is part of the core of our beingness. Culture does several things for each individual:

- It unifies and orders our experience by providing a worldview that orients our activity and interpretation of reality.

- It provides collective group identification built on shared history, symbols, and meanings.

- It institutionalizes and validates group beliefs, values, behaviors, and attitudes. (Ani, 1994)

Thus, it is at the deep-structured level of culture where the psychology of a people can best be understood, referenced, and interpreted. It is culture that describes the ethos of a people. It is culture that colors and shapes a people's design for living and patterns for interpreting reality. It is culture that provides an axiological interpretation of a people's value system that sees the following: an integrated versus a fragmented vision of the self; feelings as a emotional tone that should be expressed, rather than suppressed; a survival orientation that is collective, as opposed to individualistic and competitive; a sense of time that is fluid, as opposed to linear; a relationship to the universe that is in harmony with, instead of in control of; and a sense of worth that is based on contribution to one's community, as opposed to the acquisition of material wealth and possessions (Nobles, 1972; Parham, 1993; Parham et al., 1999; White, 1984).

Thus, if one's quest to understand the psychohistory and culture of African-descent people is real, then our focus and discussion must extend beyond how Black people persevered through American psychology programs to earn advanced degrees and how African people generally reacted to and/or resisted our oppression and dehumanization. This includes the collective activity of creating our own institutions when traditional organizations and membership within them left African-descent psychologists and students frustrated with the status quo and angry about the misapplication of psychological principles and techniques that created more harm than good in Black communities all across the United States. Here, reference is first made to Dr. Francis Sumner, who in 1920 became the first person of African descent to be awarded a doctorate in psychology, having graduated from Clark University in Massachusetts (Guthrie, 1976). Guthrie (1976) also noted that Sumner was joined at Clark University by a number of notable psychologists and sociologists, including Henry Alston (MA Psychology, 1920) and E. Franklin Frazier (MA Sociology, 1920), and across the country at Northwestern University by Herman Canady, who would later receive his BA (1927), MA (1928), and PhD (1941).

Reference is also made, as Guthrie (1976, 1998) reminds us, to the formation of the Psychology Caucus of the American Teachers Association, an all-Black caucus and organization formed in 1938 at a conference in Tuskegee, Alabama, after Black psychologists, primarily in teaching positions, expressed their frustration with the American Psychological Association. Additionally, it is important to recognize the formation of the national Association of Black Psychologists (ABPsi) in 1968, when a group of committed Black Psychologists broke away from the American Psychological Association (APA) at APA's convention in San Francisco (Belgrave & Allison, 2006; Guthrie, 1998; Parham et al., 1999). In the intervening 40 years, the ABPsi has, until very recently, been the only autonomous ethnic psychological association in the United States. It has its own headquarters; its own newsletter (*Psych Discourse*); its own journal (the *Journal of Black Psychology*); and its own convention, which meets annually. The ABPsi has also extended its reach by defining and framing the discourse on issues such as testing Black children; educating Black students; training counselors and psychologists; and providing primary, secondary, and tertiary levels of intervention and care to Black clients and patient populations. Indeed, members of the ABPsi have been a vital force in creating better conditions for people of African descent, and they continues in that role today.

It is no wonder, then, why many students and professionals alike consider the awarding of Sumner's degree or the formation of the ABPsi as the foundation and genesis of not just the contemporary Black Psychology movement but also the discipline of African Psychology as a whole. This is not surprising given the level of activity in which the organization has engaged over the past 40 years, the relative absence of a major movement of Black psychologists (despite some very significant individual contributions) in the preceding 50-plus years before 1968, and the lack of historical reference to psychology's African roots traditional psychology makes in the training of most psychologists. My task in this chapter, however, is to connect those two endpoints, highlight ancient psychology's past and contemporary presence in the field, and then develop a speculative road map about where the discipline of African-centered psychology might be going in the future. Accordingly, I now turn to psychology's ancient Kemetic roots.

African Psychology's Kemetic Roots

The centering of our analysis in ancient Africa's past is critically important, because traditional psychology has been focused on analyzing human behavior, measuring differences, and classifying people with diagnostic labels that characterize their deviation from a cultural norm that is Eurocentric in orientation (Kambon, 1992; Nobles, 1972; Parham et al., 1999; White, 1972; White et al., 1980). This tendency to use a European American norm as a standard by which normal behavior in different cultural groups is measured is not only the epitome of arrogance on the part of our European American brothers and sisters, but it is just plain incorrect. In addition, using Eurocentric norms as a template from which to measure the thoughts, feelings, and behaviors of people of African descent places Black people at a conceptual disadvantage, resulting in a tendency to characterize our behaviors as pathological (White & Parham, 1990). White (1972), in his seminal article "Toward a Black Psychology," was very clear in this regard when he argued that it was inappropriate to use traditional psychological theories, that were developed by White psychologists to explain the behaviors of White people, on Black folks. When this occurs, White argued, people of African descent are labeled with diagnostic conclusions that are weakness dominated and inferiority oriented.

Belgrave and Allison (2006), in their seminal and comprehensive contribution titled *African American Psychology: From Africa to America,* similarly argued that any attempts to study the psychology of African-descent people from other than a perspective that is African centered can lead to gross omissions of necessary information as well as distortions in the phenomenon one is attempting to study. Their book is a must-read for students and professionals alike looking to familiarize themselves with the contributions of a Black psychological perspective to the literature. Belgrave and Allison provided what might be one of the most comprehensive analyses of the discipline of African/Black Psychology that has ever been written, and yet, while arguing for the correctness of an African-centered perspective, their coverage of psychology's ancient Kemetic (Egyptian) roots is somewhat limited. If we are going to understand the psychohistory and culture of people of African descent, then I believe it important to reorient our compass and begin our journey toward enlightenment with an analysis of ancient Kemetic life. It is there, among civilizations past, that we will find the true psychology.

Why is ancient Kemetic (Egyptian) history important? Perhaps Clarke (1996), in his award-winning documentary film *John Henrik Clarke: A Great and Mighty Walk,* said it best. He reminds us that history is a clock that people use to tell their political and cultural time of day. He concluded by suggesting that the relationship of history to a people is like the relationship of a mother to her child. Hilliard (1997), in his must-read scholarly work titled *SBA: The Reawakening of the African Mind,* also is clear in this regard as he argues that a people's indigenous culture anchors them to reality and must be the starting point for all learning. Similarly, Karenga (1990), in support of Diop's (1974) work, contended that ancient Egypt was the key to classical African civilization given its abundance of documents, its level of achievement in various areas of culture and human knowledge, and its resultant significance to other African cultures as well as world cultures. Bynum (1999) also weighed in by documenting the historical, anthropological, developmental, and evolutionary neurobiological trends and evidence of ancient Africa's gifts to the rest of the world.

If one examines what was indigenous to African folks before contamination from European influences, one realizes that there is a wealth of information, knowledge, and wisdom that African Psychology and African-centered psychologists have helped us reclaim. Looking back across space and time, African Psychology, like African thought, was concerned primarily with the development of one's consciousness and with the development and sustaining of positive relationships. It is clear that the ancients thought these elements of consciousness and proper conduct in relationships were central to sustaining a "right ordering" of the world.

African Psychology also provided a tool through which one could view the soul. The focus here, as Asante (2000) explained, was not on the individual personality of the human being but rather on how each individual's thoughts, emotions, behaviors, and spiritual energy aligned with a principle of truth. That fundamental principle is called *Ma'at*. In discussing the sacred principle of Ma'at, Karenga (1990) explained that any discussion of African Kemetic spirituality must begin with Ma'at, because it was a fundamental principle of the Divine, natural, and social orders, established by RA, who was God at the time of creation. Hilliard (1997), like Obenga (1996) before him, highlighted the fact that Ma'at was concerned with all of the spheres of reality, including the Divine, or sacred world; the cosmos, or the universe; the state, or the governance; the society, or human community; and the human being, which also included the family. I (Parham, 2002) also reminded us that Ma'at was defined as a code of conduct and a standard of aspiration for the ancient Africans, and it was characterized by seven cardinal virtues: (1) truth, (2) justice, (3) righteousness, (4) harmony, (5) order, (6) balance, and (7) propriety.

In illustrating this principle, it is important to understand that Ma'at was a conceptual template through which each individual could view his or her relationships with others in his or her immediate and extended circles. The aim, then, was to establish in each relationship the conditions for Ma'at to reign. Thus, individuals interacting with one another were bound to engage at a level where competition, jealousy, aggressiveness, and a quest for material acquisition were secondary or nonexistent in the face of truth, justice, righteousness, and proper conduct. It is interesting that Obenga's (1996) work has documented that there is linguistic evidence for the term Ma'at and for its meaning in many parts of Black Africa, including Egypt, Ethiopia, The Congo, Central African Republic, Equatorial Guinea, South Cameroon, and Gabon. This analysis, I believe, constitutes the first assessment of what was and is mentally healthy for people of African descent throughout the various regions of the continent, or in African Psychology, what is referred to as *ordered behavior*.

Although the science and practice of psychology in ancient times were fundamentally about the study of the soul or the spirit, these elements were never meant to be viewed as static entities. On the contrary, a proper ordering of the world and one's psyche required a movement and sustained momentum characterized by the alchemic notion of "being and becoming." The notion of "being" related to a conscious understanding of where one was at any given moment in time, in one's life. The notion of "becoming" recognized that humans have an innate desire to continue to grow and that growth represented the actualization of the transformative possibilities of the human spirit. Thus, elevated human consciousness (i.e., mental health) was related to a mastery of fundamental sets of knowledge and skill that signified a person's growth and development represented by engaging in the highest forms of human endeavor.

This process of growth, development, and mastery in ancient African Psychology has been illustrated by both Nobles (1986) and Akbar (1994); each described the various divisions of the psychic nature. In ancient Kemetic metaphysics, the psyche, or soul, comprised seven interrelated dimensions. First, the psyche was composed of the *KA*, or the physical structure of an individual's humanity. This body each individual inhabited, without spirit or energy, would deteriorate into those earthly elements from which it came at the end of one's life. The second dimension of the psyche was the *BA*, or the breath of life. This energy or life force was believed to be transmitted by the Creator and ancestors into each individual and was seen as the essence of all things that have life. The third dimension of the psyche was represented by the *KHABA*, which represented emotion and motion. *Motion* in this regard related to the natural order of things, including rhythmic patterns characterized by blood circulation.

The fourth dimension of the psyche was the *AKHU*, which represented the seat in intelligence or the capacity for thought and mental perception. It was characterized by judgment, analysis, and mental reflection. The fifth dimension is the *SEB*, or eternal soul. This element of the psyche was thought to manifest itself once an individual reached adolescence or puberty and was characterized by the self-creative power/ability to reproduce one's own kind. The sixth dimension of the psychic nature was the *PUTAH*, and it represented the union of the brain with the conscious mind. Differing from the capacity for thought, it was characterized by mental maturity. The seventh dimension of the psychic nature is known as the *ATMU*. It was considered the Divine or eternal soul, characterized by the breadth of everlasting life (energy, life force). As we come back around, in summary, to understand these dimension of the soul or psychic nature, Nobles (1986) and Akbar (1994) also have remind us and helped us understand that the KA is also thought of as a sum of all of the dimensions described earlier, enwrapping all of the various elements.

It is also important to understand that the seven dimensions just described were not separate domains but instead should be viewed as integral parts of a whole that functioned in an interrelated way. In essence, these elements of the psychic nature represent a unity between the human and the Divine and, at some level, maintain a reciprocal interdependence. In this regard, I mean to suggest that the human being is the form, whereas the spiritual energy is the force. Although the spiritual energy gives life and force to the material body, the human body provides a form for the force of life's energy, which is spirit, to manifest (Ani, 1980). In essence, this is what Myers (1988), Nobles (1986), Akbar (1994), Parham, (1993, 2002), Hilliard (1997), and others have discussed when characterizing life as a spiritual material union. This concept is fundamental to an African Psychology and foundational to the psychohistory and culture of African people.

Historical African Roots

To really gain an appreciation of African Psychology, it is important here to reinforce the need to view the discipline as a landscape that cuts across space and time. *Time*, of course, refers to reference points in ancient Kemet, historical Africa, and even contemporary African America. Space in this regard refers to the fact that the emotional tone and cultural worldview discussed earlier is not only anchored in the spaces of Kemetic (Egyptian) civilization, but can also be found throughout the entire African continent from ancient times through the present. Accordingly, what Black psychologists advance as an African-centered approach to mental health and psychology is reflective of perspectives that can be found in North, Central, South, East, and West Africa.

Grills (2002) provided an informative discussion of this idea by arguing that the African-centered perspective advanced by African scholars and thinkers across the Diaspora reflects a historical continuity, historical consciousness, and a cultural unity with respect to what it means to be African and, by extension, what constitutes ordered (i.e., mentally healthy) behavior. The essential features of this unity of thought and continuity of perspective reflect notions of self-definition, spirit and spirituality, the harmonious interrelationship between man and woman, the Divine, nature, the reality of metaphysical interconnectedness, and the importance of communal order and self-knowledge.

Grills and Ajei (2002) added to this discussion by highlighting, for example, the essential features of an Akan (Ghana, West Africa) conceptualization of the person. They described how the Akan system recognized God as the source of all being; that existence has both visible and invisible realms; that the universe contains a hierarchy of beings, including God, deities, ancestral spirits, humans, animals, and physical objects, which are all interconnected; and that the universe is endowed with varying degrees of force or power, which extends from the Creator. Bynum's (1999) work reinforces this perspective as he commented on the striking parallels between Egyptian cosmology and the West African Ifa worldview. He traced the concepts of energy and life force, the notion of vitalism, ideas of rhythm and natural order, notion of communal consciousness, and other values from their ancient Kemetic roots throughout various parts of the African continent and beyond.

This unity of thought across the continent is also reflected in the work of Fu-Kiau (1991). In his text, *Self Healing Power and Therapy* (which should be considered essential reading for those interested in conducting therapy with African American populations), he describes the Bantu–Kongo teaching of life describe the individual as spirit, the various realms of reality in which the spirit reigns, that human beings are seeds of divinely inspired possibility, the need for balance and harmony of energy in one's life, the innerconnectedness between all things in the universe, the importance of the collective, and that each person is endowed with a self-healing power.

Using this "unity of thought" as a conceptual template from which to view the psychohistory and culture of people of African descent, the principles that form the foundation of Black or African Psychology become much more crystallized. They include a belief that African Psychology is a dynamic manifestation of African-centered principles where these ideas are used in the understanding of ordered and disordered behaviors in people of African descent. Relying on the principle of harmony within the universe as the natural order of human experience, these core elements of an African-centered psychology include the following:

- The **spiritness** that permeates everything that exists in the universe,
- The notion that everything in the universe is **interconnected**,
- The idea that the **collective** is the most salient element of existence, and
- The idea that **self-knowledge** (know thyself) is the key to mental health. (Parham, 2002, p. xv)

Within this framework, it is easy to see how many of the major theorists in African American Psychology have anchored their theories in the worldview of an African-centered ideology. Baldwin (1986), for example, argued that African Psychology is a system of knowledge concerning the nature of the social universe from the perspective of African cosmology. He further argued that this culturally specific discipline seeks to uncover, articulate, operationalize, and apply principles of an African reality structured to understand various psychological phenomenon. Myers (1988) similarly argued that an Afrocentric conceptual analysis provides an "optimal" worldview from which to view the psychology of people of African descent. In her work, she discussed the notion of ancient Kemetic metaphysics, the union of the spiritual with the material, the relationship between individuals and the Divine, and the necessity of being clear about who one is at the core of his or her being. She went on to suggest that her theory is not relegated to African people alone in some sort of racial matching but rather represents a conceptual template that might be applicable across cultural groups.

Fundamental Principles and Questions

The discipline of African Psychology has provided a set of principles or core constructs that serve as a foundation from which to study and understand persons of African descent. In addition to principles such as culture, Ma'at, spirituality, consciousness, relationships, collective, and innerconnectedness, Fanon (1967) introduced us to three fundamental questions. These questions serve almost as an accountability loop for the discipline in that once the knowledge base has been established, there was a need to examine and explore the relationship between conscious recognition of an idea and how that principle was operationalized into the life space of each individual.

Fanon's three critical questions include (1) "Who am I?" (2) Am I who I say I am?" and (3) "Am I all I ought to be?" "Who am I?" is a question of identity, in challenging each person to understand who he or she is at the core of his or her being. It invites a deep exploration into each person's nature, essence, and character in the human family. The question of "Am I who I say I am?" is fundamentally a question of congruence or authenticity, in trying to ascertain the relationship between who people are and how they conduct their affairs within the geographical spaces they occupy. In other words, it is a question of do they practice what they preach? The question of "Am I all I ought to be?" is a question of actualizing potential. Here, each person is challenged to examine all of the talents and gifts with which he or she has been blessed and whether those gifts are being used to their fullest potential.

Fanon's (1967) questions provide an important conceptual template from which people can determine how each should respond to the reality of a particular situation or circumstance, and psychologists can determine whether those responses constitute ordered or disordered behavior from the perspective of an African-centered psychological worldview. For example, the man or woman who elevates the needs of his or her extended family members above his or her own needs, and derives satisfaction from attending to and caring for others who are very high maintenance, might be considered codependent, in an individually focused psychological template. Conversely, such a person might be perceived as living in harmony (congruent) with his or her own cultural dispositions where survival is much more collective and attending to the needs of the group or tribe is the essence of good character.

Perspectives That Helped African Psychology Lose Its Way

One perspective that helped African Psychology lose its way is *scientific colonialism*. The challenge of maintaining one's sanity or mental health rests with preserving one's sense of agency or power over a particular situation or circumstance. That ability to confront the inevitable challenges life throws at you, and to do so with confident assurance, is key to managing those dilemmas. The personal power referred to here has less to do with extreme financial resources or military might; instead, the power I speak about here has to do with defining and framing the discourse in ways that support one's perceptions of reality.

One of the ways I have observed persons of African descent giving away their power is in allowing others—in this case, primarily White society—to define and frame the way one should look at his or her circumstances. According to Nobles (1986), a situation in which one's ability to define and frame reality and make others respond to that definition as if it were their own is diminished or taken away is the essence of power. Similarly, the psychohistory of African Psychology has been forced to yield some of its power by allowing traditional European American psychology to frame the discipline, with African Psychology acting only as an invisible partner. This is the essence of Nobles's concept of scientific colonialism, whereby the process involving the political control of knowledge is carried out by a deliberate and sophisticated act of falsifying the production of information and ideas.

Social Pathology of American Life

Another factor that has helped African-centered psychology lose its way is the prevalence of a social pathology that contaminates the lives of people of African descent. Woodson (1933) was clear indeed when he commented that allowing another people to control the way one thinks will result in an adoption of an inferior status mentality even before one can be assigned to you by your oppressor. Perhaps no author captures for me the essence of America's contradictions regarding her citizens of African descent than that famed public intellectual Dr. Cornel West. His prophetic scholarship provides an intellectual flavor to a description of Black social misery that is unparalleled in our contemporary times. Among the many contributions he has authored, perhaps no piece is more descriptive of African Americans' ability to psychologically adapt to and confront the social pathology of American life than his essay titled "Black Strivings in a Twilight Civilization" (1999). Like Du Bois (1903), Woodson (1933), Ellison (1952), Elijah Muhammad (1965), and others, he articulates the conditions of Black suffering with an uncompromising clarity, describing America as a "chamber of Horrors." The horrors to which he speaks include the consistent and vicious attacks on Black people's beauty, intelligence, moral character, behavior, capability, and life itself. These are all elements that African/Black Psychology have spent a lifetime defending.

The reason why West's work is so profound is reflected in his ability to capture the essence of psychological adaptation in which people of African descent engage while attempting to carve out a slice of life for themselves. West speaks to the emotional tone of a people (ethos), introduced earlier, who construct for themselves affective and even cognitive spaces from which to pull on the reservoir of energy used to help them cope with life's circumstances and absurdities. *Black Strivings*, as he called them, are creative and complex structures of meaning, purpose, and feeling that allowed people of African descent to both maintain their sanity in the context of insane conditions as well as carve out for themselves strategies to sustain their needs for growth, regeneration, and self-preservation. All the while, these strategies are birthed from the womb of African psychological and cultural traditions that help them improvise on, transcend, and sometimes transform their social circumstance. We refer here, for example, to the art forms of African invention of singing the blues when times were hardest; of singing gospel as a way of keeping the faith and keeping hope alive, and of using gallows humor in comedy as a way to laugh to keep from crying. All of these help to create a cathartic effect similar to that which Black people experience in their therapy sessions with mental health professionals. This is the essence of a Black Psychology perspective, where ideas of self, recognitions of where and who one is in the world, and strategies to help sustain some movement and momentum in the face of adversity are all part of normal and ordered behavior for a people whose environmental circumstances have been so hostile. This ability to cope and adapt, to seek truth in the midst of falsehood and deceit, to find hope in the midst of despair, to maintain one's sense of African consciousness in the face of hostile threat, and to "keep on keepin' on" despite life's hardships is characteristic of the most profound display of African Psychology in action.

Balancing Two Competing Worldviews

My references to the work of West (1999) and others are no accident, because the study of the psyche in people of African descent is not only an exploration of the psyche's composition but also a study in adaptation. Cross (1991, 2001) has helped illustrate this point as he argued that the psyche of each individual interacts with the sociocultural environment, which helps to shape the characteristic ways in which people adjust to their surroundings. Within the course of normal or ordered development, each individual should engage with an environmental space that allows for a nurturing and supportive experience. In that context, individual personalities blossom into a full expression of each person's humanity. The psychohistory of African Psychology has been at the forefront of helping our discipline and the rest of the world understand that.

Unfortunately, the dynamics of White supremacy and other oppressive forces conspire to deprive many African Americans of an opportunity to grow, develop, and prosper in ways that conform to patterns that are normal and ordered for people of African descent. When this occurs, individuals react in ways that are ultimately functional but sometimes maladaptive. This is certainly true for people who experience some level of anxiety in attempting to cope with the duality of navigating at least two culturally different worldviews.

With regard to identity states, Du Bois (1903) is perhaps best known for labeling this duality, whereby life becomes an intricate dance of maneuvering in two worlds: one White and American and the other Black and African centered. His classic text *The Souls of Black Folk* ably articulates the challenges of being a person of African descent in an American experience that has proved harsh, destructively discriminatory, brutally oppressive, and anything but supportive for most Black people. Consequently, there should be no surprise that Du Bois's work has been so influential in the articulation of this struggle for identity congruence in persons of African descent. In some respects, Du Bois's work underscores the dilemma of what it means to be Black in America. What is interesting about Du Bois's work, however, is not simply the intellectual constructs he advances (e.g., the notion of "double consciousness"), or his belief in a "talented tenth" notion scholars are fond of quoting. For me, Du Bois's life is a mirror in which is reflected the deep pain, psychic scars, and behavioral blisters of trying himself to successfully confront the most fundamental question of that day and this: "To be African or not to be"? In that struggle are the dueling sentiments of courage and fear, despair and optimism. On one hand, he courageously argued for the redress of the problems of all Black people, while simultaneously fearing that the masses of Black people were incapable of participating in their own liberation struggle, hence his "talented tenth" notion. On the other, his own upbringing instigated in him a sense of hope and optimism about a people's ability to rise above their current circumstance while ultimately giving in to a personal climate of despair about the race condition in America and the nation's refusal to confront the issues openly and honestly. This despair ultimately influenced his decision to leave the United States and establish a new home in Ghana, West Africa.

Within Du Bois's (1903) work, one can see the psychic struggle to both achieve social progress in ways that do not prove too antagonistic to the broader White community while simultaneously staying true to a legacy of African history and culture that in spite of its challenges never forgot that being African was at the core of human authenticity. Du Bois's struggle, in some respects, is no different than the one African-descent people in contemporary America must face. They receive very little validation and affirmation for being their authentic Black selves. They love their Blackness at the core of their being, but they learn to disguise it in certain situations and circumstances so as not to antagonize or make uncomfortable their White colleagues, neighbors, and/or social acquaintances. They wear it as a badge of cultural pride and yet realize that doing so might antagonize their culturally different colleagues, resulting in restricted access to opportunities in the larger White world. They struggle with both self-imposed and socially imposed notions of invisibility. They confront what I (Parham, 1989) described as the essential question of how one maintains a sense of cultural integrity in a world that neither supports nor affirms one's humanity as a person of African descent. It is this struggle that is so clearly captured in the Nigrescence writings of C. Thomas (1971); Cross (1971, 1991); Parham (1989); Cross, Parham, and Helms (1998); Spenser and Markstrom-Adams (1990); Stevenson (1995), and others, as they sought to describe the dynamics associated with the identity resolution process. African Psychology has devoted considerable time to this area, and I would expect that to continue into the short- and long-term future.

Equally interesting is the cyclical way in which themes of struggling with identity resolution, notions of invisibility, and psychological adaptation continue to appear on the landscape of the study of the psychology of people of African descent. Like Ellison's (1952) *Invisible Man*, A. J. Franklin's (2006) analysis of the "invisibility syndrome" is right on target in describing both how society views persons of African descent and how they in turn experience the chronic assaults on their humanity. These assaults, or *microaggressions*, as they were characterized by the psychological (A. J. Franklin, 1999) and psychiatric (Pierce, 1988) literature, further enhance the psychic tension and struggle African Americans face in seeking recognition, valuation, and validation of both who they are in the world and how they participate in their familial, social, occupational, academic, and even religious endeavors. The psychology of people of African descent continues to chronicle this struggle in the books, monographs, and journal articles.

Another important contribution to the African/Black Psychology literature that is beginning to gather some momentum is Leary's (2005) work, *Post Traumatic Slave Syndrome*. In it, she chronicled the role that a history of slavery, racism, oppression, denigration, and social misery has played on persons of African descent. She goes on to explain how patterns of psychological adaptation and survival influenced by that history have been handed down to succeeding generations who continue to think, feel, and behave in ways that are both consistent with generations past and indicative of a psychological maladjustment that is detrimental to their future. The book sought to provide the reader with greater insight into the African American psyche and the keys to aligning African thoughts, emotions, and behaviors with what is considered culturally congruent with the best of African traditions. It also provided the research arm of the discipline with a challenge to explore how this posttraumatic slave syndrome impacts various aspects of African people's lives. It also provided the more applied arm of the discipline with another diagnostic category with which to assess the ways in which psychic debilitations continue to plague persons of African descent.

AFRICAN PSYCHOLOGY: RECENTERING ONE'S ANALYSIS

One of the more important perspectives to keep in mind when reviewing the field of African Psychology is the idea of *within-group variability*. This concept, while often used in discussions of identity development, has applicability in analyzing the discipline of African/Black Psychology as well. Particular attention is paid to this idea here because of the temptation to categorize African American people—and, by extension, African-centered psychology—as homogeneous. This would be a serious mistake, for just as diversity exists among persons of

African descent, so too does diversity of thought reign within the discipline. Even as the various racial designation labels (colored, Negro, Black, Afro-American, African American) have transcended the last four to five decades in the Black community, so too has the psychohistory of African Psychology experiences a parallel transformation.

There are some theories and theorists who, in analyzing the psychology of Black people, would consider the use of traditional psychology's norms and paradigms as proper and legitimate. These scholars argue for a universality of psychological and personality constructs that should be applied equally across samples being studied (Jenkins, 1982). Jenkins's (1982) well-thought-out textbook and application of the humanistic approach to understanding the psychology of people of African descent is an example that comes to mind. Some scholars, on the other hand, would insist that to use Eurocentric perspectives in the analysis of Black psychological functioning is a major error, arguing instead for an analysis that is more African centered in orientation (Akbar, 1992; Kambon, 1992; Nobles, 1986). There is perhaps even a third school of thought, if you will, that would argue for a need to synthesize the two perspectives, taking the best of both into account when analyzing psychological functioning, as Belgrave and Allison (2006) did in their most recent work.

From my standpoint, the question is not simply one of preference but one of perspective. Traditional psychology has a sordid past that has proved itself biased with respect to analyzing the spiritual, intellectual, emotional, biological, and behavioral perspectives of people of African descent. The limitation here is not simply in the way Eurocentric theories have been applied to African-descent people by biased behavioral scientists but also in the construct or theory itself that is normed on a different cultural group. However, much of the early scholarship around the discipline of Black Psychology was very reactionary in its posture, as theorists sought to dispel some of the racist ideology advanced by traditional psychology. Although the intent here was and is honorable, the result potentially leads to the creation of a "Black norm" that does not engage the study of the psychology of people of African descent from a deep structured analysis and uses analyses of current Black behaviors and thoughts in certain situations as "normal" for Black people. As a consequence, Parham et al. (1999) argued, as Akbar (1992, 1994) did before us, that analysis of current psychological functioning of people of African descent helps us understand ways in which people have adapted to America's "chamber of horrors" but may not be indicative of what is normal and healthy for people of African-descent from their own indigenous cultural worldview. Thus, the weighting of my scholarship over the past several years has been biased toward trying to understand healthy psychological functioning from the level of the cultural deep structure, and I would argue that this is a direction in which African American Psychology needs to continue as they chart a course for the discipline's future.

Conclusion

The African American psychohistory and culture has left to the world a rich legacy of scholarship and information from which to draw. Crossing the vast recesses of space and time, this knowledge and wisdom have made the world better by increasing our exposure to new and alternate perspectives, enhancing our understanding of ideas and constructs previously misunderstood, and illuminating critical elements of information that heretofore had been rendered dormant by traditional psychology's collusion with an ideology of White supremacy and a conceptual shackling that refused to venture out of its own cultural worldview to understand people from other racial, ethnic, and cultural groups.

The utility of a body of knowledge, however, does not rest with its mere existence. African American Psychology as a science and art dates back thousands of years, so time is certainly not the issue. Instead, the utility of this knowledge base rests with the ability of contemporary generations of scholars and researchers to harness the information and use it to open minds, enlighten intellects, and change lives. One of the best examples of this commitment and practice is reflected in the work of Fred Phillips and Laurence Jackson, at the Progressive Life Centers in the greater Washington, D.C., and Maryland areas. Phillips's NTU Psychotherapy model is an African-centered approach to therapy and treatment that is used to deliver a broad range of treatment services, which include individual, group, and family therapy; treatment of youth in the foster care system; case management for community residents in need of social services; and a range of culturally specific programming designed to teach participants knowledge and skills that can help them lead more healthy and functional lives. Furthermore, NTU therapy utilizes the principles of Nguzo Saba as guidelines for harmonious living. Basic principles of NTU therapy include: Harmony; Balance; Interconnectedness; Cultural Awareness; and Authenticity. The role of the NTU therapist is based on a spiritual relationship with the client system since NTU therapy recognizes that the healing process is a natural process in which the therapist assists the client system to rediscover natural alignment. The five phases of NTU psychotherapy are (1) Harmony, (2) Awareness, (3) Alignment, (4) Actualize, and (5) Synthesis (Jackson, Gregory, & Davis, 2004; Phillips, 1990).

Another equally powerful example is reflected in the work of Dr. Michael Connor, who developed the Role Of Men program as a way of teaching responsible fathering to African American men in the southern California area. His program provides outreach and recruitment, screening and selection, therapy, as well as training and follow-up for the men involved with the program, as he seeks to render African-centered psychological principles relevant is helping to build stronger Black families and stronger father–child connections (Connor & White, 2006). Indeed, this is African-centered psychology in action.

I developed another innovative approach to working with African American youth (Parham, 2006), by introducing the Bakari Project. The model, influenced by African-centered ideology and African Psychology principles, seeks to instruct and guide youth in the development of responsible adulthood attitudes and behaviors. The model is designed as a didactic and experiential teaching tool, using six areas of mastery taught across 4 years of programmatic intervention. The program is utilized by The 100 Black Men of Orange County, California, and the College Bound program in the greater Los Angeles, California, area, and it is being utilized in working with adjudicated youth in the criminal justice systems in San Luis Obispo, California, and New York City areas.

The application of African-centered psychological principles can also be useful in issues of both educating and socializing African American students at all grade levels. The reports on the educational disparities in achievement, promotion, college eligibility, and dropout rates for African American children and adolescents, when compared with their other ethnic and racial counterparts, continue to be alarming. However, I am convinced that one of the major keys to addressing this issue is confronting the mental shackles that conceptually incarcerate the thinking of young African American people. It is there that the struggle to instill pride in their cultural beingness, enhance their sense of efficacy, expose them to their divine talents and gifts, correct their often-distorted sense of identity, and create a sense of hope and optimism about their futures, must be waged.

The social engineering aspects of African-centered psychology must continue to wrestle with the social pathology of racism, sexism, classism, and other oppression and use its intellectual pulpit to advocate for continued and sustained social change. What was true decades ago is still true today: that much of the psychic debilitations African American clients in therapy experience is less about an intrapsychic disturbance and more about reactions to social cultural and environmental disorder. As a consequence, I have continuously argued that therapeutic interventions must be focused on helping clients navigate their way to more empowered lives while also addressing the social ills that so impact their ability to support and sustain their own personal growth and development (Parham et al., 1999; White & Parham 1990).

Social engineering and advocacy strategies must also be directed at society's institutions that have major impact of the lives of people of African descent. One of those institutions that is in critical need of change is the U.S. criminal justice system and prison industrial complex. In light of the extraordinary numbers of people of African descent in the system, particularly those who are eligible for release back into the communities, African Psychology must design structured interventions that rehabilitate the psyches and reorient the consciousness of prior offenders, such that they become more fully functioning, productive, and prosperous members of their community. We cannot just treat those who have made mistakes as disposable capital. We as African-centered psychologists cannot be a healing presence in our communities if we lose the capacity to believe in the transformative possibilities of the human spirit or that people with challenging pasts can elevate themselves to rightful places of rulership and mastery over their own circumstances.

Finally, the social engineering responsibilities of the discipline must extend to agencies that deliver less than adequate health care to community populations; federal, state, and municipal governments that provide social services to children and families in need; print and electronic media outlets that present society with distorted and irresponsible images of people of African descent; and to the community institutions that attend to the socialization of children, adolescents, and adults in ways that do not validate and affirm the dignity and humanity of each member of the human family.

NOTE

1. *Maafa* is a Swahili term popularized in America by Marimba Ani (1994). It is defined as a great disaster of death and destruction that is beyond human comprehension and convention. The chief feature of the Maafa is the systematic denial of the humanity of people of African descent, which occurs in many ways and across numerous situational circumstances.

REFERENCES

Akbar, N. (1992). *Chains and images of psychological slavery*. Tallahassee, FL: Mind Productions.
Akbar, N. (1994). *Light from ancient Africa*. Tallahassee, FL: Mind Productions.
Ani, M. (1980). *Let the circle be unbroken*. New York: Nkonimfo Publications.
Ani, M. (1994). *Yurigu: An African centered critique of European cultural thought and behavior*. Trenton, NJ: African World Press.
Asante, M. (2000). *The Egyptian philosophers: Ancient African voices from Imhotep to Akhenaten*. Chicago: African American Images.
Baldwin, J. A. (1986). Black Psychology: Issues and synthesis. *Journal of Black Studies, 16*, 235–249.
Banks, J. A., & Grambs, J. D. (1972). *Black self concept*. New York: McGraw-Hill.
Belgrave, F. Z., & Allison, K. W. (2006). *African American Psychology: From Africa to America*. Thousand Oaks, CA: Sage.
Bennett, L., Jr. (1966). *Before the Mayflower: History of Black America*. Chicago: Johnson.
Billingsley, A. (1968). *Black families in White America*. New York: Prentice Hall.
Bynum, E. B. (1999). *The African unconscious: Roots of ancient mysticism and modern psychology*. New York: Teachers College Press.
Carter, R. T., & Helms, J. E. (1987). Relationship of Black values orientations to racial identity attitudes. *Measurement and Evaluation in Counseling Development, 19*, 185–195.
Clarke, J. H. (1996). *John Henrik Clarke: A great and mighty walk* [Documentary]. New York: The Cinema Guild.
Connor, M. E., & White, J. L. (2006). *Black fathers: An invisible presence in America*. Mahwah, NJ: Lawrence Erlbaum.
Cross, W. E. (1971). The Negro to Black conversion experience. *Black World, 209*, 13–27.
Cross, W. E. (1980). Models of psychological Nigrescence: A literature review. In R. L. Jones (Ed.), *Black Psychology* (2nd ed., pp. 81–98). New York: Harper & Row.
Cross, W. E. (1991). *Shades of Black: Diversity in African American identity*. Philadelphia: Temple University Press.
Cross, W. E. (2001). Encountering Nigrescence. In J. G. Ponterotto, J. M. Casas, L. A. Suzuki, & C. M. Alexander (Eds.), *Handbook of multicultural counseling* (2nd ed., pp. 30–44). Thousand Oaks, CA: Sage.
Cross, W. E., Parham, T. A., & Helms, J. E. (1998). Nigrescence revisited: Theory and research. In R. L. Jones (Ed.), *African American identity development* (pp. 3–71). Hampton, VA: Cobb & Henry.
Diop, C. A. (1974). *The African origins of civilizations: Myth or reality*. Westport, CT: Lawrence, Hill & Company.
Du Bois, W. E. B. (1903). *The souls of Black folks*. New York: Signet Classic.
Ellison, R. (1952). *The invisible man*. New York: Random House.
Fanon, F. (1967). *Black skin, White masks*. New York: Grove Press.
Fernald, L. D., & Fernald, P. S. (1978). *Introduction to psychology* (4th ed.). Boston: Houghton Mifflin.
Franklin, A. J. (1999). Invisibility syndrome and racial identity development in psychotherapy and counseling African American men. *The Counseling Psychologist, 29*, 761–793.
Franklin, A. J. (2006). *From brotherhood to manhood: How Black men rescue their relationships and dreams from the invisibility syndrome*. Hoboken, NJ: Wiley.
Franklin, J. H. (1974). *From slavery to freedom*. New York: Knopf.
Fu-Kiau, K. K. (1991). *Self healing power and therapy: Old teachings from Africa*. New York: Vantage Press.

Grills, C. (2002). African-centered psychology: Basic principles. In T. A. Parham (Ed.), *Counseling persons of African descent: Raising the bar of practitioner competence* (pp. 10–24). Thousand Oaks, CA: Sage.

Grills, C., & Ajei, M. (2002). African-centered conceptualizations of self and consciousness: The Akan model. In T. A. Parham (Eds), *Counseling persons of African descent: Raising the bar of practitioner competence* (pp. 75–99). Thousand Oaks, CA: Sage.

Guthrie, R. V. (1976). *Even the rat was white: A historical view of psychology*. New York: Harper & Row.

Guthrie, R. V. (1998). *Even the rat was white: A historical view of psychology* (2nd ed.). Needham Heights, MA: Allyn & Bacon.

Hilliard, A. G. (1997). *SBA: The reawakening of the African mind*. Gainesville, FL: Marare Press.

Jackson, L., Gregory, H., & Davis, M. (2004). NTU psychotherapy and African American youth. In J. R. Ancis (Ed.), *Culturally responsive interventions: Innovative approaches to working with diverse populations* (pp. 49–70). New York: Brunner-Routledge.

Jenkins, A. H. (1982). *The psychology of the Afro-American: A humanistic approach*. New York: Pergamon Press.

Jones, F. (1972). The Black psychologist as consultant and therapist. In R. L. Jones (Ed.), *Black Psychology*. New York: Harper & Row.

Jones, R. L. (1972). *Black Psychology*. New York: Harper & Row.

Jones, R. L. (1980). *Black Psychology* (2nd ed.). New York: Harper & Row.

Kambon, K. K. (1992). *The African personality in America: An African centered framework*. Tallahassee, FL: Nubian Nation.

Karenga, M. (1990). *The book of coming forth by day: The ethics of the declaration of innocence*. Los Angeles: University of Sankore Press.

Khatib, S. (1980). Black studies and the study of Black people: Reflections on the distinctive characteristics of Black Psychology. In R. L. Jones (Ed.), *Black Psychology* (2nd ed., pp. 48–55). New York: Harper & Row.

Leary, J. D. (2005). *Post traumatic slave syndrome*. Milwaukie, OR: Uptone Press.

McAdoo, H. P. (1981). *Black families*. Beverly Hills, CA: Sage.

Muhammad, E. (1965). *Message to a Black man*. Chicago: Muhammad Mosque #2.

Myers, L. J. (1988). *Understanding the Afrocentric worldview: Introduction to an optimal psychology*. Dubuque, IA: Kendall Hunt.

Nobles, W. W. (1972). African philosophy as a foundation for Black Psychology. In R. L. Jones (Ed.), *Black Psychology* (pp. 18–32). New York: Harper & Row.

Nobles, W. W. (1986). *African Psychology*. Oakland, CA: Institute for Black Family Life and Culture.

Obenga, T. (1996). *Icons of Maat*. Philadelphia: The Source Editions.

Parham, T. A. (1989). Cycles of psychological Nigrescence. *The Counseling Psychologist, 17*, 187–226.

Parham, T. A. (1993). *Psychological storms: The African American struggle for identity*. Chicago: African American Images.

Parham, T. A. (Ed.). (2002). *Counseling persons of African descent: Raising the bar of practitioner competence*. Thousand Oaks, CA: Sage.

Parham, T. A. (2006). *The Bakari Project* [DVD]. Irvine, CA: KenTay Productions.

Parham, T. A., & Helms, J. E. (1981). Influence of Black students' racial identity attitudes on preferences for counselor race. *Journal of Counseling Psychology, 28*, 250–256.

Parham, T. A., & Helms, J. E. (1985). Relation of racial identity to self-actualization and affective states in Black students. *Journal of Counseling Psychology, 32*, 431–440.

Parham, T. A., White, J. L., & Ajamu, A. (1999). *The psychology of Blacks: An African centered perspective*. Englewood Cliffs, NJ: Prentice Hall.

Phillips, F. (1990). NTU psychotherapy: An Afrocentric approach. *Journal of Black Psychology, 17*, 215–222.

Pierce, C. (1988). Stress in the workplace. In A. F. Coner-Edwards and & J. Spurlock (Eds.), *Black families in crisis: The middle class* (pp. 27–34). New York: Brunner/Mazel.

Pugh, R. (1972). *The psychology of the Black experience*. Monterey, CA: Brooks/Cole.

Spenser, M. B., & Markstrom-Adams, C. (1990). Identity process among racial and ethnic minority children in America. *Child Development, 61*, 290–310.

Stevenson, H. C. (1995). Relationship of adolescent perceptions of racial socialization to racial identity. *Journal of Black Psychology, 21*, 49–70.

Sue, S. (1978). *Ethnic minority research: Trends and directions*. Paper presented at the National Conference on Minority Group Alcohol, Drug Abuse, and Mental Health Issues, Denver, CO, May 22–24.

Thomas, A., & Sillen, S. (1972). *Racism in psychiatry*. Secaucus, NJ: Citadel Press.

Thomas, C. (1971). *Boys no more*. Beverly Hills, CA: Glencoe Press.

Thomas, C. (1972). Psychologist, psychology, and the Black community. In R. L. Jones (Ed.), *Black Psychology* (pp. 375–383). New York: Harper & Row.

Van Sertima, I. (1976). *They came before Columbus: The African presence in ancient Africa.* New York: Random House.

West, C. (1999). *The Cornel West reader.* New York: Basic Cervitas Books.

White, J. L. (1972). Toward a Black Psychology. In R. L. Jones (Ed.), *Black Psychology* (pp. 43–50). New York: Harper & Row.

White, J. L. (1984). *The psychology of Blacks.* New York: Prentice Hall.

White, J. L. & Parham, T. A. (1990). *The psychology of Blacks: An African American perspective* (2nd ed.). Upper Saddle River, NJ: Prentice Hall.

White, J. L., Parham, W. D., & Parham, T. A. (1980). Black Psychology: The Afro-American tradition as a unifying force for traditional psychology. In R. L. Jones (Ed.), *Black Psychology* (2nd ed., pp. 56-66). New York: Harper & Row.

Williams, C. (1974). *The destruction of Black civilization: Great issues of a race 4500 B.C. to 2000 A.D.* Chicago: Third World Press.

Williams, R. L. (1972). Abuses and misuses of testing Black children. In R. L. Jones (Ed.), *Black Psychology* (pp. 77–91). New York: Harper & Row.

Williams, R. L., & Mitchell, H. (1980). The testing game. In R. L. Jones (Ed.), *Black Psychology* (2nd ed., pp. 186–195). New York: Harper & Row.

Woodson, C. G. (1933). *The miseducation of the Negro.* Trenton, NJ: African World Press.

2

SANKOFA

History of and Aspirations for Black Psychology Through the Eyes of Our Elders

M. NICOLE COLEMAN AND ADANNA J. JOHNSON

It was 40 years ago that a group of African American psychologists at the 1968 annual meeting of the American Psychological Association (APA) expressed their outrage and dissatisfaction with the current state of affairs in White-dominated, mainstream psychology. These pioneers had the fortitude to demand changes in the operations of APA and the noble vision to develop their own organization of Black psychologists. The primary mission of the Association of Black Psychologists (ABPsi) would be to address the psychological needs of Black people throughout the Diaspora from a perspective that honors and respects African and African American culture. In this chapter, we recount the vibrant—and at times, turbulent—history of the field of Black Psychology provided through the oral histories of five prominent elders.

Sankofa is an Akan term that references the sentiment of looking back in order to go forward. It is rooted in the notion that knowing one's history is fundamental to the proper orientation of one's future. The notion of Sankofa also implies that all we do is interconnected and cyclical. We embraced this perspective in shaping the focus of this chapter. Moreover, we synthesized the historical information provided by each elder by reflecting on the lived experiences and the wisdom each shared. As such, this historical perspective is more of a contextual accounting of Black Psychology based on five biographical interviews rather than a detailed chronological one. We chose this historical accounting because we were interested in learning about the rich experiences of those who have been so instrumental in shaping the discipline of Black Psychology. Learning about the circumstances, challenges, and supports that shaped their professional development would also allow us to learn about the forces that shaped the discipline as a whole. We refer readers to previously published volumes that include an exhaustive recounting of the development of Black Psychology, including Guthrie (2003); Jones (2004); and Black, Spence, and Omari (2004).

Specifically, we interviewed Dr. Janet Helms, Dr. Linda James Myers, Dr. Joseph White, Dr. Daniel Williams, and Dr. Robert Williams, inquiring about their professional experiences, personal reflections, and hopes for the future of Black Psychology. We selected these individuals because of their profound, long-standing influence on the discipline as academicians, practitioners, and university administrators. They have been hailed as the most renowned scholar of racial identity measurement and theory, the innovator of optimal psychology, the "father of Black Psychology," an expert clinician and forensic psychologist, and "Dr. Ebonics," respectively. In our conversations with these prominent psychologists we sought to discover, from their unique perspectives, what Black Psychology, as a distinct discipline, is and where the discipline should be heading.

To that end, we asked each of our distinguished interviewees to share their professional journey, reflecting on where they started as early professionals to where they are currently with respect to their primary roles and responsibilities as professionals. In reflecting on their unique journeys, we asked them what had been specific supports of and challenges to their professional development. We also asked each of them to intimate their thoughts about their respective noteworthy contributions to the field. We have synthesized the information from each of these interviews and present them here. More germane to this volume, we asked each distinguished elder to define Black Psychology and to identify future directions of Black Psychology over the next 10 years. We first provide a brief biography of each of these illustrious elders, followed by an integrated discussion of their professional journeys. Then, we share their reflections on what Black Psychology is, followed by an integrated discussion of their desires for and opinions about the future goals and direction of the discipline. The chapter concludes with our specific recommendations of avenues and strategies for bringing those future goals and direction into fruition.

Elder Biographies

Dr. Janet Helms

Janet Helms received her PhD in counseling psychology from Iowa State University in 1975. Currently, she is the Augustus Long Professor of Counseling Psychology and is founder and director of The Institute for the Study and Promotion of Race and Culture at Boston College. In addition to this role, Dr. Helms also serves as the president-elect for Division 17, the Society for Counseling Psychology, in the APA. Dr. Helms specializes in the areas of racial identity, psychological testing and assessment, and racial and cultural counseling and psychotherapy.

Dr. Helms is most well known in the field of psychology for her distinctive work on Black and White racial identity development theory and research. Her proliferation as a scholar has led to more than 60 theoretical and empirical articles and 4 books on the topics of racial identity and cultural influences on assessment and counseling practice. Her 1992 book, *A Race Is a Nice Thing to Have: A Guide to a White Person or Understanding the White Persons in Your Life*, is one of the most popular titles in the area of White racial identity. In 2007, she was recognized as a Distinguished Psychologist by ABPsi for her influential work on Black racial identity.

Dr. Linda James Myers

Linda James Myers received her PhD in clinical psychology from The Ohio State University (OSU) in 1975. Currently, she serves as the executive director of The Center for Optimal Thought and holds dual professor positions at OSU and The New College of California. Dr. Myers's scholarship focuses on moral, spiritual, and identity development and the inclusion of traditional healing practices in psychotherapeutic processes. She is best known for her work in the development of a theory of optimal psychology and her theory of divine consciousness grounded in the wisdom tradition of African deep thought.

Dr. Myers is a past president of ABPsi (1990) and received their highest honor for excellence in research and scholarship, having been named Distinguished Psychologist in 1992. She has received numerous accolades in her professional career, including the Winter Roundtable on Cross-Cultural Psychology and Education Social Justice Action Award in 2007. She has published many books, including *Understanding an Afrocentric World View: Introduction to an Optimal Psychology* (1988, 1992) and *Blessed Assurance: Deep Thought and Meditations in the Tradition and Wisdom of Our Ancestors* (2004).

Dr. Joseph White

Joseph White received his PhD in child clinical psychology from Michigan State University in

1961. He is currently professor emeritus of psychology and psychiatry at the University of California, Irvine, and has been retired since 1994. Dr. White's scholarship focuses on the instruction, consultation, and practice in the areas of African American studies and cross-cultural programming. As part of his continual professional consultation, he is a member of the Board of Trustees of The Menninger Foundation in Houston, Texas, and a consultant to several colleges and to a comprehensive health care system.

Dr. White became the first licensed African American clinical psychologist in the state of California in the early 1960s. In addition, he was one of the founding members of ABPsi and has remained an active member of that organization throughout its existence. Dr. White has become well known in the field for his work as a teacher, mentor, administrator, clinical supervisor, writer, consultant, and practicing psychologist. Known by some in the field as the "father of Black Psychology," Dr. White has authored a number of articles and four books in the area of African American and ethnic psychology, including two editions of *The Psychology of Blacks*.

Dr. Daniel Williams

Daniel Williams received his PhD in clinical psychology from St. John's University in 1968. Currently, Dr. D. Williams has an active private practice in New Jersey and serves on the executive board of the New Jersey chapter of ABPsi. Most of Dr. D. Williams's career has focused on teaching, clinical practice, professional service, and social activism. He has been a licensed, practicing psychologist since 1972 and became certified by the American Board of Professional Psychology in 1977. In addition, Dr. D. Williams taught at Montclair State University in New Jersey for more than 20 years; he developed its first Affirmative Action plan. This eventually led to the university's development of the Educational Opportunity Office.

Dr. D. Williams became a member of ABPsi in 1970 and has been an influential and active part of the organization since that time. Recently, he served as an Elder of Elders at the national level for the organization. Notably, he served as president of ABPsi in 1980; he was also the founding president of the New Jersey chapter and served as the chapter president five times. Throughout his career, Dr. D. Williams has provided expert testimony as a forensic psychologist numerous times. In his role as the National President of ABPsi, Dr. D. Williams and his wife were invited to the White House by then-President Jimmy Carter and First Lady Rosalynn Carter. The invitation was extended because of the President's decision to sign the Mental Health Systems Act of 1980 into law.

Dr. Robert L. Williams

Robert L. Williams received his PhD in clinical psychology from Washington University in Saint Louis, Missouri, in 1961. Currently, Dr. R. L. Williams has been retired for almost 15 years. He retired as professor of African American Studies from Washington University after being recruited there to develop their African American Studies program almost 30 years ago. Since his retirement, Dr. R. L. Williams has continued to focus on his writing and scholarship. He specializes in the areas of cultural bias in testing, racism, race relations, Black language, and program evaluation. Dr. R. L. Williams is a founding member of ABPsi and served as the organization's president in 1969. During his tenure as president, he began a number of initiatives that still have an impact on the field of Black Psychology today. Most notable of these was his "10-Point Program," which outlined the need for and strategies to increase the enrollment of Black students in graduate psychology programs.

However, Dr. R. L. Williams is most well known for coining the term *Ebonics* and developing the Black Intelligence Test of Cultural Homogeneity (1972). He was asked to provide expert testimony to a U.S. Senate Congressional Panel in 1997 about his groundbreaking research on Ebonics, Black children's learning processes, intelligence testing, and cultural bias in testing. In addition, he has published more than 60 professional articles and books; his most recent publication is the book *Racism Learned at an Early Age Through Racial Scripting* (2007).

Contextual Factors

Black Psychology has been shaped by external social and political forces since its beginning. In the interviews, each of the elders shared with us how the social and political context of the time shaped their career paths, their specific interests in Black Psychology, and their respective worldviews on Blacks throughout the Diaspora. Moreover, these specific worldviews have had a significant influence on their overlapping yet distinct definitions of the goals and functions of Black Psychology, their assessments of the noteworthy advances in the field, and their respective suggestions and hopes for the future of the discipline. In this section, we highlight some of the salient contextual factors shared in the interviews. Although there are nuances in each individual's definition of Black Psychology, there seems to be consensus that the inception of the ABPsi in 1968 was one of the most significant events in defining the discipline. Although we use this marker as a point in designating the formal inception of Black Psychology, we want to note that Black scholars had long been present in the field of psychology. Furthermore, and of great significance, we give credence to the wisdom of the healing traditions of Africa that included addressing issues of the mind long before the notion of Western psychology began to evolve as a science. In particular, we highlight that Black people in the United States have continued to use these African traditions to persevere through the horrors of the Maafa (the transatlantic slave trade), Jim Crow laws, the Civil Rights Movement, up to the present.

During the 1960s, the primary psychological models that were used to define, and purportedly explain, but served to functionally limit, the experiences of Black people were the *deficit* or *deficiency models*. In essence, these models proposed that Black people were deficient in a number of domains, including intelligence and achievement, and even in terms of social structures when compared with Whites a group (Parham, White, & Ajamu, 2000). One of the most insidious ways these models shaped the experiences of our interviewees was the widely accepted notion, by mainstream psychology, of the intellectual inferiority of Black people. During this period, there was a focus among Black scholars in psychology on addressing the literary, philosophical, and scientific biases of Western psychology. Specifically, Black scholars challenged the racist assertions and "science" that pathologized people of African descent and other non-European ethnic groups as being less intelligent as well as animalistic and degenerate.

However, even earlier in the 20th century, Black psychologists met at the American Teachers' Association meeting, in Tuskegee, Alabama, in 1938 (Guthrie, 2003). During this time, the majority of Black psychologists were employed as teachers, and they were angry and discontent about the unfair and unequal treatment of Black psychologists. They then held a 2-day psychology program at the convention, which yielded valuable discussion about the needs of the profession. Unfortunately, the organization did not continue beyond this meeting because the beginning of World War II directed attention away from the organization's cause (Guthrie, 2003). The founding of the ABPsi in 1968 was the first time since the 1930s that Black psychologists from throughout the nation gathered to address the needs of this group of professionals and the mental health of Blacks in the United States. The student-led rebellion at the 1968 meeting of the APA, fueled by a consistent frustration that they did not have a voice in the broader field of psychology, subsequently led to the founding of the ABPsi. For a detailed accounting of the history of ABPsi, we refer readers to B. H. Williams's doctoral dissertation, *Coming Together: The Founding of the Association of Black Psychologists* (1997).

Two of the interviewees for this chapter were present at the 1968 APA meeting: Drs. Joseph White and Robert Williams. The other psychologists present at the founding were Joseph Awkward, Wiley Bolden, Alvis Caliman, Norman Chambers, Harold Dent, Aubrey Escoffery, Florence Farley, Jane Fort, George Franklin, Alvin Goins, Robert Green, Robert V. Guthrie, William Harvey, Leslie Hicks, Anna Jackson, Walter Jacobs, Adelbert Jenkins, Reginald Jones, Melvin King, Lonnie Mitchell, Dalmas Taylor, David Terrell, and Ernestine Thomas. Against this backdrop, two of our interviewees were pursuing their doctoral degrees and starting their careers during the height of the Civil Rights Movement. Dr. R. L. Williams recalled that it was a surreal experience for many of the staff when he began working as a psychologist in the Arkansas State Hospital, because he was the first African American to do so. He states they were "shocked and surprised, you know, that here was this young Black man coming in applying for a position at a state hospital" (R. L. Williams, personal communication, September 10, 2007) because at that time, in 1955, all of the facilities were still segregated. The other three interviewees were beginning their professional development in the midst of the Black Power Movement of the late 1960s and 1970s. Dr. White was in the beginning of his career as a teacher and clinician at a children's clinic when the 1965 Los Angeles race riots occurred. Dr. White states, "The brothers burned up the community for four days" (personal communication, September 12, 2007). During that tumultuous time, he recounts that some White people burned a cross on his front lawn. In 1965, he was the only African American PhD-level licensed psychologist in California, and as such, he was sought out by the media to share his viewpoint on the underlying reasons for the riot. Dr. White reflected on that experience as a turning point in his career. He expressed that during the interview, he felt that the moment was a call to action and that his original career goals were no longer the intended path for him: "There was nowhere for me to go but to be Black."

It was shortly after this that the inaugural ABPsi meeting took place. The founders decided to meet separately from, but during the same time period as, the annual meeting of the APA in San Francisco. Dr. D. Williams graduated from his doctoral program the same year that ABPsi was formed, and although he was unable to attend the initial meeting of the organization, he got involved during its second year. It was clear that this initial coalition of Black psychologists as a unified voice in psychology had a significant impact on Dr. D. Williams's career development. In their indictment of the APA, Dr. R. L. Williams reported that the initial concerns of the founding members were that the APA should implement the following four practices: (1) racially integrate its own workforce, (2) facilitate the entry of more Blacks into the graduate programs in psychology, (3) eliminate racist theory and research from its journals, and (4) establish a program within which psychologists of color's concerns about psychology could be expressed. Through this process, the ABPsi established itself as a distinct organization and made its formal indictment to the APA for its apathetic at best and, in most instances, racist policies and practices. It was at this point that the founding members began to articulate a specific agenda for Black Psychology as a discipline.

One of the first tasks of the newly formed ABPsi was developing a moratorium against culturally biased tests. This influenced the agenda for the 1973 National Conference of Levels and Patterns of Training in Professional Psychology in Vail, Colorado (Guthrie, 2003). Prior to the Vail conference there had been unspoken acceptance of the "science" of old in the research, training, and practice of psychology. It was the perseverance of the ABPsi that called for conscious denouncement of these deficit models of psychology and demanded development of research, training, and practice models that acknowledged diversity, not deficiency.

Drs. R. L. Williams, White, D. Williams, and Helms shared that their lived experience countered every aspect of the racist notion of Blacks' intellectual inferiority. This disparity between their real experiences and the rhetoric of the mainstream served as a major motivation for their pursuit of psychology. They discussed how they wanted to become psychologists because, among other reasons, they wanted to pursue research and scholarship that would not only pointedly counter this fallacious perspective but to also assert their accurate, valid perspective of Black people. In this manner, one could argue that all Black Psychology is, on some level, social action. As with any social change, there is inherent challenge and struggle.

Dealing With Adversity

In their discussion of their professional journeys, the elders shared with us specific barriers that were posed by these contextual factors as well as the supports that were available to them (and some that they created) in their pursuit of graduate studies and career development. Inherent to being a pioneer is the experience of operating in uncharted territory, and this was the experience of most of the elders we interviewed. This also implies that they were creating theory, research, and their own professional structure and support where there was none. Specifically, we identified four themes among their experiences, including (1) being the only one/lack of role models, (2) dealing with racism, (3) limited support in their professional development, and (4) lack of validation or acknowledgment of their contributions.

Being the only one/lack of role models. A theme throughout the interviews was the experience of being either the "first of" or the "only to." As a result of their professional careers burgeoning during the time frame of the Civil Rights

Movement and the Black Power Movement of the late 1960s and early 1970s, each of the psychologists interviewed represents the first African American to pursue and complete myriad professional accomplishments in the field of psychology. In fact, Dr. R. L. Williams was the first African American to earn a PhD in psychology from Washington University. He shared that his interview for doctoral admissions took place outside of a train station in Little Rock, Arkansas, because the train station itself was segregated at the time. Because of the Jim Crow laws of the time, he was disallowed from meeting with the faculty member in the "Whites Only" section, and the faculty member refused to sit in the section reserved for African Americans. Despite these less-than-optimal beginnings, Dr. R. L. Williams went on to successfully complete his doctoral studies in 4 years. Prior to his doctoral studies, Dr. R. L. Williams worked as a psychologist in the Arkansas State Hospital and was the first African American to do so. Dr. White discussed the impact of not having any Black psychologists as role models; he could foresee himself as a lawyer because he knew one, but he never thought that being a psychologist was a viable option for him: "The first Black Ph.D. I ever saw in clinical psychology was when I came home from my dissertation orals and I looked in the mirror and saw myself" (personal communication, September 12, 2007).

Dealing with racism/oppression. From the interviews, it became excruciatingly clear that barriers posed by institutional racism and sexism were significant to our elders' professional development; specifically, they discussed their experiences of racism in the form of barriers to access higher education and different challenges once in graduate school. Although all of our interviewees were drawn to careers in psychology at early points in their lives, few had access to avenues that would allow them to do so. Both Drs. R. L. Williams and White shared that there were barriers to their entering college. Ironically, Dr. R. L. Williams had taken an intelligence test in high school, and because of low scores, the school counselor discouraged him from pursuing college as an option. This experience speaks directly to the biased data that were used by mainstream psychology to bolster their deficit–deficiency models. Dr. Helms reported that during her education, she wondered, "Why is it that people think that White people are much smarter than Black people?" (personal communication, September 13, 2007), and Dr. White noted, "We started from the premise of, all right, American society said that we were inferior and we said, 'no way we would believe that.' So, we start from the premise that Black people had psychological strengths" (personal communication, September 12, 2007).

Once in graduate school, the elders continued to come up against a variety of barriers and challenges. Dr. Myers shared,

> One of the frustrations that I think in graduate school was that, you know, it was difficult oftentimes to find support for wanting to do something that was focused on African Americans or Native Americans or any persons of color for that matter. You always needed a White sample to compare things of that nature. So, I really spent a lot of my career trying to create this space for scholars to step outside the boundaries of the mainstream. (personal communication, September 25, 2007)

Dr. D. Williams said he feels that racism played a part in his career as a clinician. He noted that, given his credentials and years of professional experience, he could be earning a great deal more money if he were a White psychologist. In addition, he intimated that White clients do not seek him out for services in the same way that he would expect them to if he were a White clinician with his same level of credentials and experience.

In addition to the barriers and challenges due to racism, two of our interviewees discussed the intersection of race and gender as playing a role in their professional development. For these women, whose experiences within the academy and within the discipline of Black Psychology were additionally challenged by virtue of them being women, it was oftentimes difficult to tease apart the influence of racism and sexism. Drs. Helms and Myers discussed their unique challenges as Black women in the academy:

> [W]ith White women, they see them as theirs in some way, either they are theirs because they remind them of a family member or they are theirs because if they can have sexually intimate relations with them that somehow bolsters their self-esteem. I'm not in either of those categories,

so what that means is that, I don't get the same kind of mentoring that my white female peers get. (J. Helms, personal communication, September 13, 2007)

Dr. Myers echoed Dr. Helms's experiences in the academy but also spoke about the gender bias within the field of Black Psychology. She expressed that she felt her biggest challenge was trying to "grapple with the gender bias that for many African Americans is unconscious or not ever confronted." Drs. Helms and Myers were the only Black women in their doctoral programs for their tenures throughout their respective programs. The unique position of being both an African American psychologist and a woman facilitates an experience of being isolated within the academy but also, perhaps, within the discipline of Black Psychology. Furthermore, as Dr. Myers intimated, the experiences with sexism within the community oftentimes goes unchallenged, perhaps in deference to the more significant need to establish clear boundaries between Black Psychology and Western psychology.

Lack of support. We believe it is important to highlight that not only were there challenges posed by racism and sexism for our interviewees but that there also was a simultaneous lack of support. It is one experience to be challenged, but it is even more daunting to be challenged without having support in the institutions and systems one is navigating. It is noteworthy that when the elders were asked, "Can you share about any supports you had in your professional development?" almost all of them responded with incredulity and sarcasm. For example, Dr. Helms retorted, "I would be making it up."

In fact, it may be more accurate to describe these elders' experiences in graduate school as degrees of indifference or apathy rather than support. Dr. Myers's experience in her doctoral studies illustrates this point. During her tenure as a doctoral student at OSU, the broader environmental culture of her department was one in which critiques of traditional views of mental illness and psychotherapy was widely accepted. She noted, "Well, you know, I came to a particular window that was open. Ohio State at the time was really attracting in its clinical program these people that were really critiquing mainstream psychology" (L. J. Myers, personal communication, September 25, 2007). So, in this environment, she felt as if she "could pull together enough people who at least had enough interest and sensitivity to support my intentions." Drs. Helms and R. L. Williams were able to cite only one or two faculty members during their time in graduate studies who were supportive of their professional development; overall, there was little faculty support for them to pursue their research interests as doctoral students. Both of them were interested in studying cultural bias in testing and assessment but ended up studying physiological psychology and psychometrics, respectively. Dr. Helms reported that although she had graduate assistantships at Iowa State University, none of the faculty wanted to work with her, so she would have conversations with fellow graduate students "about what they were doing so I would learn vicariously through their activities." Our interviewees consistently noted that they received minimal and sporadic support from within the institutions of which they were a part. As a consequence, most of the support they noted came from their family, friends, and other networks outside of those institutions. They spoke warmly of support they received from family, friends, and their growing network of Black psychologists as they progressed in their careers.

Lack of validation or acknowledgment of their contributions. As they began to enter the professional world, our interviewees faced another set of challenges. Each of their stories is fraught with examples of how they had to make a place for themselves in the academy and psychology as a discipline where there was none. It was a common experience to feel as if their scholarship and clinical contributions were acknowledged as legitimate by mainstream psychology. During their early careers, Western psychology was quite opposed to the notion that a different philosophy was necessary to appropriately assess and treat psychological problems faced by African Americans. Neither was Western psychology open to the idea that racial inequality and oppression experienced by African Americans had much bearing on those psychological problems and their treatment. Therefore, many of the elders interviewed were not only isolated in their professional pursuits but also were forced to justify the relevance and legitimacy of their unique perspectives on the psychology of Blacks. For instance, in 1981, Dr. Helms and her then-advisee, Dr. Thomas Parham, developed the Racial Identity Attitude Scale (Parham & Helms, 1981) to measure racial identity for Black Americans. However, Dr. Helms shared that there was difficulty publishing their initial research using the scale because reviewers for journals to which she submitted the work "would say, 'Well, we don't understand why you study Black identity, you need to prove that there's a difference between Black people and White people. Why don't you study White people's identity?'" (personal communication, September 13, 2007).

Even Dr. R. L. Williams's most significant contribution, his work on Ebonics, struggled to gain legitimacy within the academy and within the Black community. He notes that he coined the term in 1973 but that it did not gain much currency until the mid-1990s, when the Oakland School District proposed to use Ebonics in their instructional methods. It was at this point that a great deal of controversy erupted over the term and its use, mostly due to the media's misrepresentation of the construct and the scholarship that existed to support its use. Dr. R. L. Williams noted that it was not until White linguists repackaged Ebonics as *African American Vernacular English* that the construct was accepted by the academy at large. In addition to the misrepresentation in the media, the term was picked up by popular comedians at the time, which served to further delegitimize the construct. He went on to say that once he began to communicate with the Black community, specifically, about Ebonics and its relevance, there was more widely spread acceptance.

Dr. R. L. Williams wrote in his report to the APA Council of Representatives that "men do not build for others; they build for themselves" (1970, p. xxvii). In this instance, he was speaking directly to the formation of the ABPsi in an act of divestment from the APA; however, his words have broader import for the field of Black Psychology as a whole. Indeed, the men and women we interviewed helped to build, maintain, and care for their own house. Their perseverance and success in spite of Black Psychology's collective challenges is testament to their commitment to the Black community and the discipline of Black Psychology.

What Is Black Psychology?

Toward a Black Psychology

In 1970, Dr. White brought the notion of Black Psychology to mainstream Black America when "Toward a Black Psychology" was published in *Ebony* magazine (White, 1970/2004). In it, he introduced the necessity for Black psychological perspectives on the experiences of Black people. Dr. White criticized the theories of White psychologists that pathologized and denigrated Blacks and characterized Blacks as culturally deficient (White, 1970/2004), and he proposed that these models were grounded in racist and oppressive thought, not ethical scientific exploration. He demanded that Black Psychology theories replace these notions and be utilized to address the unique experiences of Blacks.

It should be noted that the development of Black Psychology as a discipline was not the only significant professional gain made within the Black community during this time. The Black Power and Civil Rights Movements also inspired Black scholars in disciplines such as history, philosophy, and anthropology. African Studies (also known as *Black Studies*) departments emerged in the late 1960s. Scholars who have written about African philosophy (Asante, 1988; Mbiti, 1970) and African worldview (Diop, 1974), for example, have been cited countless times in African psychology literature. Considering the contemporary development of Africana Studies and Black/African psychology, we recognize that these disciplines have mutually influenced one another.

Since the publication of Dr. White's work in *Ebony,* the concept of Black Psychology has expanded. Scholars in psychology and other disciplines have addressed the concept of Black Psychology, and the discipline has undergone several distinct shifts in its continued development. Early in its conception, much of the theory and research conducted in Black Psychology fit into what Karenga (1982) defined as the *Traditional School* of Black Psychology. He suggested that the Traditional School of psychology was a reactive, defensive, critical approach that sought to change White theories that lacked focus and sought to create replacements for problematic theories. This reactive approach was vital in that it voiced the shortcomings of traditional psychology. After asserting that traditional psychology had egregiously failed to address the psychological functioning and needs of people of African descent, there emerged a new perspective in Black Psychology that not only pointed out the flaws of traditional psychology but also proposed culturally relevant and appropriate theories and modalities of treatment. As attempts were made to address the nature of Black psychological functioning, scholars began to look to historical, philosophical, and religious foundations of Africa. Particularly during the 1970s, scholars began calling for a sole focus on the need for social change for people of African descent and said this change must occur through use of Africentric ideology, proposing "analysis, treatment and transformation of Black people . . . with roots in an African world view" (Karenga, 1982, p. 325).

Although there may be other ways of categorizing theories of Black Psychology, these distinctions appear to be fitting when examining the body of Black Psychology literature. In general, the Traditional School of thought appears to be antiquated, and it has been replaced with models that are reformist and/or radical in their approach. Although no formal best practice model has been endorsed by the ABPsi, the organization has agreed that models that recognize the African roots for Blacks throughout the Diaspora are preferred over those that ignore the cultural significance of Africa.

Defining Black Psychology

Our interviewees have varied perspectives on the nuances of the theory and practice of Black Psychology; however, the common theme among their responses was that Black Psychology can be defined as theory development, research, and practice that recognize the importance of the Black cultural experience and seeks to ameliorate the mental health state of Black people. Specifically, Black Psychology includes the axiology, concepts of self, time orientations, human goals, and epistemology grounded in the sociohistorical context of people of African descent. Furthermore, Black Psychology seeks to address the mental health of people of African descent, recognizing the influence of racism and oppression and how experiences with these ills have shaped the psychology of Blacks throughout the Diaspora.

In discussing this general view, Dr. R. L. Williams suggested it should be about "developing of and/or liberating Black people; developing programs, theories, research that would be for Black people and by Black people" (personal communication, September 10, 2007). Dr. White stated that, in addition to theory development and practice, training is essential. He noted that one of the significant goals of the ABPsi was to develop models of practice and training to create a "pipeline to bring the younger people into the field" to ensure its longevity.

How Definitions Have Evolved

Drs. Helms, Myers, R. L. Williams, and White all acknowledged that Black Psychology originally was a critique of and response to Western psychology's approach to theory, research, and practice with Blacks. Dr. Helms feels that "historically we've been trying to prove to people that we exist," but she suggested that we have proved our existence and that now we need to move forward to use what we know to help make positive change in people's lives. The overall historical shift appears to have been from pointing out the oppressive and erroneous nature of traditional psychology in explaining Black psychological functioning to addressing the needs of Blacks in a manner that honors our unique experience in America and throughout the Diaspora (including a focus on theories and treatment grounded in an African worldview) to inclusive models that focus on a more multicultural perspective and that address issues of racism and oppression in mainstream society, not only the Black community.

The importance of Black Psychology representing the community was the impetus behind Dr. White's perspective on Black Psychology. As defined by Dr. White, Black Psychology is built on the principle that Black people have significant strengths and we must create models of practice and training that address seven primary themes: improvisation, resilience, connectedness to others, spirituality, emotional vitality, gallows humor (serious humor), and a healthy suspicion of White people. As Black Psychology developed in the late 1960s, Dr. White stated that pioneers wanted it to "represent the voice of the people, not the voice of the university"; thus, they went to churches, dances, funerals, and beauty parlors to develop theory. The development of the seven primary themes was the result of community exploration.

Dr. White believes that that primary functions and goals of Black Psychology are "to help Black people who grow up in America, in what is a toxic environment for Black people, to help them discover and rediscover those seven core themes. And then internalize those themes and utilize them in their daily life" (personal communication, September 12, 2007). When asked about experiences that grounded the field of Black Psychology, Dr. White commented that the experiences of growing up "in the 'hood" for the pioneers in the field and "connecting [that experience] to Africa" was one of the significant aspects in that process.

Similarly, Dr. D. Williams purports that the goal of Black Psychology is to resurrect our cultural beliefs and use them to establish our self-concept. He suggested that we have focused, both as a collective community and within the discipline of Black Psychology, with aligning ourselves with European cultural standards. Although he struggles to incorporate specific African theory and modalities of therapy into his own practice, he stated that he consistently uses culture to guide therapy. Overall, he believes that therapists must align themselves with an individual's culture to be responsive.

Conversely, Dr. Helms suggested that African-centered ideals need not be central to Black psychological theory and practice in order to be effective with Black people. She stated that the differences in the socialization of Blacks in the United States compared to Blacks on the Continent and other parts of the Diaspora underscores the idea the Black Psychology does not have to be African. Dr. Helms's perspective seems to be that of understanding the unique experiences of African Americans in the United States. Essential to her definition of Black Psychology is the notion we should "not [be] appropriating anyone else's culture, rather finding out what defines us, and then, if we know what defines us, we know how we overlap with people and how we don't" (personal communication, September 13, 2007).

Dr. Myers's perspective on Black Psychology is grounded in an African worldview yet offers to address mental health issues of people of color and Whites. Although Dr. Myers agrees with mainstream definitions of Black Psychology, she has her own research and theory. Dr. Myers indicated that she, like many other early Black psychologists, began with an interest in critiquing existing Western theory. As she began her professional career, she became engaged in research about worldview, and she began to develop psychological theory from an African perspective, what she titled *Optimal Psychology*. She views Black Psychology as "the articulation, clarification and the integration of this holistic perspective that yields or contributes to oneness as well as illumination or enlightenment" (personal communication, September 25, 2007). Dr. Myers argued that the African holistic perspective of Black Psychology offers opportunity for unification of all cultures. She explained that as we have increased our knowledge (in the West), our paradigms have shifted (e.g., Newtonian physics to quantum physics); similarly, "Western science has... caught up with African common sense," and we have begun to integrate basic African thought principles into the practice of science, including psychology. She believes that the use of an African deep thought paradigm can be central to the amelioration of the spiritual, psychological, and physical health of society at large. Our interviewees hold some differing beliefs about what is significant in the practice of Black Psychology. In reviewing their thoughts, it appears that the paramount idea is the Black Psychology is about the forward movement of Black people, meaning that Black psychological models for research, practice, and training must undoubtedly contribute to the betterment of Black people throughout the Diaspora. It has been the focus on this forward movement that has contributed not only to the advancement of the field of Black Psychology but also to the field of psychology at large.

Significant Milestones in Black Psychology

It is important to highlight some of the significant advancements in theory, research, and practice as a means of describing the history of Black Psychology. Two themes stood out across all of the interviews. The first is the recognition of Black Psychology moving from a place of a critique of Western psychology to a place of self-definition. The second is the profound and pervasive influence that Black Psychology has had on the development of ethnic studies by other groups of people of color and the movement of multiculturalism within mainstream psychology. In its initial state, Black Psychology focused mainly on distinguishing the psychology of Black people from the limited, pathological perspective that Western psychology had imposed on the group for so long. This meant that most of the early literature was on a critique of Western psychology for Blacks as compared to a composition of a specific psychology for Black people. As Dr. R. L. Williams states, "When we first started, we were more or less dealing with criticizing Eurocentric psychology." This sentiment was echoed by Drs. Helms and Myers. Therefore, it was when Black Psychology began to be defined itself by Black scholars for Black people that the discipline really took shape as a distinctive perspective in the broader field of psychology. Drs. D. Williams and R. L. Williams specifically cite the publications of African psychology/philosophy by Drs. Nobles, Kambon, and Akbar as being particularly significant in the process of developing a Black Psychology. This was further reinforced by the publication of Dr. Reginald Jones's first edition of *Black Psychology* (1972).

Furthermore, it was this process of distinguishing Black Psychology from mainstream psychology that directly impacted the second aforementioned theme: ethnic psychology and multiculturalism. Dr. White noted that

> We had to fight the profession to establish the legitimacy of [Black Psychology] and then what happened was while they were arguing with us, the Asian dude turned around and said that they didn't like how they were being defined in psychology and they didn't like the invisibility and they were going to write their own psychology and then the Chicano dude and the Chicano sister wanted to set up and do the same thing. (personal communication September 12, 2007)

Drs. Myers and R. L. Williams echoed these sentiments. In fact, Dr. Myers stated that a great deal of the ideas and perspectives that have been present in Black Psychology from its beginning have been incorporated into mainstream psychology in some broader way:

> So, in some ways if you look at the field of Black Psychology you can really see they are the precursor to a lot of developments that now have been kind of absorbed as part of mainstream, so

that, the so-called multicultural psychology was predated by African-centered psychology.
(L. J. Myers, personal communication, September 25, 2007)

Another noteworthy advancement has been the impact of Black Psychology on the Black community. All of our interviewees highlighted the imperativeness that Black Psychology was not only developed by Black people but also that it is used for the benefit of Black people. Drs. D. Williams and White in particular noted that the clinical and social activist work they and other Black psychologists have done in the community were pivotal to the relevance and success of Black Psychology. Dr. D. Williams stated, "You know the people who'll remember me are the clients with whom I've worked. I know I have an impact on clients all the time." He went on to say, "My mission, the reason I'm here is to have an impact on you" (personal communication, October 10, 2007). In addition, Dr. White discussed the significance of psychologists having to "roll up your sleeves and be a part of social change, you can't just stand up in your classroom all day." He also mentioned that Black Psychology has always had a tradition that psychology should "belong to the people." It was also evident in Drs. R. L. Williams's, Helms's, and Myers's interviews that they firmly believe that one of the foundational strengths of Black Psychology has been its dedication to helping Black people in the community.

Where Does Black Psychology Go From Here?

Within the discussion of their definition of Black Psychology, the elders all shared their visions for the future direction of the discipline. They provided suggestions for continued theory development, research, practice, and training for the next generation of Black psychologists. We agree that they have established a solid foundation for the next generation of activists, scholars, teachers, and clinicians. Therefore, the most common theme among the elders was a focus on training future Black psychologists to play pivotal roles in the academy, Black communities, a variety of mental health settings, and other decision-making institutional positions. Along with this common theme, there was a general sentiment that the field of

Black Psychology is well positioned to make monumental contributions to the field of psychology, for those people of African descent throughout the Diaspora, and to the world. In essence, the elders encouraged us to dream big and feel empowered by the groundwork they have laid to bring those goals into fruition.

With this in mind, Drs. R. L. Williams, D. Williams, White, and Myers all suggested that the creation and institutionalization of think tanks in Black Psychology are imperative to the continuation of the field. As Dr. R. L. Williams stated, there should be a place "where some of the younger Black psychologists can go and just sit and think and create" (personal communication, September 10, 2007). He went on to share that there needs to be more coalition and integration among the work that we do as Black psychologists. In other words, there are great training programs, rigorous research, and efficacious practice but that goal should be to coalesce that shared knowledge and skill in a cohesive manner. The elders also suggested more specific suggestions for the future of Black Psychology. In this next section, we delineate some specific strategies that can be developed in tangible ways for the field on the basis of the elders' suggestions. We have categorized these suggestions in three areas: (1) training, (2) practice, and (3) scholarship.

Suggestions for Training

1. *Think tanks.* We agree with the elders' suggestions of establishing Black Psychology think tanks to sustain the long-standing tradition of scholarship and deep thought in the field.

2. *Mentorship.* Although we recognize that informal mentorship occurs regularly, we suggest that formal mentorship systems should be institutionalized in our professional organizations. In addition, this mentorship should take place on multiple levels, with elders mentoring early career professionals and graduate and undergraduate students. The Jegnaship Program within ABPsi is a current mechanism, as is Links and Shoulders, offered by Division 45, Society for the Psychological Study of Ethnic Minority Issues, within the APA. However, these programs can be strengthened by creating a centralized database of mentors and mentees; taking advantage of the Internet and electronic resources to foster long-distance mentoring relationships; building in a system of accountability so that, once paired, mentors and mentees can better maintain their relationship; and including early career professionals as mentees.

3. *Recruitment and retention.* In 1970, Dr. R. L. Williams submitted his 10-Point Program to increase the enrollment of Black doctoral students and the production of PhD graduates, yet Black PhD-level psychologists remain significantly underrepresented. We suggest that Black psychologists within the academy may benefit from reviewing the 10-Point Program (R. L. Williams, 1974) and reexamine the need to continue to work within their respective institutions to increase enrollment and foster retention of Black graduate students.

4. *Specific training programs.* One specific recommendation is to develop training in traditional African healing methods and therapeutic interventions. Use of traditional African healing methods is highly congruent with ABPsi's African-centered organizational mission and an Afrocentric framework of Black Psychology.

5. *Grant funding.* Opportunities for funding should be vigorously pursued to establish institutionalized training programs for Black psychologists by Black psychologists. This type of focused training is highly consistent with our continual effort to firmly establish ourselves as a distinct discipline to provide culturally congruent mental health services to Black people.

Suggestions for Practice

1. *Social activism.* Black Psychology has always been influenced by—and, in turn, has influenced—the social political landscape of the United States. We believe that the practice of Black Psychology should inherently and explicitly include social activism. Along this vein, we suggest that Black psychologists should continue to do the following:

   a. Develop, implement, and evaluate community interventions. Furthermore, we suggest that these community interventions should always be a collaborative effort between the so-called professionals and the people in the community. In addition, we stress the importance of evaluating the effectiveness of community interventions in an effort to contribute to further activism.

b. Get and stay involved in local, national, and international social and political movements that directly impact the lives of Black people.

c. Secure positions of power within institutions of which we are a part and that have a direct impact on the lives of Black people.

2. *Empirically validated treatments.* Black psychologists should work toward establishing empirically validated treatment interventions for work with Black people. In this manner, effective interventions (in areas of prevention, individual, or group therapy) with Black people can be used by all psychologists and mental health practitioners that serve Black people. Furthermore, these treatments can be adapted to serve people of African descent throughout the Diaspora.

Suggestions for Research

1. *Intervention research.* Consistent with the previous suggestions for practice, there should be rigorous, ongoing evaluation of treatment interventions for Black people. In addition, there should also be rigorous research examining the related outcomes for interventions.

2. *Antecedent research.* In addition to the research on effective interventions, we suggest that there needs to be continued research on the antecedents to and protective factors from poor mental health in people of African descent throughout the Diaspora.

Conclusion

As it stands, Black Psychology as a unique discipline has a substantial and solid foundation. In keeping with our framework of Sankofa, that foundation serves a reflection of the brilliance and abundance of the future of the discipline. As we were able to engage in the process of Sankofa (looking back) with our elders, we are reminded of the vision, strength, and wisdom of our elders. The emergence of Black Psychology and ABPsi has had a profound impact on the Black community and the training, research, and practice of all psychologists. Although there have been some considerable gains in the presence of Blacks in the discipline of psychology and representation of culturally relevant theory and research, prodigious tasks still lie ahead. We agree that Black Psychology must ultimately address the needs of the Black community, and we must not allow our differences in the nuances of how this mission should be accomplished to cloud our vision. There continues to be a need for increased representation in training programs, academia, and clinical practice with collaboration between academicians and clinicians to further research to inform clinical practice and for clinical practice to help us solidify theory. This can occur through continued social activism, obtaining grant funding to conduct our research intervention and antecedent research, and the development of manualized treatment.

In closing, we would like to extend sincere gratitude to our elders for sharing their time, wisdom, and warmth with us for these interviews. We hope that our contribution in this chapter is a true accounting of their words and experiences. We felt validated in our burgeoning professional development, and we have become more focused in our professional journeys because of the conversations we had with these pioneering men and women. It is our sincerest wish that readers feel the same way.

References

Asante, M. K. (1988). *Afrocentricity*. Trenton, NJ: Africa World Press.

Black, S. R., Spence, S. A., & Omari, S. R. (2004). Contributions of African Americans to the field of psychology. *Journal of Black Studies, 35,* 40–64.

Diop, C. A. (1974). *The African origin of civilization: Myth or reality.* New York: Lawrence Hill.

Guthrie, R. V. (2003). *Even the rat was white: A historical view of psychology* (2nd ed.). Boston: Allyn & Bacon.

Helms, J. E. (1992). *A race is a nice thing to have: A guide to being a White person or understanding the White persons in your life.* Topeka, KS: Content Communications.

Jones, R. L. (1972). *Black Psychology.* New York: Harper & Row.

Jones, R. L. (Ed.). (2004). *Black Psychology* (4th ed.). Hampton, VA: Cobb & Henry.

Karenga, M. (1982). *Introduction to Black studies.* Inglewood, CA: Kawaida.

Mbiti, J. S. (1970). *African religions and philosophies.* Garden City, NY: Anchor Books, Doubleday.

Myers, L. J. (1988). *Understanding an Afrocentric world view: Introduction to an optimal psychology.* Dubuque, IA: Kendall/Hunt.

Myers, L. J. (1992). *Understanding an Afrocentric world view: Introduction to an optimal psychology* (2nd ed.). Dubuque, IA: Kendall/Hunt.

Myers, L. J. (2004). *Blessed assurance: Deep thought and meditations in the tradition and wisdom of our ancestors.* Columbus, OH: Author.

Parham, T. A., & Helms, J. E. (1981). The influence of Black students' racial identity attitudes on preferences for counselor's race. *Journal of Counseling Psychology, 28,* 250–257.

Parham, T. A., White, J. L., & Ajamu, A. (2000). *The psychology of Blacks: An African-centered perspective* (3rd ed.). Upper Saddle River, NJ: Prentice Hall.

White, J. L. (2004). Toward a Black Psychology. In R. L. Jones (Ed.), *Black Psychology* (4th ed., pp. 5–16). Hampton, VA: Cobb & Henry. (Original work published 1970)

Williams, B. H. (1997). *Coming together: The founding of the Association of Black Psychologists.* Unpublished doctoral dissertation, St. Louis University.

Williams, R. L. (1970). Report to the APA council of representatives. *American Psychologist, 25,* xxvii–xxviii.

Williams, R. L. (1972). Manual of directions for the Black Intelligence Test of Cultural Homogeneity. *Journal of Black Psychology, 4,* 77–92.

Williams, R. L. (1974). A history of the Association of Black Psychologists: Early formation and development. *Journal of Black Psychology, 1,* 9–24.

Williams, R. L. (2007). *Racism learned at an early age through racial scripting.* Bloomington, IN: AuthorHouse.

PART II

AFRICAN/BLACK PSYCHOLOGY

3

Theoretical and Conceptual Approaches to African and African American Psychology

Linda James Myers

In this chapter, I discuss theoretical and conceptual approaches developed in the literature described as African American, Black, and African Psychology. Just like the people and culture, a psychology so designated has faced special challenges, as well as advantages. For the most part, the challenges have been the result of the denigrating influence of the tradition common to the dominant culture of socialization in U.S. society. Some of the advantages can be traced to the robust strengthening that occurs in the face of such trials. However, as I discuss in this chapter, many are the result of the comprehensiveness, coherence, and cohesion afforded to people and cultural orientations grounded in a multidimensional reality connecting and available to all of humanity. The expansiveness of African cultural worldviews and traditions acknowledge many levels and aspects of reality so uncommon, if not unfamiliar, in Western culture that they are ignored or potentially dismissed. Because of the nature of its assumptions, the prevailing Western cultural framework is incapable of holding and making understandable those aspects of consciousness beyond which the five senses are informed, even though their value has been made increasingly evident by the height of its scientific investigations into neuroscience and quantum physics. The purpose of this chapter is met in part by exploring the complex determinants influencing the theoretical and conceptual approaches to human psychology as we know it. The challenges to deepening our understanding of humanity and human potential are greatest when we fail to appreciate the contributions of all cultural groups to the greater good of the whole.

Culture and Psychology

Our understanding of humanity is culture bound. *Culture* is the social force that informs our designs for living and patterns of interpreting reality. Thus, legitimate psychological study of humanity can be facilitated by giving appropriate regard to the cultural underpinnings informing our perceptions and shaping our interpretations as knowers. Included in the self-critical analyses should be considerations of the ways the nature of reality, knowledge, development, axiology, cosmology, and so forth are conceived. Not requiring such considerations can yield for the field of psychology un–self-conscious propagation of noninterrogated assumptions that might be assumed universal and the only valid measures for the area of study. Such a stance has made difficult acknowledgment, much less appreciation, of competing alternate cultural frames of reference that would be helpful in expanding our understandings of humanity and the human condition, as well as pathways to health and well-being, individually and collectively.

As scholars utilizing sociocultural frames of reference nondominant in the West are heard, the breadth and depth of knowledge available to meet human needs can be increased; however, resistance to such expansion has existed since the emergence of mainstream Western psychology. Theorists and researchers whose subject matter and interests, perspectives, and cultural frames of reference differ distinguishably from those dominant in mainstream Western psychology are marginalized, limiting the scope and depth of inquiry available to the field of study.

As should be expected, each cultural group embraces its own perspectives and understandings of the world. The difficulty with embracing one's own cultural frame of reference lies for the most part in the prohibitions the perspective might hold against exploring and honoring the perspectives of other cultural groups. This difficulty mounts in accordance with the extent to which the other cultural group is one that has historically been perceived as inferior, exploited, dehumanized, and disenfranchised legally, socially, economically, educationally, and politically by the dominant cultural group. When a cultural worldview supports the construction of such a social reality without critical self-awareness and consciousness of its own character and biases, access to more complete knowledge of humankind is limited. Further compounding the difficulty is that when the dominant cultural worldview is fragmented in its own orientation to life, disciplinary boundaries may prevent the synthesis of knowledge into a comprehensive, coherent, cohesive whole, leaving gaps in scientific knowledge, such as ignoring the proactive role of consciousness in human experience and its subjective nature, which fosters a distorted view.

Western psychology has historically been particularly handicapped by the nature of its monocultural perspective when it comes to people acknowledging African descent and their cultural inheritances. However, despite these tests, Black Psychology has reemerged in contemporary times to bring to bear an abundance of ideas, perspectives, and theories to enrich and advance this human enterprise. Some of the most noteworthy contributions have been from scholars engaging their own cultural traditions and embracing nondominant and non-Western models, conceptions, and perspectives. The road of African/Black/African American Psychology has not been easy in light of the history of psychology in the West, and in the United States in particular, but that history has itself become "grist for the mill" in many ways that are useful to our understanding of humankind.

Over the past 50 years, we have seen the descriptors for the discipline change, as have the self-designations of the people whose psychology it is often used to describe. Thus, we have seen similar bodies of knowledge referred to as *Black Psychology*, *African American Psychology*, *African Psychology*, *Afrocentric Psychology*, and *African-centered Psychology*. That we witness these changes reflects in part not only the complications of development in a hostile and oppressive, racist and culturally biased social reality and ethnic consciousness but also the resilience of a long-standing cultural tradition and orientation to life that is dynamic and sustainable. Interestingly, this bias is supported by a failure to recognize or acknowledge the historical legacy and heritage from which Western thinking emerges; for example, the African roots of Western philosophy are seldom identified (Bernal, 1987; James, 1953). For the purposes of this chapter, I use the terms *African(a)* or *Black* to express the multiple and varied dimensions of the field devoted to the study of people acknowledging African descent, as well as the study of all humanity from a cultural frame of reference rooted in African cultural traditions and worldviews.

Despite the antagonistic nature of the larger social context, the field of study known as African American, African or African(a), and Black Psychology has forged ahead to give us insights into all of humanity, such is the purpose of theory building in the human sciences in general and the psychological sciences in particular. Identifying themselves ethnically and acknowledging the cultural perspective of their work, scholars and researchers in the field have brought to bear approaches and conceptualizations much needed for investigating and solving the many complex and complicated concerns facing persons who acknowledge African descent and those who do not acknowledge their African heritage, distant though it may be.

When exploring the theoretical and conceptual appproaches in African(a) Psychology, it is important to be mindful of the role that culture plays in the evolution of psychology and the various schools of thought that have emerged and their relationship to cultural orientation. The relationship to the source culture and cultural worldview being relyed on will be the key point of reference used to differentiate theoretical approaches and conceptions in this chapter. Depending on the scholar being read, it becomes clear that perceptions of the social context are not homogeneous within cultural groups. For the purposes of this chapter, I explore the major theories and conceptions developed in the field by dividing them along the lines of relationship to identified mainstream Western cultural norms versus those commonly identified with an African American, Black, and African cultural worldview.

The four categories I am suggesting are (1) *pre-assimilation*, those works either preceding or not conforming to mainstream Western cultural orientations; (2) *assimilation*, which includes works reflecting the adoption of the dominant mainstream European American cultural orientation; (3) *bicultural reform*, meaning the works that adopt some mainstream Western cultural assumptions but also make transitional movement toward self-definition and identification; and (4) *cultural congruence*, which includes works with interest in and emphasis on authenticating or being grounded in an African-centered cultural frame of reference. These categories can then be divided further in terms of the assumed universality of their subject matter or specialized applicability to only those persons acknowledging African descent.

In searching for descriptors of the categories, depending on perspective, all categories could be seen as sharing the qualities of being, or being intended to be, corrective and prescriptive and/or reactive and proactive, blurring the complexities and limiting capacity to benefit from an understanding of the Black experience(s) that could be liberatory and healing. Value judgments appear unavoidable; liberation and healing are in themselves value judgments. No pejorative judgment is intended by the names of the categories assigned in this chapter; each is intended to offer a fair descriptor of the impact the theoretical and conceptual approaches have had in all of their complexity. A basic presumption on which the orientation of this chapter is founded is that all approaches are good, necessary, and contribute to the greater good of the whole. All theoreticians are correct to the limits of their knowledge, wisdom, and understanding, and by nature of being human, there will be limits for everyone, and there is value for all in interrogating those limits (Myers, 1999a, 1999b).

PSYCHOLOGICAL SCIENCE AND THE AMERICAN SOCIAL CONTEXT

In engaging in an examination of theoretical and conceptual approaches to African(a) Psychology, or any so-called ethnic minority psychology, attention to the larger contemporary social context within which theories and conceptions emerge is warranted. Theories and conceptual approaches to the various aspects of our being as humans manifest within sociocultural contexts with attributes that inform and shape their focus, assumptions, and conclusions. In this society in particular, it matters whether you came to the United States as a voluntary or involuntary immigrant and the extent to which you have assimilated or internalized the dominant cultural worldview. Also, when trained in the United States, although the field of study identified as psychology is more accurately European American, White, European Psychology, it is seldom, if ever, acknowledged as such.

To date, European American, White, European psychologists have defined the discipline to reflect the belief that Western thinking is universally applicable to, relevant to, and representative of all of humanity. Heretofore, this influential cultural minority has imposed its vision globally, resulting in the study of "psychology" in the West not being culturally self-reflective because it fails to recognize and acknowledge its critical grounding or biases.

The prevailing cultural attributes in the West support a consciousness that is grounded in the "myth of objectivity" and fragmentation. Disregarding the primary and proactive role of consciousness in human experience and its subjective nature, social constructions are often created out of unconscious needs and fears collectively shared without awareness or acknowledgment of any role in the creation process. Such conditions have made suspect the relevance and applicability of its models and theories to populations of color in particular. Other specific events in the history of psychology in the United States make evident the depth and breadth of the problem.

European, White, European American Psychology: The Modern Historical Context

Mainstream American psychology cannot be separated from the social context within which it emerges; it has historically been Eurocentric and plagued by blatant racism characteristic of the times (Richards, 1997). In 1797, Dr. Benjamin Rush, the reputed "father of American psychiatry," declared that the color of Black people was caused by a congenital disease akin to leprosy. The only evidence of a cure was when the skin turned white. Dr. Edward Jarvis, a specialist in mental disorders, used the 1840 census to purportedly prove that the condition of freedom in the North was so unnatural to Blacks it made them more prone to mental illness, thus justifying the enslavement of African people by the flawed premise that it provided a shield for Black people from what he considered the liabilities and dangers of active self-determination. These positions taken by the medical and mental health establishments of the day clearly illustrate the complementary and intimate relationship between the perspectives of the mental health professionals and the prevailing sociocultural predispositions of the larger society.

The inability to see Black people as fully human permeates the foundations of mainstream American, European, European American, White Psychology. The cultural lens used by those developing the field had been so fractured that healthy, efficacious behaviors on the part of Black people were perceived and defined as insane. In 1851, Dr. Samuel Cartwright published an article in a professional journal of his time claiming that he had discovered two new mental diseases peculiar to Black people: (1) *drapetomania*, which caused Black people to have the uncontrollable urge to run away from their slave captors and (2) *dysaesthesia aethiops*, evidenced by disobedience, answering disrespectfully, and refusing to work. The commonly prescribed cures were beating them mercilessly and forcing the captive to undertake even more taxing and difficult labor. The historical and social context is one in which the field of mainstream American, European, European American, White psychology discredits and totally impedes its capacity to discern and define mental health and illness, not only for people acknowledging African descent but for members of their own cultural group as well.

The first president of the American Psychological Association, G. Stanley Hall, theorized that Africans, Indians, and Chinese were members of "adolescent races" and in the stage of "incomplete growth" (Richards, 1997) and that therefore it was Western psychology's role and responsibility to save these adolescent races from the liabilities of freedom. The alleged intellectual inferiority of Blacks has been a long-standing premise of American psychologists throughout the 20th century, from Popenoe's (1929) assertion that intelligence is determined by the amount of white blood to Herrnstein and Murray's (1999) more recent variations on the same theme at the dawn of the 21st century.

Evolving African(a), African American, Black Psychology

The evolution of the field of Black Psychology has progressed from ancient to modern/postmodern times in a consistent pattern. The history of Black Psychology can be traced to the beginnings of human culture and civilization in classical African civilization or ancient Kmt (known in the West as Egypt), a period in human history in which Africans first produced an "organized system of knowledge (philosophy, definitions, concepts, models, procedures, and practices) concerning the nature of the social universe" (Baldwin, 1986, as cited in Belgrave & Allison, 1996, p. 5). Classical African civilization was rife with literature concerned with matters psychological in nature, that is, concerned with the nature of human consciousness, heart, mind, soul, and beyond. A full appreciation of the relationship between the meaning of that history and African(a) psychology in contemporary times requires an understanding of the cosmology and cultural worldview from which both emerge (Azibo, 1996; Grills, 2002; Nobles, 2005). The challenges to such an appreciation are great in the West, given the marked differences in the prevailing cultural assumptions. However, despite those differences, the heights of Westerns scientific knowledge are converging around assumptions consistent with African cosmology and cultural worldview (Myers, 1988, 1992, 2003). However, the sociocultural gap between Western scientific knowledge and information structuring everyday life is quite large; as a consequence, African(a) Psychology can play a pivotal role in bridging the gap and further transforming Western society and culture, if the restricting cultural biases can be overcome.

Grills and Rowe (1998) described African(a) Psychology as incorporating several fundamental concepts: worldview and the corresponding metaphysical basis of African science, concepts of consciousness, conceptualizations of the person and human beingness, concepts of health and wellness, and models of the healing exchange or process. Thus, as Africanist scholar Obenga (2005) pointed out, an African-centered perspective is not restricted to a particular ethnic group; instead, it reflects a basic historical continuity, consciousness, and cultural unity. Because of the differences in the deep structure of cultural worldview, the scope of African(a) Psychology is potentially much larger than that of Western psychology. When the concerns of the person and community in everyday life are grounded in spirit/mind/soul and multidimensional, all cycles of life—including death, the afterlife, ancestorhood, rebirth, resurrection, creation, and transformation—are of interest from the outset. Universal order, metaphysics, and divine consciousness all fit within the purview of African(a) Psychology, along with the examination of such things as the personality mind, heart, thought, will, memory, speech, individual and collective health and behavior, and human development around issues including the moral and spiritual dimensions of life.

Therefore, as the Bantu Kongo proverb states, "One cannot dance with ease in a borrowed wrap," it is impossible to fit African(a) Psychology into the prevailing Western cultural frames, although this is the context within which we have seen the reemergence of African(a) Psychology in the West in modern times. African(a), African American, Black Psychology did not start in the West with the chattel enslavement of Africans by Europeans; instead, its history can be traced to the beginnings of human culture and civilization and forward to contemporary times.

Schools of Thought in African(a), African American, Black Psychology

Given this history, it is not surprising that the reemergence of African(a) Psychology within this antagonistic sociocultural context would be fraught with challenges unknown to theorists whose cultural stance is supported institutionally by congruent, hegemonic structures. Despite the adversity, Black psychologists, aware of the extreme hypocrisy and incapacity to address the mental health needs of Black people—and, consequently, all people—stepped forward to declare the status quo unacceptable and to commit themselves to finding their own way on the basis of their cultural realities and experiences. Thus, in 1968, a number of Black psychologists withdrew from the American Psychological Association (APA) to form their own professional organization, the Association of Black Psychologists.

Although Black Psychology's history can be traced to the beginnings of human culture and civilization as described in the ancient texts of classical African civilization, with regard to the most recent encounters with the West in the past 400 years, Black Psychology can be described as fitting different schools of thought. All schools of thought are reflective of the experiences, exposures, and meanings made by the scholars doing the research and theory building; thus, all perspectives have value for others who share the same worldview.

One system of categorization used by Daudi Azibo has been to divide the perspectives between *pro-Black* perspectives, which focus on the Western experience of Africans without using their worldview and cultural congruence, and *pro-Africentric* perspectives, which view African philosophy and worldview as essential to understanding the psychology of Black/African people. Kambon (1998) made a similar distinction between Black Psychology and African(a) Psychology, conceiving Black Psychology as a reactionary response to Western psychology and concerned with the psychological consequences of being a Black American. At the same time, Kambon acknowledged that because African people predate European people as a distinct cultural group with an extant psychology, irrespective of when and where it was put forward, Black Psychology *is* African Psychology.

Another area distinction often mentioned is whether the theories of African(a) Psychology are deemed to be universally applicable to all people or conceived as applicable only to people who acknowledge African descent. Belgrave and Allyson (2006) made the point that the psychology of African Americans can be conceptualized around convergent viewpoints that involve organized, structured, systematic approaches to a broad and diverse scope and content that will have implications for self-definition and self-determination.

In the next section, I further grapple with some of the complexities and challenges associated with these issues in regard to theoretical and conceptual approaches in African(a) Psychology and their relationship to culture, social context, and worldview. In addition to providing examples of theories and conceptual approaches associated with each school, I highlight and describe their implications and areas of future research.

Insight into the contemporary evolution of African(a) Psychology, or any psychology, is facilitated by exploring the characteristics of the historical context and the dominant cultural climate within which the various theoretical and conceptual approaches develop. Unless particular theorists have specifically designated use of a particular term to characterize their work, the interchangeable use of the various terms will be continued. Below, I provide a few research examples characterizing the four schools of thought (i.e., pre-assimilation, assimilation, bicultural reform, and cultural congruence) and recommendations for future development. Although this treatment is by no means intended to be exhaustive, it does provide an overview that attempts to give a reflexive picture of the evolution of the field.

Pre-Assimilation

One of the earliest treatises on psychological processes can be found in the *Book of Knowing: The Creation of Ra as Ptah*, translated from hieroglyphics by Karenga (1989). Estimated to have been written around 2500 BC, this text presents a foundational interpretation of an African-centered understanding of the role of cognition, affect, and language in human functioning:

> It is Ptah, the Most Great, who has given existence to all the divine powers and to their essences through his heart, mind and tongue. Thus it came to pass that the heart, mind and tongue ruled all the other members through teaching that Ptah is within every body, as heart and mind, and within every mouth, as tongue, of all the divine powers, of all humankind, of cattle, of all creeping things and of all living things. And He thinks as heart and mind and commands as tongue whatever He wishes. . . . The seeing of the eyes, the hearing of the ears and the breathing of the nose are communicated to the heart and mind, and the heart and mind cause all perceptions to come forth. And what the heart and mind think and wish is declared by the tongue. So were all divine powers created and the company of divine powers complete. (Karenga, 1989, p. 24)

Focusing on the transformation of the source of life or creator (Ra, symbolized by the sun) into divine human consciousness (Ptah), the text suggests that, for the most part, reality is created by what we think, feel, and say. Although tracing the evolution of this theoretical or conceptual approach across thousands of years is beyond the scope of this chapter, its theme is picked up in contemporary times by the African-centered theorists in the cultural congruence school, which I discuss later.

Turning now to the reemergence of Black Psychology in the West, one of the first psychological treatises written by an African examining the experience of European chattel enslavement and exploring its devastating impact was an autobiographical text by former captive, Olaudah Equiano (1797/2001). His work still stands today as a testimony of the will of African people to give voice to the social realities created by the dominant cultural group.

Edward R. Blyden (1856) was one of the first scholars to examine the psychological and social damage caused by the colonization of Africa by the Europeans. Blyden sought to prove that Africa and Africans have a worthy history and culture. He rejected the prevailing notion of the inferiority of the Black man but accepted the view that each major race has a special contribution to make to world civilization. He also examined the impact of Westernized religion on the African. Blyden's text was perhaps one of the first books written in the English language to use critical theory and "deconstruction" to challenge the then-widespread notion of African inferiority.

Carter G. Woodson (1933), a prophetic scholar and educator, analyzed the negative impact of the formal educational system on Black people, leading to the miseducation that would ensure their continued subjugation as a race. The seminal works of these early thinkers contributed to the foundation of a body of knowledge on which Black Psychology is built in the West. Their conceptual approaches are culturally congruent and avoid identification with the primacy of the mainstream American cultural worldview. This school of thought reemerged in the late 1970s and early 1980s, as evidenced in the cultural congruence school among scholars fully exposed to mainstream American psychology.

When, in the late 1960s and early 1970s, the social, cultural, and political conditions made it possible for African Americans to be trained in the discipline of Western psychology, they immediately began to identify the limitations inherent in their training with regard to Black people. Their critiques of the field pointed out mainstream psychology's contribution to the continued oppression and dehumanization of people acknowledging African descent. The Association of Black Psychologists did not believe APA, given its history and prevailing monocultural views, had the capacity to effectively identify, much less meet the mental health needs of people who acknowledge African descent. Although that view is still widely held in the field of Black Psychology, there are various approaches that address the inadequacies of mainstream American psychology. Adopting a strategy of identifying with the cultural mainstream has its costs and benefits, as does stepping outside the box of mainstream dominant culture. Two years after the formation of the Association of Black Psychologists, the first and only African American was elected APA president: Kenneth Clark.

Assimilation: Conforming to Mainstream American

Within the literature identified as Black Psychology, the approaches that adhere to a mainstream American cultural worldview and perspectives are identified here as belonging to the assimilation school. Theoretical perspectives and conceptual approaches are shaped by the larger social context within which they emerge, and the scholars of the genre, having been trained in the Western tradition of psychology, bring forward perspectives influenced by that training, as well as their orientation to and basis for cultural identification. In exploring the diversity of perspectives within Black Psychology, we can see the role of sociocultural influences and can better identify, appreciate, and understand the multiple forces shaping the realities informing each perspective.

The research of Kenneth Clark and Mamie Phipps Clark fits within the assimilation school and has been credited with helping shape the 1954 landmark Supreme Court decision *Brown v. Board of Education of Topeka, Kansas*, which ruled public school segregation unconstitutional. The Clarks' research concluded that Black children had negative self-concepts, due largely to the impact of segregated formal educational systems on them. The research of Kenneth and Mamie Phipps Clark challenged the notion of differences in the mental abilities of Black and White children. The cultural frame of reference of this research is grounded in assimilation. The long-term consequences of the research have not been proven to yield the outcomes in educational achievement for the masses of Black children that were desired. In addition, the self-concepts of Black children have not been shown to improve with school desegregation.

In terms of future research, still to be addressed are in-depth longitudinal analyses of the costs and benefits of assimilation into the American educational mainstream. What are the costs, as well as benefits, of assimilation into a formal educational system that has its primary goal the indoctrination of the students into a dominant cultural worldview that has historically denigrated them and the perpetuation of a status quo that has historically disenfranchised them? To what extent does valid cultural mistrust interfere with the capacities of students to adopt and adapt to the information being taught? How are the abilities of the progeny of involuntary-immigrant African-descent American students influenced educationally by the utilization of a cultural worldview and pedagogy that are alien to their cultural realities and experiences? In what ways are current social policies and practices designed to provide opportunity for low-income students to get access to higher education, contributing to an untenable status quo for the communities of these African American students? What is, and how does one measure, educational success for this population?

These and other questions must be addressed if Black Psychology is to fully realize its intention and potential. Given the prophetic cautions of Woodson (1933) in the early 20th century, it would appear that the "mis-education of the Negro" remains a pervasive problem. More culturally congruent research has demonstrated that the educational success of all children, and Black children in particular, are best met in warm, nurturing environments where the expectation for success is high and is matched with instruction in accordance with the learning styles appropriate for the children being taught (Hilliard, 1991; Wilson, 1992).

A valuable contemporary assimilation-oriented view was presented by Charisse Jones and Kumea Shorter-Gooden (2003) in their treatment of the psychological process they called *shifting*. Their research identified and described the revelation that a large number of Black women experience pressure to compromise their true selves in order to fit in to American society. They reported changing inwardly and outwardly—that is, shifting to "White," then to "Black" again, or shifting to "corporate," and so on. Jones and Shorter-Gooden see this process as a coping and survival skill that diminishes the joys of living an authentic life and that can have a devastating effect on the woman's body and soul, making women susceptible to an array of psychological problems, including anxiety, low self-esteem, disordered eating, depression, and self-hatred.

With many Black women reported as left feeling conflicted, weary, and alone, while attempting to make others feel comfortable and themselves acceptable, the solution Jones and Shorter-Gooden (2003) offered for this deplorable condition is catharsis by encouraging the women to share their stories and give voice to their pain. Although a necessary first step, the strategy proffered is restricted by the assimilation orientation, which may support women's ability to adapt to compromising but does not provide the women with a means to move toward authenticity and sustainable health.

These fine researchers have identified important problems and issues to be addressed. What is "good mental health" for Black women, and how can it best be achieved? Liberation from the dominant culture's worldview and adoption of a culturally congruent perspective would provide one viable healing solution (Myers, 1992, 2003). Research looking at the career paths, challenges, and successes of African Americans who choose not to "shift" seems warranted. The assimilation school has contributed strategies for working with the critical issues and concerns facing Black people within the system that created and supports them.

Bicultural Reform

A number of researchers' work fits the bicultural reform approach. In part, the approach to the subject matter intends more knowledge by emphasizing the duality of the Black experience but at the same time moving toward clearer self-definition. One area of research in which this approach has proliferated is that which looks at racial identity. One of the most widely used models of racial identity development is the one commonly associated with William Cross. He and his colleagues conceptualized a model of Black identity development referred to as the *psychological Nigrescence model*, which has been revised (Cross, 1971, 1995). The model starts with a stance conforming to the dominant culture's norms with the intention of predicting movement toward a positive racial identity, which would be a position counter to that perpetuated by the dominant culture. The racial identity research and instrument development done by Helms and her students has contributed greatly to the study and elaboration of this model (e.g., Helms & Cook, 1999). The Negro-to-Black conversion model has been criticized because the determinants of the person's worldview are dominated by Euro-American sociocultural constructs, which are believed to cause the individual to degrade or deny Blackness. While this progression may be accurate for those who start from a position of internalized oppression and racism, this trajectory may not be the starting point for many Blacks who have recognized and understood the misguided nature of the larger social context.

Questions remain regarding whether it is truly a developmental process, because little evidence for the progressive sequencing through the model's stages has been found, and little empirical support has been found for the "encounter" stage. Movement from internalization of the dominant culture's views and negative stance toward to a positive identity has been of great interest to many scholars and researchers. Its relevance can be noted in the number of groups for whom this model has resonated, those who also inhere a human diversity marker for which they are oppressed by the dominant culture, including gays and lesbians, Hispanics/Latinos, Asian Americans, and feminists.

Future research should include exploration of a model that is designed to take into account individuals who do not begin in their developmental process toward the achievement and sustaining of a positive racial identity in a hostile social context with internalized oppression or conforming to the determinants of the dominant culture's worldview. In addition, defining with specificity the following concerns is requisite: What does it mean to be Black?; what would a truly positive and sustainable Black identity look like?; what are the characteristics of the culminating stage of positive racial identity development?; how it would function?; and how is it sustained in a social context in which the dominant worldview has not changed? Many researchers have contributed greatly to these clarifications; however, more work needs to be done in the areas mentioned.

A number of Black psychologists have used their experiences and exposures to inform the bicultural reform approach, which is designed to both critique mainstream psychology and offer directives that could lead toward alternative paradigms. The part autobiography and part history of psychology research of Robert V. Guthrie, author of *Even the Rat Was White* (1998), documents and informs the scope and growth of African American Psychology from the time of its emergence in America. Joseph L. White and James H. Cones III, authors of *Black Man Emerging: Facing the Past and Seizing the Future* (1999), used their personal views and experiences struggling with oppression and case histories and biographical sketches of other Black men to describe effective strategies for dealing with racism and healing communities. Joseph L. White is one of the earliest African American psychologists to address the issues faced by African American men in America. Reginald Jones, editor of *Black Psychology* (1991, 1994) and numerous other key texts instrumental to the advancement of Black Psychology (R. Jones, 1999a, 1999b), is a third researcher who has contributed significantly to the literature of Black Psychology that could be described as bicultural reform, providing that transitional bridge to the more self-determining cultural congruent stance of common to African(a) Psychology. The texts edited by Jones are typically inclusive of multiple schools of thought. Future research conducted by African American women would be of great benefit to the field and bring forward voice and balance seen less often than that of men, although there seem to be more women in the field. A number of researchers' work is making significant contributions to the field by utilizing the research methods of mainstream American psychology to inform understandings about persons of African descent that would otherwise be unavailable. Particularly significant has been the work of Madonna Constantine, Suzette Speight, Nancy Boyd Franklin, Shawn Utsey, Faye Belgrave, and their students, as well as others too numerous to mention.

Cultural Congruence

There are several scholars in the school focusing on cultural congruence and the development of alternative paradigms based on African-centered cultural realities and experiences; a few are mentioned here to provide examples of the genre. Kobi Kambon (formerly known as Joseph Baldwin) was one of the first African American psychologists to develop an African self-consciousness scale to explore the many facets of African American identity. Baldwin went beyond the mainstream cultural definitions to theoretical positions that allowed the interrogation of constructs beyond the conscious and cognitive self. Akbar (1995, 2003), trained as a clinical psychologist in a psychodynamically oriented program, focuses his research on increasing understanding of the mental health needs of African Americans. His categories of mental disorder, designed to provide the appropriate cultural frame for more validly assessing and diagnosing African American mental functioning, has been a major contribution to the field, along with the nosology developed by Azibo.

Nobles (1986, 2005) argued that because Western psychology has misunderstood and distorted the essence of African thought, it has also failed to acknowledge the human being as an entity that comprises spiritual as well as physical attributes. Because in ancient African thought the universe is perceived as being interconnected and communal, Nobles's work focuses on the essential nature of the family in terms of the existence of the individual and the spiritual nature of the human being. Thomas Parham's (2002) edited text, *Counseling Persons of African Descent: Raising the Bar of Practitioner Competence*, includes a number of chapters by researchers discussing the deepening of our understanding of the origins of African identity, value systems, and worldview. Through the African worldview the contemporary lives of African Americans can be improved and much of the trauma healed. My own work (Myers, 1988, 1992) builds on the assumptions of this worldview to develop a theory of Optimal Psychology that fully embraces and acknowledges the primary role of consciousness in human experience and it subjective nature to inform an understanding of humanity that allows for the primacy of spirit and its illumination toward the realization of divine consciousness. E. Bruce Bynum's (1999) *The African Unconscious*, a seminal work on the African roots of psychology and many spiritual disciplines, represents another major step in the development of the cultural congruence school literature.

The cultural congruence school faces the challenge of what I (Myers, 2003) refer to as *fearless studies*, that is, embarking on the interrogation of subject matter heretofore perceived as esoteric, mysterious, or unknowable by Western standards. According to my analysis and that of other scholars in this school, the depth and breadth of the African worldview opens up levels of consciousness not otherwise generally pursued in the West, as well as new understandings of what it means to be human, the purpose and meaning of life, and the multiple levels of consciousness. Still to be grappled with are the role and value of African metaphysics in the mental functioning and health of people who acknowledge African descent. Furthermore, the boundaries of currently surrounding our conceptions of the nature of human consciousness must be expanded. Questions for future research in the field of Black Psychology are many and varied, and each school has its own special pieces to contribute. Essential questions and issues remain for all to address. One area yet to be fully interrogated is the question of what mental health is, individually and collectively, for a people existing in a hostile social context in which healthy, efficacious behaviors have historically been seen as insane.

This and other questions hold great promise for future conceptual and theoretical approaches in the field of Black Psychology. Black Psychology in this context is concerned with the future and evolution of all of humanity, as the interdependence and interrelatedness of all is appreciated. A holistic perspective encourages the examination of the hard question. For example, why has the leadership offered by the West in general and the United States in particular, despite its contributions, led humanity and the world as we know it to the brink of destruction in terms of depletion of resources, destruction of the environment, global wars, human alienation, and so on? What factors and forces pushed the early development of psychology as a discipline in the United States from a commitment to a deeper understanding of and interest in the soul to that of behavior, a limited conception of mind, and the objectification of the researcher?

The current human condition offers the opportunity to explore the simultaneous interweavings of individual and collective factors and forces that function to create the realities and histories humanity has experienced to date. A culturally congruent Black Psychology will continue to provide new lenses through which to view the status of things. The idea that all is in everything takes us out of the box of either–or reasoning to a place of observing the degree and functioning of what is, yielding both–and conclusions. With this in mind, the subject matter of Black Psychology is not limited. Although all pursuits are assumed of value, learning more about the sociocultural, historical, personal, and other factors contributing to sustainable human triumph and diminishing human suffering is essential.

Summary and Conclusion

The problem of cultural orientation in psychology may not be in having a strong cultural preference for one's own heritage itself—it may be in the nature of the assumptions, designs for living, and patterns of interpreting reality that characterize the cultural worldview. When the cultural worldview encourages the devaluing and dehumanization of other cultural groups, attributing little or no positive value to the differences perceived and identifying them as deficiencies relative to their own cultural norms, the result is a monocultural hegemony that is damaging and destructively nonsustainable across cultures and humanity. Cultures with such characteristics run the risk of becoming monoculturally hegemonic. Such cultural traditions typically define cultural differences as deficiencies and tend not to be oriented toward the discernment of interrelatedness and interdependence. This kind of cultural tradition presents particular challenges to nondominant members of the society, including academicians and researchers, who are members of cultural groups perceived as deficient or who do not embrace the dominant cultural perspective. The need for understanding and insight into the human personality and the collective humanity has not decreased over time; neither has the cumulative impact of increased information gleaned by the "human sciences" yielded improved human relations, either intrapersonally or interpersonally, as one might expect.

As the literature of Black Psychology has been reviewed, the direct relationship between the proximity to mainstream values and worldview determinants of the scholarship, and mainstream psychology's reception to the scholarship, becomes apparent. This relationship is readily accounted for by the interrelated and interdependent nature of psychology and its sociocultural context that was discussed earlier. Nonconforming ideas or radical departures from the dominant cultural worldview often are not published in mainstream journals or by mainstream presses; therefore, the broader mainstream audience's access to much of this important psychology literature is limited. Only recently has there been increased interest in psychology as developed in other cultural groups, but that interest has mostly been focused on so-called Eastern philosophies; little attention has yet been paid to Africa, and even less has been paid to the involuntary African immigrants whose cultural heritage and traditions have continued to be honored. In some cases, the decision to publish outside of the mainstream has been the preference of the scholar, because the target audience is not mainstream America and/or the freedom to speak the truth as known is cherished over mainstream acceptance.

In focusing on the field of African(a) Psychology, it is evident that great strides have been made in developing theories that hold tremendously insightful implications for all of humankind and that have been utilized by other cultural psychologies. However, the dominant cultural worldview in the West still devalues alternate cultural frames of reference, designs for living, and patterns of interpreting reality, particularly African/African American ones (Parham, 2002). When examined, the theoretical and conceptual developments in the field over the course of its history can be seen to reflect the cycles of time and knowledge that are coming full circle to present a picture of humanity that is comprehensive, cohesive, and coherent.

References

Akbar, N. (1995). *Natural psychology and human transformation.* Tallahassee, FL: Mind Productions.

Akbar, N. (2003). *Akbar papers in African Psychology.* Tallahassee, FL: Mind Productions.

Azibo, D. A. (1996). *African Psychology in historical perspective and related commentary.* Trenton, NJ: African Third World Press.

Belgrave, F. Z., & Allison, K. W. (2006). *African American Psychology: From Africa to America.* Thousand Oaks, CA: Sage.

Bernal, M. (1987). *Black Athena: The Afroasiatic roots of classical civilization (The fabrication of ancient Greece 1785–1985): Volume 1.* Newark, NJ: Rutgers University Press.

Blyden, E. W. (1856). *A voice from bleeding Africa.* Cambridge, MA: Classic Books.

Bynum, E. B. (1999). *The African unconscious: Roots of ancient mysticism and modern psychology.* New York: Teachers College Press.

Cross, W. E. (1971). The Negro-to-Black conversion experience. *Black World, 20,* 13–27.

Cross, W. E. (1995). The psychology of Nigrescence: Revising the Cross model. In J. Ponterrotto, J. Casas, L. Suzuki, & C. Alexander (Eds.), *Handbook of multi-cultural counseling* (pp. 93–122). Thousand Oaks, CA: Sage.

Equiano, O. (2001). *The interesting narrative of the life of Olaudah Equiano, or Gustavus Vassa, the African, written by himself.* New York: Broadview Press. (Original work published 1789)

Grills, C. (2002). African-centered psychology: Basic principles. In T. A. Parham (Ed.), *Counseling persons of African descent: Raising the bar of practitioner competence* (pp. 10–24). Thousand Oaks, CA: Sage.

Grills, C., & Rowe, D. (1998). African traditional medicine: Implications for African-centered approaches to healing. In R. L. Jones (Ed.), *African American mental health: Theory, research and intervention* (pp. 71–100). Berkeley, CA: Cobb & Henry.

Guthrie, R. V. (1998). *Even the rat was white: A historical view of psychology* (2nd ed.). Needham Heights, MA: Allyn & Bacon.

Helms, J., & Cook, D. (1999). *Using race and culture in counseling and psychotherapy: Theory and process.* Needham Heights, MA: Allyn & Bacon.

Herrnstein, R. J., & Murray, C. (1999). *The bell curve: Intelligence and class structure in American life.* New York: Free Press.

Hilliard, A. G. (1991). *Testing African American students.* Chicago: Third World Press.

James, G. G. M. (1953). *Stolen legacy.* New York: Africa World Press.

Jones, C., & Shorter-Gooden, K. (2003). *Shifting: The double lives of Black women in America.* New York: HarperCollins.

Jones, R. L. (1991). *Black Psychology.* Hampton, VA: Cobb & Henry.

Jones, R. L. (1994). *Black Psychology* (2nd ed.). Hampton, VA: Cobb & Henry.

Jones, R. L. (Ed.). (1999a). *Advances in African American Psychology.* Hampton, VA: Cobb & Henry.

Jones, R. L. (Ed.). (1999b). *African American mental health.* Hampton, VA: Cobb & Henry.

Kambon, K. K. K. (1998). *African/Black Psychology in the American context: An African-centered approach.* Tallahassee, FL: Nubian Nation.

Karenga, M. (1989). *Selections from the Husia: Sacred wisdom of ancient Egypt.* Los Angeles: University of Sankore Press.

Myers, L. J. (1988). *Understanding the Afrocentric world view: Introduction to Optimal Psychology.* Dubuque, IA: Kendall/Hunt.

Myers, L. J. (1992). *Understanding the Afrocentric world view: Introduction to Optimal Psychology* (2nd ed.). Dubuque, IA: Kendall/Hunt.

Myers, L. J. (1999a). Therapeutic processes for health and wholeness in the 21st century: Belief systems analysis and the paradigm shift. In R. L. Jones (Ed.), *Advances in African American Psychology* (pp. 313–358). Hampton, VA: Cobb & Henry.

Myers, L. J. (1999b). Transforming psychology: An African American perspective. In R. L. Jones (Ed.), *Advances in African American Psychology* (pp. 9–26). Hampton, VA: Cobb & Henry.

Myers, L. J. (2003). *Our health matters: Guide to an African (indigenous) American psychology and cultural model for creating a climate and culture of optimal health.* Columbus: Ohio Commission on Minority Health.

Nobles, W. W. (1986). *African Psychology: Towards its reclamation, reascension, & revitalization.* Oakland, CA: The Institute for the Advanced Study of Black Family Life and Culture.

Nobles, W. W. (2005). *Seeking the Sakhu: Foundational writings for an African Psychology.* Chicago: Third World Press.

Obenga, T. (2005). *African philosophy: The Pharaonic period: 2780–330 BC.* London: Karnak House.

Parham, T. A. (2002). *Counseling persons of African descent: Raising the bar of practitioner competence.* Thousand Oaks, CA: Sage.

Popenoe, P. B. (1929). *The child's heredity.* New York: Williams & Wilkins.

Richards, G. (1997). *Race, racism and psychology: Towards a reflexive history.* New York: Routledge.

White, J. L., & Cones, J. H., III. (1999). *Black man emerging: Facing the past and seizing the future.* New York: Routledge.

Wilson, A. (1992). *Awakening the natural genius of Black children.* New York: Afrikan World Infosystems.

Woodson, C. G. (1933). *The mis-education of the Negro.* Washington, DC: The Associated Publishers.

4

AFRICAN PSYCHOLOGY, OR *SAHKU SHETI*

An Application of the Art of Spiritual Liberation and Illumination of African People

EZEMENARI M. OBASI AND ANTHONY J. SMITH

The field of African Psychology stands on the shoulders of a rich legacy that ranges from ancient KMT (i.e., Egypt) to the Black Power movement of the 1960s. It is multidisciplinary in nature yet has an interdependent relationship with the advancement of the Africentric paradigm largely associated with prominent scholars in Black Studies programs. Although a comprehensive history of African Psychology is beyond the scope of this chapter, the reader is encouraged to read some of the seminal writings that have shaped the current trajectory of this filed (Akbar, 1979, 1981, 1984, 1985; Asante, 1987, 1988; Clark, McGee, Nobles, & Weems, 1975; Grills, 2004; Kambon, 1998; Karenga, 1982; Karenga & Carruthers, 1986; Myers, 1987, 1988; Nobles, 1972, 1973, 1976, 1986, 1998). This chapter instead is designed to provide a primer of African Psychology, first by revisiting the philosophical assumptions that guide the discipline. This includes a critical discussion of the constructs of worldview, human beingness, health, and illness. We also will advance a set of principles and interventions that can be used in the healing process. Finally, we present a case illustration in the spirit of providing an example of how a healer trained in psychology might translate some of these principles into practice.

According to the African Psychology Institute of the Association of Black Psychologists, African-Centered Psychology is defined as

> the dynamic manifestation of the unifying African principles, values and traditions. It is the self-conscious centering of psychological analysis and applications in African reality, culture, and epistemology. African-Centered Psychology examines the process that allows for the illumination and liberation of the spirit. Relying on the principles of harmony within the universe as a natural order of existence, African-Centered Psychology recognizes: the Spirit that permeates everything that is; the notion that everything in the universe is interconnected; the value that the collective is

the most salient element of existence; and the idea that communal self-knowledge is the key to mental health. (Parham, White, & Ajamu, 1999, p. 95)

On the basis of this formulation, African-Centered Psychology represents a first step toward designing a discipline that is concerned with addressing the mental health needs of people of African descent from a self-empowering vantage point. This definition represents a radical redefinition of psychology in a way that embraces the ethnocultual worldview, experience, and metaphysical humanity of African people. As a result, it rejects the Western doctrine of materialism and embraces the possibilities associated with a spirit-based ontological system.

To date, there has been a healthy debate that raises the question of whether African-Centered Psychology is a functional scientific discipline that has the capacity to address the plight of African people throughout the Diaspora. To be a functional discipline, African-Centered Psychology would first have to have a critical mass of elders and *jegnas*—protectors of the tradition—who are responsible for keeping the ancestral wisdom that has been passed down from generation to generation, adapting such ideas to be relevant under present conditions, and infusing into this rich depository new ideas that uphold the tradition's mission. This would be consistent with the *Akan* proverb that recognizes the notion that one head does not store all wisdom ("Ti-korɔ mu nni nyansa"). According to Ajamu (2004), such a scientific discipline should include a systematicity of deep thought, theoretical construction and consistency, methodological precision, and paradigmatic coherence. Thus, culturally congruent methodology would have to be developed with the intention of protecting the discipline's philosophical models from falsification (Banks, 1992). Such methodology must be well thought out and in harmony with the African *Utamawazo*—or worldview.

In addition, there would need to be an institutionalized mechanism from which such wisdom and art are disseminated to future custodians of the tradition. This then begs a series of logistical questions, such as Where will these institutions be located? How will they be funded? What process will be used to determine who will be initiated into this system? What pedagogy will be used to develop future generations of deep thinkers and healers? What is the scope of services that will be provided? To what ethical code will the initiates of this system be bound? In the end, a system will need to be in place that is both regenerative and consistent with the African *Utamawazo*.

Ultimately, an appropriate name needs to be adopted that speaks to the essence of such a discipline. The term *African-Centered* is typically used to articulate an alignment with the African *Utamawazo*. In contrast, psychology is defined as the study of the human mind and behavior. Given technological advances in the area of neuroscience (e.g., functional magnetic resonance imaging, magnetoencephalography, electroencephalography), it is not uncommon for neuronal activity to be used as a materialistic surrogate for the immaterial mind. Psychology's ontological position is rooted in materialism and embraces logical positivism (or empiricism) as the method for justifying and protecting its ideas. Such an antimetaphysical approach is in direct conflict with the African *Utamawazo*. An alternative to the term *African-Centered Psychology* is *Sahku Sheti*—from ancient KMT. According to Nobles (1998), *Sahku* is defined as understanding, the illuminator, the eye of the soul, and that which inspires. *Sheti* involves the deep exploration of a subject, to study profoundly, to penetrate deeply. Therefore, *Sahku Sheti* represents the deep penetration into the understanding, illumination, and inspiration of the soul.

An *Akan* proverb reminds us that one does not exchange the feather of an eagle for that of a vulture ("Obi mfa ne kɔreɛ takra nkɔsesa pɛtɛ takra"). *Sahku Sheti* represents a liberating alternative to the field of psychology. As a result, it is imperative that its keepers resist the urge to develop psychological accoutrements that are disguised as *Sahku Sheti*. Doing so would be tantamount to spray painting Socrates black and calling him Imhotep. Akbar (1984) reminds us that

> African social scientists have failed to come to grips with the fact that the tools that they have acquired in the course of their training in the Western social science tradition have ill-equipped them to deal with the fundamental task of liberating African people—socially, politically, economically, and psychologically. (p. 395)

A challenge for the elders and *jegnas* of *Sahku Sheti* involves the mental cleansing needed to free its custodians of the conceptual incarceration that comes as a function of 20-plus years of Western schooling and minimal African education. The mission of *Sahku Sheti* ultimately involves the arduous teleological thrust toward the spiritual, mental, physical, and social liberation of African people throughout the Diaspora. Although many people of African descent may have lost a conscious connection to their history, culture, worldview, and spiritual essence, it is not forbidden when you go back and take that which you forgot ("Wo wɛrɛ firi na wosane kɔfa a, yɛnkyi"). *Sankɔfa!*

UTAMAWAZO

Utamawazo (Ani, 1994) is a Kiswahili term that refers to the culturally structured thought—or worldview—that is determined by the primordial essence of a people. It determines the way in which people are socialized to perceive, think, and experience the world (Myers, 1988). *Utamawazo* represents the culmination of philosophical beliefs that have been sharpened through the historical trial of experience, and it serves as the navigational system that guides human behavior.

Similar to the African-centered Psychology question, there is an ongoing debate regarding whether an African philosophy exists as a discipline (Gyekye, 1995; Hountondji, 1983; Wiredu, 1980). Given the futility of such a debate, there is no question that African deep thought—or posing questions that reflect the fundamental aspects of the human life experience—is prevalent throughout the African continent (Obasi, 2002). This can be seen in the folktales, proverbs, and spiritual systems that are inseparable from traditional African life. In order to actualize *Sahku Sheti* as a legitimate discipline that has the capacity to engender the spiritual liberation and illumination of African people throughout the Diaspora, the keepers of the discipline must have an understanding of African deep thought. Nobles (1972) argued that African philosophy—or deep thought—is quintessential to understanding the African experience. The African *Utamawazo* also serves as the survival toolkit for African people.

It is important to note that the African continent is filled with thousands of indigenous groups living in diverse geographic areas. Furthermore, centuries of migration—both forced and voluntary—have resulted in African people living all over the world. As a result, it would be irresponsible to assume that all of these communities operate and experience the world in an indistinguishable manner. This begs the question of whether there is a universal African *Utamawazo* that can be meaningfully applied to African people throughout the Diaspora. Many social scientists and philosophers have identified important commonalities that are woven in the African cultural fabric that cannot merely be dismissed as coincidence (Akbar, 1979, 1984, 1985; Ben-Jochannon, 1971/1988, 1972/1989; Billingsley, 1968; Diop, 1974, 1978; Kambon, 1998; Mbiti, 1970; Nobles, 1972, 1976; Williams, 1976). However, such customary ethos may be expressed differently in response to geographic specific stressors (i.e., nature, colonization, slavery, oppression, missionaries, etc.). The constructs of cosmology, epistemology, ontology, axiology, and teleology historically have been used to articulate the African *Utamawazo*.

Cosmology. Cosmology refers to the study of the nature of the universe. More specifically, cosmology examines the structure of reality. The African *Utamawazo* contends that the universe is a creation of the Supreme Being; thus, it is divine in nature. The universe is understood to be a harmonious system in which all of its residing elements are understood to be interdependent and governed by a natural order. Furthermore, human beings are understood to be organically related to all things in the universe (Nobles, 1998). Therefore, the same forces and natural order that permeate and govern the cosmic universe also permeate and govern the life of people.

Epistemology. Epistemology is concerned with understanding the foundations of human knowledge. Within the African *Utamawazo*, perceptions are not limited to space, time, and the five senses. Spiritual mediumship in the forms of divination, telepathy, clairvoyance, precognition, and dreams are all forms in which knowledge can be obtained about the past, present, or the future. Gyekye (1995) asserted that some aspects of knowledge are understood to be intuitive ("Obi nkyere abofra Nyame" ["No one teaches a child God"]) and dependent on experience

("Nneema nyinaa dan sua" ["All things depend on experience"]). Knowledge is derived from active participation with and experience in the universe (Nobles, 1998). Emotion and affect are also important sources of knowledge (Akbar, 1984).

Ontology. Ontology can be understood as assigning a meaning to the essential nature of reality. The African *Utamawazo* employs a spiritual basis of reality. As a result, knowledge is connected to reality through the functions of the Supreme Being, departed ancestors, human beings, and spiritual energy permeating the entire universe (Gyekye, 1995; Mbiti, 1970). African ontology is both idealistic (i.e., has a spiritual basis of reality) and naturalistic (i.e., has a physical basis of reality). In the African *Utamawazo,* scientific causality is regarded as incomplete because it answers only the "how" question (Mbiti, 1970) and leaves chance, or probability, unanswered. Gyekye (1995) stated that African causality is generally explained in terms of spiritual phenomenon.

Axiology. Axiology describes a fundamental value system that defines the relationships between people and their environment. The value system associated with the African *Utamawazo* is determined by divine law (i.e., the Seven Cardinal Virtues of Maat: truth, justice, righteousness, harmony, balance, order, and reciprocity; Carruthers, 1995; Hilliard, 1998) and is witnessed in the works of nature. Human relationships are characterized as being driven by communalism, cooperation, harmony with nature, and survival of the group, to name a few (Kambon, 1998, Nobles, 1976). Gyekye (1995) stated that undergoing shame, disgrace, or dishonor that results from unethical behavior is a serious sanction in African moral conduct ("Aniwu ne owu, na efanim owu" ["Given a choice between disgrace and death, one had better choose death"]). Therefore, interpersonal relationships with nature and other human beings become essential in defining what it means to be human. Within the African *Utamawazo,* the ancestors are venerated, elders are respected, and all adults are responsible and held accountable for the moral and spiritual development of the children. According to the *Akan,* if a minor breaks nine taboos, he or she is held responsible for five ("Abɛ̈fraɛ̈b mmusuo nkron a, ɛ̈fa mu num"), while the rest is shouldered by the family, elders, and broader community.

Teleology. Teleology refers to the science of becoming, or the theory that everything acts for an end purpose. It investigates an object's sense of directedness, definite ends, and ultimate purpose. The African *Utamawazo* is concerned with the "alchemical process of human transformation" (Nobles, 1986), where spiritual illumination transcends physical desires. Nobles (1986) described African human development as

> a) a sense of "self," which gives it some understanding of its own integrity; b) motion, which implies its changing nature; c) order, which defines the natural connections and separations of its integrity; d) form, which outlines its integrity and marks the point of distinction; and e) direction, which identifies its purpose and mission. (p. 95)

Part of what it means to be human also involves an active engagement in a community and the pursuit of one's destiny through the exhibition of good character. Poverty of friendship is worse than material poverty ("Ago-hia sene hia pa"). In the end, the life cycle is patterned by nature (birth, growth, reproduce, grows old, dies, rebirth...) and can best be characterized as comprising cycles that represent the progression and digression of the soul's development across time.

Research. To date, there is a dearth of empirical evidence to substantiate the universality and applicability of such claims. In part, this is due to conceptual incarceration (Nobles, 1986) whereby Western science dictates what epistemology and methodology are deemed credible for uncovering ontological relationships. Given this imposed etic (cultural universal) that is inherent to Western science, limitations in researching African deep thought become inevitable when epistemological and ontological relationships rooted in consubstantiation (spirit as the first principle) come into conflict with research methods that are fundamentally grounded in a Western worldview. In summary, it is difficult to impossible to use research methods grounded in materialism and logical positivism to uncover spiritual phenomena.

Given the limitations in such methodology, historical, anthropological, and social science research has consistently illustrated the vast amount of basic cultural similarities between Africans born in Africa and their descendents throughout the Diaspora (Akbar, 1979, 1984, 1985; Ben-Jochannon, 1971/1988, 1972/1989; Billingsley, 1968; Diop, 1974, 1978; Du Bois, 1903; Grills & Livingston, 2001; Herskovits, 1958/1970; Janheinz, 1961; Kambon, 1998; Karenga, 1982; Nobles, 1972, 1976; Parham, White, & Ajamu, 1999; Williams, 1976). Much of this qualitative work has consisted of field interviews and observations; archeological excavations; and the review of archival documents, artwork, folktales, and proverbs, to name a few. More recently, some quantitative research using Western-based scale construction techniques have illustrated a strong connection that contemporary African people residing in the United States have with the African *Utamawazo* and culture (Baldwin & Bell, 1985; Baldwin & Hopkins, 1990; Montgomery, Fine, & Myers, 1990; Obasi, Flores, & Myers, in press; Utsey, Adams, & Bolden, 2000).

Human Beingness

One cannot begin to appreciate the scope of *Sahku Sheti* without having a clear understanding of what it means to be human. Within the African *Utamawazo* the notion of human beingness is not confined to the physical aspect of a person. Neither does the classification of being a Homo sapien automatically qualify a person as being human. To be human involves an active engagement with a community. It represents an organic relationship among human beings, nature, and the universe as whole. We present an *Akan* and *Yorùbá* conception of human beingness to provide examples of what it means to be human from two different African viewpoints. Such comparisons could have been made with other African communities (e.g., Bantu-Kongo, Dogon, Ga, Igbo, Lebou, Mende, Nuer, Zulu), but this is beyond the scope of this chapter. Although different in meaningful ways, the presentation of at least two cultural systems allows for the illustration of overarching similarities that are worth noting.

Akan. The *Akan* (an African ethnic group in Ghana) conception of the person has been reviewed previously in the literature (Appiah-Kubi, 1981; Danquah, 1968; Ephirim-Donkor, 1997; Fisher, 1998; Grills, 2004; Grills & Ajei, 2002; Gyekye, 1995; Nobles, 1998; Obasi, 2002; Opoku, 1978). According to *Akan* metaphysics, the person is understood to be both spiritual and physical in nature. More specifically, the person is conceptualized though the interchange among the *Ɔkra, sunsum,* and *nipadua.*

The *Ɔkra*—or soul—is understood to originate from and be a manifestation of the Supreme Being, *Onyankopon.* It represents the divine essence of the person that gives an existential meaning to life and is often referred to as the *living soul* (*Ɔkrateasafo*). The *Ɔkra* is the embodiment and transmitter of a person's destiny (*nkrabea*), and it resides only in human beings. *Honhom*—or breath of life—is evidence that the *Ɔkra* is currently manifested inside of the body (*nipadua*). Therefore, the *Akan* believe that the *Ɔkra* cannot leave the body without resulting in the physical death of the *nipadua*. Once the body experiences a cessation of breath, the *Ɔkra* leaves the *nipadua* and returns back to its origin, *Onyankopon.* It is at this point that the *Ɔkra* then accounts for its deeds.

Another important immaterial dimension of the person is *sunsum,* or spirit. It is important to note that the *Akan* understand *sunsum* to be the primary building block that permeates all natural things in the universe. It is an immaterial power, or force, that is manifested in human beings and in nature (trees, rocks, rivers, mountains, etc.). When applied to the person, *sunsum* is the intangible element that accounts for character (*suban*), intelligence (*nyansa*), disposition, and individuality. Unlike the *Ɔkra, sunsum* has the capacity to leave the person without resulting in physical death. In fact, it is the *sunsum* that is understood to be the actor—or persona—that travels and experiences during dreams. *Sunsum* is thought to be a direct correlate of health. In fact, a strong *sunsum* is thought to be a strong protector from illness.

In addition to *Ɔkra* and *sunsum* the *Akan* also recognize the importance of the material—or physical—aspect of the person. The *nipadua*, or body, is the house of vital entities such as the heart (*koma*), brain (*adwene*), and blood (*mogya*). *Mogya* is thought to be the most vital part of the *nipadua*, and it is understood to be passed down to the child through the mother. As a result, *mogya* represents a physiological bond to one's mother and an interdependent membership into her clan (*abusua*), or maternal lineage. Similarly, the child receives *ntro* from the father through his semen. The *ntro* also represents a paternal group membership. Both *mogya* and *ntro* represent biogenetic materials that are responsible for the character and phenotypic traits that a child inherits from the parents. Upon physical death, the *nipadua* returns to its origins—Mother Earth (*Asase Yaa*).

Yorùbá. The *Yorùbá* (an African ethnic group in Nigeria) conception of the person has also received a lot of attention in the literature (Bascom, 1991; Gbadegesin, 1991; Idowu, 1995; Lucas, 1996; Nobles, 1998; Obasi, 2002; Opoku, 1978). Consistent with the *Akan* model just presented, *Yorùbá* metaphysics also understands the person to be both spiritual and physical in nature. More specifically, the person is conceptualized through the interchange among *ara, èmí, orí, okàn,* and *ojiji*.

According to the *Yorùbá*, the *ara* is described as the physical/material body that is sculptured by the divinity, *Orìsà-nlá*. More specifically, the *ara* represents the flesh, bones, organs, and so on that give agency to our senses and allow people to interact with the physical environment. Given the physical nature of the *ara*, it will disintegrate back into the elements of the earth upon physical death. Once the *ara* is formed, the divinity *Olórun* animates the *ara* with the life-giving force of *èmí*, or spirit. *Èmí* is divine in nature and comes directly from the Supreme Being—*Olódùmarè*. Once *èmí* is activated throughout the *ara*, the body now has *èémí* (breath) and begins to *mí* (breathe). Given the essence of *èmí*, it does not perish during physical death. Instead, it returns back to *Elèmí*—the Owner of the Spirit—and accounts for its deeds.

Dimensions of the person that transcend a simplistic spiritual versus material classification include the *orí* and *okàn*. The *orí* is understood to be the physical head and is responsible for the personality of the person. Like the *Akan* notion of ɔ*kra*, the *orí* is the bearer of one's destiny. Additionally, *orí* is understood to be the guardian protector of the person that guides day-to-day decision making and is closely related to *èmí*. The *okàn* literally translates as the heart. However, it is much more than this English translation. For example, the *okàn* is more accurately understood as the heart–soul. It is understood to be the seat of intelligence, emotion, psychic energy, thought, and action. Similar to the *Akan* notion of *sunsum*, the *okàn* is thought to leave the body during sleep and experience what is understood to be a dream.

Finally, the *Yorùbá* recognize *ojiji*—shadow—as a constant companion of the person. The *ojiji* is a visible representation of the *okàn* that ceases to exist when the *ara* dies.

In summary, any conception of health and illness for people of African descent must take into account the metaphysical nature of what it means to be human. Both the *Akan* and the *Yorùbá* show an appreciation for the physical and spiritual aspects of the person. In fact, a holistic approach to healing must take this extended self (Nobles, 1976) into account. To address this belief, these communities regularly partake in rituals that are designed to keep both the body and soul strong. For example, the *Akan* participate in a ritual called ɔ*kraguare*. This is an ɔ*kra* cleansing that is performed to wash away filth that may have been accumulated on the soul through day-to-day life. With a substantial amount of importance placed on such rituals, the *Akan* elucidate the importance of maintaining both the physical and spiritual facets of the *onipa* (human being) to bring about a holistic notion of health. This is captured in the belief that unless the soul heals, the body will not respond to physical treatment (Gyekye, 1995).

Health and Disease

The African *Utamawazo* conceptualizes the notion of health from a holistic perspective. According to the *Bântu-Kôngo* deep thought, the prospect of being healthy involves a balance in life, or *kinenga kianzîngila* (Fu-Kiau, 1991). This conception of balance includes all aspects of the person, environment, and larger universe. Furthermore, they believe all people have a package of energy, or self-healing power (*ngolo*), that is biogenetically endowed by one's parents at the moment of conception (*va ngyakulu*). For the *Yorùbá*, the term *àlàáfíá* is used to describe health. *Àlàáfíá* is similar to the *Bântu-Kôngo* conception of health in that it takes into consideration a person's physical, spiritual, social, and psychological well-being. A person cannot claim to have *àlàáfíá* if he or she is experiencing an imbalance in any of these domains.

On the basis of these holistic conceptions of health, it makes sense that illness occurs at the juncture when one's *ngolo* begins to diminish and the person reaches a state of disequilibrium in life. According to the *Akan*, disease is a state of disharmony in the physical, psychological, emotional, social, environmental, and/or spiritual aspects of the person (Appiah-Kubi, 1981). As a result, unidimensional approaches to healing (spiritual or physical) are inadequate. Given this cosmic conceptualization of disease, *Akan* ontological interventions often involve a humble approach that calls on the Supreme Being (*Oyankopon*), Mother Earth (*Asase Yaa*), deities (*Ɔbosom*), and/or the ancestors (*Nananom Nsamanfo*) for answers. This can been seen in the *Akan* proverb "When the Supreme Being gives a disease, the Supreme Being prescribes the cure" ("*Oyanme ma wo yare a na wama ano aduru*"; Appiah-Kubi, 1981).

It is the role of the healer to regenerate people's self-healing power (*dikitisa ngolo*). The art of healing (*niakisa*) transcends the temptations of curing symptoms and engages in a healing process that has the propensity to restore equilibrium in the person, family, society, and nature. According to Fu-Kiau (1991), "healing wounds of the flesh is only half healing; furthermore, healing spiritual wounds, restoring individual smile and laughter, social ties and trust in the individual, self-confidence, and the normal flow of one's energy is whole healing" (p. 49).

TO BE A HEALER

Given the introduction of *Sahku Sheti* that we previously discussed, it is a natural extension to explore how to apply this perspective in a practical manner that is rooted both in the beliefs of our clients' ancestral forebears and in their subconscious archetypical images. It is important to note that one way of working with a client from an African perspective does not exist. In fact, having a variety of approaches and appealing to the intuitive art of healing is paramount for anyone who truly wants to be effective in the task of helping the African community. There is a time in the process where the academic mind must be turned off and the intuitive spiritual nature of the healer takes control. The techniques used when one is in this space cannot necessarily be quantified and are often client specific. In fact, because we are all shaped by a unique experience, our interpretation of how to work with a given individual can be quite different.

WAYS OF BEING

Within an African framework, the work of healing is multidimensional and interactive. It occurs within the healer and the client in a dynamic exchange of energy that affects both. Although the client's concerns are at the center of the therapeutic dialogue, the healer's level of balance and alignment directly informs what occurs throughout the client's experience. There are boundaries, but there is no finite disconnection between the healer and the healed—and one cannot neglect his or her own wellness and expect that neglect to not manifest in some way within the room. Before articulating practices the clinician can use to address the needs of the client, we first present a set of guidelines, as adapted from Armah's (1978) seminal novel *The Healers*, which can be used within the therapists' own practice of self-discovery and self-healing.

1. The Healer does not drink or smoke intoxicants.

One must be in a place of mental clarity in order to help others, and cannot have their mind or faculties altered in an inappropriate state. Intoxication blocks the flow of divine energy and promotes illusion. (p. 92)

2. The Healer should never call upon God to destroy anyone.

One cannot get around the fact that the concept of Spirit has a vital role of the lives of all. This is particularly important for those that we work with. Our ability to help them connect, reconnect, or strengthen their existing connection with spirit is a significant aspect of helping them reach their destiny. Regardless of the client's spiritual or religious affiliation, it is important to help them tap into their source of strength in a way that is culturally meaningful. (p. 93)

3. The Healer avoids going any place where people go to seek power over other people.

This is best understood by the phrase "power corrupts and absolute power corrupts absolutely." The need for power suggests one that feels they are "better than" others. Movement in this direction is counter to creating an egalitarian relationship that appreciates the God like qualities that inhabit us all. (p. 94)

4. Healers work to create a power based on respect.

Respect is reciprocal, with the therapist not placing themselves in a position of power or authority, instead establishing a more harmonious relationship which conveys that the client has the internal power to heal themselves. The healer serves as a mirror or a guide, to help individuals realign their soul with their destiny, or purpose. (p. 94)

5. The Healer does not heal a sick body.

Rather, the body has its own healing energies which fight the poisons and disease. The healer merely recognizes these healing energies and works to develop them to reduce the poisons of the disease. (pp. 81–82)

This suggests that healers must understand that they are merely conduits for the people they are working with. Each individual has divine qualities that can imbue them with the necessary tools for growth and development, and ultimately healing. Once healers are able to understand the person that they are working with and understand what particular healing energies are, they then can help to foster and increase those energies so that maximum growth and protection is attained. Simultaneously, healers identify those things that service as poisons and assist in the creation of remedies for these targets of intervention.

6. The Healer eschews rewards, fame, wealth, and power.

The work is hard; there is no comfort in it for the body. Occasionally, a healer might get thanks, but not typically. More often there is suspicion and hostility. Always there is contempt of those who will never understand the healer's work. (p. 91)

It takes a strong healer to remain devoted to the African art of healing despite those who threaten to attack and belittle the work that is being done. A sense of selflessness helps to facilitate this strength. *Humility* is one of the most important words on which the healer can constantly reflect. The healer must understand that he or she is merely a vessel being used by the Supreme Being to help those who come for guidance, insight, and growth.

The healer is involved with the client and feels what the client feels, but not to the extent that it becomes harmful to them. They have a healthy balance that comes from knowing thyself first. If healers have not done the work on themselves, then their mission to help others cannot manifest at a maximum level. This does not mean that the healer has to be perfect. It does suggest that healers have to be willing to constantly look at their own lives and the choices they make on their own path of evolution. In order to be grounded, it is important that healers focus on meditation or other epistemological techniques that facilitate one's capacity to get in touch with one's inner strengths. We have shown that modeling is a way in which lasting information is passed on. Thus, healers have to employ good character in an attempt to allow the light of the Supreme Being to shine through them and inspire those with whom they are working.

THE PRACTICAL HEALING PROCESS

To facilitate the healing process, there are some foundational issues, such as trust, purpose, and expertise, that are important to discuss. Trust is a key element in establishing a good therapeutic relationship with people who come for healing. One of the first barriers to treatment is getting past what may be understood as *cultural functional paranoia* (Ridley, 1984) or *healthy cultural suspicion* (Boyd-Franklin, 1989). This is especially the case when the services are being provided in a traditional mental health setting. Instead of adopting a posture of defensiveness, the healer might embrace this resistance and use it as a basis for discussion and investigation. When clients understand and intuitively feel that they do not have to explain all the nuances of racism, they are able to focus solely on the task of healing themselves. In short, trust is established by identifying with the client and allowing his or her natural fears and defensiveness to manifest and be adequately addressed.

The importance of dealing with the fundamental question of "Why?" stands out as a focus of initial involvement with the client. Asking our clients why they do what they do and what they would like to do differently provides a foundation for how the healing process will commence. Helping them to come to their own answers to the issues they bring into session is the ultimate goal. It also provides a clear operationalization of the purpose of therapy. Also, we cannot discuss African-centered approaches to treatment without largely involving spirit and intuition. The healer has to possess an intuitive faith that he or she is operating from a place of balance and *Iwa Pele*, or good character. The healer must also have a sense of humility to recognize when his or her ability ends and where the consultation/services of another healer should begin. In doing this work, healers will have a variety of tools at their disposal, the effectiveness of which will be commensurate with their natural ability and experience. In the following sections, we outline some interventions that may be incorporated into the healing process.

Using the Supreme Being in Therapy. It is impossible to deal with healing the human essence without understanding one's concept and relationship to a higher power. This is important, because the values that underscore this understanding of a Supreme Being are useful in helping individuals move toward important goals in their healing process. Often, traditional psychotherapy shies away from the inclusion of spirituality in the therapeutic process. *Sahku Sheti* understands that connecting one's concept of a Supreme Being with the use of questions and intuition can enhance the process of healing at the core of the person.

Divination. It is not uncommon for people to have questions regarding essential aspects of life (e.g., purpose, illness, relationship, job, personal crisis, decision making) whose answers seem inaccessible. Divination provides a medium where natural elements of the universe interact with the spiritual realm to provide people with important information that transcends cognitive deliberation. Although a proper divination will yield verifiable outcomes, the details of what can be obtained from a reading is a function of the person's experience with this technique. Examples of sacred implements used in divination include cowrie shells, coins, nuts, bones, coconut pieces, eggshells, sticks, and water.

Sacrificial Rites. In the spirit of reciprocity, to give and to receive should remain in harmonious balance. In order to receive specific things that a person might need, it is not uncommon for some type of sacrifice to take place. The purpose of performing a sacrifice may be to honor, commune, express gratitude, and/or appease forces that have the capacity to impact one's realty. Sacrifices can come in many forms. It could involve anything from an offering (e.g., food, drink, libation, money) to one's willingness to give up something for a specific duration of time. Sacrificial rites can target any aspect of the extended self (i.e., personal spirit, family, community, ancestors, deities, Mother Earth, or the Supreme Being) and can be a powerful technique for healing purposes. Specific rites can be identified by the individual, family, or broader community, or in consultation with a spiritual advisor.

Dreams. Dreams can be thought of as nonsense by American society. However, there is often important historical, present- and future-oriented information that can be obtained as the spirit travels while the body rests. A dream can be a warning, or it can provide information about choices that should or should not be made. Having an understanding of the symbolic meanings of dreams and how dreams affect a person's reality can be a useful tool for spiritual–emotional growth and healing.

Ancestral/Spiritual Guides. Most African traditions have a reverence for ancestors and appreciate their role in our day-to-day lives. Ancestors are able to see and understand things that we cannot. They have the capacity to provide guidance on how to negotiate challenges or barriers that exist in our lives. Ancestor altars are used to provide a sacred space in which to honor and commune with these ancestors in the spirit of receiving this information. Although we are probably all capable of tapping into a level of awareness that allows us to communicate with these ancestors or spiritual guides, our current socialization, with its emphasis on instant gratification and materialism, tends to strip us of this strength. Communing with these entities takes a level of patience and dedication that many people choose not to exercise. There may be some people whose gifts facilitate an ability to tap into this world, and all can benefit from this interaction.

Astrological Charts. Similar to the manner in which divination provides information about a person or situation on the basis of how elemental forces are manifesting in an individual's life, astrological charts map the influence of planetary cosmology onto those same elements. As humans, we fundamentally consist of the same elements that make up the universe. In the same way that the moon influences the ocean and the sun influences the earth, the position and the movement of the planets play a significant role in our personalities and significant life events. A trained astrologer—who goes beyond superficial interpretations and utilizes an authentic understanding of the dynamics of cosmos—can be quite useful in delineating personality traits, familial interactions, relationship dynamics, the cycles and patterns of obstacles, and stages of development. Although some may say it is absurd to think such forces influence our lives, the African *Utamawazo* would argue that it is absurd to think that we exist independent of the forces that direct and inform the development of the universe with which we are interdependent.

We now shift to looking at the practical application of some of these techniques in an actual session. When a client walks in the door, we can go into the session blind, with no knowledge of the presenting issues. At other times, we receive collateral information that gives us insight into the client's issues and how these have been approached previously. In the following case presentation, we were able to obtain a previous report that had been completed on the client, Donovan, a year before he came to us for treatment. We compare and contrast the different approaches utilized to understanding the client and ultimately "treat" the issues with which the client presents.

Brief Highlights of Applying Sahku Sheti. An African conception of health is holistic in nature. As previously mentioned, the notion of health—to experience *àlàáfíá*—must take into consideration a person's physical, spiritual, social, and psychological well-being. *Sahku Sheti* goes beyond the traditional medical model to address the spiritual and physical dimensions of the person. If a materialistic conception of health is sufficient, it would have been likely that Donovan's previous treatment regimen (e.g., psychotropic drugs and talk therapy) would have also been sufficient. Additionally, *Sahku Sheti* recognizes the role that the family plays in the healing process; thus, substantial limitations will be inevitable when treatment focuses solely on the individual. We now offer some brief examples of how different types of interventions can be applied to areas that are often ignored in traditional psychotherapy.

CASE STUDY: DONOVAN

Previous Evaluation and Diagnosis. Donovan is an African American adolescent who suffers from depression and anger management problems. He exhibits serious problems controlling his aggression, being disruptive, and engaging in assaultive behavior. Furthermore, his relationship with his mother has deteriorated, and his relationships with his peers are unmanageable. These problems have led to several school suspensions and are indicative of an overall inability to function in school. Donovan has an extensive history of mental health treatment that includes treatment in an inpatient unit, partial hospitalization, and various community mental health centers. He was placed on several medication cocktails (e.g., antidepressants, antipsychotics, and stimulants) that included Concerta, Strattera, Risperdal, and Desyrel. It is important to note that Donovan failed to show any significant improvements while on this medication regimen.

Axis I: Depressive reaction, not otherwise specified, mixed with anxiety reaction

Cognitive/perceptual/sensorimotor impairment with a learning disability

Axis II: An element of a conduct disorder emerging with a possible learning disability

Axis III: Generally healthy

Axis IV: Multiple stressors; developmental, educational, social and interfamily—moderate to severe

Axis V: Global Assessment of Functioning on discharge 45–50

- This evaluation is symptom focused and rooted in the medical model. A culturally informed evaluation was conducted to gain access to additional sources of information, such as strengths, worldview, extended self, family structure, spirituality, conceptions of health, cultural practices, socioeconomic context, diet, and so on.

Extended Self. Donovan resided in a single-parent household with his mother, Ms. Roberts, who worked 16-hour shifts. Thus, Donovan was often left at home unsupervised and spent the majority of his time watching videos and cartoons. He expressed some resentment toward his mother because her work schedule did not allow for him to take part in extracurricular activities (e.g., football and basketball). Ms. Roberts felt intense guilt about their situation and disclosed a lack of effective parenting strategies. Donovan's contact with his father was limited at best. He expressed anger toward his father and made statements like "He is not my father." Furthermore, he did not have direct access to additional male role models. Ultimately, he longed for a better relationship with his father and resented being away from his hometown and extended family.

- The role of Donovan's father and the extended family were explored. The impact that Ms. Roberts's guilt had on her parenting style/decision making process was explored.
- Ms. Roberts was invited to participate at the beginning of each session to provide support and corroborative information. She was also encouraged to utilize suggested interventions related to parenting.
- Ms. Roberts was given several articles and books to read to enhance her understanding of her son and their interaction.
- Ms. Roberts was encouraged to have an astrological chart done. This could provide insight into her son's specific characteristics and provide specific information regarding the type of environment that would lead to his optimal development.

Diet. Given Ms. Roberts's work schedule, the preparation of healthy, balanced meals were not part of norm. Instead, she and Donovan both ate out at fast-food restaurants on a daily basis. Furthermore, Ms. Roberts noted that Donovan probably consumed too much candy and sugar. She also felt there were times when his behavior and health had worsened as a function of him being on psychotropic medications (e.g., loss of appetite with subsequent weight loss, dry mouth, lethargy, etc.). It is important to note that Ms. Roberts was overweight (~380 lbs), did not exercise, did not report any self-care activities, and reported having poor health.

- Ms. Roberts and Donovan were assigned various literature to read, and it was suggested they watch the documentary *Super Size Me*.

- Ms. Roberts and Donovan were asked to chart Donovan's diet to get a sense of exactly what things were entering his body (e.g., Red Dye 40) and in what amounts. This was used to determine what changes in diet produced what types of changes in overall behavior, attitude, and well-being. Of note is that Ms. Roberts also decided to participate in this intervention.

Spiritual Well-Being. To address this domain, a Yorùbá *Babalawo* (African traditional healer) was consulted who had no previous knowledge of Donovan or his history. After casting a divination tool, in this case an *Opele*, the *Babalawo* asked a series of follow-up questions to the therapist: Did he have a history of abuse? (yes); Is his dad around? (no). On the basis of this divination, the *Babalawo* noted that Donovan had *Egun* problems—or issues with ancestral spirits. He stated that Donovan needed a divination reading and that previous psychological testing should be reinterpreted through a culturally sensitive lens. He also suggested asking the mother if Donovan had been a *meconium baby*—one who is born with oxygen deprivation. The *Babalawo* noted that Donovan was suffering from both organic and spiritual problems. Furthermore, having someone to talk to would have a healing effect on Donovan.

Ms. Roberts was amazed at the information that came back from the *Babalawo*. She noted that, prior to birth, Donovan had the umbilical cord wrapped around his neck, and they had to do an emergency Caesarean section because he was being deprived of oxygen. Additionally, she began to wonder why previous therapists had failed to ask these types of questions.

- Several spiritual baths were suggested to reduce negative energy and address issues with ancestral spirits. This was possible only given the level of rapport and trust that was previously established.

One might want to learn about specific outcomes regarding Donovan's response to an African-centered treatment. What is clear from an African *Utamawazo* is that healing is a process whose clock we do not control. Moreover, the process of actualizing *àlàáfíá*—health—transcends any one person or domain. Helping Donovan was much more comprehensive than constraining this treatment to a traditional individual therapy model. It was just as important for Ms. Roberts to explore and make appropriate changes to her attitudes and behaviors given the impact she has on her son's life. Because change is a very difficult undertaking, this family was able to make some progress, but they did not reach their optimal potential. Donovan was able to reduce his acting-out behavior at school and become more comfortable disclosing personal information in therapy. In addition, they were able to make improvements in their daily dietary habits. A major impediment to the healing process was rooted in their social context. As a single-parent, Ms. Roberts's extended work hours rendered her in a constant state of fatigue, and thus, she was unable to implement developed interventions in a consistent manner. Although her words and affect suggested she wanted things to be better for Donovan and her, her actions dictated a less than optimal outcome. Even when healers are able to apply those things that allow for optimal healing to take place, the client must internalize and actualize the information to bring about lasting change.

Future Directions

Some of the challenges associated with training clinicians in psychology to be actual healers capable of working most effectively with African/African American clients involve a variety of issues dealing with the prevailing paradigm. Most students in psychology are trained in the Western method, which eschews an emotional and qualitative approach in favor of "practical" quantitative studies. Also, in a traditional society's apprenticeship model, the training for a healer could last for years. This might involve an individual as early as 2 or 3 years old, learning and being trained in the ways of curative practice. A variety of things, from how to use herbs to ways of understanding spirit and the manifestations of spirit, and how to read the oracles that may come in different systems are vast areas of studies that one never knows completely. Our current educational model does not allow for any of these components in its current system. Therefore, it is incumbent on those who wish to embark on this line of healing to be studious, endure a significant amount of research outside the mainstream, and connect themselves with people who understand how this work is done.

There are a number of spiritual approaches that practitioners should study and process until they find one that resonates with their innate spirit. By so doing, they enable themselves to concurrently receive the knowledge that the academy deems necessary while also acquiring the knowledge that is indispensable for healing the population with which they are working. This is a long-term process and one that should not be taken lightly. Indeed, those who embark on it should have a steadfast spirit that can stand up in the midst of negative thoughts, comments, or critiques because the Western academy may never accept this African way of operating.

So, in response to the question of how one does this work, the answer is that one does it with an open mind, heart, and soul. One does it with the ability to consider multiple perspectives and to allow the essence of spirit to guide the course of treatment. One does it with a willingness to remain open to learning new, remarkable things and ways of being. One does it with constant consultation and interaction with others who share similar beliefs and understandings of what it means to be a healer. Ultimately, one does it with a never-ending humility that allows spirit to be the authority and us merely the vessel through which wisdom and inspiration pass.

In closing, it is important to note that *Sahku Sheti* preceded the field of psychology and will continue to exist long after psychology has exhausted its usefulness. A current challenge resides in the need for institutionalizing a long-term intergenerational dialogue to address issues of theory, research, training, and the provision of services. Such an institution would allow for the continued flow of ancient wisdom to regenerate itself in psychologists who are invested in the spiritual, mental, and physical liberation of African people throughout the Diaspora. Such an institution would be able to generate culturally informed solutions to contemporary problems.

References

Ajamu, A. A. (2004). Rekh: Prelude to an intergenerational conversation about African psychological thought. In R. L. Jones (Ed.), *Black Psychology* (4th ed., pp. 221–242). Hampton, VA: Cobb & Henry.

Akbar, N. (1979). African roots of Black personality. In W. D. Smith (Ed.), *Reflections on Black Psychology* (pp. 79–87). Washington, DC: University Press of America.

Akbar, N. (1981). Mental disorders among African Americans. *Black Books Bulletin, 7*(2), 18–25.

Akbar, N. (1984). Africentric social sciences for human liberation. *Journal of Black Studies, 14*, 395–414.

Akbar, N. (1985). Nile Valley origins of the science of the mind. In I. Van Sertima (Vol. Ed.), *Nile Valley civilizations.* New Brunswick, NJ: Journal of African Civilizations.

Ani, M. (1994). *Yurugu: An African-centered critique of European cultural thought and behavior.* Lawrenceville, NJ: Africa World Press.

Appiah-Kubi, K. (1981). *Man cures, God heals: Religion and medical practice among the Akans of Ghana.* Totowa, NJ: Allanheld, Osmun, & Co.

Armah, A. K. (1978). *The healers.* Portsmouth, NH: Heinemann.

Asante, M. K. (1987). *The Afrocentric idea.* Philadelphia: Temple University Press.

Asante, M. K. (1988). *Afrocentricity.* Trenton, NJ: African World Press.

Baldwin, J. A., & Bell, Y. R. (1985). The African Self-Consciousness Scale: An Africentric personality questionnaire. *Western Journal of Black Studies, 9*, 61–68.

Baldwin, J. A., & Hopkins, R. (1990). African-American and European-American cultural differences as assessed by the Worldviews paradigm: An empirical analysis. *Western Journal of Black Studies, 14*, 38–52.

Banks, W. C. (1992). The theoretical and methodological crisis of the Africentric conception. *Journal of Negro Education, 61*, 262–272.

Bascom, W. (1991). *Ifa divination: Communication between gods and men in West Africa.* Bloomington: Indiana University Press.

Ben-Jochannon, Y. (1988). *Africa: Mother of Western civilization.* Baltimore: Black Classic Press. (Original work published 1971)

Ben-Jochannon, Y. (1989). *Black man of the Nile and his family* (2nd ed.). Baltimore: Black Classic Press. (Original work published 1972)

Billingsley, A. (1968). *Black families in White America.* Englewood Cliffs, NJ: Prentice Hall.

Boyd-Franklin, N. (1989). *Black families in therapy: A multisystem approach.* New York: Guilford Press.

Clark, C. X., McGee, D. P., Nobles, W. W., & Weems, L. X. (1975). Voodoo or IQ: An introduction to African Psychology. *Journal of Black Psychology, 1*, 9–29.

Carruthers, J. H. (1995). *MDW NTR: Divine speech, a historical refection of African deep thought from the time of the pharaohs to the present.* London: Karnak House.

Danquah, J. B. (1968). *The Akan doctrine of God: A fragment of Gold Coast ethics and religion.* London: Frank Cass.

Diop, C. A. (1974). *The African origin of civilization: Myth or reality* (M. Cook, Ed. & Trans.). Chicago: Lawrence Hill Books.

Diop, C. A. (1978). *The cultural unity of Black Africa: The domains of patriarchy and of matriarchy in classical antiquity.* Chicago: Third World Press.

Du Bois, W. E. B. (1903). *The souls of Black folk.* Chicago: McClurg.

Ephirim-Donkor, A. (1997). *African spirituality: On becoming ancestors.* Trenton, NJ: Africa World Press.

Fisher, R. B. (1998). *West African religious traditions: Focus on the Akan of Ghana.* New York: Orbis Books.

Fu-Kiau, K. K. B. (1991). *Self-healing power and therapy: Old teachings from Africa.* New York: Vantage Press.

Gbadegesin, S. (1991). *African philosophy: Traditional Yoruba philosophy and contemporary African realities.* New York: P. Lang.

Grills, C. (2004). African Psychology. In R. L. Jones (Ed.), *Black Psychology* (4th ed., pp. 171–208). Hampton, VA: Cobb & Henry.

Grills, C., & Ajei, M. (2002). African centered conceptualization of the self and consciousness: Further elaboration on the Akan model. In T. A. Parham (Ed.), *Counseling persons of African descent: Raising the bar of practitioner competence* (pp. 75–99). Thousand Oaks, CA: Sage.

Grills, C., & Livingston, A. (2001). *Research report: The African project of consciousness project.* Submitted to the Center for Consciousness Study.

Gyekye, K. (1995). *An essay on African philosophical thought: The Akan conceptual scheme* (Rev. ed.). Philadelphia: Temple University Press.

Herskovits, M. J. (1970). *The myth of the Negro past.* Gloucester, MA: P. Smith. (Original work published 1958)

Hilliard, A. G. (1998). *SBA: The reawakening of the African mind.* Gainesville, FL: Makare.

Hountondji, P. J. (1983). *African philosophy: Myth and reality* (H. Evans, Trans.). Bloomington: Indiana University Press.

Idowu, E. (1995). *Olodumare: God in Yoruba belief* (2nd ed.). Plainview, NY: Original Publications.

Janheinz, J. (1961). *Muntu: An outline of the new African culture.* New York: Grove Press.

Kambon, K. K. K. (1998). *African/Black Psychology in the American context: An African-centered approach.* Tallahassee, FL: Nubia Nation.

Karenga, M. (1982). *Introduction to Black studies.* Inglewood, CA: Kawaida.

Karenga, M., & Carruthers, J. H. (1986). *Kemet and the African worldview: Research, rescue and restoration.* Los Angeles: University of Sankore Press.

Lucas, J. (1996). *The religion of the Yorubas.* New York: Athelia Henrietta Press.

Mbiti, J. S. (1970). *African religions and philosophy.* New York: Anchor Books.

Montgomery, D. E., Fine, M. A., & Myers, L. J. (1990). The development and validation of an instrument to assess an optimal Afrocentric world view. *Journal of Black Psychology, 17,* 37–54.

Myers, L. J. (1987). The deep structure of culture: Relevance of traditional African culture in contemporary life. *Journal of Black Studies, 18,* 72–85.

Myers, L. J. (1988). *Understanding an Afrocentric worldview: Introduction to an Optimal Psychology.* Dubuque, IA: Kendall/Hunt.

Nobles, W. W. (1972). African philosophy: Foundations for Black Psychology. In R. L. Jones (Ed.), *Black Psychology* (pp. 22–36). New York: Harper & Row.

Nobles, W. W. (1973). Psychological research and the Black self-concept: A critical review. *Journal of Social Issues, 29,* 11–31.

Nobles, W. W. (1976). Extended self: Rethinking the so-called Negro self-concept. *Journal of Black Psychology, 2,* 15–24.

Nobles, W. W. (1986). *African Psychology: Towards its reclamation, reascension, and revitalization.* Oakland, CA: Institute for the Advanced Study of Black Family Life and Culture.

Nobles, W. W. (1998). To be African or not to be: The question of identity or authenticity—Some preliminary thoughts. In R. L. Jones (Ed.), *African American identity development* (pp. 185–206). Hampton, VA: Cobb & Henry.

Obasi, E. M. (2002). Reconceptualizing the notion of self from the African deep structure. In T. A. Parham (Ed.), *Counseling persons of African descent: Raising the bar of practitioner competence* (pp. 52–74). Thousand Oaks, CA: Sage.

Obasi, E. M., Flores, L. Y., & James-Myers, L. (in press). Construction and initial validation of the Worldview Analysis Scale. *Journal of Black Studies.*

Opoku, K. A. (1978). *West African traditional religion.* Accra, Ghana: FEP International.

Parham, T. A., White, J. L., & Ajamu, A. (1999). *The psychology of Blacks: An African-centered perspective* (3rd ed.). Upper Saddle River, NJ: Prentice Hall.

Ridley, C. R. (1984). Clinical treatment of the nondisclosing Black client: A therapeutic paradox. *American Psychologist, 39,* 1234–1244.

Utsey, S. O., Adams, E. P., & Bolden, M. (2000). Development and initial validation of the Africultural Coping Systems Inventory. *Journal of Black Psychology, 26,* 194–215.

Williams, C. (1976). *The destruction of Black civilization: Great issues of race from 4500 B.C. to 2000 A.D.* (Rev. ed.). Chicago: Third World Press.

Wiredu, K. (1980). *Philosophy and an African culture.* Cambridge, UK: Cambridge University Press.

5

AFRICENTRIC THEORIES OF AFRICAN AMERICAN PERSONALITY

Basic Constructs and Assessment

KOBI KAMBON AND TERRA BOWEN-REID

Perhaps no other area of African/Black Psychology has had such a legacy of controversy and strident intellectual debate than the area of African American personality (Akbar, 2003; Azibo, 1990; Belgrave & Allison, 2006; Cross, 1991; Kambon, 1992, 1998, 2006; Nobles, 1986, 2005; Wilcox, 1971). This has been due not only to the legacy of the notorious contentiousness of the literature on African American intelligence but also to the subsequent literature on African American self-concept/racial identity and self-esteem, as well as the focus on African American motivation (e.g., achievement motivation) and antisocial behaviors such as drug abuse, delinquency, and criminality (Belgrave & Allison, 2006; Cross, 1991; Jones, 1972, 1980, 1991, 2004; Kambon, 1992, 1998). Each of these areas of the psychological study of African American personality has brought to the table its own set of controversial theoretical models, methodologies, databases, analyses, and conclusions. Through the years, and as a result of the accumulation of a relatively large amount of research data and theoretical constructs, a distinct area of study called *African American personality* has emerged within the African-centered psychological literature (Baldwin, 1976; Kambon, 1992, 1998; Nobles, 1986, 2005) that commands serious consideration in any social policies that are respectful of cultural diversity and focused on truly improving the lives of all people.

We situate the current discussion within the framework of the African-centered psychology movement. Specifically, this chapter focuses on articulating the major features of the Africentric approaches, because they have received by far the least attention in the literature and, in our opinion, represent the cutting-edge approach in this field of study. There are four models (or distinct sets of ideas about African American personality) that have emerged in the literature that meet the criteria for the Africentric approach. These models have been proposed by Na'im Akbar, Wade Nobles, Robert Williams, and Kobi Kambon (Kambon, 1998).

AFRICENTRIC THEORIES OF AFRICAN AMERICAN PERSONALITY

Wade Nobles's (1980) Extended-Self Model, Na'im Akbar's (1979) Divine or Spiritual Core Model, Robert Williams's (1981) WEUSI Model, and Kobi Kambon's (1992) African Self-Consciousness Model represent the only relatively well-developed ideas about African American personality from the Africentric perspective of which we are aware. Other models may have been proposed are more or less offshoots of one of these models. Actually, Kambon's model builds on some of the ideas of Akbar's and Nobles's models in particular, although the specifics of the models were all derived relatively independent of one another. Whereas Nobles did not actually put forth a substantive model of personality as compared with the others, Akbar's, Williams's and Kambon's models all utilized some of Nobles's ideas in developing their conceptions. The Kambon and Williams models are by far the most fully developed Africentric theories of African American personality that have been brought forth to date, and they share many more similarities than differences. A brief treatment of each of these models follows.

Wade Nobles's Extended-Self Model

The Basic Core of African/Black Personality

According to Wade Nobles (1972, 1976, 1980, 1986, 2005), the basic core of the African personality is the Black self-concept, which derives from the nature of the African worldview. The core of the African worldview emphasizes oneness with nature, interdependence, and oneness of being (Kambon, 1992, 1998). For Nobles, the African self-concept is a "We-ness" self-concept, as opposed to an "I-ness" self-concept (awareness of self as unique and separate). It recognizes that only in terms of one's people does the individual become conscious of his or her own existence. Thus, one's self-definition is dependent on the corporate definition of one's people (group), that is, a "corporate self." The collective consciousness transcends the individual consciousness, and the individual consciousness extends to include the collective consciousness in Nobles's (1972, 1980) model. This interdependence of individual and group consciousness (the "oneness-of-being" relationship) translates into an extended definition of the self in the African worldview.

The African self-concept thus extends into the collective consciousness of African people. This, according to Nobles (1972, 1980), is the nature of the Black self-concept, the core of African personality. Whatever deviations that may be observed in African people under European oppression is merely a distortion of this natural state of the African self-concept (psychological confusion). Nobles (1980) proposed that the "Negro" self-concept (the African American self-concept shaped by the forces of European American cultural oppression of Blacks).

Components of the African Self-Concept

The chief components of the African self-concept in Nobles's model are an awareness of self in terms of (a) one's historical past, (b) one's historical future (where the future is tied to/projected in reaffirmation of the past) or collective spirituality consciousness, and (c) one's physical and collective self (individual and group self-concept). In Nobles's model, then, the African self-concept derives from the evolutionary production of African consciousness across the three dimensions or planes of experience noted. No specific empirical research directly based on Nobles's model has been conducted, however. Notwithstanding the absence of any direct confirmatory research program, the cumulative body of African-centered personality research findings in general lend a preponderance of indirect empirical support for much of his thinking in this area, especially his general construct of extended self (Azibo, 1996, 2003; Kambon, 1992, 1998; Williams, 1981). Nonetheless, a more systematic and direct assessment of these ideas is ultimately desired to move the theoretical propositions beyond the mere conceptual stage.

Na'im Akbar's Divine or Spiritual Core Model

The Basic Core of African/Black Personality

According to Akbar's (1975, 1976, 1979, 2003) model, the core of the African American personality is divine substance (i.e., a spiritual substance having universal origin). It is defined by and therefore reflects nature/natural order. Because this is essentially Akbar's (1984) conception of the essence of the African worldview, then we can rightly infer that he sees African American personality as being based on the African worldview. This spiritual substance reflects a deep inner sense of self that reaches back before contact with Europeans and unites the African person with everything else in the universe.

African Personality Dynamics

Akbar (1975, 1976) has proposed that the energy system of Black personality is rhythm. Rhythm is flow (the natural and unrestricted free flowing of energy), and flow is interconnecting (the natural binding function of energy/spirit). It is the free floating and constant striving to unite the self with the universe; the striving for unity between the self and nature. In other words, it is constant striving to reaffirm oneness with nature that drives Black personality functioning. Thus, rhythm is essentially a self-transcending striving, seeking a state of shared self, a collective self or communal self, and so on.

African consciousness and Africentric functioning. In Akbar's model, the Black personality, in terms of its divine substance or spirituality, is both conscious and unconscious. It is fundamentally a collective self-consciousness that can be distorted, but not destroyed. Although it is always active, even when operating under distorted conditions, it must be conscious for effective Black psychological functioning to exist. As a conscious phenomenon, it is an awareness of the inner (Divine) core of the personality: Awareness of self enables the personality to act in terms of itself, in terms of its own enhancement, affirmation, and preservation. This awareness, of course, transcends the individual self. It is this African consciousness that forms the inner core of the African American personality in Akbar's theory.

African consciousness and African institutions. This African consciousness, if it is to be mentally alive and viable, must be maintained and reinforced through the creation and operation of self-affirming institutions, for example, religious celebrations, rituals, memorials, museums, books and literature, monuments, and so on. Akbar (1979) noted that even when the Black personality (the African consciousness) is distorted or suppressed, such as through Western slavery and oppression, the inner core of the personality still seeks expression, such as through the Negro mentality (similar to Nobles's idea of self-orientation resulting from the forces of European American cultural oppression of Blacks), but the institutions are necessary to truly awaken, release, and/or revitalize it (i.e., its authentic expression).

Akbar (1979, 2003) has further noted that previous interventions have not been effective with African Americans because they have erroneously focused on the *surface* rather than *substance* of Black personality (i.e., on the material over the spiritual/self-knowledge dimension). Therefore, for clinical intervention with African American personality disorders to be truly effective, it must focus on the spiritual/self-knowledge dimension. As with Nobles's (1972, 1980) model, no specific research has been associated with Akbar's model per se. The general body of African-centered research on the African American personality, however, has had some degree of bearing on empirical confirmation of many of his theoretical ideas. Of course, the preponderance of everyday observational evidence seems to provide a wealth of support for his conceptions by and large (Kambon, 1992, 1998). Nonetheless, a more systematic program of direct empirical support is ultimately desirable in order to buttress these very insightful theoretical propositions.

Robert L. Williams' WEUSI Model

Basic Core and Major Constructs of African/Black Personality

Williams (1981) referred to the basic core of the African American personality as "The Collective Black Mind." He identified a Kiswahili term, *WEUSI* (the combination of the English terms *We*, *Us*, and *I*), as one that best captures this authentic African psychological condition because of its holistic nature. Like Nobles's (1972, 1980) model, Williams's model also views the Black self-concept as the core of the Black personality, and it is conceptualized in terms of WEUSI. Thus, WEUSI for Williams best characterizes the African self-concept as the core of Black personality. WEUSI has three distinguishing features or qualities: (1) Blackness, (2) Collectiveness, and (3) Naturalness.

Blackness. Blackness is the most distinctive feature of WEUSI. It contains four major aspects: (1) Genetic Blackness, (2) Cultural Blackness, (3) Psychological Blackness, and (4) Spiritual Blackness. Through these four aspects, WEUSI serves as the storehouse for the basic Afrotypic features, attributes, and traits.

1. *Genetic Blackness* is inherited; thus, all Blacks possess it. In this capacity, WEUSI defines the basic biological makeup and identification of Black people throughout the world. Melanin, both skin melanin and neuro-melanin (occurring within the brain and nervous system), are critical components of Genetic Blackness.
2. *Cultural Blackness* is acquired through the socialization thrust or function of traditional Black institutions. These institutions comprise the Black family, the Black church, the Black community, historically Black colleges, barber/beauty shops, and many others of what he calls *traditional Black institutions*.
3. *Psychological Blackness* refers to Black awareness and Black consciousness. It exists as potential and must be developed through a process called *Afrocizing* (Black cultural specific socialization). Williams (1981, p. 107) defined this component as a corpus of attitudes, beliefs, preferences, and behaviors undergirded by Africentric philosophy transmitted through the other components of WEUSI (genetic, cultural, and spiritual transmitters) bound together within a system by a natural rhythm. It is one's personal Black identity developed in Afro-space and expressed through Afrotypes.
4. *Spiritual Blackness* refers to feelings of unity and oneness of being with other Blacks. It is the sense of collectivity, togetherness, and rhythm (free-flowing energy communicated in harmonious music, movement, and general expressive behavior) that Black people feel and express in regard to each other. The concept of "soul" conveys that it is a very special quality of feeling unique to Black people (demonstration of strong emotional energy in harmonious music, dance, and general expressiveness).

Collectiveness. This distinguishing feature of WEUSI refers to common or shared Africanity among Black people. At the level of the individual, WEUSI means a collective (common/shared) Black mind. At the levels of groups, institutions, and organizations, WEUSI means collective Black networks. Collectiveness, then, is a deeply rooted African part of Black people's nature at all levels of being (individual, group, community, nation, world) that essentially refers to pulling together and working toward common goals.

Naturalness. This distinguishing feature of WEUSI refers to Black-specific behavior, unlearned Black behaviors such as unity, commonality, spirituality, and rhythm. These are the purest, most unadulterated forms of Black behavior and functioning; thus, it is natural for Blacks to form families, groups, organizations, networks, and so on, that are empowering, and it is unnatural for Blacks to engage in de-empowering behaviors.

Black Personality Development

Williams advanced the concept of *developmental space* (i.e., socialization/social learning developmental space) and the "dual pathways of development" that are open to Black children to account for and articulate the parameters of African American personality development. He defined Black socialization as *Afro-typing*, which begins in the Black community within the Black family. According to Williams (1981), the developmental pathways for Black children are either the natural "Afrocizing process" of *Africentric developmental space*, consisting of Black churches, schools, and neighborhoods, or the Anglocentric (i.e., Eurocentric) modification process of *Anglocentric developmental space*. Anglocentric developmental space is dictated by the mainstream White American society consisting of racially integrated churches, schools, and neighborhoods. The natural Afrocizing process operates according to the oneness value principles of the *Nguzo Saba*, which represents the Black value system associated with the Kwanzaa celebration (Karenga, 1988; i.e., unity, self-determination, cooperative work and responsibility, cooperative economics, purpose, creativity, and faith). Williams, on the other hand, views the Anglocentric modification/socialization process operating on the contrasting principles of acceptability, duality, competition, independence, and uniqueness. He proposed the outcome of "normal" Black personality development or Afro-typing as being the development of an Africentric (pro-Black) orientation, whereas the outcome of Anglocentric modification is that of a ainstream/Anglocentric orientation. He viewed transformation from an Anglocentric to an Africentric orientation as a part of this developmental process as well.

Black Personality Assessment

Although Williams did not discuss African American personality disorder in depth, his concepts of Anglocentric modification/socialization and the developmental outcome of an Anglocentric orientation appear to have some relevance to the issue of African American mental health or suboptimal psychological functioning. He also proposed an extensive program of psychological assessment of (variability in) Black personality functioning that clearly has some implications for a conception of Black mental health. Williams has, in almost 30 years of research, developed some of the earliest psychological measures that were sensitive to an African-centered personality assessment and analysis. His repertoire of African American cultural specific measures includes the Black Preference Inventory, the Black Opinion Scale, the Themes of Black Awareness Test, and the Themes Concerning Blacks Test (see Baldwin, 1987; Wright & Isenstein, 1977). His well-known (if not infamous) Black Intelligence Test for Cultural Homogeneity (Williams, 1972) is also a part of this collection of African-centered personality measures. However, his Black Personality Questionnaire (BPQ) (Williams, 1981; Wright & Isenstein, 1977) has been the chief instrument utilized to assess his model of African American personality (see Azibo, 1996). The conceptual base from which items for the BPQ were derived was the notion of Black awareness. Williams defined *Black awareness* as "identification with Black causes and Black people...based on one's...positive and negative experiences...in this society" (1976, as, cited in Wright & Isenstein, 1977, p. 18). It further encompasses a specific response set (values, beliefs, and preferences) that predisposes Blacks to engage in certain types of behaviors (see Azibo, 1996; Baldwin, 1987; Wright & Isenstein, 1977).

The BPQ is a 50-item measure surveying African American beliefs, attitudes, and behavioral and lifestyle patterns that are organized into six major bipolar response sets: (1) a Pro-Black–Pro-White response set, (2) a Pan-African–Non-Pan-African response set, (3) a Third World–Non-Third World response set, (4) an Anti-White–Non-Anti-White response set, (5) a Non-Anti-Black–Anti-Black response set, and (6) a Non-Pro-White–Non-Pro-Black response set. An example of an item from this measure is "When Black people move into a community, it tends to become run down." The BPQ has been used most often with college students and can be individually or group administered. It requires approximately 30 to 40 minutes to complete. Responses to items on a subscale are summed to produce a subscale score. Azibo (1996) reported reliability coefficients in the .90s for the BPQ along with some relatively high convergent validity coefficients (correlating BPQ scores with African Self-Consciousness Scale [ASCS] scores) as well. Azibo (1996) also reported that a six-factor solution has been computed on the BPQ that corresponds to the six analytical BPQ subscales. However, no actual data from the factor analysis have been reported to date (see Azibo, 1996).

Interestingly, Williams's BPQ suggests that he actually views African American personality as a highly complex and culturally diverse condition. For example, he conceptualizes various combinations of the six components or subscales of Black personality, ranging from a pro-Black to an anti-Black orientation and from pro-White to anti-White orientations, as indicative of one's Black personality disposition (strong, weak, etc.).

Wright and Isenstein (1977) described the six subscales as follows:

1. Pro-White (PW) responses indicate acceptance and approval of the White standard and Whites in general.

2. Anti-Black (AB) responses indicate negativism toward/rejection of a Black/self-affirmative orientation.

3. Anti-White (AW) responses indicate a negation/rejection of Whiteness and a White/Eurocentric orientation.

4. Pro-Black (PB) responses indicate both positive Black self-identity (personal) and collective Black identity.

5. Pan-African (PA) responses indicate an orientation toward the plight of all African people (continental and [D]iasporan).

6. Third World (TW) responses indicate an orientation toward the plight of all oppressed people regardless of race. (pp. 18–19)

Although no manual for interpreting the BPQ is available (Azibo, 1996), we might cautiously speculate on what appear to be some reasonable assessment outcomes. Agreement responses to positive (toward Black awareness or Black consciousness) response set items (i.e., PB, PA, TW, AW, NAB, and NPW) are probably generally indicative of a strong–healthy Black personality orientation/Black awareness. The reverse of this scoring system can be used for negative (away from Black awareness/consciousness) response set items (i.e., PW, AB, NPA, NTW, NAW, and NPB) and may be generally indicative of a weaker–unhealthy Black personality orientation (see Azibo, 1983, 1996, 2003; Wright & Isenstein, 1977). It is unclear, however, as to whether Williams actually sees these six factors as comprising healthy–optimal Black personality or as perhaps the typical condition of African American personality under White supremacy domination (European American societal oppression), that is, as influenced or distorted by White supremacy domination (racially negative socialization, miseducation, etc.). Some research findings regarding the BPQ will be helpful in understanding how BPQ scores might be interpreted.

Azibo (1983, 1990, 1991, 1996, 2003) has been the chief researcher who has used the BPQ. In several studies with the BPQ, he has found that Blacks who score higher on the strong Black personality subscales of the BPQ display greater intrinsic motivation (personal causation), perceive a Black female as more attractive than a White female, and engage in more own-race sustaining behaviors than those who score higher on the weak Black personality subscales. Azibo (1991, 1996) also proposed the development of BPQ profiles as having possible diagnostic value in treating African American mental health problems. The profiles might be used, he noted, as an objective index of a client's Black personality state/condition. He proposed, for example, the treatment regimen can be facilitated by utilizing subscale profiles to see where the client's psychological–emotional energies are being directed. Hence, the relative proportion of AW, PW AB, PB, PA, and TW responses could be charted (perhaps as baseline measures), and appropriate subsequent changes in the profile could be used as an empirical measure of clinical improvement, successful treatment, and so on. He noted that many Black clients do suffer conflicts in some of the areas assessed by the BPQ subscales and that their inclusion in mental health treatment could therefore represent an important additional tool for African-centered therapists (Azibo, 1991, 1996, 2003).

Kobi K. K. Kambon's African Self-Consciousness Theory

Like the other theorists presented, Kambon (aka Baldwin, 1976, 1981, 1984; Kambon, 1992) takes the position that the dynamic African spirituality of communalism–collective merging or uniting into holistic synthesis is the driving energy in African American personality and, in terms of its conscious-level manifestation, forms the basis for understanding and articulating the dynamics of optimal and suboptimal African American mental health. It is a biogenetic (innate) and deeply rooted unconscious core of psychical energy that is immutable in the inner psychical functioning of the African American personality. This deeply rooted African spirituality acquires consciousness through experience, and this consciousness functions to direct, maintain, preserve, and fortify itself in the fulfillment of its inherent or genetically programmed thrust or propensity toward African affirmation–empowerment. The core features and constructs of Kambon's model provide the critical explanatory nexus of this theory. The three major constructs of the model are (1) the African Self-Extension Orientation (ASEO), (2) African Self-Consciousness (ASC), and (3) Cultural Misorientation (CM) (Kambon, 1992, 2003).

Basic Core and Major Constructs of African/Black Personality

ASEO refers to the deeply rooted, unconscious, genetically based African spirituality reflecting a continual, unending urge/striving for collective–communal expression of African cosmic (spiritual) wholeness or unity. It is the deeply rooted core of the personality that is inherited in the biogenetic condition of being born African and thus represents the most fundamental African psychological predisposition. ASC represents the conscious expression of African spirituality (ASEO) that affirms African life, survival, and self-determination. The basic traits of African personality, according to Kambon, refer to those beliefs, attitudes, and behaviors that reflect and reinforce African spirituality. These are the thoughts and behavioral qualities that are natural/indigenous to African people irrespective of social and environmental conditions. ASC consist of four key components: (1) a collective African identity, (2) a prioritization on African racial–cultural survival, (3) advocacy for and active participation in the creation and perpetuation of African-centered institutions and practices, and (4) a resolute posture of defense against anti-African forces in one's thoughts, attitudes, and behaviors or in other individuals, groups, or institutions (Kambon, 1992). Combined, these competencies define the self-affirming and self-fortification thrust of the African American personality's basic striving for collective self-empowerment.

African Personality Dynamics

Thus, Kambon sees the basic striving in African American personality as being toward the affirmation of the *African Survival Thrust* (African American affirmation, survival maintenance, and self-determination). This is the continual striving for authentic African affirmation and self-determination inherent to the African American psychical system. Although the dynamics of ASEO are more or less the same as those proposed by Akbar (1976, 1979) in relation to the rhythm aspect of spirituality (through the natural flow of energy/spirit, binding material bodies into a natural, harmonious flow reflecting deep feelings—strong emotional expression and physical-spiritual oneness—all of which is indicative of a general striving toward unity with nature or cosmic wholeness). ASC always thrusts the personality system in the sociopolitical/ideological direction of African affirmation, survival maintenance, and self-determination (i.e., collective African empowerment). Only under externally influenced conditions of distortion at the ASC level of the personality system does this thrust suffer interference, and even then, the basic thrust toward affirmation remains true—only its surface level or overt manifestation reflects distortion (as Akbar [1976, 1979] also argues in his model).

Hence, ASC can function at different levels of intensity (from weak to strong), depending on the dominant sociocultural, institutional experiences characterizing the developmental context of a young African American personality. Moderate to strong ASC represents movement toward the optimal pole of the African mental health continuum more so than weak ASC, and particularly severely weak ASC, which represents simply a much lower intensity or weaker movement toward the optimal end along the African mental health continuum, that is, from weak to moderate to strong ASC (Kambon, 1992, 2003).

African Personality Development

In regard to African personality development, Kambon's model, specifies that the overriding, overarching goal of African American personality development and functioning is the vigorous expression of ASC that affirms global Pan-African cultural nationalism and African nation-building and maintenance (Kambon, 1998). He proposed that the attainment and maintenance of an African World Order/Pan-African World Nationhood expression is the ultimate goal of African American personality development and functioning as manifested along the ASC continuum (from weak to moderate to strong ASC) among individual Blacks.

In Kambon's theory, African American personality development proceeds along the lines of African American cultural-centered socialization. He proposed a process similar to Williams's (1981) concept of culturally valenced socialization space (the Africentric developmental space construct discussed earlier). In this regard, Kambon (1992) speculated that when African American children are nurtured and socialized in African-centered environments or African-centered social learning/developmental space, involving the practice of African cultural rites and rituals, celebrations, and consistent reinforcement of African-centered values, then strong and healthy ASC will define the outcome or culmination of the developmental process. On the other hand, however, when African children are socialized in Eurocentric developmental space, or some approximation of it, then a weaker ASC condition will result and define the personality outcome. This will be commensurate with the strength of the Eurocentric emphasis in the socialization/indoctrination processes shaping the child's early psychological development. Under the more stringent emphasis of Eurocentric socialization, severely weakened or deteriorated ASC can result and effectively alter the psychological orientation of the person from an Africentric orientation to a Eurocentric one, thus representing faulty personality development (Kambon, 1992, 2003). Faulty African American personality development, then, can and does occur and can result in what Kambon

(2003) referred to as African American "personality disorder."

Cultural Misorientation as Basic African American Personality Disorder/Mental Disorder

Kambon's (1992; Baldwin, 1984, 1985) model explains the occurrence of African American personality disorder through the sociopathological process of European American cultural oppression of African Americans (Kambon, 2003). This forced (imposed) cultural indoctrination process refers to the intense, pervasive, and prolonged condition of cultural oppression of Africans in America by Eurocentric cultural domination of the society's institutional infrastructures (educational, religious, communications, economic, legal, and political institutions). This abnormal (at least for African Americans) psychosocial process can interfere with the normal developmental process of African American personality beginning in childhood and reinforced throughout an individual's life. Kambon coined the term *Cultural Misorientation* to account for the basic psychological condition of African American personality disorders that occur within this context (or that result from the cultural oppression process).

CM refers to the psychological orientation in Blacks/African Americans (i.e., all Diasporan African descendants) reflecting the *European Survival Thrust* emphasizing a materialistic, individualistic, alien and anti-self, self-destructive, and racial integration orientation in one's thoughts, attitudes, and behaviors resulting from European cultural oppression (Kambon, 2003). Under the enormous pressure of the prolonged and intense conditions of psychological and cultural oppression over African Americans' social–cultural reality, a Eurocentric consciousness overcomes ASC within the African American psyche. This in essence creates an African American person with a dominant European/Eurocentric self-consciousness. Such a person has internalized, and therefore promotes, the European survival thrust in his or her conscious everyday psychological functioning and behavior, even at the expense of African American survival (see Kambon, 1992, 1998, 2003).

As was the case with ASC, it is also proposed that CM can similarly operate at different intensities/levels, from minimal to severe CM, depending on the depth and breadth of the internalization and expressions of the European Survival Thrust. Moderate to severe CM represents a much stronger movement along the negative or suboptimal pole of the African American mental health continuum. Minimal CM, though not as severe, still represents negative movement along the European Survival Thrust of the same suboptimal dimension of the African American mental health continuum (Kambon, 1992, 2003). The CM condition therefore represents a severe deterioration of the ASC condition and comes to dominate both the conscious and subconscious levels (as opposed to the deep unconscious level) of African American personality functioning. Kambon further proposed that the European American societal and cultural institutional infrastructure nurtures, reinforces, and maintains CM throughout the vast majority of the African American population. CM ultimately leads African Americans to subordinate their natural African-centered cultural orientation (values, beliefs, rituals, customs, attitudes, etc.) to a Eurocentric/anti-African cultural orientation, thus weakening and suppressing their optimal African-centered cultural expression and empowerment (Kambon, 2003). Thus, CM is recognized in Kambon's model as "Basic African American personality disorder" primarily because it is the predisposing condition for most other personality/mental disorders that can characterize the African American psyche (Kambon, 2003).

The ASC and CM Prediction Models

As can be surmised, ASC is reflective of healthy or optimal African American personality functioning in Kambon's model, whereas CM is reflective of unhealthy or suboptimal African American personality or personality disorder (Kambon, 1992, 2003). Hence, the ASC and CM constructs constitute those aspects or components of the African American personality system that have good heuristic value and can thus be assessed through systematic empirical examination (Kambon, 1992, 1998, 2003). Thus, empirical assessment of ASC and CM and the predictions generated from these constructs, Kambon (1992, 1998) argued, should drive African-centered research on African personality and mental health in America. The assessment of ASC and CM are therefore critical to a substantive and comprehensive evaluation of contemporary African American behavior and psychological functioning according to Kambon's model (Kambon, 1992, 2003; Kambon & Rackley, 2005, 2008).

Kambon (1992, 2003) has proposed a systematic set of propositions related to both ASC and CM. The focus of these propositions, where ASC is concerned, emphasize psychological correlates of ASC that involve general psychological dispositions (self-esteem, personal causation, achievement motivation, etc.), behavioral predictions of ASC that involve self-affirming (pro-Black) behaviors and opposition to anti-African/anti-Black forces, as well as background predictors of ASC indicative of Africentric socialization experiences (Kambon, 1992; Kambon & Rackley, 2008). On one hand, the opposite predictions for the most part emanate from the CM construct. In this case, the focus of the propositions suggest, on the other, that positive relationships would be expected to occur between CM and poor or suboptimal mental health states such as low self-esteem, apathy, low motivation, high anxiety, low stress tolerance, problems in anger control, and so on, and Eurocentric measures of psychological disorder/mental illness such as depression, psychosomatic disorders, schizophrenia and psychopathic states, paranoia, and so on (Kambon, 2003; Kambon & Rackley, 2005). Some Eurocentric measures of psychological health/positive–optimal mental health within the European worldview context, such as an internal locus of control orientation, a high need for achievement, competitiveness, and aggressiveness, also would be expected to correlate positively with CM. Positive correlations may also be expected between CM and other African-centered measures of personality disorders or poor African American mental health, such as anti-Black attitudes, N-word usage, light skin preference, pro-White attitudes and behaviors, and measures of racial neutrality, among many others. At the same time, however, negative relationships would be expected to occur between CM and African-centered measures of healthy/optimal personality such as ASC, an African worldview orientation, and pro-Black attitudes and behaviors in general (Kambon, 2003; Kambon & Rackley, 2005). Accordingly, a psychologically healthy African American, as noted earlier, manifests conscious functioning and behavior reflective of the affirmation and perpetuation of an African Survival Thrust (Kambon, 1992, 1998).

Heuristically speaking, then, the core predictions emanating from Kambon's model suggest that contemporary African Americans can be found to differ individually in their psychological states/orientations related to racial–cultural identity and consciousness along these two key psychological dimensions of mental health, and certain racially/culturally focused behaviors (affirming/empowering vs. disaffirming/de-empowering behaviors) should be predictable from them. In this sense, ASC and CM should predict opposite mental health states for African Americans. Thus, moderate to strong levels of ASC should predict more pro-Black and African American culturally affirmative attitudes and behaviors than weaker levels of ASC, and moderate to severe CM levels should predict more anti-Black and culturally de-empowering attitudes and behaviors than weaker or minimal CM levels (Kambon, 1992, 2003).

The African Self-Consciousness Scale and the Cultural Misorientation Scale: Empirical Research Based on Kambon's Model

Kambon has also generated a number of instruments that are relevant to African American personality assessment, such as the Worldviews Scale (Kambon, 1992, 1998), the ASCS (Kambon, 1992, 1996), and the Cultural Misorientation Scale (CMS) (Kambon, 2003; Kambon & Rackley, 2005), among a number of other measures (Kambon, 2005). The ASCS and CMS were developed to address concerns regarding assessment of the ASC and CM constructs, respectively (see Kambon, 1992, 1996, 2003, 2005). The ASCS and CMS have therefore been utilized in various research studies involving variables such as personal causation (Kambon, 1992), psychological well-being (Chambers et al., 1998; Pierre & Mahalik, 2005), health-promoting behaviors (Thompson & Chambers, 2000), anti-Black behavior (Kambon, 2003; Kambon & Rackley, 2005), career decision making (McCowan & Alston, 1998), and male–female relationships (Kambon, 1992, 1998), among others (see Cokley, 1999; Kambon, 1992, 2003; Kambon & Rackley, 2005, 2008; Stokes, Peacock, Murray, & Kaiser, 1994).

The ASCS is a 42-item, Likert-type-format questionnaire conceptually organized around the four competency dimensions of ASC that were discussed earlier across six manifest dimensions of education, family, religion, cultural activities, interpersonal relations, and political orientation. The four ASC competencies correspond to the four ASCS subfactors/subscales that have been generated through factor analysis (Kambon, 1996): (1) Collective African Identity and Self-Fortification, (2) Resistance Against Anti-African Forces, (3) Value for African-Centered Institutions and Cultural Expressions, and (4) Value for African Culture.

> Factor 1: Collective African Identity and Self-Fortification (15 items). A psychological disposition reflecting a sense of collective African identity and a tendency to engage in activities that affirm one's African identity (e.g., pro-Black/Black-empowering actions, such as promoting African history and cultural activities, Black-organized/collective activities, Black economic and political activities/ *Nguzo Saba*).
>
> Factor 2: Resistance Against Anti-African Forces (11 items). A psychological disposition reflecting a tendency to resist, by any means necessary, any and all information that may be perceived (experienced/interpreted) as anti-African/anti-Black, or as a threat to African/Black survival in any way, shape or form (e.g., rejects White supremacy and actively combats it in all areas of experience).
>
> Factor 3: Value for African-Centered Institutions and Cultural Expressions (8 items). A psychological disposition reflecting a belief in the importance of Africentric/pro-Black-oriented/empowering organizations, institutions, practices, and so on, that are under African/Black control based on African cultural definitions (e.g., practicing African cultural rituals, celebrations, commemorations).
>
> Factor 4: Value for African Culture (5 items). A psychological disposition reflecting a firm belief in the value/importance of traditional African cultural forms (practices, products, artifacts, etc.) for Africans (in America).

A little more than 90% of the items loaded on these four factors, accounting for nearly 76% of the variability. Internal consistency reliability coefficients have been found to range from the high .70s to high .80s for the composite ASCS, and from the .50s to mid-.80s for the ASCS subfactors (Kambon, 1992, 1996, 1998; Kambon & Rackley, 2008).

The CMS consists of 56 items in a Likert-type format designed to assess the level of one's endorsement of different aspects of a European Survival Thrust (European worldview orientation) across six subscales based on the six conceptual dimensions of CM (Kambon, 2003):

CMSS1: The *Materialism Orientation* subscale (9 items) reflects a physical–material objectification emphasis through ascription of value and significance to experiences in life (emphasis on physical characteristics, clothes, money, things, etc.).

CMSS2: The *Individualism Orientation* subscale (8 items) reflects an I/Me emphasis in life, as opposed to a collective emphasis.

CMSS3: The *Alien-Self Orientation* subscale (12 items) reflects a general Eurocentric emphasis in one's self-concept and one's approach to life in general.

CMSS4: The *Anti-Self Orientation* subscale (11 items) reflects the same emphasis as the Alien-Self Orientation Subscale, with the added emphasis of negative values being ascribed and hostility directed toward Blackness/Africanity.

CMSS5: The *Self-Destructive Orientation* subscale (9 items) reflects an emphasis on self–group injurious and antisocial and/or criminal thoughts and behaviors, especially directed against Blacks (the extended self and/or others).

CMSS6: The *Integration Orientation* subscale (7 items) reflects an emphasis on the inclusion/involvement of non-Blacks (viz., Whites) in as many aspects of one's life as possible (from intimacy to the most distant/abstract aspect of experience).

The composite CMS has generated internal consistency reliabilities that range from the mid-.80s to low .90s, and the subscale reliabilities range from the low .50s to the mid-.80s. Convergent and divergent validity between the CMS and ASCS and the BPQ subscales range from the low .50s to the high .80s (Kambon, 2003; Kambon & Rackley, 2005).

The ASCS and CMS thus have psychometric support for testing the predictions of the ASC and CM models. Empirical research using the ASCS has been conducted on Kambon's model since the mid-1980s (see Kambon, 1992, 1998). This research has revealed the following:

- the ASCS has been shown to be a correlate of both general psychological health factors (self-esteem, sense of personal causation, stress coping, anger control, 16 Personality Factor Questionnaire scores, etc.) and African-centered psychological health factors and behavior (pro-Black functioning) among contemporary African Americans and Caribbean Island reared African-descendant groups, both young and older, from diverse socioeconomic and other demographic persuasions (Kambon, 1992; Kambon & Rackley, 2008);

- the ASCS has been shown to be associated with certain background profiles of African Americans such as childhood experiences with racism, parental instructions about race relations, parental education, ethnic distribution, and exposure to Black Studies curricula in elementary and/or high school (Kambon, 1992, 1998; Kambon & Rackley, 2008), as well as other measures of African American mental health, such as self-esteem, depression, psychosomatic reactions, anger experience and stress coping (Chambers, Kambon, Davis-Birdsong, Brown, Dixon & Robbins-Brinson, 1998), N-word usage, and light skin preference (Kambon & Rackley, 2005, 2008); and

- the ASCS has shown promise as an effective assessment tool in clinical interventions (as a measure of treatment progress and outcome) with both individuals and groups of adult African Americans such as recovering alcoholics, drug abusers, and abused women (Kambon, 1992, 1998, 2003; Kambon & Rackley, 2005, 2008).

The CMS, on the other hand, has enjoyed a much shorter period of research activity given its briefer history (Kambon, 2003; Kambon & Rackley, 2005). Since its development in the mid-1990s, the CMS has been shown to provide a multifactored assessment of the CM construct (Kambon, 2003; Kwate, 2001), and to have relatively good convergent and divergent validity, primarily among African American college-age adults and among smaller samples of non-college African American adults. The CMS has also been shown to be a reliable predictor of general maladaptive and psychologically disordered functioning (depression, antisocial drug use, violence) among young adult African Americans (Kambon & Rackley, 2005) as well as more culturally specific psychological disorders (i.e., more African American-centered cultural reality-based disorders), such as N-word usage, light skin preference, preference for anti-Black rap music, and so on, among African American young adults in diverse social settings (Kambon, 2003; Kambon & Rackley, 2005).

Research in the general areas of ASC and CM assessment is ongoing. Some of the ongoing studies are generating ASCS and CMS subscale profiles in relation to background and Africentric activities measures. These profiles are also being looked at in relation to other psychological attributes and behaviors among African Americans that may be regarded as presenting a more general picture of positive mental health (self-esteem, stress coping attributes, sense of personal empowerment, etc.) as well as unhealthy or negative mental health states (anti-Black attitudes and behaviors in general). Thus, empirical support for Kambon's model and the theoretical implications of some of the key aspects of the other African-centered models is steadily accumulating in the African-centered psychological literature. We strongly believe that the promise of such research in generating a much broader picture and more systematic understanding of African American personality and mental health than has heretofore been presented is unmistakably clear. The accumulation of these findings should provide tremendous help in our achieving a better understanding of this phenomenon in general and in our developing a more comprehensive view of the application of this paradigm to contemporary African American experience.

Conclusion

Overall, in this chapter we have attempted to provide a brief survey of the major paradigms that have characterized the study of African American personality across the African worldview spectrum (i.e., Africentric paradigms). In this exegesis, we specifically sought to highlight the differences and commonalities in the area of African American personality assessment theories. As the field continues to grow and wrestle with modern-day challenges, idiosyncrasies, and biases, several key questions beg consideration in projecting the future status of this vital area of psychological theory and assessment. Where are we currently, and where do we appear to be heading in the area of "African-centered theories of African American personality"? What future issues and concerns will we confront as this area of focus continues to unfold and expand its conceptual and contextual boundaries? One of the apparent critical issues for future theoretical developments in the area appears to be the need for our models to accommodate more of the variety of developmental and socialization circumstances that the contemporary African American personality might experience (e.g., predominantly Black vs. predominantly White or racially–culturally integrated environments, or Africentric vs. Eurocentric worldview-dominated socialization or biracialism). There seems to be a continual need to call for emphasis on the role of cultural reality forces in forming the conceptual framework and content of our theories. More important is that emphasis should be placed on diversifying previously studied populations, in order to generalize the empirical predictions of the Africentric models. Of course, we must also welcome the addition of more creative and innovative methodologies, instrumentation, and analyses of these models.

In addition, we also need to begin to develop educational curricula, apart from a general survey course in African/Black Psychology (Kambon, 1998), that specifically focus on theories of African American personality. This course should fundamentally incorporate a serious discussion/presentation of Diasporan African personality and Continental African personality (and, eventually, the systematic treatment of Global African personality). Thus, there appears to be an acute need to begin to extend these models or develop new ones that encompass and incorporate the Diasporan—and, most important, the wide variety of Continental African—experiences that abound in our future formulations of theories of African personality for the 21st century. Because the African experience is globally, ethnically, and socially diverse, future expansions in African personality theories must take into account this vast conceptual terrain that confronts psychological theories of the Global African experience (Bynum, 1999; Sofola, 1973). We further believe that the natural conceptual linkage between these theories and African/African American mental health must be emphasized as we seek to understand the practical utility of such models in forging an improvement of the quality of life among global African populations.

Finally, we encourage more critical discourse around the work of African American personality theories in hopes of improving the overall quality of such conceptualizations in terms of comprehensiveness, accuracy, clarity, and African-centeredness. We feel quite confident that many of these developments will make a significant contribution toward setting the agenda for theories of African and African American personality over the next half century. They will provide the springboard for our future knowledge base and the formulation of African-centered social policies that are vital to the designing of effective social and mental health intervention strategies, social and political liberation strategies, and overall quality of life improvements so desperately needed throughout the contemporary African world. Theories of African and African American personality are undoubtedly the bedrock of true African nation-building and maintenance (Kambon, 1998). African-centered personality theories and assessment naturally comprise a continually evolving area of study in African/Black Psychology (Belgrave & Allison, 2006; Kambon, 1998). Thus, we fully expect that future study and research in this area will continue to inform the various models already in existence, perhaps stimulate the development of new ones and, in the long run, increase our overall understanding of this important area.

References

Akbar, N. (1975). The rhythm of Black personality. *Southern Exposure, 3,* 14–19.

Akbar, N. (1976). Rhythmic patterns in Black personality. In L. M. King, V. Dixon, & W. W. Nobles (Eds.), *African philosophy: Assumptions and paradigms for research on Black persons* (pp. 175–189). Los Angeles: Fanon Research and Development Center.

Akbar, N. (1979). African roots of Black personality. In W. D. Smith, K. Burlew, W. Whitney, & M. Mosley (Eds.), *Reflections on Black Psychology* (pp. 136–144). Washington, DC: University Press of America.

Akbar, N. (1984). Africentric social science for human liberation. *Journal of Black Studies, 14,* 395–414.

Akbar, N. (2003). *Akbar papers in African Psychology.* Tallahassee, FL: Mind Productions & Associates.

Azibo, D. A. (1983). Perceived attractiveness and the Black personality. *Western Journal of Black Studies, 7,* 229–238.

Azibo, D. A. (1990). Advances in Black personality theories. *Imhotep: An Afrocentric Review, 2,* 22–47.

Azibo, D. A. (1991). Diagnosing personality disorder in Africans (Blacks) using the Azibo nosology: Two case studies. *Journal of Black Psychology, 17,* 1–22.

Azibo, D. A. (1996). The Black Personality Questionnaire: A review and critique. In. R. L. Jones (Ed.), *Handbook of tests and measurements for research on Black populations* (Vol. II, pp. 241–250). Hampton, VA: Cobb & Henry.

Azibo, D. A. (Ed.). (2003). *African-centered Psychology* (pp. 277–292). Durham, NC: Carolina Academic Press.

Baldwin, J. A. (1976). Black Psychology and Black personality: Some issues for consideration. *Black Books Bulletin, 4*(3), 6–11, 65.

Baldwin, J. A. (1981). Notes on an Afrocentric theory of personality. *Western Journal of Black Studies, 5,* 172–179.

Baldwin, J. A. (1984). African self-consciousness and the mental health of African-Americans. *Journal of Black Studies, 15,* 177–194.

Baldwin, J. A. (1985). The dialectics of culture: Psychological aspects of European cosmology in American society. *Western Journal of Black Studies, 9,* 216–233.

Baldwin, J. A. (1987). African Psychology and Black personality testing. *Negro Educational Review, 38*(2–3), 56–66.

Belgrave, F. Z., & Allison, K. W. (2006). *African American Psychology: From Africa to America.* Thousand Oaks, CA: Sage.

Bynum, E. B. (1999). *The African unconscious: Roots of ancient mysticism and modern psychology.* New York: Columbia University Press.

Chambers, J. W., Jr., Kambon, K., Davis-Birdsong, B., Brown, J., Dixon, P., & Robbins-Brinson, L. (1998). Africentric cultural identity and the stress experience of African American college students. *Journal of Black Psychology, 24,* 368–396.

Cokley, K. (1999). Reconceptualizing the impact of college racial composition on African American students' racial identity. *Journal of College Student Development, 40,* 235–246.

Cross, W. E. (1991). *Shades of Black: Diversity in African American identity.* Philadelphia: Temple University Press.

Jones, R. L. (Ed.). (1972). *Black Psychology.* Hampton, VA: Cobb & Henry.

Jones, R. L. (Ed.). (1980). *Black Psychology* (2nd ed.). Hampton, VA: Cobb & Henry.

Jones, R. L. (Ed.). (1991). *Black Psychology* (3rd ed.). Hampton, VA: Cobb & Henry.

Jones, R. L. (Ed.). (2004). *Black Psychology* (4th ed.). Hampton, VA: Cobb & Henry.

Kambon, K. (1992). *The African personality in America: An African-centered framework.* Tallahassee, FL: Nubian Nation.

Kambon, K. (1996). Introduction to the African Self-Consciousness Scale. In R. L. Jones (Ed.), *Handbook of tests and measurements for research on Black populations* (Vol. II, pp. 207–215). Hampton, VA: Cobb & Henry.

Kambon, K. (1998). *African/Black Psychology in the American context: An African-centered approach.* Tallahassee, FL: Nubian Nation.

Kambon, K. (2003). *Cultural misorientation: The greatest threat to the survival of the Black race in the 21st century.* Tallahassee, FL: Nubian Nation.

Kambon, K. (2005). *African-centered measures for research on Black personality and mental health.* Tallahassee, FL: Nubian Nation.

Kambon, K. (2006). *Kambon's reader in Liberation Psychology: Selected works* (Vol. 1). Tallahassee, FL: Nubian Nation.

Kambon, K., & Rackley, R. (2005). The Cultural Misorientation Scale/CMS: Psychometric assessment. In J. Conyers, Jr. (Ed.), *Afrocentric traditions: Africana studies* (Vol. 1, pp. 15–34). Edison, NJ: Transaction.

Kambon, K., & Rackley, R. (2008). *Psychometric properties and socio-political considerations associated with the African Self-Consciousness Scale.* Manuscript in preparation.

Karenga, M. R. (1988). *Kwanzaa: Origins, concepts and practice.* Los Angeles: University of Sankora Press.

Kwate, N. O. (2001). Assessing African-centered mental disorder: Validation of the Cultural Misorientation Scale. Unpublished doctoral dissertation, St. John's University.

McCowan, C., & Alston, R. (1998). Racial identity, African self-consciousness, and career decision making in African American women. *Journal of Multicultural Counseling and Development, 26,* 28–38.

Nobles, W. W. (1972). African Psychology: Foundation for Black Psychology. In R. Jones (Ed.), *Black Psychology* (pp. 18–32). New York: Harper & Row.

Nobles, W. W. (1976). African science and the consciousness of self. In L. M. King, V. Dixon, & W. W. Nobles (Eds.), *African philosophy: Assumptions and paradigms for research on Black persons* (pp. 163–174). Los Angeles: Fanon Research and Development Center.

Nobles, W. W. (1980). Extended self: Rethinking the so-called Negro self-concept. In R. L. Jones (Ed.), *Black Psychology* (2nd ed., pp. 99–105). Berkeley, CA: Cobb & Henry.

Nobles, W. W. (1986). *African Psychology: Towards its reclamation, reascension, and revitalization.* Oakland, CA: Black Family Institute.

Nobles, W. W. (2005). *Seeking the Sakhu: Foundational writings for an African Psychology.* Chicago: Third World Press.

Pierre, M., & Mahalik, J. (2005). Examining African self-consciousness and Black racial identity as predictors of Black men's psychological well-being. *Cultural Diversity and Ethnic Minority Psychology, 11,* 28–40.

Sofola, J. (1973). *African culture and the African personality.* Ibadan, Nigeria: African Resources.

Stokes, J. E., Peacock, M. J., Murray, C. B., & Kaiser, R. T. (1994). Assessing the validity and reliability of the African Self-Consciousness Construct in a general population of African Americans. *Journal of Black Psychology, 20,* 62–74.

Thompson, S., & Chambers, J. (2000). African self-consciousness and health promoting behaviors among African American college students. *Journal of Black Psychology, 26,* 330–345.

Wilcox, R. (Ed.). (1971). *The psychological consequences of being a Black American.* New York: Wiley.

Williams, R. L. (1972). *The Black Intelligence Test for Cultural Homogeneity.* St. Louis, MO: Williams & Associates.

Williams, R. L. (1981). *The collective Black mind: An Afrocentric theory of Black personality.* St. Louis, MO: Williams & Associates.

Wright, B. J., & Isenstein, V. R. (1977). *Psychological tests and minorities* (DHEW Publication No. ADM 78-482). Washington, DC: Government Printing Office.

6

ASSESSING AFRICAN-CENTERED (AFRICENTRIC) PSYCHOLOGICAL CONSTRUCTS

A Review of Existing Instrumentation

SHAWN O. UTSEY, BENITA BELVET, AND NICOLE FISCHER

African-centered psychologists have long recognized the need to have at their disposal instruments that assess constructs relevant to the psychological, behavioral, and spiritual experiences of African people.[1] To this end, a number of African-centered psychological instruments have been developed over the last 2 decades to assess a host of related constructs. For example, the African Self-Consciousness Scale (ASC; Baldwin & Bell, 1985) was developed to assess dimensions of the African personality. The Africentrism Scale (AS; Grills & Longshore, 1996) was developed to assess the degree to which African Americans embrace the Africentric principles of *Nguzo Saba* (e.g., unity, self-determination, collective work, and responsibility). The ASC and AS are just two examples of instruments that were developed to fill the void related to assessing African-centered psychological constructs. We describe these and other African-centered measures in greater detail in this chapter.

Despite some activity in the development of African-centered measures, what has been lacking, is a systematic evaluation of the psychometric properties of these instruments. Having valid and reliable instruments available to assess African-centered constructs is essential to deepening our understanding of the variables that represent the cultural reality of African-descent persons. The availability of psychometrically sound instrumentation is of paramount importance to conducting culturally relevant research with African-descent populations. How does one conduct theoretically and methodologically sound research with these populations? The most essential methodological precondition for conducting sound African-centered psychological research is to locate any analysis of the cognitive, emotive, behavioral, or spiritual processes of African-descent persons in an African reality structure (Azibo, 1999; Baldwin, 1986; Bankole, 2006; Grills, 2002).

African-centered Psychology is not a single, unitary discipline but comprises several subfields.

These subfields include, but are not limited to, time orientation, intelligence, mental health, soul/spirit, and personality (Azibo, 1989). The need for valid and reliable instruments to assess constructs within the various subfields of African-centered Psychology, however, continues to block theoretical and methodological advancements in the discipline as a whole. The purpose of this chapter, then, is to review and evaluate the current state of affairs with regard to existing instrumentation currently being used in the assessment of African-centered phenomena. First, we provide a primer on African-centered psychological theory to familiarize the reader with the major conceptual tenets of the discipline. Next, we provide some historical context to role of research and scale development in African-centered Psychology. The primary aim of this chapter is to review the development and psychometric properties of the tests and measures most commonly used in African-centered Psychology. To this end, we review the development and psychometric properties of the following instruments: the ASC, the Belief Systems Analysis Scale (BSAS; Montgomery, Fine, & Myers, 1990), the AS, the Africultural Coping Systems Inventory (ACSI; Utsey, Adams, & Bolden, 2000), the Africentric Home Environment Inventory (AHEI; Caughy, Randolph, & O'Campo, 2002), the Communalism Scale (CS; Jagers & Mock, 1995), and the Oshodi Sentence Completion Test (OSCT)/Africentric Sentence Completion Test (Oshodi, 1999). We conclude this chapter with a summary of the current state of affairs in the measurement of African-centered constructs and include several recommendations for future directions in this area.

Primer on African-Centered Psychology

African (Black) Psychology or African-centered Psychology has its origins in ancient Kemet (often misnomered *Egypt*) and is grounded in the worldview and philosophical systems of African culture (Baldwin, 1986; Bynum, 1999; Grills, 2002; Nobles, 1972, 1986, 2004). A fundamental component of African thought and worldview is the principle of *consubstantiation*, which holds that all elements of the universe are of one substance (Nobles, 2004). Furthermore, the African worldview presupposes that the essence of all things in the universe is composed of spirit (Bynum, 1999; Gyekye, 1987, 1996; Nobles, 2004; Olupona, 2000). From these ontological principles of African Cosmology come the major tenets of African (Black) Psychology. Joseph A. Baldwin (now known as Kobi K. K. Kambon), a pioneer in African personality psychology, proffered one of the earliest definitions of African-centered Psychology, which he defined as "a system of knowledge (philosophy, definitions, concepts, models, procedures, and practices) concerning the nature of the social universe from the perspective of African Cosmology" (Baldwin, 1980, p. 23). Nobles (1972, 1986, 2004) posited that African (Black) Psychology is rooted in African culture and based on indigenous (African) philosophical assumptions. Similarly, Grills (2002) defined African-centered Psychology as that which is concerned with understanding and/or explaining the psychological experiences of African-descent persons from an African reality and worldview.

Some of the essential conceptual features of African-centered Psychology include *self-definition, spirit, nature, metaphysical interconnectedness,* and *communal order and self-knowledge* (Grills, 2002). *Self-definition* is the act/process of rejecting a hegemonic European realty structure while simultaneously actualizing an authentic African identity. *Spirit* is the life force and divine essence of the Creator that is present in all matter, both animate and inanimate (Parham, 2002). *Nature* provides a framework for harmonious living, understanding the rhythms of life, and a window into the human psyche (Grills, 2002). *Metaphysical interconnectedness* represents the acknowledgment, through ritual, that individuals do not exist in the universe in isolation of divine forces. *Communal order and self-knowledge* emphasizes the reciprocal relationship between knowledge of self and connection to community (Grills, 2002). It is this African-centered conceptual model that informs our understanding of what constitutes an African reality structure, mental health and mental illness, spiritual health and well-being, interpersonal well-being, adaptive behavior, and optimal psychological functioning. Likewise, African-centered interventions are informed by our understanding of the African reality structure and cultural ethos of African people. To this end, and beginning early in the history of African (Black) Psychology, a number of African-centered scholars have sought to develop valid and reliable measures that assess the thoughts, emotions, behavior, spirit, and social relations of African-descent persons from the perspective of an African reality. A majority of the African-centered measures developed to date are aimed primarily at assessing various components of the African/Black personality structure and concomitant behavioral manifestations thereof.

African Philosophy and the Tenets of African Personality Theory

The conceptual foundation of the African/Black personality is grounded in African philosophical notions of the self. According to West African philosophical thought, and in particular the *Akan* (a major cultural group of Ghana, West Africa) conceptual system, the self comprises three interrelated elements (Abraham, 1962; Gyekye, 1987). First, there is the *okra*, which is considered the innermost self or essence of the individual and is similar to the concept of the soul in Western philosophy (Abraham, 1962). Furthermore, an individual's destiny or fate is actualized through the *okra*. The *sunsum* is believed to be that part of the self that determines the personality or character of an individual (Abraham, 1962). In Akan philosophical thought, *sunsum* is essentially spirit. According to Gyekye (1987), the *sunsum* and *okra* are distinct yet related elements of the self that serve different functions. For example, the *sunsum* is said to leave the body during dreams, whereas the *okra* leaves the body only on death. The final component of the self in the Akan system is the *honan*, which represents the physical body (Abraham, 1962). The Akan believe the physical body provides a window into the soul (Gyekye, 1987). Therefore, a person with a diseased soul will manifest physical symptoms of this condition. African philosophical conceptualizations of the self have been instrumental in the development of African-centered theories of African/Black personality.

Theories of African/Black personality have been advanced by a number of African-centered scholars. One of the earliest theorists of the African/Black personality was Joseph Baldwin, who posited that the African personality consisted of two core components he termed (1) the *African Self-Extension Orientation* (ASEO) and (2) the *African Self-Consciousness Scale* (ASC; Baldwin, 1990). The ASEO, according to Baldwin, is the basic foundation and organizing principle of the African personality. He described it as biogenetically determined (innate), unconscious, and spiritual in its essence. The ASC emanates out of the ASEO and is considered its conscious expression. Like the ASEO, the ASC is in part biogenetically determined, but because it is the conscious-level expression of the underlying core personality structure, it is also influenced by environment (see Chap. 5, this volume). It is the ASC component of the African/Black personality that gives meaning to the underlying ASEO. Moreover, individual differences (variability) in the ASC are a consequence of early (childhood) socialization experiences, sociocultural influences, and institutional/systemic forces. It is at the ASC level of the African/Black personality that current African-centered instruments are intended to assess individual differences in the personality structure of African people.

AFRICAN-CENTERED RESEARCH AND SCALE DEVELOPMENT

The study of the personality and behavior of African people in the United States by White scholars has a nefarious history and is be covered here (see Guthrie, 1998; Ponterotto, Utsey, & Pedersen, 2006; and Thomas & Sillen, 1972, for a comprehensive review of this history). The anti-African *zeitgeist* permeating American culture, including science, art, and education, had a profound negative influence on Black scholars as well. Consequently, much of the research on the personality and behavior of African people coming out of the Black academy was grounded in a deficit model that viewed African people as deviant and pathological. Even at the point when Black scholars began to reject the deficit model of African personality and behavior, many simply adopted (and, in some cases, adapted) European (White) conceptualizations of personality functioning for application to Black populations. Our brief discussion of the history and timeline of African-centered psychological research and scale development, therefore, begins with the theoretical contributions of Wade Nobles and Luther X (Weems; now known as Na'im Akbar). Nobles (1972) published a chapter titled "African Philosophy: Foundations of Black Psychology," which appeared in the first edition of R. L. Jones's *Black Psychology*. In an article on Black consciousness that appeared in the very first issue of the *Journal of Black Psychology*, Akbar ([Weems] 1974) asserted that "we are Africans (i.e., non-Western) in our basic dispositions" (cited in Weems, 1974, p. 31). In the very next issue of the *Journal of Black Psychology*, Clark, McGee, Nobles, and Weems (1974) published their classic article on African/Black Psychology, "Voodoo or IQ: An Introduction to African Psychology." Other scholars would soon follow with empirical examinations of African-centered constructs based on Weems's and Clark, McGee, Nobles, and Weems's supposition about the cultural continuity of African people.

Given the space limitations of this chapter, it is impossible to review all of the research on African-centered personality and behavior constructs, so we focus our efforts on the seminal studies in this area. We are working with a somewhat strict definition of African-centered scholarship as a way to narrow our review and make it manageable. For the purposes of this chapter, the phrase *African-centered research/scale development* means any empirical examination of personality and behavioral phenomena from the perspective of an African reality structure. Therefore, the three criteria for inclusion will be as follows: (1) the study's conceptual framework is grounded in an African-centered theoretical model; (2) the study's constructs are readily identifiable as African centered; and (3) the study is clearly empirical, employing either quantitative or qualitative research methods. With these criteria in mind, an appropriate time period to begin our review is prior to 1990.

Surprisingly, our search of the literature turned up only a few empirical studies with a focus on African-centered constructs that were conducted during this time period. There were, however, a plethora of theoretical pieces written during this time (e.g., Azibo, 1989; Baldwin, 1986; Myers, 1988; Nobles, 1972, 1986; Weems, 1974). The earliest empirical study that we were able to locate during the specified period was the development of the ASC, published in the *Journal of Black Studies* (Baldwin & Bell, 1985). Given that this instrument is described in detail later in this chapter, we provide only a cursory review of this work here. The ASC is perhaps the most widely used African-centered Black personality measure. Baldwin (Baldwin & Bell, 1985) followed up his ASC development with an empirical examination of African self-consciousness in Black students at a Historically Black College versus Black students at a Predominantly White Institution. He found that students at the Historically Black College scored higher on the ASC than students at the Predominantly White Institution and that older students scored higher than younger students, and upper-level students scored higher than lower-level students. Although no other studies meeting the criteria for review could be found dating prior to 1990, a plethora of empirical studies emerged during the 1990s. For example, a search of the *Journal of Black Psychology* alone produced 30 articles that had the word *African-centered* or *Africentric* in the title or abstract. This proliferation of African-centered scholarship is no doubt due to the pioneering efforts of Baldwin and his colleagues in the decade prior to the 1990s. It was also during the 1990s that most of the scale development occurred.

A REVIEW OF INSTRUMENTATION

African Self-Consciousness Scale

Description and Development. The ASC was developed by Baldwin and Bell (1985) to assess the respondent's attitudes, beliefs, values, and interests regarding his or her awareness and knowledge of the history, culture, and philosophical position of African Americans. The instrument consists of 42 items that reflect beliefs, attitudes, and behaviors that advance an African cultural consciousness and survival thrust. More specifically, the instrument includes four competency dimensions and six expressive dimensions. The competency dimensions include (1) awareness and recognition of one's African identity and heritage; (2) recognition of Black practices, customs, and values; (3) participation in the survival, liberation, and development of Black people and defense of their dignity, worth, and integrity; and (4) resistance to anti-Black forces. The six expressive dimensions include (1) religion, (2) family, (3) education, (4) culture, (5) interpersonal

Table 6.1   African-Centered (Africentric) Psychological Constructs and Empirical Literature

Construct (Author/Year)	Sample	Method	Finding
African Self-Consciousness Scale (Baldwin & Bell, 1985)	50 African American college students	Questionnaire	Validity estimate, $r = .70$, test–retest reliability, $r = .90$.
Stokes, Murray, Peacock, & Kaiser (1994)	147 African Americans	Questionnaire	Cronbach's $\alpha = .78$.
Dixon & Azibo (1998)	101 African American polydrug-addicted males	Questionnaire	Value for African Centered Institutions and Relationships accounted for 26% of the variance (Cronbach's $\alpha = .88$) and Value Against Affirmative Africanity accounted for 10.9% of the variance (Cronbach's $\alpha = .89$).
Chambers et al. (1998)	701 African American university students	Questionnaire	Internal consistency was high for females (Cronbach's $\alpha = .86$) and males (Cronbach's $\alpha = .89$).
Thompson & Chambers (2000)	80 African American university students	Questionnaire	Cronbach's $\alpha = .92$.
Jefferson & Caldwell (2002)	275 African American university students	Questionnaire	Cronbach's $\alpha = .88$
Oshodi Sentence Completion Index/ Africentric Sentence Completion Test (Oshodi, 1999)	107 Nigerian and American college student volunteers	Questionnaire	Cronbach's α for each of the 20 items = .98–1.00.
Africentric Home Environment Inventory (Caughy et al., 2002)	200 African American families	Home visit; observed behavior or self-reported	Cronbach's $\alpha = .88$.
	405 African American families	Home visit; observed behavior or self-reported	Cronbach's $\alpha = .92$.
Belief Systems Analysis Scale (Montgomery et al., 1990)	140 White students at private, Midwestern university	Questionnaire	Cronbach's $\alpha = .71$.
Brookins (1994)	171 African American students at predominately White university	Questionnaire	Cronbach's $\alpha = .71$.
Hatter & Ottens (1998)	67 African American students at predominately White university	Questionnaire	
Communalism Scale (Boykin et al., 1997)	Four samples of African American undergraduates. Sample 1: $N = 140$ Sample 2: $N = 57$ Sample 3: $N = 274$ Sample 4: $N = 135$	Self-report questionnaire	Cronbach's αs ranged from .83 to .89, test–retest reliability, $r = .81$. Significant correlations with subscales of the Scales of Social Interdependence.

(Continued)

Table 6.1 (Continued)

Construct (Author/Year)	Sample	Method	Finding
Africultural Coping Systems Inventory (Utsey et al., 2000)	Factor analyses	Self-report questionnaire	Cronbach's alphas for the four subscales of the measure range from .65 to .87.
Africentrism Scale (Grills & Longshore, 1996)	Factor analyses	Self-report questionnaire	Cronbach's α = .79.

relationships, and (6) political orientation. All responses to the scale are recorded on a 7-point Likert-type scale.

Psychometric Properties. The ASC demonstrated adequate evidence of reliability in the development study (test–retest, $r = .90$; Cronbach's $\alpha = .70$; Baldwin & Bell, 1985). Other studies have replicated these findings, with Cronbach's alpha coefficients that range from .61 to .88 (Jefferson & Caldwell, 2002; Kelly & Floyd, 2001; Stokes, Murray, Peacock, & Kaiser, 1994). With regard to validity evidence, a study conducted by Bell, Bouie, and Baldwin (1990) examined the relationship between ASC scores and perceptions of male–female relationships in a community sample ($N = 177$) of African Americans. The results revealed a positive correlation between ASC scores and Ideal Mate scores ($r = 44$, $p < .001$) and between ASC scores and Heterosexual Attitudes scores ($r = .53$, $p < .001$). Another study that examined ASC scores and African American male–female relationships found inverse relationships between ASC scores and partner dependability and dyadic adjustment (Kelly & Floyd, 2001). A study conducted by Thompson and Chambers (2000) revealed that ASC scores predicted the unique variance in health-promoting behaviors beyond that accounted for by health consciousness. Two other studies have found statistically significant relationships between ASC scores and measures of racial identity (Jefferson & Caldwell, 2002; Pierre & Mahalik, 2005). Both of these studies found that ASC scores were positively correlated with a more developed racial identity statuses. Dixon and Azibo (1998) examined the relationship between ASC scores and psychological misorientation (i.e., substance abuse and addiction) with a sample of 101 African American male crack cocaine users. Surprisingly, they found no differences in levels of ASC scores and antisocial behavior (selling illicit substances, theft, robbery, etc.). With regard to the ASC's factor structure, the findings have been divergent. For example, Dixon and Azibo discovered a two-factor solution, whereas Stokes et al. (1994) arrived at a four-factor solution. Cronbach's alphas ranged from .61 to .89 across the two studies.

Evaluation. Across all of the studies just reviewed, the ASC has demonstrated adequate evidence of reliability and validity as a measure of Africentric cultural consciousness. However, given the mixed findings regarding the measure's factor structure, additional research is needed to establish a stable ASC model. Although the initial purpose of the ASC was exclusively for use among African American university students in the South, it has since been utilized among other geographic locations and demographic groups. Overall, the ASC is a useful tool with moderate to strong psychometric evidence for effective use among diverse respondents. There are, however, questions about the ASC's face validity. A review of the ASC items, for example, reveals what appears to be an assessment of an individual's Black nationalism as opposed to African cultural preferences.

Communalism Scale

Description and Development. The CS was developed by Boykin, Jagers, Ellison, and Albury (1997) to assess Afrocultural communal values, such as feelings of responsibility to a social group and interdependence with others within the group. This scale was created along with a working definition of *communalism* to provide a basis for future scholarly research on the expression of communalism, especially by individuals of African heritage (Boykin et al., 1997). A panel of experts selected 46 items from an initial bank of 54 to be administered to separate samples for the purpose of initial validation. On the basis of these findings, the scale was reduced to 31 items. Five of these items were reverse keyed, and nine filler items were added to control for response bias, resulting in a 40-item, 6-point Likert-type scale ranging from *completely false* to *completely true*.

Psychometric Properties. Two additional samples of African American undergraduates were used to further evaluate the psychometric properties of the CS. These participants were administered the final 40-item version of the CS, as well as the Scales of Social Interdependence (Johnson & Norem-Hebeisen, 1979), a measure of cooperative, competitive, and individualistic views. Correlations between the CS and the Scales of Social Interdependence ranged from .35 to .59 on the Cooperative subscale and from −.29 to −.40 on the Individualistic subscale (Boykin et al., 1997). Jagers and Mock (1995) found the CS scores to be positively correlated with collectivistic behaviors, namely, with scores on the Concern for In-Group, Prosocial, Restrictive Conformity, Tradition, and Security subscales. The CS was inversely correlated with the Distance From In-Group scale, and the Self-Reliance scale was inversely correlated with the Competition scales. Test–retest reliability of the CS in a sample of 135 African American undergraduate college students was .81 (Boykin et al., 1997). Prior studies have produced Cronbach's alpha coefficients for the CS ranging from .83 to .89 (Jagers & Mock, 1995; Mattis, Hearn, & Jagers, 2002). This suggests acceptable internal consistency and stability for the measure.

Evaluation. The CS was developed out of an effort to create a working definition of *communalism* as well as an attempt to lay the groundwork for future research on the expression of this African-centered value with a reliable and valid measure. The sound psychometric properties have been established in relatively homogeneous samples (i.e., African American undergraduates), and it would be interesting to explore the way these scores compare with scores of samples from more varied populations (i.e., in respect to age, ethnicity, geography, education level; Jagers & Mock, 1995). Future research may also further establish the relationship between communal attitudes and psychological functioning as well as implications for styles of learning and work environments that may result in greater success for individuals with more group-oriented values, as indicated by the CS (Boykin et al., 1997).

Africultural Coping Systems Inventory

Description and Development. The ACSI is a 30-item factor-analytically derived self-report measure that was developed by Utsey et al. (2000) in response to the lack research and measures that tap into culture-specific, African-centered coping utilized by African Americans during times of stress. Factor analyses of this instrument revealed four specific dimensions: (1) Cognitive/Emotional Debriefing (CED; 11 items), (2) Spiritual-Centered Coping (SC; 8 items), (3) Collective Coping (CC; 8 items), and (4) Ritual-Centered Coping (3 items). The scores for each dimension of coping style are obtained by summing items across each of the subscales, with higher scores indicating increased use of a particular coping strategy. In completing this measure, participants are asked to briefly describe a recent stressful event and to keep that particular event in mind while responding to the inventory items (descriptions of coping techniques) using a 4-point Likert-type scale (range. 0 = *did not use* to 3 = *used a great deal*).

Psychometric Properties. Both exploratory and confirmatory factor analyses were conducted with two separate samples of African Americans to examine the underlying factor structure of the ACSI. On the basis of this analysis, a four-factor oblique structure emerged as best representing the ASCI factor structure. The four-factor model was confirmed using confirmatory factor analysis. Cronbach's alphas for the ACSI subscales were as follows: CED = .78–.84, SC = .79–.87, CC = .71–.82, and Ritual-Centered Coping = .65–.76 (Lewis-Coles & Constantine, 2006; Utsey et al., 2000; Utsey, Bolden, Lanier, & Williams, 2007). The CED, SC, and CC subscales of the ACSI produced statistically significant correlations with subscales of the Ways of Coping Questionnaire (Folkman & Lazarus, 1985). The CED was positively correlated with the Detachment, Seeking Social Support, and Focusing on the Positive subscales of the Ways of Coping Questionnaire; the SC was positively correlated with the Problem-Focused Coping, Seeking Social Support, and Focusing on the Positive subscales; and the CC was positively correlated with the Problem-Focused Coping, Seeking Social Support, and Focusing on the Positive.

Evaluation. Prior to the ASCI, the canon of traditional coping measures was largely Eurocentric and failed to consider the unique experiences of individuals of African descent and the ways in which these experiences influence culturally relevant coping behaviors. The ASCI is a psychometrically sound measure of unique, spiritually based, and culturally relevant coping behaviors employed by African Americans during stressful encounters with the environment (Utsey et al., 2000). This instrument aims to capture unique aspects of the Africentric worldview as it relates to African American personality and coping. Future research is needed to examine the relationship between the culture-specific coping measured by the ASCI and other indicators of the physical and mental health status of African Americans. Future research should also include participants of varied demographic backgrounds (age, ethnicity, religion, education, socioeconomic status).

Africentrism Scale

Description and Development. The Africentrism Scale (AS) was developed by Grills and Longshore (1996) to assess the degree to which a person embraces/adheres to the *Nguzo Saba* of African and African American culture: *Umoja* (unity), *Kujichagulia* (self-determination), *Ujima* (collective work and responsibility), *Ujamaa* (cooperative economics), *Nia* (purpose), *Kuumba* (creativity), and *Imani* (faith). These seven principles and related African-centered constructs were used as a guide in the development of AS scale items. The final product is a 15-item measure with a 4-point Likert-type scale ranging from *strongly agree* to *strongly disagree*.

Psychometric Properties. The AS is a factor-analytically derived measure of Africentric attitudes and behaviors. Factor analysis revealed an Individualism–Communalism dimension of the scale (Grills & Longshore, 1996). These findings were later confirmed by Kwate (2003). For initial development study, however, evidence of the AS's construct validity was established by comparing scores between groups who were known to differ on Africentric attitudes and behaviors (i.e., African Americans and Caucasians). Similarly, the study examined AS scores of African Americans who were studying African American history in comparison to those who were not (Grills & Longshore, 1996). Additional evidence of the instrument's construct validity can be observed in Kwate's study, which found that the AS was inversely correlated with the Cultural Misorientation Scale (Kambon, 1992). Another study found AS scores to be positively correlated with three subscales of the Multigroup Ethnic Identity Measure (Phinney, 1992), a measure of ethnic identity and involvement in ethnic traditions and pride. Specifically, AS scores were highly correlated with the following subscales of the Multigroup Ethnic Identity Measure: Ethnic Identity Achievement, Ethnic Behavior, and Group Affirmation. Cronbach's alphas for the AS have ranged from .71 to .83, suggesting that the scores on the measure have moderate internal consistency.

Evaluation. The AS is a self-report measure that is based on broad Africentric concepts and is meant to be easily understood and completed by individuals from varied educational backgrounds. Kwate (2003) cross-validated this measure, including a wide variety of individuals in the sample, such as Afro-Caribbean and African, as well as African American individuals of differing ages, educational levels, birthplace, and so on. This cross-validation further supported the solid internal consistency and validity of the instrument. Future research is needed to provide an examination of the test–retest reliability of this measure. A limitation of the AS is its theoretical grounding in the *Nguzo Saba*, or Seven Principles. As noted, the *Nguzo Saba* represents a set of communitarian values based in an African reality. These principles represent more of the ideal value system embraced by African Americans and not so much the actual beliefs and behaviors of this group. Consequently, little empirical evidence supporting this conceptual framework has been generated.

Oshodi Sentence Completion Index

Description and Development. The OSCI, or Africentric Sentence Completion Test, was developed by Oshodi (1999) to assess the need for achievement among African American students. This measure is based on Murray's (1973) Thematic Apperception Test and includes individualistic, materialistic, and self-oriented views of achievement characteristic of European Americans (Atkinson, 1964; McClelland, Atkinson, Clark, & Lowell, 1953). The purpose of this test is to account for achievement motives that are unique among people of African descent (e.g., spiritual, communal, nonmaterial, and holistic traits) (Asante, 1990; Baldwin, Brown, & Rackley, 1990; Bell, 1994; Mbiti, 1970; Myers, 1988; Ogbonnaya, 1994). This is done through sentence completion items that focus on an African worldview. The 20 items of the OSCI reflect an African-centered theory of motivation, or attitude: attitude toward aspiration, attitude toward obstacles, attitude toward risk taking, attitude toward persistence, attitude toward spirituality, or attitude toward communality (Oshodi, 1999). When taking the OSCI, students are instructed to complete each incomplete sentence in a way that expresses his or her personal feelings and needs. In the initial development study, Oshodi attempted to identify and reconstruct those factors that restrain or enhance achievement motives and to explore the usefulness of the OSCI as a measure of achievement.

Psychometric Properties. First, it should be noted that there are few published empirical studies utilizing the OSCI, so our focus here will be on the development study. Moreover, given the projective framework of the instrument, much of the initial validity evidence is qualitative in nature. In the initial development study, Oshodi (1999) found that responses of African American participants toward the OSCI revealed that Africentric values (e.g., collective self, spiritual supportiveness, cultural identification, and family loyalty) were the underlying motives of persistence, resilience, and aspiration toward achievement. Neutral or negative responses (e.g., need for externality and individuality, inflexibility and material dependency) were less related to Africentric constructs. Interrater reliability was established by two clinical judges with an understanding of the collective African worldview. Interrater reliability produced a kappa coefficient of .99 (Oshodi, 1999).

Evaluation. The OSCI was developed as a measure of collectivist traits common among African Americans or people of African descent. In the pilot study, the OSCI was administered to university students from Nigeria and the United States. The instrument was successful in eliciting collectivist ideas from students. Interrater reliability indices were high. The most obvious limitation of the OSCI is the absence of empirical evidence regarding its reliability and validity. There is a need for further evaluation of the OSCI, either in the context of clinical assessment or large-scale empirical research. Another major concern is the instrument being grounded in Western psychology's psychoanalytic tradition. Although the concept of the unconscious is not a Western concept per se (see Bynum, 1999), the Thematic Apperception Test, on which the OSCI is based, is. Therefore, the author must reconcile the use of instruments from Western psychology in assessing the African personality.

Belief Systems Analysis Scale

Description and Development. The BSAS was developed to assess an individual's commitment to an Afrocentric worldview (optimal) and belief system (Montgomery et al., 1990). The optimal worldview is described as holistic, nonmaterialistic, and community oriented. It is accompanied by a spiritual centeredness (Clark et al., 1974) that relates all objects and individuals to one another (Akbar, 1979). In theory, holistic unity will eliminate the seeming importance of superficial differences between people and instead emphasize the substantial character of the individual (Montgomery et al., 1990). Responses to the 31 questions are recorded on a 5-point Likert-type scale that ranges from *strongly agree* to *strongly disagree* (i.e., "The more important consideration when looking for a job is not the money offered but the people I would be working with").

Psychometric Properties. In the development study (Montgomery et al., 1990), the BSAS showed acceptable internal consistency (Cronbach's α = .80) and adequate test–retest reliability (n = 41; 1 week apart, r = .63). The BSAS was significantly correlated ($p < .001$) in the anticipated direction with the Social Interest Scale (r = .50; Crandall, 1975), the Dogmatism Scale (r = –.51; Rokeach, 1960), and the Symptom Checklist–90–R (r = –.38; Derogatis, Rickels, & Rock, 1976). The moderate size of these correlations suggests that the BSAS measured a related construct. A principal-component analysis was conducted to identify the underlying factor structure of the BSAS, and five factors accounted for 38.3% of the total variance: (1) Interpersonal Valuing, (2) Deemphasis on Appearance, (3) Integration of Opposites, (4) Nonmaterial-Based Satisfaction, and (5) Optimism. Brookins (1994) found that the BSAS correlated negatively with the Racial Identity Attitude Scale's (Helms & Parham, 1990) Preencounter subscale ($r = -.38$, $p < .001$) and positively with its Internalization subscale ($r = .17$, $p = .024$). Hatter and Ottens (1998) found the BSAS to be moderately correlated with the Student Adaptation to College Questionnaire subscale scores ($r = .28-.60$) (Baker & Siryk, 1989).

Evaluation. The normative scores for the second sample of African American college students (Brookins, 1994) was significantly higher and more stable than the previous sample of White college students (Montgomery et al., 1990). These findings suggest a discrepancy in worldview between the two samples. Although the overall BSAS demonstrated acceptable internal consistency according to Cronbach's alpha, the subscales only showed moderate alpha levels. Beyond the observations regarding the measure's empirical attributes there are concerns about its early theoretical and conceptual development. The authors used a sample of White college students from the Midwest as the initial development sample. They justified this by stating that "If we go back far enough, we are all Africans." This approach to the development of culture-specific instrumentation is not only counterintuitive but also psychometrically questionable. Therefore, it is recommended that the BSAS be reevaluated with a sample of African Americans or other African-descent persons. This reevaluation should include an examination of the measure's underlying factor structures as well as other indices of reliability and validity.

Africentric Home Environment Inventory

Description and Development. The AHEI was developed to assess observable Africentric features in the home environment. The purpose of this instrument was to determine the relationship between the family environment and social and cognitive development among African American children who are socialized among both Black and White communities (Caughy et al., 2002). The most commonly used measure of physical, social, and emotional environment influences on children is the Home Observation for Measurement of the Environment Scale (Caldwell & Bradley, 1984). A sample of 25 African American families composed the sample for the pilot study of the 10-item inventory. Afterward, it was decided that inventory scoring would include self-reports in addition to observed behavior.

Psychometric Properties. In the development study (Caughy et al., 2002), the AHEI showed acceptable internal consistency (Cronbach's $\alpha = .88$). Other studies have supported these findings (e.g., Caughy & O'Campo, 2006: $\alpha = .88$; Caughy, O'Campo, Nettles, & Lohrfink, 2006: $\alpha = .92$). The development study also included an initial factor analysis that produced a single factor that expained 44.6% of the variance in the 10 items. A confirmatory factor analysis demonstrated an excellent fit: goodness of fit index = .96, root-mean-square error of approximation = .04. The AHEI was found to be significantly correlated with the Preparation for Bias subscale of the Parent's Experience of Racial Socialization scale ($r(184) = .235$, $p < .01$) (Stevenson, 2006). In addition, as family income increased, scores on the AHEI also increased, $F(3, 184) = 10.07$, $p < .01$, and as poverty level increased, scores on the AHEI decreased, $F(2, 196) = 13.81$, $p < .01$. Higher scores were also found among more highly educated parents, $F(2, 196) = 11.15$, $p < .01$.

Evaluation. The AHEI has shown strong internal reliability throughout three studies. One interesting result was a strong association found between scores on the AHEI and family socioeconomic status. As family income increased, the probability of having items in the home that reflect distinct, African American culture also increased. Future psychometric studies of the AHEI should compare and contrast items that are measured by direct observation and those that are self-reported. In addition, interrater reliability and test–retest reliability should be examined in future studies. This is because neither has been assessed during any of the previous studies.

SUMMARY AND RECOMMENDATIONS

Empirical research and scale development has not kept pace with the theoretical and conceptual literature in African-centered psychology, which has developed at a much faster rate. Early theoretical contributions by Na'im Akbar, Kobi Kambon, Cedrick X, and Wade Nobles laid the foundation for the empirical studies that began to proliferate during the 1990s. Because of these efforts there has been a twofold increase in the number of empirically based, African-centered studies conducted for the period beginning 1990 and ending 2008. Furthermore, it was during this period that we witnessed a substantial increase in the number of studies that focused on the development and validation of instruments that assess African-centered constructs. For example, the BSAS, the AS, the CS, and the OSCI were all developed in the 1990s. Both the ACSI and the AHEI were developed during this decade. One positive consequence of this increase in the number of African-centered measures is that scholars are now provided with more tools to assess constructs related to the personality and behavior of African people. As the number of studies utilizing African-centered constructs continue to increase, so will the evidence of the psychometric properties of these various instruments.

It is above all imperative that scholars continue to develop valid and reliable instruments to assess those constructs that represent the reality of African people. Moreover, there must be a systematic effort to subject these instruments to rigorous theoretical and empirical scrutiny. In the absence of an adequate body of empirical literature with which to evaluate the evidence in favor of the psychometric utility of instruments used to assess African-centered constructs, there exists a reduced likelihood that there will be significant theoretical and conceptual advances in the discipline of African (Black) Psychology. Having reviewed seven of the most widely used measures for assessing African-centered (psychological and social) constructs, we conclude that specific recommendations for the future development and/or evaluation of these and other instruments are warranted. To this end, we make the following recommendations for the development and validation, or psychometric evaluation, of African-centered tests and measures:

1. Begin with a strong theoretical basis for the development of validation of African-centered measurement instruments. The theoretical orientation must be grounded in an authentic African reality structure and worldview.

2. Researchers should commence programs of research aimed at the development and validation of African-centered measures. Such research programs should consist of multiple-part studies or a series of studies that result in an accumulation of evidence to support the validity and reliability of a given measure.

3. Researchers must develop appropriate African-centered methodologies that facilitate the exploration of the African reality structure and worldview. This recommendation does not assume that current methodologies (i.e., paper-and-pencil measures, experimental designs, etc.) have no utility in the examination of African-centered constructs. As noted earlier in this chapter, the rejection of all forms of empiricism based on the false notion that it represents a European epistemology is ill advised.

4. Researchers would benefit from the use of more rigorous and sophisticated statistical techniques to evaluate the psychometric properties of African-centered measures. This is not to suggest that sophisticated statistical techniques should be used simply for the sake of using more advanced methods but that researchers should select data-analytic approaches that provide more flexibility for assessing the psychometric properties of tests and measures.

5. Given the theoretical supposition of African (Black) Psychology that African people share a common underlying core personality structure (Baldwin, 1986), studies that examine group invariance between Africans in the Diaspora are needed.

Conclusion

This chapter was intended to provide the reader with a review of the most commonly used measures of African-centered psychological and social constructs. We reviewed the psychometric properties of each instrument so the reader would be informed as to the strengths and limitations of each measure and therefore better positioned to make an informed decision regarding which measure to use in their own research. We concluded by providing a number of recommendations that might be useful in guiding future research in this area. We hope that African-centered scholars will continue contributing to the empirical literature so as to contribute to the literature base that will allow us to advance the theoretical range of African (Black) Psychology.

Note

1. The term *African people* is used to refer to all persons of African descent in the Diaspora (e.g., Africa, the Caribbean, North and South America, the United States, and Europe; Clark et al., 1975).

References

Abraham, W. E. (1962). *The mind of Africa.* Chicago: University of Chicago Press.

Akbar, N. (1979). African roots of Black personality. In W. D. Smith, K. Burlew, W. Whitney, & M. Mosley (Eds.), *Reflections on Black Psychology* (pp. 79–87). Washington, DC: University Press of America.

Asante, M. K. (1990). *Kemet, Afrocentricity and knowledge.* Trenton, NJ: African World Press.

Atkinson, J. W. (1964). *An introduction to motivation.* Princeton, NJ: Van Nostrand.

Azibo, D. (1989). Pitfalls and some ameliorative strategies in African personality research. *Journal of Black Studies, 19,* 306–319.

Azibo, D. (1999). Africentric conceptualizing as the pathway to African liberation. *International Journal of Africana Studies, 5,* 1–31.

Baker, R. W., & Siryk, B. (1989). *The Student Adaptation to College Questionnaire* (SACQ). Los Angeles: Western Psychological Services.

Baldwin, J. A. (1980). An Africentric model of Black personality. In *Proceedings of the 14th Annual Convention of the Association of Black Psychologists.* Washington, DC: Association of Black Psychologists.

Baldwin, J. A. (1986). African (Black) psychology: Issues and synthesis. *Journal of Black Studies, 16,* 235–249.

Baldwin, J. A. (1990). *African personality from an Afrocentric framework.* Tallahassee, FL: A&M University Press.

Baldwin, J. A., & Bell, Y. (1985). The African Self-Consciousness Scale: An Africentric personality questionnaire. *Western Journal of Black Studies, 9,* 61–68.

Baldwin, J. A., Brown, R., & Rackley, R. (1990). Some socio-behavioral correlates of African self-consciousness in African American college students. *Journal of Black Psychology, 17,* 1–17.

Bankole, K. O. (2006). A preliminary report and commentary on the structure of graduate Afrocentric research and implications for the advancement of the discipline of Africalogy, 1980–2004. *Journal of Black Studies, 36,* 663–697.

Bell, Y. R. (1994). A culturally sensitive analysis of Black learning style. *Journal of Black Psychology, 20,* 4–61.

Bell, Y. R., Bouie, C. L., & Baldwin, J. A. (1990). Afrocentric cultural consciousness and African American male–female relationships. *Journal of Black Studies, 21,* 162–189.

Boykin, A. W., Jagers, R. J., Ellison, C. M., & Albury, A. (1997). Communalism: Conceptualization and measurement of an Afrocultural social orientation. *Journal of Black Studies, 27,* 409–418.

Brookins, C. C. (1994). The relationship between Afrocentric values and racial identity attitudes: Validation of the Belief Systems Analysis Scale on African American college students. *Journal of Black Psychology, 20,* 128–142.

Bynum, E. B. (1999). *The African unconscious: Roots of ancient mysticism and modern psychology.* New York: Teachers College Press.

Caldwell, B., & Bradley, R. H. (1984). *Home Observation for Measurement of the Environment—Revised edition.* Little Rock: University of Arkansas at Little Rock.

Caughy, M. O., & O'Campo, P. J. (2006). Neighborhood poverty, social capital, and the cognitive development of African American preschoolers. *American Journal of Community Psychology, 37,* 141–154.

Caughy, M. O., O'Campo, P. J., Nettles, S. M., & Lohrfink, K. F. (2006). Neighborhood matters: Racial socialization of African American children. *Child Development, 77,* 1220–1236.

Caughy, M. O., Randolph, S. M., & O'Campo, P. J. (2002). The Africentric Home Environment Inventory: An observational measure of the racial socialization features of the home environment for African American preschool children. *Journal of Black Psychology, 28,* 37–52.

Chambers, J. W., Kambon, K., Birdsong, B. D., Brown, J., Dixon, P., & Brinson, L. R. (1998). Africentric cultural identity and the stress experience of African American college students. *Journal of Black Psychology, 24,* 368–396.

Clark, C. X., McGee, D. P., Nobles, W., & Weems, L. X. (1975). Voodoo or IQ: An introduction to African Psychology. *Journal of Black Psychology, 1,* 9–29.

Crandall, J. E. (1975). A scale for social interest. *Journal of Individual Psychology, 31,* 187–195.

Derogatis, L., Rickels, K., & Rock, A. (1976). The SCL-90 and the MMPI: A step in the validation of a new self-report scale. *British Journal of Psychiatry, 128,* 280–289.

Dixon, P., & Azibo, D. A. (1998). African self-consciousness, misorientation behavior, and a self-destructive disorder: African American male crack-cocaine users. *Journal of Black Psychology, 24,* 226–247.

Folkman, S., & Lazarus, R. S. (1985). If it changes it must be a process: A study of emotion and coping during three stages of a college examination. *Journal of Personality and Social Psychology, 48,* 150–179.

Grills, C. (2002). African-centered psychology: Basic principles. In T. Parham (Ed.), *Counseling persons of African descent: Raising the bar of practitioner competence* (pp. 10–21). Thousand Oaks, CA: Sage.

Grills, C., & Longshore, D. (1996). Africentrism: Psychometric analyses of a self-report measure. *Journal of Black Psychology, 22,* 86–106.

Guthrie, R. V. (1998). *Even the rat was white: A historical view of psychology* (2nd ed.). Boston: Allyn & Bacon.

Gyekye, K. (1987). *An essay on African philosophical thought: The Akan conceptual scheme.* Philadelphia: Temple University Press.

Gyekye, K. (1996). *African cultural values: An introduction.* Philadelphia: Sankofa.

Hatter, D. Y., & Ottens, A. J. (1998). Afrocentric world view and Black students' adjustment to a predominately White university: Does worldview matter? *College Student Journal, 32,* 672–685.

Helms, J. E., & Parham, T. A. (1990). Racial Identity Attitude Scale. In J. E. Helms (Ed.), *Black and White racial identity: Theory, research and practice* (pp. 245–247). Westport, CT: Greenwood Press.

Jagers, R. J., & Mock, L. O. (1995). The Communalism Scale and collectivistic– individualistic tendencies: Some preliminary findings. *Journal of Black Psychology, 21,* 153–167.

Jefferson, S. D., & Caldwell, R. (2002). An exploration of the relationship between racial identity attitudes and the perception of racial bias. *Journal of Black Psychology, 28,* 174–192.

Johnson, D. W., & Norem-Hebeisen, A. A. (1979). A measure of cooperative, competitive and individualistic attitudes. *Journal of Social Psychology, 109,* 253–261.

Kambon, K. K. K. (1992). *The African personality in America: An African-centered framework.* Tallahassee, FL: Nubian Nation.

Kelly, S., & Floyd, F. J. (2001). The effects of negative racial stereotypes and Afrocentricity on Black couple relationships. *Journal of Family Psychology, 15,* 110–123.

Kwate, N. O. A. (2003). Cross-validation of the Africentrism Scale. *Journal of Black Psychology, 29,* 308–324.

Lewis-Coles, M. E. L., & Constantine, M. G. (2006). Racism-related stress, africultural coping, and religious problem-solving among African Americans. *Cultural Diversity and Ethnic Minority Psychology, 12,* 433–443.

Mattis, J. S., Hearn, K. D, & Jagers, R. J. (2002). Factors predicting communal attitudes among African American men. *Journal of Black Psychology, 28,* 197–214.

Mbiti, J. (1970). *African philosophy and religion.* New York: Anchor.

McClelland, D. C., Atkinson, J. W., Clark, R. A., & Lowell, E. L. (1953). *The achievement motive.* New York: Appleton-Century-Crofts.

Montgomery, D. E., Fine, M. A., & Myers, L. J. (1990). The development and validation of an instrument to assess an optimal Afrocentric world view. *Journal of Black Psychology, 19,* 37–54.

Murray, H. A. (1973). *Thematic Apperception Test.* Cambridge, MA: Harvard University Press.

Myers, L. J. (1988). *Understanding an Afrocentric worldview: Introduction to an Optimal Psychology.* Dubuque, IA: Kendall/Hunt.

Nobles, W. W. (1972). African philosophy: Foundations for Black Psychology. In R. L. Jones (Ed.), *Black Psychology* (pp. 18–32). New York: Harper & Row.

Nobles, W. W. (1986). *African Psychology: Toward its reclamation, reascension, and revitalization.* Oakland, CA: Black Family Institute.

Nobles, W. W. (2004). African philosophy: Foundations for Black Psychology. In R. L. Jones (Ed.), *Black Psychology* (4th ed., pp. 57–72). Hampton, VA: Cobb & Henry.

Ogbonnaya, O. (1994). Person as community: An African understanding of the person as an intrapsychic community. *Journal of Black Psychology, 20,* 75–87.

Olupona, J. K. (2000). *African spirituality: Forms, meanings, and expressions.* New York: Cross Roads.

Oshodi, J. E. (1999). The construction of an Africentric Sentence Completion Test to assess the need for achievement. *Journal of Black Studies, 30,* 216–231.

Parham, T. A. (2002). Understanding African American mental health: The necessity of new conceptual paradigms. In T. Parham (Ed.), *Counseling persons of African descent: Raising the bar of practitioner competence* (pp. 10–21). Thousand Oaks, CA: Sage.

Phinney, J. S. (1992). The Multigroup Ethnic Identity Measure: A new scale for use with diverse groups. *Journal of Adolescent Research, 7,* 156–176.

Pierre, M. R., & Mahalik, J. R. (2005). Examining African self-consciousness and Black racial identity as predictors of Black men's psychological well-being. *Cultural Diversity and Ethnic Minority Psychology, 11,* 28–40.

Ponterotto, J. G., Utsey, S. O., & Pedersen, P. B. (2006). *Reducing prejudice: A guide for* counselors, educators, and parents (2nd ed.). Thousand Oaks, CA: Sage.

Rokeach, M. (1960). *The open and closed mind.* New York: Basic Books.

Stevenson, H. C. (2006). *Development and scoring of the Racial Socialization Belief and Experiences Scales for Adolescents and Parents.* Unpublished manuscript, University of Pennsylvania.

Stokes, J. E., Murray, C. B., Peacock, M. J., & Kaiser, R. T. (1994). Assessing the reliability, factor structure, and validity of the African Self-Consciousness Scale in a general population of African Americans. *Journal of Black Psychology, 20,* 62–74.

Thomas, A., & Sillen, S. (1972). *Racism and psychiatry.* New York: Citadel Press.

Thompson, S. N., & Chambers, J. W. (2000). African self-consciousness and health-promoting behaviors among African American college students. *Journal of Black Psychology, 26,* 330–345.

Utsey, S. O., Adams, E. P., & Bolden, M. (2000). Development and initial validation of the Africultural Coping Systems Inventory. *Journal of Black Psychology, 26,* 194–215.

Utsey, S. O., Bolden, M. A, Lanier, Y., & Williams, O., III. (2007). Examining the role of culture-specific coping as a predictor of resilient outcomes in African Americans from high-risk urban communities. *Journal of Black Psychology, 33,* 75–93.

Weems, L. X. (1974). Awareness: The key to Black mental health. *Journal of Black Psychology, 1,* 30–37.

PART III

CONTEXTUALIZING ATTITUDES AND BEHAVIORS

![chapter 7 banner]

RELIGION AND SPIRITUALITY

JACQUELINE S. MATTIS AND CAROLYN R. WATSON

For more than 5 decades, social scientists have examined the roles of religiosity and spirituality in the lives of African Americans (Frazier, 1963; Mays, 1969). Using a variety of methodologies (qualitative, small-scale survey studies, and large regional as well as national survey approaches), these scholars have focused on an array of topics, including African Americans' patterns of involvement in religious life, the nature and context of African American religious experience (e.g., the liturgical practices and liberationist themes in African American theological traditions), the role of religious institutions and religious leaders in preserving the well-being of African Americans, religion's role in African American family life, religion's role in the socio-moral development of African American children and youth, and the role of religion in African American youth's and adults' efforts to cope with the challenges of life. More recently, scholars have begun to map the role of religion and spirituality in the prosocial and positive psychological development of African Americans. Through a review of this extant literature, we endeavor here to address a single question: What roles do religiosity and spirituality play in influencing the psychological health of African Americans?

As a beginning point, we attend to two foundational questions: (1) What do we mean by *religiosity* and *spirituality*? (2) What do we mean by *psychological health*? Subsequently, we address two higher-order questions. First, what do existing studies reveal about the pattern of relationships between religiosity and spirituality and psychological health? Second, what are the mechanisms via which religion and spirituality are presumed to influence psychological health outcomes? We conclude by identifying limitations and future directions for the study of the link between religiosity and spirituality and mental health.

DEFINING RELIGIOSITY, SPIRITUALITY, AND PSYCHOLOGICAL HEALTH

Studies of health, religiosity, and spirituality often have proceeded without benefit of explicit definitions of these terms. As such, we often are left to infer the meanings of *religiosity*, *spirituality*, and *mental health* from the particular ways that these constructs are operationalized in research involving African Americans. Explicit definitions of these three constructs are an important launch point for exploring both the breadth and the limits of extant research on the religiosity/spirituality–health link.

Historically, the terms *religiosity* and *spirituality* have been used interchangeably. This is likely a consequence of the experiential overlap between these constructs. However, recent scholarship suggests that African Americans do make distinctions between religiousness and spirituality (Mattis, 2000). Content analyses of the written and oral narratives of African American adults indicate that *religion/religiosity* refers to one's adherence to the prescribed beliefs and ritual practices associated with the worship of God or a system of gods. In contrast, *spirituality* refers to a relationship between transcendent forces (e.g., God, spirits, ancestors) and humans that results both in the individual's recognition of the sacredness of all things and in a conscious commitment to live a life of virtue. The meanings of spirituality that emerge out of qualitative research are echoed by scholars. Indeed, Boykin and Ellison (1995), Edwards (1998), Jagers (1997), and Potts (1991) all have defined spirituality as a belief in a sacred, transcendent force that resides in all things and that infuses and directs all happenings in the human as well as nonhuman spheres. It is important to note that existing research suggests that religiosity and spirituality are concepts that exist on distinct continua. As such, individuals can describe themselves as "not at all" to "very" religious and "not at all" to "very" spiritual (as opposed to either religious or spiritual). However, the phenomenology of faith and transcendence is such that individuals can be (and often do describe themselves as) simultaneously religious and spiritual.

How we define religiosity and spirituality has implications for how we measure these constructs in social science research. For African American adherents of theistic religions (e.g., Christianity, Islam), God/Allah, Jesus Christ, and the Holy Spirit are among the ultimate manifestation(s) of the omnipresent and omniscient force that we refer to as "the sacred" or "the divine." For some people, reverence for, and a desire to know and follow the will of, the divine inspires an interest in careful and systematic study of sacred texts (e.g., the Bible, the Q'uran). These individuals may express their commitment to the divine by attending and/or holding memberships in organized faith communities in which the tenets of their faith are reinforced through sermons, scriptural readings, testimonies, songs, ritual practices (e.g., prayer), and outreach activities (e.g., care for the needy). This pattern of expression is referred to as *organizational religious involvement*. Others may not participate or hold memberships in faith communities but may demonstrate their reverence for and devotion to the divine privately (e.g., through private prayer, the consumption of religious music and literature, or by watching religious media [e.g., televised church services]). These forms of involvement are referred to as *nonorganizational involvement*. Finally, individuals may express their commitment (or lack of commitment) to faith by embracing a subjective identity as religious, spiritual, or atheist. This personal identification is referred to as *subjective religiosity* or *subjective spirituality* (see Chatters, Levin, & Taylor, 1992, for a discussion).

The word *health* is derived from the Old English words *hal* or *hoelth* (meaning "to be whole, sound, or well"). *Psychological health*, then, refers to the experience of having a psyche (mind) that is whole, sound, or well. In research and practice, psychological health typically has been constructed in one of three ways: (1) as the relative absence of subjectively reported distress (e.g., low levels of reported depressive or anxious symptomatology), (2) as the subjective report of positive individual states of being (e.g., high self-esteem), or (3) as any of an array of behaviors that reflect "normative" social functioning (e.g., avoidance of risky or antisocial activities). More recently, with the emergence of a focus on positive and optimal psychological functioning, scholars have begun to attend to positive cognitive and affective states (e.g., optimism, happiness) and positive and prosocial behaviors (e.g., emotional self-regulation, cooperation, civic engagement, volunteerism) as indices of mental health.

Religion and Psychological Health: An Overview of Findings From Correlational Studies

In spite of the great variation in the ways that religiosity, spirituality, and mental health have been conceptualized and measured in extant research, the preponderance of qualitative as well as quantitative empirical research has established that religion and spirituality do influence the psychological health of African Americans. Indeed, Levin and Taylor (1998); Ellison, Boardman, Williams, and Jackson (2001); and Jang and Johnson (2004) have found an inverse relationship between the frequency of both religious service attendance and the strength of individuals' religious beliefs and psychological distress (e.g., depression, anxiety). This inverse relationship between religiosity and distress is evident in a plethora of studies (see Black, 1999; Blaine & Crocker, 1995; Bowman, 1990; Christian & Barbarin, 2001; Coleman, 2004; Coleman & Holzemer, 1999; Levin & Taylor, 1998; Neighbors, Jackson, Bowman, & Gurin, 1983; Neighbors, Musick, & Williams, 1998; Watlington & Murphy, 2006).

The religiosity/spirituality–mental health link manifests in various ways. African American adults who regularly attend religious services report fewer family, work, and financial stresses than do their less involved counterparts (Ellison et al., 2001). However, stress is inevitable, and religiosity and spirituality play roles in African American people's efforts to negotiate stress. Adults in the African American community report that in times of stress, faith (evidenced in service attendance, prayer, use of ministerial or church supports, and the use of religious coping strategies) is central in efforts to endure mundane as well as extraordinary adversity (Mattis et al., 2007; McAdoo, 1995; Neighbors et al., 1983, 1998). Indeed, African Americans seek religious (i.e., ministerial) support for a wide array of problems, including financial problems; issues of grief and loss; physical and mental illness; emotional support; the need for emergency housing, food, clothing; and marital and family problems (Lincoln & Mamiya, 1990; Mattis et al., 2007; Neighbors et al., 1998; Taylor, Ellison, Chatters, Levin, & Lincoln, 2000; Young, Griffith, & Williams, 2003). Faith in God is key in coping with the strains and challenges of grandparenting (Gibson, 2002) and parenting (McAdoo, 1995). Religion plays a positive role in African American men's efforts to cope with the challenges that they face in fulfilling the social, emotional, and financial responsibilities in their families (Bowman, 1990; Tinney, 1981). African American couples point to religion as both a source of meaning and a means of coping with life's challenges (Blaine & Crocker, 1995; Chadiha, Veroff, & Leber, 1998; Mattis, 2002; McAdoo, 1995). Religiosity and spirituality buffer the effects of discrimination on mental health among African Americans (Bierman, 2006) and are associated with efforts to negotiate extraordinary forms of violation. They are associated, for example, with African American men's efforts to forgive race-related transgressions (Powell-Hammond, Hudson-Banks, & Mattis, 2006). Religiosity and spirituality also inform African American women's efforts to endure and make meaning of interpersonal violence (Banks-Wallace & Parks, 2004; Watlington & Murphy, 2006) as well as incest (Robinson, 2000).

For African American youth, religious beliefs and religious involvement play critical roles in resolving social and moral challenges (Cooke, 2000; Jagers, Smith, & Mock, 1997), in regulating emotions (Stevenson, 1997), and in shaping identity (Mattis, Ahluwalia, Cowie, & Kirkland-Harris, 2006). Furthermore, African American adolescents and emerging adults whose religious beliefs are salient in their everyday lives score higher than their counterparts on measures of self-esteem, life satisfaction, and perceived self-control (Blaine & Crocker, 1995), and these youth are less likely to perceive themselves as at risk of dying by suicide (Greening & Stoppelbein, 2002).

Despite the wealth of evidence regarding the link between religiosity and spirituality and positive psychological and psychosocial outcomes among African Americans, little empirical attention has been paid to mapping the pathways by which the various dimensions of religion and spirituality achieve their salutogenic effects. We endeavor here to weave together quantitative and qualitative findings from research in sociology, psychology, and cultural studies in order to bring some coherence to our understanding of the means by which religiosity and spirituality may inform well-being. Here, we pay particular attention to the complex roles of religious institutions, religious social networks, theology and belief, prayer, and subjective religious and spiritual identities in shaping positive mental health outcomes.

RELIGIOSITY, SPIRITUALITY, AND PATHWAYS TO HEALTH AND WELLNESS

Religious Institutions

The mechanisms by which religious institutions may inform well-being are myriad. First, national as well as regional surveys of African American churches have found that African American religious institutions provide an array of supports to members of African American communities, including political and civic instruction, academic instruction, health education, medical interventions, food, clothing, housing, jobs, financial support, and social and emotional support (Lincoln & Mamiya, 1990; Rubin, Billingsley, & Caldwell, 1994; Taylor, Thornton, & Chatters, 1987). Furthermore, religious institutions provide couples and family counseling, psychological and material supports to youth and adults and their families, domestic violence intervention, child care, mentoring, parenting workshops, life skills training, workshops on relationships and sexuality, and prayer and visitation for the elderly as well as for the sick and "shut in" (Billingsley, 1992, 1999; Billingsley, & Caldwell, 1991; Blank, Mahmood, Fox, & Guterbock, 2002; Caldwell, Chatters, Billingsley, & Taylor, 1995; Lincoln & Mamiya, 1990; Rubin et al., 1994). These initiatives are critical for preventing and ameliorating distress; preventing social isolation; invoking hope; and providing the spiritual, moral, and psychological guidance needed to ensure that individuals can successfully negotiate the challenges wrought by life. It is important to note that although women are more conventionally religious than men (e.g., they attend religious services more frequently; see Taylor & Chatters, 1991), scholars argue that African American men historically have (and continue to) experienced substantial direct as well as indirect benefits from organized religious life. Indeed, religious institutions provide jobs, opportunities for esteem-building leadership, educational supports (e.g., scholarships), political position and support, assistance in securing and retaining housing, business skills, and social supports to African American men, including men who are not personally affiliated with an organized faith community (Tinney, 1981).

Second, religious institutions facilitate the mental health of children, adolescents, and adults by providing concrete opportunities for involvement in constructive activities. Billingsley (1999) and Lincoln and Mamiya (1990) have noted, for example, that African American churches offer opportunities for involvement in a range of activities, including public readings of (often-memorized) scriptures, musical training and performance (e.g., choir), sports, cheerleading, Girl Scouts and Boy Scouts, and volunteer work. These opportunities provide individuals with critical venues in which to build and publicly demonstrate competencies and personal qualities that may be ignored, invisible, or actively denigrated in other settings. The positive response of members of the faith community to the competencies and values of members of their faith community may elevate self-esteem and lead to a heightened sense of self-efficacy. Furthermore, the experience of engaging in constructive activity may inspire outcomes (e.g., a sense of purpose, self-efficacy, satisfaction) that signify psychological health.

Third, religious institutions historically have promoted the psychological well-being of youth and adults by routinely, publicly celebrating the personal achievements of members of their congregations. For example, in many faith communities religious leaders publicly announce the academic achievements of youth (e.g., honor roll, scholarships, internships, college and graduate school acceptances). The warm, enthusiastic, and authentic public support that youth and adults in these settings receive from religious leaders and congregations, as well as their peers, can bolster self-esteem, create a psychological sense of connectedness, and serve as a buffer against perceived isolation, hopelessness, and despair.

Fourth, religious institutions may promote psychological health and well-being by situating African American youth and adults in an enduring and supportive multigenerational, familistic web of relationships that include ministers, an array of other religious leaders (e.g., youth ministers), authority figures (e.g., church mothers, church elders, deacons, deaconesses), and coreligionists (e.g., family, friends, and acquaintances who share the same faith background). Cook (2000) aptly noted that for youth of African descent, religious institutions and religious leaders (e.g., youth ministers) may serve as crucial sources of mentorship, moral guidance, advice, and emotional support. The tendency of African Americans to employ racialized familistic labels (e.g., "church home," "church mother," "church brother," or "church sister") to describe members of their faith community designates churches as spaces of profound and enduring intimacy and connection in which religious adherents can be recognized, welcomed, and embraced (see Moore, 1991; Townsend-Gilkes, 1997). The church family also serves as a group of people to whom individuals may turn for moral and spiritual guidance and correction and for material, spiritual, and psychological support in life's most vulnerable moments (e.g., deaths, births, extraordinary losses). This supportive network can provide instrumental assistance and can inspire optimism as well as buffer people against depression and despair in times of adversity.

It is important to note that involvement in religious institutions situates people in vital and supportive social networks that include living as well as deceased others (Banks-Wallace & Parks, 2004; Mattis, 2002; Nelson, 1997). Empirical findings lend credence to the theorized links among spirituality and religious involvement, greater perceived social support, and mental health (Brome, Owens, Allen, & Vevaina, 2000; Watlington & Murphy, 2006). For example, Jang and Johnson (2004) asserted that religious African Americans reported receiving greater levels of social support from friends and family, and this reported support mediated the relationship between religiosity and psychological distress. Furthermore, Bowman (1990) reported that religious family members (e.g., spouses) may extend greater emotional and social support to husbands and fathers who are unemployed or underemployed, and this support is crucial to these men's efforts to cope with the challenges associated with fulfilling their roles as providers. Taken together, these findings suggest that religious and spiritual individuals may not only *perceive* greater support, but also they may both *receive* greater support and be more willing to extend support to family, friends, and co-religionists. Support whether perceived, received, or extended, may help buffer against stress. However, Ellison et al. (2001) found that congregational support does not inevitably lead to an amelioration of distress. In fact, they found no association between reported level of congregational support (e.g., the frequency with which individuals receive help from members of their faith community) and reported level of psychological distress. However, the works of Cook (2000), Moore (1991), and McRae, Thompson, and Cooper (1999) suggest that there are indeed mental health benefits to involvement.

Ministers and coreligionists may help foster mistrust of and skepticism about seeking secular interventions (e.g., professional psychology, psychiatry) and a preference for faith-centered interventions. Importantly, however, there is substantial evidence that religious African Americans are especially likely to turn to religious leaders for psychological support, recent evidence suggests that greater involvement in the public aspects of faith life (e.g., religious attendance) is associated with a greater willingness to seek mental health care (Morse, Morse, Klebba, Stock, Forehand, & Panayotova, 2000). Morse et al.'s findings suggest that some individuals who are involved in faith communities may be willing to accept that there are limits to the kinds of supports that faith communities can provide. These individuals may be especially likely to augment the support that they receive from faith life with supports from secular contexts (e.g., psychologists, psychiatrists).

Consistent with this notion, in a focus group study, Mattis et al. (2007) asked African American adults about the limits to the kinds of psychological and personal concerns that they will take to ministers and about a range of factors that influence their willingness to take or not take certain concerns to ministers. Some individuals reported that they never seek support from ministers for any issue. Others refuse to seek support for family and marital concerns, sexual concerns (including matters related to sexual identity and sexual intimacy), reproductive issues, financial matters, health concerns, sexual or intimate partner violence, or substance abuse. Those who elected not to seek emotional or instrumental support from ministers identified a number of factors that influenced their unwillingness to seek ministerial support. Some individuals reported that they do not need ministerial support because they can take their concerns to God directly. Others reported that they would not seek ministerial support because of poor ministerial character (judgmental, indiscreet, unempathic ministers); lack of comfort with turning to ministers as a source of support; availability of alternative sources of support; shame; real or perceived limits to ministerial competence; the limited availability of ministers; and the seriousness of the issue at hand. Whether African Americans pursue psychological and psychiatric support through faith-centered or secular venues is likely dependent on a number of factors (e.g., the education level of religious leaders and the adherents themselves, availability of secular treatment options, and availability of faith-focused interveners with the competence to address the client's needs). However, the availability of multiple venues through which to pursue support may increase individuals' opportunities to receive the supports needed to increase or sustain mental health.

Nonorganizational Religious Involvement: Focus on Prayer

Although formal involvement in religious life is central in catalyzing and sustaining psychological well-being, religious individuals rely on a variety of noninstitutional activities and resources to sustain their faith and to help them endure life's vicissitudes. Individuals may, for example, read religious material (e.g., daily affirmations, books about faith) or listen to religious music or music that they deem has religious or spiritual significance. However, the form of nonorganizational religious activity that has received most attention in research on well-being is prayer.

A national survey of African Americans revealed that prayer is the coping resource of choice for most of them, particularly for African American women (Neighbors et al., 1983). In fact, Neighbors et al. (1983) noted that as problems become more severe, African American women tend to rely more heavily on prayer as their means of coping. Through prayer, people experience emotional and moral support and receive guidance and answers to prayers (El-Khoury et al., 2004; Mattis, 2002; McAdoo, 1995; Neighbors et al., 1998; Nelson, 1997). Prayer also is a vehicle by which people extend and demonstrate their concern and support for others who are in need.

Double-blind studies of the efficacy of intercessory prayer (prayers offered on behalf of others) suggest that even when they are unaware that they are being prayed for by strangers, individuals who are the beneficiaries of intercessory demonstrate lower levels of mortality and post-surgery morbidity (Byrd, 1988; Harris et al., 1999). The mechanisms by which prayer achieves its health effects are unclear. Neuroscientists and neurotheologists speculate that prayer and meditation may influence health by altering brain chemistry and improving immune functioning (McCullough, 1995). Prayer also may serve as a vehicle for emotional catharsis. Individuals engaged in fervent prayer may weep or laugh with abandon; they may express and confess troubles, thoughts, and feelings; they may confide thoughts and feelings that may be unknown to others; raise questions; admit confusions; and experience relief that comes from communicating without fear of being judged and with the knowledge that they can trust that their prayers have been heard by an omnipotent, omniscient, and loving being. Gerontological research suggests that it is not the frequency with which individuals pray but the trust-based expectation that God knows and does what is best for us, and that God always answers our prayers (i.e., prayer expectancies), that influences mental health (Krause, 2004).

Meaning-Making

Public, private, and subjective involvement in religious and spiritual life is important in informing the link between religiosity and spirituality and well-being. However, the link between faith and mental health/wellness is influenced powerfully by our conceptualization of the nature of the divine and by our understanding of how this force operates in our lives. Each individual, and each faith community, endorses a particular view of the divine. For some, the divine is an omniscient, omnipresent, and loving force who is an unwavering friend and ally. For others, the divine is a capricious, wrathful, and jealous figure who, although loving, is also quite punitive. Some individuals adhere to a worldview in which all events (mundane or extraordinary, positive or negative) are a part of a larger transcendent plan. For some individuals who embrace this view, the world is not an arbitrary place; instead, all events have meaning, and each of life's joys and challenges contain life lessons that promote our spiritual and material well-being and that draw us closer to our purpose or to the divine. For individuals who view the divine as unpredictable, jealous, and punitive, however, life's challenges often are experienced as punishments for having violated the mandates of the divine (e.g., sin). Those who view the divine as punitive, and who see the world as an arbitrary and painful place to be, are likely to experience greater levels of despair. Individuals who view the divine as an unconditionally loving figure, and who believe that all events have meaning and purpose, are likely to find reasons for hope and are likely to be psychologically healthy.

Theologians argue that for African Americans (particularly for those who embrace liberation theologies), hope, love, humility, forgiveness, and the capacity to survive and thrive even in the face of overwhelming suffering and evil come from the tradition of linking their plight to the plight of prominent figures from the Bible and Q'uran.

From this perspective, the Bible and the Q'uran dramatically depict God's/Allah's enduring love; omnipotence; and creative, improvisational spirit (i.e., His ability to "make a way out of no way") and assure believers that there is reason to hope because with divine favor they can endure any adversity.

Consistent with the premise that religiosity and spirituality inspire hope, Mattis and colleagues found that African American adults who perceived themselves to be spiritual and those who viewed God as a loving, forgiving, and supportive figure reported a greater level of optimism (Mattis, Fontenot, & Hatcher-Kay, 2003; Mattis, Fontenot, Hatcher-Kay, Grayman, & Beale, 2004). It is interesting that a positive view of God predicted optimism even after accounting for the deleterious effect of encounters with everyday racism. Further, people who experienced themselves as spiritual reported a lower level of pessimism (Mattis et al., 2004). Notably, those who viewed God as a punitive figure reported greater pessimism (Mattis et al., 2004). Importantly, the findings from these studies suggest that traditional indices of religious commitment (subjective religiosity, early and current involvement in the public aspects of religious life) may not be sufficient to instill optimism. Instead, for African Americans optimism may be rooted in a particular view of God as a just and loving figure who will guide and protect them (Mattis et al., 2003, 2004).

The positive ramifications of meaning-making are not limited to optimism or pessimism. Blaine and Crocker (1995) found that African Americans who make meaning-centered attributions to God (e.g., those who believe that there is a divine purpose for the negative events that occur in their lives) reported greater well-being (e.g., greater self-esteem and satisfaction). Among African Americans, those who are highly religious tend to believe that they have control over negative events (e.g., that the outcomes of life events are in their hands), and there is evidence that this belief in personal control helps ameliorate depression and anxiety (Jang & Johnson, 2004). Jang and Johnson's (2004) work suggests that perceived personal control mediates the relationship between religiosity (organizational, nonorganizational, and subjective religiosity) and psychological distress.

Recent qualitative research has identified several themes associated with the roles of religion and spirituality in meaning-making and coping among African American women. Mattis (2002) noted that religiosity and spirituality helped women question and accept reality, engage in spiritual surrender, confront and transcend limits, identify and grapple with existential questions and life lessons, recognize their purpose and destiny, act in accordance with subjectively meaningful moral principles, achieve growth in the aftermath of adversity, and trust in transcendent sources of knowledge and communication (e.g., dreams, intuition). For some individuals, the process of making meaning from adversity involves an awakened sense of gratitude for the graces of life (Black, 1999); a heightened sense of purpose, esteem, and efficacy; and a deepened experience of faith in God's goodness and love (Black, 1999; Mattis, 2002; Miller, 2005, 2007).

The process of making meaning can be painful and faith-rocking. Indeed, in the face of life's most profound challenges (e.g., personal experiences with physical or sexual violence, the suffering and death of a child or a loved one, incest, devastating loss) believers often are forced to wonder how a loving God could allow "innocents" (e.g., children) or faithful believers to endure violation, hurt, or undeserved hardship. Certainly, religious texts provide believers with powerful portrayals of life's potentially overwhelming dramas and dilemmas (e.g., grief, conflict, infidelity, trust, illness) and provide adherents with guidance regarding how to understand, respond to, and transcend mundane as well as extraordinary experiences. However, it is the subjective meaning that individuals ascribe to the events that they face that determines, in large, how they respond to such events. Rogers-Dulan (1998) demonstrated that although religion helps caregivers cope with their caregiving demands and challenges, caregivers who conceived of their children's disabilities as the result of a punishment from God tended to experience psychological distress in the forms of shame and guilt. In contrast, individuals who conceived of the events that they encountered as a calling or as a part of divine will were more likely to experience positive outcomes.

Religious Involvement and Emotional and Behavioral Control

There is some evidence that religious and spiritual ideology and involvement may inform mental health by reducing the likelihood that individuals will engage in an array of risky behaviors (Maton & Wells, 1995; Wallace & Williams, 1997). For example, Morse et al. (2000) reported that individuals who were involved in public as well as private religious activities were less likely to use alcohol and illicit substances (e.g., marijuana, street drugs) and more likely to have a positive subjective evaluation of their mental health. Similarly, religiously involved African-ancestried adolescents were significantly less likely to engage in antisocial activity, were more likely to be employed, and tended to report fewer psychological problems (Cook, 2000). As a complement to the research on risk avoidance, Jagers (1997) found that urban-residing African American children who rated their families as more spiritual, affective, and communal tended to withdraw from social situations and from community members whose behaviors were antisocial. Furthermore, Stevenson (1997) demonstrated that religious and spiritual youth were more likely than their counterparts to regulate their own emotions and behaviors; that is, they were less likely to externalize their anger and more likely to exercise control over their behavior. These findings, when considered in tandem with Woods and Jagers's (2003) finding that, among African American adolescents, spirituality is associated with greater levels of moral reasoning, suggests that the self-regulatory and self-monitoring behavior evident among religious youth and adults may result from religion's and spirituality's roles in creating a moral core from which individuals can draw. These studies collectively suggest that religiosity and spirituality may provide individuals with a moral grounding that guides choices and behaviors. For some individuals, drawing on this wellspring of morality may facilitate avoidance of risk; however, for youth who are embedded in high-risk environments, personal and familial spirituality may facilitate efforts to extricate themselves from potentially negative circumstances and to control their responses to stimuli in those environments.

Religiosity and Identity Coherence

There is compelling emerging evidence that religion and religious institutions may influence mental health by influencing the ways that religious adherents construct, understand, and experience their social identities—particularly their racial identity. Reese and Brown (1995) and Wilcox and Gomez (1990) have asserted that the ideological leanings of religious institutions inform the racial identity of members of religious institutions. These authors have noted that African American religious institutions that espouse liberationist and social justice themes (i.e., "political churches") tend to promote a heightened sense of racial identification among members of their congregations. Individuals who attend these politicized institutions tend to view larger social and political forces (instead of personality) as responsible for the predicaments of African Americans. Consistent with of the notion that Black religious institutions help to craft positive political racial and social identities among their members, Brega and Coleman (1999) indicated that African Americans who attend church more frequently are less likely to endorse negative attitudes and beliefs about African Americans as a group and of themselves as individuals. Similarly, Blaine and Crocker (1995) reported that African American emerging adults who experience religiosity as salient to their identity are more likely to evaluate their social (i.e., racial and religious) groups positively (e.g., to report being proud to be members of their racial and religious groups, and to believe that others hold positive views of their racial and religious groups). These tendencies to assign responsibility for social problems to systems rather than to individuals, and the tendency to hold one's social identity groups in positive regard, may help buffer individuals against the deleterious effects of living in racist and nihilistic society.

Although faith life appears to shape racial identity, the link among religiosity, mental health, and other social identities may be more complex and less positive. This may be particularly true for sexual identity. Douglas (1999) and Miller (2007) have aptly noted that historically churches, including the Black church, have taken a hostile and punitive stance toward lesbian, gay, bisexual, and transgendered (LGBT) individuals. The notable exception to this rule has been the church's silent "tolerance" of gay men who, in their roles as music ministers, choir directors, and/or musicians, dedicate their creative energies to advancing the music and arts ministries of Black churches (Miller, 2007). Certainly, some LGBT African Americans are members of faith communities that are explicitly welcoming and affirming of their identities. Some are driven out of religious institutions by openly hostile religious leaders. Those who remain in religious institutions that are hostile to the LGBT community often are exposed to homophobic messages that can undermine their well-being and self-worth. The social and psychological costs to LGBT individuals of crafting faith life in a hostile context cannot be ignored. Indeed, the view that the feelings and patterns of intimacy associated with LGBT identities are inherently sinful means that members of the LGBT community often are denied opportunities to seek emotional, social, or instrumental supports from religious leaders, coreligionists, and religious institutions as a whole. Furthermore, homophobia in the church may negatively impact individuals' efforts to cultivate a coherent link among their sexual, racial, and spiritual identities (e.g., individuals may be unable to healthily reconcile their identities as Black, gay, and Christian or Muslim), may undermine self-esteem, and may leave people with the despair that comes from being socially isolated and stigmatized.

LIMITS OF EXTANT RESEARCH AND FUTURE DIRECTIONS FOR EMPIRICAL RESEARCH

Several limitations to the literature on the religiosity–spirituality–mental health link are worthy of note. First, studies of the link between religiosity and spirituality and mental health typically have focused on four traditional indicators of religious involvement: (1) religious affiliation (membership in a religious institution and the denomination to which the individual belongs), (2) organizational religious involvement (e.g., service attendance), (3) nonorganizational religiosity (e.g., prayer), and (4) subjective religiosity (e.g., self-evaluation as religious). Furthermore, these studies traditionally have attended to a very localized class of indices of mental health (e.g., depression, anxiety, self-esteem). At present, there is a dire need for research that examines the extent to which a wider array of indices of mental health might be informed by other domains of religious life—namely, religious orthodoxy, spiritual values, spiritual well-being, and use of religious coping.

Second, conceptual and methodological work in the psychological and sociological study of religion and spirituality has proceeded orthogonally. Despite recent research that has outlined points of overlap and divergence in the meanings and manifestations of religiosity and spirituality, scholars continue to measure religiosity and spirituality in ways that either are conceptually fuzzy or ignore the distinctions between them. A more seamless link between conceptual literature and measurement is needed.

The issue of measurement (i.e., instrumentation) is a third point of limitation. With respect to instrumentation, seven concerns are worth noting. First, scholars use a wide array of single- as well as multi-item measures to assess religiosity and spirituality. Second, scholars continue to develop their own scales to measure these constructs, often without regard for redundancy and without regard for findings regarding the distinctions between religiosity and spirituality.

Third, the psychometric properties of these measures are not always identified (or, when they are identified, are not always adequate). Certainly, no single scale can assess all dimensions of religious or spiritual life. However, focused efforts to validate and use a limited but culturally viable set of measures may prove more useful than the present tendency to invent new scales or to use single item measures.

Fourth, the preponderance of research on the religious and spiritual lives of African Americans comes from cross-sectional analyses of small and large scale data sets. There is a dire need for longitudinal data on the religious and spiritual lives of African American youth, adolescents, and adults. Only with the aid of these data can we effectively investigate how mental health is informed by the changing religious and spiritual experiences and by the interplay between those experiences and the evolving social identities of members of the community.

Fifth, extant research on psychological health has proceeded under the assumption that the meaning of *health* is universal. However, as Constantine and Sue (2006) aptly noted, constructions of optimal mental health are culturally determined. We do not know how African Americans conceptualize health; that is, we do not know how African American youth and adults conceive of what it means to be a whole, sound, or well entity/being. Future research must interrogate the meanings of the concept of health for African Americans and must clarify whether there are indicators of health and wellness that are important in an African American cultural frame but that have gone unexplored (or underexplored) in the social science literature.

Sixth, there is a need for more substantial attention to the link between religiosity and spirituality and mental health for LGBT African American youth and adults. Because there is diversity in the extent to which African American religious communities openly welcome LGBT individuals, and because faith life is so central to the survival of African Americans, it is imperative that we elucidate the ways in which religious, spiritual, and sexual identity development intersect with each other across the life span for LGBT as well as for heterosexual individuals within the African American community.

Seventh and last, the research on the link between religiosity and spirituality and mental health among African Americans is distinctively Christ centered. As a consequence, we know virtually nothing about the link between these concepts for African Americans who are members of non-Christian religious communities (e.g., Muslims, Buddhists). This gap in knowledge is profound both because the exclusive focus on African American Christians fails to embrace the diversity within the African American community and because it leaves us unable to understand how mental health is influenced by the dual experience of being from a racial *and* a religious minority community.

References

Banks-Wallace, J., & Parks, L. (2004). It's all sacred: African American women's perspectives on spirituality. *Issues in Mental Health Nursing, 25,* 25–45.

Bierman, A. (2006). Does religion buffer the effects of discrimination on mental health? Differing effects by race. *Journal for the Scientific Study of Religion, 45,* 551–565.

Billingsley, A. (1992). *Climbing Jacob's ladder: The enduring legacy of African American families.* New York: Simon & Schuster.

Billingsley, A. (1999). *Mighty like a river: The Black church and social reform.* New York: Oxford University Press.

Billingsley, A., & Caldwell, C. (1991). The church, the family and the school in the African American community. *Journal of Negro Education, 60,* 427–440.

Black, H. (1999). Life as gift: Spiritual narratives of elderly African-American women living in poverty. *Journal of Aging Studies, 13,* 441–455.

Blaine, B., & Crocker, J. (1995). Religiousness, race, and psychological well-being: Exploring social psychological mediators. *Personality and Social Psychology Bulletin, 21,* 1031–1041.

Blank, M., Mahmood, M., Fox, J., & Guterbock, T. (2002). Alternative mental health services: The role of the Black church in the South. *American Journal of Public Health, 92,* 1668–1672.

Bowman, P. (1990). Coping with provider role strain: Adaptive cultural resources among Black husband–fathers. *Journal of Black Psychology, 16,* 1–21.

Boykin, A., & Ellison, C. (1995). The multiple ecologies of Black youth socialization: An Afrographic analysis. In R. L. Taylor (Ed.), *African American youth: Their social and economic status in the United States* (pp. 93–128). Westport, CT: Praeger.

Brega, A., & Coleman, L. (1999). Effects of religiosity and racial socialization on subjective stigmatization in African American adolescents. *Journal of Adolescence, 22,* 223–242.

Brome, D., Owens, M., Allen, K., & Vevaina, T. (2000). An examination of spirituality among African American women in recovery from substance abuse. *Journal of Black Psychology, 26,* 470–486.

Byrd, R. (1988). Positive therapeutic effects of intercessory prayer in a coronary care unit population. *Southern Medical Journal, 81,* 826–829.

Caldwell, C., Chatters, L., Billingsley, A., & Taylor, R. (1995). Church-based support programs for elderly Black adults: Congregational and clergy characteristics. In M. Kimble, S. McFadden, J. Ellor, & J. Seeber (Eds.), *Aging, spirituality and religion* (pp. 306–324). Minneapolis, MN: Fortress Press.

Chadiha, L., Veroff, J., & Leber, D. (1998). Newlywed's narrative themes: Meaning in the first year of marriage for African American and White couples. *Journal of Comparative Family Studies, 29,* 115–130.

Chatters, L., Levin, J., & Taylor, J. (1992). Antecedents and dimensions of religious involvement among older Black adults. *Journal of Gerontology, 47,* 269–278.

Christian, M., & Barbarin, O. (2001). Cultural resources and psychological adjustment of African American children: Effects of spirituality and racial attribution. *Journal of Black Psychology, 27,* 43–63.

Coleman, C. (2004). The contribution of religious and existential well-being to depression among African American heterosexuals with HIV infection. *Issues in Mental Health Nursing, 25,* 103–110.

Coleman, C., & Holzemer, W. (1999). Spirituality, psychological well-being and HIV symptoms for African Americans living with HIV disease. *Journal of the Association of Nurses in AIDS Care, 10,* 42–50.

Constantine, M., & Sue, D. (2006). Factors contributing to optimal human functioning in people of color in the United States. *The Counseling Psychologist, 34,* 228–244.

Cook, K. (2000). "You have to have somebody watching your back, and if that's God, then that's mighty big": The church's role in the resilience of inner-city youth. *Adolescence, 35,* 717–730.

Douglas, K. (1999). *Sexuality and the Black church: A womanist perspective.* Maryknoll, NY: Orbis Books.

Edwards, K. (1998). A cogno-spiritual model of psychotherapy. In R. Jones (Ed.), *African American mental health* (pp. 329–355). Hampton, VA: Cobb & Henry.

El-Khoury, M., Dutton, M., Goodman, L., Engel, L., Belamaric, R., & Murphy, M. (2004). Ethnic differences in battered women's formal help-seeking strategies: A focus on health, mental health, and spirituality. *Cultural Diversity and Ethnic Minority Psychology, 10,* 383–393.

Ellison, C., Boardman, J., Williams, D., & Jackson, J. (2001). Religious involvement, stress, and mental health: Findings from the 1995 Detroit Area Study. *Social Forces, 80,* 215–249.

Frazier, E. F. (1963). *The Negro church in America.* New York: Schocken Books.

Gibson, P. (2002). African American grandmothers as caregivers: Answering the call to help their grandchildren. *Families in Society, 83,* 35–43.

Greening, L., & Stoppelbein, L. (2002). Religiosity, attributional style, and social support as psychosocial buffers for African American and White adolescents' perceived risk for suicide. *Suicide and Life-Threatening Behavior, 32,* 404–417.

Harris, W., Gowda, M., Kolb, J., Strychacz, C., Vacek, J., Jones, P., et al. (1999). A randomized controlled trial of the effects of remote, intercessory prayer on outcomes in patients admitted to the coronary care unit. *Archives of Internal Medicine, 159,* 2273–2278.

Jagers, R. (1997). Afrocultural integrity and the social development of African American children: Some conceptual, empirical and practical considerations. *Journal of Prevention and Intervention in the Community, 16,* 7–31.

Jagers, R. J., Smith, P., & Mock, L. (1997). An Afrocultural social ethos: Component orientations and some social implications. *Journal of Black Psychology, 23,* 328–343.

Jang, S., & Johnson, B. (2004). Explaining religious effects on distress among African Americans. *Journal for the Scientific Study of Religion, 43,* 239–260.

Krause, N. (2004). Assessing the relationships among prayer expectancies, race, and self-esteem in late life. *Journal for the Scientific Study of Religion, 43,* 395–408.

Levin, J., & Taylor, R. (1998). Panel analysis of religious involvement and well-being in African Americans: Contemporaneous and longitudinal effects. *Journal for the Scientific Study of Religion, 37,* 695–709.

Lincoln, C., & Mamiya, L. (1990). *The Black church in the African-American experience.* Durham, NC: Duke University Press.

Maton, K. I., & Wells, E. A. (1995). Religion as a community resource for well-being: Prevention, healing, and empowerment pathways. *Journal of Social Issues, 51,* 177–193.

Mattis, J. (2000). African American women's definitions of spirituality: A qualitative analysis. *Journal of Black Psychology, 26,* 101–122.

Mattis, J. (2002). The role of religion and spirituality in the coping experience of African American women: A qualitative analysis. *Psychology of Women Quarterly, 26,* 308–320.

Mattis, J. S., Ahluwalia, M. K., Cowie, S.-A. E., & Kirkland-Harris, A. M. (2006). Ethnicity, culture, and spiritual development. In E. C. Roehlkepartain, P. E. King, L. Wagener, & P. L. Benson (Eds.), *The handbook of spiritual development in childhood and adolescence* (pp. 283–296). Thousand Oaks, CA: Sage.

Mattis, J. S., Fontenot, D. L., & Hatcher-Kay, C. A. (2003). Religiosity, racism, and dispositional optimism among African Americans. *Personality and Individual Differences, 34,* 1025–1038.

Mattis, J. S., Fontenot, D., Hatcher-Kay, C., Grayman, N., & Beale, R. (2004). Religiosity, optimism and pessimism among African Americans. *Journal of Black Psychology, 30,* 187–207.

Mattis, J. S., Mitchell, N., Zapata, A., Grayman, N., Taylor, R., Chatters, L., & Neighbors, H. (2007). The uses of ministerial support by African American women: A focus group study. *American Journal of Orthopsychiatry, 77,* 249–258.

Mays, B. (1969). *The Negro's church.* New York: Russell & Russell.

McAdoo, H. (1995). Stress levels, family help patterns, and religiosity in middle- and working-class African American single mothers. *Journal of Black Psychology, 21,* 424–449.

McCullough, M. (1995). Prayer and health: Conceptual issues, research review, and research agenda. *Journal of Psychology and Theology, 23,* 15–29.

McRae, M., Thompson, D., & Cooper, S. (1999). Black churches as therapeutic groups. *Journal of Multicultural Counseling and Development, 27,* 207–220.

Miller, R. (2005). Look what God can do: African American gay men, AIDS, and spirituality. *Journal of HIV/AIDS and Social Services, 4,* 25–46.

Miller, R. (2007). Legacy denied: African American gay men, AIDS, and the Black church. *Social Work, 52,* 51–61.

Moore, T. (1991). The African American church: A source of empowerment, mutual help, and social change. *Prevention in Human Services, 10,* 147–167.

Morse, E., Morse, P., Klebba, K., Stock, M., Forehand, R., & Panayotova, E. (2000). The use of religion among HIV-infected African American women. *Journal of Religion and Health, 39,* 261–276.

Neighbors, H., Jackson, J., Bowman, P., & Gurin, G. (1983). *Stress, coping, and Black mental health: Preliminary findings from a national study.* Beverly Hills, CA: Sage.

Neighbors, H., Musick, M., & Williams, D. (1998). The African American minister as a source of help for serious personal crises: Bridge or barrier to mental health care? *Health Education & Behavior, 25,* 759–777.

Nelson, T. (1997). He made a way out of no way: Religious experience in an African American congregation. *Review of Religious Research, 39,* 5–26.

Potts, R. (1991). Spirits in the bottle: Spirituality and alcoholism treatment in African-American communities. *Journal of Training & Practice in Professional Psychology, 5,* 53–64.

Powell-Hammond, W., Hudson-Banks, K., & Mattis, J. (2006). Masculinity ideology and forgiveness of racial discrimination among African American men: Direct and interactive relationships. *Sex Roles, 55,* 679–692.

Reese, L., & Brown, R. (1995). The effects of religious messages on racial identity and system blame among African Americans. *The Journal of Politics, 57,* 24–43.

Robinson, T. (2000). Making the hurt go away: Psychological and spiritual healing for African American women survivors of childhood incest. *Journal of Multicultural Counseling and Development, 28,* 160–176.

Rogers-Dulan, J. (1998). Religious connectedness among urban African American families who have a child with disabilities. *Mental Retardation, 36,* 91–103.

Rubin, R., Billingsley, A., & Caldwell, C. (1994). The role of the Black church in working with Black adolescents. *Adolescence, 29,* 251–266.

Stevenson, H. (1997). Managing anger: Protective, proactive, or adaptive racial socialization identity profiles and African American manhood development. *Journal of Prevention and Intervention in the Community, 16,* 35–61.

Taylor, R., & Chatters, L. (1991). Religious life. In J. S. Jackson (Ed.), *Life in Black America* (pp. 105–123). Newbury Park, CA: Sage.

Taylor, R., Ellison, C., Chatters, L., Levin, J., & Lincoln, K. (2000). Mental health services in faith communities: The role of clergy in Black churches. *Social Work, 45,* 73–87.

Taylor, R., Thornton, M., & Chatters, L. (1987). Black Americans' perceptions of the sociohistorical role of the church. *Journal of Black Studies, 18,* 123–138.

Tinney, J. (1981). The religious experience of Black men. In G. Lawrence (Ed.), *Black men* (pp. 269–276). Beverly Hills, CA: Sage.

Townsend-Gilkes, C. (1997). The roles of church and community mothers: Ambivalent American sexism or fragmented African familyhood? In T. Fulop & A. Raboteau (Eds.), *African American religion: Interpretive essays in history and culture* (Vol. 25, pp. 524–543). New York: Routledge.

Wallace, J., & Williams, D. (1997). Religion and adolescent health compromising behavior. In J. Schulenberg, J. Maggs, & K. Hurrelmann (Eds.), *Health risks and developmental transitions during adolescence* (pp. 444–468). Cambridge, UK: Cambridge University Press.

Watlington, C., & Murphy, C. (2006). The roles of religion and spirituality among African American survivors of domestic violence. *Journal of Clinical Psychology, 62,* 837–857.

Wilcox, C., & Gomez, L. (1990). Religion, group identification, and politics among American Blacks. *Sociological Analysis, 51,* 271–285.

Woods, L., & Jagers, R. (2003). Are cultural values predictors of moral reason in African American adolescents? *Journal of Black Psychology, 29,* 102–118.

Young, J., Griffith, E., & Williams, D. (2003). The integral role of pastoral counseling by African American clergy in community mental health. *Psychiatric Services, 54,* 688–692.

8

BLACK FAMILIES

HARRIETTE PIPES MCADOO AND SINEAD N. YOUNGE

No volume on persons of African descent residing in America is complete without a discussion of the Black[1] family. A number of scholars have laid the foundation for a strength-based, multidisciplinary, culturally relative examination of the Black family. As a result, there exists a substantial body of descriptive and empirical literature on the Black family. The purpose of this chapter is to review the contemporary literature and explore some of the emerging and understudied topics and trends. The chapter underscores an urgent need to promote the further development of culturally congruent, therapeutic practice, and programming for families of African descent. In order to gain a better understanding of the contextual underpinnings of the Black family, we also discuss the current demographic composition of the Black family.

DEMOGRAPHIC CHARACTERISTICS OF THE BLACK FAMILY

The structure of families in the United States has changed dramatically in the past several decades, and these changes have been particularly pronounced for Blacks. It is estimated that only 30% of all U.S. families conform to the traditional structure of a mother, father, and child (Donenberg, 2004). Similarly, the proportion of African Americans who live in heterosexual, married–coupled families has declined sharply over the last couple of decades such that marriage has become a minority lifestyle (Chapman, 1997). According to the U.S. Bureau of the Census, 34% of African Americans are married, 22% are widowed, divorced, or separated and approximately 4 out of every 10 African American men and women have never been married, the highest proportion of any racial category (U.S. Census Bureau, 2003). In addition, nearly one half (48%) of all African American families are maintained by women with no spouse present, and 75% of all Black children born in the last 2 decades are likely to live for some portion of their childhood with only their mothers (Bumpass & Sweet, 1989).

These demographic characteristics have important implications for socioeconomic status, because poverty is highest in families maintained by women with no spouse present. For example, 35% of African American families and 19% of White families with no spouse present live in poverty. Plausible explanations for the higher percentage among African Americans include the fact that African American women have the highest rates of marital separation (6%) and are more likely to remain separated without getting a legal divorce than are women of all other racial groups. In addition, cohabitation as an alternative to marriage is more common among Blacks, possibly because male income and employment are lower among minorities and individuals of lower socioeconomic status. Thus, male economic status remains an important determinant as to whether a man feels ready to marry and a woman wants to marry him (Popenoe & Whitehead, 2002). It is important to note, however, that despite these potential barriers and a retreat from marriage, many African Americans are able to attain middle-class status.

The demographic composition of the African American family has and continues to engender a large number of family related research. Most recently, research using *American General Social Surveys* data collected from 1973 through 2002 was conducted by the National Opinion Research Center at the University of Chicago and compiled into a report titled *The Consequences of Marriage for African Americans: A Comprehensive Literature Review* (Blackman, Clayton, Glenn, Malone-Colon, & Roberts, 2005). The report attempted to address several major research questions including: "What are the economic, psychosocial, and health-related consequences of marriage for African American men, women, and children?" and "Do the consequences of marriage differ for Blacks and Whites, and if so, why?" The findings demonstrated that the benefits of two-parent, married households were greater for African American men and children (particularly young African American male children); however, the researchers found that African American women reportedly benefited less from marriage than their White female counterparts, and in terms of economics, marriage benefited African Americans more than their White counterparts.

Characteristics of the Black Family

The Black family is confronted with a number of societal pressures, ranging from social to economic; thus, the Black family must be understood as an institution that, as Niara Sudarkasa (2007) surmised, contains "historical traditions" that set them apart as "alternative" formations that are not identical to or pathological variants of European American, middle-class family structures. Anthropologist Melville Herskovits (1930) wrote extensively about African cultural vestiges, which survived slavery and continue to play a pivotal role in the lives of African Americans, particularly the family structure.

According to Billingsley (1968), there are five general statements that characterize families of all people of African descent: They (1) are extended in form, (2) have *fictive kin*—close, nonblood family members who become as close to the family as blood kin, (3) have supportive family patterns, (4) have flexible family boundaries, and (5) have flexible gender roles in child rearing. Subsequently, in more contemporary research from an African-centered perspective, Nobles and his chief collaborator Goddard have provided an Africentric perspective of the African family in America. Nobles's (1985) model is characterized by continual flexibility in the extended family kinship structure, role flexibility, strong mother roles and family survival, the importance of children and motherhood, communalistic socialization of children, an emphasis on spiritual over material values, the role of the elderly, and a strong sense of humanness. These characteristics of African American family functioning compose an important framework for examining African American families from a culturally relative perspective.

Perspectives on the Black Family

A deficit perspective has historically been used to characterize African American families as deprived, disadvantaged, and poorly educated (Frazier, 1939/1965) This is in large part due to the release of a report called *The Negro American Family: The Case for National Action* by Daniel P. Moynihan (1965), which discussed the diminished role of the African American male and a resulting inability to provide positive socialization to children. As a result of this report, researchers assumed that two-parent households headed by males were better off than single-parent homes and that single-parent households are necessarily culturally deviant (Harris & Graham, 2007). Wade Nobles (see http://www.iasbflc.org/nobles.htm) states that the study of the Black experience in the United States has been one of the most widely and perhaps misunderstood research areas in the field of social science. Consequently, much of the traditional, and some of the contemporary, research on Black families continues to employ the deficit perspective.

Early family researchers also employed a cultural-equivalent theoretical framework that placed European American, middle-class values and practices as the barometer for normative functioning. Unfortunately, many of the empirical investigations on Black families have used European American, middle-class families as the standard of comparison. This long-standing tradition of using Whites as the standard is methodologically limited and often results in the biased interpretation of study findings. Furthermore, the development of innovative models for family research, including methodology, interventions, and the development of new theory for families of color, is warranted. As a result, an Africentric approach is increasingly being utilized to define Black psychological experiences from a perspective that demonstrates the strengths inherent in Black families and understands the problems that exist from a contextual framework (Hines & Boyd-Franklin, 1996; McAdoo, 2007; Staples, 1988).

ALTERNATIVE STRUCTURES IN THE BLACK FAMILY

Black Fathers

With the increasing number of Black children being born to single mothers, there has been a renewed interest in the role of the Black father. Much of the early research on Black children in the United States has been *matricentric*, or mother centered in character, and not until recently has there been substantive discussion about and investigation into the roles fathers play in rearing their children (Achatz & McAllum, 1994; Furstenberg & Harris, 1993; Livingston & McAdoo, 2007; McAdoo & McAdoo, 2002). African American fathers represent a significant position in the Black family despite the fact that in every decade postslavery, Black men have experienced high rates of unemployment, and lower levels of education, compared with their White counterparts, which has influenced their role as providers (Hamer, 1997).

Livingston and McAdoo (2007) noted that despite a considerable amount of research that has examined Black fathering, "there still exists a need to bring clarity to the roles that Black fathers have in rearing their children, given the tremendous economic shifts and the changing nature of marriage in the Black community" (p. 219). Traditional research on Black fathers has focused on absenteeism in the home and the resulting problems, including delinquency, economic hardship, lack of male role models, violence, and abuse. It is interesting that data from the National Survey of Families and households indicate that Black males are more likely to be single full-time fathers than males from other ethnic groups (Eggebeen, Snyder, & Manning, 1996). Therefore, although a significant proportion of African American children do indeed come from single-parent homes, a father or father figures often is present, even if he does not reside in the home with the child on a full-time basis. In a qualitative study of 38 noncustodial Black fathers conducted by Hamer (1997), the participants reported that spending time with their children was the greatest factor for being a good father. Also, although the mothers are the gatekeepers, the majority of the men felt that their role in their children's lives was important and could not be fulfilled or replaced by their children's mother. Fathers are, however, missing in the literature and accounts of daily lives of families and children (White, 2006).

Role of the Extended Family

The extended family and fictive kin are critical characteristics of the Black family. It is not uncommon for Black families to live within an intergenerational family network (Kinsey, 1999) that may contain family members outside of the nucleus, including grandparents, adult children, grandchildren, nieces, nephews, aunts, uncles, and fictive kin. In general, African American parents rely on these relatives and friends to play supportive roles in their child-rearing practices. Extended kinship support has long been characterized as a key adaptive strategy and traditional family resource for African Americans (Billingsley, 1968; Demo & Cox, 2000; Johnson, 2000; R. D. Taylor, 1996). This support is an adaptive strategy that allows for the sharing of resources and the opportunity for extended kin to provide social capital to help influence children's growth toward positive developmental pathways. Although these arrangements may be beneficial for child-rearing practices, a small but growing body of research has examined their benefits to other family members, particularly elderly family members (elders).

Elders in the Black Family

A growing number of gerontological studies are focusing on the Black family. According to the U.S. Census Bureau (2003), a comparatively high percentage of African American grandparents were living in the same household as their grandchildren (8%) compared with Whites (2%). Moreover, research demonstrates that Blacks are more likely than any other ethnic group to take care of their elderly family members, and not surprisingly, Black elders have been found to use familial support and assistance more than formal support services, which has resulted in a strong positive relationship between family involvement and life satisfaction among African American elders (Coke, 1992). Heightened family involvement may be a contributing factor in elderly African Americans' views of themselves as successful grandparents and contributing members of their families (Strom, Strom, Collinsworth, & Griswold, 1993). Johnson and Barer (1990) reported that African American elders have more active support networks than Whites and are more likely to have live-in support and assistance from distant relatives and friends (White-Means, 1993).

Grandparent-Headed Households

More than half of African American grandparents report that they are responsible for the basic needs of their grandchildren (Donenberg, 2004). Grandparent-headed households (GPHHs) cut across socioeconomic levels, but they are more likely to exist among families living in poverty. The majority of GPHHs are African American (Donenberg, 2004). Research indicates that grandparents have a positive impact on their grandchildren's psychological well-being and social adaptability among children. Research on the effects of GPHHs on the caregivers has been mixed. Some studies have found that single grandmothers caring for grandchildren are twice as likely to experience depressive symptomatology (Minkler, Fuller-Thomson, Miller, & Driver, 1997). Moreover, grandmothers report additional negative health effects, including increased anxiety, stress, and worry. The caregiving burden and negative effects have been demonstrated to be greater for European American than African American grandmothers. In contrast, some grandmothers report satisfaction, positive affect, and pride in helping to keep these children out of the foster care system. The high levels of crack use, the high levels of incarceration of both young mothers and fathers, and the increasing number of AIDS-related illnesses do not predict that grandparents will be able to lessen their burdens of child rearing (Joslin & Harrison, 1998; Minkler & Roe, 1993).

For many Black families living in intergenerational and extended family networks, the reciprocal process of helping each other and exchanging and sharing resources and support is an important cultural and survival mechanism model that can be used by social service practitioners as a cultural strength. The disruptive consequences of such arrangements must also be taken into account. Extended family members may not always provide positive support and benefits; some may at times be disruptive or act as a burden on the family, and because of the cultural practice of taking in family members in need, some Black families may feel conflicted about withdrawing their support from such a family member. Practitioners must be able to distinguish between supportive versus unsupportive methods of family functioning, without relying on traditional deficit-based models of Black family functioning.

Same-Sex Unions and Parenting

The aforementioned *Consequences of Marriage Review* (Blackman et al., 2005) did not include studies on common-law or same-sex unions. Black same-sex unions is a topic that has a dearth of literature; however, even though they are an alternative and often marginally accepted lifestyle among African Americans, these unions and families should not be ignored. To date, little is known about the experiences of the African American lesbian, gay, bisexual, and transgendered community or same-sex unions, specifically, African American same-sex families and parenting practices. The lack of data on this group may be due to a number of factors, including social and policy ones. Prior to 1973, homosexuals were regularly denied the right to adopt, which limited the number of same-sex parents (excluding those with biological children). Although legislation has changed or eased in some states, lesbian and gay parents of all races continue to face social stigmatization, particularly African Americans because of the stigma regarding homosexuality in their community, and may have fears of being too open or public about their parenting status because of custody concerns (Rooney, 2001) and the negativity associated with homosexuality.

As a result of this dearth of data on Black same-sex households, the National Gay and Lesbian Task Force Policy Institute, in collaboration with the National Black Justice Coalition, conducted an analysis of data from the 2000 U.S. Census. Data demonstrated that Black same-sex households constituted 14% of all same-sex households in the United States and, according to the 2000 U.S. Census, Black and Latino same-sex households are nearly twice as likely as White non-Hispanic same-sex households to be parenting, which means that anti-gay parenting policies directly and disproportionately affect Black and Latino same-sex couples (Dang & Frazer, 2004). U.S. Census data also demonstrate that Black male same-sex couples are almost twice as likely to be living with a biological child as White male same-sex couples. Also, Black female same-sex couples are just as likely to be living with an adopted or foster child as Black married heterosexual couples (U.S. Census Bureau, 2000). On average, Black same-sex couples earn less and are less likely to own a home than their White and heterosexual Black counterparts. Their inability to access the legal protections of marriage disproportionately impacts their earning power and diminishes their ability to provide for their children (Dang & Frazer, 2004). In addition, Black lesbian, gay, bisexual, and transgendered parents experience a double, and in some instances a triple, minority status by being confronted with racism in (majority) White gay events and homophobia in Black heterosexual organizations.

Parenting Style

Regardless of whether a child is raised in a two-parent, single-parent, intergenerational, or same-sex household, there exists some shared parenting practices among Black persons residing in the United States. Franklin and Boyd-Franklin (1985) contend that traditional African values and beliefs have been transmitted from generation to generation and continue to influence African American parenting (Cain & Combs-Orme, 2005). With respect to these commonalities in parenting practices, which may be a reaction to shared experiences, it is important to note that within-group differences do exist. Some family researchers employ a case-centered or *typological* methodological approach in which they examine simultaneously the interrelated dimensions of family functioning (Bergman, Cairns, Nilsson, & Nystedt, 2000; Mandara & Murray, 2002). Some of the most well-known typological studies are those conducted by Diana Baumrind (1971, 1972, 1996). Baumrind theorized that families are classified into variations of four prototypical family types, according to their relative level on two broad dimensions: (1) parental demandingness (control and restrictiveness) and (2) responsiveness (warmth and noncoerciveness). The four family types identified are (1) authoritative, (2) authoritarian, (3) permissive, and (4) neglectful. Although Baumrind's original conceptualization of parenting styles was based on the observations of European American families, she later went on to examine the family patterns of Black and White schoolchildren (1972). According to Baumrind's research, African Americans were generally characterized as having an *authoritarian* parenting style, which is characterized as being highly demanding and low in responsiveness—otherwise stated, low in warmth and high in control. This was in contrast to authoritative parenting which is high in demandingness and responsiveness. Authoritative parents remain receptive to the child's view but take responsibility for firmly guiding the child (Baumrind, 1996). This parenting style is also linked to positive adolescent development. Interestingly, although the authoritarian style is linked to negative outcomes such as a lack of social competence for Whites, this is not necessarily the case for African Americans. In fact, Black females in Baumrind's (1972) study were more independent and self-assertive. This suggests that Baumrind's model may be applicable to racial–ethnic minorities, but only when considered with contextual considerations. Parenting styles are qualitatively different across racial groups, and when European American family functioning is utilized as the standard for "normal family functioning" Black parenting styles may be misinterpreted (Younge & McAdoo, 2008). Moreover, parenting style must be examined within the contexts in which children are raised, taking into account the sociocultural differences within African American communities. A number of researchers have expanded on the work of Baumrind's typologies (Glasgow, Dornbusch, Troyer, Steinberg, & Ritter, 1997; Lamborn, Dornbusch, & Steinberg, 1996; Mandara & Murray, 2002; Steinberg, Dornbusch, & Brown, 1992).

In a 2002 study, Mandara and Murray developed an empirical typology of African American family functioning that included a wider range of class and income than previous studies had. Using data from the African American Families and Child Outcomes Project, Mandara and Murray examined 15-year-old African Americans ($N = 116$) and their parents in southern California. Using a cluster analytic procedure to classify families on the basis of their patterns of family functioning, the results of their study yielded three types of African American families, which they named (1) *cohesive–authoritative*, (2) *conflictive–authoritarian*, and (3) *defensive–neglectful*. The cohesive–authoritative family exhibits the highest overall level of family functioning and is characterized as having a high level of family cohesion and authoritative disciplinary styles. Members of cohesive–authoritative families are encouraged to be assertive and practice proactive racial socialization. In contrast, the conflictive–authoritarian family typology is characterized by high internal conflict, lack of communalism or commitment to other family members, and a strict authoritarian disciplinary parenting style that creates an environment in which children may not feel comfortable expressing emotion. The focus on racial socialization in this family typology is moderate. In addition, there is high emphasis on achievement. Last, the defensive–neglectful family is thought to be at greatest risk for dysfunction. This typology is characterized by neglectful and authoritarian parental disciplinary practices in addition to defensive racial socialization whereby children are socialized to dislike other racial groups and are not taught to be proud of their own racial group. Mandara and Murray found that the adolescents in the cohesive–authoritative family type had significantly higher self-esteem than the adolescents in families of the other two types. They reported that this is most likely because the parents in the cohesive family types are more likely to express to their children that they are appreciated and valued the way they are and because the other two family types are more likely to express unhappiness with their children's abilities and performance. Furthermore, the cohesive family type seems to have found a balance of control and nurturance in the way that Baumrind (1971, 1972, 1996) theorized would be most beneficial to children and adolescents. Higher levels of racial socialization demonstrated in the cohesive–authoritative family type are hypothesized to contribute to the relatively higher self-esteem found among African American adolescents in these families (Murray & Mandara, 2001). As demonstrated, no one family typology represents all Black families.

Racial and Gender Role Socialization

An important aspect of socialization for Black parents and children is racial socialization. Socialization in Black families has been defined as parents' "attempts to prepare their children for the realities of being Black in America" (R. J. Taylor, Chatters, Tucker, & Lewis, 1990, p. 994). Hughes (2003) examined the frequency and correlates of two dimensions of racial socialization messages about ethnic pride, history, and heritage and messages about discrimination and racial bias among urban African American, Puerto Rican, and Dominican parents. Hughes found that African American parents reported giving more frequent "preparation for bias" messages to their children. This demonstrates that the frequency and correlates of racial socialization depend on the parents' ethnic group membership and experiences with racial bias. The aforementioned factors are all imperative for the development of a healthy self-esteem in addition to equipping children of color for future, perhaps adverse, experiences based on race. A more thorough discussion of racial socialization is given in Chapter 14 of this volume.

William Cross (1971) outlined four stages that African Americans go through in moving from self-hatred to self-acceptance referred to as *Nigrescence*, or the process of becoming Black: (1) pre-encounter, (2) encounter, (3) immersion/emersion, and (4) internalization. In the final stage, internalization, individuals feel more positive and secure about their Black identity but also exhibit increased comfort with and acceptance of other cultures. Cross's model supports the view that affirmation toward one's ethnic group leads to a positive ethnic identity and higher levels of acceptance toward other out-groups. The model operates at all levels in Black families.

Socialization of Gender Roles in the Black Family

In addition to racial and ethnic socialization and identity development, gender roles remain a pivotal aspect of family functioning and child development in the Black family. Biological gender differences transcend race, class, and sexual orientation; however, gender roles are socially constructed and vary depending on cultural norms. Although gender does play an important role in the discourse on the African American experience, some have argued that the emphasis on race and ethnicity has eclipsed the discourse on the role of gender among African Americans. The disparate proportion of economic deprivation in the African American community, along with racism, has made it difficult and impractical for many African Americans to create sharply defined divisions between male and female gender roles. S. A. Hill (2001) postulated that Black parents have embraced many of the values of the dominant society; however, she argued that their American experiences and African heritage have led to some distinctive socialization patterns, most of which revolve around the intersection of race, class, and gender. There is evidence that many African American women have escaped the narrow confines of the restrictive gender roles assumed by a Eurocentric worldview. African American women have had to assume heavy responsibility for paid work, family, and community and have incidentally circumvented Eurocentric ideas of male privilege and power (Dill, 1988).

As a result of African American women's unique experiences in the United States, Ossana, Helms, and Leonard (1992) developed the *womanist identity model*, an adaptation from Cross's (1971) Nigrescence model. Like Cross's model, Ossana and colleagues' stages include pre-encounter, encounter, immersion/emersion and internalization. Also similar to Cross's model, the fourth and final stage is characterized by the woman defining her womanhood in her own terms and not being bound by external definitions about what it means to be a woman. There is a small but growing body of research to support women's differential identity development based on race (Boisnier, 2003). In addition to society, families play an important role in the gender role development of children. African American daughters, from an early age, are taught to assume strong family roles and to be strong, self-reliant, and independent individuals who are part of and play an integral role in a larger group, the family (Collins, 1987). Some studies support the view of gender neutrality in socializing children in Black families such that parents have similar role expectations for sons and daughters (Nobles, 1985; Peters, 1988; Scott, 1993). The child's gender does not dictate these expectations. Other scholars have argued that child rearing in the African American community is gender specific. Both hooks (1981) and Pinderhughes (1986) have written about the protective stance that many African American women take toward their fathers and brothers, husbands and sons. Institutionalized racism has made many African American women reluctant to hold African American men to a feminist standard of accountability in the private world of the family. Black parents support competence and self-reliance more in daughters than in sons (McAdoo, 2007; Staples & Johnson, 1993) and may have higher expectations for daughters because they view them as having a greater opportunity to survive and succeed in mainstream society (Staples & Johnson, 1993). Conversely, lower expectations for sons may be shaped by the "extra" barriers commonly faced by Black men. However, this stance ignores the double burden of sexism and racism that constructs the lives of African American women (Silverstein, 2006).

DISABILITY IN THE BLACK FAMILY

Almost every Black family must deal with racial and gender issues; however, an increasing number of Black families are also faced with family members who have a disability. In studying data from the National Health Interview Survey, a continuing cross-sectional survey of approximately 40,000 households conducted by the U.S. Census Bureau, Newacheck and colleagues (Newacheck, Stein, Bauman, & Hung, 2003) found that Black children had higher rates of disability from chronic conditions than did White children. They also found that the higher rates of disability among Black children were impacted by increased exposure to risk factors, namely, poverty. When working with African American individuals who have disabilities, it is important for professionals to recognize and understand the culture, various communication styles, values of African American families and the role of socioeconomic status. Although there are services designed to help families that have members with disabilities, they are often underutilized by African Americans, especially economically challenged families (Terhune, 2005). In addition to economic challenges, much of this underutilization may result from the fact that formal developmental disabilities services are often created from a European American middle-class framework that emphasizes independence (Terhune, 2005). Placing greater emphasis on the value of independence among African American individuals with disabilities may present a problem for some people, especially because African American families are known to value family, community, and group effort in solving problems (Parette, VanBiervliet, Reyna, & Heisserer, 1999). Although African American families are traditionally known for valuing the family and community, some share views of the European American norms. Despite the conflicting views, it is imperative for professionals to consider families that value independence as well as interdependence within the family and community setting when developing effective programs for African American individuals with disabilities.

As noted, at the core of many African American families are values that stress the importance of family and having a sense of community. "Families that use the value of relationships, family, and wisdom are known to deal with family members with disabilities from a *spiritual kin* discourse" (Terhune, 2005, p. 25). These individuals often view the loved one with a disability as a blessing from God, and they try their best to help the person feel loved and accepted. As demonstrated with the underutilization of formal support services by African American elderly, caretakers of persons with disabilities often take full responsibility of them, relying on professional services only when deemed absolutely necessary (Terhune, 2005). Other African American families are less likely to utilize formal developmental services because they view the services as biased or racist (Terhune, 2005, p. 24).

As African Americans families deal with loved ones with disabilities, they express values that can affect the treatment and at times be inconsistent with current social service models. Some families may underscore interdependence and use their family and the community as a support system for individuals with disabilities. Other families emphasize the value of independence, in order to allow a disabled family member to view his or her condition from a self-help perspective. Whether they endorse interdependence or independence, family values can affect how formal developmental services are used to help family members with disabilities. African American families are more likely to use services that parallel with their own values; therefore, professionals must take into account values from all spectrums of African American families when designing effective services for individuals with disabilities.

One disease that is becoming more prevalent in families is breast cancer. Black women are more likely to develop breast cancer before age 35 and to die of it before age 35 (Malveaux, 2006). Eighty-four of 100 non-Blacks survive 5 years after diagnosis, but only 69 of 100 Black women do. Medical researchers say that they do not know whether breast cancer is more aggressive in young Black women or whether it is caused by something to which they are more likely to be exposed. Researchers should especially look at stress. Black women are more likely to be poor and to head families. Too many Black women work in locations where health insurance is unavailable. Black women with breast cancer often must wait for Medicaid or rely on a clinic. Too many women wait too long to look for breast cancer. Malveaux (2006) stated the Black women must get a mammogram beginning at age 30, not 40, and must purchase health insurance.

The provision of mental health services for African American individuals and families can be complex because of the great diversity among families and the lack of clear theoretical approaches for working with this population. Also, there are a number of traditional psychological theories that are not generalizable to the dynamics of African American family dynamics (Boyd-Franklin, 1989; Parham, 2002). For instance, studies show that African Americans are far less likely than their racial counterparts to attend a family support group (Guarnaccia & Parra, 1996). As an interpersonal intervention, family therapy benefits both individuals and their families. The underlying premise of family therapy is that familial functioning impacts optimal functioning among individuals, whereas individual functioning significantly impacts current and future familial dynamics (Sanders, 2007). This circular process is based on the *systems orientation*, a central paradigm within the field of marriage and family therapy (Becvar & Becvar, 2000). From a cultural orientation, African American families, churches, and neighborhoods have buffered individuals, allowing maintenance of some sense of value and self-worth (Ellison, 1997). Within these environments the help-seeking process is comprehensive and multifaceted (Leong, Wagner, & Tata, 1995). Duncan (2003) stated that, among African Americans, a person's comfort with seeking help can serve as either a barrier to or an asset in his or her ability to access social supports. Help-seeking for informal supports occurs for a range of problems, including finances, child rearing, and emotional as well as interpersonal problems (Broman, 1996; Hofferth, 1984). Many churches have adopted what they call "outreach services and activities." Although different churches may use different terms and offer different services, the same definition applies; this help was designed for people with the same problems and/or interests to speak about their issues, trials, and tribulations to come together as a support group and/or council for one another. These church outreach groups are geared toward providing services that may not be widely available in the community, including health care and other helpful resources. A 2002 study by Pickett-Schenk revealed that church-based support groups were an effective outreach strategy for assisting African American families of persons with mental illnesses. This finding is important in a community where mental health is often stigmatized and formal support groups go underutilized. This study demonstrates that the church can normalize the process of receiving assistance and possibly act as a bridge to more formal support services.

Despite the historical and contemporary challenges endured by Blacks in the United States, the Black family remains one of the most influential, if not the most influential, institutions within the Black community. The literature is replete with examples of the resiliency and resolve of Black families. This resilience needs to be further capitalized on, and the challenges need to be confronted from a holistic and culturally relative perspective.

A Systems Approach to Studying and Working With Black Families

According to Bronfenbrenner's (1979) classic systems approach to human behavior, it is a widely accepted belief that children and families do not develop or function in isolation; they develop in a variety of contexts and environments that surround the individual and with which the child is in constant interaction (e.g., Bridge, Judd, & Moock, 1979; Bronfenbrenner, 1979). In Bronfenbrenner's sociocultural view of development, five environmental systems act as socialization agents: (1) the *microsystem* (most direct interaction agents, e.g., family, peers, school, neighborhood), (2) the *mesosystem* (relations between microsystems, e.g., family functioning can influence academic performance), (3) the *exosystem* (experiences in social setting in which an individual may not have an active role but still experience an immediate context, e.g., parental job stress), (4) the *macrosystem* (cultural attitudes/ideologies, e.g., religion), and (5) the *chronosystem* (environmental events and transitions over time). The microlevel of the ecological model of human behavior includes the immediate and earliest influences, such as the institution of the family. The relationship between these levels is multidirectional, and there exist both negative and positive factors in the social environment that influence parenting and the developmental trajectories of children. An ecological approach to examining the Black family should utilize and promote the preexisting strengths within the African American community while being careful not to dismiss, in the name of cultural relativism, the harmful effects of unhealthy family functioning.

Conclusion

Studies of traditional African practices have demonstrated that more similarities than differences exist among the various distinct ethnic groups (Mbiti, 1991) and that these vestiges continue to exist among Blacks residing in America. Although it is imperative to understand the shared experiences of Black Americans, it also is critical that within-group differences are explored and accounted for. In addition, there are a number of Eurocentric and a growing number of Africentric theories utilized to describe the experience of Black families. The current presidential administration and resulting policies have engendered an imminent need for evidence-based research.

Initiatives such as *Healthy People 2010* (see http://www.healthypeople.gov) focus primarily on physical health but have further highlighted the substantial racial disparities and factors that compromise quality of life. Factors such as social and physical environment, education, income, disability status, and so forth, all directly affect the institution of the family. The Black family has faced and continues to face a disproportionate amount of these burdens; however, what has made and continues to make the Black family so unique is its resilience. Researchers and practitioners should continue to explore the multifaceted nature of this resilience and to develop appropriate postpositivist theory based on empirical research.

Note

1. The terms *African American* and *Black* are used interchangeably throughout this chapter, depending on the terminology of the specific authors being cited.

References

Achatz, M., & McAllum, C. (1994). *Young unwed fathers: Report from the field*. Philadelphia: Public/Private Ventures.

Baumrind, D. (1971). Current patterns of parental authority. *Developmental Psychology Monographs, 4*, 1–103.

Baumrind, D. (1972). An exploratory study of socialization effects on Black children: Some Black–White comparisons. *Child Development, 43*, 261–267.

Baumrind, D. (1996). Parenting, the discipline controversy revisited. *Family Relations, 45*, 405–414.

Becvar, D., & Becvar, R. (2000). *Family therapy: A systemic integration* (4th ed.). Boston: Allyn & Bacon.

Bergman, L. R., Cairns, R. B., Nilsson, L. G., & Nystedt, L. (2000). *Developmental science and the holistic approach*. Mahwah, NJ: Lawrence Erlbaum.

Billingsley, A. (1968). *Black families in White America*. Englewood Cliffs, NJ: Prentice Hall.

Blackman, L., Clayton, O., Glenn, N., Malone-Colon, L., & Roberts, A. (2005). *The consequences of marriage for African Americans: A comprehensive literature review*. New York: Institute for American Values. Retrieved December 8, 2007, from http://americanvalues.org/consequences_report.pdf

Boisnier, A. D. (2003). Race and women's identity development: Distinguishing between feminism and womanism among Black and White women. *Sex Roles, 49*, 211–219.

Boyd-Franklin, N. (1989). *Black families in therapy: A multisystems approach*. New York: Guilford Press.

Bridge, R., Judd, C., & Moock, P. (1979). *The determinants of educational outcomes: The impact of families, peers, teachers, and schools*. Cambridge, MA: Ballinger.

Broman, C. (1996). Coping with personal problems. In H. Neighbors & J. Jackson (Eds.), *Mental health in Black America* (pp. 117–129). Thousand Oaks, CA: Sage.

Bronfenbrenner, U. (1979). *The ecology of human development: Experiments by nature and design*. Cambridge, MA: Harvard University Press.

Bumpass, L., & Sweet, J. (1989). National estimates of cohabitation. *Demography, 26*, 615–625.

Cain, D. S., & Combs-Orme, T. (2005). Family structure effects on parenting stress and practices in the African American family. *Journal of Sociology and Social Welfare, 12*(2), 19–40.

Chapman, A. B. (1997). The Black search for love and devotion: Facing the future against all odds. In H. P. McAdoo (Ed.), *Black families* (3rd ed., pp. 273–283). Thousand Oaks, CA: Sage.

Coke, M. (1992). Correlates of life satisfaction among elderly African Americans. *Journal of Gerontology, 47*, 316–320.

Collins, P. H. (1987). The meaning of motherhood in Black culture and Black mother–daughter relationships. *Sage: A Scholarly Journal on Black Women, 4*, 3–10.

Cross, W. E. (1971). The Negro to Black conversion experience: Towards the psychology of Black liberation. *Black World, 20*, 13–27.

Dang, A., & Frazer, S. (2004, December). *Black same-sex households in the United States: A report from the 2000 census* (2nd ed.). Washington, DC: National Gay and Lesbian Task Force Policy Institute, National Black Justice Coalition.

Demo, D. H., & Cox, M. J. (2000). Families with young children: A review of research in 1990s. *Journal of Marriage and the Family, 62*, 876–895.

Dill, B. T. (1988). Our mother's grief: Racial ethnic women and the maintenance of families. *Journal of Family History, 13*, 415–431.

Donenberg, G. R. (2004). *Traditional and alternative families: Strengths and challenges*. Retrieved October 15, 2007, from http://www.psych.uic.edu/hd/NonTradFam_hand.pdf

Duncan, L. E. (2003). Black male college students' attitudes toward seeking psychological help. *Journal of Black Psychology, 29,* 68–86.

Eggebeen, D., Snyder, T., & Manning, W. D. (1996). Children in single-father families in demographic perspective. *Journal of Family Issues, 17,* 441–465.

Ellison, C. (1997). Religious involvement and the subjective quality of family life among African Americans. In R. Taylor, J. Jackson, & L. Chatters (Eds.), *Family life in Black America* (pp. 117–131). Thousand Oaks, CA: Sage.

Franklin, A. J., & Boyd-Franklin, N. (1985). A psychoeducational perspective on Black parenting. In H. P. McAdoo & J. L. McAdoo (Eds.), *Black children: Social, educational, & parental environments* (pp. 194–212). Beverly Hills, CA: Sage.

Frazier, E. F. (1966). *The Negro family in the United States* (Rev. & abridged ed.). Chicago: University of Chicago Press. (Original work published 1939)

Furstenberg, F., & Harris, K. (1993). When and why fathers matter: Impacts of father involvement on children of adolescent mothers. In R. Lerman & T. Ooms (Eds.), *Young unwed fathers: Changing roles and emerging policies* (pp. 117–138). Philadelphia: Temple University Press.

Glasgow, K. L., Dornbusch, S. M., Troyer, L., Steinberg, L., & Ritter, P. L. (1997). Parenting styles, adolescents' attributions, and educational outcomes in nine heterogeneous high schools. *Child Development, 68,* 507–529.

Guarnaccia, P. J., & Parra, P. (1996). Ethnicity, social status, and families' experiences of caring for a mentally ill family member. *Community Mental Health Journal, 32,* 243–260.

Hamer, J. (1997, November–December). The fathers of fatherless Black families: What they say they do as fathers. *Journal of Families and Society,* 564–578.

Harris, Y. R., & Graham, A. J. (2007). *The African American child: Development and challenges.* New York: Springer.

Herskovitz, M. (1930). *The anthropometry of the American Negro.* New York: Columbia University Press.

Hines, P. M., & Boyd-Franklin, N. (1996). African-American families. In M. McGoldrick, J. Giordano, & J. K. Pearce (Eds.), *Ethnicity and family therapy* (pp. 66–84). New York: Guilford Press.

Hill, S. A. (2001). Class, race, and gender dimensions of child rearing in African American families. *Journal of Black Studies, 31,* 494–506.

Hofferth, S. (1984). Kin networks, race, and family structure. *Journal of Marriage and the Family, 46,* 791–806.

hooks, b. (1981). *Ain't I a woman? Black women and feminism.* Boston: South End Press.

Hughes, D. (2003). Correlates of African American and Latino parents' messages to children about ethnicity and race: A comparative study of racial socialization. *American Journal of Community Psychology, 31,* 15–33.

Johnson, C. L. (2000). Perspectives on American kinship in the later 1990s. *Journal of Marriage and the Family, 62,* 623–639.

Johnson, C. L., & Barer, B. (1990). Families and networks among older inner-city Blacks. *The Gerontologist, 30,* 726–733.

Joslin, D., & Harrison, R. (1998). The hidden patient: Older relatives raising children orphaned by AIDS. *Journal of the American Medical Women's Association, 53,* 65–71.

Kinsey, R.W. (1999) Attendance patterns in therapy across five decades. *Dissertation Abstracts International: Section B: The Sciences and Engineering, 60.*

Lamborn, S. D., Dornbusch, S. M., & Steinberg, L. (1996). Ethnicity and community context as moderators of the relations between family decision making and adolescent adjustment. *Child Development, 67,* 283–301.

Leong, F. T., Wagner, N. S., & Tata, S. P. (1995). Racial and ethnic variations in help-seeking attitudes. In J. M. Casas, J. G. Ponterotto, L. A. Suzuki, & C. M. Alexander (Eds.), *Handbook of multicultural counseling* (pp. 415–438). Thousand Oaks, CA: Sage.

Livingston, J. N., & McAdoo, J. L. (2007). The roles of African American fathers in the socialization of their children. In H. P. McAdoo (Ed.), *Black families* (4th ed., pp. 219–237). Thousand Oaks, CA: Sage.

Malveaux, J. (2006, June 15). Knowledge, access to health care is key to curbing breast cancer in Black women. *State News, 6,* 4.

Mandara, J., & Murray, C. B. (2002). Development of an empirical typology of African American family functioning. *Journal of Family Psychology, 16,* 318–337.

Mbiti, J. (1991). *Introduction to African religion.* Oxford, UK: Heinemann Educational.

McAdoo, H. P. (2007). *Black families* (4th ed.). Thousand Oaks, CA: Sage.

McAdoo, H. P., & McAdoo, J. L. (2002). The dynamics of African American fathers' family roles. In H. P. McAdoo (Ed.), *Black children: Social, educational, and parental environments* (2nd ed., pp. 3–11). Thousand Oaks, CA: Sage.

Minkler, M., Fuller-Thomson, E., Miller, D., & Driver, D. (1997). Depression in grandparents raising grandchildren: Results of a national longitudinal study. *Archives of Family Medicine, 6,* 445–452.

Minkler, M., & Roe, K. M. (1993). *Grandmothers as caregivers: Raising children of the crack cocaine epidemic.* Newbury Park, CA: Sage.

Moynihan, D. P. (1965). *The Negro family: The case for national action.* Washington, DC: Office of Policy Planning Research, U.S. Department of Labor.

Murray, C. B., & Mandara, J. (2001). Racial identity development in African American children: Cognitive and experiential antecedents. In H. P. McAdoo (Ed.), *Black children* (2nd ed., pp. 73–96). Thousand Oaks, CA: Sage.

Newacheck, P. W., Stein, R. E. K., Bauman, L., & Hung, Y. (2003). Disparities in the prevalence of disability between Black and White children. *Archives of Pediatric Adolescent Medicine, 157,* 244–248.

Nobles, W. W. (1985). *Africanity and the Black family: The development of a theoretical model* (2nd ed.). Oakland, CA: Institute for the Advanced Study of Black Family Life and Culture.

Ossana, S. M., Helms, J. E., & Leonard, M. M. (1992). Do "womanist" identity attitudes influence college women's self-esteem and perceptions of environmental bias? *Journal of Counseling and Development, 70,* 402–408.

Parette, P., VanBiervliet, A., Reyna, J. W., & Heisserer, D. (1999). *Families, culture and augmentative and alternative communication (AAC): A multimedia instructional program for related service personnel and family members.* Retrieved June, 11, 2008, from http://cstl.semo.edu/parette/homepage/database.pdf

Parham, T. A. (2002). *Counseling persons of African descent.* Thousand Oaks, CA: Sage.

Peters, M. F. (1988). Parenting in Black families with young children: A historical perspective. In H. P. McAdoo (Ed.), *Black families* (2nd ed., pp. 227–241). Newbury Park, CA: Sage.

Pickett-Schenk, S. A. (2002). Church-based support groups for African American families coping with mental illness. *Psychiatric Rehabilitation Journal, 26,* 173–180.

Pinderhughes, E. (1986). Minority women: A nodal position in the functioning of the social system. In M. Alt-Riche (Ed.), *Women and family therapy* (pp. 51–63). Rockville, MD: Aspen Systems.

Popenoe, D., & Whitehead, B. D. (2002). *Should we live together? What young adults need to know about cohabitation before marriage: A comprehensive review of recent research.* New Brunswick, NJ: National Marriage Project.

Rooney, S. C. (2001). Examining Redding's (2001) claims about lesbian and gay parenting. *American Psychologist, 57,* 298–299.

Sanders, M. M. (2007). Family therapy: A help-seeking option among middle-class African Americans. In H. P. McAdoo (Ed.), *Black families* (4th ed., pp. 263–278). Thousand Oaks, CA: Sage.

Scott, J. W. (1993). African American daughter–mother relations and teenage pregnancy: Two faces of premarital teenage pregnancy. *Western Journal of Black Studies, 17,* 73–81.

Silverstein, L. B. (2006). Integrating feminism and multiculturalism: Scientific fact or science fiction? *Professional Psychology: Research and Practice, 37,* 21–28.

Staples, R. (1988). An overview of race and marital status. In H. P. McAdoo (Ed.), *Black families* (2nd ed., pp. 187–189). Newbury Park, CA: Sage.

Staples, R., & Johnson, L. B. (1993). *Black families at the crossroads: Challenges and prospects.* San Francisco: Jossey-Bass.

Steinberg, L., Dornbusch, S. M., & Brown, B. B. (1992). Ethnic differences in adolescent achievement: An ecological perspective. *American Psychologist, 47,* 723–729.

Strom, R., Strom, S., Collinsworth, P., & Griswold, D. (1993). Helping Black grandparents help three generations. *The Education Digest, 59,* 43–46.

Sudarkasa, N. (2007). Interpreting the African heritage in African American family organization. In H. P. McAdoo (Ed.), *Black families* (4th ed., pp. 29–47). Thousand Oaks, CA: Sage.

Taylor, R. D. (1996). Adolescents' perceptions of kinship support and family management practices: Associations with adolescent adjustment in African American families. *Developmental Psychology, 32,* 687–695.

Taylor, R. J., Chatters, L. M., Tucker, M. B., & Lewis, E. (1990). Developments in research on Black families: A decade review. *Journal of Marriage and Family, 52,* 993–1014.

Terhune, P. S. (2005). African-American developmental disability discourses: Implication for policy development. *Journal of Policy and Practice in Intellectual Disabilities, 2,* 18–28.

U.S. Census Bureau. (2000). *Statistical abstract of the United States 2000: The National data book* (120th ed.). Washington, DC: Author.

U.S. Census Bureau. (2003, April). The Black population in the United States: March 2002. In J. McKinnon, *Current population reports.* Washington, DC: Author. Retrieved May, 1, 2007, from http://www.census.gov/prod/2003pubs/p20-542.pdf

White, A. (2006, February). African American feminist fathers narratives of parenting. *Journal of Black Psychology, 32,* 43–71.

White-Means, S. L. (1993). Informal home care for frail Black elderly. *Journal of Applied Gerontology, 12,* 18–33.

Younge, S. N., & McAdoo, H. P. (2008). Home and family in the development of a multicultural worldview. In J. K. Asamen, M. L. Ellis, & G. L. Berry (Eds.), *The SAGE handbook of child development, multiculturalism, and media* (pp. 101–112). Thousand Oaks, CA: Sage.

9

INTIMATE RELATIONSHIPS OF AFRICAN AMERICANS

Anita Jones Thomas, Rabiatu Barrie, and Brendesha M. Tynes

Beginning with mother and child and continuing through same-sex and early opposite sex friendships, intimate relationships provide critical training ground for future sexual behavior, decision making, and romantic relationships. As individuals reach adulthood, intimate relationships can then determine a number of psychological, emotional, economic, and social outcomes. Given the significance of intimate relationships, surprisingly little psychological literature has focused on the nature and scope of those of African Americans. The research that has been done suggests that they differ greatly from their white counterparts because of the influence of oppression on socialization, identity, and gender role expectations as well as the high value placed on communalism and strong kinship bonds in African American culture (Boyd-Franklin, 2006).

In this chapter, we summarize the literature and research on African American relationships, highlighting many of these differences. Although we acknowledge the importance of examining relationships of varying types, the focus of this chapter is on male–female relationships and their precursors. Other chapters in this volume, including Chapters 8 and 23, address issues related to same-sex couples and families. This chapter begins with a discussion of gender role socialization, the role and nature of friendships in African American youth and the relationship between friendships, intimacy and sexuality. We then address issues in male–female relationships, beginning with a discussion of mate availability, sexuality, and dating. We also include a discussion of marital couples, cohabitation, and interracial relationships. Strengths and areas of resilience identified by the research are presented. We conclude the chapter with implications and recommendations for practice, research, and policy.

FACTORS THAT INFLUENCE INTIMATE RELATIONSHIPS

Gender Role Socialization

Socialization experiences greatly influence intimacy in relationships, particularly gender role expectations. From birth, gender typing begins, and by age 4 or 5, many gender attitudes and beliefs have been internalized (Bigler, 1997; Hill, 2002). Boys are socialized to be independent, hard working, self-reliant, and ambitious while girls are socialized to be loving, interdependent, well mannered, and kind (Block, 1983). A noted strength of African Americans, however, is flexible or androgynous gender roles (Boyd-Franklin, 2003; Lawrence-Webb, Littlefields, & Okundaye, 2004). Although men and women are socialized by the dominant society in the United States according to patriarchal values that stress the supremacy of men, African Americans often receive more egalitarian messages.

For example, in Hill's (2002) interview study of 35 African American mothers and fathers, regardless of sex of parent, sex of child or social class, parents verbally supported gender equality. Participants reported communicating messages to their sons about egalitarian marital roles and domestic work and stressing the importance of independence to both boys and girls. This was even more so the case with parents who had at least some college education. In spite of the egalitarian messages that may be sent in the home, African Americans must function within American society. African American men are denigrated in this society and experience challenges to the traditional patriarchal role. Similarly, African American women experience negative stereotypes suggesting that they are unfeminine and emasculating (Lawrence-Webb et al., 2004).

African American men have faced negative stereotypes and images since the time of slavery, when they were used for hard labor and mating purposes. Men have been judged according to their physique, skin color, intelligence, and language (Franklin, 1999). The effects of the images and stereotypes of African American men have led to what Franklin (1999) termed the *invisibility syndrome*: African American men are both feared and ignored by Whites, leading men to feel as if others are treating them as if they have no worth. The invisibility syndrome is the inner struggle that one's abilities and personality are not valued. While men are socialized to be providers, they may feel frustrated by sociopolitical constraints. Because of experiences of racism and oppression, men are socialized to develop the "cool pose," a phrase coined by Majors and Billson (1993), a stance that demonstrates a quiet, emotional strength and invulnerability. The cool pose helps men reclaim their masculinity through physical posture, style, and speaking (Diemer, 2002).

Women's socialization experiences influence intimate relationships in a number of ways. African American women are socialized to be independent, self-sufficient, and strong yet are seen as too overbearing, controlling, and unfeminine in relationships (Lawrence-Webb et al., 2004; Romero, 2000). Studies suggest that African American women from childhood are socialized to be strong and independent (Browning & Miller, 1999; Thomas & King, 2007). Girls are taught that they need to take care of themselves and that they will be responsible for their families. They also are taught that men are unreliable or unavailable (Browning & Miller, 1999). This internalized message often makes it difficult for women to be vulnerable in relationships or to feel comfortable relying on their partners. The push for independence may counteract with men's need to exhibit control over and strength in the relationship. African American women are also socialized with conservative and traditional perspectives on marriage (Browning & Miller, 1999), but they may not know how to reconcile the notions of traditional marriage with the messages of being strong and independent. Many contemporary issues within male–female African American relationships stem from socialization experiences and stereotypes of men and women.

Friendship and Intimacy

The development of intimate relationships is an important social developmental task of adolescents. These relationships are commonly forged with peers as adolescents spend increasing amounts of time away from the home and with close friends. It is in early same-sex, opposite-sex, and ultimately early romantic relationships that adolescents are provided with the mechanism for observing and practicing skills for relationship development. Adolescents seek to explore romantic and more intimate relationships as a form of social support and as a precursor to developing sexuality and sexual intimacies (Harper, Gannon, Watson, Catania, & Dolcini, 2004).

Researchers have examined the demographic, individual-level, and contextual factors associated with perceived quality of general and closest same-sex friendships among ethnic minority youth from low-income families (Way, Cowal, Gingold, Pahl, & Bissessar, 2001; Way & Greene, 2006; Way & Pahl, 2001) as well as the nature of friendships. In Way and Chen's (2000) study of close and general friendships among 160 ninth-grade African American, Latino, and Asian

Americans, 73% of the participants had predominantly same-race friendship networks. More specifically, 63.9% of African Americans' peer network was of the same race. In addition, girls were more likely to have same-race/ethnic peers than boys. Participants had also maintained their relationships for an average of 6 years. The authors further noted that girls reported higher levels of friendship support than boys and that African Americans reported higher levels of friendship support than Asian Americans.

African American youth friendships tend to follow developmental trajectories and be influenced by contextual factors. For example, Way and Greene (2006) found that adolescents' perceptions of the quality of general and close friendships increases from middle to late adolescence, with boys reporting higher levels of intimacy from childhood to adolescence. Contextual factors that were significantly associated with trajectories of friendship quality were family relationships, teacher–student relations, and student–student relations in school. Similarly, Way and Pahl (2001) found that contextual factors, including school climate, were associated significantly with increases over time in perceived quality of general friendships. Perceived relationships with mothers contributed significantly to changes in perceived friendship quality.

Way et al. (2001) examined types of friendship relationships and found four: (1) ideal, (2) engaged, (3) average, and (4) disengaged. Like other ethnic minority youth, African American youth with friends in the ideal cluster typically had stable, close friendships to which they were deeply committed, with friends they had known for long periods and for whom they felt great affection and admiration. These close friendships often involved numerous conflicts but were quickly resolved, and the friendships were consistently maintained. Youth in the engaged cluster spoke with equal intensity of feeling close to and sharing everything with friends, but they focused their discussions on the fights and conflicts in those relationships, without an emphasis on the resolution of the conflicts. The most distinguishing characteristic of adolescents in the average cluster was the ambivalence with which they spoke about their closest same-sex friendships. Adolescents in the disengaged cluster reported having best friends but did not appear to experience these friendships as satisfying or supportive.

Friendship and Sexuality

According to Christopher (2001), dating and sexual relationships are formed partly on the basis of socialization experiences provided by peers, dating partners, and parents. Harper and colleagues (2004) conducted a qualitative analysis of the role of friendships in shaping intimacy and sexuality in a sample of low-income African American adolescents. They found that friends are instrumental in providing feedback and support regarding dating and sexual experiences. Gender differences were observed in that girls reported needing to be coaxed to share information or being more comfortable when friends initiated discussion, and boys were more likely to discuss their sexual activities in a competitive fashion. The girls in the study used relational terms when describing their sexual activity, whereas boys discussed it in a more egocentric fashion. Girls also spent more time making sure that the experiences were viewed as pleasurable. This finding is probably linked to concerns that girls have regarding dating violence. Both boys and girls were concerned with condom use to protect against unwanted pregnancy and sexually transmitted diseases. The authors noted that dating and sexual experiences often began within friendship circles, with friends providing feedback on relationships.

Similarly, O'Sullivan & Meyer-Bahlburg's (2003) interviewed African American 10- to 13-year-old inner-city girls about their romantic and sexual development and found that friendships provide scripts for appropriate sexual and romantic conduct. The authors found that romantic development followed a sequence of events. From 7 to 9, girls first express romantic interest in boys. It is not until between 9 and 11, however, that they begin having boyfriends. These relationships involved "hanging out" in groups and being with boyfriends during breaks at school. Little physical or social activity outside of these experiences was reported. It was also during this time that participants reported that their first experimentation with sexual activity was expected to be in group dating contexts. These included after-school parties and parks. Finally, by 12 and 14, girls indicated increasingly more private sexual participation in dating relationships and that sexual intercourse began thereafter.

O'Sullivan and Meyer-Bahlburg (2003) further noted that girls had common scripts and expectations about their relationships, including the fact that sexual activity had to occur within an affectionate relationship, that boys were less emotionally engaged in relationships, and that they needed to engage in sexual activity to sustain their relationship. These romantic relationships were a source of status for the participants and often led to competition among them. Understanding the sexual scripts of adolescent peer groups provide a window into their sexual behavior both during adolescence and in later life.

Issues Within Male–Female Relationships

Mate Availability

One area of concern for African Americans is mate availability. There seems to be a shortage of available African American men due to high rates of incarceration, unemployment, and substance use, and high mortality rates (Boyd-Franklin, 2003; Franklin, 1999; Pinderhughes, 2002). Men are more likely to prematurely die of violence or homicide (Franklin, 1999). In general, African Americans are less likely to marry or to remain married than are members of other ethnic groups (Bulanda & Brown, 2007; Goodwin, 2003), or to separate or not remarry (Cherlin, 1998). The marriage rate for African American women is particularly low and is projected to decrease (James, Tucker, & Mitchell-Kernan, 1996). African American women still have the expectation of being married, because they perceive economic and social and emotional benefits from marriage (Bulcroft & Bulcroft, 1993; Porter & Bronzaft, 1995). Mate availability does not influence women's mental health or well-being, possibly because they view the issue of mate availability as systemic and outside of their control (James et al., 1996; Tucker & Mitchell-Kernan, 1998). Men who have stable employment are more likely to marry (Pinderhughes, 2002). Research has suggested that men are less likely to find benefits from marriage, particularly in their sexual lives or peer relationships (South, 1993). Couples have to balance economic opportunities and differences in their relationships. These differences in mate availability are related to gender role expectations and socialization experiences of men and women.

Dating

Today, in the United States, more African American women are likely to be single than they have at any other time (Goodwin, 2003), leaving more women available in the dating pool. In the Spike Lee movie *Jungle Fever*, a group of women discuss concerns with dating, including the shortage of available African American men, their perception that men find more educated and successful women to be intimidating, that successful African American men are more attracted to White women, and their level of distrust for men who have a tendency toward infidelity in relationships. Popular magazines such as *Ebony*, *Essence*, and *Jet* frequently feature issues on African American intimate relationships, including the limited number of available men and the rise in educational levels and professional/managerial positions of women. Research has not explored these issues and their influence on intimacy in relationships.

The little research on dating in African Americans has focused on dating violence within relationships (Few & Bell-Scott, 2002; Salazar, Wingood, DiClemente, Lang, & Harrington, 2004; West & Rose, 2000). In a study that examined the prevalence of violence within dating relationships, West and Rose (2000) found that women are more likely to be victims, and men are more likely to engage in more serious physical and psychological aggression toward women. Dating and violence in relationships often occur as a by-product of the historical oppression and sexual victimization of African American women. Dating violence has serious consequences for women. They are more likely to endorse more adversarial sexual beliefs in male–female relationships (West & Rose, 2000) and are likely to experience psychological distress, including depression and low self-esteem (Salazar et al., 2004).

Sexuality

Few studies have examined sexuality of African Americans within the context of intimacy in relationships. The research on adolescents in this area has primarily focused on teenage pregnancy and

HIV/AIDS (Harper et al., 2004). Sexuality is influenced by socialization experiences and peer messages (Rouse-Arnett, & Long Dilworth, 2007). Stephens and Few (2007) found that girls based their sexuality and sense of physical attractiveness on their fathers' perceptions and approval and their relationships with women, along with developmental progression of racial identity. Women have reported that the information provided by parents was inadequate and less influential than that gained from peers and cultural influences (Rouse-Arnett & Long Dilworth, 2007). Boys relate to sexuality in a depersonalized fashion, seeing women, body parts, and sexual acts separately as commodities (Harper et al., 2004; Stephens & Few, 2007).

African American women develop sexual scripts based on exposure to music videos that feature images based on the historical sexualized image of Jezebel (Stephens & Few, 2007). In fact, Stephens and Phillips (2003) contended that the oversexualized stereotypes of African American women propagated in the media and in broader society have helped shape the perception of African American women's and girls' sexuality. These images, with their highly sexual connotations, influence the way others may appreciate and interact with African American girls, possibly contributing to the high rates of sexual victimization experienced among this population (Stephens & Phillips, 2005). Similarly, African American men have been characterized as sexualized. African male slaves were often described as well endowed, with sexual prowess and as potential perpetrators. The stereotype of African American men as violent and highly sexualized has been transformed into an image of strength, beginning with gangsta rap and moving to hip-hop culture (Oliver, 2006). There are three types of men portrayed in this image: (1) the tough guy/gangsta, (2) the player, and (3) the hustler/balla. These images convey the notion that African American men are powerful, controlling, and emotionally invulnerable.

There are two issues within sexuality that African Americans face: (1) the prevalence of HIV/AIDS and the (2) *down low phenomenon*, or men who have sex with men but keep the relationship a secret from others. African American women have the highest prevalence rate of new HIV cases, particularly girls between ages 15 and 24 (Centers for Disease Control and Prevention, 2005). The rise in cases is hypothesized to be a result of the sexual victimization of women, reluctance of condom use for men, and from men who secretly sleep with men.

Marriage and Intimacy

The institution of slavery changed the nature of intimate relationships because, although slaves were allowed to marry, they were not allowed the traditional rights afforded from marriage (Frazier, 1966). So, although couples may have functioned and lived as husband and wife, women were still subject to sexual exploitation by slave owners, and couples and families were torn apart when individual family members were sold from plantations. Slave owners also had the power to determine who married and who would be used for breeding purposes (Billingsley, 1968, as cited in Emery & White, 2006). Slavery and mating procedures often prohibited the expression of intimacy or romantic love among African Americans (Lawrence-Webb et al., 2004). During Reconstruction, couples and families were still affected by economic conditions as well as by racism and oppression (Pinderhughes, 2002). African American men often could not find employment or suitable wages, and African American women were more likely to work for the economic necessity of families. Tensions in relationships often occurred as men felt *role strain*, the frustration of not being able to provide adequately for families, and women felt frustrated by the inability to rely on their spouses for support (Emery & White, 2006).

Oppression and societal influences continue to influence marriage. Internalized oppression has been shown to have a negative relationship on marital satisfaction for both men and women (Taylor, 1990). Marital satisfaction is linked to psychological well-being and life satisfaction (Goodwin, 2003), which suggests that oppression may have both a direct and indirect effect on well-being and marital satisfaction (Taylor, 1990). As men and women develop their identity and gender role perspectives, they must determine how to reconcile negative images and stereotypes and experiences of oppression into their identity/self-concept. Kelly and Floyd (2001) examined the relationship among internalized negative stereotypes, Afrocentricity, and trust and adjustment of Black couples and found that greater Afrocentric beliefs among men were associated with less perceived partner dependability and satisfaction.

Interracial Relationships

Interracial relationships historically have been viewed negatively in the United States, with prevailing notions that individuals from mixed racial heritages, particularly White and Black, would have difficulty being accepted in society. It was also believed that mixing the races would "dilute" Whiteness, leading to an inferior race or group of people. In the early 1800s, interracial marriages were outlawed, and it was not until 1967 that the Supreme Court ruled that those laws were unconstitutional (Kerwin & Ponterotto, 1995). The historical legacy from slavery and Jim Crow laws that prohibited interracial relationships and marriages still has an influence on relationships today. Today, approximately 0.06% of couples in this country are interracial (Childs, 2005). Among African American interracial couples, the majority are between African American men and White women (Batson, Qian, & Lichter, 2006). Many African Americans believe that African American men choose to marry White women as a form of status (Childs, 2005). This may be a consequence of oppression, issues of colorism, and the caste system established during slavery. Some African American women blame White women for decreasing availability of eligible men for the African American community (Childs, 2005).

Attitudes toward interracial marriage are beginning to change, particularly among African American women, who view interracial marriage as an option because of decreased mate availability. In a national study of African Americans, 85% of participants approved of interracial marriage, particularly if they had more contact or friendship with Whites (Jacobson & Johnson, 2006). Findings from Childs's (2005) qualitative study of Black women suggested that the participants felt negatively about interracial marriages because of the prevalence and nature of racism, and they feel as if Whites cannot understand Black culture or experiences of racism. Perceived obstacles for interracial marriage included intragroup judgment and insensitivity from others. The women in the study indicated that they would be willing to consider interracial marriage if the man were interested in and supportive of Black culture (Childs, 2005).

Kouri and Lasswell (1993) interviewed Black-White interracial couples about their decisions for marrying, obstacles faced, and relationship satisfaction. The couples indicated that they primarily married for reasons of compatibility and were less concerned about intragroup judgment as in Childs's (2005) study. Potential differences in these findings may be due to the samples included in the study, one with Black women and other with couples who were interracial relationships. Couples in the Kouri and Lasswell study felt that the African American families were initially more supportive of the relationships compared to the White American families.

Resilience in African American Couples

Although the marriage rate for African American couples may be lower than that for other races, many couples do thrive and succeed. Women who report higher levels of marital satisfaction also report emotional health, a sense of trust and equity, physical health, and feelings of closeness with their in-laws (Goodwin, 2003). Strengths of African American couples stem from Afrocentric values. African Americans tend to be more communal in nature, valuing relationships, interconnectedness, and deriving identity from group status. Research suggests that African American couples value collaboration and mutuality in marriage (Orbuch, Veroff, & Hunter, 1998). Communalism, less independence, and the ability to have shared support all increase levels of intimacy and vulnerability in relationships (Pinderhughes, 2002). Extended family networks and kinship networks are also important for the functioning of African American couples. Social support provided by families helps couples cope with stress and oppression and can be vital for the transition to parenthood. Spirituality is another Afrocentric value that supports couples and helps to sustain relationships. Carolan and Allen (1999) interviewed midlife couples regarding their marriages, and couples reported that spirituality and a commitment to faith helped to maintain their marriages.

Conclusion and Implications

The nature and scope of intimate relationships in African Americans must be examined in the light of systemic factors, particularly the role of oppression and images that shape and influence gender role stereotypes. In the following sections, we discuss several recommendations for clinical work, research, and policy.

Clinical Implications

In general, clinicians should consider the reasons why couples present for treatment and should take into account the dynamics that occur whether the couple is married, cohabitating, or seeking premarital counseling. The most typical presenting problems revolve around social class, family secrets, workplace stress, and racism (Boyd-Franklin, 2003). Therapists who work with African American couples need to help couples to examine and deconstruct the role that oppression and societal influences have on their functioning (LaTaillade, 2006). Boyd-Franklin (2003) described how critical it is for couples to discuss the roles of workplace stress and experiences of racism. When men do not feel powerful outside of the home, and feel that their partners are also being disrespectful or invalidating, they may respond with inappropriate anger or by withdrawing from the family. Women who feel abandoned or anxious may respond by exerting more independence and power and control in the relationship (Lawrence-Webb et al., 2004). When African American women feel that they are providing more to the family and not receiving support from men, and thus not benefiting from marriage, they view marriage less favorably and feel less satisfied (Goodwin, 2003). Identifying the outside stressors and reframing the influence of racism as a joint problem can help couples connect and be more supportive of each other (Franklin & Boyd-Franklin, 2000). Clinicians must help individuals to not internalize negative societal stereotypes (Pinderhughes, 2002). Therapy can create the space for both men and women to share the stress from outside influences.

Therapy can also be an outlet for couples to discuss socialization messages and to be able to construct their roles together. This should include a discussion of tasks and chores within the home (Pinderhughes, 2002). Couples should explore their expectations and attitudes regarding marriage. Pinderhughes (2002) suggested that women seek financial security from marriage, whereas men expect more companionship. These issues are critical for African Americans because of the influence of racial and often class oppression. Clinicians also need to help couples discuss power issues and expectations, and they may provide effective role models for intimacy and emotional vulnerability in relationships. In addition to couples therapy, clinical support groups would provide valuable outlets for addressing oppression (Franklin & Boyd-Franklin, 2000). Creative and expressive therapies may be also useful for working with issues of intimacy, abuse, and violence in relationships (Few & Bell-Scott, 2002).

Prevention programs specific to the cultural needs of African American couples should be developed, funded, and researched. Although enrichment programs are useful, adding aspects on the influence of oppression, socialization experiences, and expectations regarding roles would provide a more substantive training for couples. Because many African Americans value spirituality and religion (Cheatham, 1990), these elements should be incorporated; men's religious beliefs may help with feelings of family satisfaction (Bowman, 1990).

Research and Policy

Since the 1960s, there has been an explosion of literature and research on African Americans in the field of psychology, particularly examinations of racial identity and psychological functioning as influenced by racism and oppression. Little attention has been given to intimate relationships or family functioning in African Americans, however. There is a need for more research on intimacy and cohesion, gender role expectations, communication, and functioning of couples and oppression. For example, developmental psychologists discuss the connection among friendship, intimacy, and adult relationships, but little research has examined these issues in African Americans. Harper et al. (2004) discussed how friendships and intimate relationships develop to provide social support and stated that African American youth select friends who will understand the influence of oppression. More research needs to examine how intimate relationships both are influenced by oppression and serve as a moderating variable between oppression and negative outcomes.

Research should examine how the changes in demographics, particularly African American women attaining higher levels of education and participating in professional positions, influences intimate relationships. There is a dearth of literature on interracial relationships. Because these relationships are increasingly being seen as a viable option for women, more research on the unique stressors for these types of relationships is needed. More longitudinal research needs to follow marital trajectories so as to provide more information on couples who are successfully married for long periods (Pinderhughes, 2002). Gay and lesbian African Americans face additional forms of oppression both within and outside of their race. Recent research has examined the identity development of lesbians and gay men (see Chap. 23 of this volume for a greater exploration of this issue), but again, less attention has been placed on same-sex functioning. Granting agencies and funding sources should begin to prioritize African American couples and family functioning. In addition, funds need to be allocated for strengthening intimate relationships in African Americans, particularly married couples. Past welfare legislation often served as a barrier (i.e., a loss of benefits) for couples who wished to marry. Policy makers should carefully examine policies or legislative acts that would have a negative influence on intimate relationships.

REFERENCES

Batson, C. D., Qian, Z., & Lichter, D. T. (2006). Interracial and intraracial patterns of mate selection among America's diverse black populations. *Journal of Marriage and Family, 68*, 658–672.

Bigler, R. S. (1997). Conceptual and methodological issues in the measurement of children's sex typing. *Psychology of Women Quarterly, 21*, 53–69.

Block, J. H. (1983). Differential premises arising from differential socialization of the sexes: Some conjectures. *Child Development, 54*, 1334–1354.

Bowman, P. J. (1990). Coping with provider role strain: Adaptive cultural resources among Black husband–fathers. *Journal of Black Psychology, 16*, 1–21.

Boyd-Franklin, N. (2003). *Black families in therapy: Understanding the African American experience* (2nd ed.). New York: Guilford Press.

Browning, S. L., & Miller, R. R. (1999). Marital messages: The case of Black women and their children. *Journal of Family Issues, 20*, 633–647.

Bulanda, J. R., & Brown, S. L. (2007). Race–ethnic differences in marital quality and divorce. *Social Science Research, 36*, 945–967.

Bulcroft, R., & Bulcroft, K. (1993). Race differences in attitudinal and motivational factors in the decision to marry. *Journal of Marriage and Family, 55*, 338–355.

Carolan, M. T., & Allen, K. R. (1999). Commitments and constraints to intimacy for African American couples at midlife. *Journal of Family Issues, 20*, 3–24.

Centers for Disease Control and Prevention. (2005). *HIV/AIDS surveillance in adolescents: L265 slide series (through 2003)*. Retrieved May 14, 2005, from http://www.cdc.gov/hiv/graphics/adolesnt.htm

Cheatham, H. E. (1990). Empowering Black families. In H. E. McAdoo & J. B. Stewart (Eds.), *Black families: Interdisciplinary perspectives* (pp. 373–393). New Brunswick, NJ: Transaction.

Cherlin, A. J. (1998). Marriage and marital dissolution among Black Americans. *Journal of Comparative Family Studies, 29*, 147–158.

Childs, E. C. (2005). Looking behind the stereotypes of the "angry Black woman": An exploration of Black women's responses to interracial relationships. *Gender & Society, 19*, 544–561.

Christopher, F. S. (2001). *To dance the dance: A symbolic interactional exploration of premarital sexuality*. Philadelphia: Lawrence Erlbaum Associates.

Diemer, M. A. (2002). Constructions of provider role identity among African American men: An exploratory study. *Cultural Diversity and Ethnic Minority Psychology, 8*, 30–40.

Emery, P., & White, J. C. (2006). Clinical issues with African-American and white women wishing to marry in mid-life. *Clinical Social Work Journal, 34*, 23–44.

Few, A. L., & Bell-Scott, P. (2002). Grounding our feet and hearts: Black women's coping strategies in psychologically abusive dating relationships. *Women & Therapy, 25*, 59–77.

Franklin, A. J. (1999). Invisibility syndrome and racial identity development in psychotherapy and counseling African American men. *The Counseling Psychologist, 27*, 761–793.

Franklin, A. J., & Boyd-Franklin, N. (2000). Invisibility syndrome: A clinical model of the effects of racism on African American males. *American Journal of Orthopsychiatry, 70*, 33–41.

Frazier, E. (1966). *The Negro family in the United States*. Chicago: University of Chicago Press.

Goodwin, P. Y. (2003). African American and European American women's marital well-being. *Journal of Marriage and Family, 65*, 550–560.

Harper, G. W., Gannon, C., Watson, S. E., Catania, J. A., & Dolcini, M. M. (2004). The role of close friends in African American adolescents' during dating and sexual behavior. *Journal of Sex Research, 41*, 351–362.

Hill, S. A. (2002). Teaching and doing gender in African American families. *Sex Roles, 47*(11–12), 493–506.

Jacobson, C. K., & Johnson, B. R. (2006). Interracial friendship and African American attitudes about interracial marriage. *Journal of Black Studies, 36*, 570–584.

James, A. D., Tucker, B., & Mitchell-Kernan, C. (1996). Marital attitudes, perceived mate availability, and subjective well-being among partnered African American men and women. *Journal of Black Psychology, 22,* 20–36.

Kelly, S., & Floyd, F. J. (2001). The effects of negative racial stereotypes and Afrocentricity on Black couple relationships. *Journal of Family Psychology, 15,* 110–123.

Kerwin, C., & Ponterotto, J. G. (1995). Biracial identity development: Theory and research. In J. G. Ponterotto, J. M. Casas, L. A. Suzuki, & C. M. Alexander (Eds.), *Handbook of multicultural counseling* (pp. 199–217). Thousand Oaks, CA: Sage.

Kouri, K. M., & Lasswell, M. (1993). Black–White marriages: Social change and intergenerational mobility. *Marriage and Family Review, 19,* 241–255.

LaTaillade, J. J. (2006). Considerations for treatment of African American couple relationships. *Journal of Cognitive Psychotherapy, 20,* 341–358.

Lawrence-Webb, C., Littlefields, M., & Okundaye, J. N. (2004). African American intergender relationships: A theoretical exploration of roles, patriarchy, and love. *Journal of Black Studies, 34,* 623–639.

Majors, R., & Billson, J. M. (1993). *Cool pose: The dilemmas of Black manhood in America.* New York: Touchstone Books/Simon & Schuster.

Oliver, W. (2006). "The streets": An alternative Black male socialization institution. *Journal of Black Studies, 36,* 918–937.

Orbuch, T. L., Veroff, J., & Hunter, A. (1998). Black couples, White couples: The early years of marriage. In E. M. Hetherington (Ed.), *Coping with divorce, single parenting, and remarriage: A risk and resilience perspective* (pp. 23–43). Mahwah, NJ: Lawrence Erlbaum.

O'Sullivan, L. F., & Meyer-Bahlburg, H. F. L. (2003). African American and Latina inner city girls' reports of romantic and sexual development. *Journal of Social and Personal Relationships, 20*(2), 221–238.

Pinderhughes, E. (2002). African American marriage in the 20th century. *Family Process, 41,* 269–282.

Porter, M. M., & Bronzaft, A. L. (1995). Do the future plans of educated Black women include Black mates? *Journal of Negro Education, 64,* 162–170.

Romero, R. E. (2000). The icon of the strong Black woman: The paradox of strength. In L. C. Jackson & B. Greene (Eds.), *Psychotherapy with African American women: Innovations in psychodynamic perspectives* (pp. 225–238). New York: Guilford Press.

Rouse-Arnett, M., Long Dilworth, J. E. (2007). Early influences on African American women's sexuality. *Journal of Feminist Family Therapy, 18,* 39–61.

Salazar, L. F., Wingood, G. M., DiClemente, R. J., Lang, D. L., & Harrington, K. (2004). The role of social support in the psychological well-being of African American girls who experience dating violence victimization. *Violence and Victims, 19,* 171–187.

Stephens, D. P., & Few, A. L. (2007). The effects of images of African American women in hip hop on early adolescents' attitudes toward physical attractiveness and interpersonal relationships. *Sex Roles, 56,* 251–264.

Stephens, D. P., & Phillips, L. D. (2003). Freaks, gold diggers, divas, and dykes: The sociohistorical development of adolescent African American women's sexual scripts. *Sexuality & Culture, 7,* 3–47.

Stephens, D. P., & Phillips, L. D. (2005). Integrating Black feminist thought into conceptual frameworks of African American adolescent women's sexual scripting processes. *Sexualities, Evolution and Gender, 7,* 37–55.

South, S. (1993). Racial and ethnic differences in the desire to marry. *Journal of Marriage and Family, 55,* 357–370.

Taylor, J. (1990). Relationship between internalized racism and marital satisfaction. *Journal of Black Psychology, 16,* 45–53.

Thomas, A. J., & King, C. T. (2007). Gendered racial socialization of African American mothers and daughters. *The Family Journal, 15,* 137–142.

Tucker, M. B., & Mitchell-Kernan, C. (1998). Psychological well-being and perceived opportunity among single African American, Latina and White women. *Journal of Comparative Family Studies, 29,* 57–72.

Way, N., & Chen, L. (2000). Close and general friendships among African American, Latino, and Asian American adolescents from low-income families. *Journal of Adolescent Research, 15*(2), 274–301.

Way, N., Cowal, K., Gingold, R., Pahl, K., & Bissessar, N. (2001). Friendship patterns among African American, Asian American, and Latino adolescents from low-income families. *Journal of Social and Personal Relationships, 18,* 29–53.

Way, N., & Greene, M. (2006). Trajectories of perceived friendship quality during adolescence: The patterns and contextual predictors. *Journal of Research on Adolescence, 16,* 293–320.

Way, N., & Pahl, K. (2001). Individual and contextual predictors of perceived friendship quality among ethnic minority, low-income adolescents. *Journal of Research on Adolescence, 11,* 325–349.

West, C. M., & Rose, S. (2000). Dating aggression among low income African American youth: An examination of gender differences and antagonistic beliefs. *Violence Against Women, 6,* 470–494.

10

HIP-HOP MUSIC AND CULTURE

A Site of Resiliency for the Streets of Young Black America

YASSER ARAFAT PAYNE AND LAMAR RASHAD GIBSON

Dear America—
I am only what you made me
Young, Black and fucking crazy
Please save me—
I'm dying inside
Can't you see it in my eyes . . .
Maybe if ya'll niggas [i.e., society at large] build schools instead of prisons
I'd stop living the way I'm living.

Shyne (2000)

Even though Rap was born in the ghetto, it addresses issues a lot of kids across America (and the world) are dealing with—anger, alienation, hypocrisy, sex and drugs—all the basics.

Kids of all colors, all over the world, instinctively seek to change the world. They usually have this desire because they don't want to buy into dominant values of the mainstream. Rappers want to change the world to suit their vision and to create a place for themselves in it. So kids can find a way into Hip-Hop by staying true to their instinct toward rebellion and change.

Hip-Hop has in fact, changed the world. It has taken something from the ghetto and made it global. It has become the creative touchstone for edgy, progressive, and aggressive youth culture around the world. (Simmons, 2001, pp. 8–9)

Hip-hop, in crude and innovative ways, frames Black youth's perspectives of social injustice in local communities and in their personal lives (DMX, 2002; Kelley, 1996; Lipsitz, 1994; Perkins, 1996; T. Rose, 1994a, 1994b; Ross & Rose, 1994; Simmons, 2001). Young Black America in dynamic ways use hip-hop as a cathartic space in which to discuss personal issues as well as larger social structural concerns. It is not uncommon to hear discussions on race and class based inequality in the music or for artists to talk about the importance of family and community. Although some argue that such moral postures are compromised when artists contrast family- and community-based ideals with crude tales of street wars or selling drugs, we believe that more is learned about the multiple identities, ideals, and/or messages raised in the music and culture by Black youth, as fans and artists, when giving context to the various dimensions of their lives. Placing more rigorous science behind the music and culture as well as the lived experiences of the artists and the local Black communities in which they reside not only would help to demystify some of hip-hop's complexity, but also would serve to better connect Black academics and, more specifically, Black psychologists, to poor Black communities. Put simply, hip-hop offers a nontraditional way for Black psychologists to understand the psychology of Black youth, especially those from urban environments. In this chapter, we theoretically address the following question: To what extent do Black youth engage in hip-hop music and culture as a site of resiliency as a function of young Black America's relationship to opportunity in the United States?

Theoretical Framework: Hip-Hop as a Site of Resiliency

According to Payne (2001, 2005, 2006a, 2006b, 2008), a *site of resiliency* theoretical analysis argues that a "street life" context offers particular psychological and physical spaces that operate in tandem to produce a site of strength, community, and, ultimately, resilience for street-life–oriented Black men. Although this theory could assess various street-life–oriented populations, it was explicitly conceived to frame Black men in the streets, who are at the center of various literatures concerning their relationship to and effect on education, employment, drug policy, and the criminal justice system. Furthermore, a site-of-resiliency analysis theorizes resiliency in the context of race and racism, sociohistorical patterns, and the intersection of concentrated economic poverty (capitalism) and resiliency, as well as the importance of phenomenologically based analysis to understand personal constructions of resiliency. It is our position that hip-hop music and culture, broadly defined, correspond in the lives of Black youth and young adults to the ideological value system and physical spaces of street-life–oriented Black men as framed in Payne's model. *Hip-hop* (like street life) is a phenomenological term viewed by Black youth as an ideological way of life centered on emotional catharsis, development of personal and group identity, and economic survival. Hip-hop also is conceptualized as a spectrum of behaviors that typically manifest in the following five identities: (1) MC or Rapper, (2) DJ or social organizer, (3) Dancer, (4) Street/Graffiti Artist, and (5) Knowledge Bearer or Intellectual (Keyes, 2002). These identities were established by the hip-hop community to give itself structural framing (T. Rose, 1994a). In addition, they are the necessary lens through which to understand the use of hip-hop by Black youth and adults.

We close the theoretical framing of this chapter by underscoring that our analysis of hip-hop in young Black America focuses on a genre of hip-hop: *street-life–oriented* hip-hop music and culture. With respect to the phenomenological dimension, it should be noted that hip-hop is a culture initially developed by and for street-life–oriented Black men (Boyd-Franklin & Franklin, 2000; Keyes, 2002; Payne, 2005). Specifically, hip-hop centrally is a composition of African American and Afro-Caribbean musical expressions that are grounded in the values, or *style* of street-life–oriented Black men (Dixon & Brooks, 2002; Perkins, 1996; T. Rose, 1994a). Although various populations engage in hip-hop, much of the music and culture are still centered on the experiences, stories, and overall values of street-life–oriented Black men.

Historical Origins of Hip-Hop: West Africa to the South Bronx

The spirit of hip-hop can be traced to the musical expressions of the Griots of West Africa, who often participated in the West African Bardic tradition (Aldridge & Carlin, 1993; Keyes, 2002; Powell, 1991). According to Keyes (2002), Bards were thought to hold the capacity to manifest the spirit of *nyama*—the transference of positive and/or negative energy through speech, music, and bodily movement. Also, Bards partook in a system of poetry and folklore known as the *Animal Trickster Tales* (Levine, 1977). The Animal Trickster Tales by way of the transatlantic African slave trade, made its way to the slave quarters located throughout the southern regions of the United States. In the United States, the Animal Trickster Tales evolved into the Slave Trickster Tales (Levine, 1977). These tales spoke to the core theme of the powerless (slave) developing ways to outsmart and defeat the more powerful and oppressive agent (White slaveholder). The contrast of song and dance juxtaposed against brutal forms of physical bondage all worked to produce a unique, raw, and rebellious sound that has taken root in multiple ways, in Black youth, from slavery until the present.

After the Civil War, Blacks continued to share tales or songs of oppression throughout the juke joints, taverns, "hot suppers," and churches of the South during the period of Black Reconstruction and well into the early 20th century (Butterfield, 1995; Levine, 1977). The northern Black migration in the late 1800s helped fill the northern bars, taverns, clubs, and street corners as well as churches and some political arenas with some of the richest Black musical expressions of its time (Keyes, 2002). During this period, the blues as well as the Bad Man Tales emerged and took hold as popular musical expressions in the Black community (Kelley, 1996; Levine, 1977; Roberts, 1989). Bad Man Tales, which evolved from the Animal and Slave Trickster Tale traditions, were, in essence, stories, poems, and songs consumed by low-income Black communities. These tales detailed factual and exaggerated accounts of Black men's criminal activities. The Bad Man Tales are the earliest as well as strongest examples of a musical expression, developed by street-life—oriented Black men, that matches the men's current musical expression with hip-hop.[1] Railroad Bill, Stagolee, Aaron Harris, and John Hardy are among those popular "Bad Men" in the late 19th and early 20th centuries. These men openly (and perhaps foolishly) discussed tales of gambling, drinking, and doing time in prison, as well as committing homicide. It was common for the men to brag about their "sawed-off shotgun" as well as more materialistic items like a "diamond cane" or "suede blue shoes":

> *I went down town de yudder night,*
> *A-raisin' san' an' a-wantin' a fight*
> *Had a forty dollar razzer, an' a gatlin' gun,*
> *Fer to shoot dem Niggers down one by one. . . .*
> *I'm de bad Nigger,*
> *If you wants to know . . . ;*
> *. . . I'm so bad, I don't ever want to be good, uh, huh;*
> *No I wouldn't go to heaven if I could. (Levine, 1977, p. 408)*

Interestingly enough, a song titled "Suicidal Thoughts" recorded on The Notorious B.I.G.'s (1994) first album, *Ready to Die*, in many respects mirrors the sentiments expressed in the aforementioned Bad Man Tales. Specifically, "Suicidal Thoughts" captures Biggie's challenges with anger, depression, and suicide, which leads Biggie to ask for his soul to rest in *hell*—a place Biggie perceives to be a more appropriate and comfortable resting place:

> *When I die, fuck it I wanna go to hell*
> *Cause I'm a piece of shit, it ain't hard to fuckin' tell*
> *It don't make sense, goin' to heaven with the goodie-goodies*
> *Dressed in white, I like Black Timbs (boots) and Black hoodies.*

Jive talk evolved from the Bad Man Tales and became formalized as a tradition in the Black community during the 1920s on the street corners of Chicago (Keyes, 2002). Jive talk was the first form of street slang that recording companies were able to successfully commodify. Scholars argue that jive talk emerged out of the street traditions of *signifying* (cleverly developed indirect statements or repartee), *toasting* (a long poem or story told in rhyming sequence), *playing the dozens* (making fun of another person), and/or the *Black pastoral or preaching* tradition (Dixon & Brooks, 2002). Such street-based Black expressions were captured and commodified particularly in the forms of blues and jazz in the decades that would follow (Aldridge & Carlin, 1993; Zillman et al., 1995). According to Perkins (1996), rap music is directly influenced by the singing and dance styles of low-income Blacks from the 1940s and 1950s in combination with the technology and/or disco age of the 1970s.

The Disco Hip-Hop Era (Mid-1970s–Early 1980s)

The 1970s, a period often referred to as the *Disco Era*, provided the springboard for the development of hip-hop music and culture in the Black community. Disco music and clubs sought to literately replicate the feeling of cocaine in the music. Low-income Black and Latinos often were banned from the more high-profile clubs located in downtown Manhattan. This discrimination contributed to the proliferation of local bars, lounges, and discotheques—particularly in places like Harlem and the Bronx (Keyes, 2002; T. Rose, 1994a, 1994b).

The militant sounds of The Last Poets' (1970) *When the Revolution Comes* and Gil Scott-Heron's (1970/1988) *The Revolution Will Not Be Televised*, in conjunction with the sounds of Jalal "Lightnin' Rod" Uridin's (1973) album *Hustler's Convention* added a contemporary sociopolitical element to Black music. George Clinton's contribution of "P-Funk" music, coupled with the sound of Curtis Mayfield, composed the image of the "hustler" and created a soundtrack for the "Blaxxploitation" era. The Blaxxploitation era was also formed through the literature of Donald Goines (1971, 1978) and Iceburg Slim (1969/1987) and through films starring the likes of Pam Grier, Fred Williamson, and Rudy Ray Moore (aka Dolemite). The militant sounds and "pimp narratives" of the 1970s played a significant role in directly setting the stage for hip-hop music and culture in the Black community (Kelley, 1994, 1996; Keyes, 2002).

The culmination of this raw creative energy birthed hip-hop in the mid-1970s in the streets of the south Bronx (Aldridge & Carlin, 1993; Dixon & Brooks, 2002; Dyson, 1996; Gardstrom, 1999; Keyes, 2002; Maultsby, 1991; Perkins, 1996; T. Rose, 1994a, 1994b). Graffiti, DJ-ing and break dancing during this early period were the more salient forms of the culture's expressions. Rap music became the focal point in hip-hop culture in 1979, chiefly as result of the Sugar Hill Gang. Although other hip-hop groups had released music prior to the Sugar Hill Gang, *Rappers Delight* (1979/1996) is generally credited as the first commercially successful hip-hop recording (Keyes, 2002; Perkins, 1996). Other artists who played a key role during the inception of hip-hop included Grandmaster Flash and The Furious Five, Grandwizard Theodore & the Fantastic Five, Kurtis Blow, Afrika Bambatta, Kool DJ Herc, and Busy Bee. "The Message" (1982/1994), "The Message II" (1982), and "White Lines" (1983) by GrandMaster Melle Mel (member of the Furious Five) were a set of singles that ultimately solidified the presence of street-life–oriented hip-hop music. Although *Rappers Delight* highlighted the social bonding or party aspect of the Black experience, "The Message" (1982/1994) and "White Lines" (1983) are among the first rap songs that directly addressed the illegal aspects of street life in the Black community, covering such topics as police brutality, incarceration, and the sale and use of narcotics (Keyes, 2002; Kriegel, 1997).

Social Structural Stage for the Development of Hip-Hop

Hip-hop culture was created in response to a plethora of social structural issues that deeply impacted the Black community in the late 1960s and 1970s, some of which include the following: the Vietnam war, inner-city race riots, rise and fall of the Black Power movement, a severe economic recession, the loss of factory- or labor-based employment, a major cocaine and heroin epidemic, prevalence and concentration of gang activity, and the mass incarceration of Black men (Kelley, 1996; Keyes, 2002; T. Rose, 1994a, 1994b; Wilson, 1987). Hip-hop scholars argue that the social structural challenges of the 1970s specifically resulted in the de-funding of vital art-based programs, community centers, and a variety of other community-based programs—programs that had formerly reduced Black youth's presence in the streets by offering them a way to channel and discipline their energy (Kelley, 1996, 1997; Keyes, 2002; T. Rose, 1994a, 1994b). The loss of these programs, and the subsequent closing of discotheques because of increasing levels of drug use and interpersonal violence, ultimately led to the prominence of the DJ in the 1970s. The hip-hop DJ now became exceptionally popular for "spinning" at block parties as well as social events in local parks, where oftentimes they illegally plugged their equipment into nearby lampposts (Keyes, 2002). According to T. Rose (1994a, 1994b), the social structural tension of the 1970s paradoxically provided the necessary bedrock for hip-hop to emerge. There was an even deeper concentration of oppressive social structural conditions for low-income Blacks in the 1980s under the presidency of Ronald Reagan. The negative sentiment of the people revealed itself in hip-hop music, which increasingly reflected the poverty (in the form of Reaganomics) and other forms of oppression in the Black community. Maultsby (1991) asserted that soul music in the forms of "Funk, Disco, or Rap music" are expressions of critical consciousness or repositioned African consciousness, developed in response to the social structural realities of the 1970s and 1980s.

Phases of Hip-Hop in the Black Community

Scholars as well as members of the hip-hop community have demarcated the 30 years of hip-hop into at least four waves or time periods (Keyes, 2002; Perkins, 1996; Powell, 1991). The first wave, called the *Disco Hip-Hop Era*, or what is also termed *Old School*, represents the first period of hip-hop culture and spans the mid-1970s to the early to mid-1980s. The emphasis during this period was a party or social event, thus bringing rise to the DJ, break dancer, and/or B (break)-boy and -girl. The second period of hip-hop culture is called the *First Golden Era*, and it is generally considered to span between 1983 and 1990. In the early to mid-1980s, the music and the artist made a distinct shift in image and sound. The dominant image of hip-hop during this period reflected to a greater extent the younger version of the more serious, explicitly masculine, street dimension of the Black community. The younger constituent of hip-hop, who was coming of age, could not identify with the disco sound of the 1970s and consequently decided against the disco format in favor of a sound and image considered to be more authentic to the issues of the Black community at that time (Simmons, 2001).

Furthermore, the First Golden Era generally consisted of three types of musical artist. MCs like Run DMC, Ice T, Rakim, early KRS-One, and N.W.A. generally represented the identity as well as the issues of the "street hustler,"[2] whereas more traditionally militant artists, such as Public Enemy, Poor Righteous Teachers, and X Clan, emerged later to close out the First Golden Era—entering hip-hop music and culture into an Africentric period (Allen, 1996; Dixon & Brooks, 2002; Henderson, 1996; Keyes, 2002; T. Rose, 1991, 1994a). Also during this period, more commercial, mainstream, or less confrontational acts emerged, such as Salt-n-Pepa, Kid-n-Play, Kwamè, and MC Hammer (Boyd-Franklin & Franklin, 2000; Keyes, 2002).

In the third wave of hip-hop, called the *Second Golden Era* (late 1980s to mid-1990s), "gangsta," "hardcore," or street-life–oriented hip-hop music became the mainstay (Kelley, 1996; Payne, 2005; Perkins, 1996). From this point on, the experiences of street-life–oriented Black men dominate the discourse of hip-hop music and culture. The music, now more than ever, is centered on the creative skill set of the MC and how he or she delivers truthful expressions over raw beats, which ideally are expected to mimic and capture the pain they have experienced in their life.

The late 1990s (1999–present) mark the fourth and most recent era of hip-hop music and culture—a period referred to as the *Bling-Bling Era* (Ossé & Tolliver, 2006; Perry, 2000). Although we view much of the music of this era as genuine artistic representations of the artists' lived experiences, it is important to note that the music at large is viewed as a gratuitous demonstration of materialistic, misogynistic, and violent messages. One credible distinction, nonetheless, is that during this period Black youth and young adults in larger numbers have developed an interest in more ownership of the music as well as entrepreneurial expansion in the larger entertainment industry (Carter, 2003; Chisholm, 2006; DMX, 2002; Kelley, 1996; Simmons, 2001). Although much of the profits and ultimate control of the industry rest in the hands of White corporations, hip-hop nonetheless is at present estimated to be at least a $10 billion industry (C. Rose, 2004). Giving the economic potential afforded through the markets of the hip-hop industry, more and more members of the hip-hop community are developing or successfully establishing recording, film, and clothing companies, among other ventures.

Furthermore, in addition to "street," gangsta, or "reality" rap, it should be underscored that other hip-hop genres, though not as popular, range from gospel rap to more revolutionary forms of the music sometimes described as *conscious*, *political*, or *backpack* rap. Also, there are geographically based genres of hip-hop. In the South, Black youth participate in "crunk" music as well as "chopped and screwed" music. Crunk is a subgenre made popular by Lil Jon and the Eastside Boys, and consists of a call-and-response system instead of traditional lyric stanzas. Chopped and screwed music is indigenous to Texas and was popularized by now-deceased DJ Screw. In the Bay Area (San Francisco/Oakland), the "hyphy" movement has gained mainstream notice in the past 3 years, thanks to the likes of veteran artist E-40.

There is no consensus in the hip-hop literature on the classification of rap musical genres. In many respects, scholars' characterizations of the music represent the variation and diversity found within the culture itself. Kitwana (2002) argued that rap music can be classified into three hip-hop musical genres: (1) recreational, (2) sex–violence, and (3) conscious forms of rap music. Allen (1996) expanded on the notion of "conscious rap," declaring that conscious rap can be understood in "three relatively distinct though inter-related expressions": (1) Islamic nationalism (e.g., Poor Righteous Teachers, Eric B. & Rakim), (2) cultural–political nationalism (e.g., Public Enemy, Boogie Down Productions), and (3) message-oriented expressions embedded in gangsta rap (e.g., N.W.A., The Geto Boys). Dyson's (1987) three-stage model of hip-hop music is (1) lighthearted banter, (2) social critique, and (3) pluralization (experimentation/alternative hip-hop, e.g., rock 'n' roll hip-hop). Aldridge and Carlin (1993), expanding on the second dimension (social critique) of Dyson's model, noted three genres as well: (1) gangster, (2) hardcore, and (3) activist-based genres, whereas Krims (2000) proposed at least four classifications of rap music: (1) party, (2) mack, (3) jazz/bohemian and (4) reality rap.

The Importance of Phenomenology

In general, rigorous investigations of hip-hop music and culture take notions of standpoint or phenomenology very seriously (Boyd-Franklin & Franklin, 2000; DMX, 2002; Dyson, 2001; Kelley, 1996; T. Rose, 1994a, 1994b; Scott, 2000; Shakur, 1999; Simmons, 2001). What artists have to say, and how they choose to position their voice, matters. Kelley (1996) argued that rappers are in essence "street ethnographers." Street or gangsta rappers are well known for their uncanny ability to unearth and offer rich descriptions that capture the nuances of their lived experiences and activities in the local community. Through the artist's lyrical delivery and musical sound, listeners can get a sense of what it means to sit inside the artist's mind as well as what it might mean to walk in his or her neighborhood. A phenomenological orientation forces the investigator's analysis of hip-hop to be guided by the values or theoretical lens of the hip-hop community. Given the level of misinformation about young Black America, and especially street-life–oriented Black men, investigators have insisted that studies work harder to incorporate a phenomenological component (Payne, 2006b; Spencer, 1995; Tolleson, 1997). Several factors that intersect and shape the various standpoints found within hip-hop culture are race/culture, gender, social class, geography, and developmental stage/generation.

Where Does Hip-Hop Live in the Academy? How Scholars Are Documenting the Culture of Hip-Hop

Hip-hop is a particular cultural phenomenon that all too often poses great theoretical, methodological, and empirical challenges to social scientists. Put simply, how do we responsibly think about, measure, and ultimately analyze hip-hop music and culture? The distance between scholars and hip-hop, in many respects, is representative of the relationship between larger society and young Black America. Given that most researchers have limited or guarded relationships with young Black Americans and the communities in which they live, and given that academics are not everyday fans of the music and culture, academics consequently have great difficulty understanding and reporting on hip-hop. Reflective of the divide, the hip-hop literature, largely, consist of analysis of songs from the Disco Era and First Golden Era—in general, the only periods of hip-hop in which most rap scholars actively played a role.

It has been argued that richer and more contextual analysis of hip-hop can and will be found among younger scholars who are now entering the academy in much larger numbers. Reyhan Harmanci's (2007) article, "Academic

Hip-Hop? Yes, Yes, Y'all," noted that as hip-hop enters its 30s, hip-hop studies have become some of "the most explosive subjects to hit academia in decades." Peter Monaghan, a correspondent for the *Chronicle of Higher Education*, noted that "What has been published to date doesn't tell the whole story, because a whole generation of young scholars is coming along, at the moment, and those researchers will produce a sudden gush of publishing within a few years" (quoted in Harmanci, 2007). Although there are still critics that openly question the seriousness of studying hip-hop, Ricky Vincent, member of the Hip-Hop Studies Working Group and author of *Funk: The Music, the People, and the Rhythm of the One* (1996), declared in the same article that hip-hop "is the language of this generation. If you don't want to speak it . . . you're not engaging the population that needs to be addressed the most. Remember, the academy needs Hip-Hop more than Hip-Hop needs that academy." According to a 2005 survey by Stanford University's Hip-Hop Archive, there are more than 300 courses being offered on hip-hop culture at U.S. colleges and universities (Harmanci, 2007).

It should be noted that hip-hop has no particular academic home; neither is it located in any particular academic discipline. At a fundamental level, hip-hop requires an academic home receptive of an interdisciplinary approach and/or mixed methodologies. Although chiefly classified in the social sciences, hip-hop has found homes in the classrooms and journals of Black American or Africana studies, ethnomusicology, psychology, sociology, urban education, English, anthropology, and public health. A variety of methods have been used to examine hip-hop. Theoretical, philosophical, historical, and polemical techniques have been the dominant methods used for analysis. Raw data typically are collected and analyzed using three methods, including (1) quantitative methods—specifically, randomized and nonrandomized survey and archival techniques (Epstein, Pratto, & Skipper, 1990; Fried, 1999; Gardstrom, 1999; K. Jones, 1997; Kubrin, 2006); (2) qualitative methods, which include various types of narrative and content analysis of lyrics (Kubrin, 2006; Payne, 2005, 2006a); and (3) formal experimental designs (Johnson, Jackson, & Gatto, 1995; Zillman et al., 1995). Recently, more researchers have decided to actually interview rappers and other members of hip-hop culture (Keyes, 2002; T. Rose, 1994a, 1994b). Also, hip-hop scholars are now using particular rap songs as primes for interviews (Gardstrom, 1999; Payne, 2005, 2006a) as well as intervention-based programs designed for schools and community-based organizations (Mahiri, 1996; Stephens, Braithwaite, & Taylor, 1998).

Popular topics or arguments raised by scholars generally involve discussions on identity development, masculinity, misogyny, violence, and materialism, whereas other discussions focus more on attitudes and treatment of members of the hip-hop community by police, the Black middle class, and larger White America, as well as other systems of authority. Other topics raised by scholars are more social structural in nature in that they more typically address the culture's concerns with economic poverty, unemployment, poor schooling conditions, and/or the effects of capitalism within low-income Black communities.

"DEMONIZED IMAGES": REFRAMING HIP-HOP TALES OF SEX AND VIOLENCE

It was toward the end of the First Golden Era when hip-hop received its first wave of harsh criticisms, primarily by so-called experts and community leaders in and out of the Black community (Dyson, 1987, 1996, 2001; K. Jones, 1997; T. Rose, 1994a, 1994b). Critics largely described the music as being "hyper-aggressive" and/or "hyper-sexual" (Boyd-Franklin & Franklin, 2000; K. Jones, 1997; Kelley, 1994, 1996; Keyes, 2002; T. Rose, 1994a). Tricia Rose (1994a) asserted that a responsible, informative, and complete analysis of sexism in hip-hop requires the union of two ideological perspectives that often are in opposition to one another. She profoundly noted that "Rap music and videos have been wrongfully characterized as thoroughly sexist but rightfully lambasted for their sexism" (p. 15). While directly challenging the sexism present in the music, T. Rose (1994a) ultimately argued that hip-hop as an institution or as individuals is no more sexist than any other traditional institution or set of individuals in the United States: "I am highly skeptical of the timing and strategic deployment of outrage regarding rap's sexism. Some responses to sexism in rap music adopt a tone that suggests that rappers have infected an otherwise sexism-free society" (p. 15). Dyson (2001), in his chapter

"Do We Hate Our Women?" also offered scathing criticisms of the sexism or "femiphobia" in hip-hop. However, Dyson, like T. Rose (1994a), brought real attention to "the sadistic sexism of the larger culture" (p. 187) that ultimately contextualizes, shapes, and endorses the misogynistic messages in the music. In addition, Dyson boldly noted that some women whom rappers and other industry insiders pursue often are "groupies" genuinely interested in getting involved in the activities that the men rap about—sexual or otherwise:

> It is undeniable that they encounter young women whose chief goal is to bring pleasure to rap stars and to procure, in Snoop Dogg's term, "superstar dick." Groupies are a staple not just of hip-hop but all forms of masculine endeavor, from the dugout to the pulpit, from the Blues hall to the boardroom. (2001, pp. 183–184)

Although this explanation does not excuse, justify, or condone sexist behavior or attitudes, it does shape hip-hop's promotion of distrust and sexual violence toward women as an American value not simply an African American male value. In addition, discourses that place all responsibilities on the shoulders of male consumers and producers of rap without rigorously contextualizing the role women play in a sexist society is myopic and incomplete.

Empirical research has nonetheless largely revealed the negative effects that violent and misogynistic hip-hop has on Black youth and young adults. Johnson et al.'s (1995) experimental study examined the attitudinal effects of being exposed to violent rap music videos in a sample of young Black men. Participants were placed in three conditions: (1) exposure to "violent" rap videos; (2) exposure to "nonviolent" rap music videos; and (3) the control condition, in which participants were exposed to no music videos. Black men in the violent exposure condition were more likely to accept the use of violence as well as more likely to state that they would engage in violent activity. Also, Black men in the violent condition were more apt to accept the use of violence toward women. K. Jones (1997) randomly selected 203 music videos to examine notions of sex and violence across five musical genres: (1) rap, (2) hip-hop, (3) R&B/soul, (4) country & western, and (5) pop. Jones concluded that although there were no significant differences among musical genres regarding rates of and the interaction between sexual and violent activity, rap videos were found to significantly be more violent (not sexual); specifically, rap videos were more apt to discuss guns, drugs, alcohol, and gambling. Kubrin (2006) conducted a content analysis of 403 songs recorded between 1992 and 2000 to explore how social structural inequality has led to larger numbers of Black youth adopting attitudes of nihilism. According to Kubrin, street rappers consider violence and death to be, "more prevalent in the ghetto than poverty, family disruption and limited opportunities" (p. 447). Specifically, Kubrin's analysis highlighted the following themes in relation to nihilism: (a) "pervasive violence in the ghetto" and (b) "preoccupation with death and dying."

Researchers have called for the critical analysis of seemingly targeted assaults on hip-hop. Some scholars have asserted that the image of the music has intentionally been defiled in favor for a cruder and more menacing portrayal of hip-hop culture and in particular young Black men (Dyson, 2001; Lipsitz, 1994; Payne, 2001; Perkins, 1996; T. Rose, 1994a; Henderson, 1996). Perkins (1996) wrote that "Young Black men are viewed as nihilistic, prone to anarchic violence, misogynistic, and greedy for the lucre associated with the trade in crack cocaine. This has made Black men targets and scapegoats for ... the police" (p. 16). Henderson (1996), in the same theoretical spirit, noted that influential powers across racial boundaries and political ideologies are actively seeking to suppress the rapid and aggressive development of this young Black American movement. Henderson ultimately called for the development of "Nation Conscious Rap" as a way to address the assault on hip-hop.

Oftentimes, the hip-hop artist's intention is to present a first-person narrative, authentic and exaggerated, moral and immoral, view of his or her lived experience. This narrative is coupled with the hope that those in power, through listening to the music, would be able to more easily connect the dots between social structural injustice and the manifestation of a street life orientation. The wide majority of rap music is not made merely for the sake of it. It is ironic that artists and fans alike often reframe songs that seemingly seek to bank on the economic value of sex and violence as evidence of the moral bankruptcy that permeates the nation. However, instead of their songs being harnessed and positioned for the world to earnestly observe and act on, their hip-hop testimonies are mostly ignored by traditional power structures and regarded as trivial.

In the next section, we provide a brief analysis of rap lyrics. Our intention is to provide the reader with examples of how to extrapolate evidence of injustice and disenfranchisement from rap lyrics that are generally derided as violent and misogynistic.

Lyrical Analysis: Hip-Hop's Testimonies of Street Life as a Site of Resiliency

In a time when 50% of Black men are unemployed (Eckholm, 2006; Levitan, 2004) and 50% of those incarcerated in state and federal prisons are Black men (Sentencing Project, 2006), street rappers often describe their experiences with economic poverty as well as the prison industrial complex. Krayzie Bone (2000) of the Cleveland, Ohio, group Bone, Thugs-N-Harmony, in particular argued this very point with a sultry melodic and almost hypnotic lyrical flow:

Nigga ain't seen daylight, they got me caged like, I'm runnin wild

Just for tryna' feed myself, since they act like we ain't even here

So I say, I've done no wrong, I wanna go home now....

I guess I'm payin the dues of a real true soldier

In this song "Shackled Up," for the soundtrack for the HBO prison series, *OZ*, Krayzie Bone argues that "the state" uses mechanisms of inhumanity (or keeps them "caged like") toward one trying to economically survive (or "feed myself") within the throes of an inner-city reality. Krayzie Bone understands very clearly that he is incarcerated for engaging in criminal activities. However, he is arguing for society at large, and the judicial system in particular, to understand that, by way of racist and classed practices, his incarceration is ultimately unjust. He poignantly notes that "the state" has no vested interest in understanding why he and others like him actually engage in criminal activities ("they act like we ain't even here"). Consequently, Krayzie Bone just wants to "go home" and finds some resolve by recognizing this form of social injustice is a way of "payin the dues of a real true soldier."

Cam'ron (2000), on his album *SDE* (Sex, Drugs, & Entertainment), opens with introductory remarks to the first song, titled "Killer." This song ironically exemplifies street life as a site of resiliency for Black men. Specifically, Cam'ron, in his introductory remarks, satirically noted some of the key social ingredients or conditions that produces the streets:

I am not going to sit here and watch this go on any longer. You know they put my food in the dark and then expect me to look for my plate on some Mr. Magoo shit. What the fuck I look like. I am not going to watch this go on any longer.

Cam'ron's (2000) underlying message is that he refuses to adhere to traditional middle-class standards, or behave "on some Mr. Magoo shit." He finds it nonsensical to move from a traditional value system in an inner-city environment that divests the community of key socioeconomic resources. Cam'ron calls attention to a society that has insidiously "put [his] food in the dark" or frozen opportunities for social, political and economic advancement. After his introductory remarks, falsetto voices in an operatic style rhythmically chant the word *killer*. One of Cam'ron's goals is to, through the first person, highlight for the listener how inner-city socioeconomic circumstances ultimately produce killers. So the objective, plainly stated, is to take the listener inside the mind and spirit of a killer, but for the intent of helping the listener understand the development of a killer.

Cam'ron (2000), in a song titled "Movin' Weight," described how street-life–oriented Black men strategically adapt—and attempt to work smarter, not necessarily less—to sell drugs in a community where hope and "pain" remain present, but usually at opposite ends of each other, mostly with pain having the edge.

Listen hear me out

I'm from a cocaine block

With some plain clothes cops

And the sun don't rise, cause the rain don't stop

The pain don't stop, but my brain don't stop

And no lock outs—the game don't stop

Every month you change your locks—change your spot (i.e., where you sell drugs)

Get a little smart, want to change your tops (i.e., caps of small glass vials)

rearrange your rocks (i.e., crack-cocaine).

Tupac Amaru Shakur was one of hip-hop culture's most passionate musical artists, eloquently capturing how Black men reframe engagement in street activities as a site of resiliency. Tupac (1994), on the *Thug Life* album, exclaimed that he is "Straight Ballin'!" (to live aggressively and extravagantly). Tupac's essential attitude and strategy in this song is that, given that his back is against the wall (figuratively and literally), he might as well go "head-up" against his opposition: "I'm straight ballin'!" Poignantly, Tupac's only concern with this newfound attitude is that his mother not "cry" if he prematurely dies in the streets as a result of using street-life–oriented activities to "survive":

They say, how do you survive weighing 165

in the city where the skinny niggas die

Tell mama don't cry, even if they kill me,

They can never take the game from a young G (i.e., gangster)

I'm straight ballin'!

Implicit in Tupac's (1994) message is that this aggressive attitude is necessary if one is to "survive weighing 165 in the city where the skinny niggas die." He is bringing to light how prevalent death is in his neighborhood—especially for those perceived to be weak. Admittedly, Tupac is willing to accept the negative consequences (i.e., injury, incarceration, and/or death) that come with being involved in the streets. Although a number of credible scholars have argued that such expressions or lyrics are examples of nihilism (Anderson, 1994; Kubrin, 2006; Poussaint & Alexander, 2000; West, 1993), we in fact view such lyrics as a demonstration of the artist's resiliency. Acknowledging the possibility of death is not a nihilistic act but in fact should be considered a realistic, intelligent, and resilient act. To say an artist's words are nihilistic is to ignore the central point of the artist, which is to reveal the injustice that intentionally is inflicted on these communities. Tupac, like other similar artists, forces listeners to ask, "Why are there an overwhelming number of poor Black communities in the United States that are similar to 'Third World Countries'"? (Lipsitz, 1994). In creative but very personal ways, Tupac linked the rage felt by the streets to the blocked opportunity found in poor Black communities. Tupac frequently argued that street-life–oriented Black men essentially were "American made." Ultimately, Tupac saw the United States as a White supremacist machine, intent on setting in place the conditions required for the demise of Black people.

Tupac tattooed the words *T. H. U. G. L. I. F. E.* on his stomach as a way to speak to the social structural oppression of Black America. The objective of the tattoo was to remind larger society of its role in creating the streets: *The Hate U (or You) Give Little Infants Fucks Everyone.* According to Tupac, if—by way of social, economical, political, and racial oppression—a child is filled with hate, then society should not be surprised when a generation of "infants" eventually acquires a street orientation (or "fucks everyone") to survive in an oppressive reality.

We close this chapter by addressing the question "Is hip-hop dead?" Given the increase in arguments addressing violent and misogynistic material, an imminent "death" has been pronounced for hip-hop by a number of Black community members—scholars as well as members of the hip-hop community. As opposed to being framed as an emotional and economic site of resiliency, the music recorded by artists like Krayzie Bone, Cam'ron, and Tupac are being positioned more now than ever as harmful to the community.

Is Hip-Hop Really Dead?

Hip-hop has been pronounced dead since its birth in the 1970s (Kelley, 1996; Keyes, 2002; Perkins, 1996; T. Rose, 1994a). The notion of hip-hop being dead has most recently been given a face by NaS's 2006 album release, titled *Hip-Hop Is Dead*. On this album, songs like "Where Are They Now" and "Who Killed It," as well as the title song "Hip-Hop Is Dead," speaks of how hip-hop has lost its integrity. It is unclear whether NaS actually believes hip-hop is dead, but we suppose that his intent was to act as a provocateur by posing the question to the hip-hop community. The subsequent furor has nonetheless been productive in galvanizing artists to prove that hip-hop culture is still important and relevant. The three chief concerns raised that speak to the death and not resiliency of hip-hop in general are (1) the increase in violent and misogynistic songs, (2) hip-hop's deep cooperation and collusion with corporate America, and (3) the overall declining sales of hip-hop music.

HIP-HOP AS A SITE OF ECONOMIC OPPORTUNITY

A number of people have countered the "death" thesis by noting the entrepreneurial ingenuity demonstrated by members of the hip-hop community as evidence of hip-hop's will to thrive in the face of overwhelming criticism. Artists such as Jim Jones, a self-proclaimed Blood gang member and former drug dealer, has been fortunate enough to take advantage of a number of entrepreneurial opportunities as a function of the hip-hop industry. Specifically, Jones is an artist signed to Koch Records, who has released three albums to date; the founder of two record companies (Diplomats and Byrdgang Records); purveyor of the alcoholic beverage Sizzurp; and owner of a clothing line titled Nostic. Dr. Ben Chavis, cofounder of the Hip-Hop Summit Action Network, says that Jones also attends the annual summit more regularly than any other rapper (Chisholm, 2006). Chavis, in an interview conducted for J. Jones's (2005) documentary, spoke directly to the entrepreneurial energy exhibited by Jones and the larger hip-hop community. He warns critics to learn how to galvanize the work ethic of a population largely and wrongfully characterized as lazy:

> Young people look up to Jim, not only because he's a gangster rapper, but because he stayed true to the game of gangster rapping, but at the same—been a successful business person. And I think the whole entrepreneurial spirit in Hip-Hop is something that should be lifted up. Doing for self. Going into business for self. Investing in self. (Chavis, quoted in J. Jones, 2005)

Street rappers come to hip-hop not only to express social concerns in their lives and communities but also to establish notions of resiliency through acquiring economic opportunity (Hoye & Ali, 2003). Hip-hop music as well as the larger hip-hop culture has been one of the few legal avenues that have opened up for street-life–oriented Black men in particular. As a consequence, these men pour out of the streets and prisons seeking to secure their economic futures through the hip-hop industry.

Within recent years, a number of street rappers have taken the initiative to form their own hip-hop brands and/or record companies. Such new and thriving companies include Ruff Ryders, G-Unit Records, Black Wall Street Records, and Murder Inc. Records. The newer hip-hop companies typically are more community based and understanding of the artist's needs. Oftentimes, they seek to give more creative control and economic opportunity to the local community through various forms of employment (e.g., promotional teams, talent scouts). Darrin Dean, one of the CEOs of Ruff Ryders Recordings, says in the Ruff Ryders, documentary:

> We try and do independent shit so other people can get jobs—so we can hire niggas and give them jobs. And don't have to worry about the white man trying to give us jobs cause he is going to limit us. So we got to give jobs back to the people where we grew up at, you know what I'm saying, in the hood. Everybody here is willing to work! You know, but they just don't get the opportunity . . . so we got to create opportunities. (Dean & Dean, 2001)

Jay-Z's, nèe Shawn Carter, hip-hop career is a great example of how hip-hop is pursued as an economic site of resiliency by street-life–oriented Black men. An admitted former drug dealer, Carter has developed one of the most successful business empires known to not only hip-hop but also the entertainment industry at large. Embedded in Carter's (2003) mission is making economic opportunities available to young Black America. According to Carter, contributions to the community by him and others in hip-hop, often are obscured by the sensationalism of the media:

> There is something I'm proud of that never gets written about: My company provides a lot of job opportunities. I employ so many people at Roc-A-Fella Records, Rocawear, Roc-A-Films, and Armadale Vodka—young black women and men with little to no experience in the music business.

I donated money to the Columbine effort, World Trade Center relief, Thanksgiving drives, the Jay-Z Santa Claus Toy Drive, Team Roc, and the Shawn Carter Scholarship Fund. I never give to get props (attention). I give because I can, because it's from my heart, and because I was raised right (p. 84).

In closing, we agree that there are many incendiary images and messages present in hip-hop culture. We also agree that some of these images are dangerous; however, to say that the images and messages of hyperviolence, objectification of women, and ideas of excess and grandeur are here because of hip-hop would dismiss the violent and misogynistic values present in the larger society. In some respects, hip-hop culture is suffering from the effects of nostalgia or a "mythic past." According to Kelley (1996),

> Spokespersons for these antirap movements invoke a mythic past in which middle-class values supposedly ruled. They point to a "golden age" of good behavior, when the young respected their elders, worked hard, did not live their lives for leisure, took education seriously, and respected their neighbor's property. (p. 148)

Although traditional critics would disagree, it should be underscored that negative images, street values, and/or ill-advised activities—real and imagined—have always been associated with hip-hop culture (Kelley, 1996; Keyes, 2002; T. Rose, 1994a; Simmons, 2001), even during the Disco Era (1973–1985). Keyes (2002) argues that during the Disco Era—a period of hip-hop believed by most to be nonviolent—there were approximately 315 gangs or 19,000 gang members in New York City alone. In fact, one of hip-hop's well-known pioneers, DJ Afrika Bambaata, was the leader of a highly respected and feared gang in New York City named the Black Spades before he became the leader of the hip-hop organization the Zulu Nation.

Hip-hop has been one of the few platforms that have allowed the men on the streets to describe the totality of their lived experience. Hip-hop offers a space for young Black America to respond to the criticisms raised against them. Street rappers, through songs, often challenge race- and class-based inequality in this society—and seek to describe how street life, inside this social reality, makes sense as a site of resiliency.

It is necessary for the Black community to watch which images are being identified with Black people; however, the responsibility should be from the inside out. Middle- and upper-middle-class Americans (Black and otherwise) who are neither consumers nor producers of hip-hop culture should not be at the forefront of debates about hip-hop. The artists and consumers of hip-hop, particularly from the Black community, should always take the opportunity to lead. Mos Def (1999) stated on the introduction to his album, *Black on Both Sides*, that "Hip-Hop is going wherever we are going"; thus, it is impossibly idealistic to look to hip-hop to be more positive and responsible when the world that to which it is speaking is still ignoring and diminishing young Black America's voice.

Notes

1. Although Black women also participated in the creation of these tales, this tradition more often than not were created by and grounded in the experiences of street-life–oriented Black men (Levine, 1977).

2. Although artists like Rakim and KRS-One generally are positioned by scholars as simply "conscious" rappers, we argue that much of their earlier material in fact confirms a strong relationship or identification with the streets of Black America. Rakim's "Paid in Full" (Eric B. & Rakim, 1987b) or "I Ain't No Joke" (Eric B. & Rakim, 1987a) as well as KRS-One's "9mm Goes Bang" (1987a) or "South Bronx" (1987b), for instance, explicitly reveal their involvement in the streets of New York City.

Discography

Cam'ron. (2000). "Killer." On *SDE*. Untertainment Records LLC/Epic.
Cam'ron. (2000). "Movin' Weight." On *SDE*. Untertainment Records LLC/Epic.
Eric B. & Rakim. (1987a). "I ain't no joke." On *Paid in full*. New York: 4th & B'way Recordings.
Eric B. & Rakim. (1987b). "Paid in full." On. New York: 4th & B'way Recordings.
GrandMaster Melle Mel. (1994). "The message." Rhino/Wea Records. (Original work published 1982)
GrandMaster Melle Mel. (1982). "The message II." Rhino/Wea Records.
GrandMaster Melle Mel. (1983). "White lines." Rhino/Wea Records.
Jones, J. (2005). *Harlem: Diary of a summer* [CD/DVD]. New York: Koch Recordings.
Krayzie Bone. (2000). "Shackled up." *OZ: The soundtrack*. Avatar Records.

KRS-One. (1987a). "9mm goes bang." On *Criminal minded*. New York: Jive (Landscape Germany).

KRS-One. (1987b). "South Bronx." On *Criminal minded*. New York: Jive (Landscape Germany).

The Last Poets. (1970). "When the revolution comes." On *The last poets*. New York: Revola Recordings.

Mos Def. (1999). *Black on both sides*. Priority Records.

NaS. (2006). "Hip-hop is dead." On *Hip-hop is dead* [CD]. New York: Def Jam Recordings.

Notorious B.I.G. (2004). "Suicidal thoughts." On *Ready to die* [CD]. New York: Bad Boy Recordings.

Scott-Heron, G. (1988). *The revolution will not be televised. A new Black poet: Small talk at 125th and Lenox* [Vinyl/CD]. New York: Flying Dutchman (Bluebird). (Original work published 1970)

Shakur, T. (1994). "Straight ballin'." On *Thug life: Volume 1*. Amaru Records/Jive Records/Interscope Records.

Shyne. (2000). *Shyne*. Bad Boy Records.

Sugar Hill Gang. (1996). *Rappers delight*. Rhino/Wea Records. (Original work published 1979)

Uridin, J. (1973). "Lightnin' Rod." *Hustler's convention*. New York: Celluloid.

REFERENCES

Aldridge, H., & Carlin, D. B. (1993). The rap on violence: A rhetorical analysis of rapper KRS-ONE. *Communication Studies, 44*, 102–116.

Allen, E., Jr. (1996). Making the strong survive: The contours and contradictions of message rap. In W. E. Perkins (Ed.), *Droppin' science: Critical essays on rap music and hip-hop culture* (pp. 159–191). Philadelphia: Temple University Press.

Anderson, E. (1994). The code of the streets. *The Atlantic Monthly, 273*(5), 80–92.

Boyd-Franklin, N., & Franklin, A. J. (2000). *Boys into men: Raising our African-American teenage sons*. New York: Dutton.

Butterfield, F. (1995). *All God's children*. New York: HarperCollins.

Carter, S. (2003, January). In my lifetime. *Vibe*, pp. 78–84.

Chisholm, N. J. (2006). Ballin' out of control. *The Source*, pp. 66–71.

Dean, D., & Dean, W. (2001). *Ruff ryders: The documentary* [DVD]. New York: Ruff Ryder Films.

Dixon, T. L., & Brooks, T. (2002). Rap music and rap audiences: Controversial themes, psychological effects and political resistance. *African-American Research Perspectives, 8*, 106–116.

DMX. (2002). *E. A. R. L.: The autobiography of DMX*. New York: Harper.

Dyson, M. (1987). Rap, race, and reality. *Christianity and Crisis, 47*, 98–100.

Dyson, M. E. (1996). *Between God and gangsta rap: Bearing witness to Black culture*. New York: Oxford University Press.

Dyson, M. E. (2001). *Holler if you hear me: Searching for Tupac Shakur*. New York: Basic Civitas Books.

Eckholm, E. (2006, March 20). Plight of Black men deepens, study warns. *The New York Times*. Retrieved November 6, 2007, from http://www.nytimes.com/2006/mar/20/2006

Epstein, J. S., Pratto, D. J., & Skipper, J. K., Jr. (1990). Teenagers, behavioral problems, and preferences for heavy metal and rap music: A case study of a southern middle school. *Deviant Behavior, 11*, 381–394.

Fried, C. B. (1999). Who's afraid of rap: Differential reactions to music lyrics. *Journal of Applied Social Psychology, 29*, 705–721.

Gardstrom, S. C. (1999). Music exposure and criminal behavior: Perceptions of juvenile offenders. *Journal of Music Therapy, 26*, 207–221.

Goines, D. (1971). *Dopefiend: The desperate rage and suffering of a hardcore junkie*. Los Angeles: Holloway House.

Goines, D. (1978). *Crime partners: A ghetto chieftain fights drugs, organized crime, White cops and cons*. Los Angeles: Holloway House.

Harmanci, R. (2007, March 5). Academic hip-hop? Yes, yes, y'all. *San Francisco Chronicle*. Retrieved December 15, 2007, from http://www.sfgate.com/cgi-bin/article.cgi?f=/c/a/2007/03/05/DDG3MOE3041.DTL&feed=rss.news

Henderson, E. A. (1996). Black nationalism and rap music. *Journal of Black Studies, 26*, 308–339.

Hoye, J., & Ali, K. (2003). *Tupac: Resurrection 1971–1996*. New York: Atria Books.

Iceburg Slim. (1987). *Pimp: The story of my life*. Los Angeles: Holloway House. (Original work published in 1969)

Johnson, J. D., Jackson, L. A., & Gatto, L. (1995). Violent attitudes and deferred academic aspirations: Deleterious effects of exposure to rap music. *Basic and Applied Social Psychology, 16*, 27–41.

Jones, K. (1997). Are rap videos more violent? Style differences and the prevalence of sex and violence in the age of MTV. *Howard Journal of Communications, 8*, 343–356.

Kelley, R. D. G. (1994). Check the technique: Black urban culture and the predicament of social science. In N. Dirks (Ed.), *In near ruins: Cultural theory at the end of the century* (pp. 39–66). Princeton, NJ: Princeton University Press.

Kelley, R. D. G. (1996). Kickin' reality, kickin' ballistics: Gangsta rap and postindustrial Los Angeles. In W. E. Perkins (Ed.), *Droppin' science: Critical essays on rap music and hip-hop culture* (pp. 118–158). Philadelphia: Temple University Press.

Kelley, R. D. G. (1997). *Yo' mama's disfunktional! Fighting the culture wars in urban America.* Boston: Beacon Press.

Keyes, C. L. (2002). *Rap music and street consciousness.* Chicago: University of Illinois Press.

Kitwana, B. (2002). *The hip-hop generation: Young Blacks and the crisis in African-American culture.* New York: BasicCivitas Books.

Kriegel, M. (1997, March 19). No message in madness of gangstas. (New York) *Daily News,* pp. 4, 5, 25.

Krims, A. (2000). *Rap music and the poetics of identity.* Cambridge, UK: Cambridge University Press.

Kubrin, C. E. (2006). "I see death around the corner": Nihilism in rap music. *Sociological Perspectives, 48,* 433–459.

Levine, L. W. (1977). *Black culture and Black consciousness: Afro-American folk thought from slavery to freedom.* New York: Oxford University Press.

Levitan, M. (2004, February). *A crisis of Black male employment: Unemployment and joblessness in New York City, 2003* (A Community Service Society Annual Report). New York: Community Service Society.

Lipsitz, G. (1994). We know what time it is: Race, class and youth culture in the nineties. In A. Ross & T. Rose (Eds.), *Microphone fiends: Youth music & youth culture* (pp. 17–28). New York: Routledge.

Mahiri, J. (1996). Writing, rap, and representation: Problematic links between texts and experience. In P. Mortensen & G. E. Kirsch (Eds.), *Ethics and representation in qualitative studies of literacy* (pp. 228–245). Urbana, IL: National Council of Teachers of English.

Maultsby, P. K. (1991). Africanisms in African-American music. In J. E. Holloway (Ed.), *Africanisms in American culture* (pp. 185–210). Bloomington/Indianapolis: Indiana University Press.

Ossé, R., & Tolliver, G. (2006). *Bling: The hip-hop jewelry book.* New York: Bloomsbury.

Payne, Y. A. (2001). Black men and street life as a site of resiliency: A counter story for Black scholars. *International Journal of Critical Psychology, 4,* 109–122.

Payne, Y. A. (2005). *The Street Life Project: How street life oriented U.S. born African men demonstrate notions of resiliency in the face of inadequate economic and educational opportunity.* Unpublished doctoral dissertation, City University of New York.

Payne, Y. A. (2006a). "A gangster and a gentleman": How street life oriented U. S. born African men negotiate issues of survival in relation to their masculinity. *Men and Masculinity, 8,* 288–297.

Payne, Y. A. (2006b). Participatory action research and social justice: Keys to freedom for street life oriented Black men. In J. Battle, M. Bennett, & A. J. Lemelle, Jr. (Eds.), *Free at last? Black America in the twenty first century* (pp. 265–280). New York: Transaction.

Payne, Y. A. (2008). "Street life" as a site of resiliency: How street life oriented Black men frame opportunity in the United States. *Journal of Black Psychology, 34,* 3–31.

Perkins, W. E. (1996). *Droppin' science: Critical essays on rap music and hip-hop culture.* Philadelphia: Temple University Press.

Perry, I. (2000). *Prophets of the hood: Politics and poetics in hip-hop.* Durham, NC: Duke University Press.

Poussaint, A. F., & Alexander, A. (2000). *Lay my burden down: Unraveling suicide and the mental health crisis among African-Americans.* Boston: Beacon Press.

Powell, C. T. (1991). Rap music: An education with a beat from the street. *Journal of Negro Education, 60,* 245–258.

Roberts, J. W. (1989). *From trickster to badman: The Black folk hero in slavery and freedom.* Philadelphia: University of Pennsylvania Press.

Rose, C. (2004, February 11). Russell Simmons, unplugged: Charlie Rose interviews the "Godfather of Hip-Hop." *60 Minutes II: CBS Evening News.* Retrieved February 9, 2008, from http://www.cbsnews.com/stories/2004/02/09/60II/main598970.shtml

Rose, T. (1991). "Fear of a Black planet": Rap music and Black cultural politics in the 1990s. *Journal of Negro Education, 60,* 276–290.

Rose, T. (1994a). *Black noise: Rap music and Black culture in contemporary America.* Hanover, NH: Wesleyan University Press.

Rose, T. (1994b). A style nobody can deal with: Politics, style and the postindustrial city in hip-hop. In A. Ross & T. Rose (Eds.), *Microphone fiends: Youth music & youth culture* (pp. 71–88). New York: Routledge.

Ross, A., & Rose, T. (1994). *Microphone fiends: Youth music & youth culture.* New York: Routledge.

Scott, C. (2000). *The murder of Biggie Smalls.* New York: St. Martin's Press.

Sentencing Project. (2006, December). *New incarceration figures: Growth in population continues.* Retrieved from http://www.sentencingproject.org/Admin/Documents/publications/inc_newfigures.pdf

Shakur, T. A. (1999). *The rose that grew from concrete.* New York: MTV/Pocket Books.

Simmons, R. (2001). *Life and def: Sex, drugs, money, & God.* New York: Crown.

Spencer, M. B. (1995). Old issues and new theorizing about African-American youth: A phenomenological variant of ecological systems theory. In R. L. Taylor (Ed.), *African-American youth: Their social and economic status in the U.S.* (pp. 37–69). Westport, CT: Praeger.

Stephens, T., Braithwaite, R. L., & Taylor, S. E. (1998). Model for using hip-hop music for small group HIV/AIDS prevention counseling with African American adolescents and young adults. *Patient Education and Counseling, 35,* 127–137.

Tolleson, J. (1997). Death and transformation: The reparative power of violence in the lives of young Black inner-city gang members. *Smith College Studies in Social Work, 67,* 415–431.

Vincent, R. (1996). *Funk: The music, the people, and the rhythm of the one.* New York: Macmillan.

West, C. (1993). *Race matters.* New York: Vintage Books.

Wilson, W. J. (1987). *The truly disadvantaged: The inner city, the underclass, and public policy.* Chicago: University of Chicago Press.

Zillman, D., Aust, C. F., Hoffman, K. D., Love, C. C., Ordman, V. L., Pope, J. T., et al. (1995). Radical rap: Does it further ethnic division? *Basic and Applied Social Psychology, 16,* 1–25.

11

THE ROLE OF MEDIA USE AND PORTRAYALS IN AFRICAN AMERICANS' PSYCHOSOCIAL DEVELOPMENT

BRENDESHA M. TYNES AND L. MONIQUE WARD

In many American households, time spent consuming various forms of media exceeds time spent in the classroom or socializing in the home with family and friends. This is particularly true of African American households. As a group, Black Americans consume almost twice as much television as White Americans—an average of 5 hours a day for Blacks versus 2 hours and 48 minutes for Whites (Roberts, Foehr, Rideout, & Brodie, 1999). Part of this viewing includes watching rap music videos. African American adolescent females, for example, report watching an average of 14 hours of rap music videos per week (Wingood et al., 2003). Moreover, despite the digital divide, African Americans as a group make heavy use of interactive media. Although some studies report that only 80% have access to the Internet, those who do spend an average of 5 hours per day surfing the Web compared with just less than 3 hours in the general population (Burns, 2005). And when Black youth play video games, they are likely to spend 23 minutes more per session than their White peers (see Kilman, 2005). This heavy consumption has led many scholars who study media effects to explore the psychological impact on the lives of African Americans.

This question is a critical one to ask when one considers the nature of the content to which African Americans are exposed. On television and in films, video games, and magazines, African Americans are often portrayed negatively or as stereotyped, unidimensional characters—when they are represented at all (Allen, 1993). Cortes (2003), drawing on a review of 2,300 research papers on television and human behavior, argued that media portrayals legitimize existing racial and ethnic hierarchies in society. He noted that

> when the entertainment media repeatedly depict intergroup dominance or subservience or consistently portray members of specific groups in limited spheres of action, they contribute to the formation of viewer organizational schema for perceiving those groups and absorbing future images into a meaningful and consistent, if distorted, conceptual framework. (p. 214)

Violent video games are a case in point. *Grand Theft Auto: San Andreas*, for example, depicts an African American gang member who avenges his mother's death by killing rival gang members.

These kinds of representations are believed to create racial scripts in the minds of consumers that can ultimately affect their attitudes and behavior (Entman & Rojecki, 2000). But are these dynamics that simple and direct? To what extent do the ethnic identity, age, or preexisting racial attitudes of the consumer shape his or her susceptibility to influence? Moreover, is all media content equally stereotypical and equally influential? Are all effects necessarily negative? These questions and many others have emerged over the past decades as media use has continued to grow both in number and in kind. In this chapter, we summarize findings from key studies that have attempted to address these questions. Focusing on a range of media (e.g., television, film, video games, magazines, music, and the Internet), we summarize the nature of media portrayals of African Americans and their effects on their psychosocial development, mental health, and behavior. We also explore characteristics of the consumer (e.g., gender) and of the media content (e.g., Black-oriented vs. mainstream) that affect the nature of these effects. Finally, we discuss how African Americans engage with media for their own empowerment and offer suggestions for empowering African American children and adults through media literacy.

Seminal Research

Gordon Berry and Claudia Mitchell-Kernan's edited volume *Television and the Socialization of the Minority Child* (1982) was one of the first works to focus on television's power as a socializing force for minority youth. The widely cited volume brought together leading scholars from various disciplines to shed light on the processes by which media influence the psychosocial development, attitudes, values, and behaviors of African American children (Latinos, American Indians, and Asians also were included in the text). It was instrumental in establishing a research agenda that focused on how a viewer's ethnicity may influence the way media messages are perceived, conceptualized, and evaluated and how this in turn affects social role learning and socialization processes. Consistent with the work of Alvin Poussaint (1974), who argued that minority children's sense of self is influenced by media representations, Berry and Mitchell-Kernan posited that television functions as part of the environmental feedback that shapes how African Americans view themselves.

Because these portrayals have not always been positive and have typically under- and misrepresented African Americans, concerns have been raised regarding their power in shaping Black viewers' attitudes and self-perceptions. These concerns are especially warranted given initial evidence that African American consumers may be especially open and accepting of media content. For example, early research by Greenberg and Atkin (1982) revealed that a higher proportion of African Americans (50%) than Whites (38%) reported that they watch television to learn how different people behave, talk, dress, and look. Scholars have observed that television can be so powerful that consumers change their attitudes so that they are consistent with actors viewed in this medium (Berry, 2000). Moreover, it has been argued that Black youth are more likely than White youth to believe that television portrayals are more realistic (Greenberg & Atkin, 1982; Stroman, 1991).

An essential component of early research in this area involved examination of the nature of the media content. Analyses of television programming from the 1970s reported that Blacks were commonly portrayed as poor, jobless, lazy, unintelligent, and incompetent; if they were employed, they typically held low-status blue-collar or service jobs and were less likely than Whites to be portrayed in professional or managerial positions (for reviews, see Graves, 1993, 1996; Greenberg & Brand, 1994; Merritt & Stroman, 1993). Overrepresented as criminals and as crime victims, a majority lived in ghettos and slums. Black families were portrayed as conflict ridden and female dominated and as exhibiting little supervision of and love toward their children. Such characterizations also extended to films. Donald Bogle's *Toms, Coons, Mulattoes, Mammies, and Bucks: An Interpretive History of Blacks in American Films*, first published in 1973, found rampant stereotyping of African Americans as lazy, docile, unintelligent, and aggressive. Images such as these are entrenched in the American psyche and have been reproduced in various media since as early as the 17th and 18th centuries.

Negative stereotyping was also found to extend even to supposedly objective news coverage. For example, the Kerner Report (National Advisory Commission on Civil Disorders, 1968) looked at the television coverage of the riots that followed the assassination of Dr. Martin Luther King Jr. in the late 1960s. It found that the media overestimated the damage caused by the riots, falsely portrayed the riots as Black-on-White violence, and in some instances even staged riot scenes. Concern has been expressed for how these representations affect Blacks' perceptions of themselves and for how they affect the perceptions and racial attitudes of Whites.

Other seminal research focused more specifically on educational media and on the potential instructional benefits for Black youth. In early studies of *Sesame Street* and *The Electric Company*, programs aimed largely at inner-city young children, Black viewers posted learning gains, including improvements on the Peabody Picture Vocabulary Test (Bogatz & Ball, 1971). Citing study findings, Graves (1982) reported that 3-year-olds who watched *Sesame Street* gained more than older children and that heavy viewers who were disadvantaged gained as much as their middle-class counterparts. However, among infrequent viewers, economically disadvantaged participants did not gain as much as the more advantaged participants. As for *The Electric Company* studies, lasting gains in reading ability were evident only in children who viewed the program at school (Ball & Bogatz, 1973). It is possible that these learning gains translated into more positive feelings about the self. Taken together, these early findings highlighted the complex nature of the media's psychosocial impact, a process in which type of media, social context, usage patterns, viewer characteristics, and program content all play a role.

THEORIES OF MEDIA EFFECTS

Researchers have put forth a number of theories and concepts to explain how media content affects users. Examples include social cognitive theory, cultivation theory, priming, and disinhibition effects. Recently, scholars have also begun to theorize about the role media may play in shaping racial attitudes. Instead of providing an exhaustive list, in this section, we highlight some examples of such theories.

Bandura's (1977) *social learning (cognitive) theory* is arguably the most common in the media effects literature. The theory predicts that learning can take place through observation and that the behavior modeled on television can be learned and imitated. In the case of violent television programming, for example, the behavior is said to be "learned" when aggressive thoughts and behaviors increase following exposure. A particular characteristic of this type of learning is that it occurs without the viewer's intention or awareness that learning is taking place (Anderson et al., 2003). Several criteria increase the likelihood that an observer will learn the behavior being modeled. These criteria include similarity between the viewer and the person modeling the behavior, identification with the model, and evidence that the behavior is rewarded (Bandura, 1977).

To further explain the impact of media messages, *cultivation theory* posits that television viewing has long-term effects that are small, gradual, and indirect yet still cumulative and significant (Gerbner, Gross, Morgan, & Signorielli, 1986). The expectation is that, over time, repeated exposure to the media's consistent images gradually leads viewers to accept those portrayals as representations of reality. If this theory is valid, then the extensive television exposure of African Americans might place them at special risk for negative effects. Other scholars argue that exposure does not have to be frequent in order to have significant effects: Even a single critical image can have a powerful impact, either positive or negative. This is known as the *drench hypothesis* (Greenberg, 1988), which asserts that especially powerful portrayals (e.g., Kunta Kinte in *Roots*) could shape viewers' attitudes and could drown out the messages from numerous other, regular portrayals.

Cognitive and social–cognitive psychologists argue that media have a priming effect such that exposure to certain images may activate similar concepts from an individual's memory (Bargh & Pietromonaco, 1982). Furthermore, they note that repeated exposure to these images can make schemas chronically accessible (Anderson et al., 2003). Chronic accessibility increases the likelihood that an individual will apply schemas across multiple domains when making judgments about the self and others. Media images may also influence thoughts, emotions, and behavior. Scholars who study media violence, for example, argue that repeated observations of violence can lead to emotional desensitization such that a person no longer responds with negative physiological arousal to violent imagery (Huesmann, Moise-Titus, Podolski, & Eron, 2003). This in turn increases the likelihood of engaging in or condoning violence (Huesmann et al., 2003).

With regard to interaction on the Internet, scholars have argued that the anonymity of the medium caused by reduced physical cues can cause online disinhibition effects (Kiesler, Siegal, & McGuire, 1984); that is, people engage in behaviors in which they would not normally engage during face-to-face interaction. These behaviors may include more self-disclosure and, at times, increased antisocial activity, such as hurling racial epithets. Because of these disinhibition effects, African Americans may be more susceptible to negative race-related experiences in online settings than in face-to-face encounters (Tynes, Reynolds, & Greenfield, 2004)—that is, they stand to experience racial prejudice at increased frequencies and in spaces that may be created solely for African Americans.

Recent theorizing about the role of race in interactive media potentially refutes this view. Jerry Kang's (2000) concept of *cyberrace*, for example, argues that the Internet will cause fundamental shifts in the way that race functions in American society. These shifts take place through racial schema that include the *racial categories* through which the basic concept of race is understood; the rules of *racial mapping* that are used to classify individuals into categories; and *racial meanings*, which are cognitive beliefs about and affective reactions to the categories (Kang, 2000). Textual and graphic representations of self can be more fluid and even masked in some cases. Kang argued that this, in turn, can reduce and even eliminate racial discrimination in some online interactions. Although there is little empirical evidence to support this particular theory, the theories highlighted in this section have been used to explain media effects on psychosocial development and behavior.

Media Effects

Media Use and Self-Concept

One of the chief concerns raised by the paradoxical relationship between Blacks' underrepresentation in the media and overrepresentation in the viewing audience is the impact on Black viewers' self-perceptions. In the case of film and television, for example, a group's absence from the screen may suggest that its members are unimportant and powerless (Graves, 1999; Powell, 1982). As a consequence of their media exposure, some scholars argue, Black viewers may come to feel that they are unimportant, thereby eroding their own sense of self-worth (Stroman, 1991).

Studies testing these assumptions have been mixed and slow to emerge. Research conducted with Black adults indicates that connections between media use and self-esteem depend in part on the genre or type of programming. Whereas greater exposure to mainstream entertainment programming has been associated with lower self-esteem (Allen, 1998; Tan & Tan, 1979), greater exposure to "Black-oriented" television has been associated with a stronger endorsement of positive stereotypical beliefs about Blacks (Allen, 1993; Allen, Dawson, & Brown, 1989).

A different pattern of results has emerged across studies that have tested children; some findings suggest the potential benefits of Black-oriented programming. Stroman (1986) tested associations between weekly hours of total television viewing and the self-concepts of 102 Black children in the third through sixth grades. The results indicated that greater television viewing was associated with a more positive self-concept among girls; among boys, no association was noted. McDermott and Greenberg (1984) examined associations among self-esteem, racial self-esteem, and exposure to Black programming among Black fourth- and fifth-graders. They found that more frequent viewing of Black programs and holding more positive attitudes toward Black characters were each associated with higher self-esteem. Looking more directly at viewers' media diets, Ward (2004) found that results differed according to whether Black teens viewed mainstream or Black-oriented programming. Greater exposure to mainstream programming and stronger identification with White characters were each associated with lower self-esteem, whereas stronger identification with popular Black characters was associated with higher self-esteem. Further investigation revealed that these associations were mainly relevant for youth who reported low levels of religiosity, which may suggest a weaker tie to the Black community or Black culture (i.e., via the church), weaker identity or belief systems, or other vulnerabilities. In a similar study, Gordon (2004) examined associations between music video exposure and several dimensions of self-esteem among Black high school girls. Girls who reported a higher percentage of Black music and music videos in their media diets also expressed higher self-esteem with respect to their personal appearance. Again, however, further analysis of specific subpopulations revealed that Black music video exposure was especially beneficial to youth who may have felt less connected to their racial identity or community.

Together, these findings illustrate the complex relations among Black viewers, media use, and self-concept, highlighting the impact of such factors as age, preexisting racial identity, and religiosity. Research with both Black youth and Black adults suggests that exposure to and identification with Black-oriented media may be beneficial, whereas the effects of connections to White-oriented media are less consistent and may depend on the age of the participant. Indeed, it seems likely that the self-concepts of Black adolescents may be particularly vulnerable to being shaped (positively or negatively) by media models, because adolescence is a time of intense identity exploration. All conclusions remain tentative, however, because of the limited number of studies available and because there is no experimental work to demonstrate causality.

Media Use and Black Women's Body Image

Television, magazines, and films, as visual media, focus heavily on physical appearance, presenting a steady stream of examples of idealized beauty and sexual attractiveness, especially for women. The Eurocentric beauty ideal put forth by the dominant culture enshrines European features, which for women include fair skin, long hair, light eyes, delicate features, and thinness (Perkins, 1996). Because most Black women do not share most of these features, there is concern about how frequent exposure to these mainstream ideals may affect their body image. At present, little empirical evidence exists on this point. Most studies that have tested associations between media use and women's body image have tested exclusively or predominantly White samples (for a review, see Ward & Harrison, 2005). Such studies have found that frequent exposure to media that promote the thinness ideal is, as expected, associated with internalization of this ideal, greater body dissatisfaction, and eating disorders among White girls and women. On the basis of these findings, it is commonly expected that exposure to the White beauty ideal in the media will be even more detrimental for Black women. What does the limited evidence indicate?

Overall, research suggests that the picture may not be as bleak as is often assumed. Data from focus groups and interviews suggest that Black girls do not necessarily internalize the beauty ideal presented by the mainstream media. For example, Milkie (1999) conducted surveys and interviews examining Black and White teen girls' perceptions of thin-ideal media and resulting appearance pressure. Many of the White girls expressed a desire to meet media ideals of thinness, even if they disliked the ideals themselves, because they assumed that their peers, exposed to similar media, expected them to be thin. African American girls, in contrast, appeared to be more resistant to this pressure to conform to what they perceived as a largely Anglo body ideal. Similar findings were reported by Duke (2000) in her interviews with Black and White teen girls and by Sekayi (2003) in her work with Black female undergraduates. The Black girls and women they interviewed were largely uninterested in the beauty ideals presented in mainstream teen magazines, dismissing them as irrelevant and as intended for White girls. Instead, the Black women with whom Sekayi spoke tended to define beauty using a more African-centered model that included characteristics such as self-confidence and friendliness.

Findings from survey and experimental work provide further evidence that Black viewers may not universally and unquestionably accept the White beauty ideal (e.g., Makkar & Strube, 1995). Indeed, the complex picture emerging suggests that potential effects are likely to vary based on the race of the media model and the current body image of the viewer. For example, Schooler, Ward, Merriwether, and Caruthers (2004) found that, among Black undergraduate women, more frequent viewing in high school of programming with predominantly Black casts was associated with a lower drive for thinness, fewer tendencies toward bulimia, and fewer negative thoughts about the body. Few effects were associated with their viewing of programming with predominantly White casts.

Similarly, in an experimental setting, the mood and body esteem of Black undergraduate women were not affected by exposure to magazines advertisements featuring images of White models (Frisby, 2004); however, exposure to magazine advertisements featuring African American models did diminish the body esteem of participants who had already reported low opinions of their own bodies. Black women with a more positive body image were not affected by the exposure.

At the same time, some findings suggest that Black girls and women may not be as resistant to mainstream models and comparisons as some initial investigations have suggested. In focus group interviews with Black female undergraduates, Poran (2006) found the participants to be very aware of mainstream beauty ideals and to feel pressure both from these ideals and from Black men. Although the women could describe more things that they loved than hated about their bodies, they also expressed great confusion, frustration, and anxiety about the rigid standards of beauty they felt could not be ignored. Survey data also highlight the pressures some Black women experience. For example, Botta (2000) found that among Black *and* White girls, the more the girls idealized TV images and compared themselves and their friends with those images, the stronger was their drive to be thin, and the more dissatisfied they were with their bodies. Among those who idealized TV images the most, Black girls engaged in more disordered behaviors than did White girls.

Overall, the data suggest that many (but not all) Black female viewers may reject White beauty ideals presented by the media. They may compare themselves favorably with, and may perhaps be inspired by, media images of Black women. For those who do idealize the White ideals, negative self-evaluations emerge as expected. Building on this small body of findings, future research should continue to explore individual-difference factors, such as ethnic identity and religiosity, that may make some Black women more resistant and others more vulnerable. These issues also need to be studied in relation to Black men and Black adults of various ages.

Media Use and Black Viewers' Attitudes About Men, Women, and Sexual Relationships

Among the many potential lessons that viewers can glean from media content are ideas about gender roles, sexual roles, and norms for sexual relationships. Because portrayals tend to enshrine traditional gender roles and the sexual double standard, concern has been expressed about how repeated exposure to such content may shape viewers' beliefs in these domains. Although numerous studies have investigated this question among White viewers (for reviews, see Signorielli, 2001, and Ward & Harrison, 2005), only a handful of studies have examined these notions among African Americans. Their results suggest that the media may indeed be a potent force in promoting certain types of sexual attitudes and behaviors.

First, research indicates the potential power of media exposure to affect viewers' attitudes and stereotypes about gender roles. In one of the first studies to test these questions, O'Bryant and Corder-Bolz (1978) examined whether exposure to stereotypical or counterstereotypical occupational roles would affect Black children's own stereotyping of and preferences for those jobs. Over one 4-week period, the authors exposed 23 6- to 10-year-olds to a set of commercials that featured women in either traditional roles (e.g., manicurist) or nontraditional roles (e.g., pharmacist). Posttest measures revealed that exposure to the nontraditional images increased girls' preferences for the jobs traditionally thought of as "male." However, exposure did not affect boys' job preferences, and it did not affect either girls' or boys' stereotyping of occupations. In a sample of 530 fourth- and fifth-graders that was 64% White and 21% Black, Signorielli and Lears (1992) found that, among both the White and Black students tested, more frequent TV viewing was associated with holding more stereotypical conceptions about who should do certain chores.

Second, findings from both correlational and experimental studies support associations between media use and Black viewers' sexual attitudes and stereotypes. In a 2-year longitudinal study of the media habits of 1,600 adolescents, Walsh-Childers and Brown (1993) reported that more frequent viewing of soap operas and sitcoms predicted increased acceptance of relationship stereotypes among Black teens. Similar findings emerge from experimental work. In their study of 60 inner-city Black teens, Johnson, Adams, Ashburn, and Reed (1995) found that girls who were exposed to eight sexist, nonviolent rap videos were more accepting of teen dating violence as featured in a subsequent vignette than were girls without this experimental exposure; boys' attitudes were not affected. Finally, Ward, Hansbrough, and Walker (2005) reported both correlational and experimental links between media exposure and Black teens' stereotypes about gender and sexual roles. Analyses of students' everyday media use indicated that frequent exposure either to music videos or to music (in general) was associated with holding more stereotypical notions about the sexes. Furthermore, students exposed to four stereotypical music videos offered stronger endorsement of sexual stereotypes than did students exposed to neutral videos.

Finally, research suggests a possible association between media exposure and Black adolescents' sexual behavior, although null results are sometimes reported (e.g., see Brown, L'Engle, Pardun, Guo, & Kenneavy, 2006). In a longitudinal analysis of 522 Black adolescent girls, Wingood et al. (2003) found that girls who reported higher levels of exposure to rap videos were more likely than those with less exposure to have multiple sexual partners, engage in risky sexual intercourse, test positive for a sexually transmitted disease, and report drug and alcohol use. A recent follow-up analysis revealed that girls who were more aware of sexual stereotypes in rap videos were also more likely to have multiple sexual partners, engage in binge drinking, use marijuana, and report a negative body image than did those who noticed fewer stereotypes (Peterson, Wingood, DiClemente, Harrington, & Davies, 2007). This was true even when levels of music video exposure were controlled. The psychological mechanisms behind these findings remain unknown, however, because it is not clear whether acknowledgment and awareness of the stereotypes represents internalization or more attentive viewing. Further study of the dynamics behind these intriguing connections is needed.

Taken together, these findings suggest that, among Black viewers, frequent media exposure is associated with holding more stereotypical beliefs about the sexes and about sexual roles, and that young viewers, girls especially, may be growing desensitized to some of the negative images of women because of this constant exposure. Evidence also suggests that viewing nontraditional images may reduce some of these associations, if only temporarily. Further study is needed of youth of diverse ages, of Black boys and men, and of additional aspects of their gender socialization (such as gendered appearance).

Media Violence, Risk Taking, and Aggression

Although the studies are fewer, media association also extends to Black viewers' beliefs about violence and to actual risk taking. A 1993 survey of teen media habits (Klein et al., 1993) reported that, among Black female teens, greater exposure to rap music predicted higher levels of risk taking. Among Black male teens, greater use of radio and sports magazines predicted more risk taking, but greater exposure to TV news predicted less risk taking. Using a more experimental paradigm, Johnson, Jackson, and Gatto (1995) examined African American boys' perceptions of violence after exposure to violent music videos. The participants (ages 11–16) were randomly assigned to one of three conditions—control, nonviolent, and violent—and were then asked to indicate their attitudes toward the use of violence and their own probability of engaging in violent behavior. Boys who were exposed to the violent music videos gave a higher endorsement of violent behavior and reported a higher likelihood of engaging in violence than did boys who were exposed to nonviolent videos.

A study of the associations between short- and long-term exposure to violent video games and desensitization (as measured by scores on an empathy vignette) found that long-term exposure to the violent games contributed to lower empathy scores in 5- to 12-year-olds (Funk, Buchman, Jenks, & Bechtoldt, 2003). Preexisting characteristics of the ethnically diverse sample (approximately 20% African American), such as empathy and attitudes toward violence, as well as previous exposure to violent video games, contributed to these scores.

Slater, Henry, Swaim, and Anderson (2003) examined aggressiveness in adolescents and its relation to consumption of violent action films, computer games, and video games and of visiting violence-oriented Internet sites. In their study of students from 20 middle schools, 10.4% of whom were African American, they found that aggressiveness was both a contributor to and an outcome of media use. This cross-sectional and lagged effect of violent media use on aggressiveness held even after controlling for contemporaneous effects in both directions.

Effects on Racial Attitudes

A final set of beliefs likely to be shaped by media use are beliefs about race. In our highly segregated society, an individual's opportunities to get to know people of different racial or ethnic groups are often limited. For many, the most regular "contact" they have with people from other groups may come through the media. What does repeated exposure to media portrayals teach Black viewers about race and race relations in America?

Surprisingly little published research has addressed this question. Instead, most studies on the subject have explored how media exposure—either to entertainment programming or to news coverage—affects White participants' perceptions of African Americans. They often find a priming of stereotypes (e.g., Dixon & Azocar, 2007; Entman, 1994; T. Ford, 1997; Fujioka, 1999; Gan, Zillman, & Mitrook, 1997; Givens & Monahan, 2005; Wester, Crown, Quatman, & Heesacker, 1997). Data from a handful of studies indicate that racial attitudes of Black viewers are also shaped by media exposure and that these effects vary by the nature of the content.

In a test of the positive power of the media, Tan and Kinner (1982) examined whether exposing Black youth to media images of Black and White children interacting as friends would affect their desire for similar interactions. As expected, the Black fourth-graders who were shown a 30-minute PBS film featuring such interactions expressed significantly more willingness to engage in friendly social interactions with White children than did participants in the control group. In an investigation of the negative power of the media, Johnson, Trawalter, and Dovidio (2000) examined whether listening to violent rap music influenced Black and White college students' perceptions of Black people. The results indicated that exposure to such music encouraged the students to later label a hypothetical Black target's violent behavior as due to his "violent nature," but no such effect in relation to the White target was observed. Listening to violent rap music also affected the students' perceptions of the intelligence of the Black target, but not the White target.

Other experimental research has documented the nuanced nature of these associations. Addressing the affective consequences of media exposure, Richeson and Pollydore (2002) examined whether experimental exposure to portrayals of African Americans affects Black viewers' perceptions and anxiety differently depending on whether the images are stereotypical or counterstereotypical and whether White or Black characters are present. Their results indicated that context does indeed matter. First, Black characters who behaved stereotypically in the presence of other Black characters were rated as more stereotypical than were Black characters who behaved stereotypically in the presence of Whites. Second, observations of Black characters who behaved counterstereotypically during interactions with Whites led to higher anxiety among the Black participants compared with observations of Black characters who behaved stereotypically. The authors speculated that such anxiety may have resulted from participants' identification with and empathy for these characters because the participants, Black students at a predominantly White college, may experience such interactions regularly. In a 2005 survey of 202 Black college students, Fujioka (2005) examined how students' perceptions of Black portrayals may affect their views about race. Holding more negative evaluations of Black media images was associated with judging them to be less accurate and assuming that others perceive Blacks more negatively in general. Although negative evaluations of Black media images were not related directly to participants' views on affirmative action, they were related to predictions of lower evaluations of Blacks by other ethnic groups, which in turn was related to a stronger endorsement of affirmative action.

Documenting the potential long-term effects of media exposure on Blacks' racial attitudes, Matabane (1988) found that higher levels of television viewing were related to greater acceptance of racial progress and integration. She surveyed 161 Black adults in Washington, D.C., and found that frequent television viewers were more inclined than infrequent viewers to believe that Blacks "fit in," to say that Blacks and Whites are similar, and to overestimate the size of the Black middle class. These findings suggest that frequent media consumers, at least those tested during the 1980s, were more inclined to believe that Blacks are doing well in society. Whether these associations would hold today remains to be seen.

Finally, new media have also been noted to impact racial attitudes. Byrne (2008) noted that participation in social networking sites and online discussions about race can ultimately strengthen African American youth's racial identity. In a recent online survey, African

American (and Latino) adolescents who reported high incidents of online racial prejudice were found to have higher ethnic identity scores than European Americans (Tynes, Giang, & Thompson, in press). Perhaps being a target of racial prejudice online heightened the salience of race and prompted further explorations into this aspect of participants' identity. The Internet also provides opportunities for more positive interaction and safe spaces to construct racial identity. Although it is difficult to draw general conclusions from these few published studies about the effects of media use on the racial attitudes of African Americans, there is encouraging potential for further research.

Media and Mental Health

Recent research has shown associations between early television exposure and later attention-deficit problems, although studies have yet to include a high percentage of African Americans (Christakis, Zimmerman, DiGiuseppe, & McCarty, 2004). Using data from the National Longitudinal Survey of Youth, Christakis et al. (2004) found that heavy exposure at ages 1 and 3 was related to attention-deficit problems at age 7 in a diverse sample of children that included African Americans. They suggested that television may actually restructure the brains of young children. However, other longitudinal studies based on data collected through the Early Childhood Longitudinal Study counter this claim (e.g., Stevens & Mulsow, 2006). Although Stevens and Mulsow (2006) did find associations between kindergartners' television exposure and subsequent symptoms of attention-deficit disorder when the children were in first grade, they found television viewing to be only a weak predictor of these symptoms. Methodological issues, such as participant age and measurement of attention-deficit symptoms, may account for the discrepancy in findings.

Adult media consumers have also been found to be vulnerable to mental health effects. A study of 1,008 adult residents of New York City conducted after the September 11 attacks revealed that participants who had repeatedly watched television footage of people falling or jumping from the Twin Towers had a higher prevalence of posttraumatic stress disorder (PTSD) symptoms and depression than those who did not. PTSD symptoms and depression were more than double for the heavy versus light viewers: 17.4% versus 6.2% and 14.7% versus 5.3%, respectively (Ahern et al., 2002). Similarly, a study of more than 2,000 middle-schoolers (43% African American) following the 1993 bombing of the Alfred P. Murray Federal Building in Oklahoma City revealed that degree of television exposure was related to posttraumatic stress symptomatology (Pfefferbaum et al., 2001). These studies suggest relations among exposure to negative content on television, PTSD symptomatology, and depression, for both children and adults. The results should be interpreted cautiously, however, because of the difficulty in determining causality. Furthermore, PTSD symptomatology is not the same as a diagnosis, and individuals who were directly exposed to terrorist events are likely to differ greatly from those indirectly exposed through media.

In addition to television, use of the Internet has been associated with mental health variables. Tynes, Giang, and Williams (2008) recently created the Online Victimization Scale to measure online victimization related to race, among other constructs. Preliminary findings from the Virtual Experience Project, a study of 264 adolescents ages 14 to 18, suggest that racial victimization and stress subscales are associated with depressive symptoms (Tynes, Giang, Williams, & Thompson, in press). This is not surprising, because studies of online intergroup experiences have revealed that nearly three quarters of the racially diverse adolescents interviewed reported either witnessing or being targets of online racial prejudice (Tynes, 2007). These racial incidents manifested themselves as verbal attacks, including racial epithets and threats of physical violence, and occurred up to several times per day. Although research has consistently shown that exposure to these negative events in offline settings has deleterious effects on a number of physical and mental health indicators for African Americans (cf. Clark, Anderson, Clark, & Williams, 1999), the evidence is just now mounting for the online equivalent.

In sum, researchers have found associations between media use and adverse mental health outcomes such as attention-deficit/hyperactivity disorder (ADHD), PTSD, and depressive symptomatology. The link among these factors, however, warrants further exploration. This is particularly important with regard to ADHD in light of the overrepresentation of African Americans in special education programs.

Empowerment

Although research on media effects has tended to focus on the negative consequences of media exposure, there is evidence that African Americans use media as a source of liberation and empowerment. This empowerment comes in many forms and is being used to effect change and reduce disparities in the areas of psychological and physical health, education, and parenting. Indeed, Everett (2002) argued that, contrary to popular notions of African American communities being on the wrong side of the digital divide, African Americans are forging an African Diasporic digital public sphere and masterfully using technology toward their own communities' ends. Others have made similar observations. In an early study of Black liberation on the Internet published posthumously, Beckles (2001) discussed the utility of some Black-oriented Web sites. He noted that "Black Information Gateways," or sites that provide critical information for Black communities, can serve as sites of resistance in their provision of historical, economic, agricultural, political, and military developments on the African continent or across the Diaspora. He also noted that the Black Information Gateways that are decidedly Africentric in nature can liberate Blacks by "challenging racist (re) presentations of Black identity" (p. 315) and by providing avenues for Black self-determination and unity on the Internet.

Several studies of media's uses for empowerment recount specific successes with African American children and adults. These studies have been primarily qualitative and/or mixed-method in nature and include interviews and case studies (London, Pastor, Servon, Rosner, & Wallace, 2006; Pinkett & O'Bryant, 2003), focus groups (Mehra, Merkel, & Peterson Bishop, 2004), observations, and content and discourse analyses (Beckles, 2001; Herman, Mock, Blackwell, & Hulsey; 2005; Knadler, 2001; Redd, 2003). For example, several analyses of Black students recount their use of the Internet for identity and validation. Although many Blacks often have to mask aspects of their Blackness in predominantly White settings, research indicates that African American students can create "safe houses" on the Internet in which they freely speak African American English without fear of reprobation from European American standard English speakers (Knadler, 2001; Redd, 2003). A number of studies also have described interventions designed to empower through improvement of such factors as health literacy, social support, parenting practices of Black fathers, and skill building in low- to moderate-income African American communities (Fagan & Stevenson, 2002; Herman et al., 2005; Hudson, Campbell-Grossman, Keating-Lefler, & Cline, 2008; Masi, Suarez-Balcazar, Cassey, Kinney, & Piotrowski, 2003). Studies also show that technology may allow youth to create social networks with peers and mentors and community technology centers have been noted to promote autonomy, leadership and self esteem among African American youth (London et al., 2006).

Other studies have found uses of the Internet as empowering for African American women. The MIT "Creating Community Connections" project in the Camfield Estates of Boston, for example, provides computers, training, and Internet/Intranet access to a low- to moderate-income sample of predominantly single African American female-headed households. A key goal of the project was to promote psychological empowerment in the community members in addition to community building and promoting self-sufficiency in computer skills. On the basis of interviews with participants, Pinkett and O'Bryant (2003) found that the project effected improvements in self-perceptions and attitudes about the self as a learner. Participants were also made more aware of personal and community strengths and ultimately became producers of Web content as well as Web administrators. Similar interventions in which participants were provided access to technology have reported improvements in empowerment factors such as perceived control over issues that affect personal and family health, satisfaction with control over health decisions, and influence over health decisions in the community in treatment versus control group members (Masi et al., 2003).

Finally, media literacy experts seek to train consumers to be critical of the media they consume. The ultimate goal of much of this literature and research is to lessen the harmful impacts on consumers' psychological and physical health. As media literacy curricula are adopted across the United States, many programs often have participants critique media by asking general questions such as the following (Kaiser Family Foundation, 2003):

- Who created this message, and why are they sending it?
- Who owns and profits from it?
- What techniques are used to attract and hold attention?
- What lifestyles, values, and points of view are represented in this message?
- What is omitted from this message? Why was it left out?
- How might different people interpret this message?

Going a step further, we draw from the work of Kellner (1995), who argued that dominant cultural ideologies be interrogated, and we propose that media literacy include explicit strategies for helping African Americans understand the specific role that race plays in the development of all media and the impact of the depiction of race on educational, psychological, and physical health outcomes for African Americans. Counselors, teachers, and researchers should also help African Americans understand how media affect them as individuals. In doing so, what we call *media self-knowledge profiles* should be developed. These profiles would include questions about personal media diets and how they may influence perceptions and behavior. Other questions should be related to African Americans in general. The following are examples of possible items for the race-specific component of such a profile:

- How are African Americans represented in much of the media you consume?
- Do you commonly see African Americans? Why or why not?
- What role do you think the legacy of slavery plays in the development of media?
- How would you say that African American representations differ from the ones in your community?
- What stereotypes of African Americans (males and females) are common in the media you use?
- How might the media influence your attitudes about African American women and men; attitudes about skin tone; beauty ideals?
- How do you think media representations of African Americans influence local, state, and federal policies?
- How might media affect teachers' perceptions of African American students?

Conclusion

Because African Americans spend up to twice as much time with media than their White counterparts, and because their portrayals in these media are often negative, there has been a growing concern among scholars and practitioners that media consumption has a negative impact on African Americans' psychosocial development, mental health, and behavior. In this chapter, we have shown that although media are pervasive in African American life, their impact is not consistently negative. Instead, research suggests that the nature of the effects depends on the content viewed and on the gender, religiosity, ethnic identity, and preexisting attitudes of the consumers. Frequent media exposure is associated with holding more stereotypical conceptions of gender roles and sexual roles among Black youth and with higher levels of sexual behavior, risk taking, aggression, and stereotypical racial attitudes. Yet, media use is also associated with psychological empowerment, including increased social support and the forging of positive racial identities.

Future Directions in Research

Although African Americans have been included in a number of media studies, they often make up a small percentage of the participants. Thus, our chief suggestion is to increase the quantity and widen the scope of research focusing specifically on the media use of African Americans. Very few systematic lines of research have examined media effects among Blacks, even though Blacks are the heaviest media consumers. This needs to be corrected on all fronts. Larger samples of African Americans, including people from different geographic regions and of different socioeconomic levels and sexual orientations, would allow for more nuanced analyses of how media affect this population.

More research is especially needed on how media consumption shapes Black people's beliefs about race. Nearly all of the existing research in this area has investigated how exposure to portrayals of African Americans affects White people's beliefs about Blacks. Little is known of how media use shapes Black viewers' beliefs about Blacks or Whites or about members of other ethnic groups, such as Asian Americans and Latinos.

In addition, there should be more theorizing about media effects from an African American Psychology perspective. Theories that focus specifically on the role that race *and* media play in African American psychological, social, emotional, and behavioral development are needed. These theories should focus not only how media affect African Americans but also on how African Americans engage media for their own empowerment.

Continued investigation is also needed into the nature and impact of exposure to mainstream versus Black-oriented media. Studies with experimental designs will be important for moving the study of African Americans and media forward. For example, does stereotypical content in Black-oriented media have a stronger effect on attitudes than the same content in mainstream media? Which has a more detrimental effect: exclusion, tokenism, or stereotypical portrayals? Because not all Black-oriented media are equivalent, which features or differences in content are most influential in determining effects? For example, what is the impact of portrayals of African Americans in integrated versus segregated settings? To what extent does the skin coloring of African American actors in Black-oriented media affect Black consumers' acceptance of them and their perceived relevance?

Longitudinal studies of the impact of television on brain development are sorely needed, because current studies either use data that are outdated or do not allow enough time between measurements to account for any effects. Understanding how television shapes African American children's brain development and behavior is critical in light of heavy exposure in many homes and even in some day care settings. These studies may ultimately lead to legislation that would limit the amount of television viewing, at least in child care settings.

Because heavy media use has been associated with poor health outcomes, including obesity, more research should explore these relations among African Americans. A promising counseling and behavioral intervention was recently conducted with African American children ages 7 through 12 and their families (B. S. Ford, McDonald, Owens, & Robinson, 2002). Families received counseling alone or counseling and a behavioral intervention that included an electronic television time manager. The behavioral intervention produced both decreased amounts of television viewing and significant gains in physical activity. These results are based on pilot data, and more rigorous research along these lines is needed.

Additional research should examine the role of parental involvement and mediation in shaping youth's media consumption. What do Black parents say and do to help their children process media content? Does limiting media exposure and time with media influence the extent and nature of media effects?

Scholars are just beginning to broaden the investigation of media genres beyond television sitcoms and dramas and music videos. The need for examination of the impact of movies, video games, and the Internet is particularly urgent. Future research should explore relations between online interaction and psychological well-being. For example, how might differential Internet use patterns affect African Americans' psychosocial development, attitudes, and behavior? Do negative race-related encounters online affect African Americans differently than other groups? If so, what factors influence their strategies for coping with such experiences? How does online interaction condition African Americans' racial, academic, occupational, and sexual identities? These questions and others offer intriguing avenues for future scholarship in African American Psychology and media studies.

REFERENCES

Ahern, J., Galea, S., Resnick, H., Kilpatrick, D., Bucuvalas, M., Gold, J., et al. (2002). Television images and psychological symptoms after the September 11 terrorist attacks. *Psychiatry, 65,* 289–300.

Allen, R. L. (1993). Conceptual model of an African-American belief system. In G. Berry & J. K. Asamen (Eds.), *Children and television: Images in a changing sociocultural world* (pp. 155–176). Newbury Park, CA: Sage.

Allen, R. L. (1998). Class, communication, and the Black self: A theory outline. In J. K. Asamen & G. L. Berry (Eds.), *Research paradigms, television, and social behavior* (pp. 153–202). Thousand Oaks, CA: Sage.

Allen, R. L., Dawson, M. C., & Brown, R. (1989). A schema-based approach to modeling an African-American racial based belief system. *American Political Science Review, 83,* 421–441.

Anderson, C. A., Berkowitz, L., Donnerstein, E., Huesmann, L. R., Johnson, J. D., Linz, D., et al. (2003). The influence of media violence on youth. *Psychological Science in the Public Interest, 4,* 81–110.

Ball, S., & Bogatz, G. A. (1973). *Reading with television: An evaluation of* The Electric Company. Princeton, NJ: Educational Testing Service.

Bandura, A. (1977). *Social learning theory.* Englewood Cliffs, NJ: Prentice Hall.

Bargh, J. A., & Pietromonaco, P. (1982). Automatic information processing and social perception: The influence of trait information presented outside of conscious awareness on impression formation. *Journal of Personality and Social Psychology, 43,* 437–449.

Beckles, C. A. (2001). Black liberation and the Internet: A strategic analysis. *Journal of Black Studies, 31,* 311–324.

Berry, G. L. (2000). Multicultural media portrayals and the changing demographic landscape: The psychosocial impact of television representations of the adolescent of color. *Journal of Adolescent Health, 27,* 57–60.

Berry, G. L., & Mitchell-Kernan, C. (Eds.). (1982). *Television and the socialization of the minority child.* New York: Academic Press.

Bogatz, G. A., & Ball, S. (1971). *The second year of Sesame Street: A continuing evaluation.* Princeton, NJ: Educational Testing Service.

Bogle, D. (1973). *Toms, coons, mulattoes, mammies, and bucks: An interpretive history of Blacks in American films.* New York: Viking Press.

Botta, R. A. (2000). The mirror of television: A comparison of Black and White adolescents' body image. *Journal of Communication, 50,* 144–159.

Brown, J. D., L'Engle, K., Pardun, C., Guo, G., & Kenneavy, K. (2006). Sexy media matter: Exposure to sexual content in music, movies, television, and magazines predicts Black and White adolescents' sexual behavior. *Pediatrics, 117,* 1018–1027.

Burns, E. (2005). *African American online population is growing.* Retrieved February 8, 2008, from http://www.clickz.com/show Page.html?page= 3555061

Byrne, D. N. (2008). The future of (the) "race": Identity, discourse, and the rise of computer-mediated public spheres. In A. Everett (Ed.), *Learning race and ethnicity* (pp. 15–38). Cambridge: MIT Press.

Christakis, D. A., Zimmerman, F. J., DiGiuseppe, D. L., & McCarty, C. A. (2004). Early television exposure and subsequent attentional problems. *Pediatrics, 113,* 708–713.

Clark, R., Anderson, N. B., Clark, V. B., & Williams, D. R. (1999). Racism as a stressor for African-Americans: A biopsychosocial model. *American Psychologist, 54,* 805–816.

Cortes, C. (2003). Knowledge construction and popular culture: The media as multicultural educator. In J. Banks & C. McGee Banks (Eds.), *Handbook of research on multicultural education* (2nd ed., pp. 211–227). San Francisco: Jossey-Bass.

Dixon, T., & Azocar, C. (2007). Priming crime and activating Blackness: Understanding the psychological impact of the overrepresentation of Blacks as lawbreakers on television news. *Journal of Communication, 57,* 229–253.

Duke, L. (2000). Black in a blonde world: Race and girls' interpretations of the feminine ideal in teen magazines. *Journalism & Mass Communication Quarterly, 77,* 367–392.

Entman, R. (1994). Representation and reality in the portrayal of Blacks on network television news. *Journalism Quarterly, 71,* 509–520.

Entman, R. M., & Rojecki, A. (2000). *The Black image in the White mind: Media and race in America.* Chicago: University of Chicago Press.

Everett, A. (2002). The revolution will be digitized: Afrocentricity and the digital public sphere. *Social Text, 20,* 125–146.

Fagan, J., & Stevenson, H. C. (2002). An experimental study of an empowerment-based intervention for African American Head Start fathers. *Family Relations, 51,* 191–198.

Ford, B. S., McDonald, T. E., Owens, A. S., & Robinson, T. N. (2002). Primary care interventions to reduce television viewing in African American children. *American Journal of Preventive Medicine, 22,* 106–109.

Ford, T. (1997). Effects of stereotypical television portrayals of African-Americans on person perception. *Social Psychology Quarterly, 60,* 266–278.

Frisby, C. M. (2004). Does race matter? Effects of idealized images on African American women's perceptions of body esteem. *Journal of Black Studies, 34,* 323–347.

Fujioka, Y. (1999). Television portrayals and African-American stereotypes: Examination of television effects when direct contact is lacking. *Journalism & Mass Communication Quarterly, 76,* 52–75.

Fujioka, Y. (2005). Black media images as a perceived threat to African American ethnic identity: Coping responses, perceived public perception, and attitudes towards affirmative action. *Journal of Broadcasting & Electronic Media, 49,* 450–467.

Funk, J. B., Buchman, D. D., Jencks, J., & Bechtoldt, H. (2003). Playing violent video games, desensitization, and moral evaluation in children, *Journal of Applied Developmental Psychology, 24*, 413–436.

Gan, S., Zillman, D., & Mitrook, M. (1997). Stereotyping effect of Black women's sexual rap on White audiences. *Basic and Applied Social Psychology, 19*, 381–399.

Gerbner, G., Gross, L., Morgan, M., & Signorielli, N. (1986). Living with television: The dynamics of the cultivation process. In J. Bryant & D. Zillman (Eds.), *Perspectives on media effects* (pp. 17–48). Hillsdale, NJ: Lawrence Erlbaum.

Givens, S. M. B., & Monahan, J. L. (2005). Priming mammies, Jezebels, and other controlling images: An examination of the influence of mediated stereotypes on perceptions of an African American woman. *Media Psychology, 7*, 87–106.

Gordon, M. (2004). *Media images of women and African American girls' sense of self.* Unpublished doctoral dissertation, University of Michigan.

Graves, S. B. (1982). The impact of television on the cognitive and affective development of minority children. In G. L. Berry & C. Mitchell-Kernan (Eds.), *Television and the socialization of the minority child* (pp. 37–67). New York: Academic Press.

Graves, S. B. (1993). Television, the portrayal of African Americans, and the development of children's attitudes. In G. Berry & J. K. Asamen (Eds.), *Children and television: Images in a changing sociocultural world* (pp. 179–190). Newbury Park, CA: Sage.

Graves, S. B. (1996). Diversity on television. In T. M. MacBeth (Ed.), *Tuning in to your young viewers: Social science perspectives on television* (pp. 61–86). Thousand Oaks, CA: Sage.

Graves, S. B. (1999). Television and prejudice reduction: When does television as a vicarious experience make a difference? *Journal of Social Issues, 55*, 707–727.

Greenberg, B. S. (1988). Some uncommon television images and the drench hypothesis. In S. Oskamp (Ed.), *Television as a social issue* (pp. 88–102). Newbury Park, CA: Sage.

Greenberg, B. S., & Atkin, C. K. (1982). Learning about minorities from television: A research agenda. In G. L. Berry & C. Mitchell-Kernan (Eds.), *Television and the socialization of the minority child* (pp. 215–243). New York: Academic Press.

Greenberg, B. S., & Brand, J. E. (1994). Minorities and the mass media: 1970s to 1990s. In J. Bryant & B. Zillman (Eds.), *Media effects: Advances in theory and research* (pp. 273–314). Hillsdale, NJ: Lawrence Erlbaum.

Herman, J., Mock, K., Blackwell, D., & Hulsey, T. (2005). Use of a pregnancy support website by low-income African American women. *Journal of Obstetric, Gynecologic, and Neonatal Nursing, 34*, 713–720.

Hudson, D. B., Campbell-Grossman, C., Keating-Lefler, R., & Cline, P. (2008). New Mothers Network: The development of an Internet-based social support intervention for African American mothers. *Issues in Comprehensive Pediatric Nursing, 31*, 23–35.

Huesmann, L. R., Moise-Titus, J., Podolski, C. L., & Eron, L. (2003). Longitudinal relations between children's exposure to TV violence and their aggressive and violence behavior in young adulthood: 1977–1992. *Developmental Psychology, 39*, 201–221.

Johnson, J. D., Adams, M. S., Ashburn, L., & Reed, W. (1995). Differential gender effects of exposure to rap music on African American adolescents' acceptance of teen dating violence. *Sex Roles, 33*, 597–605.

Johnson, J. D., Jackson, L. A., & Gatto, L. (1995). Violent attitudes and deferred academic aspirations: Deleterious effects of exposure to rap music. *Basic and Applied Social Psychology, 16*, 27–41.

Johnson, J. D., Trawalter, S., & Dovidio, J. F. (2000). Converging interracial consequences of exposure to rap music on stereotypical attributions of Blacks. *Journal of Experimental Social Psychology, 36*, 233–251.

Kaiser Family Foundation. (2003). *Key facts: Media literacy.* Washington, DC: Author.

Kang, J. (2000). Cyber-race. *Harvard Law Review, 113*, 1130–1208.

Kellner, D. (1995). *Media culture.* London: Routledge.

Kiesler, S., Siegal, J., & McGuire, T. W. (1984). Social psychological aspects of computer mediated communication. *American Psychologist, 39*, 1123–1134.

Kilman, C. (2005, June). *Video games: Playing against racism.* Retrieved February 8, 2008, from http://www.tolerance.org/news/article_tol.jsp?id= 1228

Klein, J. D., Brown, J. D., Walsh Childers, K., Oliveri, J., Porter, C., & Dykers, C. (1993). Adolescents' risky behavior and mass media use. *Pediatrics, 92*, 24–31.

Knadler, S. (2001). E-racing difference in e-space: Black female subjectivities and the Web-based portfolio. *Computers & Composition, 18*, 235–255.

London, R. A., Pastor, M., Servon, L., Rosner, R., & Wallace, A. (2006). *The role of community technology centers in youth skill-building and empowerment* (Center for Justice, Tolerance & Community special report). Santa Cruz, CA: Center for Justice, Tolerance & Community.

Makkar, J., & Strube, M. (1995). Black women's self-perceptions of attractiveness following exposure to White versus Black beauty standards: The moderating role of racial identity and self-esteem. *Journal of Applied Social Psychology, 25*, 1547–1566.

Masi, C. M., Suarez-Balcazar, Y., Cassey, M. Z., Kinney, L., & Piotrowski, H. (2003). Internet access and empowerment: A community-based health initiative. *Journal of General Internal Medicine, 18,* 525–530.

Matabane, P. (1988). Television and the Black audience: Cultivating moderate perspectives on racial integration. *Journal of Communication, 38,* 21–31.

McDermott, S. T., & Greenberg, B. S. (1984). Black children's esteem: Parents, peers, and television. In R. N. Bostrom (Ed.), *Communication yearbook 8* (pp. 164–177). Beverly Hills, CA: Sage.

Mehra, B., Merkel, C., & Peterson Bishop, A. (2004). The Internet for empowerment of minority and marginalized users. *New Media & Society, 6,* 781–802.

Merritt, B., & Stroman, C. A. (1993). Black family imagery and interactions on television. *Journal of Black Studies, 23,* 492–499.

Milkie, M. A. (1999). Social comparisons, reflected appraisals, and mass media: The impact of pervasive beauty images on Black and White girls' self-concepts. *Social Psychology Quarterly, 62,* 190–210.

National Advisory Commission on Civil Disorders. (1968). *Report of the National Advisory Commission on Civil Disorders.* New York: Bantam Books.

O'Bryant, S. L., & Corder-Bolz, C. R. (1978). Black children's learning of work roles from television commercials. *Psychological Reports, 42,* 227–230.

Perkins, K. (1996). The influence of television images on Black females' self-perceptions of physical attractiveness. *Journal of Black Psychology, 22,* 453–469.

Peterson, S., Wingood, G., DiClemente, R., Harrington, K., & Davies, S. (2007). Images of sexual stereotypes in rap videos and the health of African American female adolescents. *Journal of Women's Health, 16,* 1157–1164.

Pfefferbaum, B., Nixon, S., Tivis, R. D., Doughty, D. E., Pynoos, R. S., Gurwitch, R. H., et al. (2001). Television exposure in children after a terrorist incident. *Psychiatry, 64,* 202–211.

Pinkett, R., & O'Bryant, R. (2003). Building community, empowerment and self-sufficiency. *Information, Communication & Society, 6,* 187–210.

Poran, M. (2006). The politics of protection: Body image, social pressures, and the misrepresentation of young Black women. *Sex Roles, 55,* 739–755.

Poussaint, A. F. (1974, August). Building a strong self-image in the Black child. *Ebony,* 138–143.

Powell, G. J. (1982). The impact of television on the self-concept development of minority group children. In G. L. Berry & C. Mitchell-Kernan (Eds.), *Television and the socialization of the minority child* (pp. 105–131). New York: Academic Press.

Redd, T. M. (2003). "Trying to make a dolla outa fifteen cent": Teaching composition with the Internet at an HBCU. *Computers and Composition, 20,* 359–373.

Richeson, J., & Pollydore, C. (2002). Affective reactions of African American students to stereotypical and counterstereotypical images of Blacks in the media. *Journal of Black Psychology, 28,* 261–275.

Roberts, D., Foehr, U., Rideout, V., & Brodie, M. (1999). *Kids and media at the new millennium.* Palo Alto, CA: Henry J. Kaiser Family Foundation.

Schooler, D., Ward, L. M., Merriwether, A., & Caruthers, A. (2004). Who's that girl: Television's role in the body image development of young White and Black women. *Psychology of Women Quarterly, 28,* 38–47.

Sekayi, D. (2003). Aesthetic resistance to commercial influences: The impact of the Eurocentric beauty standard on Black college women. *Journal of Negro Education, 72,* 467–477.

Signorielli, N. (2001). Television's gender role images and contribution to stereotyping. In D. Singer & J. Singer (Eds.), *Handbook of children and the media* (pp. 341–358). Thousand Oaks, CA: Sage.

Signorielli, N., & Lears, M. (1992). Children, television, and conceptions about chores: Attitudes and behaviors. *Sex Roles, 27,* 157–170.

Slater, M. D., Henry, K. L., Swaim, R. C., & Anderson, L. L. (2003). Violent media content and aggressiveness in adolescents: A downward spiral model. *Communication Research, 30,* 713–736.

Stevens, T., & Mulsow, M. (2006). There is no meaningful relationship between television exposure and symptoms of attention-deficit/hyperactivity disorder. *Pediatrics, 117,* 665–672.

Stroman, C. A. (1986). Television viewing and self-concept among Black children. *Journal of Broadcasting and Electronic Media, 30,* 87–93.

Stroman, C. A. (1991). Television's role in the socialization of African American children and adolescents. *Journal of Negro Education, 60,* 314–327.

Tan, A. S., & Kinner, D. (1982). TV role models and anticipated social interaction. *Journalism Quarterly, 59,* 654–656.

Tan, A., & Tan, G. (1979). Television use and self-esteem of Blacks. *Journal of Communication, 29,* 129–135.

Tynes, B. (2007). Role-taking in online "classrooms": What adolescents are learning about race and ethnicity. *Developmental Psychology, 43,* 1312–1320.

Tynes, B., Giang, M., & Thompson, G. (in press). Ethnic identity, intergroup contact, and outgroup orientation among diverse groups of adolescents on the Internet. *Cyberpsychology and Behavior.*

Tynes, B. M., Giang, M. T., & Williams, D. R. (2008). *The Online Victimization Scale: Psychological distress and wellbeing.* Manuscript in preparation.

Tynes, B. M., Giang, M. T., Williams, D. R., & Thompson, G. (in press). Online racial discrimination and psychological adjustment among adolescents. *Journal of Adolescent Health.*

Tynes, B., Reynolds, L., & Greenfield, P. M. (2004). Adolescence, race and ethnicity on the Internet: A comparison of discourse in monitored and unmonitored chat rooms. *Journal of Applied Developmental Psychology, 25,* 667–684.

Walsh-Childers, K., & Brown, J. D. (1993). Adolescents' acceptance of sex-role stereotypes and television viewing. In B. S. Greenberg, J. D. Brown, & N. L. Buerkel-Rothfuss (Eds.), *Media, sex, and the adolescent* (pp. 117–133). Cresskill, NJ: Hampton Press.

Ward, L. M. (2004). Wading through the stereotypes: Positive and negative associations between media use and Black adolescents' conceptions of self. *Developmental Psychology, 40,* 284–294.

Ward, L. M., Hansbrough, E., & Walker, E. (2005). Contributions of music video exposure to Black adolescents' gender and sexual schemas. *Journal of Adolescent Research, 20,* 143–166.

Ward, L. M., & Harrison, K. (2005). The impact of media use on girls' beliefs about gender roles, their bodies, and sexual relationships: A research synthesis. In E. Cole & J. H. Daniels (Eds.), *Featuring females: Feminist analyses of media* (pp. 3–23). Washington, DC: American Psychological Association.

Wester, S. R., Crown, C., Quatman, G., & Heesacker, M. (1997). The influence of sexually violent rap music on attitudes of men with little prior exposure. *Psychology of Women Quarterly, 21,* 497–508.

Wingood, G. M., DiClemente, R. J., Bernhardt, J. M., Harrington, K., Davies, S. L., Robillard, A., et al. (2003). A prospective study of exposure to rap music videos and African American female adolescents' health. *American Journal of Public Health, 93,* 437–439.

12

RACISM, WHITE SUPREMACY, AND RESISTANCE

Contextualizing Black American Experiences

HELEN A. NEVILLE AND ALEX L. PIETERSE

What is racism? The word has represented daily reality to millions of black people for centuries. . . . [It consists of] the predication of decisions and polices on considerations of race for the purpose of subordinating a racial group and maintaining control over that group . . . Racism is both overt and covert . . . We call these individual racism and institutional racism. The first consists of overt acts by individuals, which cause death, injury or violent destruction of property . . . The second type originates in the operation of established and respected forces in the society, and thus receives far less public condemnation than the first type. (Carmichael & Hamilton, 1967/1992, pp. 3–4)

Racism consists of two interlocking dimensions: (a) an institutional mechanism [structural] of domination and (b) a corresponding ideological belief that justifies the oppression of people whose physical features and cultural patterns differ from those of the politically and socially dominated group—Whites. (Thompson & Neville, 1999, p. 163)

Any doctrine of superiority based on racial differentiation is scientifically false, morally condemnable, socially unjust and dangerous, and . . . there is no justification for racial discrimination, in theory or in practice, anywhere. (United Nations, 1965, p. 1)

We began this chapter with three quotes to contextualize the topic of White supremacy and racism and their influence on the lived experiences of Black people throughout the Diaspora. Stokley Carmichael (aka Kwame Ture) and Charles Hamilton, in their call for Black Power a little over 30 years ago, eloquently identified the types and processes of racism. Drawing on their arguments, the hanging of the noose at the "White" tree at Jena High School in Jena, Louisiana, in late 2006 represents an act of individual racism; however, the arrests and excessive charges against the six Black teenagers accused of beating a White male peer in the aftermath of the incident reflects racial discrimination in the justice system (a component of institutional racism). Racism clearly is more complex than outward expressions; it is part of a larger social design intended to create racial stratification consisting of a privileged race and oppressed racial groups.

In their treatise on racism and mental health, psychologists Thompson and Neville (1999) drew on the interdisciplinary literature to highlight the structural and ideological foundations of racism. They argued that beliefs about the superiority/inferiority of racial groups (ideology) and the organization of society in terms of political, economic, educational, and social institutions (structural) operate in a discursive manner to rationalize and perpetuate racial privilege and domination. Scholars across disciplines have documented the profound toll of racism on nearly every aspect of human life, ranging from psychological adjustment to educational attainment and economic security.

In this chapter, we use the terms *White supremacy* and *racism* to denote a system of racial oppression. Although the terms are similar, *racism* is broader in scope and applies to "any distinction, exclusion, restriction or preference based on race, colour, descent, or national or ethnic origin" (United Nations, 1965, p. 2). This inclusive definition encompasses multiple types of ethnic discrimination in which an ethnic group in power supports scripts of superiority/inferiority and corresponding policies and practices that reinforce the domination/subjugation of the ethnic groups in all public and private spheres, such as the oppression of Koreans in Japan and the genocide of the Black African ethnic groups by the Arabs in Sudan. Thus, we included the concept of White supremacy to underscore the type of racism most relevant to the field of African American Psychology; that is, a system in which Whites, particularly the socioeconomic elite, have established and maintained an unfair system serving to systematically exclude the full participation and development of Blacks in a given society. White supremacy also provides a framework in which to understand the uneven development of communities and their members in countries that are predominantly Black but have (partial) White control through current social capital and/or economics, such as the Republic of South Africa and the island of Bermuda.

We believe a strength of African American Psychology is the placement of human behavior within a larger context. That is why the growing theoretical and empirical work on racism in the field is not at all surprising. A search of the *Journal of Black Psychology* indicates that about 10% of the articles published in the journal focus on racism. In this chapter, we propose a psychosocial model of racism (PMR) to (a) provide an integrative framework to help organize this growing disparate, but interrelated, psychologically based research and (b) provide guidance to future research and practice. We provide an overview of the model (see Figure 12.1) and empirical literature.

Historical Context of the Psychosocial Model of Racism

Although psychologists have historically challenged racist scholarship in the field and in society, publications of the theoretical articulations of racism did not appear until the emergence of the modern Civil Rights movement in the 1950s. During this time, psychologists published tomes theorizing the characteristics of racial prejudice and its effect on both Black and Whites; this includes seminal texts such as Gordon Allport's (1954) *The Nature of Prejudice* and Kenneth Clark's (1955) *Prejudice and Your Child*. Shortly after these publications, Martiniquian psychiatrist Frantz Fanon penned *The Wretched of the Earth* (1961/1963) and *Black Skin, White Masks* (1967); these texts are arguably the most insightful and influential on the psychology of racial domination, subjugation, and liberation. In addition to emerging scholarship on racism and White supremacy, at this time, we witness the rise for Black power and the demand to legitimize the intellectual integrity of the study of Blacks throughout the Diaspora. Psychologists in the United States responded to this call in a number of ways, including the formation of the Association of Black Psychologists and subsequently the *Journal of African American Psychology*. There were curricular demands for the training of all psychologists as well. For example, Leslie Hicks (1969) urged psychology training programs to offer courses on the Black

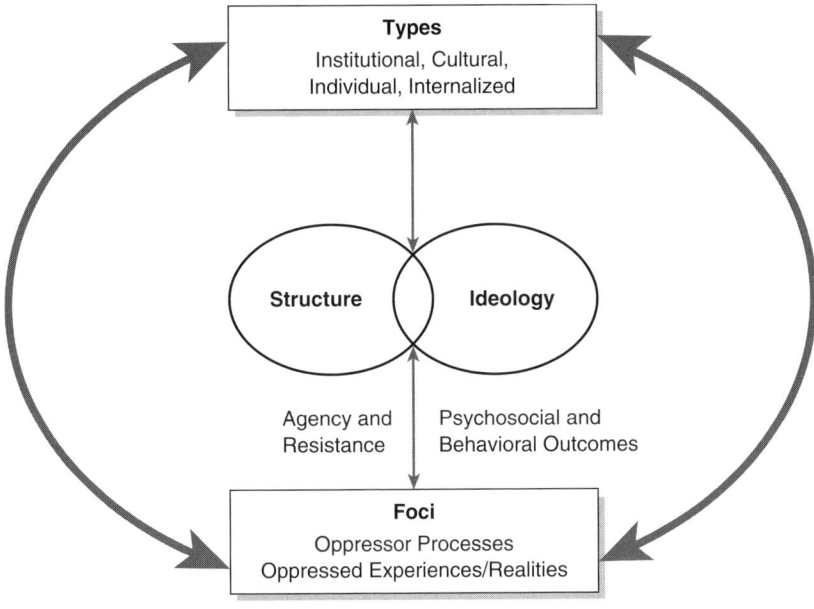

Figure 12.1 Psychosocial Model of Racism

experience, which he argued would begin with the study of racism. It was not until the 1970s that consistent scholarship on racism in the psychological literature emerged with the publications of works such as *White Racism: A Psycho-History* (Kovel, 1970), and another two decades passed before the explosion of empirical research on the association between perceived racism on psychological and physical health. Although the definitions of racism have tended to include the systemic and institutional nature on racial oppression, the research has primarily focused on individual perceptions of racism. In this regard, a model that explicitly outlines the range of psychosocial processes associated with the phenomenon of racism, and the manner in which these processes might impact the psychological functioning of Black Americans, could be of value in furthering our understanding of the manner in which racism is experienced, negotiated, and resisted.

THE PSYCHOSOCIAL MODEL OF RACISM: CONCEPTUAL TENETS AND EMPIRICAL RESEARCH

Building on the African American psychological conceptions of racism articulated by Jones (1972, 1997) and Thompson and Neville (1999), as well as the interdisciplinary research, the PMR seeks to provide a framework to place psychological research within a more systems-level analysis. Our attempt also helps address the failure of psychologists to locate the ideology of racism within a larger context of dominance and subjugation as evidenced by such global phenomenon as imperialism, patriarchy, and capitalism. The PMR recognizes that social processes are dynamic and are influenced and changed by both internal and external processes. Thus, the racial structure and ideology in the United States influence, and are influenced by, current manifestations of racism around the globe.

Racial Structure and Ideology

At the core of racism and White supremacy are those historical and contemporary systematic practices that have created a racially hierarchical society in which Whites have unearned privileges and nondominant racialized groups experience labor exploitation and disadvantage. Throughout history, a corresponding set of complex ideas and interpretative lenses have been established to rationalize and perpetuate these inhumane practices. The ideology of scientific racism served as the foundation of the eugenics movement at the turn of the 20th century and was used to justify the creation of apartheid in South Africa (e.g., publications were widely disseminated providing "justifications" for maintaining racial boundaries and inequalities). Just as the expressions of racism have changed over time, space, and location, so too have the ideologies that have been used to legitimize the racial status quo. In the post–Civil Rights movement era, color-blind racial beliefs serve as a dominant racial ideology to cover up and explain away racial disparities (cf. Bonilla-Silva, 2003); according to this framework, as a society, we have "moved beyond" race and racism, and thus, any potential group differences are due to other factors, such as culture and social class. Thus, racial categorization is no longer the fundamental cause of the inequitable distribution of resources; however, social disadvantage is more likely to be associated with cultural and language differences, poverty, and moral lapses. Also noteworthy are the spaces capturing both structure and ideology, such as the media, politics, religious institutions, and the education system; these are larger systems in which ideological beliefs are embedded, created, and transferred.

Racial Structure. Psychologists' contribution to the racism literature is a keen examination of intrapsychic processes—the ways in which individuals interpret, experience, respond to, and are affected by racism. At the same time, though, there is limited problematization of the link between social structures, institutions, broader ideological positions and individual-level processes in the psychological literature. It is not surprising, then, that the research examining institutional and structural racism centers on the stress individuals report from the awareness of institutional racism as opposed to the actual way in which society is structured. Sociological researchers, however, have theorized and empirically investigated the role of racial stratification on mental health. For example, Gabbidon and Peterson (2006), using government databases and survey research, developed an index of living while Black to explore the influence of state-level processes on the psychological adjustment of Blacks. "Living while Black" was measured as the number or percentage of African Americans in each state who were in prison, uninsured, living in poverty, or were victims of homicide or infant mortality. The results suggest that death and economic problems were significantly related to poorer quality of life among Black Americans. LaVeist (2003), using data from the National Survey of Black Americans, reported that Black individuals living in segregated communities had higher rates of mortality even after controlling for age, health status, and other factors associated with mortality. Findings such as these emphasize the role racial stratification continues to play within U.S. society, a society that remains clearly structured according to a distinct racial hierarchy.

White Supremacy and Other Racial Ideologies. In contemporary U.S. society, racial ideology works in a subtle and covert manner; it is often hidden through nonracial rhetoric such as a class analysis that ignores the fact that within the United States class is highly racialized. Furthermore, because of the inequitable distribution of resources across racial groups, nondominant racial groups tend to be lower than their White counterparts on a range of social indicators, such as level of education and occupational status. Thus, although the narrative of White superiority is now publicly disavowed, the racial hierarchy functions in such a way that nondominant groups continue to experience the deleterious effects of social inequity.

One cannot ignore, however, the influence of dominant racial stereotypes (a form of ideology) on our daily realities. African American psychologists have developed models to explain the ways in which Black individuals adhere to *dominant racial scripts* (an aspect of internalized White supremacy beliefs) and *counterracial scripts*—scripts in which individuals name racism and develop a positive identity that challenges racist assumptions and embraces racial pride. Cokley and Chapman (Chap. 21, this volume) discuss at length racial identity models, and later in this chapter we summarize the literature on internalized racism. Acknowledging that dominant beliefs about race are necessarily gendered, a number of psychologists have begun to explore the role of gender-specific racial stereotypes or dominant beliefs. For example, Thomas, Witherspoon, and Speight (2004) examined the influence of the stereotypic roles for Black women (e.g., sapphire, mammy, Jezebel) on the psychological adjustment of a community sample of African American women. The findings suggest that the internalization of these constricting roles were related to lower levels of self-esteem.

Scholars have also theorized and empirically investigated articulations of *color-blind racial ideology*, or the dominant belief that racism is a thing of the past and does not explain current racial stratification. For example, Neville, Coleman, Falconer, and Holmes (2005) examined the association between racial color-blindness and self-reported psychological false consciousness (i.e., the internalization of dominant racial beliefs in which Blacks work against their individual and collective interest). As hypothesized, findings among a sample of college students and community members indicated that greater endorsement of racial color-blindness was associated with blaming Black individuals themselves for racial inequality, a strong belief in a hierarchical social structure, and internalized oppression. Collectively, these studies provide evidence of the role of dominant and counter-hegemonic racial messages (an aspect of ideology) on Black Americans' attitudes, beliefs, and psychosocial adjustment.

Racism Types

The iterative forces of racial structures and ideologies influence the types and expressions of racism. Jones's (1972, 1997) *tripartite model of racism* is among the most well-known definition of racism in psychology; the model outlines three basic types of racism: (1) *individual* (individual or interpersonal interactions designed to injure, denigrate, or deny services/goods to individuals from racial groups defined as inferior), (2) *institutional* (policies, practices, and norms that incidentally, but inevitably, perpetuate inequality by restricting opportunities of people of color), and (3) *cultural* (symbols and practices used to reinforce a belief in the racial superiority of Whites and the inferiority of nondominant racial groups). Psychologically oriented researchers have further complicated individual racism by proposing multiple subtypes, including *everyday racism* (Essed, 1991) and *microaggressions* (Pierce, 1975). Particularly relevant to the field of African American Psychology are the ways in which Black individuals and communities make sense of the ideology of White supremacy. We argue that *internalized racism*, or the acceptance of the dominant racial ideology among some Blacks, is a particularly relevant type or outcome of racism in our community. We are not suggesting that Black individuals create racial inequalities but that some Blacks, through acceptance of the dominant framework, help to support individual, institutional, and cultural racism.

In sum, the PMR provides a framework in which to appreciate and explore the intersecting nature of types of racism, the organizing function of racial ideology, and the psychosocial correlates of racism as experienced by Black Americans. We have argued for the utilization of the PMR in order to allow psychologists to more explicitly incorporate the ideological and structural aspects of racism structural levels in both scholarship and research. It could be instructive, therefore, to review and critique current approaches to the understanding of psychological responses among Black Americans to the phenomenon of racism.

Racism-Related Stress, Conceptual Models, and Empirical Findings

The bulk of psychological research assessing the influence of racism on its targets is built on the conceptual base of *perceived racism*, or the manner in which individuals interpret and process race-related encounters. As such, models designed to explicate the psychological processes associated with racism for Black Americans focus on the individual interpretations and responses to racism-related incidents. Incidents of discrimination, prejudice, and harassment experienced by Blacks have been identified as a unique type of life stress referred to as *race-* or *racism-related stress* (Utsey & Ponterotto, 1996).

Racism-Related Stress. Although there are numerous models outlining the impact and process of racism, two contemporary models have received growing attention: (1) Rodney Clark and colleagues' (Clark, Anderson, Clark, & Williams, 1999) biopsychosocial model of racism and (2) Shelly Harrell's (2000) multidimensional model of racism-related stress. Clark and colleagues' model is grounded in an interactional stress approach and includes the psychophysiological responses to perceptions of racism as stressors. Simply stated, Clark et al.'s model of racism-related stress views environmental stimuli, such as personal prejudice against Blacks or structural aspects of racism, as exerting a response that overwhelms the individual's normal coping mechanisms, thereby producing psychological and physiological responses that are detrimental to the individual's well-being. A critical aspect of the model, however, is the extent to which the individual perceives the stimuli as reflective of racism. Also, the model incorporates contextual factors, such as socioeconomic status, individual psychological constitution, and social support, as influential variables that either exacerbate or potentially buffer the stress response. Although there is little empirical evidence supporting the model as a whole, various aspects of it have undergone empirical examination. There is now a fairly robust body of work exploring the association between racism-related stress and cardiovascular reactivity (R. Clark, 2006) and well as studies examining the moderating role of individually based variables, such as Johnny Henryism (R. Clark & Adams, 2004) and racial identity (e.g., Sellers, Caldwell, Schmeelk-Cone, & Zimmerman, 2004).

Also drawing on the interactional model of stress, S. P. Harrell (2000) defined racism-related stress as "[t]he race-related transactions between individuals or groups and their environment that emerge from the dynamics of racism, and that are perceived to tax or exceed existing individual and collective resources or threaten well-being" (p. 44). Her model consists of five broad processes: (1) antecedent variables (e.g., personal and socioenvironmental factors that influence one's potential exposure to racism); (2) familial and socialization influences, including the messages individuals receive about race and racism from family and peers; (3) sources of stress including racism-related stress, other types of group identity stress, and generic stress; (4) internal (e.g., cultural worldview, coping styles) and external mediators (e.g., available institutional support) to help buffer the potential negative effects of racism-related stress; and (5) negative outcomes across a spectrum of psychological, physical, social, and spiritual dimensions. Of particular relevance are the six types of racism-related stress she proposed: (1) racism-related life events, (2) vicarious racism experiences, (3) daily racism microstressors, (4) chronic contextual stress, (5) collective experience of racism, and (6) transgenerational transmission of group trauma. Harrell suggested that racial–cultural worldviews that are consistent with one's racial–cultural heritage and a mature racial identity could serve as a protective factor in dealing with racism-related stress.

Using S. P. Harrell's (1997) Racism and Life Experiences Scales, researchers have been able to examine the manner in which experiences of racism, as described in Harrell's (2000) model, are associated with various psychological outcomes. Measures taken from the Racism and Life Experiences Scales have been used in a range of empirical investigations (Paradies, 2006), with findings generally indicating that Black Americans perceive racism as stressful and that the experiences of racism tend to have adverse psychosocial outcomes. For example, Caughy, O'Campo, and Muntaner (2004) found, on the basis of parent reports, that preschool-age children with significant racism experiences had lower levels of well-being, and Peters (2004), in a survey of 162 African American adults, reported that experiences of racism were positively associated with anger suppression.

There are a number of additional measures of racism-related stress in the extant literature; each measure assesses different sources of perceived types of stressors. For example, Utsey and Ponterotto's (1996) Index of Race-Related Stress is the first measure of racism stress that we were able to locate. It assesses four dimensions of perceived racism influencing the individual and Black people collectively: (1) cultural racism, (2) institutional racism, (3) individual racism, and (4) collective racism. A complete review of these measures is beyond the scope of this chapter. We refer the reader to Utsey's (1998) excellent review of six race-related stress instruments and their psychometric properties.

Race-Based Traumatic Stress. Some scholars argue that the persistence of racial discrimination is not only stressful but is in fact traumatic. According to Root (1992), race-based trauma is

> insidious trauma [and] is usually associated with the social status of an individual being devalued because a characteristic intrinsic to their identity is different to what is valued by those who are in power . . . As a rule insidious trauma's effects are cumulative and directed toward a community of people. (p. 240)

Carter's (2007) race-based traumatic stress model is among the few psychological models in this area. Although acknowledging the insidious nature of trauma as described by Root, Carter defined race-based traumatic stress in more psychological terms, indicating that it is "emotional or physical pain or the threat of physical and emotional pain that results from racism in the forms of racial harassment(hostility), racial discrimination (avoidance), or discriminatory harassment (aversive hostility)" (p. 88). Carter's model therefore incorporates a conceptual frame in which to deconstruct racism-related experiences and to describe the psychological reactions to these experiences as emotionally injurious and/or traumatic.

Carter's race-based traumatic stress model consists of three data-driven categories: (1) *racial discrimination*, or those thoughts, behaviors, and policies that both intentionally and unintentionally result in the creation of distance between the dominant and nondominant racial groups; (2) *racial harassment*, which consists of strategies employed to purposefully convey to nondominant racial groups their assumed "inferior status"; and (3) *discriminatory harassment*, which includes complex experiences and reactions that exhibit both elements of discrimination and harassment. Carter and colleagues' (Carter, Forsyth, Mazzula, & Williams, 2005) findings from an open-ended survey study with 323 people of color suggested that emotional and psychological responses to racist experiences varied according to the three categories of racism, with trauma-related responses being more reflective of discriminatory harassment category. The race-based traumatic stress model provides the opportunity to further our understanding of the psychological responses to racism in that it locates specific emotional responses to specific types of racism experiences. Furthermore, by describing the emotional/psychological response as "injury," Carter emphasizes the psychological effects as racism as stemming from the sociocultural environment and not reflective of individual pathology.

Racial Microaggressions. Over the past few decades, social psychologists documented the shift in racism from the overt racism of the Jim Crow era to the more subtle process whereby White Americans, while holding onto egalitarian beliefs, continue to feel discomfort and negative feelings toward racial minorities in relation to people who are racially different, a phenomenon referred to as *aversive racism* (Gaertner & Dovidio, 1986). Thus, although intentional acts of hostility and discrimination might be disavowed, more unintentional behaviors consistent with avoidance and minimization of racial others continue to provide racism with it ubiquitous hold on American society. Pierce (1975) was one of the first authors to refer to these so-called unintentional behaviors as a type of microaggression. Later, Pierce (1995) offered the following definition and analysis of microaggressions:

> Microaggressions ... are subtle, innocuous, preconscious, or unconscious degradations, and putdowns, often kinetic, but capable of being verbal and/or kinetic. In and of itself a microaggression may seem harmless, but the cumulative burden of a lifetime of microaggressions can theoretically contribute to diminished mortality, augmented morbidity and flattened confidence. (p. 281)

A full appreciation of microaggressions, however, can stem only from a recognition of the ideology of White superiority; thus, microaggressions can be viewed as a natural and necessary product of the racial hierarchy. In order for the racial hierarchy to be maintained, individuals of African descent are essentialized and objectified. The types of microaggression offered by Sue et al. (2007) are illustrative of the manner in which Black Americans tend to be responded to or interacted with on the basis of an essentialized or objectified representation as opposed to an acknowledgement of their individualized and subjective existence.

One specific microaggression noted by A. J. Franklin (1999) pertains to the experience of invisibility among African American men. This "invisibility syndrome" is thought to be a phenomenon whereby, irrespective of accomplishments, Black men continue to be reacted to on the basis of stereotypical notions of inferior intelligence, criminality, and danger. The consistent exposure to racial microaggressions is understood to have a detrimental effect on well-being. It is important to note, however, that research exploring psychological responses to microaggressions is very much in its infancy. Methodological approaches have included qualitative inquiry and the development of a brief measure designed to assess microaggressions in the context of counseling relationships (Constantine, 2007).

It is important to note that although microaggressions can clearly have a negative effect on perceptions of the self and psychological well-being (e.g., Sue et al., 2007), by focusing on the distorted ideology and the racial hierarchy that produces microaggressions the personal impact of the aggression could potentially be blunted. A consistent recognition of racism as an organizing principle of social structure might allow Black Americans to perceive racial microaggressions as symbolic of a pathological ideology and thus blunt the power of these experiences. It also might be useful to view microaggressions as a logical outcome of the ideology of racism as opposed to a central construct. Note that the extent to which a microaggression might be traumatic is largely informed by the subjective experience of its target. Simply stated, all Black Americans experience racism; however, all Black Americans might not report experiencing microaggressions. An overemphasis on the subjective experience of racism might have the unintended consequence of moving the focus away from the effect of systemic and institutional forces that cannot be explained by perception or subjective experience (see Gee, 2002).

Internalized Racism (or Psychic Trauma). Racism has long been viewed as having significant psychological aspects. Fanon (1961/1963) spoke in terms of racism leading to alienation—alienation from self, from significant others, from one's culture and history, and from self-determination and access to various forms of social power. Arguably, one of the most powerful structures of oppression and exploitation has been the "appropriation of the means and resources of identity" (Hook, 2005, p. 482) that accompanied the historical appropriation of lands and bodies of Black populations via colonization and slavery. *Internalized racism* "refers to the acceptance by marginalized racial populations, of the negative societal beliefs and stereotypes about themselves" (Williams & Williams-Morris, 2000, p. 225). Yet, to fully appreciate the process of internalized racism, one has to appreciate the manner in which racism is maintained. Fanon interrogated racism from the perspective of systematic violence. In this regard, the linkages between racism as an economic, cultural, psychological, and social means of oppression highlights the manner in which Black Americans might come to internalize a false consciousness in relation to their individual and collective identities in comparison to Whites. Racism as a system built on colonization and slavery has included the stripping away of a cultural and historical identity—indeed, antiracism scholars have emphasized the need for Black Americans to grieve the loss of their heritage and to seek ways in which to recapture a collective identity built on common elements of their African heritage (Wallace, 2006). Thus, although significant gains have been made through the Civil Rights Movement and other forms of national independence, the ongoing devaluing of historical and cultural identities, the lack of consistently seeing cultural representations of oneself in social positions of power, mean that the mechanism through which internalized racism becomes a psychological process for Black Americans remains very much in place.

A small body of research has examined psychosocial correlates of internalized racism among African Americans. Taylor and Grundy (1996) developed the Nadanolization Scale to examine the manner in which internalized racism relates to psychological and health-related outcomes. Research in this area suggests that internalized racism is associated with such physiological processes as the development of glucose intolerance and the distribution of abdominal fat (Chambers, Tull, & Fraser, 2004), reports of decreased marital satisfaction by husbands (Washington, 1997), depressive symptoms (Taylor, Henderson, & Jackson, 1991), and increased stress levels as measured by cortisol levels (Tull, Sheu, & Butler, 2005). The extent to which internalized racism might be associated with other psychosocial outcomes is, however, unclear. To illustrate, Harper (2006) reported no association in a sample of Black male college students between internalized racism and academic performance.

Racism Foci

The research in the general discipline of psychology has traditionally focused on the articulation of types of expressions of individual-level racism or the way in which larger racial processes influence White Americans' attitudes and behaviors. The work in this area is wide ranging and includes the examination of racial prejudice (including expressions of modern, ambivalent, and aversive racism; see Devine, Plant, & Blair, 2001, for a review of this literature); racial identity (e.g., Helms, 1990); and, more recently, psychosocial costs of racism to Whites (Spanierman & Heppner, 2005; Utsey, McCarthy, Adrian, & Eubanks, 2002) and antiracism activism (Green & Sonn, 2005). This research is important in developing a critical understanding of Whiteness; however, the scholarship in African American Psychology centers on the exploration of the nature and consequences of (perceived) racism on Black populations. That is why the preceding review of types of racism and the following discussion of agency and psychological correlates focus on the experiences of Black individuals.

Psychosocial and Physical Outcomes: Correlates of Racism for Black Americans

A growing body of research indicates that experiences of racism are linked to psychological distress; decreased quality of life; and specific physiological disorders, such as hypertension (see Paradies, 2006). A review of the empirical literature provides much evidence for the association between racism-related stress and a range of general psychological, affective, and cognitive outcomes. To illustrate, perceived racism has been noted to be associated with symptoms of obsessive–compulsive disorder and somatization (Klonoff, Landrine, & Ullman, 1999), anxiety and hypervigilance (J. P. Harrell, Hall, & Talieferro, 2003), feelings of depression (e.g., Taylor & Turner, 2002), higher levels of psychological distress (e.g., Pieterse & Carter, 2007), feelings hopelessness (e.g., Nyborg & Curry, 2003), and lowered academic performance (e.g., Cohen & Steele, 2002).

Research in health-related topics also suggests that experiences of (perceived) racism have been found to be positively associated with increased cardiovascular reactivity (e.g., Guyll, Matthews, & Bromberger, 2001), glucose intolerance (e.g., Tull & Chambers, 2001), hypertension (e.g., Brondolo, Rieppi, Kelly, & Gerin, 2003), low birth weight (Collins, David, & Handler, 2004), and smoking behavior (e.g., Landrine & Klonoff, 1996). Thus, the current research indicates that perceive racism is associated with adverse health-related outcomes, particularly in the case of mental health (Carter, 2007).

A number of scholars have also examined individual and sociocultural factors that mediate and moderate the link between perceived racism and health outcomes. Shawn Utsey and his colleagues have completed several studies in this area. For example, Utsey et al. (2006) found that cognitive ability and social support conjointly moderated the link between race-related stress (particularly individual and cultural) and quality of life among a community sample of Black Americans. Utsey is also interested in understanding race-related correlates of racism. Utsey, Bolden, and Brown (2001) proposed six categories of reactions to racism to better describe the race-specific psychological responses to racism among Black Americans: (1) race-related trauma, (2) racism-related fatigue, (3) anticipatory racism reaction, (4) race-related distress, (5) racism-related confusion, and (6) racism-related frustration. These categories represent a fairly comprehensive yet untested description of the types of race-specific psychological and emotional sequelae associated with responding to, reacting to, and experiencing racist events, and it could provide a useful framework for future research.

(Black) Agency and Resistance

Although White supremacy is pervasive, people resist and challenge racial oppression at every turn. Resistance can take many forms, including responding directly to the incident at an individual or microlevel (e.g., confronting perpetrators through comments or actions, e.g., a boycott), a policy level (e.g., helping to implement policies to challenge racism on the job, in education, or in society, e.g., the passage of hate crime laws), and a macrolevel in which larger social relations are challenged (e.g., the Black Power Movement in the United States and anticolonial movements throughout the Diaspora in the 1960s and beyond). Thus, although racism and White supremacy have influenced the life experiences of people throughout the Diaspora, Blacks have individually and collectively challenged these forces to help transform interpersonal and sociopolitical conditions.

There is a growing body of literature examining the mediating and moderating role of coping in explaining the link between perceived racism and health. In her qualitative study with approximately 200 Black women, Shorter-Gooden (2004) uncovered a number of strategies women used to manage the ill effects of racism, including internal (i.e., resting on faith, standing on the shoulders of others who have gone before, valuing the self) and external strategies (e.g., leaning on the shoulders of others to gain social support) as well as specific coping strategies to deal with "isms" (including standing up and fighting back).

The coping literature has examined the ways in which people manage the stress associated with experiencing racism. The focus on agency (or self-activity) and resistance, on the other hand, speaks to actions taken to challenge and disrupt racism. We view Shorter-Gooden's (2004) findings around standing up and fighting back as exemplifying antiracism resistance activity. It is interesting that Blacks are invisible in the antiracism psychology research, as if to suggest only White individuals are engaged in doing work to challenge racism or that engagement in antiracism activity is a natural occurrence for Blacks and thus not worthy of investigation. Janet Swim and her colleagues' (Swim, Hyers, Cohen, Fitzgerald, & Bylsma, 2003) diary study began to address the gap in the literature by identifying a number of strategies (or "behavioral responses," p. 56) Black men and women use to counter experiences with everyday racist incidents. In their small sample, the majority of participants either directly confronted the perpetrator (42%) or indirectly challenged the incident (21%) through acts such as ending the interaction or boycotting the perpetrator; only one third of the participants did not indicate a behavioral response designed to disrupt the racist encounter. There is some evidence suggesting that individual-level resistance to racial discrimination is related to better health outcomes. In their large-scale prospective study of Black and White women, Krieger and Sidney (1996) found that working-class women in the sample who challenged racial discrimination reported lower levels of systolic blood pressure compared with women who did not actively challenge the incidents.

The power of racism ultimately lies in its ability to shape the social experiences of people according to their racial group membership; the power of antiracism, however, is in placing the focus of racism on challenging racial ideology, on exposing the social structures that create and/or support the ideology, and in providing Black Americans with the psychological tools claim their own liberation as opposed to requesting the oppressor to behave differently. Roderick Watts and his colleagues (Watts, Abdul-Adil, & Pratt, 2002) developed an innovative culturally appropriate program designed to increase the critical consciousness of young African American men. A central goal of the "Young Warriors" program is to increase critical thinking skills about the sociopolitical and racial landscape in which one lives; the program is also designed to increase media literacy and liberation behaviors. Thus, these community psychologists are interested in working with young men to challenge internalized racism, critically evaluate the messages they have received, and acquire skills to disrupt racism.

Conclusion and Future Directions

We presented the PMR to help organize and structure the disparate psychological research on racism and to help inform future research directions. We have argued that racial structure and ideology serve as the core of racism and White supremacy and that these overlapping processes influence the types or ways in which racism is expressed in a given society. In examining racism, researchers can focus on processes related to the dominant racial group (i.e., Whites), the experiences of nondominant racial groups, or their interaction. The PMR also accounts for self-activity and the way in which individuals and communities can participate in or challenge the racial status quo as well as the potential impact of racism and resistance on psychosocial outcomes.

Of particular interest to us in this chapter were the structural and ideological foundations of racism and White supremacy and their roles in shaping racial stratification and health disparities, primarily in the United States. Unlike the broader discipline of psychology, the crux of the research in African American Psychology serves to understand the profound influence of racism on the lives of Black individuals. As psychologists, research in our field has tended to emphasize the intrapsychic nature of racism through the exploration of perceived racism as a source of stress. A number of comprehensive racism stress models exist in the literature, albeit with limited empirical testing. A strength of the field is in the articulation of types of racism Blacks experience, including racial trauma, microaggressions, and internalized racism. This body of work is a critical step in describing the deleterious effects of racism. At the same time, other dimensions are important as well, including the ways in which Black individuals resist racism in everyday practices and larger organized efforts.

The role of structural racism and the influence of Black agency are among the least empirically examined components of the PMR. Additional state- or institutional-level analyses of racism and their influence on psychological processes are needed. This research necessarily extends beyond the examination of perceived racism to include the influence of observed racial incidents in an institution and/or specific forms of racial stratification (e.g., school achievement gap, pay inequity in a job, racial job stratification in a neighborhood) on mental health and psychological behaviors. Of particular importance to this area of inquiry is attention to developmental issues across the life span (e.g., documenting the experiences of youth, young adults, and older adults). At this point, we also know very little about the potential buffering role of antiracism activism on psychological and behavioral processes, including self-efficacy, leadership skills, career development, political behaviors, psychological adjustment, hope, authenticity, and so on.

Although there is a wealth of empirical studies documenting the association between perceived racism and health outcomes, a number of areas of inquiry are worthy of further investigation. For example, what is the role of a White supremacy or other dominant racial ideology both at the individual level and at an institutional or group level on health and related behaviors? Also, we do not have a clear sense of the differential influence of types (and manifestations) of racism on specific psychological outcomes. Some initial research indicates that everyday racism plays a more powerful role in adjustment over time than do major racial stressors. However, the question remains: Which types of everyday racism or microaggressions are the most influential, on what outcomes, and for whom? Moreover, is perceived racism more important than institutional or structural racism in regard to health outcomes?

A number of studies have included gender in their analyses, and several studies have focused on the experiences on either women or men. However, there is a paucity of investigations examining the influence of gendered racism on the health of men and women. For example, the microaggressions related to "driving while Black" or being treated as if one is a violent criminal are generally targeted toward men. What are the effects of these gendered expressions of racism? Similarly, we know almost nothing about the types of racism that gay, lesbian, and bisexual individuals experience. In essence, we argue that greater attention be paid to the ways in which intersectionality plays a role in the structure, experience, and consequences of racism.

In addition to further problematizing aspects of the PRM, more methodological development is needed. Research examining the link between racism and mental health in psychology relies on correlational designs. Mixed-method approaches, along with longitudinal designs, ethnographic inquiries, and interpretative and archival research are needed to further explore the nuances of the context and consequences of racism. In emphasizing the social context of racial hierarchies, the PRM might allow researchers to move beyond perceived racism and examine the extent to which racism has a psychological impact irrespective of one's acknowledgment of being exposed to racist experiences.

References

Allport, G. (1954). *The nature of prejudice*. Boston: Beacon Press.

Bonilla-Silva, E. (2003). *Racism without racists: Color-blind racism and the persistence of racial inequality in the United States*. Boulder, CO: Rowman and Littlefield.

Brondolo, E., Rieppi, R., Kelly, K. P., & Gerin, W. (2003). Perceived racism and bloop pressure: A review of the literature and conceptual and methodological critique. *Annals of Behavioral Medicine, 25*, 55–65.

Carmichael, S., & Hamilton, C. V. (1992). *Black power: The politics of liberation*. New York: Vintage. (Original work published 1967)

Carter, R. T. (2007). Racism and psychological and emotional injury: Recognizing and assessing race-based traumatic stress. *The Counseling Psychologist, 35,* 13–105.

Carter, R. T., Forsyth, J. M., Mazzula, S. L., & Williams, B. (2005). Racial discrimination and raced-based traumatic stress: An exploratory investigation. In R. T. Carter (Ed.), *The handbook of racial-cultural psychology and counseling* (Vol. II, pp. 447–476). Hoboken, NJ: Wiley.

Caughy, M. O., O'Campo, P. J., & Muntaner, C. (2004). Experiences of racism among African American parents and the mental health of their preschool-aged children. *American Journal of Public Health, 94,* 2118–2124.

Chambers, E. C., Tull, E. S., & Fraser, H. S. (2004). The relationship of internalized racism to body fat distribution and insulin resistance among African adolescent youth. *Journal of the National Medical Association, 96,* 1594–1598.

Clark, K. (1955). *Prejudice and your child.* Oxford, UK: Beacon Press.

Clark, R. (2006). Perceived racism and vascular reactivity in Black college women: moderating effects of seeking social support. *Health Psychology, 25,* 20–25.

Clark, R., & Adams, J. H. (2004). Moderating effects of perceived racism on John Henryism and blood pressure reactivity in Black female college students. *Annals of Behavioral Medicine, 28,* 126–131.

Clark, R., Anderson, N., Clark, V. R., & Williams, D. R. (1999). Racism as a stressor for African Americans: A biopsychosocial model. *American Psychologist, 54,* 805–816.

Cohen, G. L., & Steele, C. M. (2002). A barrier of mistrust: How negative stereotypes affect cross-race mentoring. In J. Aaronson (Ed.), *Improving academic achievement: Impact of psychological factors on education* (pp. 303–327). San Diego, CA: Academic Press.

Collins, J. W., David, R. H., & Handler, A. (2004). Very low birthweight in African American infants: The role of maternal exposure to interpersonal racial discrimination. *American Journal of Public Health, 94,* 2132–2138.

Constantine, M. G. (2007). Racial microaggressions against African American clients in cross-racial counseling relationships. *Journal of Counseling Psychology, 54,* 1–16.

Devine, P. G., Plant, E. A., & Blair, I. (2001). Classic and contemporary analyses of prejudice. In R. Brown & S. L. Gaertner (Eds.), *The Blackwell handbook in social psychology: Vol. 4. Intergroup processes* (pp. 198–217). Oxford, UK: Blackwell.

Essed, P. (1991). *Understanding everyday racism.* Newbury Park, CA: Sage.

Fanon, F. (1963). *Wretched of the earth.* New York: Grove Press. (Original work published 1961)

Fanon, F. (1967). *Black skin, White masks.* New York: Grove Press.

Franklin, A. J. (1999). Invisibility syndrome and racial identity development in psychotherapy and counseling African American men. *The Counseling Psychologist, 27,* 761–793.

Gabbidon, S. L., & Peterson, S. A. (2006). Living while Black—A state-level analysis of the influence of select social stressors on the quality of life among Black Americans. *Journal of Black Studies, 37,* 83–102.

Gaertner, S. L., & Dovidio, J. F. (1986). The aversive form of racism. In J. F. Dovidio & S. L. Gaertner (Eds.), *Prejudice, discrimination, and racism* (pp. 61–90). San Diego, CA: Academic Press.

Gee, G. C. (2002). A multilevel analysis of the relationship between institutional and individual racial discrimination and health status. *American Journal of Public Health, 92,* 615–623.

Green, M. J., & Sonn, C. S. (2005). Examining discourses of Whiteness and the potential for reconciliation *Journal of Community and Applied Social Psychology, 15,* 478–492.

Guyll, M., Matthews, K. A., & Bromberger, J. T. (2001). Discrimination and unfair treatment: Relationship to cardiovascular reactivity among African American and European American women. *Health Psychology, 20,* 315–325.

Harper, S. R. (2006). Peer support for African American male college achievement: Beyond internalized racism and the burden of "acting White." *Journal of Men's Studies, 14,* 337–358.

Harrell, J. P., Hall, S. P., & Taliaferro, J. (2003). Physiological responses to racism and discrimination: An assessment of the evidence. *American Journal of Public Health, 93,* 243–248.

Harrell, S. P. (1997). *The Racism and Life Experiences Scales.* Unpublished instrument.

Harrell, S. P. (2000). A multidimensional conceptualization of racism-related stress: Implications for the well-being of people of color. *American Journal of Orthopsychiatry, 70,* 42–57.

Helms, J. E. (Ed.). (1990). *Black and White racial identity: Theory, research, and practice.* Westport, CT: Greenwood Press.

Hicks, L. H. (1969). Black studies in psychology. *American Psychologist, 24,* 759–761.

Hook, D. (2005). A critical psychology of the postcolonial. *Theory & Psychology, 15,* 475–503.

Jones, J. (1972). *Prejudice and racism.* New York: McGraw-Hill.

Jones, J. (1997). *Prejudice and racism* (2nd ed.). New York: McGraw-Hill.

Klonoff, E. A., Landrine, H., & Ullman, J. B. (1999). Racial discrimination and psychiatric symptoms among Blacks. *Cultural Diversity and Ethnic Minority Psychology, 5,* 329–339.

Kovel, J. (1970). *White racism: A psycho-history.* New York: Pantheon.

Krieger, N., & Sidney, S. (1996). Racial discrimination and blood pressure: The CARDIA study of young Black and White adults. *American Journal of Public Health, 86,* 1370–1378.

Landrine, H., & Klonoff, E. A. (1996). The Schedule of Racist Events: A measure of racial discrimination and a study of its negative physical and mental health consequences. *Journal of Black Psychology, 22,* 144–168.

LaVeist, T. A. (2003). Racial segregation and longevity among African Americans: An individual-level analysis. *Health Services Research, 38,* 1719–1734.

Neville, H. A., Coleman, M. N., Falconer, J. W., & Holmes, D. (2005). Color-blind racial ideology and psychological false consciousness among African Americans. *Journal of Black Psychology, 31,* 27–45.

Nyborg, V. M., & Curry, J. F. (2003). The impact of racism: Psychological symptoms among African American boys. *Journal of Clinical Child and Adolescent Psychology, 32,* 258–266.

Paradies, Y. (2006). A systematic review of empirical research on self-reported racism and health. *International Journal of Epidemiology, 35,* 888–901.

Peters, R. M. (2004). Racism and hypertension among African Americans. *Western Journal of Nursing Research, 26,* 612–631.

Pierce, C. M. (1975). A report on minority children. *Psychiatric Annals, 5,* 244–246.

Pierce, C. M. (1995). Stress analogs of racism and sexism: Terrorism, torture, and disaster. In C. V. Willie, P. P. Rieker, B. M. Kramer, & B. S. Brown (Eds.), *Mental health, racism, and sexism* (pp. 277–278). Pittsburgh, PA: University of Pittsburgh Press.

Pieterse, A. L., & Carter, R. T. (2007). An examination of the relationship between general life stress, racism-related stress, and psychological health among Black men. *Journal of Counseling Psychology, 54,* 101–109.

Root, M. P. (1992). Reconstructing the impact of trauma on personality. In L. S. Brown & M. Ballou (Eds.), *Personality and psychopathology: Feminist perspectives* (pp. 229–265). New York: Guilford Press.

Sellers, R. M., Caldwell, C. H., Schmeelk-Cone, K. A., & Zimmerman, M. A. (2004). Racial identity, racial discrimination, perceived stress, and psychological distress among African American young adults. *Journal of Health and Social Behavior, 44,* 302–317.

Shorter-Gooden, K. (2004). Multiple resistance strategies: How African American women cope with racism and sexism. *Journal of Black Psychology, 30,* 406–425.

Spanierman, L. B., & Heppner, M. J. (2005). The Psychosocial Costs of Racism to Whites Scale (PCRW): Construction and initial validation. *Journal of Counseling Psychology, 51,* 249–262.

Sue, D. W., Capodilupo, C. M., Torino, G. C., Bucceri, J. M., Holder, A. M. B., Nadal, K. L., et al. (2007). Racial microaggressions in everyday life—Implications for clinical practice. *American Psychologist, 62,* 271–286.

Swim, J. K., Hyers, L. L., Cohen, L. L., Fitzgerald, D. C., & Bylsma, W. H. (2003). African American college students' experiences with everyday racism: Characteristics of and responses to these incidents. *Journal of Black Psychology, 38,* 38–67.

Taylor, J., & Grundy, C. (1996). Measuring Black internalization of White stereotypes about African Americans: The Nadanolitization Scale. In R. L. Jones (Ed.), *Handbook of tests and measurements of Black populations* (Vol. 2, pp. 217–226). Hampton, VA: Cobb & Henry.

Taylor, J., Henderson, D., & Jackson, B. B. (1991). A holistic model for understanding and predicting depression in African American women. *Journal of Community Psychology, 19,* 306–320.

Taylor, J., & Turner, R. J. (2002). Perceived discrimination, social stress, and depression in the transition to adulthood. *Social Psychology Quarterly, 65,* 213–225.

Thomas, A. J., Witherspoon, K. M., & Speight, S. L. (2004). Toward the development of the Stereotypic Roles for Black Women Scale. *Journal of Black Psychology, 30,* 426–442.

Thompson, C. E., & Neville, H. A. (1999). Racism, mental health, and mental health practice. *The Counseling Psychologist, 27,* 155–223.

Tull, E. S., & Chambers, E. C. (2001). Internalized racism is associated with glucose intolerance among Black Americans in the U.S. Virgin Islands. *Diabetes Care, 24,* 1498.

Tull, E. S., Sheu, Y., & Butler, C. (2005). Relationships between perceived stress, coping behavior and cortisol secretion in women with high and low levels of internalized racism. *Journal of the National Medical Association, 97,* 206–212.

United Nations. (1965). *International Convention on the Elimination of All Forms of Racial Discrimination.* Retrieved January 5, 2008, from http://www.unhchr.ch/html/menu3/b/9.htm

Utsey, S. O. (1998). Assessing the stressful effects of racism: A review of instrumentation. *Journal of Black Psychology, 24,* 269–288.

Utsey, S. O., Bolden, M. A., & Brown, A. L. (2001). Visions of revolution from the spirit of Frantz Fanon: A psychology of liberation for counseling African Americans confronting societal racism and oppression. In J. G. Ponterotto, J. M. Casas, L. A. Suzuki, &

C. M. Alexander (Eds.), *The handbook of multicultural counseling* (2nd ed., pp. 290–310). Thousand Oaks, CA: Sage.

Utsey, S. O., Lanier, Y., Williams, O., III, Bolden, M., & Lee, A. (2006). Moderator effects of cognitive ability and social support on the relation between race-related stress and quality of life in a community sample of Black Americans. *Cultural Diversity and Ethnic Minority Psychology, 12,* 334–346.

Utsey, S. O., McCarthy, E., Adrian, G., & Eubanks, R. (2002). White racism and sub-optimal psychological functioning among White Americans: Implications for counseling and preventing prejudice. *Journal of Multicultural Counseling and Development, 30,* 81–95.

Utsey, S. O., & Ponterotto, J. G. (1996). Development and validation of the Index of Race Related Stress. *Journal of Counseling Psychology, 43,* 490–501.

Wallace, B. C. (2006). Healing collective wounds from racism: The Community Forum model. In M. C. Constantine & D. W. Sue (Eds.), *Addressing racism: Facilitating cultural competence in mental health and educational settings* (pp. 105–123). Hoboken, NJ: Wiley.

Washington, N. C. (1997). The relationship between internalized racism, locus of control, and marital satisfaction in African-Americans. *Dissertation Abstracts International, 57*(10B), 6658.

Watts, R., Abdul-Adil, J., & Pratt, T. (2002). Enhancing critical consciousness in young African American men: A psycho-educational approach. *Psychology of Men and Masculinity, 3,* 41–50.

Williams, D. R., & Williams-Morris, R. (2000). Racism and mental health: The African-American experience. *Ethnicity and Health, 5,* 243–268.

PART IV

EDUCATIONAL ISSUES

13

AFRICAN AMERICAN CHILDREN'S EARLY LEARNING AND DEVELOPMENT

Examining Parenting, Schools, and Neighborhood

IHEOMA U. IRUKA AND OSCAR BARBARIN

School readiness and academic preparedness of African American children are a continuing concern to many, including early childhood researchers and interventionists, school administrators, policy makers, and community leaders (Johnston & Viadero, 2000; U.S. Department of Education, 2005). Recognition of the lagging educational progress and patterns of subpar achievement among African American children have given rise to a push for greater understanding of the underlying causes. There are many theories of African American underachievement, such as genetic explanations and faulty neurodevelopment, but they account for only a tiny fraction of the affected population. This chapter focuses on the key ideas that dominate the literature and that have been strongly linked to children's early schooling: parenting and the home environment, school environment, and neighborhood effects. In addition to reviewing previous research, we summarize newly analyzed relevant data from a large national study; provide recommendation for parents, teachers, and communities; and suggest future steps.

Bronfenbrenner's (2000) ecological theory framed our review. He emphasized that the child's experiences are interconnected and embedded within four systems: the (1) microsystem, (2) mesosystem, (3) exosystem, and (4) macrosystem (Bronfenbrenner, 2000). The microsystem is the closest layer to the child and consists of the closest people in the child's life, such as family members, child-care teachers, and neighbors. The mesosystem is the connection across the microsystems, such as the connection between a child's teacher and his or her parent, or the neighborhood and the school. The exosystem comprises the social settings that indirectly influence the child, such as the lowered responsivity of a parent because of stress at work or government policies that affect child development programs. The macrosystem is the broadest environment. It focuses on the cultural values and customs and norms in the system, such as a child's ethnic group or a culture's belief that a parent is solely responsible for the child's well-being, which may lead to limited resources to assist parents, thus affecting parents' functioning and connection with the child's microsystem. According to Bronfenbrenner, the interconnection and interaction of these various systems form the basis for a child's development.

The home environment is very important to children's developmental outcomes, because it is the most direct influence in a child's microsystem. Children's adjustment to and success in school is unquestionably affected by the extent to which parents create a propitious environment at home that actively promotes an expanding knowledge of their world, skilled use of language, emergent reading, academic motivation, autonomy, persistence, and adherence to social rules. Parenting is conceptualized here as intentional activities in which parents engage with or for the benefit of their children. Parenting behaviors that have been the focus of studies include warmth and nurturance (i.e., sensitive and responsive parenting), discipline, teaching/didactic strategies, language use by parents, and provision of cognitively stimulating materials in the home (see Brooks-Gunn & Markman, 2005). As proximal processes, these parenting behaviors or practices have been found to mediate the relationship between distal factors, such as socioeconomic status or maternal education and children's cognitive and social development (Linver, Brooks-Gunn, & Kohen, 2002; Mistry, Biesanz, Taylor, Burchinal, & Cox, 2004). These parental practices arguably arise from traditions passed from one generation to another, supported by cultural views of childhood and child development. Furthermore, they channel children's behavior into a range of acceptable behaviors, attitudes, and values that parents think will prepare children to successfully meet the challenges they will encounter in life (Barbarin et al., in press).

African American Parenting and Children's Development: Role of Socioeconomic Status and Parenting Style

Research has shown that there are differences between African Americans and Whites in their parenting behaviors, particularly in teaching style, discourse strategies, control, and discipline, especially in the high use of punishment. However, these findings are moderated by the family's socioeconomic status (SES), an exosystem element. In other words, the association between African Americans' parenting behavior and children's schooling success has been found to differ across SES groups (J. Lee & Bowen, 2006); for example, parents of lower income are more likely to use coercive and harsher punitive measures. Many of the findings attributed to being African American are more properly attributed to having a low SES. This is true, for example, in the case of discourse, such as the use of dialogic practices. The term *dialogic practices* refers to the use of teaching strategies, such as asking questions, commenting with new information, and directing attention to critical features of a problem that leads a child to the solution (Haden, Ornstein, Eckerman, & Didow, 2001). These practices are especially important because of their strong empirical link to children's academic and social developmental outcomes (Cervantes, 2002; Haden et al., 2001; Hart & Risley, 1992). Dialogic practices occur at different rates depending on social class and ethnicity (Portes, Cuentas, & Zady, 2000). For example, compared with lower-SES African American mothers, higher-SES African American mothers are more likely to employ question-asking routines during reading, provide more object labels, provide a wider variety of words, sustain conversation topics, contingently respond to children's speech, and elicit talk from their children (Hammer & Weiss, 1999; Hart & Risley, 1992, 1995; National Research Council, 2000).

Parenting style is another major area that has been the focus of much research on parenting and child development. Four of the parenting typologies enumerated by Baumrind (1972) are (1) authoritative, (2) authoritarian, (3) permissive, and (4) dismissive parenting. Authoritarian parenting, one of the parental styles disproportionately associated with African American parents, is characterized by highly controlling, punitive, harsh, and intrusive behaviors and low warmth and responsiveness directed toward the child. It is thought that authoritarian parenting undermines children's autonomy and confidence. High parental control and harsh punishment have been linked empirically to negative child outcomes, including problems in the self-regulation of behavior and emotions (Heller & Baker, 2000; Mistry, Melsch, & Taheri-Kenari, 2003; Rubin, Burgess, Sawyer, & Hastings, 2003) but also, more important, to lower academic achievement (Culp, Hubbs-Tait, Cuilp, & Starost, 2001). Ethnic differences across SES have been observed in the use of harsh and intrusive parenting strategies (Dornbusch, Ritter, Leiderman, Roberts, & Fraleigh, 1987; McGroder, 2000), with African American mothers more likely to use explicit direction and control practices in teaching situations and the socialization of their children (Anderson-Yockel & Haynes, 1994; Delpit, 1988). For example, African American parents have been depicted as having an intrusive and controlling style that is characterized by being highly intrusive and overly involved in conversational and teaching situations. They often select the topic of conversation or play for their child, use direct commands to guide the child's behavior, intrude on the child's effort to complete a task, and give solutions—or take over entirely—rather than giving the child time to work through the task herself (Murray & Hornbaker, 1997).

Most of the ethnic comparative research on discipline and control styles has focused on African Americans and Whites, with some limited attention to Hispanic parents By implication, comparisons of African American with White mothers often lead to conclusions that African American mothers are less effective than White mothers because of their higher use of harsh and punitive parenting (Brooks-Gunn & Markman, 2005; Garcia Coll et al., 1996; McAdoo, 1988; Phinney & Landin, 1998). Such conclusions are premature and unwarranted, because these high-control behaviors and harsh punishments are not related to socioemotional and behavioral problems in African American children's development as they are for White children (Deater-Deckard & Dodge, 1997; Ispa et al., 2004). In other words, although research demonstrates that harsh and controlling parenting is associated with more behavioral problems, lower academic achievement, and more limited school success for children from White middle-class families, this relationship is not obtained for African American children (Baldwin, Baldwin, & Cole, 1990; Dornbusch, Ritter, & Steinberg, 1991). Moreover, "harsh" and controlling parenting accompanied by warmth and support, sometimes called *no-nonsense parenting* or *tough love*, have been found to be beneficial for African American children's development (Baldwin et al., 1990; Brody & Flor, 1998; Deater-Deckard & Dodge, 1997; McLoyd & Smith, 2002; Scott-Jones, 1987).

Differential Effects of Parenting

In addition to certain parenting behaviors and typologies not being necessarily detrimental to African American children's school success, it is also not clear whether the presence of certain presumably supportive parenting behaviors have the same positive effect on children's development across ethnic groups. Considering the amount of funding and resources invested in family programs on the basis of the assumption that these practices have similar effects across ethnic groups, clarity of the effect is of great importance. Using recently analyzed data from the Early Childhood Longitudinal Study—Kindergarten Cohort (ECLS–K), Barbarin and Aikens (2006) examined whether parenting practices and beliefs (e.g., children's knowledge of the alphabet, visits to the library, contact with child's teacher, frequency of time spent reading with child, and academic expectations) predicted children's kindergarten reading ability across ethnic groups. The ECLS–K is an ongoing longitudinal study following a representative sample of more than 21,000 socioeconomically and ethnically diverse American children from the time they began kindergarten in 1998–1999 until the eighth grade in 2007 (U.S. Department of Education, National Center for Education Statistics, 2006). The ECLS–K focuses on children's school experiences and their cognitive, social, and physical development, based on information provided by children, their families, teachers, and the schools. Time spent reading and storytelling with children did not contribute as much to African American children's reading ability as it did with White and Hispanic children. Other parenting practices, such as knowledge of the alphabet, academic expectations, and number and type of books owned were related to African American and White children's kindergarten reading ability; however, the effect was smaller for African Americans. These findings lead to the conclusion that although some frequently studied practices have effects that generalize across ethnic and racial groups, the effects for African Americans are muted. This raises questions about the extent to which existing research has sufficiently illuminated the processes and the configuration of practices through which African American families facilitate their children's academic development. Thus, advocating the use of a specific parenting behavior to promote academic development in one cultural group must be done with caution if applied to a different cultural group.

Understanding Culturally Relevant Parenting Practices Predictive of African American Children's Success

To better capture proximal parenting processes that are relevant to African American children's schooling, the sociocultural environment of African Americans must be researched from African Americans' point of view instead of compared with a Western, White, middle-class standard (Brooks-Gunn & Markman, 2005). As components of the macrosystem in the ecological framework, cultural views about children, the timing and content of their learning, and culturally based socialization goals may also influence parenting behaviors. For example, African American families are hesitant to employ dialogic practices, such as explain and expand/elaborate, because they are viewed initially as undermining parental authority, and African American parents respond negatively to the idea of inviting questions and responding freely to children's queries. They interpret these practices as contributing to a distorted and upside-down power dynamic that encourages children to question parents in a way that could ultimately undercut parents' capacity to direct child behavior and command strict, immediate, and unquestioning compliance. African American parents tend to look past the cognitive benefits of dialogic practices to the implications of these practices to guide and safeguard their children. To develop in the child the expectation that parents will explain and expand/elaborate may be viewed by African American families as a slippery slope leading to a child thinking that he or she is on an equal footing with parents. Consequently, interventions must recognize that definitions of competency vary according to the cultural context, with the realization that before one promotes particular parenting behaviors one must understand why a particular parenting behavior is preferred (Keller, 2003). In other words, parental beliefs, feelings, and knowledge about child-rearing practices and child development play important roles in affecting parents' behaviors and, in turn, children's academic success (Benasich & Brooks-Gunn, 1996).

Furthermore, culture gives rise to worldviews, which shape attitudes, beliefs, and expectations, and are then transmitted to children. Culture may influence the literacy environment through families' expectations and beliefs about what children should know, the ages at which particular kinds of knowledge are appropriate, and who is responsible for directing and facilitating children's learning. Partly a consequence of environmental demands and social conditions, such as discrimination, health issues, and neighborhood concerns, families differ in socialization goals and practices that might be reflected in, for example, beliefs about how children and parents should interact or the type of parenting behaviors that should be employed (Lambert et al., 1992; Lareau, 1989; Weisz, Sigman, Weiss, & Mosk, 1993).

The Role of School in African American Children's Learning

In addition to parenting, an important component of the microsystem of influences on African American children's readiness to learn and their school success is the teacher and the school/classroom/child-care environment. The quality of the education in public schools has received a great deal of attention for its contribution to and subsequent failure to reduce the achievement gap (Johnston & Viadero, 2000). Schools are differentially effective in structuring a learning environment suitable for diverse group of children learners (Au, 1998; Pallas, Natriello, & McDill, 1989). Admittedly, public schools struggle with issues of how best to serve diverse populations, particularly in the midst of recruiting and retaining adequately prepared teachers in sufficient numbers, developing relevant and engaging curricula for culturally diverse students, and addressing issues of accountability. In addition, schools are challenged to contend with cultural values and home environments that do not mesh well with the school value and environment.

The ECLS–K was used to examine the influence of schools on children's literacy achievement from kindergarten to third grade, above and beyond family characteristics (i.e., number of books in home, home literacy environment, and involvement in child's school) and neighborhood (i.e., home neighborhood safety and problems, school neighborhood problems and cleanliness, and community support for learning). Aikens and Barbarin (2008) found that school variables, such as school poverty status, peers' reading level, and frequency of children's participation in literacy-based activities, accounted for some difference in children's reading growth during the first 4 years of school but had a minimal effect on initial reading level. In addition, the resources of schools, including qualified teachers, books, and materials, have a direct impact on children's acquisition of skills and information.

Instead of waiting for failure in early school grades, infant/toddler, preschool, and prekindergarten programs have been developed to promote early success for all children in spite of demographic characteristics that place them at risk. The Carolina Abecedarian Project in North Carolina and the Perry Preschool in Ypsilanti, Michigan, have been highly touted as exemplary models of preschool programs that have shown extensive effect of high-quality, center-based early intervention for African American children at risk of school disengagement and behavioral problems (Campbell, Pungello, Miller-Johnson, Burchinal, & Ramey, 2001; Schweinhart, 1985; Weikart, Deloria, Lawser, & Wiegerink, 1970). However, most children, particularly children from disadvantaged families, are unlikely to attend center-based programs with quality as good as the Abecedarian Project and the Perry Preschool. African Americans and low-income children are more likely to be in low-quality child-care environments (Ronsaville & Hakim, 2000; Ziegler & Finn-Stevenson, 2007). The key process and structural aspects of early educational care quality included caregiver–child interaction, interaction among children, emotional tone and warmth of the environment, availability of developmentally appropriate and enriching activities, education and training of the staff, child–caregiver ratio, group size, mix of children, safety, and parent–caregiver interaction (see Ceglowski & Davis, 2004). When African American children (Burchinal, Peisner-Feinberg, Bryant, & Clifford, 2000) and children from low-income homes (Taylor, Dearing, & McCartney, 2004) were in high-quality child care, they were more likely to benefit, as evidenced by higher cognitive scores.

Beyond preschool, the Abecedarian Project and Perry Preschool positively affected children's cognitive development, academic achievement, and employment advancement as young adults and reduced later criminal activities and teenage pregnancy (Campbell, Ramey, Pungello, Sparling, & Miller-Johnson, 2002; Schweinhart, 2000). Some of the Abecedarian and all of the Perry Preschool cognitive effects were attenuated once children entered formal schooling. This is consistent with findings from Lee, Brooks-Gunn, Schnur, and Liaw (1990), who found that the advantage African American children had from attending Head Start was attenuated by the first grade. Lee et al. speculated that this attenuation of growth may be due to African American children's high probability of attending low-SES schools and being in low-educated and academically deprived home environments, leading to fewer learning opportunities. These findings suggest that these early intervention programs alone may not be able to combat the poor-quality schools from which low-income African American children are more likely to matriculate.

However, other comprehensive preschool programs that included at-risk African American children have not shown such robust findings. For example, the Comprehensive Child Development Program and Early Head Start, which had 43% and 34%, respectively, of African American children in their samples, showed minimal or no effect of their preschool programs on children's cognitive language, language, and problem behaviors (see Abt Associates Inc., 1997, and Love et al., 2005). This was substantiated by the National Institute of Child Health and Human Development's Study of Early Child Care, a study whose purpose was to "examine how variations in early care experiences were related to children's social–emotional adjustment, cognitive and linguistic performance, and health" (National Institute of Child Health and Human Development Early Child Care Research Network, 2006, p. 101). With the mixed findings regarding the influence of the school or child care environment, more research is needed to determine what factors in child care and preschool programs contribute to African American children's optimal development.

Thus, both early childhood programs and K–12 are still grappling with ways to improve the learning of their most at-risk children and students and further reduce the academic achievement gap. Research has shown that when children's learning in the classroom is not further supported by parents and the home learning environment, little, if any, progress is made in children's academic and social development (Christenson, 2004).

The home–school partnership has been touted as a key strategy to prepare at-risk children's readiness to learn as well as to adjust to the demands of elementary school and onward. The No Child Left Behind Act incorporates and encourages home–school contact through progress and annual reports that schools and teachers provide to parents about the child's and school's progress in educating the most at-risk students, which include members of ethnic minority groups, low-SES students, students with special needs, and English language learners (Fusarelli, 2004). Morrow and Young (1997) found that by engaging in literacy activities similar to the ones in the classrooms, African American and Latino parents were able to enhance children's understanding of school materials as well as increase children's enjoyment of reading. Morrow and Young noted that teachers were an integral part of the success of the programs, and parents noted their increased confidence in attending school meetings and being more actively involved in their children's learning.

Other research has noted the ethnic and SES differences in the home–school partnership, parents' perceptions about the school, and father involvement (Lareau, 1989; McCarthey, 1997). Lareau's (1989) research suggested that working-class mothers and African American families had more distant, hands-off relationships with the school; they rarely intervened; they saw a limited role for themselves in their children's education; and they rarely sought accommodation by the school when their children experienced difficulties. Low-SES and African American fathers were rarely involved even in passive events, such as school events and meetings. In contrast, higher-SES fathers and Whites in Lareau's study had a more integrated relationship with the school, sought more information, advocated for their child's needs, and were involved in school-related decisions about their children. In her ethnographic study of five students from diverse backgrounds and five European American teachers, McCarthey (1997) found that the one possible reason for the lack of ethnic minority connection with schools and teachers is due to schools' and teachers' White, middle-class values and reinforcement of these values and devaluing of ethnic minority and non–middle-class values. McCarthey also found that classroom structures and curriculum that were intended to strengthen the home–school relationship with diverse families inadvertently discouraged these connections. For example, the choice of books in the curriculum "seemed to reflect more of the teachers' European-American, Christian backgrounds and values than those of the students" (p. 169). In addition, many of the teachers did not live in the communities they taught, and school policies forbade home visitations. The disconnect between the home and school is occurring at both the student and parent level; however, the expectations and burdens placed on teachers without the infrastructure reduce teachers' abilities to meet the needs of their diverse student body.

Thus, complaints about low parental involvement and exhortations for parents to attend school functions and meetings represent an overly simplistic formula for marshalling families as a resource. Such complaints betray a lack of understanding of the history of cultural, economic, and instrumental factors that shape parents' lives and their relationships with the educational institutions. The important question is how best to engage parents, in the home and at school, as a resource to promote their children's learning and development, and how best to help teachers understand how their values may differ from those of the students they teach and to develop culturally responsive teaching (Au, 1993).

Neighborhood Context and African American Children's Schooling

The neighborhood context, as an underresearched microsystem in comparison to the home and classroom environment, plays an important role in African American children's early learning and development. Ellen and Turner (1997) synthesized the effects of neighborhood impact on parenting and children's outcomes, providing examples of neighborhood characteristics that have a direct and indirect effect on children's early schooling. Some of the characteristics include local services, such as local public schools and preschools; socialization by adults, which affects children's view on education if they are surrounded by adults who are not working; peer influences that may contribute to children's disinterest in school and engagement; social networks that assist families in seeking jobs and finding resources; exposure to crime and violence, which has been found to be linked to victimization, injury, emotional trauma, and fewer learning opportunities and interaction with others; and physical distance and isolation, which limits one's economic opportunities, such as jobs and resources.

Poverty and African American status are often confounded, placing African American children in dangerous and undesirable neighborhoods (Duncan, Brooks-Gunn, & Klebanov, 1994; McLoyd, 1998; McLoyd & Ceballo, 1998; Skiba, Poloni-Staudinger, Simmons, Feggins-Azziz, & Chung, 2005). Duncan et al. (1994) and Klebanov, Brooks-Gunn, McCarton, and McCormick (1998) have investigated the role of the family, as well as the economic status of the neighborhood, on the early child development of high-risk children using data from the Infant Health and Development Program, a comprehensive center-based birth-to-age-3 intervention for high-risk children in eight sites around the United States. They found that residing in an affluent neighborhood was associated with higher IQs, whereas residing in a low-income neighborhood was associated with children's higher externalizing problem behaviors.

Similarly, in their book *Good Kids From Bad Neighborhoods*, Elliott et al. (2006) investigated neighborhood effects in youth living in Denver and Chicago. They found that growing up in a disadvantaged neighborhood (e.g., characterized by poverty, family disruption, rates of population turnover, and racial–ethnic heterogeneity) was related to lower personal and prosocial competence, grades, and educational expectations and to higher rates of problem behaviors and arrest. However, there was variability in the number of children from disadvantaged neighborhoods who were successful and held high educational expectations. Furthermore, when the impact of neighborhood was analyzed at the individual level, a different picture emerged, suggesting that neighborhood factors play a minimal role in children's success and that most of the neighborhood effects were due to differences between families—that is, families residing in advantaged neighborhoods are more likely to be educated and have access to economic and social resources, thus leading to better outcomes for their children. In contrast, families residing in disadvantaged neighborhoods were less likely to be educated and have access to resources. Thus, one should not assume that all children from disadvantaged neighborhoods are not able to be successful. As Elliott et al. (2006) noted, "It is the combined effects of these separate socialization contexts [neighborhood, family, school, and peer group] that produce a truly large effect on the chances for a successful course of youth development" (p. 284).

Conclusion

The school success of African American children is a public crisis that needs to be a focus of researchers, policy makers, educators, and community leaders. The academic achievement gap that persists between African American and White children should continue to be of concern and continually addressed. In this chapter, we have attempted to synthesize some of the issues as they relate to African American children's early learning and development, including parenting and the home environment, the school and preschool environment, and the neighborhood/community. In many instances, parenting behaviors and the home environment have been negatively implicated in African American children's schooling. Prominent researchers, such as Brody, Brooks-Gunn, Garcia Coll, Lareau, McLoyd, and Scott-Jones, have pushed the field forward by examining the role of culture and ethnicity in the parenting and home, school, and neighborhood experiences of children of color. These and other researchers continue to examine how various factors, such as poverty, health, economic and social opportunities, discrimination, crime, and school policies such as accountability affect the proximal processes of the home, school, and neighborhood. They further question the validity and reliability of measurements and findings based only on White, middle-class values that do not account for the culture, values, and history of African American families.

With the sociocultural issues embedded in parenting beliefs and behaviors, more research is needed to extrapolate the parenting behaviors and activities that are conducive to African American children's development while not interfering with parents' parenting or beliefs. With the changing diversity in U.S. society, the role culture plays in determining parenting behaviors, as well as in determining the parenting behaviors that are more salient for African American children, cannot be ignored. Because not every parenting behavior is as salient for African American children as it is for Whites and other cultural groups, researchers need to identify practices that are unique to African Americans and are propitious for their academic and social competence. At the same time, attention needs to be paid to parenting behaviors and practices that have been found to be salient and advantageous for African American children, which include sensitive and responsive parenting, providing an enriching home environment, and engaging in literacy-based activities. By broadening existing definitions, research can refine, redefine, and find factors that are most relevant for the optimal development of African American children.

Last, schools and neighborhoods play an incredibly important role in improving African American children's school success. Strong home–school collaborations that engage parents and teachers in discourse regarding individual children's strengths and difficulties are effective in enhancing children's optimal development. Although more limited in their impact on children's development, neighborhoods can have an indirect and lasting effect on children's academic and socioemotional functioning. Thus, strategies to limit negative neighborhood effects or to increase the positive impact of the home and the school would prove to be valuable for African American children's school success as well as reduce the White–Black achievement gap.

Recommendations for Parents

To formulate realistic strategies to increase parental investment, it is necessary to begin with an understanding of the context of families and to consider how effective forms of engagement may take root. School-based interventions must begin with some understanding of the work and context from which their pupils emerge. If we are to begin where children are, building on what they already know, then we must proceed with some understanding of the social environment that shapes their daily experiences and sets the stage for later learning. Provided in Table 13.1 are suggestions based on our own work and adapted from Comer (1991) and Swick, Brown, and Boutte (1994). The culture and diversity of African American families must be accounted for and may require that any recommendation be subjected to fine-tuning before it can be useful. With those caveats in mind, the following recommendations are offered for parents, schools, and communities.

Future Research

Potential factors that influence African American children's success have been understudied: maternal work conditions; child care environments of families, friends, and neighbors; teacher–child relationships; and mother–child relationships, particularly from the perspective of the types of relationships that are conducive for African American children's development, such as no-nonsense parenting. Focusing on these relationships from a perspective that is salient to African Americans reduces the deficient view that often characterizes African American culture. This would require interdisciplinary research across various areas, including anthropology, sociology, psychology, and education.

Research regarding African American children's success is still lacking in the inclusion of African American fathers and other adults. Currently, research is focused on mothers and single, female-headed households. The dearth of research focused on African American fathers and males may suggest that two-parent families homes do not exist in the African American community or that fathers and males are not beneficial but, as some researchers (e.g., Battle, 1998) have noted, this is not the case. However, it is paramount to show the broad spectrum of African American family and parenting characteristics that contribute to the success (and failure) of African American children, particularly in the midst of the continued academic achievement gap.

In addition, use of advanced methodological strategies and comprehensive, nationally representative, longitudinal data are needed to

Table 13.1 Suggested Strategies to Help Facilitate the Early Learning and Development of African American Children

Parents	• Provide multiple opportunities for children to exercise their emergent skills in literacy and numeracy through various activities, such as music, dance, games, and oral stories. • Review and revisit stories and events from parents' and grandparents' childhood and adolescence. Talk to children about obstacles and discrimination they may confront, and listen to the issues and difficulties they may be experiencing, particularly as it relates to their race and culture. • Use varied opportunities throughout the day for interactions with children that promote engagement and a positive attitude toward learning. • Foster self-awareness, intellectual curiosity, whimsy, joy, and interpersonal trust that lead children to desire to learn more about self, others, and the world, and to see education as one means of attaining those ends. • Go beyond words and create an environment that conveys to children that reading is valued and rewarding, such as having books and literature that engage them while enhancing their knowledge about their culture and society. • Create and maintain ritual and practices in the home around learning and education that convey the notion that school is essential for optimal development and success. • Begin a discourse with teachers about the role teachers and parents play in bringing about successful African American children in the midst of discrimination, educational and social inequality, and negative images and expectations.
School/ Communities	• Develop curriculum and instruction that include culturally relevant materials and resources and is reflective of the professional standards of the highest quality, which should also be relevant and interesting to children. The curriculum African American children experience should be equal to that of the highest quality learning environments present in the nation. • Create parental involvement programs that are compatible and reflect knowledge of the challenges, constraints, and opportunities in children's socioeconomic, sociocultural, and familial environments. School materials must draw on stories, metaphors, images, heroes and heroines, and values of the African American children. • Develop programs that are sensitive to the time constraints, resource limitations, and demands that already exist for families. • Engage parents through efforts developed for all socioeconomic status groups by noting that parents from different socioeconomic groups have different obstacles and needs and thus require different resources and opportunities. • Remove existing barriers to children's learning, such as tracking, labeling, grouping, abusive uses of tests, and many other segregational practices. Nongraded, continuous progress systems that use heterogeneous learning groups can and have fostered success for children of many cultures and backgrounds. • Create classroom learning climates where children's cultural backgrounds are not only appreciated but also integrated into the daily instructional practices, thus providing a bicultural set of experiences for children, teachers, and parents.

Sources: Adapted from Comer (1991) and Swick et al. (1994).

further move the field forward. For example, structural equation modeling would help determine whether measures are valid across groups. It is important to ensure that the same factors equally contribute to children's development or whether certain factors are more salient to particular groups of children (i.e., whether no-nonsense parenting is more relevant for African American children living in high-crime neighborhoods in comparison to White children living in rural areas). Comprehensive, longitudinal data would allow for the examination of complex models with independent multiple processes predicting multiple child and family outcomes at multiple time points. These data would help researchers begin to infer causality regarding the development of efficacious and effective interventions.

In summary, additional work is needed to ensure that factors selected to predict African American children's success are culturally relevant to the group and are not defined from a deficiency-based perspective. In combination with culturally relevant definitions, inclusion of other relevant factors, such as father involvement and work environment, as well as more rigorous analytical procedures will help provide accurate answers to determine the most salient factors that contribute to African American children's success.

REFERENCES

Abt Associates, Inc. (1997). *National impact evaluation of the Comprehensive Child Development Program.* Washington, DC: U.S. Department of Health and Human Services.

Aikens, N., & Barbarin, O. (2008). Socioeconomic differences in reading trajectories: The contribution of family, neighborhood, and school contexts. *Journal of Educational Psychology, 100,* 235–251.

Anderson-Yockel, J., & Haynes, W. O. (1994). Joint book-reading strategies in working-class African American and White mother–toddler dyads. *Journal of Speech and Hearing Research, 37,* 583–593.

Au, K. (1993). *Literacy instruction in multicultural settings.* Fort Worth, TX: Harcourt Brace.

Au, K. H. (1998). Social constructivism and the school literacy learning of students of diverse backgrounds. *Journal of Literacy Research, 30,* 297–319.

Baldwin, A. L., Baldwin, C., & Cole, R. E. (1990). Stress-resistant families and stress-resistant children. In J. Rolf, A. S. Masten, D. Cicchetti, K. Neuchterlein, & S. Weintraub (Eds.), *Risk and protective factors in the development of psychopathology* (pp. 257–280). Cambridge, UK: Cambridge University Press.

Barbarin, O., & Aikens, N. (2006). *Parental involvement and development of reading skills: Effects of SES and ethnicity.* Manuscript submitted for publication.

Barbarin, O., McCandies, T., Early, D., Clifford, R., Bryant, D., Burchinal, M., et al. (in press). Parental conceptions of school readiness: Relation to ethnicity, socio-economic status and children's academic skills. *Early Education and Development.*

Battle, J. J. (1998). What beats having two parents? Educational outcomes for African American students in single- versus dual-parent families. *Journal of Black Studies, 28,* 783–801.

Baumrind, D. (1972). An exploratory study of socialization effects of Black children: Some Black–White comparisons. *Child Development, 43,* 261–267.

Benasich, A. A., & Brooks-Gunn, J. (1996). Maternal attitudes and knowledge of child-rearing: Associations with family and child outcomes. *Child Development, 67,* 1186–1205.

Brody, G. H., & Flor, D. L. (1998). Maternal resources, parenting practices, and children competence in rural single-parent African American families. *Child Development, 69,* 803–816.

Bronfenbrenner, U. (2000). Ecological system theory. In A. E. Kazdin (Ed.), *Encyclopedia of psychology* (Vol. 3, pp. 129–133). Washington, DC: American Psychological Association.

Brooks-Gunn, J., & Markman, L. B. (2005). The contribution of parenting to ethnic and racial gaps in school readiness. *The Future of Children, 15,* 139–168.

Burchinal, M. R., Peisner-Feinberg, E. S., Bryant, D. M., & Clifford, R. M. (2000). Children's social and cognitive development and child care quality: Testing for differential associations related to poverty, gender, or ethnicity. *Applied Developmental Science, 4,* 149–165.

Campbell, F. A., Pungello, E. P., Miller-Johnson, S., Burchinal, M. R., & Ramey, C. T. (2001). The development of cognitive and academic abilities: Growth curves from an early childhood educational experiment. *Developmental Psychology, 37,* 231–242.

Campbell, F. A., Ramey, C. T., Pungello, E., Sparling, J., & Miller-Johnson, S. (2002). Early childhood education: Young adult outcome from the Abecedarian Project. *Applied Developmental Science, 6,* 42–57.

Ceglowski, D., & Davis, E. E. (2004). Assessing structural indicators of child care quality at the local level: Lessons from four Minnesota counties. *Child and Youth Care Forum, 33,* 71–93.

Cervantes, C. A. (2002). Explanatory emotion talk in Mexican immigrant and Mexican American families. *Hispanic Journal of Behavioral Sciences, 24,* 138–163.

Christenson, S. L. (2004). The family–school partnership: An opportunity to promote the learning competence of all students. *School Psychology Review, 33,* 83–104.

Comer, J. (1991). Parent involvement in schools: An ecological approach. *Elementary School Journal, 91,* 271–278.

Culp, A., Hubbs-Tait, L., Cuilp, R., & Starost, H. (2001). Maternal parenting characteristics and school involvement: Predictors of kindergarten cognitive competence among Head Start

children. *Journal of Research in Childhood Education, 15,* 5–17.
Deater-Deckard, K., & Dodge, K. A. (1997). Externalizing behavior problems and discipline revisited: Nonlinear effects and variations by culture, context, and gender. *Psychological Inquiry, 8,* 161–175.
Delpit, L. D. (1988). The silence dialogue: Power and pedagogy in educating other people's children. *Harvard Educational Review, 58,* 280–298.
Dornbusch, S. M., Ritter, P. L., Leiderman, P. H., Roberts, D. F., & Fraleigh, M. J. (1987). The relation of parenting style to adolescent performance. *Child Development, 58,* 1244–1257.
Dornbusch, S. M., Ritter, P. L., & Steinberg, L. (1991). Community influences on the relation of family statuses to adolescent school performance: Differences between African Americans and non-Hispanic Whites. *American Journal of Education, 99,* 543–567.
Duncan, G. J., Brooks-Gunn, J., & Klebanov, P. K. (1994). Economic deprivation and early childhood development. *Child Development, 65,* 296–318.
Ellen, I. G., & Turner, M. A. (1997). Does neighborhood matter? Assessing recent evidence. *Housing Policy Debate, 8,* 833–866.
Elliott, D. S., Menard, S., Rankin, B., Elliott, A., Huizinga, D., & Wilson, W. J. (2006). *Good kids from bad neighborhoods: Successful development in social context.* New York: Cambridge University Press.
Fusarelli, L. D. (2004). The potential impact of No Child Left Behind Act on equity and diversity in American education. *Educational Policy, 18,* 71–94.
Garcia Coll, C., Lamberty, G., Jenkins, R., McAdoo, H. P., Crnic, K., Wasik, B. H., et al. (1996). An integrative model for the study of developmental competencies in minority children. *Child Development, 67,* 1891–1914.
Haden, C. A., Ornstein, P. A., Eckerman, C. O., & Didow, S. M. (2001). Mother–child conversational interaction as events unfold: Linkages to subsequent remembering. *Child Development, 72,* 1016–1031.
Hammer, C. S., & Weiss, A. L. (1999). Guiding language development: How African American mothers and their infants structure play interaction. *Journal of Speech, Language, and Hearing Research, 42,* 1219–1233.
Hart, B., & Risley, T. R. (1992). American parenting of language-learning children: Persisting differences in family–child interaction observed in natural home environments. *Developmental Psychology, 28,* 1096–1105.
Hart, B., & Risley, T. R. (1995). *Meaningful differences in the everyday experiences of young American children.* Baltimore: Paul H. Brookes.
Heller, T., & Baker, B. (2000). Maternal negativity in children's externalizing behavior. *Early Education and Development, 11,* 483–498.

Ispa, J. M., Fine, M. A., Halgunseth, L. C., Harper, S., Robinson, J., Boyce, L., et al. (2004). Maternal intrusiveness, maternal warmth, and mother–toddler relationship outcomes: Variation across low-income ethnic acculturation groups. *Child Development, 75,* 1613–1631.
Johnston, R. C., & Viadero, D. (2000). Unmet promise: Raising minority achievement. The achievement gap. *Education Week, 19,* 1–23.
Keller, H. (2003). Socialization for competence: Cultural models of infancy. *Human Development, 46,* 288–311.
Klebanov, P. K., Brooks-Gunn, J., McCarton, C., & McCormick, M. C. (1998). The contribution of neighborhood and family income to developmental test scores over the first three years of life. *Child Development, 69,* 1420–1436.
Lambert, M. C., Weisz, J. R., Knight, F., Desrosiers, M., Overly, K., & Thesiger, C. (1992). Jamaican and American adult perspectives on child psychopathology: Further exploration of the threshold model. *Journal of Consulting and Clinical Psychology, 60,* 146–149.
Lareau, A. (1989). *Home advantage: Social class and parental intervention in elementary education* (Rev. ed.). New York: Rowman and Littlefield.
Lee, J., & Bowen, N. K. (2006). Parent involvement, cultural capital, and the achievement gap among elementary school children. *American Educational Research Journal, 43,* 193–218.
Lee, V. E., Brooks-Gunn, J., Schnur, E., & Liaw, F. (1990). Are Head Start effects sustained? A longitudinal follow-up comparison of disadvantaged children attending Head Start, no preschool, and other preschool program. *Child Development, 61,* 495–507.
Linver, M. R., Brooks-Gunn, J., & Kohen, D. E. (2002). Family processes as pathways from income to young children's development. *Developmental Psychology, 38,* 719–734.
Love, J. M., Kisker, E. E., Ross, C., Raikes, H., Constantine, J., Boller, K., et al. (2005). The effectiveness of Early Head Start for 3-year-old children and their parents: Lessons for policy and programs. *Developmental Psychology, 41,* 885–901.
McAdoo, H. P. (1988). *Black families* (2nd ed.). Newbury Park, CA: Sage.
McCarthey, S. J. (1997). Connecting home and school literacy practices in classrooms with diverse populations. *Journal of Literacy Research, 29,* 145–182.
McGroder, S. M. (2000). Parenting among low-income, African American single mothers with preschool-age children: Patterns, predictors, and developmental correlates. *Child Development, 71,* 752–771.
McLoyd, V. C. (1998). Socioeconomic disadvantage and child development. *American Psychologist, 53,* 185–204.

McLoyd, V. C., & Ceballo, R. (1998). Conceptualizing and assessing economic context: Issues in the study of race and child development. In V. C. McLoyd & L. Steinberg (Eds.), *Studying minority adolescents: Conceptual, methodological, and theoretical issues* (pp. 251–278). Mahwah, NJ: Lawrence Erlbaum.

McLoyd, V. C., & Smith, J. (2002). Physical discipline and behavior problems in African American, European American, and Hispanic children: Emotional support as a moderator. *Journal of Marriage and the Family, 64,* 40–53.

Mistry, R. S., Biesanz, J. C., Taylor, L. C., Burchinal, M., & Cox, M. J. (2004). Family income and its relation to preschool children's adjustment for families in the NICHD Study of Early Child Care. *Developmental Psychology, 40,* 717–745.

Mistry, R. S., Melsch, A., & Taheri-Kenari, A. (2003). *Assessing the relations among maternal employment, family processes, and preschoolers' cognitive and social adjustment for families in the Comprehensive Child Development Program (CCDP).* Paper presented at Northwestern University/University of Chicago Joint Center of Poverty Research 2002–2003, Chicago.

Morrow, L. M., & Young, J. (1997). A family literacy programs connecting school and home: Effects on attitude, motivation, and literacy achievement. *Journal of Educational Psychology, 89,* 736–742.

Murray, A. D., & Hornbaker, A. V. (1997). Maternal directive and facilitative interaction styles: Associations with language and cognitive development of low risk and high risk toddlers. *Development and Psychopathology, 9,* 507–516.

National Institute of Child Health and Human Development Early Child Care Research Network. (2006). Child-care effect sizes for the NICHD Study of Early Child Care and Youth Development. *American Psychologist, 61,* 99–116.

National Research Council. (2000). *From neurons to neighborhoods: The science of early childhood development.* Washington, DC: National Academy Press.

Pallas, A. M., Natriello, G., & McDill, E. L. (1989). Changing nature of the disadvantaged population: Current dimensions and future trends. *Educational Researcher, 18,* 16–22.

Phinney, J. S., & Landin, J. (1998). Research paradigms for studying ethnic minority families within and across groups. In V. C. McLoyd & L. Steinberg (Eds.), *Studying minority adolescents: Conceptual, methodological, and theoretical issues* (pp. 89–110). Mahwah, NJ: Lawrence Erlbaum.

Portes, P. R., Cuentas, T. E., & Zady, M. (2000). Cognitive socialization across ethnocultural contexts: Literacy and cultural differences in intellectual performance and parent–child interaction. *The Journal of Genetic Psychology, 161,* 79–98.

Ronsaville, D. S., & Hakim, R. B. (2000). Well child care in the United States: Racial differences in compliance with guidelines. *American Journal of Public Health, 90,* 1436–1443.

Rubin, K., Burgess, K., Sawyer, K., & Hastings, P. (2003). Predicting preschoolers' externalizing behaviors from toddler temperament, conflict, and maternal negativity. *Developmental Psychology, 39,* 164–176.

Schweinhart, L. J. (1985). Effects of the Perry Preschool program on youths through age 19: A summary. *Topics in Early Childhood Education, 5,* 26–35.

Schweinhart, L. J. (2000). The High/Scope Perry Preschool study: A case study in random assignment. *Evaluation and Research in Education, 14,* 136–147.

Scott-Jones, D. (1987). Mother-as-teacher in the families of high- and low-achieving low-income African American first-graders. *Journal of Negro Education, 56,* 21–34.

Skiba, R., J., Poloni-Staudinger, L., Simmons, A. B., Feggins-Azziz, L. R., & Chung, C. (2005). Unproven links: Can poverty explain ethnic disproportionality in special education? *Journal of Special Education, 39,* 130–144.

Swick, K. J., Brown, M., & Boutte, G. (1994). African American children and school readiness: An analysis of the issues. *Journal of Instructional Psychology, 21,* 183–191.

Taylor, B. A., Dearing, E., & McCartney, K. (2004). Incomes and outcomes in early childhood. *Journal of Human Resources, 39,* 980–1007.

U.S. Department of Education. (2005). *2004 National Assessment of Academic Progress: Trends in academic progress. Three decades of student performance in reading and mathematics.* Washington, DC: National Center for Education Statistics. Retrieved August 1, 2007, from http://nces.ed.gov/nations reportcard/pdf/main2005/2005463.pdf

U.S. Department of Education, National Center for Education Statistics. (2006). *ECLS-K longitudinal kindergarten–fifth grade public-use data file and electronic codebook* [CD-ROM] (NCES 2006-035). Washington, DC: Author.

Weikart, D. P., Deloria, D., Lawser, S., & Wiegerink, R. (1970). Longitudinal results of the Ypsilanti Perry Preschool Project. *Monographs of the High/Scope Educational Research Foundation, 1.*

Weisz, J. R., Sigman, M., Weiss, B., & Mosk, J. (1993). Parent reports of behavioral and emotional problem among children in Kenya, Thailand, and the United States. *Child Development, 64,* 98–109.

Ziegler, E., & Finn-Stevenson, M. (2007). From research to policy and practice: The school of the 21st century. *American Journal of Orthopsychiatry, 77,* 175–181.

14

ACADEMIC MOTIVATION AND ACHIEVEMENT OF AFRICAN AMERICAN YOUTH

Cynthia Hudley

Racial disparity in academic achievement is one of the most hotly contested educational questions of our time, and student motivation has been a prominent concern among voices on all sides of these debates. On traditional indexes of academic performance (e.g., standardized tests, educational attainment, grades), African American children and adolescents as a group underperform relative to national averages across all levels of education. From 1971 through 2004, averaged standardized test scores in reading and math for African American children in elementary school have been the lowest of any racial–ethnic group (National Center for Education Statistics [NCES], 2006). Among adolescents, SAT scores for African American students have consistently ranked below scores of any other racial–ethnic group in both critical reading and mathematics for the past 2 decades (NCES, 2007). Finally, among all African American high school sophomores in 1990, a decade later, in 2000, only 39% had enrolled in postsecondary education, and 15% had completed a bachelor's degree (NCES, 2007). Lack of participation in higher education now places greater downward pressure on the life chances of African American youth than does dropping out of high school. The average annual income disparity between workers with a high school diploma and those with a bachelor's degree is more than $24,000; in contrast, the annual income disparity between those who drop out of high school and those who earn a high school diploma or general equivalency diploma is $10,500 (U.S. Census Bureau, 2004).

The search for causes of African American students' academic underperformance is understandably both ongoing and far reaching, given the obvious benefits of academic success for both the student and our society as a whole. Unequal schooling, social inequality, and racial discrimination have been clearly implicated in academic underachievement. Inexperienced teachers, insufficient school resources (e.g., science laboratories, foreign language instruction, Advanced Placement courses) (Oakes, 1985), social stereotypes (Hudley & Graham, 2001), racism and institutional bias (Fine, 1991), neighborhood disarray (e.g., unemployment, substandard housing, crime) (Ascher, 1991), and a variety of other barriers have a significant impact on school achievement. However, academic underachievement among African American students is equally robust among urban and suburban students as well as across the full spectrum of socioeconomic status (Ogbu, 1993; University of California, Outreach Task Force, 1997). As well, many African American students at all socioeconomic status levels are quite successful in school (Hilliard, 2003), and African American students as a group have always articulated high aspirations (Kao & Thompson, 2003; Solorzano, 1992), irrespective of their measured achievement. Fortunately, the search for variables that contribute to academic success for African American students has generated an important body of research that provides insights into both causes and best practices for the successful education of African American students. Thus, we are able to look beyond obvious racial inequities in educational and economic opportunities that operate at the group level to examine variables that capture individual differences in academic achievement.

One theoretically robust and empirically fruitful area of research on individual differences in academic achievement among African American students has been the study of *academic achievement motivation*. The study of achievement motivation moves beyond the reality of inequality and oppression at the group level to take a decidedly psychological, or individual approach to the study of motivation-related attitudes, beliefs, and behaviors that influence student achievement. Although the range of motivational constructs present in the literature is broad, this review will focus on empirical research that has been published since the appearance of Graham's (1994) seminal review of African American achievement motivation. Outdated constructs, such as the achievement motive measured with projective tests (McClelland, 1961) and racial comparative research on locus of control (Rotter, 1966) and expectancy of success (Rosen, 1959), are not included here, because the study of achievement motivation in African American children has matured considerably beyond such negative theoretical formulations and empirical strategies. In this chapter, I explore the extent to which motivationally relevant variables, including self-beliefs and perceptions of barriers to success, account for individual differences in African American student achievement. However, because motivational variables can intersect with and be influenced by environmental conditions, structural and social variables also are discussed where appropriate.

Self Beliefs

Academic Self-Concept

Academic self-concept, a motivational variable that comprises attitudes and beliefs about one's academic abilities, has been conceptually distinguished from *global self-concept*, a composite of multiple dimensions of the self (e.g., social, physical, emotional) (Harter, 1999; Marsh & Shavelson, 1985) and has been investigated among African American students over the past 4 decades. Early research (Green & Farquhar, 1965) found that a measure of academic self-concept developed initially on White high school students correlated more strongly with grade point average (GPA) than did standardized test scores for African American high school students in the Midwest; for African American males, standardized test scores had no relation to GPA. Similarly, Epps (1969) found that a measure of self-concept of ability was positively correlated with both academic grades and academic expectations (i.e., how much education students expected to complete) in a sample of male and female African American high school students drawn from the northern and southern regions of the United States. More than a decade later, Jordan (1981) established that academic self-concept, but not global self-concept, significantly predicted academic GPA in a sample of low-income African American eighth-grade students attending an inner-city public middle school. Similarly, research with the Piers Harris Self-Concept Scale (Piers & Harris, 1984), a self-report instrument that measures multiple dimensions of self-concept, demonstrated that scores on the academic self-concept dimension as well as the happiness and physical attractiveness dimensions differed significantly by levels of academic achievement (as measured by GPA) in a sample of African American inner-city high school students (Haynes, Hamilton-Lee, & Comer, 1988). However, scores on the popularity and anxiety dimensions did not differ by academic achievement. More recent research continues to find a similar, positive relationship between academic self-concept and achievement but not other facets of self-concept in samples as young as preschool-age children (Justice, Lindsey, & Morrow, 1999), adolescent students (Fisher, 2000; Gordon, 1995), and college students (Cokley, 2003).

One might conclude from these data collected over the past 4 decades that when African American students, like students of all groups, feel confident about their academic abilities, they tend to experience academic success in the classroom. However, this conclusion must be tempered by parallel findings that African American students often exhibit a very positive self-concept of ability, irrespective of achievement levels that are below those of their White peers (Hare, 1980; Kugle, Clements, & Powell, 1983). Some researchers have suggested that an apparent incongruity between levels of self-concept and levels of academic achievement may reflect a different understanding of the academic self among African American students (Cokley, 2003; Graham, 1994), but such fundamental differences may be obscured by an overreliance on racial comparative research that presumes self-beliefs described by White samples are characteristic of all students.

Initial support for such an interpretation comes from psychometric studies. A measure of academic self-concept (Cokley, Komarraju, King, Cunningham, & Muhammad, 2003) and a broader measure of self-concept and motivation (Gordon-Rouse & Cashin, 2000) have both yielded different factor structures for African American students relative to White and Latino students. Therefore, although research reliably finds that African American students as a group have high levels of academic self-concept and comparatively low levels of academic achievement, the consistently positive relationship between the two variables (but not other elements of self-concept) supports the usefulness of academic self-concept as an explanation for individual differences in academic achievement. A student's beliefs about his or her own abilities can explain some of the variance in academic achievement across the age span and can sometimes predict academic achievement in adolescence (Fisher, 2000; Jordan, 1981).

Academic Efficacy

Self-efficacy, a construct at the heart of social-cognitive theory (Bandura, 1997), is similar in many ways to self-concept. Self-efficacy is a judgment about the ability of the self to pursue action that will achieve a particular goal or level of performance. Thus, academic efficacy beliefs are judgments of the ability of the self to perform an academic task at a given level. Consistent with findings concerning academic self-concept, academic efficacy beliefs among African American students significantly predict GPA and apparently serve as protective factors during periods of school transition. Students with high academic efficacy in sixth grade, as they enter middle school, have been shown to earn higher grades than their peers with lower efficacy beliefs. Conversely, GPA for low-efficacy students declines significantly during the transition to middle school (Gutman & Midgley, 2000). Very recent research examining efficacy beliefs during the transition from middle school to high school (Long, Monoi, Harper, Knoblauch, & Murphy, 2007) has found that self-efficacy beliefs moderately predicted academic grades during the last year of middle school (eighth grade) and strongly predicted academic grades during the first year of high school (ninth grade).

In addition to differences by age, research has consistently identified gender differences in the relation between efficacy and achievement. A recent study (Saunders, Davis, Williams, & Williams, 2004) demonstrated that academic self-efficacy is a significantly stronger predictor of grades for African American female high school students (explaining 28% of the variance) than for their male counterparts (explaining 8% of the variance); males also demonstrate lower levels of academic achievement and attainment overall. Self-efficacy specific to science learning also significantly predicts science achievement for both genders in middle school (Liu, Hsieh, Cho, & Schallert, 2006)—a particularly important finding given the pressing need for trained scientists and the dearth of African American students opting for scientific careers. Thus, research on academic self-efficacy, similar to findings for academic self-concept, concurs that African American students' judgments about their academic abilities are predictive of their academic achievement.

Perceived Competence

Perceived competence is another construct that captures beliefs about the abilities of the self. Motivational theory has defined multiple subdomains of perceived competence, including physical competence, social competence, and academic competence (Harter, 1999). Academic competence comprises success in schoolwork, being smart, and remembering things easily. In studies conducted with African American students, perceived academic competence was significantly related to school adjustment. For example, research on African American college undergraduates in a predominantly White institution (Chavous, Rivas, Green, & Helaire, 2002) found a significant relationship between perceived academic competence and college GPA ($r = .33$, $p < .01$). Research with low-income African American adolescents has found relationships between perceptions of competence and academic engagement, which is related to academic achievement (Connell, Halpern-Felsher, Clifford, Crichlow, & Usinger, 1995; Hudley, 1995). Hudley (1995) examined multiple dimensions of perceived competence in a group of middle school students who were enrolled in an academic academy for African American male students and a comparison group of male students not enrolled in the program. Connell et al. (1995) examined a single, composite measure of perceived competence in both male and female students in both middle school and high school. Perceptions of intellectual competence ("How smart am I") correlated significantly ($r = -.71$, $p < .01$) with attendance as a measure of engagement in Hudley's sample, but only for the students enrolled in the special program. In Connell's data, perceived competence correlated significantly with a composite measure of engagement for males ($r = .50$, $p < .001$) and for females ($r = .50$, $p < .001$).

Taken together, these findings on self-beliefs suggest a possible reciprocal mechanism through which self-perceptions of ability may influence academic achievement. When students feel competent and successful at academic tasks, they are more likely to take advantage of available learning opportunities. On the other hand, students are more likely to derive a more positive sense of self when they are successfully engaged in learning activities. Academic learning requires time on task, which typically means time spent in school and at home participating in intellectually enriching activities, and positive self-perceptions and time on task seem to support one another.

Other–Self Beliefs

Attributions. Motivational constructs that represent some combination of beliefs about the self and beliefs about the academic context have also guided studies of individual differences in academic achievement for African American students. Attribution theory has been one framework used to conceptualize a number of these studies (Graham, 1988). An attribution answers the "Why" question; for example, "Why did I fail that test?" When a person assigns a cause to the given outcome or behavior, that person has made an *attribution*. In the study of academic achievement, causes for failure (and success) have typically been classified into four categories that reflect either the self or the external environment: (1) effort, (2) innate ability or aptitude, (3) task characteristics, and (4) luck. For failure experiences, attributions of low effort are most adaptive, because effort can be controlled by the individual, and thus, the failure outcome can be changed in the future. For success, attributions to aptitude are deemed most adaptive (followed by effort attributions), because aptitude is considered to be a stable characteristic of the self, and thus, success should continue into the future and be unaffected by environmental circumstances.

A noteworthy body of literature demonstrates that causal attributions play a substantial role in academic achievement. Although relatively little of that work has examined individual differences in African American students, available findings are generally consistent with the theoretical formulation. Early research (Willig, Harnisch, Hill, & Maehr, 1983) demonstrated that low-achieving African American students in elementary school more strongly attributed academic success to external characteristics (task ease and luck). A decade later, research with low-income African American students found that high-achieving elementary school students most often attributed their success to high ability, whereas low-achieving students most often attributed their failure to low ability (Bempechat, Nakkula, Wu, & Ginsburg, 1996). A second study in this research program (Bempechat, Graham, & Jimenez, 1999) revealed that lower standardized math test scores were associated with attributing failure to lack of ability and attributing success to external factors. All of these studies demonstrate that academic achievement varies as a function of students' beliefs that success and failure are under their control instead of subject to external forces, that failure can be changed by changing one's behavior, and that success is a relatively stable characteristic of the self.

Finally, some research has investigated gender differences in middle school to determine whether attributional patterns play some role in the higher rates of achievement among African American females, particularly in the fields of math and science (McClendon & Wigfield, 1998). An interesting Sex × Achievement interaction revealed that in math, lower-achieving girls endorsed effort more strongly than lower-achieving boys, but higher-achieving boys endorsed effort more strongly than higher-achieving girls. A highly speculative interpretation is that girls who are not doing well may believe in their own efforts more so than boys who are not doing well, and so they persist in their academic strivings more so than the boys. On the other hand, boys who are doing well believe in their own efforts, consistent with theoretical predictions, but girls in math who are doing well seem less sure of their own efforts as a reason for their success. Research has consistently shown sex differences in achievement beliefs in the math domain, a subject field traditionally stereotyped as appropriate for men (e.g., Herbert & Stipek, 2005).

Stereotype Threat. *Stereotype threat* is directly relevant to African American student motivation and achievement. Blending self-beliefs and beliefs about the academic context, this motivational construct has been used to explain both group and individual differences in academic achievement. The construct is defined as a social-psychological threat in any situation or activity for which there is a negative stereotype about one's group; it has also been referred to as *spotlight anxiety* (Cross, 1991, p. 195). Such a circumstance leads one to consider the possibility of being judged or treated stereotypically and whether one is conforming to the stereotype (Steele, 1997). Given the wealth of negative stereotypes about academic abilities and intelligence and students' awareness of these stereotypes (Hudley & Graham, 2001), African Americans students may be especially likely to fear confirming negative stereotypes.

A growing body of literature using inventive study techniques has documented the negative effects of stereotype threat on academic performance of African American children as young as second grade (McKown & Weinstein, 2003); however, critiques of both the construct and the research have arisen on several fronts. Work on this construct has also begun to investigate the activation of positive stereotypes and has found positive effects on academic performance (Ambady, Shih, Kim, & Pittinsky, 2001); however, to date, none of this work has been done with African American children. For a full discussion of this construct, see Chapter 16 of this volume.

Achievement Goals. Although very little of the work on it has addressed African American student achievement, *achievement goal theory* represents a central research strand in the achievement motivation literature. Achievement goal theory is concerned with an individual's purposes for academic activities and typically delineates two distinct types of goals that differ substantially in their influences on achievement. *Mastery, learning,* or *task goals* are defined as the desire to develop or improve knowledge or ability. *Performance* or *ego goals* refer to the demonstration of ability to others. *Performance approach goals* reflect a desire to demonstrate or prove ability, whereas *performance avoidance goals* are defined as the desire to avoid demonstrating incompetence or lack of ability (Elliot, 1999). These goal orientations are theorized to be influenced by achievement settings; the organization of a classroom can have a direct effect on the achievement goals that a given student adopts (Ames, 1992). Achievement goals, in turn, strongly influence how an individual defines achievement in that setting. Mastery goals lead to adaptive learning strategies (e.g., persistence, deep processing, preference for challenging tasks), whereas performance goals foster competition, increased awareness of student differences, and heightened awareness of group status. Thus, performance goals may impede feelings of belonging for an African American student in a predominantly White class or school (Kaplan & Maehr, 1999b). As well, a classroom that facilitates performance goals may activate racial stereotypes of achievement. Motivation and achievement among African American students in such an environment might be especially debilitated due to pervasive negative stereotypes of low ability (Hudley & Graham, 2001).

The few empirical studies on achievement goal theory that have examined African American student achievement indicate that achievement goals are associated with academic achievement. For example, research in a predominantly White middle school found that African American students' personal ego goals negatively predicted GPA, whereas personal task goals positively predicted GPA (Kaplan & Maehr, 1999a). A more recent study with high school students similarly found that ego goals were negatively related to GPA for African American ninth-grade students and, controlling for eighth-grade math achievement, task goals predicted positive changes in mathematics GPA from eighth grade to ninth grade. Although not a specific measure of achievement, self-handicapping strategies (e.g., putting off studying for an exam, appearing to not try hard in school), a set of performance avoidance strategies, are also positively related to ego goals among African American students (Midgley, Arunkumar, & Urdan, 1996). Such learning strategies undermine academic success; however, they also deflect perceptions of low ability by providing alternate, effort-based explanations for failure.

Recent research on achievement goals has linked stereotype threat and goals into potentially productive models to examine individual differences in motivation and achievement (Ryan & Ryan, 2005; Seibt & Förster, 2004). Seibt and Förster (2004) initially proposed that one of several mechanisms linking stereotypes to intellectual performance involved the self-regulation goal of the perceiver (Higgins, 1997). Although *regulatory focus* is a construct in social psychology that has not been examined in research with African American children, it has been widely studied in both academic and social domains. Seibt and Förster examined the extent to which activating negative self-stereotypes leads to self-regulation goals that foreground risk-aversion and perseveration strategies when completing a task (i.e., prevention regulatory goals), whereas positive self-stereotype activation leads to self-regulation strategies that are more creative and exploratory (i.e., promotion regulatory goals). In a series of five experimental studies with White undergraduate students, these social psychology researchers were able to induce a prevention regulatory style that impaired specific kinds of functioning on cognitive tasks by creating a fictitious, race-irrelevant group to whom they imputed a negative intellectual stereotype. The authors argued that their findings describe a disturbing breadth of stereotype threat in that "negative stereotypes created within the experimental situation had the same effects as those that are culturally inherited" (Seibt & Förster, p. 52). Although these findings have not been generalized to African American students, the clear implication is that stereotype threat can influence the learning goals that a student adopts and affect how a student works on cognitive tasks. African American students who become focused on avoiding the risk of confirming a negative stereotype may use study or problem-solving strategies that limit their creative thinking and the tendency to explore multiple perspectives or solutions to a task.

Another line of theorizing examines the traditional typology of achievement goals as influences that mediate the relationship between stereotype threat and academic performance (Ryan & Ryan, 2005). This comprehensive model posits that, under stereotype threat conditions, African American students may more often adopt performance avoidance goals. These goals might lead to maladaptive cognitions during academic tasks, including anxiety, disorganized thinking, and declines in feelings of efficacy. The ability of stereotype threat to impede academic performance in this model is dependent on the extent to which an individual student adopts performance avoid goals in the face of stereotype threat. The only empirical investigation of achievement goals and stereotype threat (Kellow & Jones, 2005) was a racial-comparative study that did not yield results in the theorized direction. A sample of African American and White high school students completed a timed test of spatial reasoning. African American students' endorsements of performance avoidance goals did not differ in the stereotype threat condition compared with a nonevaluative condition. Furthermore, endorsement of performance approach goals was greater in the evaluative condition than in the nonevaluative condition and greater than performance avoidance goals in the evaluative condition, although the results were not statistically significant. It is interesting that expectancies for success were significantly greater in the nonevaluative condition than in the stereotype threat condition.

Unfortunately, this study did not include a test of the impact of goals or test condition on test performance; neither did the authors test the possibility of goals as a mediator of the effects of stereotype on performance. Thus, this study did not test the Ryan and Ryan (2005) model and did not address the question of individual differences for African American students.

Barriers to Success

In addition to self-relevant variables, other influences are uniquely relevant to motivation and achievement among African American students. The experiences of people of African descent in the United States are characterized by oppression and negative stereotypes that date from the 1600s, with the arrival of the first enslaved Africans on American soil. Although the stain of legalized slavery has been long eliminated from this country, African Americans continue to be segregated, relegated to subordinate status (Hacker, 1992), and stereotyped as lazy and intellectually inferior (e.g., Krueger, 1996; Niemann, Jennings, Rozelle, Baxter, & Sullivan, 1994). Some researchers have argued that the unique barriers faced by African American students as they attempt to access the opportunity structure play a significant role in motivation and achievement. As students begin to clearly perceive and understand the racialized nature of barriers created by institutional bias and negative stereotypes, they may respond to manifest inequality by decreasing their efforts to succeed in an arena that seems closed off to them, or by increasing their efforts to overcome such barriers. Several theories have been proposed to explain these individual differences in responses to racial barriers.

Perhaps the best known of theories to explain the achievement and motivational consequences of perceived racial inequality is John Ogbu's (1993) *cultural–ecological theory*. A complete review of this extensive literature is beyond the scope of this chapter; however, the construct of importance to this review is *oppositional identity*. According to cultural–ecological theory, students are able to observe that school success does not lead to the kind of material rewards or social acceptance that is true for members of the dominant group, because of racially biased job ceilings, lending practices, and housing opportunities (Hacker, 1992). As well, African American students may view education as a product of the system and the group that has oppressed them and their ancestors. As a result, some students may reject academic achievement striving as a threat to an African American identity and will instead adopt attitudes and behaviors that are in direct opposition to academic success. As Fordham and Ogbu's (1986) seminal study revealed, the greater the adoption of an oppositional identity, the lower will be achievement striving and academic success. However, this relationship may be moderated by social class and be less prevalent among African American students from households that are middle class and above (Ainsworth, 2002).

The empirical literature investigating cultural–ecological theory has been almost entirely qualitative and has sometimes demonstrated that African American students who develop an identity that incorporates achievement striving and success are often academically successful, whereas those students who espouse a classic oppositional identity are typically not so successful in school. Solomon's (1992) ethnographic study of West Indian students in a Toronto high school demonstrated the negative influences of an oppositional identity merged with a racial group identification.

Research that has examined African American students' attitudes toward school and expectancies for success has been generally quantitative in nature and has yielded relatively consistent findings that a positive attitude toward school and positive expectancies for success are linked to higher academic achievement. Mickelson (1990), using regression analyses with data from eight high schools, found that African American students' positive attitudes toward education were related to academic achievement, and this relationship was moderated by socioeconomic status such that working-class students' attitudes derived from daily experience (what she calls "concrete" attitudes) were significantly lower, as was their academic achievement. Data from the National Education Longitudinal Study revealed that African American students' grades were positively related to positive attitudes toward school, and those who self-reported high popularity with peers were also the highest achieving students of their racial group (Ainsworth-Darnell & Downey, 1998), a finding that conflicts sharply with cultural–ecological theory.

Finally, research that has examined males students' beliefs about school success in conjunction with attitudes about the dominant society (Irving & Hudley, 2005) has found that African American students' mistrust of the formal institutions of the dominant society (e.g., schools, the justice system, corporate America) were inversely related to students' expectations about the future benefits of educational success and their valuing of academic effort. Thus, individual differences in students' beliefs about access to the opportunity structure explained differences in student motivation. A follow-up study (Irving & Hudley, 2008) further demonstrated that academic expectancies and beliefs in the value of academics are positively related to academic achievement. Beliefs that access to the opportunity structure is limited are negatively related to achievement and, controlling for expectancy, significantly negatively predictive of GPA for African American students.

Thus, quantitative results suggest that oppositional identity, negative attitudes, and students' expectancies are useful in explaining individual differences in both motivation and achievement. The whole-group propensity toward lowered academic achievement among African American students proposed by cultural–ecological theory is not as useful in explaining these students' motivation and achievement.

Conclusion and Future Directions

In this chapter, I have examined perceptions of self as well as perceptions of society as factors that contribute to African American students' academic achievement and achievement motivation. The body of literature on African American student motivation and achievement is surprisingly scant, and much of it has focused on racial-comparative studies at the group level. Therefore, one obvious conclusion is the pressing need to more extensively examine correlates, causes, and consequences of individual differences in motivation and achievement among African American students. Potential variables of interest include the ones studied in the research reviewed in this chapter as well as other cognitive (e.g., self-regulation), contextual (e.g., teacher effects), cultural and subcultural (e.g., regional differences), and situational (e.g., access to rigorous education) influences. Group-level research is of relatively little value in efforts to construct learning environments both in school and out of school that will successfully facilitate motivation and learning for all students, because it is foolish to assume that any group of students can be characterized as a monolithic entity.

Another important conclusion that stems from the repudiation of a monolithic identity for African American students should not merit repeating, but unfortunately does. Race and ethnicity are not the superordinate explanation for attitudes and behavior of any group; however, differences in life experience by race, class, and gender are very real and must not be ignored. Such a nuanced understanding of the role of race in the life experiences of African Americans at this point in American social and cultural history requires a sophisticated level of cultural understanding and cultural competence (Hudley & Taylor, 2006) on the part of both researchers and of practitioners who work with communities of color.

Finally, as a researcher with primary interest in human development, I find the lack of research on the development of academic achievement motivation in African American students a serious omission in the literature. As described in this chapter, some work has made important contributions to our understanding of developmental issues using both qualitative (Solomon, 1992) and quantitative (Ainsworth-Darnell & Downey, 1998) approaches, but this work does not begin to approach the volume of data that we will need to fully understand motivation over the life course. For example, we know very little about how children's understanding of their own motivation changes over time, and virtually none of that work has examined individual differences in development among African American children. As well, although there are well-documented gender differences in motivation and achievement among African American students (Graham, Taylor, & Hudley, 1998) and students themselves endorse these gender differences (Hudley & Graham, 2001), we have surprisingly little understanding of how these differences in beliefs and behaviors develop or of what malleable variables might serve as the foundation for a theory-driven intervention to enhance the African American students' achievement motivation (Hudley, Graham, & Taylor, 2007). However, research on motivation and achievement in African American students may be our best hope for improving the achievement and life chances of children and thus benefit our society at large.

REFERENCES

Ainsworth, J. W. (2002). Why does it take a village? The mediation of neighborhood effects on educational achievement. *Social Forces, 81,* 117–152.

Ainsworth-Darnell, J., & Downey, D. B. (1998). Assessing the oppositional identity culture explanation for racial/ethnic differences in school performance. *American Sociological Review, 63,* 536–553.

Ambady, N., Shih, M., Kim, A., & Pittinsky, T. (2001). Stereotype susceptibility in children: Effects of identity activation on quantitative performance. *Psychological Science, 12,* 385–390.

Ames, C. (1992). Classrooms: Goals, structures, and student motivation. *Journal of Educational Psychology, 84,* 261–271.

Ascher, C. (1991). *School programs for African American male students* (Trends and Issues No. 15, Institute for Urban and Minority Education). New York: ERIC Clearinghouse on Urban Education.

Bandura, A. (1997). *Self-efficacy: The exercise of control.* New York: Freeman.

Bempechat, J., Graham, S. E., & Jimenez, N. (1999). The socialization of achievement in poor and minority students: A comparative study. *Journal of Cross-Cultural Psychology, 30,* 139–158.

Bempechat, J., Nakkula, M., Wu, J., & Ginsburg, H. (1996). Attributions as predictors of math achievement: A comparative study. *Journal of Research and Development in Education, 29,* 53–59.

Chavous, T., Rivas, D., Green, L., & Helaire, L. (2002). Role of student background, perceptions of ethnic fit, and racial identification in the academic adjustment of African American students at a predominantly White university. *Journal of Black Psychology, 28,* 234–260.

Cokley, K. (2003). What do we know about the motivation of African American students? Challenging the "anti-intellectual" myth. *Harvard Educational Review, 73,* 524–558.

Cokley, K., Komarraju, M., King, A., Cunningham, D., & Muhammad, G. (2003). Ethnic differences in the measurement of academic self-concept in a sample of African American and European American college students. *Educational and Psychological Measurement Journal, 63,* 707–722.

Connell, J., Halpern-Felsher, B., Clifford, E., Crichlow, W., & Usinger, P. (1995). Hanging in there: Behavioral, psychological, and contextual factors affecting whether African-American adolescents stay in high school. *Journal of Adolescent Research, 10,* 41–63.

Cross, W. (1991). *Shades of black: Diversity in African-American identity.* Philadelphia: Temple University Press.

Elliot, A. (1999). Approach and avoidance motivation and achievement goals. *Educational Psychologist, 34,* 169–189.

Epps, E. (1969). Correlates of academic achievement among northern and southern urban Negro students. *Journal of Social Issues, 25,* 55–70.

Fine, M. (1991). *Framing dropouts: Notes on the politics of an urban high school.* Albany: State University of New York Press.

Fisher, T. (2000). Predictors of academic achievement among African American adolescents. In S. Gregory (Ed.), *The academic achievement of minority students: Perspectives, practices, and prescriptions* (pp. 307–334). Lanham, MD: University Press of America.

Fordham, S., & Ogbu, J. (1986). African American students' school success: Coping with the burden of "acting White." *Urban Review, 18,* 176–206.

Gordon, K. (1995). Self-concept and motivational patterns of resilient African American high school students. *Journal of Black Psychology, 21,* 239–255.

Gordon-Rouse, K., & Cashin, S. (2000). Assessment of academic self-concept and motivation: Results from three ethnic groups. *Measurement and Evaluation in Counseling and Development, 33,* 91–102.

Graham, S. (1988). Can attribution theory tell us something about motivation in Blacks? *Educational Psychologist, 23,* 3–21.

Graham, S. (1994). Motivation in African Americans. *Review of Educational Research, 64,* 55–117.

Graham, S., Taylor, A., & Hudley, C. (1998). Exploring achievement among ethnic minority early adolescents. *Journal of Educational Psychology, 90,* 606–620.

Green, R., & Farquhar, W. (1965). Negro academic motivation and scholastic achievement. *Journal of Educational Psychology, 56,* 241–243.

Gutman, L. M., & Midgley, C. (2000). The role of protective factors in supporting the academic achievement of poor African American students during the middle school transition. *Journal of Youth and Adolescence, 29,* 223–248.

Hacker, A. (1992). *Two nations: Black and White, separate, hostile, unequal.* New York: Macmillan.

Hare, B. (1980). Self-perception and academic achievement: Variations in a desegregated setting. *American Journal of Psychiatry, 137*, 683–689.

Harter, S. (1999). *The construction of the self: A developmental perspective.* New York: Guilford Press.

Haynes, N., Hamilton-Lee, M., & Comer, J. (1988). Differences in self-concept among high, average, and low achieving high school sophomores. *Journal of Social Psychology, 128*, 259–264.

Herbert, J., & Stipek, D. (2005). The emergence of gender differences in children's perceptions of their academic competence. *Journal of Applied Developmental Psychology, 26*, 276–295.

Higgins, E. T. (1997). Beyond pleasure and pain. *American Psychologist, 52*, 1280–1300.

Hilliard, A. (2003). No mystery: Closing the achievement gap between Africans and achievement. In T. Perry, C. Steele, & A. Hilliard (Eds.), *Young, gifted, and Black: Promoting high achievement among African-American students.* Boston: Beacon Press.

Hudley, C. (1995). Assessing the impact of separate schooling for African-American male adolescents. *Journal of Early Adolescence, 15*, 38–57.

Hudley, C., & Graham, S. (2001). Stereotypes of achievement striving among early adolescents. *Social Psychology of Education: An International Journal, 5*, 201–224.

Hudley, C., Graham, S., & Taylor, A. (2007). Reducing aggressive behavior and increasing motivation in school. *Educational Psychologist, 47*, 251–260.

Hudley, C., & Taylor, A. (2006). Cultural competence and youth violence prevention programming. In N. Guerra & E. Smith (Eds.), *Ethnicity, culture, and youth violence prevention programming* (pp. 249–269). Washington, DC: American Psychological Association.

Irving, M., & Hudley, C. (2005). Cultural mistrust, academic outcome expectations and outcome value among African American males. *Urban Education, 40*, 476–496.

Irving, M., & Hudley, C. (2008). *Cultural identification and academic achievement among African American males.* Manuscript submitted for publication.

Jordan, T. (1981). Self-concepts, motivation, and academic achievement of Black adolescents. *Journal of Educational Psychology, 73*, 509–517.

Justice, E. M., Lindsey, L. L., & Morrow, S. F. (1999). The relationship of self perceptions to achievement among African American preschoolers. *Journal of Black Psychology, 25*, 46–60.

Kao, G., & Thompson, J. (2003). Racial and ethnic stratification in educational achievement and attainment. *Annual Review of Sociology, 29*, 417–442.

Kaplan, A., & Maehr, M. (1999a). Achievement goals and student well-being. *Contemporary Educational Psychology, 24*, 330–358.

Kaplan, A., & Maehr, M. (1999b). Enhancing the motivation of African American students: An achievement goal theory perspective. *Journal of Negro Education, 68*, 23–41.

Kellow, J. T., & Jones, B. D. (2005). Stereotype threat in African-American high school students: An initial investigation. *Current Issues in Education, 8*(20). Retrieved January 15, 2008, from http://cie.asu.edu/volume8/number20

Krueger, J. (1996). Personal beliefs and cultural stereotypes about racial characteristics. *Journal of Personality and Social Psychology, 71*, 536–548.

Kugle, C., Clements, R., & Powell, P. (1983). Level and stability of self-esteem in relation to academic behavior of second graders. *Journal of Personality and Social Psychology, 44*, 201–207.

Liu, M., Hsieh, P., Cho, Y., & Schallert, D. (2006). Middle school students' self-efficacy, attitudes, and achievement in a computer-enhanced problem-based learning environment. *Journal of Interactive Learning Research, 17*, 225–242.

Long, J., Monoi, S., Harper, B., Knoblauch, D., & Murphy, P. K. (2007). Academic motivation and achievement among urban adolescents. *Urban Education, 42*, 196–222.

Marsh, H., & Shavelson, R. (1985). Self-concept: Its multifaceted, hierarchical structure. *Educational Psychologist, 20*, 107–123.

McClelland, D. (1961). *The achieving society.* Princeton, NJ: Van Nostrand.

McClendon, C., & Wigfield, A. (1998). Group differences in African American adolescents' achievement-related beliefs about math and science: An initial study. *Journal of Black Psychology, 24*, 28–43.

McKown, C., & Weinstein, R. (2003). The development and consequences of stereotype consciousness in middle childhood. *Child Development, 74*, 498–515.

Mickelson, R. (1990). The attitude–achievement paradox among Black adolescents. *Sociology of Education, 63*, 44–61.

Midgley, C., Arunkumar, R., & Urdan, T (1996). "If I don't do well tomorrow, there's a reason": Predictors of adolescents' use of academic self-handicapping strategies. *Journal of Educational Psychology, 88*, 423–434.

National Center for Education Statistics. (2006). *NAEP 2004 Trends in Academic Progress.* Washington, DC: U.S. Department of Education, National Center for Education Statistics. Retrieved December 4, 2007, from http://nces.ed.gov/pubsearch/pubsinfo.asp?pubid=2005464

National Center for Education Statistics. (2007). *Digest of education statistics: 2006*. Washington, DC: U.S. Department of Education, National Center for Education Statistics. Retrieved December 4, 2007, from http://nces.ed.gov/programs/digest/d06/tables/dt06_131.asp?referrer=list

Niemann, Y., Jennings, L., Rozelle, R., Baxter, J., & Sullivan, E. (1994). Use of free responses and cluster analysis to determine stereotypes of eight groups. *Personality and Social Psychology Bulletin, 20,* 379–390.

Oakes, J. (1985). *Keeping track: How schools structure inequality.* New Haven, CT: Yale University Press.

Ogbu, J. (1993). Differences in cultural frame of reference. *International Journal of Behavioral Development, 16,* 483–506.

Piers, E., & Harris, D. (1984). *The Piers Harris Self Concept Scale Revised.* Los Angeles: Western Psychological Services.

Rosen, B. (1959). Race, ethnicity, and the achievement syndrome. *American Sociological Review, 24,* 47–60.

Rotter, J. (1966). Generalized expectancies for internal versus external control of reinforcement. *Psychological Monographs: General & Applied, 80,* 1–28.

Ryan, K. E., & Ryan, A. M. (2005). Psychological processes underlying stereotype threat and standardized math test performance. *Educational Psychologist, 40,* 53–63.

Saunders, J., Davis, L., Williams, T., & Williams, J. (2004). Gender differences in self-perceptions and academic outcomes: A study of African American high school students. *Journal of Youth and Adolescence, 33,* 81–90.

Seibt, B., & Förster, J. (2004). Stereotype threat and performance: How self-stereotypes influence processing by inducing regulatory foci. *Journal of Personality and Social Psychology, 87,* 38–56.

Solomon, P. (1992). *Black resistance in high school.* Albany: State University of New York Press.

Solorzano, D. (1992). Mobility aspirations among racial minorities, controlling for SES. *Sociology and Social Research, 75,* 182–188.

Steele, C. (1997). A threat in the air: How stereotypes shape intellectual identity and performance. *American Psychologist, 52,* 613–629.

University of California, Outreach Task Force. (1997). *New directions for outreach.* Berkeley: University of California Press.

U.S. Census Bureau. (2004). *American Community Survey.* Washington, DC: Author.

Willig, A., Harnisch, D., Hill, K., & Maehr, M. (1983). Sociocultural and educational correlates of success–failure attributions and evaluation anxiety in the school setting for Black, Hispanic, and Anglo children. *American Educational Research Journal, 20,* 385–410.

15

AFRICAN AMERICAN ENGLISH

ANNE HARPER CHARITY HUDLEY

An estimated 34,658,190 people, or 12.3% of the total U.S. population, are of African American heritage, according to the 2000 census (U.S. Census Bureau, 2008). Most people who self-identify as African American are assumed to have one or more linguistic features of African American English (AAE) in their speech. Speakers who do not identify as African American have also been shown to have characteristics of AAE in their speech, such that the total number of speakers who use features of AAE may be greater than those who identify as African American.

The majority of linguists now view AAE as a dialect of Standard American English (SAE), but some researchers argue that the definition of a language is more deeply rooted in the histories of social and cultural power than in linguistic reality, following the idea that "A language is a dialect with an army and navy" (Unknown). Regardless of the perspective taken on whether AAE is a dialect or a language, many of the linguistic features of AAE and Standard American English as a larger entity do overlap. The focus of this chapter and of much of the work on AAE overall is the linguistic features that differ between AAE and SAE.

In this chapter,[1] I discuss the origins of AAE and provide an overview of the specific linguistic characteristics of AAE. I then discuss the relationship between the use of AAE and racial discrimination, especially as it pertains to student populations. I address educational issues surrounding AAE with respect to reading and writing, language and assessment, and teachers' attitudes concerning student use of AAE. I conclude by suggesting future research directions, in the expectation that knowledge of AAE can enhance the learning experiences of African American students.

AFRICAN AMERICAN ENGLISH

A wide variety of terms (i.e., Ebonics, Black English, African American Vernacular English) have been used to described English as spoken by African Americans in the United States. The variety in the terminology used to describe African American language parallels the difficulty that people have had putting one name and one face on people of African descent in the United States. Most ethnic groups have been described as having unique dialects; in this respect, the term *White English* is akin to AAE. Standard English crosses ethnic categorizations and is a characterization of the English that is used by the power elite in commerce, government, and education. AAE is the more encompassing term, and it is used throughout this chapter to refer to all varieties of English used by speakers where low socioeconomic status African Americans live or historically have lived.

The term *AAE* has often been used to refer to the linguistic features of the language of African Americans that are most unlike White English. The term *Ebonics* was coined during a conversation between Robert Williams and Ernie Smith as a combination of *ebony* and *phonics* (Williams, 1975). Ebonics was widely adopted by educators and the general public following a movement in Oakland, California, in 1996 and 1997 that was designed to help teachers use AAE as a way to help students acquire the language of the school. The efforts were widely misunderstood in the media as an attempt to teach children to speak AAE in school, and thus, the educators' efforts were thwarted (Perry & Delpit, 1997).

AAE has also been called *Urban English* (especially in cities in the Northeast) and *Rural English* (especially in the South). These more general terms reflect the idea that social and economic contact between Blacks and Whites did exist historically and continues to exist. As a result of this contact, AAE and other dialects of American English, including SAE, share many characteristics. Most African Americans in the United States, and many non–African American speakers use linguistic features that have also been used, either historically or currently, in AAE. As America's borders have opened to allow greater numbers of immigrants with Caribbean and African heritage, definitions of AAE have now been expanded to include English of speakers from other countries and those who come into contact with African Americans and acquire some of their language patterns.

The Origins of African American English

There are two main theories on the development of AAE in the United States. The first one, called the *Creolist hypothesis*, states that AAE is the product of the African languages that slaves brought with them across the Atlantic during the Middle Passage (Rickford, 1998). Some linguists and historians have posited that a major component of AAE is its connection to Niger–Congo language systems and the many features common to both languages. Africanist theories regarding the origins of AAE were highlighted in the Oakland Ebonics Resolution, and the theories surrounding the formation of Ebonics caused much controversy among educators and teachers in Oakland and beyond. Theories on the origin of AAE are very difficult to verify because of the brutal nature of slavery and the intentional separation of speakers of similar African languages. There are some elements of African languages that still remain in modern AAE (Turner, 1949). The documentary *The Language You Cry In: The Story of a Mende Song* (Toepke & Serrano, 1998) shows the migration of a Mende funeral song, complete with lyrics and music, from Sierra Leone to the Gullah speakers on the sea islands of South Carolina. When the African language speakers came in contact with English speakers, Creole languages formed. In areas where speakers were more isolated, Creole languages such as Gullah, Jamaican English, and Patois still survive. In areas where speakers' isolation was not as severe, English has more heavily influenced the Creole languages that formed, resulting in dialects such as AAE.

The second theory of the development of AAE, called the *English hypothesis*, states that although Creole languages may have been used in earlier periods of forced migration and slavery, the dialect of English that is spoken today is a product of natural language variation and change among speakers in the United States. People who adhere to the English hypothesis maintain that AAE is a dialect of English rather than a Creole language unto itself. The origins of AAE may not be determined in such a binary manner, because aspects of the multiple histories of African Americans are present in the language varieties. Although the true origins of AAE remain the subject of ongoing debate, an issue of immediate and practical importance is how AAE is understood outside of the AAE-speaking community and, specifically, how practitioners understand the workings of the language and the implications of the language variety for its speakers.

Overview of Research on African American English

Much of the research on AAE had its start in psychology and education research. Scholars have operated on the premise that knowing more about the unique language patterns of students can help with the acquisition of reading and with overall school performance. The U.S.

government funded seminal studies of AAE in the 1960s and 1970s to address the academic Black–White achievement gap. AAE was examined in contrast to SAE, which is the language of education and industry. Large-scale examinations of speech communities in Detroit (Wolfram, 1969) and Harlem (Labov, 1972) provided crucial evidence for establishing that AAE is a full linguistic system and not merely a result of language impoverishment or defect.

Research on AAE in the 1980s and 1990s centered on expanding the communities in which AAE was studied and sampled as well as understanding the social and cultural ramifications of AAE on its speakers (Labov & Harris, 1986; Smitherman, 1986). As American society started to integrate, linguists questioned whether AAE was converging with other dialects of American English because of greater contact between the races or whether it was diverging from dialects spoken by White speakers (Fasold, 1987). Researchers presented evidence for both theories, but it seems that the question, just like the analysis of specific language situations, must be built on localized speech data and not on samples that are meant to be broad, sweeping, or definitive. Much of the early work centered on the speech of boys; in the late 1980s and 1990s, researchers added information about the language of women and girls (Goodwin, 1990; Morgan, 1998). Current research on AAE continues to build on knowledge of specific social groups and African American communities.

Lexical Variation in African American English

The lexicon of AAE is perhaps the feature best known to the general American public. Many of the new words in American English have come into the English language via African American speakers. A general American appreciation for inventing new words and new ways of expressing ideas has combined with American fascinations with African American culture, leading to a greater infusion of AAE into the SAE lexicon.

Many words that speakers of American English no longer think of as slang or nonstandard were once uniquely part of AAE. Major (1994) presented a historical overview of the African American lexicon. The Urban Dictionary (www.urbandictionary.com) contains a large amount of the current lexicon and is edited by AAE speakers, thus including the most current vocabulary available.

Often, the lexicon used by young African American males is emphasized and represented in popular culture, but there are other, largely unnoticed, lexical items that may have an effect on a child's understanding and success in the classroom. Scarborough, Charity, and Griffin (2003) showed that many relational terms describing space, time/order, quantity, and logic that are used in the classroom and on aptitude tests are actually acquired at school during the kindergarten and first-grade years. These functional words include relational terms such as *beginning*, *middle*, and *end* as well as *different*, *every*, and *most of*. Variation in the school lexicon can cause misunderstandings between students and teachers. For example, the more standard phrases "Turn on the lights" and "Go to the front of the line" may be represented in AAE with the forms "Cut on the lights" and "Go to the head of the line." AAE-speaking students may not be exactly sure what the teacher means, and thus, compliance with the command may be delayed or not completed at all.

Phonological Variation in African American English

Phonological features denote the sounds of the language. When great phonological variation or difference is heard by the general speaker, it is often referred to as being an *accent*. Many of the phonological features of AAE are shared by other dialects of American English, especially Southern American English. Some features that are common to AAE also appear as features in the speech of younger Southern American English speakers. Educators must be aware of the differences in the appearance of these features in different groups. Table 15.1 demonstrates consonantal variation in AAE.

African Americans for the most part do not participate in the local vowel changes that characterize the speech of White speakers outside of the South. Some vowel variations that are found among Southern White speakers, however, are found among African American speakers throughout the United States. Because of variation in the ways that vowels

Table 15.1 Consonantal Variation in African American English

Name	Examples
ask/aks alternation	I aks him a question.
ing/in alternation	He's runnin' fast.
/r/ vocalization or deletion	Occurs in words such as in *four, father, car*
/l/ vocalization or deletion	Occurs in words such as *school, cool, people*
final consonant reduction in clusters	*Find* as *fine, hand* as *han*
single final consonant absence	*Five* and *fine* as *fie*
final consonants can be devoiced	*Bad* as *bat*
initial /th/ as [d,t] and final /th/ as [d,t,s,z,f,v]	*They* as *day, with* as *whiff,* and *with* as *wit*
/s/ as [d] before /n/	*Isn't* as *idn't, wasn't* as *wadn't*
glide [j]	*Computer* as *compooter, Houston* as *Hooston*
/t/ as /k/ in a *str-* cluster	*Stream* as *scream*
syllable stress can shift from the second to the first syllable	*POlice, UMbrella*

Table 15.2 Vowel Variation in African American English

Name	Examples
pen–pin merger before nasal consonants	*Pen* as *pin, ten* as *tin*
/ij/ and /i/, /ej/ and /e/ merge before /l/	*Feel* and *fill; fail* and *fell* rhyme
diphthongs as monophthongs	*Oil* and *all; time* and *Tom* may rhyme
/er/ as ur word finally	Occurs in words such as *hair, care,* and *there*

are pronounced, it may be quite difficult for African American children to determine what rhymes, and this difficulty can interfere with phonological awareness and the acquisition of reading. Table 15.2 demonstrates vowel variation in AAE.

Grammatical Variation in African American English

The grammatical features of AAE are well studied because of their uniqueness to the language variety. Grammatical features of AAE are, to most listeners, more noticeable and distinct than the phonological features described earlier. It is important to remember, however, that despite their uniqueness, the features are nonetheless systematic and regular and not indicative of a degraded or defective form of SAE. The grammatical features described in Table 15.3 are more unique to speakers of AAE than many other English dialects.

Prosodic Variation in African American English

Many listeners report that the melody and rhythm of a speaker's voice may mark a speaker as African American even if all other aspects of the speaker's language sound standard. Rhythmic patterns are often preserved in speakers who do not use many of the more socially stigmatized lexical, phonological, and grammatical features of AAE. It is very difficult for linguists to measure and describe the unique prosodic patterns of AAE, but they are noticeable to many speakers. Intonation differences have also been found in the formation of questions in AAE. I (Charity, 2005) found differences in the way that teachers asked questions and the way that children imitated these questions in several major cities in the United States. Teachers' voices more frequently rose at the end of the question sentence, whereas many of the students' voices remained flat. Although the absence of a rise in tone at the end of the question may be a neutral

Table 15.3 Grammatical Variation in African American English (AAE)

Name	Examples
negative concord/multiple negation	*He doesn't see anything* as *He don't see nothing*
irregular verbs may be regularized	*I saw her* as *I seened/seent her*
done may be used to mark distant past tense	*He failed out ages ago* as *He done failed out*
ain't may be used as an auxiliary verb or copula	*He isn't shy* as *He ain't shy*
double modals may be used	*I could have done that* as *I might could have done that*
subject–verb agreement is not required	*They weren't there* as *They wasn't there*
the copula may be deleted where it can be contracted in SAE	*She is funny* and *She's funny* as *She funny*
stressed *bin* may be used to mark the completion of an action	*I finished long ago* as *I bin finished my homework*
the copula *be* may be used to mark habitual action	*He talks nonstop* as *He be talking all the time*
the use of *steady* and *come* to mark habitual action	*He is always talking* as *He steady talking*
the auxiliary *had* may be used with the simple past tense	*What happened was* as *What had happened was*
existential *it* and *dey* are used to mark something that exists	*There is a dog in here* as *It's a dog in here*
a plural may be unmarked	*Fifty cents* as *fifty cent*
a possessive may be unmarked	*My mama's house* as *My mama house*
third-person singular verbs may be unmarked	*He talks too much* as *He talk too much*
hypercorrected forms may occur where AAE has a variable form	*I had to go to the store* as *I hadded to go to the store*
inversion of subject and auxiliary is not obligatory in questions	*Is he behind me?* as *He is behind me?*
relative clauses are not obligatory	*You are the one that she knows* as *You the one she knows*

Note: SAE = Standard American English.

dialectal feature of AAE, flat questions are also used in SAE to mark disengagement and disinterest. The confounding of the expression of emotion in SAE with features in AAE that do not display the same emotion may cause students to be improperly evaluated academically, socially, and emotionally. Generalized qualitative evaluations of intonation are used by reading instructors to mark students' general fluency and engagement in the text (Downhower, 1997). Because of dialectal differences in rates of speech, such general measures may not be the best predictor of reading fluency.

Intonation differences may be important in interpreting emotion across dialects. The lack of melodic variation in the voice among African American students, especially males, may simply reflect dialectal variation, but it is often misinterpreted as boredom, lethargy, or an indication of a general sense of apathy. Misunderstandings regarding the expression and comprehension of emotion are possible (Collins & Nowicki, 2001).

Pragmatic Variation in African American English

Discourse-level differences in AAE have also been well documented. Smitherman (1977) and Morgan (1998) have noted verbal styles that are more frequent and prominent among AAE speakers. For example, direct commands are frequently used in AAE, such that AAE-speaking students may understand commands couched in politeness strategies as suggestions and therefore not obey them, for example, "Let's get lined up" instead of "Line up now," and "I like the way you all are talking quietly" instead of "Please (continue to) talk quietly."

Instigating, the initiation of verbal commentary or insult to provoke response, is a form of going on the offensive either in a playful or more serious manner. The great danger with instigation is that playful teasing may quickly turn into a more heated or violent argument. Instigation may cause problems in the classroom or on the playground, if the teasing is misinterpreted and used as a segue to greater forms of confrontation.

Variability Within Speakers of African American English

There are many complexities of putting one definition on AAE. AAE varies by the age, gender, region, and social class of the speaker. Most sociolinguistic studies do not examine every given feature of a dialect and, as such, it is difficult to make cross-study comparisons of feature use over space, time, and demographic group. Many of the features and characteristics of AAE that have been described thus far in the literature, however, have been measured or described for African Americans across the United States, yet differences have been reported in the frequency of use of certain features by age, gender, region, and degree of segregation of the African American population in a given area (Rickford, 1999). Examinations of social class differences are limited, but the use of AAE features has been identified in the speech of middle-class African Americans. Lower-income African Americans have been reported as having more features of AAE in their speech than do middle-class speakers, but few studies have examined the speech of middle-class speakers to see what features they do use (Horton-Ikard & Miller, 2004). The main differential in the use of AAE features is not in absolute appearance but in the frequency of appearance of features. Young male speakers have been shown in studies to use AAE features, especially stigmatized features, more frequently than female speakers (Charity, 2005).

Males also have been shown to be less likely to use features of SAE across races and social groups than females (Labov, 2001). Women may ascribe more social capital to the standard forms of language, and these are passed down from mother to daughter. Boys develop language at a slower rate than girls, and therefore they might miss these verbal/social cues in their formative years and attend more to the language of their peers (Van Hulle, Goldsmith, & Lemery, 2004). Other challenges that large numbers of African American boys face, such as discipline and attention issues, become conflated with linguistic differences, and thus, boys are subject to more frequent placement in special education courses, suspension, and expulsion than African American girls (Ferguson, 2000). Schoolteachers are disproportionately female, which also leads to the characterization of female speech as the academic standard.

Language Discrimination and Racism

All speakers have distinct features that can be described and compared with other speech varieties, yet because of the history of racism and discrimination in the United States, the language of African Americans is seen as substandard and undesirable. American schools and institutions were until the late 1960s bound by law to systematically exclude students by race, gender, and national origin. In addition, schools still marginalize those who fall outside the norm, with respect to language and all other social, cultural, and economic factors. The proposed goal, therefore, of education is to make the individual mainstream or "educated" enough to be successful in higher levels of education and in the marketplace. Many people have the misconception that AAE is slang or lazy English. Linguists have demonstrated that AAE is just as systematic and regular as any other language or variety of English. *Martin Luther King Junior Elementary School Children et al. v. Ann Arbor School District Board* (1979) provided an attempt to confront the linguistic consequences of slavery and segregation (Baugh, 2000). The case involved 11 African American children plaintiffs of low socioeconomic status in a predominately White and middle-class school in Ann Arbor, Michigan, who had been misplaced in remedial education because of their use of AAE in school (Smitherman, 1998). The families filed suit against the school district for the wrongful placement in special education and for neglecting to teach the students appropriately, because the school had disregarded cultural and linguistic differences in its evaluation process. Judge

Charles Joiner focused his ruling on the school system's "failure ... to overcome language barriers," as covered by Section 1703(f) of the Equal Employment Opportunity Commission Title 20. At the same time, however, Joiner did not address the linguistic facts brought to the trial that dispute what he considered to be the lawful policy of placing AAE speakers in speech pathology sessions as a result of their dialect. Section 1703(f) of Title 20 was originally written to support the education of bilingual individuals, but not the education of speakers of nonstandard English. Joiner's interpretation was not taken to a higher court, leaving the educational issues surrounding AAE unacknowledged by the federal government (Baugh, 2000).

Although AAE may not be a variety of English that is central to education and commerce, it should still be respected and understood. Understanding more about AAE will help educators use the language that their students bring with them to the classroom in order to help them achieve greater academic and social success. Although strides have recently been made to eliminate overt racism, discrimination based on language differences is an indirect byproduct of inequalities in American schools. Colleges' rejection of prospective students with weaker writing skills and employers' denial of jobs to speakers who do not have a voice that would successfully represent a company are acceptable under most discrimination policies. Also, although there are programs to aid English language learners' acquisition of English, there are few such programs in place to help dialect speakers; the general sentiment is that native English speakers should be able to produce SAE no matter what their background.

Psychological and Educational Issues for Speakers of African American English

Language and Identity

When children come to school speaking AAE, they are aware that it is the language of their families, friends, and neighbors. Children understand that their culture and identity are tied to their language. Delpit (2003) described this difficult tension between wanting to protect a child's cultural heritage and the desire for the child to use the standard language or "sound educated." Delpit inquired, at what point does the price become too high—what cultural price do children have to pay by speaking the standard dialect so that they will be, in a sense, protected from others' prejudices and opinions? If a child's language is devalued, then the people whom the child knows and respects most are also devalued, and in turn, the child may lose confidence in the school and in his or her teachers. In addition, misunderstandings are possible between teachers and students, particularly when each assumes the other understands and he or she is understood. For example, if a child states, "I *bin* finished my homework," it may mean that he or she finished it a long time ago, and the listener should already know that it is done. If the teacher does not understand this, a crucial transfer of information is lost. A child's use of dialect may be seen as an act of defiance or disrespect. Even though the child may not have other forms in his or her linguistic repertoire, the use of AAE may be seen as signal of rejection of the school culture and may lead to differential treatment in the classroom.

Much of the educational literature on AAE has been devoted to the concept of "sounding" and "acting" White. Many African American speakers are invested in the maintenance of what they perceive to be authentic African American speech and culture. The concept of "keeping it real" expresses the idea that although the dominant White society may prevail in most of the world, internal respect for AAE is essential. The stigmatization of the use of SAE by African Americans supports the idea that African American students who want to do well in school are often seen as acting White (Fordham & Ogbu, 1986; Ogbu, 2003).

The idea of "acting White" as a way of achieving educational success is contested. Even if African Americans speak SAE or in other ways attempt to act in a way that is seen as White, American society still recognizes the individual as Black, and the attempt to sound like a White speaker may have even more adverse effects. A standard English–speaking African American still might not get a job because he or she is African American. As James Baldwin (1979) explained:

> It is not the black child's language that is in question, it is not his language that is despised: it is his experience. A child cannot be taught by anyone who despises him, and a child cannot afford to be fooled. A child cannot afford to be taught by

anyone whose demand, essentially, is that the child repudiates his experience, and all that gives him sustenance, and enter a limbo in which he will no longer be black, and which he knows that he can never become a white. Black people have lost too many black children that way. (p. 16)

Practical Implications

Smitherman (2000) described the identity crisis of "push–pull" that African American students face. As students push harder to assimilate to the school culture in order to succeed in school, they are forced to pull away from the identity of their home communities. Schools, and society in general, do not appreciate the child's home language and experience. The schools expect the child to implicitly look down on his or her own language and culture as part of the educational process. Most people, not just African Americans with their specific social and cultural history, would personally find this message hard to accept, but African Americans must live this reality every day in their actions in order to succeed.

Wilder (2000) reported that, over the past 3 decades, White teachers have made up about 88.5% of the U.S. teaching workforce, and 30% of the children in schools in the United States are African American. Two thirds of these African American teachers work in the South, 4.8% work in the Northeast, 4.9% work in the Midwest, and 2.7% work in the West. Even those teachers who speak AAE may not look favorably on its use in the school setting, because a speaker's use of AAE is often perceived as a mark of defiance, even though students intend to use AAE as a marker of their identity.

Knowledge of AAE features is crucial to understanding how teachers can more systematically help students with issues in reading, writing, and speaking. Teachers are charged with helping students to learn the social value of language use. This is difficult for teachers of AAE speakers to do without devaluing students' home language. Studies also have indicated that teachers feel that it is inappropriate to use features of AAE in school (e.g., Blake & Cutler, 2003; Hoover et al., 1996; Taylor, 1973). Such studies, however, have not focused on which specific aspects of AAE are most stigmatized by teachers. Researchers have argued that dialectal differences themselves are not the major contributor to academic failure and instead point to extrinsic explanatory factors for low achievement, including prejudice against, and lowered educational expectations for, African American students by classroom teachers; the inappropriateness of testing procedures, and of many tests themselves, for evaluating reading and related abilities of AAE speakers; and the confounding of socioeconomic and instructional differences with dialectal variation in many studies. The contemporary work on teachers' attitudes toward AAE supports Seligman, Tucker, and Lambert's (1972) discovery of a relationship between the speech and photographs of students and the way teachers judged those students. Children who are perceived as sounding White are judged as being friendlier and, by extension, communicatively competent in the school setting. Seligman et al. noted, "We wonder just how many boys who look and sound 'unintelligent' were discouraged from continuing their education because they did not receive the appropriate feedback from their teachers" (p. 141). Thirty-three years later, similar questions remain.

Purcell-Gates (1995) suggested that direct instructions be provided for children to increase their social and metalinguistic analysis of differences between AAE and SAE without devaluing either language variety. For example, explicit instruction in contrastive analysis for children can include phrases such as "We don't use that word in school or church," "When you address Mr. Bush, be sure to look him in the eye and say, 'Pleased to meet you, sir,'" and "When you write a letter, begin with 'Dear So-and-So.'" Using this same model, teachers can instruct children about phonological and grammatical differences. Wheeler and Swords (2006) gave detailed examples of teaching contrastive analysis at the elementary school level. For example, the use of explicit directions, such as "When we are in school, we practice using our linking verbs just the same way that we sometimes practice speaking Spanish," takes the linguistic burden from the child and encourages the sentiment that school is a place for expansion and exploration instead of a place for correction and devaluation.

It is important to practically consider what teachers and other educators can know about all the language varieties that exist and how that information should be shared/imparted. Brief, yet comprehensive Web sites designed for specific practitioners include http://www

.rehabmed.ualberta.ca/spa/phonology/Features.htm (Pollock et al., 1998) for speech pathologists and http://heaski.people.wm.edu (Askin, 2007) for teachers. A comprehensive bibliography of research on AAE can be found online at http://privatewww.essex.ac.uk/~patrickp/AAVE.html (Patrick, 2007). The American Speech, Language, and Hearing Association has created a CD-ROM reference guide (Adger, Schilling-Estes, & Wolfram, 2003) to help professionals who serve AAE-speaking populations learn more about the dialect.

African American English Reading and Writing

The mismatch between AAE and written SAE may cause great challenges for an AAE speaker who is learning how to read. The use of AAE features is shown to inversely correlate with reading scores as demonstrated by the Woodcock Johnson Mastery Reading Test—Revised (Charity, Scarborough, & Griffin, 2004), and AAE has been shown to influence early spellers' ability to produce SAE written forms (Terry, 2006). Scott and Rogers (1996) provided an overview of issues that AAE-speaking students face in regard to academic writing from elementary through postgraduate schooling. Students generally use fewer AAE features when writing than when speaking, but they face challenges in the macro-level transition from oral to written styles of communication. Michaels (1987) demonstrated how the more locally centered narrative style of African American children conflicts with the expectations of academic writing. Even in the reporting of personal experience, SAE writing conventions state that writing should be neutral and speak to a general readership. Helping students understand the differences between such conventions and the ones they learned through AAE is crucial to their understanding of the academic writing process.

Assessment and Education

Many of the challenges in the assessment of AAE-speaking children are a result of teachers' ignorance of linguistic and cultural differences. Conventional testing situations have been shown to cause African American (as well as other) children to become hesitant and taciturn. The use of AAE presents special challenges to language assessment of AAE-speaking children who have other physical and mental differences (e.g., Down syndrome, fetal alcohol syndrome, and lead poisoning). These populations have no normalized samples against which to compare their language variation. Washington (1996) described the necessity of understanding the individual child's language patterns and the language patterns of the community in light of the lack of normative samples. Stockman (1996) noted that it is important to know what the accepted way of speaking in the child's community is, yet macro-level examinations of AAE are limited. AAE-speaking children may have more or less the same phonetic inventory as other children, but their frequency and use of AAE causes their language to pattern differently than that of other speakers. Many developmental guides rely on binary assessments of linguistic features in a speaker's language. Either the feature is assessed to be in the language or it is not. For example, all children may have the /th/ phoneme, but for AAE, the assessment of the feature with respect to placement in the word is essential. African American children may have the phoneme at the beginning of the word, but less frequently at the end of the word. So, if the phonetic inventory is tested using a word that asks the child to produce a -th word finally, the item may be missed in the assessment of the child's inventory.

Contemporary aptitude and achievement tests have attempted to respond to commonly known dialectal differences by including a caveat in the directions that instruct the test scorer not to take off points for dialectal differences. However, if the tester is not well versed in the features of AAE, then it is very difficult to make the needed accommodations.

FUTURE DIRECTIONS IN RESEARCH

Future research on AAE and the social and educational progress of its speakers is needed in order to understand the role that the dialect plays in the development of its speakers. Large empirical studies that would serve as general references for language variation among African Americans are greatly needed. More longitudinal quantitative studies of AAE are needed in order to document and describe the language that AAE speakers are actually using in schools and how their use of AAE affects their academic achievement. Research on the varieties of language used in school and clinical settings also is needed. Examinations of African Americans who use varying degrees of AAE features would clarify whether distinctions are drawn between the language and the race and culture of the speakers. Such studies would provide language bases on which standardized tests could be developed for dialectal sensitivity issues and would provide teachers and educators with linguistic models and references within their own communities. More effort should be spent on disseminating information that has already been gathered about AAE and on adding to this information by recording language samples in specific African American communities. It is crucial that researchers share with clinicians and practitioners what they already know. Researchers should be more involved in creating easy-to-implement, realistic language instruction models that help students understand the differences between AAE and SAE that teachers can use in the classroom with their individual students, because it is on this teacher–student level that many educational changes could occur.

Conclusion

To implement change in teacher attitudes and school policy, educators must emphasize what can be learned about language use in the school. In the classroom setting, there are a variety of students from different backgrounds and social networks, but these students are taught in very similar ways. What children say and do and what they do *not* say and do in the classroom predict so much about their future successes and what path their lives will take. A combination of efforts by educators and by scholars from various disciplines would result in instructional materials for teachers and students that will help bring the relationship between oral and written language to the forefront in the educational process. Research thus far on AAE has shown that the speech of African Americans is not unsystematic and depraved. Many listeners do not accept this fact because of the mismatch between the richness of the AAE system that linguists observe and the academic performance of the African Americans who speak it.

Note

1. This material is based on work supported by the National Science Foundation under Grant 0512005 and by the College of William and Mary. I would like to thank Carolyn Palmquist, Melissa Edwards, Christine Mallinson, Renée Price, and Chris Hudley for their feedback on earlier versions of this chapter.

References

Adger, C., Schilling-Estes, N., & Wolfram, W. (2003). *African American English: Structure and clinical implications* [CD-ROM and manual]. Rockville, MD: American Speech, Language, and Hearing Association.

Askin, H. (2007). *Language variation in the classroom: A guide for teachers.* Retrieved October 8, 2007, from http://heaski.people.wm.edu

Baldwin, J. (1979, July 29). If Black English isn't a language, then tell me, what is? *New York Times,* pp. 16–17.

Baugh, J. (2000). *Beyond Ebonics: Linguistic pride and racial prejudice.* New York: Oxford University Press.

Blake, R., & Cutler, C. (2003). AAE and variation in teachers' attitudes: A question of school philosophy? *Linguistics and Education, 14,* 163–194.

Charity, A. H. (2005). *Dialect variation in school settings among African-American children of low-socioeconomic status.* Unpublished doctoral dissertation, University of Pennsylvania.

Charity, A. H., Scarborough, H. S., & Griffin, D. M. (2004). Familiarity with school English in African-American children and its relation to early reading achievement. *Child Development, 75,* 1340–1356.

Collins, M., & Nowicki, S., Jr. (2001). African American children's ability to identify emotion in facial expressions and tones of voice of European Americans. *Journal of Genetic Psychology, 162,* 334–347.

Delpit, L. (2003). *The skin that we speak: Thoughts on language and culture in the classroom.* New York: W. W. Norton.

Downhower, S. (1997). Effects of repeated readings techniques on second-grade transitional readers' fluency and comprehension. *Reading Research Quarterly, 22,* 389–406.

Fasold, R. (Ed.). (1987). Are Black and White vernaculars diverging? [Special issue]. *American Speech, 62*(1).

Ferguson, A. (2000). *Bad boys: Public school in the making of Black masculinity.* Ann Arbor: University of Michigan Press.

Fordham, S., & Ogbu, J. (1986). Black students' school success: Coping with the "burden of 'acting White.'" *The Urban Review, 18,* 176–206.

Goodwin, M. H. (1990). *He-said–she-said: Talk as social organization among Black children.* Bloomington: Indiana University Press.

Hoover, M., Lewis, S., Politzer, R., Ford, J., McNair-Knox, F., Hicks, S., et al. (1996). Tests of African American English for teachers of bidialectal students. In R. Jones (Ed.), *Handbook of test and measurements for Black populations* (pp. 367–381). Hampton, VA: Cobb & Henry.

Horton-Ikard, R., & Miller, J. F. (2004). It is not just the poor kids: The use of AAE forms by African-American school-aged children from middle SES communities. *Journal of Communication Disorders, 37,* 467–487.

Labov, W. (1972). *Language in the inner city: Studies in the Black English vernacular.* Philadelphia: University of Pennsylvania Press.

Labov, W. (2001). The gender paradox. In *Principles of linguistic change: Social factors* (pp. 261–293). London: Blackwell.

Labov, W., & Harris, W. (1986). Defacto segregation of Black and White vernaculars. In D. Sankoff (Ed.), *Diversity and diachrony* (pp. 1–24). Philadelphia: John Benjamins.

Major, C. (1994). *Juba to jive: A dictionary of African-American slang.* New York: Penguin.

Martin Luther King Junior Elementary School Children et al. v. Ann Arbor School District Board 73 F.Supp. 1371 (E.D. Mich. 1979).

Michaels, S. (1987). Text and context: A new approach to the study of classroom writing. *Discourse Processes, 10,* 321–347.

Morgan, M. (1998). More than a mood or an attitude: Discourse and verbal genres in African-American culture. In S. Mufwene, R. Rickford, G. Bailey, & J. Baugh (Eds.), *African American English: Structure, history and use* (pp. 251–281). New York: Routledge.

Ogbu, J. (2003). *Black American students in an affluent suburb: A study of academic disengagement.* Mahwah, NJ: Lawrence Erlbaum.

Patrick, P. (2007). *African American English: A Webpage for linguists and other folks.* Retrieved October 8, 2007, from http://privatewww.essex.ac.uk/~patrickp/AAVE.html

Perry, T., & Delpit, L. (Eds.). (1997). *The real Ebonics debate: Power, language, and the education of African-American children.* Boston: Beacon Press.

Pollock, K., Bailey, G., Berni, M., Fletcher, D., Hinton, L., Johnson, I., et al. (1998). *Phonological features of African American English.* Retrieved October 8, 2007, from http://www.rehabmed.ualberta.ca/spa/phonology/Features.htm

Purcell-Gates, V. (1995). *Other people's words: The cycle of low literacy.* Cambridge, MA: Harvard University Press.

Rickford, J. (1998). The Creole origins of African American vernacular English: Evidence from copula absence. In S. Mufwene, J. Rickford, G. Bailey, & J. Baugh (Eds.), *African American English: Structure, history and use* (pp. 154–200). New York: Routledge.

Rickford, J. (1999). *African American English: Features, evolution, educational implications.* Malden, MA: Blackwell.

Scarborough, H. S., Charity, A. H., & Griffin, D. (2003, June 15). *Linguistic challenges for young readers.* Presentation given to the Society for the Scientific Study of Reading, Boulder, CO.

Scott, C., & Rogers, L. (1996). Written language abilities of African American children and youth. In A. Kamhi, K. Pollock, & J. Harris (Eds.), *Communication development and disorders in African American children: Research, assessment, and intervention* (pp. 307–332). Baltimore: Paul H. Brookes.

Seligman, C. R., Tucker, G. R., & Lambert, W. E. (1972). The effects of speech style and other attributes on teachers' attitudes toward pupils. *Language in Society, 1,* 131–142.

Smitherman, G. (1977). *Talkin and testifyin: The language of Black America.* Boston: Houghton Mifflin.

Smitherman, G. (1986, March). *Toward a national public policy on language.* Paper presented at the 37th Annual Meeting of the Conference on College Composition and Communication, New Orleans, LA.

Smitherman, G. (1998). What go round come round: King in perspective. In T. Petty & L. Delpit (Eds.), *The real Ebonics debate: Power, language, and the education of African-American children* (pp. 163–171). Boston: Beacon Press.

Smitherman, G. (2000). *Talkin that talk: Language, culture and education in African America.* London: Routledge.

Stockman, I. (1996). Phonological development and disorders in African American children. In A. Kamhi, K. Pollock, & J. Harris (Eds.), *Communication development and disorders in African-American children: Research, assessment, and intervention* (pp. 117–154). Baltimore: Paul H. Brookes.

Taylor, O. (1973). Teachers' attitudes toward Black and nonstandard English as measured by the Language Attitude Scale. In R. Shuy & R. Fasold (Eds.), *Language attitudes: Current trends and prospects* (pp. 174–201). Washington, DC: Georgetown University Press.

Terry, N. P. (2006). Relations between dialect variation, grammar, and early spelling skills. *Reading and Writing, 19,* 907–931.

Toepke, A. (Producer), & Serrano, A. (Director). (1998). *The language you cry in: The story of a Mende song* [Documentary]. Sierra Leone/Spain: California Newsreel.

Turner, L. D. (1949). *Africanisms in the Gullah dialect.* Ann Arbor: University of Michigan Press.

U.S. Census Bureau. (2008). *The Black population in the United States.* Retrieved May 1, 2008, from http://www.census.gov/population/www/socdemo/race/black.html

Van Hulle, C., Goldsmith, H., & Lemery, K. (2004). Genetic, environmental, and gender effects on individual differences in toddler expressive language. *Journal of Speech, Language, and Hearing Research, 47,* 904–912.

Washington, J. (1996). Issues in the assessing of African-American children. In A. Kamhi, K. Pollock, & J. Harris (Eds.), *Communication development and disorders in African-American children: Research, assessment, and intervention* (pp. 34–45). Baltimore: Paul H. Brookes.

Wheeler, R., & Swords, R. (2006). *Code-switching: Teaching standard English in urban classrooms.* Urbana, IL: National Council of Teachers of English.

Wilder, M. (2000). Increasing African American teachers' presence in American schools: Voices of students who care. *Journal of Urban Education, 35,* 205–220.

Williams, R. (Ed.). (1975). *Ebonics: The true language of Black folks.* St. Louis, MO: Robert L. Williams and Associates.

Wolfram, W. (1969). *A sociolinguistic description of Detroit Negro speech.* Washington, DC: Center for Applied Linguistics.

16

STEREOTYPE THREAT

A Review, Critique, and Implications

CLAYTIE DAVIS III AND CRYSTAL SIMMONS

The educational outcomes of African Americans continue to puzzle and be a source of contentious debate for educators and scholars alike (Jencks & Phillips, 1998). According to the most recent educational statistics, Black students have a higher dropout rate, complete fewer years of school, and enroll in fewer Advanced Placement/or gifted classes, than their White and Asian counterparts (U.S. Department of Education, National Center for Education Statistics, 2007).[1] Black students also score lower than all other races on the SAT Verbal and Math sections. They score, on average, 93 points lower than Whites on the SAT Verbal section and 107 points lower than Whites on the SAT Math section (see http://nces.ed.gov/programs/digest/d05). Furthermore, according to national achievement assessments, Black students score lower than their White counterparts in both reading and math. In fourth grade, the difference between Black students' and White students' math scaled scores is 20 and increases to 23 points by the eighth grade. Similarly, the difference between Black and White students' reading scaled scores is more than 26 points in both the fourth and eighth grades (U.S. Department of Education, National Center for Education Statistics, 2005). Unfortunately, given the structural and economic barriers (e.g., higher student–teacher ratios; attending underfunded schools; institutional racism) facing many African American children and their families there is little to suggest that this trend is likely to change.

Few would deny that the legacy of slavery, discrimination, segregation, and decreased socioeconomic status has had an adverse impact on the educational outcomes just listed for students of African descent (Woodson, 1933/2000). However, the legacy of racism and oppression cannot completely explain the achievement gap. Similarly, other hypotheses, such as genetic differences (Herrnstein & Murray, 1994), a desire to not "act White" (Fordham & Ogbu, 1986), "cool pose" for African American males (Majors & Billson, 1992), or test bias (Williams, Williams, & Mitchell, 2004), are not sufficient for understanding this epidemic.

So why does the achievement gap persist? Moreover, why is it that when Black and White students enter college with the same level of preparation (e.g., same SAT score, similar schooling), a pattern develops whereby Black students' grade point averages (GPAs) are lower than their White peers' GPAs? Why are White college students graduating at faster rates than

Black students? Although no one explanation is likely to explain all of the differences among various ethnic groups, the notion of *stereotype threat* is promising because of its emphasis on the individual as a member of a group instead of on genetic differences or on the test (and possible bias)—neither of which readily lend themselves to practical interventions.

Stereotype threat is defined as "being at risk of confirming as self-characteristic, a negative stereotype about one's group" (Steele & Aronson, 1995, p. 797). In this case, the stereotype is that Blacks are less intelligent (or do not perform well on standardized assessments) than their White counterparts. For example, when placed in the high-stakes situation of taking a standardized achievement test, stereotype threat theory posits that an African American's performance will be negatively impacted, in part, because of the fear of confirming the stereotype that Blacks do not do well on achievement tests. However, stereotype threat is not just about explaining the academic gap between African Americans and Whites; it is a social psychological phenomenon with implications for the field of education; that is, with the knowledge of how stereotype threat negatively impacts an individual's performance comes the opportunity to design creative interventions to mitigate the pernicious effect of stereotype threat. In this chapter, we review the stereotype threat literature. We outline Steele and Aronson's (1995) original study, critique the evidence supporting the stereotype threat effect, review proposed mediating and moderating variables of stereotype threat, and conclude with implications for research. It is our hope that readers will use the information provided to design and conduct studies that advance the field as it relates to improving the educational outcomes of African Americans.

Stereotype Threat

In an interview regarding the origins of stereotype threat (Steele, 2003) Claude Steele modestly described how the theory came to fruition. Steele reflected that he had noticed a trend whereby African American students with a certain SAT score consistently earned lower grades at the university level than other students with the same SAT score. Later, he and a colleague (Steven Spencer) found a similar pattern in the grades of women in challenging math courses (compared with their male peers). However, it was not until Steele collaborated with Joshua Aronson that he explicitly conducted studies designed to test the hypothesis that some mechanism—apprehension of confirming a negative stereotype—was depressing African American performance. The original stereotype threat article (Steele & Aronson, 1995), "Stereotype Threat and the Intellectual Test Performance of African Americans," published in the *Journal of Personality and Social Psychology*, actually consists of four studies, each building on the other. The following is a brief overview of this seminal work that informs the rest of this chapter.

In Study 1, 114 Stanford University undergraduates were randomly assigned to one of three conditions: (1) a diagnostic condition, (2) a nondiagnostic-only condition, and (3) a nondiagnostic challenge condition. In the diagnostic condition, students were told that the study was about "various personal factors involved in performance on problems requiring reading and verbal reasoning abilities" (Steele & Aronson, 1995, p. 799). In the nondiagnostic-only and the nondiagnostic challenge conditions, students were told that the study was about "psychological factors involved in solving verbal problems" (p. 799). However, for the nondiagnostic challenge condition a caveat was added that the researchers wanted to present "even highly verbal people with a mental challenge" (p. 799). The researchers speculated that presenting the test in this manner might increase motivation for the students. All students took the same test (challenging items taken from a sample Graduate Record Examination study guide), with the number of correctly solved items serving as the dependent variable. The results demonstrated a significant difference between Black students in the diagnostic condition compared with White students in the diagnostic condition; just as important, Black students in the nondiagnostic conditions scored comparably to their White peers after controlling for SAT score. However, the researchers failed to find a Race × Condition interaction; that is, there was no significant difference in scores between the Black students in the diagnostic condition and Black students in the nondiagnostic-only and nondiagnostic challenge conditions.

In Study 2, Steele and Aronson (1995) explored whether students in the stereotype threat condition evidenced increased anxiety. In this study, the nondiagnostic challenge condition was eliminated. Study 2 provided support for a Race × Diagnostic condition effect. African American students in the diagnostic condition performed fewer items correctly than did African Americans in the nondiagnostic condition. Black students in the diagnostic condition completed fewer items than Whites in the diagnostic condition and both Whites and Blacks in the nondiagnostic condition. However, there was no evidence of increased anxiety for African Americans in the threat condition compared with the nonthreatening condition.

In Study 3, the authors hypothesized that stereotype activation was taking place in stereotype threatening situations. Moreover, they expected that African Americans would be more likely to distance themselves from the stereotypes, more likely to self-handicap in a stereotype threatening situation, and less likely to indicate their race if they were concerned about the threat of confirming a negative stereotype. All four hypotheses were supported, providing the first evidence that students in the diagnostic condition think about racial stereotypes more than those students in the nondiagnostic condition and the control condition.

In Study 4, Steele and Aronson questioned whether merely activating the stereotype was enough to lead to decreased performance evidenced in the previous studies. In this study, Black and White students were assigned to one of two conditions: (1) race prime or (2) no race prime. In the race prime condition, students were asked to indicate their race immediately before taking the test (with instructions similar to Study 1 and Study 2). As predicted, Black students in the race prime condition performed significantly worse than Blacks and Whites in the unprimed condition. They also exhibited significantly more anxiety as measured by the State–Trait Anxiety Inventory (Spielberger, 1983), a finding not supported in Study 2.

Since publication of Steele and Aronson's (1995) seminal study, scores of studies conducted on the stereotype threat effect have successfully replicated the results. Just as important, researchers have provided ample support that the stereotype threat effect is not endemic to African Americans or other marginalized groups. For example, Aronson et al. (1999) demonstrated that White males in advanced math courses may experience stereotype threat when led to believe that experimenters want to know why Whites underperform compared with Asian students (stereotype threat condition); Aronson and Salinas (1997) examined stereotype threat with Latino college students and obtained similar results; and Spencer, Steele, and Quinn (1999) found that academically gifted women (i.e., who scored at or above the 85th percentile on the Math section of the SAT or ACT) underperformed, compared with their equally gifted male peers, on a difficult math examination (stereotype threat condition) but did not struggle on an easy examination (control condition). In a novel spin on previous stereotype threat studies, Stone, Lynch, Sjomeling, and Darley (1999) found that Black participants performed better when a golf task was described as being diagnostic of natural ability instead of sports intelligence; the opposite was found for White participants, who performed better when the task was described as indicative of sports intelligence. The stereotype threat effect has also been found with French students (Croizet & Claire, 1998) and with students in elementary school (Ambady, Shih, Kim, & Pittinsky, 2001).

CRITIQUE OF STEREOTYPE THREAT RESEARCH

Although stereotype threat effects on stigmatized individuals are well documented, some researchers (Sackett, Hardison, & Cullen, 2004; Sackett, Schmitt, Ellingson, & Kabin, 2001) have proposed several criticisms against this literature. Their primary concerns surround the statistical methods used to demonstrate the strength of the stereotype threat effect and the generalizability of the results found in the laboratory to more applied settings.

Statistical Methods and Strength

In their article highlighting the misinterpretation of Steele and Aronson's (1995) initial finding of stereotype threat, Sackett and his colleagues (2004) argued that the initial study, and other studies that used Steele and Aronson's design, did not show that removing stereotype threat from testing situations eliminates the Black–White test score gap. Indeed, Steele and Aronson never made this claim in their original study, and their results have been misinterpreted by other people in psychology. Instead, their research and other research using this method show that absent stereotype threat, the African American–White difference is just what one would expect based on the African American–White difference in SAT scores, whereas in the presence of stereotype threat, the difference is larger than would be expected based on the difference in SAT scores. (Sackett et al., 2004, p. 9)

Because Steele and Aronson (1995), and other replications of their study, controlled for SAT scores prior to examining the manipulation, the observed differences between Whites and Blacks in the diagnostic condition actually demonstrates that stereotype threat has an independent effect above and beyond the established test score difference between Blacks and Whites.

This clarification of stereotype threat findings raises a serious question of how to interpret studies using this method: Can stereotype threat explain a substantial portion of test score differences between Blacks and Whites? The question has largely been untested, but it is important to consider when examining what influences, other than genetic predisposition, can account for achievement and intelligence outcomes. Some researchers have argued that the stereotype threat effects in the literature are "typically very small" (Reeve & Hakel, 2002); however, other researchers have used different statistical methods to address this question. Brown and Day (2006) used a statistical method to control for within-group differences on previous test scores in their investigation of the stereotype threat phenomenon between Whites and Blacks on the Raven's Advanced Progressive Matrices (APM; Raven, Raven, & Court, 1998). This statistical control allows for a better test of stereotype threat in that it controls only for prior ability within the race and therefore is not subjected to the aforementioned critique by Sackett et al. (2001, 2004).

Brown and Day (2006) found that Blacks in the low-threat condition scored substantially higher, approximately three fourths of a standard deviation higher, than Blacks in the high-threat and standard conditions. The most important finding, however, was that, although Blacks scored lower than Whites on the ACT, Blacks in the low-threat condition performed as well as Whites in both the standard condition and the high-threat condition on the APM. Thus, when the test was framed as a problem-solving task, Blacks were capable of performing as well as Whites on the APM despite having on average lower ACT scores. Although this is only one study, it suggests the possibility that stereotype threat can explain a significant portion of the Black–White test gap.

Generalizability

A second criticism leveled against the stereotype threat literature is how well the results of the laboratory findings extend to the real-world settings. Several studies from the industrial–organizational and educational psychology literatures have investigated stereotype threat effects in real-world and simulated standardized testing situations, largely finding mixed results for stereotype threat effects (Cullen, Hardison, & Sackett, 2004; Stricker & Ward, 2004). We discuss this research literature in the following sections.

Industrial–Organizational. In the field of industrial–organizational psychology, a series of studies examined stereotype threat effects on job selection measures (Mayer & Hanges, 2003; McFarland, Lev-Arey, & Ziegert, 2003; Ployhart, Ziegart, & McFarland, 2003). All of the studies simulated a real-world testing situation but were conducted in a laboratory using a design similar to Steele and Aronson's (1995) original study. All of the studies, although aimed at determining mediating processes for stereotype threat, did not find a stereotype threat effect for performance between Blacks and Whites (Sackett, 2003). As Sackett (2003) noted, these results are surprising, considering the well-established stereotype threat effect using this method.

Educational Literature. In the educational literature, Cullen et al. (2004) used a differential prediction model[2] to determine whether SAT Math and Verbal scores could predict freshmen overall GPA the same for White and Black students. Two models that predicted nonlinear relationships between SAT and grade for Black students were tested. Model 1 posited that stereotype threat is likely to affect individuals at the upper end of the score distribution; therefore, the regression lines should be the same for Blacks and Whites with low test scores, but as test scores increase, the Black and White regression lines would separate. Model 2 posited that stereotype threat is assumed to affect only minority applicants having identified with the domain but who are so gifted in that domain that the test is not challenging. If Model 2 is true, then the test should systematically underestimate the performance of minority students in the middle range of the test distribution.

The results showed that the SAT Verbal score–GPA relationship for Black students was linear throughout the score range, which is contrary to the nonlinear relationship predicted by stereotype threat theory (Cullen et al., 2004). SAT Math and SAT Verbal scores were shown to overpredict the academic performance of Black students. Also, examination of the slope between Blacks and Whites on the SAT Math–GPA relationship revealed an apparent change in the slope, indicating that the SAT Math scores predicted performance better in the top half of the distribution and in the bottom half of the distribution. Further analyses were conducted in the top half of the distribution to see if there were any differential effects within this population, because individuals who identify strongly with the domain are predicted to be most affected by stereotype threat. However, the Black and White slopes were virtually identical, and the interaction terms that tested for the slope differences accounted for only 0.003% of the variance. In sum, on the basis of the differential predictive models outlined within Cullen et al.'s (2004) study, stereotype threat did not have a strong effect on the difference between Black and White tests scores.

Another study, conducted by Stricker and Ward (2004), used the same design reported by Steele and Aronson (1995, Study 3) to determine whether indicating one's race (and gender) before completing the Advanced Placement calculus and community college entrance examinations would produce performance differences. These researchers found that Black students in the diagnostic condition (i.e., students who indicated their race before taking the examination) did not perform significantly different than students in the nondiagnostic condition (i.e., students who indicated their race after taking the examination) on any of the measures.

However, research design interventions aimed at decreasing the effects of stereotype threat have found stereotype threat effects on performance in real-world settings. Aronson, Fried, and Good (2002) hypothesized that encouraging Black students to view intelligence as expandable was enough to improve their academic achievement.

They had one group of students write to a pen pal about the malleability of intelligence; another group of students wrote letters talking about how intelligence is composed of many abilities, not one single entity; and a third group served as the control group and did not send letters to pen pals but completed all other measures. African American students who wrote about the malleability of intelligence obtained higher grades than did the students in the control condition, reported greater enjoyment of their own educational process (compared with their peers in the other two experimental conditions), and valued academics more.

In a similar study, Good, Aronson, and Inzlicht (2003) demonstrated that changing students' explanations for academic difficulty from a negative perspective to a more promising perspective could help reduce their vulnerability to stereotype threat. Students (seventh-graders, mostly Hispanic and Black) in the *incremental* condition were encouraged to view intelligence as something that increases over time, whereas students in the *attribution* condition were encouraged to view academic difficulty as something all students deal with (but eventually can catch up). Students in the control condition received an antidrug message. The results suggest that both the incremental and attribution messages increased students' standardized test scores.

Finally, in a more recent study directed at identifying potential buffers against the negative effects of stereotype threat, Cohen, Garcia, Apfel, and Master (2006) conducted a two-part investigation with a population of seventh-graders from lower-middle-class to middle-class families. These researchers also wanted to determine whether self-affirmations could mitigate some of the stress found in stereotype threat situations. They found that African Americans in a self-affirmation group achieved significantly higher grades than those in the control group. Of interest is that lower-performing students tended to benefit from the intervention more than higher-performing students. African Americans in the affirmation conditions earned a significantly higher GPA than those in the control group. Similar to the stereotype activation in Steele and Aronson's (1995) Study 3, Cohen et al. found that students in the affirmation condition listed fewer stereotype word fragments than those in the control group.

Collectively, these studies suggest that stereotype threat can have a significant impact on the performance of females, ethnic minorities, and low-income students on standardized tests in real-life situations. If this is the case, then what can account for the disparate results among the studies? What can account for the lack of an effect in some studies and not others? Stricker and Ward (2004), Cullen et al. (2004), and Sackett (2003) have noted several factors within the real-world setting that have implications for determining the generalizability of stereotype threat effects in studies that use test score data and methods similar to those used in Steele and Aronson's (1995) original work. One of these was that the motivation to perform well was heightened in the real-world setting. One could argue that, within a naturalistic testing situation, there is an inherent incentive to do well because one's performance can determine college or job prospects (Cullen et al., 2004; Stricker & Ward, 2004). In contrast, the students in Steele and Aronson's study were simply directed to take a test. It is plausible, then, that the increased motivation to succeed in the high-stakes testing situation may override stereotype threat effects. This notion is supported by the studies from the industrial–organizational psychology literature, considering that all of these studies provided an incentive for taking the test (i.e., financial or obtaining a job), and not all of these studies support the stereotype threat effect (Sackett, 2003).

A second important distinction between the real-world setting studies and other stereotype research using Steele and Aronson's (1995) experimental design is that, within a real-life testing situation, it is readily apparent to an individual that the tests are diagnostic of ability (Sackett et al., 2001). It is possible, then, that stereotype threat was already activated for students in both the diagnostic and control conditions, which in turn resulted in similar performance between Blacks across experimental conditions. Thus, the lack of an effect found in some studies does not indicate the absence of a stereotype threat in testing situations (Cullen et al., 2004; Sackett et al., 2001). However, if a certain level of threat is always present for stigmatized individuals in testing situations, then establishing a stereotype threat effect in real-life applied settings will be very difficult, whether one uses Steele and Aronson's original method or other current statistical methods that rely on test score data. All test score data in applied settings are to some degree influenced by the stereotype threat inherently present within these settings.

Overall, then, the research shows that when a negative stereotype is activated for a member of stigmatized group, one should expect the target's performance to be adversely affected (Wheeler & Petty, 2001). Furthermore, telling students that no group differences are present on a test of cognitive ability (Wheeler & Petty), or providing opportunities for students to engage in cognitive interventions addressing stereotypes about academic performance and intelligence (Aronson et al., 2002; Cohen et al., 2006; Good et al., 2003) can eliminate poor performance among African Americans (Wheeler & Petty). Therefore, stereotype threat, in some way, does affect the performance of African Americans, and removing the stigmatized ability stereotype can lead to more positive outcomes for African Americans.

Mediators and Moderators of Stereotype Threat

The quest to determine how stereotype threat affects performance is still in the early stages. A number of mediators and moderators have been tested to determine how stereotype threat does its damage, including, but not limited to, anxiety/arousal (Blascovich, Spencer, Quinn, & Steele, 2001; Osborne, 2001; Steele & Aronson, 1995, Study 2), expectancies (Spencer et al., 1999; Stone et al., 1999), evaluation apprehension (Aronson et al., 1999; Steele & Aronson, 1995), effort (Spencer et al.; Steele & Aronson, 1995, Study 2 and Study 4), self-handicapping (Steele & Aronson, 1995, Study 3), perceptions of test fairness (Steele & Aronson, 1995, Study 3; Stone et al., 1999), racial identity (Davis, Aronson, & Salinas, 2006), stigma/stigma consciousness (Brown & Pinel, 2003), gender identity (Schmader, 2002), and stereotype activation (Davies, Spencer, & Steele, 2005; Steele & Aronson, 1995, Study 3). However, on the basis of several reviews, studies have yielded mixed results or no evidence for mediation or moderation by these variables (see Smith, 2004; Wheeler & Petty, 2001, for a review of mediators).

Because of the mixed evidence for mediating and moderating variables, researchers are focusing more on the psychosocial variables that contribute to within-group variation in stereotype effects on academic performance in African Americans. Other researchers have proposed using achievement goal theory as a theoretical framework to explain how stereotype threat and academic performance can be mediated or moderated by other variables.

Psychosocial Variables

Recent research examining the mediating or moderating role of psychosocial variables in the stereotype threat–performance relationship have focused on domain identity (Smith & White, 2001), racial identity (Davis et al., 2006; Ployhart et al., 2003), and perceived stereotype threat (Mayer & Hanges, 2003; Ployhart et al., 2003).

Domain identity, although originally hypothesized as a boundary condition for stereotype threat effects to occur (Steele & Aronson, 1995), has not been clearly investigated as a moderator of stereotype threat effects (Ployhart et al., 2003; Smith & White, 2001). As Steele and Aronson (1995) suggested in their original studies, the performance of students highly identified with the academic domain will be more affected by stereotype threat than will the performance of students who have low or no identification with the domain. Steele (1997) also discussed how stereotype threat can lead to disidentification from the academic domain over time, and Osborne (1997) found some evidence for this effect at the group level, especially in Black males. Thus, examining the relation between stereotype threat and domain identity is crucial to understanding how or whether stereotype threat can affect Black students of all academic abilities.

Most studies to date, however, have addressed the stereotype threat effect only in students highly identified with the domain of academics and have used a variety of measures to determine domain identity, including enrollment in certain math or Advanced Placement classes, SAT scores above 600, or grades that are above a certain average (Smith & White, 2001). Smith and White (2001) developed a domain identification measure to examine individual differences in stereotype threat effects for women and math achievement. They found that the domain identification measure was reliable and valid for a large sample of male and female college students and suggested that it could be modified to address any domain. The measure, however, has yet to be employed to determine how domain identity influences the stereotype threat–performance relationship.

Other research has examined individual differences in domain identity in conjunction with other variables. Ployhart et al. (2003) found that domain identity did not directly moderate the relationship between stereotype threat and test performance for African Americans. Domain identity affected performance outcomes indirectly through test-taking motivation, in that those individuals who had high domain identity scores also tended to persist more on tasks. This result is congruent with other research suggesting that individuals who are more identified with a domain will persist longer on tasks within that domain. However, these results also contradict previous research suggesting that individuals highly identified with the domain are more susceptible to stereotype threat.

In fact, recent research has found that racial identity may be a primary moderator of the stereotype threat effects in African Americans (Davis et al., 2006; McFarland et al., 2003). At the same time, the specific role that racial identity plays is unclear. For example, Davis et al. (2006) found that Black students who had a secure sense of belongingness and connectedness to their race performed significantly better on a Verbal section of the Graduate Record Examination than did their Black peers who did not identify as strongly with their racial identity. However, this finding was true only in the low-threat condition; racial identity did not protect individuals in the high-threat situations, and Davis et al. suggested that individuals who strongly identified with their race were "the ones most likely to want to disprove the negative stereotype about African Americans" (p. 413) and therefore more vulnerable to this psychological threat.

On the other hand, McFarland et al. (2003) found that Blacks who were high in both racial and domain identification performed better than Black students who were in a high-threat situation. Furthermore, they found that Black students in the high-threat situation who had high scores on the racial identity measure *before* taking the test but low scores *after* taking the test, performed the best. The authors interpreted the change in racial identity scores to suggest that in order for Blacks to perform well they had to *disidentify* themselves from their race and convince themselves that they were not "like other Black individuals" (p. 200).

The research examining racial identity as a moderator has produced mixed results; it appears that one's racial identity may both increase one's susceptibility to, or protect against, stereotype threat. However, the specific role of racial identity may also lie in when racial identity is assessed and/or the presence of other mediating variables, such as domain identification.

Finally, research on an individual's perception of stereotype threat (Mayer & Hanges, 2003; Ployhart et al., 2003) may play an important role in how African Americans approach a testing situation and their performance on tests. Current research has found that both specific perceptions about the test (i.e., stereotype specific) and general perceptions of how the larger society views an individual (i.e., stereotype general) affects an individual's test-taking motivation, which in turn influences academic performance in African Americans (Ployhart et al.). Furthermore, individuals who have high scores for stereotype-general perceptions also have high scores for stereotype-specific perceptions, suggesting that if a person perceives that society judges him or her with a negative stereotype, that person will feel more threatened in a testing situation (Mayer & Hanges, 2003).

Achievement Goal Theory and Stereotype Threat

Although a plethora of variables have been proposed and investigated as mediators between stereotype threat and performance, few attempts have been made to organize the stereotype threat research into a meaningful framework. Researchers have proposed adding achievement goal theory as an overarching framework to explain the stereotype threat–performance relationship.

Smith (2004) and Ryan and Ryan (2005) have argued that the achievement goal and stereotype threat research provide similar explanations for performance outcomes. Research in achievement goal theory has found that when a student adopts a *performance avoidant* (PAV) goal toward an academic task, his or her performance suffers (Smith, 2004; Ryan & Ryan, 2005). Similarly, stereotype threat theory postulates that students perform poorly for fear of confirming a negative stereotype. Thus, the researchers (Smith, 2004; Ryan & Ryan, 2005) posit that stereotype threat causes students to adopt a PAV goal, which in turn "leads an individual to predictably self regulate his or her behavior and motivation according to potential negative outcomes" (Smith, 2004, p. 195).

Smith's (2004) Stereotype Task Engagement Process (STEP) model outlines the mediating role of PAV goals between stereotype threat and academic performance. Specifically, the model suggests that stereotype threat engenders a PAV goal, which in turn directs how the individual behaves (e.g., whether and how he or she self-sabotages performance), feels (e.g., experiences feelings of competence; feelings of interest), and ultimately performs and persists at the task. Situations that are not high in stereotype threat cause an individual to adopt a *performance approach* goal. This goal engenders helpful self-regulation strategies, leading to positive performance outcomes.

To date, only one study (Smith, 2006) has used the STEP model to examine the relationship between PAV goal adoption and stereotype threat. In her investigation of the effects of gender stereotypes on women's performance expectancies on math tasks, Smith found that women endorsed PAV goals to a greater extent when experiencing stereotype threat compared with when the stereotype is countered. Furthermore, women seemed to endorse PAV goals more than men when taking a math test. Thus, there is evidence that stereotype threat is capable of leading to the adoption of PAV goals, at least for women in regard to math performance.

Research and Educational Implications

Although there is ample evidence to suggest that stereotype threat contributes to performance decrements for African Americans, there are still many unanswered questions as to the strength and nature of its role in contributing to the Black–White achievement gap. To provide adequate answers to these questions, future research should investigate stereotype threat effects using different statistical methods and focus on examining the role of individual-difference variables to build a theoretical framework for how stereotype threat does its damage.

Statistical Methods

Only two studies to date have supported the notion that stereotype threat can contribute in a statistically significant way to the overall Black–White achievement gap (Brown & Day, 2006; Cohen et al., 2006). Brown and Day's (2006) study provides the strongest evidence; it demonstrated that Blacks and Whites with differing SAT scores had comparable scores when the cognitive test was presented as a problem-solving task. Furthermore, Cohen et al.'s (2006) study, in which affirmation cards were used as an intervention for stereotype threat effects, shows that changing a student's cognitions about his or her academic ability can essentially close the Black–White academic achievement. Replication of these studies could provide a solid foundation from which to make judgments about the strength of the stereotype threat relationship.

In addition, using new statistical methods to examine real-world effects on the Black–White achievement gap, such as that proposed by Wicherts, Dolan, and Hessen (2005), can provide a better understanding of how stereotype threat affects the performance of African Americans. Because other methods have failed to be sensitive to the possibility that stereotype threat is always present within high-stakes settings, or that the motivation to do well may override stereotype threat effects, Wicherts and colleagues proposed measuring stereotype threat effects as a source of measurement invariance or bias. They argued that stereotype threat theory violates assumptions for analysis of covariance and that studies using this method could result in incorrect Type I error rates and distortions in the adjustment of means. More specifically, analysis of covariance does not take into account the effect that stereotype threat may have on the covariate, which in experimental studies is usually scores on a high-stakes test (i.e., SAT or ACT scores). In their study, they used structural equation modeling techniques and found a stereotype threat effect in math performance within high school students in the Netherlands. Examination of high-stakes testing data in America using this method may be able to capture stereotype threat affect on performance in African Americans and may address whether stereotype threat contributes in a robust way to the Black student achievement gap.

Building a Theoretical Framework

In determining how stereotype threat does its damage, researchers need to consider integrating the STEP model with the psychosocial variables to determine an overarching theoretical framework for the stereotype threat–performance relationship. Although the STEP model has yet to be tested with African Americans, it provides a new understanding of how stereotype threat causes performance decrements and new hypotheses to test, which is crucial to moving research forward in determining the mechanisms that mediate stereotype threat. Furthermore, any model examining stereotype threat effects in African Americans should consider including a measure of racial identity, because this variable has been found to have a significant impact on the stereotype threat–performance relationship. The specific role that racial identity plays is still unclear; however, determining its effects may be useful in designing interventions around the promotion of a healthy racial identity.

Similarly, an individual's perceptions or expectations of being stereotyped play an important role in academic outcomes. Expecting to be stereotyped may undermine a person's confidence in his or her abilities or even motivation with the task, and consequently his or her academic performance could suffer (Stangor, Carr, & Kiang, 1998). The expectation of being stereotyped may also be related to contextual cues in the environment that heighten the presence of stereotype threat. In their work on the relationship of solo status and stereotype threat, Sekaquaptewa and Thompson (2003) found that women taking a test (as the only female) with a group of men performed worse on a test of math material in the stereotype threat condition. Researchers may find this useful in testing the effect of solo status in relation to stereotype perceptions and expectations, because these results may have implications for stereotype threat effects on the performance of Black students enrolled in Advanced Placement or gifted classes (and even their reluctance to enroll in these courses).

Researchers also need to consider at what age African American students begin to be effected by stereotype threat. Ambady et al. (2001) studied Asian American children and found evidence for stereotype threat in elementary school age students; however, whether their results generalize to African Americans is unclear. There is reasonable evidence, though, that African American children can be at risk of experiencing threat at a young age. McKown and Weinstein (2003) found that, between the ages of 6 and 10, children are able to infer the stereotypes that others hold of them; children become increasingly aware of broadly held stereotypes as they get older; and that stigmatized children (African Americans and Latinos) at all ages are more aware of broad stereotypes than their less stigmatized counterparts (Whites and Asians). Thus, children's awareness of stereotypes may make them vulnerable to stereotype threat at an early age, potentially causing early disidentification from the academic domain and, consequently, lower achievement scores. This hypothesis, however, needs to be empirically validated.

Conclusion

A considerable amount of research has assessed the effects of stereotype threat on performance. However, most of the work confirming the existence of stereotype threat either has been performed in a decontextualized laboratory setting or has focused on the gender and math achievement gap. It is evident from the research that has studied stereotype threat within the real-world environment that different processes are operating within the real-life testing situations, processes that laboratory studies have not or may not ever adequately capture. Despite these limitations, the research shows that stereotype threat can lead to decrements in performance in academic achievement and cognitive ability testing for African Americans. It has also demonstrated that building interventions from this theory have led to successful outcomes for African American students (Cohen et al., 2006).

It is our hope that this chapter stimulates readers to conduct their own studies to either replicate the findings of earlier studies or to test new mediators and moderators of stereotype threat. Many of the studies described in this chapter demonstrate that intervention programs do not have to entail significant intrusions in the lives of students. Thus, unlike many theories attempting to explain the achievement gap between Black and White students, stereotype threat offers unlimited possibilities for designing interventions that allow equally prepared Black students to perform at levels comparable to those of their peers.

Notes

1. We use *Black* and *African American* interchangeably throughout this chapter; however, unless otherwise noted, we are referring only to individuals of African descent living in the United States. It is also important to note that stereotype threat focuses on the individual; thus, we do not address larger issues, such as poverty, discrimination, expectations of teachers, and so on, all of which are significant contributors to the troubling educational outcomes for African Americans.

2. This approach is the established method of determining whether a test exhibits predictive bias when used to predict a given criterion. Under this approach, a regression line resulting from regressing a criterion of interest (e.g., GPA) on the test of interest (e.g., the SAT) is computed separately for the subgroups being compared. The researchers posited that stereotype threat theory results in a set of testable predictions about the expected pattern of regression lines for different subgroups.

References

Ambady, N., Shih, M., Kim, A., & Pittinsky, T. L. (2001). Stereotype susceptibility in children: Effects of identity activation on quantitative performance. *Psychological Science, 12,* 385–390.

Aronson, J., Fried, C. B., & Good, C. (2002). Reducing the effects of stereotype threat on African American college students by shaping theories of intelligence. *Journal of Experimental Social Psychology, 38,* 113–125.

Aronson, J., Lustina, M., Good, C., Keough, K., Steele, C. M., & Brown, J. L. (1999). When White men can't do math: Necessary and sufficient factors in stereotype threat. *Journal of Experimental Social Psychology, 35,* 29–46.

Aronson, J., & Salinas, M. F. (1997). *Stereotype threat, attributional ambiguity, and Latino underperformance.* Unpublished manuscript, University of Texas.

Blascovich, J., Spencer, S. J., Quinn, D., & Steele, C. (2001). African Americans and high blood pressure: The role of stereotype threat. *Psychological Science, 12,* 225–229.

Brown, R. P., & Day, E. A. (2006). The difference isn't Black and White: Stereotype threat and the race gap on Raven's Advanced Progressive Matrices. *Journal of Applied Psychology, 91,* 979–985.

Brown, R. P., & Pinel, E. C. (2003). Stigma on my mind: Individual differences in the experience of stereotype threat. *Journal of Experimental Social Psychology, 39,* 626–633.

Cohen, G. L., Garcia, J., Apfel, N., & Master, A. (2006, September 1). Reducing the racial achievement gap: A social-psychological intervention. *Science, 313,* 1307–1310.

Croizet, J. C., & Claire, T. (1998). Extending the concept of stereotype threat to social class: The intellectual underperformance of students from low socioeconomic backgrounds. *Personality and Social Psychology Bulletin, 24,* 588–594.

Cullen, M. J., Hardison, C. M., & Sackett, P. R. (2004). Using SAT–grade and ability–job performance relationships to test predictions derived from stereotype threat theory. *Journal of Applied Psychology, 89,* 220–230.

Davies, P. G., Spencer, S. J., & Steele, C. M. (2005). Clearing the air: Identity safety moderates the effects of stereotype threat on women's leadership aspirations. *Journal of Personality and Social Psychology, 88,* 276–287.

Davis, C., III, Aronson, J., & Salinas, M. (2006). Shades of threat: Racial identity as a moderator of stereotype threat. *Journal of Black Psychology, 32,* 399–417.

Fordham, S., & Ogbu, J. (1986). Black students' school success: Coping with the "burden of 'acting White.'" *Urban Review, 18,* 176–206.

Good, C., Aronson, J., & Inzlicht, M. (2003). Improving adolescents' standardized performance: An intervention to reduce the effects of stereotype threat. *Applied Developmental Psychology, 24,* 645–662.

Herrnstein, R. J., & Murray, C. (1994). *The bell curve: Intelligence and class structure in American life.* New York: Simon & Schuster.

Jencks, C., & Phillips, M. (Eds.). (1998). *The Black–White test score gap.* Washington, DC: Brookings Institution.

Majors, R., & Billson, J. M. (1992). *Cool pose: The dilemmas of Black manhood in America.* New York: Lexington Books.

Mayer, D., & Hanges, P. J. (2003). Understanding the stereotype threat effect with "culture-free" tests: An examination of its mediators and measurement. *Human Performance, 16,* 207–230.

McFarland, L. A., Lev-Arey, D. M., & Ziegert, J. C. (2003). An examination of stereotype threat in a motivational context. *Human Performance, 16,* 181–205.

McKown, C., & Weinstein, R. (2003). The development and consequences of stereotype consciousness in middle childhood. *Child Development, 74,* 498–515.

Osborne, J. W. (1997). Race and academic disidentification. *Journal of Educational Psychology, 89,* 728–735.

Osborne, J. W. (2001). Testing stereotype threat: Does anxiety explain race and sex differences in achievement? *Contemporary Educational Psychology, 26,* 291–310.

Ployhart, R. E., Ziegert, J. C., & McFarland, L. A. (2003). Understanding racial differences on cognitive ability tests in selection contexts: An integration of stereotype threat and applicant reactions research. *Human Performance, 16,* 231–259.

Raven, J. C., Raven, J., & Court, J. H. (1998). *A manual for Raven's Progressive Matrices and Vocabulary Scales.* London: H. K. Lewis.

Reeve, C. L., & Hakel, M. D. (2002). Asking the right questions about g. *Human Performance, 15,* 47–74.

Ryan, E. R., & Ryan, A. M. (2005). Psychological processes underlying stereotype threat and standardized math test performance. *Educational Psychologist, 40,* 53–63.

Sackett, P. R. (2003). Stereotype threat in applied selection settings: A commentary. *Human Performance, 16,* 295–309.

Sackett, P. R., Hardison, C. M., & Cullen, M. J. (2004). On interpreting stereotype threat as accounting for African-American–White differences on cognitive tests. *American Psychologist, 59,* 7–13.

Sackett, P. R., Schmitt, N., Ellingson, J. E., & Kabin, M. B. (2001). High-stakes testing in employment, credentialing, and higher education: Prospects in a post–affirmative action world. *American Psychologist, 56,* 302–318.

Schmader, T. (2002). Gender identification moderates stereotype threat effects on women's math performance. *Journal of Experimental Social Psychology, 38,* 194–201.

Sekaquaptewa, D., & Thompson, M. (2003). Solo status, stereotype threat, and performance expectancies: Their effects on women's performance. *Journal of Experimental Social Psychology, 39,* 68–74.

Smith, J. L. (2004). Understanding the process of stereotype threat: A review of mediational variables and new performance goal directions. *Educational Psychology Review, 16,* 177–206.

Smith, J. L. (2006). The interplay among stereotypes, performance-avoidance goals, and women's math performance expectations. *Sex Roles, 54,* 287–296.

Smith, J. L., & White, P. H. (2001). Development of the domain identification measure: A tool for investigating stereotype threat effects. *Educational and Psychological Measurement, 61,* 1040–1057.

Spencer, S. J., Steele, C. M., & Quinn, D. M. (1999). Stereotype threat and women's math performance. *Journal of Experimental Social Psychology, 35,* 4–28.

Spielberger, C. D. (1983). *Manual for the State–Trait Anxiety Inventory*. Palo Alto, CA: Consulting Psychologists Press.

Stangor, C., Carr, C., & Kiang, L. (1998). Activating stereotypes undermines task performance expectations. *Journal of Personality and Social Psychology, 75,* 1191–1197.

Steele, C. M. (1997). A threat in the air: How stereotypes shape intellectual identity and performance. *American Psychologist, 52,* 613–629.

Steele, C. M. (2003). Through the back door to theory. *Psychological Inquiry, 14,* 314–317.

Steele, C. M., & Aronson, J. (1995). Stereotype threat and the intellectual test performance of African-Americans. *Journal of Personality and Social Psychology, 69,* 797–811.

Stone, J., Lynch, C. L., Sjomeling, M., & Darley, J. M. (1999). Stereotype threat effects on Black and White athletic performance. *Journal of Personality and Social Psychology, 77,* 1213–1227.

Stricker, L. J., & Ward, W. (2004). Stereotype threat, inquiring about test takers' ethnicity and gender, and standardized test performance. *Journal of Applied Social Psychology, 34,* 665–693.

U.S. Department of Education, National Center for Education Statistics. (2005). *2005 Mathematics assessment results*. Retrieved May 1, 2008, from http://nces.ed.gov/nationsreportcard/pdf/main2005/2007468_3.pdf

U.S. Department of Education, National Center for Education Statistics. (2007). Status dropout rates by race/ethnicity. In *The condition of education 2007* (Report No. NCES 2007-064). Retrieved May 1, 2008, from http://nces.ed.gov/programs/coe/2007/section3/indicator23.asp

Wheeler, S. C., & Petty, R. E. (2001). The effects of stereotype activation on behavior: A review of possible mechanisms. *Psychological Bulletin, 127,* 797–826.

Wicherts, J. M., Dolan, C. V., & Hessen, D. J. (2005). Stereotype threat and group differences in test performance: A question of measurement invariance. *Journal of Personality and Social Psychology, 89,* 696–716.

Williams, R. A., Williams, R. L., & Mitchell, H. (2004). The testing game. In R. L. Jones (Ed.), *Black Psychology* (4th ed., pp. 465–485). Hampton, VA: Cobb & Henry.

Woodson, C. G. (2000). *The mis-education of the Negro*. Chicago: African American Images. (Original work published 1933)

17

RACIAL IDENTITY AND PEER PRESSURES AMONG GIFTED AFRICAN AMERICAN STUDENTS

Issues and Recommendations

DONNA Y. FORD AND GILMAN W. WHITING

Although a large body of literature exists on gifted children in general, few publications have focused on the affective and psychological needs of students who are both gifted and racially and culturally diverse. In essence, one body of research has focused on gifted students with scant attention to race and culture, and another body of work has focused on culturally diverse students with little attention to those who are gifted. For instance, studies have examined the effects of labeling on gifted students' self-image and their feelings about being gifted (e.g., Robinson, 1989), as well as whether gifted students have unique needs by virtue of being gifted and whether they contend with more affective and psychological issues than other students (e.g., Neihart, Reis, Robinson, & Moon, 2002). Likewise, separate studies have explored the affective and psychological needs of African American students, particularly how such needs influence their achievement (e.g., Fordham, 1988, 1991; Steele, 1997, 1999).

In this chapter,[1] we focus on the literature related to gifted African American students, paying particular attention to identification and achievement issues related to their affective and psychological development (for a general discussion, see resources by the National Association for Gifted Children, Council for Exceptional Children [Talented and Gifted Division; e.g., http://www.nagc.org] as well as Neihart et al., 2002, and Coleman and Cross, 2001). Within this discussion, we rely extensively on the most widely researched theory of racial identity development (Cross, 1971, 1995; Cross & Vandiver, 2001) as the foundation of our discussion. Using this theory, we draw implications from research and conceptual perspectives on African American students in general to gifted African American students. This chapter concludes with suggestions for prevention and intervention appropriate for use with gifted African American students.

Gifted Education and African American Students: An Overview

At least a half century of data (see Jenkins, 1936) indicates that, since their creation, gifted programs have lacked the presence of African American students, even when they have high test scores (Ford, 1996, 1998). Regardless of the year or decade under scrutiny, African American students remain underrepresented in gifted education programs (and Advanced Placement [AP] classes). Despite myriad efforts to reverse this problem, percentages do not seem to be changing, even as we write this chapter. For example, in 1993, African American students were underrepresented in gifted education by 50%: They represented approximately 16.2% of the school district but comprised only 8.4% of gifted programs (see Ford, 1998). As of 2002, African American students remain underrepresented by approximately 60% (U.S. Department of Education, 2002). It is disturbing to note that, when examined by gender, African American males are more underrepresented than African American females.

Although many explanations have been advanced for the unrelenting and widespread underrepresentation problem, Ford (1994, 1996) and colleagues (Ford, Harris, Tyson, & Frazier Trotman, 2002; Ford, Grantham, & Whiting, in press) have contended that the primary variables contributing to the underrepresentation of African Americans in gifted education programs are low teacher referral, low student test scores, and student and family choice to not participate in gifted education, respectively. Although other barriers have been identified, these three are the primary hindrances.

Teacher Referral Issues

For most school districts, the identification and placement process begins with teacher referral followed by a student taking an intelligence and/or achievement test. This policy is highly problematic given data indicating that teachers tend not to refer African American students for screening and placement in gifted programs. Given that most school districts use teacher referral as the initial step in the placement process (e.g., Colangelo & Davis, 2003; Davis & Rimm, 2004), the use of teacher referrals serves as a definitive gatekeeper, thereby denying them access to appropriately challenging classes, programs, and services.

The topic of teachers as referral sources for gifted education assessment and placement falls under the realm of the teacher expectations or perceptions and subsequent student achievement and outcomes (see Merton, 1948; Rosenthal & Jacobson, 1968). This body of work refers to the degree to which a teacher's a priori judgment of a student's achievement and/or potential corresponds to the student's eventual achievement (e.g., grades) or performance on some formal and objective measure (Rist, 1996; Zucker & Prieto, 1977). Since the 1920s, researchers have examined the efficacy of teacher judgment when making referrals for gifted education screening, identification, and placement (e.g., Cox & Daniel, 1983; Gagne, 1994; Gear, 1976; Hoge & Coladarci, 1989; Pegnato & Birch, 1959; Terman, 1925); only more recently have studies focused on teacher referral and African American students. Research results have varied; some studies have found teachers to be rather accurate in their referrals, whereas others have found them to be inaccurate and ineffective. At least four factors appear to contribute to the differential findings: (1) different instruments used to validate the teacher's judgment; (2) different referral forms, checklists, and other forms used by teachers; (3) different populations of gifted students being evaluated (e.g., gifted vs. highly gifted, male vs. female, high vs. low income); and (4) different methods (e.g., use of vignettes vs. actual case studies).

One body of scholarship has shown that some teachers have negative stereotypes and inaccurate perceptions about the abilities of African American students and their families, even when the children have been identified as gifted or high achieving (e.g., Boutte, 1992; Harmon, 2002; Huff, Houskamp, Watkins, Stanton, & Tavegia, 2005; Louie, 2005; Rist, 1996; Shumow, 1997). Specifically, it is feasible to conclude that teachers (the vast majority of whom are White) are more effective at identifying giftedness among White students but less effective at identifying gifted African American students.

Two recent studies have continued this line of research on teacher referral and culturally diverse students. Elhoweris, Mutua, Alsheikh, and Holloway (2005) examined the effects of students' race–ethnicity on teachers' decision making using three vignettes of gifted students. Only the race–ethnicity of the student in the vignette changed. This impacted teacher referrals; specifically, "elementary school teachers treated identical information contained in the vignettes differently and made different recommendations despite the fact that the student information was identical in all ways except for ethnicity" (p. 29). Last, in a study of referral sources using all elementary students in the state of Georgia, McBee (2006) reported that teacher referrals were more effective (i.e., accurate) for White and Asian students than for African American and Hispanic/Latino students. McBee concluded, "The results suggest inequalities in nomination, rather than assessment, may be the primary source of the underrepresentation of minority ... students in gifted programs" (p. 103). Furthermore, he noted that the findings could be interpreted in several ways, one being that "the low rate of teacher nomination could indicate racism, classism, or cultural ignorance on the part of teachers" (p. 109). Ford et al. (in press; Ford & Grantham, 2003) have attributed such lack of referral to *deficit thinking* (see Menchaca, 1997; Valencia, 1997), in which educators focus on students' perceived differences and weaknesses instead of their strengths. Professionals who see such differences as weaknesses, or "deficits," do not refer those students for gifted education services. Deficit thinking can be attributed to educators seldom having the formal preparation and informal experiences to work effectively with African American students in general and those who are gifted in particular.

Testing Issues

African American students are also underrepresented in gifted education because they tend to score lower on standardized tests than White students. The countless reasons for differential test performances between African American and White students are discussed here. Two camps seem to be in opposition: (1) the *hereditarian orientation*, which supports and promotes the position that intelligence is hereditary, and (2) the *environmental position*, which argues that social variables—education, exposure, and opportunity—matter most and that thus intelligence is dynamic, not static. In the first position, African Americans are often deemed genetically less endowed than Whites. As we write this chapter, the debate about White supremacy continues with DNA founder James Watson charging that he was "inherently gloomy about the prospect of Africa'" because "all our social policies are based on the fact that their intelligence is the same as ours—whereas all the testing says not really." ("Science museum," 2007). Likewise, supremacist views were espoused by Herrnstein and Murray (1994), who polemically misinterpreted and misrepresented their data so as to confirm prejudices and stereotypes and to change social policy. Although such thinking was prevalent in earlier centuries, the fact that researchers in the 21st century also hold such views is obviously disturbing. As Gould (1981) noted, the hereditarian theory of IQ is as American as apple pie; it is "a home-grown American product that persists in contemporary practices of testing, sorting, and discarding" (pp. 74, 158).

It is not surprising, then, that controversy abounds regarding the efficacy of using traditional, standardized tests with African American and other ethnically culturally diverse populations. In a monograph on this topic, Ford (2004) argued that static theories and notions of both intelligence and testing hinder the equitable identification and placement of African American students. The impact of hereditarian thinking on gifted education is clear when one considers how *giftedness* and *intelligence* are used interchangeably, how both are subjective and value-laden terms, and how prized gifted programs are among the educational elite and middle class. We have argued elsewhere (Ford & Whiting, 2006; Naglieri & Ford, 2003; Whiting & Ford, 2006) that the use of biased tests, policies, and procedures can hinder the representation of African American students in gifted education. However, few schools seem proactive or willing to change the tests and instruments (e.g., checklists, nomination forms, referral forms) they use. They have been reticent and slow to adopt alternative tests; therefore, we see the persistent use of traditional, verbally loaded tests (Ford, 1994)—and few changes in the demographics of gifted education. In essence, like teacher referrals, deficit thinking seems to be associated with views about intelligence, how scores are interpreted and used, and how the instruments are selected.

Student and Family Choice

The third major representation barrier is the choice that African American students and their families make regarding participation in gifted education and AP classes. Some African American students and their families have chosen not to participate in gifted programs because of social–emotional and psychological concerns. This issue falls under the larger umbrella of negative peer pressures, a problem facing all racial and ethnic groups and students of all achievement levels. Specifically, some African American students choose not to be in gifted programs because of negative peer pressures and concerns about being isolated from their African American peers (Ford, 1992, 1996; Fordham, 1988, 1991, 1996; Fordham & Ogbu, 1986) and because of concerns about being alienated from and rejected by White students in their gifted education classes (Ford, 1994, 1996). In the first instance, African American students may underachieve if accused of "acting White" by African American peers. This notion was also vividly illustrated in July 1999 when the ABC news program *20/20* aired a segment called "Acting White" (Redmond, 1999). In this documentary, high-achieving African American high school students complained about negative peer pressures because of their high grades, participation in gifted programs, speaking Standard English, and other stipulations.

It is this phenomenon—African American students accusing other African American students of acting White—that heavily informs the remainder of this chapter. We recognize the debates and critiques of the acting-White hypothesis; although the majority of research appears to support the hypothesis, some refutes it (e.g., Cokley, 2003). We contend that too much has been about written African American students being accused of acting White to ignore it. Recognizing these tensions and different opinions and research findings, we nonetheless propose that African American students who do not have a positive or healthy self-image (i.e., self-esteem, self-concept, racial identity) are more likely to succumb to negative peer pressures than others, as evidenced by underachievement and underrepresentation in gifted education (Ford, 1996). Few studies have focused on the peer pressures and experiences of gifted African American students. Ford, Grantham, and Whiting (2008) sought to address this shortage, following up on studies by Ford in the 1990s.

Ford et al. (2008) surveyed 166 African American students (Grades 5–12) identified as gifted regarding the peer pressures they experience specifically related to accusations of acting White. They also studied the students' experiences with and perceptions of "acting Black." The students were recruited from two school districts in Ohio; they are similar in racial diversity (both have 70% Black students) but are different in other ways. One middle school, from District A, an urban school, participated in the study. The district has more than 17,000 students; it is inner city, of low socioeconomic status, and one of the lowest performing districts in the state. At the time of the study (2005), the district was in academic emergency, having passed only 1 of 18 state standards and with a little more than half of the students (54%) graduating from high school. All of the middle school students from District A who participated in the study were Black and of low socioeconomic status, as indicated by free or reduced-price lunch status.

District B is suburban, with a student population of approximately 6,800 students. Students from five middle and high schools were surveyed. This district is higher performing than District A, having passed 6 of the 18 state standards. According to its annual report (2002–2003 school year), the district received several awards for student achievement, including almost 30 AP scholars (17 national, 4 with distinction, and 8 with honors). The graduation rate is 88%.

In District A, 189 students completed the survey; there were 183 completed surveys from District B. Of these, there were 166 gifted Black students, with the majority attending District B ($n = 142$, 85.5%). In Ohio, students are identified as cognitively gifted if they have an IQ score of 127 or higher; academically gifted students are identified at the 98th percentile or higher on an achievement test. Most of the students were in Grades 6 ($n = 75$, 45%), 7 ($n = 34$, 21%), or 8 ($n = 36$, 22%). There were 80 males (48%) and 86 females (52%).

The researchers made comparisons across gender, grade level, and school performance (i.e., grades, grade point average). Regardless of these variables, the sample from both school settings was rather homogeneous in their responses and experiences. Over 80% had heard of acting White and acting Black, and most had been accused of acting White. The majority of students equated acting White with (a) being intelligent, (b) speaking Standard American English, (c) being a high achiever and caring about school, and (d) having mainly White friends. The opposite or reverse was found for their perceptions of acting Black: (a) being unintelligent; (b) speaking non-Standard English; (c) showing disinterest in school and learning, low achievement; (d) being "thuggish" and having "bad" behaviors and attitudes; and (e) showing a preference for hip-hop culture in dress and music.

As researchers, we recognize that the findings are not generalizable to all gifted African American students. Questions have been raised about how peer pressures, including accusations of acting White, vary by school demographics: (a) African Americans in predominantly White schools, (b) African Americans in racially balanced schools, and (c) African Americans in predominantly African American schools. Likewise, questions focus on how peer pressures vary in public versus private versus magnet versus parochial schools, and across income and socioeconomic status levels. We have yet to find research that has been conducted across these settings. It should be noted that students in Ford et al.'s (2008) study differed in the type of school attended (urban vs. suburban), achievement status (high- vs. low-performing school), and income levels (e.g., free or reduced-price lunch status), but the schools were similar in their racial makeup, with the majority being African American; however, the findings were quite similar for both settings. More work on context is essential to shed light on how peer pressure varies and affects students.

The discussion of peer pressure in the form of accusations of acting White is incomplete without attention to racial identity. How individual African American students respond to such a charge may depend on the stage and strength of their racial identity. In the next section, we apply one racial identity development theory to the gifted African American students.

Psychological Issues of African American Students: Racial Identity Development

Smith (1989) advanced the theory that racial identity development as a process of coming to terms with one's racial group membership as a salient reference group. Attention to racial identity among African American students dates back to the early work of Clark and Clark (1940), who used African American and White dolls to examine the extent to which African American children recognized themselves as racial or ethnic beings and how they felt about being African American or different from Whites. The findings, used in the *Brown v. Board of Education* (1954) case, indicated that most of the preschoolers showed a preference for White dolls; they often equated being "good" and "pretty" with the White dolls and "bad" and "ugly" with the African American dolls; equally troubling is that most of these young children thought they looked like the White dolls.

Several decades later, many studies have replicated this work and/or examined some aspect of racial identity with African American adults and children. Many of these studies have concluded that African Americans are more likely than White students to encounter barriers to healthy racial identity development (e.g., Helms, 1989; Parham, 1989; Parham & Helms, 1985; Smith, 1989; Spencer & Markstrom-Adams, 1990). *Racial identity* concerns the extent to which people of color are aware of, understand, and value their racial features, background, and heritage. Smith (1989) argued that race creates a bond—feelings of peoplehood—among members; accordingly, individuals often define themselves in terms of racial membership in a particular group. She asserted that a healthy regard for one's racial status is psychologically important for racially diverse groups. Race has an effect on one's social-emotional and psychological health in noteworthy ways, because the complexity of racial identity development increases as a function of skin color and other physical features (e.g., hair length and texture, body type).

Although research has explored the relationship between self-concept and achievement, and between self-esteem and achievement, Ford (1996) argued that culturally diverse populations have been shortchanged in theories of self-perception, because these theories have neglected to reflect on racial identity in the context of self-concept, self-esteem, and overall self-perception. As we discuss next, Whiting (2006); Ford, Harris, and Schuerger (1993); Ford et al. (2008, in press); Smith (1989); and Exum and Colangelo (1981) have proposed that, for African American youth, racial identity has a significant impact on achievement, motivation, and attitudes toward academic achievement. For instance, in the earlier stages of racial identity development, described in the next section, African American youth may deliberately underachieve and choose not to participate in gifted programs and AP classes to avoid peer pressures and accusations that they are acting White and/or to avoid rejection by White peers, or they may camouflage their abilities to be accepted socially by their same-race peers (Fordham, 1988, 1991; Fordham & Ogbu, 1986; Ogbu, 2003; Ogbu & Simmons, 1998).

Nigrescence Theory: One Theory of Racial Identity Development

The most studied theory of racial identity was introduced by Cross in 1971. Since then, the theory has undergone three revisions. In the most recently revised model, titled *Nigrescence theory*, also referred to as the "process of becoming African American," Cross and Vandiver (2001) presented eight identity types clustered into three major stages: (1) pre-encounter, (2) immersion–emersion, and (3) internalization. Each stage and identity type has substantive implications for working with and meeting the needs of gifted African American students.

Pre-Encounter Stage

Three identity types are present in the pre-encounter stage; all have in common the belief that "White is right" and some level of detachment (i.e., low salience) from one's identity as an African American. Thus, when accused of acting White, individuals in this stage may feel complimented.

Assimilation. The first identity type describes an African American whose social identity is organized around his or her sense of being an American and an "individual." This individual places little emphasis or salience on racial group identity or affiliation and, consequently, is not engaged in the African American community and culture. His or her primary identity is being an "American"—unqualified.

Miseducation. This identity type is representative of an African American who accepts the negative images, stereotypes, and historical misinformation about African Americans. This person sees little strength in the African American community, hesitates to engage in solving problems or resolving issues in the African American community, and distances him- or herself from the African American community. Furthermore, he or she often holds the attitude "That's the way *they* act, but *I* am different."

Racial Self-Hatred. People reflecting this identity type experience profound negative feelings and severe self-loathing because of being African American. Cross and Vandiver (2001) contended that this sense of group hatred limits the person's positive engagement of African American problems and African American culture.

Immersion–Emersion Stage

The second stage of identity, immersion–emersion, comes into play when African Americans face encounters or *microaggressions*—racial insults and offenses (see Sue et al., 2007). Sue et al. (2007) provided nine cogent examples of microaggressions that serve to effectively remind African Americans that the may be viewed by other groups as inferior. These insults can be direct or indirect, and small (so to speak) or large. Examples include being told that "You speak well," being questioned about one's ability to purchase an expensive item, being ignored by a salesclerk, and watching an African American on television being abused and/or beaten by police.

This stage is characterized by two identity types, both of which are associated with some form of anti-White sentiment. When accused of acting White, an individual in this stage is likely to feel angry, and he or she may stop displaying the characteristic(s) associated with the accusation (e.g., start to dress or talk differently, disengage from academics).

Anti-White. The African American here is nearly consumed by a hatred of White people and society, and all that Whiteness represents. He or she is engaged in African American problems and culture but is frequently full of fury and pent-up rage associated with social injustices.

Intense African American Involvement. The individual often holds a simplistic, romanticized, and obsessive dedication to all things African

American. He or she engages in "African American-ness" in a hypervigilant, cultlike fashion. This person, for a range of reasons, may exaggerate or distort his or her sense of what is means to be African American.

Internalization Stage

The final racial identity stage, internalization, comprises three identity types. The underlying characteristics among them are a strong and positive sense of racial pride, high racial salience, and a sense of wholeness. There is also a keen sense of social justice, equality, and equity. An individual in the internalization stage is not likely to succumb to accusations of acting White; it has little to no effect on his or her psyche and performance.

Internalization Nationalist. An individual of this identity type emphasizes an Afrocentric perspective about him- or herself, other African Americans, and the world. This individual proactively and assertively engages in and contributes to the African American community, endeavoring to decrease social injustices facing African Americans.

Internalization Biculturalist. This type represents an African American who gives equal importance and salience to being an African American *and* an American. He or she is able to celebrate being both and is able to engage positively in both cultures without identity conflicts, doubt, and self-questioning.

Internalization Multiculturalist. This type represents the exemplar of an African American whose identity fuses two or more social categories or frames of reference. He or she is interested in resolving issues that address multiple oppressions and is confident and comfortable in multiple groups and settings. Racial salience and pride as an African American are positive in all settings.

Cross (1995) maintained that individuals can stop at one stage or type, or even regress after progressing to a higher and healthier stage. Whether an individual regresses, becomes stagnant, or progresses through the stages of racial identity depends heavily on one's personality, support systems, resources, and experiences. For example, when encounters or microaggressions (Sue et al., 2007) are intense and ongoing, one can remain in the immersion–emersion stage. Cross did not place any age limitations in his theory; for example, one can experience a negative racial encounter at the age of 3, 13, 43, or 63.

Several qualifications are in need of attention at this point. First, we must consider that African Americans in predominantly White settings (e.g., gifted and AP classes) may experience more negative racial encounters than those in predominantly African American settings (Ford, 1992; Ford et al., 2008, in press; Smith, 1989). Second, African Americans in predominantly White settings also may experience such encounters at an earlier age than African Americans in predominantly African American settings A third consideration is that, because of characteristics often associated with giftedness (e.g., insightfulness, intuitiveness, sensitivity, keen sense of justice), gifted African American students may be particularly aware of and sensitive to racial injustices (e.g., encounters and microaggressions). Finally, one's stage of racial identity may be related to achievement (Ford, 1996; Ford et al., 1993); specifically, there may be a curvilinear relationship between racial identity and achievement, with those in the earliest stage (pre-encounter) and those in the last stage (internalization) having the highest achievement orientation and being less vulnerable to peer pressures. Achievement orientations and academic performance may be similar between those in the different stages (earliest vs. latest), but the extent to which the individual is perceived as acting White or "selling out" is different. Pre-encounter individuals, because of their low salience and/or anti–African American attitudes, are likely to be rejected by some members of the African American community; conversely, individuals in the immersion–emersion and internalization stages, because of their strong and positive racial identity and salience, bicultural stance, and pluralistic perspectives, seem more likely to be accepted by members of the African American community. Some individuals in the middle stages of racial identity (i.e., immersion–emersion) appear so subsumed with finding and validating their identity that academic achievement may have low significance in their lives; the need for affiliation may be stronger than the need for achievement (Whiting, 2006).

Implications for Students Who Are Both Gifted and African American

It is our experience and belief that African Americans encounter more barriers to identity development, particularly racial identity development, than White students (Helms, 1989; Parham, 1989; Parham & Helms, 1985; Smith, 1989; Spencer & Markstrom-Adams, 1990). Moreover, gifted African American students may experience more psychological and emotional problems than African American students not identified as gifted (Colangelo & Exum, 1979; Exum & Colangelo, 1981; Ford, 1996). Lindstrom and San Vant (1986) argued that gifted children who are African American students often find themselves in a dilemma whereby they must choose between academic success and social acceptance—the need for achievement versus the need for affiliation. They quoted one gifted African American student who said, "I had to fight to be gifted and then I had to fight because I am gifted" (p. 584). In some situations, gifted or high-achieving minority students may perceive academic achievement as a pyrrhic victory (Fordham, 1988; Ogbu, 2003). They win in one respect—academically—but lose in other respects—socially, affectively, and/or psychologically. Feelings of loneliness, isolation, and rejection increase, and the need for affiliation begins to outweigh the need for achievement (Ford, 1996; Whiting, 2006). When caught in this psychological and social-emotional battle, some African American students attempt to sabotage their achievement (e.g., procrastinating, failing to do assignments, exerting little effort, refusing to be in gifted education and advanced-level classes; Ford, 1996; Ogbu, 2003; Ogbu & Simmons, 1998). Their efforts and priorities shift, with psychological energy devoted to seeking and securing social acceptance or approval. Because of the numerous and complex problems that influence the psychological well-being of African American students, and because of our limited understanding of these problems, attention to racial identity development in educational (and all) settings is essential.

Discussion and Recommendations

Scholars have explored the affective and psychological needs and development of African Americans. Although the various conceptual, theoretical, and data-based works have been helpful and insightful, few studies have explored the racial identities of students who are gifted and African American. Proactive and aggressive prevention and intervention are needed to promote achievement among gifted African American students and to increase their representation in gifted education and AP classes. In the following sections, we present an overview of key recommendations.

Multicultural Counseling

African American students experiencing racial identity difficulties and/or conflicts can benefit from multicultural counseling. They need opportunities to share their concerns with other students who have had similar experiences. Sessions may focus on such topics as coping with peer pressures, family pressures, and low teacher expectations, as well as improving study habits, asking for help, and communicating effectively with teachers and other adults (see Ford, 1995, 1996). In terms of providing students with overall assistance, we suggest supportive, intrinsic, and remedial intervention strategies. The purpose of such strategies is to provide students with the support they need to feel confident in their abilities, to feel motivated, and to overcome academic shortcomings. Specifically, intrinsic strategies are designed to enhance African American students' belief in their ability (and right) to succeed in gifted education classes; supportive strategies are designed to help them to understand the benefits of participating in gifted education and AP classes; and remedial strategies help students to improve their academic performance, engagement, and work ethic in the specific area or areas of difficulty.

Social and Communal Experiences. Educators can also use small group and cooperative learning experiences to facilitate sharing and communication among African American students. These strategies provide gifted African American students with opportunities to establish friendships with White and other culturally diverse peers and to decrease feelings of isolation and alienation. African American students should also be encouraged to participate in extracurricular activities that promote racial pride, social interaction, and leadership. In essence, social and group experiences will give them opportunities to talk about their lives and concerns as racial and cultural beings. Questions worth discussion include, for example, "To whom can I, as a gifted African American student, turn to for emotional, psychological, social, and academic support?"; "How do I feel about being identified and placed in gifted education and AP classes?"; "How do I make friends with White students and those whose backgrounds are different from my own?"; "Am I 'inadequate' for having these needs and concerns?"; "How do I cope with social injustices in school and other settings?"

Mutual understanding and respect between White and African American students and between White school personnel and African American students is necessary. In order to build such relationships, educators must spend time—quality time—getting to know these students, their dreams, interests, values, and cultural traditions. Suggestions for providing all students with a multicultural education, building positive relationships between African American and White students, and building positive student–teacher relationships have been described by Ford (1996), Ford and Harris (1999), Ford and Milner (2006), and Ponterotto and Pedersen (1993) and have appeared in several multicultural books and articles (e.g., Banks, 2006; Lee, 1997; Ponterotto, Casas, Suzuki, & Alexander, 1995; Sue & Sue, 1990).

Racial Identity Development Focus

Psychological and counseling strategies and initiatives must help gifted African American students with poor or weak racial identities (i.e., being in the pre-encounter and immersion–emersion stages of identity) to understand and appreciate their dual identities of being both gifted and African American. White educational professionals must also understand that students in the pre-encounter and immersion–emersion stages of racial identity may resent and reject their help. These students may generalize negative perceptions of Whites in general to White educators (Exum & Colangelo, 1981). Educators will need to be patient and persistent in earning the trust of these students. As we describe shortly, a mentor or role model may be helpful in advancing African American students in the pre-encounter and immersion–emersion stages into higher and more positive and healthy stages of racial identities. Finally, a mentor or role model can also help students in the higher racial identity stages to maintain their positive, healthy, balanced self-perception (Whiting, 2006).

Exposure to Mentors and Role Models

Mentors can work with gifted African American students by focusing on at least two major strategies: (1) discussions and (2) exposure/experiences.

1. *Discussions.* Gifted African American students may think that they have no one to talk with about their concerns. Mentors can talk with them about the academic and social advantages and disadvantages of being in gifted programs, including some long- and short-term benefits. Ultimately, the most important focus of such discussions should be on increasing gifted African American students' sense of empowerment, improving their problem-solving and decision-making skills, and clarifying their goals for the future to give them a sense of direction and purpose. Discussions can take place with mentors and/or with African American students who were successful students in gifted programs:

   a. *Conversations with mentor about social injustices.* It is important that mentors have sincere and authentic conversations with mentees about real issues, specifically, social injustices. How did mentors cope with social injustices, including peer pressures, when they were students? How do mentors now cope with social injustices as adults?

   b. *Conversations with mentor about motivation and persistence.* It is essential that mentors hold discussions with gifted African American students about the fact that life is a series of compromises; in this light, students need to know about possible sacrifices they may have to make because of their participation in gifted programs (e.g., fewer African American classmates, more schoolwork, less time with peers).

   c. *Interviews with former students who are successful.* These persons can be African American students enrolled in college, African American adults who have their own business, and so on. Ideally, these persons will have participated in gifted programs as youth.

2. *Exposure and experience.* This recommendation is designed to increase the experiences gifted African American students have with

mature, academic-oriented persons. Second, these experiences are designed to give the students experiences in settings where African Americans are doing well academically, fiscally, and socially. Finally, such exposure is designed to help gifted African American students to develop effective coping and problem-solving skills.

a. *Academic extracurricular activities.* Exposure to and participation in extracurricular activities that focus on achievement can help to motivate and keep gifted African American students focused on doing well in school. For example, mentees should be encouraged to take advantage of tutoring, being on debate and chess teams, being a member of honor societies, and to participate in any activity or organization that promotes achievement.

b. *Black fraternities and organizations.* Member of fraternities can be asked to conduct workshops with gifted African American students on the importance of doing well in school, coping with peer pressures, building relationships with school personnel, acquiring scholarships, selecting a college and major, and finding internships. The goal here is to give them exposure to slightly older African Americans who are succeeding.

c. *College tours, including historically Black colleges and universities.* Students who are not aware of local and national colleges and universities are less likely to have higher education aspirations, and they may be hesitant about applying to the more elite institutions. By exposing gifted African American students to colleges, mentors are able to increase these students' awareness. Such experiences can be motivating, increasing the awareness of these students about the vital need to do well in their classes as well as to get the challenge they need by participating in gifted and AP classes.

d. *Shadowing and internships.* Depending on their socioeconomic status, African American students may have limited knowledge of the numerous careers that exist, the academic courses and strengths needed to pursue certain careers, and other career-related issues and topics. Thus, a student who wants to be an engineer can gain extensive information from shadowing an engineer and learning about job requirements and duties and pros and cons of the engineering professions.

e. *Reading books on African Americans who have faced barriers and been successful.* It is common knowledge that many gifted students enjoy reading. Given this fact, mentors can read books with mentees about African American students who have faced barriers and succeeded. Ford et al. (Ford, Howard, & Harris, 1999; Ford, Tyson, Howard, & Harris, 2000) have suggested multicultural bibliotherapy as an important strategy for use with these students and have provided a list of recommended multicultural books that have gifted individuals as the main character.

f. *Anger management skills.* This strategy may be especially necessary for gifted African American students in the pre-encounter and immersion–emersion stages of racial identity, both of which are characterized by confusion and anger.

g. *Conflict resolution skills.* Although many African American students face negative peer pressures when they achieve, they seldom know how to cope with these pressures, and they often succumb. Conflict resolution skills provide students with ways to cope with negative pressures from peers, teachers, family members, and other children and adults.

Multicultural Education

School personnel must also (re)evaluate the extent to which their curriculum and instruction affirm African American students' racial identities, while increasing all students' knowledge and acceptance of the nation's multicultural history (see Ford & Harris, 1999). How does the curriculum promote negative or positive images of African Americans? Does the curriculum (e.g., topics and books) promote racial pride in gifted African American students? Do the lessons plans promote positive achievement orientations among gifted African American students? Do they see themselves often in the lesson plans and books?

According to Banks (2006) and Banks and Banks (1995, 2004, 2006), few schools infuse multicultural content into the curriculum, thereby leaving gifted African American students feelings unconnected to what is being taught and read. When students—regardless of achievement level and racial background—do not see the curriculum as personally and culturally relevant, they are likely to become disinterested and unmotivated and thus to underachieve. Multicultural content can be infused into curriculum in at least four ways (Banks, 2006). The lowest and most common level is the *contributions approach*, followed by the *additive approach*. At both levels, multicultural content is elementary and somewhat superficial, with a focus on multicultural heroes, holidays, and traditions. Substantive issues of diversity and inequity are ignored, minimized, or trivialized because of the superficial nature of these levels. For example, controversial people of color and events are likely to be ignored in lesson plans. Furthermore, multicultural topics tend to be reserved for special days and events (e.g., Black History Month). Accordingly, Banks and Banks (1995, 2006) have advised schools to focus less on the contributions and additive approaches and more on the *transformation* and *social action approaches*. In the higher levels, students are consistently exposed to substantive multicultural topics; thus, every day and every subject area lend themselves to having a multicultural focus. At the transformation level, students are presented more than one perspective on a person, topic, or event; they are asked to view all issues from multiple perspectives in order to avoid stereotyping and polemic thinking, for example. At the social action level, students are taught and encouraged to address social issues and to confront, for instance, discrimination in school texts, discussions, and the media.

In their work with gifted African American students, Ford and Harris (1999) not only saw the need to ensure that gifted students were exposed to high levels of multicultural content, as proposed by Banks and Banks (1995), but they also saw the need ensure that such work was challenging and promoted higher-level thinking skills. Thus, they included the work of Bloom (1995), whose taxonomy focuses on higher-level thinking.

Multicultural Training for School Personnel

Ultimately, to work effectively with gifted African American students, school personnel require multicultural training. Such training is available through more than 700 ethnic studies and multicultural programs at colleges and universities (Banks & Banks, 1995, 2005). Counselors require an understanding of self-perceptions that goes beyond self-esteem and self-concept when working with African American and other racially and culturally diverse students. Several professional counseling associations (e.g., the American Counseling Association, the Association for Multicultural Counseling and Development, the American Psychological Association) have guidelines and position statements regarding multicultural competencies. Counselors and psychologists who wish to build a positive and trusting relationship with minority students can take multicultural counseling courses offered at colleges and universities, attend multicultural workshops and conferences offered by professional associations, seek internships in urban communities, and subscribe to publications that address issues of diversity (see Ford & Frazier Trotman, 2001; Ford & Harris, 1999).

Family Education

The majority of this chapter has focused on the role of school personnel in promoting strong racial identities among gifted African American students and helping them deal constructively with peer pressures and social injustices. We acknowledge that the roles and responsibilities of families cannot be overlooked. Few families have formal education and training in self-concept and racial identity theories. Although some African American families may be aware of the need to develop their children's self-concept and self-esteem, they may not know that the focus on self-concept must include racial identity. Educators who have multicultural training are in an ideal position to provide training to African American families on this topic. For instance, families can be taught how to discuss prejudice and discrimination with their children, discuss negative peer pressures and resolving conflicts with their children, and select books and movies that promote strong racial pride (see Ford & Harris, 1999, and Ford & Milner, 2006, for a list).

SUMMARY

African Americans live in a world and learn in schools that seldom affirm their dignity and worth as racial beings. Many of these students, like adults, struggle to develop a healthy sense of self, which includes views about their personal worth, their academic worth, and their social worth as racial beings. These damaging messages and associated challenges and struggles seem particularly difficult or complicated for

African American students who are identified as gifted. These students frequently face negative peer pressures relative to doing well in school: They are often accused of acting White, and they are frequently alienated and isolated from African American and White students alike. When African American students develop healthy racial identities (viz., the internalization stage), they are freer to focus on the need to achieve, and when gifted African American students develop positive, healthy racial identities they are less likely to succumb to negative peer pressures and social injustices.

People are not born with a self-concept, self-esteem, or racial identity; these perceptions of self are developed over time, as we interact with others, read, and watch or listen to the news and entertainment media. Racial identities are formed in multiple settings—at home, by the media, in day care centers, in preschools, and during the kindergarten through the higher education process. Thus, school personnel must proactively and aggressively seek to understand the powerful influence that self-perception has on students' achievement and motivation. When the student is culturally different, the focus must necessarily be on students' racial identity.

Note

1. This chapter builds and expands upon an earlier article: Grantham and Ford (2003).

References

Banks, J. A. (2006). *Cultural diversity in American education*. Boston: Allyn & Bacon.

Banks, J. A., & Banks, C. A. M. (Eds.). (1995). *Handbook of research on multicultural education*. New York: Simon & Schuster Macmillan.

Banks, J. A., & Banks, C. A. M. (Eds.). (2004). *Multicultural education: Issues and perspectives*. Hoboken, NJ: Wiley.

Banks, J. A., & Banks, C. M. (Eds.). (2006). *Multicultural education: Issues and perspectives* (6th ed.). Hoboken, NJ: Wiley.

Bloom, B. A. (1995). *Developing talent in young people*. New York: Random House.

Boutte, G. S. (1992). Frustrations of an African-American parent—A personal and professional account. *Phi Delta Kappan, 73,* 786–788.

Clark, K. B., & Clark, M. K. (1940). Skin color as a factor in racial identification of Negro preschool children. *Journal of Social Psychology, 11,* 159–169.

Cokley, K. (2003). What do we know about the academic motivation of African American college students? Challenging the "anti-intellectual myth." *Harvard Educational Review, 73,* 524–558.

Colangelo, N., & Davis, G. A. (2003). *Handbook of gifted education.* Boston: Allyn & Bacon.

Colangelo, N., & Exum, H. A. (1979, January–February). Educating the culturally diverse gifted: Implications for teachers, counselors, and parents. *Gifted Child Today, 22–23,* 54–55.

Coleman, L. J., & Cross, T. L. (2001). *Being gifted in school: An introduction to development, guidance, and teaching.* Waco, TX: Prufrock Press.

Cox, J., & Daniel, N. (1983, May–June). Identification: Special problems and special populations. *Gifted Child Today, 30,* 54–61.

Cross, W. E., Jr. (1971, July). Toward a psychology of Black liberation: The Negro-to-Black conversion experience. *Black World,* 13–27.

Cross, W. E., Jr. (1995). The psychology of Nigrescence: Revising the Cross model. In J. G. Ponterotto, J. M. Casas, L. A. Suzuki, & C. M. Alexander (Eds.), *Handbook of multicultural counseling* (pp. 93–122). Thousand Oaks, CA: Sage.

Cross, W. E., Jr., & Vandiver, B. J. (2001). Nigrescence theory and measurement: Introducing the Cross Racial Identity Scale (CRIS). In J. G. Ponterotto, J. M. Casas, L. A. Suzuki, & C. M. Alexander (Eds.), *Handbook of multicultural counseling* (2nd ed., pp. 30–44). Thousand Oaks, CA: Sage.

Davis, G. A., & Rimm, S. B. (2004). *Education of the gifted and talented* (5th ed.). Boston: Allyn & Bacon.

Elhoweris, H., Mutua, K., Alsheikh, N., & Holloway, P. (2005). Effects of children's ethnicity on teachers' referral and recommendation decisions in gifted and talented programs. *Remedial and Special Education, 26,* 25–31.

Exum, H. A., & Colangelo, N. (1981). Culturally diverse gifted: The need for ethnic identity development. *Roeper Review, 3,* 15–17.

Ford, D. Y. (1992). Determinants of underachievement as perceived by gifted, above-average, and average Black students. *Roeper Review, 14,* 130–136.

Ford, D. Y. (1994). *The recruitment and retention of Black students in gifted programs.* Storrs: National Research Center on the Gifted and Talented, University of Connecticut.

Ford, D. Y. (1995). *A study of achievement and underachievement among gifted, potentially gifted, and average African-American students.* Storrs: National Research on the Gifted and Talented, University of Connecticut.

Ford, D. Y. (1996). *Reversing underachievement among gifted Black students: Promising practices and programs.* New York: Teachers College Press.

Ford, D. Y. (1998). The under-representation of minority students in gifted education: Problems and promises in recruitment and retention. *Journal of Special Education, 32,* 4–14.

Ford, D. Y. (2004). *Intelligence testing and cultural diversity: Concerns, cautions, and considerations.* Storrs: National Research Center on the Gifted and Talented, University of Connecticut.

Ford, D. Y., & Frazier Trotman, M. (2001). Teachers of gifted students: Suggested multicultural characteristics and competencies. *Roeper Review, 23,* 235–239.

Ford, D. Y., & Grantham, T. C. (2003). Providing access for gifted culturally diverse students: From deficit thinking to dynamic thinking. *Theory Into Practice, 42,* 217–225.

Ford, D. Y., Grantham, T. C., & Whiting, G. W. (2008). Another look at the achievement gap: Learning from the experiences of gifted Black students. *Urban Education, 43,* 216–239.

Ford, D. Y., Grantham, T. C., & Whiting, G. W. (in press). Under-representation of culturally and linguistically diverse students in gifted education: A review of recruitment and retention. *Exceptional Children.*

Ford, D. Y., & Harris, J. J., III. (1999). *Multicultural gifted education.* New York: Teachers College Press.

Ford, D. Y., Harris, J. J., III, & Schuerger, J. M. (1993). Racial identity development among gifted Black students: Counseling issues and concerns. *Journal of Counseling and Development, 71,* 409–417.

Ford, D. Y., Harris, J. J., III, Tyson, C. A., & Frazier Trotman, M. (2002). Beyond deficit thinking: Providing access for gifted African American students. *Roeper Review, 24,* 52–58.

Ford, D. Y., Howard, T. C., & Harris, J. J., III. (1999). Using multicultural literature in gifted education classrooms. *Gifted Child Today, 22,* 14–21.

Ford, D. Y., & Milner, H. R. (2006). Counseling high achieving African Americans. In C. C. Lee (Ed.), *Multicultural issues in counseling: New approaches to diversity* (pp. 63–78). Alexandria, VA: American Counseling Association.

Ford, D. Y., Tyson, C. A., Howard, T. C., & Harris, J. J., III. (2000). Multicultural literature and gifted Black students: Promoting self-understanding, awareness, and pride. *Roeper Review, 22,* 235–240.

Ford, D. Y., & Whiting, G. W. (2006). Underrepresentation of diverse students in gifted education: Recommendations for nondiscriminatory assessment (Part 1). *Gifted Education Press Quarterly, 20*(2), 2–6.

Fordham, S. (1988). Racelessness as a factor in Black students' school success: Pragmatic strategy or pyrrhic victory? *Harvard Educational Review, 58,* 54–84.

Fordham, S. (1991). Peer-proofing academic competition among Black adolescents: "Acting White" Black American style. In C. E. Sleeter (Ed.), *Empowerment through multicultural education* (pp. 69–93). Albany: State University of New York Press.

Fordham, S. (1996). *Blacked out: Dilemmas of race, identity, and success at Capital High.* Chicago: University of Chicago Press.

Fordham, S., & Ogbu, J. U. (1986). Black students' school success: Coping with the "burden of 'acting White.'" *Urban Review, 18,* 176–203.

Gagne, F. (1994). Are teachers really poor talent detectors? Comments on Pegnato and Birch's (1959) study of the effectiveness and efficiency of various identification techniques. *Gifted Child Quarterly, 38,* 124–126.

Gear, G. H. (1976). Accuracy of teacher judgment in identifying intellectually gifted children: A review of the literature. *Gifted Child Quarterly, 20,* 478–489.

Gould, S. J. (1981). *The mismeasure of man.* New York: Norton.

Grantham, T. C., & Ford, D. Y. (2003). Beyond self-concept and self-esteem for African-American students: Improving racial identity improves achievement. *High School Journal, 87,* 18–29.

Harmon, D. (2002). They won't teach me: The voices of gifted African American inner-city students. *Roeper Review, 24,* 68–75.

Helms, J. E. (1989). Considering some methodological issues in racial identity counseling research. *The Counseling Psychologist, 17,* 227–252.

Herrnstein, R. J., & Murray, C. (1994). *The bell curve: Intelligence and class structure in American life.* New York: Free Press.

Hoge, R. D., & Coladarci, T. (1989). Teacher-based judgments of academic achievement: A review of literature. *Review of Educational Research, 3,* 297–313.

Huff, R. E., Houskamp, B. M., Watkins, A. V, Stanton, M., & Tavegia, B. (2005). The experiences of parents of gifted African American children: A phenomenological study. *Roeper Review, 27,* 215–221.

Jenkins, M. D. (1936). A socio-psychological study of Negro children of superior intelligence. *Journal of Negro Education, 5,* 175–190.

Lee, C. (Ed.). (1997). *Multicultural issues in counseling: New approaches to diversity* (2nd ed.). Alexandria, VA: American Counseling Association.

Lindstrom, R. R., & San Vant, S. (1986). Special issues in working with gifted minority adolescents. *Journal of Counseling and Development, 64,* 583–586.

Louie, J. (2005). *We don't feel welcome here: African Americans and Hispanics in Metro.* Cambridge, MA: The Civil Rights Project at Harvard University.

McBee, M. T. (2006). A descriptive analysis of referral sources for gifted identification screening by race and socioeconomic status. *Journal for Secondary Gifted Education, 17,* 103–111.

Menchaca, M. (1997). Early racist discourses: The roots of deficit thinking. In R. Valencia (Ed.), *The evolution of deficit thinking* (pp. 13–40). New York: Falmer.

Merton, R. K. (1948). The self-fulfilling prophecy. *Antioch Review, 8,* 193–210.

Naglieri, J. A., & Ford, D. Y. (2003). Addressing under-representation of gifted minority children using the Naglieri Nonverbal Ability Test (NNAT). *Gifted Child Quarterly, 47,* 155–160.

Neihart, M., Reis, S. M., Robinson, N. M., & Moon, S. M. (2002). *The social and emotional development of gifted children.* Waco, TX: Prufrock Press.

Ogbu, J. U. (2003). *Black students in an affluent suburb: A study of academic disengagement.* New York: Lawrence Erlbaum.

Ogbu, J. U., & Simmons, H. D. (1998). Voluntary and involuntary minorities: A cultural–ecological theory of school performance with some implications for education. *Anthropology and Education Quarterly, 29,* 155–188.

Parham, T. A. (1989). Cycles of psychological Nigrescence. *The Counseling Psychologist, 17,* 187–226.

Parham, T. A., & Helms, J. E. (1985). Relation of racial identity attitudes to self-actualization and affective states of Black students. *Journal of Counseling Psychology, 32,* 431–440.

Pegnato, C. W., & Birch, J. W. (1959). Locating gifted children in junior high schools: A comparison of methods. *Exceptional Children, 48,* 300–304.

Ponterotto, J. G., Casas, J. M., Suzuki, L. A., & Alexander, C. M. (Eds.). (1995). *Handbook of multicultural counseling.* Thousand Oaks, CA: Sage.

Ponterotto, J. G., & Pedersen, P. B. (1993). *Preventing prejudice: A guide for counselors and educators.* Newbury Park, CA: Sage.

Redmond, L. (Producer). (1999). Acting White. [Television series episode]. In *20/20.* New York: American Broadcasting Company.

Rist, R. C. (1996). Color, class, and the realities of inequality. *Society, 33,* 2–36.

Robinson, A. (1989). Gifted: The two-faced label. *Gifted Child Today, 12,* 34–26.

Rosenthal, R., & Jacobson, L. (1968). *Pygmalion in the classroom: Teacher expectation and pupils' intellectual development.* New York: Rinehart and Winston.

Science museum bans DNA genius at centre of race row. (2007, October 18). *Daily Mail.* Retrieved May 1, 2008, from http://www.dailymail.co.uk/pages/live/articles/news/news.html?in_article_id=488232&in_page_id=1770

Shumow, L. (1997). Daily experiences and adjustment of gifted low-income urban children at home and school. *Roeper Review, 20,* 35–38.

Smith, E. M. J. (1989). Black racial identity development. *The Counseling Psychologist, 17,* 277–288.

Spencer, M. B., & Markstrom-Adams, C. (1990). Identity processes among racial and ethnic children in America. *Child Development, 61,* 290–310.

Steele, C. M. (1997). A threat in the air: How stereotypes shape the intellectual identities and performance of women and African Americans. *American Psychologist, 52,* 613–629.

Steele, C. M. (1999). Thin ice: "Stereotype threat" and Black college students. *Atlantic Monthly, 284*(2), 50–54.

Sue, D. W., Capodilupo, C. M., Torino, G. C., Bucceri, J. M., Holder, A. M. B., Nadal, K. L., et al. (2007). Racial microaggressions in everyday life: Implications for clinical practice. *American Psychologist, 62,* 271–286.

Sue, D. W., & Sue, D. (1990). *Counseling the culturally different: Theory and practice* (2nd ed.). New York: Wiley.

Terman, L. M. (1925). *Genetic studies of genius: Vol. 1. Mental and physical traits of a thousand gifted children.* Stanford, CA: Stanford University Press.

U.S. Department of Education. (2002). *Office for Civil Rights survey redesign: A feasibility survey.* Retrieved June 29, 2008, from http://nces.ed.gov/surveys/frss/publications/92130

Valencia, R. (Ed.). (1997). *The evolution of deficit thinking.* New York: Falmer.

Whiting, G. W. (2006). Enhancing culturally diverse males' scholar identity: Suggestions for educators of gifted students. *Gifted Child Today, 39,* 46–50.

Whiting, G. W., & Ford, D. Y. (2006). Under-representation of diverse students in gifted education: Recommendations for nondiscriminatory assessment (Part 2). *Gifted Education Press Quarterly, 20*(3), 6–10.

Zucker, S. H., & Prieto, A. G. (1977). Ethnicity and teacher bias in educational decisions. *Journal of Educational Psychology, 4,* 2–5.

18

THE TALENT QUEST MODEL AND THE EDUCATING OF AFRICAN AMERICAN CHILDREN

A. WADE BOYKIN AND CONSTANCE M. ELLISON

The educational plight of African American children and youth has been well documented (Hollins, King, & Hayman, 1994; Jencks & Phillips, 1998; King, 2005). This is a concern that cries out for immediate, sustained, and profound attention. Until our schools do a substantially better job of educating Black students, to the very highest levels of achievement and attainment, then Black communities in particular and U.S. society in general will fail to realize a vast reservoir of human talent that our communities and society at large will greatly need—indeed, require—in the years and decades ahead. To address this concern proactively and substantially, nothing short of a shift in the paradigm of schooling must take place. New purposes and functions for our schools are needed. New bases are needed for determining what programs and practices are to occur in schools. New processes are called for in terms of what is to transpire inside classrooms. New outcomes should be expected of our students in comparison to what is asked of them now, or what has been asked in the past. New relationships are required among schools, families, and communities. In this chapter, we present such a paradigm of schooling.

Although the calls to reform our schools and to raise educational achievement have continued unabated over the last half of a century, the problematics of school achievement have not dissipated. Indeed, at present they are just as evident, and the achievement gap between majority and certain minority groups has remained virtually unchanged across this period. There are striking, rather persistent achievement gaps between the performance of Black students, both boys and girls, and their White counterparts. These gaps show up even before students start formal schooling—for example, in terms of knowledge of vocabulary words children are likely to see in a formal school curriculum (Jencks & Phillips, 1998). Gaps in tested achievement have been documented at the beginning of kindergarten, and these gaps widen over the course of this year in school (Barbarin, 2002). Gaps grow even wider with the same cohort of children by the third grade, with the disparities relatively more pronounced in higher-order skill domains such as deriving meaning from text and drawing inferences beyond the literal text for reading, or in understanding rate and measurement in mathematics (Murname, Willett, Bub, & McCartney, 2006; U.S. Department of

Education, National Center for Education Statistics, 2004). Gaps show up in grade point averages and in the taking of rigorous courses in high school (G. Cohen, Garcia, Apfel, & Master, 2006; Ryan & Ryan, 2005). Black–White achievement gaps have been captured over time in the results from the "Nation's Report Card" in the periodic National Assessment of Educational Progress (U.S. Department of Education, 2005). Over the last 30 years, test score disparities have shown up in successive cohorts of 9-, 13-, and 17-year-olds in reading, mathematics, and science.

Even more noteworthy, however, is that when American students in general are compared with those of other nations, especially in Europe and Asia, on tests of achievement in reading, mathematics, and science, they fall in the middle of the pack, suggesting that there is room for improvement for American students in general. For example, data from The Trends in International Mathematics and Science Study (Institute of Education Sciences, 2003; Mullis, Martin, Gonzalez, & Chrotowski, 2003) show that, of fourth- and eighth-grade American students, either or both fall significantly behind the math performance levels of students from nations such as Singapore, South Korea, Japan, Belgium, the Netherlands, Hungary, Russia, Slovenia, and the Slovak Republic.

Moreover, American students must acquire increasingly higher-level numeracy and literacy skills as well as higher-level critical thinking skills. They must go beyond such academic skills as the accumulation of facts, rules, algorithms, and basic expository information. They must come to be not only knowledge consumers but also knowledge producers. They must generate and create and be adept at the application of knowledge to social and civic settings that are more complex than what we have witnessed in the past or witness today. They must be more adept at reflecting on what they know. They will live in an age more greatly dominated by information. Indeed, the production, processing, transmission, interpretation, and utilization of information will be major commodity products.

Closing the achievement and attainment gaps is for certain a laudable goal for us as a society. However, the gap is at least two leveled. Consequently, whatever methods we deploy to address this academic challenge should not merely be about catching up Black (and Latino students) to the levels of their White counterparts per se. Closing the current majority–minority group gap in achievement should be done in ways that raise achievement for all students so that we can not only close the gaps between the performance of American students and their counterparts from other parts of the world but also, simultaneously, raise levels at a steeper rate for certain students of color. This should be our goal (Hilliard, 2003).

Current societal trends certainly justify such an educational tack. In the years ahead, American society can ill afford not to educate all of its students to high levels of attainment, given the rising intellectual, technological, social, and global demands that the future will place on them. Thus, meeting the challenges of educating students from historically disenfranchised groups should be a major societal goal. To accomplish such ends, nothing short of a reformulation of the nature and purposes of schooling, and the substance of the educational process, is required. Educational reform requires change—substantive change, if any sustainable effects are to occur. Adherence to the old culture is widespread, but schools must be willing to let go of the status quo and venture into new territory before positive effects of reform can be realized. It goes without saying that learning does not occur in a vacuum; neither does it happen without a plan representing a clear and consistent vision for increasing the students' and stakeholders' role in the improvement process. We believe that most efforts of the past have excluded from discussions of program development many important stakeholder voices, have been insufficiently based on a solid scientific foundation, have been focused on too limited a set of educational goals, have not been sufficiently informed by the human dynamics attendant to teaching and learning, and have too often been driven more by a focus on deficits than assets.

A Model to Guide Change: The Talent Quest Approach

We are well aware of the challenges attendant to school reform interventions. We have come to appreciate that the school is a significant socialization agency in the lives of African American and other disenfranchised children. There can be implicit if not explicit resistance to this schooling process and subsequent dampening of these children's educational prospects by virtue of the attitudes and expectations directed at them (Tenenbaum & Ruck, 2007). We have also come to appreciate how implementing an effective change process is at least as important as the content of the reform model's components themselves. We recognize the importance of mutual ownership of the change process and the informed buy-in of a renewed reform model by school personnel. We appreciate that authentic and sustained school reform classroom interventions entail changing the "core" of educational practice, enhancing school leadership, and establishing a sense of professional community; consequently, our efforts have incorporated these insights through the implementation of the Talent Quest Model for Comprehensive School Reform (TQM; LaPoint, Ellison, & Boykin, 2006). This model was developed by the authors and their colleagues at the Capstone Institute for School Reform at Howard University. The TQM initially evolved from a talent development approach to school reform that is predicated on the presumption that virtually all students can learn to high standards given that they are provided a demanding yet supportive environment and that all of the school's stakeholders are accountable for attaining this objective (Boykin, 2000).

The TQM resonates through six key interconnected, operative principles: (1) overdetermination of success, (2) co-construction, (3) evidence-based framework, (4) continuous improvement, (5) multiple outcomes, and (6) optimizing classroom transactions. We now discuss each of these principles. Table 18.1 represents elements of the TQM principles and associated classroom practices.

Overdetermination of Success

The TQM seeks to *overdetermine* success for students. This can be accomplished by ensuring that multiple activities are in place, such as programs as well as school and classroom practices and structures that become multiple pathways for success. The redundancy of such activity will reduce substantially the possibility that children fall through the cracks of failure. Overdetermining success is enacted through the simultaneous implementation of multiple activities and programs, any of which could stand alone and lead to enhanced outcomes but that together can have an even greater effect on student success. For us, this means implementing activities and programs in the areas of leadership support and support for the change process; classroom teaching and learning; teacher professional development with classroom follow-up; academic support involving tutorials, academic acceleration, and enrichment; student support services, including youth development programs; school–family–community partnerships; and support of assessment and evaluation.

Co-Construction

A second key element of the TQM is a focus on *co-construction* of the implementation at a school site. Co-construction entails paying heed to the social and cultural dynamics at school sites that will affect implementation of the TQM components and ensuring that there is authentic practitioner input into how these components are tailored to the unique dynamics, social context, and organizational features of a given school. Co-construction underlies our approach to all facets of the school reform intervention, including teacher professional development, school–family–community partnerships, and so forth. Moreover, as a classroom intervention tool, co-construction implies that students in the company of other students in a given setting are in the process of constructing their own knowledge acquisition and contributing to the construction of others in that setting. All the participants in that setting are simultaneously contributing to the collective understanding of the meaning and purpose of that setting through the consumption, and even production, of new information available in the setting and then augmenting prior information with it; interpreting it from a particular point of view, prior understanding, or learning; and then incorporating it into an existing knowledge base. Consequently, co-construction means multiplying this effect by and across the participants in the setting.

Evidence-Based Activities

Comprehensive school reform work that decisively addresses the kinds of challenges for educating African American students to high, 21st-century standards poses daunting challenges. Successfully pursuing our task, however, becomes

Table 18.1   Talent Quest Model (TQM) Key Operating Principles

Operative TQ Principles	Definition of Principles	Definition (continued)	Implementation Examples
Overdetermine success: Implementing multiple activities	• Create redundancy for success by having multiple pathways to success. • Every success pathway by itself can lead to enhanced student outcomes.	• By having multiple such pathways, the probability of student failure is minimized.	• Teacher professional development • Learning community (planning time support) • Instructional coaching • Supplemental programs (after-school tutoring) • Family/community involvement • Capacity building • Administration/leadership development
Optimizing classroom transaction: Integrity-based educational interventions	• Embrace interpersonal interactions inside classrooms that transpire across the school day and regularly between students and teachers that form the fundamental basis of everyday teaching and learning activities. • Facilitate meaningful learning by building on students' past experiences and prior knowledge and making connections to significant experiences in their lives. • Incorporate cultural resources by building positively on the cultural, family, and community assets and practices that students bring with them to the classroom.	• Enhance the learning community by enabling collaborative intellectual exchanges among students and ensuring that all students are actively involved in the learning process. • Provide information management and scrutiny by directly teaching students problem-solving and learning strategies and promoting higher order thinking and deep understanding. • Facilitate constructive social interactions by providing a socially supportive learning environment that is still academically demanding and rewards excellence, effort, and improvement.	• Making connections through students' lives and experiences • Collaboration among and between teachers and students • Promotion of fundamental, functional, and pop cultural themes • Demonstration of high expectations in a supportive learning environment
Multiple outcomes and barometers for success	• Transformation of school in reference to school and classroom climate. • Enhancement in staff quality of life and professional well-being. • Enhancement of neighborhood and family involvement and support.	• Enhance student achievement through improvement in standardized test scores, critical thinking skills, creative problem solving, motivation, and positive schooling behavior.	• Cognitive skills development and enhancement • Academic optimism • Academic efficacy • Enabling rather than toxic overall schooling environment • Broad stakeholder buy-in
Co-construction	• Entails understanding the social and cultural dynamics at school sites that will impact the implementation of the TQ intervention components.	• Ensure that there is authentic practitioner input into how these components are tailored to the unique dynamics, social context, and organizational features of a school. • Secure stakeholder voice in the change process.	• Collaborating with support and administrative staff regarding expressed school needs that are accompanied by co-constructive meetings
Evidence-based activities	• Select interventions based on best available evidence. • Provide required enabling conditions and resources. • Rigorously assess implementation quality.	• Determine and assess relevant outcomes. • Link outcomes to practice, conditions, and resources. • Make necessary changes to guide subsequent interventions.	• Application of research literature • Formative assessment • Gauging of implementation quality • Outcomes assessment • Data-driven instruction
Continuous improvement	• Attending/responsive to present and future educational challenges. • Striving for culture of improvement.	• See lack of success as a growth opportunity.	• Seeking and providing constructive feedback • Ongoing professional development • Sustained benchmark assessments across all programs and practices

Source: Copyright © 2008 Capstone Institute, Howard University.

more realistic when we embrace an evidence-based framework. Even today, too much of educational practice, too many educational programs, are based on hearsay, on what sounds good, on how things have always been done—even on who knows whom. We must build educational practices and capacity-building initiatives on sound and rigorous research, and on systematic evidence; evidence not only of what works but also on how and why things work, where things work, and for whom they work.

What does an evidence-based framework entail? Several ingredients come to mind. First, it is imperative to scrutinize the research literature to glean the best available findings that can help shape and direct the practices to be implemented. Three general rules should govern what qualifies as best evidence. First, did the obtained findings actually result from the practices that were implemented, or could there be plausible alternative explanations for the outcome(s)? Second, are there indications that the results have been repeated and are not just one-time occurrences? Third, have the results been obtained at other sites beyond the place of origin; that is, is there evidence for similar findings occurring more generally and not just under a special circumstance, or with a unique situation? These three rules are familiar to research methodologists and have been correspondingly labeled as matters of *internal validity*, *reliability*, and *external validity* (or generalizability).

Just because a positive result is reported in the literature does not mean that a given program or practice will work, only that it can work. An evidence-based approach also calls for implementers to gather data at the local site of focus as well. Therefore, effective staff preparation must be done, and the quality of implementation of the program or practice has to be assiduously gauged. Outcomes, both short and long term, need to be ascertained, and they should be assessed with regularity to determine trends across time and linked to preparation and implementation quality. Short-term outcomes could be in the form of scores on weekly quizzes or level of student classroom engagement. Long-term outcomes could be in the form of district-level standardized achievement tests. By linking preparation and implementation quality to outcomes, we can discern the operative factors that account for what is working, or what modifications should be made to better ensure that the program or practice will be successful in the future.

Continuous Improvement

It is seductively easy to presume that a school in the throes of reform is dysfunctional, that real student learning is elusive at best, and that effective teaching and teachers are virtually nonexistent. The goal of school reform, then, is not a matter of repairing or replacing the poor-quality elements and processes that are currently manifested and the ensuing assumption that when this is done, school reform will be judged a success. Such a presumptive mind set has fatal limitations. Even in the worst performing schools, there are pockets of excellence, and there are strengths and assets distributed among students and teachers alike. School reform should not be conceived as a trip that a school and its protagonists take from a state of "unreformed" to an achieved state of "now reformed." Given the complex dynamics at play; given the diversity among, for example, teachers and students in their current and potential assets; and given the resistance to change that comes from the presumptions of incompetence, school reform, in our opinion and experiences, is best construed as a journey of continuous improvement. So it should not matter if a teacher is a "poor" one or a "good" one, a novice or a veteran; there should always be room for improvement. It shouldn't matter if a student is a "poor" one or a "good" one; the student can always get better in his or her understanding of the academic material. A school should never rest on its laurels, because excellence, even when apparently achieved, must be sustained.

Multiple Outcomes
(Focus on the Whole Child)

In this era of high-stakes testing, in which student, teacher, and school accountabilities are linked to test score outcomes more emphatically than ever, it is temptingly easy to see the testing tail as wagging the educational dog. Yet, especially for African American students from marginalized social backgrounds, such a narrow focus on test scores may do more harm than good and may not ultimately accomplish the objective of greater achievement. It is crucial that we focus on the whole child (LaPoint et al.,

2006). Consequently, we must aim to foster educational optimism among the students, such that they come to set high expectations for themselves and become more positive about their educational futures. The aim is to enhance students' self- and collective efficacy so that they come to believe that their genuine efforts will pay positive academic dividends. They will also come to have positive academic identities so that it is important to them to be good in math and that they see themselves as good readers. It is crucial that they enhance their social and emotional competence, and these should be linked to such expressions as healthy conflict-resolution skills and healthy and mature social decision-making skills as they put a premium on being good classroom citizens. In essence, it seems crucial that for socially marginalized and educationally disenfranchised children, there should be an interlocking network of success domains to facilitate actualization of an interlocking network of successful outcomes. One could argue that focusing only on closing test score gaps is too narrow and myopic; closing achievement gaps is also simply not enough. Indeed, we must also close other gaps, including expectation, social positioning, contextually appropriate behavioral competency, and social belief system gaps.

Multiple outcomes also transcend student performance. Multiple stakeholders are involved in a paradigm-shifting school reform effort. Success outcomes should be tied to the realities of this broad participation. Other such outcomes would include enriching the school leadership's capacity to manage the change process, enhancing the professional quality of life for instructional staff, garnering informed and sustained buy-in from family and community stakeholders, and embracing collective responsibility among all stakeholders for a school's success.

Optimizing Classroom Transactions

Of all the principles, this is the one that we believe truly sets TQM apart from virtually all other approaches, or at least gives it its distinctive signature flavor. Perhaps it is also the one factor that may be most difficult for the concerned reader to fully understand and embrace. It is, in our estimation, the most central to school reform success and what is often the missing ingredient in other approaches to school improvement, and for this reason we believe this principle requires the greatest elaboration.

A persuasive case can be made that we must direct more intensive attention to changing the *educational core* of schooling. Elmore (1996) conceptualized the core as the fundamental ways teachers think about the nature of knowledge along with teachers' and students' roles in teaching and learning. Mounting evidence supports that factors that are close at hand, in particular those having to do with the ongoing daily transactions that transpire between teachers and students, and among students within classrooms, are educational core considerations that explain a sizable portion of the variation in student achievement outcomes (D. K. Cohen, Raudenbush, & Ball, 2003; Marzano, Pickering, & Pollock, 2001; Wang, Haertel, & Walberg, 1993). Such classroom contextual dynamics encompass students' prior experiences, attitudes, knowledge bases, values, goals and agendas; attendant interpersonal interactions, and the imputed and extrapolated voices and interests of other concerned stakeholders in the educational enterprise not physically present in the classroom (D. K. Cohen et al., 2003; Ellison, Boykin, Towns, & Stokes, 2000). In addition, many educators are currently attempting to change the core, some by focusing on the curriculum as a tool for teaching and learning, others by focusing on the practices of teaching, and others by focusing on the sociocultural development of students' thinking and learning processes (Boykin, Ellison, Wallace, & Slavin, in press).

Evidence has now increasingly pointed to a class of transactional practices that not only are identified with raising achievement levels for students but also, simultaneously, are likely to be particularly effective in closing the achievement gaps between minority group and majority group students. We have labeled these *integrity-based strategies*, and they are incorporated substantially into the core of teaching and learning activities within the TQM. A focus on integrity is in contradistinction to the more prevalent focus on the deficit perspective that is all too often invoked as the basis for solving the educational challenges of African American students.

Integrity, by definition, means that there is complexity, coherence, and texture contained in people's life experiences (Boykin & Allen, 2004). Therefore, these experiences are not simply characterized by deficiencies, inadequacies, and pathologies, even when the experiences are those of people from low-income, marginalized social backgrounds. This ethos posits that we hold high expectations for all to reach demanding standards, that there is emphasis placed on individual and collective accountability and responsibility, and that all stakeholders have a voice and choice. Moreover, this ethos implies that we build on people's social and cultural assets, draw on their existing knowledge and prior experiences, and encourage continual striving for improvement through effort. Evidence supports that enacting elements of this integrity-based ethos in classroom practices has beneficial effects for low-income minority children, especially African American children (Balfanz & Byrnes, 2006; Guthrie et al., 2004; Ladson-Billings, 2001; Langer, 2001; Lee, 2006).

It should be emphasized that building on children's integrity for educationally beneficial purposes is not a strategy that uniquely applies to African American (and Latino) children. The present argument is that building on integrity has been going on all along for the preponderance of mainstream European American students, whereas there has been denial or rejection that displays of integrity even exist to be built upon for most Black and Brown children (Valencia, 1997). Furthermore, the evidence to date suggests that although all children benefit from the deployment of integrity-based strategies, the improvement slope is steeper for African American and Latino children.

Implementation of diversity-sensitive, integrity-based pedagogy or other schooling activities has certain implications. Instead of dwelling on children's deficits, or what they can't do, won't do, don't do, don't know, and presumably don't get at home, one could compellingly argue that integrity-based strategies and practices draw their potency in no small measure from linking student learning and performance functionally to students' assets. Indeed, construing the diversity in children's backgrounds as a source of assets, if not strengths, is another hallmark of the Talent Quest approach to schooling. Integrity-based strategies are composed to build upon the assets that children from diverse backgrounds bring with them into learning settings, or to provide conditions in classrooms that allow the expression of such assets to be encouraged, or at least not be stifled; or in cases where pertinent assets do not exist, rather than penalizing children for not doing or knowing, to help create academically relevant assets for students in school settings. So what constitutes "assets" from this perspective? These would entail students' interests and preferences; motivational inclinations; passions and commitments; prior experiences and knowledge; existing or emerging understandings; existing or emerging skills and competencies; personal, family, and cultural values; family traditions and practices; attitudes, beliefs, and opinions; and self-perceptions and personal or collective identities.

An additional challenge that we acknowledge here is adequately differentiating between those experiences and their consequences that can and those that cannot be built upon (or even that get in the way) and under what conditions incorporating such factors would be beneficial or not. These are undeniably thorny issues, whose resolution (and perhaps others in this chapter) cannot be sufficiently addressed given page limitations. However, this is fertile territory for debate and research. This caveat notwithstanding, integrity-based schooling activities fall roughly into five interrelated yet distinct categories: (1) meaningful learning, (2) cultural resources, (3) constructive social interactions, (4) learning community, and (5) information management and scrutiny.

The term *meaningful learning* conveys strategies that, for example, make connections among different curriculum topics, connections to students' own personal experiences and future endeavors, connections to their prior knowledge, and pedagogical connections to the larger world in which they live (G. Cohen et al., 2006). In teaching reading to children, tying the reading text to personalized questions, such as "What you have done in this setting?" or "What would you tell your mother about this story?" would be another practical example (Guthrie et al., 2004).

Cultural resources refer to individual, family, and community experiences that give rise to funds of knowledge, values, inclinations, beliefs, and practices that link to the ways people prioritize, interpret, and negotiate their everyday lives. Ladson-Billings's (2001) work on culturally relevant pedagogy is worthy of mention in regard to examining cultural factors whose incorporation can likely lead to enhanced outcomes for African American students. She demonstrated that the successful teachers of African American are ones who include in their instruction community-based issues and challenges that children and their families must confront and negotiate. Academic lessons could center on the subtexts of power and privilege in American society and link concretely students' real-life community-based experiences to the official curriculum. An example Ladson-Billings provided is a teacher who had students conduct a project on how vacant land use in their community could be put to better use than as a magnet for drug users. This effort, then, is tied to topics and skills acquisition in the actual curriculum.

The work of Bell and Clark (1998) is exemplary. They found greater reading comprehension and story recall for African American elementary school children when text material was punctuated with practices representing cultural themes that have been traditionally associated with African American family and community experiences. These practices included ones that emphasized respect for eldership, flexibility in family roles, highly active and rhythmic games, and a focus on affective and social bonds. Of interest is that no effect on recall and comprehension was obtained as a function of the race of story characters.

Over the years, research has specified potential cultural values or themes that may manifest more prominently in certain populations than in others and that may be conduits for operationalizing learning contexts to enhance learning and performance outcomes for these populations. One such identified theme is *communalism* (Boykin, 1986; Boykin & Ellison, 1995). Communalism as a cultural theme implies that a premium is placed on collaborative interdependence as an intrinsic value. If this is the case for many Black Americans, then this could be one possible account of the especial receptiveness to collaboration learning for Black students that is found in the research literature. Moreover, if communalism is truly a culturally meaningful theme, then performance enhancements in group settings would occur even in the absence of individual incentives to perform well in collaborative settings and in the absence of the necessity to structure the collaborative setting, as is the case, for example, in reciprocal peer tutoring. This notion has been put to the test in several experimental investigations that have generally backed up these claims (e.g., Dill & Boykin, 2000; Hurley, Boykin, & Allen, 2005; Serpell, Boykin, Madhere, & Nasim, 2006).

Recently, Coleman (2003) was able to successfully train teachers of low-income third- and fourth-grade Black students to use a systematic guess-and-check strategy in the teaching of a 4-week unit that focused on identifying, adding, and subtracting fractions. The guess-and-check strategy consisted of allowing students to explore a given problem first and then to rely on their prior knowledge to guess at an answer. Later, after working the problem, students were to check to see how well that guess fits the conditions of the problem and then to use this information to make an improved guess the next time. For half of the intervention classrooms, this strategy was yoked to an individualistic learning condition, and for the other half, it was yoked to a communal learning condition. Although the individual learning condition produced significantly better performance on the fractions unit test than a standard/control learning condition, the communal context for learning produced significantly higher test performance than did the individual learning condition.

A third integrity-based strategy is referred to as *constructive social interactions*. This has to do with providing a supportive yet demanding learning environment, that is, one where encouragingly high expectations are set and in which effort and improvement are promoted, along with an emphasis on sustained excellence. The focus is on gaining mastery and understanding of the material instead of on rivaling and surpassing others per se, and on teacher support for student learning such that the classroom is an enabling rather than toxic environment.

In keeping with this strategy, Kaplan and Maehr (1999) found, in a sample of sixth-grade African American students from low-income backgrounds, that the more strongly classroom goals focused on students gaining understanding and emphasized effort and improvement (constructive social interactions), the higher were the students' reported levels of academic self-confidence, and the less there was reported disruptive classroom behavior. Conversely, the more classrooms were devoted to discerning which students performed the best, as they competed against each other to achieve the highest academic outcomes, the lower was the reported emotional tone, and the more problematic were reported peer relationships in the classrooms.

Yet, a fourth integrity-based approach is referred to as *learning community*. The intent here is to create academically productive collaborative exchanges among students. The theme is inclusiveness in a quality education instead of such an education being in the reach of only a chosen few. Evidence certainly points to the beneficial effects of deploying various cooperative or collaborative learning strategies, especially for African American and Latino students. (Rohrbeck, Ginsburg-Block, Fantuzzo, & Miller [2003] provided an excellent meta-analysis of the literature between 1996 and 2002.) A particularly noteworthy strategy, which has proved to be particularly beneficial for African American students, is Numbered Heads Together (Maheady, Mallette, & Harper, 1991). Here, students in mixed-skill groups study together without knowing ahead of time on whom from the group the teacher is going to call. Group members are prompted to ensure that all participants understand the material at hand.

The fifth integrity-based based approach is labeled *information management and scrutiny*. This actually entails a family of strategies, all geared toward creating academically relevant assets that will serve students well in formal learning settings. Here, the emphasis is on directly teaching students learning and thinking strategies to equip them with explicit tools and academic road maps that allow for deep, constructive, and appropriately focused engagement with the relevant academic tasks (Fuchs et al., 2004; Wasik & Bond, 2001). This would include deploying Venn diagrams for teaching similarities and differences, or story maps and story grammar schemes for critically apprehending cause-and-effect relationships (Marzano et al., 2001). This would further include other means to accentuate and deepen understanding of subject matter content to impart effective critical thinking skills, information processing, and long-term retention. Also under this umbrella would be multiple practice opportunities and opportunities to grasp material through multiple representations and vantage points.

A particularly striking research example that substantiates the merit of implementing several of the integrity-based strategies in actual classroom settings can be found in the work of Langer (2001). She documented the instructional strategies of teachers who "beat the odds," by increasing test scores for low-income, primarily African American and Latino children who closed achievement gaps with their White counterparts. These teachers are highly likely to use strategies consistent with several of these integrity-based domains. More particularly, teachers who teach skills by integrating them into the context of a larger, more purposeful activity (meaningful learning); who make connections within lessons, across lessons, and between in-school and out-of-school experiences (meaningful learning); who overtly teach enabling strategies, such as planning, organization, and reflection (information management and scrutiny); and who provide opportunities for students to work together in authentically collaborative ways that foster real intellectual exchanges (learning community) are more likely to be ones who beat the odds.

PUTTING IT ALL TOGETHER: THE TALENT QUEST MODEL OF SCHOOL REFORM

Although the intertwined notions of *integrity* and *assets* were originally and primarily conceived with respect to their positive application to student learning in classroom contexts, these principles should very likely apply to any learning context and thus for any learner. Other stakeholders involved in the schooling process also take on the role as learners themselves. For example, teachers participate in professional development. Principals take part in leadership development regimens, and there are educational activities in which parents participate as well. It stands to reason that in these settings we should build upon these participants' assets, prior knowledge, and cultural resources. We should involve them in collaborative learning activities and hold high expectations for them. It makes intuitive sense that teachers cannot effectively impart critical thinking skills if they are not themselves prepared to be critical thinkers.

Indeed, many of the key components of TQM should permeate most, if not all, facets of the schooling enterprise. By way of summary, the components of the TQM are depicted in Figure 18.1. Inside the large oval are the three key elements that must be included in any school reform effort. These are leadership development

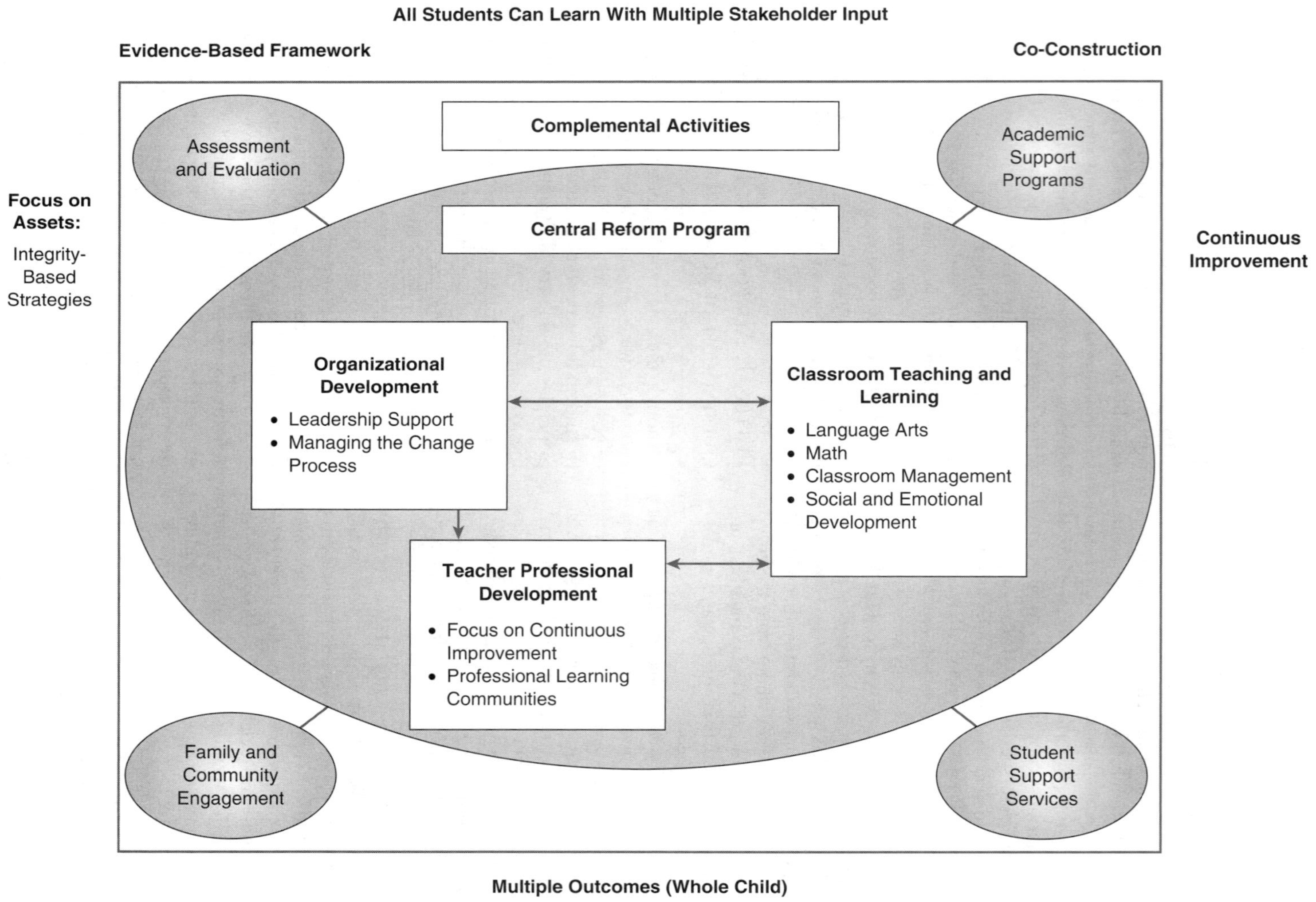

Figure 18.1 Talent Development Context

Source: Adapted from LaPoint, Ellison, and Boykin (2006, p. 378). Copyright © 2008 Capstone Institute, Howard University.

and support to ensure that the change process is effectively managed; classroom learning and teaching to encompass literacy, math, classroom management, and social/emotional competence; and teacher professional development. Capstone has developed program, practices, and materials to enact these elements according to a talent development perspective. Surrounding these components are crucial, complementary activities that, when added to the central components, ensure *overdetermination of success*. These are academic support programs; student support services, including youth development programs; and school–family–community partnerships to ensure that schools function to support families and communities while families and communities function to support positive schooling outcomes. Assessment and evaluation activities are organic to the school reform endeavor as well. The outer edge of this diagram lists the other key elements of our talent development paradigm. They are positioned there to emphasize that these factors are to inform all of the relevant schooling programs and practices. For all facets, the activities are to be evidence based and informed by co-constructive processes. A commitment to continuous improvement should be pervasively present. Multiple outcomes should be sought in all components, and professionals in all programs should be mindful that the whole child is in focus. Finally, the integrity of all stakeholders is to be acknowledged, and there is to be a relentless focus on assets.

But Does It Work? Impact of Talent Quest Educational Interventions

On the surface, the TQM may appear to be sensible, and intuitively plausible, but does it work? In classrooms where Talent Quest interventions have been implemented, students do learn, and learn well. They understand and remember the contents of the curriculum. They can perform classroom tasks that show us what they know and are able to do. Students often construct knowledge rather than recite information. They draw conclusions from their work by elaborating on their understanding by connecting the classroom topics to their own lived experience. Yet, a proverbial question that remains is whether these students do well on high-stakes standardized tests mandated by the states. Research shows that test scores have increased in both reading and mathematics. To illustrate the enhancement in standardized test performance in math and reading, Talent Quest interventions were employed over a 1-year period for low-achieving

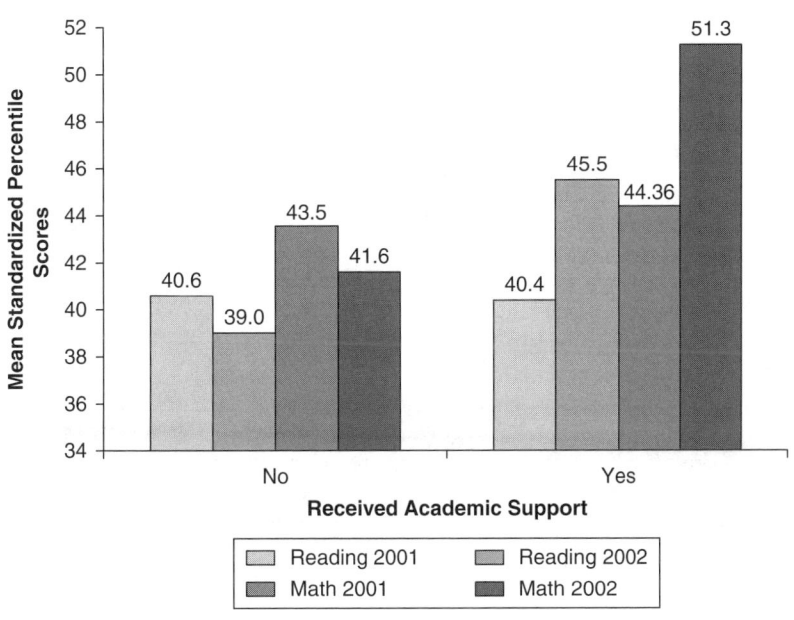

Figure 18.2   Kasper Elementary School (Pseudonym) Academic Support Program (Grades 3–6) Stanford Achievement Test Matched-Samples Comparisons (2001–2002)

students enrolled in Capstone's After School Program (ASP) and performance was compared with a matched sample (based on the previous year's Stanford Achievement Test [9th ed.] scores) of non-ASP students. This was at an inner-city school with a 98% African American student population. From 2001 to 2002 (see Figure 18.2), there was actually a drop in the math and reading scores of similar students who were not participants in the ASP. For the ASP participants, Stanford Achievement Test performance in reading and math rose 13% and 16%, respectively, from 2001 to 2002. Similar results were obtained in other years at this school and at other sites with similar demographics. Participation in the TQM ASP clearly is linked to improvements in both reading and math.

Additional research highlights related findings. For example, in 2003, one school deployed elements of the TQM as the state put this school on the "watch" list for reconstitution. Over 95% of this school's student enrollment consisted of African American students from low-income backgrounds. That year, only 30% and 34% of the students performed at or above the proficiency level on the state achievement test in reading and math, respectively. After 3 years, 68% and 64% of the students had reached proficiency in reading and math, respectively (see Figure 18.3).

Regarding the TQ integrity-based instructional practices, when correlating the observational rating of the teacher's use of integrity-based strategies and student reading and math performance on the standardized achievement tests, we found at several sites over the years that the more teachers implemented these TQM evidence-based practices in their classrooms, the higher were the test performance levels for their students (as an example, see Table 18.2).

Future Research Directions

The true effectiveness of this paradigm of schooling for enhancing academic outcomes for African American students (if not all students) is certainly far from a settled matter. Numerous questions still need to be addressed. More and better research still needs to be done. Promising results have been attained at certain sites and in communities of great need. Accumulating findings from the research literature continue to point in the directions that the paradigm pursues. However, can these effects be sustained over time? Can they be sustained when school and district leadership change? Can they be sustained under differing school demographic circumstances, or when student demographics change? Can the school reform efforts be scaled up beyond relatively isolated occurrences for more widespread implementation?

Moreover, many of the findings to date are encouraging, but they are based on correlational

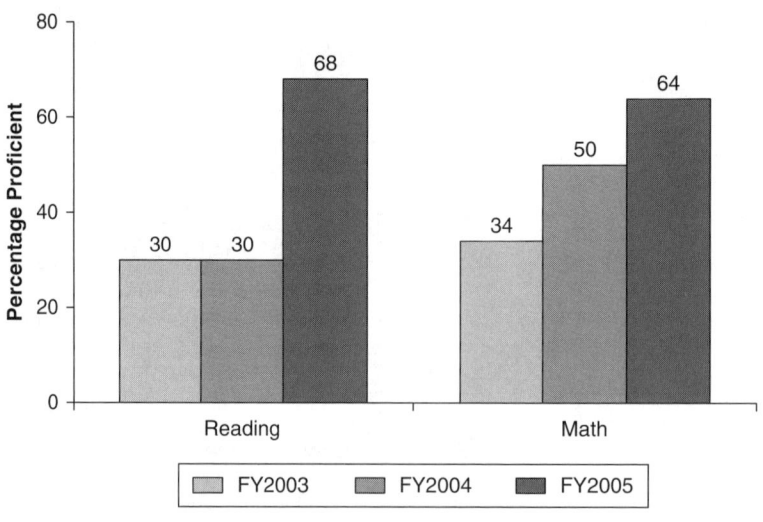

Figure 18.3 Goodwork Elementary School (Pseudonym) Student Performance in Reading and Math (2003–2005)

Table 18.2 Covington Elementary School (Pseudonym) Correlations Between Teacher Observations and Stanford Achievement Test Performance (2003–2004)

Subscale	Reading Scores	Math Scores
Meaningful Learning	.297**	.341**
Cultural Resources	.524**	.522**
Constructive Social Interactions	.233*	.285**
Learning Community	.361**	.368**
Information Management and Scrutiny	.265**	.292**

* $p < .05$. ** $p < .01$.

data instead of on data gleaned from more rigorous research designs, under more controlled conditions, and under conditions in which alternative explanations can be confidently ruled out. This must be rectified. Some of the findings pertaining to the enhancing role that culture may play for African American students have been obtained under controlled and rigorous conditions, but can these same outcomes be obtained under the more complex and nuanced conditions of daily classroom life? Can effective, culturally relevant pedagogy for Black students be successfully enacted by teachers who may not share or value or understand these cultural inclinations?

Beyond this, what are the most effective professional development/capacity-building strategies to ensure implementation accuracy and sufficient dose levels of the programs and practices? Recent research suggests that teachers' existing belief systems vary concerning the nature and purpose of learning and the potential for all students to learn to high standards. Teachers whose own learning and teaching ideologies are at odds with those inherent to a reform program will be resistant to change and to carrying out the new strategies (Manouchehri, 2004). How should this be taken into consideration in the implementation of school reform?

These are but a few of the challenges and questions that must be addressed—and they will be addressed. Our children, our communities, and our society at large require nothing less.

Rhetoric to Reality:
Some Concluding Comments

Solving the educational challenges faced by African American students remains a persistent and vexing concern for Black communities in particular and for American society at large. In spite of apparently concerted national attention to this matter, over recent decades, the achievement gap between Black and White American students remains unacceptably large. This is further complicated by the reality of another persistent achievement gap such that American students in general don't fare as well as those from several other nations in the world. These educational disparities must also be reconciled with the goal of having an educated citizenry with the learning, thinking, and problem-solving skills needed to make a meaningful contribution to an increasingly complex and dynamically changing society; we must provide all American students the tools that they will need to be productive in an increasingly demanding, globally interdependent world.

We have argued in this chapter that many of the previous efforts at school reform have fallen short, for a variety of reasons. They have underestimated the nature and scope of the extant educational challenges that must be successfully addressed. They have pursued change more from an outside in methodology rather than from the inside out. The pursuit of technocratic solutions has been more the rule than the exception. Starting change from the inside of schooling is what Elmore (1996) referred to as changing the "educational core." The starting focal point should be supporting students in the process of classroom learning on a day-by-day basis and then restructuring the remaining elements of the schooling context so they are explicitly designed to assist this process by, for example, altering the organization of teacher and staff time and the roles and responsibilities of teachers, school administrators, parents, and other interested stakeholders. These other elements would include programs and practices that allow for success to be overdetermined so that it becomes difficult for students to fall short in their learning outcomes. This change process also must not operate from a top-down approach whereby the outside experts, or even the educational powers that be, impose the transformations on those who must bear the brunt of their enactment. We have learned that change imposed is change opposed; therefore, change must start with and be accompanied by a co-constructive process that involves the voices of a broad spectrum of individuals with stakes in seeing enhanced educational outcomes.

Moreover, the pursuit of enhanced educational outcomes must be substantially informed by evidence. It must be driven by systematic and rigorous research that illuminates not necessarily what we want to hear but what we must do to ensure success, and this evidence should lead us down the path of continuous improvement such that improvement becomes not just a means to an educational end but a continuous goal in its own right. It is crucial also to appreciate that enhancing student test performance should not be the only goal for a successful school. Especially for students from disenfranchised backgrounds, enhancing the whole child should be the focus; beyond this, success indicators need to be in place for all stakeholders, so that there are multiple barometers encompassed in a school of success.

At the center of this reform enterprise must be optimizing transactions inside classrooms between teachers and students and among students themselves. The evidence clearly indicates that such transactions are facilitated not when the task is approached via an attempt to fix broken children or repair their deficits per se but when we treat diversity as an asset on which to build. Honoring the integrity of the learner would lead to discerning integrity in the life experiences of students and of the families that send their sons and daughters to the school. Thus, instruction must be built on students' out-of-school experiences, and teachers need to allow students to use these experiences as starting points for learning. Moreover, helping students build on their knowledge base is facilitated when teachers learn more about students' home cultures and adapt their teaching approach to incorporate students' cultural inclinations and salient cultural experiences (Boykin & Allen, 2004; Lee, 2006; Tharp & Gallimore, 1989). Classroom teaching and learning must transpire under supportive, high-expectation conditions, where students sustain each other by participating in collaborative learning opportunities. Indeed, the notion of collaboration should transcend the classroom such that all stakeholders participate in communities of learning.

Furthermore, classroom teaching and learning should not be conceived as a pouring-in and pouring-out process; instead, there should be a premium attached to promoting more effective and efficient ways for students (if not all learners) to more deeply and more thoroughly process subject matter content so they are not just knowledge consumers but also knowledge producers.

Our TQM for schooling incorporates these considerations, and we have drawn optimism from the encouraging and promising results yielded by our efforts to date. Although many challenges still remain, and more research needs to be done, we believe we have charted a compelling direction for the schooling of African American students, if not all students.

Finally, school leaders must accept their share of the responsibility for lifting achievement while closing achievement gaps, by crafting a set of deliberate action strategies that focus on the dismantling of inequitable schooling practices such that African American students, for example, are given greater access to opportunities to learn. School leaders, guided by systematic evidence, must stay the course in pursuit of school-wide improvements instead of being swayed by the latest educational fads. To be sure, one other challenge school leaders must address proactively will be how to change, or at least minimize, the entrenched attitudes and beliefs of some practitioners that children from certain familial or ethnic backgrounds simply cannot or will not learn well to achieve at high levels.

TQM intervention strategies are designed to be comprehensive, coherent, and sustainable over time, yet this will happen only if the preponderance of school stakeholders truly believe that excellent outcomes can be achieved at their schools. If there is any hope of narrowing or eliminating the achievement gaps at the school or broader level, it is clear that educational stakeholders must be truly willing to accept responsibility for educating to high levels every child and placing all students at promise for educational success.

References

Balfanz, R., & Byrnes, V. (2006). Closing the achievement gap in high-poverty middle schools: Enablers and constraints. *Journal of*

Education for Students Placed At Risk, 11, 143–159.

Barbarin, O. (2002). The Black–White achievement gap in early reading skills: Familial and sociocultural context. In B. Bowman (Ed.), *Love to read: Essays in developing and enhancing early literacy skills of African American children* (pp. 1–15). Washington, DC: National Black Child Development Institute.

Bell, Y., & Clark, T. (1998). Culturally relevant reading material as related to comprehension and recall in African American children. *Journal of Black Psychology, 24,* 455–475.

Boykin, A. W. (1986). The triple quandary and the schooling of Afro-American children. In U. Neisser (Ed.), *The school achievement of minority children* (pp. 57–93). Hillsdale, NJ: Lawrence Erlbaum.

Boykin, A. W. (2000). The talent development model of schooling: Placing students at promise for academic success. *Journal of Education for Students Placed At Risk, 5,* 3–25.

Boykin, A. W., & Allen, B. (2004). Cultural integrity and schooling outcomes of African American schoolchildren from low-income backgrounds. In P. Pufall & R. Unsworth (Eds.), *Rethinking childhood* (pp. 104–120). New Brunswick, NJ: Rutgers University Press.

Boykin, A. W., & Ellison, C. (1995). The multiple ecologies of Black youth socialization. In R. Taylor (Ed.), *African American youth: Their social and economic status* (pp. 93–128). Westport, CT: Praeger.

Boykin, A. W., Ellison, C., Wallace, M., & Slavin, R. (Eds.). (in press). *Promoting high achievement for all children: Evidence based programs, practices, and procedures.* Alexandria, VA: Stylus Press.

Cohen, D. K., Raudenbush, S. W., & Ball, D. L. (2003). Resources, instruction, and research. *Educational Evaluation and Policy Analysis, 25,* 119–142.

Cohen, G., Garcia, J., Apfel, N., & Master, A. (2006, September 1). Reducing the racial achievement gap: A social-psychological intervention. *Science, 313,* 1307–1310.

Coleman, S. (2003). *Mathematics classroom performance as a function of communal versus individualistic learning contexts.* Unpublished doctoral dissertation, Howard University.

Dill, E., & Boykin, A. W. (2000). The comparative influence of individual, peer tutoring, and communal learning contexts on the text recall of African American children. *Journal of Black Psychology, 26,* 65–78.

Ellison, C., Boykin, A. W., Towns, D. P., & Stokes, A. (2000). *Classroom cultural ecology: The dynamics of classroom life in schools serving low-income African American children* (Technical Report No. 44). Baltimore and Washington, DC: Johns Hopkins University and Center for Research on the Education of Students Placed At Risk, Howard University.

Elmore, R. (1996). Getting to scale with good educational practice. *Harvard Educational Review, 66,* 1–26.

Fuchs, L. S., Fuchs, D., Prentice, K., Hamlett, C. L., Finelli, R., & Courey, S. J. (2004). Enhancing mathematical problem solving among third-grade students with schema-based instruction. *Journal of Educational Psychology, 96,* 635–647.

Guthrie, J., Wigfield, A., Barbosa, P., Perencevich, K., Taboada, A., Davis, M. H., et al. (2004). Increasing reading comprehension and engagement through concept-oriented instruction. *Journal of Educational Psychology, 96,* 403–423.

Hilliard, A. (2003). No mystery: Closing the achievement gap between Africans and excellence. In T. Perry, C. Steele, & A. Hilliard (Eds.), *Young, gifted, and Black: Promoting high achievement among African-American students* (pp. 131–165). Boston: Beacon Press.

Hollins, E., King, J., & Hayman, W. (Eds.). (1994). *Teaching diverse learners: Formulating a knowledge base.* Albany: State University of New York Press.

Hurley, E. A., Boykin, A.W., & Allen, B. A. (2005). Communal vs. individual learning of a math-estimation task: African American children and the culture of cooperative learning contexts. *Journal of Psychology: Interdisciplinary & Applied, 139,* 513–527.

Institute of Education Sciences. (2003). *Trends in International Mathematics and Science Study.* Washington, DC: Author.

Jencks, C., & Phillips, M. (1998). *The Black–White test score gap.* Washington, DC: Brookings Institution Press.

Kaplan, A., & Maehr, M. (1999). Achievement goals and student well-being. *Contemporary Educational Psychology, 24,* 330–358.

King, J. (Ed.). (2005). *Black education: A transformative research and action agenda for the new century.* Mahwah, NJ: Lawrence Erlbaum.

Ladson-Billings, G. (2001). The power of pedagogy: Does teaching matter? In W. Watkins, J. Lewis, & V. Chou (Eds.), *Race and education* (pp. 73–88). Boston: Allyn & Bacon.

Langer, J. (2001). Beating the odds: Teaching middle and high school students to read and write well. *American Educational Research Journal, 38,* 837–880.

LaPoint, V., Ellison, C., & Boykin, A. W. (2006). Educating the whole child: The talent quest model for educational policy and practice. *Journal of Negro Education, 75,* 373–388.

Lee, C. (2006). "Every good-bye ain't gone": Analyzing the cultural underpinnings of classroom talk. *International Journal of Qualitative Studies in Education, 19,* 305–327.

Maheady, L., Mallette, R., & Harper, G. (1991). Accommodating cultural, linguistic, and academic diversity: Some peer-mediated instructional options. *Preventing School Failure, 36,* 26–31.

Manouchehri, A. (2004). Implementing mathematics reform in urban schools: A study of the effect of teachers' motivation style. *Urban Education, 39,* 472–508.

Marzano, R., Pickering, D., & Pollock, J. (2001). *Classroom instruction that works: Research-based strategies for increasing student achievement.* Alexandria, VA: Association for Supervision and Curriculum Development.

Mullis, I., Martin, M., Gonzalez, E., & Chrotowski, S. (2003). *Findings from IES's Trends in International Mathematics and Science Study (TIMSS) at fourth and eighth grades.* Chestnut Hill, MA: TIMSS and PIRLS International Study Center, Boston College.

Murname, R., Willett, J., Bub, K., & McCartney, K. (2006). Understanding trends in the Black–White achievement gap during the first years of school. *Brookings Wharton Papers on Urban Affairs, 7,* 97–135.

Rohrbeck, C. A., Ginsburg-Block, M. D., Fantuzzo, J. W., & Miller, T. R. (2003). Peer-assisted learning interventions with elementary school students: A meta-analytic review. *Journal of Educational Psychology, 94,* 240–257.

Ryan, K., & Ryan, A. (2005). Psychological processes underlying stereotype threat and standardized math test performance. *Educational Psychologist, 40,* 53–63.

Serpell, Z., Boykin, A. W., Madhere, S., & Nasim, A. (2006). The significance of contextual factors in African American students' transfer of learning. *Journal of Black Psychology, 32,* 442–454.

Tenenbaum, H. R., & Ruck, M. D. (2007). Are teachers' expectations different for racial minority than for European American students? A meta-analysis. *Journal of Educational Psychology, 99,* 253–273.

Tharp, R., & Gallimore, R. (1989). *Rousing minds to life: Teaching, learning and schooling in social context.* New York: Cambridge University Press.

U.S. Department of Education. (2005). *National Assessment of Education Progress.* Washington, DC: Author.

U.S. Department of Education, National Center for Education Statistics. (2004). *Early Childhood Longitudinal Study (K–Third Grade).* Washington, DC: Author.

Valencia, R. (1997). *The evolution of deficit thinking: Educational thought and practice.* London: Falmer.

Wang, M. C., Haertel, G. D., & Walberg, H. J. (1993). Toward a knowledge base for school learning. *Review of Educational Research, 63,* 249–294.

Wasik, B., & Bond, M. (2001). Beyond the pages of a book: Interactive book reading and language development in preschool classrooms. *Journal of Educational Psychology, 93,* 243–250.

PART V

GROUP IDENTITY

19

RACIAL SOCIALIZATION

Roots, Processes, and Outcomes

KEISHA L. BENTLEY, VALERIE N. ADAMS, AND HOWARD C. STEVENSON

Keep aware of who you are: "a tree without roots"—if you don't have roots, you will be cut off; be reminded of who you are and where you are coming from . . . you need to provide the correctives and don't be so much in awe of the place and "whatever they do to my child is good." You need to provide correctives.

—An African American parent responds to questions of how she engages in racial socialization
(Arrington & Stevenson, 2006, p. 13)

Throughout our lives, we are exposed to verbal, visual, and tacit messages that shape our self-perceptions as well as our interpretations of our place in the world. As Black families are faced with the temperamental whims of acceptance by mainstream society, parents may use racial socialization to counter and protect their children from malicious stereotypes that may limit their opportunities as well as to promote healthy functioning through adulthood. In this chapter, we discuss the historical and current issues in racial socialization research and propose new directions for conceptualizing future research.

CONCEPTUALIZING RACIAL SOCIALIZATION: AN UNFINISHED JOURNEY

Bush and Simmons (1990) defined *socialization* (without racial framing) as "the ways in which individuals learn skills, knowledge, values, motives, and roles appropriate to their position in a group or society" (p. 134). As a starting point, current research has sought in bits and pieces to examine how thoughts, emotions, behaviors, and interactions are influenced by racial socialization, but defining racial socialization has been a challenging journey across sociological, biological, psychological, and political disciplinary terrains (Lesane-Brown, 2006). The term *racial socialization* has been used interchangeably with *ethnic* or *cultural socialization* and a host of other terms. We propose that each of these terms should follow Boykin and Toms's (1985) *triple-quandary framework* of mainstream, minority, and cultural explanations of Black culture and should constitute different forms of socialization that have distinct and overlapping characteristics that can be explored independently or collectively, depending on the research needs (Stevenson, Bentley, & Adams, 2007). The triple-quandary framework, which is perhaps the most quoted frame for contexts of racial socialization, posits that all three are situated within family socialization, yet our measurement and conceptual models to date tend to focus on them as separate. Our goal in this brief review of the field of racial socialization is to encourage future work on racial socialization to integrate these different contexts, but with some adjustments.

In the current literature, race, culture, and ethnicity are not well distinguished. Cultural socialization has included messages that reflect cultural pride and that reinforce the historical knowledge of a specific cultural group. It is often the most frequently acknowledged type of socialization provided by parents and received by children (Hughes & Chen, 1997; McLoyd, Cauce, Takeuchi, & Wilson, 2000; A. J. Thomas & Speight, 1999). Although racism may be discussed in cultural socialization, it tends to be based on uplift from challenging sociohistorical contexts, such as slavery and the Civil Rights movement, but without raising oppression as the most salient aspect of those contexts. Cultural socialization has also been described as a transmission of knowledge of and respect for Diasporic accomplishments, communalism, and spiritual connections.

Ethnic socialization reinforces the values and strengths of a specific ethnic group and teaches preparation for the biases or stereotypes that may be faced as a result of membership of this group. For instance, research that examines the socialization of African American, Caribbean, African, or Hispanic Blacks would serve as a function of ethnic socialization. The ethnic pride messages may be more linked to their distinct cultural traditions and demonstrate a nationalistic, geographic, or family-of-origin connectedness. Therefore, the pride or bias they display or promote may be less about being Black than it is about being proud of being, for example, Haitian, or Nigerian. Both racial and ethnic pride may coexist; however, one may be at the foreground or background, depending on the context. There is an assumption that African Americans do not receive ethnic socialization. On the contrary, African Americans often use a geographical connection that includes the appropriate ways of being and how their family traditions and historical perspectives impact current situations. Thus far, most research that specifically targets Black ethnic socialization investigates the between group differences in messages and racial identity (Anglin & Whaley, 2006). Although recent research by T. L. Brown and Krishnakumar (2007) focused on the ethnic socialization of African Americans, there remains a lack of within-group socialization studies of Black ethnic groups—both as immigrants in America and throughout the Black Diaspora.

In racial socialization, we see greater attention given to messages about preparation for bias, which include ideas about societal racism, assimilation, biculturalism, spirituality, and egalitarianism (McHale et al., 2006; Stevenson, Cameron, Herrero-Taylor, & Davis, 2002). Whereas cultural and ethnic socialization focuses on a rich cultural heritage that looks within and is enhancing of the group, racial socialization includes an emphasis on how others will perceive you and influences your interactions and strategic maneuvering as well. Messages transmitted that include within-group internalized racism would also be incorporated in racial socialization in that they are a perpetuation of others' divisive belief systems. Researchers have documented that African American parents are more likely than parents from other ethnic groups to engage in racial socialization (Coard & Sellers, 2005; Stevenson, 1995). In our review of the literature, two types of socialization have been identified most frequently and with greatest agreement among researchers: (1) *cultural socialization* and (2) *preparation for bias* (Hughes et al., 2006).

Seminal Work

The following review of selected foundational research provides the background and framing for current research on racial socialization theory and measurement from multiple perspectives.

Parental racial socialization research over the last 2 decades has focused on its conceptualization and development, its impact on child racial attitudes, its differential manifestations and types, and its interpretation from adolescent perspectives. It is important to return from our journey to the roots of racial socialization conceptualization by examining what Boykin and Toms (1985) described as "triple consciousness" and the "dynamic interplay among three competing contexts of socialization" (p. 46). Boykin's triple quandary (Boykin, 1983, 1984; Boykin & Toms, 1985) is a conceptual framework suggesting how African Americans struggle to balance child rearing among three contexts of socialization (mainstream, minority, and Black cultural). Because it is inevitable that African Americans will be exposed to White mainstream values, Black families continue to judge themselves against White middle-class barometers of success, which develops into a mainstream orientation. A minority orientation includes the acknowledgment and development of strategies that attempt to negotiate American racial hierarchies. Black cultural orientation is not necessarily about imparting racial knowledge; instead, it is more about transmitting a Black way of being that is rooted in West African culture, but it has been amended through the Black American experience. Boykin and Toms speculated that when there is compatibility between family and societal socializing forces (school, the media, cultural norms, etc.), these external forces serve to reinforce and fortify the values and ideas of the family.

Margaret Beale Spencer (1983) was among the first researchers to directly assess the influence of parental child rearing about racial matters. A major assumption and influence of Spencer's work was that Black children's behaviors and attitudes are susceptible to adult interpretations and motivations. Using a revision of the Clark and Clark (1947) doll study framework, she targeted three groups of children: (1) 3- to 5-year-olds; (2) 4- to 6-year-olds and (3) 3-, 5-, 7-, and 9-year-olds. She used postcards depicting Black and White children/objects to determine not only racial preferences but also color connotations and racial attitudes. Moreover, she explored whether the parents' transmission of racial matters and their estimation of their child's racial knowledge and attitudes was predictive of their child's racial orientation. Spencer found that parental reports of giving (or not giving) specific messages did indeed predict children's racial identity outcomes. For instance, racial attitudes were predicted by socialization regarding civil rights and preparation for discrimination, with a lack of both of these predicting higher Eurocentric attitudes. In addition, when parents reported that their children had good knowledge of Black history, their children were also significantly more likely to have higher Afrocentric preferences and color connotations. Approximately two thirds of the parents discussed racial issues before their children inquired about these issues. Spencer's work was pivotal in racial socialization research in that it demonstrated its prevalence in the African American community and linked it with specific psychosocial outcomes.

Diane Hughes and her colleagues have conducted several significant studies examining the influences and motivations of mothers and fathers as they racially socialize their children (Hughes & Chen, 1997, 1999; Hughes et al., 2006). Hughes and Chen (1997) revealed that the most frequent form of racial socialization was cultural socialization, followed by preparation for bias and promotion of mistrust, respectively. However, as their children grew older, parents conferred significantly more racial socialization messages, especially regarding preparation for bias. Parent characteristics, such as age and level of education, proved to have a significant impact on racial socialization practices as well. Also, there were moderate but significant increases in preparation-for-bias and promotion-of-mistrust messages for respondents who reported race-related job stress.

Howard Stevenson and his colleagues have developed a different line of research that focused on the measurement and psychological outcomes of adolescent reception and reporting of parental racial socialization messages rather than parental perspectives on the topic (Stevenson, 1994b, 1995, 1997; Stevenson et al., 2002; Stevenson, Reed, Bodison, & Bishop, 1997). Research showed that different types of racial socialization led to differential psychological adjustment outcomes and that gender, neighborhood factors, and racism experience mediated these outcomes. By understanding youth perspectives on parental racial socialization, future research might understand socialization as socially interactive and mutually influenced by parents and youth rather than generated from parents alone. This line of work also points to how racial socialization might be internalized, retranslated, or misunderstood by youth.

CURRENT RESEARCH

Why Is Racial Socialization Necessary? For Protection, Meaning, and Launching

With the end of de jure segregation and the expansion of opportunities for Blacks, some feel not only that racial socialization is unnecessary but also that youth about racism will lead to paranoia and hopelessness that may hinder their academic and social development. However, Black progress has not eliminated the blaring health, economic, and social disparities that continue to plague Black communities (Farmer & Ferraro, 2005). The insidious nature of racism has shifted from overt to covert institutionalized expressions and racial microaggressions (Franklin & Boyd-Franklin, 2000; Sue et al., 2007), which has also forced a shift in racial socialization messages (T. N. Brown & Lesane-Brown, 2006). Specifically, researchers have studied racial socialization from both parental transmission and youth acquisition perspectives.

Parenting and Youth Perspectives

Parenting Perspectives. Youth's concepts of identity, colorism, and racial preferences are received from a variety of societal cues and sources, as well as from parents (Spencer, 1983; Stevenson, 1994a). For parents, the overall role of socialization is to provide the knowledge and tools to children that will enable them to become appropriately independent and functional in society (Spencer, 1983). On the other hand, one could argue that socialization from the wider society (i.e., media, social norms) is more likely to motivate youth to subscribe to the status quo and social hierarchies that may not benefit their developmental growth and emotional health. A parent's ability to filter mainstream messages to promote healthy identity and outcomes may be dependent on his or her racial identity and trust/belief/endorsement of these ideas and concepts (Boykin & Toms, 1985). For example, parents who are knowledgeable about Black exploitation in the news and entertainment media would be better equipped to explain and identify Black cultural phenomenon that has been absorbed by the mainstream in a way that empowers their children.

Halgunseth, Ispa, Csizmadia, and Thornburg's (2005) study of maternal parenting indicated that the mother's racial identity influenced the type of messages they shared with their children. African American parents who score high on the internalization stage of racial identity are more likely than other African American parents to view racial socialization as an integral part of child rearing (D. S. G. Thomas & Shaw, 1999). Thornton, Chatters, Taylor, and Allen (1990) found mothers to be more involved in day-to-day conversations about race, and fathers were more likely to engage in conversations with boys (McHale et al., 2006).

Youth Perspectives. Stevenson (1994b) distinguished racial socialization messages and communications that emphasize reactions to racial oppression (*protective messages*) from those that de-emphasize oppression and instead focus on cultural strengths and character (*proactive messages*). The combination of these two forms has been defined as *adaptive racial socialization.* Because African American children will encounter racism at some point in their lives, they may require both antagonistic coping strategies for protection and cultural-empowering messages for uplift that validate ethnic standards of beauty and cultural norms that lead to healthy functioning (Hill, 2001; Scott, 2003). Adaptive racial socialization messages have been associated with greater psychological adjustment compared with either proactive or protective messages alone (Stevenson, 1997). These forms of racial socialization can be characterized as positive in that they serve as buffers for African American children, particularly when skin color and stereotypes impose inevitable restrictive social parameters that result in Black children being labeled "high risk" (e.g., at school; Spencer, 1995; Spencer & Markstrom-Adams, 1990; Spencer & Swanson, 2000).

It must also be recognized that some socialization messages are maladaptive in that they may be less supportive of healthy public or private racial regard and represent messages of internalized racism (Coard & Sellers, 2005). Internalized racism is often viewed as a form of self-hatred, but a more reasonable definition is "[the] . . . acceptance by members of the stigmatized races of negative messages about their own abilities and intrinsic worth. It is characterized by their not believing in others who look like them, and not believing in themselves" (Jones, 2000, p. 1214).

Cokley (2002) defined *racialism* as not necessarily a reflection of self-hatred but a belief in negative stereotypes that may be the result of prolonged marginalization and reflect an acceptance of societal views of Blacks. More research is necessary to illuminate the interplay among protective, protective, and maladaptive racial socialization as they influence social and behavioral functioning.

Adolescent experiences of racial socialization have been linked to behavioral adjustment across multiple domains of academic and social competence (Davis & Stevenson, 2006; Phinney & Chavira, 1995; Stevenson et al., 2002; Stevenson et al., 1997; D. E. Thomas, Townsend, & Belgrave, 2003). Most research that has investigated the connection between racial socialization and achievement has focused on academic indicators such as cognitive competency (Caughy, O'Campo, Randolph, & Nickerson, 2002) and academic efficacy (Constantine & Blackmon, 2002). Very few researchers have concentrated on concrete academic outcomes, such as grades (Neblett, Philip, Cogburn, & Sellers, 2006; Oyserman, Bybee, & Terry, 2003) or test scores. Using the Teenager Experiences of Racial Socialization (TERS; Stevenson et al., 2002) measure, Constantine and Blackmon (2002) found that endorsement of mainstream racial socialization was inversely related to school self-esteem: Respondents who received more messages about the importance of engaging in White or mainstream institutions and values suffered from lower academic self-efficacy. They also found that racial socialization was inversely related to problem behavior, but it had no significant relationship to academic achievement. More research is needed that looks at the relationship between racial socialization and concrete academic variables using more robust racial socialization measurement.

Research on the effects of preparation for bias socialization has revealed conflicting relationships with emotional and behavioral outcomes (Christian & Barbarin, 2001; Davis & Stevenson, 2006; McHale et al., 2006; Oyserman, Harrison, & Bybee, 2001; D. E. Thomas, Coard, Stevenson, Bentley, & Zamel, 2007). In their research of African American children throughout the Midwest, Christian and Barbarin (2001) attributed race-based claims of injustice to parental socialization messages regarding bias. They found that higher expectations of bias were associated with maladaptive behavior. Conversely, D. E. Thomas and colleagues (2007) demonstrated that adolescent boys with histories of aggression who reported receiving socialization regarding alertness to discrimination were more likely to control their anger and less likely to be labeled as overactive by their teachers. Oyserman et al. (2001) established that for boys, specifically, knowledge of racism was a positive predictor of academic achievement.

Gender Dynamics. In addition to racial attitudes, parenting and youth processes are central to the transmission and acquisition of gender attitudes, but the literature has not as yet distinguished gender-specific messages from race-specific messages or how they may be integrated. Despite this omission, it is still important to understand how gender may play a role in the ways parents raise their children. Hesse-Biber, Howling, Leavy, and Lovejoy (2004) found that African American mothers taught racial and gender socialization by "doing gender"—modeling the behaviors they believed and verbally expressed were preferred and of importance for their daughters. Black parents encourage their daughters to work hard; persevere; show tenacity, self-reliance, and resistance to conformity; and strive for sexual equality (Buckley & Carter, 2005; Hill, 2001, 2002). Black women are more likely to resist mainstream messages of beauty and instead rely on their cultural group's standards of beauty, passing these perspectives on to their children (Hesse-Biber et al., 2004; Hill, 2001, 2002; Stephens & Phillips, 2005; Yasui, Dorham, & Dishion, 2004). African American daughters receive messages framed by the reality that beauty standards and roles traditionally relegated to women do not readily apply to them (Buckley & Carter, 2005; Hill, 2001, 2002). During adolescence, when popularity is predicated on the attractiveness of one's physical features as much as personality, a reliance on culturally specific standards of beauty appears to serve as a protective mechanism for adolescent girls (Hesse-Biber et al., 2004).

African American boys are also encouraged to do well academically and to work hard, but their messages are saturated with strategies on how to self-regulate their behavior and defuse racial encounters that may occur. They receive more messages about overcoming racism. African American boys and girls who experience early ("big-boned") maturation undergo enormous societal misperceptions. Often those "big-boned" youth are inaccurately assessed and treated as adults. Prepubescent growth spurts result in additional height, deeper voices, and muscle mass definition compared with their White male counterparts

(Spencer, Dupree, Swanson, & Cunningham, 1998). Therefore, parents teach youth practical strategies to manage racially charged crises without sustaining physical or psychological injury (Stevenson, 1997).

Whereas the early physical maturation of Black boys is often exploited in the media through the promotion of hypermasculine behaviors and attitudes, the early maturation of Black girls tends to manifest itself in an image of hypersexuality that serves the needs of others. These examples are particularly poignant in music videos (Stephens & Phillips, 2003).

Measurement

How Do You Know It If You Saw It? Although racial socialization measurement has varied in format and context, there has been a consistent focus on determining the prevalence and frequency of its transmission or reception. In its early development, racial socialization data were primarily collected qualitatively (Bowman & Howard, 1985; Harris, 1995; Hughes & Chen, 1997; Peters, 1985; Thornton et al., 1990). Some researchers believe that qualitative measurements continue to provide a comprehensive, multidimensional, and accurate method of data collection analysis (Caughy et al., 2002; Coard, Wallace, Stevenson, & Brotman, 2004). Qualitative research benefits from allowing participants s to speak of their own experiences without possible interference from researcher assumptions. On the other hand, the nature of classifying responses can be ambiguous, resulting in less generalizability to other measures and a difficulty in making associations with outcomes. To counter these concerns, the use of quantitative methodologies is growing and becoming multifaceted in nature (Lesane-Brown, Brown, Caldwell, & Sellers, 2005; Spencer, 1983; Stevenson, 1994a; Stevenson et al., 2002). Many quantitative measures of racial socialization may be seen as too essentialistic or suffer from low reliability. An essentialistic perspective in measurement may narrow the conceptualization and range of the Black experience. Both qualitative and quantitative research identify specific types of racial socialization (cultural legacy appreciation, alertness to racism, etc.) that provide important contributions to the literature; agreement across methods about the most important elements will strengthen the body of available research.

Quantitative Measurement of Racial Socialization

Lesane-Brown et al. (2005) provided a thorough review of racial socialization measures to demonstrate the variability of racial socialization constructs; however, most racial socialization measures lack reliability and depth and are overly simplistic through the use of dichotomous (yes/no) responses or broad, generalized questions. There is debate in the field whether cursory knowledge from brief measurement is more valuable than in-depth knowledge from extended measures. Although most research identifies subtypes of racial socialization (cultural legacy appreciation, alertness to racism, mainstream socialization, etc.), no consensus exists about whether to focus on these subtypes or the higher order factors they represent (preparation for bias and cultural socialization).

Racial Socialization Measure. The Racial Socialization Measure (Hughes & Chen, 1997) includes 16 items to measure parental racial socialization that comprise three dimensions: (1) Preparation for Bias, (2) Cultural Socialization, and (3) Promotion of Mistrust. Parents were first asked whether they practiced a specific behavior. Affirmative responses were followed up with a question of frequency in the last year. The measure yielded two reliable factors, (1) Preparation for Bias ($\alpha = .91$) and (2) Cultural Socialization ($\alpha = .84$), and one marginally reliable factor, Promotion of Mistrust ($r = .68$).

Teenager Experiences of Racial Socialization and the Scale of Racial Socialization. The TERS (Stevenson et al., 2002) measures the frequency with which Black adolescents experience specific racial socialization messages. This 40-item measure targets teenage (Constantine & Blackmon, 2002; Stevenson et al., 2002) and college-age (Anglin & Whaley, 2006; Bynum, Burton, & Best, 2007) African Americans. Stevenson and colleagues performed an exploratory factor analysis on the TERS that revealed five reliable racial socialization constructs: (1) Cultural Coping With Antagonism, (2) Cultural Pride Reinforcement, (3) Cultural Legacy Appreciation, (4) Cultural Alertness to Discrimination, and (5) Cultural Endorsement of the Mainstream. The TERS was developed as a revision and supplement to Stevenson's (1994b, 1996) Scale of

Racial Socialization (SORS), a 45-item beliefs survey that measures the degree to which Black adolescents agree with racial socialization statements regarding African American cultural issues and interactions. Both the TERS and the SORS have been widely accepted as valued measurements of racial socialization, in large part because of their consistently acceptable reliability estimates (TERS: $\alpha = .91$, SORS: $\alpha = .75$; Anglin & Wade, 2007; Bennett, 2006; Bynum et al., 2007; Constantine & Blackmon, 2002; Fischer & Shaw, 1999; Leary, Brennan, & Briggs, 2005; Lesane-Brown et al., 2005).[1]

Parent Experiences of Racial Socialization. The Parent Experiences of Racial Socialization (PERS; Stevenson, 1999) is the parent version of the aforementioned TERS; it asks parents to report how frequently they have told their children a set of 40 statements about how to handle racial issues in school, their neighborhood, or society. The PERS also has psychometric support, with the four subscale (Promotion of Mistrust, Preparation for Bias, Racial Pride, and Spirituality) coefficients ranging from .76 to .86 (Caughy et al., 2002).[2]

Qualitative Measurement of Racial Socialization

Some researchers believe that because of the multidimensional nature of racial socialization that qualitative measurements provide the most comprehensive and accurate method of data collection analysis (Coard et al., 2004; Peters, 1985). The racial socialization component of the National Survey of Black Americans has been used multiple times to predict and correlate an assortment of variables, including socioeconomic factors (Thornton et al., 1990), racial identity (Demo & Hughes, 1990; Harris, 1995), and church involvement (Harris, 1995). Research from Bowman and Howard (1985) has served as a guide with the use of four themes of socialization: (1) racial barriers, (2) self-development, (3) racial pride, and (4) egalitarianism. Using interview data from a sample of 2,107 African Americans, Bowman and Howard, working at the University of Michigan, asked adults ages 17 through 101 whether their parents told them what it meant to be Black and how to deal with White people. They also were asked whether there were things that they had told their children about what it meant to be Black and how to deal with White people. These lead questions were followed up with an open-ended question of what the specific message included, and responses were operationalized and classified on the basis of the analytical needs of respective researchers.

In a mixed-method study of 225 African American adults, Sanders-Thompson (1994) used Likert scale and open-ended questions to assess retrospective experiences of racial socialization and labeled her findings to fit the familiar constructs of racial pride, self-development, racial barrier awareness, and egalitarianism identified earlier by Bowman and Howard (1985).

Despite the growth in racial socialization measurement, the field has failed to make concise distinctions among cultural, ethnic, and racial processes. Moreover, as measurement becomes more sophisticated, research questions will have to determine whether racial socialization manifests itself through behavior, racial knowledge, attitudes, skills, and coping, or some combination.

FUTURE DIRECTIONS AND CONCLUSION

Racial socialization helps strengthen African American youth's level of resiliency and coping; it is an essential value-added component of the identity development experience (Simpson, Hughes, Kopaska-Merkel, & Ludvigsen, 2005; Spencer, 1990; Spencer, 1999; Stevenson, 1995). Hughes et al.'s (2006) review of racial socialization validates the swell of interest in parent's racial socialization practices. Their synthesis of recent research provides further validation of how racial socialization influences self-esteem, coping behaviors, and externalizing and internalizing behaviors (Simpson et al., 2005), providing persuasive evidence that studies integrating racial socialization and identity are prime opportunities for contributing to the literature. This review also incorporates discussion of many of the challenges evident in the research reviewed for this chapter: consensus of defined terminology, sample diversity, sample power, and conceptualization of the study.

There are challenges to creating an integrated framework for decreasing unexplained variance and offering concrete explanations for study findings. We believe that researchers, when investigating racial socialization, struggle with what research question to ask because of the lack of a theoretical conceptualization that clearly defines, identifies, and unites the salient variables involved in racial, ethnic, and/or cultural identity and socialization. Without clear, consistent conceptualization and inclusion of items to measure the disparate but important elements, researchers will remain puzzled about unexplained variance. Developing a theory of racial socialization that is detailed, inclusive of all salient variables, and that can provide a reliable foundation for measurement and analysis is no easy feat, but the future of this field depends on such an endeavor. This work undoubtedly lends itself to research on other developmental processes that affect African Americans.

Also, Boykin and Toms (1985) posed a significant question that has yet to be sufficiently answered. If the goal of socialization is to prepare a child to be a self-sufficient and adapted adult, then what constitutes an appropriately adapted African American adult? What are the consequences of an African American who has been completely indoctrinated with mainstream values and perspectives? Does this type of socialization equate to economic success and a seamless acceptance by wider, more specifically White American society and isolation from Black social circles? Will this person be ignorant of Black racial or ethnic knowledge, experiences, and styling? What about bicultural/shifting or more Afrocentric orientations? Can a complete indoctrination in any specific orientation be harmful? How does being perceived as having a specific orientation or indoctrination impact how one is treated or mistreated in society? This highlights the multifaceted nature of the Black experience. Therefore, using a purely essentialist perspective on Black racial socialization may be misinformed and naïve. However, there are certain essentialist contexts within Black life based on socially constructed images of racial hegemony that may determine mainstream success or failure. These constructs lead to specific socializing strategies to counter or challenge stereotypes in the broader world depending on the multigenerational familial background.

Adjustments to the Triple Quandary: Kernels for Future Theory Development

Although the triple-quandary framework has been foundational to racial socialization research for 3 decades, reducing confusion for future racial socialization researchers necessitates an appreciation of how the field has grown with American advancement and retrenchment in local, national, and international civil rights; an imperialistic foreign policy; and philanthropic politics. Just as *Black* means something different from *African American* to many, so too do preparation for bias and pride development dynamics within racial, ethnic, and cultural identity processes. At the risk of adding to the confusion, we propose several adjustments to racial socialization as a research area. One adjustment is to redefine mainstream, minority, and cultural contexts as racial, ethnic, and cultural contexts. These continua are distinctly defined by foci on the politics of socially constructed racial hierarchy interactions (race), within-subcultural group interactions (ethnicity), and Black Diasporic symbolic interactions (culture). On the basis of a greater belief in the pervasiveness of discrimination, we propose that the politics and interactions of both mainstream and minority contexts fit within the dimension of socially constructed racial hierarchy. We further propose that within-subcultural group dynamics are more likely to define socialization messages and outcomes in which oppression is a background rather than a foreground dynamic. Being a numerical minority, for example, may be relevant to that oppression more or less, depending on one's geography, country, or family of origin. This adjustment is also meant to embrace recent advances in our understanding of international and immigrant models of ethnic identity.

The second adjustment is that each context (racial, ethnic, cultural) can include mechanisms of self-preservation that range from empowering (persistence through inter- and intraracial adversity) to diminishing (compromised self-efficacy due to stigma internalization). It is important to recognize the current literature's focus on bias preparation and cultural pride infusion as two enduring themes that might fit on either end of the modified triple-quandary continua. A potential third theme might encompass negative socialization, in which internalized racism can be adopted as a powerful force within Black child rearing (Coard & Sellers, 2005).

Third, it is important that researchers come to an agreement on the purpose of socialization within race, ethnicity, and cultural contexts if thinking and behavior are the targets. Moreover, we recommend that researchers in the field adopt Cross, Parham, and Helms's (1991) three positive functions of racial identity for racial socialization (protection/defensiveness, social/existential anchoring and meaning, and critical transcendental coping; Stevenson, 1995) to guide researchers in clarifying why parents and youth engage in these processes.

Fourth, we propose that there are four targets of socialization influence (thinking and behaving)—beliefs, knowledge, experiences, and behaviors—and that the integration of all four represent identity coping (see Figure 19.1). Each may embody similar intra-/intergroup, political, and social emphases, but they differ depending on which are foregrounded or backgrounded within the socialization interactions, communications, or modeling.

Fifth, we propose that despite the foundational nature of these traditional and modified triple-quandary contexts of socialization, they will still be defined differently because of individual researchers' intellectual theoretical or ideological frames that have not been as yet articulated in the current research on racial/ethnic/cultural socialization. Some theoretical frames might posit different research questions than others. *Critical race theory* posits several assumptions., including that racism and discrimination are enduring facets of American life that invest in the persistent economic and social domination by White people and that Whites accept and support equality as long as it does not interfere with the venerable comforts and access to power/wealth/opportunity to which they are accustomed as a result of the legacy of slavery (Ladson-Billings & Tate, 1995; Taylor, 1998). The critical race theory perspective would assert that messages from societal and media sources would fortify ideas and behaviors that are divisive in the Black community (e.g., internalized racism) and validate the American racial/wealth hierarchy (meritocracy and color-blind messages). Theoretical frameworks that do not posit the permanence or structure of systemic racism might lead to a downplaying of the measurement or complexity of bias preparation socialization.

These three socialization contexts of socially constructed racial hierarchy, within-ethnic group dynamics, and Black cultural symbolic interactions are similar in that they all acknowledge that children acquire behaviors, knowledge, perceptions, values, and attitudes through direct or indirect messages and modeling from the important people (peers and family) around them as well as from external societal and community sources (Stevenson, 1998). It is our assertion that all three forms of socialization facilitate an individual's identity development and degree of racial–ethnic salience. These factors enable them to perceive their racial–ethnic self positively or negatively and determine whether they view themselves as a cohesive member or outsider of their respective racial group (Coard et al., 2004; Stevenson, 1995; Stevenson et al., 1997). The beliefs, knowledge, experiences, behaviors, and coping goals or outcomes of these various forms of socialization differ in meaningful ways, have implications for the consequent expression of coping and identity, and provide guidelines for psychological or community intervention development (see Figure 19.1). We point to these issues briefly here; a fuller discussion of this model can be found elsewhere (Stevenson et al., 2007). The roots of racial, ethnic, and cultural socialization rest within the triple-quandary framework and early researchers' quest to explain how children come to know they are different. The future of racial, ethnic, and cultural socialization research is promising, and we have recommended here the beginnings of a framework for consolidating disparate ideas within the literature as well as projecting future research questions that are testable. We caution future researchers against parceling out different components of racial socialization (focus on bias preparation and not cultural pride, or vice versa) because this will serve to direct the field away from multidimensional understandings of these processes.

In this chapter, we have examined the measurement, processes, and forms of expression of racial socialization. It should be understood that the prevalence of racial socialization is not in question. Even when parents choose not to discuss racial hierarchies and cultural pride with their children, they are still bombarded with direct and tacit illustrations of Blackness from society that fortify social and wealth structures. Knowing what Blacks have been told in their youth about their place in the world can provide insight on psychological, behavioral, academic, and health outcomes. This knowledge can serve as a guide for

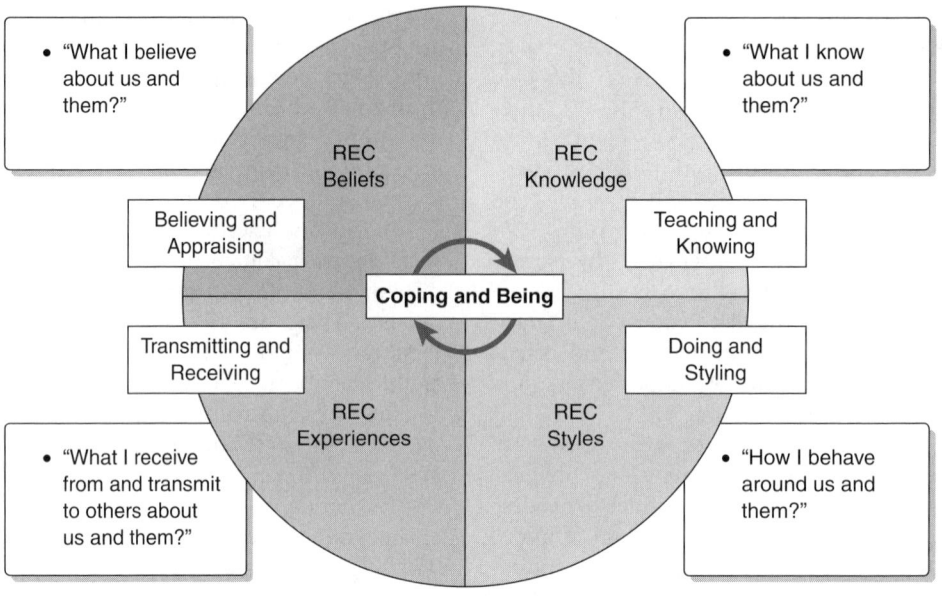

Figure 19.1 Transmission and Reception of Racial, Ethnic, and Cultural (REC) Experience, Knowledge, Beliefs, and Styles

the development of curricula and psychosocial interventions targeting Black youth.

> *A people without the knowledge of their past history, origin and culture is like a tree without roots.*
>
> —Marcus Garvey

Notes

1. The TERS has recently been updated to reflect advances in the field in a multidimensional measure called the Cultural and Racial Experiences of Socialization (CARES). The CARES adds to field by controversially acknowledging that all messages received may not be positive or promote healthy adjustment (internalized racism messages).

2. The PERS has been updated and revised as the Parent-CARES, which comprises three individual measures. The first measure, Parental Transmission Frequency, determines the frequency with which parents transmit racial socialization messages to their children. The second measure, Parental Reception Frequency, determines the frequency with which parents received racial socialization messages while they were growing up. Last, the Parent-CARES measures the gender-specific direction of racial socialization messages based on the importance parents place on specific items for their daughters or sons.

References

Anglin, D. M., & Wade, J. C. (2007). Racial socialization, racial identity, and Black students' adjustment to college. *Cultural Diversity and Ethnic Minority Psychology, 13,* 207–215.

Anglin, D. M., & Whaley, A. L. (2006). Racial/ethnic self-labeling in relation to group: Socialization and identity in African-descended individuals. *Journal of Language and Social Psychology, 25,* 457–463.

Arrington, E., & Stevenson, H. C. (2006). *Final report for the Success of African American Students (SAAS) in Independent Schools Project.* Philadelphia: University of Pennsylvania Press.

Bennett, M. D. (2006). Culture and context: A study of neighborhood effects on racial socialization and ethnic identity content in a sample of African American adolescents. *Journal of Black Psychology, 32,* 479–500.

Bowman, P. J., & Howard, C. (1985). Race-related socialization, motivation, and academic achievement: A study of Black youths in three-generation families. *Journal of the American Academy of Child Psychiatry, 24,* 134–141.

Boykin, A. W. (1983). The academic performance of Afro-American children. In J. Spence (Ed.), *Achievement and achievement motives* (pp. 323–371). San Francisco: Freeman.

Boykin, A. W. (1984). Reading achievement and the social-cultural frame of reference of Afro-American children. *Journal of Negro Education, 53,* 464–473.

Boykin, A. W., & Toms, F. D. (1985). Black child socialization: A conceptual framework. In H. P. McAdoo & J. L. McAdoo (Eds.), *Black children: Social, educational, and parental environments* (Vol. 72, pp. 33–51). Beverly Hills, CA: Sage.

Brown, T. L., & Krishnakumar, A. (2007). Development and validation of the Adolescent Racial and Ethnic Socialization Scale (ARESS) in African American Families. *Journal of Youth and Adolescence, 36,* 1072–1085.

Brown, T. N., & Lesane-Brown, C. L. (2006). Race socialization messages across historical time. *Social Psychology Quarterly, 69,* 201–213.

Buckley, T. R., & Carter, R. T. (2005). Black adolescent girls: Do gender role and racial identity: Impact their self-esteem? *Sex Roles, 53,* 647–661.

Bush, D. M., & Simmons, R. G. (1990). Socialization processes over the life course. In M. Rosenberg & R. Turner (Eds.), *Social psychology: Sociological perspectives* (pp. 133–164). Piscataway, NJ: Transaction.

Bynum, M. S., Burton, E. T., & Best, C. (2007). Racism experiences and psychological functioning in African American college freshmen. Is racial socialization a buffer? *Biennial Convention of the Society for Research on Adolescence 2006, 13*(1), 64–71.

Caughy, M. O. B., O'Campo, P. J., Randolph, S. M., & Nickerson, K. (2002). The influence of racial socialization practices on the cognitive and behavioral competence of African American preschoolers. *Child Development, 73,* 1611–1625.

Christian, M. D., & Barbarin, O. A. (2001). Cultural resources and psychological adjustment of African American children: Effects of spirituality and racial attribution. *Journal of Black Psychology, 27,* 43–63.

Clark, K. B., & Clark, M. K. (1947). Racial identification and preferences in Negro children. *Personality and Social Psychology Bulletin, 5,* 420–437.

Coard, S. I., & Sellers, R. M. (2005). African American families as a context for racial socialization. In V. C. McLoyd, N. E. Hill, & K. A. Dodge (Eds.), *African American family life: Ecological and cultural diversity* (pp. 264–284). New York: Guilford Press.

Coard, S. I., Wallace, S. A., Stevenson, H. C., & Brotman, L. M. (2004). Towards culturally relevant preventive interventions: The consideration of racial socialization in parent training with African American families. *Journal of Child and Family Studies, 13,* 277–293.

Cokley, K. (2002). Testing Cross's revised racial identity model: An examination of the relationship between racial identity and internalized racialism. *Journal of Counseling Psychology, 49,* 476–483.

Constantine, M. G., & Blackmon, S. K. M. (2002). Black adolescents' racial socialization experiences: Their relations to home, school, and peer self-esteem. *Journal of Black Studies, 32,* 322–335.

Cross, W. E., Jr., Parham, T. A., & Helms, J. E. (1991). The stages of Black identity development: Nigrescence models. In R. L. Jones (Ed.), *Black Psychology* (3rd ed., pp. 319–338). Berkeley, CA: Cobb & Henry.

Davis, G. Y., & Stevenson, H. C. (2006). Racial socialization experiences and symptoms of depression among Black youth. *Journal of Child and Family Studies, 15,* 303–317.

Demo, D. H., & Hughes, M. (1990). Socialization and racial identity among Black Americans. *Social Psychology Quarterly, 53,* 364–374.

Farmer, M. M., & Ferraro, K. F. (2005). Are racial disparities in health conditional on socioeconomic status? *Social Science & Medicine, 60,* 191–204.

Fischer, A. R., & Shaw, C. M. (1999). African Americans' mental health and perceptions of racist discrimination: The moderating effects of racial socialization experiences and self-esteem. *Journal of Counseling Psychology, 46,* 395–407.

Franklin, A. J., & Boyd-Franklin, N. (2000). Invisibility syndrome: A clinical model of the effects of racism on African-American males. *American Journal of Orthopsychiatry, 70,* 33–41.

Halgunseth, L. C., Ispa, J. M., Csizmadia, A., & Thornburg, K. R. (2005). Relations among maternal racial identity, maternal parenting behavior, and child outcomes in low-income, urban, Black families. *Journal of Black Psychology, 31,* 418–440.

Harris, D. (1995). Exploring the determinants of adult Black identity: Context and process. *Social Forces, 74,* 227–241.

Hesse-Biber, S. N., Howling, S. A., Leavy, P., & Lovejoy, M. (2004). Racial identity and the development of body image issues among African American adolescent girls. *The Qualitative Report, 9,* 49–79.

Hill, S. A. (2001). Class, race and gender dimensions of child rearing in African American families. *Journal of Black Studies, 31,* 494–508.

Hill, S. A. (2002). Teaching and doing gender in African American families. *Sex Roles 47,* 493–506.

Hughes, D., & Chen, L. (1997). When and what parents tell children about race: An examination of race-related socialization among African American families. *Applied Developmental Science, 1,* 200–214.

Hughes, D., & Chen, L. (1999). *The nature of parents' race-related communications to children: A developmental perspective.* New York: Psychology Press.

Hughes, D., Rodriguez, J., Smith, E. P., Johnson, D. J., Stevenson, H. C., & Spicer, P. (2006). Parents' ethnic–racial socialization practices: A review of research and directions for future study. *Developmental Psychology, 42,* 747–770.

Jones, C. P. (2000). Levels of racism: A theoretic framework and a gardener's tale. *American Journal of Public Health, 90,* 1212–1215.

Ladson-Billings, G., & Tate, W. F. I. V. (1995). Toward a critical race theory of education. *Teachers College Record, 97,* 47–68.

Leary, J. D., Brennan, E. M., & Briggs, H. E. (2005). The African American Adolescent Respect Scale: A measure of a prosocial attitude. *Research on Social Work Practice, 15,* 462–469.

Lesane-Brown, C. L. (2006). A review of race socialization within Black families. *Developmental Review, 26,* 400–426.

Lesane-Brown, C. L., Brown, T. N., Caldwell, C. H., & Sellers, R. M. (2005). The Comprehensive Race Socialization Inventory. *Journal of Black Studies, 36,* 163–190.

McHale, S. M., Crouter, A. C., Kim, J.-Y., Burton, L. M., Davis, K. D., Dotterer, A. M., et al. (2006). Mothers' and fathers' racial socialization in African American families: Implications for youth. *Child Development, 77,* 1387–1402.

McLoyd, V. C., Cauce, A. M., Takeuchi, D., & Wilson, L. (2000). Marital processes and parental socialization in families of color: A decade review of research. *Journal of Marriage and the Family, 62,* 1070–1093.

Neblett, E. W., Jr., Philip, C. L., Cogburn, C. D., & Sellers, R. M. (2006). African American adolescents' discrimination experiences and academic achievement: Racial socialization as a cultural compensatory and protective factor. *Journal of Black Psychology, 32,* 199–218.

Oyserman, D., Bybee, D., & Terry, K. (2003). Gendered racial identity and involvement with school. *Self and Identity, 2,* 307–324.

Oyserman, D., Harrison, K., & Bybee, D. (2001). Can racial identity be promotive of academic efficacy? *International Journal of Behavioral Development, 25,* 379–385.

Peters, M. F. (1985). Racial socialization of young Black children. In H. P. McAdoo & J. L. McAdoo (Eds.), *Black children: Social, educational, and parental environments* (pp. 169–183). Beverly Hills, CA: Sage.

Phinney, J. S., & Chavira, V. (1995). Parental ethnic socialization and adolescent coping with problems related to ethnicity. *Journal of Research on Adolescence, 5,* 31–53.

Sanders-Thompson, V. L. (1994). Socialization to race and its relationship to racial identification among African Americans. *Journal of Black Psychology, 20,* 175–188.

Scott, L. D., Jr. (2003). The relation of racial identity and racial socialization to coping with discrimination among African American adolescents. *Journal of Black Studies, 33,* 520–538.

Simpson, A. G., Hughes, N. C., Kopaska-Merkel, D. C., & Ludvigsen, R. (2005). Development of the caudal exoskeleton of the pliomerid trilobite *Hintzeia plicamarginis* new species. *Evolution Development, 7,* 528–541.

Spencer, M. B. (1983). Children's cultural values and parental child rearing strategies. *Developmental Review, 3,* 351–370.

Spencer, M. B. (Ed.). (1990). *Black families: Interdisciplinary perspectives.* New Brunswick, NJ: Transaction.

Spencer, M. B. (1995). Old issues and new theorizing about African American youth: A phenomenological variant of ecological systems theory. In R. L. Taylor (Ed.), *Black youth: Perspectives on their status in the United States* (pp. 37–69). Westport, CT: Praeger.

Spencer, M. B. (1999). Social and cultural influences on school adjustment: The application of an identity-focused cultural ecological perspective. *Educational Psychologist, 34,* 43–57.

Spencer, M. B., Dupree, D. V., Swanson, D. P., & Cunningham, M. (1998). The influence of physical maturation and hassles on African American adolescents' learning behaviors. *Journal of Comparative Family Studies, 29,* 189–200.

Spencer, M. B., & Markstrom-Adams, C. (1990). Identity processes among racial and ethnic minority children in America. *Child Development, 61,* 290–310.

Spencer, M. B., & Swanson, D. P. (2000). Promoting positive outcomes for youth: Resourceful families and communities. In J. Waldfogel & S. Danzinger (Eds.), *Securing the future* (pp. 182–204). New York: Russell Sage Foundation.

Stephens, D. P., & Phillips, L. (2005). Integrating Black feminist thought into conceptual frameworks of African American adolescent women's sexual scripting processes *Sexualities, Evolution & Gender, 7,* 37–55.

Stephens, D. P., & Phillips, L. D. (2003). Freaks, gold diggers, divas, and dykes: The sociohistorical development of adolescent African American women's sexual script. *Sexuality & Culture: An Interdisciplinary Quarterly, 7,* 3–49.

Stevenson, H. C. (1994a). Racial socialization in African American families: The art of balancing intolerance and survival. *Family Journal, 2,* 190–198.

Stevenson, H. C. (1994b). Validation of the Scale of Racial Socialization for African American adolescents: Steps toward multidimensionality. *Journal of Black Psychology, 20,* 445–468.

Stevenson, H. C. (1995). Relationship of adolescent perceptions of racial socialization to racial identity. *Journal of Black Psychology, 21,* 49–70.

Stevenson, H. C. (1996). Development of the Scale of Racial Socialization for African American Adolescents. In R. L. Jones (Ed.), *Handbook of tests and measures for Black populations* (Vol. 1, pp. 309–326). Hampton, VA: Cobb & Henry.

Stevenson, H. C. (1997). Managing anger: Protective, proactive, or adaptive racial socialization identity profiles and African-American manhood development. *Journal of Prevention & Intervention in the Community, 16,* 35–61.

Stevenson, H. C. (1998). Raising safe villages: Cultural–ecological factors that influence the emotional adjustment of adolescents. *Journal of Black Psychology, 24,* 44–59.

Stevenson, H. C. (1999). *Parent experience of racial socialization.* Unpublished manuscript, University of Pennsylvania.

Stevenson, H. C., Bentley, K. B., & Adams, V. N. (2007). *Theory of racial, ethnic, and cultural socialization: Making meaning of situations, interactions, and targets of influence.* Unpublished manuscript, University of Pennsylvania.

Stevenson, H. C., Cameron, R., Herrero-Taylor, T., & Davis, G. Y. (2002). Development of the Teenager Experience of Racial Socialization Scale: Correlates of race-related socialization frequency from the perspective of Black youth. *Journal of Black Psychology, 28,* 84–106.

Stevenson, H. C., Reed, J., Bodison, P., & Bishop, A. (1997). Racism stress management: Racial social beliefs and the experience of depression and anger in African American youth. *Youth & Society, 29,* 197–222.

Sue, D. W., Capodilupo, C. M., Torino, G. C., Bucceri, J. M., Holder, A. M. B., Nadal, K. L., et al. (2007). Racial microaggressions in everyday life: Implications for clinical practice. *American Psychologist, 62,* 271–286.

Taylor, E. (1998). A primer on critical race theory. *Journal of Blacks in Higher Education, 19,* 122–124.

Thomas, A. J., & Speight, S. L. (1999). Racial identity and racial socialization attitudes of African American parents. *Journal of Black Psychology, 25,* 152–170.

Thomas, D. E., Coard, S. I., Stevenson, H. C., Bentley, K. L., & Zamel, P. C. (2007). *Race and emotional factors predicting teachers' perceptions of classroom behavioral adjustment for urban African American male youth.* Manuscript submitted for publication.

Thomas, D. E., Townsend, T. G., & Belgrave, F. Z. (2003). The influence of cultural and racial identification on the psychosocial adjustment of inner-city African American children in school. *American Journal of Community Psychology, 32,* 217–228.

Thomas, D. S. G., & Shaw, P. A. (1999). Late Cainozoic drainage evolution in the Zambezi basin—Geomorphological evidence from the Kalahari Rim. *Journal of African Earth Sciences and the Middle East, 8*(2), 40–42.

Thornton, M. C., Chatters, L. M., Taylor, R. J., & Allen, W. R. (1990). Sociodemographic and environmental correlates of racial socialization by Black parents. *Child Development, 61,* 401–409.

Yasui, M., Dorham, C. L., & Dishion, T. J. (2004). Ethnic identity and psychological adjustment: A validity analysis for European American and African American adolescents. *Journal of Adolescent Research, 19,* 807–825.

20

RACIAL IDENTITY DEVELOPMENT DURING CHILDHOOD

DENA PHILLIPS SWANSON, MICHAEL CUNNINGHAM,
JOSEPH YOUNGBLOOD II, AND MARGARET BEALE SPENCER

In this chapter, we explore the development of racial identity and its implications during childhood, focusing on preschool through late childhood. The primary purpose is to review psychosocial processes that facilitate competent development of African American children. The overall review provides developmental perspectives in facilitating the synthesis and interpretation of the presented themes and issues.

The chapter is organized into five sections. The first section is devoted to a historical overview of research on racial identity processes in childhood. In the following section, we address the developmental progression of racial identity during this period of development. In the next section, we focus on theoretical perspectives and research that has shaped the field of study, addressing implications of children's racial attitudes on general school experiences and behavioral outcomes. In the fourth section, we address academic and behavioral implications for African American children, and in the final section, we explore promising areas of research that remain underdeveloped.

Racial identity refers to the attitudes, perceptions, and beliefs that an individual holds toward his or her racial group in relation to the majority racial group (Arroyo & Zigler, 1991).

Racial identity among children is conceptualized, and generally assessed, as racial awareness, attitudes, preferences, and socialization (Katz & Kofkin, 1997). Racial awareness subsequently influences racial preferences and attitudes but, as research since the 1940s reflects, is also developmentally and culturally influenced. Differentiating between early knowledge of the self and later identity-formation processes provides an understanding of these constructs relevant to children's development.

HISTORICAL OVERVIEW

Research regarding the association of racial awareness in African American children can be traced back to theoretical perspectives associated with Charles H. Cooley (1902, 1908), George Herbert Mead (1934), Kurt Lewin (1935), and G. W. Allport (1937). These perspectives provided the foundation for much of the research over the subsequent 4 decades that focused on self-development. They emphasized that understanding self-development represented the basis for understanding how individuals evolve a sense of personal uniqueness as distinct from other individuals. Although these theoretical perspectives were useful in their broader contribution to conceptualizing psychological processes, they were not generally utilized in the conceptualization of research conducted on African American children. Kenneth and Mamie Clark (1939) were pioneers in using these theoretical perspectives to empirically examine self-identification in African American preschool children. Their research focused on the emerging awareness of the self associated with racial membership. Their initial research indicated that African American preschool boys could identify themselves as distinct individuals from other groups by age 5. This finding laid the foundation for their future work in which they examined preschoolers' knowledge of the self with value judgments made regarding their racial preferences (see K. B. Clark & Clark, 1947).

Between the early 1940s and 1980s, research frequently found African American children to report White (Eurocentric) preferences when assigning personal attributes to Black and White pictures or dolls. There have been numerous writings and studies based on the work of K. B. Clark and Clark (1939, 1947), as well as many replications of their ground-breaking studies involving Black preschool children's racial preference. Their work, which was also instrumental in the *Brown v. Board of Education* decision of 1954, catapulted research interest in children's psychosocial development and racial identity. Although it would take several decades to unpackage the processes and the findings, the Clarks' work was groundbreaking and firmly imbedded the relevance and evaluation of race on children's development in psychology (Philogene, 2004).

Developmental Progression of Racial Identity in Childhood

Children demonstrate age-related developmental progression of race conception beginning with knowledge of color categories and culminating with conceptual awareness of racial categories. Early research on young children, however, did not differentiate between their personal (i.e., self-concept) and group identity (i.e., racial awareness). As such, racial awareness and racial preferences were treated as impacting children's personal identity. Children's awareness of race reflects their cognitive ability to differentiate individuals on the basis of racial characteristics. Children 3 to 4 years old, for example, are able to categorize by racial group based on color (brown or pink skin color), and 5- to 6-year-olds are capable of accurately identifying racial labels based on socially constructed skin color identifiers (black or white). Similarly, children associate socially constructed positive attributes with white and negative attributes with black, thus reflecting research findings associated with their Eurocentric, or White-oriented, racial preferences. Racial preferences were often methodologically based on children's responses to dolls or pictures requiring a forced-choice option between a Black or White child with whom they would want to play or have as a friend. Of particular concern regarding children's Eurocentric preferences was the implication that children internalized these preferences, subsequently resulting in a poor self-concept and self-hatred. Later research, however, consistently documented neither racial preference nor attitude about one's membership in their racial group was a significant predictor of self-concept (Lerner & Buehrig, 1975; Spencer, 1985).

Using research techniques similar to those the Clarks (1939, 1947) used, Spencer (1982a) presented African American preschool children with a racial attitude and preference procedure that was designed for preschool children by Williams and Roberson (1967). Students were presented with picture cards of a "dark-skinned" (African American) versus a "light-skinned" (White) person. Similar to the research with Black and White dolls used by the Clarks, the preschoolers were asked to identify the "smart" person. The study demonstrated that "contrary to previous theoretical expectations (see Pettigrew, 1964), that racial stereotyping for minority group children during the preoperational period is not necessarily internalized to the affective domain or to one's personal identity" (Spencer, 1982b, p. 284). Plainly stated, African American preschool children can choose a "White" image as the "smart" image and not internalize these feelings toward themselves.

Spencer (1982b) further noted that African American preschoolers' White preference is not necessarily associated with their self-concept. In fact, African American preschool children have "White" preference for dolls or "White" images and have high self-concepts. This point is especially important to emphasize. Although the Clarks' (1939, 1947) empirical research and Pettigrew's (1964) theorizing suggested that African American children showed a negative association between their Eurocentric preference and self-concept, the latter construct was rarely measured. As Spencer (1982b) demonstrated, African American preschoolers can have both a Eurocentric preference and a high self-concept. Recent studies further support the intraindividual variability that correlates with shifts in cognitive development. C. B. Murray and Mandara's (2002) research revealed that Black and White children between the ages of 3 and 6 display White-biased choice behavior, whereas older Black children (age 9) display Black preference while their White counterparts remain Eurocentric. Whaley's (1993) literature review on self-concept and cultural identity in African American children noted limitations of the social-psychological perspective and the need to consider cognitive– developmental and cultural factors.

Self-concept and cultural identity are independent aspects of personal identity, yet they follow a normative cognitive–developmental course. As development proceeds, older children acquire greater cognitive differentiating abilities than younger children. By age 8, for example, children understand racial classification beyond simple physical features and characteristics, and by age 10, they recognize social stereotypes associated with racial groups. During middle to late childhood, there is greater variability in dissonance reported between social stereotypes and the impact this understanding has on the child's personal identity. Self-esteem, once considered a global self-concept construct, becomes compartmentalized as children develop. This process of personality development clarifies differential findings of the impact of racial attitudes and self-esteem among older children. The utilization of domain-specific self-esteem contributes to inferences that distinguish between how children view themselves within different contexts, for example, valued at home but not at school. The school context provides feedback about the self consistent with larger societal perceptions, thus contributing to greater variability in findings that report correlations between self-esteem and racial attitudes in older children. In addition, children whose parents socialize them regarding racial history and values report more positive self-concept than children who lack an intervention that protects against unchallenged and pervasive stereotypes. As such, older children's racial attitudes and preferences are influenced by their social cognitive abilities in conjunction with their socialization experiences.

Spencer's research on children's racial preferences highlights the need to consider both personal identity and reference group orientation. The Personal Identity–Racial Group Orientation (PI–RGO) perspective has been criticized by scholars who use a traditional Afrocentric perspective (see Baldwin, Brown, & Hopkins, 1991). Arguing that the PI–RGO perspective is situated within a European worldview, Baldwin et al. (1991) presented an Afrocentric perspective as an alternative. They argued that understanding of the self is inexplicably associated with the group. The rationale is that individuals cannot understand themselves without understanding their group. While not negating this perspective, we do emphasize that understanding one's self as associated with a group requires advanced cognitive abilities, which, as previously noted, are not yet developed in preschool children. In fact, the two perspectives are not too distinct from each other. For example, a critical examination of classic empirical studies conducted by scholars who subscribe to the PI-RGO perspective (see McAdoo, 1985; Semaj, 1980, 1985; Spencer, 1982a, 1982b) helps explain the different perspectives. In each of the aforementioned studies, there were preschool children who did not choose the Eurocentric image as the more positive image. One explanation is that the children had significant adults reinforcing positive Black, Afrocentric, or African American images. Thus, when these children were presented with a choice of a Eurocentric (White) or an African American (Black) image, they had the cognitive schemas to choose the Black image as more positive.

The distinction can also be explained from a cognitive development perspective. Just as Vygotsky's (1962) zone of proximal development advanced Jean Piaget's (1929) theorizing regarding what children could learn at young ages, parents and/or significant adults can use scaffolding techniques to foster African American cultural pride in young children. This racial socialization is important to consider when critically analyzing the two perspectives. Racial socialization is also a complex phenomenon and has been critically reviewed elsewhere (see Hughes et al., 2006). Thus, in acknowledging the critique of the PI-RGO perspective, the research is further suggested as situated within the context of children's development. The evolution of research on racial awareness and preferences supports a developmental perspective demonstrating that preoperational-thinking children obtain cultural stereotypes from social learning experiences, although the more subtle cultural differentiation, integration, and categorization are more directly predicted by later cognitive development.

Two major questions emerged from the findings of earlier research, both concerned with the psychological implications for children that would impact the focus and direction of research in this area: (1) How are racial attitudes shaped and (2) what mechanisms and factors contribute to these processes? The first question has a rich history in exploring the role of racial socialization and contextual influences, primarily within the home but also with implications for other socializing contexts. The second question reframes the literature through the application of a theoretical frame that shifted the paradigm from one of deficit-oriented thinking to developmental and contextual considerations. In the next section, we explore the role of four theoretical perspectives in shaping research and findings on African American children's racial identity.

Conceptual Foundation of Research

Several theoretical orientations have been particularly relevant to understanding children's racial awareness and the implications for their development. Developmental theories, as already presented, afforded the opportunity to explore individual processes that consider developmental needs and transitions. Theories addressing cognitive development, social cognition, perspective taking, and symbolic interaction were instrumental in shifting atheoretical paradigms of earlier research conducted on African American children and youth. Other perspectives—life span, ecological, and a phenomenological variant of ecological systems theory—afford special insights into the unique experiences and adaptive responses of children. They also provide a framework for understanding childhood precursors that impact identity formation during adolescence. Research studies are discussed within each of the other perspectives to illustrate the application of the theoretical premises but do not necessarily represent the broader theoretical orientation espoused by the authors of the work presented.

Life Span Perspective

The life span perspective conceptualizes human behavior as influenced by developmental processes across biological, historical, sociocultural, and psychological factors from conception to death (Lerner, 2002). It extended the theoretical focus of historically traditional developmental psychology, with a focus on intraindividual processes, to incorporate sociocultural influences. This allows researchers to evaluate the impact of social experiences on psychosocial processes and behavioral outcomes of African American children. Some of the most prolific work that exemplifies this perspective focuses on the role of racial socialization and intergenerational communication on children's racial attitudes and preferences. Socialization opportunities exist in contexts where children have experiences and receive feedback about the explicit and implicit meanings regarding behavior and expectations. These include, for example, home, school, church, and recreational facilities. For illustrative purposes, we highlight studies that have addressed parental socialization practices on children's racial identity.

McAdoo's (1985) study with preschool children modified their racial attitudes using operant learning conditions. Mechanisms contributing to Afrocentric (in contrast to Eurocentric) attitudes and preferences were central to understanding the process. Parental teaching about racial history and strategies for addressing discrimination influences children's Afrocentric racial attitudes and preferences (S. A. Hill, 2006). Social scientists remain increasingly interested in the nature of communications from parents to children regarding ethnicity and race and the role these communications play in shaping or modifying racial identity attitudes. Race-related messages (racial socialization) contribute significantly to children's identity development and well-being. Stevenson (1994) posited that racial socialization was necessary to ameliorate the impact of racial hostilities and for African American children to achieve and develop positive self-images. Studies have frequently examined these processes through two broad dimensions that represent messages about cultural socialization (e.g., ethnic pride and heritage) and preparation for bias (e.g., discrimination and racial bias).

Research has shown that Black parents embrace both American and African-based values and endeavor to instill both value systems in their children. Given the historical factors explored under a life span perspective, parents' values and history of sociocultural experiences with discrimination affect the socialization strategies they use (Hughes & Johnson, 2001). Black parents value honesty, academic success, and family responsibility, and they teach these values to their children. In addition, they are likely to embrace culturally distinct values, which include kin networks, respect for the elderly, and mutual cooperation and sharing (S. A. Hill, 2001; Murry et al., 2005). Parents emphasize humanistic values over more ethnic-specific parenting practices and values (Marshall, 1995). African American parents want to raise children with values and expectations common for all parents. They come to understand, however, that although they may raise their children to treat others with respect, they will not always encounter respect from others. As such, racial and ethnic minority parents report more frequent cultural socialization than preparation for bias for their school-age children (Hughes, 2003).

The life span perspective provides a framework for exploring multidimensional processes that impact individual developmental outcomes. The focus allows greater understanding of the fluidity of development over time and an opportunity to consider the impact of contextual influences. Contextual theories, however, provide a broader conceptualization of exploring the influence of context on the development of African American children.

Ecological Perspective

Ecological or contextual perspectives emphasize the relation between the individual (e.g., the demands or presses) and the structural characteristics of the individual's context. The work of Bronfenbrenner (1979) and Garbarino (1982) provide mechanisms for examining the interaction of the individual and the various levels of the environment. Particular attention is given to the constraints and opportunities afforded by the individual and the context (Lerner, 2002). N. E. Hill, Murry, and Anderson (2005), for example, addressed families' sociocultural contexts as including social, political, and economic factors. These broader ecological conditions, however, have significant implications for family functioning and child-rearing efforts (e.g., racial socialization).

In describing contextual challenges in America, Schorr (1997) enumerated "the decline of manufacturing, the disappearance of well-paid jobs for the unskilled, racial discrimination ... [depleted neighborhoods] ... inferior and overwhelmed schools and services ... have all combined to form [places] inhospitable to healthy human development" (p. 305). Additionally, the impact of community conditions in determining individual outcomes has accelerated the need for intervention initiatives.

The complexity of these ecological processes is exacerbated when one considers the growing chasm between wealthy and impoverished families that heightens within (ethnicity–race) group complexities and tensions. Bronfenbrenner (2005) asserted that although these broader conditions influence the social conditions that support development, it is the more proximal contexts that have the most immediate impact on developmental processes. Accordingly, a nurturing context for child development, along with parental provisions of psychosocial assistance and support, is nested in the community.

Smith, Atkins, and Connell (2003) suggested that family, school, and community are each important factors in children's racial attitudes and academic performance. Using path analyses, they found associations between children living in communities with a high proportion of college-educated residents and children with teachers who demonstrated racial trust and perceived few racial barriers. In benefiting from both supportive centers, these children demonstrated more trust and optimism and exhibited more positive racial attitudes, and their racial attitudes contributed to better academic performance. In contrast, racial distrust and perception of barriers due to race were related to poorer academic performance. Similarly, Johnson (2005), using a mixed-methods design, explored the multiple contextual influences of racial socialization on the racial coping outcomes of African American children and found similar results.

The studies presented here not only emphasize the breadth of empirical options, particularly when focusing on the same context, but also note the importance of specificity in reporting contextual details relevant to understanding children's racial attitudes in ecologically based research. In expanding the ecological perspective, a comprehensive theory that accounts for normative developmental processes and specific risks faced by African Americans is presented in Spencer's (1995, 1999, 2006) Phenomenological Variant of Ecological Systems Theory (PVEST) model which situates human development in cultural context.

Phenomenological Variant of Ecological Systems Theory

PVEST integrates an explicitly phenomenological perspective with Bronfenbrenner's (1989) ecological systems theory, linking context with perception. In determining how African American children view and comprehend family, peer, and societal expectations, various theoretical positions—including psychosocial, ecological, self-organizational, and phenomenological models—are integrated, with an emphasis on self-appraisal processes relevant to the children's racial identity development (Swanson, Spencer, & Peterson, 1998). The approach takes into account structural and contextual barriers to identity formation and their implication for psychological processes, such as self-appraisal. It consists of five components (see Figure 20.1) linked by bidirectional processes; conceptualized as systems theory, it is a cyclic, recursive model that describes identity development throughout the life course.

The first component of PVEST, *net vulnerability level*, represents risk contributors and protective factors that may predispose children to adverse outcomes. The net balance between risk contributors and proactive factors is inextricably linked to social–cognitive abilities that provide the framework for interpreting external information (detailed in Figure 20.2). Children have the capacity to interpret societal assumptions and biases about what it means to be African American, male or female, or overweight. The research, as previously noted, has demonstrated the undifferentiated cognitive processing of preschool children that is subsequently not integrated into the concept of the self. With cognitive maturation, however, children's capacity to internalize biases increases unless there is active (and consistent) intervention to minimize the influence. In addition, adults who provide racial socialization may facilitate children's more advanced cognitive interpretations of race and color in the United States.

The second component of PVEST, *net stress engagement*, refers to experiences that challenge (i.e., produce dissonance, e.g., being called a racial epithet) or support children in negotiating the risks encountered (i.e., preparation for bias). During childhood, this has been most directly linked to parental socialization (both racial and gender) and to incorporation of culturally relevant materials and activities into children's school experiences (e.g., positive African American images in textbooks). Adaptive strategies are important for minority-status individuals independent of age; however, the potential consequences are significant during the middle to late childhood years because of the foundation they provide for successfully addressing developmental needs during adolescence.

Net stress engagement contributes to *reactive coping strategies* as adaptive or maladaptive. Children whose challenges outweigh their support might adopt maladaptive coping strategies (e.g., acting out due to negative school experiences). Alternatively, children's whose supports outweigh the challenges are able to negotiate challenges of positive Black identity within a social context. For example, as an explanation for the achievement gap between White and African American students, it has been proposed that African American students would do better if they adopted a Eurocentric cultural values system. This deficit-oriented perspective denies African American students (and other children of color) their own culturally specific normative developmental perspective. To illustrate, Spencer, Noll, Stoltzfus, and Harpalani (2001) examined students ages 11 through 16 years on multiple dimensions of PVEST. The students, in contrast to the traditionally offered acting-White assumption, demonstrated high self-esteem and achievement goals in conjunction with high Afrocentricity. In addition, students with a Eurocentric perspective scored lower on self-esteem and achievement measures. Thus, an explanation for diverse outcomes is explained by using a more comprehensive theoretical perspective that explicitly addresses race and human development simultaneously (see Spencer, 2006).

20. Racial Identity Development During Childhood 275

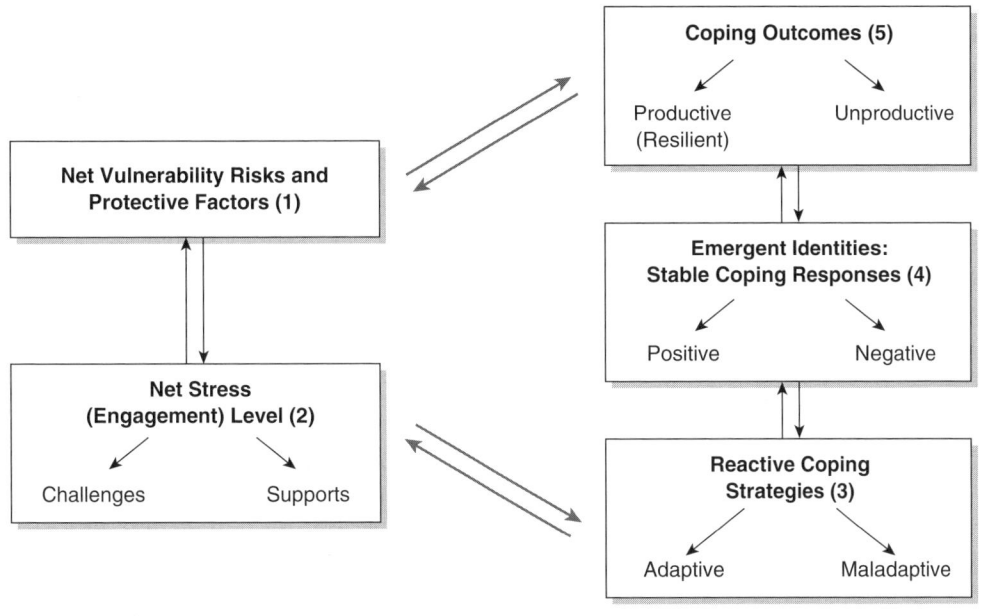

Figure 20.1 Phenomenological Variant of Ecological Systems Theory

Source: Spencer, M. B. "Old Issues and New Theorizing About African American Youth: A Phenomenological Variant of Ecological Systems Theory." In R. L. Taylor (Ed.), *Black Youth: Perspectives on Their Status in the United States.* Copyright © 1995 by Praeger. Reproduced with permission of Greenwood Publishing Group, Inc., Westport, CT.

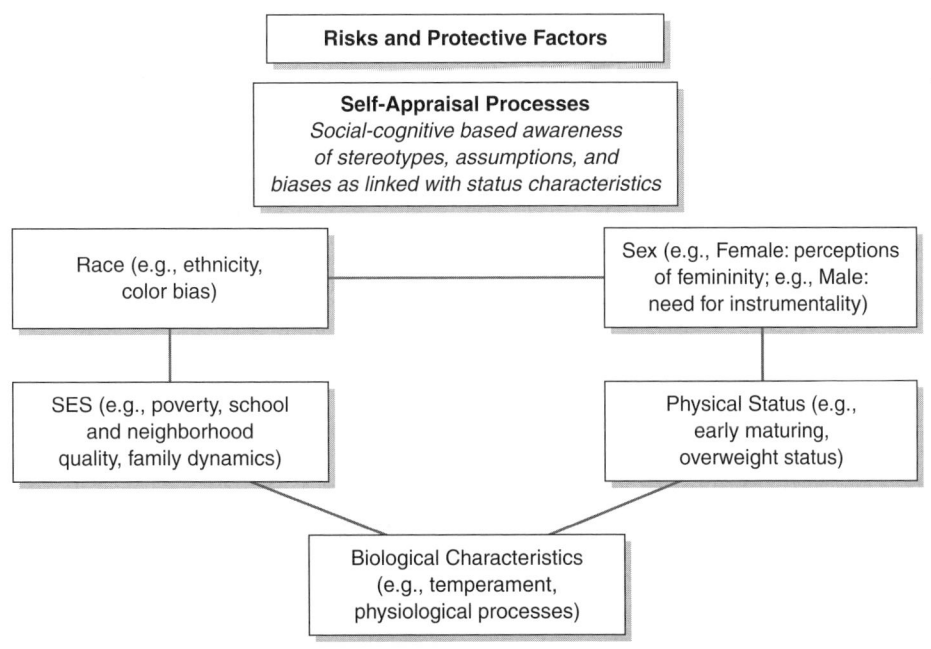

Figure 20.2 Phenomenological Variant of Ecological Systems Theory: Factors Contributing to Self-Appraisal Processes

Self-appraisal processes impact identity development (*emergent identities*) that contributes to future perception and behavior, yielding adverse or productive *coping outcomes* across various contexts. For African American children, the presence and engagement of structural racism poses risks embedded in their socializing contexts that influence their understanding of how to effectively negotiate within their world. PVEST, foundationally, incorporates developmental and cultural themes with ecological theorizing by Bronfenbrenner (1979) and Erikson's (1968) perspectives regarding life-course identity processes. Thus, life-course perspectives of normative developmental processes are relevant not only for research but also for evaluating practices which influence development (e.g., classroom practices, after-school or recreational programming). In essence, PVEST offers implications for understanding and enhancing children's long-term development.

Racial Identity and Child Outcomes

A primary premise up to this point has been to demonstrate the impact of racial identity formation for African American children and the necessity for understanding it from a theoretical perspective that considers contextual influences. Identity formation is the primary psychosocial goal of adolescence, but developing a sense of competence during childhood precedes this psychosocial challenge. Given the cognitive and contextual aspects of competence, two conditions are proposed as relevant for children (Anderson & Messick, 1974): the ability (1) to initiate action and direct behavior within given environmental constraints and (2) to recognize that different roles are required in different situations and contexts and therefore demonstrate behavior that reflects the incorporation of these expectations. Whaley (1993) suggested that the concept of competence provides a more integrative perspective on the interactions of social experiences, cultural factors, and cognitive development in the process of identity formation for African American children.

Academic disengagement, maladaptive coping strategies, and alcohol and tobacco use are behaviors whose etiology lies in middle childhood. In examining the impact of racial identity on children's drug use, Belgrave et al. (1994) found children's Afrocentric values to influence their understanding drug attitudes and suggest the integration of Afrocentric values in drug prevention programs and efforts (see Thomas, Townsend, & Belgrave, 2003). Other research has consistently demonstrated a decline in children's school general and academic self-esteem beginning in second grade, followed by another significant decline in fourth grade.

Using data from a statewide Beginning School Study (which had more lower-income Blacks than Whites), Entwisle and Alexander (1990) found that the groups were equivalent on academic skills at first grade. After analyzing the data by group, they found that Black males outperformed Black females in math reasoning; however, White males did not outperform White females. Statistically significant gender differences were not found until Entwisle and Alexander considered parents' economic resources. Other research, conducted by Patterson, Kupersmidt, and Vaden (1990), found that Black male elementary students were more vulnerable to teacher ratings of low academic performance, conduct problems, and peer relations than were Black females or White males and females.

Slaughter-Defoe and Rubin (2001) noted how an ecological context is associated with academic outcomes. In following a group of Head Start–eligible children from preschool until late adolescence, they found that teachers had more of an influence on child outcomes from middle to late childhood than parents. Their research echoes earlier research and observations that African American boys and girls have different school experiences. Irvine (1990) highlighted the interactions between teachers and students: "The White teachers directed more verbal praise, criticism, and nonverbal praise toward males than towards females. In contrast, they directed more nonverbal criticism toward Black males than toward Black females, White females, or White males" (p. 59). Thus, by early childhood, cognitive egocentrism can no longer protect African American males from negative teacher perceptions (Spencer, 1985). In fact, African American males become more aware of how others perceive them as they develop into adolescents (see Cunningham, 1999; Swanson, Cunningham, & Spencer, 2003). Thus, identity process for African American children must include both an understanding of their basic developmental processes and a consideration of how development is associated with one's gender and context.

The sociocultural context of African American children can enhance or compromise productive outcomes. Given such issues, there is a particular need to incorporate development and context when examining behavioral or academic outcomes and implementing prevention strategies. The long-term influence of unsupportive contexts on the future outcomes for African American children remains staggering in contrast to the incredibly talented children who transition into adolescence with a clearly defined identity base. An understanding and interpretation of such outcomes require an integrated knowledge of adaptation, both normative and non-normative, in the context of development (Masten & Coatsworth, 1998).

Methodological Considerations

Despite the fact that earlier research did not differentiate personal and group identity, the negative self-concept and self-hatred interpretation of racial preferences prevailed for decades. While focusing on one or both constructs, the research frequently ignored developmental transitions, parental racial socialization, and societal and historical traditions that stress racial membership as a determinant of group and individual experiences. Nevertheless, the literature showed a consistent pattern of Eurocentric preferences among African American preschool children, with greater variability among older school-age children. Given the history of research on racial attitudes and preferences, the interpretation of research findings initially raised concerns regarding the validity of the use of forced-choice instruments (e.g., puppets, dolls, pictures) to explore the relationship between racial attitude and self-esteem (M. L. Clark, 1982, 1992).

When other methods were used, the findings were less Eurocentric than the results of studies that used forced-choice options. Banks and Rompf (1973), for example, had 6- to 8-year-olds evaluate the performance of a Black and White player in a ball-tossing game. Although Black children rewarded the White player more frequently, they chose the Black player more frequently as the winner. In finding no consistent preference toward Whites, the authors reported no support for "self-rejection" among Black children. Belgrave et al. (1994) developed the 9-item Children's Black Identity Scale for use with a fifth-grade sample. The measure assesses children's affective, cognitive, and behavioral components of racial identity using a 3-point scale with reasonable reliability. Their findings, although consistent with studies that took a developmental perspective, showed personal and racial identity among this older group to have a positive relationship.

In addition to considering assessment approaches, recent advances in theoretical applications have contributed to complexities in analytic strategies. Studies that have examined the influence of various contexts (e.g., multilevel models), have gained in popularity over recent decades. When designing and conducting studies that examine contextual factors, it is critical to address any differences in units of analyses when using this perspective. Mixed methods, path modeling, and hierarchical linear modeling relevant to multilevel modeling provide greater support for using this perspective. In studies that use an ecological perspective, the context should be adequately described to provide information about the contextual level being examined (i.e., meso vs. exo, degree of mbeddedness). In cases with a developmental focus, individual factors should be provided to situate the person (i.e., child, parent) within a specific context at a given period.

Recent prominence is particularly noted in the reported used of mixed-methods research designs. Cross (2005) provided a historical perspective on the use of mixed methods to study identity among African Americans. He pointed out that, although valuable new constructs were added over time in the research on Black identity, self-report questionnaires were the primary method of assessment. Multiple ethnic identities and situational and developmental changes in identity are clearly important, and therefore the use of mixed methods extends knowledge of identity processes across contexts. While using the strengths of quantitative and qualitative methods, it is also important to address potential pitfalls by adopting greater vigilance in design and implementation of the research than typically required in using one primary method. However, when approached from a conceptually based framework it offers numerous advantages in addressing the complex questions now emerging around racial identity and in providing greater translation of the research for practice purposes (see Weisner, 2004, for a compilation of mixed-methods studies conducted with ethnic minority children and families).

Future Directions

We have documented substantial gains in the focus on children's racial identity over several decades. Many of these gains represent paradigm shifts and theoretical applications used to clarify the constructs and empirically explore underlying processes. Future research can enhance our current knowledge base and provide greater applicability of the research to practice (see Quintana et al., 2006, for a detailed review). Among areas of future interest, some to consider include clarification of cultural meaning for African American families (particularly given the implications of racial socialization on children's racial identity), influences of technological advances in video gaming, and the translation of research into practice.

Considering assumptions about what constitutes African American culture and its potential role in identity processes, N. E. Hill et al. (2005) proposed the need for scholars to examine the current meaning of culture among African American families. As part of this process, we recommend also exploring what constitutes models of culture that are transmitted to their children. Black churches, for example, have been instrumental in instilling not only a sense of spiritual understanding but also of history and community (Lincoln, 1995): "In the African American experience ... [religious] belief(s) and practice was sufficiently common to the African American minicultures to provide a framework of reference from which a common identity could reasonably be inferred" (Lincoln, 1995, p. 219). The Black church became the chief index of identification, not because it transcended "race-rooted ... values and behaviors" but because it was an opportunity to express, transmit, and validate cultural identity. A critical direction is therefore an exploration of what constitutes culture and what context, if not the church, is considered a significant context for defining, instilling, and validating cultural values.

There is a long history of research on the impact of the news and entertainment media on African American children's psychosocial development. With the emergence of accessible video games with advanced programming potential, there is now a new "context" offering opportunities for children's identity development. Current advances in video game technology now allow children to generate *avatars*, personalized computer-generated images for use in game playing. Avatars are hypothesized to impact identity formation as a potential resource for the child's presentation of the self in his or her social context. Although this research is gaining prominence in the broader literature on children and media influences (Turkle, 1995; Walkerdine, 1998), research is needed to explore the implications of this expanded context on African American children's personal and racial identity.

A final note regarding research direction is in reference to the work required for translating research into practice. While continuing to make institutional and system-based inroads, research scholars can facilitate the translation of the breadth of research for those who work directly with and subsequently impact the lives of African American children. This work is taking place in varying forms, including program development and professional training. The move by funding agencies toward requiring dissemination plans for research findings emphasizes this need. The ability to translate research is particularly appropriate when sufficient research is available to identify processes and outcomes: This is certainly the case for racial identity for African American children. Continuing research is necessary to address effects of social trends, but sufficient data have been available and replicated to provide the necessary translation. We have seen some of this take place over the past couple of decades in children's television programming, school readiness programming, and select professional training seminars. What remains lacking, however, is an ongoing integration of this knowledge into teacher training programs, school curriculum and classroom practices, training for community and mental health providers working with African American children, and integration into higher education courses that address child development. Institutions that train professional and other service personnel can use the research to strengthen their focus and impact on child development.

There is a wide breadth of research available on African American children's racial identity that contributes to a significant basis of knowledge. The utilization of theoretical perspectives that facilitate the direction and interpretation of research has provided a rich source of information on which to build and to translate in the ongoing effort to maximize the psychosocial development of African American children.

REFERENCES

Allport, G. W. (1937). *Personality: A psychological interpretation.* New York: Holt.

Anderson, S., & Messick, S. (1974). Social competency in young children. *Developmental Psychology, 10,* 282–293.

Arroyo, C., & Zigler, E. (1991). Racial identity, academic achievement, and the psychological well-being of economically disadvantaged adolescents. *Journal of Personal and Social Psychology, 69,* 903–914.

Baldwin, J. A., Brown, R., & Hopkins, R. (1991). The Black self-hatred paradigm revisited: An Afrocentric analysis. In R. L. Jones (Ed.), *Black Psychology* (pp. 28–44). Berkeley, CA: Cobb & Henry.

Banks, W. C., & Rompf, W. J. (1973). Evaluative bias and preference behavior in Black and White children. *Child Development, 44,* 776–783.

Belgrave, F. Z., Cherry, V. R., Cunningham, D., Walwyn, S., Letdaka-Rennert, K., & Phillips, F. (1994). The influence of Africentric values, self-esteem, and Black identity on drug attitudes among African American fifth graders: A preliminary study. *Journal of Black Psychology, 20,* 143–156.

Bronfenbrenner, U. (1979). *The ecology of human development.* Cambridge, MA: Harvard University Press.

Bronfenbrenner, U. (1989). Ecological systems theory. In R. Vasta (Ed.), *Annals of child development* (Vol. 6, pp. 187–251). Greenwich, CT: JAI Press.

Bronfenbrenner, U. (2005). Ecological systems theory (1992). In U. Bronfenbrenner (Ed.), *Making human beings human: Bioecological perspectives on human development* (pp. 106–173). Thousand Oaks, CA: Sage.

Clark, K. B., & Clark, M. K. (1939). The development of consciousness of self and the mergence of racial identity in Negro preschool children. *Journal of Social Psychology, 10,* 591–599.

Clark, K. B., & Clark, M. K. (1947). Racial identification and preference in Negro children. In T. Newcomb & E. L. Hartley (Eds.), *Readings in social psychology* (pp. 602–611). New York: Holt.

Clark, M. L. (1982). Racial group concept and self-esteem in Black children. *Journal of Black Psychology, 8,* 75–88.

Clark, M. L. (1992). Racial group concept and self-esteem in Black children. In A. K. H. Burlew, W. C. Banks, H. P. McAdoo, & D. A. Azibo (Eds.), *African American Psychology: Theory, research, and practice* (pp. 159–172). Newbury Park, CA: Sage.

Cooley, C. H. (1902). *Human nature and the social order.* New York: Scribner's.

Cooley, C. H. (1908). A study of the early use of self-words by a child. *Psychological Review, 6,* 339–357.

Cross, W. E. (2005). Ethnicity, race, and identity. In T. S. Weisner (Ed.), *Discovering successful pathways in children's development: Mixed methods in the study of childhood and family life* (pp. 171–182). Chicago: University of Chicago Press.

Cunningham, M. (1999). African American males' perceptions of their community resources and constraints: A longitudinal analysis. *Journal of Community Psychology, 27,* 568–588.

Entwisle, D. R., & Alexander, K. L. (1990). Beginning school math competence: Minority and majority comparisons. *Child Development, 61,* 454–471.

Erikson, E. H. (1968). *Identity, youth, and crisis.* New York: W. W. Norton.

Garbarino, J. (1982). *Children and Families in the social environment.* New York: Aldine de Gruyter.

Hill, N. E., Murry, V. M., & Anderson, V. D. (2005). Sociocultural contexts of African American families. In V. C. McLoyd, N. E. Hill, & K. A. Dodge (Eds.), *African American family life: Ecological and cultural diversity* (pp. 21–44). New York: Guilford Press.

Hill, S. A. (2001). Class, race, and gender dimensions of child rearing in African American families. *Journal of Black Studies, 31,* 494–508.

Hill, S. A. (2006). Racial socialization. In G. Handel (Ed.), *Childhood socialization* (2nd ed., pp. 89–111). New Brunswick, NJ: Aldine Transaction.

Hughes, D. (2003). Correlates of African American and Latino parents' messages to children about ethnicity and race: A comparative study of racial socialization. *American Journal of Community Psychology, 31,* 15–33.

Hughes, D., & Johnson, D. (2001). Correlates in children's experiences of parents' racial socialization behaviors. *Journal of Marriage and Family, 63,* 981–995.

Hughes, D., Rodriquez, J. R., Smith, E. P., Johnson, D. J., Stevenson, H. C., & Spicer, P. (2006). Parents' ethnic–racial socialization practices: A review of research and directions for future study. *Developmental Psychology, 42,* 747–770.

Irvine, J. J. (1990). *Black students and school failure: Policies practices, and prescriptions.* New York: Greenwood Press.

Johnson, D. J. (2005). The ecology of children's racial coping: Family, school, and community influences. In T. S. Weisner (Ed.), *Discovering successful pathways in children's development: Mixed methods in the study of childhood and family life* (pp. 87–109). Chicago: University of Chicago Press.

Katz, P. A., & Kofkin, J. A. (1997). Race, gender, and young children. In S. S. Luthar, J. A. Burack, D. Cicchetti, & J. R. Weisz (Eds.), *Developmental psychopathology: Perspectives on adjustment, risk, and disorder* (pp. 51–74). New York: Cambridge University Press.

Lerner, R. M. (2002). *Concepts and theories of human development* (3rd ed., pp. 48–85). Mahwah, NJ: Lawrence Erlbaum.

Lerner, R. M., & Buehrig, C. J. (1975). The development of racial attitudes in young Black and White children. *Journal of Genetic Psychology, 127,* 45–54.

Lewin, K. (1935). *Dynamic theory of personality.* New York: McGraw-Hill.

Lincoln, E. C. (1995). Black religion and racial identity. In H. W. Harris, H. C. Blue, & E. E. H. Griffith (Eds.), *Racial and ethnic identity: Psychological development and creative expression* (pp. 208–221). New York: Routledge.

Marshall, S. (1995). Ethnic socialization of African American children: Implications for parenting, identity development, and academic achievement. *Journal of Youth and Adolescence, 24,* 377–396.

Masten, A. S., & Coatsworth, J. D. (1998). The development of competence in favorable and unfavorable environments: Lessons from research on successful children. *American Psychologist, 53,* 205–220.

McAdoo, H. P. (1985). The village talks: Racial socialization of our children. In H. P. McAdoo & J. L. McAdoo (Eds.), *Black children: Social, educational, and parental environments* (pp. 47–55). Beverly Hills, CA: Sage.

Mead, G. H. (1934). *Mind, self, and society.* Chicago: University of Chicago Press.

Murray, C. B., & Mandara, J. (2002). Racial identity development in African American children: Cognitive and experiential antecedents. In H. P. McAdoo (Ed.), *Black children: Social, educational, and parental environments* (2nd ed., pp. 73–96). Thousand Oaks, CA: Sage.

Murry, V. M., Brody, G. H., McNair, L. D., Luo, Z., Gibbons, F. X., Gerrard, M., et al. (2005). Parental involvement promotes rural African American youths' self-pride and sexual self-concepts. *Journal of Marriage and Family, 67,* 627–642.

Patterson, C. J., Kupersmidt, J. B., & Vaden, N. A. (1990). Income level, gender, ethnicity, and household composition as predictors of children's school-based competence. *Child Development, 61,* 485–494.

Pettigrew, T. F. (1964). *A profile of the Negro American.* Princeton, NJ: Van Nostrand.

Philogene, G. (Ed.). (2004). *Racial identity in context: The legacy of Kenneth B. Clark.* Washington, DC: American Psychological Association.

Piaget, J. (1929). *The child's conception of the world.* New York: Harcourt, Brace Jovanovich.

Quintana, S. M., Aboud, F. E., Chao, R. K., Contreras-Grau, J., Cross, W. E., Hudley, C., et al. (2006). Race, ethnicity, and culture in child development: Contemporary research and future directions. *Child Development, 77,* 1129–1141.

Schorr, L. B. (1997). *Common purpose: Strengthening families and neighborhoods to rebuild America.* New York: Anchor.

Semaj, M. T. (1980). The development of racial development and preference: A cognitive approach. *Journal of Black Psychology, 6,* 59–79.

Semaj, M. T. (1985). Afrikanity, cognition and extended self-identity. In M. B. Spencer, G. K. Brookins, & W. R. Allen (Eds.), *Beginnings: The social and affective development of Black children* (pp. 173–184). Hillsdale, NJ: Lawrence Erlbaum.

Slaughter-Defoe, D. T., & Rubin, H. (2001). A longitudinal case study of Head Start eligible children: Implications for urban education. *Educational Psychologist, 36,* 31–44.

Smith, E. P., Atkins, J., & Connell, C. M. (2003). Family, school, and community factors and relationships to racial–ethnic attitudes and academic achievement. *American Journal of Community Psychology, 32,* 159–173.

Spencer, M. B. (1982a). Personal and group identity of Black children: An alternative synthesis. *Genetic Psychology Monographs, 106,* 59–84.

Spencer, M. B. (1982b). Preschool children's social cognition and cultural cognition: A cognitive developmental interpretation of race dissonance findings. *Journal of Psychology: Interdisciplinary and Applied, 112,* 275–286.

Spencer, M. B. (1985). Black children's race awareness, racial attitudes, and self-concept: A reinterpretation. *Annual Progress in Child Psychiatry and Child Development, 71,* 616–630.

Spencer, M. B. (1995). Old issues and new theorizing about African American youth: A phenomenological variant of ecological systems theory. In R. L. Taylor (Ed.), *Black youth: Perspectives on their status in the United States* (pp. 37–69). Westport, CT: Praeger.

Spencer, M. B. (1999). Social and cultural influences on school adjustment: The application of an identity-focused cultural ecological perspective. *Educational Psychologist, 34,* 43–57.

Spencer, M. B. (2006). Phenomenology and ecological system theory: Development of diverse groups. In W. Damon & R. Lerner

(Eds.), *Handbook of child psychology* (6th ed., Vol. 1, pp. 829–893). New York: Wiley.

Spencer, M. B., Noll, E., Stoltzfus, J., & Harpalani, V. (2001). Identity and school adjustment: Revisiting the "acting White" assumption. *Educational Psychologist, 36,* 21–30.

Stevenson, H. C., Jr. (1994). Racial socialization in African American families: The art of balancing intolerance and survival. *The Family Journal, 2,* 190–198.

Swanson, D. P., Cunningham, M., & Spencer, M. B. (2003). Black males' structural conditions, achievement patterns, normative needs, and "opportunities." *Urban Education, 38,* 608–633.

Swanson, D. P., Spencer, M. B., & Petersen, A. (1998). Identity formation in adolescence. In K. Borman & B. Schneider (Eds.), *Ninety-seventh yearbook of the National Society for the Study of Education: Pt 1. The adolescent years: Social influences and educational challenges* (pp. 18–41). Chicago: University of Chicago Press.

Thomas, D. E., Townsend, T. G., & Belgrave, F. Z. (2003). The influence of cultural and racial identification on the psychosocial adjustment of inner-city African American children in school. *American Journal of Community Psychology, 32,* 217–228.

Turkle, S. (1995). *Life on the screen: Identity in the age of the Internet.* New York: Simon & Schuster.

Vygotsky, L. S. (1962). *Thought and language.* Cambridge: MIT Press.

Walkerdine, V. (1998). Children in cyberspace: A new frontier. In K. Lesnik-Oberstein (Ed.), *Children in culture: Approaches to childhood* (pp. 231–247). Basingstoke, UK: Macmillan.

Weisner, T. S. (2004). *Discovering successful pathways in children's development: Mixed methods in the study of childhood and family life.* Chicago: University of Chicago Press.

Whaley, A. L. (1993). Self-esteem, cultural identity, and psychosocial adjustment in African American children. *Journal of Black Psychology, 19,* 406–422.

Williams, J. E., & Roberson, J. K. (1967). A method of assessing racial attitudes in preschool children. *Educational and Psychological Measurement, 27,* 671–689.

21

RACIAL IDENTITY THEORY
Adults

KEVIN COKLEY AND COLLETTE CHAPMAN

Psychologists have long been interested in issues of identity with African Americans. Dating back to the studies of Eugene and Ruth Horowitz in the mid-1930s, there has been a persistent concern about the socio-psychological identity issues of African Americans (Cross, 1991). Specifically, there has been a focus on how African Americans define themselves (e.g., self-concept) and feel about themselves (e.g., self-esteem) in the context of a racist and White supremacist country (i.e., the United States) where negative messages about their humanity are part of the history and cultural fabric. The marginalized and oppressed social status of African Americans has historically resulted in periodic attempts to name themselves in an effort to bolster their collective racial self-concept and racial self-esteem. History shows that Americans of African descent have called themselves, or been called, *African, colored, negro/Negro, Black, Afro-American*, and *African American* (Holloway, 1990). Each label used is a reflection of a change in sociopolitical consciousness (Holloway, 1990) and racial identity. The underlying psychological processes associated with the construction of racial identity remains an enormously popular focus in African American Psychology. It is one of the most frequently researched and debated topics in African American Psychology as well as the multicultural counseling and psychology literature at large (Cokley, 2002, 2005). Given the amount of attention, disagreement, and debate that researchers and scholars have dedicated to the study of racial identity of African Americans, this topic is foundational in any discussion of African American Psychology.

The organization of the chapter is as follows: (a) historical context, (b) seminal models, (c) analysis of key racial identity theories, (d) literature review, (e) methodological issues, and (f) trends, debates, and future directions.

HISTORICAL CONTEXT

A review of the seminal racial identity theories would be incomplete without placing them in proper historical context. In the 1903 book *Souls of Black Folks*, W. E. B. Du Bois introduced the concept of *double consciousness*, a psychological state in which African Americans struggled to balance the tensions between their American (i.e., White) and African (i.e., Black) "souls." This can be considered a precursor to the modern idea of racial identity. The intellectual foundation of racial identity theories can be traced back to the 1930s' French Négritude movement and the 1920s and 1930s' Harlem Renaissance. *Négritude*, whose closest English translation is "blackness," was a literary and political movement developed by Aime Cesairé, Léopold Senghor, and Léon Damas. Cesairé, Senghor, and Damas were Black students from the French colonies of Senegal, Martinique, and Guyana, respectively, who sought the development of a common Black identity that rejected French colonial racism. The Négritude movement was greatly influenced by the Harlem Renaissance, a literary period during which Black American authors focused on Black life from a Black perspective. The Négritude movement's emphasis on Africa and restoring and/or creating a global African identity is clearly the direct intellectual predecessor of Molefi Asante's Afrocentry as well as Afrocentric psychology, popularized by individuals such as Wade Nobles, Na'im Akbar, and Asa Hilliard. Although racial identity theories were clearly influenced by the Négritude movement, their intellectual and ideological kinship perhaps lies closest with the Harlem Renaissance, which fostered a new Black cultural identity that acknowledged and at times embraced, but not necessarily emphasized, the influences of African cultures on Black Americans. This comes as no surprise given that both the Harlem Renaissance and the creation of racial identity theories are American phenomena whose writers were Black Americans, whereas the Négritude movement included writers representing a more Diasporic, pan-African perspective.

Seminal Models

The seminal models of racial identity were produced in the early 1970s by Charles Thomas (1971), William Cross (1971), and Bailey Jackson (1976). The initial groundwork for these models can be traced to an article published by Thomas (1969), first president of the Association of Black Psychologists, in *The American Behavioral Scientist*. In this article, Thomas laid the foundation for racial identity models through his discussions of how "Black people accommodated and internalized their astoundingly oppressive society" (p. 39), "the felt meaning of blackness is akin to one's first physical sexual encounter or a deep religious conversion," (p. 40), "the developmental view of man . . . can be used for understanding the psychological and social experience of which black people have been a part" (p. 40), and "few blacks can claim that they were always black" (p. 41). Later, Thomas (1970) introduced the concept of *Negromachy* as a form of mental illness for Black Americans involving racial rejection. Thomas then developed a five-stage model of Negromachy that reflected stages of transition from racial rejection to racial acceptance (Thomas, 1970, 1971).

According to Bailey Jackson (2001), Thomas's work influenced him and William Cross. In the seminal and now highly cited article published in *Black World*, Cross (1971) constructed a model, originally referred to as *the Negro-to-Black conversion experience*, which described five stages of psychological *Nigrescence*, or the process of becoming Black. Bailey Jackson's (2001) model of racial identity was developed with the goal of understanding the range of views Black people hold about their Blackness so that interventions and techniques could be developed to facilitate the development of individuals, groups, and systems. According to Jackson, his five-stage model of Black identity development was developed independent of Cross in the early 1970s but was not published until 1976.

Out of these three models, Cross's (1971) Nigrescence model has received the most scholarly and empirical attention. This is primarily because an instrument, the Racial Identity Attitudes Scale (RIAS; Parham & Helms, 1981), was developed to explicitly operationalize Cross's Nigrescence model. Since the publication of Parham and Helms's (1981) influential article, the RIAS has become the most widely used racial identity instrument in the literature, and it has allowed researchers to test the viability of Cross's Nigrescence theory. As more researchers began to use the RIAS, some became more critical of its theoretical assumptions, which are rooted in Nigrescence theory. The criticisms included Nigrescene theory's narrow description of pre-encounter attitudes (e.g., individuals do not necessarily have to be "self-hating" to de-emphasize their Blackness) and its pejorative description of Black Nationalism (Cross, 1991). In response to the criticisms, Cross (1991, 1995; Cross & Vandiver, 2001) revised his model as presented in Table 21.1.

Helms, greatly influenced by Cross's (1971) original Nigrescence model, can be credited with conducting an extensive program of empirical research during a time when empirical research on racial identity was scant. Having used Nigrescence theory in her work, Helms (1986) eventually amended the theory to make it more reflective of her beliefs about racial identity. In her amendments, Helms considered each stage to be a distinct worldview that people use to organize and make sense of racial information about the world around them. In later writings, Helms (1996) referred to racial identity stages as

Table 21.1 Racial Identity Theory

	Model (Author, Model Type)				
Model Characteristics	Negromachy (Thomas, 1971): Stage Model	Psychological Nigrescene & Psychological Nigrescene Revised (Cross, 1971, 1991): Stage Model	Black Identity Development (Jackson, 1976): Stage Model	Psychodiagnostic Model Of Racial Identity Development (Helms, 1990): Ego Status Model	Multidimensional Model of Racial Identity (Sellers, 1998): Typology Model
Keys to conceptualization	Five-stage model based on the concept of Negromachy that Thomas (1970) introduced as mental illness for Black Americans involving racial rejection. Stages of Negromachy reflected transition from racial rejection to racial acceptance.	Five-stage model that describes the process of becoming Black. Model originally referred to as the Negro-to-Black conversion experience (Cross, 1971).	Five-stage model developed with the goal of understanding the range of views Black people hold about their Blackness. Model aimed to help facilitate the development of interventions and techniques to foster the advancement of individuals, groups, and systems (Jackson, 2001).	Credited with conducting extensive empirical research on racial identity particularly for use in applied settings. Influenced by Cross's psychological Nigrescene model.	Focuses on conceptualizing social identities in relation to racial identity development.
Description	Stage 1: Withdrawal—Characterized by temporary isolation and verbalizing frustrations about Whites while trying to get a better understanding of Negromachy. Stage 2: Testifying—Characterized by testimonies and confessions about the	Stage 1: Pre-encounter—Characterized by attitudes that degrade Blackness and a worldview that is dominated by White references. Revision: The pre-encounter stage is more complex than originally conceptualized. It can be represented by three attitudes or identities: assimilation, miseducation, and self-hatred. Stage 2: Encounter—Related to a troubling personal or social event that	Stage 1: Naïve—Marked by lack of a Black identity and/or social consciousness. Stage 2: Acceptance—Characterized by the uncritical acceptance of White people's perceptions and beliefs about Black people.	Individual's racial identity consists of three interacting components: ascribed identities, personal identity, and reference-group identities. Components are influenced by factors related to environmental reactions to proximal characteristics (Helms, 1990).	Model assumes that African Americans have several social identities, including race, which is hierarchically ordered. Focuses on the belief that African Americans have about the significance of race in terms of how they define themselves and the qualitative meaning the assign to belonging to a racial group (Sellers et al., 1997, 1998).

(Continued)

Table 21.1 (Continued)

Model Characteristics	Model (Author, Model Type)				
	Negromachy (Thomas, 1971): Stage Model	Psychological Nigrescene & Psychological Nigrescene Revised (Cross, 1971, 1991): Stage Model	Black Identity Development (Jackson, 1976): Stage Model	Psychodiagnostic Model Of Racial Identity Development (Helms, 1990): Ego Status Model	Multidimensional Model of Racial Identity (Sellers, 1998): Typology Model
Description	individual person's pain, which is due racial self-denial. Stage 3: Information Processing About Cultural Heritage—Involves processing information about the African background of Black Americans' cultural heritage and the Black contribution to America. Stage 4: Activity—Concerned with working through Black subgroups to become a larger part of the Black experience. Stage 5: Transcendental—Individual no longer has problems related to race, transcending race into ideas about people as a part of the human race.	challenges the beliefs and attitudes of the individual. Stage 3: Immersion–emersion—Emotionally charged stage characterized by deifying Black culture and Black people while demonizing all things associated with White people. Then follows an emergence from the intense emotions. Revision: Immersion–emersion consists of two conceptually separate identities: anti-White and Black involvement. Stage 4: Internalization—Marked by a decline and eventual resolution of anti-White feelings as well as a secure, nonreactionary sense of one's Blackness. Revision: Internalization is more complicated and consists of three attitudes or identities: Black Nationalist, biculturalist, and multiculturalist. Stage 5: Internalization-Commitment—Characterized by an active involvement in activities that promote social justice. Revision: Internalization-commitment removed, thus reducing the model to four stages.	Stage 3: Resistance—Involves the rejection of White people's views about Blacks and the valuing of the Black culture. Stage 4: Redefinition—Involves the positive reaffirmation of one's racial identity and sense of Blackness. Stage 5: Internalization—Marked by the integration of a redefined racial identity into one's self-concept.	The ways in which people organize and make sense of racial information is characterized by a person's worldview. Model supposes that worldview is embedded in factors such as personal attributes, sociocultural factors, and systematic influences.	Model consists of four dimensions: Dimension 1: Salience of identity—Refers to the importance of the individual's race is in that person's self-concept at a specific moment in time. Dimension 2: Centrality of identity—Refers to how dominant and stable an individual's race is in that person's self-concept. Dimension 3: Racial ideology associated with identity—Marked by beliefs, attitudes, and opinions an individual has about how members or a race should act. Dimension 4: Regard (public and private)—Public regard refers to the degree to which an individual thinks the public feels positively or negatively about African Americans. Private regard refers to the degree to which an individual feels positively or negatively toward African Americans and being African American.

Source: Adapted from Cross and Vandiver (2001).

"ego statuses" to "encourage mental health workers who use racial identity models to conceive of the process of development as involving dynamic evolution rather than static personality structures or types" (Helms & Cook, 1999, p. 84). Helms also went into detail in describing the emotional, behavioral, and cognitive expressions associated with each ego status. It is important to note that although she has made these amendments, they do not fundamentally change the basic tenets of Nigrescence theory, as evidenced by the fact that she continues to use most of the original Nigrescence theory stage names.

Although the Nigrescence model has been the dominant racial identity model used by counseling and clinical psychology researchers, social psychologists have also long been interested in racial identity and other social identities. In spite of attempts to modify the Nigrescence model, some researchers have sought to reconceptualize racial identity altogether. The most prominent of these efforts is the work of Robert Sellers. Sellers and his research team created the Multidimensional Inventory of Black Identity (MIBI) to address what they believed were inconsistencies in the racial identity literature using the Nigrescence model (Sellers, Rowley, Chavous, Shelton, & Smith, 1997). The MIBI is based on the Multidimensional Model of Racial Identity (MMRI; Sellers, Smith, Shelton, Rowley, & Chavous, 1998). Influenced by the work of social identity theorists, Sellers et al. (1997, 1998) believe that although race is a very important identity, it is only one of many social identities that are of significance to an individual's self-concept. Therefore, the MMRI assumes that African Americans have several social identities, including race, which are hierarchically ordered. The MMRI focuses on the beliefs that African Americans have about the significance of race in terms of how they define themselves and the qualitative meaning they assign to belonging to a racial group (Sellers et al., 1997, 1998).

ANALYSIS OF THE KEY RACIAL IDENTITY THEORIES

The Nigrescence model has proved to be particularly appealing to researchers and clinicians alike because of its seemingly developmental thrust. As a heuristic, the Nigrescence model has mass appeal because it seems to capture a psychological phenomenon that is believed to be a historical theme in the history and lives of African Americans. One example in history is Malcolm X, who in his teenage years held a somewhat naïve optimism about his goals because he was smart, through his hustling days as Detroit Red, to his days as the charismatic Black nationalist leader Malcolm X, to his attitudinal change toward Whites as a result of his trip to Mecca, seems to exemplify all the stages of psychological Nigrescence (Parham, 1989). However, one persistent criticism of the model is its assumption that most Blacks experience pre-encounter attitudes because of internalized negative beliefs and attitudes about Blacks. It has been pointed out that many Blacks have been raised in predominantly Black communities where they have attended predominantly Black schools and Black churches and have always been socialized with positive messages about being Black. These individuals conceivably never experience pre-encounter attitudes because negative messages about Blacks were not a part of their reality. A related criticism is that the model is not truly a developmental stage model, because all African Americans do not proceed through all the stages in the linear, hierarchical manner that is required by true developmental theories. These criticisms notwithstanding, the model continues to enjoy widespread appeal in the counseling literature, apparently because it lends itself to clinical case conceptualization. The model also maintains its broad appeal because it appears to be applicable to other marginalized social groups who also struggle with developing positive collective identities in the midst of societal oppression.

Unlike Nigrescence theory, which focuses on the *process* of how an individual's racial identity changes over time, the MMRI focuses on the *content* (i.e., dimensions) of the individual's racial identity. Also unlike Nigrescence theory, the MMRI does not assume that any one racial ideology (i.e., nationalist, oppressed minority, humanist, assimilationist) is most optimal for African Americans' mental health and overall psychological well-being; common interpretation of the Nigrescence theory is that higher stages of racial identity (i.e., internalization attitudes) are more optimal than lower stages (i.e., pre-encounter attitudes). Another major difference of the MMRI in comparison to Nigrescence theory is that the MMRI explicitly acknowledges that race may not be a central aspect of a person's identity; therefore, the MMRI allows researchers conducting racial identity research to always assess whether race is important to the individual's self-concept rather than assuming it is. Consistent with social psychological research, the MMRI was conceptualized in such a way as to allow for easier experimental manipulations (e.g., assigning individuals to "high" or "low" race centrality groups). A limitation of the MMRI is that it does not indicate what constitutes optimal mental health for African Americans. Thus, under the model, it is possible for an individual to have low racial centrality and to have negative feelings about being African American, yet still be considered mentally healthy.

Literature Review

Over the past 20 years, there has been an explosion of literature on racial identity. Early empirical studies in the 1980s and early 1990s were conducted primarily by counseling psychologists and focused on the relationship between racial identity and preferences for counselor race (Parham & Helms, 1981), self-actualization (Parham & Helms, 1985b), self-esteem (Parham & Helms, 1985a), attitudes toward counseling (Ponterotto, Anderson, & Grieger, 1986), and psychological functioning (Carter, 1991). Later, empirical studies in the 1990s examined the relationship between racial identity and Afrocentric values (Brookins, 1994), psychological feelings of closeness (Brookins, Anyabwile, & Nacoste, 1996), self-esteem (Speight, Vera, & Derrickson, 1996), academic self-efficacy and school achievement (Witherspoon, Speight, & Thomas, 1997), and ethnic identity and self-esteem (Goodstein & Ponterotto, 1997). During this time, as racial identity research began to grow in popularity, there was also growing concern about measurement issues. The first article regarding psychometric concerns was published in 1987 (Ponterotto & Wise, 1987). This was followed by several other articles in the 1990s (Tokar & Fischer, 1998; Yanico, Swanson, & Tokar, 1994). It should be noted that similar concerns were also being expressed about the measurement of White racial identity (Swanson, Tokar, & Davis, 1994; Tokar & Swanson, 1991). The conceptual underpinning of all these early empirical Black racial identity studies was Cross's (1971) Nigrescence model. In the late 1990s, an alternative model of racial identity was introduced (Sellers et al., 1997, 1998), with empirical studies soon following (e.g., Cokley, 1999; Rowley, Sellers, Chavous, & Smith, 1998).

A comprehensive review of the burgeoning literature after 2000 is beyond the scope of this chapter. Instead, we identify and describe selected studies to provide a representative snapshot of the types of studies currently being conducted that examine the various correlates of racial identity.

Mental Health

In a continuing search to find mental health correlates of racial identity, one study examined racial identity as a predictor of psychological defenses (Nghe & Mahalik, 2001). Using the RIAS–Brief Version (RIAS–B), the authors found that lower racial identity statuses (preencounter and encounter stages) were related to less healthy psychological defenses, whereas immersion was related to immature psychological defenses and emersion was related to mature psychological defenses.

As mentioned earlier, Carter (1991) examined whether racial identity attitudes were predictive of psychological functioning of African American students attending a predominantly White university and found that pre-encounter and immersion–emersion attitudes predicted negative psychological symptomatology. In a replication of the study at a historically Black university, Gilbert, So, Russell, and Wessel (2006) used the Black Racial Identity Attitude Scale (BRIAS; Helms, 1990) and found that racial identity attitudes were not predictive of psychological functioning. They concluded that racial identity may be predictive of psychological functioning for African Americans only when they are in the minority.

Revisiting the theme of racial identity, psychological distress, and psychological well-being, Franklin-Jackson and Carter (2007) examined both race-related stress and racial identity attitudes as predictors. Using the RIAS, they found that racial identity attitudes were stronger predictors of psychological distress and well-being than race-related stress. In another study, Banks and Kohn-Wood (2007) used the MIBI to examine the relations among mental health outcomes, discrimination, and racial identity profiles. They found that racial identity moderates the relation between depressive symptoms and discrimination.

Another aspect of racial identity research that is gaining momentum is the relation of racial identity to perceived discrimination. In one study, researchers using the MIBI found that racial centrality was related to perceived discrimination (Sellers & Shelton, 2003). They also found that racial ideology moderated the relationship between perceived discrimination and psychological distress.

The link between racial identity and internalized racialism also has been examined (Cokley, 2002). Cokley (2002) conducted the first published canonical correlation using the Cross Racial Identity Attitudes Scale (CRIS; Vandiver, Cross, Worrell, & Fhagen-Smith, 2002) and found that racial identity stages are more or less comparable to degrees of internalized racialism, which is the degree to which individuals internalize both negative and positive stereotypes about their race.

Over the past 2 to 3 years, research on psychological well-being, racial identity, and gender-related constructs with African Americans has increased. In one study, Carter, Williams, Juby, and Buckley (2005) used the long form of the BRIAS and found that racial identity "fully" mediated the relationship between gender role conflict and psychological symptoms in a sample of Black men. Specifically, they reported that immersion–emersion attitudes were the only racial identity attitudes that significantly predicted psychological symptoms (as measured by the Global Severity Index) "when the other variables were held constant" (p. 479). It should be mentioned that some questions remain about the authors' analysis, namely, that racial identity variables were kept in the analysis even though they did not meet the requirements for testing mediation (i.e., being related to the independent variable) because the authors "chose to keep them in the analysis for the subsequent procedure due to the exploratory nature of the study" (p. 479). Furthermore, the claim of full mediation appears to be doubtful, because no Sobel's test was reported and the reduction of beta to zero, which is required for a true full mediation, is not reported. Another study using the CRIS found that self-hatred racial identity attitudes partially mediated the relation between gender role conflict and psychological distress (Wester, Vogel, Wei, & McLain, 2006). Using the bootstrap approach to detect indirect effects, the authors found that pre-encounter self-hatred attitudes were the only racial identity attitudes that partially mediated the relationship between gender role conflict and psychological distress.

Academic

One aspect of racial identity research that has captured the imagination of researchers is the association of racial identity and academic achievement. An interesting study was published in 2003 that examined the relationship of racial identity scores (as measured by the BRIAS) and grade point average (Lockett & Harrell, 2003). The authors found that racial identity contributed minimally in the prediction of grades and that most of the little that racial identity did contribute was actually best explained by self-esteem. Another recent study found that racial identity (as measured by the CRIS) did not significantly contribute to the prediction of Verbal Graduate Record Examination scores or grades (Awad, 2007).

In a novel study that examined racial identity as a possible moderator of stereotype threat, Davis, Aronson, and Salinas (2006) found a significant interaction between racial identity attitudes and type of threat condition. Specifically, students in the low stereotype threat condition who were high in internalization attitudes correctly solved more Graduate Record Examination Verbal items than students who were lower in internalization attitudes.

Attitudes

A special issue of the *Journal of Black Psychology* examined the relationship of racial identity and drug attitudes (Belgrave, Brome, & Hampton, 2000; Burlew et al., 2000; Townsend & Belgrave, 2000). The conceptual foundation for these research studies appear to be a derivative of Cross's (1971) Nigrescence model. Collectively, the results showed only modest support for the link.

Racial identity has been examined as a predictor of attitudes toward affirmative action among African American students (Schmerund, Sellers, Mueller, & Crosby, 2001). Using the MIBI, Schmerund et al. (2001) found that race centrality, private regard, and oppressed minority status ideology were all significant predictors.

In a preliminary study, Pope-Davis, Liu, Ledesma-Jones, and Nevitt (2000) were the first researchers to examine the link between racial identity and African American enculturation (misnamed *acculturation* in their study). Using the RIAS–B, Pope-Davis et al. found that three of the RIAS subscales (Dissonance, Immersion, and Emersion) accounted for a significant amount (18%) of the variance of "acculturation" scores. In a follow-up study using the CRIS, Cokley and Helm (2007) found that pre-encounter assimilation, pre-encounter miseducation, pre-encounter self-hatred, immersion–emersion anti-White attitudes, and internalization Afrocentricity and three demographic variables predicted 26% of the variance of enculturation scores.

Psychometric Studies

Psychometric investigations have not been limited to the RIAS scales. As the MMRI slowly grew in popularity, the MIBI came under closer scrutiny. In the only psychometric study conducted independent of the creators of the scale, Cokley and Helm (2001) conducted a confirmatory factor analysis and found limited support for the structural validity of the scale, reporting an original comparative fit index value of .68 that only marginally improved to .71 with model respecification. Item analysis also revealed several conceptually problematic items. The strongest support for the scale was theoretically consistent correlations with the African Self-Consciousness Scale (Baldwin, 1996), which was evidence of concurrent validity.

The year 2002 produced perhaps the most rigorous racial identity validation study to date. Beverly Vandiver and a team of researchers published a comprehensive scale validity study involving the CRIS (Vandiver et al., 2002). Using both exploratory and confirmatory factor analysis (a combination lacking in most previous racial identity validation studies), Vandiver et al. demonstrated that the CRIS produces valid scores.

Within-Group Differences

As evidenced throughout this chapter, there is a vast body of literature suggesting that racial identity among African Americans is related to a variety of outcomes and topics of scientific inquiry. It stands to reason that one of the many psychological consequences of being Black is the development of a racial identity, the degree of which should vary with one's life experiences and social roles (Demo & Hughes, 1990). Several studies have examined the multidimensional construct of racial identity, investigating factors such as socialization, age, gender, and socioeconomic status. Thus, in discussing within-group differences, it is important to consider the ways in which research questions and statistical outcomes are explored because of the multifaceted nature of African American identity. Often, investigating within- and between-group differences are foundational to the quality and meaning of group comparisons (Lubke, Dolan, Kelderman, & Mellenbergh, 2003). Researchers often describe racial identity as a dichotomous construct (e.g., high or low, strong or weak), and they often overlook within-group heterogeneity. Examination of within-group differences allows for a more careful interpretation of individual differences within a group. For example, using data from a national sample of adult African Americans, Broman, Neighbors, and Jackson (1988) found that racial group identification is strongest among older Blacks and poorly educated Blacks in urban areas. Findings like the aforementioned reveal that factors such as age and status may have an impact on one's racial group identification and racial identity. Although the literature is replete with theoretical models that explore racial identity and related topics, research investigating within-group heterogeneity is still largely emerging. In the following sections, we discuss a brief sampling of research on within-group differences, or lack thereof, in four areas: (1) gender, (2) skin tone, (3) age, and (4) socialization.

Gender. A few within-group examinations of gender differences among adults do exist (e.g., Caldwell, Kohn-Wood, Schmeelk-Cone, Chavous, & Zimmerman, 2004; Cokley, 2001). Using the MIBI, Cokley (2001) found that there were no gender differences in the centrality of race; however, there were differences in how racial centrality related to academic variables. Racial identity played a more pivotal role in academic psychosocial development for females than males, as evidenced through significant correlations for females but not males. Cokley suggested that as African American males become increasingly disenchanted with the educational process, their racial identities become detached from academics.

In a study that examined racial discrimination and racial identity as risk or protective factors of violent behaviors in young African American adults, researchers used the MIBI to find that the safeguarding effects of racial identity were more salient for men than women (Caldwell et al., 2004). More specifically, there was an inverse relationship between racial centrality and engaging in violent behaviors. Males who exhibited low centrality of race were likely to engage in more violent behaviors, whereas violent behaviors were not associated with high centrality males.

Age. Yip, Seaton, and Sellers (2006) used the MIBI-S and the MEIM (Phinney, 1992) to examine racial identity across three periods of development: (1) adolescence (13–17 years), (2) young adulthood (18–23 years; college students), and (3) adulthood (27–78 years). The study provides evidence for Phinney's (1989) four theorized identity statuses (diffused, foreclosed, moratorium, and achieved). Briefly defined, the *diffused identity status* is characterized by one having neither explored the meaning of his or her ethnicity nor committed to an identity meaning. The *foreclosed identity status* describes one who has firmly committed to a definition of what ethnicity means to him or her without engaging in the exploration process. Individuals of *moratorium identity status* are described as actively exploring definitions of ethnicity yet not having committed to a specific definition. Finally, the *achieved identity status* refers to individuals who have actively explored and committed to a particular definition of what ethnicity means. Using Phinney's model of ethnic identity development and the MMRI as a framework, the authors reported that diffused young adults had higher depressive symptoms than achieved young adults. Furthermore, the researchers found that the foreclosed identity status was more prevalent in the adolescent group than the other developmental age groups.

In another study of racial identity attitudes across the lifespan, Plummer (1996) used the RIAS to explore Nigrescence in three life stages: (1) adolescence, (2) young adulthood, and (3) middle adulthood. Study participants ranged in age from 14 to 59. Of interest is that this study revealed that racial identity attitudes differed across each developmental stage. The pattern of results indicated that as individuals increased in age they were less likely to endorse immersion attitudes. Furthermore, adolescents and middle adults primarily endorsed internalization attitudes, whereas young adults endorsed encounter attitudes.

Skin Tone. Although to our knowledge not many studies have explored the relations between skin tone and racial identity, a few have explored skin tone in a variety of ways that relate to the construct of racial identity. Within-group variation exists not only in demographic factors, such as age and gender, but also in physical characteristics, such as skin tone. Myriad studies have indicated that, in earlier generations, Blacks with lighter skin tones tended to have higher status than Blacks with darker skin tones and that Blacks with darker skin tones incurred more difficulty attaining status in the Black community (Harvey, LaBeach, Pridgen, & Gocial, 2005; Keith & Herring, 1991; Landry, 1987). As Harvey et al. (2005) noted, "the degree to which African Americans' skin tone places them at the margin or the center of their group also has important implications for their identification with their racial group" (p. 240). Hence, this growing body of literature suggests that one's level of racial identification and racial identity attitudes is, to some degree, related to complexion.

In a study that examined the significance of skin color as it relates to life chances, mate selection, and Black consciousness, researchers found that skin color was related to several outcomes (Hughes & Hertel, 1990). Particularly relevant to this discussion are the findings concerning Black consciousness. Using several items from the National Survey of Black Americans, Hughes and Hertel (1990) found a weak yet significant correlation of skin color with Black identity and Black consciousness. Darker skin among women and older men was associated with a stronger Black identity. On the other hand, for younger males, lighter skin was associated with higher levels of Black identity. These findings reveal gender, age, and skin tone differences, thus illustrating the complexity and the heterogeneous nature of racial identity among Blacks.

Moreover, in a study of intragroup stigmatization Harvey et al. (2005) found that the salience of skin tone in the university setting was largely related to racial context—a historically

Black institution as compared with a predominantly White institution. The researchers measured racial identity by modifying the Multigroup Ethnic Identity Measure (Phinney, 1990) and substituting the word *race* for the term *ethnic group*. Although there are some conceptual and methodological problems with this, the results of this study revealed that darker skin tone was associated with higher levels of racial identity in both university settings. Moreover, skin tone and racial identity appeared to be more important in the predominately White university setting.

Socialization. Another important source of within-group variation that shapes one's level of racial identification is *familial socialization*. Studies suggest that the quality of familial interactions and societal exposure should be important determinants of Black racial identity. Researchers examining social structures and racial identity have found that primary parental messages concerning the meaning of being Black was an important factor of one's level of racial identification (Demo & Hughes, 1990; see also Chap. 19, this volume). They found that group identity is often shaped by the content of parental socialization. Blacks who experienced or grew up in homes that presented assertive messages about being Black tended to have stronger feelings of racial identity as compared with those who did not remember their parents telling them anything about being Black.

In summary, although it is promising that racial identity researchers are beginning to study within-group differences, much more work needs to be done in this area. Racial identity theories could benefit from considering more carefully differences within groups (e.g., age and gender) on the basis that exploring heterogeneity within groups provides a more tailored way of interpreting outcomes. Thus, the study of within-group differences has important implications for developing more concise and robust findings in racial identity research.

METHODOLOGICAL ISSUES

Given the popularity of racial identity research among students and professionals, it is important that attention be paid to methodological issues, with the ultimate goal being to improve the quality and influence of the research conducted. Broadly speaking, the challenges in this area of research involve methods (i.e., the tools used to conduct scientific investigations, e.g., instruments and surveys) and methodology (i.e., the principles that are used to determine how the tools are used and interpreted). Specifically, many methodological problems involve psychometrics and include the misuse, misapplication, or selective application of principles associated primarily with quantitative research. The major psychometric issues can be summarized under the following themes—factor structure, (b) internal consistency, and (c) skewed distributions—and the major research challenges include an excess of overly simplistic research questions that result in an underutilization of more sophisticated research methods and advanced statistical techniques such as mediation, moderation, path analysis, and structural equation modeling.

Measurement. Psychometric concerns about racial identity instruments have been a recurring theme in the literature. One of the earliest psychometric studies of a racial identity instrument noted problems with the measurement of encounter scores using the RIAS (Ponterotto & Wise, 1987). Specifically, a factor analysis derived a three-factor solution (i.e., Pre-Encounter, Immersion–Emersion, Internalization) that did not include the encounter stage. Furthermore, Cronbach's alpha for the Encounter subscale was a lowly .37, and the three-factor solution accounted for only 23.3% of the total variance. The authors suggested that "encounter attitudes are difficult to conceptualize and measure" (p. 222) and recommended that serious modification of the scale should take place.

In another psychometric investigation, a factor analysis again revealed support for a three-factor solution that accounted for only 20.1% of the total variance and did not include the Encounter subscale, which had a Cronbach's alpha of .47 (Yanico et al., 1994). As a result, the authors recommended that use of the Encounter subscale be discontinued. Furthermore, the authors noted that the distributions of scores on the Pre-Encounter subscale were positively skewed (i.e., low item endorsement) and were negatively skewed (i.e., high item endorsement) for the Internalization subscale. These results were consistent with previous studies (Parham

& Helms, 1981; Ponterotto et al., 1986) and are consistent with more recent studies using the RIAS (Carter et al., 2005; Johnson & Arbona, 2006). As a result of skewed distributions, Yanico et al. (1994) stated the following: "In interpreting previous studies, it is essential to understand that respondents with 'high Preencounter scores' did not necessarily agree with Preencounter items; they simply disagreed less with Preencounter items than did other participants" (p. 231). The authors followed up by speculating that causes of the skewed distributions may be because college students in the samples do not truly have pre-encounter attitudes. The authors also cited Ponterotto's (1989) suggestion that the RIAS may be anachronistic in its language and that the language may be too obvious to capture the subtleties of pre-encounter racial attitudes.

In yet another psychometric study of the RIAS, Tokar and Fischer (1998) conducted a confirmatory factor analysis on the newest version of the RIAS–L (long form) and found that a four-factor model was a poor fit to the data. Instead, consistent with previous studies, they found that a three-factor solution (excluding the Encounter subscale, which had a Cronbach's alpha of .34) provided a better fit to the data. They also found evidence of extreme positive skewness for the Pre-Encounter subscale and extreme negative skewness for the Internalization subscale. This same team of researchers also found mixed evidence for the convergent and discriminant validity of the RIAS–L (Fischer, Tokar, & Serna, 1998). They also found evidence that social desirability adversely affects Pre-Encounter subscale scores.

Beyond psychometric concerns, there are additional concerns about simplistic research questions that lead to the underutilization of more advanced statistical techniques such as tests of mediation and moderation, path analysis, and structural equation modeling. The use of these techniques is usually evidence that an area of research has reached a certain level of theoretical maturity and sophistication (Frazier, Tix, & Barron, 2004). Outside of psychometric studies, which use primarily exploratory and confirmatory factor analyses, the majority of racial identity research (using the RIAS or CRIS) uses correlations and regressions, with the occasional canonical correlation, profile, and cluster analysis. Psychometric studies aside, the majority of research using the MIBI uses correlations, tests of moderation, and cluster analysis. Because the MIBI was developed by social psychologists, there is more emphasis on trying to determine causality through research design than research conducted using the RIAS or CRIS, which tends to be correlational in nature. In addition, research conducted using the RIAS is often described as "exploratory" or "preliminary," with researchers often exploring relationships with variables that do not appear to have a strong theoretical foundation for doing so. As the body of racial identity literature grows, so too does the expectation that researchers will be guided by theory and increasingly employ more sophisticated statistical techniques and research designs to answer questions that establish racial identity in a larger nomological network of relationships (Cokley, 2005).

Trends, Debates, and Future Directions

The racial identity literature, more than any other topical area within African American Psychology, arguably has generated among the most intense criticism and debate. The criticisms and debates can be characterized as ideological, methodological, and theoretical in nature, and usually a combination of all three. The exact contribution of each is virtually impossible to determine and probably is in the eye of the beholder.

Among the most pointed theoretical criticisms has been that of Afrocentric psychologists. Azibo and Robinson (2004) argued that racial identity as conceptualized using the Nigrescence model is an abnormal process. Specifically, they argued that what is supposed to be the advanced stage of racial identity (i.e., internalization) is nothing more than a "sophisticated regression to a 'deracinated,' psychologically misoriented orientation" (p. 249). In short, they believe that individuals who hold internalization attitudes are still "Negroes" who happen to be more sophisticated but who still do not prioritize the defense and promotion of African life and culture. Other criticisms by Afrocentric psychologists, such as Nobles (1989) and Akbar (1989), focus on the reactionary and non-Afrocentric basis of Nigrescence theory.

Methodological and ideological tensions led to the recently published special section in the *Journal of Counseling Psychology* titled "Conceptual and Methodological Issues in the Study of Race and Ethnicity." In one of the lead articles, Cokley (2007) argued that the study of racial identity has been slowed by ideologically driven adherence to psychometrically problematic instruments. He specifically drew attention to the RIAS and challenged attempts to defend the instrument that employ what he believes to be dubious logic about internal consistency regarding Cronbach's alpha. In the other lead article, Helms (2007) argued that researchers have used poor practices when conducting research with racial identity scales. She argued, among other things, that Cronbach's alpha was not intended to measure the reliability of a multidimensional measure, that in most cases it is the wrong statistic to use, and that a low alpha might, in some cases, be attributed to an "aberrant" sample.

Conclusion

Theoretical and psychometric debates indicate that interest in racial identity continues to remain as high as ever. This review supports the belief that, in spite of the limitations of racial identity research, it most likely will continue to remain popular among researchers, especially African American researchers. We believe that racial identity research has reached a level of maturity that warrants more sophisticated research questions that will require the use of more sophisticated statistical analyses and research designs. Descriptive and correlational studies are important and have their place; however, as Frazier et al. (2004) pointed out, it is important to move beyond basic correlational and even causal questions to questions that address the conditions under which relationships exist or why relationships exist (e.g., moderator and mediator effects). For example, are there conditions under which certain racial identity attitudes or ideologies may be positively or negatively related to mental health or educational outcomes? Do specific racial identity attitudes explain relationships between other variables? In addition, it is important that researchers judiciously use racial identity theory to guide all hypotheses regarding the linkages between racial identity and other psychological constructs, as required by path analysis and structural equation modeling. As racial identity research continues to capture and maintain the interest of researchers, it is our ultimate hope that future research will result in therapeutic and educational interventions that prove to be efficacious in the lives of clients and students with whom we work.

References

Akbar, N. (1989). Nigrescence and identity: Some limitations. *The Counseling Psychologist, 17,* 258–263.

Awad, G. (2007). The role of racial identity, academic self-concept, and self-esteem in the prediction of academic outcomes for African American students. *Journal of Black Psychology, 33,* 188–207.

Azibo, D. A., & Robinson, J. (2004). An empirically supported reconceptualization of African–U.S. racial identity development as an abnormal process. *Review of General Psychology, 8,* 249–264.

Baldwin, J. A. (1996). An introduction to the African Self-Consciousness Scale. In R. Jones (Ed.), *Handbook of test and measurements for Black populations* (pp. 207–215). Berkeley, CA: Cobb & Henry.

Banks, K. H., & Kohn-Wood, L. P. (2007). The influence of racial identity profiles on the relationship between racial discrimination and depressive symptoms. *Journal of Black Psychology, 33,* 331–354.

Belgrave, F. Z., Brome, D. R., & Hampton, C. (2000). The contribution of Afrocentric values and racial identity to the prediction of drug knowledge, attitudes, and use among African American youth. *Journal of Black Psychology, 26,* 386–401.

Broman, C., Neighbors, H. W., & Jackson, J. S. (1988). Racial group identification among Black adults. *Social Forces, 67,* 146–158.

Brookins, C. C. (1994). The relationship between Afrocentric values and racial identity attitudes: Validation of the Belief Systems Analysis Scale on African American college students. *Journal of Black Psychology, 20,* 128–142.

Brookins, C. C., Anyabwile, T. M., & Nacoste, R. (1996). Exploring the links between racial identity attitudes and psychological feelings of closeness in African American college students. *Journal of Applied Social Psychology, 26,* 243–264.

Burlew, K., Neely, D., Johnson, C., Hucks, T., Purnell, B., Butler, J., et al. (2000). Drug attitudes, racial identity, and alcohol use among African American adolescents. *Journal of Black Psychology, 26,* 402–420.

Caldwell, C.-H., Kohn-Wood, L.-P., Schmeelk-Cone, K.-H., Chavous, T.-M., & Zimmerman, M.-A. (2004). Racial discrimination and racial identity as risk or protective factors for violent behaviors in African American young adults. *American Journal of Community Psychology, 33,* 91–105.

Carter, R. T. (1991). Racial identity attitudes and psychological functioning. *Journal of Multicultural Counseling and Development, 19,* 105–114.

Carter, R. T., Williams, B., Juby, H. L., & Buckley, T. R. (2005). Racial identity as mediator of the relationship between gender role conflict and severity of psychological symptoms in Black, Latino, and Asian men. *Sex Roles, 53,* 473–486.

Cokley, K. (1999). Reconceptualizing the impact of college racial composition on African American students' racial identity. *Journal of College Student Development, 40,* 235–245.

Cokley, K. O. (2001). Gender differences among African American students in the impact of racial identity on academic psychosocial development. *Journal of College Student Development, 42,* 480–487.

Cokley, K. O. (2002). Testing Cross's revised racial identity model: An examination of the relationship between racial identity and internalized racialism. *Journal of Counseling Psychology, 49,* 476–483.

Cokley, K. O. (2005). Racial(ized) identity, ethnic identity, and Afrocentric values: Conceptual and methodological challenges in understanding African American identity. *Journal of Counseling Psychology, 52,* 517–526.

Cokley, K. O. (2007). Critical issues in the measurement of ethnic and racial identity: A referendum on the state of the field. *Journal of Counseling Psychology, 54,* 224–234.

Cokley, K. O., & Helm, K. (2001). Testing the construct validity of scores on the Multidimensional Inventory of Black Identity. *Measurement and Evaluation in Counseling and Development, 34,* 80–95.

Cokley, K. O., & Helm, K. (2007). The relationship between African American enculturation and racial identity, *Journal of Multicultural Counseling and Development, 35,* 142–153.

Cross, W. E., Jr. (1971). The Negro-to-Black conversion experience. *Black World, 20,* 13–27.

Cross, W. E., Jr. (1991). *Shades of black: Diversity in African-American identity.* Philadelphia: Temple University Press.

Cross, W. E., Jr. (1995). The psychology of Nigrescence: Revising the Cross model. In J. Ponterotto, J. M. Casas, L. A. Suzuki, & C. M. Alexander (Eds.), *Handbook of multicultural counseling* (pp. 93–122). Thousand Oaks, CA: Sage.

Cross, W. E., & Vandiver, B. J. (2001). Nigrescence theory and measurement: Introducing the Cross Racial Identity Scale (CRIS). In J. Ponterotto, J. M. Casas, L. A. Suzuki, & C. M. Alexander (Ed.), *Handbook of multicultural counseling* (2nd ed., pp. 371–393). Thousand Oaks, CA: Sage.

Davis, C., III, Aronson, J., & Salinas, M. (2006). Shades of threat: Racial identity as a moderator of stereotype threat. *Journal of Black Psychology, 32,* 399–417.

Demo, D.-H., & Hughes, M. (1990). Socialization and racial identity among Black Americans. *Social Psychology Quarterly, 53,* 364–374.

Du Bois, W. E. B. (1903). *The souls of Black folks.* New York: Signet Classic.

Fischer, A. R., Tokar, D. M., & Serna, G. S. (1998). Validity and construct contamination of the Racial Identity Attitude Scale–Long Form. *Journal of Counseling Psychology, 45,* 212–224.

Franklin-Jackson, D., & Carter, R. T. (2007). The relationships between race-related stress, racial identity, and mental health for Black Americans. *Journal of Black Psychology, 33,* 5–26.

Frazier, P. A., Tix, A. P., & Barron, K. E. (2004). Testing moderator and mediator effects in counseling psychology research. *Journal of Counseling Psychology, 51,* 115–134.

Gilbert, S. C., So, D., Russell, T. M., & Wessel, T. R. (2006). Racial identity and psychological symptoms among African Americans attending a historically Black university. *Journal of College Counseling, 9,* 111–122.

Goodstein, R., & Ponterotto, J. G. (1997). Racial and ethnic identity: Their relationship and their contribution to self-esteem. *Journal of Black Psychology, 23,* 275–292.

Harvey, R. D., LaBeach, N., Pridgen, E., & Gocial, T. M. (2005). The intragroup stigmatization of skin tone among Black Americans. *Journal of Black Psychology, 31,* 237–253.

Helms, J. E. (1986). Expanding racial identity theory to cover counseling process. *Journal of Counseling Psychology, 33,* 62–64.

Helms, J. E. (1990). *Black and White racial identity: Theory, research, and practice.* Westport, CT: Greenwood Press.

Helms, J. E. (1996). Toward a methodology for assessing "racial identity" as distinguished from "ethnic identity." In G. R. Sodowsky & J. C. Impara (Eds.), *Multicultural assessment in counseling and clinical psychology* (pp. 143–192). Lincoln, NE: Buros Institute of Mental Measurement.

Helms, J. E. (2007). Some better practices for measuring racial and ethnic identity constructs. *Journal of Counseling Psychology, 54,* 235–246.

Helms, J. E., & Cook, D. A. (1999). *Using race and culture in counseling and psychotherapy: Theory and process.* Needham Heights, MA: Allyn & Bacon.

Holloway, J. E. (1990). *Africanisms in American culture.* Bloomington: Indiana University Press.

Hughes, M., & Hertel, B. R. (1990). The significance of color remains: A study of life chances, mate selection, and ethnic consciousness among Black Americans. *Social Forces, 68,* 1105-1120.

Jackson, B. W., III. (1976). Black identity development. In L. H. P. Golubchick (Ed.), *Urban, social, and educational issues* (pp. 158–164). Dubuque, IA: Kendall/Hunt.

Jackson, B. W., III. (2001). Black identity development: Further analysis and elaboration. In C. L. J. I. Wijeyesinghe (Ed.), *New perspectives on racial identity development: A theoretical and practical anthology* (pp. 8–31). New York: New York University Press.

Johnson, S. C., & Arbona, C. (2006). The relation of ethnic identity, racial identity, and race-related stress among African American college students. *Journal of College Student Development, 47,* 495–507.

Keith, V.-M., & Herring, C. (1991). Skin tone and stratification in the Black community. *American Journal of Sociology, 97,* 760–778.

Landry, B. (1987). *The new Black middle class.* Berkeley and Los Angeles: University of California Press.

Lockett, C. T., & Harrell, J. P. (2003). Racial identity, self-esteem, and academic achievement: Too much interpretation, too little supporting data. *Journal of Black Psychology, 29,* 325–336.

Lubke, G.-H., Dolan, C.-V., Kelderman, H., & Mellenbergh, G.-J. (2003). On the relationship between sources of within- and between-group differences and measurement invariance in the common factor model. *Intelligence, 31,* 543–566.

Nghe, L. T., & Mahalik, J. R. (2001). Examining racial identity statuses as predictors of psychological defenses in African American college students. *Journal of Counseling Psychology, 48,* 10–16.

Nobles, W. (1989). Psychological Nigrescence: An Afrocentric review. *The Counseling Psychologist, 17,* 253–257.

Parham, T. A. (1989). Cycles of psychological Nigrescence. *The Counseling Psychologist, 17,* 187–226.

Parham, T. A., & Helms, J. E. (1981). The influence of Black students' racial identity attitudes on preferences for counselor's race. *Journal of Counseling Psychology, 28,* 250–257.

Parham, T. A., & Helms, J. E. (1985a). Attitudes of racial identity and self-esteem of Black students: An exploratory investigation. *Journal of College Student Personnel, 26,* 143–147.

Parham, T. A., & Helms, J. E. (1985b). Relation of racial identity attitudes to self-actualization and affective states of Black students. *Journal of Counseling Psychology, 32,* 431–440.

Phinney, J. S. (1989). Stages of ethnic identity in minority group adolescents. *Journal of Early Adolescence, 9,* 34–49.

Phinney, J. S. (1990). Ethnic identity in adolescents and adults: Review of research. *Psychological Bulletin, 108,* 499–514.

Phinney, J. S. (1992). The Multigroup Ethnic Identity Measure: A new scale for use with diverse groups. *Journal of Adolescent Research, 7,* 156–176.

Plummer, D.-L. (1996). Black racial identity attitudes and stages of the life span: An exploratory investigation. *Journal of Black Psychology, 22,* 169–181.

Ponterotto, J. G. (1989). Expanding directions for racial identity research. *The Counseling Psychologist, 17,* 264–272.

Ponterotto, J. G., Anderson, W. H., & Grieger, I. Z. (1986). Black students' attitudes toward counseling as a function of racial identity. *Journal of Multicultural Counseling and Development, 14,* 50–59.

Ponterotto, J. G., & Wise, S. L. (1987). Construct validity study of the Racial Identity Attitude Scale. *Journal of Counseling Psychology, 34,* 218–223.

Pope-Davis, D. B., Liu, W. M., Ledesma-Jones, S., & Nevitt, J. (2000). African American acculturation and Black racial identity: A preliminary investigation. *Journal of Multicultural Counseling and Development, 28,* 98–112.

Rowley, S. J., Sellers, R. M., Chavous, T. M., & Smith, M. A. (1998). The relationship between racial identity and self-esteem in African American college and high school students. *Journal of Personality and Social Psychology, 74,* 715–724.

Schmerund, A., Sellers, R., Mueller, B., & Crosby, F. (2001). Attitudes toward affirmative action as a function of racial identity among African American college students. *Political Psychology, 22,* 759–774.

Sellers, R. M., Rowley, S. A., Chavous, T. M., Shelton, J., & Smith, M. A. (1997). Multidimensional Inventory of Black Identity: A preliminary investigation of reliability and construct validity. *Journal of Personality and Social Psychology, 73,* 805–815.

Sellers, R. M., & Shelton, J. (2003). The role of racial identity in perceived racial discrimination. *Journal of Personality and Social Psychology, 84,* 1079–1092.

Sellers, R. M., Smith, M. A., Shelton, J., Rowley, S. A., & Chavous, T. M. (1998). Multidimensional model of racial identity: A reconceptualization of African American racial identity. *Personality and Social Psychology Review 2,* 18–39.

Speight, S. L., Vera, E. M., & Derrickson, K. B. (1996). Racial self-designation, racial identity, and self-esteem revisited. *Journal of Black Psychology, 22,* 37–52.

Swanson, J. L., Tokar, D. M., & Davis, L. E. (1994). Content and construct validity of the White Racial Identity Attitude Scale. *Journal of Vocational Behavior, 44,* 198–217.

Thomas, C. W. (1969). Boys no more: Some social psychological aspects of the new Black ethic. *American Behavioral Scientist, 12,* 38–42.

Thomas, C. W. (1970). Different strokes for different folks. *Psychology Today, 4,* 48–53.

Thomas, C. W. (1971). *Boys no more: A Black psychologist's view of community.* Beverly Hills, CA: Glencoe.

Tokar, D. M., & Fischer, A. R. (1998). Psychometric analysis of the Racial Identity Attitude Scale—Long Form. *Measurement and Evaluation in Counseling and Development, 31,* 138–149.

Tokar, D. M., & Swanson, J. L. (1991). An investigation of the validity of Helms's (1984) model of White racial identity development. *Journal of Counseling Psychology, 38,* 296–301.

Townsend, T. G., & Belgrave, F. Z. (2000). The impact of personal identity and racial identity on drug attitudes and use among African American children. *Journal of Black Psychology, 26,* 421–436.

Vandiver, B. J., Cross, W. E., Jr., Worrell, F. C., & Fhagen-Smith, P. E. (2002). Validating the Cross Racial Identity Scale. *Journal of Counseling Psychology, 49,* 71–85.

Wester, S. R., Vogel, D. L., Wei, M., & McLain, R. (2006). African American men, gender role conflict, and psychological distress: The role of racial identity. *Journal of Counseling & Development, 84,* 419–429.

Witherspoon, K. M., Speight, S. L., & Thomas, A. J. (1997). Racial identity attitudes, school achievement, and academic self-efficacy among African American high school students. *Journal of Black Psychology, 23,* 344–357.

Yanico, B. J., Swanson, J. L., & Tokar, D. M. (1994). A psychometric investigation of the Black Racial Identity Attitude Scale–Form B. *Journal of Vocational Behavior, 44,* 218–234.

Yip, T., Seaton, E.-K., & Sellers, R.-M. (2006). African American racial identity across the lifespan: Identity status, identity content, and depressive symptoms. *Child Development, 77,* 1504–1517.

22

CULTURAL MISTRUST

A Core Component of African American Consciousness

FRANCIS TERRELL, JEROME TAYLOR,
JEFFERY MENZISE, AND RONALD K. BARRETT

Unique to people of African descent is that, for the most part, this ethnic group was transported to the United States against their will, enslaved, and treated brutally by a dominant culture once they arrived. This mistreatment continues to the present. These people of African descent brought with them their own language; food preferences; dress styles; musical preferences; and other values, customs, and traditions. For many of them, these customs continue to be prominent. In addition, as a result of being discriminated against by Whites, African Americans began to develop beliefs about Whites and what they perceived to be essential behaviors for them to survive and thrive in U.S. society. For more than 2 decades, researchers have argued that the study of African Americans would be incomplete if one did not take into consideration the tendency of this ethnic group to mistrust Whites (Harrell & Harris, 1984; Whaley, 1997, 1998, 2002). One belief is that Whites could not be trusted. We refer to this belief as *cultural mistrust*. In this chapter,[1] we describe the etiology, some issues regarding cultural mistrust, the results of research, some practical implications based on these findings, and some suggested directions for additional inquiry into what seems to be this common tendency among many African Americans not to trust Whites.

DEFINITION OF *CULTURAL MISTRUST*

Blacks who do not trust Whites tend to avoid sharing information with them, avoid interacting with them, and are apprehensive when asked to share information with them for fear of being betrayed or exploited. Some, but not all Blacks, have not been treated as badly as others. Therefore, as in the past, not all Blacks mistrust Whites to the same extent. Those who are more trusting of Whites tend to be more willing to interact with them as well as to share their thoughts and feelings with Whites. In contrast, cultural mistrust is the belief acquired by African Americans, due to past and ongoing mistreatment related to being a member of that ethnic group, that Whites cannot be trusted. Blacks have endured a pattern of deception and mistreatment throughout the history of their presence in the United States. As a result of racism, the tendency of Blacks to mistrust Whites now seems to be deeply embedded in their psyche and has become a part of their culture. Perhaps the status of the extent to which Blacks mistrust Whites and White-related institutions can best be summarized by a statement by a Black client. In a moment of frustration with the quality of mental health services he was receiving from White therapists, this client spontaneously blurted out: "I don't even trust these White people enough to tell them that I don't trust them."

Evolution of the Tendency of Blacks Not to Trust Whites

It has long been recognized that the way a person behaves toward others is, to some extent, a function of whether they trust the other person, organization, or institution. When an individual does not trust others, that individual may not share accurate information, avoid interacting with those he or she does not trust, and engage in a wide array of behaviors designed to avoid being exploited. Extensive empirical data indicate that Blacks do not trust Whites, and this belief influences how they behave in a number of different situations (Lightsey & Barnes, 2007; F. Terrell, Terrell, & Nickerson, 1996).

The tendency of Blacks to not trust Whites in the United States can be traced back to the institution of chattel slavery when, for survival purposes, Blacks gravitated toward not trusting Whites, White-oriented establishments, and people of any race who seemed to have adopted a White-oriented ideology. This tendency could be seen by the use of codes among Blacks in their songs, the language they used, and even the content of what they taught their children. Thus, children were taught religious songs that oftentimes contained disguised messages, words that had subtle meanings, or to become noncommunicative in some social situations. In other instances, Blacks were taught to not share information with Whites about their financial and other assets, and they were admonished to be extremely cautious in the presence of legal authorities.

Over time, spokespersons acceptable to the Black community have addressed this issue. Dick Gregory (1971), the comedian turned activist, pointed this out in his speeches and writings. Indeed, it is not often realized that in Martin Luther King Jr.'s famous speech during the March on Washington (i.e., the "I Have a Dream" speech), he made as the centerpiece of his message that Blacks had been given a promissory note that had never been honored by American society. Although subtle, this statement clearly implied that from the foundation of this nation up to that point, Whites could not be trusted to keep their commitments.

Perhaps the first scholarly attempt to examine this tendency was made by two Harvard psychiatrists, Grier and Cobbs (1968), who referred to this tendency as *cultural paranoia*. These authors used numerous examples and case studies to demonstrate the tendency of Blacks to mistrust Whites in a variety of areas of their lives. The systematic study of the extent to which Blacks mistrust Whites and the impact that it has on the behavior of Blacks began in the late 1970s and began to accelerate in the 1980s (F. Terrell & Terrell, 1981, 1984).

Controversies Related to Cultural Mistrust

Early in the efforts to explore the tendency of Blacks to mistrust Whites, at least two issues emerged. The first focused on what terminology would be most appropriate. Other researchers have used terms similar to Grier and Cobbs's (1968) *cultural paranoia*, including *mild paranoia*. As we were formulating our own thoughts about the appropriate terminology for this construct, our immediate reaction to the use of terms like *paranoia* was that other cultural groups had already coined a plethora of pathological terms to explain a wide range of behaviors commonly seen among Blacks and that this community did not need anymore of these condescending labels. We therefore rejected *paranoia* and other terms that imply pathology. Blacks' view that Whites cannot be trusted is in many instances not based on a false belief. Instead, this perception is often based on actual direct and indirect experiences. We continue to vigorously oppose the use of words that suggest that Blacks' tendency to mistrust Whites is indicative of a delusional disorder or any other form of mental illness (see Whaley, 2001, 2002).

In addition to the debate regarding appropriate terminology, another, somewhat related controversy has centered on whether the tendency to mistrust Whites is indicative of a delusion or some form of mental illness. If the use of words connoting pathology is inappropriate, and the Black mistrust of Whites is actually a manifestation of an acquired tendency based on experience, then it follows that individuals who have been discriminated against should be more mistrustful of Whites.

Whether the mistrust by Blacks of Whites is acquired through exposure to racial discrimination is an empirical question. Several studies have examined this hypothesis. Phelps, Taylor, and Gerard (2001) administered the Cultural Mistrust Inventory (F. Terrell & Terrell, 1981) to African American, West Indian, and Caribbean college students. African Americans had significantly higher mistrust scores than either of the other two groups. Other studies have produced similar findings. Combs et al. (2006), for example, examined the relations between perceived racism and a variety of indexes of mistrust among African American college students. Racism was found to be related to cultural mistrust but not clinical paranoia.

Conceptual Models of Cultural Mistrust

Theory is essential to guiding inquiry into the merits of any construct. Several theories regarding the cause of cultural mistrust and how it can best be conceptualized have been proposed. Among the earliest theorists to propose that mistrust was a component of Black consciousness were Jerome Taylor and his colleagues. Taylor and Brown (1984) argued that Blacks do not enter this life with an inherent predisposition to mistrust Whites; instead, this apprehension of Whites originates from previous experiences with Whites. Thus, being African American almost implies that many, but not all, Blacks will be discriminated against and acquire a mistrust of Whites. These authors then suggested that the extent to which Blacks mistrust Whites can be altered by eliminating racial discrimination in U.S. society. F. Terrell and Terrell, (1996, 1999) agree with Taylor and Brown. They also suggested that the tendency of Blacks to be suspicious of Whites has its origins in being discriminated against by, or observing other Blacks being subjected to racial discrimination by, White individuals, organizations, or institutions. Furthermore, because this belief is acquired, and because Black children are often discriminated against in their schools and other contexts, this mistrust can often be seen in very young African American children.

Adopting another perspective, Neville and Mobley (2001) suggested that cultural mistrust can be conceptualized using what they refer to as an *ecological model*. They proposed that there is an ongoing interaction between the effects the environment has on the individual and, in turn, the effects of a person's response to a particular situation. Therefore, they proposed that one must be familiar with a person's culture before one is able to fully understand that person's behavior. Within this ecological model, they proposed a macrosystem. They suggested that a person's experience within a broad situation influences that person's behavior in more specific situations. Using this reasoning, Neville and Mobley suggested that, because racism is so pervasive, the tendency of Blacks to mistrust Whites is so common that it should be considered a part of the African American culture. These "mistrust" models are complementary; that is, it seems as if the mistrust of Whites by Blacks may be acquired as a result of previous experience, as suggested by Taylor and Brown (1984); is related to being mistreated and deceived in a variety of different situations, as proposed by F. Terrell and Terrell (1999); and is a major component of the Black experience, or what is also often referred to as *Black consciousness*, as has been suggested in the combined ecological approach (Neville & Mobley, 2001).

Measurement of Cultural Mistrust

If a credible effort is to be made to study the existence and extent to which Blacks mistrust Whites (or any construct, for that matter), a psychometrically sound method for measuring that construct must first be devised. Several measures of mistrust among Blacks exist (Landrine & Klonoff, 1994; LaVesit, Nickerson, & Bowie, 2000; F. Terrell & Terrell, 1981). Landrine and Klonoff's (1994) measure of cultural mistrust consists of items derived primarily from the Cultural Mistrust Inventory (CMI; F. Terrell & Terrell, 1981) and is part of an inventory designed to measure the extent to which Blacks identify with their culture. To the best of our knowledge, that set of items has been used only by the authors of that inventory. The measure of mistrust developed by LaVesit et al. (2000) was designed for the limited purpose of measuring the extent to which Blacks mistrust Whites in medical settings. Like the items used by Landrine and Klonoff, to the best of our knowledge, this measure has been used only on a limited basis by LaVesit et al.

The oldest, most comprehensive, and commonly used measure is the CMI. In the process constructing of this instrument, considerable care was taken to create a measure that would provide a global indication of the extent to which Blacks mistrust Whites as well as estimates of the extent to which Blacks seemed to mistrust Whites in four relatively specific areas: (1) Education and Training settings, (2) Interpersonal Relations, (3) Business and Work situations, and (4) Politics and Law.

Although standard scale construction methods were used to develop the CMI, this inventory was not factor analyzed at the time it was published. Whaley (2002) conducted a factor analytic study of the CMI using a sample of Black inpatient men in a mental hospital located in the Northeast. Overall, as expected, the items of the four scales did load most heavily on their own scale. Clark (2003) also factor analyzed the CMI using a sample of Black college students residing in the South. In addition to high intratest reliability scores, a general factor, as well as four factors consistent with the four subscales of the CMI, was extracted. Bell and Tracey (2006) administered the CMI as well as a measure of self-efficacy and outcome expectations to African American students attending a large, predominately White, state university located in the Midwest. Through confirmatory factor analysis, the subscales of the CMI were confirmed. Bell and Tracey also found significant positive correlations between moderately high CMI scores and measures of levels of self-efficacy, academic adjustment, social adjustment, and personal–emotional adjustment.

Meta-analysis can also be used to explore the validity of assessment instruments. Whaley (2001) compared the findings of more than 20 independent studies that had used the CMI and different behaviors among Blacks. He found four factors consistent with the subscales of the CMI and determined that total score on the CMI was a good predictor of the behavior of Blacks in general. Other studies further support the construct validity of the CMI as well as suggest some practical implications for working with Blacks. Lee (2003) noted that the gap between the proportion of African Americans and Whites who obtained bachelor's degrees has continued to increase. He speculated that one of the reasons Blacks did not complete college as often as Whites was because of a mistrust of Whites to provide them with appropriate guidance while receiving their education. To explore this hypothesis, Black students were administered the CMI, a measure of university alienation, and a measure of academic self-efficacy. Black students with higher CMI scores tended to have higher feelings of alienation and were less willing to seek academic help. The reliability and validity of the CMI has also been independently evaluated by others (e.g., Mosley, Treed, Bullard, & Gold, 2007; Sabnani & Ponterotto, 1992). Collectively, these studies not only support the construct validity of the CMI but also indicate that the mistrust of Whites by Blacks exists in different regions of the country and is found among Blacks of different educational levels.

Group Correlates of Cultural Mistrust

Gender and Cultural Mistrust

If mistrust of Whites is related to membership in a specific cultural group, then this tendency should be found among both genders. Several studies have found that cultural mistrust exists among both Black males and females, and this belief in turn is related to a variety of behaviors. Fyffe (2000) examined the effects of different levels of cultural mistrust on Black college women's perceptions of racially similar versus dissimilar counseling dyads. After completing the CMI, participants watched one of eight videotapes of counseling sessions containing racially sensitive versus nonsensitive sessions. Black women with a low level of cultural mistrust perceived counselors in a nonracially sensitive context as being trustworthy. In contrast, highly mistrustful women did not perceive White counselors as being trustworthy in either the racially sensitive or nonsensitive situations. Similarly, Wright (2004) found that African American college women with higher levels of cultural mistrust tended to share beliefs and engage in behaviors commonly seen among African Americans. Furthermore, participants with higher levels of cultural mistrust, as assessed by the CMI, did not report a higher level of psychological and physical distress than those with lower levels of cultural mistrust scores. Cultural mistrust does not indicate the presence of a manifestation of mental illness.

Cultural mistrust has also been found to exist among Black males. Research highlights the link between cultural mistrust and help-seeking behaviors (e.g., L. D. Scott & Davis, 2006). For example, Nickerson, Helms, and Terrell (1994) explored the relations among distrust of Whites, opinions about mental illness, and help-seeking attitudes among Black male college students. Greater mistrust of Whites was associated with more negative general attitudes about seeking help from clinics staffed primarily by Whites. Their results also revealed that participants with higher mistrust scores believed that the services rendered by White counselors would be less satisfactory.

Socioeconomic Level and Cultural Mistrust

It is often assumed that there are more differences in beliefs and values between upper and lower socioeconomic groups, regardless of ethnicity, than there are differences between Blacks and Whites. Although this may be an accurate assumption regarding some variables, cultural mistrust seems to be found among Blacks regardless of their socioeconomic and educational levels. Duncan (2003) explored the association among age, socioeconomic status, cultural mistrust, Afrocentricity, and attitudes about seeking psychological help among a sample of Black male college students. He found that individuals with higher levels of cultural mistrust as well as higher levels of Afrocentricity tended to have more negative attitudes about seeking counseling. He did not report any significant differences in cultural mistrust levels as a function of socioeconomic levels.

CULTURAL MISTRUST IN HEALTH SETTINGS

Cultural Mistrust in Mental Health Settings

By far, the most extensive study of cultural mistrust in the mental health field has consisted of exploring whether the extent to which Blacks mistrust Whites is related to their perceptions of mental health system and their willingness to seek services. An ongoing problem confronted by mental health professionals consists of motivating Blacks to seek and remain in treatment. Earlier in this chapter, we speculated that one possible reason for this lack of participation in the mental health system might be that Blacks mistrust the mental health system or those assumed to be in charge of it.

General research suggests that Blacks who mistrust Whites and were seen by a White mental health professional had the lowest probability of remaining in treatment (F. Terrell & Terrell, 1984), seeking mental health services (Watkins & Terrell, 1988), and believing that they would benefit from treatment (Watkins, Terrell, Miller, & Terrell, 1989). Following these initial findings, numerous studies were conducted by other investigators with different samples from other geographical regions. Gardiner (2005), for example, explored the association between cultural mistrust and counselor preference. The CMI was administered to Black college students attending a historically Black college. A significant relation was found between cultural mistrust and preference for a Black counselor (e.g., Townes, 2003). In an early study, Poston, Craine, and Atkinson (1991) asked Black adults using services at an African American community center to first read bogus resumés and letters of application for vacancies open at the center. Participants then completed the CMI, the Counselor Effectiveness Rating Scale, and a self-disclosure scale that measured the extent to which respondents were willing to share their thoughts and feelings with a White counselor. Participants with high mistrust levels reported significantly less willingness to disclose to White counselors. Almost all of the studies that have explored the relations between cultural mistrust and attitudes toward the counseling setting have used an analogue design. It may be that findings from these simulated studies may not completely generalize to actual counseling settings. Thus, more studies with respondent samples consisting of actual Black clients with actual counselors from different ethnic groups would be optimal. However, given the consistency of findings across the studies that have been done, it seems reasonable to assume that Blacks with high cultural mistrust scores would indeed be less willing to seek counseling; remain in counseling; and believe that they can benefit from counseling, especially with White counselors.

Cultural Mistrust in Medical Settings

Extensive research has explored the link between cultural mistrust and the behavior of Blacks in U.S. medical settings. F. Terrell and colleagues (Terrell, Mosley, Terrell, & Nickerson, 2004) found that Blacks with high mistrust scores were less willing to either donate their organs or the organs of relatives. Benkert, Peters, Clark, and Keves-Foster (2006) collected data from 145 African American clients receiving primary care at a local hospital. The results suggest that, as participants' level of perceived discrimination increased, their level of mistrust increased, and their level of satisfaction with the services they were receiving decreased. Similarly, Mosley et al. (2007) found that Black parents with the highest level of cultural mistrust tended to be the most apprehensive about the quality of medical care that their children would receive.

Mistrust may not play as an important role in all aspects of the medical system. For example, Alston (2003) compared the CMI scores of African Americans who were receiving services from a public rehabilitation agency whose files were closed successfully versus those whose files were closed unsuccessfully. No differences were found between these groups on CMI scores.

COGNITIVE AND EDUCATIONAL CORRELATES OF CULTURAL MISTRUST

An area of ongoing concern among educators and mental health professionals has been the lower levels of academic performance of Black children. When working with young Black children, we have observed that a number of Black children are not motivated to perform at their maximum potential on cognitive tasks. In fact, what we see is that these Black students tend to be nonresponsive or to give brief, nonelaborative answers to interview and test questions in evaluative situations. Therefore, early in our research efforts we set about exploring some possible contributors to this seeming lack of motivation on the part of these children. We theorized that one possible reason for the lack of motivation for Black students to perform at their best on cognitive tasks and in classes might be due to the belief that White teachers would not give them a fair evaluation. After meeting with some of these students and listening to them state why they did not try harder in school, a recurring theme was the belief that teachers treat them unfairly regardless of their effort or intellect, and thus there was no real compulsion to demonstrate their abilities. To explore the possibility that Black children did not trust their teachers to treat them fairly, a series of studies exploring correlates of cultural mistrust and Black student performance on standardized cognitive tests were conducted. In our early research, Black adolescents were partitioned into groups consisting of those with either high or low levels of mistrust. Students were then administered a standardized intelligence test. Follow-up studies consistently found that Black youth with high levels of cultural mistrust tended to obtain lower scores (see F. Terrell et al., 1996, for a summary of these findings).

More recent research has reported findings consistent with this early work. Irving and Hudley (2005) explored the relation between expectations for academic success and cultural mistrust among African American high school males. Individuals with high levels of mistrust had lower levels of academic achievement and lower expectations that they would be successful in school. Chase (2000) administered the Education and Training scale of the CMI, as well as the California Safety and School Climate Survey, and conducted focus groups with African American high school students attending a predominately White school. Chase found that as cultural mistrust scores increased, students reported more dissatisfaction with the school climate and the extent to which they felt safe. A common theme of the focus groups was that these students did not trust their school authorities, and they felt hopeless about the possibility of circumstances improving.

In another study, Irving and Hudley (2005) hypothesized that a negative perception of the dominant cultural group would increase one's level of cultural mistrust and negatively affect academic outcome expectations and academic achievement values among African American male high school students attending an urban, predominantly White school. A significant inverse relationship was found between cultural mistrust and outcome expectations; that is, Black college students with higher mistrust levels believed that they would be less successful in college and tended to minimize the importance of receiving a college education. The results reported by Chase (2000) and by Irving and Hudley (2005) are inconsistent with the work of Bell and Tracey (2006), who found that Black students with higher mistrust scores tended to function better in college and had higher levels of contentment with their schools than did Blacks with lower mistrust scores. One possible reason for this conflicting finding is that the combination of both high levels of cultural identification and cultural mistrust increases the probability of success among Blacks, at least in higher education situations.

Cultural Mistrust and Interpersonal Relations

The CMI was designed to assess the extent to which Blacks mistrust Whites in general. Many, but not all, Blacks will encounter Whites in specific situations in which they will be deceived or discriminated against by Whites in work, school, medical, neighborhood (etc.) settings. In addition to being suspicious of Whites, Blacks who have been mistreated by Whites may also be wary of other Blacks who share values similar to those of Whites. There are many Blacks who, for one reason or another, have been treated favorably by Whites and have internalized similar negative views about African Americans as those held by Whites. Thus, cultural mistrust can be manifested in the presence of Blacks who hold negative views about African Americans. The military has long been viewed of as, not prejudice free, but one of the least racist organizations in U.S. society, because promotions and pay rate are based, to some extent, on a set of objective criteria. Also, regardless of socioeconomic level, gender, or ethnicity, individuals are required to adhere to directives given by a person of higher rank. Indeed, over the years, many Blacks have gravitated toward entering the military both because of its financial benefits and because it offers a situation that is essentially race neutral. If what has been suggested by others is learned as a result of racial discrimination in U.S. society, then it follows that by being in an environment in which racism is relatively low, cultural mistrust should also be low, or a less influential predictor of the behavior of Blacks. Using this reasoning, Coker (2002) explored whether one's level of mistrust decreased as a function of interacting with Whites. Blacks with less than 6 years of military service and stationed in Germany were administered the Interpersonal Relations subscale of CMI as well as a faith maturity inventory. No significant differences were found between cultural mistrust level and the extent to which Blacks were willing to socialize with Whites.

In another line of reasoning, some individuals have speculated that a healthy environment contributes to feelings of well-being. Bell and Tracey (2006) explored the association between scores on the CMI and psychological health among African American students. Moderate scores on the CMI were found to be the most strongly correlated with the highest level of psychological health. Burrow, Tubman, and Gil (2007) argued that negative experiences associated with perceived discrimination may lead to maladaptive externalized behaviors, such as substance abuse, delinquency, and risky sexual behavior. A large sample of Black adolescents was given the CMI and a measure of ethnic orientation. Participants also were asked questions related to their sexual and substance abuse history. No significant relations were found between either scores on the CMI or measures of ethnic identity and sexual and substance abuse history. Although Burrow et al. expressed surprise at the lack of a significant relationship between mistrust and either substance abuse or risky sexual behavior, this finding should not be unexpected: There is no reason to believe that simply because one mistrusts Whites, there will be an increased engagement in maladaptive behaviors.

Implications for Application

Taken collectively, the literature does seem to indicate that there is a strong relation between the extent to which Blacks trust Whites and the behavior of African Americans in various situations. These findings have a number of implications for working with African Americans in a variety of different contexts. Within the mental health field, it is important to consider the possibility that a Black client might be mistrustful of Whites and, when attempting to interpret test results or conducting therapy, to understand that this may gave influenced the client's performance or behavior. If a client is apprehensive during the evaluation process, this should be noted in the report. In counseling settings, if it seems as the client does not trust Whites, this should be noted in the charts and the possibility of transferring the African American client to another mental health professional who is familiar with the African American culture should be considered. In educational settings, as in the field of mental health, when achievement and cognitive evaluations are done, the possibility that the results may have been influenced by a mistrust of Whites should be considered.

Recommendations for Future Inquiry

To the best of our knowledge, this chapter represents the first relatively comprehensive survey of research that has explored correlates between the behaviors of African Americans and their tendency to not trust Whites. Most of these studies found significant relationships between cultural mistrust and the behaviors of Blacks in mental health, medical, and educational settings. These studies necessarily are correlational in design; therefore it would be improper to assume, on the basis of empirical studies, that cultural mistrust is a cause of the behaviors of Blacks. However, given the consistency of findings across a broad range of situations, it seems reasonable to assume that mistrust is a major contributor to the way African Americans behave in many situations.

Despite the accumulation of data supporting the suggestion that the extent to which Blacks mistrust Whites plays an important role in their lives, several areas remain almost unexplored. One area that requires attention is the possible role cultural mistrust might play in the business and financial activities of Blacks. Isimbabi (1999) reported that people in American society prefer to take somewhat of an aggressive, risky approach to money management and financial decisions.

In contrast, a relatively deeply entrenched tradition within the Black community is that Blacks tend to engage in what we refer to as a *defensive* or *conservative* approach when it comes to money management. The reason for the lack of more extensive participation by African Americans in the economic system could be due to a number of variables. Among these could be discriminatory practices by financial institutions, a lack of resources on the part of Blacks necessary to improve one's financial status, and a lack of knowledge about economics and finances. However, we believe that all of these examples are, at least to some extent, latent manifestations of the tendency of Blacks to mistrust Whites when it comes to the accumulation of wealth. An understanding of whether cultural mistrust might play a role in the prudent financial behavior of Blacks may have important implications for the financial prosperity of African Americans.

A well-documented finding is that the crime rate tends to be relatively high in predominantly Black neighborhoods, especially ones of lower socioeconomic levels (Y. M. Scott, 2001). This finding is generally interpreted to mean Blacks are more tolerant of crime or actually engage in more crime. Another possible explanation is that Blacks do not trust Whites to respond appropriately. As a consequence, they may not report some criminal activities in the Black community to legal authorities for fear that these authorities will either not believe them, distort what they have said, or use the information received to betray them.

This perception regarding the belief that the White-dominated "justice" system cannot be relied on has a factual basis. There are numerous examples of Blacks being erroneously convicted of committing crimes based on the deception of that person (Y. M. Scott, 2001). Indeed, a common theme heard among some of these individuals is that when they were forthcoming with members of the legal system, their statements were distorted, and then used against them. In other instances, Blacks who observe crimes being committed often report that they decide to keep silent instead of seeking assistance from the legal system. Thus, it is possible that those who are not forthcoming in legal situations do so because they tend to distrust Whites, not because they are tolerant of crime. To attenuate this dilemma, it may be worthwhile for Blacks to have a rapport with other Blacks (i.e., in the criminal justice system) who can be available to prevent such circumstances from occurring and to reassure those who wish to report crimes from being exploited.

Most of the research in the area of cultural mistrust has consisted of a study of the relations between cultural mistrust and behavior among Black adolescents and young adults. A population that has not been scrutinized extensively is younger, school-age children. Younger children are often subjected to being bullied and teased in school. In fact, it is not uncommon for Black children living in predominantly White neighborhoods to frequently be tormented by their White racist classmates (Lee & Cohen, 2008; Whitted & Dupper, 2008). Black children who do not trust Whites, including White teachers, may be apprehensive about reporting these problems to teachers. They may be especially unwilling to report these problems when the problems consist of racial slurs and racial harassment by White students. It seems important to study the extent to which cultural mistrust exists in this very vulnerable population of Blacks and the role it has on their behavior.

At a broader, more speculative level, over the years that we have been involved in the study of African Americans, and followed the findings of others, three variables seem to have emerged as being highly predictive of the behavior of African Americans as well as highly related to each other: (1) the extent to which Blacks identify with their ethnic group, (2) Blacks' level of religiosity and spirituality, and (3) the extent to which Blacks trust Whites. The relations among these three constructs have consistently produced strong, positive correlations. We are now persuaded that the combination of high scores on measures of Afrocentricity, religion, and spirituality, and higher scores of cultural mistrust level (in the typical the range of 120–160 points on the CMI) can be highly predictive of the success among Blacks who are successful, especially when criteria such as academic and economic success are used. Conversely, low scores on a combination of measures in these three areas may place a person at risk for not being as successful, especially when the outcome variables consist of potential for school dropout and substance and alcohol abuse. We hope that future researchers will begin to explore whether the extent to which a combination of these three variables are predictive of behaviors of Blacks in various situations. In addition to theory development, these results could have important implications for both intervention and prevention if the findings are in the direction anticipated.

To date, empirical findings indicate that many Blacks do not trust Whites, and this is related to their behavior in a variety of situations. However, differences in level of the extent to which Blacks mistrust Whites may exist within groups of Blacks. Therefore, we suggested that future research compare possible cultural mistrust differences among Blacks as a function of gender and socioeconomic differences. Such information would be especially useful in applied situations when it is important to anticipate whose behavior is most likely to be affected because of a mistrust of Whites. Also, much of the research in the area of cultural mistrust has consisted of data collected from college students. Therefore, the extent to which these findings can be generalized to Blacks in noncollege populations may be limited. To improve the extent to which these results might be applicable to a broader range of Blacks, we suggest that additional studies survey Blacks who vary in age and educational level and who reside in different geographical regions.

Conclusion

In the process of preparing this chapter, we reviewed more than 125 studies which examined correlates of cultural mistrust and different behaviors among Blacks. Unfortunately, we could review only some of them in this chapter. We limited our discussion in this chapter to findings that were either reported relatively recently or that offered insights into different areas in which cultural mistrust might play a role. Insofar as this last criterion is concerned, we hoped that by doing so, we could stimulate others to explore other important situations and conditions in which this variable might be related to behavior. Almost all of those studies we reviewed reported findings consistent with what would be expected among Blacks—across gender, socioeconomic status, age, and context—who mistrust Whites. Overall, empirical findings suggest that the extent to which Blacks mistrust Whites is related to the behavior of Blacks in many aspects of their lives. We found no studies that reported contradictory relations between cultural mistrust and what was predicted or would be theoretically expected.

As a final word, it has been rewarding to us to observe that Black psychologists have taken a leadership role in investigating the nature of cultural mistrust and the relationship this construct seems to have on a wide range of behaviors commonly observed among African Americans. We encourage the continuation of these efforts. This should be followed by appropriate proposals for policy implementation.

Note

1. We are indebted to Arthur Whaley for his invaluable suggestions in the preparation of this chapter. Francis Terrell would especially like to express his appreciation to Robert L. Williams for his support during the early stages of his research in cultural mistrust.

References

Alston, R. J. (2003). Racial identity and cultural mistrust among African-American recipients. *International Journal of Rehabilitation Research, 4,* 289–295.

Bell, T., J., & Tracey, T. J. G. (2006). The relation of cultural mistrust and psychological health. *Journal of Multicultural Counseling and Development, 34,* 2–10.

Benkert, R., Peters, R., M., Clark, R., & Keves-Foster, K. (2006). Effects of perceived racism, cultural mistrust and trust in providers satisfaction with care. *Journal of the National Medical Association, 98,* 1532–1540.

Burrow, A. L., Tubman, J. G., & Gil, A. G. (2007). Heterogeneity in patterns of sexual risk behaviors among African-American youth: Associations with general and race-specific factors. *Journal of Community Psychology, 35,* 447–462.

Chase, M. A. (2000). *An examination of cultural mistrust in a school-based context for African American adolescents*. Unpublished doctoral dissertation, University of California, Santa Barbara.

Clark, S. L. T. (2003). *A further examination of the Cultural Mistrust Inventory*. Unpublished doctoral dissertation.

Coker, H. E. B. (2002). *The impact of cultural and spiritual mentoring on the development of African American young adults in a military setting*. Unpublished doctoral dissertation, Oral Roberts University.

Combs, D. R., Penn, D. L., Cassisi, J., Michael, C., Wood, T., Wanner, J., et al. (2006). Perceived racism as a predictor of paranoia among African Americans. *Journal of Black Psychology, 32,* 87–104.

Duncan, L. E. (2003). Black male college students' attitudes toward seeking psychological help. *Journal of Black Psychology, 29,* 68–86.

Fyffe, D. C. (2000). *Effects of trust, cultural mistrust, counselor's race and race-sensitive orientation on perceived trustworthiness in Black college women*. Unpublished doctoral dissertation, Hofstra University.

Gardiner, C. L. (2005). *Examining the influence of racial identity, ethnicity, ethnic identity, cultural mistrust, and self-esteem of students of African descent on their preferences for counselors' ethnicity*. Unpublished doctoral dissertation, Texas Southern University.

Gregory, D. (1971). *No more lies: The myth and the reality of American history*. New York: Harper & Row.

Grier, W. H., & Cobbs, P. M. (1968). *Black rage.* New York: Basic Books.

Harrell, J. P., & Harris, C. (1984, August). *Cultural mistrust and Black nationalism: Evidence of a positive relationship*. Paper presented at the 92nd Annual Convention of the American Psychological Association, Toronto, ON, Canada.

Irving, M. A., & Hudley, C. (2005). Cultural mistrust, academic outcome expectations and outcome values among African American adolescent men. *Urban Education, 40,* 476–496.

Isimbabi, M. J. (1999). *Capital entrepreneurship and Black progress*. Washington, DC: The Black Progress Network.

Landrine, J., & Klonoff, E. A. (1994). The African American Acculturation Scale: Development, reliability, and validity. *Journal of Black Psychology, 20,* 104–127.

LaVesit, T. A., Nickerson, K. J., & Bowie, J. (2000). Attitude about racism, medical mistrust, and satisfaction with care among African Americans and White cardiac patients. *Medical Care Research and Review, 57,* 146–151.

Lee, D. R., & Cohen, J. W. (2008). Examining strain in a school context. *Youth Violence and Juvenile Justice, 6,* 115–135.

Lee, E. E. (2003). *Cultural mistrust, university alienation, academic self-efficacy and academic help seeking in African American college students*. Unpublished doctoral dissertation, University of Arkansas.

Lightsey, O. R., Jr., & Barnes, P. W. (2007). Discrimination, attributional tendencies, generalized self-efficacy, and assertiveness as predictors of psychological distress among African Americans. *Journal of Black Psychology, 33,* 27–50.

Mosley, K. L., Treed, G., Bullard, C. M., & Gold, S. D. (2007). Measuring African-American parents' cultural mistrust while in a healthcare setting: A pilot study. *Journal of the National Medical Association, 99*, 15–21.

Neville, H. A., & Mobley, M. (2001). Social identities in contexts: An ecological model of multicultural counseling psychology processes. *The Counseling Psychologist, 29*, 471–486.

Nickerson, K. L., Helms, J. E., & Terrell, F. (1994). Cultural mistrust, opinions about mental illness and Black students' attitudes toward seeking psychological help from White counselors. *Journal of Counseling Psychology, 41*, 378–385.

Phelps, R. E., Taylor, J. D., & Gerard, P. A. (2001). Cultural mistrust, ethnic identity, racial identity, and self-esteem among ethnically diverse Black university students. *Journal of Counseling and Development, 79*, 209–216.

Poston, W. S. C., Craine, M., & Atkinson, D. R. (1991). Counselor dissimilarity conformation, client cultural mistrust, and willingness to disclose. *Journal of Multicultural Counseling and Development, 19*, 65–73.

Sabnani, H. B., & Ponterotto, J. G. (1992). Racial/ethnic minority-specific instrumentation in counseling research: A review, critique, and recommendations. *Measurement and Evaluation in Counseling and Development, 24*, 161–187.

Scott, L. D., & Davis, L. (2006). Young, Black, and male in foster care: Relationship of negative social contextual experiences to factors relevant to mental health services, *Journal of Adolescence, 29*, 721–736.

Scott, Y. M. (2001). *Fear of crime among inner-city African Americans*. New York: LFB Scholarly Publishing.

Taylor, J., & Brown, A. (1984). *Discrimination and the development of distrust among African Americans*. Unpublished manuscript.

Terrell, F., Mosley, K. L., Terrell, A. S., & Nickerson, K. J. (2004). The relationship between motivation to volunteer, gender, cultural mistrust, and willingness to donate organs among Blacks. *Journal of the National Medical Association, 96*, 53–60.

Terrell, F., & Terrell, S. L. (1981). An inventory to measure cultural mistrust among Blacks. *Western Journal of Black Studies, 5*, 180–185.

Terrell, F., & Terrell, S. L. (1984). Race of counselor, client sex, cultural mistrust level, and premature termination from counseling among Black clients. *Journal of Counseling Psychology, 31*, 371–375.

Terrell F., & Terrell S. L. (1996). The Cultural Mistrust Inventory: Development, findings, and implications. In R. L. Jones (Ed.), *Handbook of test and measurements for Black populations* (Vol. 1, pp. 326–329). Hampton, VA: Cobb & Henry.

Terrell, F., & Terrell, S. L. (1999). Cultural identification and cultural mistrust: Some findings and implications. In R. L. Jones (Ed.), *Advances in African American Psychology* (Vol. 2, pp. 217–228). Berkeley, CA: Cobb & Henry.

Terrell, F., Terrell, S. L., & Nickerson, K. J. (1996). Cultural identification and cultural mistrust: Some findings and implications. In R. L. Jones (Ed.), *Advances in Black Psychology*. Berkeley, CA: Cobb & Henry.

Townes, D. L. (2003). *The impact of cultural mistrust, racial identity, and attitudes for seeking professional psychological help on prospective Black clients' preference for their counselor's race*. Unpublished doctoral dissertation, University of Louisville.

Watkins, C. E., & Terrell, F. (1988). Mistrust level and its effects on counseling expectations in Black client–White counselor relationships: An analogue study. *Journal of Counseling Psychology, 35*, 194–197.

Watkins, C. E., Terrell, F., Miller F., & Terrell, S. L. (1989). Cultural mistrust and its effects on expectational variables in Black client–White counselor relationships. *Journal of Counseling Psychology, 36*, 447–450.

Whaley, A. L. (1997). Ethnicity/race, paranoia, and psychiatric diagnoses: Clinician bias versus sociocultural differences. *Journal of Psychopathology and Behavioral Assessment, 19*, 1–20.

Whaley, A. L. (1998). Black psychiatric patients' reaction to the Cultural Mistrust Inventory. *Journal of the National Medical Association, 90*, 676–678.

Whaley, A. L. (2001). Cultural mistrust and mental health services for African Americans: A review and meta-analysis. *The Counseling Psychologist, 29*, 513–531.

Whaley, A. L. (2002). Psychometric analysis of the Cultural Mistrust Inventory with a Black psychiatric inpatient sample. *Journal of Clinical Psychology, 58*, 383–396.

Whitted, K. S., & Dupper, D. R. (2008). Do teachers bully students? Findings from a survey of students in an alternative education setting. *Education and Urban Society, 40*, 329–341.

Wright, S. (2004). *Racial gender role socialization of the African American female: Development and validation of the socialization internalization scale*. Unpublished doctoral dissertation, University of Missouri–Columbia.

23

AFRICAN AMERICAN LESBIANS AND GAY MEN

Life Between a Rock and a Hard Place

BEVERLY GREENE

This chapter focuses on African American lesbians and gay men as a group that reflects the spectrum of diversity among African Americans. Neither the (African American) psychological literature nor the lesbian, gay, and bisexual psychological literature has much to say about members of this group (Greene, 2000; Hall & Greene, 1996). My colleagues and I (Greene, 2000; Greene & Boyd-Franklin, 1996) have observed that African Americans were somewhat of a footnote in American psychology, and African American lesbians and gay men receive even less attention.

AFRICAN AMERICAN LESBIANS AND GAY MEN: GENERAL CONSIDERATIONS

African American lesbians and gay men are a large and diverse group whose members are represented in all social class, education, geographical region, age, sex, and gender presentations and other groups that exist among African Americans. That diversity must be considered in any attempt to understand both the psychological vulnerabilities and strengths of members of this group. This is a reflection of the multiple identities of group members, no single one of which can be assumed to be ubiquitously more important than any other across a group that is so diverse. Because this group is so diverse, the material in this chapter should be considered general and not absolute in its description of them.

Lesbians and gay men are considered to constitute 4% to 17% of the general population; however, 10% is usually considered an acceptable estimate (Gonsiorek & Weinrich, 1991). Similar numbers within African Americans as a group suggest that although they represent a minority group, they are not an inconsiderable population. It is likely that most African Americans have someone in their family who is lesbian or gay, although they may not necessarily be aware of that reality given the propensity of many African American lesbians and gay men to conceal that aspect of their identity or remain "closeted."

African American lesbians and gay men are part of a diverse ethnic group whose cultural origins are rooted in members of West African tribes who were stolen and forcibly transported to the United States as slaves (Boyd-Franklin, 1989; Greene, 1986, 1990b, 1994a, 1994c, 1997, 2000).

One can observe among African American lesbians and gay men many of the same African cultural derivatives that are seen in their heterosexual counterparts. These cultural derivatives include the presence of strong family ties in both nuclear and extended family networks of mutual obligation and support (Boyd-Franklin, 1989; Greene, 1986, 1994a, 1997, 2000; Icard, 1986). They also reflect more flexible gender roles than White and other ethnic minority groups; however, that does not negate the presence of sexism and behaviors that are derivative of patriarchal ideologies in some African American families and communities. Their gender role flexibility may be explained by multiple factors. One factor is the need to adapt to the institutional racism that forced African American women to assume more active roles as breadwinners (Boyd-Franklin, 1989; Greene, 1997, 2000). First, slavery and then the lack of employment opportunities that were a function of racism made it difficult for African American men to conform to the Western ideal of male as the sole family provider. This meant that African American women were forced to work outside the home from the very moment they arrived on these shores to a greater degree than their White counterparts. This reverse arrangement of gender roles often resulted in a view of African American men and women as defective. Other factors include cultural values that stress interdependence and a greater gender egalitarianism in some precolonial African tribes (Greene, 2000).

The absence of research with significant numbers of African American lesbians and gay men has important implications for our understanding of all African Americans. Bell and Weinberg (1978); Bass-Hass (1968); Mays and Cochran (1988); Jackson and Brown (1996); and Mays, Cochran, and Rhue (1993) have conducted a few of the published empirical studies that include all, or significant numbers of, group members. The findings yielded by these studies suggest that African American lesbians are more likely to have children, to maintain close relationships with their biological and extended families, to depend more on family members or other African American lesbians for support than their White counterparts, and to have greater contact with men and heterosexual peers than their White counterparts. African American lesbians and bisexual women have also been observed to have a greater likelihood of experiencing tension and loneliness but were less likely to seek professional help (Greene & Boyd-Franklin, 1996). This combination may leave them more vulnerable to the effects of chronic stressors and perhaps a higher rate of negative psychological outcomes when they finally do seek help (Greene, 1994a, 1998a, 2000).

Understanding the reality of being an African American lesbian or gay man requires a careful exploration of the impact of factors such as ethnic identity, gender, social class, minority sexual orientation, and the dynamic interactions of these within the individual. The nature of the traditional gender role stereotypes within African Americans, the ways those stereotypes have been shaped by institutional racism and its ethnosexual stereotypes of both men and women, and the role of religion and spirituality in the lives of African Americans are important factors in shaping the reality of group members. Such factors may be used to mitigate or reinforce societal heterosexism and homophobia among African Americans. These factors also contribute to the wide range of diversity among African American lesbians and gay men as a group.

African Americans were sexually objectified during slavery, which reinforced images of them as being sexually promiscuous, morally loose, and out of control sexually and otherwise (Clarke, 1983; Collins, 1990; Greene, 1986, 1990a, 1990c, 2000; Icard, 1986; Loiacano, 1989). Internalization of these images among African Americans has important implications for how they view themselves and their lesbian and gay members as well as how the latter view themselves. Although the strength of family ties can often mitigate against the outright rejection of lesbian and gay family members, what may appear to be acceptance it is usually based on their silence about their sexual orientation. The African American community is viewed by its lesbian and gay members as extremely homophobic, generating the pressure for many lesbians and gay men to remain closeted (e.g., Greene, 1990a, 1994a, 1994c, 1995a, 1998a, 2000, 2007; Jackson & Brown, 1996; Nettles, 2007). Research conducted by the National Black Justice Coalition suggests that upwards of two thirds of Black Americans oppose same-sex marriage as well as civil unions (Lynsen, 2008).

African American communities across the United States are often very different from one another. There are great differences in the stressors and the resources of urban versus rural locales as well as differences in the degree to which racism restricts as well as punishes those who do not obey racial rules. Those rules and restrictions also vary across time in both formal and informal ways. The components of racism and other forms of institutional discrimination will not be identical across time and locale, so the psychological survival strategies required to manage it will vary as well. Hence, African American lesbians and gay men will have different experiences of what it means to be an African American and what it means to be gay or lesbian that are often a function of these variables. Where an individual was raised and socialized is an important contextual element in the shaping of his or her responses to these aspects of his or her identity.

Another relevant factor is the person's degree of acculturation or assimilation into a dominant cultural community, as well as how that person's family values or disparages assimilation and to what degree. Other factors include the person's class or educational standing and the degree to which it is similar or significantly different from that of other family members. If these things are different, how family members feel about the differences, as well as what and how they communicate those feelings to lesbian and gay family members, also is relevant. For other African American lesbians and gay men, their work, social class, and/or education may place them in the work and social environments of the primarily dominant culture. The feelings that family members and peers have about a lesbian or gay person's sexual orientation may be mediated by the extent to which that individual is different from them, not just by virtue of that individual's sexual orientation but also by virtue of the class, education, racial identity of his or her colleagues or social peers from the family members who are heterosexual. It is not uncommon for African American family members and peers to respond to disclosures about a family member's lesbian or gay sexual orientation with the charge that they "acquired" this "sickness" from "decadent White practices." African American lesbians and gay men who work, live, or play in predominantly White environments are more vulnerable to taking seriously this challenge to their authenticity as African Americans. The concept of lesbian or gay sexual orientation as "the White man's disease" may seem deceptively harmless; however, it is often connected to more pernicious beliefs about lesbian and gay sexual orientations and a level of denial about lesbian and gay members in African American communities that is destructive to both those communities and individuals. Such beliefs support the development of heterosexism and internalized homophobia that can lead to violence against lesbian and gay members. This issue and its connection to those beliefs are explored more comprehensively later in this chapter.

African American lesbians and gay men are not inevitable psychological cripples, despite the challenges they face. When analyzing the history of discrimination of any ethnic group, it is essential to consider the group members' understanding of their oppression and their sense not only of how they cope but also of where and how they learned to do so. African American lesbians and gay men often use the successful strategies they have developed to negotiate racism, to manage homophobia and heterosexism, and to appropriately locate the problem in social pathology, not in themselves. A person's capacity to effectively cope with one form of discrimination can be a most potent psychological resource if that person confronts multiple layers of discrimination, as commonly occurs with African American lesbians and gay men (Greene, 2000).

Another important dimension that must be considered is how culture shapes attitudes about what are considered appropriate forms of sexuality and gender expression (Greene, 2000). Espin (1984) observed that in most cultures, a range of sexual behaviors are tolerated, whereas others are not. In clinical practice, when making assessments of sexual behavior it is important for the clinician to determine where the client's behavior fits along the spectrum of sexual behavior for African Americans in general (Espin, 1984; Greene, 1996b, 2000). In exploring the range of sexuality tolerated by African Americans, one needs to know whether, or to what extent, formally forbidden practices are tolerated as long as they are not discussed and labeled (and to what degree), or if they are not tolerated under any circumstances.

It is also important to determine the relationship of the *ethnosexual mythologies* applied to African American lesbians and gay men's understandings of their sexuality and the degree to which they have internalized racial and sexual stereotypes of group members

(Greene, 1996b, 2000). Ethnosexual myths were created and perpetuated by the dominant culture and often represent a complex combination of racial and sexual stereotypes. These negative stereotypes are employed to objectify African American men and women, to isolate and degrade them in comparison to their idealized White counterparts, and to promote their sexual exploitation and control (Cohen, 1999; Collins, 1990; Greene, 1994a, 1994c, 1996b, 2000; hooks, 1981). The symbolism of these stereotypes and its interaction with stereotypes held about lesbians and gay men play an important role in the stereotypes and myths perpetrated against and often internalized by African American lesbians and gay men. I return to the discussion of ethnosexual stereotypes after I briefly review characteristics of African American families that are relevant to African American lesbian and gay men's lives.

African American Family of Origin: Refuge or Gilded Cage?

The African American family has functioned as an important refuge to protect group members from the racism of the dominant culture. It has also served as an important socializing tool for African Americans as an oppressed group in a hostile environment. African American families teach their young about how to accurately recognize and negotiate racial barriers and offer them powerful positive cultural mirroring to mitigate internalization of negative images of themselves. Greene (2007), Greene and Boyd-Franklin 1996), Jackson and Brown (1996), Nettles, (2007), and A. Smith (1997) have observed that the importance of African American family and community as a survival tool makes the coming-out process for African American lesbians and gay men fraught with greater difficulty and the perception of greater risk than that of their White counterparts. Although this perception is not unusual, it is important to understand that it is not ubiquitous. African American families vary in the range of tolerance and acceptance they display for lesbian and gay members. Some families may be harsh and rejecting; others are loving and supportive. Despite this, the caution and apprehension expressed by lesbian and gay members is still warranted. The stakes, if they are wrong about their families' reaction, are very high.

Because of the strength of family ties, there may be a reluctance to formally expel a lesbian or gay member from the family despite an undisputed rejection of that person's sexual orientation. This may represent varying levels of tolerance for nonconformity, denial of the person's sexual orientation, or even culturally distinct ways of conveying negative attitudes about a family member's sexual orientation (Greene, 1994a, 1994c, 1998a, 2000). In African American families, lesbians and gay men are not formally disowned to the extent that their White counterparts may be. This may be a reflection, in some families, of the importance of family members to one another and the sense that family members, no matter what they do, are not expendable. It may also represent the degree to which many African American families depend on all of the resources of all family members to survive. African American families are also diverse from within. Whereas some family members may be hostile and rejecting, others may be accepting. Villarosa (1993, cited in Brownworth, 1993) observed that instead of throwing someone out of the family, they "keep you around to talk you out of it" (p. 18). Overall, there is the potential for a wide range of different responses from family members and peers.

Coming Out: A Developmental Challenge

Coming out represents the acknowledgment of a lesbian or gay sexual orientation to oneself and disclosure to others. For lesbians and gay men, coming out is a lifelong developmental challenge. Because people are presumed to be heterosexual until they say otherwise, and because sexual orientation cannot be accurately discerned solely on the basis of physical characteristics or features, every new event, job, or social situation may represent an occasion during which one is confronted with individuals who do not know, and a decision must be made about whether to tell them, what the consequences may be, and how to reveal that status.

The fact that many African American families are accepting and tolerant of a family member's gay or lesbian sexual orientation does not warrant the assumption that it constitutes approval or that there are no African American families who do throw out or disown a lesbian or gay family member. In African American families, there is often a kind of quiet tolerance for lesbian and gay members; however, it is contingent on that person's silence about their sexual orientation. Serious conflicts may occur within the family or between family members if a lesbian or gay family member openly discloses his or her sexual orientation or demands that the family recognize it or his or her relationships. For example, a lesbian or gay family member's partner may have been "accepted" in the family in ways that may appear to be informed acceptance. Things may go along smoothly until the relationship is openly labeled. This labeling can result from behavior at one end of the spectrum, overt disclosure, to the other end of the spectrum, for example, when the lesbian or gay family member simply moves out of the family's household and establishes a household with his or her partner. There is a wide range of other behaviors in between. When a gay or lesbian family member directly discloses his or her sexual orientation to family members the family's response may be hostile.

Even when family members are accepting and supportive, the broader African American community or the person's heterosexual peers may not be (Greene, 1996b, 1998a, 2000; Walters, 1996). Because of the extended nature of African American families, close and emotionally intense ties between adult women are common. There is a culturally defined role within the African American community for the nonrelated adult girlfriend who has an often very intense but nonsexual, spiritual, and emotionally connected relationship with an African American woman friend and her family (Greene, 2000; Greene & Boyd-Franklin, 1996). This is reflected in the greeting "girlfriend," which acknowledges and confers kinshiplike status on a close adult female friend who is not blood related but is experienced as intensely as such. These women are often informally adopted by the family and are referred to by children and younger family members with terms such as *aunt*. Sometimes, there is a formal aspect to this relationship, as, for example, when this person is a godparent to a child in the family.

The role of the close female friend among adult women in African American culture can make it even easier for African American families to avoid acknowledging the lesbian nature of a relationship between two adult women, even when it is right within their midst (Greene & Boyd-Franklin, 1996). African American lesbian women can sometimes collude in this denial by never actually saying anything to pierce the family's denial. Others may not keep the information a secret but still never fully come out to their family members. Other men and women may come out to their families and find that the family continues to pretend that the relationship does not exist, accepting the lover in the culturally accepted role of "girlfriend" for women, or just friend, for men. Conversely, family members may, for a variety of reasons, disapprove of two adult women who have a close nonsexual relationship. Despite the nonsexual nature of the relationship, family members may attempt to disrupt such friendships by implying that they are lesbians. These accusations can be terrifying for heterosexual women and, as such, can be used successfully to weaken kinship bonds between women.

Consistent with gender role norms that are different for men and women, close personal friendships between women are generally treated with much less suspicion than those of their male counterparts, and women who violate gender role norms are not vilified to the extent that their male counterparts are disparaged. This does not mean that lesbians are not targets of homophobic violence; however, men who violate masculine gender role norms of heterosexuality seem to evoke a heightened level of viciousness than women.

In psychotherapies with African American lesbians and gay men who are exploring the possibility of coming out to loved ones, it is important that the therapist explore the potential responses of specific persons in the family, rather than the family as a whole group. The prospect of coming out to the entire family at once can be overwhelming and is not necessary (Greene, 2000; Greene & Boyd-Franklin, 1996). Psychotherapy can assist men and women who are contemplating coming out to anticipate potentially painful reactions to the disclosure, which may be more likely if the individual is a part of an interracial relationship. In interracial relationships, the other partner's race may become a more comfortable target for the family's anger about the disclosure (Greene, 2000; Greene & Boyd-Franklin, 1996).

The man or woman who is poised to disclose his or her sexual orientation to a family member or peer is at a very different developmental stage than the person to whom they come out. The individual's personal acceptance of his or her own lesbian or gay sexual orientation has rarely taken place without hesitation or private doubts; neither, typically, will it for loved ones. Its absence at the stage of coming out means not that it can never take place but that it may require time to develop (Greene, 1994a, 2000; Greene & Boyd-Franklin, 1996). Psychotherapies can assist individuals at this developmental juncture in anticipating and preparing for the worst as well as the best scenarios and to engage in anticipatory problem solving. In spite of the most thoughtful preparation, outcomes will be as diverse as African American families themselves.

Challenges to Relationships of African American Lesbians and Gay Men

There is great diversity among African American lesbians and gay men as far as their relationships are concerned. Those relationships are as diverse as those of heterosexual relationships, except many of them exist under a veil of secrecy and are openly disapproved of, challenged, and may even be undermined by family and friends. The lack of support that traditionally accompanies their heterosexual counterparts' relationships and the contentiousness they may elicit from family members and heterosexual friends seriously challenges their capacity to function optimally and may be a significant source of stress. Even when their relationships are known and accepted by family members and peers, they do not uniformly receive the same acceptance or legal protections that heterosexual relationships routinely acquire. Some of these individuals form lifelong partnerships in which they may be out or closeted. Some may formalize their relationships when possible as civil unions, domestic partnerships, and even legal marriage. Others may have serial monogamous relationships or a series of short-lived relationships. Still, others may knowingly engage in heterosexual relationships and marriages with a lesbian or gay "spouse" so that each may conceal their sexual orientation from others. Many also function in heterosexual marriages while conducting clandestine lesbian or gay relationships that are not divulged to their heterosexual spouse. Those who formalize their relationships are more likely to be out, because the act of formalizing the relationship mitigates against keeping the relationship a secret. Formalizing the relationship may also evoke greater hostility from family and friends who do not accept the relationship and may evoke hostility from families who are accepting of the relationship as long as it does not require formal acknowledgment.

The secrecy and deception that surround lesbian and gay relationships can be directly attributed to the ill treatment accorded lesbians and gay men who openly self-identify as such, treatment that continues despite what appears to be evolving as a more accepting social environment. This greater acceptance is reflected in the gradual evolution of marriage and domestic partnership rights in the last 5 years. Despite that progress, however, African American lesbians and gay men still face the potential for verbal and physical harassment and job loss as well as rejection from family members and heterosexual peers if they are out.

King (2004) and Boykin (2005) have offered commentaries on men who have sex with men but do who not consider themselves gay as being on the *down low*. Although discussions about the down low usually focus on African American men, it is by no means limited to or characteristic of them. There is no evidence to support the notion that African American men engage in down low behavior any more than their White counterparts. Men who are married or in relationships with women and who have unprotected sex with men contribute to higher rates of sexually transmitted diseases among their female partners; however, there is no evidence to suggest that they do this any more so than married heterosexual men who have unprotected sexual relationships with other women. Clandestine unprotected sexual relationships, not sexual orientation, are the problem.

The race–ethnicity of the partner of an African American lesbian or gay man can greatly affect the dynamics of the relationship as well as its visibility/invisibility and therefore how it is perceived and received by the African American family and community. For the most part, African American lesbians and gay men's relationships are largely unsupported outside of the broader, predominantly White lesbian community and the smaller African American lesbian and gay community. The latter may be nonexistent outside of large urban centers where there are few open, healthy models of such relationships. Like their sexual orientation, their relationships' acceptance may be marked by an often-conspicuous collusion of silence, ambivalence, and denial. Neither can they assume that their families will empathize with their appropriate distress if the relationship is troubled or ends. For some family members, the end of a lesbian or gay relationship may be met with rejoicing. This is compounded upon seeking professional assistance, where many African American lesbians and gay men find few, if any, therapists who have been trained in lesbian and gay relationship issues with women and men who are not White (Greene, 1994a, 1994b, 1994c; 2000; Greene & Boyd-Franklin, 1996).

African American lesbians and gay men in general have relationships with same-sex partners who are not members of their same ethnic group to a significantly greater degree than their White counterparts (Greene, 2000; Greene & Boyd-Franklin, 1996; Mays & Cochran, 1988; Tafoya & Rowell, 1988). This has been attributed in part to a larger pool of White lesbians and gay men than their African American counterparts (Tafoya & Rowell, 1988). Although heterosexual interracial relationships often lack the support of each member's family and community, lesbian and gay interracial relationships face even greater challenges to a situation already fraught with difficulty (Greene, 1994a, 1994c, 1995b, 2000; Greene & Boyd-Franklin, 1996).

An interracial lesbian or gay couple is more publicly visible and recognizable as a couple than two women or two men who are members of the same ethnic group and thus has a greater potential to elicit homophobic reactions. Both may be perceived by others as lacking loyalty to their own racial–ethnic group and may even feel ashamed of their involvement with someone who is not African American (Clunis & Green, 1988; Falco, 1991; Greene, 1994a, 1998a, 2000; Greene & Boyd-Franklin, 1996). This complicates both the resolution of issues within the relationship and intensifies the complex web of loyalties and estrangements for the African American partner.

Although racial issues and cultural differences between partners offer realistic challenges to lesbian and gay relationships, they are not responsible for every problem within them. Visible differences such as ethnoracial identity may be scapegoated as the cause of problems simply because they are so visible. Choices of partners and feelings about those choices may, but do not automatically, reflect an individual's personal conflicts about racial and ethnic identity either. African American lesbians and gay men who experience themselves as racially or culturally deficient or ambiguous may seek a partner from their own ethnic group to compensate for their perceived deficiency or to demonstrate their cultural loyalty. There may also be a tendency for an African American lesbian or gay person in a relationship with another African American lesbian or gay man to expect greater levels of similarity between them than is realistically warranted.

Exclusive choices in this realm may also reflect a person's tendency to idealize people who are like them and devalue those who are not. When this is the case, the reality often does not live up to the fantasy, resulting in the individual's intense disappointment and feeling of betrayal and/or failure. It is important to remember that such decisions and preferences have many different determinants that are often made outside of a person's conscious awareness (Greene, 1994c, 2000).

The Role of Ethnosexual Stereotypes in Heterosexism

Since their origins in America as objects of the U.S. slave trade (Greene, 1990b, 1994a, 1994c, 2000), African American men and women were considered to be property, and forced sexual relationships were the norm. Ethnosexual stereotypes about African American men and women originate in images created by a White society that struggled to reconcile the contradictions between its ideals and espoused values and its inhuman treatment of African Americans (Greene, 1996b, 2000). African American women clearly did not fit the traditional stereotypes of women as fragile, weak, and dependent. They were viewed in ways that are consolidated in the "Mammy" figure. The "Mammy", symbolic of African American women, is domineering and strong, characteristics that define men in patriarchal cultures and are the antithesis of femininity (West, 1995). Assertiveness in African American females was depicted as castrating, and even antimale. African American men could not protect their women or children from the sexual abuse of White slave masters, or from being sold away from them; neither could they protect themselves from routine ethnoracial humiliation.

African American gay men are the focus of hostility from heterosexual African American women who view them as culpable in the shortage of marriage-eligible African American men and as less than "real men" if they do not fit the traditional masculine stereotype of dominant male. Many African Americans, including lesbians and gay men, have internalized these myths. Their internalization intensifies the negative psychological effects of heterosexism on them and further compromises their ability to be affirming of themselves, to protect themselves, and to obtain support from the larger African American community (Cohen, 1999; Collins, 1990; Greene, 1994a, 1994c, 1996b, 2000; Monroe, 1998).

African American men and women who have internalized the racism, sexism, and heterosexism inherent in the patriarchal values of Western culture may scapegoat any men or women who defy traditional gender role norms. Those norms explicitly embed erotic attraction to members of the other gender as normative. African American lesbians and gay men violate that norm.

Multiple Jeopardies: Psychological Challenges to the Optimal Development of African American Lesbians and Gay Men

African American lesbians and gay men develop, work, play, and love in a climate of ubiquitous hostility toward them. The need to negotiate pervasive environmental antagonism and discrimination creates a range of psychological challenges to the optimal development and functioning of this group's members. Despite the odds against them, they are not inevitable psychological cripples. Therapists must appreciate the tenacity of their resilience under most challenging circumstances. The antagonism that confronts African American lesbians and gay men comes from personal, family, and institutional sources. These sources have historically included psychotherapy and institutional mental health.

The underpinnings of traditional approaches to psychology and psychotherapy are replete with racist, sexist, classist, and heterosexist biases (Garnets & Kimmel, 1991; Glassgold, 1992, 1995; Greene, 1994a, 1994c, 1996b, 1998a, 1998b, 2007). These approaches often reinforce rather than mitigate the beliefs and rationales that support the multiple levels of discrimination that African American lesbians and gay men routinely encounter.

The view that reproductive sexuality is normative mirrors the long-standing bias against lesbian and gay sexual orientations in the broader culture, in Western psychology, and in much of organized mental health. It was not until 1973 that the American Psychiatric Association removed the diagnosis of homosexuality from the *Diagnostic and Statistical Manual of Mental Disorders.* Similarly, it was not until 1975 that the American Psychological Association adopted its official policy that homosexuality per se implied no psychological impairment. Although psychodynamic theories and practice have not been alone in taking views that pathologize lesbian and gay sexual orientations, they have been the slowest of organized mental health professions, training programs, and theoretical perspectives to alter the view that a lesbian sexual orientation is a result of a developmental arrest or trauma and that its expression is pathological. In 1998, the American Psychoanalytic Association finally altered its official policy on the subject. Despite official changes in the diagnostic nomenclature negative bias and misinformation continues to infuse the practice of psychotherapy with lesbians (Brown, 1996; Garnets, Hancock, Cochran, Goodchilds, & Peplau, 1991; Garnets & Kimmel, 1991; Greene, 2000).

The legacy of pervasive bias and discrimination against lesbians and gay men, women, and people of color, among other socially disadvantaged group members in society creates a wealth of challenges to their optimal development as well as their optimal treatment in psychotherapy. This is particularly true for African American women and men who are sexual minorities. Before changes were made in the diagnostic nomenclature, most practitioners would engage in unquestioned attempts to convert lesbian or gay clients to heterosexual sexual orientation in what are known as the *conversion* and *reparative* therapies. These attempts represent one of many manifestations of institutional bias against lesbian and gay clients. Haldeman (2000) reviewed the history and discussed the ethical implications of conversion therapies. For most clients, psychotherapy would be expected to provide a safe, nonjudgmental haven to explore the ramifications of life's challenges. Lesbian and gay clients, however, could expect to find themselves pathologized and ill treated by the very professionals we would expect to be helpful to them. In addition to the discrimination they face in day-to-day life, bias against lesbians and gay men in the basic theoretical and practical structures of organized mental health institutions leaves members of this population at psychological risk.

It is fair to say that the needs of African American women and men of all sexual orientations have been ill considered in American mental health. It is also fair to say that these institutions have often contributed to the stigma associated with these identities. They also have facilitated the development of biased attitudes in therapists in the form of negative countertransference. Although a comprehensive discussion of the various manifestations of these issues and their resolution is beyond the scope of this chapter, readers are referred to Greene (1994a, 1994c, 1995b) and Greene and Boyd-Franklin (1996).

Overall, an exclusive focus on intrapsychic dynamics runs the risk of ignoring important social and cultural realities that shape the lives and functioning of men and women as well as the interactions between those realities. Therapists who have a personal need to avoid the anxiety this material may often evoke in them may deem inquiries about intrapsychic material more important as if they have a universal context. It is safe to assume that the relationship between childhood trauma and adult pathology has many determinants and that the very notion of pathology itself is socially and culturally determined (Altman, 1995; Chodorow, 1989; Glassgold, 1992, 1995; Gould, 1995; Kassoff, Boden, deMonteflores, Hunt, & Wahba, 1995; Maracek & Hare-Mustin, 1991; Thompson, 1987).

Institutional mental health has played a distinct role in supporting heterosexist beliefs and values. These beliefs often result in misconceptions about lesbians and gay men and appear to be as common among people of color as they are in the dominant culture. Some of these questionable beliefs are that lesbians either want to be or naturally look like men (Taylor, 1983); are unattractive or less attractive than heterosexual women (Dew, 1985); are less extroverted than heterosexual individuals (Kite, 1994); are unable to get, or have had traumatic experiences with, men that presumably "turned" them against men; or are simply defective females (Christian, 1985; Collins, 1990;

Greene, 1994a, 1994c; Kite, 1994). Similarly, African American gay men are presumed to be more like, or want to be, women; are weak when men should be strong; and, similar to African American lesbians, are defective men. African American communities often share with the dominant culture the same assumptions about what constitutes normal sexual attraction and a range of equally inaccurate assumptions. Acceptance of such assumptions often leads to a range of equally inaccurate conclusions. One of the most significant assumptions is that reproductive sexuality is the only form of sexual expression that is both psychologically normal and morally correct (Garnets & Kimmel, 1991; Glassgold, 1992, 1995; Greene, 1994a, 1996b, 1998a, 2000), that there is a direct relationship between sexual orientation and conformity to traditional gender roles and physical appearance within the culture (Kite & Deaux, 1987; Newman, 1989; Whitley, 1987). These assumptions are also used to threaten men and women with the stigma of being labeled lesbian or gay if they do not adhere to the traditional gender role stereotypes of the African American community in which males are dominant and females are submissive (Collins, 1990; Gomez & Smith, 1990; Greene, 2000; Monroe, 1998; B. Smith, 1982). This often occurs in African American communities despite the history and tradition of gender role flexibility within African American families.

Being labeled a lesbian or gay can inhibit men and women, whether they are lesbian or gay or not, from seeking nontraditional roles or engaging in nontraditional behaviors. This leads to a discussion of homophobia in African Americans. Homophobia among African Americans has multiple determinants. I explore them in detail as I contend that there is often a connection between homophobia and the internalized racism that resides in the psyches of many African Americans. Both are psychologically destructive to individuals as well as the African American community.

Homophobia and Heterosexism Among African Americans: The Challenge From Within

West (1999) observed that to talk about the history of heterosexism and homophobia is to talk about the ways in which various institutions and persons have promoted unjustified suffering and unmerited pain. I do not assume that homophobia is greater among African Americans than among other people of color or that African Americans have greater resistance to civil rights for lesbians and gay men. It is possible that the homophobic voices are the loudest in the public arena but are not necessarily representative of African Americans as a group. Nonetheless, homophobic rhetoric and behavior harms African American lesbians and gay men and ultimately harms African American communities (Greene, 2000; Hall & Greene, 2002).

Boykin (1998), Clarke (1983), and Jeffries (1992) have observed that there was once a greater tolerance for lesbians and gay men in some poor African American communities, such as Harlem, New York, in the 1940s through 1950s. Clarke explained this tolerance as "seizing the opportunity to spite the white man" Jeffries attributed it to the empathy African Americans experienced, as oppressed people, toward members of another oppressed group. However, a strong component to this tolerance was the relative invisibility of homosexuals within the African American community and the dominant culture. The heightened visibility of lesbians and gay men in contemporary environments may place greater tension on the invisibility and denial that have been components of that tolerance (Greene, 1994a, 1994c, 1996b, 2007).

Oppressed groups that have been the object of genocide—for example, African Americans and Native Americans—accord reproductive sexuality great importance (Greene, 1994a, 1996b, 2000). Many group members view it as the way to guarantee their continued presence in a society that wants to be rid of them and uses racist and genocidal practices to accomplish that goal. Nonreproductive sexual practices are seen by many African Americans as another way that the group's survival is threatened (Monroe, 1998). Some consider lesbian and gay sexual orientation to be a part of a larger scheme on the part of White America to accomplish this goal (Monroe, 1998). In this view, women's primary roles are to reproduce. Women and men who reject this role are viewed as traitors to the race (Cohen, 1999; Monroe, 1998). Kanuha (1990) referred to these beliefs as "fears of extinction" (p. 176). Although fears of genocidal practices against African Americans as a group are warranted, this view scapegoats lesbian and gay members of the community instead of the more appropriate targets: racist practices and institutions. Furthermore, having a lesbian or gay sexual orientation is not synonymous with not having children, particularly among African American and other lesbians of color. However, the internalization of this view may make it harder for African American lesbians and gay men who wish to have children to reconcile this desire with that of their sexual orientation. It may also be used as a barrier between members of the African American community affecting the kind and degree of support a lesbian or gay man may obtain (Cohen, 1999; Greene, 1994a, 1996b, 1998a, 2000; Monroe, 1998).

Homophobia can assume many diverse forms, and they are usually based on distortions of lesbian and gay sexuality. One form of homophobia is represented in the belief that lesbian and gay sexual orientation is a chosen lifestyle. When viewed in this manner, homophobia is rendered an inconvenience that does not compare with the protracted, involuntary hardship of being African American (Gates, 1993). The belief that lesbian and gay sexual orientations are chosen and that race is not is a function of the resentment expressed by many African Americans at comparisons between racial discrimination and homophobia. These attitudes grossly underestimate the destructive impact of homophobia.

The relative visibility of race–ethnicity among African Americans and the invisibility of sexual orientation plays a significant role in the belief that lesbian and gay sexual orientations are chosen or that, if they are invisible, they can and should be concealed. When individuals choose to reveal same-sex relationships, they are treated as if they deserve the ill treatment directed at them. Unlike racial identity, sexual orientation is viewed as something that can and should be concealed, making homophobia appear to be more controllable than racism. There is also the assumption that there is no cost in remaining silent or "passing" for heterosexual. This position is a stark representation of heterosexual privilege among African Americans who hold such beliefs and stands in sharp contradiction to what we know about the cost of invisibility, hiding, and passing for White. The lesbian and gay psychological literature and the African

American psychological literature have long documented the negative psychological effects of passing for White as a long-term mechanism for managing discrimination (Gomez, 1999; West, 1999). Aside from the stress that is part of the constant fear of discovery, there is also the physical and psychic energy that a person is forced to expend if he or she lives a fraudulent life or if he or she is forced, out of fear, to conceal significant aspects of their lives from significant persons. Although there is a choice about telling, there is not a corollary choice about being lesbian or gay.

The assumption that race is always visible among African Americans ignores the presence of light-skinned African Americans throughout history who have passed for White to avoid discrimination. Those who do so are often the objects of scathing contempt. Indeed, biracial African Americans who do not declare monoracial loyalty are often equally disparaged. This suggests that African Americans associate claiming African heritage with a level of integrity and authenticity. The same principle, however, is not applied to sexual orientation and in this manner exercises a form of heterosexual dominance that declares claiming ethnic heritage a healthy imperative while deeming being out as a lesbian or gay man as something that invites abuse and is deserving of it. In this schema, when people are harmed by racial discrimination, racism is the problem, but when a lesbian or gay man is harmed by discrimination, the person's disclosure is viewed as the problem. Although African Americans are a disadvantaged group, these examples inform us that all group members are not equally disadvantaged.

Religiously Derived Prejudice and Homophobia

Another more pernicious form of homophobia among African Americans is based on religious and theological grounds. One of the most frequent sources of internalized homophobia among African American lesbians and gay men, and a frequent source of conflict between them and other family members, is an objection to their sexual orientation on religious grounds. Family members may report that their acceptance of the lesbian or gay family member's sexual orientation is a betrayal or repudiation of their faith and that a lesbian or gay relationship violates the teachings in Biblical scripture and God's law or intent. Many individuals themselves report feeling conflicted about how they can be practicing lesbian/gay and good Christians simultaneously. The degree and intensity of these feelings of conflict or ambivalence about being a lesbian or gay man may vary with the individual's family's degree of involvement (present or past) with formal religion. For strict adherents to Western Christian theology, selective interpretations of Biblical scripture have been historically used to reinforce homophobic attitudes (Claybourne, 1978; Gomes, 1996; Greene, 1994a, 1994c, 2000, 2008; Icard, 1986; Monroe, 1998; Moses & Hawkins, 1982; Weatherford & Weatherford, 1999). African Americans have a strong Christian spiritual and religious orientation (Boyd-Franklin, 1989). It is no surprise that religious derivatives are often a part of the conflict for clients who are ambivalent about or do not accept their sexual orientation, particularly those who seek solace from their church. Weatherford and Weatherford (1999) observed, "The African American church sweeps eroticism under the rug, but most congregations don't even give homosexuality a foot in the door" (p. 21).

Although the Black church has served as a haven for many African Americans in their struggles with racism, and has often been a potent force in liberation theology, it has been less than hospitable toward its lesbian, gay, and bisexual members. Silvera (1991) wrote that when her grandmother discovered that she was a lesbian, she took out her Bible and explained "This was a t'ing only people of mixed blood was involved in" (p. 16). Shaka-Zulu (1996) reflected on her life and struggles as an African American lesbian growing up in a Black Fundamentalist church. She offers that a "don't ask, don't tell" policy of denial was a part of an atmosphere in which compulsory heterosexuality was strictly enforced (Shaka-Zulu, 1996).

There is a great variance among African American mainstream denominations in their official policies on homosexuality (Weatherford & Weatherford, 1999). The Weatherfords wrote that the Roman Catholic, Southern Baptist, and Pentecostal denominations maintain the most conservative positions on the subject, and the United Church of Christ was deemed most welcoming to lesbian and gay members. Others fit in between these extremes. Many congregations that belong to national religious organizations have a measure of local autonomy in their execution of the organization's policies (Weatherford & Weatherford, 1999); hence, there may actually be some latitude in the degree to which official denominational policies are followed. Certain non-Christian religious sects view homosexuality as a decadent Western practice as well. Readers are referred to Weatherford and Weatherford (1999) for more detailed information about the official policies of other specific denominations.

For adherents to Western Christian religiosity, Biblical scripture may be selectively used to express a family member's discomfort with other aspects of the lesbian or gay family member's person or life choices. Objections to lesbian sexual orientation can mask difficulty that parenting or other figures may experience over the loss of control or healthy separation individuation of an adult child. There is great potential for this when a lesbian or gay member is establishing a family with another woman or man and leaves the household of her family of origin. If parenting figures are not ready for healthy separation, it may be easier to target sexual orientation as the focus of their distress instead of separation, and they may get more support for doing so. Leaving the home to marrying or establish a life with a person from the other sex would be a normal developmental expectation, and parental objections might be more easily recognized as the parent's problem, not the adult child's problem. Family objections may also mask a family member's characterological discomfort with his or her own sexuality or with sexual matters altogether. These and other forms of discomfort may be expressed via the rationale of religious conviction with the assumption that behavior based on religious belief is beyond question.

Biblical scripture can be selectively used in the service of homophobia and the status quo of heterosexism. There is no uniform way that Christian theologians or Biblical scholars interpret these issues. Psychotherapy can be useful in determining how the Scripture or belief is being used defensively instead of arguing the specifics of the interpretation with either a client or a family member. For example, is the belief being used in the interest of bringing family members together in a peaceful and mutual reconciliation, or is the belief being used to further split family members into "good" and "bad" camps, exacerbating preexisting conflicts between members or between other factions of the family? Gomes (1996) observed that legitimizing violence against lesbians and gay men, Jews, women, and Blacks is derived from the perspective that if the Bible stigmatizes people, it is acceptable for us to harm them, a practice that has devastating consequences.

Gomes (1996) and Weatherford and Weatherford (1999) have written that no credible case against homosexuality or homosexuals can be made from the Bible unless one chooses to interpret Scripture in ways that presume the preexisting prejudices against homosexuality are true. Gomes argued that the subject of homosexuality is not even mentioned in the early texts of the Bible and that the word *homosexual* itself, an invention of the late 19th century, is never mentioned until the 1946 Revised Standard version. Gomes and Weatherford and Weatherford have challenged the notion that the Bible's failure to mention homosexual relationships warrants condemnation of them. They pointed out that the Bible does not discuss celibacy, the single state, friendships, or other kinds of relationships that we do not hold in contempt. That heterosexuality is dominant does not warrant the assumption that it is the only form of sexuality that is morally correct.

Dyson (1996), Cone (1990), and Fielding-Stewart (1994) have observed that the African American church espouses a "profoundly" conservative theological position on sexuality in general and that this "rigid" perspective creates a repressive climate within the church itself. It is within that repressive climate that African Americans are taught *not* to question, or apply a critical analysis to Biblical scriptures or religious doctrines. Instead of questioning interpretations of Scripture, they are expected by church authority to accept what is given at face value, particularly about sexual matters (Greene, 2000, 2008). Because many people in Black communities are not literate, they are not able to read the Biblical Scriptures themselves; instead, they depend on others to interpret for them. Monroe (1998) suggested that this conservative theology regarding sexual matters is a derivative of a legacy of slavery, misogyny, and racism. I contend that theological homophobia, often expressed in the rejection of lesbians and gay men in both the Black church and the African American community, is also connected to internalized racism and sexism among African Americans.

Monroe (1998) and Simmons (1999, cited in Weatherford & Weatherford, 1999, p. 32) have observed that gay-friendly roles (the choirmaster, etc.) in the Black church, and, by extension, in the Black community, are tolerated as long as they are nonthreatening and as long as there are no open displays of homosexual behavior. As long as open lesbians and gay men are not a part of the governing, administrative, or power hierarchy, and as long as they are silent about who they are, they are tolerated. Monroe described the ministry of misogyny and homophobia in the Black church as one in which social action is predicated on the devaluation of women, and of lesbian, gay, bisexual, and transgendered people. In Monroe's thesis, this practice rests on the belief that Black men are the most endangered members of the Black community and that they must be protected by, and at the expense of, African American women as well as other members of the community. Male superiority and dominance are active ingredients in homophobia in that they support the preservation of traditional gender roles and the hierarchies that accompany them (Greene, 1996b, 2000, 2008; Monroe, 1998). Roles and hierarchies that maintain female subordination are not viewed appropriately as a construction of society but instead are seen as God's will. In this analysis, African American lesbians and gay men are blamed for not upholding what are perceived to be roles given by God rather than the dictates of a patriarchal society.

One of the explanations of homophobia among African Americans says that because African Americans are largely a part of the Christian traditions, their discomfort with lesbian and gay sexual orientations is understandable, as if that position is universally accepted in all Christian congregations. This is a curious argument devoid of the realistic history of African Americans who came to the United States not as Christians but as slaves. Slaves were pieces of property, regarded as creatures devoid of souls. They were the focus of an evil enterprise that was supported by mainstream Christian denominations. Indeed, many holding pens for slaves and auctions were held on church property. This is not an indictment of Christianity per se; instead, it serves as another potent example of how religion can be hijacked and used to support the selective abuse of people in society who are unpopular, who make others uncomfortable, or for whom there is a desire to exploit their labor, territory, or possessions without their consent or adequate compensation. Furthermore, Christian theology has been an important source of strength and support for African Americans in their struggle against racism. This clearly illustrates the capacity for African Americans and other groups to use religious doctrine as a form of liberation theology in ways that affirm social justice rather than the social status quo of dominance and subordination exemplified in homophobic rhetoric and behavior.

The "White Man's Disease"

Lesbian and gay sexual orientations among African Americans have long been attributed to too much assimilation, a disease of the White man or a product of too much Western assimilation. These are positions that have enjoyed the support of the hierarchy of organized Black churches.

There Were No Gay People in Africa: Fact or Fiction?

Smith (in Riggs, 1995) suggested that homophobic beliefs among African Americans are also a function of Black Nationalists' efforts to claim an African heritage. These beliefs, however, are based on the assertion that there was no homosexuality in Africa. Myths are created about an Africa and an African past to which most contemporary African Americans have no connection, whose history has been obscured, and, depending on the period of African and American history one examines, was alternately devalued and then idealized.

I briefly address the contention that lesbian (and gay) sexual orientations are inauthentic in African-descended people on the basis of the assertion that there is no evidence of them in Africa. Overall, this view is not supported by the anthropological study of African peoples (Blackwood & Wieringa, 1999; Wekker, 1993). It is important to note, however, that the way a culture defines sexuality will determine whether the African and Western constructs of sexual orientation are conceptually equivalent. What we in the West mean when we label someone lesbian, gay, or bisexual is often based on conceptualizations of gender that are constructed differently in other cultures and may be less visible to the Western observer.

Gevisser (1998) and Potgieter (1997) have observed that as more African nations turn to democracy lesbian and gay Africans have become more visible and assertive, despite the fact that it places them in conflict with conservative African leaders. Indeed, South Africa under the leadership of Nelson Mandela was the first and for some time the only nation to include protection from sexual orientation discrimination in its constitution (Potgieter, 1997). Anthropological evidence reveals that there have always been forms of what in the West would be considered homosexuality in African and in all other human cultures (Blackwood & Wieringa, 1999; Gevisser, 1998; Murray & Roscoe, 1998; Potgieter, 1997). In some parts of southern Africa, lesbians are often considered traditional healers (as they were in many Native American tribes). Their "difference" in some cultures is seen as something that gives them a special connection to the supernatural (Gevisser, 1998). The healer status also means that they do not have to marry. Not having to marry allows them to live independent lives as unattached women (Gevisser, 1998; Kendall, 1998). It is important to understand the economic structure of a society and its role in defining marriage as a factor that is interrelated with gender roles. Women who must marry men in order to attain economic viability may construct their relationships with other women differently than the lesbian couples structure we observe in the West (Kendall, 1998). It is also important to consider the effect of colonization on indigenous cultural practices. In Africa, the advent of Christianity and the influx of Christian missionaries who facilitated Africa's colonization stigmatized the kinds of people and relationships whom Westerners would currently regard as lesbian or gay. If and when they were stigmatized, punishment by death was often the price paid for this identity. For this reason, many became hidden members of society.

Although many contentions about contemporary and precolonial Africa are more representative of social fiction than reality, many African Americans believe them, forgetting that they are social creations to begin with. Nonetheless, because of the important role these ideas play in the psyche of African Americans, and the degree to which they are accepted as fact among many African Americans, I think it is important to briefly address them. Many of these beliefs are significant ingredients in both the internalized racism and homophobia in the African American community as well as internalized homophobia among African American lesbians. As such, this warrants the serious attention of clinicians.

We must begin by asking what are the psychological consequences, for African Americans, of developing in a society that objects to and negatively stigmatizes significant elements of their sexual and other identities? The sexuality of African Americans has been defined and created by the dominant culture as abnormal, bestial, and it conjures up the image of lascivious, out-of-control beasts who require external control and are to be feared. Images of "reckless, irresponsible, dangerous, Black sexuality" are used to maintain stigmatized images of African American women and men and simultaneously support and sustain their exploited position in the social hierarchy (Cohen, 1999; Greene, 2000; Monroe, 1998; West, 1993). Although race plays a role in defining Black sexuality, sexuality has always played an important role in defining Blackness. This is evident in the ethnosexual mythologies used to stigmatize African American sexuality (Greene, 1996b, 2000; Wyatt, Strayer, & Lobitz, 1976).

Cohen (1999), Higginbotham (1993), and West (1993) have observed that in the minds of many African Americans, respectability and acceptance by the dominant group came to be equated with distancing oneself from any image or behavior found in racist stereotypes of African Americans. This of course meant distancing oneself from any members of the African American community who refuse to attempt to live up to the dominant culture's proscription for respectability. West (1993) wrote:

> Black survival required accommodation with and acceptance from white America.... Struggling black institutions made a Faustian pact with white America: avoid any substantive engagement with black sexuality and your survival on the margins of American Society is, at least, possible. (p. 86)

West (1993) conceptualized behavior that in psychological terms can be seen as an attempt to act against a stereotype. Some individuals who behave as West described do not necessarily believe the essence of the stereotypes that degrade Black sexuality. They may, however, feel required to give the appearance of imitating the dominant culture's norms, regardless of whether they believe in the superiority of those norms. However, other individuals who engage in this behavior do so because they do believe that degrading stereotypes or elements of them are true. For those who believe the degrading stereotypes of Black sexuality, and who behave as West described, this can be understood as a form of psychological defense against the belief that one is actually inferior. The belief in stereotypes of one's own inferiority represents a form of internalized racism.

For African Americans who have internalized the negative stereotypes of their sexuality constructed and held by the dominant culture, sexual behavior outside of dominant societal norms can be experienced as a negative reflection on all African Americans. There may be an exaggerated desire to model "normalcy" to the dominant culture (Clarke, 1983; deMonteflores, 1986; Gomez, 1983; Greene, 1986, 1994a , 1994c, 1996a, 1996b, 1998a, 2000; Higginbotham, 1993; Wyatt et al., 1976). This form of defensive response to attacks on African American sexuality is reflected in part and supported by the African American church's demonization of sexuality and idealization of the need for sexual purity (Monroe, 1998; Higginbotham, 1993; Weatherford & Weatherford, 1999). Because acceptance of lesbian and gay sexual orientations is inconsistent with the dominant culture's ideal, lesbians and gay men may be experienced as an embarrassment to persons who strongly identify with the dominant culture (Cohen, 1999; Greene, 1994a, 2000; Poussaint, 1990; West, 1993). Indeed, the only names for lesbians and gay men in the African American community—"funny women," "bulldagger-women," "faggots," "fairies"—are derogatory (Jeffries, 1993, p. 44; Omosupe, 1991).

Homophobia allows the African Americans who have internalized sexual and racial stereotypes to distance themselves personally, and the Black community in general, from the sexual stigma that the dominant culture has associated with Black identity, particularly Black sexuality (Cohen, 1999; West, 1993). This allows some segments of the African American community to maintain their hope for legitimacy and full incorporation into the dominant culture's power structure (Cohen, 1999; Monroe, 1998). For other African Americans, distancing from lesbian and gay members is based on a distortion of African cultures and African descendency. This distortion, intended to "normalize" Africans, appears to be based on the assumption that the presence of lesbian and gay members of one's ethnic group is a bad thing. Hence, claims of African conformity to exclusive heterosexuality represents a denial of the realistic presence of lesbian, gay, bisexual, and transgendered people among Africans as they are present among every other human group. Although same-gender sexual attractions and relationships occur in all cultures, they may be constructed and understood differently than the Western concept of lesbian and gay identities.

The notion of a monolithic racial identity that excludes lesbian and a gay sexual orientation, represents an attempt to exercise an oppressive form of social control for unilateral group conformity (Cohen, 1999; Gates, 1991; Greene, 2000; Monroe, 1998; West, 1993). However, this mythical uniformity is maintained by keeping elements of the community and group silenced, invisible, and denied. If a model of the community requires that members of the African American community be silenced, or their presence denied, we are left with a model of the group that is neither authentic nor representative. Lesbian and gay members of the African American community who attempt to deny healthy parts of themselves—in this case, by denying their sexuality—to fit within this inauthentic framework of "Blackness" commit a form of psychological suicide. This behavior at its core represents a derivative of internalized racism, a kind of pathology in the group that will neither tolerate nor accept the realistic diversity of its members. The lesbian or gay individual is not pathological for failing to live up to a false cultural standard. Despite this reality, many lesbians and gay men express great conflict around which community warrants their allegiance and support and whether their "Blackness" is authentic if they are lesbian or gay.

One of the methods for silencing nonconforming group members who are lesbian or gay is the accusation of racial disloyalty, lack of authenticity, or incompatibility of lesbian or gay sexual orientation and "Blackness." Such accusations often lead individuals to experience conflicts between their "loyalty" to the African American community or the lesbian/gay community, which is perceived as the White community. This leaves them in a psychological no-win situation as they are forced to compartmentalize and conceal different parts of themselves depending on the context (Greene, 1994a, 1996b, 2000, 2007; Nettles, 2007; Walters, 1996). The concept of racial loyalty presumes that a lesbian or gay sexual orientation is incompatible with a Black identity, or at least an authentic one.

The charge of being racially disloyal or not "Black enough" is extremely painful for many African Americans. Those who organize other aspects of their identity around being African American are particularly vulnerable. These issues should not be regarded as frivolous or tangential. It is important to understand what it is like for an African American lesbian or gay person to face the stated or implied charge of racial disloyalty. A person who is African American and lesbian or gay is a member of a visible, oppressed ethnic group as well as a less visible, oppressed minority, in a racially hostile society. Most members of these groups have other identities as well, and those multiple identities further complicate their dilemma. Because of the racism in the predominantly White lesbian and gay community, those identities are no substitute for the protective function of the African American family and community. However, African American lesbians and gay men may be forced to be silent about their sexual orientation to obtain the protection and support offered by the African American community and their families. It is important to understand what happens when an individual is relegated to the margins or pushed outside of the group that has been necessary to their survival and, worse yet, when they are then accused of belonging to the enemy camp, a confused traitor to his or her race. African American lesbians and gay men who internalize these beliefs are indeed between a rock and a hard place. The loss of tangible and emotional support, the special buffering function and protection from racism that is withdrawn from some African American lesbian and gay members on disclosure, is real, and its impact should not be underestimated. However, we must ask why these assertions of racial disloyalty carry such emotional weight and are so painful to many clients when, on the surface, their manipulative function may appear obvious. Gates (1993) observed that

> Blacks across the economic and ideological spectrum are often astonishingly vulnerable to charges of in-authenticity or disloyalty to the race.... [T]his vulnerability and the pain associated with it attests to the enduring strength of our feelings of guilt, and our anxiety about having been or having the potential to be false to our people, having sinned against our innermost identity. (p. 118)

One explanation for this heightened sensitivity to accusations of disloyalty resides in African Americans' own psyche as descendants of Africans, a group that was far from monolithic. A part of their heritage is that of being descendants of stolen people, an identity that most African Americans readily claim. They are also, however, descendants of the Africans who sold other Africans, an ancestry that there is no rush to claim. The participation of some Africans and African tribes in the selling of Africans into slavery does not relieve the dominant culture in America for its establishment and operation of institutional, chattel slavery, or of the responsibility for the destructive effects of hundreds of years of American apartheid and institutional racism. It does, however, mean that African Americans have a complicated history and legacy.

African Americans share a complex legacy, not an ideal legacy. Indeed, no ideal legacy exists for any other ethnic group; neither is one required to demonstrate human worth. The attempt to construct an edited version of African ancestry, devoid of sexuality that is condemned by the West, is understandable. It is a logical defense against the overwhelming barrage of negative images and distortions of Africa and African descendants and the harsh treatment based on those depictions. Similarly, the attempt to maintain distance from community members who appear to fulfill negative stereotypes of the dominant culture about Black sexuality begin, at least, as understandable attempts at accommodation and survival. The danger is that they lead communities to deny the realistic and deserved presence of many of their members and lead those members to deny or to experience shame about important parts of themselves. Furthermore, these attempts do not leave African Americans with a realistic legacy of the African past, or understanding of contemporary African America. In the long run, they do not serve the interests of the African American community as the diverse community that it really is.

Baldwin (1984, cited in Goldstein, 1984) observed, "There is nothing in me that is not in everybody else, and nothing in everybody else that is not in me" (p. 182). Baldwin's eloquence draws our attention to the reality that African Americans have all the potential in behavior and emotions that all other human beings have and that are a part of being totally human. Distortions of what it means to be "authentically" Black that rest on silencing elements of African American contemporary communities and eradicating pieces of our history, particularly when internalized by lesbian and gay clients, must be deconstructed. Just as there is no ideal family, there is no ideal nation family, and none is warranted.

Psychological health is predicated on the acceptance and integration of the disparate elements of the self and family, in both the biological and nation or ethnic sense. Thus, assisting clients, when appropriate, in identifying and acknowledging healthy, nurturing, and toxic elements in the family, among or within loved and trusted as well as hated figures, is an active component of most psychotherapies. It includes both the repudiation or appropriate management of toxic or unhealthy elements of the self, family, and community. The spiritual and emotional reconciliation of those disparate elements, as well as individual's own ambivalence about them, must take place in order for a healthy development or therapeutic transformation to occur. In psychotherapy, this is an appropriate goal. Just as reconciliation takes place in psychotherapy around mixed and multiple legacies among one's family of origin, it may for some individuals need to take place when it applies to the nation family that they have internalized as well. This is particularly important when it is connected to such beliefs about core aspects of the person's identity. This means accepting in the nation context, just as one must in the family and in the self, a mixed heritage. The identities of African Americans' ancestors and descendants need not be distorted to be redeemable or to demonstrate their worth. When reconciliation is successful, there is no need to distort and silence members of the community or elements of the self that do not maintain images borne of shame or defensiveness. The internalized racism that is a significant ingredient in the need for the distortions discussed can be transformed into a healthy acceptance of a wider range of ways of being in the world that do not mitigate the authenticity of one's identity as an African-descended person.

African American lesbians and gay men who struggle with these issues have the opportunity in psychotherapies of having their accurate perceptions of discrimination and unfair treatment validated by identifying and understanding the conscious and unconscious methods they employ in confronting and negotiating systemic and personal barriers, by analyzing the effectiveness of their methods, and by developing a wider range of personally compatible options.

Conclusion

For African American lesbians and gay men, the effects of racism, sexism, and heterosexism (among other identities) cannot be neatly separated from one another; neither can they be understood in isolation from one another or the social context. Racism affects African American heterosexual individuals, lesbians, and gay men differently. Being an African American shapes the construction and understanding of an individual's sexuality in a reciprocal fashion; it also shapes the construction and manifestations of heterosexism and internalized homophobia. Gender, race, social class, and sexual orientation oppression interact with one another in particular ways, and all shape and interact with the personality dynamics of each individual. Any analysis that fails to take into account this complex interaction of experiences and their effects can neither sensitively nor appropriately grasp the complex nuances of experience as well as the perils and pleasures of life as members of multiple minority groups that comprise African American lesbians and gay men.

References

Altman, N. (1995). *The analyst in the inner city: Race class and culture through a psychoanalytic lens.* New York: Analytic Press.

Bass-Hass, R. (1968). The lesbian dyad: Basic issues and value systems. *Journal of Sex Research, 4,* 126.

Bell, A., & Weinberg, M. (1978). *Homosexualities: A study of human diversity among men and women.* New York: Simon & Schuster.

Blackwood, E., & Wieringa, S. E. (1999). Sapphic shadows: Challenging the silence in the study of sexuality. In E. Blackwood & S. E. Wieringa (Eds.), *Same sex relations and female desires: Transgender practices across cultures* (pp. 39–63). New York: Columbia University Press.

Boyd-Franklin, N. (1989). *Black families: A multisystems approach to family therapy.* New York: Guilford Press.

Boykin, K. (1998). Gay and lesbian movements in the United States. In K. A. Appiah & H. L. Gates, Jr. (Eds.), *Microsoft Encarta Africana: Comprehensive encyclopedia of Black history and Black culture* [CD-ROM]. Redmond, WA: Microsoft.

Boykin, K. (2005). *Beyond the down low: Sex, lies and denial in Black America.* New York: Carroll & Graf.

Brown, L. S. (1996). Preventing heterosexual bias in psychotherapy and counseling. In E. Rothblum & L. Bond (Eds.), *Preventing heterosexism and homophobia* (pp. 36–58). Thousand Oaks, CA: Sage.

Brownworth, V. A. (1993, June). Linda Villarosa speaks out. *Deneuve, 3*(3), 16–19, 56.

Chodorow, N. J. (1989). *Feminism and psychoanalytic theory.* New Haven, CT: Yale University Press.

Christian, B. (1985). *Black feminist criticism: Perspectives on Black women writers.* New York: Pergamon Press.

Clarke, C. (1983). The failure to transform: Homophobia in the Black community. In B. Smith (Ed.), *Home girls: A Black feminist anthology* (pp. 197–208). New York: Kitchen Table–Women of Color Press.

Claybourne, J. (1978). Blacks and gay liberation. In K. Jay & A. Young (Eds.), *Lavender culture* (pp. 458–465). New York: Jove/Harcourt Brace Jovanovich.

Clunis, M., & Green, G. D. (1988). *Lesbian couples.* Seattle, WA: Seal Press.

Cohen, C. (1999). *The boundaries of Blackness: AIDS and the breakdown of Black politics.* Chicago: University of Chicago Press.

Collins, P. H. (1990). Homophobia and Black lesbians. In *Black feminist thought: Knowledge, consciousness, and the politics of empowerment* (pp. 192–196). Boston: Unwin/Hyman.

Cone, J. (1990). *A Black theology of liberation: Twentieth century edition.* Maryknoll, NY: Orbis Books.

deMonteflores, C. (1986). Notes on the management of difference. In T. Stein & C. Cohen (Eds.), *Contemporary perspectives on psychotherapy with lesbians and gay men* (pp. 73–101). New York: Plenum Press.

Dew, M. A. (1985). The effects of attitudes on inferences of homosexuality and perceived physical attractiveness in women. *Sex Roles, 12,* 143–155.

Dyson, M. E. (1996). *Race rules.* New York: Addison-Wesley.

Espin, O. (1984). Cultural and historical influences on sexuality in Hispanic/Latina women: Implications for psychotherapy. In C. Vance (Ed.), *Pleasure and danger: Exploring female sexuality* (pp. 149–163). London: Routledge & Kegan Paul.

Falco, K. L. (1991). *Psychotherapy with lesbian clients.* New York: Brunner/Mazel.

Fielding-Stewart, C. (1994). *African American church growth: 12 principles for prophetic ministry.* Nashville, TN: Abington Press.

Garnets, L., Hancock, K. A., Cochran, S. D., Goodchilds, J., & Peplau, L. A. (1991). Issues in psychotherapy with lesbian and gay men: A survey of psychologists. *American Psychologist, 46,* 964–972.

Garnets, L., & Kimmel, D. (1991). Lesbian and gay male dimensions in the psychological study of human diversity. In J. Goodchilds (Ed.), *Psychological perspectives on human diversity in America* (pp. 137–192). Washington, DC: American Psychological Association.

Gates, H. L., Jr. (1991, April 29–May 6). The charmer. *The New Yorker,* 116–131.

Gates, H. L., Jr. (1993, May 17). Blacklash. *The New Yorker, 69,* 42–44.

Gevisser, M. (1998). Homosexuality in Africa: An interpretation. In K. A. Appiah & H. L. Gates, Jr. (Eds.), *Microsoft Encarta Africana: Comprehensive encyclopedia of Black history and culture* [CD-ROM]. Redmond, WA: Microsoft.

Glassgold, J. (1992). New directions in dynamic theories of lesbianism: From psychoanalysis to social constructionism. In J. Chrisler & D. Howard (Eds.), *New directions in feminist psychology: Practice, theory and research* (pp. 154–163). New York: Springer.

Glassgold, J. (1995). Psychoanalysis with lesbians: Self reflection and agency. In J. Glassgold & S. Iasenza (Eds.), *Lesbians and psychoanalysis: Revolutions in theory and practice* (pp. 203–228). New York: Free Press.

Goldstein, R. (1984). Go the way your blood beats: An interview with James Baldwin. In Q. Troupe (Ed.), *James Baldwin: The legacy* (pp. 173–186). New York: Simon & Schuster.

Gomes, P. J. (1996). The Bible and homosexuality: The last prejudice. In *The Good Book: Reading the Bible with mind and heart* (pp. 144–172). New York: William Morrow.

Gomez, J. (1983). A cultural legacy denied and discovered: Black lesbians in fiction by women. In B. Smith (Ed.), *Home girls: A Black feminist anthology* (pp. 120–121). New York: Kitchen Table–Women of Color Press.

Gomez, J. (1999). Black lesbians: Passing, stereotypes, and transformation. In E. Brandt (Ed.), *Dangerous liaisons: Blacks, gays and the struggle for equality* (pp. 161–177). New York: New Press.

Gomez, J., & Smith, B. (1990). Taking the home out of homophobia: Black lesbian health. In E. C. White (Ed.), *The Black women's health book: Speaking for ourselves* (pp. 198–213). Seattle, WA: Seal Press.

Gonsiorek, J., & Weinrich, J. (1991). The definition and scope of sexual orientation. In J. Gonsiorek & J. Weinrich (Eds.), *Homosexuality: Research implications for public policy* (pp. 1–12). Newbury Park, CA: Sage.

Gould, D. (1995). A critical examination of the notion of pathology in psychoanalysis. In J. Glassgold & S. Iasenza (Eds.), *Lesbians and psychoanalysis: Revolutions in theory and practice* (pp. 3–17). New York: Free Press.

Greene, B. (1986). When the therapist is White and the patient Black: Considerations for psychotherapy in the feminist heterosexual and lesbian communities. *Women and Therapy, 5*, 41–66.

Greene, B. (1990a, December). African American lesbians: The role of family, culture and racism. *BG Magazine, 6*, 26.

Greene, B. (1990b). Stereotypes of African American sexuality: A commentary. In S. Rathus, J. Nevid, & L. Fichner-Rathus (Eds.), *Human sexuality in a world of diversity* (p. 257). Boston: Allyn & Bacon.

Greene, B. (1990c). Sturdy bridges: The role of African American mothers in the socialization of African American children. *Women and Therapy, 10*, 205–225.

Greene, B. (1994a). Ethnic–minority lesbians and gay men: Mental health and treatment issues. *Journal of Consulting and Clinical Psychology, , 62*, 243–251.

Greene, B. (1994b). Lesbian and gay sexual orientations: Implications for clinical training, practice and research. In B. Greene & G. Herek (Eds.), *Psychological perspectives on lesbian and gay issues: Vol. 1. Lesbian and gay psychology: Theory, research, and clinical applications* (pp. 1–24). Thousand Oaks, CA: Sage.

Greene, B. (1994c). Lesbian women of color: Triple jeopardy. In L. Comas-Diaz & B. Greene (Eds.), *Women of color: Integrating ethnic and gender identities in psychotherapy* (pp. 389–427). New York: Guilford Press.

Greene, B. (1995a). An African American perspective on racism and antisemitism within feminist organizations. In J. Adleman & G. Enguidanos (Eds.), *Racism in the lives of women* (pp. 303–313). New York: Haworth Press

Greene, B. (1995b). Lesbian couples. In K. Jay (Ed.), *Dyke life: From growing up to growing old—A celebration of the lesbian experience* (pp. 97–98, 100–101, 103–104, 106). New York: Basic Books.

Greene, B. (1996a). African American women: Considering diverse identities and societal barriers in psychotherapy. In J. A. Sechzer, S. M. Pfafflin, F. L. Denmark, A. Griffin, & S. Blumenthal (Eds.), *Annals of the New York Academy of Sciences: Vol. 789. Women and mental health* (pp. 191–209). New York: New York Academy of Sciences.

Greene, B. (1996b). Lesbians and gay men of color: Ethnosexual mythologies in heterosexism. In E. Rothblum & L. Bond (Eds.), *Preventing heterosexism and homophobia* (pp. 59–70). Thousand Oaks, CA: Sage.

Greene, B. (1997, June). Psychotherapy with African American women: Integrating feminist and psychodynamic models. *Smith College Studies in Social Work, 67*, 299–322.

Greene, B. (1998a). Family, ethnic identity and sexual orientation among African American lesbians and gay men. In C. Patterson & A. D. Augelli (Eds.), *Lesbian, gay and bisexual identity: Psychological research and social policy* (pp. 40–52). New York: Oxford University Press.

Greene, B. (1998b). Sexual orientation. In M. Hersen & A. Bellack (Eds.), *Comprehensive clinical psychology: Vol. 10. Sociocultural and individual differences* (pp. 207–232). Oxford, UK: Elsevier Science and Pergamon Press.

Greene, B. (2000). African American lesbian and bisexual women in feminist-psychodynamic psychotherapies. In L. Jackson & B. Greene (Eds.), *Psychotherapy with African American women: Innovations in psychodynamic perceptives and practice* (pp. 82–125). New York: Guilford Press.

Greene, B. (2007). Homophobia/heterosexism in communities of color. In *Communique: Psychological perspectives on sexual orientation in communities of color* (pp. xxv–xxviii). Retrieved from http://www.apa.org/pi/oema/special_section_august%202007_communique.pdf

Greene, B. (2008). African American women, religion and oppression: The use and abuse of spiritual beliefs. In C. A. Rayburn & L. Comas-Diaz (Eds.), *Womansoul: The inner life of women's spirituality* (pp. 153–166). Westport, CT: Praeger.

Greene, B., & Boyd-Franklin, N. (1996). African American lesbians: Issues in couples therapy. In J. Laird & R. J. Green (Eds.), *Lesbians and gay men in couples and families: A handbook for therapists* (pp. 251–271). San Francisco: Jossey-Bass.

Haldeman, D. (2000). Therapeutic responses to sexual orientation: Psychology's evolution. In B. Greene & G. L. Croom (Eds.), *Education, research, and practice in lesbian, gay, bisexual and transgendered psychology* (pp. 244–262). Thousand Oaks, CA: Sage.

Hall, R. L., & Greene, B. (1996). Sins of omission and co mission: Women, psychotherapy and the psychological literature. *Women & Therapy, 18,* 5–31.

Hall, R. L., & Greene, B. (2002). Not any one thing: The complex legacy of social class on African American Lesbian relationships. *Journal of Lesbian Studies, 6,* 65–74.

Higginbotham, E. (1993). *Righteous discontent: The women's movement in the Black Baptist Church, 1880–1920.* Cambridge, MA: Harvard University Press.

hooks, b. (1981). *Ain't I a woman: Black women and feminism.* Boston: South End Press.

Icard, L. (1986). Black gay men and conflicting social identities: Sexual orientation versus racial identity. *Journal of Social Work and Human Sexuality, 4,* 83–93.

Jackson, K., & Brown, L. B. (1996). Lesbians of African heritage: Coming out in the straight community. *Journal of Gay & Lesbian Social Services, 5*(4), 53–67.

Jeffries, I. (1992, February 23). Strange fruits at the purple manor: Looking back on "the life" in Harlem. *NYQ, 17,* 40–45.

Kanuha, V. (1990). Compounding the triple jeopardy: Battering in lesbian of color relationships. *Women & Therapy, 9,* 169–183.

Kassoff, B., Boden, R., deMonteflores, C., Hunt, P., & Wahba, R. (1995). Coming out of the frame: Lesbian feminism and psychoanalytic theory. In J. Glassgold & S. Iasenza (Eds.), *Lesbians and psychoanalysis: Revolutions in theory and practice* (pp. 229–263). New York: Free Press.

Kendall, K. (1998). Women in Lesotho and the Western construction of homophobia. In E. Blackwood & S. E. Wieringa (Eds.), *Same sex relations and female desires: Transgender practices across cultures* (pp. 157–178). New York: Columbia University Press.

King, J. L. (2004). *On the down low: A journey into the lives of straight Black men who sleep with men.* New York: Broadway Books.

Kite, M. (1994). When perceptions meet reality: Individual differences in reactions to lesbians and gay men. In B. Greene & G. Herek (Eds.), *Lesbian and gay psychology: Theory, research and clinical applications* (pp. 25–53). Thousand Oaks, CA: Sage.

Kite, M., & Deaux, K. (1987). Gender belief systems: Homosexuality and the implicit inversion theory. *Psychology of Women Quarterly, 11,* 83–96.

Loiacano, D. (1989). Gay identity issues among Black Americans: Racism, homophobia and the need for validation. *Journal of Counseling and Development, 68,* 21–25.

Lynsen, J. (2008, July 11). Black opposition to gay marriage remains strong. *Washington Blade.* Retrieved July 30, 2008, from http://www.washblade.com/print.cfm?content_id=12917

Maracek, J., & Hare-Mustin, R. (1991). A short history of the future: Feminism and clinical psychology. *Psychology of Women Quarterly, 15,* 521–536.

Mays, V., & Cochran, S. (1988). The Black's Women Relationship Project: A national survey of Black lesbians. In M. Shernoff & W. Scott (Eds.), *The sourcebook on lesbian/gay health care* (2nd ed., pp. 54–62). Washington, DC: National Lesbian and Gay Health Foundation.

Mays, V., Cochran, S., & Rhue, S. (1993). The impact of perceived discrimination on the intimate relationships of Black lesbians. *Journal of Homosexuality, 25*(4), 1–14.

Monroe, I. (1998). Louis Farrakhan's ministry of misogyny and homophobia. In A. Alexander (Ed.), *The Farrakhan factor: African-American writers on leadership, nationhood, and Minister Louis Farrakhan* (pp. 275–298). New York: Grove Press.

Moses, A. E., & Hawkins, R. (1982). *Counseling lesbian women and gay men: A life issues approach.* St. Louis, MO: Mosby.

Murray, S. O., & Roscoe, W. (Eds.). (1998). *Boy wives and female husbands: Studies of African homosexualities.* New York: St. Martin's Press.

Nettles, R. (2007). Challenges to healthy African American lesbian, gay bisexual or transgender status. In *Communique: Psychological perspectives on sexual orientation in communities of color* (pp. xiv–xvii). Retrieved from http://www.apa.org/pi/oema/special_section_august%202007_communique.pdf

Newman, B. S. (1989). The relative importance of gender role attitudes toward lesbians. *Sex Roles, 21,* 451–465.

Omosupe, K. (1991). Black/lesbian/bulldagger. *differences: A Journal of Feminist Cultural Studies, 2,* 101–111.

Potgieter, C. (1997). From Apartheid to Mandela's constitution: Black South African lesbians in the nineties. In B. Greene (Ed.), *Psychological perspectives on lesbian and gay issues: Vol. 3.*

Ethnic and cultural diversity among lesbians and gay men (pp. 88–116). Thousand Oaks, CA: Sage.

Poussaint, A. (1990, September). An honest look at Black gays and lesbians. *Ebony,* 124, 126, 130–131.

Riggs, M. (Producer/Director). (1995). Interview with bell hooks and Barbara Smith. *Black is . . . Black ain't* [videotape]. Available from California Newsreel, 149 Ninth Street, #420, San Francisco, CA 94103.

Shaka-Zulu, N. (1996). Sex, race and the stained glass window. *Women & Therapy, 19*(4), 27–35.

Silvera, M. (1991). Man royals and sodomites: Some thoughts on the invisibility of Afro-Caribbean lesbians. In M. Silvera (Ed.), *Piece of my heart: A lesbian of color anthology* (pp. 14–26). Toronto, ON, Canada: Sister Vision Press.

Smith, A. (1997). Cultural diversity and the coming out process: Implications for clinical practice. In B. Greene (Ed.), *Ethnic and cultural diversity among lesbians and gay men* (pp. 279–300). Thousand Oaks, CA: Sage.

Smith, B. (1982). Toward a Black feminist criticism. In G. Hull, P. Scott, & B. Smith (Eds.), *All the women are White, all the Blacks are men, but some of us are brave* (pp. 157–175). Old Westbury, NY: Feminist Press.

Tafoya, T., & Rowell, R. (1988). Counseling Native American lesbians and gays. In M. Shernoff & W. A. Scott (Eds.), *The sourcebook on lesbian/gay health care* (pp. 63–67). Washington, DC: National Lesbian and Gay Health Foundation.

Taylor, A. T. (1983). Conceptions of masculinity and femininity as a basis for stereotypes of male and female homosexuals. *Journal of Homosexuality, 9,* 37–53.

Thompson, C. (1987). Racism or neuroticism: An entangled dilemma for the Black middle class patient. *Journal of the American Academy of Psychoanalysis, 15,* 395–405.

Walters, K. (1996). Negotiating conflicts in allegiances among lesbians and gays of color: Reconciling divided selves and communities. In G. Mallon (Ed.), *Foundations of social work practice with lesbian and gay persons* (pp. 47–75). New York: Harrington Park Press.

Weatherford, R. J., & Weatherford, C. B. (1999). *Somebody's knocking at your door: AIDS and the African American Church.* New York: Haworth Press.

Wekker, G. (1993). Mati-ism and Black lesbianism: Two idealtypical expressions of female homosexuality in Black communities of the diaspora. *Journal of Homosexuality, 24*(3–4), 11–24.

West, C. (1993). *Race matters.* New York: Vintage Books.

West, C. (1995). Mammy, Sapphire, and Jezebel: Historical images of Black women and their implications for psychotherapy. *Psychotherapy, 32,* 458–466.

West, C. (1999). Cornel West on heterosexism and transformation. In E. Brandt (Ed.), *Dangerous liaisons: Blacks, gays and the struggle for equality* (pp. 290–305). New York: New Press.

Whitley, E. B., Jr. (1987). The relation of sex role orientation to heterosexual attitudes toward homosexuality. *Sex Roles, 17,* 103–113.

Wyatt, G., Strayer, R., & Lobitz, W. C. (1976). Issues in the treatment of sexually dysfunctioning couples of African American descent. *Psychotherapy, 13,* 44–50.

PART VI

PSYCHOLOGICAL, PHYSICAL, AND BEHAVIORAL HEALTH

24

BLACK AMERICANS AND MENTAL HEALTH STATUS

Complexities and New Developments

TARA R. EARL AND DAVID R. WILLIAMS

Racial disparities in health are embedded within the historical, social, environmental, and political contexts that shape the lives of individuals and groups (Williams, Yu, Jackson, & Anderson, 1997); however, disparities in mental health are often inconsistent with those for physical health status and are neither simple nor straightforward. When we look at current evidence on the prevalence of mental health problems, such as studies of anxiety, mood, substance abuse (comorbidity), and psychotic disorders, findings for Blacks are inconsistent and not well understood (Neighbors, 1984; Williams & Earl, 2007). The best available evidence suggests that the pattern of racial differences varies depending on the indicator of mental health status. Accordingly, whether African Americans are disadvantaged in regard to mental health care compared with Whites depends on whether the focus is on measures of mental health symptoms, psychotic disorders, psychological distress, or psychological well-being.

In this chapter,[1] we provide an overview of the evidence on the mental health status of Blacks in the United States and highlight some of the complexities of the findings that are possibly related to their social context. We review evidence on the prevalence of multiple indicators of mental health status, such as anxiety disorders, mood disorders, substance abuse, psychotic disorders, psychological distress, and psychological well-being. We then highlight the extent of disparities for Blacks in terms of the severity of mental health problems. We also review evidence for racial differences in access to mental health services and the quality of mental health care. We conclude the chapter with a consideration of recent developments in research on Black mental health and a review of the challenges that remain for Black mental health research.

PREVALENCE OF MENTAL HEALTH DISORDERS

There are large racial differences on physical health status that are pervasive across outcomes and persistent over time (Williams, 2005). For most measures of physical health status, Blacks

335

have higher rates for morbidity and mortality than Whites. There is growing evidence that stress and poor social conditions may play a role in the higher rates of illness in socially disadvantaged populations (Williams, 1999). There has been a general assumption that socially disadvantaged groups, such as African Americans, would be at elevated risk of mental health problems. Early studies of mental disorders, though not without controversy, suggested that Blacks had higher rates of mental illness than Whites (Williams & Harris-Reid, 1999). A major limitation the earlier research was the focus on persons in treatment as opposed to those in the community.

The development of community-based psychiatric epidemiology studies provided an opportunity to obtain a more comprehensive picture of mental illness in society. Prior to the last 3 decades, little information was available to ascertain the prevalence of treated and untreated mental disorders in broad-based populations, because there was no standardized criteria on which to base a proper diagnosis. Interest in psychiatric disorders flourished after the inclusion of specific diagnostic criteria in the *Diagnostic and Statistical Manual of Mental Disorders, Third Edition* (*DSM–III*; American Psychiatric Association, 1980) and the operationalization of these criteria in lay-administered instruments. The Epidemiologic Catchment Area Study (ECA), one of the largest mental health studies of its time, was conducted in the 1980s and provided data on the rates of mental illness for about 20,000 adults, both in and out of treatment, in four different communities in the United States. Surprisingly, the ECA found that Blacks did not have higher rates of most common psychiatric disorders than Whites (Robins & Regier, 1991). A decade later, the first national study of psychiatric disorders in the United States, called the *National Comorbidity Study* (NCS), was conducted (Kessler et al., 1994). Findings about lifetime and 12-month prevalence estimates of 14 *DSM–III–R* (American Psychiatric Association, 1987) psychiatric disorders from the NCS indicated that rates of mental illness were high in the United States: Nearly 50% of the respondents had experienced at least one lifetime disorder, and about 30% were affected by at least one 12-month disorder. Surprisingly, this study also found that Blacks had lower rates of commonly occurring psychiatric disorders than Whites (Kessler et al.). Similar findings were revealed by the recent National Comorbidity Study—Replication (NCS–R; Breslau et al., 2006), which was conducted a decade later.

We now turn to a more detailed review of the studies of racial differences on specific classes of psychiatric disorders.

Anxiety Disorders

Approximately 29% of adults are reported to have had an anxiety disorder within their lifetime, making this class of disorders the most prevalent in the United States (Kessler, Chui, et al., 2006). As noted earlier, the ECA study found that Blacks tended not to have higher rates of psychiatric disorders than Whites. One exception to this pattern was anxiety disorders, for which Blacks had higher rates than Whites, especially for phobias. However, the true relationship between race and anxiety disorders was unclear. First, there was some skepticism about the validity of the ECA findings for Blacks because of problems linked to its assessment of phobias (Neal & Turner, 1991). The NCS, which had a better assessment of phobias, found that Blacks had slightly lower rates of anxiety disorders than Whites (Kessler et al., 1994). Lifetime prevalence of any anxiety disorder for Blacks was 23.8%, compared with 24.9% for Hispanics and 29.4% for Whites. Second, racial disparities appear to differ for specific disorders within the anxiety disorders category. Using NCS data, Breslau, Kendler, Su, Gaxiola-Aguilar, and Kessler (2005) found that Blacks reported higher lifetime prevalence rates of posttraumatic stress disorder than both Hispanics and Whites (7.1% compared with 5.9% and 6.8%, respectively). These findings remained significant after the researchers adjusted for cohort variations, age of onset, and sociodemographic differences. Third, more detailed analyses of the NCS revealed a striking interaction among race, gender and phobia (Magee, 1993). White men had higher rates of phobias than their Black counterparts, and White women had lower rates of phobias than their Black peers.

Mood Disorders

Mood disorders are the second most prevalent class of psychiatric disorders with lifetime and 12-month prevalence estimates of 21% and

10%, respectively, for the general population (Kessler, Akiskal, et al., 2006). The most commonly occurring mood disorders are major depressive disorder (MDD), dysthymic disorder, and bipolar disorder I or II (Kessler et al., 2005). Given the suggestions that mood disorders are linked to the social and environmental conditions under which people live and work (see G. Brown, 2005; Turner & Lloyd, 2004; Williams & Neighbors, 2006), one could assume that Blacks and other economically vulnerable groups would fair poorly compared with Whites.

Evidence from national psychiatric epidemiological studies spanning more than 15 years continue to show that Blacks consistently report lower rates of any mood disorder than Whites (Breslau et al., 2006; Somervell et al., 1989; Williams, Gonzalez, et al., 2007). Using ECA data, Somervell et al. (1989) concluded that, after controlling for age and household income, Blacks from New Haven, Connecticut; Baltimore, Maryland; and the Piedmont area of North Carolina had lower lifetime prevalence of major depressive disorder than Whites. The NCS–R revealed rates of lifetime prevalence to be lower between Blacks and Whites for dysthymic disorder and MDD (Breslau et al., 2006). The most recent data come from the National Survey of American Life (NSAL), the largest study of Black mental health ever conducted in the United States. It found that lifetime and 12-month prevalence of MDD was higher for Whites than for Blacks (Williams, Gonzalez, et al., 2007). The NSAL study also highlights the diversity of the Black population.

In the NCS–R, bipolar disorder was the only mood disorder for which Blacks differed significantly from Whites. Lifetime prevalence of bipolar disorder for Blacks was 4.9% as compared with 3.2% for Whites (Breslau et al., 2006). Other data from the NCS–R indicate that, for the general U.S. population, the odds of being affected with bipolar disorder are generally greater in the presence of other disorders (Merikangas et al., 2007).

Substance Abuse Disorders

Research on the prevalence of substance abuse disorders reveals that approximately 15% of the general population will have had a substance abuse disorder within their lifetime, and about 4% will have had a substance abuse disorder within the past 12 months (Kessler, Adler, et al., 2006). Several studies have reported that Blacks have substantially lower prevalence rates of substance abuse disorders than do Whites (Grant, 1996; Kessler et al., 1994; Robins & Regier, 1991). Findings from the National Longitudinal Alcohol Epidemiological Survey showed that although Whites were more likely than Blacks to use drugs within their lifetime, Blacks were significantly more likely to persist in their drug dependence than Whites (Grant, 1996). The National Longitudinal Alcohol Epidemiological Survey addressed some of the limitations of the ECA study and the NCS by including a nationally representative sample, which improved on the ECA study, and it included adults over age 55, thus including a broader adult age range than the NCS (Grant, 1996). These findings are counterintuitive, because indicators of socioeconomic status (SES) have been significantly associated with higher prevalence of substance abuse disorder, and Blacks are a socially disadvantaged group with values on indicators of SES that are lower than those of Whites (Kessler et al., 1994; Yu & Williams, 1999). Recent data show that the pattern of substance use and dependence are similar to that of most mood disorders: Blacks have significantly lower rates of substance use and dependence than Whites.

Race and Psychotic Disorders

There are several reasons why prevalence estimates of psychotic disorders for Blacks should be interpreted with caution. Racial differences in psychotic disorders are unclear. Early studies based on data from state psychiatric hospitals reported that Blacks had higher rates of schizophrenia than Whites; however, these studies did not comprehensively cover schizophrenia cases (Barnes, 2004). Researchers have noted potential problems with these data that stemmed from the fact that most study participants were in inpatient settings, and some evidence suggests that Blacks are overdiagnosed with schizophrenia and underdiagnosed with depression (Adebimpe, 1994; Baker & Bell, 1999). In contrast to the early studies that relied on small, nonrepresentative samples, the ECA study offered a large, population-based sample. It found little to no differences in Blacks versus Whites for psychiatric disorders in general, but the rate of schizophrenia for Blacks was slightly higher than that of

Whites (Robins & Regier, 1991). The racial difference was reduced to nonsignificance when adjusted for SES and other demographic variables. Despite the large population-based sample size of the ECA study, the absence of clinical judgment was a major limitation. Clinical validation studies show that clinical judgment is important for the valid assessment of psychotic disorders (Kessler et al., 2005).

In light of the limitations of the ECA study, the NCS–R included a clinical reappraisal interview in which clinicians used a structured diagnostic instrument to reinterview respondents who had earlier completed a psychosis screen (Kessler et al., 2005). From this, Blacks seemed to have higher rates of nonaffective psychosis than Whites, but this estimate was based on an extrapolation of only 73 clinical reinterviews. Thus, these analyses had limited statistical power, and there are serious reservations regarding their generalizability.

The *DSM–IV* Field Trial for Schizophrenia and Other Psychotic Disorders study was designed to test the reliability and concordance of several diagnostic criteria sets for psychotic disorders to be included in the *DSM–IV* (American Psychiatric Association, 1994). It found that Blacks were more likely to receive a *DSM–III–R* diagnosis of schizophrenia and were less likely to be diagnosed with psychotic depression than White patients (Strakowski, Flaum, Amador, & Bracha, 1996). In addition, first-rank symptom presentation (e.g., severe auditory hallucinations, paranoia, delusions of thought insertion or withdrawal, thoughts of being controlled by an external force) was more common for Black patients compared with White patients. Finally, Strakowski et al. (1996) discussed the implication of the historical association of psychosis or schizophrenia with Blacks, which, in their opinion, could subconsciously have influenced or biased the rating of symptoms. They also pointed out that "the prominent use of first-rank symptoms as diagnostic criteria may lead to racially disproportionate rates of diagnosing schizophrenia, suggesting that further study is needed to clarify racial and cultural differences in the expression of psychosis" (p. 122).

Race and Psychological Distress

Findings from studies of psychological distress for Blacks are inconsistent. For example, in an earlier assessment, Barbara and Bruce Dohrenwend (Dohrenwend & Dohrenwend, 1969) reviewed eight community-based psychiatric epidemiological studies: Four showed higher rates of mental health problems for Blacks, and the other four showed higher rates for Whites. A review of subsequent studies also found higher rates of psychological distress for Blacks and Whites, but the racial differences were reduced to nonsignificance when adjusted for SES (Neighbors, 1984). Other reviews of the literature on race and psychological distress indicate that Blacks report lower levels of psychological distress than Whites in some studies, whereas in other studies, the opposite occurs. Some recent studies have found no racial differences at all. Racial differences in rates of distress were thought to be due to low SES (Warheit, Holzer, & Arey, 1975) but, after controlling for indicators of SES (income and education), the differences were later found to be minimal or nonexistent (Vega & Rumbaut, 1991). However, other research has documented an interaction between race and SES, with low-SES Blacks having higher rates of distress than their White counterparts (Kessler & Neighbors, 1986).

Race and Psychological Well-Being

For racial and ethnic minorities, studies of psychological well-being (i.e., satisfaction and happiness) have assessed the extent to which membership within a racial group predicts levels of well-being. Measures have sought to make judgments about an individual's positive and negative affect, level of satisfaction, and the lack of strain that characterizes his or her quality of life in multiple domains (Andrews & Withey, 1976; Wilson & Williams, 2004). An early review of the evidence by Bracy (1976) found that Blacks were significantly less satisfied than Whites, even after controlling for family income, education, occupation, geographic residence, household size, and age. Racial differences were also significant between lower-SES Blacks and Whites, with Blacks reporting lower life satisfaction than Whites. Similar analyses of the General Social Survey (GSS) data, a national survey on demographic data and attitudes of the U.S. population, have continued to support Bracy's conclusion that Blacks continually report significantly lower levels of satisfaction or well-being than Whites. Michael Hughes and Melvin

Thomas conducted two investigations, 12 years apart, using GSS data to examine Black–White differences in psychological well-being. The first study, which used GSS data between 1972 and 1985, suggested that subjective well-being for Blacks was significantly and consistently lower than that for Whites, even after controlling for SES, age, and marital status (Thomas & Hughes, 1986). The follow-up study, which used GSS data from 1972 to 1996, found that Blacks' psychological well-being continued to be worse than that of Whites (Hughes & Thomas, 1998).

Race and Flourishing as "Positive" Mental Health

There is a lot of interest in expanding the definition of mental health to include positive aspects of mental well-being. The term *flourishing* is fairly new to the field, but the concept of focusing on the positive aspects mental health, as compared with the problems related to illness, was one of the major themes in the U.S. Surgeon General's 1999 report on Mental Health (Kennedy, 1999; U.S. Department of Health and Human Services, 1999). *Flourishing* is defined as the absence of mental illness and the presence of mental health (Keyes, 2007). To be diagnosed as flourishing in life, "individuals must exhibit high levels on at least one measure of hedonic well-being [positive emotions towards one's life] and high levels on at least six measures of positive functioning" (Keyes, 2007, p. 98). On the other end of the mental health spectrum, individuals who exhibit low levels on at least six measures of positive functioning are diagnosed as languishing in life (Keyes, 2007, p. 98).

Keyes (2007) provided a detailed description of the dimensions that reflect mental health flourishing. Some examples of the ways in which positive functioning was assessed include areas such as self-acceptance, having purpose in life, positive relations with others, social coherence, and social integration. Keyes found that Blacks reported higher levels of flourishing than Whites. Before and after controlling for education, income, and other demographic variables, Blacks were significantly advantaged over Whites on measures of psychological well-being or flourishing. Moreover, after controlling for perceived discrimination, the rate of psychological well-being for Blacks increased, suggesting that if discriminatory experiences were reduced or eliminated, Blacks could potentially be able to achieve complete mental health (Keyes, 2007).

To summarize, understanding the complexity of mental problems for Blacks requires researchers to examine indicators of mental health status to better understand the issues. There are some consistencies in the data, but they vary across indicators on mental health status. Compared with Whites, Blacks continue to report lower prevalence for commonly occurring psychiatric disorders (anxiety, mood, and substance abuse disorders), and lower levels of psychological well-being, but more often than not, they also have higher rates of psychological distress. For schizophrenia, the data are not quite clear, but Blacks may have higher rates than Whites. At the same time, Blacks also report higher levels of flourishing or being free of mental disorder and having higher levels of positive well-being than Whites (Keyes, 2007).

SEVERITY OF MENTAL HEALTH PROBLEMS

On initial review, readers might be tempted to conclude that the mental health of Blacks is either similar to or even better than Whites in terms of the prevalence of mental health problems. However, we need to look not only at the prevalence of disorders but also at racial differences in severity and chronicity. A closer look at the available psychiatric epidemiological data reveals that Blacks tend to have significantly higher levels of the persistence and severity of mental disorders than Whites. Using data from the NCS, Breslau et al.'s (2005) analysis showed significant racial differences in the persistence of disorders. The NCS defined *persistence* as the onset of a disorder at least 2 years prior to the interview and having symptoms within 12 months prior to the survey among persons with a lifetime history of the disorder. This study found that Blacks had higher risk of being persistently ill than Whites. After controlling for age and gender, about 74% of Blacks with a lifetime history of a disorder still had the disorder at the time of the study, compared with approximately 61% for Whites. The pattern remained after adjusting for SES.

Williams, Gonzalez, and colleagues (2007) explored the prevalence and persistence of MDD among African Americans, Caribbean

Blacks, and Whites based on data from the NSAL study. Severity of MDD was higher for both African Americans (56.5%) and Caribbean Blacks (56.0%) than for Whites (38.6%). On average, African Americans had higher scores for all correlates of depression than did Caribbean Blacks, but the differences were not significant, a finding that was attributed to low statistical power.

On the basis of these studies, it appears that although the U.S. Black population has lower lifetime risk of suffering from mental disorders, when they actually experience a disorder, the episode is more debilitating and severe, and it persists longer than other groups. In light of the recent findings, future research is needed to further investigate the quality and presence of treatment differences that operate at or after onset of disorder for Blacks (Breslau et al., 2005).

Disparities in Mental Health Treatment

Access and Service Utilization

Blacks are almost twice as likely to be uninsured, compared with Whites (Smedley, Stith, & Nelson, 2003). The Surgeon General's report on race, ethnicity, culture, and mental health documented disparities in access to mental health care and appropriate services that have created a greater overall burden for Blacks and other racial and ethnic minorities compared with Whites (U.S. Department of Health and Human Services, 2001). Earlier studies of mental health service use indicated underutilization of specialty mental health services for all Americans, but disparities were greater for need and use of services among Blacks and Hispanics (Cheung & Snowden, 1990; Sussman, Robins, & Earl, 1987). Analysis of the ECA data for individuals with symptoms of depression revealed racial differences in service use between general medical settings compared with specialty mental health settings (Cooper-Patrick, Crum, & Ford, 1994). Compared with other groups, Blacks were more likely to be seen in general medical settings for mental health problems than in specialty mental health settings. Researchers have also suggested that Blacks are more likely to utilize services differently than Whites, with higher usage of non–health care professionals (e.g., pastors or other faith-based resources) compared with formal, specialized care, such as psychiatrists or other mental health specialists (Neighbors, 1988; Neighbors & Jackson, 1984).

Nonetheless, compared with the general population, Blacks appear to underutilize services overall. The prevalence rates of 12-month mental health service patterns from two population studies that used the same assessment instruments—the NSAL (Neighbors et al., 2007) and the NCS–R (Wang et al., 2005)—are provided in Table 24.1. The NCS–R provides an estimate for the U.S. adult population, not emphasizing any particular racial or ethnic group, whereas the NSAL study provides national estimates for two Black groups (African Americans and Caribbean Blacks). Both studies indicate the proportion of persons diagnosed with any *DSM–IV* disorder who sought treatment. Service use included general medicine, mental health specialty services, and nonhealth services. Compared with the national estimate, both Black groups had lower levels of any service use any health care and general medical care use. The differences were small for any mental health service use, and Caribbean Blacks had lower levels of non–health care use than both Americans in general and African Americans in particular.

Disparities in Quality of Mental Health Care

Research reveals that racial and ethnic minorities not only have lower levels of access to mental health care but also are less likely to receive adequate care. For example, researchers have found that, after initiating mental health care, Blacks were less likely than Whites to receive the best available treatments for some disorders, but not for others (Wang, Demler, & Kessler, 2002; Young, Klap, Sherbourne, & Wells, 2001). Research reveals that when Blacks enter the mental health system, they are more likely than Whites to receive inferior access to needed services and to receive poorer quality of care, despite insurance coverage (Cooper-Patrick et al., 1997, 2002; Smedley et al., 2003; van Ryn & Fu, 2003).

There are multiple determinants of the receipt of poorer quality care by Blacks. Compared with Whites, Blacks have higher rates of morbidity, comorbidity, and mortality (Smedley et al., 2003). These differences suggest a high level of need that can be exacerbated by a

Table 24.1 Prevalence of 12-Month Mental Health Service Use by 12-Month *DSM–IV*/WMH Composite International Diagnostic Interview Disorders Among National Comorbidity Study–Replication (NCS–R)[1] and National Survey of American Life (NSAL)[2] Populations

	Any Services		Any Health Care Service		General Medical		Any Mental Health Specialty		Any Non-Health Care		
	%	SE	%	SE	%	SE	%	SE	%	SE	n
NCS-R (National Data)[1]											
Anxiety Disorders											
Panic Disorder	65.4	3.3	59.1	3.3	43.7	3.3	34.7	2.6	17.3	2.3	251
Agoraphobia w/o Panic	52.6	7.4	45.8	7.0	NA		NA		NA		79
Social Phobia	45.6	1.9	40.1	1.9	25.3	1.7	24.7	1.5	13.4	1.1	632
GAD	52.3	2.9	43.2	3.0	31.7	2.6	25.5	2.9	21.7	3.5	247
PTSD	57.4	3.3	49.9	3.3	31.3	2.5	34.4	2.9	19.7	2.4	203
Any Anxiety Disorder[3]	42.2	1.3	36.9	1.4	24.3	1.0	21.7	1.2	13.5	0.7	1036
Mood Disorders											
MDD	56.8	2.2	51.7	2.2	32.5	2.3	32.9	1.6	16.8	1.7	623
Dysthymia	67.5	4.1	61.7	4.5	39.6	5.1	36.8	4.1	17.5	3.9	135
Bipolar I and II Disorders	55.5	3.0	48.8	2.7	33.1	3.0	33.8	2.3	21.6	3.2	244
Any Mood Disorder[3]	56.4	1.8	50.9	1.8	32.8	1.8	32.9	1.3	18.1	1.6	884
Substance Disorders											
Alcohol Abuse	37.2	2.6	33.4	2.5	16.4	2.1	25.6	2.3	12.8	2.2	176
Alcohol Dependence	48.4	5.4	43.6	4.9	19.3	3.7	35.1	4.4	19.6	3.9	76
Drug Abuse	43.1	4.8	40.5	4.9	21.8	4.1	32.8	4.9	14.2	5.5	79
Drug Dependence	51.5	9.9	49.8	9.8	23.9	7.3	42.9	10.0	6.0	3.6	24
Any Substance Disorder	38.1	2.7	34.5	2.6	18.1	1.7	26.2	2.5	13.7	2.6	219
Any Disorder[3]	41.1	1.0	36.0	1.1	22.8	0.9	21.7	0.9	13.2	0.7	1443
No Disorder	10.1	0.6	8.3	0.5	4.7	0.3	4.4	0.4	3.0	0.3	4249
NSAL (National Black Data)											
Total African American	10.1	0.7	8.0	0.5	4.3	0.4	5.6	0.5	4.1	0.5	3412
Anxiety Disorders											
Panic Disorder	41.3	7.2	36.0	7.1	22.4	5.8	24.3	5.9	15.4	5.7	76
Agoraphobia w/o Panic	30.9	6.9	13.9	6.6	9.5	5.4	13.9	6.6	18.5	5.9	46
Social Phobia	37.6	5.4	26.8	5.9	16.8	3.3	21.4	5.4	19.7	3.5	140
GAD	42.8	6.8	35.4	6.9	19.8	5.7	31.0	6.1	21.4	5.8	75
PTSD	36.7	6.2	29.3	5.9	21.3	5.6	20.1	4.9	14.9	3.8	134
Any Anxiety Disorder[3]	35.8	3.0	28.6	2.5	17.6	2.2	20.5	2.9	15.2	2.1	356
Mood Disorders											
MDD	45.0	3.3	35.8	3.0	21.8	3.5	26.1	3.2	20.4	3.2	197
Dysthymia	46.9	7.8	38.6	7.1	19.5	5.5	26.0	7.1	15.2	5.5	70
Bipolar I and II Disorder[3]	43.5	3.2	34.6	3.1	21.0	2.8	25.7	3.4	20.5	2.8	245
Substance Disorders											
Alcohol Abuse	26.2	5.7	19.7	5.2	5.9	2.0	18.3	5.3	10.0	3.6	77
Alcohol Dependence	38.2	9.3	35.9	9.5	6.9	2.5	35.9	9.5	9.5	4.1	42
Drug Abuse	39.8	9.2	37.4	8.4	10.2	5.1	37.4	8.4	15.6	6.4	40
Drug Dependence	37.2	12.9	37.9	12.9	11.1	5.3	37.2	12.9	10.3	6.4	20
Any Substance Disorder	29.7	5.6	24.9	4.9	7.2	2.1	23.8	5.0	10.8	3.2	103
Any Disorder[3]	32.0	2.1	25.5	1.9	15.1	1.6	18.7	2.0	13.6	1.5	619
No Disorder	5.4	0.6	4.3	0.4	2.0	0.3	2.8	0.3	2.1	0.4	2793

(Continued)

Table 24.1 (Continued)

	Any Services		Any Health Care Service		General Medical		Any Mental Health Specialty		Any Non-Health Care		
	%	SE	%	SE	%	SE	%	SE	%	SE	n
Total Caribbean Black	10.1	2.0	8.5	2.0	3.7	1.5	5.9	2.0	1.8	0.5	1579
Anxiety Disorders											
Panic Disorder	44.1	6.1	41.5	6.9	36.5	9.9	7.7	7.5	3.4	3.1	25
Agoraphobia w/o Panic	7.1	6.8	7.1	6.8	7.1	6.8	NA		NA		12
Social Phobia	30.8	17.4	29.6	17.3	22.5	17.2	8.9	6.2	1.6	1.1	58
GAD	11.3	6.0	10.0	5.7	5.8	4.4	5.1	2.9	2.1	1.6	27
PTSD	52.2	19.0	50.9	19.2	21.7	16.6	30.3	21.8	1.3	0.9	41
Any Anxiety Disorders[3]	31.0	11.9	29.4	11.9	12.2	7.1	18.8	12.2	2.1	0.9	133
Mood Disorders											
MDD	24.3	12.1	21.5	11.9	14.0	11.5	20.1	11.8	3.6	2.1	79
Dysthymia	3.5	3.4	2.0	2.1	0.9	1.1	1.1	1.4	1.6	1.7	12
Bipolar I and II Disorder	25.2	11.2	24.3	11.1	2.7	2.7	24.3	11.1	4.1	2.9	30
Any Mood Disprder[3]	22.9	10.8	20.4	10.6	12.5	10.3	19.2	10.5	3.6	1.9	97
Substance Disorders[4]											
Any Substance Disorder	38.8	4.8	38.8	4.8	29.7	7.6	11.3	10.9	0.6	0.7	23
Any Disorder[3]	29.9	8.5	27.4	8.4	11.5	5.3	21.4	9.3	3.2	1.1	250
No Disorder	4.8	1.3	3.6	1.1	1.8	0.8	2.0	1.0	1.4	0.6	1329

1. Data presented from Table 1 of the Wang et al., 2005 article in the Archives of General Psychiatry.
2. Data presented from Table 3 of the Neighbors et al., 2007 article in the Archives of General Psychiatry.
3. In some of the categories, there were more disorders in NSAL than NCS-R.
4. The sample of Caribbean Blacks with alcohol and other drug abuse or dependence was too small to report in the article.

Note: DSM-IV = Diagnostic and Statistical Manual of Mental Disorders; WMH = World Mental Health; GAD = generalized anxiety disorder; PTSD = posttraumatic stress disorder; MDD = major depressive disorder.

severely fragmented system of mental health care and the challenges that Blacks face in obtaining high-quality care. In the face of greater needs, a disjointed mental health care system is unlikely to adequately address them, because problems of accessing the right services at the right time by an appropriate provider can be insurmountable. Provider behavior is another source of inadequacies in quality of care. In recent years, provider behavior has been garnering a lot of interest and has been related to quality of care (Cooper-Patrick et al., 1997; Smedley et al., 2003). Some researcher suggests that unconscious or unthinking discrimination by providers is a contributor to observed racial and ethnic disparities in the quality of medical care (Smedley et al, 2003; van Ryn & Fu, 2003). This research is consistent with a large body of social-psychological research on stereotypes and unconscious bias. Research reveals that when an individual holds a negative stereotype about a group, and meets someone from that group, he or she will discriminate against that individual, without conscious awareness of doing so (van Ryn & Fu, 2003).

Patient behavior is also likely to be a contributor to gaps in the quality of care. Issues of mistrust and perceived discrimination, for example, have been linked to lower quality care. When sociocultural differences are not explored, appreciated, or understood, the patient can become less engaged in treatment, which can lead to poor mental health outcomes, which in turn can perpetuate the cycle of health care disparities (Atdjian & Vega, 2005; Whaley, 1997). If a patient does not feel or sense some form of respect, acceptance, trust, or understanding from the provider or the system of care, he or she may be less likely to adhere to or comply with treatment, which is another, less researched, but valuable contribution to the scope of understanding disparities.

Some evidence suggests that increased availability of Black clinicians would reduce inadequate medical care of Blacks. Studies of medical care reveal that Black physicians are more likely than White physicians to spend more time treating Black patients (Freiman, Cunningham, & Cornelius, 1994). Other data indicate that Black patients perceive the quality of their care to be higher when they see providers of the same racial and ethnic background (Cooper-Patrick et al., 2002; LaVeist & Nuru-Jeter, 2002; Malat, 2001). LaVeist and Nuru-Jeter (2002) found that Blacks and other racial and ethnic minority patients reported higher levels of satisfaction with their providers when the provider was of the same racial and ethnic background. Cooper-Patrick et al. (2002) found that Black patients who were in racially concordant settings significantly rated their visits to be more participatory than those who were in racially discordant settings. Finally, Malat (2001) found race concordance to be strongly associated with Black patients feeling as if the provider treated them with higher levels of respect than for White patients.

Diversity Among Black Americans

There is increasing attention to the heterogeneity of the Black population and to the implications that such variation may have for mental health. Although there are common or shared experiences across the Black community, there are also important within-group distinctions that should also be considered. Understanding the mental health status of Black Americans requires moving beyond a monolithic approach. Multiple factors can contribute to variations in mental health. Differences in geographic location, SES, and patterns of migration can all contribute to varying mental health risks (Williams & Neighbors, 2006). Ethnicity is one of those dimensions that have been addressed in recent research.

In the 2000 census, approximately 12.9% of the U.S. population (out of about 36 million) identified themselves as Black or African American (McKinnon, 2001). It is also important to note that the terms *Black* and *African American* are not necessarily synonymous. Being "Black" in the United States includes individuals who are of West Indian, African, or other foreign-born heritages; some of them identify with the term *African American*, but many of them, appropriately (as recent immigrants, they are not American citizens), do not. Approximately 6% of the Black U.S. population is foreign born, and about 10% have parents who were born in other countries (Jackson et al., 2004). Over the past few decades, the patterns of Black immigration have contributed to the diversity of this population (Takeuchi, Alegria, Jackson, & Williams, 2007). Caribbean Blacks are the largest group of Black immigrants (Pierre-Pierre, 1993). Some estimates suggest that the Black population of Caribbean or West Indian ancestry alone may account for at least 10% of the Black population in the United States (Williams, Haile, et al., 2007). Although it is important to start by evaluating Black–White differences in indicators of mental health status, it is equally important to understand within-group variations of different subpopulations of Black Americans (Ajani ya Azibo, 1991; Wilson & Williams, 2004).

Lucas, Bar-Anderson, and Kington (2005) used data from the 1992 through 1995 National Health Interview Surveys to analyze Black–White differences in health status and documented that variables linked to migration history and status predict variations in physical health. They noted that foreign-born Blacks had higher SES levels than the U.S.-born Blacks. Fifty-seven percent of foreign-born Black families had a household income above $20,000, compared with 45% of their U.S.-born counterparts. In addition, 64% of foreign-born Blacks were currently employed, compared with 57% of U.S.-born Blacks (Lucas et al., 2005). Moreover, differences in physical health status between foreign-born and U.S.-born Black persons paralleled the differences in SES, such that the health of foreign-born Blacks was substantially better than that of U.S.-born Blacks. Over 67% of the foreign-born Black population assessed their health as being excellent or very good. This was significantly greater than the 52% of their U.S.-born counterparts who assessed their health as excellent or very good and similar to the proportions of U.S.- and foreign-born White persons who rated their health at that level (69% and 62%, respectively). In general, in the 1992 through 1995 National Health Interview Surveys, the health of foreign-born Blacks was comparable to that of U.S.-born White persons in most cases, and, in some cases, better than the health of foreign-born White persons.

The NSAL has been instrumental in moving forward research to be able to shed light on differences in the prevalence, severity, and impairment of psychiatric disorders for ethnic subgroups of the Black U.S. population (Jackson et al., 2004). The NSAL includes a nationally representative sample of Blacks of Caribbean ancestry, as well as other Blacks. It also included a sample of Whites who reside in the residential contexts where Blacks are concentrated.

For indicators of mental health, researchers recently have looked at differential prevalence rates among the Black population. Williams, Gonzalez, and colleagues (2007) examined rates of depression among U.S. Blacks using data from the NSAL. The researchers compared African Americans and Caribbean Blacks, using non-Hispanic Whites as a comparison group. They documented striking patterns of similarity and differences of the two ethnic Black groups compared with Whites. Both African Americans (10.4%) and Caribbean Blacks (12.9%) had a lower lifetime prevalence of MDD than Whites (17.9%). Both Black groups' depression was also more likely to be persistent, severe, and disabling than Whites' depression. At the same time, rates of depression were higher among women than men for both African Americans and Whites; the same was not true for Caribbean Blacks. In addition, although depressed persons in both Black groups were less likely to be treated than Whites, the level of past-year treatment among Caribbean Blacks (25%) was markedly lower than that of African Americans (45%).

Complex patterns of interaction of ethnicity with gender also were evident in the NSAL. Whereas Caribbean men had higher rates of psychiatric disorders than African American men, Caribbean women had lower prevalence rates than African American women (Williams, Haile, et al., 2007). Furthermore, when researchers looked within the Black Caribbean population they found that risk of disorder varied by migration history and status variables. For example, first-generation Caribbean Blacks had substantially lower risk for a psychiatric disorder than those who were born in the United States, with length of stay in the United States and lengthening generational status increasing the risk of disorder. The single most disadvantaged subgroup in the NSAL were the third-generation Caribbean Blacks, who had a markedly elevated risk of disorder. Ethnic differences were also evident within the Black Caribbean sample. Black men from the Spanish Caribbean and Haitian men had lower rates of mood disorders than did men from the English-speaking Caribbean, whereas Black Hispanic women had higher rates of mood and anxiety disorders than their peers from the English Caribbean (Williams, Haile, et al., 2007). Future research needs to attend to the gendered nature of the Black immigrant experience and must take into account both ethnic variation and ethnic differences into the context of reception into the United States.

More generally, attending to the ethnic diversity of Blacks allows for the identification of distinctive cultural profiles of mental health that may have important implications for intervention, treatment, and service planning for Blacks.

Challenges That Remain for Black Mental Health Research

A number of challenges remain in relation to Black mental health status. Some have called attention to the added influence of both vulnerability factors issues, such as racism and discrimination (Phyllis-Jones, 2000; Williams & Williams-Morris, 2000), and resilience factors, such as spirituality or religion (Williams & Neighbors, 2006) as contributing factors for explaining health and mental health status for Blacks. In the next few sections, we highlight additional issues that affect Black mental health status and may provide information to enhance our understanding.

Racism, Perceived Discrimination, and Mental Health Status

Racism operates at multiple levels to affect the mental health status of racial and ethnic populations (Phyllis-Jones, 2000; Williams & Williams-Morris, 2000). Phyllis-Jones (2000) defined and illustrated examples of individual, internalized, and institutionalized racism. *Individual racism* refers to prejudice and discrimination, whereas *prejudice* means differential assumptions about the abilities, motives, and intentions of others according to their race, and *discrimination* means differential actions toward others according to their race. *Internalized racism* occurs when there is acceptance of negative messages by members of stigmatized groups about their abilities and intrinsic worth. Through this form of racism, individuals might embrace forms of "Whiteness," such as straightening their hair, stratifying by skin tone individuals within their community, rejecting their ancestral culture, or resigning themselves to feelings of hopelessness and no longer believing in their personal self-expression or value. *Institutionalized racism* is defined as differential access to goods, services, and opportunities by individuals based on their race. Having disparate access to goods, services, and opportunities can often go unnoticed, because a lot of what happens is viewed as normative.

Some of the major consequences of racism for mental health status lie within the structural nature of racism. Issues of *structural racism* involve mechanisms that are so embedded into the norms, legal system, and customs of society that it is difficult to identify a single perpetrator. These are practices, such as housing, education, or income structures, that have evolved in such a way that observed institutional advantages and disadvantages between groups are seemingly inherent to the structure of society. Thus, when we think about these issues in relation to health and mental health status, the true impact is often not well understood (Williams & Williams-Morris, 2000).

Racial residential segregation has arguably been identified the central determinant among institutional mechanisms of race in the United States (Massey & Denton, 1993; Williams & Collins, 2001). *Racial residential segregation* refers to the physical separation of people of different racial groups into separate residential areas. Although the laws supporting segregation were abandoned in the 1960s, the levels of segregation have declined only slightly in recent decades. Moreover, the declines in segregation have not reduced the high concentration of Blacks in urban and suburban areas and the concentration of Black poverty (Williams & Collins, 2001). Residential segregation determines access to education, employment, commerce, and health care, which ultimately leads to diminished opportunities of socioeconomic mobility for Blacks and other disadvantaged groups. Segregation also creates distinctive residential contexts that have high levels of stress, including neighborhood disorder and crime and reduced access to a broad range of goods and services, including medical care.

Perceived discrimination is one aspect of racism that has been empirically examined in terms of mental health. Reviews of this literature indicate that mental health status is the most frequently assessed indicator of health studies of discrimination (Paradies, 2006; Williams, Neighbors, & Jackson, 2003). Experiences of discrimination for Blacks and other racial and ethnic populations have been related to psychological distress, psychiatric disorders, and psychological well-being. A review of this literature concluded that about 80% of the 47 associations explored in the literature between measures of discrimination and indicators of mental health status show that poor mental health status is related to high levels of discrimination (Williams et al., 2003). Using the 2002 and 2003 New Hampshire Racial and Ethnic Approaches to Community Health 2010 Initiative data, Gee, Ryan, and Laflamme (2006) found that adults of African descent (U.S. or foreign born) who scored lower on the Mental Component Summary, Short Form (Ware, Kosinski, & Keller, 1998) were strongly associated with self-reporting the worst mental health care status and greater perceptions of discrimination than other groups.

Much of the extant literature has been limited to cross-sectional study designs, which presents a challenge to adequately capture exposure to discrimination and assess the cumulative or long-term burden that it may have on an individual's psychological state (Williams et al., 2003). For instance, Broman, Mavaddat, and Hsu (2000) conducted an exploratory study to investigate the link between experiences of racial discrimination and personal outcomes for a sample of Blacks living in Michigan. Their findings suggest that discriminatory experiences affect a person's sense of mastery and thus create or exacerbate psychological distress. Recently, Shultz et al. (2006) used longitudinal models to examine self-reported health and everyday discrimination over time for changes in self-reported symptoms of depression with a group of Black women in the Detroit, Michigan, area. They found that exposure to discriminatory experiences over time was significantly associated with an increase in reports of depressive symptoms and declining self-rated health and mental health status for Black women. These findings remained after controlling for income, education, and occupation.

The larger racialized sociopolitical environment may also affect mental health. T. N. Brown, Wallace, and Williams (2001) assessed the distribution of race-related worry and pessimism to subjective well-being in a national sample of high school seniors and found that worrying about race relations and perceiving problematic race relations were significantly associated with low levels of satisfaction and happiness. In addition, simply being Black, or a member of another socially disadvantaged group; living in an oppressed society; and perceiving forms of injustice, discrimination, and racism could trigger feelings of paranoia or distrust that can lead to higher levels of unhappiness and life dissatisfaction. Blazer, Hays, and Salive (1996) pointedly noted that, for Blacks, expressing symptoms of paranoia may represent an appropriate response to a hostile environment rather than a psychopathic trait. Other studies provide support for this notion (Whaley, 2001, 2004). This suggests that there may be culture-specific factors that affect the risks of mental health problems for Blacks and that may also affect the profile of presumed mental health symptoms.

Future research needs to help us understand how multiple risk factors relate to each other and combine to affect the mental health of Blacks in the United States. The ECA study found that, for both Blacks and Whites, the likelihood of having a psychiatric disorder was three times greater for individuals of low SES (based on a composite measure of income, education, and occupation), compared with those of higher SES (Robins & Regier, 1991; Williams, Takeuchi, & Adair, 1992). The NCS found that persons in lower categories of income and education were twice as likely as those in higher levels to meet criteria for a psychiatric disorder (Kessler et al., 1994). At the same time, low-SES Black males had higher levels of disorder than low-SES White males (Williams et al., 1992). On the other hand, other research indicates that low-SES Blacks have higher rates of psychological distress than their White peers (Kessler & Neighbors, 1986). We need a better understanding of how multiple risks, at the level of the individual, household, and community, accumulate over the life course to affect the onset, severity, and course of mental health problems.

Religion and Spirituality and Mental Health Status

Religion and spirituality play an important and role in the mental health status of the Black community (Williams, 1994; Williams & Neighbors, 2006). Religious institutions provide emotional and social support and a feeling of connectedness and belonging. Also, religious beliefs and values can enable an individual to interpret or contextualize stressors. Religious beliefs also can provide mechanisms to cope with adversity and potentially reduce risk-taking behavior. At the same time, religious beliefs and participation can also generate stress and role conflicts that can adversely affect mental health. For example, if a person engages in an activity that he feels is in opposition to his religious values or beliefs, then he may experience negative emotions and ultimately become ill.

Research reveals that religious involvement can buffer or reduce the negative effects of stress on mental health (Williams & Neighbors, 2006). At present, we do not know how much of this effect is due to the social aspects of religious participation and how much is linked to the particular religious beliefs. Aspects of some religious services may also facilitate the reduction of tension and the release of emotional distress (Williams & Neighbors, 2006). For example, studies of Wednesday evening prayer meetings at Black churches in New Haven, Connecticut, revealed that all the key elements of a therapeutic encounter between a client and a clinician existed in the liturgy and ritual of these religious services (Griffith, Young, & Smith, 1984). Griffith et al. (1984) concluded that these services can function as an alternative form of therapy for Blacks. There is still much to learn about the ways in which religious beliefs and involvement can affect mental health status. There also is a need to expand our conceptualization and assessment of spirituality and religion and identify the multiple pathways by which they can affect mental health.

Conclusion

Our brief review of the available evidence suggests that association between race and mental health is complicated. Blacks in the United States function better on some indicators of mental health than Whites, but worse on others. The overall pattern nonetheless indicates that the mental health of African Americans is better than expected given their high levels of exposure to social risk factors for mental health problems. These findings highlight the importance that future studies on race and mental health pay attention to the strengths, resources, and resilience factors in the Black community equal to the attention given to the risk factors and exposure to adversities. We need to obtain greater clarity regarding what the various indicators of mental health status really capture and of the combinations of risk and resources that undergird them. Our review also highlights that there is a pressing need to more systematically disentangle subpopulation differences by ethnicity, region, and culture within the Black population of the United States. This work must also attend to the various ways in which subpopulations of Blacks are assessed and diagnosed, as well as how their mental health is affected by the quality of their social environment.

At the same time, our review provides striking evidence that race matters a lot for the mental health of Blacks. Although Blacks have lower levels of the common psychiatric disorders, once diagnosed they are disadvantaged compared to Whites on every indicator of severity, persistence, and the treatment. This suggests that racism institutionalized in the structures of society continue to shape the quality and life experiences of Blacks. Thus, the mental health of Blacks provides a lens through which to view both the resistance and resilience of an oppressed population as well as a need to dismantle the persisting structures of injustice.

NOTE

1. This chapter was supported by a National Institute of Mental Health Minority/Diversity Supplement to Research Grant P50 MH73469-01.

REFERENCES

Adebimpe, V. R. (1994). Race, racism, and epidemiological surveys. *Hospital and Community Psychiatry, 45,* 27–31.

Ajani ya Azibo, D. (1991). Towards a metatheory of the African personality. *Journal of Black Psychology, 17,* 37–45.

American Psychiatric Association. (1980). *Diagnostic and statistical manual of mental disorders* (3rd ed.). Washington, DC: Author.

American Psychiatric Association. (1987). *Diagnostic and statistical manual of mental disorders* (3rd ed., revised). Washington, DC: Author.

American Psychiatric Association. (1994). *Diagnostic and statistical manual of mental disorders* (4th ed.). Washington, DC: Author.

Andrews, F., & Withey, S. (1976). *Social indicators of well-being: Americans' perceptions of life quality.* New York: Plenum Press.

Atdjian, S., & Vega, W. (2005). Disparities in mental health treatment in U.S. racial and ethnic minority groups: Implications for psychiatrists. *Psychiatric Services, 56,* 1600–1602.

Baker, F. M., & Bell, C. C. (1999). Issues in the psychiatric treatment of Blacks. *Psychiatric Services, 50,* 362–368.

Barnes, A. (2004). Race, schizophrenia, and admission to state psychiatric hospitals. *Administration and Policy in Mental Health, 31,* 241–252.

Blazer, D. G., Hays, J. C., & Salive, M. E. (1996). Factors associated with paranoid symptoms in a community sample of older adults. *Gerontologist, 36,* 70–75.

Bracy, J. (1976). The quality of life experience of Black people. In *The quality of American life: Perceptions, evaluations, and satisfactions* (pp. 443–464). New York: Russell Sage Foundation.

Breslau, J., Aguilar-Gaxiola, S., Kendler, K., Su, M., Williams, D., & Kessler, R. C. (2006). Specifying race–ethnic differences in risk for psychiatric disorder in a USA national sample. *Psychological Medicine, 36,* 57–68.

Breslau, J., Kendler, K., Su, M., Gaxiola-Aguilar, S., & Kessler, R. (2005). Lifetime risk and persistence of psychiatric disorders across ethnic groups in the United States. *Psychological Medicine, 35,* 317–327.

Broman, C., Mavaddat, R., & Hsu, S. (2000). The experience and consequences of perceived racial discrimination: A study of African Americans. *Journal of Black Psychology, 26,* 165–180.

Brown, G. (2005). Social origins of depression and the role of meaning. In A. F. Heath, J. Ermisch, & D. Gallie (Eds.), *Understanding social change* (pp. 255–291). Oxford, UK: Oxford University Press.

Brown, T. N., Wallace, J. M., & Williams, D. R. (2001). Race-related correlates of young adults' subjective well-being. *Social Indicators, 53,* 97–116.

Cheung, F., & Snowden, L. (1990). Community mental health and ethnic minority populations. *Community Mental Health Journal, 26,* 277–291.

Cooper-Patrick, L., Crum, R., & Ford, D. (1994). Identifying suicidal ideation in general medical patients. *Journal of the American Medical Association, 272,* 1757–1762.

Cooper-Patrick, L., Gallo, J., Gonzales, J., Vu, H., Powe, N., Nelson, C., et al. (2002). Race, gender, and partnership in the patient–provider relationship. In T. LaVeist (Ed.), *Race, ethnicity, and health: A public reader* (pp. 609–625). San Francisco: Jossey-Bass.

Cooper-Patrick, L., Powe, N., Jenckes, M., Gonzales, J., Levine, D., & Ford, D. (1997). Identification of patient attitudes and preferences regarding treatment of depression. *Journal of General Internal Medicine 12,* 431–438.

Dohrenwend, B., & Dohrenwend, B. (1969). *Social status and psychological disorder: A causal inquiry.* New York: Wiley-Interscience.

Freiman, M., Cunningham, P., & Cornelius, L. (1994). *Use and expenditures for treatment of mental health problems* (Publication No. 94-0085). Rockville, MD: Agency for Health Care Research.

Gee, G., Ryan, A., & Laflamme, D. J. (2006). Self-reported discrimination and mental health status among African descendants, Mexican Americans, and other Latinos in New Hampshire: REACH 2010 initiative. The added dimension of immigration. *American Journal of Public Health, 96,* 1821–1828.

Grant, B. (1996). Prevalence and correlates of drug use and *DSM–IV* drug dependence in the United States: Results of the National Longitudinal Alcohol Epidemiologic Survey. *Journal of Substance Abuse, 8,* 195–210.

Griffith, E. E., Young, J. L., & Smith, D. L. (1984). An analysis of the therapeutic elements in a Black church service. *Hospital and Community Psychiatry, 35,* 464–469.

Hughes, M., & Thomas, M. (1998). The continuing significance of race revisited: A study of race, class, and quality of life in America, 1972 to 1996. *American Sociological Review, 63,* 785–795.

Jackson, J., Torres, M., Caldwell, C., Neighbors, H., Nesse, R., Taylor, R., et al. (2004). The National Survey of American Life: A study of racial, ethnic and cultural influences on mental disorders and mental health. *International Journal of Methods in Psychiatric Research, 3,* 196–207.

Kennedy, R. (1999). Surgeon General's first report on mental health. *Medscape General Medicine, 1*(3). Retrieved August 25, 2008, from http://www.medscape.com/viewarticle/430603

Kessler, R., Adler, L., Barkley, R., Biederman, J., Conners, C., Demler, O., et al. (2006). The prevalence and correlates of adult ADHD in the United States: Results from the National Comorbidity Survey Replication. *American Journal of Psychiatry, 163,* 716–723.

Kessler, R., Akiskal, H., Ames, M., Birnbaum, H., Greenberg, P., Hirschfeld, R., et al. (2006). Prevalence and effects of mood disorders on work performance in a nationally representative sample of U.S. workers. *American Journal of Psychiatry, 163,* 1561–1568.

Kessler, R., Birnbaum, H., Demler, O., Falloon, I., Gagnon, E., Guyer, M., et al. (2005). The prevalence and correlates of non-affective psychosis in the National Comorbidity Survey Replication (NCS-R). *Biological Psychiatry, 58,* 668–678.

Kessler, R., Chiu, W., Jin, R., Ruscio, A., Shear, K., & Walters, E. (2006). The epidemiology of panic attacks, panic disorder, and agoraphobia in the National Comorbidity Survey Replication. *Archives of General Psychiatry, 63,* 415–424.

Kessler, R., McGonagle, K., Zhao, S., Nelson, C. B., Hughes, M., Eshleman, S., et al. (1994). Lifetime and 12-month prevalence of *DSM–III–R* psychiatric disorders in the United States: Results from the National Comorbidity Study. *Archives of General Psychiatry, 51,* 8–19.

Kessler, R., & Neighbors, H. W. (1986). A new perspective on the relationship among race, social class, and psychological distress. *Journal of Health and Social Behavior, 27,* 107–115.

Keyes, C. (2007). Promoting and protecting mental health and flourishing: A complementary strategy for improving national mental health. *American Psychologist, 62,* 95–108.

LaVeist, T. A., & Nuru-Jeter, A. (2002). Is doctor–patient race concordance associated with greater satisfaction with care? *Journal of Health and Social Behavior, 43,* 296–306.

Lucas, J. W., Barr-Anderson, D. J., & Kington, R. S. (2005, July). *Health status of non-Hispanic U.S. born and foreign born Black and White persons: United States, 1992–95* (Vital and Health Statistics Series 10, No. 226). Hyattsville, MD: U.S. Department of Health and Human Services.

Magee, W. J. (1993). *Psychological predictors of agoraphobia, simple phobia, and social phobia onset in a U.S. national sample.* Unpublished doctoral dissertation, University of Michigan.

Malat, J. (2001). Social distance and patients' rating of healthcare providers. *Journal of Health and Social Behavior, 42,* 360–372.

Massey, D. S., & Denton, N. (1993). *American apartheid: Segregation and the making of the underclass.* Cambridge, MA: Harvard University Press.

McKinnon, J. (2001). *The Black population 2000: Census 2000 brief.* Washington, DC: U.S. Department of Commerce, U.S. Census Bureau.

Merikangas, K., Akiskal, H., Angst, J., Greenberg, P., Hirschfeld, R., Petukhova, M., et al. (2007). Lifetime and 12-month prevalence of bipolar spectrum disorder in the National Comorbidity Survey Replication. *Archives of General Psychiatry, 64,* 543–552.

Mills, T. (2001). Comorbid depressive symptomatology: Isolating the effects of chronic medical conditions on self-reported depressive symptoms among community-dwelling older adults. *Social Science & Medicine, 53,* 569–578.

Neal, A. M., & Turner, S. M. (1991). Anxiety disorder research with African Americans: Current status. *Psychological Bulletin, 109,* 400–410.

Neighbors, H. (1984). Professional help among Black Americans: Implications for unmet need. *American Journal of Community Psychology, 12,* 551–566.

Neighbors, H. (1988). Needed research on the epidemiology of mental disorders in Black Americans. In A. Harrison, J. Jackson, C. Munday, & N. Bleiden (Eds.), *A search for understanding: The Michigan Research Conference on Mental Health Services for Black Americans* (pp. 49–60). Detroit, MI: Wayne State University Press.

Neighbors, H., Caldwell, C., Williams, D., Nesse, R., Taylor, R., Bullard, K., et al. (2007). Race, ethnicity, and the use of services for mental disorders: Results from the National Survey of American Life. *Archives of General Psychiatry, 64,* 485–494.

Neighbors, H., & Jackson, J. (1984). The use of informal and formal help: Four patterns of illness behavior in the Black community *American Journal of Community Psychology,* 12, 629–644.

Paradies, Y. C. (2006). Defining, conceptualizing, and characterizing racism in health research. *Critical Public Health, 16,* 143–157.

Phyllis-Jones, C. (2000). Levels of racisms: A theoretic framework and a gardener's tale. *American Journal of Public Health, 90,* 1212–1215.

Pierre-Pierre, G. (1993, September 6). West Indians adding clout to the ballot box. *New York Times,* pp. 17, 19.

Robins, L., & Regier, D. (Eds.). (1991). *Psychiatric disorders in America: The Epidemiologic Catchment Area Study.* New York: Free Press.

Shultz, A. J., Gravlee, C. C., Williams, D. R., Israel, B. A., Mentz, G., & Rowe, Z. (2006). Discrimination, symptoms of depression, and self-rated health among African American women in Detroit: Results from a longitudinal analysis. *American Journal of Public Health, 96,* 1265–1270.

Smedley, B., Stith, A., & Nelson, A. (2003). *Unequal treatment: Confronting racial and ethnic disparities in health care.* Washington, DC: Institute of Medicine, National Academies Press.

Somervell, P. D., Kaplan, B. H., Heiss, G., Tyroler, H. A., Kleinbaum, D. G., & Obrist, P. A. (1989). Psychologic distress as a predictor of mortality. *American Journal of Epidemiology, 130,* 1013–1023.

Strakowski, S., Flaum, M., Amador, X., & Bracha, H. (1996). Racial differences in the diagnosis of psychosis. *Schizophrenia Research, 21,* 117–124.

Sussman, L., Robins, L., & Earl, F. (1987). Treatment-seeking for depression by Black and White Americans. *Social Science & Medicine, 12,* 187–196.

Takeuchi, D., Alegria, M., Jackson, J., & Williams, D. (2007). Immigration and mental health: Diverse findings in Asian, Black, and Latino populations. *American Journal of Public Health, 97,* 11–12.

Thomas, H., & Hughes, M. (1986). The continuing significance of race: A study of race, class, and quality of life in America, 1972–1985. *American Sociological Review, 51,* 830–841.

Turner, R., & Lloyd, D. (2004). Stress burden and the lifetime incidence of psychiatric disorder in young adults: Racial and ethnic contrasts. *Archives of General Psychiatry, 61,* 481–488.

U.S. Department of Health and Human Services. (1999). *Mental health: A report of the Surgeon General.* Rockville, MD: Author.

U.S. Department of Health and Human Services. (2001). Mental health care for African Americans. In *Surgeon General's report* (pp. 51–69). Rockville, MD: Author.

van Ryn, M., & Fu, S. (2003). Paved with good intentions: Do public health and human service providers contribute to racial/ethnic disparities in health? *American Journal of Public Health, 93,* 248–255.

Vega, C., & Rumbaut, R. (1991). Ethnic minorities and mental health. *Annual Review of Sociology, 17,* 351–383.

Wang, P., Berglund, P., Olfson, M., Pincus, H., Wells, K., & Kessler, R. (2005). Failure and delay in initial treatment contact after first onset of mental disorders in the National Comorbidity Survey Replication. *Archives of General Psychiatry, 62,* 603–613.

Wang, P., Demler, O., & Kessler, R. (2002). Adequacy of treatment for serious mental illness in the United States. *American Journal of Public Health, 92,* 92–98.

Ware, J. E., Kosinski, M., & Keller, S. D. (1998). *SF-12: How to score the SF-12 Physical and Mental Summary Scales* (3rd ed.). Lincoln, RI: QualityMetric.

Warheit, G., Holzer, C., & Arey, S. (1975). Race and mental illness: An epidemiologic update. *Journal of Health and Social Behavior, 16,* 243–256.

Whaley, A. (1997). Ethnicity/race, paranoia, and psychiatric diagnoses: Clinician bias versus sociocultural differences. *Journal of Psychopathology and Behavioral Assessment, 19,* 1–20.

Whaley, A. (2001). Cultural mistrust and mental health services for African Americans: A review and meta-analysis. *Counseling Psychologist, 29,* 513–531.

Whaley, A. (2004). Ethnicity/race, paranoia, and hospitalization for mental health problems among men. *American Journal of Public Health, 94,* 78–81.

Williams, D. R. (1994). The measurement of religion in epidemiologic studies: Problems and prospects. In J. Levin (Ed.), *Religion, aging and* health: Theoretical foundations and methodological frontiers (pp. 125–148). Thousand Oaks, CA: Sage.

Williams, D. R. (1999). Race, SES, and health: The added effects of racism and discrimination. In N. Adler, M. Marmot, B. McEwen, & J. Stewart (Eds.), *Annals of the New York Academy of Sciences: Vol. 896. Socioeconomic status and health in industrial nations: Social, psychological and biological pathways* (pp. 173–188). New York: New York Academy of Sciences.

Williams, D. R. (2005). Health of U.S. racial and ethnic populations. *Journal of Gerontology, 60B,* 53–63.

Williams, D. R., & Collins, C. (2001, September/October). Racial residential segregation: A fundamental cause of racial disparities in health. *Public Health Reports, 116,* 404–416.

Williams, D. R., & Earl, T. R. (2007). Race and mental health: More questions than answers. *International Journal of Epidemiology, 36,* 758–760.

Williams, D. R., Gonzalez, H., Neighbors, H., Nesse, R., Abelson, J., & Sweetman, J. (2007). Prevalence and distribution of major depressive disorder in African Americans, Caribbean Blacks, and non-Hispanic Whites: Results from the National Survey of American Life. *Archives of General Psychiatry, 64,* 305–315.

Williams, D. R., Haile, R., Gonzalez, H., Neighbors, H., Baser, R., & Jackson, J. (2007). The mental health of Black Caribbean immigrants: Results from the National Survey of American Life. *American Journal of Public Health, 97,* 52–59.

Williams, D. R., & Harris-Reid, M. (1999). Race and mental health: Emerging patterns and promising approaches. In A. Horwitz & T. Scheid (Eds.), *Handbook for the study of mental health* (pp. 295–314). Cambridge, MA: Cambridge University Press.

Williams, D. R., & Neighbors, H. W. (2006). Social perspectives on mood disorders. In D. Stein, D. Kupfer, & A. Schatzberg (Eds.), *The American Psychiatric Publishing textbook of mood disorders* (pp. 145–158). Washington, DC: American Psychiatric Publishing.

Williams, D. R., Neighbors, H. W., & Jackson, J. S. (2003). Racial/ethnic discrimination and health: Findings from community studies. *American Journal of Public Health, 93,* 200–208.

Williams, D. R., Takeuchi, D., & Adair, R. (1992). Socioeconomic status and psychiatric disorder among Blacks and Whites. *Social Forces, 71,* 179–194.

Williams, D. R., & Williams-Morris, R. (2000). Racism and mental health: The African American experience. *Ethnicity & Health, 5,* 243–268.

Williams, D. R., Yu, Y., Jackson, J. S., & Anderson, N. B. (1997). Racial differences in physical and mental health: Socioeconomic status, stress, and discrimination. *Journal of Health Psychology, 2,* 335–351.

Wilson, C., & Williams, D. (2004). *Mental health of African Americans.* Westport, CT: Praeger.

Young, A., Klap, R., Sherbourne, C., & Wells, K. (2001). The quality of care for depressive and anxiety disorders in the United States. *Archives of General Psychiatry, 58,* 55–61.

Yu, Y., & Williams, D. R. (1999). Socioeconomic status and mental health. In *Handbook of sociology and mental health* (pp. 151–166). New York: Kluwer/Plenum.

25

PSYCHOLOGICAL HEALTH IN SCHOOL-AGE POPULATIONS

FRANK C. WORRELL

Although the 2000 U.S. Census (U.S. Census Bureau [USCB], 2001b) indicated that Black Americans are the second largest minority group in the country, with Hispanics now constituting the largest group, Black Americans are still the largest *racial* minority group in the country (Worrell, 2005), and Black children and youth make up 15% of the U.S. population under the age of 18. Moreover, African Americans "occupy a unique niche in the history of America and in contemporary national life," given "the legacy of slavery and the historical and discrimination" (U.S. Department of Health and Human Services [USDHHS], 2001, p. 53). Thus, any discussion of the psychological health of African Americans must take into account the historical and social context of life in America (Dillard, 2005).

The issue of psychological health is far reaching and impossible to address fully in one short chapter. Moreover, there is limited information available on the psychological health of school-age African Americans (Dillard, 2005; USDHHS, 2001), with even less information available on children than on adolescents, because much of the literature on these topics focuses on adult and majority populations. Indeed, in a recent text highlighting the crisis in youth mental health, race is mentioned only in connection with housing (Rusk, 2006). Thus, the goal in this chapter is to provide brief overviews of the extant literature across the wide range of perspectives that make up psychological health. The review is structured around the two major classification systems most frequently used in assessing the mental health of children and adolescents: (1) the *Diagnostic and Statistical Manual of Mental Disorders* (4th ed., text revision; *DSM–IV–TR*; American Psychiatric Association, 2000) and (2) the Individuals with Disabilities in Education Improvement Act of 2004 (IDEIA). In the discussions of each category, I present information on promising interventions. However, before discussing the classification systems, I begin with a brief overview of other factors related to the psychological health of African American youth.

FACTORS RELATED TO PSYCHOLOGICAL HEALTH

Factors related to the psychological health of African Americans fall into several categories, including demography, education, biology, and social psychology. One of the most potent demographic factors is socioeconomic status (SES), in part because of the number of constructs encompassed by this variable. SES, which can include income, social class or status, educational attainment, and standard of living, has a potent impact on the amount of resources that families can bring to bear on problems and the societal supports that can be accessed. The strong relationship between number of years of schooling and lifetime earnings warrants mentioning educational attainment as an important variable in its own right. In 2000, 79% of African Americans over 25 had graduated from high school, but only 17% of this group had a college degree (USCB, 2001b). Consequently, 45% of African Americans have annual incomes less than $25,000, and poverty rates for African Americans in general and for African Americans under age 18 are 23.6% and 33.1%, respectively. At 44%, female-headed families constitute a substantial segment of the African American community (USCB, 2001a), and the poverty rate in these families is 35.2% (USCB, 2003a).

African Americans are also more likely to live in segregated communities (Massey, 2000; USCB, 2003b) located in the urban cores of major cities (USCB, 2000) where crime rates are higher and social services more limited; both the segregation and lack of resources are mirrored in the schools that African American children attend. African Americans are overrepresented in populations with high mental health needs, including the homeless ($\approx$40%; USDHHS, 2001), adults and juveniles in prison ($\approx$40–50%), individuals exposed to violence (U.S. Department of Justice, 2002), children in the foster care ($\approx$45%; Child Welfare Information Gateway, 2005), and children in households on welfare ($\approx$45%; USDHHS, 2001).

Physical health is often related to psychological health, and there are several areas in which African Americans have greater physical health challenges than their majority counterparts across the life span (Belgrave & Allison, 2006; USDHHS, 2001; Worrell, 2005). African Americans have higher rates of diabetes, heart disease, stroke, prostate cancer, and female breast cancer than Whites. Infant mortality rates are also highest for African Americans (Foundation for Child Development, 2007), who also have the highest rates of low-birthweight infants and sudden infant death syndrome. The AIDS epidemic has had a disproportionate impact on the African American community, with African Americans constituting over 33% of the males age 13 and over who die from HIV/AIDS. The percentages for African American females age 13 and over and African American children under age 13 who die from HIV/AIDS are 60.5% and 61.4%, respectively (Miniño, Arias, Kochanel, Murphy, & Smith, 2002). Not surprisingly, African Americans have the highest death rates in the United States (National Center for Health Statistics, 2006; Worrell, 2005) and the lowest life expectancy rates (Belgrave & Allison, 2006).

It is not difficult to conceive of the impact on the psychological health of African American children and adolescents that these statistics reflect, and the high death rates of adults contribute both to the number of African American youth in the foster care system and psychosocial stress in this community. However, in spite of the dire statistics, African American children of school age are not the group most at risk in many categories of psychological disorders. Indeed, studies of prevalence rates indicate that when social class is controlled, African American youth are often at lower risk than their majority counterparts (Angold et al., 2002; Roberts, Roberts, & Xing, 2006). Research also indicates that African American youth generally have higher self-esteem and expectations for the future than their counterparts (Mello, in press). To date, the resilience manifested by African American youth is not fully understood. Explanations have included extended family networks, religious participation, a grounding in Afrocentric principles, racial socialization, and positive racial identity attitudes (Woodland, 2008). However, the empirical evidence for all of these explanations is inconclusive, highlighting the need for further research on this topic.

CATEGORICAL DISORDERS

Although the *DSM–IV–TR* has a list of several disorders that are often diagnosed in childhood or adolescence, some of these are more typically associated with conceptions of psychological health than others. These include the developmental disorders and attention-deficit and disruptive behavior disorders. In addition, children and youth are diagnosed with other *DSM–IV* disorders (American Psychiatric Association,

1994) that are not included in the childhood and adolescent section (e.g., anxiety disorders, eating disorders). Many of the *DSM–IV* disorders have similar names in the special education classification system (e.g., *mental retardation, developmental delays*). An additional category used in education and of importance to African Americans is serious emotional disturbance (IDEIA, 2004). However, this special education category subsumes anxiety, behavioral, mood, and personality disorders, which are not listed separately in IDEIA, and is not discussed separately in this chapter.

Brief overviews of our knowledge base in the categories that are most applicable to African American school-age populations follow. Not surprisingly, there is more information available on anxiety, behavioral disorders, and learning disorders, which are the most frequently diagnosed problems in children and adolescents (Doll, 1996), but even in these categories, there are far fewer studies on African Americans than on their majority counterparts.

Anxiety Disorders

As indicated earlier, there is a limited knowledge base on psychological disorders in the African American population and on children and adolescents more specifically (Angold et al., 2002; A. M. Neal & Ward-Brown, 1994; Roberts et al., 2006; USDHHS, 2001). The literature on anxiety disorders is illustrative in this regard. A search of the major databases using *anxiety disorders* as the keyword yields 10,355 peer-reviewed articles and 310 books. Adding *African Americans* and/or *Blacks* as keywords reduces the yield to 67 articles and 2 books, and adding *children, adolescent,* and/or *youth* results in 19 studies. The lack of information is more extreme in many of the other categories related to psychological health.

Much of the early research in this area focused on identifying the types of fears reported by African American youth from small convenience samples (e.g., A. M. Neal & Ward-Brown, 1994; Treadwell, Flannery-Schroeder, & Kendall, 1995). The results from many of these early studies indicated that African American children's fears were "relatively stable over time" (A. M. Neal & Ward-Brown, 1994, p. 69) and that African American and White children had generally similar types and levels of fears. Some researchers (e.g., A. M. Neal & Ward-Brown, 1994) have indicated that school-based fears are less common, and simple phobias more common, in African American youth, and fear intensity, frequency, and number are higher in African American children aged 8 to 11.

Several large-scale studies of psychiatric disorder prevalence in youth have included African Americans. In 2002, Angold et al. conducted a telephone interview with a representative sample of parents of 3,613 youth aged 9 through 17 in four rural North Carolina counties and follow-up in-person interviews with 920 of these families. Fifty-four percent of those interviewed by telephone, and 60% of those interviewed in person, were African American. Prevalence rates for African American children and youth ($n = 541$) were generally low for anxiety disorders: generalized anxiety (0.9%), panic disorder (0.9%), separation anxiety (2%), social phobia (0.6%), obsessive–compulsive disorder (0.1%), and agoraphobia (0.7%). In a study of teenagers in the Houston, Texas, metropolitan area, Roberts et al. (2006) reported a similar rate (7.9%) for anxiety disorders generally in their African American subsample ($n = 1,479$). When these researchers coded for at least moderate impairment using two different methods, prevalence rates decreased to 3.3% and 1.4%.

There is a growing literature on urban African American youth's exposure to high rates of violence and its relationship to elevated levels of posttraumatic stress disorder (PTSD) in both observers and victims (Foster, Kuperminc, & Price, 2004; Paxton, Robinson, Shah, & Schoeny, 2004). Exposure to violence also is positively associated with elevated behavioral problems and other negative outcomes. Although boys and girls report witnessing violence and being victims of violence at similar rates, girls report higher rates and levels of anxiety and depression in response to violence than boys. Paxton et al. (2004) reported that social support did not moderate the relationship between violence exposure and depression or PTSD symptoms; however, Jones (2007) found that formal social support by family and spirituality acted as a protective factor against developing PTSD symptoms. As in much of the literature, these findings are based on convenience samples, and larger scale studies need to be conducted.

Reliability and validity are properties of scores in specific samples or populations. Thus, researchers need to assess the validity of instruments' scores, specifically in African American samples. For example, Lambert, Cooley, Campbell, Benoit, and Stansbury (2004) reported that the factor structure of the Childhood Anxiety Sensitivity Index (Silverman, Fleisig, Rabian, & Peterson, 1991) in Black children is different from its structure in White children. Similarly, White and Farrell (2001) have proposed using a different structure on the Revised Children's Manifest Anxiety Scale (Reynolds & Richmond, 1985) for African Americans than the empirically derived one proposed by the authors. Currently, the Fear Survey Schedule for Children—II (Burnham, & Gullone, 1997) is the most promising measure for assessing fears in children and adolescents. However, despite a growing recognition that culture plays a role in the fears that youth manifest, there is no extant literature on this instrument with African American samples.

Treadwell et al. (1995) reported that after treatment involving a 16-session cognitive–behavioral therapy (CBT) protocol, African American children "reported less anxious symptomatology and fewer fears and worries than they did at pretreatment" (p. 380) based on both teacher and parent reports. CBT interventions have demonstrated positive results with African American children and adolescents in other studies (e.g., Cooley, Boyd, & Grados, 2004), and a recent report indicates that attachment-based family therapy also has promise (Diamond, 2005).

Attention-Deficit and Disruptive Behavioral Disorders

A review of the literature indicates differences in prevalence rates of behavioral disorders reported by parents and children on the one hand, and teachers on the other, for African American youth. On the basis of parent and child reports, Angold et al. (2002) reported lower or comparable prevalence rates for rural African American youth and White youth on attention-deficit/hyperactivity disorder (ADHD; 2.1% vs. 3.2%), conduct disorder (CD; 5.3% vs. 5.6%), oppositional defiant disorder (ODD; 1.1% vs. 2.7%), and comorbid CD and ODD (1.7% vs. 4.2%). In another study of urban adolescents ($N = 4,175$), Roberts et al. (2006) reported a similar trend in prevalence rates for ADHD and disruptive behavior disorders—5.7% and 7.2%, respectively, for African Americans and Whites without impairments, and 2.0% to 4.5% and 3.2% to 6.4%, respectively, for African Americans and Whites with impairments. In one of the largest studies of ADHD ($N = 20,401$) based on data from the National Health Institute Survey of parents, Pastor and Reuben (2005) reported prevalence rates for African Americans ($n = 3,562$) for ADHD and ADHD comorbid with learning disabilities of 2.2% and 4.0% respectively. Rates for non-Hispanic Whites were 4.1% and 3.5%.

However, teacher reports consistently yield higher rates of disruptive behavior disorders for African American children and youth. McDermott and Spencer (1997) examined prevalence rates based on teacher reports on the nationally representative sample ($N = 1,400$) used for norming the Adjustment Scale for Children and Adolescents (McDermott, Marston, & Stott, 1993). They reported on several syndromes, including ADHD, solitary aggressive provocative disorder, solitary aggressive impulsive disorder, ODD, diffident disorder, and avoidant disorder. McDermott and Spencer reported numbers "1.5 times expectancy" on "impulsive aggression and opposition defiance" and "significantly less diffidence" for African Americans (p. 396). In another study ($N = 3,006$), which used *DSM–IV* referenced rating scales completed by teachers, Nolan, Gadow, and Sprafkin (2001) indicated that screening prevalence rates for African Americans were higher than their White counterparts at all age levels: 36% versus 16% in the 3- to 5-year-olds, 44% versus 15% in the 6- to 12-year-olds, and 40% versus 13% in the 13- to 18-year-olds. Rates of ODD and CD in preschool-age children also were higher for African Americans; however, the Nolan et al. sample had small numbers of African Americans, suggesting caution in interpreting the results.

The higher prevalence rates for African Americans, and especially African American males, on behavioral disorders based on teacher reports have raised concerns about potential bias in both respondents and assessment tools (Harry & Anderson, 1994; Reid, 1995), and a substantial, albeit inconclusive, literature has developed around potential reasons for this bias. In 2003, L. I. Neal, McCray, Webb-Johnson, and Bridgest reported on a study in which 136 teachers judged videotapes of Black and White students walking into a classroom. Students used either a stroll associated with African Americans or a standard stroll. Teachers rated both Black and White students using the African American stroll as lower in achievement and higher in aggression, and teachers were more likely to indicate that they would refer these students to be assessed for special education. However, teachers rated the African American students using the standard stroll as higher in achievement than Whites using the standard stroll, and there was no main effect of ethnicity in either ratings of aggression or likelihood of referral for special education assessment. These results suggest that teachers have a negative stereotype of a type of stroll associated with African Americans such that everyone using that walk, including majority students, is subject to negative perceptions but that the same teachers do not negatively stereotype African Americans students, a finding that raises questions about what the source of the bias is. Thus, this study reflects the conflicting results in this literature that Neal et al. acknowledged in their introduction.

Scholarship on ADHD specifically has also yielded results that are not clear cut. For example, Spencer and Oatts (1999) argued in a position paper that African Americans with ADHD may be misdiagnosed with CD. In a more recent study, using a vignette method, Hartnett, Nelson, and Rinn (2004) found that in the unprimed condition, 77% of a group of counselors rated a student's behaviors as indicative of an ADHD diagnosis, but that in a primed condition, only 45% rated the same behaviors as indicative of ADHD, with 14% rating the behaviors as indicating giftedness and 32% diagnosing both ADHD and giftedness. These studies suggest that the same behaviors may lead to students being classified as having ADHD, CD, or being gifted. Similarly, Reid et al. (1998) suggested that scores on some ADHD scales may not perform similarly across ethnic groups (Reid et al., 1998). However, when Epstein et al. (2005) compared teacher ratings and classroom observations of White and African American children diagnosed with ADHD and a matched sample of children in the same classroom who were not diagnosed, their findings did not provide support for "a negative response bias among teachers" (p. 432).

The conflicting findings highlight the need for ongoing research on the issue of bias in special education diagnosis and assignment; however, they also raise some concerns about how this research is conducted. First, referral to special education does not guarantee being assigned to special education, and a substantial proportion of the students who are referred for special education assessment are not given a special education classification. Second, the actual decision to classify a student is made by a multidisciplinary team, not a teacher, and in many states, the common individual on the team is the school psychologist, not the counselor or a specific teacher, in part because school psychologists administer and interpret the psychological tests that are used as part of the diagnostic material. Thus, researchers interested in the issue of bias in placement should be studying school psychologists and, more important, multidisciplinary teams.

There is a growing body of literature available on the treatment of ADHD in African American youth. Jurbergs, Palcic, and Kelley (2007) found that school home notes, both with and without response cost, were effective in increasing academic productivity and on-task behavior in a sample of low-income African American children diagnosed with ADHD. Research also suggests that ADHD treatments have comparable effectiveness outcomes in African American youth (Arnold et al., 2003) but also indicate that African Americans are less likely to seek and receive treatments because of unfamiliarity with ADHD (Bailey & Owens, 2005), concerns about overdiagnosis and misdiagnosis (Bailey & Owens, 2005), less private insurance coverage, and fewer concerns about the academic impact of the diagnosis.

African Americans are also more likely to receive treatment in the school setting (Bussing et al., 2005), which will reduce the probability of medical interventions. The majority of information available on the treatment of disruptive behavior disorders is based on samples of White children; however, Capage, Bennett, and McNeil (2001) reported comparable outcomes for African American and White American children between 3 and 8 years old who received parent–child interaction therapy.

Pervasive Developmental Disorders

There is a dearth of literature on pervasive developmental disorders (e.g., autism, Asperger's, or Rett's disorder) in the literature on African

American populations. Croen, Grether, and Selvin (2002) examined the records of more than 3.5 million births in California between 1989 and 1994. They examined maternal characteristics related to children diagnosed as autistic ($n = 4,381$; prevalence = 12.3/10,000 live births) within the first 3 years of life. The risk for Black mothers having a child diagnosed as autistic was 1.6 times that of their White counterparts, after controlling for place of birth and other factors. However, in a study in Philadelphia, White children were diagnosed with autism at age 6.3 on average, as opposed to Black children, who were diagnosed at age 7.9, on average (Mandell, Listerud, Levy, & Pinto-Martin, 2002). Mandell et al.'s (2002) study suggests that Black children spend more time in treatment before being diagnosed.

In a third study, conducted in metropolitan Atlanta, Georgia, Yeargin-Allsopp et al. (2003) reported prevalence rates of 3.4 per 1,000 for both Black and White children. However, they also noted that schools played a bigger role in diagnosing Black children, as well as children of younger mothers and children whose mothers had not completed high school. The latter two groups often have a higher proportion of African Americans. Treatment options for autism are limited, and early diagnosis and intervention are crucial. Thus, African Americans are currently at greater risk for poor outcomes.

Learning Disorders and Mental Retardation

There is a substantial literature on the achievement gap between Blacks and Whites, a gap that is present as early as the kindergarten years and extends through college (Jencks & Phillips, 1998), and this gap is reflected in the overrepresentation of African American students in the mental retardation and developmental delay categories and their underrepresentation in gifted and talented programs (McCray, Webb-Johnson, & Neal, 2003; Worrell, 2003). However, African Americans are not overrepresented in the specific learning disability category (McCray et al., 2003), even though this category accounts for over 50% of the students in special education.

Although the issue of bias cannot be discounted, in disability categories related to learning, specifically, one cannot interpret over- and underrepresentation without taking the achievement gap into account and some of the reasons for that gap, including many of the issues mentioned at the beginning of this chapter (e.g., poverty; low birthweight; greater exposure toxins, such as lead, early in development; poorer nutrition [Donovan & Cross, 2002]). The overrepresentation in the area of developmental delays highlights the importance of early intervention and access to *quality* preschool education, because African American children attend preschools at rates that are equivalent or greater than their White counterparts (National Center for Education Statistics, 2002). For more information on the achievement gap and African Americans, see Blanchett (2006), Lee (2002), and Losen and Orfield (2002).

Eating Disorders

More than 90% of individuals diagnosed with eating disorders are female and at least in the adolescent period, and the prevalence rates are generally low (anorexia nervosa = 0.5%, bulimia nervosa = 1%–3%; American Psychiatric Association, 2000). The results on adult prevalence rates have been mixed, with most research indicating lower rates for African Americans (e.g., Falconer, 2006). Adams et al. (2000) found that Black fourth- and seventh-grade students had larger ideal adult body sizes than their White counterparts, and Botta (2000) found that watching a lot of television had a greater negative impact White adolescents' eating behaviors than on Blacks' eating behaviors. Adolescent female athletes, who are often studied as a special group, show the same patterns, with Latinas and Whites exhibiting higher rates of disordered eating and attitudes towards eating than African Americans (Pernick et al., 2006). There is currently little research on treatment specific to African Americans in the literature, but Falconer (2006) indicated that there are no differences "in the likelihood of obtaining treatment" (p. 167).

Mood Disorders

Angold et al. (2002) reported that rural African Americans youth aged 9 to 17 had lower prevalence rates on major depression (0.5% vs. 1.5%), dysthymia (0.2% vs. 0.3%), and minor depression (0.7% vs. 2.8%) than Whites of the same age. Prevalence rates for urban adolescents were 3.2%, 2.0%, and 3.4% for European Americans, African Americans, and Mexican Americans, respectively. As with other disorders, the literature is mixed, with other studies reporting no differences among groups and some reporting higher rates for African Americans (McLauglin, Hilt, & Nolen-Hoeksema, 2007). There also are claims that differences in rates disappear when sociodemographic factors (e.g., income, education level) are controlled (Doi, Roberts, Takeuchi, & Suzuki, 2001).

Suicidal ideation and suicide attempts are often associated with depression. African Americans have historically had considerably lower suicide rates than Whites (USDHHS, 2001). The suicide rates among African American youth began to increase in the mid-1980s, peaked in the mid-1990s, and reached historic lows in 2003 (approximately 4, 6, and 8 deaths per 100,000 for Blacks, Hispanics, and Whites, respectively). The rates have begun to increase again (Foundation for Child Development, 2007). There are nuances, however, that the completed suicide rates do not reveal. In 2005, African American high schoolers reported feeling sad or helpless at rates comparable to Whites, although still lower than Hispanics, and the rates for attempted suicides were similar for African Americans (7.6%) and White students (7.3%; Centers for Disease Control and Prevention, 2006). Both CBT (Kennard, Stewart, Hughes, Patel, & Emslie, 2006) and attachment-based family therapy (Diamond, 2005) have been found to be effective for African American youth. Antidepressants have been found to have the potential to increase suicide risk (Goodman, Murphy, & Lazoritz, 2006) and should be used with caution.

Substance Use

Angold et al. (2002) reported that substance use was one of the most prevalent disorders in their sample of rural youth, with rates of 5.4% and 4.0% for Blacks and Whites, respectively. Roberts et al. (2006) reported rates of 6.2%, 2.2%, and 6.4% for urban European American, African American, and Mexican American youth. Alcohol is the drug most frequently used by African American youth (with 70% having used it by Grade 12), followed by cigarettes (50%), marijuana (25%), and cocaine (< 2%;

Wallace et al., 1999). Despite these apparently high numbers, several studies with substantial sample sizes indicate that Black youth are less likely to use alcohol (Welte & Barnes, 1987); cigarettes (Kelder et al., 2003); and illicit drugs (Wallace et al., 1999), including inhalants (Siqueira & Crandall, 2007) and methamphetamines (Springer, Peters, Shegog, White, & Kelder, 2007). African American usage rates for some substances match and exceed Whites in the 25-and-older age range (Belgrave & Allison, 2006). Treatment programs include teaching youth to resist peer pressure, teaching skills to enhance coping and competence, and exposing youth to African American cultural experiences to bolster identity (Belgrave & Allison).

Other Disorders

There are several disorders for which there is little or no information available on African American adults or youth. These tend to be low-incidence conditions, and they include adjustment disorders, dissociative disorders, factitious disorders, gender identity disorders, impulse control disorders, personality disorders, somatoform disorders, and schizophrenia and psychotic disorders. Angold et al. (2002) reported prevalence rates of 2.7% and 0.3% for functional enuresis and encopresis, respectively, but there are few other studies available. There is one study on sleep disorders that suggests that African Americans are twice more likely than Whites to experience hypersomnia, but there were no differences across the groups on insomnia (Roberts, Robert, & Chen, 2000).

GAY AND LESBIAN YOUTH

The dearth of literature on gay and lesbian issues in regard to African American youth is even more extreme. The copious literature on racial identity attitudes in African Americans highlights the importance of minority identity issues, but this attention has not been focused on lesbian, gay, bisexual, transgendered, and questioning (LGBTQ) youth, and most of the literature in this area is on White youth. Of course, sexual orientation is an invisible identity and, given its stigma in society, is difficult to study in nonadult populations (Miller, Forte,

Wilson, & Greene, 2006). Moreover, the African American community has often been less tolerant of sexual minorities, framing LGBTQ youth as making an immoral choice (Froyum, 2007). However, there is an increasing recognition on the part of the larger society that sexual orientation is not a free choice, as evidenced by the success of mainstream movies with gay protagonists and legal same-sex marriage in countries such as Canada and Spain.

In 1990, Hunter reported violent attacks on lesbian and gay adolescents at rates of greater than 40% and noted that these attacks were also associated with elevated rates of suicide attempts. Not surprisingly, the negative responses to gay and lesbian youth result in a high level of nondisclosure. For example, in a study of 37 gay Black male adolescents, Edwards (1996) found that although all of them reported being comfortable with their sexuality, "all of them were passing as heterosexuals" (p. 334). In a more recent study, Black gay youth reported more positive attitudes toward homosexuality over time than their White counterparts, but they also reported participating in fewer gay-related social activities; more discomfort about others knowing they were gay; and, consequently, less disclosure about their sexual orientation (Rosario, Schrimshaw, & Hunter, 2004). As these data make clear, Black LGBTQ youth (especially males) are at greater risk of isolation or marginalization in both Black-majority and other schools (McCready, 2004), and they may need psychosocial supports from mental health professionals.

Access to Mental Health Services

Despite the needs in the African American community, access to health care is limited by several factors. As indicated previously, African American youth are overrepresented in high-need populations that have fewer socioeconomic resources (USDHHS, 2001), and they are less likely to be diagnosed with some disorders (e.g., autism). Second, as a group, they are more dependent on the school system for diagnoses. African Americans have lower rates of insurance in general and lower rates of employer-based insurance (USDHHS, 2001), as well as less access to private practitioners. Third, low rates of education often result in a lack of information on the nature of disorders and the longer term consequences if the disorders are not treated.

However, even when resources are not the issue, African Americans are less likely to access health care because of issues of cultural mistrust. Concerns about overdiagnosis and misdiagnosis, and fears about being deliberately infected (Belgrave & Allison, 2006), make African Americans less likely to seek out treatment. The relatively low numbers of African American medical practitioners and the lack of cultural competence on the part of many practitioners also contribute to lower than ideal rates of accessing services. All of these concerns are exacerbated for children and adolescents, who often must depend on adults to make the decision to get them services.

Conclusion

African Americans make up approximately 12% of the U.S. population but constitute 17% of the school-age population. In addition to the achievement gap and the negative stereotypes about African American educational competence, African American children are more likely than their majority counterparts to live in poverty, to be exposed to violence, to live in a single-parent home, and to experience the death of someone they know. Despite the dire statistics presented in this chapter, the trends in psychological well-being for African American youth are not universally negative. Although African American youth have higher rates of ADHD, their rates of other disruptive behavior disorders and of most anxiety disorders are comparable to those of other groups. They are also less likely to engage in substance use. Thus, it is fair to say that African American youth are remarkably resilient in the face of multiple risk factors.

There is, however, a clear need for research in a number of areas. Success in school plants the seeds for adult success and for decreasing risk in subsequent generations. Thus, it is important to address the overrepresentation of African Americans in learning and behavioral difficulties categories. There is also a critical need for research on assessment, diagnosis, and treatment of psychological disorders in African American youth and for culturally competent practitioners. Medical doctors, who may see a child on multiple occasions before the child begins school, can diagnose many psychological disorders. These individuals must be trained to recognize signs of psychopathology in African American youth so that the latter do not have to wait until they start school to be diagnosed. Researchers must develop strategies to reduce mistrust and to educate African Americans so that they are more likely to seek out mental health services earlier, and systems and policies need to change so that high-need populations have equal access to services of which they are more in need than those who do have access.

In the school setting, there is also a clear need for better training of mental health professionals. Counselors and school psychologists working in school settings need basic training in cultural competence. They must be prepared to treat cultural background as one important individual-difference characteristic that must be considered without engaging in stereotyping. They must pay attention to issues of reliability and validity of scores on the assessment tools that are used African American students and to the caveats that are necessary when the only tools that are available have not been validated with this population. Most important, they need to recognize that a free and appropriate public education is more than a legal right; it is also a public health concern. This framing requires mental health professional working with school-age populations to recognize that both prevention activities and the education of other professionals in schools (e.g., teachers, principals) are critical and necessary components of their work that may be of greater importance for their African American students and other clientele from marginalized groups.

References

Adams, K., Sargent, R. G., Thompson, S. H., Richter, D., Corwin, S. J., & Rogan, T. J. (2000). A study of body weight concerns and weight control practices of 4th and 7th grade adolescents. *Ethnicity & Health, 5,* 79–94.

American Psychiatric Association. (1994). *Diagnostic and statistical manual of mental disorders* (4th ed.). Washington, DC: Author.

American Psychiatric Association. (2000). *Diagnostic and statistical manual of mental disorders* (4th ed., text revision). Washington, DC: Author.

Angold, A., Erkanli, A., Farmer, E. M. Z., Fairbank, J. A., Burns, B. J., Keeler, G., et al. (2002). Psychiatric disorder, impairment, and service use in rural African American and White youth. *Archives of General Psychiatry, 59,* 893–904.

Arnold, L. E., Elliott, M., Sachs, L., Bird, H., Kraemer, H. C., Wells, K. C., et al. (2003). Effects of ethnicity on treatment attendance, stimulant response/dose, and 14-month outcome in ADHD. *Journal of Consulting and Clinical Psychology, 71,* 713–727.

Bailey, R. K., & Owens, D. L. (2005). Overcoming challenges in the diagnosis and treatment of attention-deficit/hyperactivity disorder in African Americans. *Journal of the National Medical Association, 97,* S5–S10.

Belgrave, F. Z., & Allison, K. W. (2006). *African American Psychology: From Africa to America.* Thousand Oaks, CA: Sage.

Blanchett, W. J. (2006). Disproportionate representation of African American students in special education: Acknowledging the role of White privilege and racism. *Educational Researcher, 35,* 24–28.

Botta, R. A. (2000). The mirror of television: A comparison of Black and White adolescents' body image. *Journal of Communication, 50,* 144–159.

Burnham, J. J., & Gullone, E. (1997). The Fear Survey Schedule for Children—II: A psychometric investigation with American data. *Behaviour Research and Therapy, 35,* 491–496.

Bussing, R., Zima, B. T., Mason, D., Hou, W., Garvan, C. W., & Forness, S. (2005). Use and persistence of pharmacotherapy for elementary school students with attention deficit/hyperactivity disorder. *Journal of Child and Adolescent Psychopharmacology, 15,* 78–87.

Capage, L. C., Bennett, G. M., & McNeil, C. B. (2001). A comparison between African American and Caucasian children referred for treatment of disruptive behavior disorders. *Child and Family Behavior Therapy, 23,* 1–14.

Centers for Disease Control and Prevention. (2006). Youth risk behavior surveillance—United States, 2005. *Morbidity and Mortality Weekly Report, 55*(SS-5).

Child Welfare Information Gateway. (2005). *Foster care.* Washington, DC: U.S. Department of Health and Human Services.

Cooley, M. R., Boyd, R. C., & Grados, J. J. (2004). Feasibility of an anxiety preventive intervention for community violence exposed African-American children. *Journal of Primary Prevention, 25,* 105–123.

Croen, L. A., Grether, J. K., & Selvin, S. (2002). Descriptive epidemiology of autism in a California population: Who is at risk? *Journal of Autism and Developmental Disorders, 32,* 217–224.

Diamond, G. S. (2005). Attachment-based family therapy for depressed and anxious adolescents. In J. L. Lebow (Ed.), *Handbook of clinical family therapy* (pp. 17–41). Hoboken, NJ: Wiley.

Dillard, J. M. (2005). Scope of mental health issues among African Americans. In D. A. Harley & J. M. Dillard (Eds.), *Contemporary mental health issues among African Americans* (pp. 3–18). Alexandria, VA: American Counseling Association.

Doi, Y., Roberts, R. E., Takeuchi, K., & Suzuki, S. (2001). Multiethnic comparison of adolescent major depression on the *DSM–IV* criteria in a U.S.–Japan study. *Journal of the American Academy of Child and Adolescent Psychiatry, 40,* 1308–1315.

Doll, B. (1996). Prevalence of psychiatric disorders in children and youth: An agenda for advocacy by school psychology. *School Psychology Quarterly, 11,* 20–47.

Donovan, M. S., & Cross, C. T. (Eds.). (2002). *Minority students in special and gifted education.* Washington, DC: Committee on Minority Representation in Special Education, National Research Council.

Edwards, W. J. (1996). A sociological analysis of an in/visible minority group: Male adolescent homosexuals. *Youth and Society, 27,* 334–355.

Epstein, J. N., Willoughby, M., Valencia, E. Y., Toney, S. T., Abikoff, H. B., Arnold, L. E., et al. (2005). The role of ethnicity in the relationship between teacher ratings of attention-deficit/hyperactivity disorder and observed classroom behavior. *Journal of Consulting and Clinical Psychology, 73,* 424–434.

Falconer, J. (2006). Eating disorders. In Y. Jackson (Ed.), *Encyclopedia of multicultural psychology* (pp. 165–167). Thousand Oaks, CA: Sage.

Foster, J. D., Kuperminc, G. P., & Price, A. W. (2004). Gender differences in posttraumatic stress and related symptoms among inner-city minority youth exposed to community violence. *Journal of Youth and Adolescence, 33,* 59–69.

Foundation for Child Development. (2007). *Child and youth well-being index (CWI), 1975–2005, with projections for 2006.* New York: Author.

Froyum, C. M. (2007). "At least I'm not gay": Heterosexual identity making among poor Black teens. *Sexualities, 10,* 623–622.

Goodman, W. K., Murphy, T. K., & Lazoritz, M. (2006). Risk of suicidality during antidepressant treatment of children and adolescents. *Primary Psychiatry, 13,* 43–50.

Harry, B., & Anderson, M. G. (1994). The disproportionate placement of African American males in special education programs: A critique of the process. *Journal of Negro Education, 63,* 602–619.

Hartnett, D. N., Nelson, J. M., & Rinn, A. N. (2004). Gifted or ADHD? The possibilities of misdiagnosis. *Roeper Review, 26,* 73–76.

Hunter, J. (1990). Violence against lesbian and gay male youths. *Journal of Interpersonal Violence, 5,* 295–300.

Individuals with Disabilities Education Improvement Act of 2004. Pub. L. No. 108-446, 20 U.S.C. 1400 Stat. 2647 (2004).

Jencks, C., & Phillips, M. (Eds.). (1998). *The Black–White test score gap.* Washington, DC: Brookings Institution Press.

Jones, J. M. (2007). Exposure to chronic community violence: Resilience in African American children. *Journal of Black Psychology, 33,* 125–149.

Jurbergs, N., Palcic, J., & Kelley, M. L. (2007). School–home notes with and without response cost: Increasing attention and academic performance in low-income children with attention-deficit/hyperactivity disorder. *School Psychology Quarterly, 22,* 358–379.

Kelder, S. H., Prokhorov, A., Barroso, C. S., Murray, N., Orpinas, P., & McCormick, L. (2003). Smoking differences among African American, Hispanic, and White middle school students in an urban setting. *Addictive Behaviors, 28,* 513–522.

Kennard, B. D., Stewart, S. M., Hughes, J. L., Patel, P. G., & Emslie, G. J. (2006). Cognitions and depressive symptoms among ethnic minority adolescents. *Cultural Diversity and Ethnic Minority Psychology, 12,* 578–591.

Lambert, S. F., Cooley, M. R., Campbell, K. D. M., Benoit, M. Z., & Stansbury, R. (2004). Assessing anxiety sensitivity in inner-city African American children: Psychometric properties of the Childhood Anxiety Sensitivity Index. *Journal of Clinical Child and Adolescent Psychology, 33,* 248–259.

Lee, J. (2002). Racial and ethnic achievement gap trends: Reversing the progress toward equity? *Educational Researcher, 31,* 3–12.

Losen, D. J., & Orfield, D. (Eds.). (2002). *Racial inequity in special education.* Cambridge, MA: Harvard Educational Press.

Mandell, D. S., Listerud, J., Levy, S. E., & Pinto-Martin, J. A. (2002). Race differences in the age at diagnosis among Medicaid-eligible children with autism. *Journal of the American Academy of Child and Adolescent Psychiatry, 41,* 1447–1453.

Massey, D. S. (2000). The residential segregation of Blacks, Hispanics, and Asians, 1970–1990. In G. D. Jaynes (Ed.), *Immigration and race: New challenges for American democracy* (pp. 44–73). New Haven, CT: Yale University Press.

McCray, A. D., Webb-Johnson, G., & Neal, L. I. (2003). The disproportionality of African

Americans in special education: An enduring threat to equality and opportunity. In C. C. Yeakey & R. D. Henderson (Eds.), *Surmounting the odds: Education, opportunity, and society in the new millennium* (pp. 455–485). Greenwich, CT: Information Age.

McCready, L. T. (2004). Understanding the marginalization of gay and gender non-conforming Black male students. *Theory Into Practice, 43,* 137–143.

McDermott, P. A., Marston, N. C., & Stott, D. H. (1993). *Adjustment scales for children and adolescents.* Philadelphia: Edumetric and Clinical Science.

McDermott, P. A., & Spencer, M. B. (1997). Racial and social class prevalence of psychopathology among school-age youth in the United States. *Youth and Society, 28,* 387–414.

McLaughlin, K. A., Hilt, L. M., & Nolen-Hoeksema, S. (2007). Racial/ethnic differences in internalizing and externalizing symptoms in adolescents. *Journal of Abnormal Child Psychology, 35,* 801–816.

Mello, Z. R. (in press). Racial/ethnic group and socioeconomic status variation in educational and occupational expectations from adolescence to adulthood. *Journal of Applied Developmental Psychology.*

Miller, L. M, Forte, D., Wilson, B. D. M., & Greene, G. J. (2006). Protecting sexual minority youth from research risks: Conflicting perspectives. *American Journal of Community Psychology, 37,* 341–348.

Miniño, A. M., Arias, E., Kochanel, K. D., Murphy, S. L., & Smith, B. L. (2002, September). Deaths: Final data for 2000. *National Vital Statistics Reports, 50*(15). Hyattsville, MD: National Center for Health Statistics.

National Center for Education Statistics. (2002). *The condition of education, 2002.* Washington, DC: Government Printing Office.

National Center for Health Statistics. (2006). Preliminary data for 2004, Table 1: Deaths and death rates by Hispanic origin, race, age, and sex. *National Vital Statistics Reports, 54*(19), 8–15.

Neal, A. M., & Ward Brown, B. J. (1994). Fears and anxiety disorders in African American children. In S. Friedman (Ed.), *Anxiety disorders in African Americans* (pp. 65–75). New York: Springer.

Neal, L. I., McCray, A. D., Webb-Johnson, G., & Bridgest, S. T. (2003). The effects of African American movement styles on teachers' perceptions and reactions. *Journal of Special Education, 37,* 49–57.

Nolan, E. E., Gadow, K. D., & Sprafkin, J. (2001). Teacher reports of *DSM–IV* ADHD, ODD, and CD symptoms in schoolchildren. *Journal of the American Academy of Child and Adolescent Psychiatry, 40,* 241–249.

Pastor, P. N., & Reuben, C. A. (2005). Racial and ethnic differences in ADHD and LD in young school-age children: Parental reports in the national health interview survey. *Public Health Reports, 120,* 383–392.

Paxton, K. C., Robinson, W. L., Shah, S., & Schoeny, M. E. (2004). Psychological distress for African-American adolescent males: Expose to community violence and social support as factors. *Child Psychiatry and Human Development, 34,* 281–295.

Pernick, Y., Nichols, J. F., Rauh, M. J., Kern, M., Ji, M., Lawson, M. J., et al. (2006). Disordered eating among a multi-racial/ethnic sample of female high school athletes. *Journal of Adolescent Health, 38,* 689–695.

Reid, R. (1995). Assessment of ADHD with culturally different groups: The use of behavioral rating scales. *School Psychology Review, 24,* 537–560.

Reid, R., DuPaul, G. J., Power, T. J., Anastopoulos, A. D., Rogers-Adkinson, D., Noll, M., et al. (1998). Assessing culturally different students for attention deficit hyperactivity disorder using behavior rating scales. *Journal of Abnormal Child Psychology, 26,* 187–198.

Reynolds, C. R., & Richmond, B. O. (1985). *Revised Children's Manifest Anxiety Scale manual.* Los Angeles: Western Psychological Services.

Roberts, R. E., Roberts, C. R., & Chen, I. G. (2000). Ethnocultural differences in sleep complaints among adolescents. *The Journal of Nervous and Mental Disease, 188,* 222–229.

Roberts, R. E., Roberts, C. R., & Xing, Y. (2006). Prevalence of youth-reported *DSM–IV* psychiatric disorders among African, European, and Mexican American adolescents. *Journal of the American Academy of Child and Adolescent Psychiatry, 45,* 1329–1337.

Rosario, M., Schrimshaw, E. W., & Hunter, J. (2004). Ethnic/racial differences in the coming-out process of lesbian, gay, and bisexual youths: A comparison of sexual identity development over time. *Cultural Diversity and Ethnic Minority Psychology, 10,* 215–228.

Rusk, D. (2006). Housing policy is school policy. In N. F. Watt, C. Ayoub, R. H. Badley, J. E. Puma, & W. A. LeBoeuf (Eds.), *The crisis in youth mental health: Critical issues and effective programs* (pp. 53–80). Westport, CT: Praeger.

Siqueira, L. M., & Crandall, L. A. (2007). Inhalant use in Florida youth. *Substance Abuse, 27,* 27–35.

Silverman, W. K., Fleisig, W., Rabian, B., & Peterson, R. A. (1991). Childhood Anxiety Sensitivity Index. *Journal of Clinical Child Psychology, 20,* 162–168.

Spencer, L. E., & Oatts, T. (1999). Conduct disorder vs. attention-deficit/hyperactivity disorder: Diagnostic implications for African American adolescent males. *Education, 119,* 514–518.

Springer, A. E., Peters, R. J., Shegog, R., White, D. L., & Kelder, S. H. (2007). Methamphetamine use and sexual risk behaviors in U.S. high school students: Findings from a national risk behavior survey. *Prevention Science, 8,* 103–113.

Treadwell, K. R. H., Flannery-Schroeder, E. C., & Kendall, P. C. (1995). Ethnicity and gender in relation to adaptive functioning, diagnostic status, and treatment outcome in children from an anxiety clinic. *Journal of Anxiety Disorders, 9,* 373–384.

U.S. Census Bureau. (2000, September). *The Black population in the United States, March 1999: Population characteristics.* Washington, DC: Author.

U.S. Census Bureau. (2001a, February). *Black population in the U.S. March 2000: List of tables (PPL-142).* Washington, DC: Author.

U.S. Census Bureau. (2001b, April). *Census 2000 PHC-T-6: Population by race and Hispanic or Latino origin for the United States, regions, divisions, states, Puerto Rico, and places of 100,000 or more population.* Washington, DC: Author.

U.S. Census Bureau. (2003a, April). *Current population survey, March 2002.* Washington, DC: Author.

U.S. Census Bureau. (2003b, May). Residential segregation of Blacks or African Americans: 1980 to 2000. In U.S. Census Bureau, *Housing patterns* (pp. 58–73). Washington, DC: Author.

U.S. Department of Health and Human Services. (2001). *Mental health: Culture, race, and ethnicity—A supplement to* Mental Health: A Report of the Surgeon General. Rockville, MD: Author.

U.S. Department of Justice. (2002). *Demographic trends in jail populations: Jail incarceration rates by race and ethnicity, 1990–2000.* Retrieved from http://www.ojp.usdoj.gov/bjs/glance/tables/jailrairtab.htm

Wallace, J. M., Jr., Forman, T. A., Guthrie, B. J., Bachman, J. G., O'Malley, P. M., & Johnston, L. D. (1999). The epidemiology of alcohol, tobacco, and other drug use among Black youth. *Journal of Studies on Alcohol, 60,* 800–809.

Welte, J. W., & Barnes, G. M. (1987). Alcohol use among adolescent minority groups. *Journal of Studies on Alcohol, 48,* 329–336.

White, K. S., & Farrell, A. D. (2001). Structure of anxiety symptoms in urban children: Competing factor models of Revised Children's Manifest Anxiety Scale. *Journal of Consulting and Clinical Psychology, 69,* 333–337.

Woodland, M. H. (2008). Whatcha doin' after school? A review of the literature on the influence of after-school programs on young Black males. *Urban Education, 43,* 537–560.

Worrell, F. C. (2003). Why are there so few African Americans in gifted programs? In C. C. Yeakey & R. D. Henderson (Eds.), *Surmounting the odds: Education, opportunity, and society in the new millennium* (pp. 423–454). Greenwich, CT: Information Age.

Worrell, F. C. (2005). Cultural variation within American families of African descent. In C. L. Frisby & C. R. Reynolds (Eds.), *Comprehensive handbook of multicultural school psychology* (pp. 137–172). Hoboken, NJ: Wiley.

Yeargin-Allsopp, M., Rice, C., Karapurkar, R., Doernberg, N., Boyle, C., & Murphy, C. (2003). Prevalence of autism in a US metropolitan area. *Journal of the American Medical Association, 289,* 49–55.

26

CONCEPTUALIZING MENTAL HEALTH FOR AFRICAN AMERICANS

SUZETTE L. SPEIGHT, SHA'KEMA M. BLACKMON,
DESMOND ODUGU, AND J. COREY STEELE

What exactly is mental health? According to the Surgeon General's Report, mental health is

a state of successful performance of mental function, resulting in productive activities, fulfilling relationships with other people, and the ability to adapt to change and to cope with adversity. Mental health is indispensable to personal well-being, family and interpersonal relationships, and contribution to community or society. (U.S. Department of Health and Human Services, 1999, p. 4)

Mental health is more than the simple absence of mental disorder or illness. On the other end of the continuum, *mental disorders* "are health conditions that are characterized by alterations in thinking, mood or behavior (or some combination thereof) associated with distress and/or impaired functioning" (U.S. Department of Health and Human Services, 1999, p. 5). Critical to this particular discussion of mental health and mental illness and African Americans is that "what it means to be mentally healthy is subject to many different interpretations that are rooted in value judgments that may vary across cultures" (U.S. Department of Health and Human Services, 1999, p. 5). Mental health (and mental illness, for that matter) is context dependent and can be understood only by exploring the reciprocal interaction of the person with his or her environment. Accordingly, mental health in men and women of African descent may in fact look different from mental health in men and women from other racial or ethnic groups because of the continuing significance of race in U.S. society.

However, the dominance of a Euro-Western perspective within psychology has typically resulted in a universalistic approach to the definition of mental health. Belgrave and Allison (2006) aptly summarized how Euro-Western psychology has defined mental health and maladjustment from a variety of theoretical perspectives. For instance, a developmental perspective emphasizes deviations from "normal" development as arrests that prevent an individual from achieving the expected and necessary skills. A behavioral perspective defines dysfunction on the basis of learning maladaptive behaviors through reinforcement or modeling. A humanistic perspective sees inner conflicts as causing maladjustment, and a family systems perspective sees ineffective family functions and interactions as responsible for individuals' problems. The medical model seeks the underlying biological causes of mental illness. Recognizing the interactive effect of biology, psychology, and society on mental health, a biopsychosocial perspective emphasizes the reciprocal influences of each of these systems on each other.

There also have been models developed that enumerate multiple qualities or characteristics of mental health from a Euro-Western perspective. Early on, Jahoda (1958) described major categories of functioning that distinguish psychological health: positive and realistic attitudes toward the self, growth and development, integration and balance, autonomy, an accurate perception of reality, and environmental mastery and capacity for adaptation. Lazarus's (1975) review of various Euro-Western models of mental health identified several common themes, including accurate reality testing; the capacity for altruistic love, a sense of belonging; acceptance of oneself and others; and autonomy and independence. Obviously, these Euro-Western conceptualizations of mental health, although presumed universal, arose from and are based in their particular cultural contexts.

C. E. Thompson and Neville (1999) criticized "the assumption of universality and the omission of cultural values" inherent in these various Euro-Western definitions and models of mental health (p. 171). Lazarus (1975) cautioned how important it is to recognize that "mental 'health' as a concept is inextricably tangled up with personal values, that is, judgments of what is good and bad, or desirable and undesirable" (p. 19). Because the mental health of African Americans has often been examined from a pathological and not culturally congruent perspective (Landrum-Brown, 1990), some African American scholars have attempted to define the mental health of African Americans from a culturally specific framework.

A culturally specific perspective is critical for understanding the individual and collective mental health of African Americans through an examination of "the larger social context, its social institutions, and the nature of the social environment" (Myers, Young, Obasi, & Speight, 2003, p. 13). Thus, within the U.S. context, understanding the influence of the historical and contemporary manifestations of multilayered oppression and the resilient African cultural values are central to an accurate conceptualization of the mental health of African Americans.

For instance, in an overview of treatment recommendations for persons of African descent, the Association of Black Psychologists asserted that "pathology in the individual is presumed to be reflective of dysfunction in the larger social group and context" (Myers et al., 2003, p. 13). Thus, definitions of mental health cannot ignore racism, a potential root cause of psychological problems that also creates environmental circumstances conducive to the development of mental health problems (Brown, 2003). Any comprehensive model or definition of African American mental health must examine the oppressive social context of psychological development.

Although there is no one specific, agreed-on definition or model of African American mental health, there have been several significant attempts to define optimal African American mental health. One paradigm commonly employed to examine African American mental health links experiences of racism with a stress and coping process, delineating the psychological consequences of oppression. This racism/stress camp examines the psychological, social, and physical effects of perceived racism. Another paradigm employed to examine African Americans' mental health has arisen from an African-centered perspective. Africentric theorists have conceptualized African heritage as essential to positive psychological functioning. Finally, there are models and definitions of African American mental health that attempt to describe the combination of the oppressive U.S. society and African cultural heritage. In the following sections, we present selective reviews of these three perspectives on mental health to identify elements key to conceptualizing African American mental health.

Racism/Stress Definitions and Models of Mental Health

According to Williams and Williams-Morris (2000), racism exacts its deleterious toll on mental health in three important ways: (1) by restricting socioeconomic mobility, leaving African Americans disproportionately poor; (2) through stressful discrimination experiences; and (3) through the development of internalized feelings of inferiority. Thus, positive mental health for African Americans hinges on their successful management of racism. Clark, Anderson, Clark, and Williams (1999) presented a comprehensive biopsychosocial model for understanding perceived racism's effects on mental and physical health. In this model, structural and interpersonal racism may be experienced as sources of stress, depending on personal psychological factors and sociodemographic factors (e.g., socioeconomic status, gender). The impact on various health outcomes of the stress of perceived racism is mediated by the adaptive or maladaptive coping responses used by the individual.

Ramseur (1991) was concerned about how African Americans could be healthy within an oppressive environment. Ramseur suggested that the ability to negotiate multiple domains of mental health was the best indicator of mental health for African Americans. The domains Ramseur proposed as most pertinent to African American mental health are a positive sense of self, positive attitudes toward other African Americans, accurate perception of the social environment, the ability to adapt to African American and European American culture in a healthy manner, developing and sustaining positive relationships with others, and having a sense of competence. Ramseur suggested that it is important to understand how individuals variously confront and achieve adaptive balance among the multiple domains.

Anderson, Eaddy, and Williams (1990) uniquely placed competence at the center of their model of African American mental health. They asserted that an examination of transactional processes via a competency model attends to both the sociocultural and psychological aspects of the African American experience. Anderson et al. highlighted the disparity between African Americans and Whites in terms of their ability to influence their environment and concluded that, for African Americans, major coping resources are necessary in negotiating the environment. Extending Ramseur's (1991) concept of negotiation and recognizing within-group variation, Anderson et al. suggested that whether an African American is competent depends on the particular individual's process of problem solving, available alternatives to deal with current conditions, the malleability of the environment, and the outcome of the chosen response. Overall, Anderson et al.'s model suggested that a combination of internal and external factors contribute to African American mental health. These factors include perception, language, problem solving, coping, vigilance, self-esteem, locus of control, nuclear and extended family support, social institutions, and group identification.

Similarly, Brown (2003), a sociologist, used *critical race theory* to explain how racial stratification (i.e., racism) influences mental health. Brown described four psychological problems among African Americans that may result from racial stratification. The first, *nihilistic tendencies*, refers "to self-defeating attempts to survive... where individuals are their own worst enemy, acting with intent to destroy themselves" (p. 296). Second, some African Americans show *anti-self issues*. They "feel estranged from their racial selves... have internalized negative notions about being black and thus feel disdain for their racial group" (p. 296). The third problem, *suppressed anger expression*, occurs when the "denial of anger and aggression becomes normative" (p. 297) because of the societal restrictions on African Americans' expression of their anger. The fourth problem, *delusional denial tendencies*, involves repressing the painful realities of racism.

There exists a significant body of literature examining the links between racism and stress. Several excellent and exhaustive reviews of the literature on racism and mental health are available for readers (cf. Carter, 2007; Harrell, 2000; C. E. Thompson & Neville, 1999; Williams & Williams-Morris, 2000). Only within the past 20 years has research begun to document the actual mental and physical health effects of racism and racial discrimination on African Americans. In summary, the racism/stress perspective not only emphasizes the deleterious oppressive environment's effect on mental health but also prioritizes successful adaptation and coping as key features of optimal health for African Americans.

Africentric Definitions and Models of Mental Health

Africentric scholars such as Azibo (1989), Akbar (1991), and Nobles (1991) have offered views of what constitutes normal, health Black personality from African-centered perspectives. According to Nobles, if one examines the African worldview and compares it with the European worldview, one can readily note the differences and the resulting implications for understanding Black self-conception. According to Nobles, a Eurocentric worldview emphasizes survival of the fittest and control over nature. The African worldview emphasizes the general guiding principles of survival of the tribe and being one with nature. The values and customs consistent with the African worldview reflect a sense of cooperation, interdependence, and collective responsibility. Thus, the proper understanding of Black mental health must be based on African values and assumptions and must incorporate African-based analyses and conceptualizations. Baldwin (1984) suggested that "non-Africentric" theories explain the personality of African Americans in terms of oppression experiences. Conversely, "Africentric" theories conceptualize the personality of African Americans in terms of a natural condition with an African reality base. Mental health is then seen as moving toward an African identity, with integrity and survival tendencies. Being grounded in an African-centered worldview becomes the most natural and self-actualized state for people of African descent. The degree to which one's worldview and subsequent self-concept is Eurocentric in nature rather than Afrocentric defines the degree of pathology one may experience (Baldwin, 1984).

Azibo constructed the *Azibo Nosology* (Atwell & Azibo, 1992) as a diagnostic system to conceptualize both normal and abnormal African personality. According to Atwell and Azibo (1992), normal African personality exists when an individual of African descent's

> beliefs, values, attitudes, and behaviors are oriented: (a) to recognize himself or herself as an African, (b) to prioritize African interests, survival, and proactive development, (c) to respect and perpetuate all things that are African, and (d) to support a standard of conduct that neutralizes people and things that are anti-African. (p. 302)

The presence of these qualities is deemed *correct orientation*. Correct orientation is described as "genetic Blackness plus psychological Blackness" (Azibo, 1989, p. 182). On the other hand, the Azibo Nosology (Atwell & Azibo, 1992) also accounts for personality disorder (i.e., mental illness) within African personality.

The most fundamental disorder is known as *psychological misorientation*, which is manifest when an African proceeds, or negotiates the environment, from a conceptual base without African-centered psychological and behavioral elements. *Misorientation* is described as "genetic Blackness minus psychological Blackness" (Azibo, 1989, p. 184). Unfortunately, little research has investigated the validity of the Azibo Nosology aside from the case studies presented by Atwell and Azibo (1991).

Similarly, Akbar (1991) conceptualized that mental disorders among African Americans are due to functioning within an alien and pathological society. The oppression that African Americans experience serves to diminish the sense of self, interrupts and distorts culturally defined gender roles, diminishes self-determination, and reduces one's ability to predict events within the environment (Akbar, 1991). He further suggested that mental health is based on an individual's ability to maintain mental growth and awareness within a society that is hindering that growth. Akbar classified mental disorder into four categories: (1) alien self disorder, (2) anti-self disorder, (3) self-destructive disorder, and (4) organic disorder. Alien self disorders are defined as behaviors and attitudes that reflect significant identification with European American mores, values, and behaviors that are counterproductive to the self. Anti-self disorders are characterized by unfavorable attitudes toward other African Americans. Self-destructive disorders manifest in relation to one's ability to live in a society that denies individuals access to the varying structures of opportunities that exist in society. Individuals engage in behaviors that are not only self-destructive but also destructive to the African American community. Organic disorders include conditions that manifest at the biological level that occur as a function of the disorder that exists in society and can be related to both alien self and anti-self disorders (Akbar, 1991).

Nobles (1991) stated that Africans in the Americas find themselves in a situation that involves the domination and imposition of a fundamentally European system of reality onto a non-European people. This situation has caused psychological confusion among Africans in the Americas, resulting in a pseudo-entity referred to as the "Negro." The concept of "Negro" refers to the African person who attempts to, is forced to, or convinced to deny the philosophical basis of his or her Africanity, even though the psychological fact of his or her Africanity is recognizable. This denial, it is believed, is due to the person being caught in the contradiction between two conflicting philosophical systems (i.e., African and European American; Nobles, 1991).

Kambon (aka Baldwin; Baldwin & Bell, 1985) attempted to operationalize the expression of the African personality through the development of African Self-Consciousness Scale (Kambon, 1992) College students attending historically Black colleges and universities were found to have higher degrees of African self-consciousness (Baldwin, Duncan, & Bell, 1992). Additional research on African self-consciousness has found that it is predictive of health behaviors such as stress management and spiritual growth (S. N. Thompson & Chambers, 2000).

In summary, the Africentric perspective is mostly theoretical or conceptual, and it warrants more research. Africentric theorists emphasize the inherent African-ness of individuals raising a compelling existential question: "To be African or not to be?" (Cooke & Parham, 2007). From an Africentric perspective, positive mental health cannot be attained by someone who does not acknowledge African cultural identity, because the embracing of African heritage is essential for positive mental health.

Models With Both Racism/ Stress and Africentric Elements

Jones (2003) proposed a theory of behavior (TRIOS) that incorporates African cultural foundations and their evolution, adaptation, and transformation in the Diasporic context of African American life. The elements of TRIOS include a special notion of time (T), a unique disposition to rhythm (R), high capacity for improvisation (I), general proclivity to orality (O), and a profound sense of spirituality (S). Cultural racism constitutes the context that necessitates and informs the distinctive African American psyche represented in TRIOS. There exist "self-enhancing motivations," or the orientation to detect the occurrence of, protect oneself from, avoid the anticipation of, and conquer if confronted with racism, as well as "self-enhancing motivations," or the orientation to sustain, defend, and enhance one's self-worth and humanity (Jones, 2003, p. 220). The cultural identity and psychological health of African Americans within the context of American life is formed around the negotiation of these self-protective and self-enhancing motivations and the resolution of these conflicts.

Negotiating these forces requires that the individual African American harness resilient elements of traditional African cultures along with the ethos of the American life and experience. It was the "abject loss of freedom resulting from enslavement [that] generated a primary psycho-cultural motivational system designed to gain control over one's body and over one's life" (Jones, 2003, p. 223). Cultural racism has transformed its many blatant forms to more subtle expressions; thus African Americans' psychocultural identity has been a continuously evolving articulation of traditional African values and contemporary American culture. TRIOS is, therefore, an effort to articulate a psychologically meaningful and historically grounded set of components defining African American psychological well-being. Faced with a new and challenging reality, Africans in America continued to progressively utilize elements of African cultural patterns in their processes of resistance, coping, and adaptation, drawing on two worlds. Jones (2003) described the development of a scale to measure TRIOS elements and found that African Americans scored higher than other racial groups, suggesting they uphold a TRIOS-ic worldview.

An extension of the dual process underlying Jones (2003), Boykin (1986), and Boykin and Allen (in press) proposed a triple-process model. Boykin's formulation incorporates the traditional African and contemporary American elements. In addition, a third element—the oppressed minority identity—is included as unavoidable in constructing this integrative view of African American cultural identity and personality. Boykin contended that the dual-process models (e.g., TRIOS) neglect the fact that the traditional African and the American cultures are not equally valued by non-Africans, and sometimes by Africans. Africa's checkered history and contacts with Europe (and, later, America) have generated a mode of thinking that denigrates whatever is culturally and traditionally African. In the United States, Africans have continued to suffer discrimination and oppression on the basis of their African origin and history. Identifying the need to merge elements of the African culture and the European American cultures without underscoring the ethnocentric (even racist) undertones of such exercise downplays the psychological, social, and cultural conflicts it presents for African Americans. Boykin emphasized that in addition to a mainstream American experience and a Black cultural experience based in African heritage, African Americans still have to articulate an oppressed minority experience to form a psychologically healthy personality and identity.

In summary, Jones's (2003) TRIOS and Boykin's (1986) efforts are attempts to address the shortcomings seen in the Africentric and the racism/stress approaches to understanding the African American experience. Although the Africentric approach underscores the strength of the traditional African cultural values, it fails to adequately recognize the impediments of African American unique minority cultural repertoire and experiences. Correspondingly, the racism/stress approach, while emphasizing the institutional roadblocks to the healthy development and full actualization of African Americans, appears to underestimate the strengths and resilience of traditional African cultures and the adaptability of African Americans. Thus, the combination perspectives strive to synthesize the strengths of both the racism/stress and Africentric perspectives.

Accounting for Within-Group Similarities and Differences

As is the case with most efforts to reclaim a resurgent African culture from the pangs of Western ethnocentrism, the Africentric and combination perspectives make the assumption that all African Americans share the same cultural origins and heritage. But anthropologists and students of African cultures understand that Africa is a very diverse continent with equally diverse cultures and traditions. To assume that all African Americans inherited the same cultural values glosses over the multiplicity of their cultural roots.

It is important, however, to make a distinction between cultural *uniformity* and cultural *similarity*. Although African societies do not have a uniform culture, an examination of traditional African cultures shows sufficient similarity among the many cultures to warrant that African culture is the referent (Onwubiko, 1991, Stewart, 2004). The suggestion that African Americans are heirs of the African culture is appropriate when construed in terms of similarity, not uniformity. Moreover, a close study of the transatlantic slave trade reveals that more Africans were taken from the Gold Coast (i.e., West Africa) than from other parts of the continent. The obvious implication is that a majority of the enslaved Africans originated from the same region; therefore, their descendants share a close cultural heritage.

Still, it is important to draw on the long debate among African philosophers on the utility (or lack thereof) of attempting to define what constitutes an African identity (Oguejiofor, 2001). For one, the identification of particular elements characteristic of all African cultures suggests essentialist conceptions of culture and identity. However, culture changes with time. The dynamics of cultural evolution show that at one time, certain cultural elements are celebrated; at other times, they are dropped or discredited; at another time, completely forgotten; and at yet at another time, unearthed, refurbished, and celebrated again. It is difficult, therefore, to talk about cultural elements as ontological characteristics of an entity as large as a continent. It is interesting that the continent of Africa is still undergoing reconfigurations in the face of neocolonialism and globalization following economic, cultural, and social changes within and among developed and developing nations. Although Africa is not one place, or one culture fixed in time and space, neither are the African descendants in America a monolith.

Moreover, our understanding of African American mental health must be nuanced by accounting for the within-group differences among African Americans. For example, the mental health needs of an African American heterosexual female may be both similar to and different from those of an African American lesbian because of varying experiences of stigmatization and community support (Bowleg, Craig, & Burkholder, 2004). These women's experiences may become further contextualized by issues of social class, racial identity, racial–ethnic socialization experiences, skin color, size, age, education, and living environment.

Empirical research further highlights that variability of experience is important to African American mental health. For instance, Postmes and Branscombe (2002) found significant differences for African Americans living in racially segregated environments versus those in desegregated environments on a number of domains relevant to mental health. Specifically, living in a racially segregated environment had an indirect causal effect on well-being and collective self-esteem. Mediating factors consisted of in- and out-group rejection, self-categorization, and social identification. Living in a segregated environment was related to feelings of acceptance by and identification with other African Americans, suggesting the likelihood of increased opportunity for social support and greater opportunities to be exposed to African American culture.

Likewise, Link and Phelan (1995) asserted that research has consistently demonstrated a significant causal role for social conditions as causes of illness in general, and mental illness in this instance. For instance, poverty involves not only a lack of income but also a lack of access to resources to avoid risks and to minimize the consequences of physical and mental difficulties once they occur.

Americans of African descent are a diverse group; thus, conceptualizing their mental health is complicated by, for example, the influences of developmental level, gender, sexual orientation, spirituality/religion, ability status, and social class.

Conceptualizing Mental Health for African Americans

Defining mental health for African Americans is a difficult enterprise. As C. E. Thompson and Neville (1990) aptly stated, "Mental health is an important yet nebulous abstraction" (p. 176). Examining elements of African American mental health that are common across the three perspectives we have reviewed might aid our attempt to conceptualize African American mental health. It appears that the racism/stress, Africentric, and combination perspectives all emphasize the importance of positive identity as well as successful negotiation with or adaptation to an oppressive environment.

According to Erikson (1968), identity is formed at the nexus of the individual and the society. The contemporary and historical social context within which identity develops for African Americans is characterized by oppression. Du Bois (1903) talked about African American's "double-consciousness, this sense of always looking at one's self through the eyes of others, of measuring one's soul by the tape of a world that looks on in amused contempt and pity" (p. 3). There is a natural tendency to look to the larger society to inform one's sense of self. However, in a society characterized by oppression, there will be little positive reinforcement for African American identity. In actuality, the society provides distorted images of "Blackness" and "African-ness" that negate and denigrate African American identity. These images created by the oppressive environment are constant indicators of African Americans' subordinate place within society and can easily become internalized. For African Americans, ever conscious of the inherent duality of their identity, there exists a "longing to merge [the] double self into a better and truer self" (Du Bois, 1903, p. 3). Obviously, positive identity is difficult to develop and maintain within an oppressive society, yet positive identity is seen as a critical ingredient in African Americans' mental health. Each of the perspectives considers a racially positive sense of one's self to be an important feature of mental health for African Americans. The Africentric perspective is distinct in that it is prescriptive in its view of identity, contending that identity must be grounded in African heritage and be African in nature.

In terms of successful negotiation with or adaptation to an oppressive environment, each of the perspectives reviewed (i.e., racism/stress, Africentric, and combination) focuses on the need to neutralize the negative influence of the oppressive society on one's mental health. The racism/stress perspective encourages healthy coping as a means to deal with the negative oppressive environment. The Africentric perspective proposes the adoption of an African-centered worldview as a means of resisting the oppressive environment. The combination perspective would suggest some fusion of these two options to counteract the oppressive environment. Although the methods may differ, the aim of thwarting the damaging effects of the oppressive environment is similar across the perspectives.

The racism/stress, Africentric, and combination perspectives all emphasize important yet competing constructs representing what Jones (2003) deemed *reactionary* and *evolutionary* mechanisms. These mechanisms may provide the foundation underlying the progression of African American culture from its African origins to the present. Reactionary mechanisms emerged over time to address the environmental challenges faced by African Americans. Evolutionary mechanisms are those expressions of African core cultural ethos. Applying Jones's observations, it seems apparent that the Africentric definitions of mental health and racism/stress definitions of mental health reflect the evolutionary and reactionary mechanisms, respectively.

The Africentric models emphasize the importance of African cultural heritage, whereas the racism/stress models emphasize the negative influence of the oppressive context of the United States. Thus, for the Africentric models, optimal mental health is derived from the acknowledgment and expression of African heritage. On the other hand, the racism/stress models suggest that optimal mental health is derived from healthy adaptation and coping with an oppressive environment. According to Jones (2003), these seemingly conflicting mechanisms actually comprise a dynamic, dual-adaptation process that promotes physical and psychological survival and psychological well-being. Thus, an issue vital to the mental health of African Americans may be the effective synthesis of the influences of traditional African cultural values with the unique experience of being a member of an oppressed minority group in order to negotiate the American context.

It seems clear that any valid conceptualization of African Americans' mental health must utilize a robust framework incorporating the dual influences—African heritage and American context—on culture, identity, and, ultimately, psychological well-being. There is a dynamic vibrancy to mental health that White (1984) captured in his description of a mentally health African American as a someone who

> has internalized an attitude towards self, other, and life in general characterized by vitality, interdependence, mastery of the oral tradition, resourcefulness, and an appreciation of the Afro-American heritage ... is able to maintain a zest and enthusiasm for living that is brought about by being open to the renewal experiences of joy, comedy, sensuality, caring and strength in the face of adversity ... is open to self, in touch with others, and willing to reach out and establish close relationships. He or she draws strength from the realization of not being alone, of being part of a larger, shared cultural heritage, and can identify with the liberation struggle of Black Americans ... [is] resourceful, inventive, imaginative, and enterprising in their approach to life. (pp. 160–161)

Taken together, two key features of positive mental health for African Americans emerge from the key constructs of the models and definitions reviewed here. First, mentally healthy African Americans possess a positive African American identity grounded in African cultural values. In other words, mentally healthy African Americans know who they are. Second, mentally healthy African Americans are able to accurately perceive, assess, and generate creative and flexible mechanisms to resist their oppressive conditions. In other words, mentally healthy African Americans know where they are and how to deal with their environment. Drawing on the strengths inherent in the cultural values of enslaved Africans and their progeny, positive mental health includes an African and African American core that provides a foundation from which to confront the contemporary needs, challenges, and experiences of the current sociocultural context.

FUTURE DIRECTIONS FOR DEFINING AFRICAN AMERICAN MENTAL HEALTH

One of the important next steps is to conduct more research examining the mental health of African Americans. Research is warranted to determine the components of optimal mental health of African Americans. It would be very interesting to utilize qualitative methodologies with clinicians who work within the African American community, asking them to define mental health. Similarly, community samples of African Americans could also provide a lay definition of mental health. In order to triangulate research findings, published experts on African American mental health could also be asked to describe elements of optimal mental health for African Americans.

Another important step is the development and implementation of prevention, outreach, educational, and remedial interventions within African American communities to promote positive mental health. Specifically, these interventions could provide sound historical and contemporary knowledge of the experiences of African Americans, facilitate the development of positive African American identity grounded in traditional African values, encourage the development of critical consciousness regarding oppression, and develop or strengthen a sense of social responsibility to and connection with the African American community (Shade, 1990).

These types of community outreach programs seem especially important for African American children and adolescents, who may be particularly vulnerable to negative societal messages. Children must be taught by significant adults about race and racism. *Racial socialization* is defined as the process by which African American parents raise children to have positive self-concepts in an environment that is racist and sometimes hostile (Stevenson, 1995; Thomas & Speight, 1999). Racial socialization includes exposure to cultural practices, promotion of racial pride, development of knowledge of African American culture, and preparation for bias and discrimination (Hughes et al., 2006). Racial socialization processes have been linked to positive outcomes in children and adolescents, such as higher academic motivation (Sanders, 1997) and less depression (Davis & Stevenson, 2006). Thus, community outreach efforts to promote positive mental health could provide support to and a sense of belonging in children while affirming African American identity within an oppressive context.

The idea of community outreach is not new: Baldwin (1989) urged African American psychologists to utilize their skills to become change agents and leaders in the struggle to liberate African Americans. In fact, recent research suggests that psychologists of color can be effective "cultural brokers" promoting mental health among populations of color (Kim, 2006). By using the cultural capital they have obtained within mainstream contexts, coupled with their own cultural identity, these cultural brokers can be genuinely vital bridges.

Conceptualizing mental health for African Americans is a complicated endeavor. Mental health is a multifaceted and multidetermined entity, ever changing, transforming, and being improvised to meet new environmental demands. Understanding the key elements critical for mental health will facilitate the development of effective interventions for enhancing and promoting positive mental health for African Americans.

References

Akbar, N. (1991). Mental disorders among African Americans. In R. Jones (Ed.), *Black Psychology* (pp. 339–352). Berkeley, CA: Cobb & Henry.

Anderson, L. P., Eaddy, C. L., & Williams, E. (1990). Psychosocial competence: Toward a theory of understanding positive mental health among Black Americans. In D. S. Ruiz (Ed.), *Handbook of mental health and mental disorder among Black Americans* (pp. 255–271). New York: Greenwood Press.

Atwell, I., & Azibo, D. (1992). Diagnosing personality disorders in Africans using the Azibo Nosology: Two case studies. In A. K. Burlew, W. C. Banks, H. P. McAdoo, & D. A. Azibo, *African American Psychology: Theory, research, and practice* (pp. 300–320). Newbury Park, CA: Sage.

Azibo, D. A. (1989). African-centered theses on mental health and a nosology of Black/African personality disorder. *Journal of Black Psychology, 15,* 173–214.

Baldwin, J. A. (1984). African self-consciousness and the mental health of African-Americans. *Journal of Black Studies, 15,* 177–194.

Baldwin, J. A., (1989). The role of Black psychologists in Black liberation. *Journal of Black Psychology, 16,* 67–76.

Baldwin, J. A., & Bell, Y. (1985). The African Self-Consciousness Scale: An Africentric personality questionnaire. *Western Journal of Black Studies, 9,* 61–68.

Baldwin, J. A., Duncan, J. A., & Bell, Y. R. (1992). Assessment of African self-consciousness among Black students from two college environments. In A. K. H. Burlew (Ed.), *African American Psychology: Theory, research and practice* (pp. 283–299). Newbury Park, CA: Sage.

Belgrave, F. Z., & Allison, K., W. (2006). *African American Psychology: From Africa to America.* Thousand Oaks, CA: Sage.

Bowleg, L., Craig, M. L., & Burkholder, G. (2004). Rising and surviving: A conceptual model of active coping among Black lesbians. *Cultural Diversity and Ethnic Minority Psychology, 10,* 229–240.

Boykin, A. (1986). The triple quandary and the schooling of Afro-American children. In

U. Neisser (Ed.), *The school achievement of minority children* (pp. 57–92). Hillsdale, NJ: Lawrence Erlbaum.

Boykin, A. W., & Allen, B. (in press). Culture matters in the psychological experiences of African-Americans: Some conceptual, process and practical considerations. *Teachers College Record.*

Brown, T. N. (2003). Critical race theory speaks to the sociology of mental health: Mental health problems produced by racial stratification. *Journal of Health and Social Behavior, 44,* 292–301.

Carter, R. T. (2007). Racism and psychological and emotional injury: Recognizing and assessing race-based traumatic stress. *The Counseling Psychologist, 35*(1), 13–105.

Clark, R., Anderson, N. B., Clark, V. R., & Williams, D. R. (1999). Racism as a stressor for African Americans: A biopsychosocial model. *American Psychologist, 54,* 805–816.

Cooke, B. G., & Parham, T. A. (2007). Reflections on Baba Asa G. Hilliard III, Ed.D. *Psych Discourse, 41*(6), 12–13.

Davis, G. Y., & Stevenson, H. C. (2006). Racial socialization experiences and symptoms of depression among Black youth. *Journal of Child and Family Studies, 15,* 303–317.

Du Bois, W. E. B. (1903). *The souls of Black folks.* Chicago: A. C. McClurg.

Erikson, E. H. (1968). *Identity: Youth and crisis.* New York: W. W. Norton.

Harrell, S. P. (2000). A multidimensional conceptualization of racism-related stress: Implications for the well-being of people of color. *American Journal of Orthopsychiatry, 70,* 42–57.

Hughes, D., Rodriguez, J., Smith, E. P., Johnson, D. J., Stevenson, H. C., & Spicer, P. (2006). Parents' ethnic–racial socialization practices: A review of research and directions for future study. *Developmental Psychology, 42,* 747–770.

Jahoda, M. (1958). *Current concepts of positive mental health.* New York: Basic Books.

Jones, J. M. (2003). TRIOS: A psychological theory of the African legacy in American culture. *Journal of Social Issues, 59,* 217–242.

Kambon, K. K. (1992). *The African personality in America: An African-centered framework.* Tallahassee, FL: Nubian Nation.

Kim, J. M. (2006). Ethnic minority counselors as cultural brokers: Using the self as an instrument to bridge the gap. In G. R. Walz, J. C. Bleuer, & R. Yep (Eds.), *Vistas: Compelling perspectives on counseling 2006* (pp. 77–79). Alexandria, VA: American Counseling Association.

Landrum-Brown, J. (1990). Black mental health and racial oppression. In D. S. Ruiz (Ed.), *Handbook of mental health and mental disorder among Black Americans* (pp. 113–132). Westport, CT: Greenwood Press.

Lazarus, R. S. (1975). The healthy personality—A review of conceptualizations and research. In L. Levi (Ed.), *Society, stress and disease: Childhood and adolescence* (Vol. 2, pp. 6–35). New York: Oxford University Press.

Link, B. G., & Phelan, J. (1995). Social conditions as fundamental causes of disease. *Journal of Health & Social Behavior, 30,* 80–94.

Myers, L. J., Young, A., Obasi, E., & Speight, S. L. (2003). Recommendations for the psychological treatment of persons of African descent. In Council of National Psychological Associations for the Advancement of Ethnic Minority Issues (Ed.), *Psychological treatment of ethnic minority populations* (pp. 13–18). Washington, DC: Association of Black Psychologists.

Nobles, W. (1991). Extended self: Rethinking the so-called Negro self-concept. In R. L. Jones *Black Psychology* (pp. 295–304). Berkeley, CA: Cobb & Henry.

Oguejiofor, J. O. (2001). *Philosophy and the African predicament.* Ibadan, Nigeria: Hope Publications.

Onwubiko, O. A. (1991). *African thoughts, religion and culture.* Enugu, Nigeria: Snapp Press.

Postmes, T., & Branscombe, N. R. (2002). Influence of long-term racial environmental composition on subjective well-being in African Americans. *Journal of Personality and Social Psychology, 83,* 735–751.

Ramseur, H. P. (1991). Psychologically healthy Black adults. In R. L. Jones (Ed.), *Black Psychology* (pp. 353–378). Berkeley, CA: Cobb & Henry.

Sanders, M. G. (1997). Overcoming obstacles: Academic achievement as a response to racism and discrimination. *Journal of Negro Education, 66,* 83–93.

Shade, B. J. (1990). Coping with color: The anatomy of positive mental health. In D. S. Ruiz (Ed.), *Handbook of mental health and mental disorder among Black Americans* (pp. 273–290). New York: Greenwood Press.

Stevenson, H. C. (1995). Relationship of adolescent perceptions of racial socialization to racial identity. *Journal of Black Psychology, 21,* 49–70.

Stewart, P. E. (2004). Afrocentric approaches to working with African American families. *Families in Society: The Journal of Contemporary Social Services, 85,* 221–228.

Thomas, A. J., & Speight, S. L. (1999). Racial identity and racial socialization attitudes of African American parents. *Journal of Black Psychology, 25,* 152–170.

Thompson, C. E., & Neville, H. A. (1999). Racism, mental health, and mental health practice. *The Counseling Psychologist, 27,* 155–223.

Thompson, S. N., & Chambers, J. W. (2000). African self-consciousness and health promoting behaviors among African American college students *Journal of Black Psychology, 26,* 330–345.

U.S. Department of Health and Human Services. (1999). *Mental health: A report of the Surgeon General.* Rockville, MD: Author.

White, J. L. (1984). *The psychology of Blacks.* Englewood Cliffs, NJ: Prentice Hall.

Williams, D. R., & Williams-Morris, R. (2000). Racism and mental health: The African American experience. *Ethnicity & Health, 5,* 243–268.

27

POSITIVE PSYCHOLOGY

African American Strengths, Resilience, and Protective Factors

A. Toy Caldwell-Colbert, Fayth M. Parks, and Sussie Eshun

The story of African people's relationship to psychology begins in the late 19th century as psychology emerged as the new science, claiming ownership of the study of human beings mental and behavioral processes. During this era, psychology and anthropology became intimate partners. In his classic book on the history of psychology, titled *Even the Rat Was White*, Guthrie (2004) explained that the Western belief of racial and cultural superiority was supported by human science methodology that provided evidence for the view that non-White peoples were primitive and backward in their ways. He explained how comparative psychology divided humankind on the basis of skin color, temperament, customs, and habits. The path and purpose of psychology's interest in race and ethnicity were legitimized by a structured methodological stance. Guthrie asserted that psychological inferiority was assigned to darker skinned people and supported by philosophical discourse and romanticism in American classic literature. He pointed out that inferiority included traits such as deviousness, slackness, and slow mental ability.[1]

Guthrie's (2004) point is even more important when the writings of African-centered scholars are considered. In his book, *African Psychology: Reclamation, Reascension and Revitalization*, Wade Nobles (1986) argued that many of the theories of Western philosophy and psychology can be traced to the teachings of ancient Africa, particularly Egypt. Although many theories can be traced to teachings of ancient Africa, Nobles emphasized that by focusing on human behavior as a sole entity, Western psychology misses the essence of African thought, which takes more of a comprehensive view and typically considers the spiritual, physical, and biological attributes of an individual. The general idea behind African psychology is that African thought focuses on community because of the view that the universe is interconnected: Family is therefore crucial to the existence of the individual. As Nobles noted in his book, implications for a Western psychology that highlights individualism and independence more strongly than other attributes is that, for African Americans and Africans, a failure to acknowledge the connection among the spiritual, mental, and physical aspects contributes to ineffective intervention strategies when working with African American clients.

Throughout the 19th and the mid-20th centuries, rationalism and scientific objectivity dominated psychology theory. Any phenomena that did not fit into Western scientific scheme were interpreted negatively or labeled as some form of pathology. During the 1960s and 1970s, seismic shifts in America's political and social consciousness, such as the Vietnam War protests and the Civil Rights Movement demanded mainstream society address race, class, and gender inequities, which resulted in federal programs, for example, antipoverty initiatives in education (e.g., Head Start Programs) and human services (e.g., Comprehensive Employment and Training Act programs). Psychology's methodological stance was also under fire. Established in 1963, activist organizations such as the Association of Black Psychologists were founded to address behavioral and social science bias in research, training, and practice (Williams, 1974).

Psychological science was challenged to discard old assumptions and revise theories about ethnic/minority people's mental and behavioral processes. Modern theories and practice approaches needed to incorporate ethnic and cultural diversity with a focus on culture-bound states and traits reflecting strengths (Caldwell-Colbert & Williams, 2003). Accordingly, the American Psychological Association (2003) created multicultural guidelines to set standards for psychological science, education, and practice. The guidelines reflect changes in society and address cultural and sociopolitical contexts relevant to groups that historically have been marginalized and disenfranchised.

The inequities of race, class, gender, and poverty are forms of pressure that have posed diverse threats to African American mental health. Forms of optimal functioning and positive personal traits have continually evolved within the context of well-documented barriers due to external circumstances such as racism and poverty. In this chapter, we address positive subjective experience for African Americans. We first ask the following question: What is positive psychology? Positive psychology is a growing movement in contemporary psychology that seeks to promote positive human strengths and living well. We then address positive psychology in a multicultural context, provide a historical overview of strength-based research, and explore neuropsychological aspects of an applied psychology of hope. Empirical investigations, with attention to protective factors, resilience, optimal functioning, hope, and faith as strength-based resources across the life span, are discussed in a positive psychology context. The chapter concludes with a summary and recommendations for future research.

What Is Positive Psychology?

Positive psychology is defined as a science of positive subjective experience: well-being and satisfaction; happiness; joy and flow; and positive cognitions about the future, such as optimism, hope, and faith (Seligman, 2005). Past president of the American Psychological Association Martin P. Seligman popularized positive psychology as a field of inquiry as one of his initiatives. Seligman observed that, since World War II, psychology had focused a great deal of its efforts on human problems and how to resolve them (Peterson, 2006). Psychology's illness-based focus and disease model has resulted in research on psychological disorders and negative environmental stressors that have led to effective evidence-based treatments to relieve human suffering. However, Seligman (2005) reminded us that "Treatment is not just fixing what is wrong; it is also building what is right" (p. 4).

As a result of Seligman's initiative, there has been a flow of research and writing on the subject, assisted by the establishment of the peer-reviewed *Journal of Positive Psychology*. In the *American Psychologist* (2000) millennial special issue on happiness, excellence, and optimal human functioning, 15 articles discuss subjects such as happiness, optimism, emotional states and health, and wisdom as an expert knowledge system concerned with the practical aspects of living. Seligman and Csikszentmihalyi (2000) introduced readers to the field of positive psychology:

> A science of positive subjective experience, positive individual traits, and positive institutions promises to improve quality of life and prevent pathologies that arise when life is barren and meaningless. The exclusive focus on pathology that has dominated so much of our discipline

results in a model of the human being lacking the positive features that make life worth living. Hope, wisdom, creativity, future mindedness, courage, spirituality, responsibility, and perseverance are ignored or explained as transformations of more authentic negative impulses. (p. 5)

In his *New York Times* bestseller *Authentic Happiness,* Seligman (2002) stated that positive psychology has three pillars: (1) the study of human emotion; (2) the study of positive traits, among them strengths and virtues and abilities such as intelligence; and (3) the study of positive institutions, such as democracy and strong families. He asserted that these pillars support the positive emotions of confidence, hope, and trust, for example, which serve us best when life is difficult.

The assertions of positive psychology and its focus on building strengths has received even more support because of brain research that points to a neural network that may generate our tendency to be optimistic. Sharot, Riccardi, Raio, and Phelps (2007) used functional magnetic resonance imaging to explore how the brain functions while participants thought about positive as well as negative future life events. Sharot et al. observed that when participants were focused on positive events, there was significant activation in the rostral anterior cingulate cortex and amygdala. They further noted that there may be a neurobiological purpose for optimistic bias: "the tendency to engage in the projection of positive future events, suggesting that the effective integration and regulation of emotional and autobiological information supports the projection of positive future events in healthy individuals and is related to optimism" (p. 102). Specifically, participants in their study tended to expect positive events to occur closer in the future, while distancing themselves from imagining negative events. Other studies, using samples of mice, have identified that vulnerable mice, when under excessive stress, had higher rates of impulse firing cells that make the neurotransmitter dopamine (Krishnan et al., 2007). Adaptive mice, on the other hand, produced potassium, which lowered firing rates of the neurotransmitter. This result points to a biological ability for resilience.

Positive Psychology From a Multicultural Perspective

We must first state that positive psychology from a multicultural perspective is a broad subject. Thus far, positive psychology has emphasized protective factors, assets, resources, and strengths, with minimal attention to multicultural context (Lopez et al., 2005). The literature on this subject suggests various ideas and approaches toward the aim of a more diverse and inclusive examination of positive emotion and strength-based models (Snyder & Lopez, 2007). Acknowledgment of negative interpretations of racial and ethnic differences and deficit models is a step in the right direction; however, caution must be raised to not promote multicultural positive psychology out of the context of the historical oppression that has affected marginalized groups. We are at risk of interpreting culturally derived meanings, coping strategies, and philosophical foundations outside of the historical context where unhealed wounds and generations of damage are still unacknowledged by the majority culture. This could unintentionally result in cultures and traditions being misunderstood or in constructions of meaning oversimplified.

The impact of sociopolitical viewpoints, such as pan-Africanist, nationalist, integrationist, or post-Black, is also important as we consider African Americans' ability to thrive and face adversity, mental health, and strength-based approaches in a positive psychology context. If we are not mindful of this, we run the risk of omitting more than 40 years of research and investigation that oppose deficit models and illuminate what works and contributes to resilience, self-efficacy, well-being, and protective factors, for example, optimism and hope for African Americans.

Positive Psychology: An African American Perspective

Positive psychology conveys a message of optimism, hope, and survival. As we discuss later in this chapter, this message is easily applicable to the cultural values of African Americans. Unlike earlier models, which perceived variations in worldview and coping as a deviation and indicative of weakness, the views held by positive psychology indicate a shift toward a real focus on the values and norms of other cultures. A truly African American positive psychology will require that researchers and scholars explore the role of African American culture as a way of building protective factors. For example, instead of assuming that virtues espoused by the majority culture are equally important to African Americans, it is important to look into their history to identify traditional African virtues, such as beneficence, improvisation, forgiveness, and justice (Ryff & Singer, 1998).

A series of readings that capture the essence of positive psychology for African Americans can be found in Elsie J. Smith's (2006a, 2006b) monographs on strength-based counseling published in *The Counseling Psychologist*. Smith expanded the strength-based model and explained that it typifies a paradigm shift from focusing on clients' deficits or weaknesses to focusing on their strengths. Strengths are culturally expressed, in that a quality perceived as a strength in one culture may be viewed as a weakness in another (E. J. Smith, 1985). For instance, Nobles (1986) noted that ancient African thought emphasized community because it viewed the world as interconnected, and thus the family was considered a crucial factor for the existence of the individual. Overall, many of the strengths identified by Peterson and Seligman (2004) and summarized by E. J. Smith (2006a) resonate with core African American values. These include wisdom, relational and nurturance abilities, survival skills, and hope.

African American Strengths and Protective Factors: Historical Overview

As buffers against life's difficult times and in celebration of life's joys, elevating attributes of inner strength, resilience, hope and optimism has been an African American response individually and collectively since the first Africans were brought to American shores (Berry & Blassingame, 1982; J. H. Franklin & Moss, 2000). Is there any more powerful symbol for elevating inner strength, resilience, hope, and optimism as buffers against imposed external circumstances than the North Star? As a symbol of freedom by faith, the North Star offered hope and optimism that life had more to offer than the unspeakable suffering of bondage and enslavement. Faith, courage, hope, and optimism were individual and collective strengths called on to overcome fear, violence, and pain of fractured families and communities. These strengths are an important legacy in African American Psychology today. Think about the character strengths and virtues called on by the late Civil Rights leader Rev. Dr. Martin Luther King Jr.'s use of the concept "beloved community." In a beloved community, homelessness, poverty, and violence are not tolerated because of a global standard of justice and human decency. King's strength-based concept was a global vision that called on positive virtues, such as love and trust, to prevail over fear and violence.

During the 1960s and 1970s, Black Psychology as a field of study was thrust forward by scholars' self-determination when their critique of conventional psychology observed its negative interpretations and lack of regard for Black psychological perspectives, concepts, cultural themes, and practices. In an effort to deconstruct deficit models and promote an African source of consciousness, scholarship centered on African principles and concepts as a center of Black Psychology (Nobles, 1991; White, 1970). Theories of Black identity development and personality conceptualized aspects of positive psychological functioning (Baldwin, 1992; Cross, 1991; Helms, 1990; Parham, 1993). In 1988, Linda James Myers offered a conceptualization of the conditions for optimal psychology and Afrocentric worldview. Myers and her colleagues further suggested positive features of optimal functioning, such as peace, love, joy, and increased well-being, as a philosophical basis of identity development theory (Myers et al., 1991). Theoretical writings and research that regard positively Black experiences and that capture constructs that meaningfully reflect Black life are regularly published in the *Journal of Black Psychology*, founded in 1974, and in edited books such as *Black Psychology* (Jones, 1991), *Mental Health in Black America* (Neighbors & Jackson, 1996), and *African American Psychology: Theory, Research, and Practice* (Burlew, 1992). Many of these edited books are in their second, third, and fourth editions.

In addition, scholars have consistently focused on resiliency and strength-based approaches rooted in adaptive strategies in Black families and communities (Billingsley, 1992; A. J. Franklin & Jackson, 1990; Neighbors & Jackson, 1996;

McAdoo, 2007; McCreary, Cunningham, Ingram, & Fife, 2006). For example, Hill's (1999) 20-year investigation of strengths of Black families, and Boyd-Franklin's (2003) ever-present reminder of lessons in survival, present evidence-based models that optimize family functioning. Boyd-Franklin offered a multisystems model based on the concept of *circularity*. Working effectively with individuals and families requires flexibility and exploration of family subsystems such as extended family, nonblood kinship, church, and community resources. African American resilience and strength-based approaches are anchored in positive racial and cultural identity and familial and social support.

COMMON THREADS: AFRICENTRIC WORLDVIEW, RESILIENCE, SPIRITUALITY, STRENGTHS, COPING, AND WELL-BEING

There is a rich body of literature on resilience, protective factors, coping, and well-being. A PsycINFO search on the terms *African Americans* and *resilience* or *resiliency* yielded more than 100 hits; *protective factors* yielded more than 80 hits, *strengths* yielded 73 hits, and *coping* and *well-being* yielded more than 300 hits each. These are common threads through the life span. The following literature review highlights some salient findings and research trends.

In the previous section, we provided a brief overview of the history behind the move toward positive psychology among African Americans. The general consensus is that African Americans as a group have learned to overcome oppression, obstacles, and other challenges because they hold on to a culture that encourages resilience, communal support, and spiritual growth. In fact, spirituality has been identified as an important source of resilience and coping mechanism (Banerjee & Pyles, 2004). African American spirituality stems from a social and political environment of oppression and therefore focuses on the need to be optimistic and hopeful about deliverance from the oppressor. This view can be summarized in a popular scripture that is read quite often in traditional religious services: "We are troubled on every side, yet not destroyed; Perplexed, but in despair; Persecuted, but not forsaken; Cast down, but not destroyed" (2 Corinthians 4:8, 9, King James Version of *The Holy Bible*). In this section, we review and summarize some of the empirical studies in this area.

Africentric Values and Racial Identity

Several studies have focused on Africentric cultural values as a strength or protective factor for African Americans. Africentric cultural values have been defined as "a set of beliefs, values, and assumptions that is founded on African cultural traditions and that relate to definitions of the self, others, and the relationship of the self with the environment" (Constantine, Alleyne, Wallace, & Franklin-Jackson, 2006, p. 142). They are typically derived from the seven main principles of Kwanzaa, namely, (1) unity, (2) self-determination, (3) collective work and responsibility, (4) cooperative economies, (5) purpose, (6) creativity, and (7) faith (Karenga, 1965). More recently, some scholars have included values such as spirituality, harmony, and balance and authenticity (for a review, see Mattis & Jagers, 2001).

In their study of the relationship between Africentric cultural values and positive mental health, Constantine et al. (2006) reported that adherence to Africentric cultural values were predictive of high self-esteem, and high self-esteem was predictive of greater life satisfaction. Their findings confirm earlier studies that reported a positive association between Africentric values and high self-esteem as well as overall good mental health (Akbar, Chambers, & Thompson, 2001; Arroyo & Zigler, 1995; Dubois, 1999).

Among adolescents, racial identity and racial socialization can be buffers against high-risk environments (Caldwell, Kohn-Wood, Schmeelk-Cone, Chavous, & Zimmerman, 2004; E. P. Smith & Hasbrouck, 2006) and promote academic achievement (Miller, 1999; Prelow, Bowman, & Weaver, 2007; Spencer, 2005). In an investigation of adolescent males, Swanson, Cunningham, and Spencer (2003) reviewed the integration of affective and cognitive processes for preschool- and elementary school–age boys to illustrate how structural conditions provide opportunities for vulnerable and successful academic outcomes and resiliency. As an offset to negative stereotyping and reactive coping, they found that proactive opportunities for affirming self-beliefs of positive aspects of manhood;

support from parents, teachers, and other school personnel and administrators (with an emphasis on training educators to facilitate achievement by creating a supportive environment); and cultural socialization by parents provides positive options as a protective factor.

Resilience

Resilience is another aspect of positive psychology that has been studied extensively. It has been defined as "positive adaptation despite negative environmental influences" (Miller & MacIntosh, 1999, p. 159). In general, an individual's ability to develop resilience depends on internal and external factors associated with exposure to risky or harsh environments and his or her ability to cope because of protective factors that have developed over the course of his or her life (Rutter, 1993). As discussed earlier, in their environment, African Americans struggle with many challenges stemming from racism, discrimination, poverty, and a general lack of available resources (McLoyd, 1990). Although they would be expected to succumb to their challenges, it is amazing how many of them are able to see beyond and rise up against the challenges.

Among African American families, resilience is a protective factor that involves raising a child strive for a healthy balance between the demands of life in general and the challenges of institutional and individual prejudice, which is an added burden for the child. This extra calling for African American parents typically places a burden on them to hammer the reality home to the child that their race and/or ethnicity may pose challenges, and that they need to be equipped to navigate those challenges (Miller & MacIntosh, 1999). One of the factors that have been found to develop resilience among African Americans is racial identity. For instance, Miller and Macintosh (1999) found that, among African American adolescents, a positive racial identity has a buffering effect and that "this variable can provide protection from and maintain competence in the presence of adversity" (p. 164).

Further investigations of African American resiliency have shown that racial socialization messages and an individual's perception that he or she has social support account for a significant proportion of the variance in resiliency levels (Brown, 2008). Earlier studies confirm that racial socialization is associated with positive academic outcome (Hughes et al., 2006) social support from the nuclear and extended families, as well as the community and church (Boyd-Franklin, 2003), and translates into their ability to overcome adversity (Pipes-McAdoo, 2002).

Spirituality

The important role of religion and spirituality in the lives of African Americans has been studied from different perspectives. Overall, findings from various researchers and scholars indicate that spiritual beliefs mold the lives of African Americans. As summarized eloquently by Mattis, Fontenot, Hatcher-Kay, Grayman, and Beale (2004), "African Americans have cultivated particular traditions of Biblical interpretation that metaphorically link Black oppression to the oppression suffered by Biblical Israel. In their interpretative scheme, God is seen as the ultimate ally of the oppressed" (p. 191). Given the extensive research findings that religion promotes positive mental health and physical well-being (Taylor, Ellison, Chatters, Levin, & Lincoln, 2000), an important, although limited, finding is that it shapes our cognitive appraisals and the meanings we attach to life's challenges (Mattis, 2002). This is a crucial protective factor for this chapter's focus on positive psychology.

In a study of spirituality and racial attribution as resources for adjustment among African American children, Christian and Barbarin (2001) found that the children of parents who attended church weekly had significantly fewer problems than their counterparts who were not frequent church attenders. Their results were linked to earlier studies that explained that religious family values may prepare children to be mature and demonstrate self-discipline by teaching them to delay immediate gratification and to exercise appropriate restraint in given circumstances (Barbarin, 1993). Other researchers have linked religiosity or spirituality to lower pro-suicide ideology and fewer suicide attempts in African American samples (Stack & Wasserman, 1995).

Mattis et al. (2004) explored the relationship among religiosity, optimism, and pessimism in a sample of 307 African Americans. Their results indicated that among subjective spirituality and a positive relationship with God were key predictors of optimism; also, subjective spirituality was negatively related to pessimism. In other words, these researchers confirmed assertions made by scholars that for African Americans, a positive relationship with God and increased levels of spirituality were significantly, positively associated with high levels of optimism and negatively associated with pessimism. Such findings are crucial and need to be explored further, because optimism and spirituality are among the key components of positive psychology and optimal functioning.

Conclusion and Future Directions

Culture plays a crucial role in the process of healing and coping with challenges. In spite of the numerous stressors African Americans encounter in today's society, they continue to persist. Risk and protective factors for urban youth in a study by Li, Nussbaum, and Richards (2007) include similar findings, for example, exposure to violence and poverty as risks and confidence, family support, and positive neighborhoods (i.e., neighborhood involvement and neighborhood cohesion) as protective factors.

Neighbors, Jackson, Bowman, and Gurin (1983) identified protective factors for African Americans to include prayer and religious commitment, facing the problem directly, and "keeping busy." Aside from spirituality, other protective factors include ethnic and racial identity, Africentric values (Brook & Pahl, 2005), and culture-specific coping (Utsey, Bolden, Lanier, & Williams, 2007). Overall, Africentric cultural patterns, such as importance of social support, kinship bonds, and spirituality, are positive aspects of collectivist cultures (Nobles, 1991; Triandis, 1995) and therefore important to African Americans. These protective factors have been identified as significant predictors of resilience in high-risk urban communities.

The information summarized in this chapter has implications for counseling African Americans and other clients from the African Diaspora. Counselors need to view their clients through special lenses that will help them acknowledge their clients' strengths within a given context. Review of historical and empirical information suggests that all cultural groups, and African Americans in particular, benefit from therapeutic interventions that empower them by identifying and recognizing their capabilities. E. J. Smith (2006b) noted that identifying and recognizing clients' strengths help them "come to believe that good things can happen and that they can be the engineer summoning and directing those good things in their lives" (p. 136).

Implications for research also are noteworthy. Although most researchers in the field of psychology would agree that culture is a crucial factor for successfully working with ethnic minority groups, few endeavors to engage in systematic investigations of the role of culture in behavior have been made. As some scholars have argued, we seem to be asking the wrong research questions: A paradigm shift from deficit models to strength models means that we redirect our focus from weakness and pathology to more routinely investigate strengths and protective factors. In order to ask the type of research questions that highlight strength models, we need culturally relevant measures and clinical assessment instruments of African American strengths. Unfortunately, the number of these instruments is meager, and thus more research in the area is needed.

There is a need for African Americans and others interested in the influence of culture and ethnicity to rise up and research factors that have a direct impact on them individually and corporately. Failure to do that would be an endorsement of Seligman's observations of learned helplessness in response to adversity. From their African roots, traditional African American culture is filled with messages of encouragement, optimism, community support, and resilience: That is the more reason why positive psychology is ripe and needs to be embraced with a passion. As Jesse Jackson so often empowers us through his Rainbow Coalition slogan, "Keep Hope Alive!"

Note

1. See Robert V. Guthrie's classic book *Even the Rat Was White: A Historical View of Psychology* (2004), originally published in 1976. Now available in its second edition, Guthrie's critique of the structural biases in psychology provides evidence that illustrates its impact on society today, particularly psychological science and formal education.

References

Akbar, M., Chambers, J. W., Jr., & Thompson, V. L. S. (2001). Racial identity, Africentric values, and self esteem in Jamaican children. *Journal of Black Psychology, 27,* 341–358.

American Psychological Association. (2003). Guidelines on multicultural education, training, research, practice, and organizational change for psychologists. *American Psychologist, 58,* 377–402.

Arroyo, C. G., & Zigler, E. (1995). Racial identity, academic achievement, and the psychological well-being of economically disadvantaged adolescents. *Journal of Personality and Social Psychology, 69,* 903–914.

Baldwin, J. (1992). *The African personality in America: An African-centered framework.* Tallahassee, FL: Nubian Nation.

Banerjee, M. N., & Pyles, L. (2004). Spirituality: A source of resilience for African American women in the era of welfare reform. *Journal of Ethnic & Cultural Diversity in Social Work, 13*(2), 45–70.

Barbarin, O. A. (1993). Coping and resilience: Exploring the inner lives of African American children. *Journal of Black Psychology, 19,* 478–492.

Berry, M. F., & Blassingame, J. W. (1982). *Long memory: The Black experience in America.* New York: Oxford University Press.

Billingsley, A. (1992). *Climbing Jacob's ladder: The enduring legacy of African-American families.* New York: Simon & Schuster.

Boyd-Franklin, N. (2003). *Black families in therapy: Understanding the African American experience* (2nd ed.). New York: Guilford Press.

Brook, J. S., & Pahl, K. (2005). The role of ethnic and racial identity and aspects of an Africentric orientation against drug use among African American young adults. *Journal of Genetic Psychology, 166,* 329–345.

Brown, D. L. (2008). African American resiliency: Examining racial socialization and social support as protective factors. *Journal of Black Psychology, 34,* 32–48.

Burlew, K. A. (1992). *African American Psychology: Theory, research, and practice.* Newbury Park, CA: Sage.

Caldwell, C. H., Kohn-Wood, L. P., Schmeelk-Cone, K. H., Chavous, T. M., & Zimmerman, M. A. (2004). Racial discrimination and racial identity as risk or protective factors for violent behaviors in African American young adults. *American Journal of Community Psychology, 33,* 91–105.

Caldwell-Colbert, A. T., & Williams, V. M. (2003). Treating ethnic minority clients. In D. K. Freedlheim (Ed.), *Handbook of psychology: Vol. 1. History of psychology* (pp. 501–502). Hoboken, NJ: Wiley.

Christian, M. D., & Barbarin, O. A. (2001). Cultural resources and psychological adjustment of African American children: Effects of spirituality and racial attribution. *Journal of Black Psychology, 27,* 43–63.

Constantine, M. G., Alleyne, V. L., Wallace, B. C., & Franklin-Jackson, D. C. (2006). Africentric cultural values: Their relation to positive mental health in African American adolescent. *Journal of Black Psychology, 32,* 141–154.

Cross, W. E. (1991). *Shades of black: Diversity in African American identity.* Philadelphia: Temple University Press.

Dubois, K. E. (1999). Racial identity, Afrocentric orientation and well-being among African American women. *Dissertation Abstracts International, 59*(9-B), 5077.

Franklin, A. J., & Jackson, J. S. (1990). Factors contributing to positive mental health among Black Americans. In D. Ruiz (Ed.), *Handbook of mental health and mental disorder among Black Americans* (pp. 291–308). Westport, CT: Greenwood Press.

Franklin, J. H., & Moss, A. A. (2000). *From slavery to freedom: A history of African Americans.* New York: McGraw-Hill.

Guthrie, R. L. (2004). *Even the rat was white: A historical view of psychology* (2nd ed.). Boston: Allyn & Bacon.

Helms, J. E. (1990). *Black and White racial identity: Theory, research, and practice.* New York: Praeger.

Hill, R. B. (1999). *The strengths of African American families: Twenty-five years later.* Lanham, MD: University Press of America.

Hughes, D., Rodriguez, J., Smith, E. P., Johnson, D. J., Stevenson, H. C., & Spicer, P. (2006). Parents' ethnic–racial socialization practices: A review of research and directions for future study. *Developmental Psychology, 42,* 747–770.

Jones, R. L. (Ed.). (1991). *Black Psychology.* Hampton, VA: Cobb & Henry.

Karenga, M. R. (1965). *Nguzo saba.* San Diego, CA: Kawaida.

Krishnan, V., Han, M., Graham, D., Berton, O., Renthal, W., Russo, S., et al. (2007). Molecular adaptations underlying susceptibility and resistance to social defeat in brain reward regions. *Cell, 131,* 394–404.

Li, S. T., Nussbaum, K. M., & Richards, M. H. (2007). Risk and protective factors for urban African American youth. *American Journal of Community Psychology, 39,* 21–35.

Lopez, S. J., Prosser, E. C., Edwards, L. M., Magyar-Moe, J. L., Neufeld, J. E., & Rasmussen, H. N.

(2005). Putting positive psychology in a multicultural context. In C. R. Snyder & S. J. Lopez (Eds.), *Handbook of positive psychology* (pp. 700–714). New York: Oxford University Press.

Mattis, J. S. (2002). Religion and spirituality in the meaning-making and coping experiences of African American women: A qualitative analysis. *Psychology of Women Quarterly, 26,* 308–320.

Mattis, J. S., Fontenot, D. L., Hatcher-Kay, C. A., Grayman, N. A., & Beale, R. L. (2004). Religiosity, optimism, and pessimism among African Americans. *Journal of Black Psychology, 30,* 187–207.

Mattis, J. S., & Jagers, R. J. (2001). A relational framework for the study of religiosity and spirituality in the lives of African Americans. *Journal of Community Psychology, 29,* 519–539.

McAdoo, H. P. (Ed.). (2007). *Black families* (4th ed.). Thousand Oaks, CA: Sage.

McCreary, M. L., Cunningham, J. N., Ingram, K. M., & Fife, J. E. (2006). Stress, culture, and racial socialization: Making an impact. In P. Wong & L. Wong (Eds.), *Handbook of multicultural perspectives on stress and coping* (pp. 487–513). New York: Springer.

McLoyd, V. C. (1990). The impact of economic hardship on Black families and children: Psychological distress, parenting, and socioeconomic development. *Child Development, 61,* 311–346.

Miller, D. B. (1999). Racial socialization and racial identity: Can they promote resiliency for African American adolescents? *Adolescence, 34,* 493–501.

Miller, D. B., & MacIntosh, R. (1999). Promoting resilience in urban African American adolescents: Racial socialization and identity as protective factors. *Social Work Research, 23,* 159–169.

Myers, J., Speight, S. L., Highlen, P. S., Cox, C. I., Reynolds, A. L., Adams, E. M., & Hanley, P. (1991). Identity development and worldview: Toward an optimal conceptualization. *Journal of Counseling and Development, 70,* 54–63.

Myers, L. J. (1988). *Understanding an Afrocentric worldview: Introduction to an optimal psychology.* Dubuque, IA: Kendall/Hunt.

Neighbors, H. W., & Jackson, J. S. (Eds.). (1996). *Mental health in Black America.* Thousand Oaks, CA: Sage.

Neighbors, H., Jackson, J., Bowman, P., & Gurin, G. (1983). Stress, coping, and Black mental health: Preliminary findings from a national study. In R. Hess & J. Hermalin (Eds.), *Innovations in prevention* (pp. 5–29). New York: Haworth Press.

Nobles, W. (1986). *African psychology: Toward its reclamation, reascension, and revitalization.* Oakland, CA: Black Family Institute.

Nobles, W. (1991). African philosophy: Foundations of Black Psychology. In R. L. Jones (Ed.), *Black Psychology* (3rd ed., pp. 47–63). Hampton, VA: Cobb & Henry.

Parham, T. (1993). *Psychological storms: The African American struggle for identity.* Chicago: African American Images.

Peterson, C. (2006). *A primer in positive psychology.* New York: Oxford University Press.

Peterson, C., & Seligman, M. E. P. (2004). *Character strengths and virtues: A handbook and classification.* Washington, DC: American Psychological Association.

Pipes-McAdoo, H. (2002). Diverse children of color: Research and policy implications. In H. Pipes (Ed.), *Black children: Social, educational, and parental environments* (2nd ed., pp. 13–26). Thousand Oaks, CA: Sage.

Prelow, H. M., Bowman, M. A., & Weaver, S. R. (2007). Predictors of psychosocial well-being in urban African American and European American youth: The role of ecological factors. *Journal of Youth and Adolescence, 36,* 543–553.

Rutter, M. (1993). Resilience: Some conceptual considerations. *Journal of Adolescent Health, 14,* 626–631.

Ryff, C. D., & Singer, B. (1998). The contours of positive human health. *Psychological Inquiry, 9,* 1–28.

Seligman, M. E. P. (2002). *Authentic happiness.* New York: Free Press.

Seligman, M. E. P. (2005). Positive psychology, positive prevention, and positive therapy. In C. R. Snyder & S. J. Lopez (Eds.), *Handbook of positive psychology* (pp. 3–9). New York: Oxford University Press.

Seligman, M. E. P., & Csikszentmihalyi, M. (Eds.). (2000). Happiness, excellence, and optimal human functioning [Special issue]. *American Psychologist, 55*(1).

Sharot, T., Riccardi, A. M., Raio, C. M., & Phelps, E. A. (2007, November 1). Neural mechanisms mediating optimism bias. *Nature, 450,* 102–106.

Smith, E. J. (1985). Ethnic minorities: Life stress, social support, and mental health issues. *The Counseling Psychologist, 13,* 537–579.

Smith, E. J. (2006a). The strength-based counseling model. *The Counseling Psychologist, 34,* 13–79.

Smith, E. J. (2006b). The strength-based counseling model: A shift in psychology. *The Counseling Psychologist, 34,* 134–144.

Smith, E. P., & Hasbrouck, L. (2006). Preventing youth violence among African American youth: The sociocultural context of risk and protective factors. In N. Guerra & E. Phillips (Eds.), *Preventing youth violence in a multicultural* society (pp. 169–197). Washington, DC: American Psychological Association.

Snyder, C. L., & Lopez, S. J. (Eds.). (2007). *Positive psychology: The scientific and practical explorations of human strengths.* Thousand Oaks, CA: Sage.

Spencer, M. B. (2005). Crafting identities and accessing opportunities post *Brown*. *American Psychologist, 60,* 821–830.

Stack, S., & Wasserman, I. (1995). The effect of marriage, family, and religious ties on African American suicide ideology. *Journal of Marriage and Family, 57,* 215–222.

Swanson, D. P., Cunningham, M., & Spencer, M. B. (2003). Black males' structural conditions, achievement patterns, normative needs, and "opportunities." *Urban Education, 38,* 608–633.

Taylor, R., Ellison, C., Chatters, L., Levin, J., & Lincoln, K. (2000). Mental health services in faith communities: The role of clergy in Black churches. *Social Work, 45,* 73–87.

Triandis, H. C. (1995). The self and social behavior in differing cultural contexts. In N. R. Goldberger & J. B. Veroff (Eds.), *Culture and psychology reader* (pp. 326–365). New York: New York University Press.

Utsey, S. O., Bolden, M. A., Lanier, Y., & Williams, O. (2007). Examining the role of culture-specific coping as a predictor of resilient outcomes in African Americans from high-risk urban communities. *Journal of Black Psychology, 33,* 75–93.

White, J. (1970, September). Toward a Black Psychology. *Ebony,* pp. 44–52.

Williams, R. L. (1974). A history of the Association of Black Psychologists: Early formation and development. *Journal of Black Psychology, 1,* 9–24.

28

BEHAVIORAL AND EMOTIONAL STRENGTHS IN PEOPLE OF AFRICAN HERITAGE

Theory, Research, Methodology, and Intervention

MICHAEL CANUTE LAMBERT AND WILLIAM K. SMITH

The contemporary and research literature base on persons of African Heritage (used interchangeably with *Blacks*) is replete with deficits in Black children,[1] adolescents, adults, and families. Although we could extensively report on this focus, literature from the last few decades has thoroughly addressed this history and decried its existence (e.g., see McAdoo, 2007, for a review). We therefore focus on the theoretical literature that addresses the behavioral and emotional strengths[2] Blacks possess, the factors that contribute to these strengths, and the effects of these strengths on their functioning. In addition, we evaluate whether existing research tests and supports or refutes such theories. Recognizing that most of the existing literature base focuses on Blacks in the United States, we also explore the scant research base in other world regions, such as the Caribbean. Finally, we address issues in need of further research, such as the availability of culturally appropriate measures needed to assess and study strengths in Blacks.

DEFINITION AND CLASSIFICATION OF STRENGTHS

In most disciplines, the first step toward understanding and researching a specific construct is naming and defining it. Unfortunately, the strength-based literature has a plethora of labels for strengths, including *assets* (Taylor et al., 2004); *psychosocial adjustment* (e.g., Thomas, Townsend, & Belgrave, 2003); *resilience* (e.g., Horning & Gordon-Rouse, 2002; Markstrom, Marshall, & Tyron, 2000); *social capital* (e.g., Caughy & O'Campo, 2006; Varon & Riley, 1999); *social functioning* (Varon & Riley, 1999); and, of course, *strengths* (e.g., Lambert, Rowan, Kim, Kirsch, & Williams, 2005; Maton & Hrabowski, 2004). Although names and definitions of strengths must vary according to the groups (e.g., communities, schools, families, religious organizations) or individuals (e.g., children vs. adolescents) of focus, even when descriptions focus on similar or identical groups the names and descriptions of strengths differ considerably.

Focusing on adolescents as an example, Markstrom (1999) defined *strength* as resilience and described it as comprising of protective factors used by at-risk youth. Using Werner and Smith's (1982) and Masten and Coatsworth's (1998) work as a backdrop, Horning and Gordon-Rouse (2002) viewed experiences with adversity as a prerequisite for resiliency. Thomas et al. (2003) adopted a more psychosocial view. Defining strengths from an Africentric perspective, they placed strengths in the context of family as well as individual beliefs and values, including spirituality, a deep sense of kinship, harmony, and identification with the collective. This perspective differs from the European perspective of individuality (see Stevenson & Renard, 1993, for further review). Littlejohn-Blake and Darling (1993) defined strengths similarly. While recognizing their African origins, they underscored that the strengths contemporary Blacks possess today are partly due to their adaptation to multiple racism-related challenges in contemporary societies (e.g., North America).

The bulk of descriptions regarding strengths emerged from a literature base in which scholars who study African Americans conceptualize their strengths or make inferences about them on the basis of their research findings. Lambert et al.'s (2005) approach to defining and understanding the strengths people of African heritage possess differ from these approaches. They emphasize the power of close collaboration between themselves and communities within the African Diaspora. Consistent with this approach, researchers have asked persons of the African Diaspora to describe the strengths they observed in themselves and in persons within their community to reflect their voice and the realities (Kline, 2005) of their lives. Many of the strengths they identified overlap with those conceptualized in the existing literature base. For example, adolescents and adults in the focus groups identified strengths reflective of psychosocial emphasis on collectivism (e.g., getting along with children and adults, respecting authority). They also described other types of strength-related behavior that are not necessarily evident in the literature, such as having one's "head on straight," having appropriate values, and taking a keen interest in their culture and communities. Lambert et al. (2005) replicated these findings with adults in a Caribbean context, which suggests that strengths might not only transcend regions where members of the African Diaspora reside but also might be similar across different developmental groups.

Historical and Contemporary Contributors to Strengths in Blacks

Prior to forced colonization of their motherland and forcible removal and migration to the Americas, Blacks were members of African cultures in which families and communities were tightly bound together and in which a strong emphasis on the survival and the well-being of family and the entire community was paramount. These cultures imbued a strong sense of duty and fervent values regarding achievement, wisdom, respect (especially for one's elders and peers), justice, and spirituality (see McAdoo, 2007). This cultural foundation was assailed during the period of slavery and forced colonization by Europeans, and it continues to receive tremendous battering within contemporary U.S. society. Yet, the central beliefs just described have endured, providing sources of strength that have sustained people of African descent through a difficult history, challenging present, and in societies that deliberately promulgate race-based challenges well into the foreseeable future. For example, Black children and adults must confront not only the developmental challenges that their White counterparts face but also the additional challenges that the United States and other nations present them. That Blacks have survived—and, in many cases, thrived—in such situations is a testament to the incredible strengths within them and the micro- and macrosystems that support them. These systems, such as the widely extended family, including blood and nonblood relatives, communities, and organizations (e.g., faith-based groups), have been well documented as contributing factors to the resiliency of people of African heritage (see Barnes, 2001, for a more thorough review).

Theories and Theoretical Models Regarding Strengths and Its Effects on Adjustment

It is important to recognize that most of the theories regarding strengths in Blacks are based on scholarly conceptualizations and do not necessarily represent comprehensive theoretical models (Littlejohn-Blake & Darling, 1993). Most of the earlier conceptualizations addressing strengths in persons of African heritage are based on the Black family, individuals within the context of their families, or the family within the context of the community. This might be due to the collectivistic nature of persons of African heritage, in which a focus on individuals is not paramount.

Most scholars who conceptualize the origins of strengths in persons of African heritage point out that appreciable amounts of culture-specific behavior in Blacks is rooted in the Africentric worldview (Thomas et al., 2003). Scholars (e.g., Akbar, Asante) who ascribe to the Africentric viewpoint have posited that values and behavioral practices emerged primarily from the cultural mores in sub-Saharan and Middle Western coastal regions of Africa. They state that beliefs and practices (e.g., spirituality and religious practices), as well as strong kinship bonds extending across blood relatives outside the immediate family and others not related by blood or marriage, are examples of the communal nature of societies from which persons of African heritage originated (Barnes, 2001; Bryant & Zimmerman, 2003; Scott, 2004).

Other scholars, such as Ogbu (2003) and Garcia Coll et al. (1996), have underscored that although persons of African heritage do have strengths that have African origins (e.g., a sense of spirituality), the enhancement of existing strengths and the development of new strengths originate from the challenges their societies present them. Ogbu further stated that many persons of European heritage mistakenly judge such strength-based behavior as being problematic. He hypothesized that Blacks adaptively respond to the countless challenges that societies present them; for example, Black parents within European-dominated nations such as Great Britain and the United States are encumbered with the essential task of racially socializing their children and protecting them from racially hostile environments (Caughy, Nettles, O'Campo, & Lorfink, 2006; Scott, 2004). Racial socialization includes racial pride, preparation for racism, and learning how to relate to the dominant European group (see Caughy et al.). This indoctrination often results in the biculturalism/multiculturalism and bilingualism/multilingualism that we believe are behavioral strengths. Persons in the Caribbean, for example, often speak two different languages. One language, or *dialect*, as they call it, is rife with words and expressions that are rooted in Africa, England, France, and Spain and is used in everyday communication among family members and acquaintances. In nations where the official language is English, citizens refer to the *Queen's English* as the other language and reserve its use for formal interactions (e.g., education and business contexts). Similarly, African Americans often speak a specific language among themselves (Williams [2007] referred to it as *Ebonics*), but they often use American English in more formal interactions, especially with European Americans.

Conceptualizations Versus Theory

The strength-based literature on Blacks is dominated by theoretical conceptualizations and generally does not fully address the interrelations between such concepts (Littlejohn-Blake & Darling, 1993). This focus is important for educating Blacks regarding the strengths of their people. Nevertheless, we echo Littlejohn-Blake and Darling's (1993) call for genuine theory construction that links concepts to one another instead of the burgeoning conceptualization-based literature.

Theory construction is painstaking work, but it can have a major impact on research and intervention. A theoretical literature base focused on the strengths of persons of the African Diaspora will better operationalize the development of theoretical constructs (see Littlejohn-Blake & Darling, 1993). Such constructs can guide us toward developing testable theoretical models. Empirically testing these models could assist us in understanding the complexities between antecedents to strengths; the strengths these antecedents generate; and the effects of these strengths on the Black family, community, and individual. Theoretical models could examine single and multiple effects these systems have on one another as well as their bidirectional, multidirectional, mediating, and moderating relationships. Well-designed and theoretically guided research can inform policy decisions, empirically based multisystemic prevention and intervention procedures to promote survival, and even help Blacks thrive despite societal-induced challenges directed toward their very existence.

Strength-Based Research on People of African Heritage

The majority of the studies we have reviewed focused on the effects of strengths on adjustment. *Adjustment* is defined in multiple ways, for example, well-being (e.g., Bryant & Zimmerman) and maladaptive behavior (e.g., suicidal behavior) that might be indicative of severe psychopathology (e.g., Molock, Puri, Matlin, & Barksdale, 2006). Most of the earlier strength-based research focused primarily on adults, but a growing portion of more recent studies has focused both on children and especially on adolescents. For example, Scott's (2004) research revealed a positive association between how well African American parents prepare their children to handle future racism and their effectiveness in coping with racial discrimination. Varon and Riley's (1999) work showed that if adolescents' mothers attend church services (at least weekly), the adolescents have better socioemotional adjustment than adolescents whose mothers do not attend church services. Molock et al. (2006) showed a negative relationship between religious coping and suicidal behaviors. A recent study of first-grade African American children revealed that children from homes rich in African culture had better cognitive outcomes than those lacking this attribute (Caughy et al., 2003). Underscoring the importance of strengths existing in widely extended African American families, a qualitative study conducted by Brown, Cohon, and Wheeler (2002) revealed that children in the foster care system who are placed with individuals who are related to them are more resilient than children who are placed with strangers. These positive effects are potentiated when the foster parent reports high levels of support from their extended families.

In the context of evidence-based practice, we are troubled by the virtual absence of strength-based intervention outcomes research in the empirical literature we have reviewed thus far. Research that addresses whether harnessing strengths in intervention planning and execution is useful is critically important, yet we found only one study that empirically demonstrated that drawing on the strengths in African American young adults and harnessing the strengths within the Black community can enhance success at the highest academic levels. Identifying and using strengths (e.g., collectivism, strong family and community ties) within persons of the African Diaspora, and providing support in a manner that maximizes the utility of these strengths, can significantly increase recruitment, retention, and graduation rates of African Americans in the sciences and engineering (Maton & Hrabowski, 2004).

We believe that Maton and Hrabowski's (2004) program evaluation procedures and research show significant promise and might be replicated across other academic disciplines. Furthermore, we believe that their evidence-based programming might be applied in intervention-related settings. By advocating this approach, we note that we do not posit that intervention programs that harness culture-specific strengths in Blacks are nonexistent; indeed, we applaud our colleagues and professional organizations for their heavy emphasis on Africentric education and intervention. Research and evaluation of existing programs using methodologically robust procedures can document whether programming and procedures used are effective and thus help us to embrace effective programming and discard ineffective programming.

There is also a dearth of published research documenting the relationship between strengths and the factors that contribute to them. We are convinced that research documenting the link between strengths and psychosocial adjustment is extremely important; we also believe that empirical work documenting the relationship between factors that contribute to or hinder strength development is equally important. Existence of well-developed strengths is critical for appropriate adjustment and for effective strength-based intervention. Empirically based knowledge about factors that contribute to, or hinder, strength development can inform policy that guides effective intervention strategies that buttress existing strengths and foster development of nonexistent ones.

STATISTICAL CONCERNS

The usefulness of research in informing appropriate policy and effective practice decisions rests on the scientific rigor with which this research is conducted. Three areas that challenge the robustness of strength-based research findings are (1) addressing issues associated with missing data, (2) instituting procedures that control for chance effects in multiple analyses, and (3) providing information on the sizes of significant effects. To most effectively address these concerns, we have selected studies from the empirical strength-based literature. We have not singled these studies out because they are worse than other studies; we merely use them as examples to illustrate our point.

Handling Missing Data

Many studies (e.g., Scott, 2004) do not report refusal rates, but this will not be the focus of our discussion. Instead, our focus is on how well researchers deal with participants within their samples who provide only partially completed data. Most researchers describe procedures they used to protect the rights, welfare, and autonomy of their participants. As part of the informed-consent process, researchers report that they informed their participants that they could choose not to answer questions without the risk of coercion and with impunity. It is therefore improbable that all participants in the majority of the studies we reviewed would have complete data. Few researchers provide information on missing data (e.g., Thomas et al., 2003), and many of these researchers sometimes report that they removed cases with missing data (e.g., Hess, Papas, & Black, 2002; Varon & Riley, 1999). Most studies (e.g., Markstrom et al., 2000; Thomas et al., 2003) do not report whether they had missing data. An extremely low probability exists that some studies have no missing data, although, even if all participants studied supply complete data, the researcher is responsible for informing readers that this is the case. Not reporting missing data is consequential, because it is difficult for others to replicate these studies or interpret the results from newer studies within the context of earlier studies.

Also problematic is removing cases with missing data. Researchers sometimes report that they tested whether participants with missing data differed from participants with complete data according to demographic variables. If these participants did not differ, the researchers usually justify removing individuals with missing data from their analyses. Unfortunately, the number of demographic variables used is often few and finite. Moreover, dropping participants is inefficient and can produce biased estimates (Alison, 2003), because participants who are excluded from further study might provide important data. A more suitable approach is the use of statistical (e.g., the maximum likelihood) procedures to impute missing data. Stand-alone software applications that accurately impute missing values are readily available for purchase and even as freeware (e.g., NORM; Schafer, 1999). Similar applications might be included as add-ins in widely used statistical software, such as SPSS.

Addressing Chance Effects in Multiple Analyses

Another of our concerns about the research literature on strengths in persons of the African Diaspora is that researchers often conduct multiple analyses but fail to address the implications of this practice. We do not always endorse stringent criteria for chance effects, because they could result in Type II errors, but we find it troubling that these concerns are seldom addressed. In one study, we found at least 10 analyses for which the traditional alpha levels of $< .05$ and $< .01$ were used. Employing typical controls for chance effects (e.g., Bonferroni; see Agresti & Franklin, 2007) would result in a critical alpha level of .005 if the traditional .05 alpha level is used and .001 if .01 is the target.

We admit that studies on the strengths of Blacks represent a new area of investigation; therefore, it might be important to identify particular areas as foci for future research. We observed instances in which researchers clearly stated that their purpose was exploratory. In other studies, researchers posited specific hypotheses, but rarely did they address chance effects. An alternative is to reduce chance effects by using more omnibus tests, such as the multivariate analysis of covariance (e.g., Thomas et al., 2003) that do not have as high a risk for Type I error as multiple analyses of variance (ANOVAs) (e.g., Markstrom, 1999).

Effect Sizes

We will not provide a lesson on power or effect sizes (ESs), but we will list some of our concerns (for more thorough discussion, see Cohen, 2003). Many authors provide information on the type of statistical test used, whether an effect was significant, and the values and degrees of freedom for such statistics. It is, however, rare that they provide information on the amount of variance their significant effects explained. It is relatively easy to judge ESs by eyeballing the results from certain statistical tests, such as the standardized regression weights or product–moment correlations, but it is often difficult to do so from the presentation of other types of analyses, such as ANOVAs/analyses of covariance/multivariate analyses of covariance, which are widely used in combination or individually in strength-based research (e.g., Bryant & Zimmerman, 2003; Strom et al., 2002). We therefore find it difficult to evaluate whether the findings are robust enough to even be regarded as a small ES. Absence of ES information can also lead research consumers to ignore findings that might have extensive consequences for policy and practice decisions.

Measurement Concerns in Strength-Based Research

To trust findings derived from strength-based studies, it is important that the measures used are psychometrically sound, that is, that they have documented reliability and validity. Space limitations preclude a detailed discussion of psychometric concerns (see Haynes, Nelson, & Blaine, 1999, for a succinct review), but we address the most glaring measurement concerns we have observed in strength-based research on persons of the African Diaspora. We divide our discussion into three areas: 1) general overview of measurement, (2) measurement- related concerns in the literature, and (3) strength measures used in the literature. Under a separate heading, we describe some of our early work on measuring strengths in persons of African heritage and how its psychometric rigor might be a model for measuring strength constructs in them.

General Measurement Overview

Haynes et al. (1999) stated that construct validity is the superordinate validity, because it comprises all the evidence supporting the trustworthiness of a measure. Acknowledging that evidence of different forms of reliability (e.g., test–retest, interrater) and validity (e.g., content, convergent, criterion-referenced, divergent) is an iterative process, they underscored that a preponderance of evidence pointing to the psychometric soundness must be present before one can trust assessment and research findings derived from a purportedly valid measure.

We add that evidence should also point to cultural validity when measures are used to assess Blacks and other groups of color. *Cultural validity*, which is related to content validity, on which other forms of validity are scaffolded, purports that measures are written in the language and the realities of the persons they assess. Cultural validity is extremely important, because the realities, customs, and lifestyles of Black people differ from those of persons of European heritage, who design and validate most measures primarily on their people.

Measurement-Related Concerns in the Existing Literature

Our review of the strength-based research literature revealed little or no psychometric information on the measures used for any group (e.g., Barnes, 2001; Strom et al., 2002). Moreover, in most studies we found few psychometric indices for Blacks. With cultural validity as a backdrop, our greatest concern is the virtual absence of measures of strengths designed for Blacks. Also disconcerting is a dearth of studies that examine the psychometric appropriateness of using measures not designed for Blacks in research that addresses Black people's functioning. Information on the psychometric properties reported for these measures is sparse, making it difficult to trust findings derived from research that uses such measures.

Most studies we reviewed reveal that, at best, researchers report coefficient alphas only for the samples on which the measures were normed (usually not focused on Blacks) and in some cases for their sample of persons of African heritage. Many studies also inappropriately use coefficient alphas, because researchers often refer to them as being indices of reliability. Even more troubling is the inference that higher alpha values are indicative that the measures are applicable to the population from which researchers survey (e.g., Caughy & O'Campo, 2006). We note that an alpha value is just an index of the intercorrelations among items and is an insufficient basis for proclaiming the measurement's reliability or unidimensionality (see Schmitt, 1996).

Most researchers could successfully argue that measures specifically designed for and standardized on persons of African heritage are difficult, if not impossible, to access. We concur; however, we do not believe it excuses researchers from addressing this concern in their studies. Although it would not fully address our concerns regarding validity, and cultural validity in particular, at the very least researchers should explore whether the factorial model of the measures used are appropriate for people of African heritage. Confirmatory factor analysis can address whether the measures possess configural invariance, that is, whether the measure's factor models are configured appropriately for persons of African heritage and, if they are not, to establish a more appropriate model. If the aim is to include or compare different groups, then metric invariance tests that simultaneously estimate parameters across such groups are more critical.

Measures of Strengths

The majority of studies we reviewed used indicators including standardized measures of achievement and intelligence (Caughy et al., 2006), ego strengths (Markstrom et al., 2000), and even level of psychopathology as a proxy for well-being (Bryant & Zimmerman, 2003). One study (Farmer et al., 2005) used the Behavioral and Emotional Rating Scale (BERS; Epstein & Sharma, 1998), a multidimensional instrument that measures behavioral and emotional strengths in children and adolescents. Although not designed specifically for Blacks, the BERS has been well researched and has acceptable psychometric properties for children throughout the United States. An examination of the BERS's configural invariance for the children Farmer et al. studied could further strengthen this research.

A Model for Developing Measures for Persons of African Heritage

This section focuses on our efforts at developing measures of strengths and difficulties (i.e., what others classify as problems) for persons of African heritage. One set of measures includes the Parent-, Teacher-, and Adolescent Self-Report forms of the Behavioral Assessment for Children of African Heritage (BACAH) (Lambert et al., 2005). Detailed descriptions regarding the procedural steps we used to ensure the cultural appropriateness of measures, and to substantiate that they are reliable and valid for the assessment of children of African heritage, are documented elsewhere (see Lambert et al., 2005; Lambert, Rowan, Longhurst, & Kim, 2006). We, however, believe that the processes we used to ensure appropriate cultural and content validity and the modern psychometric procedures we used to ensure reliability and validity are worthy of discussion. These procedures might be used as models or scaffolds for the development of measures that assess various constructs in people of African heritage.

The Behavioral Assessment for Children of African Heritage

Before describing the measures and their use, we first acknowledge that diversity exists within the Black community and that it is impossible to fully account for this diversity in any measure we design. Nevertheless, we also believe that there are specific cultural characteristics (e.g., minority group status, African heritage) that almost universally influence Black children and adolescents in the United States. As we briefly discussed earlier, an example of customs and practices that undergird most Black families' lives are an emphasis on immense collectivism, interdependence, and less autonomy than majority groups (Boyd-Franklin, 2003). Having good-quality relationships with biological and other relatives, including family members, godparents, fictitious kin, peers, and elders, is an expected behavioral characteristic for many Black children and adolescents (Boyd-Franklin, 2003). The absence of appropriate content in existing measures that address these and other strengths and difficulties experienced and exhibited by Black children make it difficult to confidently assess these areas of their functioning.

Development of the forms. Focusing on Black children and the adults who closely interact with them (e.g., parents, teachers, clinicians, and other professionals), we conducted focus groups in eight Midwestern cities with sizable Black populations to obtain their perspectives and write the measures in their "voice" and realities (Kline, 2005). Participants with child assessment experience, including those who administered or completed existing measures, noted that most traditional measures omit behavioral and emotional strengths for most children as well as difficulties that are particularly salient to Black children. They stated that the strengths typically omitted include "spirituality," "cooperation," "respect for others," "interest in one's history and culture" and "a sense of humor."

Behavioral and emotional difficulties not addressed include a child's experience (or other informants' perceptions) of "feeling/being strung out," "playing yo' mama jokes," "lacking in optimism/no sense of the future," and "wearing overly revealing clothing." These examples, and other items, they believed, are often critical to understanding the functioning of Black youth. Parents and youngsters noted that because of the content and the manner in which test items are presented (e.g., language style) they were sometimes unsure of the meaning of the items on the measures they completed and had little confidence that their responses matched the test authors' intent. Addressing issues of cultural validity, some African American adolescents in one of the focus groups mentioned that the hobby stamp collecting, an example of an item on one of the popularly used measures they completed, "would not go over well in our 'hood ... [or] even for those of us living in the suburbs."

Focus group participants also suggested the inclusion of items assessing the *effects* of the strengths the youngster possesses and how, within certain contexts, strengths could produce negative effects for a child (e.g., an academically competent child being accused of "acting White"). In other situations, difficulties might produce effects that are not particularly bothersome to the child or to others in the child's surroundings. In addition to focus group information, we obtained behavioral and emotional difficulty items from a clinic record survey of more than 1,500 Black children (see Lambert, Rowan, & Lyubansky, 2002).

To provide information from different informants and different settings (e.g., home vs. school), the BACAH consists of four strength forms: (1) a parent-report form, for ages 4 to 18; (2) a teacher-report form, for ages 5 to 18; (3) an adolescent self-report form, for ages 11 to 18; and (4) an interview schedule, for ages 6 to 10. Besides the strength forms, which include more than 50 behavioral and emotional strength items, the BACAH difficulties forms also have more than 150 items addressing difficulties. The forms also include questions regarding the youngster's history, such as experience with or exposure to physical abuse and violence, history of mental health intervention the child received, and history of mental health concerns in the child's family. These items are not scored as part of the measures, but they might be useful in clinical evaluation. Each form can be administered by computerized adaptive testing or in paper-and-pencil format.

On the left side of each item on parent-, teacher-, and self-report forms, informants rate strengths and difficulties items as 0 = not true (as far as they know), 1 = somewhat or sometimes true, and 2 = very true or often true. On the right side, parents, teachers, and adolescents rate each strength item as having a negative effect (−1), no effect (0), or a positive effect (+1) on the child. The left-side rating scale is similar for parent-, teacher-, and self-report behavioral and emotional difficulties forms. On the right side of each form, informants rate whether the difficulty rated for each item is (0) of no concern, (1) of some concern, or (2) of great concern. The interview form has the left-side rating scale only; it is presented graphically to facilitate the child's communication of strength and difficulty levels.

Psychometrics. The psychometric properties of the measures were established from responses derived from more than 1,500 respondents who rated Black children's functioning and are detailed elsewhere (see Lambert, Essau, Schmitt, & Samms-Vaughan, 2007; Lambert et al., 2005). In brief, exploratory and confirmatory factor analyses of the strength forms have yielded two cross-informant (identical across informants) dimensions labeled Resilience and Self-Regulation and Prosocial Behavior. The content of the Resilience factor includes academic achievement and the activities related to achievement, adaptation to the environment, appropriate role models, spirituality, positive self-regard, and sense of humor. The second factor, Self-Regulation and Prosocial Behavior, includes content that reflects values of the Black community, such as being able to control one's wishes and impulses for the benefit of one's family, peers, and community and the ability to appropriately interact and develop relationships within the family and others in the youngster's community. The dimensions for the difficulties forms are grouped according to six major diagnostic categories in the *Diagnostic and Statistical Manual of Mental Disorders* (4th ed., text revision; American Psychiatric Association, 2004; Attention and Hyperactivity, Anxiety, Conduct Difficulties, Mania, Depression, Oppositional Defiant, and Psychosis).

It is important to note that the psychometric properties for all dimensions of the BACAH, which are detailed elsewhere (see Lambert et al., 2005, 2006, 2007), were established using modern measurement theory-driven (i.e., item response theory) procedures. These procedures, which address the validity of using the forms across different groups of Black youth, demonstrate that the different forms are unbiased across different age, gender, and socioeconomic groups. Bias emerged for a few items across type of informant (i.e., parents, teachers, adolescents), whether the child was identified as having behavioral and emotional difficulties, and across the ratings regarding the presence of the behavior versus its level of distress. Item response theory was used to link items across these groups and permits unbiased assessment across these items as well as unbiased score comparisons across children identified as troubled (i.e., with behavioral and emotional difficulties or referred for clinical services) and those in the general population, informants, and across the ratings on the presence versus the effect of the item (i.e., for strengths) or how bothersome (i.e., for problems) the item is to the child.

Flexibility derived from item response theory–based psychometric properties, makes the BACAH forms adaptable and valid for clinical evaluation, treatment planning, and for program evaluation and research projects that compare children identified as having behavioral and emotional concerns with their well-adjusted peers. This flexibility extends to administration of left-side rating scales only and to separate administration of items on any one or more scales without risk of invalid use of the measures. Its computerized adaptive test delivery capabilities allow single and multiple user on-site administration and secure remote delivery though the Internet. To illustrate its comprehensiveness and flexibility, we next present a case in which three forms of the BACAH were used.

Sample Psychological Evaluation Based on the Behavioral Assessment for Children of African Heritage

Background and History

Hassan Abdulla is a 14-year-old male of African heritage who is currently a client of a child guidance clinic in a midwestern state. Hassan completed the self-report measure with the help of an interviewer. Both Hassan's grandmother and his parole officer completed the parent- and teacher-report BACAH measure, respectively, by self-administration. This examiner did not meet with Hassan or any other BACAH informants and has no access to his clinical or other records. All information in this psychological report was derived from the BACAH measures. We inferred from the BACAH parent report measure that Hassan lives with his grandparents, although it is impossible to determine whether they are his maternal or paternal grandparents. Although his grandmother provides no information on his grandfather's or her own employment status or their employment histories, Hassan states that both grandparents are unemployed and that both have no previous employment. On the parent-report measure, Hassan's grandmother describes her own and Hassan's ethnicity as Black, but she reports that his father is multiracial. All three informants, however, describe Hassan as Black.

All informants note that Hassan is in the ninth grade, but no information is provided on whether his academic achievement is below, matches, or supersedes his ninth-grade educational placement. Hassan describes himself as having no learning or other school-related difficulties and states that he has neither been retained in any grade nor received special education services. His grandmother, however, reports that he has experienced grade retention.

Although each measure requests that all informants write about behavioral and emotional difficulties Hassan exhibits that might be of concern to him or them, no informant responded to this question. The history regarding Hassan's behavioral and emotional functioning is sketchy. Hassan, however, reports that his father has a history of mental illness and that his mother has a history of legal problems. Although Hassan states that he has never received mental health services, his grandmother reports that he has received such services in the past. Hassan reports that in 2002, he witnessed severe acts of violence against his grandmother. His grandmother also reports that Hassan has been a victim of violence. Nevertheless, neither Hassan nor his grandmother provides information regarding the perpetrator of this violence. It is also unclear whether this violence has been continuous or whether Hassan or his grandmother is currently being victimized. Hassan reports that he has experienced no physical or sexual abuse.

Hassan's grandmother omits information on whether he is taking prescription drugs. She did, however, state that he is taking nonprescription drugs, but she did not provide the name of these drugs. Hassan omits information regarding his use of nonprescription drugs but states that he is taking two different prescribed medicines. One drug he lists is Prilosec, but his handwriting describing the other drug was illegible.

Test Results

A profile of Hassan's test scores is presented in Figure 28.1. The BACAH measures reveal that Hassan's self-report and his parole officer's ratings indicate that he has average strength levels. They also report the effects of Hassan's strengths on him are not considerably different form the levels of strengths they report. Hassan's grandmother, by contrast, reports his strength levels as being considerably above average across the dimensions of Resilience and Self-Regulation and Prosocial Behavior. She also rates the effects of his strength in these domains, especially resilience, as being considerably lower than the magnitude of strengths she reports. These findings suggest that she might view people in Hassan's environment as not being supportive of his strengths. It might also suggest that her ratings regarding his strengths are somewhat inflated or that she does not perceive considerable benefits from his strength levels.

We now shift the focus to difficulties. Hassan's test results reflect a risk for self-destructive behavior that might be exacerbated by moderate levels of difficulties reflecting impulsivity in the areas of hyperactive and manic/hypomanic behavior. This risk factor might be evident in the form of potential suicide attempts or less readily observable self-destructiveness. In the case of the latter, Hassan's behavior might not reflect obvious suicide attempts but that he might be placing himself in contexts, such as hanging out in dangerous environments, that might subject him to harm. Nevertheless, Hassan's scores on other dimensions reveal that he might have the capacity to appropriately manage behavior that could increase his risk for self-destructiveness; that is, his grandmother's ratings of concern regarding his self-destructiveness potential are at considerably higher levels than her ratings of the magnitude of self-destructive behavior. A similar trend is evident for oppositional/defiant and manic/hypomanic behavior, two areas of difficulties that might be regarded as evidence for impulsive behavior. Although the levels of behavior in these domains are at average levels, Hassan expresses considerably higher levels of concern regarding them than their severity levels. His alarm suggests healthy anxiety regarding his behavioral and emotional difficulties and a motivation to take steps to reduce them.

Viewed within the context of the difficulties discussed, Hassan's scores also suggest that although his strength levels could benefit from intervention that increases their magnitude, the strength levels he possesses might be used to partly inoculate him from self-destructive behavior. These findings also indicate that Hassan might have some of the characteristics necessary to assist him in taking steps toward further intellectual and psychosocial growth. Finally, Hassan's strength levels and his levels of concern as they relate to his behavioral and emotional difficulties could be due in part to the effects of previous intervention provided for Hassan and his family.

Strength-Based Recommendations

It is important to conduct further evaluation to determine whether Hassan is currently at risk for self-destructive behavior. If this risk is confirmed, then an investigation of the form in which this behavior is being exhibited now and in the future might be important. A thorough clinical interview with Hassan's grandmother regarding her ratings on the negative effects of his strengths she reports is indicated. This interview might focus on the types of reinforcement she perceives that he is receiving from others in his environment for the above-average strength levels

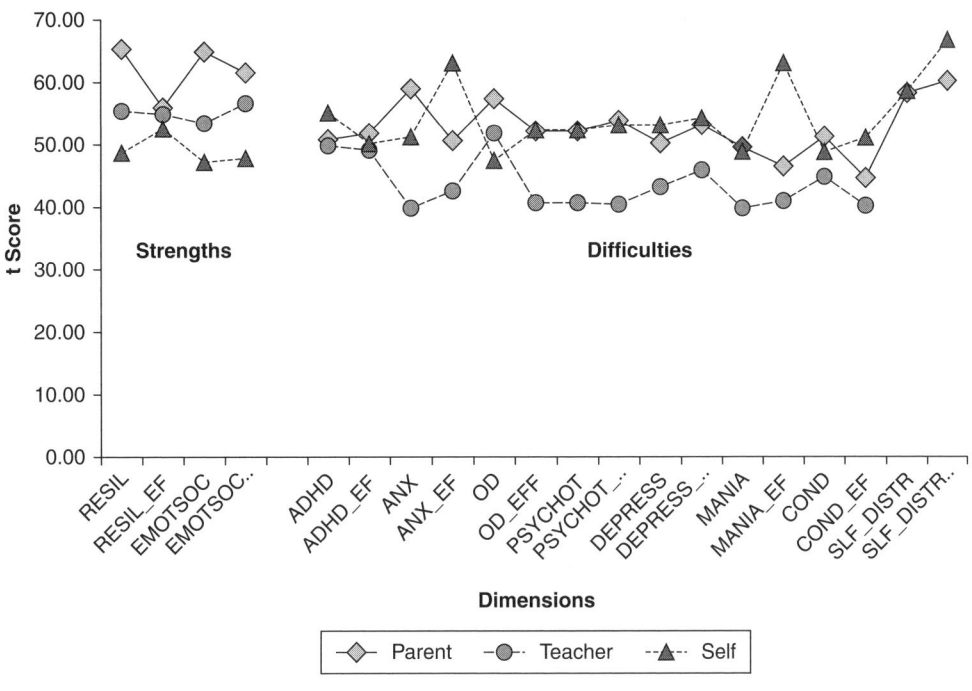

Figure 28.1   Behavioral Assessment for Children of African Heritage Report for Hassan Abdulla

Notes: RESIL = Resilience; RESIL_EF = Effects of Resilience; EMOTSOC = Emotional Control and Prosocial Behavior; EMOTSOC... = Effects of Emotional Control and Prosocial Behavior; ADHD = Attention Deficit Hyperactive Behavior; ADHD_EF = Concern Regarding Attention Deficit Hyperactive Behavior; ANX = Anxiety; ANX_EF = Concern Regarding Anxiety; OD = Oppositional Defiant Behavior; OD_EFF = Concern Regarding Oppositional Defiant Behavior; PSYCHOT − Psychotic Behavior; PSYCHOT_... − Concern Regarding Psychotic Behavior; DEPRESS = Depression; DEPRESS_... Concern Regarding Depression; MANIA = Hypomanic and Manic Behavior; MANIA_EF = Concern Regarding Hypomanic and Manic Behavior; COND = Difficulties With Conduct; COND_EF = Concern Regarding Difficulties With Conduct; SLF_DISTR = Self-Destructive Behavior; SLF_DISTR... = Concern Regarding Self-Destructive Behavior.

she identifies in him. It should also focus on how Hassan's grandmother and other adults react to different types of behavior Hassan exhibits, including whether they effectively communicate positive responses to his reported strengths.

It is important to further evaluate Hassan's moderately high anxiety and depression levels, including whether they are a result of the effects of intervention and are producing healthy levels of anxiety regarding his difficulties. It is also important to evaluate whether Hassan is underreporting the intensity of his more internalized difficulties, especially within the context of the Black male culture within which he lives and interacts. This cultural context could inhibit the reporting of anxiety, depression, and other internally based difficulties by deeming the expression of such concerns a reflection of weakness. These cultural standards could be forcing Hassan to present himself as a fearless, tough, and asymptomatic individual. If this assumption is correct, then his scores on dimensions such as anxiety and depression might not be fully reflective of his distress. His parole officer's report of significantly lower than average anxiety levels might further support the inference that Hassan's behavior reflects the "cool pose" phenomenon when in the presence of others and whereby he feels anxiety and other aversive affect but works hard at hiding them.

We now turn to recommendations for intervention during Hassan's tenure within the clinical facility. It might be important to demonstrate acceptance of and value for his strengths and to provide opportunities for growth in these domains. His clinician might focus on recognizing, reinforcing, and further enhancing the development of Hassan's strengths. His level of resilience suggests that with support for, and emphasis on, increasing his adaptive functioning, his prognosis is good. Therefore, it is important to provide positive reinforcement for Hassan's strength levels first by communicating that others recognize them. For example, the therapist might recognize and communicate to Hassan that his levels of emotional control and prosocial behavior suggest that he is able to control his emotions and impulsivity. His resilience also suggests his capability of adapting to, and recovering from, his difficulties, leadership skills, and the potential for academic achievement. Providing opportunities for success in these domains in the therapeutic milieu and in other settings could stimulate social and emotional growth, higher strength levels, and greater impulse control capabilities. The effects of intervention on strength development and reduction in difficulties might be tracked by the BACAH forms and other evaluation procedures.

Case Discussion

If we place Hassan's case study in the context of psychometrically sound assessment, we note that, similar to other Black youth who might be suffering from severe behavioral and emotional difficulties, and even legal troubles, Hassan possesses appreciable amounts of strengths. The cross-informant reports on these strengths not only provide different contexts in which they occur but also arm the professional with information regarding whether the strengths are costly or beneficial to the youngster. The professional can therefore make well-informed decisions regarding whether there is a need to focus on increasing this child's strengths and whether intervention is needed in the context of where the youngster presents his strengths.

Informant responses regarding Hassan's difficulties and the levels of distress he experiences regarding such difficulties might also assist the professional in effectively formulating and executing intervention plans. For example, it would be helpful to know that a youngster who might be presenting difficulties in defiance and in conduct is experiencing little or no distress regarding these difficulties. The professional who plans and executes intervention might wish to focus both on raising the levels of concern (i.e., constructive levels of appropriate anxiety) in the youngster or other informants as well as reduction of the youngster's difficulties.

Strength-based assessment information for this youngster might also provide the professional with further information regarding treatment concerns. Using the context of high levels of strengths with negative impact on the child, as noted in the case study, the child might receive little reinforcement for possessing and using behavioral and emotional strengths but might unintentionally or even intentionally receive reinforcement for exhibiting behavioral and emotional difficulties. This information might guide the professional toward buttressing the youngster's strengths, addressing cognitive distortions the youngster might have internalized regarding these strengths, and making changes in the youngster's environment to support intervention and thus produce lasting effects.

We close this section by noting that we are aware that there are no perfect measures. We have, however, taken all available and relevant steps to reduce measurement error and promote psychometric soundness. Equally important is that although we do address difficulties, our work and our measures include a strong emphasis on strength-based assessment and on using the results of this assessment to guide intervention planning and execution. Our emphasis on psychometric soundness also makes our system highly relevant for inclusion in program evaluation and treatment outcome projects.

Extending Measurement Development Procedures Internationally

In this section, we briefly describe how we have extended our strengths-based assessment to other persons of the African Diaspora. First we note that the BACAH parent-, self-, and interview forms were translated and used in research in southern Africa. Furthermore, we note that we provided the researchers with items not only from our measure but also from other widely used measures. They chose the BACAH forms because they saw it as being more relevant to their populations. Similarly, the parent- and self-report forms have been used to study Sudanese adolescent refugees.

Extending the methodologies we used in measurement development for African American children, we note that because of a need to develop comprehensive measures of behavioral and emotional functioning, we were asked by the Jamaican Ministry of Health to develop a comprehensive set of measures capable of assessing strengths and difficulties adults in the general population residing in Jamaica as well as for individuals who are referred for psychological services.

Similar to our BACAH development procedure, we recruited adults in urban and rural regions of Jamaica for focus groups and requested that they describe behaviors they might observe in a well-functioning adult in their nation. There was remarkably considerable overlap between the behavioral and emotional strengths emerging from the BACAH work that we did in the United States. Similarly, we obtained items reflecting difficulties from the focus groups and from a survey of the clinic records of more than 300 individuals. We therefore constructed two forms that measure strengths and difficulties in Jamaica that we call the *Caribbean Strength and Difficulties Checklist* (see Lambert et al., in press). One form is a self-report that is completed by the person targeted for assessment. The other is a third-party form that can be filled out by individuals who know the target individual well. We have conducted analyses that are similar to those we conducted for the BACAH.

These forms have been reviewed by professionals and persons from the general populations across Caribbean nations. Individuals in different nations have agreed that some items need translation to match the idiomatic expression of their people. With these translations, we have also used these forms in a study across the nations of Barbados, Jamaica, and Trinidad. One-way ANOVAs conducted on unequated problem scores across the nations revealed differences in strengths and difficulties (e.g., aggression), underscoring the importance of addressing invariance by equating items on the self-report form of the measures across the three nations. Equated responses revealed no differences and suggest the findings from the earlier analyses might be related to measurement artifact. Furthermore, this shows the consequences of ignoring this issue, because indicating that adolescents and adults in one nation are more likely to be aggressive than adolescents and adults in another nation could have a major impact on policy and intervention focused on the country deemed "most aggressive." For countries in the Caribbean Basin, where resources are often scarce, an unequal distribution of resources to one nation that has no difference in behavioral and emotional concerns comprises a sacrifice of resources to other nations.

Conclusion and Recommendations

We summarize our synthesis of strengths in persons of African heritage by pointing out that a comprehensive literature base with more complex theories regarding strengths, their antecedents, and their impact on adjustment is lacking. This literature should also focus on defining what the strengths are and on producing appropriate definitions that can guide the development of strengths constructs. These constructs can be the backbone of measures designed to assess them and can generate research that establishes their psychometric properties. Robust measures of these constructs can permit the testing of complex models that hypothesize the relationships between contributors to strengths and the relationship between these contributors, as well as the effects of strengths on adjustment in Blacks. Equally important is that these measures can also be used in clinical assessment and thus guide strength-based intervention. The national (Lambert et al., 2005) and international work that we and our colleagues (Lambert et al., in press) have amassed might form a scaffold for some of this research. Such efforts will move us beyond mere conceptualization of strengths and stabs in the dark at studying them and using them in the intervention with our people. Most important is that coherent theoretical work, a body of empirical research, and rigorously validated measures that can guide evidence-based practice can move us beyond the era of simpler conceptual models.

Notes

1. *Children* is used to refer to persons age birth to 18 with the exception of when adolescents are the specific focus.

2. *Strengths* is used hereafter to reflect behavioral and emotional strengths.

References

Agresti, A., & Franklin, C. (2007). *Statistics: The art and science of learning from data.* Upper Saddle River, NJ: Pearson Prentice Hall.

Alison, P. D. (2003). Missing data techniques for structural equation modeling. *Journal of Abnormal Psychology, 112,* 545–557.

American Psychiatric Association. (2004). *Diagnostic and statistical manual of mental disorders* (4th ed., text revision). Washington, DC: Author.

Barnes, S. L. (2001). Stressors and strengths: A theoretical and practical examination of nuclear single parent, and augmented African American families. *Families in Society: The Journal of Contemporary Human Services, 5,* 449–460.

Boyd-Franklin, N. (2003). *Black families in therapy: An African-American experience* (2nd ed.). New York: Guilford Press.

Brown, S., Cohon, D., & Wheeler, R. (2002). African-American extended families and kinship care: How relevant is the foster care model for kinship care. *Children and Youth Service, 24,* 53–77.

Bryant, A. L., & Zimmerman, M. A. (2003). Role models and psychosocial outcomes among African American adolescents. *Journal of Adolescent Research, 18,* 36–67.

Caughy, M. O., Nettles, S. M., O'Campo, P. J., & Lohrfink, K. F. (2006). Neighborhood matters: Racial socialization of African American children. *Child Development, 77,* 1220–1236.

Caughy, M. O., & O'Campo, P. J. (2006). Neighborhood poverty, social capital and the cognitive development of African American preschoolers. *American Journal of Community Psychology, 37,* 141–154.

Caughy, M. O., O'Campo, P. J., & Muntaner, C. (2003). When being alone might be better: Neighborhood poverty, social capital, and child mental health. *Social Science & Medicine, 57,* 227–237.

Cohen, J. (2003). A power primer. In A. E. Kazdin (Ed.), *Methodological issues and strategies in clinical research* (3rd ed., pp. 427–436). Washington, DC: American Psychological Association.

Epstein, M. H., & Sharma, J. (1998). *Behavioral Emotional Rating Scale: Strength-based approach to assessment.* Austin, TX: Pro-Ed.

Farmer, T. W., Clemmer, J. T., Leung, M., Goforth, J. B., Thompson, J. H., Keagy, K., et al. (2005). Strength-based assessment of rural African American early adolescents: Characteristics of students in high and low groups on the Behavioral and Emotional Rating Scale. *Journal of Child and Family Studies, 14,* 57–69.

Garcia Coll, C., Lamberty, G., Jenkins, R., McAdoo, H. P., Crnic, K., & Wasic, B. J. (1996). An integrated model for the study of developmental competences and minority children. *Child Development, 67,* 1891–1914.

Haynes, S. N., Nelson, K., & Blaine, D. D. (1999). Psychometric issues in assessment research. In P. C. Kendall, J. N. Butcher, & G. N. Holembeck (Eds.), *Handbook of research methods in clinical psychology* (pp. 125–154). New York: Wiley.

Hess, C. R., Papas, M. A., & Black, M. M. (2002). Resilience among African American adolescent mothers: Predictors of positive parenting in early infancy. *Society of Pediatric Psychology, 27,* 619–629.

Horning, L. E., & Gordon-Rouse, K. A. (2002). Resilience in preschoolers and toddlers from low-income families. *Early Childhood Education Journal, 29,* 155–159.

Kline, T. J. B. (2005). *Psychological testing: A practical approach to design and evaluation.* Thousand Oaks, CA: Sage.

Lambert, M. C., Essau, C. A., Schmitt, N., & Samms-Vaughan, M. E. (2007). Dimensionality and psychometric invariance of the Youth Self-report Form of the Child Behavior Checklist in cross-national settings. *Assessment, 14,* 231–245.

Lambert, M. C., Lambert, C. T. M., Hickling, F., Douglas, K., Samms-Vaughan, M. E., Chang, C., et al. (in press). Development and use of a culturally relevant measure to assess behavioral and emotional functioning and to identify the contributors to severe psychopathology in a Caribbean nation. In F. Hickling & R. Gibson (Eds.), *Caribbean handbook of psychology.*

Lambert, M. C., Rowan, G. T., Kim, S., Rowan, S. A., An, A. S., Kirsh, E. A., et al. (2005). Assessment of behavioral and emotional strengths in Black children: Development of the Behavioral Assessment for Children of African Heritage (BACAH). *Journal of Black Psychology, 31,* 321–351.

Lambert, M. C., Rowan, G. T., Longhurst, J., & Kim, S. (2006). Strengths as the foundation for intervention with Black youth. *Reclaiming Children & Youth: The Journal of Strength-Based intervention, 15,* 147–154.

Lambert, M. C., Rowan, G. T., & Lyubansky, M. (2002). Behavior and emotional problems of clinic-referred African American children and adolescents: Parent reports for ages 4–18. *Journal of Child and Family Studies, 11,* 271–285.

Littlejohn-Blake, S. M., & Darling, C. A. (1993). Understanding the strengths of African American families. *Journal of Black Studies, 23,* 460–471.

Markstrom, C. A. (1999). Religious involvement and adolescent psychosocial development. *Journal of Adolescence, 22,* 205–221.

Markstrom, C. A., Marshall, S. K., & Tryon, R. J. (2000). Resiliency, social support, and coping in rural low-income Appalachian adolescents from two racial groups. *Journal of Adolescence, 23,* 693–703.

Masten, A. S., & Coatsworth, J. D. (1998). The development of competence in favorable and unfavorable environments: Lessons from research on successful children. *American Psychologist, 53,* 205–220.

Maton, K. I., & Hrabowski, F. A. (2004). Increasing the number of African American PhD's in the sciences and engineering: A strengths-based approach. *American Psychologist, 59,* 547–556.

McAdoo, H. P. (2007). *Black families* (4th ed.). Thousand Oaks, CA: Sage.

Molock, S. D., Puri, R., Matlin, S., & Barksdale, C. (2006). Relationship between religious coping and suicidal behaviors among African American adolescents. *Journal of Black Psychology, 32,* 366–389.

Ogbu, J. U. (2003). *Black American students in an affluent suburb: A study of academic disengagement.* Mahwah, NJ: Laurence Erlbaum.

Schafer, J. L. (1999). NORM: Multiple imputation of incomplete multivariate data under a normal model (version 2.03) [Software for Windows 95/98/NT]. Retrieved from http://www.stat.psu.edu/~jls/misoftwa.html

Schmitt, N. (1996). Uses and abuses of coefficient alpha. *Psychological Assessment, 8,* 350–353.

Scott, L. D. (2004). Correlates of coping with perceived discriminatory experiences among African American adolescents. *Journal of Adolescence, 27,* 123–137.

Stevenson, H. C., & Renard, G. (1993). Trusting ole' wise owls: Therapeutic use of cultural strengths in African American families. *Professional Psychology: Research and Practice, 24,* 433–442.

Strom, R., Dohrmann, J., Strom, P., Griswold, D., Beckert, T., Strom, S., et al. (2002). African American mothers of early adolescents: Perceptions of two generations. *Youth & Society, 33,* 394–417.

Taylor, C. S., Lerner, R. M., Eye, A. V., Bobek, D. L., Dowling, E. M., & Anderson, P. M. (2004). Internal and external developmental assets among African American male gang members. *Journal of Adolescent Research, 19,* 303–322.

Thomas, D. E., Townsend, T. G., & Belgrave, F. Z. (2003). The influence of cultural and racial identification on the psychosocial adjustment of inner city African American children in school. *American Journal of Community Psychology, 32,* 217–228.

Varon, S. R., & Riley, A. W. (1999). Relationship between maternal church attendance and adolescent mental health and social functioning. *Psychiatric Services, 50,* 799–805.

Werner, E., & Smith, R. (1982). *Vulnerable but invincible: A longitudinal study of resilient children and youth.* New York: Adams, Bannister, and Cox.

Williams, R. L. (2007). *Racism learned at an early age through racial scripting.* Bloomington, IN: AuthorHouse.

29

FROM ANXIETY AND DEPRESSION TO SUICIDE AND SELF-HARM

RHEEDA L. WALKER AND LORA ROSE HUNTER

Emotional and psychological distress accompanied by shifts in mood, sleeplessness, poor memory and concentration, and unexplained stomach problems are often dismissed or temporarily alleviated by painkillers and over-the-counter interventions. However, these are also possible symptoms of anxiety and depression, common motivators among African Americans for seeking mental health care. African American adults who have sought treatment have specifically cited depression and suicidal ideation as legitimate reasons for psychotherapy (Thompson, Bazile, & Akbar, 2004). However, progress toward systematically diagnosing and treating these debilitating problems is lagging, and sufficient prevention models for self-harm behavior, a frequent consequence of untreated depression and anxiety, may be even further from reality. Advances in mental health research for people of African descent in the United States have been hindered by inadequate definitions of mental health and mental illness. Any legitimate effort to categorize and ameliorate the psychological ills that burden African people must begin with an understanding of who African people are in America and how coping (both adaptive and maladaptive) has evolved as a function of this reality. In this chapter, we provide an overview of the extant empirical and theoretical literature on African American anxiety, depression, and suicide; outline methodological challenges; and propose directions for advancing these important areas of African American mental health.

ANXIETY IN AFRICAN AMERICANS

According to data from the National Comorbidity Survey–Replication (NCS–R), anxiety disorders are the most prevalent class of mental disorders in the United States (Kessler et al., 2005) such that 28.8% of the population will suffer from a clinically significant anxiety disorder at some point in their lifetime. *Anxiety* is defined as "the apprehensive anticipation of future danger or misfortune accompanied by dysphoria or somatic symptoms of tension" (American Psychiatric Association, 2000, p. 820). These disorders include panic disorder, specific phobias, social phobia, generalized anxiety disorder, posttraumatic stress disorder (PTSD), and obsessive–compulsive disorder (OCD). All are marked by persistent and debilitating fear. These disorders are frequently characterized by early onset and, without treatment, have a chronic course and high rates of comorbidity with other conditions, such as substance abuse disorders and depression (Kessler et al., 2005). Unfortunately, anxiety disorders in African Americans have been grossly understudied (Carter, Sbrocco, & Carter, 1996; Neal & Turner, 1991).

Prevalence, Patterns, and Characteristics

Neal and Turner's (1991) review has been a seminal work in the area of African Americans and anxiety disorders. Most studies, and the epidemiological data of the time, concluded that African Americans experienced higher rates of anxiety disorders than European Americans. However, the available data were said to have been overrepresented by individuals from low socioeconomic status (SES) brackets and failed to provide useful insights for upper-SES subgroups. The NCS, a nationally representative study of mental health, found that African Americans have lower rates of anxiety disturbance relative to European Americans, although anxiety disorders in African Americans have a more chronic course (Breslau, Kendler, Su, Gaxiola-Aguilar, & Kessler, 2005). Some researchers have suggested that the chronicity of disease is due to sparse coping resources at the onset of an anxiety disorder. When symptoms of anxiety, such as trembling, chest pain, or dizziness, develop abruptly and dissipate without treatment, fears of future "attacks" are heightened. Fear of negative consequences, such as job loss and inability to access services (Breslau, Gaxiola-Aguilar, et al., 2005), further compound the negative emotional outcome. In the long run, such consequences can lead to severe depressive reactions in the absence of appropriate coping and problem-solving intervention.

Given available data, Neal and Turner (1991) discussed notable phenomenological patterns in anxiety psychopathology that implicated increased rates of isolated sleep paralysis in African Americans with panic disorder (Bell, Dixie-Bell, & Thompson, 1986; Bell, Hildreth, Jenkins, & Carter, 1988). Unfortunately, these data have not been replicated recently, and few of the other findings mentioned in the review were empirically well supported. On the basis of ethnographic studies, some people have speculated that the prevalence of African American anxiety might be obscured by poorly constructed cross-cultural research (Heurtin-Roberts, Snowden, & Miller, 1997)

Differential Symptomatology and Diagnosis

African Americans may demonstrate a unique experience of anxiety that is yet to be articulated in diagnostic texts. Studies show that panic disorder characterized by recurrent unexpected panic attacks, persistent concern about having another attack, and the implications and consequences of the panic attacks is uniquely presented among African Americans. As an example, African Americans with panic disorder are said to demonstrate higher rates of isolated sleep paralysis and more frequent and intense panic symptoms involving tingling, numbness, and hot and cold flashes, in addition to fears of going crazy (Freidman & Paradis, 2002). African Americans with panic disorder tend to report more comorbid PTSD symptomatology relative to members of other ethnic groups who report PTSD symptoms (Smith, Friedman, & Nevid, 1999).

PTSD is the development of severe symptoms of anxiety following exposure to an extremely traumatic event. Studies have found that, despite having no differences in preexisting trauma, combat trauma, or comorbid diagnoses, African American veterans are more likely than other veterans to receive a diagnosis of a comorbid psychotic disorder (Frueh et al., 2002; Monnier, Elhai, Frueh, Sauvageot, & Magruder, 2002). It is possible that this outcome reflects differentially higher levels of psychotic symptoms in African Americans, but more likely it is the result of differences in either descriptive language of symptoms or clinical bias. In either case, it suggests that African Americans experience PTSD and undergo assessment differently than members of other ethnic groups.

African Americans may be at systematically greater risk for the development of PTSD as a function of SES. For example, Perilla, Norris, and Lavizzo (2002) interviewed 404 southern Florida residents 6 months after Hurricane Andrew. In this sample, 23% of African American participants were experiencing clinically significant PTSD, compared with 15% of European American participants and 38% of Latinos. In this case, the lack of resources available to African American communities made it less likely that they would be able to participate in recovery-related activities such as rebuilding homes and neighborhoods. Some initial reports in the aftermath of Hurricane Katrina have identified factors such as proximity to the coast and female gender that are associated with immediate symptoms of PTSD (Weems et al., 2007). However, as time goes by and disadvantaged individuals are less able to rebuild or remain displaced, PTSD symptoms are likely to be more closely associated with minority ethnic group status. Moreover, the initial anger and distrust that resulted because of the U.S. government's lack of response to the crisis (see Cordasco, Eisenman, Glik, Golden, & Asch, 2007) will likely mature into a sense of hopelessness that puts both victims and sympathetic African Americans nationwide at greater risk for developing symptoms of anxiety and depression.

Neal and Turner (1991) posited that systematic underreporting of symptoms may be at play. Consider that the essential features of OCD are recurrent intrusive thoughts and/or a feeling of being driven to perform repetitive behaviors aimed at reducing anxiety or distress. African American individuals with OCD may be misdiagnosed because of an inclination to report only physical symptoms of distress (Friedman et al., 2003). Anecdotal evidence suggest that the underreporting of cognitive symptoms of OCD by African Americans is due in part to higher levels of shame, fears of going crazy, and a sense of uniqueness relative to European Americans with OCD. To illustrate, K. E. Williams, Chambless, and Steketee (1998) presented a case study of two African American women with OCD. Both of the women demonstrated classic presentations of OCD symptoms and responded well to conventional cognitive–behavioral therapy that consisted of exposure to the stressor with response prevention. However, the authors noted that both women were excessively concerned with being considered crazy or psychotic. For example, one of the clients said,

> If white people get anxious, they can be neurotic and get better with a little therapy. All of you are going to a (outpatient) therapist. But when a black person gets anxious, people think she's crazy and ought to be put away. (p. 166)

This statement likely reflects higher rates of perceived and real stigmatization of mental illness, a significant barrier to treatment seeking.

Similarly, pathological worry, which is the essential feature of generalized anxiety disorder, has been found to have a different factor structure in African American samples relative to other ethnic groups (Carter et al., 2005); that is, worry in African Americans is believed to consist of a component that represents a more conscious effort to dismiss unwanted cognitions.

A Theoretical Conceptualization

There is some evidence for a developmental model of anxiety informed by racial and cultural factors. Carter et al. (1996) concluded that racial identity and acculturation were predictive of symptom manifestation, views about help seeking attitudes and behavior, and treatment outcome in African Americans. *Racial identity* was described as "belongingness to the African American group culture" (pp. 456–457) by both recognition of one's African descent, including shared values and traditions, and the historical turbulence of the African presence in European America. *Acculturation* was defined as the adoption of characteristics and participation in activities and traditions originating from European American culture, including beliefs about psychological disturbances. According to Carter et al., racial identity, together with acculturation, led to one of four possible classifications that yielded significantly different outcomes. As an example, individuals high in racial identity and low in acculturation were expected to have difficulty recognizing symptoms of anxiety and to be more likely attribute anxiety to physical or spiritual causes. Consequently, this group would be more likely to see a medical doctor and be resistant to psychological interventions but more receptive to nontraditional (e.g., spiritual) intervention.

Of note, Carter et al.'s (1996) model suggested that African Americans who are more acculturated and less accepting of African and African American mores will manifest *all* psychological disorders, including anxiety and other psychiatric problems, in a way that is similar to the majority culture. In many ways, this is akin to African Psychology models that posit that a strong African identity is protective against psychopathology. Baldwin (1984) asserted that by embracing a value system based on interdependence and actively resisting European American value systems, African Americans are less likely to develop mental illness.

African American Depression

Much of the depression literature relevant to African Americans has been characterized by conflicting reports that yield an unclear picture of the prevalence, risks, and severity of symptoms associated with depression in African Americans. According to the U.S. Surgeon General (U.S. Department of Health and Human Services, 2001), clinical depression and other mental illnesses are as common in African Americans as they are in European Americans. Robins and Regier (1991) emphasized that African Americans report comparable levels of clinical depression but more depressive symptomatology relative to other ethnic groups. The seemingly invisible symptoms that do not meet criteria for a diagnosis can lead to life-threatening consequences.

The National Survey on American Life has offered the most comprehensive assessment of major depressive disorder (MDD) in African Americans to date (see D. R. Williams et al., 2007). In this national probability sample, the lifetime prevalence rate of MDD was estimated as approximately 10%, which was less than rates for both Caribbean Blacks (12.9%) and European Americans (17.9%). D. R. Williams and colleagues (2007) observed, importantly, that depression is more persistent and more debilitating for African Americans and for Caribbean Americans. Furthermore, only 1 in 2 African Americans with severe depression was reported to receive treatment. Studies show that African women, including those between the ages of 18 and 24 (Somervell, Leaf, Weissman, Blazer, & Bruce, 1989), middle-aged women (Bromberger, Harlow, Avis, Kravitz, & Cordal, 2004), those with moderate to high incomes (Brown & Keith, 2003), and college students (Brown, Parker-Dominguez, & Sorey, 2000), tend to report greater levels of depression and dysthymia compared with European American women. Unfortunately, these findings have not been tested in African American men.

There exist systematic challenges to quantifying African American depression. The Surgeon General's report acknowledged that syndromal levels of depression may be underestimated in African Americans, who are often excluded from epidemiological surveys because of overrepresentation in psychiatric and penal institutions. Coyne and Marcus (2006) noted that insistence on clinical significance of depressive symptoms undermines referrals for treatment and contributes to health disparities. Relative to Hispanic and non-Hispanic White adults, non-Hispanic Black[1] adults demonstrated lower rates of lifetime MDD (Kessler et al., 2003). However, non-Hispanic Black Americans reported higher 12-month incidence of MDD than non-Hispanic Whites.

Challenges in Diagnosis and Measurement

Differential expression of depressive symptoms has been raised as a potential confound to reliable measurement and depression diagnosis. Kleinman and Good (1985) highlighted a tendency within research to overlook racial variation in the expression of mental disorders when developing nosological categories. They argued that there is an assumption that psychiatric symptoms are manifested in a uniform manner across all cultural groups. Investigations that clarify racial differences in the manifestation of depression may shed light on the etiology and treatment of mood disorders and improve assessment for Blacks and Whites.

Some studies indicate that the differences in psychiatric symptomatology are systematic, such that African Americans endorse more somatic symptoms than cognitive symptoms. In a study of Black and White college students, Walker et al. (2008) found that although the overall cognitive–somatic factor structure for depression that has been found in previous studies held up, Black students did not similarly endorse certain somatic items (e.g., difficulties with sleep, indecision) despite reporting the same level of depression as their White peers. Studies have demonstrated systematic racial differences in depression symptom expression such that Black adults emphasized somatic problems whereas White adults reported cognitive disturbances (Weissman, Bruce, Leaf, Florio, & Holzer, 1991). However, these findings have not always held up (Gallo, Cooper-Patrick, & Lesikar, 1998). An important source of potential bias in assessing racial differences in the expression of depression is the set of actual items included for the assessment of depression; that is, if there are items that differentiate Blacks and Whites on depression, current depressive scales may not adequately represent such items. In this regard, there have been few investigations of the validity of depressive scales or checklists as applied to Black American populations.

A universal taxonomy (beyond rigid somatic and cognitive difficulties) that is potentially accompanied by semantic flexibility is needed to articulate depressive symptoms and syndromes in African American people. A qualitative study of Black male college students noted that they were more comfortable with day-to-day jargon (rather than formal language) to describe mental health problems (Watkins & Neighbors, 2007). "Getting beat" (p. 277) was one example used to describe poor mental health. Jones and Shorter-Gooden (2003) explored gender and race realities for African American women. In doing so, they posited a framework for depression characterized by the emotional strain of "shifting," in ways that include shifting from satisfying self to placating White America, from functioning successfully and independently to tolerating sexism and abuse, and from experiencing emotional difficulty to denying any psychological need. They noted that a Black woman who is "working very hard and seems disconnected from her own needs" and who "may be busy around the clock, constantly on the go, unable to relax, and often compromising her sleep for household, child-care, and job tasks" may be staving off debilitating sadness (p. 125). Jones and Shorter-Gooden also noted that (a) overeating and (b) obsessive attention to outward appearance accompanied by (c) excessive time and financial resources allocated to shopping are potential attempts to avoid depressive realities. These signs of depression along with the physical manifestations of stomach problems and other unexplainable bodily aches can obscure and conceal depression.

Sociocultural Factors Across the Life Span

Findings from the National Survey on American Life demonstrate that youth, female gender, marital status, and geographic residence were associated with MDD in that younger adults and women were more likely to be diagnosed with MDD. However, individuals who were married, living in the rural United States, or residing in the southern and western U.S. regions were less likely to demonstrate evidence of a depressive disorder. Some studies have concluded that African Americans' vulnerability to depressive symptoms was associated with difficulties meeting basic needs for food and/or shelter as well as insufficient social support (Plant & Sachs-Ericsson, 2004). Of interest is that Myers et al. (2002) found differences in symptomatology at the assessment level such that African American women self-reported more depressive symptoms than were assessed by trained interviewers. Myers et al. attributed the discrepancies to limitations in self-report relative to the interviewer ratings and to factors such as age, employment status, and overall burden of medical disease instead of depression per se. Of note, SES was controlled for and was not a factor in the findings.

The factors that lead to depression vary across age and generational subgroups. Elder African Americans are said to demonstrate higher risk for depressive symptoms when activities of daily living such as driving and meal preparation are limited (see Cummings, Neff, & Husaini, 2003). However, religious activities and adequate support systems are believed to mitigate the negative impact of limited functioning. In a study of disadvantaged Black women, those born outside the United States were more likely to report depression (Miranda, Siddique, Belin, & Kohn-Wood, 2005). Of importance is that depressive symptoms increased as length of U.S. residence increased.

AFRICAN AMERICAN SUICIDE

Untreated symptoms of anxiety and depression can lead to suicide and self-harm behavior for African American adults and youth. As it is currently defined, suicide remains a nebulous and peculiar phenomenon for lay African Americans. The widely accepted, Eurocentric understanding of suicide is "death from injury, poisoning, or suffocation where there is evidence (either explicit or implicit) that the injury was self-inflicted and that the decedent intended to kill himself/herself" (O'Carroll, Berman, Maris, & Moscicki, 1996, pp. 246–247). Suicidal behavior includes the continuum of suicidal ideation; parasuicidal behavior, such as cutting; and fatal and nonfatal attempts to intentionally end one's life. Although African American suicide is not well understood, there has been a surge of literature prompted in part by the swell in suicide rates for African American male youth observed in the 1980s and 1990s. Pierson (1977) noted that, rather than accepting enslavement, hanging and drowning were the most common methods that captured Africans used to end one's life. In the contemporary United States, suicide has been relegated primarily to European American populations. However, studies show that African American suicide death rates have been poorly documented and obscured by underreporting and mislabeling (e.g., suicide deaths listed as "accidents"; Rockett, Samora, & Coben, 2006).

Prevalence, Patterns, and Characteristics

According to Crosby and Molock (2006), suicide is the 16th leading cause of death for African Americans; 6 African Americans die by suicide each day. This rate masks the seriousness of the problem, because some African American subgroups are seemingly protected from suicide, whereas others are at relatively high risk. As an example, the Institute of Medicine of the National Academies (Goldsmith, Pellmar, Kleinman, & Bunney, 2002) cited a suicide rate for African American men (24/100,000) that was comparable to that of White men (25.6/100,000) in the 25- to 34-year age group during the 1980s and 1990s. In other studies, African American women have been said to attempt suicide at rates comparable to European American women (Nisbet, 1996).

National probability data for Black suicide risk (i.e., ideation and attempts) provide some insights into the prevalence, course, and risk for suicidal ideation and attempts (Joe, Baser, Breeden, Neighbors, & Jackson, 2006). Joe et al. (2006) estimated lifetime prevalence for suicidal ideation as 11.7% and suicide attempts as 4.1%. Further assessment of individuals at risk revealed that more than one third of those who had considered suicide made plans to attempt suicide. Of those who attempted suicide, more than 40% indicated that their attempt would have been fatal had it not been for "luck that [they] did not succeed" (Joe et al., 2006, p. 2115). Otherwise, 45% endorsed that the attempt was a "cry for help" in which the attempter did not intend to die. These statistics are intriguing in light of the low reported suicide rates among African Americans; that is, some poorly conceived "cries" that resulted in death may be labeled as "accidental" deaths. Herein lies evidence of the need for more concise coroner and medical examiner investigations of death among African Americans. Although there has been a decline in suicide deaths among African American men similar to that observed in European American men and women during the period 1996 to 2002 (see Minino, Arias, Kochanek, Murphy, & Smith, 2002), suicidality in this group remains a public health concern. Suicide attempts (including those that require serious medical attention) among African American males continue to surpass attempts for both White males and White females in the United States (Centers for Disease Control and Prevention, 2004).

The current profile for African American suicide is not like that of other ethnic groups in the United States. As an example, the African American male suicide death rate peaks much earlier—25 to 34 years compared with age 75 to 84 years for European American men (cf. Joe, 2006; Lester, 1998). African Americans who die by suicide are said to have demonstrated less "known risk factors," including history of depression, financial stressors, chronic disease, substance abuse (Abe, Mertz, Powell, & Hanzlick, 2004), and family history of suicide (Roy, 2003). Willis, Coombs, Drentea and Cockerhan (2003) noted that African Americans are more likely to die in urban areas than in rural areas. In Fulton County, Georgia, 62% of all suicide deaths for individuals age less than 19 years were African American (Garlow, Purselle, & Heninger, 2005). Of those, the overwhelming majority (82%, $n = 49$) were cocaine and alcohol free at the time of autopsy. Despite the persistently unique profile for African American suicide, no systematized psychological autopsy studies have been conducted to better understand African American suicide.

There is some evidence that the highest risk for onset of suicidal ideation and attempts occurs during the teenage and early 20s age bracket (Joe et al., 2006). Individuals in this age cohort were said to be more likely to develop a plan for suicide and attempt suicide. According to Joe and colleagues (2006), sociodemographic factors associated with risk were said to include less than high school education level, midwestern residence, and single marital status. Despite indications that risk increased given less education, Wasserman and Stack (2000) noted in another study that suicide risk *increased* as a function of increased occupational status in one midwestern state. Relevant to psychiatric status, there is evidence that risk for suicide increased substantially given the presence of an anxiety disorder (i.e., panic disorder, PTSD, OCD), mood disorder (e.g., depression that lasts for 2 years or more), history of drug dependence, and anorexia (Joe et al., 2006). When controlling for sex and other sociodemographic factors, anxiety seemed to be a stronger risk factor than depression. This finding is important to pursue in future postmortem studies given that depression is said to be the strongest clinical precipitant to suicide attempts and death (E. C. Harris & Barraclough, 1997). Although Joe et al.'s study presents the first nationally representative study of suicidal ideation and attempts, recall bias and social demand may have skewed the findings. More studies are needed that probe determinants of medically serious suicide attempts as well as culturally informed protective factors.

Contemporary Notions of African American Suicide

The increase in African American male youth suicide has, theoretically, been attributed to cultural shifts (Willis, Coombs, Cockerham, & Frison, 2002). Willis and colleagues (2002) suggested that suicide death rates have reflected profound societal changes; that is, African Americans were believed to benefit from homogeneous African American communities in which they were not exposed to the stress of minority group status. Furthermore, employment opportunities for uneducated and unskilled workers were in seeming abundance. Changes in employment security, in turn, disrupted familial ties. Others have similarly pointed to deindustrialization and economic inequality as causes of Black males' suicidal behavior (Burr, Hartman, & Matteson, 1999; Joe, 2006). However, the shifts in advantage do not account for the stability of suicide rates in African American women and girls and in African Americans who benefit from higher economic status who are seemingly unprotected (Wasserman & Stack, 2000). Stack (1998) reported that whereas suicide rates decrease with education for White males, deaths by suicide for African American males are more likely to increase.

Walker (2007) proposed a multivariate model of African American suicide that presupposes that untreated psychological problems (e.g., anxiety and depression) that are (a) preceded or exacerbated by race/ethnicity-related tensions and poor sociocultural cohesion and identity and that are also (b) unregulated by cultural buffers are most likely to lead to suicide-related behaviors. As such, racism and cultural isolation are believed to activate depressive or anxious symptoms, and these symptoms are escalated by the strain of navigating racism and dual (mainstream and African American) cultures. Suicide is a cultural phenomenon. Given the relatively low rates of suicide among African Americans, one might speculate that African American cultural ties in a sense inoculate those who might otherwise be at risk. A sense of belongingness and attachment to the African/African American ethnocultural group is believed to be important for individual well-being and necessary for the collective well-being of African people. Lack of acculturation in the African American community is potentially devastating. When persons of African descent increasingly minimize the importance of African cultural tenets, their capacity for protection is compromised, and problem-solving options (e.g., suicide death) that were once shunned may now, in contemporary times, seem less taboo. Even more, the notion of negotiating dual cultures presents a strain (i.e., acculturative stress) that often leads to depressive and anxious symptoms. There was a time when "I'm Black and I'm proud" rang true. Now, some African-descended people vehemently exclaim why they are "Black, not African American" (McWhorter, 2004).

Empirically Supported Determinants of Suicidal Behavior

It is interesting that several studies have found no significant association of suicide with depression in African Americans (Kung, Pearson, & Wei, 2005; Willis et al., 2003). Because no psychological autopsy or systematic postmortem investigations have specifically examined African American suicide deaths, investigations in African American suicide deaths have been limited to proxy reports by next of kin and close others. In some representative and population-based studies, suicide has been most likely associated with marijuana use; access to firearms; and use of mental health services—a proposed proxy for the presence of psychological distress (Kung et al., 2005). Similar to previous reports, Kung et al. (2005) noted that proxy reports of depressive symptoms and heavy alcohol use were not characteristic of African American suicide in decedents age 15 through 64 years. Thus, behavioral risks, such as access to firearms and marijuana use, were more readily disclosed and identified than decedent reports of depressive symptoms (see Kung et al., 2005).

Juon and Ensminger (1997) followed the developmental paths of more than 1,200 African American youth beginning at Grade 1 and concluding when the participants were 32 years old. They found sex differences such that, for males, being in a single-parent family, childhood psychopathology, and single marital status were associated with suicidal behaviors, whereas for females aggressive tendencies were a risk factor. Kaslow and colleagues (Anderson, Tiro, Price, Bender, & Kaslow, 2002; Kaslow, Jacobs, Young, & Cook, 2006; Kaslow et al., 1998) have consistently cited partner abuse and childhood physical and sexual abuse as factors in suicide risk for low-income African American women who have attempted suicide.

Sociocultural Factors Across the Life Span

In nonprobability studies that focus on culturally relevant variables, suicide protection is associated with commitment to Christian values, particularly in African American adolescents, even more so than internalized religious beliefs (Greening & Stoppelbein, 2002). In African American college students, resilience to suicide is related to familial support, suicide unacceptability, and collaborative religious problem solving (T. Harris & Molock, 2000; Marion & Range, 2003).

Walker, Utsey, Bolden, and Williams's (2005) investigation of sociocultural risk factors generated some unexpected outcomes in which suicidality (i.e., suicide-related thoughts and beliefs) among persons of African descent was associated with religious participation (but not social support). Their findings also indicated that religiosity was a better predictor of suicidality than acculturation, another variable of interest. Future studies should examine the importance of religious participation as a predictor of suicide with some attention to level of acculturation or acculturative stress as possible mediators. Walker and Bishop (2005) noted that more refined examinations of religious and other factors are overdue. Studies that explore religious activities (e.g., church attendance, prayer) and how these behaviors affect psychological health and coping are much more informative than epidemiological summaries indicating that African Americans are simply more religious than other ethnocultural groups (see Chap. 7, this volume). Religiosity may come at a price (cf. Hill & Pargament, 2003), and although it seems true that African Americans (including youth) are more religious than others, this "protection" may not differentially protect them from suicidal behavior.

Older African American adults seem to be most resilient to suicide-related behavior. One study of adults age 55 through 96 years found 2.5% and 1.4% rates of passive and active suicidal ideation, respectively (Cook, Pearson, Thompson, Black, & Rabins, 2002). Passive suicidal ideation characterized by "thoughts of death" was associated with older age, lower educational level, depressive symptoms, and poorer cognitive functioning. These individuals were likely to have discussed problems with a health care provider. Active suicidal ideation, in which an individual considered taking his or her own life, was observed for respondents who had previously received mental health services and who lacked assistance with daily life tasks. Cook and colleagues (2002) noted that, in the larger sample, active suicidal ideation was more likely to be observed for European Americans than for African Americans. Suicide deaths are said to be so rarely observed for elderly African American women that the precise incidence is unknown.

An Alternative Conceptualization of Suicide

Suicide, characterized as intentional self-injury, is dismissed by lay African Americans. Such behavior is described as "alien to the Black experience" and is said to "run directly counter to all that is implicit to what it means to be African American (Early & Akers, 1993, p. 283). Yet, suicide is a reality in the African American community. Unfortunately, it is unlikely to be identified through standard definitions. As an example, Wolfgang (1959) found that a significant proportion of deaths classified as homicides were more likely suicide deaths. Early and Akers (1993) distinguished "real" suicide from "slow" suicide in which drug use was thought of as slow suicide but an understandable response to socioeconomic and political conditions; real suicide was described as unthinkable. Although the previously accepted conceptualization of suicide has been updated (see Silverman et al.,

2007), the revision was not broad enough to include the "slow" suicide described by Early and Akers. Contemporary studies are needed to operationalize self-destructive behavior across the life span in African American communities. Inclusion of self-destructive behavior in its many forms (e.g., alcohol and drug abuse, victim-precipitated homicide) in response to interpersonal, sociopolitical, and psychological difficulty should be considered in conceptualizations of suicide. Doing so raises questions regarding intentionality in the event of a possible suicide death. However, minimizing these self-destructive behaviors and other slow suicides (e.g., obesity-related illness) confers a certain complicity in premature death for people of African descent in the United States.

Suicide might be characterized as one of many preventable public health problems that plague Black Americans. Although efforts to address heart disease and diabetes management have received some attention in African American communities, suicide has received no such attention in regard to prevention efforts. Nevertheless, personal neglect in the face of a life-threatening illness and experiences of hopelessness can reap despair and subsequent self-harm behavior, especially in the absence of interpersonal support and psychological resilience. As such, these factors are critical in generating a new understanding of suicide and reinvigorating efforts to prevent foreseeable death. Given better definitions, current assessment strategies would do well to include indexes of depression and anxiety as well as physical health in determining suicide risk as well as to assess protective factors, such as familial cohesion and absence of familial conflict. Epidemiological data add to a more accurate profile of suicide by disaggregating suicide by region, across the life span, and by sex, among other demographic constants.

ANXIETY, DEPRESSION AND SUICIDALITY IN GAY, LESBIAN, BISEXUAL, AND TRANSGENDERED AFRICAN AMERICANS

A growing body of research suggests that demographic subsets of the African American community, particularly gay, lesbian, bisexual, and transgendered (GLBT) African Americans, are at greater risk for anxiety, depression, and associated psychological distress. Cochran and Mays (1994) examined rates of depression and suicidal thoughts in 829 African American men and 603 African American women who were active in same-sex relationships. In this sample, rates of depression and depressive symptoms were higher than previously reported. In addition, the findings suggest that African American women who self-identified as lesbian, gay, or bisexual were as distressed as gay African American men infected with HIV. The "triple stigma" associated with ethnic minority status, sexual orientation, and gender may result in a specific vulnerability to chronic stress and depression for women (Mays, Cochran, & Roeder, 2003).

Factors such as HIV status, identity reconciliation, and overt discrimination are particularly problematic. Symptomatic HIV is said to contribute to significantly more distress for gay men relative to those who are infected but asymptomatic, those who are HIV-antibody negative, and those whose HIV status is unknown to them (Cochran & Mays, 1994). The emotional strain of sexual identity, which includes coming out and encounters with stigma and discrimination, can be incapacitating. For example, Herek, Gillis, Cogan, and Glunt (1997) found that in a sample of 147 African American lesbian, gay, and bisexual individuals, over 40% reported experiencing bias-related criminal victimization, and almost 10% reported that they had been the victims of attempts at violent victimization. Research studies have suggested that these types of stressors can lead to symptoms of anxiety, conduct problems, and substance use, in addition to depression (Rosario, Rotheram-Borus, & Reid, 1996).

Some potentially useful protective factors have been identified. At least one study suggests that, for African American gay men, dual-identity development, or positive self-identification as both African American and gay, is associated with higher self-esteem and life satisfaction, stronger social support, and HIV prevention self-efficacy (Crawford, Allison, Zamboni, & Soto, 2002). Psychosocial resources are believed to be important in that they mediate the effects of life stressors on depression symptoms for African American men regardless of whether they are gay, bisexual, or heterosexual (Peterson, Folkman, & Bakeman, 1996). This suggests that social supports are protective regardless of sexual identity status. However, GLBT African American individuals may be more vulnerable to depression and anxiety, because the stigma associated with minority sexual identity often affects available social support networks and belongingness. Coping strategies identified as protective for the general African American community can be equally useful for GLBT individuals. One qualitative study of spirituality in African American gay men living with AIDS revealed that spirituality was "interactive, integrative, and protective" and a resource for coping that was actually strengthened by adversity (Miller, 2005, p. 42).

Future Directions

When available, the scholarly literature provides some compelling insights to anxiety, depression, and suicide in African Americans. However, the need for more empirical research that includes well-defined and culturally informed research questions, representative samples of African American participants, and appropriate statistical analyses and conclusions remains. The current literature promotes conventional notions of mental illness that were originally developed for, delivered to, and administered by European Americans and do not adequately capture psychological phenomena for individuals of African descent, a very heterogeneous group. Increased diversity in research studies is directly associated with the accumulated knowledge about anxiety disorders, depression, and suicide in African Americans. The appropriateness of conventional measures in African American samples is a significant domain of concern. Several studies have indicated that conventional measures of risk factors and symptoms, when applied to African Americans, may not appropriately capture the constructs they were designed to measure (Carter, Miller, Sbrocco, Suchday, & Lewis, 1999; Carter et al., 2005; Lambert, Cooley, Campbell, Benoit, & Stansbury, 2004; Walker et al., 2008). Possible research questions are specifically highlighted (see Table 29.1) and should be considered in context of social and economic status and moderating effects of ethnic identity and acculturation strategies.

Future studies must generate better surveillance data for suicidal acts, anxiety pathology, and depressive profiles. As one example, well-designed postmortem investigations, also known as *psychological autopsy projects*, are key to understanding the influence of emotional distress, severe psychopathology, and other determinants of suicide in the African American community.

Suicide deaths are relatively difficult to predict, and fatal attempts are even less predictable in the African American community. Research projects that include interviews with adults and youth who have survived near-fatal attempts are essential to developing culturally meaningful interventions. Such interventions would be informed by those most at risk in the community.

Neal and Turner's (1991) review, a seminal work in the area of anxiety disorders, cited negative perceptions of research and differences in help-seeking behaviors for emotional distress as reasons for the small number of studies that have investigated pathology in African Americans. There is compelling evidence that (a) mistrust of health care and research institutions and (b) the tendency to handle mental health problems at home or within the African American community significantly limit the number of African Americans in clinical studies (e.g., Whaley, 2001).

It is additionally problematic that available studies have rarely assessed ethnic and cultural differences within the Black American population. In one example, Friedman and Paradis (2002) prompted participants to identify themselves as African American or Afro-Caribbean in a study of panic disorder to compare specific ethnic differences. Although they found no ethnic group differences in the experience of panic disorder, the investigators acknowledged the diversity of African peoples. To our knowledge, no other published anxiety studies have done so. Future studies should systematically consider variables beyond race, including ethnicity and level of acculturation.

Kwate (2005) astutely summarized the problem that continuously plagues our legitimacy as African American mental health scholars and practitioners: the marginalization of African-centered psychology in characterizing mental health problems for persons of African descent. According to Kwate and others, the nosology set forth by the family of *Diagnostic and Statistical Manuals of Mental Disorders* (e.g., American Psychiatric Association, 2000) are ill equipped to designate psychological and spiritual sickness. The current manual presents a grossly oversimplified profile of psychiatric problems that disregards social context and cultural milieu. For example, self-harm and slow suicides may be best characterized by Akbar's (1991) articulation of self-destructive behavior in which the individual struggles with survival and adaptation in

Table 29.1 Example Research Questions for Advancing Mental Health Study Associated With Suicide, Depression, and Anxiety in African Americans

Category	Research Questions
Suicide	What is the most comprehensive definition of suicide/self-harm behavior for African American men, women, and youth?
	What are the suicide risk factors for African American males age 18 to 45?
	Are African Americans less likely to preempt a possible suicide attempt of a family member or friend if suicide is believed to be "unthinkable" in the community?
	Given the high homicide rates among African men, might there be some association of the sense of hopelessness that leads to suicide death and the sense of haplessness that leads to "victim-precipitated" homicide deaths?
Depression	Should overeating, unexplained physical illness, and other stress indicators be weighed differently in depression evaluations for African American women and men?
	Are measures such as the Beck Depression Inventory–II, Center for Epidemiologic Studies Depression Scale (CES–D), and Hamilton Rating Scale for Depression (HAM–D) valid measures of depressive symptoms?
	Which subgroups (elderly; chronically ill; lesbian, gay, bisexual, transgendered; women) of African Americans are most at risk for depression?
	How does spirituality affect the impact of depressive symptoms and decision making for seeking treatment?
Anxiety	How does one characterize anxiety etiology for African Americans?
	Do African American combat veterans experience more profound symptoms of posttraumatic stress disorder relative to other combat veterans despite seemingly comparable exposure to adverse situations? Does worldview affect perception of combat?
	Does level of acculturation significantly affect one's self-reported anxiety symptoms?
	Does shame impact one's willingness to disclose symptoms of anxiety and depression?

a hostile society. As Kwate asserted, African psychology must "broaden its scope to a larger stage or risk permanent suppression" (p. 232). The consequence of disregarding a psychological science that is relevant to African Americans is prolonged assignment to poor emotional health and physical health outcomes.

NOTE

1. The ethnic label *African American* and racial label *Black* are used interchangeably in this chapter, in some cases to retain the level of identification observed in the research and articles that were reviewed. For the purposes of this discussion, both labels represent persons of African descent living in the United States.

REFERENCES

Abe, K., Mertz, K., Powell, K., & Hanzlick, R. (2004, April). *Characteristics of Blacks and Whites committing suicide—Fulton County, Georgia, 1988–2002.* Poster session presented at the Epidemic Intelligence Service Conference of the Centers for Disease Control and Prevention, Atlanta, GA.

Akbar, N. (1991). Mental disorders of African Americans. In R. Jones (Ed.), *Black Psychology* (3rd ed., pp. 339–352). Hampton, VA: Cobb & Henry.

American Psychiatric Association. (2000). *Diagnostic and statistical manual of mental disorders* (4th ed., text rev.). Washington, DC: Author.

Anderson, P. L., Tiro, J. A., Price, A. W., Bender, M. A., & Kaslow, N. J. (2002). Additive impact of childhood emotional, physical, and sexual abuse on suicide attempts among low-impact African American women. *Suicide and Life-Threatening Behavior, 32,* 131–138.

Baldwin, J. A. (1984). African self-consciousness and the mental health of African-Americans. *Journal of Black Studies, 15,* 177–194.

Bell, C. C., Dixie-Bell, D. D., & Thompson, B. (1986). Further studies on the prevalence of isolated sleep paralysis in Black subjects. *Journal of the National Medical Association, 75,* 649–659.

Bell, C. C., Hildreth, C. J., Jenkins, E. J., & Carter, C. (1988). The relationship of isolated sleep paralysis and panic disorder to hypertension.

Journal of the National Medical Association, 80, 289–294.

Breslau, J., Gaxiola-Aguilar, S., Kendler, K. S., Su, M., Williams, D., & Kessler, R. C. (2005). Specifying race–ethnic differences in risk for psychiatric disorder in a USA national sample. *Psychological Medicine, 35,* 1–12.

Breslau, J., Kendler, K. S., Su, M., Gaxiola-Aguilar, S., & Kessler, R. C. (2005). Lifetime risk and persistence of psychiatric disorders across ethnic groups in the United States. *Psychological Medicine, 35,* 317–327.

Bromberger, J. T., Harlow, S., Avis, N., Kravitz, H., & Cordal, A. (2004). Racial/ethnic differences in prevalence of depressive symptoms among middle-aged women: The Study of Women's Health Across the Nation (SWAN). *American Journal of Public Health, 94,* 1378–1385.

Brown, K. A., & Keith, V. M. (2003). The epidemiology of mental disorders and mental health among African American women. In D. R. Brown & V. M. Keith (Eds.), *In and out of our right minds: The mental health of African American women* (pp. 23–58). New York: Columbia University Press.

Brown, K. A., Parker-Dominguez, T., & Sorey, M. (2000). Life stress, social support, and well-being among college-educated African American women. *Journal of Ethnic and Cultural Diversity, 9,* 55–72.

Burr, J. A., Hartman, J. T, & Matteson, D. W. (1999). Black suicide in U.S. metropolitan areas: An examination of the racial inequality and social integration–regulation hypotheses. *Social Forces, 77,* 1049–1081.

Carter, M. M., Miller, O., Sbrocco, T., Suchday, S., & Lewis, E. L. (1999). Factor structure of the Anxiety Sensitivity Index among African American college students. *Psychological Assessment, 11,* 525–533.

Carter, M. M., Sbrocco, T., & Carter, C. (1996). African Americans and anxiety disorders research: Development of a testable theoretical framework. *Psychotherapy, 33,* 449–463.

Carter, M. M., Sbrocco, T., Miller, O., Suchday, S., Lewis, E. L., & Freedman, R. E. (2005). Factor structure, reliability, and validity of the Penn State Worry Questionnaire: Differences between African-American and White-American college students. *Anxiety Disorders, 19,* 827–843.

Centers for Disease Control and Prevention. (2004). Youth risk behavior surveillance—United States, 2003. *Morbidity and Mortality Weekly Report, 53*(SS-2), 1–96.

Cochran, S. D., & Mays, V. M. (1994). Depressive distress among homosexually active African American men and women. *American Journal of Psychiatry, 15,* 524–529.

Cook, J. M., Pearson, J. L., Thompson, R., Black, B. S., & Rabins, P. V. (2002). Suicidality in older African Americans: Findings from the EPOCH Study. *American Journal of Geriatric Psychiatry, 10,* 437–446.

Cordasco, K. M., Eisenman, D. P., Glik, D. C., Golden, J. F., & Asch, S. M. (2007). "They blew the levee": Distrust of authorities among Hurricane Katrina evacuees. *Journal of Health Care for the Poor and Underserved, 18,* 277–282.

Coyne, J. C., & Marcus, S. C. (2006). Health disparities in care for depression possibly obscured by the clinical significance criterion. *American Journal of Psychiatry, 163,* 1577–1579.

Crawford, I., Allison, K. W., Zamboni, B. D., & Soto, T. (2002). The influence of dual-identify development on the psychosocial functioning of African-American gay and bisexual men. *Journal of Sex Research, 39,* 179–189.

Crosby, A. E., & Molock, S. D. (2006). Introduction: Suicidal behaviors in the African American community. *Journal of Black Psychology, 32,* 253–261.

Cummings, S. M., Neff, J. A., & Husaini, B. A. (2003). Functional impairment as a predictor of depressive symptomatology: The role of race, religiosity, and social support. *Health & Social Work, 28,* 23–32.

Early, K. E., & Akers, R. L. (1993). "It's a White thing": An exploration of beliefs about suicide in the African American community. *Deviant Behavior: An Interdisciplinary Journal, 14,* 277–296.

Friedman, S., & Paradis, C. (2002). Panic disorder in African-Americans: Symptomatology and isolated sleep paralysis. *Culture, Medicine, and Psychiatry, 26,* 179–198.

Friedman, S., Smith, L. C., Halpern, B., Levine, C., Paradis, C., Viswanathan, R., et al. (2003). Obsessive–compulsive disorder in a multi-ethnic urban outpatient clinic: Initial presentation and treatment outcome with exposure and ritual prevention. *Behavior Therapy, 34,* 397–410.

Frueh, B. C., Hamner, M. B., Bernat, J. A., Turner, S. M., Keane, T. M., & Arana, G. W. (2002). Racial differences in psychotic symptoms among combat veterans with PTSD. *Depression and Anxiety, 16,* 157–161.

Gallo, J. J., Cooper-Patrick, L., & Lesikar, S. (1998). Depressive symptoms of Whites and African Americans aged 60 years and older. *Journals of Gerontology Series B: Psychological Sciences and Social Sciences, 53B,* 277–286.

Garlow, S., Purselle, D., & Heninger, M. (2005). Ethnic differences in patterns of suicide across the life cycle. *American Journal of Psychiatry, 162,* 319–323.

Goldsmith, S. K., Pellmar, T., Kleinman, A., & Bunney, W. E. (Eds.). (2002). *Reducing suicide: A national imperative.* Washington, DC: National Academies Press.

Greening, L., & Stoppelbein, L. (2002). Religiosity, attributional style, and social support as psychosocial buffers for African American and White adolescents' perceived risk for suicide. *Suicide and Life-Threatening Behavior, 32,* 404–417.

Harris, E. C., & Barraclough, B. (1997). Suicide as an outcome for mental disorders: A meta-analysis. *British Journal of Psychiatry, 170,* 205–228.

Harris, T., & Molock, S. D. (2000). Cultural orientation, family cohesion and family support in suicide ideation and depression among African American college students. *Suicide and Life-Threatening Behavior, 30,* 341–353.

Herek, G. M., Gillis, J. R., Cogan, J. C., & Glunt, E. K. (1997). Hate crime victimization among lesbian, gay, and bisexual adults. *Journal of Interpersonal Violence, 12,* 195–215.

Heurtin-Roberts, S., Snowden, L., & Miller, L. (1997). Expressions of anxiety in African Americans: Ethnography and the Epidemiological Catchment Area Studies. *Culture, Medicine, and Psychiatry, 21,* 337–363.

Hill, P. C., & Pargament, K. I. (2003). Advances in the conceptualization and measurement of religion and spirituality. *American Psychologist, 58,* 64–74.

Joe, S. (2006). Explaining changes in the patterns of Black suicide in the United States from 1981–2002: An age, cohort, and period analysis. *Journal of Black Psychology, 32,* 262–284.

Joe, S., Baser, R. E., Breeden, G., Neighbors, H. W., & Jackson, J. S. (2006). Prevalence of and risk factors for lifetime suicide attempts among Blacks in the United States. *Journal of the American Medical Association, 296,* 2112–2123.

Jones, C., & Shorter-Gooden, K. (2003). *Shifting: The double lives of Black women in America.* New York: HarperCollins.

Juon, H., & Ensminger, M. E. (1997). Childhood, adolescent, and young adult predictors of suicidal behaviors: A prospective study of African Americans. *Journal of Child Psychology and Psychiatry, 38,* 553–563.

Kaslow, N. J., Jacobs, C. H., Young, S. L., & Cook, S. (2006). Suicidal behavior among low-income African American women: A comparison of first-time and repeat suicide attempters. *Journal of Black Psychology, 32,* 349–365.

Kaslow, N. J., Thompson, M. P., Meadows, L. A., Jacobs, D., Chance, S., & Gibb, B. (1998). Factors that mediate and moderate the link between partner abuse and suicidal behavior in African American women. *Journal of Consulting and Clinical Psychology, 66,* 533–540.

Kessler, R. C., Berglund, P., Demler, O., Jin, R., Koretz, D., Merikangas, K. R., et al. (2003). The epidemiology of major depressive disorder: Results from the National Comorbidity Survey Replication (NCS–R). *Journal of the American Medical Association, 23,* 3095–3105.

Kessler, R. C., Berglund, P., Demler, O., Jin, R., Merikangas, K. R., & Walters, E. E. (2005). Lifetime prevalence and age-of-onset distributions of *DSM–IV* disorders in the National Comorbidity Survey Replication. *Archives of General Psychiatry, 62,* 593–602.

Kleinman, A. M., & Good, B. J. (1985). Introduction: Culture and depression. In A. Kleinman & B. Good (Eds.), *Culture and depression: Studies in the anthropology and cross-cultural psychiatry of affect and disorder* (pp. 1–33). Berkeley and Los Angeles: University of California Press.

Kung, H., Pearson, J. L., & Wei, R. (2005). Substance abuse, firearm availability, depressive symptoms, and mental health service utilization among White and African American suicide decedents aged 15 to 64 years. *Annals of Epidemiology, 15,* 614–621.

Kwate, N. A. (2005). The heresy of African-centered psychology. *Journal of Medical Humanities, 26,* 215–235.

Lambert, S. F., Cooley, M. R., Campbell, K. D. M., Benoit, M. Z., & Stansbury, R. (2004). Assessing anxiety sensitivity in inner-city African American children: Psychometric properties of the Childhood Anxiety Sensitivity Index. *Journal of Clinical Child and Adolescent Psychology, 33,* 248–259.

Lester, D. (1998). *Suicide in African Americans.* Hauppauge, NY: Nova Science.

Marion, M. S., & Range, L. M. (2003). African American college women's suicide buffers. *Suicide and Life Threatening Behavior, 33,* 33–43.

Mays, V. M., Cochran, S. D., & Roeder, M. R. (2003). Depressive distress and prevalence of common problems among homosexually active African American women in the United States. *Journal of Psychology & Human Sexuality, 15,* 27–46.

McWhorter, J. (2004). Getting over identity. In T. Jacoby (Ed.), *Reinventing the melting pot: The new immigrants and what it means to be American* (pp. 249–258). New York: Basic Books.

Miller, R. L. (2005). Look what God can do: African American gay men, AIDS, and spirituality. *Journal of HIV/AIDS and Social Services, 4,* 25–46.

Minino, A., Arias, E., Kochanek, K., Murphy, S., & Smith, B. (2002). *Deaths: Final data for 2000* (National Vital Statistics Reports, 50, DHHS

Publication No. PHS 2001-1120). Hyattsville, MD: National Center for Health Statistics.

Miranda, J., Siddique, J., Belin, T., & Kohn-Wood, L. P. (2005). Depression prevalence in disadvantaged young Black women. *Social Psychiatry and Psychiatric Epidemiology, 40,* 253–258.

Monnier, J., Elhai, J. D., Frueh, B. C., Sauvageot, J. A., & Magruder, K. M. (2002). Replication and expansion of findings related to racial differences in veterans with combat-related PTSD. *Depression and Anxiety, 16,* 64–70.

Myers, H. F., Lesser, I., Rodriguez, N., Mira, C. B., Hwang, W., Camp, C., et al. (2002). Ethnic differences in clinical presentation of depression in adult women. *Cultural Diversity and Ethnic Minority Psychology, 8,* 138–152.

Neal, A. M., & Turner, S. M. (1991). Anxiety disorders research with African Americans: Current status. *Psychological Bulletin, 109,* 400–410.

Nisbet, P. A. (1996). Protective factors for suicidal Black females. *Suicide and Life-Threatening Behavior, 26,* 325–341.

O'Carroll, P., Berman, A., Maris, R., & Moscicki, E. (1996). Beyond the Tower of Babel: A nomenclature for suicidology. *Suicide and Life-Threatening Behavior, 26,* 237–252.

Perilla, J. L., Norris, F. H., & Lavizzo, E. A. (2002). Ethnicity, culture, and disaster response: Identifying and explaining ethnic differences in PTSD six months after Hurricane Andrew. *Journal of Social and Clinical Psychology, 21,* 20–45.

Peterson, J. L., Folkman, S., & Bakeman, R. (1996). Stress, coping, HIV status, psychological resources, and depressive mood in African American gay, bisexual, and heterosexual men. *American Journal of Community Psychology, 24,* 461–487.

Pierson, W. D. (1977). White cannibals, Black martyrs: Fear, depression, and religious faith as causes of suicide among new slaves. *Journal of Negro History, 62,* 147–159.

Plant, E. A., & Sachs-Erisson, N. (2004). Racial and ethnic differences in depression: The roles of social support and meeting basic needs. *Journal of Consulting and Clinical Psychology, 72,* 41–52.

Robins, L., & Regier, D. (1991). *Psychiatric disorders in America: The Epidemiologic Catchment Area Study.* New York: Free Press.

Rockett, R. H., Samora, J. B., & Coben, J. H. (2006). The Black–White suicide paradox: Possible effects of misclassification. *Social Science & Medicine, 63,* 2165–2175.

Rosario, M., Rotheram-Borus, M. J., & Reid, H. (1996). Gay-related stress and its correlates among gay and bisexual male adolescents of predominantly Black and Hispanic background. *Journal of Community Psychology, 24,* 136–159.

Roy, A. (2003). African American and Caucasian attempters compared to suicide risk factors: A preliminary study. *Suicide and Life-Threatening Behavior, 33,* 443–447.

Silverman, M. M., Berman, A. L., Nels, D., Sanddal, M. S., O'Carroll, P. W., & Joiner, T. E., Jr. (2007). Rebuilding the Tower of Babel: A revised nomenclature for the study of suicide and suicidal behaviors. Part 2: Suicide-related ideations, communications, and behaviors. *Suicide and Life-Threatening Behavior, 37,* 264–277.

Smith, L. C., Friedman, S., & Nevid, J. (1999). Clinical and sociocultural differences in African American and European American patients with panic disorder and agoraphobia. *Journal of Nervous and Mental Disease, 187,* 549–560.

Somervell, P. D., Leaf, P. J., Weissman, M. M., Blazer, D. G., & Bruce, M. L. (1989). The prevalence of major depression in Black and White adults in five United States communities. *American Journal of Epidemiology, 130,* 725–735.

Stack, S. (1998). Education and risk for suicide: An analysis of African Americans. *Sociological Focus, 31,* 295–302.

Thompson, V. L., Bazile, A., & Akbar, M. (2004). African Americans' perceptions of psychotherapy and psychotherapists. *Professional Psychology: Research and Practice, 35,* 19–26.

U.S. Department of Health and Human Services. (2001). *Mental health: Culture, race, and ethnicity—A supplement to* Mental Health: A Report of the Surgeon General. Rockville, MD: Public Health Service, Office of the Surgeon General.

Walker, R. L. (2007). Acculturation as a risk factor for suicidality among African Americans. *American Journal of Orthopsychiatry, 77,* 386–391.

Walker, R. L., & Bishop, S. (2005). Examining a model of the relation between religiosity and suicidal ideation in a sample of African American and White College Students. *Suicide and Life-Threatening Behavior, 35,* 630–639.

Walker, R. L., Utsey, S. O., Bolden, M. A., & Williams, O. (2005). Do sociocultural factors predict suicidality among persons of African descent living in the U.S.? *Archives of Suicide Research, 9,* 203–217.

Walker, R. L., Van Horn, L., Tinsley, S. C., Northrup, T., Sachs-Ericsson, N., & Joiner, T. E. (2008). *Measurement invariance and the Beck Depression Inventory: Testing racial group differences.* Manuscript submitted for publication.

Wasserman, I. M., & Stack, S. (2000). The relationship between occupation and suicide among African American males, Ohio, 1989–1991. In R. W. Maris, S. S. Canetto, J. L. McIntosh, & M. M. Silverman (Eds.), *Review of suicidology* (pp. 242–251). New York: Guilford Press.

Watkins, D. C., & Neighbors, H. W. (2007). An initial exploration of what "mental health" means to young Black men. *Journal of Men's Health and Gender, 4,* 271–282.

Weems, C. F., Watts, S. E., Marsee, M. A., Taylor, L. K., Costa, N. M., Cannon, M. F., et al. (2007). The psychosocial impact of Hurricane Katrina: Contextual differences in psychological symptoms, social support, and discrimination. *Behaviour Research and Therapy, 45,* 2295–2306.

Weissman, M. M., Bruce, M. L., Leaf, P. J., Florio, L. P., & Holzer, C. (1991). Affective disorders. In D. A. Regier & L. N. Robins (Eds.), *Psychiatric disorders in America: The Epidemiologic Catchment Area Study* (pp. 53–80). New York: Free Press.

Whaley, A. L. (2001). Cultural mistrust and mental health services for African Americans: A review and meta-analysis. *The Counseling Psychologist, 29,* 513–531.

Williams, D. R., Gonzalez, H. M., Neighbors, H., Nesse, R., Abelson, J., Sweetman, J., et al. (2007). Prevalence and distribution of major depressive disorder in African Americans, Caribbean Blacks, and Non-Hispanic Whites. *Archives of General Psychiatry, 64,* 305–315.

Williams, K. E., Chambless, D. L., & Steketee, G. (1998). Behavioral treatment of obsessive–compulsive disorder in African Americans: Clinical issues. *Journal of Behavior Therapy, 29,* 163–170.

Willis, L. A., Coombs, D. W., Cockerham, W. C., & Frison, S. L. (2002). Ready to die: A postmodern interpretation of the increase of African American adolescent male suicide. *Social Science & Medicine, 55,* 907–920.

Willis, L. A., Coombs, D. W., Drentea, P., & Cockerham, W. C. (2003). Uncovering the mystery: Factors of African American suicide. *Suicide and Life-Threatening Behavior, 33,* 412–427.

Wolfgang, M. E. (1959). Suicide by means of victim-precipitated homicide. *Journal of Clinical and Experimental Psychology, 20,* 335–349.

30

PSYCHOSOCIAL ASPECTS OF SICKLE CELL DISEASE

A Primer for African American Psychologists

SHAWN M. BEDIAKO

The term *sickle cell disease* (SCD) refers to a group of hemoglobinopathies (genetic blood disorders) that affect over 250 million people worldwide. Although SCD occurs with varying frequency among diverse racial and ethnic groups (Castro, Chicoye, Greenberg, Haynes, & Peterson, 1994), it is generally perceived to be a condition that is exclusive to persons of African descent (Barbarin & Christian, 1999; Wailoo, 2001). It is not surprising that this perception is dominant in the United States, where nearly 1 out of 400 African Americans (compared to 1 out of 1,400 Latinos and 1 out of 10,000 non-Hispanic Whites) currently cope with some type of SCD, including sickle cell anemia, sickle hemoglobin C disease, or sickle beta thalassemia (Ballas, 2001). It is ironic that, despite the public perception of SCD as a "Black" disease, there is evidence that a sophisticated understanding of the condition is lacking, particularly in communities of color[1] (Ogamdi, 1994; Treadwell, McClough, & Vichinsky, 2006).

Concomitantly, a similar perception of SCD exists among health policy makers and researchers. Although a 1972 congressional mandate provided funds for SCD research and established a program of comprehensive research centers that existed until 2008, SCD remains peripheral to the broader dialogue on race, health care access, and health disparities (Bediako & Griffith, 2007; Bediako, Lavender, & Yasin, 2007; Kirschstein & Ruffin, 2001). Given this current milieu of genomic advances, community health activism, and emphasis on racial and cultural dimensions of health, it is quite remarkable that the relations among race, health disparities, and SCD remain untenable. Furthermore, compared with other chronic conditions, SCD has historically received less attention in the scientific research literature (R. B. Scott, 1970a, 1970b; Smith, Oyeku, Homer, & Zuckerman, 2006)—especially that which examines psychological and behavioral medicine aspects. An average of only 12 peer-reviewed articles per year was published on psychosocial-related aspects of SCD between 1983 and 2007. Such production is hardly adequate to generate a useful body of knowledge on which to develop and implement comprehensive interventions.

Taken together, these facts suggest a critical need for an enhanced knowledge of and sensitivity to the unique demands of SCD, especially among psychological researchers and practitioners. In this chapter, I aim to introduce and summarize selected themes from psychosocial research in SCD to African American psychologists and those who work with African American populations. I first review the literature on psychological, interpersonal, and sociocultural aspects of SCD; a brief discussion follows, in which I highlight the therapeutic implications of these findings. Finally, I offer suggestions that encourage psychologists to develop innovative conceptual frameworks that may potentially improve health outcomes and inform ways to promote psychological adjustment for individuals and families who cope with SCD.

PAIN: THE HALLMARK CHARACTERISTIC OF SICKLE CELL DISEASE[2]

The most commonly reported complication in SCD is recurrent, unpredictable, and severe pain episodes, commonly referred to as *crises* (Grant, Gil, Floyd, & Abrams, 2000). Vaso-occlusive pain crises are the chief reason that individuals with SCD seek medical care (Epstein, Yuen, Riggio, Ballas, & Moleski, 2006; Gil et al., 2004). Psychological factors, such as stress, anxiety, and negative mood are often implicated as precursors to SCD pain (Gil et al., 2003; Porter, Gil, Carson, Anthony, & Ready, 2000; Porter et al., 1998). SCD pain management is often complex because of the interaction between pain and psychological symptoms. Edwards and colleagues (2005), for example, noted that whereas SCD pain contributes to psychological symptoms such as depression and anxiety, it is also the case that psychological symptoms reduce the ability to effectively cope with pain. SCD is perhaps best seen, then, as a condition in which both psychosocial and physiological factors equally exert significant influences on the course of the disease and the concomitant illness experience. Thus, psychologists could play a much more prominent role in contributing to patient adjustment to SCD pain.

SCD pain is often at the core of interpersonal misunderstandings among patients, their families, and health care providers (Barbarin & Christian, 1999). For example, adults may unwittingly acclimate to their experience of SCD pain and blunt their emotional responses to severe pain in ways that do not resemble the typically expected expressions of frowning, grimacing, or sighing when one is in pain. Family members and medical professionals might misinterpret this lack of emotional response as indicating that the individual with SCD is not in severe pain when, in fact, the opposite is true. Such interpersonal conflicts can potentially amplify the SCD pain experience and have deleterious consequences. The cognitive and social psychological implications are obvious in that reliance on heuristics and stereotypes about SCD pain by medical staff, caregivers, or others can have a direct impact on the stress experienced by patients—principally during vaso-occlusive pain episodes. Thus, not only must individuals with SCD contend with physiological and psychological aspects of the disease, but they also face uncertainties about its social perception and the stigma that often accompanies such fears. This is certainly an area in which additional research is needed. A more comprehensive view of SCD can be obtained when more is known about three particular areas: (1) the psychological consequences of the condition, (2) the interpersonal processes involved in adjustment, and (3) sociocultural variables that shape psychological and behavioral adaptation. These issues are gaining more interest among federal funding agencies (National Heart Lung & Blood Institute, 2002), and African American psychologists could potentially play an important role in advancing research in these emerging domains.

PSYCHOLOGICAL CONSEQUENCES OF SICKLE CELL DISEASE

Several studies suggest that the experience of SCD pain may contribute to depression, stress, and an overall poorer quality of life (Schaeffer, Gil, & Porter, 1999). Depressive symptoms are the most commonly reported marker of psychological status in SCD (Alao & Cooley, 2001; Molock & Belgrave, 1994). Rates of clinical depression in samples of youth and adults with SCD range from 30% to 44% in most studies, which are significantly higher than those reported in control samples or the general African American population (Hasan, Hashmi, Alhassen, Lawson, & Castro, 2003; Jenerette, Funk, & Murdaugh, 2005). Although there are mixed findings on whether more stringent cutoff scores yield increased validity in detecting clinical levels of depression in adults with SCD (Grant et al., 2000; Schaeffer, Gil,

Burchinal, et al., 1999), ample empirical evidence suggests that persons who report more frequent and more intense pain episodes are more likely to report depressive symptoms (Barbarin, Whitten, & Bonds, 1994; Hasan et al., 2003; Key, Brown, Marsh, Spratt, & Recknor, 2001; Schaeffer, Gil, Burchinal, et al., 1999).

The stressful aspects of SCD pain have also been underscored in the research literature (Anie & Steptoe, 2003; Barbarin, Whitten, Bond, & Conner-Warren, 1999; Leavell & Ford, 1983). Several studies have reported the negative impact of stress from SCD on patients and families (Anyanwu & Anyanwu, 2001; Brown et al., 2000; Hocking & Lochman, 2005; Noll, Swiecki, Garstein, & Vannatta, 1994; Rao & Kramer, 1993; Thompson, Gil, Abrams, & Phillips, 1992; Thompson, Gil, Burbach, & Keith, 1993), and most of these studies implicitly endorse a causal link that presumes SCD pain as the driving mechanism of increased stress. However, questions about the pain–stress association have arisen over the last decade because of methodological advances, namely the use of daily diaries to assess pain and psychological outcomes (Porter et al., 1998). For example, Porter and colleagues (2000) examined daily diaries among adults with SCD who reported their pain, stress, mood, health care use, and medication use for an average of 94 days. They found that both stress and mood were significantly related to same-day pain ratings in the expected directions. Stress and mood were also associated with health care and medication use during painful episodes. Moreover, the longitudinal nature of the daily diary method allowed these researchers to observe that painful episodes were usually *preceded* by increases in stress 2 days earlier (Porter et al., 2000), suggesting that life stress may play a role in the onset of SCD pain. A subsequent study that used the same method found that the reverse was true for adolescents—SCD pain was predictive of higher stress and lower positive mood on subsequent days (Gil et al., 2003). Gil and colleagues (2004) found similar results in a daily diary study of 41 African American adults with SCD: Pain appeared to be the more potent instigating variable in the pain–mood and pain–stress cycles. It also was observed that positive mood was negatively associated with both same-day and subsequent-day pain, suggesting that positive emotions may counter harmful consequences of pain and other illness symptoms (Gil et al., 2004). To conclude, future research on pain and stress in SCD should emphasize three things: (1) contextual variables that modify the temporal nature of the pain–mood/pain–stress relation; (2) the range of variables that contribute to adolescent versus adult pain, stress, and psychological adjustment; and (3) the role of positive psychological variables, such as optimism, resilience, hope, and psychological well-being. The last point is important given that the majority of psychosocial research in SCD emphasizes morbid, pathological outcomes (e.g., depression, anxiety, and stress). An unintended consequence of such an emphasis is that it precludes examination of factors that promote adjustment and resilience. The literature is replete with examples that paint pejorative portraits of SCD patients, but there is relatively little information about those who cope effectively and their means of adaptation (Abrams, Phillips, & Whitworth, 1994). African American psychologists who study well-being and adjustment could potentially broaden our knowledge on this understudied issue.

Interpersonal Processes

The impact of SCD on interpersonal processes and social relationships has not been fully explicated. For example, some findings suggest that individuals with SCD are at increased risk for social isolation and withdrawal (Atkin & Ahmad, 2001; Noll, Vannatta, Koontz, & Kalinyak, 1996; Rodrigue, Streisand, Banko, & Kedar, 1996; Thomas & Taylor, 2002). Very little research, however, has examined the influence of these factors over time. One area of particular significance concerns the mechanisms by which social withdrawal and isolation limit the career options of young adults and adults with SCD (Day & Chismark, 2006). Financial hardships are sure to be experienced among individuals with SCD who have low levels of academic achievement (which limit earning potential) and restrictions on strenuous physical activity (which limit options for maintaining certain types of employment). Given that there is a general link between employment status and health (Ahs & Westerling, 2006; Elstad, 1995; Sadava, O'Connor, & McCreary, 2000), these issues are essential for understanding SCD outcomes in their proper context. Some researchers have noted employment difficulties among persons with SCD (Davis, 1995; Yardley-Jones, 1999) and higher rates of unemployment compared to African Americans without SCD (Laurence, George, & Woods, 2006). However, there are no current data that describe either the general academic achievement or employment status levels of individuals with SCD. More research is needed that examines the impact of SCD on academic aspirations and educational achievement; the adherence of educational institutions and employers to the provisions of the Americans with Disabilities Act—a federal policy that prohibits discrimination based on disability; and the effects of unemployment and underemployment on the health of adults with SCD.

Other areas of emerging interest that are related to interpersonal processes are concerned with gender and reproductive decision making. With regard to gender, there is little evidence to suggest male–female differences in pain and other pain-related behaviors. One study of 226 adults with SCD in Virginia found no significant differences between men and women in the percentage of days that they experienced pain, the number of pain episodes reported over a 6-month period, or average pain scores (McClish et al., 2006). Yet, in a recent presentation given by researchers developing a health-related quality of life instrument for adults with SCD (Treadwell, Levine, Moucheraud, & Werner, 2006), a common theme expressed in focus groups of men involved concerns that SCD interfered with their idea of "manhood." Anecdotally, in July 2006, I interviewed a 24-year-old African American man who had been recently discharged from the hospital with a severe SCD pain episode. When asked why he had made the decision to play in an outdoor summer league basketball game—despite knowing that being overheated and dehydrated would cause a pain episode—the young man responded that he did not want to be perceived as being "weak" by his friends. Even though he was well aware that such vigorous physical activity in hot weather could lead to a pain episode in which he might be hospitalized, he stated that it was more important to "maintain my status with my boys." Despite the growing interest in masculinity and Black men's health (Courtenay & Keeling, 2000; Hammond & Mattis, 2005; Stibbe, 2004), there are few empirical studies that have explored the experiences of men with SCD. Although most sickle cell research studies related to manhood and masculinity emphasize priapism (Douglas, Fletcher, & Serjeant, 1990; Jagadheesan, Thakur, & Akhtar, 2004; Sirota & Bogdanov, 2000; Wang, Kao, Chen, Tung, & Lung, 2006) or other issues concerning sexual functioning (Chavis & Norman, 1993; Shilalukey et al., 1997), future research should examine broader aspects of gender and masculinity in the context of SCD and should explore their associations with pain, self-care, and adherence to medical regimens.

Similarly, women with SCD must make choices on whether to focus on their health or fulfill a common, socially proscribed gender role—child bearing (Asgharian, Anie, & Berger, 2003; Hill, 1994). In the absence of a cure, the primary means for reducing transmission of SCD comes about by making informed reproductive choices.[3] However, it is sometimes difficult for partners to discuss these issues (Neal-Cooper & Scott, 1988) and even more difficult for women to negotiate the topic. To illustrate, Ashgarian and colleagues (2003) explored reproductive decision-making in women with the sickle cell trait to gain insight into issues surrounding reproductive choices. Thirty-five women were interviewed; not only did the women find it very difficult to talk about their trait status with their partners before they became pregnant, but many women also reported that it was simpler to risk giving birth to an affected child than to commence discussions that could potentially lead to rejection, the likely loss of a relationship, or the opportunity to reproduce. Genetic counseling, although especially relevant to individuals with both the sickle cell trait and SCD, is often perceived negatively in the African American community (Matthews et al., 2000). African American psychologists can potentially assist genetic counselors in understanding the cultural nuances of attitudes toward genetics and reproduction and offer culturally appropriate techniques that individuals with the sickle cell trait and SCD can use to become more skilled in discussing their status with prospective partners or when asking questions to determine their partner's sickle cell trait status.

Sociocultural Influences

Few researchers explicitly consider the direct or indirect influence of sociocultural factors on SCD. In most studies of psychosocial adjustment, sociocultural variables are often *discussed* as important factors in SCD outcomes (Baskin et al., 1998; Christian & Barbarin, 2001; Kaslow & Brown, 1995; K. D. Scott & Scott, 1999), but are rarely *analyzed*. Sociocultural factors are important to assess in SCD because such factors can either strengthen an individual's resolve to overcome debilitating pain or generate anxiety and stigma that undermine effective coping (Barbarin & Christian, 1999). Three areas that show particular promise in this regard pertain to (1) perceived racism, (2) racial identity, and (3) spirituality.

Because SCD has primarily been conceptualized as a "Black" disease, it is reasonable to anticipate that racialized perceptions of health and health care could wield considerable influence on the health-seeking behaviors (Barbarin & Christian, 1999; Tapper, 1999; Wailoo, 2001). One early study examined perceptions of health care quality among parents/guardians of children and young adults who had SCD and medical staff at a treatment clinic (Chestnut, 1994). Results showed that Whites were perceived as receiving better service than Blacks, young children were perceived as receiving better service than the elderly, and the elderly were perceived as getting better service than middle-age adults. The extent to which these perceptions about quality care inhibit health care utilization for sickle cell-related problems is not as well known compared with other studies of racialized perceptions (Benkert & Peters, 2005; F. M. Chen, Fryer, Phillips, Wilson, & Pathman, 2005; Ma & Stafford, 2005; Voils et al., 2005).

Even though some have argued that there is insufficient evidence to propose that racial–ethnic perceptions influence health care (Satel & Klick, 2005), studies conducted with medical professionals suggest otherwise. For example, Telfair, Myers, and Drezner (1998) examined whether 227 multidisciplinary health care providers perceived the race of persons with SCD as an influence in the delivery of health care. The results indicated that African American providers were more likely to perceive race as an influence, whereas White and other-race providers did not. The impact of these perceptions on patients was not directly evaluated in this particular study. However, in another study that explored the hospital experiences of 27 African and African-Caribbean adults with SCD who were previously admitted during a painful episode, Harris, Parker, and Barker (1998) reported evidence of pronounced global psychological distress, depression, and anxiety among those who perceived negative attitudes from hospital staff. Future areas of inquiry in this domain include assessing patient perceptions of respect and trust toward medical staff and the influence of such perceptions on health care utilization and resolution of painful episodes (Beach et al., 2005).

Another vantage point from which to enhance our understanding of the sociocultural context of SCD involves exploring the role of racial identity. Barbarin (1999) compared the family functioning of 71 parents who had children with SCD with that of 50 healthy control participants matched for race and socioeconomic status. He found that, in general, functioning within SCD and control families did not differ, yet racial consciousness, religiosity, and emotional support enhanced the ways that parents coped with the adverse effects of SCD.

More recently, attention has turned to the influence of racial identity variables as predictors of health outcomes in SCD. For example, my colleagues and I (Bediako et al., 2007) tested an exploratory model of the confluence of racial centrality, pain, psychological variables, and health care use in a sample of African American adults with SCD. The results indicated that participants who reported more frequent pain episodes tended to use more health care services and that those who endorsed a highly central African American identity utilized fewer health care services (Bediako et al., 2007). In general, these findings suggest a need for expanded thinking about determinants of health care use in this population beyond psychological and physiological variables. Further exploration of the sociocultural context of SCD is needed that includes highlighting the complex relationships among multidimensional aspects of racial identity and health care use.

Finally, there is a need to examine the impact of religion and spirituality in SCD. Christian and Barbarin (2001) examined the effect of parental religiosity and racial identity on parental reports of child behavioral problems in a sample of 40 low-income African American children from Ohio and southeastern Michigan who had SCD. The results demonstrated the importance of religion as a central sociocultural resource by showing that children whose parents attended church at least weekly had fewer problems compared with those whose parents attended less frequently. In another study that evaluated the role of spirituality on pain in SCD, 71 patients completed a questionnaire addressing their ability to cope with the pain of SCD and their degree of spirituality (Cooper-Effa, Blount, Kaslow, Rothenberg, & Eckman, 2001). The results indicated that participants exhibited high levels of spirituality and religiosity, but the influence of these feelings on coping with SCD was variable: Although spiritual well-being was associated with life control (but not with perceived pain), existential well-being was significantly related to general coping ability. Harrison et al. (2005) purported that religious involvement plays an important role in altering the SCD pain experience. They examined three domains of religiosity/spirituality (i.e., church attendance, prayer/Bible study, intrinsic religiosity) in a sample of 50 SCD patients (Harrison et al., 2005) and found that church attendance was inversely related to measures of pain, even after controlling for age, gender, and disease severity. Although these studies clearly suggest a relation between cognitive aspects of spirituality and behavioral aspects of religiosity, research on other aspects of the spiritual experience and its link to pain and psychosocial outcomes is warranted. I (Bediako, 2005) recently explored the influence of daily spiritual experiences and optimism on self-reported pain severity and perceived stress among 83 adults with SCD. The analyses showed no main effects for spirituality but indicated that higher levels of optimism were associated with lower levels of stress. Although optimism did not moderate the relation between spiritual experiences and both outcomes, trends in the data suggested that when optimism was minimal, spiritual experiences were weakly related to pain and perceived stress and that when optimism was greater, the influence of spiritual experiences on pain and stress was stronger. Overall, these studies imply that even though individuals may report high levels of spiritual experiences, such as closeness to God or finding comfort in their religion, it is important to assess the extent to which patients expect positive things to happen in the future.

Exploration of other within-group differences, such as those due to social class and socioeconomic status, is complicated in SCD research because of an implicit selection bias; that is, most of the research on SCD has been conducted with samples recruited primarily from research hospitals or comprehensive centers that collectively serve only a small percentage of the estimated 115,000 persons with SCD in the United States (Hassell, 2007). Therefore, little is known about the experiences of those who have private insurance, those who are seen at other types of clinics and medical facilities, or those who do not regularly utilize traditional healthcare services. Creative methodological approaches are needed to address this major concern.

Therapeutic Implications

This cursory review of psychosocial aspects of SCD yields several therapeutic implications for clinical and counseling psychologists. First, with regard to pain management, there is a need for culturally appropriate approaches that facilitate effective coping. Psychologists who can effectively impart to clients specific techniques to reduce stress and improve adjustment to pain could perhaps have the greatest impact on altering the pain–stress cycle in SCD. Interventions currently exist that utilize a range of cognitive–behavioral modalities, including biofeedback, meditation/guided imagery, or mindfulness-based stress reduction practices (Gil et al., 2000). It should be noted that these techniques are not inconsistent with an African worldview or other Africultural coping strategies (Lewis-Coles & Constantine, 2006; Utsey, Adams, & Bolden, 2000). However, if these practices were to be integrated within explicitly African-centered frameworks, such as NTU psychotherapy (Gregory, 1997; Mitchell-Jackson, 2006; Phillips, 1990), then perhaps their cultural appeal and overall effectiveness could be broadened. Second, because interpersonal misunderstandings are also central elements in the SCD pain experience, two ways in which psychologists may intervene to promote efficacious outcomes among SCD patients include offering communication skills training and using pertinent family therapy techniques (Boyd-Franklin, Smith Morris, & Bry, 1997). Finally, psychological symptoms such as depression and anxiety may be related to larger interpersonal issues (e.g., employment difficulties, inadequate housing, and problematic social relationships) rather than

SCD pain. Psychologists who are able to enhance coping with such issues would be valuable members of multidisciplinary teams that provide comprehensive care to SCD patients.

Conclusion

Major biomedical advances over the last 2 decades have significantly reduced SCD mortality rates, and a need persists for incorporating a broader range of psychological knowledge into health care protocols. Given that the SCD population is growing both larger and older, there is certainly a need for more research on psychological and social aspects of coping with the illness. Psychologists who are expert in the physiological, psychosocial, and cultural exigencies of SCD will be poised to assume a leadership role in expanding research paradigms. Specifically, African American psychologists could contribute by

- determining optimal ways to provide mental health services to individuals with SCD,
- developing SCD-specific instruments to assess quality of life and psychosocial outcomes,
- assessing the utility of gender-specific transition programs from pediatric to adult care,
- using popular media to counter stigmatization and stereotypes about SCD,
- modifying attitudes toward genetics education and genetic counseling, and
- integrating sociocultural variables into research programs, where appropriate.

While the search for a SCD cure continues, it is imperative to find ways to promote an optimal quality of life for individuals who are currently managing the illness. In this chapter, I have highlighted psychosocial aspects of adapting to SCD pain and contended that psychologists will play a prominent role in improving the provision of effective pain management protocols and developing novel interventions for enhancing psychological adaptation. However, until a critical mass of informed psychologists begin to truly understand SCD, treatment strategies will continue to have a one-dimensional pathophysiological focus.

Notes

1. The commonly held perception that SCD evolved in Africa as a mechanism to reduce malaria is not wholly accurate. Hemoglobin AS (sickle cell trait) and SS (sickle cell anemia) are more resistant to malaria parasites; thus, individuals with one or two sickle alleles are less likely to die from malaria. Conversely, those with "normal" hemoglobin AA do not have the same protections and therefore have higher mortality from malaria. The greater proportion of AS and SS in malaria-prone areas, then, appears to result from natural selection effects on the gene pool.

2. A comprehensive review of the etiology, pathophysiology, and treatment of SCD pain is beyond the scope of this chapter, but several excellent examples provide a concise background of these issues (e.g., Ashley-Koch, Yang, & Olney, 2000; E. Chen, Cole, & Kato, 2004; Edwards et al., 2005).

3. An individual with SCD (Hb SS) cannot have a child with SS if his or her partner has "normal" Hb AA. All children from such unions will have sickle cell trait (Hb AS). However, if a person with SS has a child with a person with AS, there is a 50% chance with each pregnancy that the child will have AS or SS. For two individuals with Hb AS, there is a 50% chance of having a child with AS and a 25% chance of having a child with either AA or SS with each pregnancy.

References

Abrams, M. R., Phillips, G. Jr., & Whitworth, E. (1994). Adaptation and coping: A look at a sickle cell patient population over age 30—An integral phase of the life long developmental process. *Journal of Health & Social Policy, 5,* 141–160.

Ahs, A., & Westerling, R. (2006). Self-rated health in relation to employment status during periods of high and of low levels of unemployment. *European Journal of Public Health, 16,* 294–304.

Alao, A. O., & Cooley, E. (2001). Depression and sickle cell disease. *Harvard Review of Psychiatry, 9,* 169–177.

Anie, K. A., & Steptoe, A. (2003). Pain, mood and opioid medication use in sickle cell disease. *Hematology Journal, 4,* 71–73.

Anyanwu, I., & Anyanwu, E. (2001). Assessment of the psychosocial impacts of sickle cell disease on adolescents and how parents and relatives cope with pain in the family. *International Journal of Adolescent Medicine and Health, 13,* 131–143.

Asgharian, A., Anie, K. A., & Berger, M. (2003). Women with sickle cell trait: Reproductive decision-making. *Journal of Reproductive and Infant Psychology, 21,* 23–33.

Ashley-Koch, A., Yang, O., & Olney, R. S. (2000). Sickle hemoglobin (HbS) allele and sickle cell disease: A HuGE review. *American Journal of Epidemiology, 151,* 839–845.

Atkin, K., & Ahmad, W. I. U. (2001). Living a "normal" life: Young people coping with thalassaemia major or sickle cell disorder. *Social Science & Medicine, 53,* 615–626.

Ballas, S. K. (2001). Sickle cell disease: Current clinical management. *Seminars in Hematology, 38,* 307–314.

Barbarin, O. A. (1999). Do parental coping, involvement, religiosity, and racial identity mediate children's psychological adjustment to sickle cell disease? *Journal of Black Psychology, 25,* 391–426.

Barbarin, O. A., & Christian, M. (1999). The social and cultural context of coping with sickle cell disease: I. A review of biomedical and psychosocial issues. *Journal of Black Psychology, 25,* 277–293.

Barbarin, O. A., Whitten, C. F., Bond, S., & Conner-Warren, R. (1999). The social and cultural context of coping with sickle cell disease: III. Stress, coping tasks, family functioning, and children's adjustment. *Journal of Black Psychology, 25,* 356–377.

Barbarin, O. A., Whitten, C. F., & Bonds, S. M. (1994). Estimating rates of psychosocial problems in urban and poor children with sickle cell anemia. *Health & Social Work, 19,* 112–119.

Baskin, M. L., Collins, M. H., Brown, F., Griffith, J. R., Samuels, D., Moody, A., et al. (1998). Psychosocial considerations in sickle cell disease (SCD): The transition from adolescence to young adulthood. *Journal of Clinical Psychology in Medical Settings, 5,* 315–341.

Beach, M. C., Sugarman, J., Johnson, R. L., Arbalaez, J. J., Duggan, P. S., & Cooper, L. A. (2005). Do patients treated with dignity report higher satisfaction, adherence, and receipt of preventive care? *Annals of Family Medicine, 3,* 331–338.

Bediako, S. M. (2005, September). *Spirituality and optimism in sickle cell disease.* Paper presented at the 33rd annual convention of the Sickle Cell Disease Association of America, Baltimore, MD.

Bediako, S. M., & Griffith, D. M. (2007). Eliminating racial/ethnic health disparities: Reconsidering comparative approaches. *Journal of Health Disparities Research and Practice, 2,* 49–62.

Bediako, S. M., Lavender, A., & Yasin, Z. (2007). Racial centrality and health care utilization among African American adults with sickle cell disease. *Journal of Black Psychology, 33,* 422–438.

Benkert, R., & Peters, R. M. (2005). African American women's coping with health care prejudice. *Western Journal of Nursing Research, 27,* 863–889.

Boyd-Franklin, N., Smith Morris, T., & Bry, B. H. (1997). Parent and family support groups with African American families: The process of family and community empowerment. *Cultural Diversity and Mental Health, 3,* 83–92.

Brown, R. T., Lambert, R., Devine, D., Baldwin, K., Casey, R., Doepke, K., et al. (2000). Risk-resistance adaptation model for caregivers and their children with sickle cell syndromes. *Annals of Behavioral Medicine, 22,* 158–169.

Castro, O., Chicoye, L., Greenberg, J., Haynes, J., & Peterson, K. (1994). Brighter horizons for sickle cell disease. *Patient Care, 28,* 26–44.

Chavis, W. M., & Norman, G. S. (1993). Sexuality and sickle cell disease. *Journal of the National Medical Association, 85,* 113–116.

Chen, E., Cole, S. W., & Kato, P. M. (2004). A review of empirically supported psychosocial interventions for pain and adherence outcomes in sickle cell disease. *Journal of Pediatric Psychology, 29,* 197–209.

Chen, F. M., Fryer, G. E., Phillips, R. L., Wilson, E., & Pathman, D. E. (2005). Patients' beliefs about racism, preferences for physician race, and satisfaction with care. *Annals of Family Medicine, 3,* 138–143.

Chestnut, D. E. (1994). Perceptions of ethnic and cultural factors in the delivery of services in the treatment of sickle cell disease. *Journal of Health & Social Policy, 5,* 215–242.

Christian, M. D., & Barbarin, O. A. (2001). Cultural resources and psychological adjustment of African American children: Effects of spirituality and racial attribution. *Journal of Black Psychology, 27,* 43–63.

Cooper-Effa, M., Blount, W., Kaslow, N., Rothenberg, R., & Eckman, J. (2001). Role of spirituality in patients with sickle cell disease. *Journal of the American Board of Family Practice, 14,* 116–122.

Courtenay, W. H., & Keeling, R. P. (2000). Men, gender, and health: Toward an interdisciplinary approach. *Journal of American College Health, 48,* 243–246.

Davis, C. (1995). Sickle cell anemia: An overview posing an employment quandary. *Vocational Evaluation & Work Adjustment Bulletin, 28,* 20–23.

Day, S., & Chismark, E. (2006). The cognitive and academic impact of sickle cell disease. *Journal of School Nursing, 22,* 330–335.

Douglas, L., Fletcher, H., & Serjeant, G. R. (1990). Penile prostheses in the management of impotence in sickle cell disease. *British Journal of Urology, 65,* 533–535.

Edwards, C. L., Scales, M. T., Loughlin, C., Bennett, G. G., Harris-Peterson, S., Decastro, L. M., et al. (2005). A brief review of the pathophysiology, associated pain, and psychosocial issues in sickle cell disease. *International Journal of Behavioral Medicine, 12,* 171–179.

Elstad, J. I. (1995). Employment status and women's health: Exploring the dynamics. *Acta Sociologica, 38,* 231–249.

Epstein, K., Yuen, E., Riggio, J. M., Ballas, S. K., & Moleski, S. M. (2006). Utilization of the office, hospital and emergency department for adult sickle cell patients: A five-year study. *Journal of the National Medical Association, 98,* 1109–1113.

Gil, K. M., Carson, J. W., Porter, L. S., Ready, J., Valrie, C., Redding-Lallinger, R., et al. (2003). Daily stress and mood and their association with pain, health-care use, and school activity in adolescents with sickle cell disease. *Journal of Pediatric Psychology, 28,* 363–373.

Gil, K. M., Carson, J. W., Porter, L. S., Scipio, C., Bediako, S. M., & Orringer, E. (2004). Daily mood and stress predict pain, health care use, and work activity in African American adults with sickle-cell disease. *Health Psychology, 23,* 267–274.

Gil, K. M., Carson, J. W., Sedway, J. A., Porter, L. S., Schaeffer, J. J. W., & Orringer, E. (2000). Follow-up of coping skills training in adults with sickle cell disease: Analysis of daily pain and coping practice diaries. *Health Psychology, 19,* 85–90.

Grant, M. M., Gil, K. M., Floyd, M. Y., & Abrams, M. (2000). Depression and functioning in relation to health care use in sickle cell disease. *Annals of Behavioral Medicine, 22,* 149–157.

Gregory, S. D. P. (1997). "Of mind, body, and spirit": Therapeutic foster care—An innovative approach to healing from an NTU perspective. *Child Welfare Journal, 76,* 127–142.

Hammond, W. P., & Mattis, J. S. (2005). Being a man about it: Manhood meaning among African American men. *Psychology of Men & Masculinity, 6,* 114–126.

Harris, A., Parker, N., & Barker, C. (1998). Adults with sickle cell disease: Psychological impact and experience of hospital services. *Psychology, Health & Medicine, 3,* 171–179.

Harrison, M. O., Edwards, C. L., Koenig, H. G., Bosworth, H. B., Decastro, L., & Wood, M. (2005). Religiosity/spirituality and pain in patients with sickle cell disease. *Journal of Nervous and Mental Disease, 193,* 250–257.

Hasan, S. P., Hashmi, S., Alhassen, M., Lawson, W., & Castro, O. (2003). Depression in sickle cell disease. *Journal of the National Medical Association, 95,* 533–537.

Hassell, K. (2007, September). *Sickle cell disease population estimation: Application of available contemporary data to traditional methods.* Paper presented at the 35th annual convention of the National Sickle Cell Disease Program and the Sickle Cell Disease Association of America, Washington, DC.

Hill, S. A. (1994). Motherhood and the obfuscation of medical knowledge: The case of sickle cell disease. *Gender & Society, 8,* 29–47.

Hocking, M. C., & Lochman, J. E. (2005). Applying the transactional stress and coping model to sickle cell disorder and insulin-dependent diabetes mellitus: Identifying psychosocial variables related to adjustment and intervention. *Clinical Child and Family Psychology Review, 8,* 221–246.

Jagadheesan, K., Thakur, A., & Akhtar, S. (2004). Irreversible priapism during olanzapine and lithium therapy. *Australian and New Zealand Journal of Psychiatry, 38,* 381.

Jenerette, C., Funk, M., & Murdaugh, C. (2005). Sickle cell disease: A stigmatizing condition that may lead to depression. *Issues in Mental Health Nursing, 26,* 1081–1101.

Kaslow, N. J., & Brown, F. (1995). Culturally sensitive family interventions for chronically ill youth: Sickle cell disease as an example. *Family Systems Medicine, 13,* 201–213.

Key, J. D., Brown, R. T., Marsh, L. D., Spratt, E. G., & Recknor, J. C. (2001). Depressive symptoms in adolescents with a chronic illness. *Children's Health Care, 30,* 283–292.

Kirschstein, R. L., & Ruffin, J. (2001). A call to action. *Public Health Reports, 116,* 515–516.

Laurence, B., George, D., & Woods, D. (2006). Association between elevated depressive symptoms and clinical disease severity in African-American adults with sickle cell disease. *Journal of the National Medical Association, 98,* 365–369.

Leavell, S. R., & Ford, C. V. (1983). Psychopathology in patients with sickle cell disease. *Psychosomatics, 24,* 23–37.

Lewis-Coles, M. E. L., & Constantine, M. G. (2006). Racism-related stress, Africultural coping, and religious problem-solving among African Americans. *Cultural Diversity and Ethnic Minority Psychology, 12,* 433–443.

Ma, J., & Stafford, R. S. (2005). Quality of U. S. outpatient care: Temporal changes and racial/ethnic disparities. *Archives of Internal Medicine, 165,* 1354–1361.

Matthews, A. K., Cummings, S., Thompson, S., Wohl, V., List, M., & Olopade, O. I. (2000). Genetic testing of African Americans for susceptibility to inherited cancers: Use of focus groups to determine factors contributing to participation *Journal of Psychosocial Oncology, 18,* 1–19.

McClish, D. K., Levenson, J. L., Penberthy, L. T., Roseff, S. D., Bovbjerg, V. E., Roberts, J. D., et al. (2006). Gender differences in pain and healthcare utilization for adult sickle cell patients: The PiSCES project. *Journal of Women's Health, 15,* 146–154.

Mitchell-Jackson, A. (2006). The Black patient and traditional psychotherapy: Implications and possible extensions. *Journal of Community Psychology, 11,* 303–307.

Molock, S. D., & Belgrave, F. Z. (1994). Depression and anxiety in patients with sickle cell disease: Conceptual and methodological considerations. *Journal of Health & Social Policy, 5,* 39–53.

National Heart Lung & Blood Institute. (2002). *Workshop on adults with sickle cell disease: Meeting unmet needs.* Retrieved November 3, 2005, from http://www.nhlbi.nih.gov/meetings/scdmtg/execsum.htm

Neal-Cooper, F., & Scott, R. B. (1988). Genetic counseling in sickle cell anemia: Experiences with couples at risk. *Public Health Reports, 103,* 174–178.

Noll, R. B., Swiecki, E., Garstein, M., & Vannatta, K. (1994). Parental distress, family conflict, and role of social support for caregivers with or without a child with sickle cell disease. *Family Systems Medicine, 12,* 281–294.

Noll, R. B., Vannatta, K., Koontz, K., & Kalinyak, K. (1996). Peer relationships and emotional well-being of youngsters with sickle cell disease. *Child Development, 67,* 423–436.

Ogamdi, S. O. (1994). African American students' awareness of sickle cell disease. *Journal of American College Health, 42,* 234–236.

Phillips, F. B. (1990). NTU psychotherapy: An Afrocentric approach. *Journal of Black Psychology, 17,* 55–74.

Porter, L. S., Gil, K. M., Carson, J. W., Anthony, K. K., & Ready, J. (2000). The role of stress and mood in sickle cell disease pain: An analysis of daily diary data. *Journal of Health Psychology, 5,* 53–63.

Porter, L. S., Gil, K. M., Sedway, J. A., Ready, J., Workman, E., & Thompson, R. J. (1998). Pain and stress in sickle cell disease: An analysis of daily pain records. *International Journal of Behavioral Medicine, 5,* 185–203.

Rao, R. P., & Kramer, L. (1993). Stress and coping among mothers of infants with a sickle cell condition. *Children's Health Care, 22,* 169–188.

Rodrigue, J. R., Streisand, R., Banko, C., & Kedar, A. (1996). Social functioning, peer relations, and internalizing and externalizing problems among youths with sickle cell disease. *Children's Health Care, 25,* 37–52.

Sadava, S. W., O'Connor, R., & McCreary, D. R. (2000). Employment status and health in young adults: Economic and behavioural mediators? *Journal of Health Psychology, 5,* 549–560.

Satel, S., & Klick, J. (2005). The Institute of Medicine report: Too quick to diagnose bias. *Perspectives in Biology and Medicine, 48,* S15–25.

Schaeffer, J. J. W., Gil, K. M., Burchinal, M., Kramer, K. D., Nash, K. B., Orringer, E., et al. (1999). Depression, disease severity, and sickle cell disease. *Journal of Behavioral Medicine, 22,* 115–126.

Schaeffer, J. J. W., Gil, K. M., & Porter, L. S. (1999). Sickle-cell disease. In A. R. Block, E. F. Kremer, & E. Fernandez (Eds.), *Handbook of pain syndromes: Biopsychosocial perspectives* (pp. 569–588). Mahwah, NJ: Lawrence Erlbaum.

Scott, K. D., & Scott, A. A. (1999). Cultural therapeutic awareness and sickle cell anemia. *Journal of Black Psychology, 25,* 316–335.

Scott, R. B. (1970a). Health care priority and sickle cell anemia. *Journal of the American Medical Association, 214,* 731–734.

Scott, R. B. (1970b). Sickle cell anemia: High prevalence and low priority. *New England Journal of Medicine, 282,* 164–165.

Shilalukey, K., Kaufman, M., Bradley, S., Francombe, W. H., Amankwah, K., Goldberg, E., et al. (1997). Counseling sexually active teenagers treated with potential human teratogens. *Journal of Adolescent Health, 21,* 143–146.

Sirota, P., & Bogdanov, I. (2000). Priapism associated with risperidone treatment. *International Journal of Psychiatry in Clinical Practice, 4,* 237–239.

Smith, L. A., Oyeku, S. O., Homer, C., & Zuckerman, B. (2006). Sickle cell disease: A question of equity and quality. *Pediatrics, 117,* 1763–1770.

Stibbe, A. (2004). Health and the social construction of masculinity in *Men's Health* magazine. *Men and Masculinities, 7,* 31–51.

Tapper, M. (1999). *In the blood: Sickle cell anemia and the politics of race.* Philadelphia: University of Pennsylvania Press.

Telfair, J., Myers, J., & Drezner, S. (1998). Does race influence the provision of care to persons with sickle cell disease? Perceptions of multidisciplinary providers. *Journal of Health Care for the Poor and Underserved, 9,* 184–195.

Thomas, V. J., & Taylor, L. M. (2002). The psychosocial experience of people with sickle cell disease and its impact on quality of life: Qualitative findings from focus groups. *British Journal of Health Psychology, 7,* 345–363.

Thompson, R. J., Gil, K. M., Abrams, M. R., & Phillips, G. (1992). Stress, coping, and psychological adjustment of adults with sickle cell disease. *Journal of Consulting and Clinical Psychology, 60,* 433–440.

Thompson, R. J., Gil, K. M., Burbach, D. J., & Keith, B. R. (1993). Psychological adjustment of mothers of children and adolescents with sickle cell disease: The role of stress, coping methods, and family functioning. *Journal of Pediatric Psychology, 18,* 549–559.

Treadwell, M. J., Levine, R., Moucheraud, C., & Werner, E. (2006, September). *Sickle cell disease health-related quality of life questionnaire development project.* Paper presented at the 34th annual convention of the Sickle Cell Disease Association of America, Dallas, TX.

Treadwell, M. J., McClough, L., & Vichinsky, E. (2006). Using qualitative and quantitative strategies to evaluate knowledge and perceptions about sickle cell disease and sickle cell trait. *Journal of the National Medical Association, 98,* 704–710.

Utsey, S. O., Adams, E. P., & Bolden, M. (2000). Development and initial validation of the Africultural Coping Systems Inventory. *Journal of Black Psychology, 26,* 194–215.

Voils, C. I., Oddone, E. Z., Weinfurt, K. P., Friedman, J. Y., Schulman, K. A., & Bosworth, H. B. (2005). Who trusts healthcare institutions? Results from a community-based sample. *Ethnicity & Disease, 15,* 97–103.

Wailoo, K. (2001). *Dying in the city of the blues: Sickle cell anemia and the politics of race and health.* Chapel Hill: University of North Carolina Press.

Wang, C. S., Kao, W. T., Chen, C. D., Tung, Y. P., & Lung, F. W. (2006). Priapism associated with typical and atypical antipsychotic medications. *International Clinical Psychopharmacology, 21,* 245–248.

Yardley-Jones, A. (1999). What are the implications of sickle cell anaemia? *Occupational Medicine, 49,* 55–56.

PART VII

Practice:
Prevention and Interventions

31

COUNSELING AND PSYCHOTHERAPY WITH AFRICAN AMERICANS

MADONNA G. CONSTANTINE, REBECCA M. REDINGTON, AND SHEILA V. GRAHAM

Studies (e.g., Swartz et al., 1998) have shown that African Americans are only half as likely as Whites to seek mental health services. When African Americans do engage in services, they engage in shorter periods of treatment and have higher premature termination rates from treatment (e.g., Sue, Fujino, Hu, Takeuchi, & Zane, 1991). In fact, the National Comorbidity Survey (Kessler, 1994) reported that only 16% of African Americans with a diagnosable mood disorder saw a therapist, and less than one third saw a health care provider of any kind. Within college populations, African Americans also are less likely to use mental health services (e.g., Constantine, Chen, & Ceesay, 1997).

In general, the level of psychopathology for African Americans often is overestimated, whereas their prognosis tends to be underestimated (Ridley, 2005). Various studies (e.g., Barnes, 2004; Loring & Powell, 1988) have reported that African Americans are consistently overdiagnosed with schizophrenia and underdiagnosed with depression. Individuals diagnosed with schizophrenia received this diagnosis more than Latino and White patients, even when there was no difference in symptom presentation (Mukherjee, Shukla, Woodle, Rosen, & Olarte, 1983). These data suggest that racism directed at African Americans exists strongly within the field of psychology.

In an effort to encourage psychologists to be culturally competent in working with African Americans and other socially oppressed groups, the American Psychological Association (2003) put forth the "Guidelines on Multicultural Education, Training, Research, Practice, and Organizational Change for Psychologists." These guidelines serve as a framework from which psychologists and other mental health professionals learn to understand the role of cultural forces (e.g., race and ethnicity) in their practice. Furthermore, they advocate for participation in social justice work in order to advance cultural knowledge among those in the psychology profession. Despite these guidelines, African Americans continue to have less access to mental health services and are less likely to get their mental health needs met as compared with Whites (U.S. Department of Health and Human Services, 2001).

The stigma associated with seeking psychological help certainly influences the extent to which African Americans use formal mental health services (Wallace & Constantine, 2005). For example, many African American college students are more likely to seek academic and vocational counseling, rather than interpersonal counseling, in light of the perceived stigma associated with the interpersonal counseling. Similarly, Sanders Thompson, Bazile, and Akbar (2004) found that African Americans were more comfortable engaging in counseling when it was termed *counseling* rather than *psychotherapy* because of the increased stigma associated with the latter. In addition, because spirituality is central in the lives of many African Americans, oftentimes they would prefer to discuss their concerns with religious leaders or within the confines of their own personal faith (Martin, 2007). Moreover, many African Americans believe it is inappropriate to speak frankly about their problems in public, particularly in places such as mental health organizations (Boyd-Franklin & Franklin, 2000).

In this chapter, we review theoretical writings and empirical research focused on issues relevant to mental health practice with African Americans, including a discussion of African Americans' views of mental health and within group differences. We also discuss Africentric cultural values because, in providing effective treatment, clinicians working with African American clients must consider the extent to which their clients adhere to these values and the ways in which the values can be integrated into their treatment plans. Finally, we discuss approaches and interventions that could assist counselors and psychologists to better meet the mental health needs of African Americans.

African Americans and Mental Health

The fields of counseling and psychology historically have been dominated by the teachings and theories of White psychologists (Sue & Sue, 2008). As a result, counseling conceptualizations over the past century have been rooted primarily in Eurocentric ideals and perspectives of mental health functioning (e.g., individuality, direct verbal communication, emotional expressiveness, etc.). Despite greater attention paid to counseling culturally diverse populations over the past several years, and despite increased scholarly writings and research concerning the experiences of African Americans in recent decades, there remains a relative dearth of literature focused on African Americans in the fields of counseling and psychology.

Of the mental health research that does exist, investigators have found that African Americans' opinions about counseling contributed to their greater reluctance than White individuals to seek psychological counseling (Hall & Tucker, 1985; Snowden, 2001). Prior to their utilization of mental health services, African Americans tend to report more positive attitudes about counseling services than do White people (Diala et al., 2000). After services have commenced, however, many African Americans tend to report more negative attitudes than do White individuals (Diala et al., 2000; Hall & Tucker, 1985). Some African Americans' negative attitudes about counselors and the counseling process may derive from feelings of cultural mistrust, racial identity attitudes, and expectations about therapists' treatment of race and racism in the context of therapeutic relationships.

Cultural Mistrust

Theoretical literature regarding cultural mistrust suggests that African Americans harbor a generalized suspicion of White people, which stems from a long history of oppression and race-related injustices (see Chap. 22, this volume, for a review). Thus, researchers (e.g., Duncan, 2003; Nickerson, Helms, & Terrell, 1994; Watkins, Terrell, Miller, & Terrell, 1989; Whaley, 2001) have investigated the extent to which cultural mistrust restricts the willingness of African Americans to establish working relationships with White counselors. Watkins et al. (1989) found that Blacks who were more mistrustful of Whites had lower and more negative expectations for therapy. Black individuals also were found to perceive White counselors as less credible (Poston, Craine, & Atkinson, 1991) and less cross-culturally competent (Fyffe, 2000), and they were more likely to prematurely terminate mental health services (Terrell & Terrell, 1984).

In their study of Black college students, Nickerson et al. (1994) found that cultural mistrust was the most consistent and powerful predictor of help-seeking attitudes. Students with higher levels of cultural mistrust had negative attitudes about undergoing counseling with a staff of primarily White counselors. They expected therapy with these counselors would be less relevant, effective, and satisfying. There was no significant relationship between attitudes about mental illness and attitudes about seeking counseling. A study of African Americans with severe mental illnesses revealed that high levels of cultural mistrust were associated with a preference for ethnically and racially similar counselors, even though they asserted that White clinicians were better trained than African American counselors (Whaley, 2001). Ridley (2005) concurred with these researchers, suggesting that, because of cultural mistrust attitudes, Black clients may be reluctant to disclose personal information to their therapists. Cultural mistrust certainly may represent a strong barrier to effective mental health care for some African Americans.

Racial Identity Attitudes

Research (e.g., Bosch & Cimbolic, 1994; Ponterotto, Alexander, & Hinkston, 1988) has indicated that as African Americans reach more advanced racial identity statuses, they become more inclined to prefer counselors of their same race. Want, Parham, Baker, and Sherman (2004) found that, as African Americans endorsed encounter attitudes (i.e., those stemming from a crisis or an event that challenges how one interprets the world) and immersion–emersion attitudes (i.e., those that cause withdrawal from the dominant culture and immersion in African American culture), their preference changed from White counselors to African American counselors. In Want et al.'s study, participants' low favorability ratings for White counselors were not dependent on the racial consciousness of the counselors, whereas their high favorability for African American counselors was dependent on levels of racial awareness. Campbell-Flint (2000) supported these findings in her study of Black male inmates; inmates who had higher immersion–emersion or internalization attitudes also had strong preferences for Black counselors. Research clearly points to the need for counselors to understand how racial identity attitudes affect their African American clients. However, it is essential that these findings do not overshadow the importance of White counselors being aware of their own racial identity development and attitudes.

Counselors and psychologists are not able to make effective decisions regarding therapeutic interventions without the knowledge and awareness of the racial identity variables in the interaction between them and their clients. Such interventions include discussions of the dynamics of race within the counseling dyad. Discussions of race play an important role in the development of the therapeutic alliance between therapists and their clients. Thompson and Jenal (1994) determined that counselors who avoided the topic of race with their African American clients missed a therapeutic connection and instead provoked avoidance or hostility in their clients.

Expectations About Issues of Race and Racism in Counseling

Raising the issue of race early in the therapeutic relationship conveys cultural sensitivity and may address clients' concerns about a racially different counselor. In dyads with racially responsive counselors, clients deem therapy more effective overall (Ward, 2005). Knox, Burkard, Johnson, Suzuki, and Ponterotto (2003) found that European American counselors reported that they typically discussed race only when clients raised it. These participants also stated that they did not typically discuss race in racially unmatched dyads. In fact, unlike African American therapists, European American therapists reported feelings of discomfort when discussions of race arose in cross-racial dyads.

Furthermore, some scholars (e.g., Constantine, Lewis, Conner, & Sanchez, 2000) have addressed counselors' reluctance to explore religious or spiritual issues in therapy with African Americans and the implication that many African Americans thereby avoid seeking psychological help. The inability of White counselors to effectively process racial and religious dynamics in the room with their clients underlies the preference of African American clients for racially similar counselors and points to the increasing need for greater multicultural education for counseling trainees. Many people of color rate Black American and Latino American counselors as more culturally competent than White American counselors (Constantine, 2001). Low ratings of multicultural competence have been associated with lower levels of a working alliance, therapist empathy, therapist expertness, attractiveness, and trustworthiness, and satisfaction with therapy (Constantine, 2002b; Fuertes et al., 2006).

Among some of the challenges African Americans face in counseling is the lack of multicultural competence reflected in covert forms of racism, in particular, *racial microaggressions*, which are subtle forms of racism that take the shape of communicating insulting and demeaning messages to people of color (Solórzano, Ceja, & Yosso, 2000). Constantine (2007) found that manifestations of racial microaggressions within White therapist and African American client counseling dyads had deleterious effects for African American clients. Her research indicated that perceived racial microaggressions were negatively correlated with White therapists' general counseling abilities and multicultural counseling competence. In addition, African American clients exposed to racial microaggressions in treatment perceived a weakened therapeutic alliance between themselves and their White counselors. Constantine also indicated that the perpetration of racial microaggressions may be especially detrimental within the confines of the counseling relationship in light of the helping nature of the counseling profession. Thus, their effects may be even more harmful when committed by helping professionals than when committed by individuals outside of this context.

Within-Group Differences Among African Americans

Gender

In general, African American women have been found to uphold more positive help-seeking attitudes than do African American men (Wallace & Constantine, 2005). The "Superwoman" syndrome imposed on many African American women, however, also has been found to contribute to the depression, exhaustion, and stress-related illnesses experienced by this subgroup (Coker, 2004). Believed to be rooted in survival mechanisms necessary during times of slavery, African American women today continue to suffer from a perpetuation of the Superwoman syndrome, which may prevent them from seeking treatment when needed.

Gender influences African American women's utilization of mental health services in yet another unique way. African American women have to contend not only with racism but also with sexism, from people both within and outside of their own community. However, because of the unified position against racism by African American men and women, it sometimes is difficult for African American women to challenge African American men about their sexist remarks and actions. African American women may not want to isolate themselves from men within their ethnic group. However, by silencing the impact of sexism they are ignoring a force of oppression that is very real and painful (Sanchez-Hucles & Jones, 2007). Therapists who do not recognize both systems of oppression are not treating African American women in their entirety; neither are they addressing the totality of these women's experiences.

Negative effects of socialization and discrimination on African American men also are pervasive. African American men are expected to fulfill gender roles that emphasize job stature and financial success, yet they live in a society that places limits on these goals for them. Furthermore, they are socialized and expected to express their emotions through competition instead of by exposing and discussing their feelings. Stereotypic associations of Black men and violence also require a hypervigilance and intrapsychic energy on the part of Black men in an attempt to ameliorate the fear their presence may evoke in others (Franklin & Boyd-Franklin, 2000). Often cited as evidence of the discrimination experienced by Black men in society is the overrepresentation of this population in incarceration and unemployment statistics (Pieterse & Carter, 2007). The *invisibility syndrome* (Franklin & Boyd-Franklin, 2000) has been used to describe a set of processes and outcomes used by African Americans to manage the personal stress caused by racial slights and a subjective experience of invisibility. These ongoing stressors are believed to produce within African American men a cluster of debilitating symptoms (e.g., frustration focused on racial injustices, anger, jaded outlook, pervasive discontent and disgruntlement, depression, loss of hope). Achieving visibility while maintaining dignity and integrity within a racist society, however, is also a stressful psychological process and a difficult feat to maintain. Because pressures in society affect African American men and women in unique ways, mental health professionals must be aware and prepared to incorporate the lived experiences of both genders into treatment.

Lesbian, Gay, and Bisexual Populations

Lesbian, gay, and bisexual (LGB) African Americans also must negotiate more than one oppressed identity. For example, these individuals struggle to claim their sexual identity because they fear losing support from their families and communities (Chung, 2007). Victims of covert and overt racism, LGB African Americans do not want to risk separation from the people who support and understand them. Furthermore, many are unwilling to sacrifice their heterosexist privilege. It is particularly difficult for African American men, who are trying to fulfill gender role stereotypes of what a Black man should be, to openly reveal their sexual identity to others (Sanchez-Hucles & Jones, 2007). For LGB members of the African American community who wish to take part in religious activities, rejection on the part of the church denies access to the religious as well as the emotional and social support often provided to members of congregations (Miller, 2007). If counselors and psychologists are not aware of the intricate ways in which race and sexual orientation interact, they will not be effective when working with African American LGB clients.

Social Class and Age

Research exploring the role of social class in the help-seeking behaviors of individuals has been inconsistent. Studies have found no significant differences among individuals from various social classes regarding help-seeking behaviors. However, most studies that have examined social class and counseling have used between-group analyses in which different racial groups have been compared with each other. There is a lack of research on help-seeking and social class that examines within-group differences; however, in one such study, the results indicate a significant difference. In an investigation of help-seeking behaviors of 631 Black men and women, Neighbors (1991) found that low-income Black individuals were 1.5 times more likely to use mental health services than high-income Black individuals, regardless of their presenting problems. Younger participants in this study (18- to 24-year-olds) also were found to be less likely to seek counseling services than older, adult Black males.

In another study focusing on social class and race, Duncan (2003) determined that older Black college students of lower socioeconomic status held more positive beliefs about seeking mental health services than did younger students of higher socioeconomic status. Psychologists (e.g., Ali, Friedman, Hall, & Leathers, 2007; Constantine, 2002a) have pointed to the lack of awareness among mental health practitioners regarding the intersections of social class and race and have encouraged practitioners to consider how their clients of color negotiate both of these social contexts. African American clients whose class issues are not attended to in counseling may be reluctant to return for more services. Further research investigating the variables of social class and age within the African American population, as well as other groups of people of color, is warranted to better understand their impact on counseling.

Africentric Cultural Values

To understand the ways in which people of African descent view and approach the world, counselors and psychologists must be familiar with the philosophical framework reflected in their values, attitudes, and customs (Utsey, Adams, & Bolden, 2000). The values and behaviors of African Americans today have been found by scholars to be a mixture of African traditions and philosophies bequeathed through generations from the descendants of African slaves in the United States. This set of beliefs and assumptions founded in African cultural traditions and through which people of African descent define themselves, others, and the world around them, has been termed *Africentric cultural values* (Belgrave, Brome, & Hampton, 2000; Brook & Pahl, 2005; Constantine, Alleyne, Wallace, & Franklin-Jackson, 2006; Morris, 2001). Africentrism emphasizes, among other things, communalism, interdependence, spirituality, and cooperation (Brook & Pahl, 2005).

Spirituality

Spirituality has been defined as a belief in the existence of a force greater than oneself that is more important than material goods (Randolph & Banks, 1993). In an Africentric worldview, spirituality also is a means of self-definition and a primary coping resource. Lewis-Coles and

Constantine (2006) defined *religious problem-solving styles* as patterns of coping within a larger spiritual and religious system that attributes responsibility for coping with problems to the self and/or a higher power. Individuals enacting problem-solving coping styles that also are collaborative and religious believe that they, along with a higher power, are collectively responsible for the resolution of a particular problem.

Understanding the importance of spirituality within the African American community helps elucidate the intricate role of the church as a resource for spiritual, personal, and political support (Morris, 2001; see also Chap. 7, this volume, for a review). When confronting serious personal difficulties and adversity, African Americans more frequently employ various forms of religious and spiritual coping or problem solving, more so than any other racial–ethnic group (Lewis-Coles & Constantine, 2006). In a sample of African American young adults, religiosity, in the form of church attendance, also was found to be related to less deviance and familial tolerance of deviance (Brook & Pahl, 2005). Not only may spirituality provide a sense of power in acknowledging each individual's ability to transform and transcend his or her circumstances, but it also provides an assured sense of purpose by highlighting the connections between one's consciousness and destiny (Cervantes & Parham, 2006).

Communalism

Communalism emphasizes the importance of human relationships and the interrelatedness of people. This belief recognizes the value and uniqueness of every member of the community and places an emphasis on unity and not uniformity (Cokley, 2005). Similarly, *collectivism* prioritizes group, family, and ethnic group goals above those of the individual, all the while maintaining interdependence within a family or ethnic group (Cokley, 2005; Wallace & Constantine, 2005). A combination of African cultural traditions and the importance of kinship relationships, which often were broken during years of slavery, resulted in a reliance on support networks of both biological and nonbiological relationships that now is called *communalism*. Brook and Pahl (2005) further noted that this value may be more salient in low-income urban communities than in middle-class suburban communities.

Communalism appears to play an intricate role in the well-being of African Americans. In a sample of African American adolescent girls, Constantine, Alleyne, and colleagues (2006) found perceived social support from peers to be positively predictive of self-esteem. This may suggest that aspects of communalism could help buffer negative mental health indices. When African Americans experience distress, family members, close friends, and community members are viewed as primary resources of assistance, and such resources generally are exhausted before formal mental health systems are accessed (Wallace & Constantine, 2005). More unfamiliar formal services also may be avoided because of shame and embarrassment associated with psychological concerns and may be reserved for use by persons with more severe mental illnesses (Sanders Thompson et al., 2004).

Harmony

People of African descent tend to value *harmony* (Morris, 2001), or the belief that all aspects of one's life must be balanced and interconnected (Belgrave et al., 2000). This perspective is reminiscent of *consubstantiation*, a philosophy that posits that everything in the universe is functionally connected and that people are an extension of their environment and the collective consciousness. Because this consubstantiative worldview emphasizes harmony with nature, effective coping for many African Americans may require an ability to harmonize life's events with the surrounding environment. Coping may therefore be viewed as an effort to maintain a balance among one's physical, metaphysical, collective/communal, and spiritual/psychological existences (Cervantes & Parham, 2006; Utsey et al., 2000). This balance, however, also must be maintained during times of hardship. Although family members, close friends, and trusted community members are the first tier of access when in duress, African Americans may not immediately disclose their problems to even the closest members of their communities in order to preserve harmony and avoid burdening loved ones (Wallace & Constantine, 2005).

Other Africentric Cultural Values

Belgrave et al. (2000) summarized several additional Africentric cultural values. For example, time as a social phenomenon is the belief that time is created as a consequence of interpersonal interaction and is not in itself an entity. Sensitivity to emotional cues, or *affect sensitivity*, is the belief that feelings are an essential method of getting to know or being in tune with other's experiences. Oral communication also is valued over written ideas and thoughts. Learning through multimodal or multidimensional methods, such as visual, aural, tactile, and modal methods, also is preferred over unimodal methods. Finally, for many African Americans value is placed on their ability to interpret negative situations from a positive viewpoint.

African Americans today exhibit and endorse any combination of the values outlined above (Constantine, Alleyne et al., 2006; Morris, 2001), and the ways in which they are employed may be as diverse as the population itself. Much research has linked the presence or absence of these values to the mental health of African Americans (Lewis-Coles & Constantine, 2006; Liddle, Jackson-Gilfort, & Marvel, 2006; Wallace & Constantine, 2005). In the following section, we explore more in-depth the role Africentric values play in the maintenance of mental health for the African American community.

Maintaining Mental Health and Well-Being

As noted earlier, formal mental health services (e.g., individual and group counseling) are generally underutilized in the Black community. After controlling for sociodemographic factors, African Americans are only half as likely as European Americans to receive formal mental health services (Sanders Thompson & Alexander, 2006), are generally more likely to attend fewer counseling sessions, and have a tendency to terminate therapy prematurely (Sue & Sue, 2003). Furthermore, African Americans have been found to be more likely to seek emergency mental health services in emergency departments during times of crisis as opposed to therapeutic prevention or ongoing treatment (Morris, 2001).

A variety of explanations have been posed to better understand this underutilization of services. It has been suggested, for example, that members of the Black community may associate mental health care services with psychopharmacology and psychiatric concerns (Dana, 2002) and thus view them as secondary to community-based supports, such as family, friends, and relationships built through religious activities (Constantine et al., 2000). The underutilization of traditional mental health services by African Americans also may be a reflection of alternate coping mechanisms that are activated to cope with psychological and environmental stressors. When confronted with stressful situations, for example, African Americans have been found to rely on family, community, and social support networks, often employing coping strategies reflective of the religious and/or spiritual belief systems outlined earlier (Daly, Jennings, Beckett, & Leashore, 1995). Research has also shown that the adherence to Africentric cultural values has been found to be positively associated with moral judgment and peer and adult relationships in African American adolescents (Woods & Jagers, 2003). Furthermore, the endorsement of Africentric values have resulted in a reduction of psychological symptoms such as depression, anxiety, and anger, as well as a promotion of a greater sense of well-being (Constantine, Alleyne, et al., 2006). In studies with Black female adolescents, Africentric values were found to be positively correlated with self-esteem (Akbar, Chambers, & Sanders Thompson, 2001; Constantine, Alleyne, et al., 2006), a factor known to protect against problematic behaviors and negative mental health outcomes (Thomas, Townsend, & Belgrave, 2003). In a culturally diverse adolescent sample, Morsi (1999) found that prosocial resiliency factors, such as perceived social support, ameliorated the detrimental effects of exposure to violent and traumatic life events. Other coping strategies enacted during times of stress include prayer, seeking guidance, and forming affiliations with other African Americans (Utsey et al., 2000). It is clear that in order to successfully meet the mental health needs of African Americans, mental health treatments must draw from the principles of Africentric values most beneficial and attractive to this community.

Nontraditional forms of mental health treatment, such as Brody and colleagues' (2006) family-centered preventive intervention program (i.e., the Strong African American Families

Program), are necessary. This model operates from a strength-based "competence-promoting perspective" wherein families, not experts, are assumed to possess the required skills and competencies to raise children. The use of this program with a sample of 332 rural African American families with children showed a significant increase in targeted parenting behaviors and regulated, communicative parenting. High-risk behavior among the youth in the sample also decreased significantly. In addition, Corneille, Ashcroft, and Belgrave (2005) examined the effectiveness of cultural curricula within various interventions for African American adolescents. They determined that African American adolescent girls who participated in Project Napa, an intervention designed to increase resiliency factors pertaining to ethnic identity, scored significantly higher on Africentric cultural values, racial identity, and self-concept related to body image than those whose intervention was not infused with a cultural curriculum. In Corneille et al.'s study, African American female youth enrolled in the Cultural Experiences in Prevention Project, a culturally enhanced drug prevention program, showed significantly higher drug and alcohol refusal self-efficacy than a comparison group of girls enrolled in a noncultural drug prevention program. However, more interventions grounded in Africentric values and designed to meet specific needs of the African American population are needed. In the following section, we suggest interventions that may be employed by individual practitioners or mental health centers serving the African American community.

Suggested Approaches and Interventions

Despite the increased emphasis placed on multicultural counseling over the last couple of decades, mental health professionals must make a greater commitment to working with African Americans in culturally appropriate and relevant ways. Research (e.g., Botvin, Schinke, Epstein, Diaz, & Botvin, 1995) has shown that culturally responsive therapy has enhanced clinical outcomes for African Americans and led to longer stays in treatment. In a study of antisocial African American adolescents, Liddle et al. (2006) outlined seven factors that contributed to the success of an empirically based treatment. These factors serve as a model for other culturally based individual and group treatment processes. These recommendations, phrased to apply to African Americans of all ages and with various presenting concerns, are as follows:

1. The Eurocentric nature and values of the fields of counseling and psychology likely contribute to the lower frequencies with which African Americans seek mental health treatment. Incorporating accurate cultural knowledge and attending to cultural factors in clients' lives therefore would reflect cultural awareness in treatment approaches.

2. The use of multiple systems and theoretical counseling frameworks might further meet the diverse mental health needs within the African American community.

3. Focusing on risk and protective factors for African American clients acknowledges existing contextual barriers, such as institutional, cultural, and individual racism (J. M. Jones, 1997), that this population routinely experiences.

4. Because many African Americans have come to mistrust formal mental health services, actively involving clients in forming goals for therapy likely will facilitate the development of trust in therapeutic situations.

5. To lengthen periods of active treatment and decrease premature treatment termination rates with African American clients, counselors and psychologists should use cultural themes to encourage client engagement in the therapeutic process.

6. Encouraging and advocating for African American clients to connect with mentors and role models within their communities might further incorporate the value of communalism outlined earlier.

7. Counselors and psychologists can have a greater impact on the well-being of their African American clients by acting as social change agents, acknowledging the systemic barriers faced by many African Americans, and teaching these clients skills to help them negotiate the systems in which they live.

In the following section, we elaborate on the preceding seven points and suggest additional tools for counselors who work with African American clients.

Effective Counseling Skills When Working With African American Clients

In light of the Africentric cultural values held by many African Americans, there are concrete strategies clinicians can employ throughout the duration of treatment to help reduce the disparities in mental health services provided to this population. Although clinicians generally are encouraged to expediently engage clients in a therapeutic alliance, therapists who work with African American clients should approach this process cautiously and temper the pace at which they expect the alliance to be formed. Counselors can attend to observed verbal and nonverbal cues expressed by the client, thereby allowing the client to set the pace of the interaction (Boyd-Franklin, 1989; Parham, 2002). This slower pace is particularly important given the level of mistrust that African American clients may experience when encountering the mental health system. It also is essential that therapists openly acknowledge this mistrust and discuss it in a way that helps legitimize clients' experiences. Furthermore, counselors should be cognizant of the behaviors they use to form the therapeutic alliance. For people of African descent, connections are often symbolized through the exchange of energy. Counselors should expand on traditional introductory behaviors, such as a formal handshake, when greeting their clients to acknowledge the energy that is exchanged in a relationship between two individuals (Parham, 2002). Alternative greeting behaviors could take many forms depending on the various aspects of the client (e.g., gender, sexual orientation) but may include an embrace or a verbal ritual to invite ancestors into the shared space.

Overall, it is imperative that clinicians consider multiple aspects of spirituality when working with African American clients. African American clients may define their concerns spiritually, attributing their problems to the will of God (Hines & Boyd-Franklin, 2005). In these cases, counselors should be careful not to invalidate the impact of spirituality on everyday experiences. Alternatively, counselors should not make assumptions regarding the extent to which spirituality plays a role in the life of their clients, because African Americans may express spiritual values in different ways. Therapists should engage their clients in dialogue around their specific spiritual beliefs and practices and address how they would like spirituality to be integrated in their treatment (Martin, 2007). Sometimes, counselors may be required to take a more passive role given their clients' belief that God will serve as the primary entity in dealing with their concerns. Phillips (1998) called therapists' attention to the term *NTU* (pronounced "in-to"), a central African Bantu term representative of a universal force/energy believed to be responsible for all creation, incorporating health, life, spirituality, and energy. Therapy incorporating this traditional African philosophy focuses on four central principles (i.e., harmony, balance, authenticity, and interconnectedness). In NTU-focused psychotherapy, the therapist serves as a spiritual guide whose primary goal is to assist the client in stimulating his or her own healing. To accomplish these tasks, the therapist must remain aware of his or her own energy, all the while remaining in harmony with the spirit-energy of the client. The therapist also is encouraged to stay centered and connected to the healing relationship in order to "experience authentic love" toward the client. NTU represents a specific framework for acknowledging the importance of allowing the client's spiritual values to guide the work of the therapeutic relationship.

In assessing clients' concerns, therapists should be mindful to focus not solely on psychopathology and debilitating aspects of clients' presenting concerns, but to also address the strength and resilience exhibited by these clients (Parham, 2002). This strength-based focus is a necessary foundation to the integration into the therapeutic work of institutionally based barriers African Americans face on a daily basis. It is essential that counselors address these social and environmental barriers in the course of treatment, because they may play an important role in the way in which clients understand their presenting concerns. African tradition emphasizes that psychological well-being and harmony occur within the context of relationships and the community (Fletcher, 1998). By extension, distress occurs not only interpsychically but also is represented in the connections African American clients have with their macro-systems (Sue & Sue, 2003).

Therapists need to acknowledge their language, as well as the language used by their clients, in discussing and assessing various psychological disorders (Mitchell & Herring, 1998). For example, when assessing feelings of depression and suicide with African American clients counselors can get a more accurate response if culturally acceptable terms are used. Discussing feelings of depression as "the blues" (a culturally accepted musical term) may enable African American clients to more comfortably discuss their feelings of sadness and hopelessness (Mitchell & Herring, 1998).

As with terminology, diagnoses should be made with culturally appropriate instruments. In a meta-analytical study, R. T. Jones, Brown, Davis, Rosell, and Shenoy (1998) reported that some of the most frequently used psychological assessment tools may not be valid measures when used with African Americans despite psychometrically sound instrumentality. These assessments, however, are widely used in studies with African American subsamples and in clinical practice with this population. The Diagnostic Interview Schedule, for example, which is widely used with African American clients, has been argued to be less accurate in capturing their symptomatology. Jones et al. clearly conveyed the importance of counselors' awareness of the shortcomings of commonly used assessment tools and emphasized the need for counselors to interpret results cautiously when using these instruments with African American clients. Counselors should examine the norming samples of instruments before using them and locate diagnostic tools normed on African American samples for use with their African American clients.

Within the course of therapy, African American clients will best be served by counselors and psychologists who are flexible in their theoretical orientation. These mental health professionals should be willing to incorporate aspects of orientations that are best suited to the needs of the client with whom they are working. Furthermore, counselors should recognize the unique cultural assumptions inherent in all theoretical orientations (Parham, 2002). For example, many theoretical orientations call on therapists to be objective (e.g., not offering advice or opinions, not self-disclosing therapist information) in working with clients. When working with African American clients, however, it may be important to be somewhat subjective from time to time, by providing advice to clients when warranted. Although traditional psychological orientations also promote the value of having an internal locus of control, it is imperative that counselors recognize the external and potentially oppressive systems influencing the experiences of African American, such that operating solely from an internal locus of control would be difficult or nearly impossible. When setting goals with their clients, counselors should recognize that some desired life changes may need to be considered in the context of institutional barriers (Sue & Sue, 2003). Mental health professionals are further encouraged to expand their work beyond the traditional confines of individual practice by adopting flexible roles, including that of advocate and social change agent, in response to diverse clients' needs (Constantine et al., 2002; Morris, 2001). Clinicians may be called on to educate members of the African American community in local institutions and churches about mental health concerns and available services. They can further partake in public policy initiatives that address barriers to equity in service and access and increase the visibility of mental health care services to communities of color.

Encouraging the use of community support systems inherent in African American communities can be a simple yet effective form of treatment intervention. Morris (2001) recommended that psychologists and other mental health professionals do the following: adopt flexible roles; be sensitive to cultural idiosyncrasies and be willing to discuss racial differences; include the church and extended family in the assessment and therapy process; consider the relevance of problem-solving approaches that address clients' daily stresses; focus not on deficits but on the client's social, emotional, and cultural strengths; and use clients' cultural contexts as the foundation for diagnostic clarification and inquiry.

Flexibility in the role as counselor also extends to the setting of the therapeutic relationship. When working with African American clients, the office may not always serve as the best location for therapy (Parham, 2002); counselors should be imaginative with their clients in determining the most comfortable spaces to engage the process (e.g., clients' homes or outdoor spaces). Furthermore, counselors may invite their clients to incorporate culturally relevant music, poetry, and other art forms into the therapeutic process, because these creative forms of expressions may facilitate clients' discussion of their concerns. The presence of cultural artifacts in the therapeutic setting, both within the therapy room and in waiting areas, also may increase the comfort level of African American clients (Parham, 2002).

In addition to attending to the therapeutic locale, counselors must attend to the structure of the therapy session itself. Many Western-based theoretical orientations call for 45- to 50-minute therapy sessions to maintain rigid boundaries around time, and clients who arrive late for a session often are labeled *resistant* to the process (Hines & Boyd-Franklin, 2005). However, many African American clients who are unfamiliar with and mistrustful of the mental health system may equate it to the medical system, where long waiting periods, despite appointment times, are the norm. Thus, reviewing the norms and expectations for therapy with clients at the onset of counseling will enable counselors to better interpret their behaviors.

Mental health professionals who endorse Western values of individualism and autonomy may unintentionally cast African American clients operating from a communalistic/collectivistic value orientation as troubled, enmeshed, or dependent. Knowledge of Africentric values and awareness of the psychotherapeutic processes through which they define and evaluate psychological functioning are therefore essential. The use of books, journals, and resources that focus specifically on the population of African Americans, such as the *Journal of Black Psychology*, will better enable mental health professionals to begin to understand African consciousness and African-centered community interventions.

Most important, counselors and psychologists must acknowledge the existence of racism in both its overt and covert forms. They must recognize that racism is not a factor external from themselves but one they may unknowingly perpetuate in their own counseling practices. Exploration of one's own racial identity is a critical component in becoming more culturally competent in working with people of color. Without this level of self-awareness, counselors and psychologists will not be able to effectively address race and racism in the context of their work with clients. Also, as discussed earlier, ignoring such issues within therapeutic dyads significantly contributes to the premature termination and reluctance for African Americans to engage in counseling in order to address their concerns and struggles.

References

Akbar, M., Chambers, J. W., Jr., & Sanders Thompson, V. L. (2001). Racial identity, Africentric values, and self-esteem in Jamaican children. *Journal of Black Psychology, 27,* 341–358.

Ali, S. R., Friedman, A., Hall, T., & Leathers, L. (2007). Social class considerations. In M. G. Constantine (Ed.), *Clinical practice with people of color* (pp. 198–211). New York: Teachers College Press.

American Psychological Association. (2003). Guidelines on multicultural education, training, research, practice, and organizational change for psychologists. *American Psychologist, 58,* 377–402.

Barnes, A. (2004). Race, schizophrenia, and admission to state psychiatric hospitals. *Administration and Policy in Health, 31,* 241–252.

Belgrave, F. Z., Brome, D. R., & Hampton, C. (2000). The contribution of Africentric values and racial identity to the prediction of drug knowledge, attitudes, and use among African American youth. *Journal of Black Psychology, 26,* 386–401.

Bosch, R., & Cimbolic, P. (1994). Black students' use of college university counseling centers. *Journal of College Student Development, 25,* 212–216.

Botvin, G., Schinke, S. P., Epstein, J. A., Diaz, T., & Botvin, E. M. (1995). Effectiveness of culturally focused and generic skills training approaches to alcohol and drug abuse prevention among minority adolescents: Two-year follow-up results. *Psychology of Addictive Behaviors, 9,* 183–194.

Boyd-Franklin, N. (1989). *Black families in therapy.* New York: Guilford Press.

Boyd-Franklin, N., & Franklin, A. J. (2000). *Boys into men: Raising our African American teenage sons.* New York: Dutton.

Brody, G. H., Murray, V. M., Gerrard, M., Gibbons, F. X., McNair, L., Brown, A. C., et al. (2006). The

Strong African American Families Program: Prevention of youths' high-risk behavior and a test of a model of change. *Journal of Family Psychology, 20,* 1–11.

Brook, J. S., & Pahl, K. (2005). Protective role of ethnic and racial identity and aspects of an Africentric orientation against drug use among African American young adults. *Journal of Genetic Psychology, 3,* 329–345.

Campbell-Flint, M. E. C. (2000). Relation of level of Black identity to destructive behaviour, emotional disturbance, mental health attitudes and help-seeking behaviours: A study of Black male inmates. (Doctoral dissertation, Virginia Commonwealth University, 2000). *Dissertation Abstracts International, 60*(11-B), 5764.

Cervantes, J. M., & Parham, T. A. (2006). Toward a meaningful spirituality for people of color: Lessons for the counseling practitioner. *Cultural Diversity and Ethnic Minority Psychology, 11,* 69–81.

Chung, Y. B. (2007). Lesbian, gay, and bisexual people of color. In M. G. Constantine (Ed.), *Clinical practice with people of color* (pp. 143–161). New York: Teachers College Press.

Coker, A. (2004). *Counseling African American women: Issues, challenges, and intervention strategies.* Retrieved August 10, 2007, from http://counselingoutfitters.com/vistas/vistas_2004_Title.htm

Cokley, K. O. (2005). Racial(ized) identity, ethnic identity, and Afrocentric values: Conceptual and methodological challenges in understanding African American identity. *Journal of Counseling Psychology, 52,* 517–526.

Constantine, M. G. (2001). Predictors of observer ratings of multicultural therapy competence in Black, Latino, and White American trainees. *Journal of Counseling Psychology, 48,* 456–462.

Constantine, M. G. (2002a). The intersection of race, ethnicity, gender, and social class in counseling: Examining selves in cultural contexts. *Journal of Multicultural Counseling and Development, 30,* 210–215.

Constantine, M. G. (2002b). Predictors of satisfaction with counseling: Racial and ethnic minority clients' attitudes toward counseling and ratings of their counselors' general and multicultural counseling competence. *Journal of Counseling Psychology, 49,* 255–263.

Constantine, M. G. (2007). Racial microaggressions against African American clients in cross-racial counseling relationships. *Journal of Counseling Psychology, 54,* 1–16.

Constantine, M. G., Alleyne, V. L., Wallace, B. G., & Franklin-Jackson, D. C. (2006). Africentric cultural values: Their relation to positive mental health in African American Adolescent girls. *Journal of Black Psychology, 32,* 141–154.

Constantine, M. G., Chen, E. C., & Ceesay, P. (1997). Intake concerns of racial and ethnic minority students at a university counseling center: Implications for developmental programming and outreach. *Journal of Multicultural Counseling and Development, 25,* 210–218.

Constantine, M. G., Kindaichi, M., Arorash, T. J., Donnelly, P. C., & Jung, K. K. (2002). Clients' perceptions of multicultural counseling competence: Current status and future directions. *The Counseling Psychologist, 30,* 407–416.

Constantine, M. G., Lewis, E. L., Conner, L. C., & Sanchez, D. (2000). Addressing spiritual and religious issues in counseling African Americans: Implications for counselor training and practice. *Counseling and Values, 45,* 28–38.

Corneille, M. A., Ashcroft, A. M., & Belgrave, F. Z. (2005). What's culture got to do with it? Prevention programs for African American adolescent girls. *Journal of Health Care for the Poor and Underserved, 16,* 38–47.

Daly, A., Jennings, J., Beckett, J. O., & Leashore, B. R. (1995). Effective coping strategies of African Americans. *Social Work, 40,* 240–248.

Dana, R. H. (2002). Mental health services for African Americans: A cultural/racial perspective. *Cultural Diversity and Ethnic Minority Psychology, 8,* 3–18.

Diala, C., Muntaner, C., Walrath, C., Nickerson, K. J., LaVeist, T. A., & Leaf, P. J. (2000). Racial differences in attitudes towards professional mental health care and in the use of services. *American Journal of Orthopsychiatry, 70,* 455–464.

Duncan, L. E. (2003). Black male college students' attitudes toward seeking psychological help. *Journal of Black Psychology, 29,* 68–86.

Fletcher, B. J. (1998). Spirituality, grieving and mental well-being. In R. L. Jones (Ed.), *African American mental health* (pp. 135–149). Hampton, VA: Cobb & Henry.

Franklin, A. J., & Boyd-Franklin, N. (2000). Invisibility syndrome: A clinical model of the effects of racism on African-American males. *American Journal of Orthopsychiatry, 70,* 33–41.

Fuertes, J. N., Stracuzzi, T. L., Bennett, J., Scheinnholtz, J., Mislowack, A., Hersh, M., et al. (2006). Therapist multicultural competency: A study of therapy dyads. *Psychotherapy: Theory, Research, Practice, Training, 43,* 480–490.

Fyffe, D. C. (2000). Effects of trust, cultural mistrust, counselor's race and race sensitive orientation on perceived trustworthiness in Black college women (Doctoral dissertation, Hofstra University, 2000). *Dissertation Abstracts International, 61,* 3-B.

Hall, L. E., & Tucker, C. M. (1985). Relationships between ethnicity, conceptions of mental illness, and attitudes associated with seeking psychological help. *Psychological Reports, 57,* 907–916.

Hines, P. M., & Boyd-Franklin, N. (2005). African American families. In M. McGoldrick, J. Giordano, & N. Garcia-Preto (Eds.), *Ethnicity and family therapy* (pp. 87–100). New York: Guilford Press.

Jones, J. M. (1997). *Prejudice and racism.* New York: McGraw-Hill.

Jones, R. T., Brown, R., Davis, M., Rosell, J., & Shenoy, U. (1998). African Americans in behavioral therapy and research: The need for cultural considerations. In R. L. Jones (Ed.), *African American mental health* (pp. 135–149). Hampton, VA: Cobb & Henry.

Kessler, R. C. (1994). The national comorbidity study of the United States. *International Review of Psychiatry, 6,* 365–376.

Knox, S., Burkard, A. W., Johnson, A. J., Suzuki, L. A., & Ponterotto, J. G. (2003). African American and European American therapists' experiences of addressing race in cross racial psychotherapy dyads. *Journal of Counseling Psychology, 50,* 466–481.

Lewis-Coles, M. E., & Constantine, M. G. (2006). Racism-related stress, Africultural coping, and religious problem-solving among African Americans. *Cultural Diversity and Ethnic Minority Psychology, 12,* 433–443.

Liddle, H. A., Jackson-Gilfort, A., & Marvel, F. A., (2006). An empirically supported and culturally specific engagement and intervention strategy for African American adolescent males. *American Journal of Orthopsychiatry, 75,* 215–225.

Loring, M., & Powell, B. (1988). Gender, race, and DSM–III: A study of the objectivity of psychiatric diagnostic behavior. *Journal of Health and Social Behavior, 29,* 1–22.

Martin, J. (2007). African American populations. In M. G. Constantine (Ed.), *Clinical practice with people of color* (pp. 33–45). New York: Teachers College Press.

Miller, R. L. (2007). Legacy denied: African American gay men, AIDS, and the Black Church. *Social Work, 52,* 51–61.

Mitchell, A., & Herring, K. (1998). *What the blues is all about: Black women overcoming stress and depression.* New York: Perigee Books.

Morris, E. F. (2001). Clinical practices with African American juxtaposition of standard clinical practices and Africentricism. *Professional Psychology: Research and Practice, 32,* 563–572.

Morsi, D. S. (1999). Adolescent exposure to violence: Antecedents and consequences. *Dissertation Abstracts International, 59*(10-B), 5312.

Mukherjee, S., Shukla, S., Woodle, J., Rosen, M. A., & Olarte, S. (1983). Misdiagnosis of schizophrenia in bipolar patients: A multiethnic comparison. *American Journal of Psychiatry, 140,* 1571–1574.

Neighbors, H. W. (1991). Mental health. In J. Jackson (Ed.), *Life in Black America* (pp. 221–237). Newbury Park, CA: Sage.

Nickerson, K. J., Helms, J. E., & Terrell, F. (1994). Cultural mistrust, opinions about mental illness and Black students' attitude toward seeking psychological help from White counselors. *Journal of Counseling Psychology, 41,* 378–385.

Parham, T. A. (2002). *Counseling persons of African descent: Raising the bar of practitioner competence.* Thousand Oaks, CA: Sage.

Phillips, F. B. (1998). Spirit-energy and NTU psychotherapy. In R. L. Jones (Ed.), *African American mental health* (pp. 135–149). Hampton, VA: Cobb & Henry.

Pieterse, A. L., & Carter, R. T. (2007). An examination of the relationship between general life stress, racism-related stress, and psychological health among Black men. *Journal of Counseling Psychology, 54,* 101–109.

Ponterotto, J. G., Alexander, C. M., & Hinkston, J. A. (1988). Afro-American preference for counselor characteristics: A replication and extension. *Journal of Counseling Psychology, 33,* 175–182.

Poston, C. W., Craine, M., & Atkinson, D. R. (1991). Counselor dissimilarity confrontation, client cultural mistrust and willingness to self-disclose. *Journal of Multicultural Counseling and Development, 19,* 65–73.

Randolph, S. M., & Banks, D. H. (1993). Making a way out of no way: The promise of Africentric approaches to HIV prevention. *Journal of Black Psychology, 19,* 204–214.

Ridley, C. R. (2005). *Overcoming intentional racism in counseling and therapy: A practitioner's guide to intentional intervention* (2nd ed.). Thousand Oaks, CA: Sage.

Sanchez-Hucles, J., & Jones, N. (2007). Gender issues. In M. G. Constantine (Ed.), *Clinical practice with people of color* (pp. 183–197). New York: Teachers College Press.

Sanders Thompson, V. L., & Alexander, H. (2006). Therapists' race and African American client's reactions to therapy. *Psychotherapy, Theory, Research, Practice, Training, 43,* 99–110.

Sanders Thompson, V. L., Bazile, A., & Akbar, M. (2004). African Americans' perceptions of psychotherapy and psychotherapists. *Professional Psychology: Research and Practice, 35,* 19–26.

Snowden, L. R. (2001). Barriers to effective mental health services for African Americans. *Mental Health Services Research, 3,* 181–187.

Solórzano, D., Ceja, M., & Yosso, T. (2000). Critical race theory, racial microaggressions, and campus racial climate: The experiences of African American college students. *Journal of Negro Education, 69,* 60–73.

Sue, S. Fujino, D., Hu, L., Takeuchi, D., Zane, N. (1991). Community mental health services for ethnic minority groups: A test of the cultural responsiveness hypothesis. *Journal of Consulting and Clinical Psychology, 59,* 533–540.

Sue, D. W., & Sue, D. (2003). *Counseling the culturally diverse* (4th ed.). Hoboken, NJ: Wiley.

Sue, D. W., & Sue, D. (2008). *Counseling the culturally diverse* (5th ed.). Hoboken, NJ: Wiley.

Swartz, M. S., Wagner, H. R., Swanson, J. W., Burns, B. J., George, L. K., & Padgett, D. K. (1998). Comparing use of public and private mental health services: The enduring barriers of race and age. *Community Mental Health Journal, 34,* 133–144.

Terrell, F., & Terrell, S. (1984). Race of counselor, client sex, cultural mistrust level, and premature termination from counseling among Black clients. *Journal of Counseling Psychology, 31,* 371–375.

Thomas, D. E., Townsend, T. G., & Belgrave, F. Z. (2003). The influence of cultural and racial identification on the psychosocial adjustment of inner-city African American children in school. *American Journal of Community Psychology, 32,* 217–228.

Thompson, C. E., & Jenal, S. T. (1994). Interracial and intraracial quasi-counseling interactions when counselors avoid discussing race. *Journal of Counseling Psychology, 41,* 484–491.

U.S. Department of Health and Human Services. (2001). *Mental health: Culture, race and ethnicity—A supplement to* Mental Health: A Report of the Surgeon General. Rockville, MD: Public Health Office, Office of the Surgeon General.

Utsey, S. O., Adams, E. P., & Bolden, M. (2000). Development and initial validation of the Africultural Coping Systems Inventory. *Journal of Black Psychology, 26,* 194–215.

Wallace, B. C., & Constantine, M. G. (2005). Africentric cultural values, psychological help-seeking attitudes, and self-concealment in African American college students. *Journal of Black Psychology, 31,* 369–385.

Want, V., Parham, T. A., Baker, R. C., & Sherman, M. (2004). African American students' ratings of Caucasian and African American counselors varying in racial consciousness. *Cultural Diversity and Ethnic Minority Psychology, 10,* 123–136.

Ward, E. C. (2005). Keeping it real: A grounded theory study of African American clients engaging in counseling at a community mental health agency. *Journal of Counseling Psychology, 52,* 471–481.

Watkins, C. E., Terrell, F., Miller, F., & Terrell, S. (1989). Cultural mistrust and its effects on expectational variables in Black client-White counselor relationships. *Journal of Counseling Psychology, 36,* 447–450.

Whaley, A. L. (2001). Cultural mistrust of White mental health clinicians among African Americans with severe mental illness. *American Journal of Orthopsychiatry, 71,* 252–256.

Woods, L. N., & Jagers, R. J. (2003). Are cultural values predictors of moral reasoning in African American adolescents. *Journal of Black Psychology, 29,* 102–118.

32

THERAPY WITH AFRICAN AMERICAN MEN AND WOMEN

KUMEA SHORTER-GOODEN

One of the challenges in exploring the psychology of African Americans is the problem of assuming or conveying that all African Americans are alike, the tendency to overlook the tremendous within-group variability, the danger of overgeneralizing. Psychologists have increasingly been calling our attention to the importance of multiple identities (Reid, 2002). Gender, in particular, is a core aspect of most people's sense of self. In the United States, race–ethnicity and gender together tend to be the most salient characteristics contributing to one's sense of identity (Reid & Comas-Díaz, 1990) and thus to one's worldview.

Even though both African American men and women must contend with racism, the lens of gender means that how Black women experience racial bias and bigotry may be different from the way that Black men experience it (V. G. Thomas, 2004). Understanding the "intersectionality" of identities is critical (Reid & Comas-Díaz, 1990).

The focus of this chapter is on gender issues in psychotherapy with African Americans, with particular attention to both the psychological themes and issues with which Black women and men wrestle and approaches and considerations for effective therapy. Because of the breadth of this topic, this review is limited to counseling and psychotherapy with adult African Americans.

One danger in focusing on gender differences is in implying that there are few similarities between African American men and women. Meta-analyses of research on the general U.S. population reveal that there are tremendous similarities between men and women (Hyde, 2005). Hyde (2005) cautioned against overinflating gender differences when in fact there are so many commonalities. Thus, the task here is to illuminate gender differences, in order to develop a more differentiated understanding of Black men and women, without conveying that Black men and Black women hail from different planets.

I begin with a brief look at what gender is, and then I explore gender differences in African Americans' psychological challenges and problems. This is followed by a discussion of gender differences in treatment considerations and approaches. I conclude the chapter with a critique of the literature and recommendations for future scholarship. Throughout, I use the terms *African American* and *Black* interchangeably to refer to people of African descent who grew up in and are living in the United States, and I use the terms *ethnicity* and *race* interchangeably.

What is gender, and what is race? Sex differences are biologically determined and present at birth, whereas gender, although typically (but not always) associated with biological sex, is learned; it is *enculturated* (Hansen, Gama, & Harkins, 2002). Gender has to do with the "culturally determined attitudes, cognitions, and belief systems about females and males" (Robinson, 2005, p. 150). It is socially constructed. Yee, Fairchild, Weizmann, and Wyatt (1993) posited a similar analysis of race. Although social scientists sometimes use the terms *gender* and *race* as if they are permanent, biologically given ways of being, it is important not to essentialize gender or race and to recognize that they are social constructs that are dynamic and responsive to historical and contemporary social, cultural, and political contexts (Williams, 2005).

This understanding of gender and race as social constructs leads to another important point: An exploration of the impact of gender in African Americans requires a contextual, ecological approach whereby attention is paid to how the person is impacted by his or her environment—by the family and community as well as by broader societal forces, including "-isms" and discrepancies in power, privilege, and status (Reid, 2002). Thus, a contextual, social constructionist framework is utilized in this literature review.

CORE PSYCHOLOGICAL ISSUES OF AFRICAN AMERICAN MEN AND WOMEN

There are a number of core psychological issues with which both African American men and women must contend by virtue of living in a racist society with a history of enslavement and the subsequent cultural, political, and economic disempowerment of people of African descent. Both African American men (P. D. Johnson, 2006) and women (Greene, 1997) have to contend with negative, demeaning stereotypes, although the specific stereotypical attributes can vary on the basis of gender. Furthermore, both Black men and women are disproportionately exposed to violence-related traumas (Harris, 2005). Some consequences are that many Black women and men struggle with developing a healthy racial identity (Franklin, 2004; S. Y. Jenkins, 1996), risk internalizing racism (Franklin, 2004; Williams, 1999), wrestle with establishing and maintaining positive self-esteem (Lee, 1999; M. J. Taylor, 1999), and are at high risk for posttraumatic stress disorder (Harris, 2005).

However, although the aforementioned represent significant challenges that are common to both African American men and women, there are gender differences in the specific manifestations of these themes, in the ensuing coping responses, and in the symptoms and diagnostic disorders that sometimes result.

Men

Although both African American men and women are faced with racial oppression, Black men appear to experience more severe bigotry in a number of areas, for example, in education, in the criminal justice system, and as retail customers (Sidanius & Pratto, 1999). Black men are often stereotyped as animalistic, violent, hypersexual, and sexually predatory (P. D. Johnson, 2006); as a result, they are frequently feared and avoided (Franklin, 2004) or treated as if they are criminals (Gayles, Alston, & Staten, 2005). A review of the extant literature revealed four core psychological issues in the lives of many Black men: (1) gender role strain, (2) invisibility syndrome, (3) challenges in handling anger, and (4) reliance on a "cool pose."

Gender Role Strain. African American men are at risk for *gender role strain*, a consequence of the contradiction between the roles men are expected to play in U.S. society, as provider and protector, and the reality of limited opportunities to fulfill these roles (Franklin, 1998). In other words, many Black men are caught in a bind. To "be a man" in American society typically means to have a job and to provide financially for one's family, yet institutional racism and inequities make it difficult for many Black men to achieve this. (These analyses draw on Pleck's [1985, cited in Franklin, 1998] notion of a *gender role strain paradigm*.) Staples (1998) highlighted the double bind faced by Black men, who, often unemployed, underemployed, or underpaid, are denigrated for failing to fulfill the ideal of "manhood" and yet who are simultaneously castigated for being too macho—for effecting a persona that is too traditionally male. A consequence of gender role strain is that Black men may experience chronic stress, negative self-image, low self-esteem, difficulties in developing a healthy male identity, and substance abuse problems (Gayles et al., 2005; Lee, 1999; Wade, 2006).

Invisibility Syndrome. A. J. Franklin (2004) posited that because of the history of racism, and because of the experience of daily *microaggressions*—subtle slights and devaluing interactions—African American men are at risk for the *invisibility syndrome*, defined as a cluster of potentially debilitating symptoms that compromise one's emotional well-being. Franklin (1992) wrote that African American men are at risk for internalizing the societal message that they are unacceptable and unworthy—a message that creates a sense of invisibility. The relative lack of access to educational and job opportunities reinforces the sense of invisibility, creating a feeling of being invalidated and rejected—of being "dissed." What is ironic is that African American men are both invisible and highly visible. They are often unseen and unacknowledged by the mainstream society, yet simultaneously, they are targeted and scapegoated. Men who fall prey to the invisibility syndrome are at risk for low self-esteem; internalized rage; oppositional behaviors; disillusionment; depression; substance abuse; and stress-related disorders, such as headaches and hypertension (Franklin, 2004). These symptoms often reflect coping strategies gone awry.

Challenges in Handling Anger. A frequent and understandable by-product of being denigrated and feeling invisible is anger/rage (Franklin, 1992). In Grier and Cobbs's (1968) seminal book on African American personality, *Black Rage*, they highlighted the importance of oppression-related anger in the psychological functioning of African Americans and noted that although both African American men and women must find ways to deal with ofttimes intense and chronic feelings of anger related to their devalued status, for Black men this is a particularly salient issue. Lee (1999) proposed that some Black men may have "problems of aggression and control" (p. 40), which can manifest in one of three ways: (1) too much control over frustration and anger, leading to emotional constriction and being cut off from meaningful and genuine connections with others; (2) "inappropriate channeling processes" (p. 40), whereby emotions are directed inward, contributing to internalizing disorders, such as hypertension and substance abuse; and (3) too little control over strong feelings, leading to immature and potentially destructive acting-out behaviors.

The literature on African American men focuses mostly on the problem of too little control and the problems that can ensue.

Too little control over one's anger can contribute to violent and criminal behavior both in or outside of the home. Acting out angrily can be a way of dealing with one's invisibility (Franklin, 1992)—a way of discharging the feelings related to being diminished or shamed, and a way of being seen. The anger that is stirred up by racism and oppression sometimes spills over into the home, disrupting family relationships and increasing the risk of family violence (Gibbs, 1994). Those who are nearby—family, friends, and acquaintances—are most at risk for being targets. In fact, Black men are disproportionately both perpetrators of violence and victims of violence (Harris, 2005). As a result of too little anger control, African American men sometimes become involved in the criminal justice system. There they are likely to be revictimized, because they are at the mercy of a racist bureaucracy that tends to demonize Black men while disregarding the psychological challenges that contributed to their acting out in the first place (Head, 2004).

Some Black men who act out their rage experience a sense of cultural alienation and assume an identity based on being an "outlaw" or "outsider" (Lee, 1999). They disconnect from meaningful societal roles and personal relationships. Prevented by racism from being "insiders," they are able to forge an alternate identity, albeit one that is fraught with risks to themselves and others.

It is important to note that the outward expression of anger by Black men is not always what it appears to be. It often conceals hurt, disappointment, and feelings of depression (Wade, 2006). The norms and values of African American culture make it more consonant for Black men to be "mad and bad" (Head, 2004, p. 46) than to be "hurt and sad." Thus, an angry persona and aggressive acting out sometimes serve as a defense, protecting Black men from acknowledging and facing their inner distress and pain. It is notable that suicide rates for Black males, especially adolescents and young adults, have risen dramatically since the 1980s (Poussaint & Alexander, 2000); meanwhile, clinical depression, which is a major risk factor for suicide, is often hidden or masked (Head, 2004; Poussaint & Alexander, 2000), making it more difficult for Black men who are in despair to get the support and professional help that they need (see also Chap. 29, this volume, for a more detailed description).

Reliance on a "Cool Pose." Richard Majors and his colleagues coined the term *cool pose* to refer to "an exaggerated or ritualistic form of masculinity" that Black men use as a coping strategy to deal with the discrimination and the inequities that they experience (Majors, Tyler, Peden, & Hall, 1994, p. 250). Head (2004) stated that African American men are taught that manhood requires that they silence their feelings, withhold emotion, and not appear weak. Acting cool is a form of impression management aimed at conveying that one has power, is in control, is competent, and is proud. Through mannerisms, speech, gestures, style of walking and moving, clothing, and hairstyles, African American men can symbolically express their masculinity. Despite the fact that they are devalued by the larger society and may be unable to fulfill societal expectations of a career and financial success, cool pose provides a way for Black men to create their own identity and to shore up their self-esteem and confidence—to develop within the Black subculture what the dominant society has denied them. Majors et al. (1994) made direct connections between the evolution of cool pose and Black men's "frustration and pain from restricted opportunities" (p. 247; which is associated with gender role strain) and their experience of invisibility.

However, although cool pose can serve a positive, healthy, self-esteem–boosting function, helping to compensate for feelings of shame and guilt, the "cool pose" stance has liabilities (Majors et al., 1994). Cool pose requires that one hide one's real feelings and emotions; the aim is to be smooth, seemingly unruffled, no matter how dangerous the situation. The cool pose is designed to garner respect, and overt displays of toughness and bravado can help to achieve this. Thus, men who affect a cool pose often get involved in risk taking, sometimes leading to violent and self-destructive behaviors. As a result, Black boys and men who affect a cool pose are at risk for engaging in gang behavior, for being physically and emotionally abusive with female partners, and for being marginalized and stigmatized by teachers and other authorities (Majors et al., 1994).

In the cool pose subculture, which typically is an adolescent and young adult subculture, Black men who do not define their masculinity and their identity using this same set of narrow über-male behaviors are at risk for being seen as "punks" (Majors et al., 1994) or for being disparaged as "gay" (A. G. Johnson, 1997). Black gay, bisexual, and transgender men, as well as heterosexual men who do not subscribe to the "compulsive masculine alternative," may be scorned, harassed, and even physically assaulted by men who subscribe to a cool pose, creating an additional psychological challenge for them.

Summary. The literature on African American men reveals four core psychological challenges that many Black men face: (1) gender role strain, (2) invisibility syndrome, (3) challenges in handling anger, and (4) reliance on a cool pose. These are not four fully distinct issues; they are interrelated. An angry persona and a cool pose often emerge as coping mechanisms that men sometimes invoke, consciously and/or unconsciously, to reduce gender role strain and to thwart the sense of invisibility. In putting forth these themes, there is the danger of reifying stereotypes, for example, the stereotype of the angry Black man. It also is possible that the literature is skewed toward a focus on anger and other negative characteristics because of the prevalent unflattering stereotypes. There clearly are substantial differences among African American men. What is in fact remarkable is that, in spite of the psychological challenges that they face, the majority of Black men demonstrate positive mental health (Anderson, Eaddy, & Williams, 1990). A growing body of research on resilience in African Americans reveals that protective factors, such as positive racial identity, spirituality, and family and social support networks, often serve as buffers or mitigating factors, diminishing the negative impact of experiences of oppression (see Anderson et al., 1990; Utsey, Bolden, Lanier, & Williams, 2007). For Black men in particular, informal community networks, such as barbershops, churches, and social clubs, may be especially important resources in managing the stress of bias and discrimination (Elligan & Utsey, 1999). As an example, affiliation with a Black church can ameliorate gender role strain by providing a context in which a Black man, regardless of educational or professional accomplishments, can assume a leadership role, for example, as a deacon or lay leader, and feel competent and valued in his male identity (W. E. Gooden, personal communication, December 27, 2007).

Women

Although African American men may experience particularly severe and brutal racism, African American women must contend with racism, sexism, and the intersection of these two (V. G. Thomas, 2004). In spite of the 1960s women's liberation movement and significant strides in the past 4 decades, the United States continues to be a patriarchal society in which men, relative to women, are privileged and empowered (A. G. Johnson, 1997), and where Black women continue to be victims of both racism and sexism. An analysis of the existing literature reveals three core psychological issues with which African American women contend: (1) sexual devaluation and victimization, (2) struggles with beauty and self-image, and (3) adoption of the "strong Black woman" persona. In addition to these themes, in a separate section, I focus on clinical symptoms and mental health disorders in Black women.

Sexual Devaluation and Victimization. African American women live in a society where demeaning and denigrating messages about their sexuality are commonplace and potentially affect how they see themselves as well as how others view and interact with them. West (1995) described an image, which originated during slavery but is still being perpetuated, of the Black woman as a morally unconstrained, hypersexual, and promiscuous Jezebel. This stereotype has been revitalized in many contemporary gangsta rap music videos, where Black women are often scantily clad, available only to provide sexual pleasure to men, and are referred to as "bitches" and "hos." A. J. Thomas, Witherspoon, and Speight (2004) demonstrated empirically that the Jezebel stereotype exists in the perceptions of contemporary African American women. Bethea-Whitfield (2005) argued that there is a strong connection between the media's promotion of degrading images of Black women and other forms of violence against Black women.

West (2002a, 2004) has reported that African American girls and women do, in fact, experience high rates of child sexual abuse, dating violence, intimate partner violence, sexual harassment, and sexual assault, and that very often women experience multiple forms of violence during their lifetimes. Similarly, research by Wyatt and colleagues provides empirical evidence for high rates of sexual harassment and sexual abuse in African American females (see, e.g., Wyatt, 1997). It is important to note that racial differences in rates of partner abuse are confounded by differences in socioeconomic status (SES); women of lower SES are more likely to be victimized than are women of higher SES (West, 2004). However, there is some evidence that racism and sexism sometimes intersect to create particularly severe and egregious forms of sexual victimization (see, e.g., J. Adams, 1997).

Some of the consequences of sexual victimization are depression; substance abuse; suicidality; and somatic complaints, such as headaches (West, 2002a). Moreover, Black women who have been victimized often come to feel less in control of their sexuality and thus are at heightened risk for subsequent abuse, for unprotected consensual sexual involvement, and as a result for sexually transmitted diseases, including HIV (West, 2002a). What makes the experience of abuse even more problematic is the tendency of Black women to remain silent about it. Although this is also an issue for other women, as well as for men who are sexually abused, for Black women, there are particular factors that can induce silence. If the perpetrator is a Black male, Black women are sometimes reluctant to report him to an employer or to a criminal justice system that they know is discriminatory (Jones & Shorter-Gooden, 2003; West, 2002a). Furthermore, Black women who see themselves as having fulfilled the Jezebel stereotype may blame themselves and experience great shame. Daniel (1995) discussed the "double victimization" that many Black women endure when they are sexually abused and then feel silenced about their experience of victimization.

Struggles With Beauty and Self-Image. Black women live in a society where there is a strong demand for women to be physically beautiful (Wolf, 1991) and where, in spite of some diversification in the past 4 decades, the standard of beauty is still primarily Eurocentric (Greene, 1997). Women who have lighter skin; longer, straighter hair; and more European facial features are privileged over those who look more traditionally African (Greene, 1997). Furthermore, femininity is associated with the White female ideal of attractiveness, and not meeting the ideal means being seen as unfeminine (M. J. Taylor, 1999). As a result, many Black women wrestle with their self-image, with feeling good about their physical appearance, and with whether they meet the dominant culture female ideal (Jones & Shorter-Gooden, 2003).

Although darker-skinned Black women receive the brunt of the impact of colorism, lighter-skinned Black women are sometimes the victims of reverse color bias—not trusted, resented, and viewed as not "Black" enough (S. Y. Jenkins, 1996; West, 1995). Even within one family, differences in skin color and hair length and texture can be a source of significant pain and alienation (Greene, White, & Whitten, 2000). As a result, it is not uncommon for Black women, wherever they fall along the color spectrum, to internalize some of the racist/sexist messages about beauty, to harbor feelings of shame, and to struggle with maintaining feelings of self-worth (Greene, 1997; M. J. Taylor, 1999).

Adoption of the "Strong Black Woman" Persona. During slavery, Black women had to be strong in order to survive and protect their children in a violent, brutal environment of forced servitude where Black families were routinely torn apart (McNair, 1992). Since emancipation, the racism, sexism, and lack of economic opportunities have likely further contributed to Black women's toughness, fortitude, independence, and resilience. African American women commonly deem themselves, and are seen by others, as strong—able to take care of and handle whatever comes there way (Romero, 2000). However, although in many ways a virtue, the Black woman's strength becomes a problem when she is unable to acknowledge pain or vulnerable feelings, when she is unwilling to ask for help, or when she feels undeserving of support (Romero, 2000; Thompson, 2000). To compound the problem, adopting a persona of invulnerability and imperviousness can be an attractive and welcomed antidote to the sense of powerlessness and helplessness that are typical by-products of oppression.

One variant of the "strong Black woman" persona is perhaps connected to the historical image of Mammy—the nurturing, self-sacrificing, family-centered caregiver (West, 1995). Mammy is all things to all people all the time, while denying her needs—a Black superwoman. Thompson (2000) wrote that many Black women engage in *moral masochism*, which she defined as a "level of excessive personal sacrifice that assumes pathological proportions" (p. 241). Abdullah (1998) coined the term *Mammy-ism* to denote a mental disorder when Black women internalize racism, spurn their culture and roots, and are self-sacrificing and accommodating to Whites—for example, in the workplace. Abdullah posited that a negative self-image and low self-esteem are consequences of this pattern, and an empirical study by A. J. Thomas et al. (2004) supports this notion.

Other scholars focus on the role strain that is endemic to being the consummate caregiver (see, e.g., West, 1995). Role strain occurs when people have multiple role obligations that they are unable to fulfill (West, 1995). African American women are more likely to be in the labor force than are White or Latina women, are more likely to work full time, and are more likely to be raising children as single parents (Jones & Shorter-Gooden, 2003). In addition to the cultural or psychological predisposition they have toward being a "strong Black woman," the realities of their lives often push for selflessness and untiring attentiveness to others' needs—a recipe for role strain.

A second variant of the "strong Black woman" persona is perhaps associated with another historical image—Sapphire, who is depicted as caustic, hostile, aggressive, domineering, and emasculating (McNair, 1992; West, 1995). Whereas Mammy's strength-through-selflessness is sometimes seen as a positive representation of womanhood; Sapphire's strength-through-aggression is reviled. Sapphire is presumably the "much-too-strong Black woman." One of the messages here is that African American women have relatively limited degrees of freedom for "acceptable" behavior. Black lesbian women, who are often seen as "masculinized females," also have to contend with these narrow definitions and with the message that they are "defective females" (Greene, 1997, p. 313). A. J. Thomas et al. (2004) found that Black women whose attitudes reflected the Sapphire stereotype were more likely to have low self-esteem than those whose attitudes were less confirming of the stereotype.

However, the challenge with regard to the "strong Black woman" persona is not simply in how others pigeonhole and judge African American women: it also has to do with how Black women perceive themselves, how they treat themselves, and what they demand of themselves. Can she find a way to feel strong and capable, yet also be attached to and interdependent with partners and friends? Can she acknowledge her own needs and vulnerability? Shorter-Gooden and Jackson (2000) pointed out that Black women who assume the "strong Black woman" persona are often frightened of attachment and dependency, which they experience as a dangerous loss of strength. The result can be chronic loneliness and emotional isolation.

Clinical Symptoms and Mental Disorders. Particular attention has been paid in the literature to exploring emotional disorders in Black women and to theorizing about clinical disorders or patterns of expression that may be unique to Black women. Abdullah's proposed disorder—Mammy-ism—was discussed earlier. I now very briefly summarize other available literature in this area.

African American women have higher rates of depressive symptoms, though not higher rates of clinically diagnosable depression, than other women (Brown, 1990), and the rate of clinical depression is twice as high in U.S. women as in men. Jones and Shorter-Gooden (2003) posited a *Sisterella complex* whereby African American women manifest depression due to the internalization of society's negative stereotypes and/or the accommodation to limiting racist/sexist notions of their roles. They assert that depression, because it is culturally incongruent with being strong, is often masked in Black women and as a result may present in indirect ways, such as through emotional overeating and somatization.

In fact, for African American women, to a greater degree than for other women, being overweight is associated with depressive feelings (Siegel, Yancey, & McCarthy, 2000), and binge eating appears to be a particular problem for depressed Black women (Striegel-Moore, Wilfley, Pike, Dohm, & Fairburn, 2000). In addition, in a major epidemiological study, Black women were found to have higher rates of somatic symptoms and somatization disorder than all other groups (Swartz, Landerman, George, Blazer, & Escobar, 1991). For Black women who feel they must be emotionally strong and who, as a result, disdain the notion of being depressed, physical symptoms may be a more acceptable way to express their emotional distress. Another cover-up for feelings of depression are feelings of anger. M. J. Taylor (1999) stated that it is common for African American women to mask their feelings of depression with anger, which may be more ego syntonic but which may also be difficult or risky to express. Of note is that, in a qualitative study, Waite and Killian (2007) found that clinically depressed African American women described their depression with terms like *upset, anger, exhaustion, stressed,* and *sick* (p. 165), instead of with more typical expressions of "hopelessness, sadness, and depressed mood" (p. 167).

Although exact rates of anxiety disorders in African American women are not available, it is known that Black women's rates of anxiety disorder and phobia are higher than that of Black men (U.S. Department of Health and Human Services, 2001). Neal-Barnett (2003) proposed that Black women are at significant risk for anxiety disorders, including generalized anxiety disorder, panic attacks, social phobia, specific phobias, and obsessive–compulsive disorder. She attributed this to chronic stress, which itself is often attributable to prejudice and discrimination; to the need to be hyper-alert and on guard to manage bias and bigotry; and to the pressure to be emotionally strong and "keep it in" (p. 20).

Summary. The literature suggests three core psychological themes for African American women: (1) sexual devaluation and victimization, (2) struggles with physical image, and (3) the "strong Black woman" persona. The "strong Black woman" stance is a cultural coping strategy on which many Black women draw as a way of responding to the sexual devaluation and to the message that they are not physically attractive. Depression, anxiety, binge eating, and somatization, with the latter two sometimes serving as stand-ins for depression, are at times the unfortunate outcomes of Black women's emotional challenges.

Just as for Black men, it is important to acknowledge the cultural strengths and resilience of African American women, which allow most women to survive emotionally and sometimes to thrive in spite of the environmental threats and challenges. As an example, the rate of completed suicide for Black women is lower than that of Black men or White men and women (American Association of Suicidology, 2000), a statistic that quite likely is due to Black women's resilience. In a qualitative study, Shorter-Gooden (2004) found that Black women have numerous strategies for coping with racial and gender bias: relying on their faith, connecting with the experiences of their ancestors, actively working to value and nurture themselves, relying on others for social and emotional support, adapting flexibly to different behavioral roles, avoiding toxic people and situations, and directly fighting back. Williams (2005) discussed the importance of Black women's "reliance on women-centered networks of emotional support and caregiving, spiritual faith, and a healthy construction of self" (p. 281). These scholars have homed in on cultural strengths that are somewhat different from the generic coping strategies that have been highlighted in the mainstream literature that focuses on coping in White men and women.

Therapeutic Considerations and Approaches

In this section, I address the literature on therapeutic considerations, strategies, and theoretical approaches to working with African American men and women. Black men and women have both been consistently documented as underutilizers of mental health services (Morris, 2001). A significant portion of the underutilization is due to inaccessible and/or culturally insensitive services (Morris, 2001; Whaley, 2001) and to an understandable cultural mistrust or "healthy cultural paranoia" based on the long history of oppression (Whaley, 2001). However, this pattern of underutilization may also be explained by the tendency to see vulnerability as weakness, the consequent difficulty in disclosing one's vulnerabilities to a therapist, and the fear of feeling out of control (Franklin, 1992; Lee, 1999). Black men and Black women often adopt strategies—for example, "the cool pose" and the "strong Black woman"—as a way of coping with oppression; yet, these same strategies can get in the way of getting help with the problems that racism and sexism have helped to create.

There is considerable convergence around a number of general therapeutic considerations in working with both Black women and men. Scholars agree that it is important for therapists to place the African American client's experience in a sociohistorical context (see, e.g., Bethea-Whitfield, 2005; Caldwell & White, 2005) in order to better understand the client and to educate the client to distinguish between internal conflicts and external oppressive forces (see, e.g., Franklin, 1998; Williams, 2005). Therapists working with Black women and men need to be knowledgeable about African American history and culture (see, e.g., Thorn & Sarata, 1998; West, 1995) and integrate Afrocentric values and worldview in the treatment (see, e.g., Morris, 2001), for example, through the use of literature, art, music, and proverbs (see, e.g., Caldwell & White, 2005; Williams, 1999).

A number of clinicians recommend consideration of more flexible roles on the part of the therapist (see, e.g., Morris, 2001), including a more interpersonal, collaborative, psychoeducational orientation and the judicious use of self-disclosure (see, e.g., Lee, 1999). Some suggest a more problem-oriented focus given the potential for ambivalence about therapy as well as the pressing external issues with which many African Americans contend (see, e.g., Morris, 2001).

A number of therapists highly recommend building on the personal and cultural assets of the Black client—in other words, not solely focusing on deficits or pathology but instead working to enhance the client's strengths, resilience, and sense of competence (see, e.g., Caldwell & White, 2005; Williams, 1999). To this end, the therapist should integrate and draw on the client's spiritual beliefs (see, e.g., Lee, 1999; Utsey et al., 2007), work to enhance the client's familial and community support systems (see, e.g., Utsey et al., 2007), consider the use of group interventions (given the importance of the extended family and community in African American culture; see, e.g., Elligan & Utsey, 1999; Williams, 1999), and encourage the client's social activism (see, e.g., West, 2002b; Williams, 2005). The aim is to facilitate the client's empowerment.

Also, numerous scholars have discussed the critical importance of clinicians' ongoing examination of their own assumptions, stereotypes, and biases about African Americans and of their own identity, power, and privilege (see, e.g., J. M. Adams, 2000; Lee, 1999), as well as a willingness to directly acknowledge and nondefensively discuss racial issues with the client, including a racial difference between the therapist and client (see, e.g., Morris, 2001).

Although there are many commonalities in the recommended therapeutic approaches with Black men and women, the literature reveals some gender differences as well.

Men

A central consideration in working with African American male clients is the importance of attention to the development of rapport, given the potential cultural mistrust of therapy and the struggles that many Black men have with needing to feel in control (Gayles et al., 2005; Lee, 1999). It is important for the therapist to facilitate a slow, careful process of engagement and to not make interpretations prematurely, before trust has developed (Franklin, 1992). The careful building of rapport may be especially important if the therapist is not Black (Gayles et al., 2005). Given the negative stereotypes of African American men and the tendency of non-Blacks to be fearful, intimidated, and thus avoidant of Black men, the issues of problematic countertransference may be particularly present when working with Black male clients and are likely to impede the development of a healthy therapeutic alliance if not carefully attended to.

The literature on therapeutic approaches and orientations specific to Black men is rather limited. Given the difficulties with rapport building, Lee (1999) detailed an interpersonally oriented five-stage process for facilitating a Black male client's movement from "initial contact" to "commitment" and "engagement." White and Cones (1999) described an array of "Black masculinity approaches" that can be utilized either as therapy or community interventions and that are aimed at educating African American men about the oppressiveness of cultural and media images and helping them redefine their identity in a positive, healthy way. There has been some exploration of African-centered approaches to therapy with Black men, and Caldwell and White (2005) advocated the application of NTU therapy for work with Black men. Developed by Phillips (1990), NTU therapy is based on an African-centered worldview and uses the seven principles of Kwanzaa, the *Nguzo Saba*, as guidelines for living. P. D. Johnson (2006) recommended use of a "contextualized humanistic" perspective, which integrates an understanding of the sociocultural context with the humanistic emphasis on person-centeredness in order to understand the particular individual's phenomenological perception of reality. Because space does not permit a discussion of these approaches here, readers are referred to the cited works.

Women

A lot more attention has been paid in the literature to proposed considerations and theoretical orientations when working with African American women in contrast to men. The considerations for psychotherapy with Black women focus on the importance of three things: (1) the therapeutic alliance, (2) attention to the intersection of race and gender, and (3) integrating religiosity and spirituality. I now sketch these out briefly.

For Black women, it is the "strong Black woman" posture that can complicate the building of a trusting relationship (McNair, 1992; Romero, 2000). Romero (2000) wrote that oftentimes, in keeping with the cultural ideal of invulnerability, Black women feel impelled to present as competent and successful in therapy. This pressure can make it more difficult to open up about one's sadness; moreover, the client may feel that she needs to take care of the therapist or to protect the therapist from the client's real feelings. For therapists, an auxiliary strategy to help Black female clients find spaces where they can share openly is to encourage and assist them in developing social support networks or "sister circles" (Bethea-Whitfield, 2005; West, 2002b).

A number of scholars have emphasized the necessity of focusing on the intersection of race and gender and of racism and sexism in psychotherapy with Black women (Greene, 1997; Williams, 1999.) Too often, there is a tendency to see and respond to the client as only Black or, conversely, as only female, instead of attending to the client's dual status. These scholars admonish therapists to use dual lenses to make sense of African American women's experiences, and in particular to focus on the intersection of these identities. Also, of course, race and gender are not the only identities that Black women (or Black men) have. The intersecting identities of sexual orientation, SES, religion, spirituality, age, and ability need to be carefully acknowledged and considered.

Empirical studies indicate that most African American women are highly religious and spiritual (see, e.g., R. J. Taylor, Mattis, & Chatters, 1999), and although attention to spirituality is important for both Black men and women, it is especially important for therapists to be aware of the importance that religious (usually, though not always, Christian) and/or spiritual beliefs hold for many Black women, to provide room for the client to share her beliefs, and to assist the client in utilizing her religious/spiritual resources as a source of support in the therapeutic process (J. M. Adams, 2000; Williams, 2005). Religious and spiritual beliefs and practices can provide a tremendous source of primary or adjunctive healing (Jones & Shorter-Gooden, 2003), but it is also important to note that it is not uncommon for Black women to wrestle with doubt, uncertainty, and conflicts related to their beliefs (J. M. Adams, 2000). Black women who enter therapy may be angry at or feel betrayed by God, and they need to be able to explore these painful thoughts and feelings (J. M. Adams, 2000), which may be particularly difficult to disclose.

A number of therapeutic orientations have been recommended for Black female clients. Afrocentric–feminist/womanist approaches (in other words, woman-centered and woman-affirming approaches that include attention to race and racism; V. G. Thomas, 2004; Williams, 1999); psychodynamic approaches that incorporate a focus on the intersection of race and gender (Greene, 1997; Shorter-Gooden & Jackson, 2000); and Stone Center relational/cultural theory (Y. M. Jenkins, 2000) have been the most prominently addressed in the literature. For discussions of these approaches, readers are referred to the cited works.

Summary

The literature on therapeutic considerations and approaches is more developed with respect to African American women than men. For both men and women, there has been a focus on the challenge of developing a positive therapeutic alliance, on utilizing psychoeducational approaches that elucidate the impact of societal oppression, and on the importance of client empowerment. For women, attention has also been paid to the importance of the intersection of race and gender, and there has been a more focused consideration of the integration of religiosity and spirituality. For Black male clients, the use of a carefully staged process of engagement, Black masculinity approaches, NTU therapy, and a contextualized humanistic approach have been recommended; whereas, for Black women, the emphasis has been on Afrocentric–feminist/womanist therapy, culturally informed psychodynamic therapy, and relational/cultural therapy.

CRITIQUE OF THE LITERATURE AND RECOMMENDATIONS FOR FUTURE SCHOLARSHIP

There are a number of strengths in the literature on gender issues in therapy with African Americans. There has been a fair amount of attention given to, and consensus around, core psychological issues of Black women and Black men as well as around important therapeutic considerations in working with Black women and Black men. However, a critical evaluation of the literature reveals significant unaddressed issues and gaps. I now discuss limitations in two main areas—(1) the use of a gender analysis and (2) the utilization of an array of methodological approaches for knowledge generation—and I propose areas for future scholarship.

Although I have discussed gender throughout this review, the use of the term has been quite broad and undifferentiated. In the clinical reports and empirical studies that have been discussed, *gender* typically refers to human beings who self-identify or are identified by others as male or female. The reviewed literature implicitly addresses gender as a bimodal construct: One presumably identifies as either male or female. The focus has been on a forced-choice, either–or gender *identification,* not on a continuum of gender *identity.* In empirical studies, gender has typically been measured by asking participants to check off "M" or "F" (Hansen et al., 2002). Differences among Black men or among Black women in the social construction of gender, the degree of identification with maleness and femaleness, and the salience of gender at different times and in different arenas have rarely been addressed. The danger here is of essentializing gender and of treating socially constructed, context-driven differences as fundamental, unchangeable givens (Williams, 1999). Moreover, the lack of attention to gender as a continuum puts us at risk for disregarding the experiences and needs of individuals who are not gender conforming. African American heterosexuals as well as lesbians, gays, and bisexuals who may not subscribe to traditional bimodal gender norms may be marginalized or made invisible, as can Blacks who are transgendered, a population about which there is virtually no psychotherapy literature.

Although there is a small body of empirical literature on gender issues in clinical diagnoses of African American men and women and in mental health help-seeking behavior, the majority of the literature on psychological themes in the lives of Black men and women and on the experience of gender in therapy relies on clinicians' theoretical assertions and clinical reports. This is an important and rich source of information, but the limited number of alternative sources is striking. There are relatively few empirical studies of the therapeutic experiences of African Americans in general (Constantine, 2007), and even fewer that have focused on gender-specific issues in therapy (Thorn & Sarata, 1998). Also, although there are a few studies on the effectiveness of therapy with African Americans, no research has explored the impact of a therapeutic approach specifically for Black women or Black men (Sue & Lam, 2002). There is no definitive information on evidence-based practice with African Americans. The existing literature on the psychological challenges of African American men and women loads heavily toward the clinical, anecdotal, and theoretical, with very limited empirical confirmation of assertions. Additional quantitative and qualitative empirical research is sorely needed.

The following questions need to be addressed in future scholarship on gender issues in therapy with African American clients: How does gender affect symptom presentation? How does gender affect the therapist–client relationship and interactions? Are race- and gender-matched therapeutic pairs more effective than race-and/or gender-different pairs? How does the therapist's gender identity impact his or her response to the client's gender identity? Do therapists convey to Black clients a narrow, rigid set of gender roles? For example, do therapists collude with the invisibility of Black men or with the "strong Black woman" persona?

To what extent are specific theoretical orientations important in providing effective therapy to Black men and Black women? The extant literature suggests that a multiplicity of theoretical orientations may be of value in the treatment of Black men and women, as long as the impact of race and gender is a significant consideration and modifications are made to the therapy to address these key factors. However, empirical studies are needed to confirm or disconfirm this hypothesis.

Moreover, how do race and gender intersect with other areas of identity—for example, sexual orientation—to impact treatment considerations and the treatment process?

The literature on African American men in therapy is much more limited than that on African American women. The reason for this needs to be explored, and the paucity of literature needs to be rectified. Is this another manifestation of Black male invisibility?

Limitations of the Review and Conclusion

This review of the literature has focused on gender differences in African American adults in psychotherapy, with particular attention given to core psychological challenges and important considerations and approaches to therapy. The review has several limitations: One is that the focus on challenges that Black men and women face as a group may tend to obscure the fact that, as Greene (1997) put it, "rarely is race or gender bias the exclusive source of a client's difficulty" (p. 316). African Americans enter therapy with the same garden variety of problems as other populations; however, their relationship problems, feelings of anxiety or depression, and existential crises are often, to varying degrees, triggered or exacerbated by experiences of oppression. The core psychological themes that have been addressed in this chapter are more likely to underlie the presenting problem than to be served up as it.

A second limitation is that attention to differences between Black men and women may inadvertently veil substantial similarities. In addition, space limitations made it difficult to focus in this chapter on sexual orientation, social class, religious, and other differences among Black men and Black women. Another limitation is that, by positing core psychological themes, there is a risk of conveying that there is a prototypical Black man or Black woman. Of course, there is none. Although there are some common experiences and perceptions, heterogeneity reigns. Yet, another limitation is the concentration on the psychological challenges and problems of Black men and women, with lesser attention to the population's considerable and documented strengths and psychological resilience. It is important to note that, in general, Blacks do not have higher rates of mental disorders than Whites, and with respect to a number of mental disorders, their rates are lower than those of Whites (Zhang & Snowden, 1999). Moreover, there are countless examples of emotionally healthy Black men and women who have taken on the challenge of "-isms" and won.

In spite of the limitations of this review, my hope is that this chapter increases scholars' awareness of and sensitivity to gender issues in African Americans, offers therapists a set of hypotheses and considerations in providing psychotherapy to African American women and men, and inspires empirical researchers and clinicians to actively address the gaps in our understanding in order to enhance our capacity to provide much-needed, effective treatment.

REFERENCES

Abdullah, A. S. (1998). Mammy-ism: A diagnosis of psychological misorientation for women of African descent. *Journal of Black Psychology, 24,* 196–210.

Adams, J. (1997). Sexual harassment and Black women: A historical perspective. In W. O'Donohue (Ed.), *Sexual harassment: Theory, research, and treatment* (pp. 213–224). Needham Heights, MA: Allyn & Bacon.

Adams, J. M. (2000). Individual and group psychotherapy with African American women: Understanding the identity and context of the therapist and patient. In L. C. Jackson & B. Greene (Eds.), *Psychotherapy with African American women: Innovations in psychodynamic perspectives and practice* (pp. 33–61). New York: Guilford Press.

American Association of Suicidology. (2000). *Suicide data page: 2000.* Retrieved May 28, 2007, from http://www.suicidology.org/associations/1045/files/2000datapg.pdf

Anderson, L. P., Eaddy, C. L., & Williams, E. A. (1990). Psychosocial competence: Toward a theory of understanding positive mental health among Black Americans. In D. S. Ruiz (Ed.), *Handbook of mental health and mental disorder among Black Americans* (pp. 255–271). New York: Greenwood Press.

Bethea-Whitfield, P. (2005). African American women and mental health. In D. A. Harley & J. M. Dillard (Eds.), *Contemporary mental health issues among African Americans* (pp. 35–47). Alexandria, VA: American Counseling Association.

Brown, D. R. (1990). Depression among Blacks: An epidemiologic perspective. In D. S. Ruiz (Ed.), *Handbook of mental health and mental disorder among Black Americans* (pp. 71–93). New York: Greenwood Press.

Caldwell, L. D., & White, J. L. (2005). African-centered therapeutic and counseling interventions for African American males. In G. E. Good (Ed.), *The new handbook of psychotherapy and counseling with men: A comprehensive guide to settings, problems, and treatment approaches* (pp. 737–753). San Francisco: Jossey-Bass.

Constantine, M. G. (2007). Racial microaggressions against African American clients in cross-racial counseling relationships. *Journal of Counseling Psychology, 54,* 1–16.

Daniel, J. H. (1995). The discourse on Thomas v. Hill: A resource for perspectives on the Black woman and sexual trauma. *Journal of Feminist Family Therapy, 7,* 103–117.

Elligan, D., & Utsey, S. (1999). Utility of an African-centered support group for African American men confronting societal racism and oppression. *Cultural Diversity and Ethnic Minority Psychology, 5,* 156–165.

Franklin, A. J. (1992). Therapy with African American men. *Families in Society: The Journal of Contemporary Human Services, 73,* 350–355.

Franklin, A. J. (1998). Treating anger in African American men. In W. S. Pollack & R. F. Levant (Eds.), *New psychotherapy for men* (pp. 239–258). New York: Wiley.

Franklin, A. J. (2004). *From brotherhood to manhood: How Black men rescue their relationships and dreams from the invisibility syndrome.* New York: Wiley.

Gayles, T. A., Alston, R. J., & Staten, D. (2005). Understanding mental illness among African American males: Risk factors and treatment parameters. In D. A. Harley & J. M. Dillard (Eds.), *Contemporary mental health issues among African Americans* (pp. 49–59). Alexandria, VA: American Counseling Association.

Gibbs, J. T. (1994). Anger in young Black males: Victims or victimizers? In R. G. Majors & J. U. Gordon (Eds.), *The American Black male* (pp. 127–143). Chicago: Nelson-Hall.

Greene, B. (1997). Psychotherapy with African American women: Integrating feminist and psychodynamic models. *Smith College Studies in Social Work, 67,* 299–322.

Greene, B., White, J. C., & Whitten, L. (2000). Hair texture, length, and style as a metaphor in the African American mother–daughter relationship: Considerations in psychodynamic psychotherapy. In L. C. Jackson & B. Greene (Eds.), *Psychotherapy with African American women: Innovations in psychodynamic perspectives and practice* (pp. 166–193). New York: Guilford Press.

Grier, W. H., & Cobbs, P. M. (1968). *Black rage.* New York: Basic Books.

Hansen, L. S., Gama, E. M. P., & Harkins, A. K. (2002). Revisiting gender issues in multicultural counseling. In P. B. Pedersen, J. G. Draguns, W. J. Lonner, & J. E. Trimble (Eds.), *Counseling across cultures* (5th ed., pp. 163–184). Thousand Oaks, CA: Sage.

Harris, R. P. (2005). The impact of violence, crime, and gangs in the African American community. In D. A. Harley & J. M. Dillard (Eds.), *Contemporary mental health issues among African Americans* (pp. 175–190). Alexandria, VA: American Counseling Association.

Head, J. (2004). *Black men and depression: Understanding and overcoming depression in Black men.* New York: Broadway Books.

Hyde, J. S. (2005). The gender similarities hypothesis. *American Psychologist, 60,* 581–592.

Jenkins, S. Y. (1996). Psychotherapy and Black female identity conflicts. *Women & Therapy, 18,* 59–74.

Jenkins, Y. M. (2000). The Stone Center theoretical approach revisited: Applications for African American women. In L. C. Jackson & B. Greene (Eds.), *Psychotherapy with African American women: Innovations in psychodynamic perspectives and practice* (pp. 62–81). New York: Guilford Press.

Johnson, A. G. (1997). *The gender knot: Unraveling our patriarchal legacy.* Philadelphia: Temple University Press.

Johnson, P. D. (2006). Counseling African American men: A contextualized humanistic perspective. *Counseling and Values, 50,* 187–196.

Jones, C., & Shorter-Gooden, K. (2003). *Shifting: The double lives of Black women in America.* New York: HarperCollins.

Lee, C. C. (1999). Counseling African American men. In L. E. Davis (Ed.), *Working with African American males: A guide to practice* (pp. 39–53). Thousand Oaks, CA: Sage.

Majors, R., Tyler, R., Peden, B., & Hall, R. E. (1994). Cool pose: A symbolic mechanism for masculine role enactment and coping by Black males. In R. G. Majors & J. U. Gordon (Eds.), *The American Black male* (pp. 245–259). Chicago: Nelson-Hall.

McNair, L. (1992). African American women in therapy: An Afrocentric and feminist synthesis. *Women & Therapy, 12,* 5–19.

Morris, E.F. (2001). Clinical practices with African Americans: Juxtaposition of standard clinical practices and Africentricism. *Professional Psychology: Research and Practice, 32*(6), 563–572.

Neal-Barnett, A. (2003). *Soothe your nerves: The Black woman's guide to understanding and overcoming anxiety, panic, and fear.* New York: Fireside.

Phillips, F. B. (1990). NTU psychotherapy: An Afrocentric approach. *Journal of Black Psychology, 17,* 55–74.

Pleck, J. H. (1985). The gender role strain paradigm: An update. In R. F. Levant & W. S. Levant (Eds.), *A new psychology of men* (pp. 11–32). New York: Basic Books.

Poussaint, A. F., & Alexander, A. (2000). *Lay my burden down: Unraveling suicide and the mental health crisis among African-Americans.* Boston: Beacon Press.

Reid, P. T. (2002). Multicultural psychology: Bringing together gender and ethnicity. *Cultural Diversity and Ethnic Minority Psychology, 8,* 103–114.

Reid, P. T., & Comas-Díaz, L. (1990). Gender and ethnicity: Perspectives on dual status. *Sex Roles, 22,* 397–408.

Robinson, T. L. (2005). *The convergence of race, ethnicity, and gender: Multiple identities in counseling* (2nd ed.). Upper Saddle River, NJ: Pearson Prentice Hall.

Romero, R. (2000). The icon of the strong Black woman: The paradox of strength. In L. C. Jackson & B. Greene (Eds.), *Psychotherapy with African American women: Innovations in psychodynamic perspectives and practice* (pp. 225–238). New York: Guilford Press.

Shorter-Gooden, K. (2004). Multiple resistance strategies: How African American women cope with racism and sexism. *Journal of Black Psychology, 30,* 406–425.

Shorter-Gooden, K., & Jackson, L. C. (2000). The interweaving of cultural and intrapsychic issues in the therapeutic relationship. In L. C. Jackson & B. Greene (Eds.), *Psychotherapy with African American women: Innovations in psychodynamic perspectives and practice* (pp. 15–32). New York: Guilford Press.

Sidanius, J., & Pratto, F. (1999). *Social dominance: An intergroup theory of social hierarchy and oppression.* New York: Cambridge University Press.

Siegel, J. M., Yancey, A. K., & McCarthy, W. J. (2000). Overweight and depressive symptoms among African-American women. *Preventive Medicine, 31*, 232–240.

Staples, R. (1998). Stereotypes of Black male sexuality: The facts behind the myths. In M. S. Kimmel & M. A. Messner (Eds.), *Men's lives* (4th ed., pp. 466–471). Boston: Allyn & Bacon.

Striegel-Moore, R. H., Wilfley, D. E., Pike, K. M., Dohm, F., & Fairburn, C. G. (2000). Recurrent binge eating in Black American women. *Archives of Family Medicine, 9*, 83–87.

Sue, S., & Lam, A. G. (2002). Cultural and demographic diversity. In J. C. Norcross (Ed.), *Psychotherapy relationships that work: Therapist contributions to responsiveness to patients* (pp. 401–421). New York: Oxford University Press.

Swartz, M., Landerman, R., George, L. K., Blazer, D. G., & Escobar, J. (1991). Somatization disorder. In L. N. Robins & D. A. Regier (Eds.), *Psychiatric disorders in America: The Epidemiologic Catchment Area Study* (pp. 220–257). New York: Free Press.

Taylor, M. J. (1999). Changing what has gone before: The enhancement of an inadequate psychology through the use of an Afrocentric-feminist perspective with African American women in therapy. *Psychotherapy, 36*, 170–179.

Taylor, R. J., Mattis, J., & Chatters, L. M. (1999). Subjective religiosity among African Americans: A synthesis of finding from five national samples. *Journal of Black Psychology, 25*, 524–543.

Thomas, A. J., Witherspoon, K. M., & Speight, S. L. (2004). Toward the development of the Stereotypic Roles for Black Women Scale. *Journal of Black Psychology, 30*, 426–442.

Thomas, V. G. (2004). The psychology of Black women: Studying women's lives in context. *Journal of Black Psychology, 30*, 286–306.

Thompson, C. L. (2000). African American women and moral masochism: When there is too much of a good thing. In L. C. Jackson & B. Greene (Eds.), *Psychotherapy with African American women: Innovations in psychodynamic perspectives and practice* (pp. 239–250). New York: Guilford Press.

Thorn, G. R., & Sarata, B. P. V. (1998). Psychotherapy with African American men: What we know and what we need to know. *Journal of Multicultural Counseling and Development, 26*, 240–253.

U.S. Department of Health and Human Services. (2001). *Mental health: Culture, race, and ethnicity—A supplement to* Mental Health: A Report of the Surgeon General. Rockville, MD: Public Health Service, Office of the Surgeon General.

Utsey, S. O., Bolden, M. A., Lanier, Y., & Williams, O., III. (2007). Examining the role of culture-specific coping as a predictor of resilient outcomes in African Americans from high-risk urban communities. *Journal of Black Psychology, 33*, 75–93.

Wade, J. C. (2006). The case of the angry Black man. In M. Englar-Carlson & M. A. Stevens (Eds.), *In the room with men: A casebook of therapeutic change* (pp. 177–196). Washington, DC: American Psychological Association.

Waite, R., & Killian, P. (2007). Exploring depression among a cohort of African American women. *Journal of the American Psychiatric Nurses Association, 13*, 161–169.

West, C. M. (1995). Mammy, Sapphire, and Jezebel: Historical images of Black women and their implications for psychotherapy. *Psychotherapy, 32*, 458–466.

West, C. M. (2002a). Battered, Black, and blue: An overview of violence in the lives of Black women. *Women & Therapy, 25*, 5–27.

West, C. M. (2002b). "I find myself at therapy's doorstep": Summary and suggested readings on violence in the lives of Black women. *Women & Therapy, 25*, 193–201.

West, C. M. (2004). Black women and intimate partner violence: New directions for research. *Journal of Interpersonal Violence, 19*, 1487–1493.

Whaley, A. L. (2001). Cultural mistrust: An important psychological construct for diagnosis and treatment of African Americans. *Professional Psychology: Research and Practice, 32*, 555–562.

White, J. L., & Cones, J. H. (1999). *Black man emerging: Facing the past and seizing a future in America.* New York: Freeman.

Williams, C. B. (1999). African American women, Afrocentrism and feminism: Implications for therapy. *Women & Therapy, 22*, 1–16.

Williams, C. B. (2005). Counseling African American women: Multiple identities—multiple constraints. *Journal of Counseling and Development, 83*, 278–283.

Wolf, N. (1991). *The beauty myth: How images of beauty are used against women.* New York: Anchor Books.

Wyatt, G. E. (1997). *Stolen women: Reclaiming our sexuality, taking back our lives.* New York: Wiley.

Yee, A. H., Fairchild, H. H., Weizmann, F., & Wyatt, G. E. (1993). Addressing psychology's problems with race. *American Psychologist, 48*, 1132–1140.

Zhang, A. Y., & Snowden, L. R. (1999). Ethnic characteristics of mental disorders in five U.S. communities. *Cultural Diversity and Ethnic Minority Psychology, 5*, 134–146.

33

SOCIAL AND CULTURAL FACTORS IN THE COGNITIVE AND CLINICAL ASSESSMENT OF AFRICAN AMERICAN ADULTS

DEIDRE M. ANGLIN AND NAA OYO A. KWATE

At its most basic level, psychological assessment identifies areas of cognitive, social, or emotional strength and weakness and thereby serves as a critical first step in any ensuing intervention and treatment. For many African American clients and patients, commonly used assessment practices are not always successful in these endeavors. Although a number of gains have been made in the attention that is paid to culture in clinical practice, assessment practices continue to reflect an orientation that emphasizes natural science epistemology and acontextualism, as is often the case with psychology in general (Rozin, 2001). Without careful attention to cultural context, assessment practices may yield quantitatively rigorous profiles with little meaning about the capabilities and vulnerabilities of individuals.

Psychological tests and clinical assessment procedures have long been developed using a Eurocentric cultural orientation and with predominantly European American populations. This bias is true of psychological research in general. Research subjects are often White (Graham, 1992), and yet, they are not always described as such: "Authors often simply [describe] the participants as 'subjects,' assuming the reader will know that they are White" (Wong, 1994, p. 137). In common discourse, Whites are in fact not *just* "white"; instead, they are "normal and customary" (Feagin, 2001), and empirical research shows that Whites are perceived as best embodying the concept "American" (Devos & Banaji, 2005).

Psychology has generally shown relatively little interest in studying culture for its own sake. Culture has historically been considered a methodologically unsound construct presenting "noise" that needs to be controlled for in analyses (J. M. Jones & Rhee, 2004). Perhaps for that reason, many of the most prolific scholars who published in ethnic minority psychology between 1993 and 1999 are themselves of color (Nagayama Hall & Maramba, 2001). In this chapter, we examine culturally relevant assessment in the context of neuropsychological, clinical, and psychiatric assessments. Our review is meant not to be exhaustive of all the relevant concerns pertaining to assessment but to discuss three key areas of psychological functioning. We conclude the chapter with directions for future research and for areas of improvement in African American assessment.

Neuropsychological Assessment

Intelligence Testing

For African Americans, the propensity for inaccurate and harmful outcomes from the standard intelligence testing paradigm has long been discussed (Helms, 1992; Hilliard, 1979; Kwate, 2001). African Americans have been characterized as intellectually inferior to European Americans for as long as intelligence tests have existed, and some have sought to create intelligence tests based on African American culture (e.g., The Black Intelligence Test of Cultural Homogeneity; R. L. Williams, 1972). At issue are how intelligence is construed and the underrepresentation of the African American experience in standardization samples and test construction (R. L. Williams & Mitchell, 1991). Given the extensive literature on the psychometric issues related to cultural bias, we do not review that here; however, it is important to briefly underscore the long history of the testing enterprise in psychology, and its impact on African Americans, particularly because the intelligence testing paradigm has fostered the concept of ranking groups of people to determine their worth and to use these measurements to determine policy.

As early as the late 1800s, psychology was beginning to define constructs of intelligence, still regarded the sole province of the discipline. By the early 1900s, Charles Spearman introduced the two-factor theory of intelligence, and Binet and Simon constructed their intelligence test. In 1916, Terman revised the Binet scales and claimed that "Spanish-Indians," Mexicans, and Blacks were dull and that this characteristic appeared to be racial in etiology. As these tests began to be used with children of African descent, pronouncements of their intellectual inferiority rapidly multiplied.

During World War I, group intelligence tests were administered to Army draftees (Guthrie, 2004), which to an extent was borne of an attempt to demonstrate psychology's scientific rigor and technological similarity to the physical sciences. The results of the program were used to propose that Black adults possessed inferior intelligence. Many of these psychology examiners, such as Terman, Yerkes, and Wechsler, went on to create civilian business corporations involved in intelligence testing, and African Americans were not allowed to participate at any level (Guthrie, 2004). Research on intelligence between 1916 and 1930 was significantly informed by the two perspectives of the "mulatto hypothesis": one held that racially "pure" individuals were superior to those of mixed background; the other held that individuals with mixed ancestry were superior (Guthrie, 2004). Toward the end of that period, a quarter of more than 100 psychologists and scholars believed that researchers conclusively demonstrated that Blacks have inferior mental abilities.

While psychologists and others investigated the proposed intellectual deficiencies of Black people, eugenicists in the late 1920s were vigorously arguing that government programs should be developed to reduce the Black birth rate (D. Roberts, 1997). By 1930, 24 states enacted sterilization laws based on eugenic data, and more than 10,000 people were sterilized. Psychology took an active role in this process by using the Stanford–Binet intelligence test as the primary measure of deficiency (Guthrie, 2004).

Most people would believe that contemporary scientific ideas about race and intelligence would not rest on ideologically driven political and social goals. However, eugenicist ideas and inquiries into and arguments for the racial–genetic bases of intelligence persist and are even published in top (e.g., American Psychological Association) journals (e.g., Gottfredson, 2005). Psychology has been reluctant to grapple with the question of who is helped or harmed when psychologists categorize intelligence. Instead, the discipline has historically spent far more energy trying to define, operationalize, and categorize intelligence instead of considering the import of these actions for society.

Race and Neuropsychology

The field of neuropsychology has been similarly insensitive to the impact of race on neuropsychological assessment procedures (Nell, 2000). We must note here that we use *race* to refer to the embodied social experience of a society stratified by skin color, which includes relative access to resources, privileges, and other social experiences. We do not use *race* to connote a biological construct. An examinee's performance and behavior on neuropsychological tests are used to draw inferences about brain functioning and the extent and root causes of brain dysfunction (Lezak, 1995). These standardized tests are usually used in conjunction with intelligence testing, and they measure memory and learning style; executive functions such as cognitive flexibility, fluency, control of attention, and inhibition; expressive and receptive language skills; sensorimotor skills; and visuomotor skills. Neuropsychological testing is often used to diagnose cognitive disorders among elderly individuals (e.g., dementia) and among those with traumatic brain injury. Testing also generally determines specific cognitive strengths and weaknesses, especially among persons with neurological illness (e.g., epilepsy, tumors).

In more recent years, the amount of empirical research devoted to understanding the role of race on the process of neuropsychological assessment has increased (see Manly & Jacobs, 2002, for an extensive review). These tests make comparisons between an examinee's performance and a standardized sample and thus assume equality in educational experiences across test takers. Researchers have critically examined whether, for African Americans, neuropsychological measures accurately detect brain dysfunction (i.e., sensitivity) and accurately reject a diagnosis of brain dysfunction where there is none (i.e., specificity; Evans, Miller, Byrd, & Heaton, 2000). In general, the literature suggests that current neuropsychological practices are suboptimal for the assessment of African Americans (Nabors, Evans, & Strickland, 2000). Specifically, current testing procedures are more likely to incorrectly label African Americans as cognitively impaired. For example, in one study, 22% of cognitively intact African Americans were misclassified as impaired on the Visual Naming Subtest (R. J. Roberts & Hamsher, 1984). More recently, Manly, Jacobs, et al. (1998) found the false-positive rate of impairment in cognitively normal African Americans was high (more than 30%) in 10 out of 16 tests in a commonly used neuropsychological battery (i.e., Halstead–Reitan Battery).

Consistent with patterns found in intelligence testing, African Americans tend to score lower than European Americans on several different neuropsychological measures. For example, differences have been found on the Boston Naming Test (Lichtenberg, Ross, & Christensen, 1994), a word finding task of language and executive function; and on the Benton Visual Retention test (Anger et al., 1997), which measures visual memory. Whether these group differences are directly related to true differences in brain function has been questioned because of concerns about the content validity and cultural equivalence of the items and testing approach, the use of education-corrected norms, and the underrepresentation of African Americans in normative samples.

Cultural Equivalence and Relevance

R. N. Jones (2003) found that much of the variance in racial group differences in a brief cognitive screening questionnaire was accounted for by differential item functioning. Several items were highly discrepant in favor of White participants. Similarly, cognitive approaches required by many neuropsychological tests may favor approaches more common in White mainstream culture. For example, many instruments of attention and information processing place high value on speed and embed this element into the task demands. African Americans have been reported to perform lower than Whites on timed tasks (Diehr, Heaton, Miller, & Grant, 1998), and in general, the African American cultural approach to time is less rushed than that of White mainstream culture (J. M. Jones, 1988). Byrd, Touradji, Tang, and Manly (2004) suggested that this cultural approach to time may affect performance on timed tasks by guiding the cognitive style used to complete the task. In other words, relative to Whites, the cognitive approach taken by African Americans may deemphasize speed in favor of maximizing accuracy. Moreover, African Americans have been found to categorize information such as word lists, pictures, and situations differently than Whites (Shade, 1991). The organization approach may vary according to the extent to which it is more holistic versus detail oriented and functional versus descriptive (Manly & Jacobs, 2002).

The relationship between acculturation and neuropsychological performance among African Americans supports the supposition that these tests favor more mainstream cultural experiences. *Acculturation*, which for African Americans has been defined as the level at which an individual shares the values, language, and cognitive styles of his or her own ethnic community (Manly, 2006), has been shown to affect neuropsychological performance in African Americans. Less acculturated African Americans (i.e., defined as those who endorse values and behaviors traditional to those in the African American South) perform lower on neuropsychological measures of verbal skills (e.g., Boston Naming Test; Manly, Miller, et al., 1998); executive functioning (e.g., Wisconsin Card Sorting Test; Kennepohl, Shore, Nabors, & Hanks, 2004); psychomotor speed (e.g., Grooved Pegboard; Kennepohl et al., 2004); and memory (Delayed Recall on Wechsler Memory Scales; Manly, Miller, et al., 1998).

Education-Corrected Norms

Researchers have identified that the use of education-corrected norms tend to overestimate the quality of education for African Americans by assuming education levels are equivalent in African Americans and Whites (Baker, Johnson, Velli, & Wiley, 1996; Hilliard, 1979; Manly et al., 1999; R. L. Williams, 1971); consequently, many standardized neuropsychological instruments tend to overestimate pathology in African Americans, especially in individuals over age 65. The commonly used practice of education-corrected norms may not be appropriate among seniors because their educational environment was not equal to that of many of their European American counterparts with the same amount of education. The quality of school equipment, infrastructure, teachers, and teaching methods were markedly different in African American and White schools, particularly prior to 1954 (Manly, Jacobs, Touradji, Small, & Stern, 2002; Rohit et al., 2007). Cognitively normal older African Americans are therefore more likely to be misdiagnosed in the impaired range (Ford-Booker et al., 1993; Manly, Jacobs, et al., 1998; Nabors et al., 2000).

Some studies suggest that reading skill is a more accurate reflection of educational experience (e.g., Byrd, Jacobs, Hilton, Stern, & Manly, 2005; Manly et al., 2002; Ryan et al., 2005), because it is highly correlated with measures of quality of education, such as teacher:student ratios (Wilkinson, 1993). When determining standard scores using education-corrected norms, it is best to use education levels obtained from reading-level grade equivalents than to use actual completed years of education. The discrepancy between self-reported education grade level and reading-level grade equivalents is larger for African Americans compared with European Americans (Manly et al., 2002; O'Bryant, Schrimsher, & O'Jile, 2005). Use of reading-level grade equivalents tends to attenuate racial differences between African and European Americans on a number of neuropsychological tasks, including visuospatial, abstract reasoning, and memory tasks (Manly et al., 2002; Ryan et al., 2005), and on visual attention and psychomotor measures (i.e., the Trail Making Test Parts A and B, and the Grooved Pegboard Test—dominant hand (Rohit et al., 2007).

Ethnicity among individuals of African descent is rarely specified in the neuropsychology literature; that is, it usually is unclear whether the African Americans in research samples were immigrants of either a first or second generation from such regions as the Caribbean, or whether their families have lived in the United States for several generations. There is little literature in this area, but preliminary work (e.g., Byrd, Sanchez, & Manly, 2005) suggests it may be important to distinguish different ethnicities of African descent. Byrd and colleagues (2005) examined whether the influence of demographic factors on cognitive test performance was equitable for the Caribbean-born and U.S.-born African American elders. They demonstrated that for Caribbean-born, but not U.S.-born, African Americans, performance on tests of memory, language, and executive functioning was largely unrelated to demographic factors known to influence cognitive ability (i.e., age and educational level). The authors suggested neuropsychological tests may have diminished construct validity in Afro-Caribbean immigrants.

Gonzalez and colleagues (2007) used the Symbol Digit Modalities Test (Smith, 1982), which measures attention, visual scanning, and psychomotor speed, to compare performance in a nationally representative sample of Caribbean- and U.S.-born African Americans and Whites. On average, Caribbean-born African Americans scored lower than U.S.-born African Americans and Whites. Although these differences in performance could represent real differences in cognitive functioning, they may be artifacts of differential item functioning among the groups. Again, the preliminary findings from both studies (i.e., Byrd et al., 2005; Gonzalez et al., 2007) highlight the need to critically examine the role of ethnicity in African American neuropsychological test performance further.

Clinical and Psychiatric Assessment

A primary concern in the clinical and psychiatric assessment of African Americans is the potential for misdiagnosis, which is influenced by several factors. In particular, misdiagnosis is thought to result from such factors as social distance and clinician biases (e.g., Whaley & Geller, 2003). White clinicians tend to prefer talking about White patients (Flaherty & Meagher, 1980) and spend less time on assessment tasks for Black patients compared with other patients (Segal, Bola, & Watson, 1996). In practice, most clinical assessments entail an unstructured clinical interview in which clinical judgment guides the interview process and analysis of the presenting complaints and symptoms. Although clinical judgment is based on the skills and expertise of individual clinicians, it is also subject to biases that clinicians may hold for different racial–ethnic groups, perceived socioeconomic statuses, and genders. These biases are often stronger the more dissimilar clinicians are from their patients or clients (Adebimpe, 1981), and the tremendous pressure to assess patients and clients expeditiously amplifies the propensity to rely on stereotypes.

Misdiagnosis may also occur because the cultural backgrounds of African Americans may create variability in clinical presentations that are not well understood by clinicians from the dominant culture. Without adequate information about underlying cultural dynamics in the African American community, clinicians may not ask culturally relevant questions that would elicit more accurate and relevant information. In the following sections, we review literature on difficulties assessing schizophrenia, mood disorders, and anxiety disorders, conditions that have been examined by the most empirical work.

Schizophrenia

African Americans are more likely than Whites to be diagnosed with schizophrenia in a variety of clinical settings (e.g., Lawson, Hepler, Holladay, & Cuffel, 1994; Strakowski, Shelton, & Kolbrener, 1993), and many of these African Americans are in fact misdiagnosed (see Neighbors, 1997, and Neighbors, Jackson, Campbell, & Williams, 1989, for extensive reviews). In a psychiatric emergency service, schizophrenia and substance abuse were more commonly assigned as principal diagnoses in African American patients, and agreement between the psychiatric emergency room diagnosis and structured clinical interview diagnosis was lower for patients who were not White (Strakowski et al., 1997). Once diagnosed, Black patients are more likely to receive depot preparations (a controlled release process that helps administer a dosage of drug over time) of antipsychotic medication (Valenstein, Copeland, Owen, Blow, & Visnic, 2001) and are more frequently involuntarily committed and physically restrained.

Mood Disorders

African Americans are less likely than Whites to receive a diagnosis of bipolar disorder in clinical settings (Strakowski, McElroy, Keck, & West, 1996; Strakowski et al., 1993) and a diagnosis of major depressive disorder in community settings (Kessler et al., 2003; D. R. Williams et al., 2007). However, recent epidemiological evidence suggests that the chronicity of major depression is significantly worse for African Americans compared with Whites (D. R. Williams et al., 2007). African Americans have long been regarded as too jovial to be depressed or too impoverished to experience object losses (Prange & Vitols, 1962), and bipolar disorder was thought to occur more frequently among individuals in the upper and middle classes (Faris & Dunham, 1939; Parker, Spielberger, Wallace, & Becker, 1959). Since then, other researchers have sought to demonstrate that affective disorders are prevalent, but often underdiagnosed, among African Americans (Baker, 2001; B. E. Jones & Gray, 1986).

Recent epidemiological evidence suggests that even though some African Americans may not meet full criteria for major depression, they may still be experiencing symptoms consistent with major depression. To receive the diagnosis, patients must describe a level of impairment that significantly impedes functioning and/or exhibit a level of distress that is extremely overwhelming. Using these *Diagnostic and Statistical Manual of Mental Disorders* (4th ed.: *DSM–IV*; American

Psychiatric Association, 1994) criteria may not allow the experience of depression experienced by African Americans to be adequately captured. Using the National Health Interview Survey, Coyne and Marcus (2006) critically examined the relationship between race–ethnicity and the major depression diagnostic category in a sample of more than 30,000 participants. When limiting the diagnosis of depression to symptom criteria alone, the authors found that the rate of depression did not differ between African American and White participants; however, when a criterion about functional impairment was introduced, the rate of major depression for African Americans was substantially reduced. Many African Americans have financial constraints and familial obligations that may make them less likely to exhibit the role impairment typical of depression (e.g., missing days at work). Furthermore, any impairment or negative emotion experienced may be viewed as a consequence of other difficult contextual factors (e.g., discrimination at work), not depression. These results emphasize that the current system of psychiatric classification (*DSM–IV*) may not be appropriate or sufficient in the assessment of depression in African Americans.

Some scholars believe the underdiagnosis of affective disorders in African Americans is related to the overdiagnosis of schizophrenia. In clinical settings, it is possible that clinicians who are less familiar with African American patients misinterpret hallucinations often seen with severe depression among African Americans (Adebimpe, 1981; Baker & Bell, 1999) as schizophrenia. In addition, clinicians may misinterpret manic symptoms. For example, Mukherjee, Shukla, Woodle, Rosen, and Olarte (1983) found that in an outpatient sample of bipolar patients significantly more African Americans had a previous misdiagnosis of schizophrenia, despite similar symptom distributions among racial groups. Higher frequencies of schizophrenia among African American patients compared with Whites are seen, despite similar rates of affective symptoms, and specifically psychotic mania (Strakowski et al., 1996).

Anxiety Disorders

Cultural variations in symptom expression also occur in anxiety disorders, but as recently as 1991, little research had investigated African Americans' experience with anxiety disorders (Neal-Barnett & Smith, 1997). *Isolated sleep paralysis*—or, as many African Americans with origins in the South refer to it, "Witch riding" (Neal-Barnett, 2003)—is a feeling of paralysis on falling asleep or waking up. This experience is reported more frequently among African American women compared with other groups (Neal-Barnett, 2003) and is more likely to accompany panic attacks in African Americans than in Whites (Friedman & Paradis, 2002). Other variations in the expression of anxiety among African Americans include the stronger tendency to view anxiety symptoms as a component of a physical disorder, such as hypertension; to experience these symptoms as part of everyday worry about stressful life situations (e.g., racism); and to seek help from primary care physicians instead of mental health professionals.

Conclusion

In this chapter, we have discussed several important factors that influence the neuropsychological and clinical assessment of African Americans. Psychological assessment has the power to change the lives of individuals, families, and even communities, because results have the potential to stamp people with enduring labels about cognitive abilities, brain impairment, or psychiatric disorders. Therefore, accuracy and contextual validity in the utility of assessment practices is paramount. The universal, culture-free approach to neuropsychological assessment with African Americans is unsatisfactory. Analyses of the complexities involved in balancing sensitivity and specificity of existent measures are needed to move the field forward overall.

Studies should continue to refine the areas of neuropsychological assessment that are most related to systematic bias related to race. For example, existing measures of executive functioning and language functioning, as opposed to psychomotor functioning, may be more susceptible to poor construct validity among African Americans, especially those from the Caribbean, because of systematic differences in educational experiences. In addition, neuropsychological assessments are increasingly being used to inform theories about the etiological role of cognition in psychiatric illness, particularly schizophrenia. It is thought that psychopharmacological treatments can be tailored to improve cognitive deficits among schizophrenia patients. Neuropsychological assessment practices that are more likely to find cognitive impairment where there is none in African Americans will introduce error in these influential psychiatric studies.

In general, assessing clinical symptoms in African Americans out of cultural context is a risky enterprise. Clinical judgment is susceptible to stereotypes and prejudices, which may increase the overdiagnosis of psychosis and underdiagnosis of affective disorders. Some researchers have suggested that the use of structured diagnostic instruments during the clinical interview may reduce the probability of misdiagnosis (Neighbors et al., 1999), as could the addition of culturally tailored modules. The general goal of such remedial strategies centers on creating greater equivalency in the measurement process for standard diagnostic outcomes. It is important to recognize, however, that the standard outcomes themselves should be interrogated. Although African Americans are often underdiagnosed with depression, some argue that depression itself as a construct has retained less conceptual clarity and integrity over time. Normal feelings of sadness associated with loss or other painful circumstances are now inseparable from disordered sadness, or depression (Horwitz & Wakefield, 2007). Horwitz and Wakefield (2007) contended that other than bereavement, normal sadness is not recognized in the *DSM*, but it can emerge in response to distinct losses or from persistent and chronically stressful social situations. These could include long-term economic hardships or a continuing inability to achieve important goals; also, in the United States, African Americans regularly contend with social inequality. In that vein, some of what is characterized as depression may in fact be the expression of normal sadness, and all sadness, even if it meets all the diagnostic criteria for major depression, is not inherently pathological (Horwitz & Wakefield).

With regard to improving clinical and psychiatric assessment, culture-specific phenomena, such as isolated sleep paralysis in panic disorder, should continue to receive more attention. Adebimpe (2004) made several suggestions to improve assessment: Ambiguous data should be clarified through the use of family members and other key informants; clinicians should demonstrate a clear awareness and empathy regarding the racially based stresses with which African American patients live; clinicians should collect suggestive family history data and extensive information on the course of symptoms; and clinicians should distinguish between mental illness and physical problems. Researchers could improve the functional impairment criteria assessments by making them more relevant to specific psychiatric disorders and by considering the ways in which African Americans with significant occupational or extended kin responsibilities may exhibit functional impairment.

Across all domains of psychological assessment, the field should continue to move towards deconstructing "African American" and "Black" into meaningful components that capture critical variation in sociocultural experience. Assessment should include questions about racial socialization, acculturation, and ethnicity as part of demographic background and history. Particular attention should be paid to making sure assessment tools are measuring phenomena in African American clients that they are meant to measure. Areas of psychological functioning that are most vulnerable to cultural biases (e.g., aspects of cognition) should be assessed with at least two different instruments, and existing psychometric instruments and standard interviews should be supplemented with qualitative questions relevant to African Americans. These changes ultimately will bring us closer to the ideal assessment, in which areas of relative strength and weakness among African Americans are identified in the most accurate and culturally appropriate manner.

References

Adebimpe, V. R. (1981). Overview: White norms and psychiatric diagnosis of Black patients. *American Journal of Psychiatry, 138*, 279–285.

Adebimpe, V. R. (2004). A second opinion on the use of White norms in psychiatric diagnosis of Black patients. *Psychiatric Annals, 34*, 543–562.

American Psychiatric Association. (1994). *Diagnostic and statistical manual of mental disorders* (4th ed.). Washington, DC: Author.

Anger, W. K., Sizemore, O. J., Grossmann, S. J., Glasser, J. A., Letz, R., & Bowler, R. (1997). Human neurobehavioral research methods: Impact of subject variables. *Environmental Research, 73*, 18–41.

Baker, F. M. (2001). Diagnosing depression in African Americans. *Community Mental Health Journal, 37,* 31–38.

Baker, F. M., & Bell, C. C. (1999). Issues in the psychiatric treatment of African Americans. *Psychiatric Services, 50,* 362–368.

Baker, F. M., Johnson, J. T., Velli, S. A., & Wiley, C. (1996). Congruence between education and reading levels of older persons. *Psychiatric Services, 47,* 194–196.

Byrd, D. A., Jacobs, D. M., Hilton, H. J., Stern, Y., & Manly, J. J. (2005). Sources of errors on visuoperceptual tasks: Role of education, literacy, and search strategy. *Brain and Cognition, 58,* 251–257.

Byrd, D. A., Sanchez, D., & Manly, J. J. (2005). Neuropsychological test performance among Caribbean-born and U.S.-born African American elderly: The role of age, education and reading level. *Journal of Clinical and Experimental Neuropsychology, 27,* 1056–1069.

Byrd, D. A., Touradji, P., Tang, M., & Manly, J. J. (2004). Cancellation test performance in African American, Hispanic, and White elderly. *Journal of the International Neuropsychological Society, 10,* 401–411.

Coyne, J. C., & Marcus, S. C. (2006). Health disparities in care for depression possibly obscured by the clinical significance criterion. *American Journal of Psychiatry, 163,* 1577–1579.

Devos, T., & Banaji, M. R. (2005). American = White? *Journal of Personality and Social Psychology, 88,* 447–466.

Diehr, M. C., Heaton, R. K., Miller, W., & Grant, I. (1998). The Paced Auditory Serial Addition Task (PASAT): Norms for age, education, and ethnicity. *Assessment, 5,* 375–387.

Evans, J. D., Miller, S. W., Byrd, D. A., & Heaton, R. K. (2000). Cross-cultural applications of the Halstead–Reitan Batteries. In E. Fletcher-Janzen, T. L. Strickland, & C. R. Reynolds (Eds.), *Handbook of cross-cultural neuropsychology* (pp. 287–303). Dordrecht, Netherlands: Kluwer Academic.

Faris, R. E., & Dunham, H. W. (Eds.). (1939). *Mental disorders in urban areas.* Chicago: University of Chicago Press.

Feagin, J. R. (2001). *Racist America: Roots, current realities, and future reparations.* New York: Routledge.

Flaherty, J. A., & Meagher, R. (1980). Measuring racial bias in inpatient treatment. *American Journal of Psychiatry, 137,* 679–682.

Ford-Booker, P., Campbell, A., Combs, S., Lewis, S., Ocampo, C., Brown, A., et al. (1993). The predictive accuracy of neuropsychological tests in a normal population of African Americans. *Journal of Clinical and Experimental Neuropsychology, 15,* 64.

Friedman, S., & Paradis, C. (2002). Panic disorder in African Americans: Symptomatology and isolated sleep paralysis. *Culture, Medicine and Psychiatry, 26,* 179–198.

Gonzalez, H. M., Whitfield, K. E., West, B. T., Williams, D. R., Lichtenberg, P. A., & Jackson, J. S. (2007). Modified-symbol digit modalities test for African Americans, Caribbean Black Americans, and non-Latino Whites: Nationally representative normative data from the National Survey of American Life. *Archives of Clinical Neuropsychology, 22,* 605–613.

Gottfredson, L. S. (2005). What if the hereditarian hypothesis is true? *Psychology, Public Policy, and Law, 11,* 311–319.

Graham, S. (1992). "Most of the subjects were White and middle class": Trends in published research on African Americans in selected APA journals, 1970–1989. *American Psychologist, 47,* 629–639.

Guthrie, R. V. (2004). *Even the rat was white: A historical view of psychology* (2nd ed.). Upper Saddle River, NJ: Pearson Education.

Helms, J. E. (1992). Why is there no study of cultural equivalence in standardized cognitive ability testing? *American Psychologist, 47,* 1083–1101.

Hilliard, A. G. (1979). Standardization and cultural bias impediments to the scientific study and validation of "intelligence." *Journal of Research and Development in Education, 12,* 47–58.

Horwitz, A. V., & Wakefield, J. C. (2007). *The loss of sadness: How psychiatry transformed normal sorrow into depressive disorder.* New York: Oxford University Press.

Jones, B. E., & Gray, B. A. (1986). Problems in diagnosing schizophrenia and affective disorders among Blacks. *Hospital & Community Psychiatry, 37,* 61–65.

Jones, J. M. (1988). Cultural differences in temporal perspectives: Instrumental and expressive behaviors in time. In J. E. McGrath (Ed.), *The social psychology of time: New perspectives* (pp. 21–38). Newbury Park, CA: Sage.

Jones, J. M., & Rhee, E. (2004). The dialectics of race: Academic perils and promises. In J. M. Darley, M. P. Zanna, & H. L. Roediger III (Eds.), *The compleat academic: A career guide* (2nd ed., pp. 295–310). Washington, DC: American Psychological Association.

Jones, R. N. (2003). Racial bias in the assessment of cognitive functioning of older adults. *Aging & Mental Health, 7,* 83–102.

Kennepohl, S., Shore, D., Nabors, N., & Hanks, R. (2004). African American acculturation and neuropsychological test performance following traumatic brain injury. *Journal of the International Neuropsychological Society, 10,* 566–577.

Kessler, R. C., Berglund, P., Demler, O., Jin, R., Koretz, D., Merikangas, K. R., et al. (2003). The epidemiology of major depressive disorder: results from the National Comorbidity Survey Replication (NCS-R). *Journal of the American Medical Association, 289,* 3095–3105.

Kwate, N. O. (2001). Intelligence or misorientation? Eurocentrism in the WISC–III. *Journal of Black Psychology, 27,* 221–238.

Lawson, W. B., Hepler, N., Holladay, J., & Cuffel, B. (1994). Race as a factor in inpatient and outpatient admissions and diagnosis. *Hospital & Community Psychiatry, 45,* 72–74.

Lezak, M. D. (1995). *Neuropsychological assessment* (3rd ed.). New York: Oxford University Press.

Lichtenberg, P. A., Ross, T., & Christensen, B. (1994). Preliminary normative data on the Boston Naming Test for an older urban population. *Clinical Neuropsychologist, 8,* 109–111.

Manly, J. J. (2006). Deconstructing race and ethnicity: Implications for measurement of health outcomes. *Medical Care, 44*(11, Suppl. 3), S10–S16.

Manly, J. J., & Jacobs, D. M. (2002). Future directions in neuropsychological assessment with African Americans. In F. R. Ferraro (Ed.), *Minority and cross-cultural aspects of neuropsychological assessment* (pp. 79–96). Lisse, Netherlands: Swets & Zeitlinger.

Manly, J. J., Jacobs, D. M., Sano, M., Bell, K., Merchant, C. A., Small, S. A., et al. (1998). Cognitive test performance among nondemented elderly African Americans and Whites. *Neurology, 50,* 1238–1245.

Manly, J. J., Jacobs, D. M., Sano, M., Bell, K., Merchant, C. A., Small, S. A., et al. (1999). Effect of literacy on neuropsychological test performance in nondemented, education-matched elders. *Journal of the International Neuropsychological Society, 5,* 191–202.

Manly, J. J., Jacobs, D. M., Touradji, P., Small, S. A., & Stern, Y. (2002). Reading level attenuates differences in neuropsychological test performance between African American and White elders. *Journal of the International Neuropsychological Society, 8,* 341–348.

Manly, J. J., Miller, S. W., Heaton, R. K., Byrd, D., Reilly, J., Velasquez, R. J., et al. (1998). The effect of African-American acculturation on neuropsychological test performance in normal and HIV-positive individuals. *Journal of the International Neuropsychological Society, 4,* 291–302.

Mukherjee, S., Shukla, S., Woodle, J., Rosen, A. M., & Olarte, S. (1983). Misdiagnosis of schizophrenia in bipolar patients: A multiethnic comparison. *American Journal of Psychiatry, 140,* 1571–1574.

Nabors, N. A., Evans, J. D., & Strickland, T. L. (2000). Neuropsychological assessment and intervention with African Americans. In E. Fletcher-Janzen, T. L. Strickland, & C. R. Reynolds (Eds.), *Handbook of cross-cultural neuropsychology* (pp. 31–42). Dordrecht, Netherlands: Kluwer Academic.

Nagayama Hall, G. C., & Maramba, G. G. (2001). In search of cultural diversity: Recent literature in cross-cultural and ethnic minority psychology. *Cultural Diversity and Ethnic Minority Psychology, 7,* 12–26.

Neal-Barnett, A. (2003). *Soothe your nerves: The Black woman's guide to understanding and overcoming anxiety, panic, and fear.* New York: Fireside Books.

Neal-Barnett, A. M., & Smith, J. (1997). African Americans. In S. Friedman (Ed.), *Cultural issues in the treatment of anxiety* (pp. 154–174). New York: Guilford Press.

Neighbors, H. (1997). The (mis)diagnosis of mental disorder in African Americans. *African American Research Perspectives, 3,* 1–11.

Neighbors, H. W., Jackson, J. S., Campbell, L., & Williams, D. (1989). The influence of racial factors on psychiatric diagnosis: A review and suggestions for research. *Community Mental Health Journal, 25,* 301–311.

Neighbors, H. W., Trierweiler, S. J., Munday, C., Thompson, E. E., Jackson, J. S., Binion, V. J., et al. (1999). Psychiatric diagnosis of African Americans: Diagnostic divergence in clinician-structured and semistructured interviewing conditions. *Journal of the National Medical Association, 91,* 601–612.

Nell, V. (2000). *Cross-cultural neuropsychological assessment: Theory and practice.* Mahwah, NJ: Lawrence Erlbaum.

O'Bryant, S. E., Schrimsher, G. W., & O'Jile, J. R. (2005). Discrepancies between self-reported years of education and estimated reading level: Potential implications for neuropsychologists. *Applied Neuropsychology, 12,* 5–11.

Parker, J. B., Jr., Spielberger, C. D., Wallace, D. K., & Becker, J. (1959). Factors in manic-depressive reactions. *Diseases of the Nervous System, 20,* 505–511.

Prange, A. J., Jr., & Vitols, M. M. (1962). Cultural aspects of the relatively low incidence of depression in southern Negroes. *International Journal of Social Psychiatry, 8,* 104–112.

Roberts, D. (1997). *Killing the Black body: Race, reproduction and the meaning of liberty.* New York: Pantheon.

Roberts, R. J., & Hamsher, K. D. (1984). Effects of minority status on facial recognition and naming performance. *Journal of Clinical Psychology, 40,* 539–545.

Rohit, M., Levine, A., Hinkin, C., Abramyan, S., Saxton, E., Valdes-Sueiras, M., et al. (2007).

Education correction using years in school or reading grade-level equivalent? Comparing the accuracy of two methods in diagnosing HIV-associated neurocognitive impairment. *Journal of the International Neuropsychological Society, 13,* 462–470.

Rozin, P. (2001). Social psychology and science: Some lessons from Solomon Asch. *Personality and Social Psychology Review, 5,* 2–14.

Ryan, E. L., Baird, R., Mindt, M. R., Byrd, D., Monzones, J., & Morgello, S. (2005). Neuropsychological impairment in racial/ethnic minorities with HIV infection and low literacy levels: Effects of education and reading level in participant characterization. *Journal of the International Neuropsychological Society, 11,* 889–898.

Segal, S. P., Bola, J. R., & Watson, M. A. (1996). Race, quality of care, and antipsychotic prescribing practices in psychiatric emergency services. *Psychiatric Services, 47,* 282–286.

Shade, B. J. (1991). African American patterns of cognition. In R. L. Jones (Ed.), *Black Psychology* (3rd ed., pp. 231–247). Berkeley, CA: Cobb & Henry.

Smith, A. (1982). *Symbol Digit Modalities Test manual* (Rev. ed.). Los Angeles: Western Psychological Services.

Strakowski, S. M., Hawkins, J. M., Keck, P. E., McElroy, S. L., West, S. A., Bourne, M. L., et al. (1997). The effects of race and information variance on disagreement between psychiatric emergency service and research diagnoses in first-episode psychosis. *Journal of Clinical Psychiatry, 58,* 457–463.

Strakowski, S. M., McElroy, S. L., Keck, P. E., Jr., & West, S. A. (1996). Racial influence on diagnosis in psychotic mania. *Journal of Affective Disorders, 39,* 157–162.

Strakowski, S. M., Shelton, R. C., & Kolbrener, M. L. (1993). The effects of race and comorbidity on clinical diagnosis in patients with psychosis. *Journal of Clinical Psychiatry, 54,* 96–102.

Valenstein, M., Copeland, L. A., Owen, R., Blow, F. C., & Visnic, S. (2001). Adherence assessments and the use of depot antipsychotics in patients with schizophrenia. *Journal of Clinical Psychiatry, 62,* 545–551.

Whaley, A. L., & Geller, P. A. (2003). Ethnic/racial differences in psychiatric disorders: a test of four hypotheses. *Ethnicity & Disease, 13,* 499–512.

Wilkinson, G. S. (1993). *Wide Range Achievement Test 3 administration manual.* Wilmington, DE: Jastak Associates.

Williams, D. R., Gonzalez, H. M., Neighbors, H., Nesse, R., Abelson, J. M., Sweetman, J., et al. (2007). Prevalence and distribution of major depressive disorder in African Americans, Caribbean Blacks, and non-Hispanic Whites: Results from the National Survey of American Life. *Archives of General Psychiatry, 64,* 305–315.

Williams, R. L. (1971). Abuses and misuses in testing Black children. *The Counseling Psychologist, 2,* 62–73.

Williams, R. L. (1972). *The BITCH-100: A cultural specific test.* St. Louis, MO: Williams & Associates.

Williams, R. L., & Mitchell, H. (1991). The testing game. In R. L. Jones (Ed.), *Black Psychology* (3rd ed., pp. 193–205). Berkeley, CA: Cobb & Henry.

Wong, L. M. (1994). Di(s)-secting and dis(s)-closing "whiteness": Two tales about psychology. *Feminism & Psychology, 4*(1), 133–153.

34

DRUG USE AMONG AFRICAN AMERICAN YOUTH

Implications for Prevention

FAYE Z. BELGRAVE, TRENETTE CLARK, AND AASHIR NASIM

Drug use and abuse are of concern in the African American community for several reasons. Overall, African Americans do not use more drugs than other racial and ethnic groups, yet they face more severe consequences from such use. Tobacco, alcohol, and other drug use and abuse contribute greatly to health disparities among African Americans. These health disparities include lung cancer and other cancers, HIV and STD infections, tuberculosis, cardiovascular disease, and other chronic and health-comprising conditions. The use, sale, and distribution of illicit drugs affect the well-being of African American communities in that illicit drug use generally co-occurs with problems of crime, violence, and low economic viability.

We focus this chapter[1] on factors related to the overall reduction and prevention of drug use, because of the social and health consequences associated with drug use and abuse among African Americans. We begin our discussion with brief definitions, followed by an overview of drug use prevalence. We then turn our attention to the etiology of drug use. Attention is given to what factors (i.e., individual, family, peer, community) are known to cause drug use (i.e., risk factors), as well as what factors are known to prevent drug use and abuse (i.e., promotive and protective factors) among African American youth. Knowledge of risk and protective factors for alcohol, tobacco, and other drug use has been instrumental in informing the development of successful prevention interventions for African American youth. Thus, we discuss universal and culturally appropriate prevention strategies for African American youth. We conclude with a brief discussion of prospective research in the field of drug use and offer some recommendations for prevention programming.

DEFINITIONS OF DRUG USE AND ABUSE

A *drug* is any chemical compound that is used in the prevention, diagnosis, treatment, or cure of disease; for the relief of pain; or to control or improve any physiological or pathological disorder in humans or animals (NDI Foundation, 2007). Drugs may be consciousness altering and habit forming, including those whose use is restricted or illegal, such as cocaine, heroin, marijuana, and amphetamines (Merriam-Webster Medical Dictionary on Medline Plus, 1998). *Illicit drug use* refers to the use of illegal and controlled drugs, such as marijuana, cocaine, or heroin (Centers for Disease Control and Prevention, 2007). *Drug abuse* is the use of a substance to modify or control mood or state of mind in a manner that is illegal or harmful to oneself or others (National Institute on Drug Abuse, 2005).

Prevalence of Drug Use

The National Survey on Drug Use & Health (NSDUH) provides information on the prevalence of tobacco, alcohol, and illicit drug use among youth ages 12 to 17 (see Table 34.1; Substance Abuse and Mental Health Services Administration, 2006). The NSDUH gathers data from a national sample of the civilian noninstitutionalized population age 12 and older on patterns of drug use among different age, gender, and ethnic groups (Substance Abuse and Mental Health Services Administration, 2002).

As can be seen in Table 34.1, African American youth engage in tobacco use and alcohol use less than Whites. Illicit drug use is slightly higher for African American youth than for White youth. Lower drug use prevalence among African American youth is notable because African American youth are disproportionately exposed to contextual disadvantages. Wallace and Muroff (2002) speculated that it may be the influence of the family that accounts for the relatively low level of drug use among younger African American youth. Families monitor and structure activities, shape antidrug attitudes, and promote norms that are intolerant of drug use. However, when African American youth grow older and leave home, the protection the family affords against drug use may diminish. We discuss the consequences of drug use next.

Consequences of Drug Use for African Americans

Although overall rates of drug use are lower for African American youth than for White youth, there are noted variations in drug use patterns that increase African Americans' susceptibility to chronic health conditions. Prevalence use data show that African American youth have a later age of onset than Whites for cigarette use. Whereas youth who initiate cigarette use in late adolescence are less likely to develop drug dependence into adulthood than those who have an earlier age of onset, the trend for cigarette use among African Americans is just the opposite. In fact, late onset is associated with greater cigarette use persistence into adulthood among African Americans (Kandel, 2006). This phenomenon has been described as the *crossover effect* (Geronimus, Neidert, & Bound, 1993).

The consequences of drug use for African Americans span health (e.g., physical and psychological) and social (e.g., intrapersonal and interpersonal) domains. Rates of smoking-related health problems, such as lung and heart disease, are 20% to 40% higher for African Americans than for White Americans (Centers for Disease Control and Prevention, 2002). Lung cancer kills more African Americans than any other cancer. African American smokers have more difficulty in quitting than other ethnic groups (Kiefe et al., 2001). Difficulty in quitting may be due to the fact that African Americans are three times more likely than Whites to prefer mentholated cigarettes (Kabat & Hebert, 1991). Smokers of mentholated cigarettes have higher nicotine dependence, which makes it more difficult to quit and increases adverse heath effects.

African American and Hispanic youth also show higher prevalence of drug-related social problems than do Whites, despite higher drug use among White youth (Barnes & Welte; 1986; Wallace & Muroff, 2002). For instance, for every ounce of alcohol consumed, African American youth have increasingly more social and academic problems when compared with White youth (Barnes & Welte). Other social and academic consequences from drug use among African American youth include higher rates of school failure, juvenile detention and incarceration, and employment problems (Wallace & Muroff). These increased problems may be due to fewer treatment and intervention resources available to assist African American youth when needed.

Finally, illicit drugs, especially crack cocaine, have contributed largely to incarceration of African American men and, more recently, women. More than 20 years ago, Congress passed an anti–drug-abuse bill that resulted in large sentencing discrepancies for possession and distribution of crack versus cocaine (King & Mauer, 2006). For example, an individual can possess 100 times the amount of powder cocaine as crack and receive the same mandatory sentence. African Americans are much more likely

Table 34.1 Prevalence of Selected Substances in the Past Month by Age and Ethnicity

	Ages 12–17		Ages 18–25		Ages 26 & Over	
	Black (Non-Hispanic)	White (Non-Hispanic)	Black (Non-Hispanic)	White (Non-Hispanic)	Black (Non-Hispanic)	White (Non-Hispanic)
Cigarettes	6.5	12.8	28.7	44.2	27.0	24.8
Alcohol	11.6	18.5	48.3	66.8	43.6	57.5
Heavy Alcohol [a]	0.6	3.2	5.9	19	4.8	6.3
Illicit Drugs [b]	11	10.1	18.21	22.9	7.8	5.9

Source: Substance Abuse and Mental Health Services Administration, Office of Applied Studies (2005).
a. Five or more drinks on the same occasion at least once in the past month.
b. Includes marijuana/hashish, cocaine (including crack), heroin, hallucinogens, inhalants, or any prescription-type psychotherapeutic agent used nonmedically.

than Whites to possess crack rather than the powder form of the drug. The harsh sentence for crack cocaine remained for many years in spite of the numerous calls for its repeal, including the 1995 recommendation from the U.S. Sentencing Commission to reduce penalties for crack offenders. In December 2007, the U.S. Supreme Court ruled, in a 7–2 vote, that the disparity in sentencing of crack and cocaine offenders is unjust. At the time of this writing, it is expected that the Sentencing Commission will suggest revisions regarding the minimum/maximum laws for crack and cocaine.

RISK AND PROTECTIVE FACTORS FOR DRUG USE AMONG AFRICAN AMERICAN YOUTH

Several theories and conceptual frameworks have been used to account for drug use among adolescent populations. There is not any single theory of adolescent substance use that predominates the research literature, and extensive reviews of such theories have been conducted elsewhere (e.g., McGuire, 1991; Petraitis, Flay, & Miller, 1995). However, one well-known conceptual framework is risk and protective factors for adolescent drug use (Hawkins, Catalano, & Miller, 1992). *Risk factors* have been defined as indexes or markers that exacerbate the negative effects of the risk condition (Luthar, Cicchetti, & Becker, 2000). *Protective factors* are characteristics that can influence outcomes either directly or indirectly, by buffering against risk factors. Research shows that not one factor, but several different factors—both risk and protective—contribute to drug use among youth. These factors can be categorized under the individual, family, peer, school, and community domains.

Although Hawkins et al. (1992) provided a laundry list of risk and protective factors for youth, we concentrate our discussion on factors that have contributed to the reduction or enhancement of drug use among African American adolescents. It is important to note that previous research on drug prevention have been based on two implicit assumptions: (1) that the risk factors for substance use are identical for African American and White youth and (2) that African American and White youth experience similar levels of risk exposure and vulnerability (Wallace & Muroff, 2002). Current studies, however, show that the relationships between risk and protective factors and drug use differ across ethnic groups. In this section, we briefly review risk and protective factors within individual, family, peer, school, and community domains. We also discuss factors within a cultural domain that have been shown to protect against African American adolescent drug use.

Individual Factors

Individual protective factors include social and problem-solving skills, positive attitude, positive temperament, emotional stability, positive self-concept, high intelligence, and low childhood stress (Grover, 1998). Individual risk factors for adolescent substance use may include a sensation-seeking orientation, poor impulse control, attention deficits, and hyperactivity (Jenson, 2004). Genetics or biological factors are also believed to play a role in drug use. Researchers have found that offspring of alcoholic parents who have been adopted show more alcoholism than those whose biological parents are not alcoholic (Center for Substance Abuse Prevention, 1993).

Family Factors

Family risk factors for substance use include family conflict, poor family management practices, dysfunctional family communication patterns, parent and sibling substance use, and poor parent–child bonding (Jenson, 2004; Windle, 2000). Family protective factors include being a firstborn child, being raised in a small family, low parental conflict, caring relationships with siblings, caring relationships with extended family members, and attachment to parents. Parental influence may be a stronger determinant than peer influence of substance use, especially for younger teens (Wallace & Muroff, 2002; Windle, 2000). High family cohesiveness and a positive parent–adolescent relationship are associated with less drug use and intolerant drug attitudes, especially under conditions of high neighborhood risk (Bray, Adams, Greg, & Baer, 2001; Grover, 1998). In a study of 155 African American sixth-grade females, Boyd, Ashcraft, and Belgrave (2006) found that positive father–daughter relationships were associated with higher levels of drug refusal self-efficacy. Previous research has also shown that children whose parents or siblings engage in serious alcohol or illicit drug use are themselves at greater risk for these behaviors (Biederman, Faraone, Monuteaux, & Feighner, 2000).

Peer Factors

Youth whose peers use drugs are more likely to use drugs than those whose peers do not (Hawkins et al., 1992). Youth try their first drugs with peers, model drug-using behaviors, and influence their peers' attitudes toward drugs. Association with drug-using friends is among the strongest predictor of adolescent substance use (Reinherz, Giaconia, Carmola Hauf, Wasserman, & Paradis, 2000). In a study of African American 10th-graders, Farrell and White (1998) found that both peer pressure and peer drug use were related to the frequency of drug use.

School Factors

Several school risk factors contribute to drug use, including academic failure, truancy, and special placements (McCluskey, Krohn, Lizotte, & Rodriguez, 2002). High academic performance and school involvement are associated with lower levels of drug use (Dekovic, 1999; Wallace & Muroff, 2002). The relationship between academic success and drug use might be different for African Americans and other ethnic groups. Wallace and Muroff (2002) found that whereas White youth generally perform better academically, they were more vulnerable than African Americans to the impact of school-related risk factors. Another study found that academic failure was not a predictor of drug use for African American adolescents (Saint-Jean & Crandall, 2004). More research on the risk or protection afforded by academic and school environment is needed to further understand this relationship.

Community/Neighborhood Factors

Neighborhood context is another predictor of substance use among African American adolescents (Lambert, Brown, Phillips, & Ialongo, 2004). Protective factors, such as neighborhood cohesion, neighborhood resources, and economic viability in neighborhoods, are associated with lower adolescent substance use (Plybon, Edwards, Butler, Belgrave, & Allison, 2003). Neighborhood risk factors, such as neighborhood disorganization, low neighborhood attachment, high rates of residential mobility, high levels of crime, and high population density, are risk factors and influence adolescent substance use (Gruenewald, Millar, Ponicki, & Brinkley, 2000). Limited community resources may contribute to lowered motivation to avoid behaviors that have negative consequences (Corneille & Belgrave, 2007). This may occur when youth in these social environments develop negative beliefs about who they are and who they can become.

Moreover, the effect of neighborhood on drug use may vary as a function of rural versus urban residence. Nasim and colleagues (2007) examined the influence of community and family as predictors of substance use among youth who lived in rural and urban communities. They found that community context (i.e., neighborhood crime) was a significant predictor of drug use among African American adolescents who lived in urban environments, but not among those who lived in rural environments. Family factors were stronger predictors of drug use among African Americans who lived in rural compared with urban environments.

Cultural Factors

Certain cultural characteristics found predominantly among African Americans may protect against substance use. Two factors that have been found to be associated with lower levels of substance use are ethnic identity (Corneille & Belgrave, 2007) and religiosity (Wills, Yaeger, & Sandy, 2003). Risk factors for drug use include racism and discrimination. Ethnic identity may buffer against drug use through its positive effect on adaptive behaviors and attitudes. Across several studies, high ethnic identity has been shown to be directly and indirectly associated with lowered drug use and antidrug attitudes in African American adolescents (Belgrave, Brome, & Hampton, 2000; Townsend & Belgrave, 2000).

High levels of religiosity among African Americans also serve as a protective factor for drug use. Belgrave, Townsend, Cherry, and Cunningham (1997) found that African American youth who attend church and who discuss religious topics within the home are less likely to use drugs than those with fewer religious practices. Booth, Curran, and Han (2004) and Wallace, Brown, Backman, and Laveist

(2003) found that adolescents who report being highly religious are less likely to use alcohol and other substances than are less religiously oriented youth. Using a sample of rural African American youth, Nasim, Utsey, Corona, and Belgrave (2006) found that religious beliefs and practices demonstrated both a promotive (i.e., associated with decreases in substance use) and a protective–stabilizing effect (i.e., religious beliefs functioned to maintain youth's low susceptibility to substance use across worsening contexts) for youth. Adolescents who adhered to religious beliefs and practices were less likely to use substances even under conditions of high community risk.

Risk factors for substance use are racism and discrimination. Perceived racism and discrimination are linked to increased use of several substances, including cigarettes and alcohol (Curtis-Boles & Jenkins-Monroe, 2000). Using a prospective design, Gibbons, Gerrard, Cleveland, Wills, and Brody (2004) examined the effect of perceived discrimination and substance use among African American parents and their children. Interviews were conducted separately for parents and children at two points in time. The researchers found that discrimination was prospectively linked with drug use for both parent and child. Participants who perceived discrimination to be high at Time 1 reported less of a decline in use over time or more of an increase in drug use. The authors noted that Time 1 discrimination had the highest correlation with parental use of any of the variables assessed at either period, including a number of additional common risk and protective factors, such as social support and social relationship problems, financial strain, optimism, religious beliefs, and perceived control. The patterns for adults were similar to those for the children. Gibbons et al. concluded that discrimination appears to be linked to substance use indirectly through its relationship with stress.

Substance Abuse Prevention Interventions

Substance abuse prevention interventions have been based on several theoretical perspectives. *Social-cognitive* approaches to substance abuse prevention provide youth with the knowledge and skills to resist peer pressure to use drugs (Belgrave et al., 2004b; Griffin, Botvin, & Nichols, 2006). *Problem behavior theory* assumes that drug use is part of a constellation of deviant and problematic behaviors; these programs address substance use by increasing social competencies and addressing underlying social and psychological factors (Collins & Ellickson, 2004b), Jessor & Jessor, 1977). *Peer cluster theory* considers that socialization factors that are associated with adolescent development interact to produce peer clusters that encourage or discourage drug use. Interventions based on peer cluster theory address drug use by changing peer networks and/or peer influence within networks (Oetting & Beauvais, 1987). *Stress coping theories* assume that youth use drugs to cope with stressors that can be due to interpersonal and environmental challenges (Schinke & Schwinn, 2005). Adaptive strategies for managing stress are used in these types of prevention interventions. *Ecological* and *family theories* assume that the route to drug prevention is through strengthening the family and community context of youth (Bronfenbrenner, 1979; Kumpfer, Alvarado, & Tait, 2007).

Substance abuse prevention programs have primarily targeted adolescents, although some programs are targeted at children, adults, and families. Among adolescents, preadolescence and early adolescence (ages 10–14) are the age groups most likely to be targeted, because this is the most common age at which drug initiation occurs. A January 2008 review of the Substance Abuse Mental Health Services Administration's National Registry of Evidence-based Programs and Practices revealed 13 substance abuse prevention interventions for African American youth ages 6 through 17 (http://www.nrepp.samhsa.gov/listofprograms). The majority of these programs target youth 11 through 14 years of age and youth in middle or junior high schools. These prevention interventions are most likely to be implemented within school settings, followed by family sessions. These prevention interventions are designed to prevent and delay drug use and also improve drug refusal or resistance skills, negative and intolerant drug attitudes and norms, prosocial behaviors and social competence, intrapersonal and psychological well-being, communication and decision-making skills, and family bonding and cohesion. The intervention programs listed on the National Registry of Evidence-based Programs and Practices are universal programs and are implemented with all racial–ethnic groups. However, as we discuss next, prevention interventions for African American youth must consider their culture and context.

Culturally Appropriate Approaches to Substance Abuse Prevention

The most effective substance abuse prevention interventions for African American youth consider cultural and contextual factors. Research suggests that cultural adaptations to universal programs may be effective in reducing alcohol and drug use (Belgrave et al., 2004a; Botvin, 1995; Burlew et al., 2000). Cultural adaptations must consider both the structure and format (i.e., the way in which the program is delivered) and the content (i.e., the lessons and the messages received). Chipungu, Hermann, and Sambrano (2000) identified several strategies used in culturally congruent programs for African American youth. They examined 47 culturally specific programs for African American youth funded by the Center for Substance Abuse Prevention. Their sample consisted of more than 10,000 participants. The majority of the African American programs (83.3%) reported using culturally focused content in their prevention interventions. These programs used one or more of the following three strategies: (1) They had participants review contemporary mainstream culture and see how this culture affected African American youth, families, and communities; (2) they discussed issues such as racism, negative media images, the contemporary condition of African American families, and consumer culture; and (3) they emphasized positive Africentric ideology, values, traditions, history, cultural appreciation, and rituals that support values indigenous to African people. Along with these topics, the interventions also targeted drug refusal skills through drug prevention curricula.

Chipungu and colleagues (2000) identified three different types of cultural programs. Although not mutually exclusive, there were unique features of each program. The first program type addressed how cultural traditions and values, such as family and spirituality, could protect youth from using substances such as cigarette, alcohol, and other drugs. An example of this type of cultural program is the use of the seven principles of *Nguzo Saba* and African proverbs. For example, the principle of *Ujima* (collective work and responsibility) might be used to provide a framework for discussing responsibilities that African American youth have for keeping their communities drug free. The Akan proverb "When the cock is drunk, he forgets about the hawk" illustrates the danger of being intoxicated. These programs emphasize that not using drugs is for the good of not only the individual but also of the family and community.

The second type of program exposed participants to the history and historical contributions of people of African descent to prime racial identity and positive affirmation. This program type emphasized the contributions of African American and African history as a way of promoting pride in one's ethnic and racial group. These programs involved youth in field trips to African-centered places and institutions and used African and African American art forms (i.e., drumming and dance). Rites-of-passage programs typically use this program format.

The third type of program addressed contemporary issues among African Americans and topics related to external risk factors. The current circumstances of African Americans and the historical impact of racism and oppression and how this affected substance use were addressed in this type of program. Participants learned about the marketing of alcohol and tobacco in the African American community and the negative impact of drugs within communities. Another example of a topic discussed in these programs is the sentencing differential between crack and crack cocaine offenders.

These three types of cultural programs have different benefits and functions. The first program type encourages a meaningful focus on positive differentiation and identity as a person of African descent. Values articulated in the cultural tradition encourage the development of beliefs in self, family, collectiveness, and interdependence. These programs provided a meaningful way in which participants develop prosocial and antidrug attitudes and behaviors. A substance abuse prevention curriculum might, for example, include a discussion of how using drugs is inconsistent with community and family values.

The second program type focused on African and African American history. These programs provided a resource in which to increase youth's identity and pride and thus make them more resistant to using drugs. Youth, especially those from low-resource communities, had opportunities to see examples of accomplishments of people of African descent. The third program type focused on the circumstances of African Americans in the United States and provided the context in which to increase the youth's awareness of community- and societal-level risk factors for drugs. Such awareness and education were believed to help inoculate youth against drugs and other negative forces in their communities. Chipungu and colleagues (2000) examined differences in program satisfaction and perceived relevance among African American youth who were in the Africentric programs and the non-Africentric programs. They found that the Africentric programs contributed to higher rates of satisfaction and perceived program importance and, subsequently, program retention.

A few efforts have been made to tailor or integrate generic or universal curricula to make them more culturally relevant for African American youth (Belgrave et al., 2004a; Botvin, Schinke, Epstein, & Diaz, 1994). Botvin et al. (1994) adapted their Life Skills Training Curriculum for African American and Latino youth. The sample was composed of 639 seventh-graders from six New York City public schools. Schools were assigned to a culturally tailored intervention (CTI), a generic intervention, or a control group. The adapted Life Skills Training Curriculum did not use the types of Africentric programming described by Chipungu and colleagues (2000) but included cultural adaptations relevant to African American and Latino youth. These include a reading level to better "fit" the culture, the use of culturally relevant names, role play scenarios, and the incorporation of cultural myths and legends. Botvin et al. found that the culturally adapted intervention showed more promising results than a generic life skills curriculum for all participants.

In a 2-year follow-up of these students, Botvin (1995) reported that students in both the CTI and the generic intervention reported lower intentions to drink alcohol than students in the control group. Students in the CTI also reported less current alcohol use, and lower intentions to drink beer or wine, than those in the generic and control groups. This study focused not specifically on Africentric programming but on cultural adaptations. Also, the study did not include measures of cultural constructs, so the mechanism linking cultural variables to lowered drug use could not be examined.

Belgrave et al. (2004b) evaluated the effectiveness of a culturally integrated drug prevention curriculum versus an activity control. Ninety-two girls with a mean age of 12 were recruited from after-school Boys and Girls Clubs in a southeastern city. Girls in the intervention group received 1.5-hour curriculum sessions once a week for 17 weeks. The program used portions of Botvin et al.'s (1994) Life Skills Training Curriculum (discussed previously), which focuses on drug refusal efficacy, and Belgrave, et al.'s (2004a) Sisters of Nia Curriculum, a cultural curriculum for African American girls. The drug prevention curriculum addressed decision- making, coping, and assertiveness skills and how to resist peer pressure to use drugs. The Sisters of Nia Curriculum attended to both ethnicity and gender. To provide culturally similar role models, African American female adults (graduate students and advanced undergraduate students) facilitated the groups. Examples of session topics included relationships, Africa and African culture, critical consciousness, and African and African American women in leadership To strengthen a relational and Africentric approach, girls worked in and made decisions in small groups called *Jaamas* (Kiswahili for "family"). Girls in the comparison group participated in arts and crafts activities twice a week.

Because of the young age of the girls and the low levels of drug use, drug refusal efficacy instead of drug use was used as the outcome measure. The results showed a significant difference between groups at posttest in refusal efficacy, with girls in the intervention group reporting high refusal efficacy for both alcohol and other drugs than girls in the activity comparison group.

Culturally integrated substance abuse prevention programs have also targeted African American families. Kumpfer, Alvarado, Smith, and Bellamy (2002) reported the results of five studies that compared a generic Strengthening Families Program (SFP) to a culturally modified SFP. The SFP is a 14-session, evidence-based parenting skills, children's life skills, and family life skills training program specifically designed for high-risk families. Parents and children participate in SFP both separately and together. Cultural adaptations included using culturally relevant examples, graphics, and stories at a reduced reading level. The adapted programs also included local videos, holding sessions in African American churches, and discussing topics that address participants' basic living needs. The evaluation showed that the culturally adapted SFP increased program retention by 40%. Among rural Alabama participants, retention of African American drug-abusing mothers who attended 12 of the 14 sessions improved from 61% to 92% after cultural adaptations. In Detroit, Michigan, completion rates increased from 45% to 85% after the cultural adaptations were made.

Chipungu and colleagues (2000) reported that culturally congruent drug prevention programs contribute to meaningful involvement of participants, thereby increasing retention. Program participants report higher satisfaction and perceived program importance. Aktan (1999) also reported that program modifications, designed to increase the cultural consistency of a prevention program, resulted in improvements in group dynamics, interaction quality, increased spontaneity, and enthusiasm in program sessions. These few studies suggest that culturally integrated prevention programs will provide some benefits over generic or universal programs. However, more research is needed to examine the mechanism that links increased retention to specific drug attitudes and behaviors. Longitudinal studies that assess how cultural constructs change over time, and how this change is linked to drug use or nonuse, are suggested. We next provide an example of a prevention intervention that is culturally specific to African American youth.

A Culturally Specific Substance Abuse Prevention Program

Both content and implementation methods define an intervention program's cultural integration. Corneille, Ashcraft, and Belgrave (2005) and Belgrave et al. (2004b) described ways they have integrated culture in their drug prevention interventions with African American girls. Africentric values of communalism and collectiveness were infused in the programs through use of cooperative and interdependent learning strategies (e.g., role plays, team-building activities, and group problem-solving activities). Opening and closing *unity circles* were used to further encourage unity. The unity circle included a libation ritual that encouraged the girls to consider their own spirituality, the importance of ancestors, and connectedness to the past. By incorporating music, poetry, and dance, the program attended to the African worldview dimensions of orality, rhythm, and verve. Expression through rhythmic and creative activities facilitated sensitivity to different learning styles.

To promote ethnic identity development, the prevention programs used cultural activities such as Kwanzaa celebrations, spoken-word poetry, hip-hop dance, and field trips to African American institutions. Participants also learned the culture and history of people of African descent throughout the Diaspora. A central feature of the prevention intervention was the use of supportive African American adult group leaders. These facilitators, referred to as *mzees* (Kiswahili for "respected elders"), modeled positive and collaborative interactions and relationships with each other and with participants.

Given the urban community context in which many African American youth live, it also is important for youth to see possibilities of whom they can become. Many African American youth reside in underresourced communities where possibilities are not always apparent. To broaden participants' perspectives of possibilities, these prevention programs used African American leaders who were entrepreneurs, business owners and managers, and who had various levels of educational attainment. Because the programs were targeted to girls, females were guest presenters.

The prevention intervention described by Corneille et al. (2005) also included an evidence-based drug prevention intervention (Botvin et al.'s [1994] Life Skill Training Curriculum). These culturally integrated programs show that the participant's culture can be used to strengthen prevention efforts. Corneille et al. were able to attend to the culture of being of African descent, female, adolescent, and urban while simultaneously increasing drug refusal efficacy and reducing drug use.

RECOMMENDATIONS FOR PREVENTION INTERVENTIONS WITH AFRICAN AMERICAN YOUTH

As noted, for prevention interventions to be most effective, culture and context must be attended to. Culturally tailored interventions attend to both the *method*, or the way in which the prevention messages are delivered, and the *content* of the message. Other suggestions for improving prevention interventions for African American youth are derived from the research literature. One suggestion is that, given a later onset of drug initiation for African American youth, prevention interventions should be extended to late adolescence and early adulthood. Interventions can be implemented at colleges and other settings where young African American adults live and work. A second suggestion is that, because drug use generally occurs later in adolescence for African American youth, the family may have provided protection against drug use; therefore, prevention interventions with African American youth may want to emphasize ways in which the family can continue to exert influence as the youth grows older. Most family-based prevention programs are designed for families with elementary and middle school children. Family programs that include high school age youth should be considered. A third suggestion is that prevention interventions consider the fact that African American youth will likely encounter life stressors, including race-related stressors. Interventions should target healthy ways of coping with these stressors. A fourth suggestion is based on research that has found that resilience among African American youth can be attributed to structured social environments, such as the church and other community organizations. Therefore, prevention interventions should consider incorporating protective factors of organized institutions into their model.

Directions for Future Research

Although there is much available information about how to prevent drug use among African American youth, considerable work is needed in terms of theory development, research, and prevention interventions. Few theoretical perspectives exist—in particular, domain and classification approaches of risk and protective factors—that offer insight on how multiple influences interact to affect behavior. Current risk and protective frameworks are too general, thus making it difficult to develop and test meaningful sociocultural models for adolescent drug use. More attention should be afforded to developing specific and testable risk–protective factor models. For instance, Flay's (2005) *quadratic influence system*—an expansion of the *theory of triadic influence* (Flay & Petraitis, 1994)—presents a novel approach to conceptualizing the biological, psychological, social, and cultural influences of adolescent drug use via interactive (sub)streams of ultimate, distal, and proximal influence. Given the contribution of cultural factors in the prevention and reduction of drug use, theories should address the interactive and multiplicative function of cultural factors in relation to other factors and drug use.

In terms of research, a considerable amount of the published work on African American adolescent drug use is based on cross-sectional studies. Longitudinal studies could provide greater insight into the etiology of drug use via the identification of sociocultural and contextual causes of behavior. Longitudinal studies, for example, might provide insight into how the protection afforded by the family diminishes as African American youth grow older.

African Americans are not a homogeneous group, although they do share a set of predominant as well as salient cultural themes that transcend geography. Therefore, research that explores intra- as well as intergroup differences among Diasporic Africans is needed to appropriately match participants to the most effective interventions. These studies could examine patterns of drug use and intervention strategies as a function of geographical residence, gender, socioeconomic class, and community type, as well as generational status.

Both theory and research can inform the development of effective prevention interventions for African American adolescent drug use. Some have already begun a concerted effort to address translation issues (i.e., from bench to bedside) in the field of prevention research (e.g., Flay, 2005). Further development and evaluation of interventions that target the reduction of risk factors and the promotion of protective factors would also be useful. These interventions might, for example, simultaneously target the enhancement of cultural attributes and drug refusal skills while increasing academic competence, family wellness, and community responsibility.

Conclusion

Drug use among African American youth is generally lower than drug use among youth from other ethnic groups. However, as African Americans age into adults, drug use increases, and so do the consequences. Drug use is influenced by several factors, including individual, family, peer, school, and neighborhood factors. Ethnic identity and religiosity are protective factors for drug use, and racism and discrimination are risk factors. Drug prevention interventions that attend to culture in format and content are likely to see better results than those that do not.

Note

1. The authors thank the Special Population Office at the National Institute of Drug Abuse for their support of Faye Z. Belgrave in preparation of this chapter, as well as Khai Nyugen, for editorial assistance.

References

Aktan, G. B. (1999). A cultural consistency evaluation of substance abuse prevention program with inner city African-American families. *Journal of Primary Prevention, 19*, 227–239.

Barnes, G. M., & Welte, J. W. (1986). Patterns and predictors of alcohol use among 7th–12th grade students in New York State. *Journal of Studies on Alcohol, 47*, 53–62.

Belgrave, F. Z., Brome, D., & Hampton, C. (2000). The contributions of Africentric values and racial identity to the prediction of drug knowledge, attitudes and use among African American youth. *Journal of Black Psychology, 26*, 386–401.

Belgrave, F. Z., Reed, M. C., Plybon, L. E., Butler, D. S., Allison, K. W., & Davis, T. (2004a). Sisters of Nia: A cultural program for African American girls. *Journal of Black Psychology, 30*, 329–343.

Belgrave, F. Z., Reed, M. C., Plybon, L. E. Corneille, M. (2004b). The impact of a culturally enhanced drug prevention program on drug and alcohol refusal efficacy among urban African American girls. *Journal of Drug Education, 34*, 267–279.

Belgrave, F. Z., Townsend, T. G., Cherry, V. R., & Cunningham, D. M. (1997). The influence of an Africentric world-view and demographic variables on drug knowledge, attitudes, and use among African American youth. *Journal of Community Psychology, 25*, 421–433.

Biederman, J., Faraone, S. V., Monuteaux, M. C., & Feighner, J. A. (2000). Patterns of alcohol and drug use in adolescents can be predicted by parental substance use disorders. *Pediatrics, 106*, 792–797.

Booth, B. M., Curran, G. M., & Han, X. (2004). Predictors of short-term course of drinking in untreated rural and urban at-risk drinkers: Effects of gender, illegal drug use and psychiatric comorbidity. *Journal of Studies on Alcohol, 65*, 63–74.

Botvin, G. J. (1995). Principles of prevention. In R. H. Coombs & D. Ziedonis (Eds.), *Handbook on drug abuse prevention: A comprehensive strategy to prevent the abuse of alcohol and other drugs* (pp. 19–44). Boston: Allyn & Bacon.

Botvin, G., Schinke, G., Epstein, J., & Diaz, T. (1994). Effectiveness of culturally focused and generic skills training approaches to alcohol and drug abuse prevention among minority youth. *Psychology of Addictive Behavior, 8*, 116–127.

Boyd, K., Ashcraft, A., & Belgrave, F. Z. (2006). The impact of mother–daughter and father–daughter relationships on drug refusal self-efficacy among African American adolescent girls in urban communities. *Journal of Black Psychology, 32*, 29–42.

Bray, J. H., Adams, G. J., Greg, G. J., & Baer, P. E. (2001). Developmental, family, and ethnic influences on adolescent alcohol usage: A growth curve approach. *Journal of Family Psychology, 15*, 301–314.

Bronfenbrenner, U. (1979). *The ecology of human development.* Cambridge, MA: Harvard University Press.

Burlew, K., Neely, D., Johnson, C., Hucks, T. C., Purnell, B., Butler, J., et al. (2000). Drug attitudes, racial identity, and alcohol use among African American adolescents. *Journal of Black Psychology, 26*, 402–420.

Centers for Disease Control and Prevention. (2002). Recent trends in mortality rates for four major cancers by sex and race/ethnicity—United States, 1990–1998. *Morbidity and Mortality Weekly Report, 51*(3), 49–53.

Centers for Disease Control and Prevention. (2007). *Illicit drug use.* Hyattsville, MD: U.S. Department of Health and Human Services.

Center for Substance Abuse Prevention. (1993). *Prevention strategies based on individual risk factors for alcohol and other drug abuse.* Rockville, MD: Office of Scientific Analysis.

Chipungu, S., Hermann, J., & Sambrano, S. (2000). Prevention programming for African American youth: A review of strategies in CSAP's national cross-site evaluation of high risk youth programs. *Journal of Black Psychology, 26,* 360–385.

Collins, R. L., & Ellickson, P. L. (2004). Integrating four theories of adolescent smoking. *Substance Use & Misuse, 39,* 179–209.

Corneille, M. A., Ashcraft, A. M., & Belgrave, F. Z. (2005). What's culture got to do with it? Prevention programs for African American adolescent girls. *Journal of Health Care for the Poor and Underserved, 16,* 38–48.

Corneille, M., & Belgrave, F. Z. (2007). Ethnic identity, neighborhood risk, and adolescent drug and sex attitudes and refusal efficacy: The urban African American girls' experience. *Journal of Drug Education, 37,* 177–190.

Curtis-Boles, H., & Jenkins-Monroe, V. (2000). Substance abuse in African American women. *Journal of Black Psychology, 26,* 450–469.

Dekovic, M. (1999). Risk and protective factors in the development of problem behavior during adolescence. *Journal of Youth and Adolescence, 28,* 667–685.

Farrell, A. D., & White, K. S. (1998). Peer influences and drug use among urban adolescents: Family structure and parent–adolescent relationships as protective factors. *Journal of Consulting and Clinical Psychology, 66,* 248–258.

Flay, B. R. (2005, September). *Integrating theories of adolescent behavior: The theory of triadic influence.* Paper presented at the NAS/IOM Workshop "Science of Adolescent Health and Development," Washington, DC.

Flay, B. R., & Petraitis, J. (1994). The theory of triadic influence: A new theory of health behavior with implications for preventive interventions. In G. S. Albrecht (Ed.), *Advances in medical sociology: Vol. IV. A reconsideration of models of health behavior change* (pp. 19–44). Greenwich, CT: JAI Press.

Geronimus, A., Neidert, L., & Bound, J. (1993). Age patterns of smoking in US Black and White women of childbearing age. *American Journal of Public Health 83,* 1258–1264.

Gibbons, F. X., Gerrard, M., Cleveland, M. J., Wills, T. A., & Brody, G. (2004). Perceived discrimination and substance use in African American parents and their children: A panel study. *Journal of Personality and Social Psychology, 86,* 517–529.

Griffin, K. W., Botvin, G. J., & Nichols, T. R. (2006). Effects of a school-based drug abuse prevention program for adolescents on HIV risk behavior in young adulthood. *Prevention Science, 7,* 103–112.

Grover, P. L. (1998). *Preventing substance abuse among children and adolescents: family-centered approaches* (DHHS Publication No. 3223).

Rockville, MD: Substance Abuse and Mental Health Services Administration.

Gruenewald, P. J., Millar, A., Ponicki, W. R., & Brinkley, G. (2000). Physical and economic access to alcohol. In R. A. Wilson & M. C. Dufour (Eds.), *The epidemiology of alcohol problems in small geographic areas* (National Institute on Alcohol Abuse and Alcoholism Research Monograph 36 [NIH Pub. No. 00-4357], pp. 163–212). Bethesda, MD: National Institutes of Health.

Hawkins, J. D., Catalano, R. F., & Miller, J. Y. (1992). Risk and protective factors for alcohol and other drug problems in adolescence and early adulthood: Implications for drug use prevention. *Psychological Bulletin, 112,* 64–105.

Jenson, J. M. (2004). Risk and protective factors for alcohol and other drug use in adolescence. In M. W. Fraser (Ed.), *Risk and resiliency in childhood: An ecological perspective* (2nd ed., pp. 183–208). Washington, DC: National Association of Social Workers.

Jessor, R., & Jessor, S. L. (1977). *Problem behavior and psychosocial development: A longitudinal study of youth.* New York: Academic Press.

Kabat, G. C., & Hebert, J. R. (1991). Use of mentholated cigarettes and lung cancer risk. *Cancer Research, 51,* 6510–6513.

Kandel, D. (2006, November 13). *Developmental trajectories of drug use among African Americans.* Presentation given at the National Institute on Drug Abuse Conference "Drug Use Trajectories Among African Americans," Bethesda, MD.

Kiefe, C. I., Williams, O. D., Lewis, C. E., Allison, J. J., Sekar, P., & Wagenknecht, L. E. (2001). Ten-year changes in smoking among young adults: Are racial differences explained by socioeconomic factors in the CARDIA study? *American Journal of Public Health, 91,* 213–218.

King, R. S., & Mauer, M. (2006). *Sentencing with discretion: Crack cocaine sentencing after Booker.* Washington, DC: The Sentencing Project. Available at http://www.sentencing project.org

Kumpfer, K. L., Alvarado, R., Smith, P., & Bellamy, N. (2002). Cultural sensitivity in universal family-based prevention interventions. *Prevention Science, 3,* 241–244.

Kumpfer, K. L., Alvarado, R., & Tait, C. (2007). The Strengthening Families Program: An evidence-based, multicultural family skills training program. In P. Tolan, J. Szapocznik, & S. Sambrano (Eds.), *Preventing youth substance abuse: Science-based programs for children and adolescents* (pp. 159–181). Washington, DC: American Psychological Association.

Lambert, S., Brown, T. L., Phillips, C. M., & Ialongo, N. F. (2004). The relationship between perceptions of neighborhood characteristics and substance use among urban African American adolescents. *American Journal of Community Psychology, 34,* 205–218.

Luthar, S., Cicchetti, D., & Becker, B. (2000). The construct of resilience: A critical evaluation and guidelines for future work. *Child Development, 71,* 543–562.

McCluskey, C. P., Krohn, M. D., Lizotte, A. J., & Rodriguez, M. L. (2002). Early substance use and school achievement: An examination of Latino, White, and African American youth. *Journal of Drug Issues, 2,* 921–944.

McGuire, W. J. (1991). Using guiding-idea theories of the person to develop educational campaigns against drug abuse and other health-threatening behavior. *Health Education Research, 6,* 173–184.

Merriam-Webster Medical Dictionary on Medline Plus. (1998). *Drug.* Retrieved November 17, 2007, from http://www2.merriamwebster.com/cgi-bin/mwmednlm?book=Medical&va=drug

Nasim, A., Corona, R., Utsey, S., Townsend, T. G., Panigrahi, B., Alleyne, R., et al. (2007). *Predictors of drug refusal efficacy for African Americans across urban and rural contexts.* Unpublished manuscript.

Nasim, A., Utsey, S. O., Corona, R., & Belgrave, F. Z. (2006). Religiosity, drug refusal efficacy, and substance use among African Americans. *Journal of Ethnicity in Substance Abuse, 5*(3), 27–48.

National Institute on Drug Abuse. (2005). *Diagnosis and treatment of drug abuse in family practice.* Retrieved November 3, 2007, from http://www.drugabuse.gov/Diagnosis-Treatment/diagnosis2.html

NDI Foundation. (2007). *Drug.* Retrieved January 21, 2008, from http://www.ndif.org/terms/6764-drug

Oetting, E. R., & Beauvais, F. (1987). Peer cluster theory, socialization characteristics, and adolescent drug use: A path analysis. *Journal of Counseling Psychology, 34,* 205–213.

Petraitis, J., Flay, B. R., & Miller, T. Q. (1995). Reviewing theories of adolescent substance abuse: Organizing pieces of the puzzle. *Psychological Bulletin, 117,* 67–86.

Plybon, L. E., Edwards, L., Butler, D., Belgrave, F. Z., & Allison, F. (2003). Examining the link between neighborhood cohesion and school outcomes: The role of support coping among African American adolescent girls. *Journal of Black Psychology, 29,* 393–407.

Reinherz, H. X., Giaconia, R. M., Carmola Hauf, A. D., Wasserman, M. S., & Paradis, A. D. (2000). General and specific childhood risk factors for depression and drug disorders by early childhood. *Journal of the American Academy of Child and Adolescent Psychiatry, 39,* 223–231.

Saint-Jean, G., & Crandall, L. A. (2004). Ethnic differences in the salience of risk and protective factors for alcohol and marijuana: Findings from a statewide survey. *Journal of Ethnicity in Substance Abuse, 3*(1), 11–27.

Schinke, S., & Schwinn, T. (2005). Gender-specific computer-based interventions for preventing drug abuse among girls. *American Journal of Drug and Alcohol Abuse, 31,* 609–616.

Substance Abuse and Mental Health Services Administration. (2002). *2002 National Survey on Drug Use and Health.* Rockville, MD: U.S. Department of Health and Human Services.

Substance Abuse and Mental Health Services Administration. (2006). *Results from the 2005 National Survey on Drug Use and Health: National findings.* Rockville, MD: U.S. Department of Health and Human Services. Retrieved May 9, 2007, from http://oas.samhsa.gov/nsduh/2k5nsduh/2k5results.pdf

Townsend, T. G., & Belgrave, F. Z. (2000). The impact of personal identity and racial identity on drug attitudes and use among African American children. *Journal of Black Psychology, 26,* 421–436.

Wallace, J. M., Brown, T. N., Backman, J. G., & Laveist, T. A. (2003). The influence of race and religion on abstinence from alcohol, cigarettes and marijuana among adolescents. *Journal of Studies on Alcohol, 64,* 843–849.

Wallace, J. M., & Muroff, J. R. (2002). Preventing substance abuse among African American children and youth: Race differences in risk factor exposure and vulnerability. *Journal of Primary Prevention, 22,* 235–261.

Wills, T. A., Yaeger, A. M., & Sandy, J. M. (2003). Buffering effect of religiosity for adolescent substance use. *Psychology of Addictive Behaviors, 17,* 24–31.

Windle, M. (2000). Parental, sibling, and peer influence on adolescent substance use and alcohol problems. *Applied Developmental Science, 4,* 98–110.

35

BLACK LIBERATION PSYCHOLOGY AND PRACTICE

CHALMER E. THOMPSON AND DORIENNA M. ALFRED

On the basis of professional codes of ethics (American Psychological Association, 2002) and a variety of specialty standards, psychologists are advised to be knowledgeable about all matters that have bearing on the well-being of individuals, including societal problems. *Liberation psychologists* have long embraced this responsibility, but instead of having a principal focus on change in individuals, they concern themselves equally with promoting the well-being of individuals and society. With specific attention to racial oppression, adherents of Black Liberation Psychology (BLP) work as theorists, researchers, and practitioners to help remove both tangible and psychological obstructions to life fulfillment and thus help "liberate" African-descended people from the stranglehold of racism and White supremacy. Although they do not ignore the needs of the many, they target their work on helping Blacks specifically to overcome the plights of racial oppression, frequently studying and/or implementing strategies that can ignite in Blacks a consciousness of emancipation. More broadly, they seek to "create just societies, strengthen self-determination [among the dispossessed], and heal the effects of oppression" (Watts & Serrano-Garcia, 2003, p. 74). The origin of BLP is often traced to the writings of Martinquean psychiatrist Frantz Fanon (1963, 1967; see also Bulhan, 1985; Utsey, Bolden, & Brown, 1995), and although key elements of Fanon's writings are practiced by those who do not call themselves liberation psychologists, there is a clear body of scholarship that informs existing and future practices of psychological emancipation. The ubiquitous oppression of African Americans has strengthened the call for approaches that promote their social, psychological, economic, spiritual, and political freedom and that obliterate systemic domination (Hilliard, 1998; Myers, 1992; Nobles, 1991).

In this chapter, we attempt to advance an understanding of BLP as a necessary, inevitable, and powerful counterstrike against racial oppression. We show how its presence is much more than a reaction to a racist status quo but instead, is a collection of research, theory, and praxis that responds creatively to the need for "new ways of operating" (Watts, Williams, & Jagers, 2003). In the following, we begin by providing a fuller description of BLP and then present six patterns that characterize the oppression of African Americans. We next identify what we believe to be best practices in BLP theory, research, and interventions, and we conclude with some recommendations for strengthening this vitally important work.

Black Liberation Psychology: Key Features

The writings of Frantz Fanon and, arguably, of W. E. B. Du Bois (see Gaines & Reed, 1995; Rabaka, 2006) and Carter G. Woodson, provide a foundation from which BLP has evolved. In these writings, we find several noted themes, including the notion that Blacks and other oppressed groups are affected not only by overt and clandestine acts of bigotry and hatred on a personal level but also by institutional practices that mount doubts about the value of their racial/cultural heritage and the worth of African-descended people. Distortions in the news and entertainment media and in formal education outlets, including the omission of information on how African-descended people have created civilizations and endured oppression in spite of meager material resources, help generate internalized beliefs about Black inferiority. Furthermore, these writers have pointed to the counterpart of the Black inferiority myth: the myth of White superiority, which is embedded into racial socialization. White superiority is the dissemination of ideas, beliefs, and attitudes about White people and White culture as being inherently more moral, intelligent, and "cultured" relative to the cultures of people of color. This reality of mythical superiority is communicated in many ways and thrives in a climate that tolerates a diminished view of racial oppression.

Theoretically, BLP adherents believe that this double-edged sword—which has on one side the adoption of beliefs about Black inferiority and on the other an internalization of White superiority—leads to ruptures in relationships, particularly with other African/Black people; a personal sense of being overwhelmed; hopelessness; and a host of other psychological problems, such as low self-esteem, fear of success, and disengagement from collective social action (Bulhan, 1985). A cadre of scholars, including Ajani ya Azibo; Linda James Myers; William E. Cross, Jr.; Janet E. Helms; and Joseph Baldwin, have developed conceptualizations of how Blacks have responded to racial oppression and have formed ideas about themselves and their worth based in part on their association with other African-descended people. In general, these theorists believe that a path to liberation is for Blacks to disrupt these distorted appraisals by seeking truth about history and sociopolitical reality and, for certain theorists, by developing a deep connection with one's African ancestry (Ajani ya Azibo, 2004; Baldwin, 1986; Kambon, 1996). According to some theorists, Black people are unhealthiest when they expend time and effort disassociating themselves from other Blacks whom they perceive as deficient and seek approval and/or rewards from Whites whom they view as "normal" or superior. At their healthiest, they feel a strong sense of worth in their association with other African-descended people, and they no longer fear or idealize White people.

BLP adherents believe that in the absence of pervasive, inclusive measures to end the oppression, structural oppression unfolds over time and reproduces itself dialectically and almost unconsciously. They advocate for justice and implement strategies that buck systems of oppression. Their focus is to end oppression primarily by helping prepare oppressed people to dismantle the obstructive forces to optimal living. A primary set of tools used to help equip oppressed groups is in illuminating the roots of oppression and strengthening the "will to act." Being empowered to act for justice is a key component of BLP. Although the attention of BLP adherents is focused on racism and White supremacy, Blacks ostensibly are affected by all forms of oppression; consequently, many BLP adherents explain how the confluence of different forms of oppression—for example, the confluence of racial and gender oppression—has, and continues to have, an impact on Black people (e.g., see White, 2006).

It is worth noting that in examining the lives of Frantz Fanon (see Bulhan, 1985) and W. E. B. Du Bois, one learns of the risks entailed in joining the fight against oppression. Each of these scholars participated in liberation movements and, apparently, was willing to die in order to realize some level of progress for African-descended people. The same level of risk was true of their Latin American liberation counterparts, Paulo Freire and Ignacio Martín-Baró. Even when the risks do not seemingly involve threats of physical harm or death, adherents of BLP face other risks that can make their advocacy-professional roles both tumultuous and psychologically taxing. They can face rejection from peers, jeopardize their employment status, be shunned by people, or face threats of harm (e.g., "Noose shocker," 2007). Also, because the vast majority of psychology programs do not offer training in social justice advocacy (Helms,

2003), BLP advocates may not have the skill base that can make them as effective as they can be. Taking on a liberation perspective requires qualities of strength and perseverance. These qualities can also rewarded by those who see the need for Black liberation.

What is the eventual goal of BLP adherents? The abruption of racial oppression in the near future is not likely, so BLP adherents set their sights on shorter term goals at the personal and group levels. They seek to help increase critical consciousness, improved relationships, social and political organizing, positive mental health functioning, self-care, and academic achievement. They also look for evidence of impact at the community and societal levels: the passage of legislature that concern all oppressed people; the adoption of textbooks at the state level that adroitly address U.S. history from a nonracist perspective; federal legislation against hate crimes; any dramatic measures to jostle business-as-usual in response to the disproportionate numbers of Blacks serving time in prison; increased attention to the murder rate of Black men; and the curtailing of the alarmingly high dropout rate among Black students. Because of the intractable nature of social problems, they recognize that race-related reform is bred under certain conducive social conditions. The longevity that comes in achieving lofty goals does not diminish their level of involvement.

From the very earliest of writers to contemporary scholars, it is evident that BLP adherents view psychologically healthy Black people as those who live and function in environments in which they are not constantly at battle to survive and prove their worth. Adherents know that for Blacks to be mentally healthy in oppressive environments, they need to recognize and fight against the forces that inhibit their lives as Black people. Stated positively, adherents believe that Blacks need to (re)discover their humanity—their ability to endure, wax brilliantly, create masterpieces of art, feel worthy because they are human, and act on behalf of injustice. For some adherents, this (re)discovery includes a connection with their African ancestry; to others, the spiritual manifestation of God or Goddess (see Myers, 1992). For Black liberation psychologists in general, the direct focus on Blacks is not with the belief that Whites have nothing to do with ending racial oppression—indeed, Whites are instrumental to ending this form of oppression.

The focus on Blacks, however, is with the understanding that forging bonds among the oppressed has been historically a formidable strategy of change. This empowering act of organizing with and on behalf of other Blacks is a source of healing in and of itself (Thompson, Murry, Harris, & Garcia, 2005).

Next we discuss six patterns of African/Black oppression to offer readers an idea of the scope of the problems.

Patterns of Black Oppression

Moane (2003) addressed the relevance of liberation psychology to the Irish context but presented six patterns or mechanisms of control that characterize the oppression that many groups experience at the macro level. We believe these general mechanisms of control offer a useful template for describing African Americans' experiences in the United States.

The first among the patterns of control or domination is the presence of *violence* in its various pervasive forms. In Utsey et al.'s (1995) examination of the African *Maafa*, or "Great Disaster," the authors described the alarming, relentless violence committed against African-descended people, beginning with the brutal kidnapping of human bodies; the savage passage of Africans from Africa to enslaving countries aboard ships; to the rapes, beatings, and killings that Black lives endured for generations because they were Black. Moreover, according to Moane (2003), "Violence is structured at the macro level in that agencies charged with the prevention, detection, and punishment of crimes of violence often fail to discharge their duty in the case of violence against minority and oppressed groups" (p. 94). This structural violence can be witnessed in the disparities that exist between Blacks and White relative to media attention directed primarily at school violence when the victims are White and less when the victims are non-White; the sanctions given to Afrikaner police in apartheid South Africa to brutally torture and kill Blacks; and the more severe and lengthier prison sentences accorded Blacks relative to Whites (see Thompson & Carter, in press).

Bulhan (1985) advocated that violence needs to be examined as a phenomenon that extends beyond that which yields physical injury or death. According to Bulhan, violence can be thought of as any set of processes or conditions that prevents people from achieving or maintaining the capacity for physical and psychological growth. Consequently, social analyses that aim to discern how oppression is enacted in local contexts ultimately entail examinations of the processes and conditions surrounding the violence. Researchers who attempt to glean the extent of the violence that emerges from these processes and conditions will need to direct their attention to such matters as the exposure of Blacks and other people of color to environmental toxins, a component of environmental racism (see Thompson & Neville, 1999). In keeping with Bulhan's definition, violence also was exacted in the U.S. government's neglect of Hurricane Katrina victims, the large majority of whom were poor and Black.

The second pattern Moane (2003) described was *political exclusion*, defined as structural factors that either deprive people of the vote or, in more subtle forms, cultivate attitudes and expectations about the oppressed group and their capacity for political action. We add to this category *legal and social injustice*, to account for the long history of duplicitous decision making in cases related to Blacks and other non-Whites (e.g., Bell, 1992). There are numerous contemporary examples of political exclusion, both covert and overt, that add to the plethora of historical accounts. For example, few African Americans will forget the 2000 U.S. presidential election, in which 54% of 180,000 "spoiled" votes, which were thus not counted, in the State of Florida belonged to African Americans (White, 2001). Explanations ranged from insufficient numbers of voting locations and working equipment and eligible voters being turned away because of voter registration flaws. None of these explanations, however, adequately addresses or changes the disenfranchisement experienced by thousands of African American voters silenced in that election.

A recent example of a legal injustice involving African Americans—more specifically, Black men—is the case that involved excessive charges of attempted murder handed to six African American male high school students in Jena, Louisiana, for allegedly assaulting a White student. Although the penalty for fighting on school grounds would typically involve suspension from school, these young men were criminally charged and faced several years in prison if convicted. The three White males who admitted hanging a noose on the "White tree" after Black students decided to sit under the tree—the incident that spurred the aforementioned fight—received in-school suspensions, detentions, and mandatory evaluations for their crimes. Unfortunately, there are far too many political exclusions and injustices that impact African Americans to note within the scope of this chapter. Each of these instances, however, is evidence that African Americans' political and legal power continues to be usurped by structures of oppression that simply must be addressed.

Economic exploitation, the third pattern, refers to structural manifestations related to the groups that are consistently represented in poverty or are underemployed (Moane, 2003). These structural manifestations related to economic exploitation include the nature of work (e.g., temporary, and low-paying jobs) as well as the lack of educational and training facilities, promotional opportunities, material resources, and the psychological problems associated with these factors, especially in a wealthy, and highly consumerist culture such as the United States (Kasser & Kanner, 2003). Economic exploitation continues to have an insidious impact on many African Americans in this country, especially for women. African American women maintain lower earning power, have fewer opportunities for career advancement, and hold fewer positions of prestige in comparison to Whites and, to a lesser degree, Black men (C. Jones & Shorter-Gooden, 2003). When we consider the impact of earning potential on African American female single-headed households, it becomes evident that their economic deprivation has implications for families and entire communities.

The fourth pattern that is surfaced in oppressive environments like the United States is *control of sexuality* (Moane, 2003). Pertaining primarily to women in countries throughout the world, this pattern refers to laws and other institutions that impose decisions about women's bodies as well as portrayals of how men and women "ought" to behave. Moane contended that laws regulating sexual relations, abortion, and birth control contribute to this oppressive pattern.

Control of African American men and women's sexuality has been historically, and continues to be, a detriment to their social, psychological, and physical well-being. Depictions of Black women as loose and wanton historically have perpetuated stereotypes of them as objects, and hypermasculinized images of Black men, particularly in portrayals as criminals or "thugs," stem the tide of fear. The curious nature of stereotyping—for example, with prevailing images of Black women as oversexualized in certain periods but as asexual (e.g., the Mammy) in others, can contribute to identity development at early ages. Intermingling race and gender issues, Black girls may feel prone to associate or refrain from associating with other Black girls if they do not conform to certain stereotypical expectations. For boys, efforts to be seen in ways that counter the thug stereotype can result in questions about their "Blackness" and their "maleness." When Blacks try to align with the stereotypes of hypersexuality by engaging in sex prematurely or without prudent judgment, they increase their likelihood of contracting communicable diseases, such as AIDS. Rigid adherence to criminal or hardened images can lead to dangerous lifestyles.

The fifth pattern, *cultural control*, involves "the many ways in which oppressed people are deprived of a voice and excluded and marginalized through control of mass media and culture" (Moane, 2003, p. 95). This pattern relates to the evident hegemony in the ownership and funding of media, publishing houses, and other institutions of media and culture that absents women and persons of color from positions of power in these institutions (Thompson & Neville, 1999). Also important to this pattern is the evidence of demeaning stereotypes that fuel negative images for the masses and, notably, promulgates feelings of low self-worth, anger, shame, and so forth among oppressed groups.

Moane's (2003) final pattern is *fragmentation*, a term that refers to the various ways oppressed people are divided. The processes that relate to divisiveness include a suppression of cultural traditions through erasure of history. Traditional school curricula promote teaching of "great wars" and aspects of U.S. and European history that feature Whites prominently, rendering imperialist violent conflict as normative and non-White aspects of history and culture as having relatively lesser significance. Although this form of divisiveness can emerge as conflicts between Blacks and Whites, the hegemony conveyed about the value of certain heritages can have an impact on the interactions of many groups, such as émigrés from the Caribbean relative to their interactions with U.S. Blacks and the interaction between Blacks and Latinos (see Thompson & Carter, in press). In small communities, or in certain political and occupational settings, these divisions can reveal themselves in cases of *tokenism*, "where members of the oppressed group are promoted into positions of power and thence, creating competition among the oppressed" (Moane, p. 95). Notions like the "model minority"—as a descriptor of Asian Americans as a racial group people who have enjoyed more successes in terms of educational advancement and economic attainment relative to other non-Whites—denies the structural disadvantages that continue to besiege all people of color and suggests that hard work alone is the solution to "minority" problems.

Drawing from the work of Fanon and other key liberation writers, Moane (2003) noted that a key psychological pattern that arises out of all of these mechanisms of control is *internalized oppression*: the adoption of beliefs, attitudes, values, and behavior about the "naturalness" or inevitability of one's oppressed status. In the following section, we elaborate on the concept of internalized oppression, which is encompassed in many of the developmental theoretical models.

Best Practices

To have an impact in transforming people and society, BLP praxis should be ecological in nature; conceptually "tight," thus driven by coherent thinking and proven methods; and sustained over time. We extract a few of these works as a way to highlight programmatic research that approaches the goals of BLP.

The theories mentioned in an earlier section serve as explications of Black consciousness (i.e., awareness of self as African-descended) or racial identity (one's response to racism based in part on one's identification with other Blacks). The most popular theory researched in the literature is *racial identity theory*. Several authors have contributed to this conceptualization in important ways, including the creation, modification, and expansion of measures to assess the construct as well as the relationship of racial identity (as measured attitudinally) to a number of outcome variables (e.g., Cross & Vandiver, 2001; H. Jones, Cross, & DeFour, 2007; Sellers &

Shelton, 2003; Sellers, Smith, Shelton, Rowley, & Chavous, 1998). We believe that racial identity theories provide a valuable base for describing and assessing "personality" characteristics of Black people, but we also believe that research that can lend itself to optimal praxis comprises studies that extend this individual focus to ecological contexts. Helms's (1995) *racial interaction model*, a conceptualization of how influential people (teachers, organizational and community leaders, etc.) advance change in groups within different ecological settings, stands as an excellent guide in promoting racial identity development and is consistent with BLP elements of multilevel ecological change (see also Thompson & Carter, 1997, in press). To date, there has been limited research on the psychological–ecological application of the theory.

Several studies have served to enrich our understanding of psychological processes experienced by Blacks that relate to racial oppression, such as race-related stress and trauma (e.g., Carter, 2007; Clark, Anderson, Clark, & Williams, 1999; Franklin & Carter, 2007; Harrell, 2000; Pieterse & Carter, 2007); racial ideological beliefs (e.g., Smalls, White, Chavous, & Sellers, 2007); and perceptions as moderated by contextual factors (e.g., Brody et al., 2006; Caldwell, Kohn-Wood, Schmeelk-Cone, Chavous, & Zimmerman, 2004), cultural mistrust (see Chap. 22, this volume), and stereotype threat (see Chap. 16, this volume). These researchers take into account the multiple factors that relate to individual processes yet are influenced by structural racism forces. Another important psychological process to study is *coping* (e.g., Lawson & Thomas, 2007), with the understanding by researchers that Blacks often have stood together in solidarity, endured oppression by developing fictive kinship and grassroots efforts to enact change, and worshiped in churches that were sites for political resistance. Consequently, research of Black coping mechanisms needs to include some attention to the extent to which sources that have historically served Blacks continue to have an impact on their ability or willingness to take care of themselves psychologically. For example, one study examined coping among Black youth and whether African cultural characteristics, often delineated in BLP writings as an important ingredient of Black mental health, play a role in how these teenagers cope: Constantine, Donnelly, and Myers (2002) found that, among Black teenagers, those with higher *public collective self-esteem*—the belief that others feel positively about their cultural group—reported use of spiritual-centered Africultural coping styles in dealing with stressful situations. The authors also found that the higher the importance placed on *identity collective self-esteem* (e.g., the belief that their cultural group is an important part of their self-concept), the greater use of collective reliance of group-centered activities to cope with stressful situations. To achieve a better understanding of how African cultural characteristics influence the promotion of health, it is important that researchers determine exactly *how* such qualities do so.

We point to the program of research by Roderick Watts, of George State University, and his colleagues, which includes the emergent conceptualization of a construct; empirical evidence of the construct; and thoughtful reflections about the findings of the research, especially as relating to practice and the marriage of research and practice. For example, Watts, Adbul-Adil, and Pratt (2002) described the Young Warriors program, a weekly and semiweekly intervention for Black males between the ages of 11 and 21 in several midwestern schools. These students of these programs had been labeled as management problems by school staff. Facilitators tried to foster and enhance critical consciousness and *sociopolitical identity development*, which the authors defined as the "process of growth in a person's knowledge, analytical skills, emotional faculties, and capacity for action in political and social systems" (Watts et al., 2003, p. 185). Watts et al. also advanced the idea that this development is essential to the liberation process in that it facilitates movement from understanding oppression to taking action against oppression and consequently inciting meaningful social change. Another intervention, concerning math literacy, carries forward the same objective of facilitating sociopolitical development in youth (Watts & Guessous, 2006). Essential to this line of research is the provision of activism skills to the groups with whom the researchers work. The groups take on their knowledge of sociopolitical identity development to anticipate where group members are and thereby anticipate the skills that need to be taught as well as the strengths with which group members possess. Such a developmental view of empowerment was proposed by Kieffer (1984) and is compatible with Freire's (1972) understanding of liberation in which he proposes that the oppressed begin taking action within the confines of their limiting situation and "through dialogue and action develop a broader analysis, and from there engage in a broader arena and ultimately with social structures" (Kieffer, 1984, p. 30). The developmental view, and the emphasis on agency in liberation psychology, highlights the importance of allowing groups to develop their own strategies for action, ones that suit their capacities and interests and that give them a sense of control and agency.

Others have examined practices in which African cultural approaches are emphasized (e.g., Foster, Phillips, Belgrave, Randolph, & Braithwaite, 1993; Jagers & Mock, 1993; Phillips, 1990), as well as group support (Turner-Musa & Lipscomb, 2007). In regard to interventions that target issues of violence (notable studies that can optimally inform interventions are Barbarin, Richter, & deWet, 2001; J. Jones, 2007), Potts (2003) noted that school-based violence prevention programs tend to focus on anger management and the resolution of interpersonal conflicts and neglect to consider the violence embedded in institutional and cultural processes. Such institutional processes often go unnoted in prevention problems, for example, in the introduction and infiltration of cocaine in African American communities by the CIA, FBI, and drug enforcement agencies. Citing Fanon (1963), Potts noted that this "vertical violence" likely contributes the unleashing of "horizontal violence," whereby oppressed group members commit overt, physical acts against others in their community or themselves. We believe that this attention to violence in intervention is of considerable importance given the degree to which violence has threaded racial/cultural socialization in the United States. An exemplary case of this inclusion in an intervention is the emancipatory education model used at the Benjamin E. Mays Institute (BEMI) in Hartford, Connecticut, where Black teachers engage students by explicitly addressing social oppression, thus situating community problems in historical context; acknowledging students as agents of social change; and affirming African cultural resources for healing and social transformation (Potts). In "reclaiming historical memory" (Martin-Baró, 1994), educators at the institute utilize written African wisdom teachings to address the problem of violence. They teach students how to prevent interpersonal violence as well as violence in society as a whole, with an emphasis on greed of the populations. As Potts noted, these teachings "(re)connect students with ancestral figures from their cultural legacy while providing them with valuable insights on the nature of violence" (p. 81).

Conclusion and Recommendations

Although liberation psychology is practiced at different ecological levels, we reemphasize the calls by several authors (e.g., Bulhan, 1985; Watts & Serrano-Garcia, 2003) that interventions that occur at individual levels need to be scaled up and thus directed also at meso- and macro-systems levels. We believe this scaling up needs to be applied also to traditional forms of family and group approaches in which a focus on cohesion among family and group members need not entail liberation concepts. To us, the attention to "more than" individual interventions reflects much more than the rejection of traditional approaches to psychology. This scaling up reflects a cosmology in which collective ways of being and knowing are honored over individualistic ones. Discovering this cosmology can occur in a study of African philosophy, as Azibo (2001) theorized for Black liberation.

We believe Black liberation psychologists should pursue research that takes into consideration not only the contexts relevant to the social environment but also various methodological frameworks for conducting participatory action research. In particular, we acknowledge the contributions of critical qualitative research that brings a rich tradition of considering power, language, agency, collaboration, and the art of social criticism in the design and implementation of participatory action research. The principles that oppressed groups guide the research, while researchers facilitate the process, and that consciousness-raising is the catalyst for change are consistent with paradigms of Black liberation psychology. Consequently, we do not argue that research with a liberation agenda ought to be exclusively qualitative but maintain instead that critical qualitative research is more consistent with Black liberation psychology principles and thus has much to offer us.

The attention to Africa is an important one, because racist theories have promulgated beliefs about Africans as having no history, having no religion and therefore needing the light of Christianity, not being able to claim ownership of their land, being unable to rule themselves because of their primitive irresponsibility, and so forth (see Mengara, 2001). These beliefs have served to justify territorial occupation of African lands and the enslavement of Africans and inculcate images of primitivism that would "permanently justify [their] violent exploitation and enslavement on the basis of the God-given right to conquer those who need God's salvation and the light of Christian 'humanism'" (Mengara, 2001, p. 6). Yet, it is also important that BLP adherents not fall into the process of expropriating Africa, as Europeans have done, by seeing African people as a single monolith instead of a continent comprising multiple ethnic groups divided by European conquest. There is no homogeneous "way of knowing" that is African; consequently, the use of Kwanzaa principles, as one example, may reflect some form of this expropriation. Furthermore, African-descended people, including U.S. Blacks, need to address not only Africa's ancient history but also contemporary problems and the multiple sources of current strife and endurance. For example, creating partnerships between schools in different regions within the African Diaspora can help young people learn specifically about the culture and language of their partners as well as the history and sociopolitical contexts that have shaped them. The interventions we have highlighted in this chapter focus primarily on young people, yet it seems vitally important that interventions be directed as well to adults.

Blacks can be accused of being preoccupied with the study of race. The implication laden in these criticisms is that Blacks are unable to see beyond race and racism and need to take into account the vast complexity that exists in people. That *some* Blacks become preoccupied with race and racism to the neglect of other issues is a factor that does not dissuade BLP adherents from their work but instead creates concern for them, because such preoccupation is an outgrowth, at least to some degree, of the hard-hitting and perpetuating nature of racism. Given this concern, it seems wise to learn how best to approach individuals who are preoccupied in order to help them. In approaching those who seem fixed on racism, while also working alongside other Blacks who respond variously to racism and White supremacy, BLP adherents know that it is often useful to begin with talk about racism before later moving on to others "-isms" that affect functioning and the will to act.

It is important to note that we believe that the insistence, subtle or otherwise, that racism ought not occupy much space in discourse on oppression, is a silencing that can leave Blacks feeling awkward about talking about racism or uncomfortable in gathering with other Black people. Consistent with the various theories already described, we believe that examining racism and its impacts are means to working through these responses. This is why it is essential that BLP adherents continue to be emboldened in researching and theorizing about race and in carrying forward interventions in which racial discourse is prized. A rich discourse is characterized by an understanding of why there are prohibitive forces and discussions of the other forces that frustrate the liberation of Black people. Developmental models can be useful guides to in determining when some people are ready to address intersecting forces of oppression and thereby become more and more inclusive in the liberation process.

Process therapy research can offer an important look at the construction of racism discourse. In a recent study conducted by Constantine (2007), Black clients identified offensive statements that occurred in their counseling interactions with White counselors. Constantine referred to these statements as *microaggressions* to denote the extent of psychological assault conveyed in these statements. Of note is that these statements can be viewed in racist society as acceptable, even gracious or "liberal." Process research like Constantine's study can present ways to address racism in therapy in order that racial stimuli are approached meaningfully and thus point clearly to the substance of what should constitute good therapy with Blacks. We believe that when people begin to study therapy process from a BLP perspective they will begin to realize how necessary it is to integrate sociocultural and sociopolitical issues into the counseling and therefore to witness the unfolding of a therapeutic discourse of liberation.

Earlier, we addressed the issue of violence as a process of oppression and an aspect to address in the struggle for liberation. We urge practitioners and any person involved in invoking change to consider the toll that loss has exacted on the people with whom they work and on themselves. The impact of violence can thwart effective social action efforts by prompting people to behave in extreme ways (e.g., using violence) or to not act at all. In news accounts, some Blacks who were interviewed about whether they would support Barack Obama for the Democratic Party nomination for U.S. President, commented that they feared that if Obama were elected he would be a target for assassination and, by implication, too risky a candidate to support (Rev. Ajabu, personal communication, January 6, 2008). Dealing with loss requires some acknowledgment of one's vulnerability and hence can be a valuable route to self-healing.

Consider the succession of losses experienced by oppressed people. These are the losses that people experience as a result of losing loved ones through violent acts and from early deaths due to poor self-care, substandard living conditions, and/or a health care system that disadvantages the poor. These are the losses that occur because of AIDS, which disproportionately affects Black women. Also, after Blacks have made decisions to leave neighborhoods that were once reserved for them, or have exercise their option of living in communities primarily populated by Whites, they can experience loss in a connection with less-than-prosperous family members. This loss is not solely physical but also cognitive and affective, a process Lott (2002) called "distancing" that becomes part of the socialization that all people are exposed relative to their ideas about poor people. Losses can also occur with ruptures in relationships, through substance abuse and addiction of family members, and with disproportionate numbers of Blacks in penal institutions (and the growing disproportion incarceration of Black women). It is loss from physical abandonment, in that there is an increase of Black children in child welfare systems, as well as the emotional/psychological abandonment that comes when people witness Blacks who abrogate their association as Black people.

Part of the healing that needs to occur with the persistence of oppression is an understanding of how we as liberation psychologists respond to loss or the threat of loss in our lives. Do we readily dismiss people, cut ourselves off from people in hurtful ways, or allow healthy boundaries to be crossed? For the purpose of facilitating the healing for the grander purpose of societal well-being, we need to take strides to be exemplars of self-care by acknowledging that the likelihood of rejection and disapproval is great when we are working to create ways to transform structures.

We end with a passage from Derrick Bell's (1992) *Faces at the Bottom of the Well*, in a story he titled "Afrolantica." Bell described a mythical land that emerged from the ocean, replete with natural resources, such as livestock, fertile soil, and precious minerals, and where only African Americans could survive. Nearly a year is spent on debates over whether Blacks should abandon the United States to migrate to the new land, as well as violent scuffs by Whites (and those non-Whites who supported them) who were threatened by this opportunity and its meaning to their (Whites') relative stature over the generations. Stated another way, the nature of these conflicts were that Whites felt envious of Blacks' opportunity and that their departure flew in the face of the "normalcy" of a racial status quo in which Whites were seen as superior to Blacks. The opportunity created a crisis in the fabric of American life! Not all Blacks decide to embark on the journey, and they disagree widely about the basis of their decision, but all are supportive of the émigrés. In the end, the émigrés, as they approach the new land with enthusiasm, witness Afrolantica sinking back into the ocean. Bell also wrote that the men and women on board felt neither grief nor despair, but rather

> felt deep satisfaction . . . in having gotten this far in their enterprise, in having accomplished it together. As the great ships swung around in the ocean to take them back to America, the miracle of Afrolantica was replaced by a greater miracle. Blacks discovered that they themselves actually possessed the qualities of liberation they had hoped to realize on their new homeland. Feeling this was, they all agreed, an Afrolantica Awakening, a liberation—not of place but of mind. . . . Their faces glowed with self-confidence, as they walked, erect and proud, down the gangplanks the next day when the ships returned to their home ports. The spirit of cooperation that had engaged a few hundred thousand blacks spread to others, as they recalled

the tenacity for humane life which had enabled generations of blacks to survive all efforts to dehumanize or obliterate them. Infectious, their renewed tenacity reinforced their sense of possessing themselves. (pp. 45–46)

Afrolantica is a "place" of liberation in which individuality in other Blacks is appreciated alongside the awareness that a spirit of cooperation is crucial to mental health. This spirit of cooperation, contrary to caricatured images, is not misguided idealism about African culture; neither is it a zealous scheme to reverse oppression, to wrest control from Whites in revenge of past and ongoing wrongs. Instead, we see this spirit as a discovery of humanity. It is the discovery of the humanity of a people too often cast off as inferior and unworthy and of those whose worth is inflated; too, it is a simultaneous discovery of one's own humanity. Like Ajani ya Azibo's (2004) contention that identity progression is toward the affirmation of an African identity, Afrolantica inspirits a renewed love of one's African-ness. Black people do not seek out acceptance from Whites; neither are they mystified with some quixotic notion of harmony that ultimately means a compromising of their selves, their *groupness*. They achieve harmony from within the group, and from this place there will likely be conflict and turmoil that can lead eventually to the regard they deserve as a people.

Black liberation psychologists cannot alone achieve this end result of which Bell (1992) wrote, but as more and more psychologists become fully aware of the impacts of racism and other forms of oppression on their well-being as a people, the greater the likelihood that Black people will refuse to tolerate oppression for themselves or anyone.

References

Ajani ya Azibo, D. (2004). An empirically supported reconceptualization of African–U.S. racial identity development as an abnormal process. *Review of General Psychology, 8*, 249–264.

American Psychological Association. (2002). *Ethical principles of psychologists and code of conduct.* Retrieved from http://www.apa.org/ethics/code2002.html

Azibo, D. (2001). *Liberation psychology: An introduction to the African personality construct.* Tallahassee, FL: Author.

Baldwin, J. (1986). African (Black) psychology: Issues and synthesis. *Journal of Black Studies, 16*, 235–249.

Barbarin, O. A., Richter, L., & deWet, T. (2001). Exposure to violence, coping resources, and psychological adjustment of South African children. *American Journal of Orthopsychiatry, 71*, 16–25.

Bell, D. (1992). *Faces at the bottom of the well: The permanence of racism.* New York: Basic Books.

Brody, G., Chen, Y., Murry, V., Simons, R., Ge, X., & Gibbons, F. (2006). Perceived discrimination and the adjustment of African American youths: A five-year longitudinal analysis with contextual moderating effects. *Child Development, 77*, 1170–1189.

Bulhan, H. A. (1985). *Frantz Fanon and the psychology of oppression.* New York: Plenum Press.

Caldwell, C. H., Kohn-Wood, L. P., Schmeelk-Cone, K., Chavous, T. M., & Zimmerman, M. (2004). Racial discrimination and racial identity as risk or protective factors for violent behaviors in African American young adults. *American Journal of Community Psychology, 33*, 91–105.

Carter, R. T. (2007). Racism and psychological and emotional injury: Recognizing and assessing race-based traumatic stress. *The Counseling Psychologist, 35*, 13–105.

Clark, R., Anderson, N. B., Clark, V. R., & Williams, D. R. (1999). Racism as a stressor for African Americans: A biopsychosocial model. *American Psychologist, 54*, 805–816.

Constantine, M. G. (2007). Racial microaggressions against African American clients in cross-racial counseling relationships. *Journal of Counseling Psychology, 54*, 1–16.

Constantine, M. G., Donnelly, P. C., & Myers, L. J. (2002). Collective self-esteem and Africultural coping styles in African American adolescents. *Journal of Black Studies, 32*, 698–710.

Cross, W. E., Jr., & Vandiver, B. J. (2001). Nigrescence theory and measurement. In J. G. Ponterotto, J. M. Casas, L. A. Suzuki, & C. M. Alexander (Eds.), *Handbook of multicultural counseling* (2nd ed., pp. 371–393). Thousand Oaks, CA: Sage.

Fanon, F. (1963). *The wretched of the earth.* New York: Grove Press.

Fanon, F. (1967). *Black skin, white masks.* New York: Grove Weidenfeld.

Foster, P. M., Phillips, F., Belgrave, F. Z., Randolph, S. M., & Braithwaite, N. (1993). An Africentric model for AIDS education, prevention, and psychological services within the African American community. *Journal of Black Psychology, 19*, 123–141.

Franklin, D. C., & Carter, R. T. (2007). Race related stress, racial identity and psychological health for Black Americans. *Journal of Black Psychology, 33,* 1–22.

Freire, P. (1972). *Pedagogy of the oppressed.* Harmondsworth, UK: Penguin.

Gaines, S. E., Jr., & Reed, E. S. (1995). Prejudice: From Allport to DuBois. *American Psychologist, 50,* 96–103.

Harrell, S. P. (2000). A multidimensional conceptualization of racism-related stress: Implications for the well-being of people of color. *American Journal of Orthopsychiatry, 70,* 42–57.

Helms, J. E. (1995). An update of Helms's White and people of color racial identity models. In J. G. Ponterotto, J. M. Casas, L. A. Suzuki, & C. M. Alexander (Eds.), *Handbook of multicultural counseling* (pp. 181–198). Thousand Oaks, CA: Sage.

Helms, J. E. (2003). A pragmatic view of social justice. *The Counseling Psychologist, 31,* 305–313.

Hilliard, A. (1998). *The awakening of the African mind.* Gainesville, FL: Makare.

Jagers, R. J., & Mock, L. O. (1993). Understanding the strengths of African American families. *Journal of Black Studies, 23,* 460–471.

Jones, C., & Shorter-Gooden, K. (2003). *Shifting: The double lives of Black women in America.* New York: HarperCollins.

Jones, H., Cross, W. E., Jr., & DeFour, D. C. (2007). Race-related stress, racial identity attitudes, and mental health among Black women. *Journal of Black Psychology, 33,* 208–231.

Jones, J. (2007). Exposure to chronic community violence: Resilience in African American children. *Journal of Black Psychology, 33,* 125–149.

Kambon, K. (1996). The Africentric paradigm and African-American psychological liberation. In D. Azibo (Ed.), *African psychology in historical perspective and related commentary* (pp. 57–70). Trenton, NJ: Africa World Press.

Kasser, T., & Kanner, A. (2003). *Psychology and consumer culture: The struggle for a good life in a materialistic world.* Washington, DC: American Psychological Association.

Kieffer, C. H. (1984). Citizen empowerment: A developmental perspective. In J. Rappaport, C. Swift, & R. Hess (Eds.), *Studies in empowerment: Steps toward understanding and action* (pp. 9–36). New York: Haworth Press.

Lawson, E. J., & Thomas, C. (2007). Wading in the waters: Spirituality and older Black Katrina survivors. *Journal of Health Care for the Poor and Underserved, 18,* 341–354.

Lott, B. (2002). Cognitive and behavioral distancing from the poor. *American Psychologist, 57*(2), 100–110.

Martín-Baró, I. (1996). *Writings for a liberation psychology.* Cambridge, MA: Harvard University Press.

Mengara, D. M. (2001). *Images of Africa: Stereotypes and realities.* Trenton, NJ: Africa World Press.

Moane, G. (2003). Bridging the personal and political: Practices for a liberation psychology. *American Journal of Community Psychology, 31,* 91–101.

Myers, L. J. (1992). *Understanding an Afrocentric world view: Introduction to an optimal psychology* (2nd ed.). Dubuque, IA: Kendall/Hunt.

Nobles, W. W. (1991). African philosophy: Foundations for Black Psychology. In R. L. Jones (Ed.), *Black Psychology* (3rd ed., pp. 47–63). Berkeley, CA: Cobb & Henry.

Noose shocker for Black Columbia prof. (2007, October 10). *New York Post.* Retrieved from http://www.nypost.com/seven/10102007/news/regionalnews/noose_shocker-for-black-columb.htm

Phillips, F. B. (1990). NTU psychotherapy: An Afrocentric approach. *Journal of Black Psychology, 17,* 55–74.

Pieterse, A. L., & Carter, R. T. (2007). An examination of the relationship between general life stress, racism-related stress and psychological health among Black men. *Journal of Counseling Psychology, 54,* 101–109.

Potts, R. G. (2003). Emancipatory education versus school-based prevention in African American communities. *American Journal of Community Psychology, 31,* 173–183.

Rabaka, R. (2006). The souls of Black radical folk: W. E. B. Du Bois, critical social theory, and the state of Africana studies. *Journal of Black Studies, 36,* 732–763.

Sellers, R. M., & Shelton, J. N. (2003). The role of racial identity in perceived discrimination. *Journal of Personality and Social Psychology, 84,* 1079–1092.

Sellers, R. M., Smith, M. A., Shelton, J. N., Rowley, S. A., & Chavous, T. M. (1998). Multidimensional model of Black identity: A re-conception of African American racial identity. *Personality and Social Psychology Review, 2,* 18–39.

Smalls, C., White, R., Chavous, T., & Sellers, R. M. (2007). Racial ideological beliefs and racial discrimination experiences as predictors of academic engagement among African American adolescents. *Journal of Black Psychology, 33,* 299–330.

Thompson, C. E., & Carter, R. T. (1997). *Racial identity theory: Applications to individual, group, and organizational interventions.* Mahwah, NJ: Lawrence Erlbaum.

Thompson, C. E., & Carter, R. T. (in press). *Racial identity theory: Applications to individual, group, and organizational interventions* (2nd ed.). Mahwah, NJ: Lawrence Erlbaum.

Thompson, C. E., Murry, S. L., Harris, D., & Garcia, P. (2005). A transformative endeavor: The implementation of racial identity theory at the community level. In R. Toporek, L. Gerstein, N. Fouad, G. Roysircar, & T. Israel (Eds.), *Handbook on social justice in counseling psychology: Leadership, vision, and action* (pp. 100–116). Thousand Oaks, CA: Sage.

Thompson, C. E., & Neville, H. A. (1999). Racism, mental health, and mental health practice. *The Counseling Psychologist, 27,* 155–123.

Turner-Musa, J., & Lipscomb, L. (2007). Spirituality and social support on health behaviors of African American undergraduates. *American Journal of Health Behavior, 31,* 495–501.

Utsey, S. O., Bolden, M. A., & Brown, A. L. (1995). Visions of revolution from the spirit of Frantz Fanon: A psychology of liberation for counseling African Americans confronting societal racism and oppression. In J. G. Ponterotto, J. M. Casas, L. A. Suzuki, & C. M. Alexander (Eds.), *Handbook of multicultural counseling* (pp. 311–336). Thousand Oaks, CA: Sage.

Watts, R., Abdul-Adil, J., & Pratt, T. (2002). Enhancing critical consciousness in young African American men: A psycho-educational approach. *Psychology of Men and Masculinity, 3,* 41–50.

Watts, R. J., & Guessous, O. (2006). *Civil rights activists in the information age: The development of math literacy workers* (Center for Information and Research on Civic Learning and Engagement Working Paper 50). Available at http://www.civicyouth.org

Watts, R. J., & Serrano-Garcia, I. (2003). The quest for a liberating community psychology: An overview. *American Journal of Community Psychology, 31,* 73–78.

Watts, R. J., Williams, N. C., & Jagers, R. J. (2003). Sociopolitical development. *American Journal of Community Psychology, 31,* 185–194.

White, A. M. (2006). Racial and gender attitudes as predictors of feminist activism among self-identified African American feminists. *Journal of Black Psychology, 32,* 455–478.

White, J. (2001, March 10). *U.S. commission on civil rights charges "voter disenfranchisement...at heart" of Bush victory in Florida.* Retrieved October 17, 2007, from http://www.wsw.org/articles/2001/mar2001/vote-m10.shtml

PART VIII

TRENDS AND FUTURE DIRECTIONS

36

AFRICAN AMERICAN PSYCHOLOGY

Trends and Future Directions

HELEN A. NEVILLE, BRENDESHA M. TYNES, AND SHAWN O. UTSEY

The collection of chapters in the handbook paint a picture of a vibrant, dynamic field, one in which researchers are producing transformative theories and research. The goal of these works is not only to improve psychological science but also to create culturally grounded knowledge that can be used to inform practices and policies to improve the day-to day lives of individuals, families, and communities of African descent. Although competing theories and approaches on a wide range of topics were presented in the collection, a number of trends emerged. These common threads highlight areas of convergence in the fields of African and African American/Black Psychology. In this chapter, we outline key trends identified in the narrative of the chapters. In addition, we pose several future directions that in part emerged from the content and suggestions presented by the authors and from our own independent analysis of the field.

It is not surprising that most of the chapters placed the topic within a sociocultural historical context, which is often overlooked within the broader discipline of psychology. Building on the tradition of African and African American/Black Psychology, the authors addressed critical questions related to the importance of the topic to society as a whole and to the field specifically, development of the issue in society and subsequent research on the issue, seminal works, and current (interdisciplinary) examinations of the topic. The authors understand that human behavior, attitudes, and experiences cannot be examined in a vacuum. The lead chapter in the handbook, for example, provided a rich discussion of the context in which the field developed, spanning from ancient Kemet, to the establishment of the Association of Black Psychologists in 1968, to recent developments. In Part IV, the authors related their review of the literature to key educational outcomes and policies. Other chapters, such as Chapter 21, by Cokley and Chapman, identified key historical research and concepts that were the precursors to Black racial identity studies. Nearly all of the authors also considered the role of the social, cultural, and political location of Black Americans in either the expression or development of the issue (e.g., the emergence of hip-hop culture, risk and protective factors related to a given phenomenon) and the articulation of practical implications. Thus, African American attitudes, cognitions, and behaviors were considered within a larger context and not limited to the domain of psychology.

All of the chapters incorporated discussions of conceptual models and/or theoretical frameworks. Many of these models/frameworks consistently applied either principles of an African

American approach (i.e., one in which Black American attitudes and behaviors are primarily rooted within the experiences shaped by African American communities and the larger U.S. context) or an African-centered approach (i.e., one in which Black American attitudes and behaviors are part of a cultural constellation with roots in Africa). Several authors, on the other hand, incorporated both African American and African-centered approaches in their analyses. What this communicates is less rigid adherence to one identified approach and instead a thoughtful consideration of the range of conceptual insights that may shed light on complex human phenomena.

Speight et al.'s examination of mental health in Chapter 26 exemplifies this effort. They presented multiple perspectives of mental health and, moreover, identified commonalities among these perspectives. They highlighted the ways in which previous researchers have combined various African American and African-centered theories to inform conceptualizations of mental health (practices). Although there are several other examples in the handbook, Thompson and Alfred concluded Part VII with an excellent illustration of this theoretical eclecticism. They incorporated the historical works of scholars such as Franz Fanon and W. E. B. Du Bois with contemporary researchers who adopt an African American (e.g., William Cross and Janet Helms) or African-centered approach (e.g., Daudi Ajani ya-Azibo, Linda James Myers, and Kobi Kambon) to develop a nuanced and compelling discussion of Black liberation psychology.

In addition to synthesizing the literature on the varying conceptualizations of mental health, many of the chapters in this volume outline the role race and culture can play in influencing mental health outcomes. The planning of the fifth version of the *Diagnostic and Statistical Manual of Mental Disorders (DSM–V)* is now well underway, and it will provide a particular way of viewing psychological health and illness that in some ways is inconsistent with conceptions put forth in this handbook. Scholars and practitioners who ultimately use the *DSM–V* to inform their research and practice might consider viewing the mental health of African Americans through the more diverse cultural lens provided in this handbook.

It seems particularly important at this historic juncture that we abandon dichotomous and often-hostile ideological divisions within the field and find common points of unity across our unique areas of inquiry. We are not arguing to ignore tensions within the field. Instead, like a number of the scholars in the handbook, we suggest increasing the dialogue and consideration of multiple perspectives in our theorizing about complex issues related to improving the psychological, physical, and educational health of African Americans.

The chapters in this book speak to both the growing theoretical development of the field across a range of perspectives and the increasing methodological sophistication of the research. The chapters highlighted theoretical developments, primarily over the last several decades, as illustrated in discussions related to racial identity, family, African American personality, cultural mistrust, racial socialization, and so on. Researchers are increasing the methodological sophistication of testing these theoretical assertions. The research on stereotype threat reflects advancements in theory and research methods; these works are grounded in the theoretical refinements and tested using experimental designs.

In Chapter 28, Lambert and Smith summarized a body of theoretically grounded and methodologically sound research on assessing behavioral and emotional strengths among African-descended youth and adults. This work addressed both the trend to increase the methodological sophistication of research and the trend related to increasing the development of strength-based approaches. Building on one of the core tenets of African American Psychology, most of the chapters in this handbook adopted a strengths-based approach. The field of African American Psychology was built on the fundamental understanding that Black Americans have a host of positive strengths that can serve as protective factors against the ills of oppression and, moreover, we have at our disposal a range of internal and external resources contributing to our ability to thrive and survive. Several of the chapters focused specifically on strengths, encouraging new and innovative examinations of protective factors in Black Americans' lives and the strengths on which we rely to promote healthy psychological, physical, and educational outcomes. For example, in Chapter 27, A. Toy Caldwell-Colbert and her colleagues reclaimed positive psychology and situated the examination of well-being and psychosocial strengths within the tradition of African American Psychology.

The chapters also consistently addressed implications of the theories and research for multilevel interventions. Psychological interventions traditionally have been viewed as individual-level activities to address personal concerns. When one thinks of the work of a psychologist, the image of one-on-one individual therapy often comes to mind. Occasionally, couples, group, or family therapy may be acknowledged. The work of psychologists, especially African American psychologists, is broader than the confines of the 50-minute therapy hour. In this collection, the authors encourage us to conceptualize the broader implications of theories and research in the field to intervene on individual, family, school, community, and societal levels. For example, Part IV covered a range of teacher- and school-level interventions along with educational policies needed to transform the educational experiences of African American youth. Belgrave and her colleagues also highlight, in Chapter 34, the importance of developing culturally relevant prevention interventions to address critical societal needs, such as reducing substance use and abuse. A number of the authors additionally noted the need to find ways to increase a critical consciousness of oppression as the key to liberation (mental, psychological, spiritual, etc.). These practices underscore the multiple uses of African American psychological theory and research in counseling, school, community, and policy interventions.

Modern African American Psychology grew out of struggle—struggle for inclusion, legitimacy, and representation of thought and bodies. It is not surprising, then, that a unifying thread throughout this handbook is one of social justice. Authors identified critical concerns facing Black Americans (e.g., the education gap, racial oppression) as well as factors of resiliency (e.g., coping, positive racial identity or African American personality). At the same time, these authors mentioned ways in which society can promote greater social justice by reducing racial disparities in psychological and physical health and promoting access to quality, culturally relevant health and educational services.

In addition to the trends that emerged across the chapters, several important future directions become evident via an analysis of the collection. Next, we outline several of these future directions that we hope will guide theoretical and empirical work. Interestingly, most of the recommendations build on ways to further develop the common emerging threads discussed earlier. Further development of theoretical and methodological approaches captures many of the recommendations. Many studies in the field use correlational designs; a few employ longitudinal or qualitative designs. To understand the complex nature of many phenomena of interest (e.g., what factors promote academic engagement; what are effective ways to prevent suicide; how can parents further promote healthy development; what is the meaning of psychological liberation, and how can we measure it?), researchers should use a range of methods available. Prospective longitudinal designs are needed to better understand the course and consequences of psychological processes. In addition, the use of advanced statistical techniques is needed to test the complexity of theoretical models that are proposed in this collection.

Similar to the broader field of psychology, only recently are African American Psychology researchers employing qualitative designs to explore research questions. These designs are needed to further describe the psychological and educational experiences of Black Americans. Qualitative designs can assist in theory refinement and meaning-making; these designs can also help complicate common understandings and help articulate the ways in which intersecting identities (e.g., race, class, and gender) influence experiences. We especially encourage researchers to explore mixed-methods approaches in which multiple sources of data are used to examine human behavior. This approach may be particularly helpful in evaluating intervention and prevention efforts. Similarly, with notable exception, researchers have traditionally overrelied on self-report survey data. We encourage the use of other sources of data with which to paint a more comprehensive picture of specific research areas; these sources include observations, physiological or health indicators (e.g., blood pressure, functional magnetic resonance imaging, cortisol levels), parent or other reports, culturally relevant assessments, records/documents, interviews, focus groups, census data, narratives (e.g., journals, Internet postings, and essays), and so on.

The contributing authors included a discussion of within-group differences throughout the text, and two chapters focused specifically on intersecting identities (race and gender and race and sexuality). These discussions exposed a limitation in the extant literature. Although some theorizing has been given to the intersection of two identities, typically race and one other identity, we know very little about how multiple identities influence experiences; moreover, there is a dearth of empirical research supporting initial theoretical assertions. Greater and more systematic consideration of within-group differences on psychosocial experiences are needed, especially the consideration of gender, class, geographic location, age, sexuality, skin color, ethnicity, and their intersections with race.

There are several glaring omissions with respect to intersecting identities in the literature. For example, there is a scant theoretical and empirical literature specifically examining the experiences of Black men; we need more explorations of gender issues related to a range of issues for Black men (e.g., experiences as fathers; issues related to academic engagement; resiliency factors; symptoms and outcomes of psychological distress, including depression and suicidal behavior; articulations of social support). Exploration of economic class also is underdeveloped in our work. Refinement of the way in which *class* is defined or conceptualized in a study and its measurement are particularly important. Special attention is needed to tease apart the influence of class from race, especially when working in urban communities. Although this collection included explorations of psychosocial and educational research across the life span, gaps exist in our knowledge. Noticeably absent from this collection was a consideration of the elderly. Building on a disparate work in the field, more coordinated research is needed to understand the unique experiences of Black older adults in terms of lifelong education, recreation, psychological well-being, health, experiences with and resistance to racism, racial identity, spirituality or religious practices, and so on.

Although there is a strong theoretical base in some areas of African American Psychology (e.g., racial identity), theory development is needed in other areas, such as new media. Just as existing theories developed to explain European American behavior in offline settings, for example, do not easily translate into African American offline contexts, the same is true for explaining African American experiences with new media. There is now a burgeoning literature on African Americans' access to and use of the Internet, but we are just beginning to understand the psychological correlates of Internet use. What factors influence the development of African American identity in online settings? How do African Americans develop intimate relationships online? How might Internet use promote the development of cognitive skills, aspects of social cognition? More research is also needed on children and adolescents' intra- and intergroup interactions, the impact of race- and gender-related online victimization, and how stereotypic images in online games and social networking sites impact African American youth. Future research is also needed on online therapeutic uses of the Internet to treat such mental health conditions as depression and substance abuse. Because African Americans utilize mental health services less than the general population, perhaps the Internet context can reduce this disparity. Methodologically speaking, the use of the Internet can dramatically increase the sample size in research studies. This will afford researchers the opportunity to explore questions about within-group differences in greater depth.

Chapter authors identified a number of ways in which African/Black Psychology has grown, especially in terms of theory development. Researchers adopting an African-centered approach rely on a broad range of literatures, including works published on the continent (i.e., Africa) and in the United States. At this point in its development, we encourage further exploration in a couple of ways. One way is to further refine theoretical assertions to consider similarities and differences in Africans on the continent and throughout the Diaspora, with special attention given to issues related to nationality or ethnicity, language, sociohistory, gender, class, cultural practices, and so on. In addition to the methodological recommendations provided in the discussion of African American Psychology, we encourage greater cross-cultural research with African populations in the Diaspora. Using quantitative, qualitative, and various interpretive methods, findings from cross-cultural research can further support theoretical assertions related to the similarities in experiences. Such findings can also uncover diversities among relevant psychosocial experiences.

The newly developed Association of Black Psychologists Board Certification in African-centered/Black Psychology further illustrates the development of African/Black Psychology over the past decade. The board certification helps to standardize acceptable, culturally relevant mental health practices with persons of African descent from an African-centered perspective. Additional work is needed to further connect theory, research, and practice to the proposed competencies.

We also encourage attention to additional training issues. What are the best practices in training mental health workers to adopt cultural competencies in working with African Americans across the life span that include both African American and African/Black Psychology perspectives? Rigorous studies of training researchers, teachers, counselors, and social workers in African American Psychology are thus needed. This is especially true in the case of training teachers to understand the developmental needs of African Americans. Recently, the National Institute of Child Health and Human Development and the National Council for Accreditation for Teacher Education released a report outlining the need for teachers to be trained in child and adolescent development (National Institute of Child Health and Human Development & National Council for Accreditation for Teacher Education, n.d.). Research on best practices might facilitate quality training on a national level. Also, at this point there is little articulation of what it means to be a culturally competent researcher in the field and how we train future professionals along these lines. Further articulations are also needed in training culturally competent professionals to interface with the community—what are culturally relevant community interventions, and what are best practices in terms of knowledge dissemination to individuals most affected by the scholarship (e.g., parents, grandparents, youth in the schools, workers, and community members)?

Since the formation of African American Psychology, the field has struggled to find ways to improve the lived realities of Black Americans. Working as researchers and practitioners over the decades, we have individually and collectively attempted to address a number of questions, including the following: What is the role of African American Psychology in addressing societal ills—racism, economic and gender exploitation, educational and health disparities, and so on? How can our research be used to inform policies and practices related to social issues including the education gap, wealth and health disparities, and access concerns (e.g., quality, culturally relevant health services)? In what ways can our research inform practices and policies that promote positive well-being across the life span, particularly in the areas of psychological, physical, educational, and spiritual health? What are the specific contributions of African American Psychology in addressing these concerns, and how can these contributions manifest themselves in interdisciplinary research and practice efforts? Also, in what ways is the knowledge in the field being shared with and refined by the community? We encourage the field to continue along this path to deepen our theoretical understanding of the complexities of psychological and educational processes of African Americans and the methodological sophistication in addressing research questions. Moreover, we encourage the field to introduce and support policies that will increase the pipeline of scholars and practitioners in African American psychology as well as funding priorities for critical research and applied initiatives related to the priorities set forth in this book.

References

National Institute of Child Health and Human Development & National Council for Accreditation of Teacher Education. (n.d.). *Child and adolescent research development and teacher education: Evidence-based pedagogy, policy, and practice* (Summary of roundtable meetings, December 1–2, 2005, and March 20–21, 2006). Washington, DC: National Council for Accreditation of Teacher Education. (ERIC Document Reproduction Service No. 496495). Retrieved July 28, 2008, from http://eric.ed.gov

AUTHOR INDEX

Abdul-Adil, J., 168
Abdullah, A. S., 450
Abe, K., 406
Abelson, J., 337, 339, 344, 404, 463
Abikoff, H. B., 355
Aboud, F. E., 278
Abraham, W. E., 77
Abrams, M., 418
Abrams, M. R., 419
Abramyan, S., 462
Achatz, M., 105
Adair, R., 346
Adams, E. M., 378
Adams, E. P., 51, 76, 80t, 81, 82, 422, 435, 436, 437
Adams, G. J., 472
Adams, J., 449
Adams, J. H., 163, 164
Adams, J. M., 453, 454
Adams, K., 356
Adams, M. S., 148
Adams, V. N., 256, 263
Adebimpe, V. R., 337, 463, 464
Adger, C., 207
Adler, L., 337
Adrian, G., 167
Agresti, A., 389
Aguilar-Gaxiola, S., 336, 337
Ahern, J., 151
Ahluwalia, M. K., 93
Ahmad, W. I. U., 419
Ahs, A., 419
Aikens, N., 177, 179
Ainsworth, J. W., 193
Ainsworth-Darnell, J., 193, 194
Ajamu, A., 5, 6, 7, 14, 15, 22, 48, 51
Ajani ya Azibo, D., 343, 484
Ajei, M., 9, 51
Akbar, M., 401, 432, 436, 437
Akbar, N., 5, 8, 9, 14, 43, 47, 48, 49, 50, 51, 61, 62, 63, 67, 83, 293, 365, 366, 379, 410
Akers, R. L., 408
Akhtar, S., 420
Akiskal, H., 337
Alao, A. O., 418
Albury, A., 79t, 80, 81

Aldridge, H., 129, 130, 132
Alegria, M., 343
Alexander, A., 136, 447
Alexander, C. M., 231, 433
Alexander, H., 437
Alexander, K. L., 276
Alhassen, M., 418, 419
Ali, K., 137
Ali, S. R., 435
Alison, P. D., 389
Allen, B., 243, 244, 250, 367
Allen, E., Jr., 131, 132
Allen, K., 95
Allen, K. R., 122
Allen, R. L., 143, 146
Alleyne, R., 473
Alleyne, V. L., 379, 435, 436, 437
Allison, F., 473
Allison, J. J., 470
Allison, K. W., 38, 40, 61, 72, 352, 357, 358, 363, 409, 475, 476
Allport, G., 160, 269
Alsheikh, N., 225
Alston, R., 69
Alston, R. J., 304
Altman, N., 319
Alvarado, R., 474, 476
Amador, X., 338
Amankwah, K., 420
Ambady, N., 191, 213, 219
Ames, C., 191
Ames, M., 337
An, A. S., 385, 386, 391, 397
Anastopoulos, A. D., 355
Anderson, C. A., 145
Anderson, E., 136
Anderson, L. L., 149
Anderson, L. P., 365, 448
Anderson, M. G., 354
Anderson, N. B., 151, 335, 365
Anderson, P. L., 408
Anderson, P. M., 385
Anderson, S., 276
Anderson, V. D., 273, 278
Anderson, W. H., 288, 293

Anderson-Yockel, J., 177
Andrews, F., 338
Anger, W. K., 461
Anglin, D. M., 256, 260, 261
Angold, A., 352, 353, 354, 356
Angst, J., 337
Ani, M., 4, 6, 9, 49
Anie, K. A., 419, 420
Anthony, K. K., 418, 419
Anyabwile, T. M., 288
Anyanwu, E., 419
Anyanwu, I., 419
Apfel, N., 215, 216, 219, 238, 243
Appiah-Kubi, K., 51, 53
Arana, G. W., 402
Arbalaez, J. J., 421
Arbona, C., 293
Arey, S., 338
Arias, E., 352, 406
Armah, A. K., 53
Arnold, L. E., 355
Aronson, J., 212, 213, 214, 215, 216, 217, 289
Arorash, T. J., 440
Arrington, E., 255
Arroyo, C., 269
Arroyo, C. G., 379
Arunkumar, R., 192
Asante, M., 8, 26, 47, 83
Asch, S. M., 403
Ascher, C., 187
Asgharian, A., 420
Ashburn, L., 148
Ashcraft, A., 472
Ashcraft, A. M., 477
Ashcroft, A. M., 438
Ashley-Koch, A., 423
Askin, H., 207
Atdjian, S., 342
Atkin, C. K., 144
Atkin, K., 419
Atkins, J., 273
Atkinson, D. R., 303, 432
Atkinson, J. W., 83
Atwell, I., 366
Au, K., 178, 180
Aust, C. F., 129, 133
Avis, N., 404
Awad, G., 289
Azibo, D. A., 38, 61, 62, 65, 66, 75, 76, 78, 80, 293, 365, 366, 489
Azocar, C., 150

Bachman, J. G., 357
Backman, J. G., 473
Baer, P. E., 472

Bailey, G., 207
Bailey, R. K., 355
Baird, R., 462
Bakeman, R., 409
Baker, B., 177
Baker, F. M., 337, 462, 463, 464
Baker, R. C., 433
Baker, R. W., 84
Baldwin, A. L., 177
Baldwin, C., 177
Baldwin, J. A., 10, 51, 61, 65, 66, 68, 75, 76, 77, 78, 79t, 80, 83, 205, 271, 290, 366, 367, 378, 403, 484
Baldwin, K., 419
Balfanz, R., 243
Ball, D. L., 242
Ball, S., 145
Ballas, S. K., 417, 418
Banaji, M. R., 459
Bandura, A., 145, 189
Banerjee, M. N., 379
Banko, C., 419
Bankole, K. O., 75
Banks, C. A. M., 232, 233
Banks, D. H., 435
Banks, J. A., 5, 231, 232, 233
Banks, K. H., 288
Banks, W. C., 48, 277
Banks-Wallace, J., 93, 95
Barbarin, O., 176, 177, 179, 237, 259, 380
Barbarin, O. A., 417, 418, 419, 421, 489
Barbosa, P., 243
Barer, B., 106
Bargh, J. A., 145
Barker, C., 421
Barkley, R., 337
Barksdale, C., 388
Barnes, A., 337, 431
Barnes, G. M., 357, 470
Barnes, P. W., 300
Barnes, S. L., 386, 387, 390
Barraclough, B., 407
Barr-Anderson, D. J., 343
Barron, K. E., 293
Barroso, C. S., 357
Bascom, W., 52
Baser, R., 343, 344
Baser, R. E., 406, 407
Baskin, M. L., 421
Bass-Hass, R., 312
Batson, C. D., 122
Battle, J. J., 182
Baugh, J., 204, 205
Bauman, L., 109
Baumrind, D., 107, 108, 176
Baxter, J., 193

Bazile, A., 401, 432, 436
Beach, M. C., 421
Beale, R., 97
Beale, R. L., 380
Beauvais, F., 474
Bechtoldt, H., 149
Becker, B., 472
Becker, J., 463
Beckert, T., 390
Beckett, J. O., 437
Beckles, C. A., 152
Becvar, D., 110
Becvar, R., 110
Bediako, S. M., 417, 418, 419, 421, 422
Belamaric, R., 96
Belgrave, F. Z., 4, 6, 7, 14, 38, 40, 61, 72, 259, 276, 277, 289, 352, 357, 358, 363, 385, 386, 387, 389, 418, 435, 436, 437, 438, 472, 473, 474, 475, 476, 477, 489
Belin, T., 405
Bell, A., 312
Bell, C. C., 337, 402, 464
Bell, D., 486, 491
Bell, K., 461, 462
Bell, T. J., 302, 305
Bell, Y. R., 51, 75, 78, 79t, 80, 83, 244, 367
Bellamy, N., 476
Bell-Scott, P., 120, 123
Bempechat, J., 190
Benasich, A. A., 178
Bender, M. A., 408
Ben-Jochannon, Y., 49, 51
Benkert, R., 304, 421
Bennett, G. G., 418, 423
Bennett, G. M., 355
Bennett, J., 433
Bennett, L., Jr., 4
Bennett, M. D., 261
Benoit, M. Z., 354, 410
Bentley, K. B., 256, 263
Bentley, K. L., 259
Berger, M., 420
Berglund, P., 340, 401, 402, 404, 463
Bergman, L. R., 107
Berkowitz, L., 145
Berman, A., 405
Berman, A. L., 408
Bernal, M., 36
Bernat, J. A., 402
Bernhardt, J. M., 143, 149
Berni, M., 207
Berry, G. L., 144
Berry, M. F., 378
Berton, O., 379
Best, C., 260, 261

Bethea-Whitfield, P., 449, 452, 453
Biederman, J., 337, 473
Bierman, A., 93
Biesanz, J. C., 176
Bigler, R. S., 117
Billingsley, A., 49, 51, 94, 104, 105, 378
Billson, J. M., 118, 211
Binion, V. J., 465
Birch, J. W., 224
Bird, H., 355
Birdsong, B. D., 79t
Birnbaum, H., 337, 338
Bishop, A., 257, 259, 263
Bishop, S., 408
Bissessar, N., 118, 119
Black, B., 408
Black, H., 97
Black, M. M., 389
Black, S. R., 19
Blackman, L., 104, 106
Blackmon, S. K. M., 259, 260, 261
Blackwell, D., 152
Blackwood, E., 323, 324
Blaine, B., 93, 97, 98
Blaine, D. D., 390
Blair, I., 167
Blake, R., 206
Blanchett, W. J., 356
Blank, M., 94
Blascovich, J., 216
Blassingame, J. W., 378
Blazer, D. G., 346, 404, 451
Block, J. H., 117
Bloom, B. A., 233
Blount, W., 422
Blow, F. C., 463
Blyden, E. W., 40
Boardman, J., 92, 93, 95
Bobek, D. L., 385
Boden, R., 319
Bodison, P., 257, 259, 263
Bogatz, G. A., 145
Bogdanov, I., 420
Bogle, D., 144
Boisnier, A. D., 109
Bola, J. R., 463
Bolden, M., 51, 76, 80t, 81, 82, 163, 167, 381, 408, 422, 435, 436, 437, 448, 452, 483, 485
Boller, K., 179
Bond, M., 245
Bond, S., 419
Bonds, S. M., 419
Bonilla-Silva, E., 162
Booth, B. M., 473
Bosch, R., 433

Bosworth, H. B., 421, 422
Botta, R. A., 148, 356
Botvin, E. M., 438
Botvin, G., 438, 476, 477
Botvin, G. J., 474, 475
Bouie, C. L., 80
Bound, J., 470
Bourne, M. L., 463
Boutte, G., 182, 183, 224
Bovbjerg, V. E., 420
Bowen, N. K., 176
Bowie, J., 301, 302
Bowleg, L., 368
Bowler, R., 461
Bowman, M. A., 379
Bowman, P., 93, 95, 96, 123, 381
Bowman, P. J., 261
Boyce, L., 177
Boyd, K., 472
Boyd, R. C., 354
Boyd-Franklin, N., 54, 105, 107, 110, 117, 118, 120, 123, 128, 131, 132, 133, 258, 311, 312, 314, 315, 316, 317, 319, 321, 379, 391, 422, 432, 434, 439, 441
Boykin, A. W., 79t, 80, 81, 92, 239, 241, 242, 243, 244, 246, 250, 255, 256, 257, 258, 262, 367, 368
Boykin, K., 316, 320
Boyle, C., 356
Bracha, H., 338
Bracy, J., 338
Bradley, R. H., 84
Bradley, S., 420
Braithwaite, N., 489
Braithwaite, R. L., 133
Brand, J. E., 144
Branscombe, N. R., 369
Bray, J. H., 472
Breeden, G., 406, 407
Brega, A., 98
Brennan, E. M., 261
Breslau, J., 336, 337, 339, 340, 402
Bridge, R., 111
Bridgest, S. T., 354
Briggs, H. E., 261
Brinkley, G., 473
Brinson, L. R., 79t
Brodie, M., 143
Brody, G., 474, 488
Brody, G. H., 177, 273, 437
Broman, C., 111, 290, 345
Bromberger, J. T., 167, 404
Brome, D., 95, 289, 473
Brome, D. R., 435, 436, 437
Brondolo, E., 167
Bronfenbrenner, U., 111, 175, 273, 274, 276, 474

Bronzaft, A. L., 120
Brook, J. S., 381, 435, 436
Brookins, C. C., 79t, 84, 288
Brooks, T., 128, 129, 130, 131
Brooks-Gunn, J., 176, 177, 178, 179, 181
Brotman, L. M., 260, 261, 263
Brown, A., 301, 462
Brown, A. C., 437
Brown, A. L., 163, 167, 483, 485
Brown, B. B., 107
Brown, D. L., 380
Brown, D. R., 451
Brown, F., 421
Brown, G., 337
Brown, J., 69, 71, 79t
Brown, J. D., 148, 149
Brown, J. L., 213, 216
Brown, K. A., 404
Brown, L. B., 312, 314
Brown, L. S., 318
Brown, M., 182, 183
Brown, R., 83, 98, 143, 146, 271, 440
Brown, R. P., 214, 216, 219
Brown, R. T., 419
Brown, S. L., 120
Brown, T. L., 256, 473
Brown, T. N., 258, 260, 261, 345, 364, 365, 473
Browning, S. L., 118
Brownworth, V. A., 314
Bruce, M. L., 404
Bry, B. H., 422
Bryant, A. L., 387, 388, 390, 391
Bryant, D., 176
Bryant, D. M., 179
Bub, K., 237
Bucceri, J. M., 165, 166, 228, 229, 258
Buchman, D. D., 149
Buckley, T. R., 259, 289, 293
Bucuvalas, M., 151
Buehrig, C. J., 270
Bulanda, J. R., 120
Bulcroft, K., 120
Bulcroft, R., 120
Bulhan, H. A., 483, 484, 485, 489
Bullard, C. M., 302, 304
Bullard, K., 340
Bumpass, L., 103
Bunney, W. E., 406
Burbach, D. J., 419
Burce, M. L., 404
Burchinal, M., 176, 179, 419
Burgess, K., 177
Burkard, A. W., 433
Burkholder, G., 368
Burlew, K., 289, 378, 475

Burnham, J. J., 354
Burns, B. J., 352, 353, 354, 356, 431
Burns, E., 143
Burr, J. A., 407
Burrow, A. L., 305
Burton, E. T., 260, 261
Burton, L. M., 256, 258, 259
Bush, D. M., 255
Bussing, R., 355
Butler, C., 166
Butler, D., 473
Butler, D. S., 475, 476
Butler, J., 289, 475
Butterfield, F., 129
Bybee, D., 259
Bylsma, W. H., 168
Bynum, E. B., 7, 9, 44, 72, 76, 83
Bynum, M. S., 260, 261
Byrd, D. A., 461, 462
Byrd, R., 96
Byrne, D. N., 150
Byrnes, V., 243

Cain, D. S., 107
Cairns, R. B., 107
Caldwell, B., 84
Caldwell, C., 94, 340, 343, 344
Caldwell, C. H., 164, 260, 261, 290, 291, 379, 488
Caldwell, L. D., 452, 453
Caldwell, R., 79t, 80
Caldwell-Colbert, A. T., 376
Cameron, R., 256, 257, 259, 260
Camp, C., 405
Campbell, A., 462
Campbell, F. A., 179
Campbell, K. D. M., 354, 410
Campbell, L., 463
Campbell-Flint, M. E. C., 433
Campbell-Grossman, C., 152
Campo, P. J., 164
Cam'ron, 135
Cannon, M. F., 403
Capage, L. C., 355
Capodilupo, C. M., 165, 166, 228, 229, 258
Carlin, D. B., 129, 130, 132
Carmichael, S., 159
Carmola Hauf, A. D., 473
Carolan, M. T., 122
Carr, C., 219
Carruthers, J. H., 47, 50
Carson, J. W., 418, 419, 422
Carter, C., 402, 403
Carter, M. M., 402, 403, 410
Carter, R. T., 5, 165, 167, 259, 288, 289, 293, 365, 434, 485, 488

Carter, S., 131, 137
Caruthers, A., 147
Casas, J. M., 231
Casey, R., 419
Cashin, S., 189
Cassey, M. Z., 152
Cassisi, J., 301
Castro, O., 417, 418, 419
Catalano, R. F., 472, 473
Catania, J. A., 118, 119, 121, 123
Cauce, A. M., 256
Caughy, M. O., 76, 79t, 84, 164, 259, 260, 261, 385, 387, 388, 391
Ceballo, R., 181
Ceesay, P., 431
Ceglowski, D., 179
Ceja, M., 434
Cervantes, C. A., 176
Cervantes, J. M., 436
Chadiha, L., 93
Chambers, E. C., 166, 167
Chambers, J., 69
Chambers, J. W., 79t, 80
Chambers, J. W., Jr., 69, 71, 379, 437
Chambless, D. L., 403
Chance, S., 408
Chang, C., 397
Chao, R. K., 278
Chapman, A. B., 103
Charity, A. H., 201, 202, 204, 207
Chase, M. A., 304, 305
Chatters, L., 92, 93, 94, 95, 108, 258, 260, 261, 380
Chatters, L. M., 454
Chavira, V., 259
Chavis, W. M., 420
Chavous, T., 190, 488
Chavous, T. M., 287, 288, 290, 291, 379, 488
Cheatham, H. E., 123
Chen, C. D., 420
Chen, E., 423
Chen, E. C., 431
Chen, F. M., 421
Chen, I. G., 357
Chen, L., 118, 256, 257, 260
Chen, Y., 488
Cherlin, A. J., 120
Cherry, V. R., 276, 277, 473
Chestnut, D. E., 421
Cheung, F., 340
Chicoye, L., 417
Childs, E. C., 122
Chipungu, S., 475, 476, 477
Chisholm, N. J., 131, 137
Chismark, E., 419
Chiu, W., 336

Cho, Y., 189
Chodorow, N. J., 319
Christakis, D. A., 151
Christensen, B., 461
Christenson, S. L., 180
Christian, B., 319
Christian, M., 93, 417, 418, 421
Christian, M. D., 259, 380, 421
Christopher, F. S., 119
Chrotowski, S., 238
Chung, C., 181
Chung, Y. B., 435
Cicchetti, D., 472
Cimbolic, P., 433
Claire, T., 213
Clark, C. X., 47, 78, 83
Clark, K., 160
Clark, K. B., 228, 257, 270, 271
Clark, M. K., 228, 257, 270, 271
Clark, M. L., 277
Clark, R., 151, 163, 164, 304, 365
Clark, R. A., 83
Clark, S. L. T., 302
Clark, T., 244
Clark, V. B., 151
Clark, V. R., 365
Clarke, C., 312, 320, 325
Clarke, J. H., 7
Claybourne, J., 321
Clayton, O., 104, 106
Clements, R., 189
Clemmer, J. T., 391
Cleveland, M. J., 474
Clifford, E., 190
Clifford, R., 176
Clifford, R. M., 179
Cline, P., 152
Clunis, M., 317
Coard, S. I., 256, 258, 259, 260, 261, 263
Coatsworth, J. D., 277, 386
Cobbs, P. M., 300, 447
Coben, J. H., 406
Cochran, S., 312, 317
Cochran, S. D., 318, 409
Cockerham, W. C., 406, 407
Cogan, J. C., 409
Cogburn, C. D., 259
Cohen, C., 314, 318, 320, 324, 325
Cohen, D. K., 242
Cohen, G., 238, 243
Cohen, G. L., 167, 215, 216, 219
Cohen, J., 390
Cohen, J. W., 307
Cohen, L. L., 168
Coke, M., 106
Cokely, K., 69
Coker, A., 434
Coker, H. E. B., 305
Cokley, K., 189, 226, 258, 283, 288, 289, 290, 293, 436
Coladarci, T., 224
Colangelo, N., 224, 227, 230, 231
Cole, R. E., 177
Cole, S. W., 423
Coleman, C., 93
Coleman, L., 98
Coleman, L. J., 223
Coleman, M. N., 163
Coleman, S., 244
Collins, C., 345
Collins, J. W., 167
Collins, M., 203
Collins, M. H., 421
Collins, P. H., 109, 312, 314, 318, 319
Collins, R. L., 474
Collinsworth, P., 106
Comas-Díaz, L., 445
Combs, D. R., 301
Combs, S., 462
Combs-Orme, T., 107
Comer, J., 182, 183, 188
Cone, J., 322
Cones, J. H., III, 43
Connell, C. M., 273
Connell, J., 190
Conner, L. C., 433, 437
Conners, C., 337
Conner-Warren, R., 419
Connor, M. E., 15
Constantine, J., 179
Constantine, M. G., 81, 99, 166, 259, 260, 261, 379, 422, 431, 433, 434, 435, 436, 437, 440, 455, 488, 490
Contreras-Grau, J., 278
Cook, D., 42
Cook, D. A., 285, 286, 287
Cook, J. M., 408
Cook, S., 408
Cooke, B. G., 367
Cooley, C. H., 269
Cooley, E., 418
Cooley, M. R., 354, 410
Coombs, D. W., 406, 407
Coook, K., 93, 94, 95, 98
Cooper, L. A., 421
Cooper, S., 95
Cooper-Effa, M., 422
Cooper-Patrick, L., 340, 342, 343, 404
Copeland, L. A., 463
Cordal, A., 404

Cordasco, K. M., 403
Corder-Bolz, C. R., 148
Corneille, M., 473, 474, 476, 477
Corneille, M. A., 438, 477
Cornelius, L., 343
Corona, R., 473, 474
Cortes, C., 143
Corwin, S. J., 356
Costa, N. M., 403
Courey, S. J., 245
Court, J. H., 214
Courtenay, W. H., 420
Cowal, K., 118, 119
Cowie, S. A. E., 93
Cox, C. I., 378
Cox, J., 224
Cox, M. J., 105, 176
Coyne, J. C., 404, 464
Craig, M. L., 368
Craine, M., 303, 432
Crandall, J. E., 83
Crandall, L. A., 357, 473
Crawford, I., 409
Crichlow, W., 190
Crnic, K., 177, 387
Crocker, J., 93, 97, 98
Croen, L. A., 356
Croizet, J. C., 213
Crosby, A. E., 406
Crosby, F., 289
Cross, C. T., 356
Cross, T. L., 223
Cross, W. E., 5, 12, 13, 42, 61, 108, 109, 191, 277, 278, 284, 286, 288, 378
Cross, W. E., Jr., 223, 228, 263, 283, 285, 286, 289, 290, 487
Crouter, A. C., 256, 258, 259
Crown, C., 150
Crum, R., 340
Csikszentmihalyi, M., 376
Csizmadia, A., 258
Cuentas, T. E., 176
Cuffel, B., 463
Culip, R., 177
Cullen, M. J., 213, 214, 215, 216
Culp, A., 177
Cummings, S., 420
Cummings, S. M., 405
Cunningham, D., 189, 276, 277
Cunningham, D. M., 473
Cunningham, J. N., 379
Cunningham, M., 260, 276, 379
Cunningham, P., 343
Curran, G. M., 473
Curry, J. F., 167

Curtis-Boles, H., 474
Cutler, C., 206

Daly, A., 437
Dana, R. H., 437
Dang, A., 107
Daniel, J. H., 449
Daniel, N., 224
Danquah, J. B., 51
Darley, J. M., 213, 216
Darling, C. A., 386, 387
David, R. H., 167
Davies, P. G., 216
Davies, S. L., 143, 149
Davis, C., 420
Davis, C., III, 216, 217, 289
Davis, E. E., 179
Davis, G. A., 224
Davis, G. Y., 256, 257, 259, 260, 371
Davis, K. D., 256, 258, 259
Davis, L., 189, 303
Davis, L. E., 288
Davis, M., 15, 440
Davis, M. H., 243
Davis, T., 475, 476
Davis-Birdsong, B., 69, 71
Dawson, M. C., 143, 146
Day, E. A., 214, 219
Day, S., 419
Dean, D., 137
Dean, W., 137
Dearing, E., 179
Deater Deckard, K., 177
Deaux, K., 319
Decastro, L. M., 418, 422, 423
DeFour, D. C., 487
Dekovic, M., 473
Deloria, D., 179
Delpit, L. D., 200, 205
Demler, O., 337, 338, 340, 401, 402, 404, 463
Demo, D. H., 105, 261, 290, 292
DeMonteflores, C., 319, 325
Denton, N., 345
Derogatis, L., 83
Derrickson, K. B., 288
Desrosiers, M., 178
Devine, D., 419
Devine, P. G., 167
Devos, T., 459
Dew, M. A., 319
DeWet, T., 489
Diala, C., 432
Diamond, G. S., 354, 357
Diaz, T., 438, 476, 477
DiClemente, R. J., 120, 143, 149

Didow, S. M., 176
Diehr, M. C., 461
Diemer, M. A., 118
Dill, B. T., 109
Dill, E., 244
Dillard, J. M., 351
Diop, C. A., 7, 26, 49
Dishion, T. J., 259
Dixie-Bell, D. D., 402
Dixon, P., 69, 71, 79t, 80
Dixon, T., 150
Dixon, T. L., 128, 129, 130, 131
DMX, 128, 131, 132
Dodge, K. A., 177
Doepke, K., 419
Doernberg, N., 356
Dohm, F., 451
Dohrenwend, B., 338
Dohrenwend, B., 338
Dohrmann, J., 390
Doi, Y., 357
Dolan, C. V., 219, 290
Dolcini, M. M., 118, 119, 121, 123
Doll, B., 353
Donenberg, G. R., 103, 106
Donnelly, P. C., 440, 488
Donnerstein, E., 145
Donovan, M. S., 356
Dorham, C. L., 259
Dornbusch, S. M., 107, 177
Dotterer, A. M., 256, 258, 259
Doughty, D. E., 151
Douglas, K., 98, 397
Douglas, L., 420
Dovidio, J. F., 150, 165
Dowling, E. M., 385
Downey, D. B., 193, 194
Downhower, S., 203
Drentea, P., 406, 407
Drezner, S., 421
Driver, D., 106
Dubois, K. E., 379
Du Bois, W. E. B., 11, 12, 13, 51, 283, 369
Duggan, P. S., 421
Duke, L., 147
Duncan, G. J., 181
Duncan, J. A., 367
Duncan, L. E., 111, 303, 432, 435
Dunham, H. W., 463
DuPaul, G. J., 355
Dupper, D. R., 307
Dupree, D. V., 260
Dutton, M., 96
Dykers, C., 149

Dyson, M., 130, 132, 133, 134
Dyson, M. E., 322

Eaddy, C. L., 365, 448
Earl, F., 340
Earl, T. R., 335
Early, D., 176
Early, K. E., 408
Eckerman, C. O., 176
Eckholm, E., 135
Eckman, J., 422
Edwards, C. L., 418, 422, 423
Edwards, K., 98
Edwards, L., 473
Edwards, L. M., 377
Edwards, W. J., 358
Eggebeen, D., 105
Eisenman, D. P., 403
Elhai, J. D., 402
Elhoweris, H., 225
El-Khoury, M., 96
Ellen, I. G., 180
Ellickson, P. L., 474
Elligan, D., 448, 452
Ellingson, J. E., 213, 214, 216
Elliot, A., 191
Elliott, A., 181
Elliott, D. S., 181
Elliott, M., 355
Ellison, C. M., 79t, 80, 81, 92, 93, 95, 111, 112, 239, 241, 242, 244, 246, 380
Ellison, R., 11, 13
Elmore, R., 242, 249
Emery, P., 121
Emslie, G. J., 357
Engel, L., 96
Ensminger, M. E., 408
Entman, R., 144, 150
Entwisle, D. R., 276
Ephirim-Donkor, A., 51
Epps, E., 188
Epstein, J., 476, 477
Epstein, J. A., 438
Epstein, J. N., 355
Epstein, J. S., 133
Epstein, K., 418
Epstein, M. H., 391
Equiano, O., 40
Eric B. & Rakim, 131
Erikson, E. H., 276, 369
Erkanli, A., 352, 353, 354, 356
Eron, L., 146
Escobar, J., 451
Eshleman, S., 336, 337, 346
Espin, O., 313

Essau, C. A., 392
Essed, P., 163
Eubanks, R., 167
Evans, J. D., 461, 462
Everett, A., 152
Exum, H. A., 227, 230, 231
Eye, A. V., 385

Fagan, J., 152
Fairbank, J. A., 352, 353, 354, 356
Fairburn, C. G., 451
Fairchild, H. H., 446
Falco, K. L., 317
Falconer, J., 356
Falconer, J. W., 163
Fallon, I., 337
Fanon, F., x, 5, 10, 160, 166, 483, 489
Fantuzzo, J. W., 245
Faraone, S. V., 473
Faris, R. E., 463
Farmer, E. M. Z., 352, 353, 354, 356
Farmer, M. M., 258
Farmer, T. W., 391
Farquhar, W., 188
Farrell, A. D., 354, 473
Fasold, R., 201
Feagin, J. R., 459
Feggins-Azziz, L. R., 181
Feighner, J. A., 473
Ferguson, A., 204
Fernald, L. D., 3
Fernald, P. S., 3
Few, A. L., 120, 121, 123
Fhagen-Smith, P. E., 289, 290
Fielding-Stewart, C., 322
Fife, J. E., 379
Fine, M. A., 51, 76, 79t, 83, 84, 177, 187
Fineli, R., 245
Finn-Stevenson, M., 179
Fischer, A. R., 288, 293
Fisher, R. B., 51
Fisher, T., 189
Fitzgerald, D. C., 168
Flaherty, J. A., 463
Flannery-Schroeder, E. C., 353, 354
Flaum, M., 338
Flay, B. R., 472, 478
Flesig, W., 354
Fletcher, B. J., 440
Fletcher, D., 207
Fletcher, H., 420
Flor, D. L., 177
Flores, L. Y., 51
Florio, L. P., 404
Floyd, F. J., 80, 121

Floyd, M. Y., 418
Foehr, U., 143
Folkman, S., 81, 409
Fontenot, D. L., 97, 380
Ford, B. S., 154
Ford, C. V., 419
Ford, D., 340, 342
Ford, D. Y., 224, 225, 226, 227, 229, 230, 231, 232, 233
Ford, J., 206
Ford, T., 150
Ford-Booker, P., 462
Fordham, S., 193, 205, 211, 223, 226, 228, 230
Forehand, R., 95, 98
Forman, T. A., 357
Forness, S., 355
Forte, D., 357
Förster, J., 192
Forsyth, J. M., 165, 167
Foster, J. D., 353
Foster, P. M., 489
Fox, J., 94
Fraleigh, M. J., 177
Francombe, W. H., 420
Franklin, A. J., 13, 107, 118, 120, 123, 128, 131, 132, 133, 165, 258, 378, 432, 434, 446, 447, 452, 453
Franklin, D. C., 488
Franklin, J. H., 4, 378
Franklin-Jackson, D., 288
Franklin-Jackson, D. C., 379, 435, 436, 437
Fraser, H. S., 166
Frazer, S., 107
Frazier, E. F., 91, 104, 121
Frazier, P. A., 293
Frazier Trotman, M., 224, 233
Freedman, R. E., 403, 410
Freiman, M., 343
Freire, P., 489
Fried, C. B., 133, 215, 216
Friedman, A., 435
Friedman, J. Y., 421
Friedman, S., 402, 403, 410, 464
Frisby, C. M., 148
Frison, S. L., 407
Froyum, C. M., 358
Frueh, B. C., 402
Fryer, G. E., 421
Fu, S., 340, 342
Fuchs, D., 245
Fuchs, L. S., 245
Fuertes, J. N., 433
Fujino, D., 431
Fujioka, Y., 4150
Fu-Kiau, K. K., 9, 52, 53

Fuller-Thomson, E., 106
Funk, J. B., 149
Funk, M., 418
Furstenberg, F., 105
Fusarelli, L. D., 180
Fyffe, D. C., 302

Gabbidon, S. L., 162
Gadow, K. D., 354
Gaertner, S. L., 165
Gagne, F., 224
Gagnon, E., 337
Gaines, S. E., Jr., 484
Galea, S., 151
Gallimore, R., 250
Gallo, J., 340, 343
Gallo, J. J., 404
Gama, E. M. P., 446, 454
Gan, S., 150
Gannon, C., 118, 119, 121, 123
Garbarino, J., 273
Garcia, J., 215, 216, 219, 238, 243
Garcia Coll, C., 177, 387
Gardiner, C. L., 303
Gardstrom, S. C., 130, 133
Garlow, S., 404
Garnets, L., 318, 319
Garstein, M., 419
Garvan, C. W., 355
Gates, H. L., Jr., 320, 325, 326
Gatto, L., 133, 134, 149
Gaxiola-Aguilar, S., 336, 339, 340, 402
Gayles, T. A., 446, 453
Gbadegesin, S., 52
Ge, X., 488
Gear, G. H., 224
Gee, G., 345
Gee, G. C., 166
Geller, P. A., 463
George, D., 420
George, L. K., 431, 451
Gerard, P. A., 301
Gerbner, G., 145
Gerin, W., 167
Geroniumus, A., 470
Gerrard, M., 273, 437, 474
Gevisser, M., 324
Giaconia, R. M., 473
Giang, M., 151
Gibb, B., 408
Gibbons, F., 488
Gibbons, F. X., 273, 437, 474
Gibbs, J. T., 447
Gibson, P., 93
Gil, A. G., 305

Gil, K. M., 418, 419, 422
Gilbert, S. C., 288
Gillis, J. R., 409
Ginsburg, H., 190
Ginsburg-Block, M. D., 245
Givens, S. M. B., 150
Glasgow, K. L., 107
Glasser, J. A., 461
Glassgold, J., 318, 319
Glenn, N., 104, 106
Glik, D. C., 403
Glunt, E. K., 409
Gocial, T. M., 291
Goforth, J. B., 391
Goines, D., 130
Gold, J., 151
Gold, S. D., 302, 304
Goldberg, E., 420
Golden, J. F., 403
Goldsmith, H., 204
Goldsmith, S. K., 406
Goldstein, R., 327
Gomes, P. J., 321, 322
Gomez, J., 319, 321, 325
Gomez, L., 98
Gonsiorek, J., 311
Gonzales, J., 340, 342, 343
Gonzalez, E., 238
Gonzalez, H., 337, 339, 343, 344
Gonzalez, H. M., 404, 462, 463
Good, B. J., 404
Good, C., 213, 215, 216
Goodchilds, J., 318
Goodman, L., 96
Goodman, W. K., 357
Goodstein, R., 288
Goodwin, M. H., 201
Goodwin, P. Y., 120, 121, 122, 123
Gordon, K., 189
Gordon, M., 147
Gordon-Rouse, K., 189
Gordon-Rouse, K. A., 385, 386
Gottfredson, L. S., 460
Gould, D., 319
Gould, S. J., 225
Gowda, M., 96
Grados, J. J., 354
Graham, A. J., 104
Graham, D., 379
Graham, S., 187, 188, 189, 190, 191, 192, 194, 459
Graham, S. E., 190
Grambs, J. D., 5
GrandMaster Melle Mel, 130
Grant, B., 337
Grant, I., 461

Grant, M. M., 418
Grantham, T. C., 224, 225, 226, 227, 229, 234
Graves, S. B., 144, 145, 146
Gravlee, C. C., 345
Gray, B. A., 463
Grayman, N., 93, 95, 97
Grayman, N. A., 380
Green, G. D., 317
Green, L., 190
Green, M. J., 167
Green, R., 188
Greenberg, B. S., 144, 145, 146
Greenberg, J., 417
Greenberg, P., 337
Greene, B., 311, 312, 313, 314, 315, 316, 317, 318, 319, 320, 321, 322, 323, 324, 325, 326, 446, 449, 450, 453, 454, 455
Greene, G. J., 358
Greene, M., 118, 119
Greenfield, P. M., 146
Greening, L., 93, 408
Greg, G. J., 472
Gregory, D., 300
Gregory, H., 15
Gregory, S. D. P., 422
Grether, J. K., 356
Grieger, I. Z., 288, 293
Grier, W. H., 300, 447
Griffin, D. M., 201, 207
Griffin, K. W., 474
Griffith, D. M., 417
Griffith, E., 93
Griffith, E. E., 346
Griffith, J. R., 421
Grills, C., 9, 38, 39, 47, 51, 75, 76, 80t, 82
Griswold, D., 106, 390
Gross, L., 145
Grossmann, S. J., 461
Grover, P. L., 472
Gruenwald, P. J., 473
Grundy, C., 166
Guarnaccia, P. J., 110
Guessous, O., 488
Gullone, E., 354
Guo, G., 149
Gurin, G., 93, 96, 381
Gurwitch, R. H., 151
Guterbock, T., 94
Guthrie, B. J., 357
Guthrie, J., 243
Guthrie, R. L., 375, 381
Guthrie, R. V., 4, 5, 6, 19, 22, 23, 43, 77
Gutman, L. M., 189
Guyer, M., 337

Guyll, M., 167
Gyekye, K., 49, 50, 51, 52, 76, 77

Hacker, A., 193
Haden, C. A., 176
Haertel, G. D., 242
Haile, R., 343, 344
Hakel, M. D., 214
Hakim, R. B., 179
Haldeman, D., 318
Halgunseth, L. C., 177, 258
Hall, L. E., 432
Hall, R. E., 448
Hall, R. L., 311, 320
Hall, S. P., 167
Hall, T., 435
Halpern, B., 403
Halpern-Felsher, B., 190
Hamer, J., 105
Hamilton, C. V., 159
Hamilton-Lee, M., 188
Hamlett, C. L., 245
Hammer, C. S., 176
Hammond, W. P., 420
Hamner, M. B., 402
Hampton, C., 289, 435, 436, 437, 473
Hamsher, K. D., 461
Han, M., 379
Han, X., 473
Hancock, K. A., 318
Handler, A., 167
Hanges, P. J., 214, 217, 218
Hanks, R., 462
Hanley, P., 378
Hansbrough, E., 147, 149
Hansen, L. S., 446, 454
Hanzlick, R., 406
Hardison, C. M., 213, 214, 215, 216
Hare, B., 189
Hare-Mustin, R., 319
Harkins, A. K., 446, 454
Harlow, S., 404
Harmanci, R., 132, 133
Harmon, D., 224
Harnisch, D., 190
Harpalani, V., 274
Harper, B., 189
Harper, G., 245
Harper, G. W., 118, 119, 121, 123
Harper, S., 177
Harper, S. R., 166
Harrell, J. P., 167, 289, 299
Harrell, S. P., 163, 164, 365, 488
Harrington, K., 120, 143, 148, 149
Harris, A., 421

Harris, C., 299
Harris, D., 188, 260
Harris, E. C., 407
Harris, J. J., III, 224, 227, 229, 231, 232, 233
Harris, K., 105
Harris, R. P., 446, 447
Harris, T., 408
Harris, W., 96, 201
Harris, Y. R., 104
Harrison, K., 148, 259
Harrison, M. O., 422
Harrison, R., 106
Harris-Peterson, S., 418, 423
Harris-Reid, M., 336
Harry, B., 354
Hart, B., 176
Harter, S., 188, 190
Hartman, J. T., 407
Hartnett, D. N., 355
Harvey, R. D., 291
Hasan, S. P., 418, 419
Hasbrouck, L., 379
Hashmi, S., 418, 419
Hassell, K., 422
Hastings, P., 177
Hatcher-Kay, C. A., 97, 380
Hatter, D. Y., 79t, 84
Hawkins, J. D., 472, 473
Hawkins, J. M., 463
Hawkins, R., 321
Hayman, W., 237
Haynes, J., 417
Haynes, N., 188
Haynes, S. N., 390
Haynes, W. O., 177
Hays, J. C., 346
Head, J., 447, 448
Hearn, K. D., 81
Heaton, R. K., 461, 462
Hebert, J. R., 470
Heesacker, M., 150
Heiss, G., 337
Heisserer, D., 110
Helaire, L., 190
Heller, T., 177
Helm, K., 290
Helms, J. E., 5, 13, 20, 26, 42, 84, 109, 167, 228, 230, 263, 284, 285, 286, 287, 288, 293, 303, 378, 432, 460, 484, 488
Henderson, D., 166
Henderson, E. A., 131, 134
Heninger, M., 406
Henry, K. L., 149
Hepler, N., 463
Heppner, M. J., 167

Herbert, J., 191
Herek, G. M., 409
Herman, J., 152
Hermann, J., 475, 476, 477
Hernstein, R. J., 38, 211, 225
Herrero-Taylor, T., 256, 257, 259, 260
Herring, C., 291
Herring, K., 440
Hersh, M., 433
Herskovits, M. J., 51, 104
Hertel, B. R., 291
Hess, C. R., 389
Hesse-Biber, S. N., 259
Hessen, D. J., 219
Heurtin-Roberts, S., 402
Hickling, F., 397
Hicks, L. H., 160
Hicks, S., 206
Higginbotham, E., 324, 325
Higgins, E. T., 192
Highlen, P. S., 378
Hildreth, C. J., 402
Hill, K., 190
Hill, N. E., 273, 278
Hill, P. C., 408
Hill, R. B., 379
Hill, S. A., 109, 117, 258, 259, 272, 273, 420
Hilliard, A. G., 3, 7, 8, 9, 42, 50, 188, 238, 460, 462, 483
Hilt, L. M., 357
Hilton, H. J., 462
Hines, P. M., 105, 439, 441
Hinkin, C., 462
Hinkston, J. A., 433
Hinton, L., 207
Hirschfeld, R., 337
Hocking, M. C., 419
Hofferth, S., 111
Hoffman, K. D., 129, 133
Hoge, R. D., 224
Holder, A. M. B., 165, 166, 228, 229, 258
Holladay, J., 463
Hollins, E., 237
Holloway, J. E., 283
Holloway, P., 225
Holmes, D., 163
Holzemer, W., 93
Holzer, C., 338, 404
Homer, C., 417
Hook, D., 166
Hooks, B., 109, 314
Hoover, M., 206
Hopkins, R., 51, 271
Horing, L. E., 385, 386
Hornbaker, A. V., 177

Horton-Ikard, R., 204
Horwitz, A. V., 465
Hou, W., 355
Hountondji, P. J., 49
Houskamp, B. M., 224
Howard, C., 261
Howard, T. C., 232
Howling, S. A., 259
Hoye, J., 137
Hrabowski, F. A., 385, 388
Hsieh, P., 189
Hsu, S., 345
Hu, L., 431
Hubbs-Tait, L., 177
Hucks, T., 289
Hucks, T. C., 475
Hudley, C., 187, 190, 191, 192, 194, 278, 304, 305
Hudson, D. B., 152
Hudson-Banks, K., 93
Huesmann, L. R., 145, 146
Huff, R. E., 224
Hughes, D., 108, 256, 257, 260, 261, 272, 273, 371, 380
Hughes, J. L., 357
Hughes, M., 261, 290, 291, 292, 336, 337, 339, 346
Hughes, N. C., 261
Huizinga, D., 181
Hulsey, T., 152
Hunt, P., 319
Hunter, A., 122
Hunter, J., 358
Hurley, E. A., 244
Husaini, B. A., 405
Hwang, W., 405
Hyde, J. S., 445
Hyers, L. L., 168

Ialongo, N. F., 473
Icard, L., 312, 321
Iceburg Slim, 130
Idowu, E., 52
Ingram, K. M., 379
Inzlicht, M., 215, 216
Irvine, J. J., 276
Irving, M., 194
Irving, M. A., 304, 305
Isenstein, V. R., 65, 66
Isimbabi, M. J., 306
Ispa, J. M., 177, 258
Israel, B. A., 345

Jackson, B. B., 166
Jackson, B. W., III, 284, 285, 286
Jackson, J., 92, 93, 95, 96, 340, 343, 344
Jackson, J. S., 290, 335, 345, 378, 381, 406, 407, 462, 463, 465

Jackson, K., 312, 314
Jackson, L., 15
Jackson, L. A., 133, 134, 149
Jackson, L. C., 451, 454
Jackson-Gilfort, A., 437, 438
Jacobs, C. H., 408
Jacobs, D., 408
Jacobs, D. M., 461, 462
Jacobson, C. K., 122
Jagadheesan, K., 420
Jagers, R. J., 76, 79t, 80, 81, 92, 93, 98, 379, 437, 483, 486, 489
Jahoda, M., 364
James, A. D., 120
James, G. G. M., 36
Jang, S., 92, 95, 97
Janheinz, J., 51
Jefferson, S. D., 79t, 80
Jeffries, I., 320, 325
Jenal, S. T., 433
Jenckes, M., 340, 342
Jencks, C., 211, 237, 356
Jencks, J., 149
Jenerette, C., 418
Jenkins, A. H., 4, 5, 14
Jenkins, E. J., 402
Jenkins, M. D., 224
Jenkins, R., 177, 387
Jenkins, S. Y., 446, 450
Jenkins, Y. M., 454
Jenkins-Monroe, V., 474
Jennings, J., 437
Jennings, L., 193
Jenson, J. M., 472
Jessor, R., 474
Jessor, S. L., 474
Ji, M., 356
Jimenez, N., 190
Jin, R., 336, 401, 402, 404, 463
Joe, S., 406, 407
Johnson, A. G., 448, 449
Johnson, A. J., 433
Johnson, B., 92, 95, 97
Johnson, B. R., 122
Johnson, C., 289, 475
Johnson, C. L., 105, 106
Johnson, D., 273
Johnson, D. J., 256, 257, 261, 272, 273, 371, 380
Johnson, D. W., 81
Johnson, I., 207
Johnson, J. D., 133, 134, 145, 148, 149, 150
Johnson, J. T., 462
Johnson, L. B., 109
Johnson, P. D., 446, 453
Johnson, R. I., 421

Johnson, S. C., 293
Johnston, L. D., 357
Johnston, R. C., 175, 178
Joiner, T. E., 404, 410
Joiner, T. E., Jr., 408
Jones, B. D., 192
Jones, B. E., 463
Jones, C., 42, 405, 449, 450, 454, 486
Jones, C. P., 258
Jones, F., 5
Jones, H., 487
Jones, J., 137, 161, 163, 489
Jones, J. M., ix, 353, 367, 368, 370, 438, 459, 461
Jones, K., 133, 134
Jones, N., 434, 435
Jones, P., 96
Jones, R. L., 5, 19, 29, 43, 61, 378
Jones, R. N., 461
Jones, R. T., 440
Jordan, T., 188, 189
Joslin, D., 106
Juby, H. L., 289, 293
Judd, C., 111
Jung, K. K., 440
Juon, H., 408
Jurbergs, N., 355
Justice, E. M., 189

Kabat, G. C., 470
Kabin, M. B., 213, 214, 216
Kaiser, R. T., 69, 79t, 80
Kalinyak, K., 419
Kambon, K. K., 7, 14, 39, 47, 49, 50, 51, 61, 62, 63, 66, 67, 68, 69, 70, 71, 72, 79t, 82, 367, 484
Kandel, D., 470
Kang, J., 146
Kanner, A., 486
Kanuha, V., 320
Kao, G., 188
Kao, W. T., 420
Kaplan, A., 191, 192, 244
Kaplan, B. H., 337
Karapurkar, R., 356
Karenga, M., 7, 8, 26, 27, 40, 47, 51, 64, 379
Kaslow, N., 422
Kaslow, N. J., 408, 421
Kasser, T., 486
Kassoff, B., 319
Kato, P. M., 423
Katz, P. A., 269
Kaufman, M., 420
Keagy, K., 391
Keane, T. M., 402
Keating-Lefler, R., 152
Keck, P. E., 463
Keck, P. E., Jr., 463, 464

Kedar, A., 419
Keeler, G., 352, 353, 354, 356
Keeling, R. P., 420
Keith, B. R., 419
Keith, V. M., 291, 404
Kelder, S. H., 357
Kelderman, H., 290
Keller, H., 178
Keller, S. D., 345
Kelley, M. L., 355
Kelley, R. D. G., 128, 129, 130, 131, 132, 133, 136, 138
Kellner, D., 153
Kellow, J. T., 192
Kelly, K. P., 167
Kelly, S., 80, 121
Kendall, K., 324
Kendall, P. C., 353, 354
Kendler, K., 336, 337, 339, 340
Kendler, K. S., 402
Kennard, B. D., 357
Kenneavy, K., 149
Kennedy, R., 339
Kennepohl, S., 462
Keough, K., 213, 216
Kern, M., 356
Kerwin, C., 122
Kessler, R. C., 336, 337, 338, 339, 340, 346, 401, 402, 404, 431, 463
Keves-Foster, K., 304
Key, J. D., 419
Keyes, C., 339
Keyes, C. L., 128, 129, 130, 131, 133, 136, 138
Khatib, S., 4
Kiang, L., 219
Kiefe, C. I., 470
Kieffer, C. H., 488, 489
Kiesler, S., 146
Killian, P., 451
Kilman, C., 143
Kilpatrick, D., 151
Kim, A., 191, 213, 219
Kim, J. M., 371
Kim, J. Y., 256, 258, 259
Kim, S., 385, 386, 391, 393, 397
Kimmel, D., 318, 319
Kindaichi, M., 440
King, A., 189
King, C. T., 118
King, J., 237
King, J. L., 316
King, R. S., 470
Kington, R. S., 343
Kinner, D., 150
Kinney, L., 152

Kinsey, R. W., 105
Kirkland-Harris, A. M., 93
Kirschstein, R. L., 417
Kirsh, E. A., 385, 386, 391, 397
Kisker, E. F., 179
Kite, M., 319
Kitwana, B., 132
Klap, R., 340
Klebanov, P. K., 181
Klebba, K., 95, 98
Klein, J. D., 149
Kleinbaum, D. G., 337
Kleinman, A., 406
Kleinman, A. M., 404
Klick, J., 421
Kline, T. J. B., 386, 392
Klonoff, E. A., 167, 301
Knadler, S., 152
Knight, F., 178
Knoblauch, D., 189
Knox, S., 433
Kochanek, K., 406
Kochanel, K. D., 352
Koenig, H. G., 422
Kofkin, J. A., 269
Kohen, D. E., 176
Kohn-Wood, L. P., 288, 290, 291, 379, 405, 488
Kolb, J., 96
Kolbrener, M. L., 463
Komarraju, M., 189
Koontz, K., 419
Kopaska-Merkel, D. C., 261
Koretz, D., 404, 463
Kosinski, M., 345
Kouri, K. M., 122
Kovel, J., 161
Kraemer, H. C., 355
Kramer, K. D., 419
Kramer, L., 419
Krause, N., 96
Kravitz, H., 404
Krayzie Bone, 135
Kriegel, M., 130
Krieger, N., 168
Krims, A., 132
Krishnakumar, A., 256
Krishnan, V., 379
Krohn, M. D., 473
KRS-One, 131, 138
Krueger, J., 193
Kubrin, C. E., 133, 134, 136
Kugle, C., 189
Kumpfer, K. L., 474, 476
Kung, H., 407, 408
Kuperminc, G. P., 353

Kupersmidt, J. B., 276
Kwate, N. A., 410
Kwate, N. O., 71, 82, 460

LaBeach, N., 291
Labov, W., 201, 204
Ladson-Billings, G., 243, 263
Laflamme, D. J., 345
Lam, A. G., 455
Lambert, C. T. M., 397
Lambert, M., 178
Lambert, M. C., 385, 386, 391, 392, 393, 397
Lambert, R., 419
Lambert, S., 473
Lambert, S. F., 354, 410
Lambert, W. E., 206
Lamberty, G., 177, 387
Lamborn, S. D., 107
Landerman, R., 451
Landin, J., 178
Landrine, H., 167
Landrine, J., 301
Landrum-Brown, J., 364
Landry, B., 291
Lang, D. L., 120
Langer, J., 243, 245
Lanier, Y., 81, 167, 381, 448, 452
LaPoint, V., 239, 241, 246
Lareau, A., 178, 180
Lasswell, M., 122
Last Poets, The, 130
Laswon, M. J., 356
LaTaillade, J. J., 123
Laurence, B., 420
LaVeist, T. A., 162, 343, 432
Laveist, T. A., 473
Lavender, A., 417, 421
LaVesit, T. A., 301, 302
Lavizzo, E. A., 402
Lawrence-Webb, C., 118, 121, 123
Lawser, S., 179
Lawson, E. J., 488
Lawson, W., 418, 419
Lawson, W. B., 463
Lazarus, R. S., 81, 364
Lazoritz, M., 357
Leaf, P. J., 404, 432
Lears, M., 148
Leary, J. D., 13, 261
Leashore, B. R., 437
Leathers, L., 435
Leavell, S. R., 419
Leavy, P., 259
Leber, D., 93
Ledesma-Jones, S., 290
Lee, A., 167

Lee, C., 231, 243, 250
Lee, C. C., 446, 447, 452, 453
Lee, D. R., 307
Lee, E. E., 302
Lee, J., 176, 356
Lee, V. E., 179
Leiderman, P. H., 177
Lemery, K., 204
L'Engle, K., 149
Leonard, M. M., 109
Leong, F. T., 111
Lerner, R. M., 270, 272, 273, 385
Lesane-Brown, C. L., 255, 258, 260, 261
Lesikar, S., 404
Lesser, I., 405
Lester, D., 406
Letkaka-Rennert, K., 276, 277
Letz, R., 461
Leung, M., 391
Lev-Arey, D. M., 214, 217
Levenson, J. L., 420
Levin, J., 92, 93, 380
Levine, A., 462
Levine, C., 403
Levine, D., 340, 342
Levine, L. W., 129, 138
Levine, R., 420
Levitan, M., 135
Levy, S. E., 356
Lewin, K., 269
Lewis, C. E., 470
Lewis, E., 108
Lewis, E. L., 403, 410, 433, 437
Lewis, S., 206, 462
Lewis-Coles, M. E., 435, 436, 437
Lewis-Coles, M. E. L., 81, 422
Lezak, M. D., 461
Li, S. T., 381
Liaw, F., 179
Lichtenberg, P. A., 461, 462
Lichter, D. T., 122
Liddle, H. A., 437, 438
Lightsey, O. R., Jr., 300
Lincoln, C., 93, 94
Lincoln, E. C., 278
Lincoln, K., 93
Lindsey, L. L., 189
Lindstrom, R. R., 230
Link, B. G., 369
Linver, M. R., 176
Linz, D., 145
Lipscomb, L., 489
Lipsitz, G., 128, 134, 136
List, M., 420
Listerud, J., 356

Littlefields, M., 118, 121, 123
Littlejohn-Blake, S. M., 386, 387
Liu, M., 189
Liu, W. M., 290
Livingston, A., 51
Livingston, J. N., 105
Lizotte, A. J., 473
Lloyd, D., 337
Lobitz, W. C., 324, 325
Lochman, J. E., 419
Lockett, C. T., 289
Loiacano, D., 312
London, R. A., 152
Long, J., 189
Long Dilworth, J. E., 121
Longhurst, J., 386, 391, 393
Longshore, D., 75, 80t, 82
Lopez, S. J., 377
Loring, M., 431
Losen, D. J., 356
Lott, B., 491
Loughlin, C., 418, 423
Louie, J., 224
Love, C. C., 129, 133
Love, J. M., 179
Lovejoy, M., 259
Lowell, E. L., 83
Lubke, G. H., 290
Lucas, J., 52
Lucas, J. W., 343
Ludvigsen, R., 261
Lung, F. W., 420
Luo, Z., 273
Lustina, M., 213, 216
Luthar, S., 472
Lynch, C. L., 213, 216
Lynsen, J., 312
Lyubansky, M., 392

Ma, J., 421
MacIntosh, R., 380
Madhere, S., 244
Maehr, M., 190, 191, 192, 244
Magee, W. J., 336
Magruder, K. M., 402
Magyar-Moe, J. L., 377
Mahalik, J., 69
Mahalik, J. R., 80, 288
Maheady, L., 245
Mahiri, J., 133
Mahmood, M., 94
Major, C., 201
Majors, R., 118, 211, 448
Makkar, J., 147
Malat, J., 343

Mallette, R., 245
Malone-Colon, L., 104, 106
Malveaux, J., 110
Mamiya, L., 93, 94
Mandara, J., 107, 108, 271
Mandell, D. S., 356
Manly, J. J., 461, 462
Manning, W. D., 105
Manouchehri, A., 249
Maracek, J., 319
Maramba, G. G., 459
Marcus, S. C., 404, 464
Marion, M. S., 408
Maris, R., 405
Markman, L. B., 176, 177, 178
Markstrom, C. A., 385, 386, 389, 391
Markstrom-Adams, C., 13, 227, 230, 258
Marsee, M. A., 403
Marsh, H., 188
Marsh, L. D., 419
Marshall, S., 273
Marshall, S. K., 385, 391
Marston, N. C., 354
Martin, J., 431, 439
Martin, M., 238
Martín-Baró, I., 489
Marvel, F. A., 437, 438
Marzano, R., 242, 245
Masi, C. M., 152
Mason, D., 355
Massey, D. S., 345, 352
Masten, A. S., 277, 386
Master, A., 215, 216, 219, 238, 243
Matabane, P., 150
Matlin, S., 388
Maton, K. I., 98, 385, 388
Matteson, D. W., 407
Matthews, A. K., 420
Matthews, K. A., 167
Mattis, J., 454
Mattis, J. S., 81, 92, 93, 95, 96, 97, 379, 380, 420
Mauer, M., 470
Maultsby, P. K., 130, 131
Mavaddat, R., 345
Mayer, D., 214, 217, 218
Mays, B., 91
Mays, V., 312, 317
Mays, V. M., 409
Mazzula, S. L., 165, 167
Mbiti, J. S., 26, 49, 50, 83, 111
McAdoo, H. P., 5, 93, 96, 105, 107, 109, 177, 271, 272, 379, 386, 387
McAdoo, J. L., 105
McAllum, C., 105
McBee, M. T., 225

McCandies, T., 176
McCarthey, S. J., 180
McCarthy, E., 167
McCarthy, W. J., 451
McCartney, K., 179, 237
McCarton, C., 181
McClelland, D. C., 83, 188
McClendon, C., 191
McClish, D. K., 420
McClough, L., 417
McCluskey, C. P., 473
McCormick, L., 357
McCormick, M. C., 181
McCowan, C., 69
McCray, A. D., 354, 356
McCready, L. T., 358
McCreary, D. R., 419
McCreary, M. L., 379
McCullough, M., 96
McDermott, P. A., 354
McDermott, S. T., 146
McDill, E. L., 178
McDonald, T. E., 154
McElroy, S. L., 463, 464
McFarland, L. A., 214, 217, 218
McGee, D. P., 47, 78, 83
McGonagle, K., 336, 337, 346
McGroder, S. M., 177
McGuire, T. W., 146
McGuire, W. J., 472
McHale, S. M., 256, 258, 259
McKinnon, J., 343
McKown, C., 191, 219
McLain, R., 289
McLaughlin, K. A., 357
McLoyd, V. C., 177, 181, 256, 380
McNair, L., 437, 450, 453
McNair, L. D., 273
McNair-Knox, F., 206
McNeil, C. B., 355
McRae, M., 95
McWhorter, J., 407
Mead, G. H., 269
Meadows, L. A., 408
Meagher, R., 463
Mehra, B., 152
Mellenbergh, G. J., 290
Melsch, A., 177
Memmi, A., x
Menard, S., 181
Menchaca, M., 225
Mengara, D. M., 490
Mentz, G., 345
Merchant, C. A., 461, 462
Merikangas, K., 337, 463

Merikangas, K. R., 401, 402, 404
Merkel, C., 152
Merritt, B., 144
Merriwether, A., 147
Merton, R. K., 224
Mertz, K., 406
Messick, S., 276
Meyer-Bahlburg, H. F. L., 119
Michael, C., 301
Michaels, S., 207
Mickelson, R., 193
Midgley, C., 189, 192
Milkie, M. A., 147
Millar, A., 473
Miller, D., 406
Miller, D. B., 379, 380
Miller, F., 303, 432
Miller, J. F., 204
Miller, J. Y., 472, 473
Miller, L., 402
Miller, L. M., 357
Miller, O., 403, 410
Miller, R., 97, 98
Miller, R. L., 410, 435
Miller, R. R., 118
Miller, S. W., 461, 462
Miller, T. Q., 472
Miller, T. R., 245
Miller, W., 461
Miller-Johnson, S., 179
Milner, H. R., 231, 233
Mindt, M. R., 462
Minino, A., 406
Miniño, A. M., 352
Minkler, M., 106
Mira, C. B., 405
Miranda, J., 405
Mislowack, A., 433
Mistry, R. S., 176, 177
Mitchell, A., 440
Mitchell, H., 5, 211, 460
Mitchell, N., 93, 95
Mitchell-Jackson, A., 422
Mitchell-Kernan, C., 120, 144
Mitrook, M., 150
Moane, G., 485, 486, 487
Mobley, M., 301
Mock, K., 152
Mock, L., 93
Mock, L. O., 76, 81, 489
Moise-Titus, J., 146
Moleski, S. M., 418
Molock, S. D., 388, 406, 408, 418
Monahan, J. L., 150
Monnier, J., 402
Monoi, S., 189

Monroe, I., 318, 319, 320, 321, 322, 323, 324, 325
Montgomery, D. E., 51, 76, 79t, 83, 84
Monuteaux, M. C., 473
Monzones, J., 462
Moock, P., 111
Moody, A., 421
Moore, E., 390
Moore, T., 94, 95
Morgan, M., 145, 201, 203
Morgello, S., 462
Morris, E. F., 436, 437, 440
Morrow, L. M., 180
Morrow, S. F., 189
Morse, E., 95, 98
Morse, P., 95, 98
Morsi, D. S., 437
Moscicki, E., 405
Mos Def, 138
Moses, A. E., 321
Mosk, J., 178
Mosley, K. L., 302, 304
Moss, A. A., 378
Moucheraud, C., 420
Moynihan, D. P., 104
Mueller, B., 289
Muhammad, E., 11
Muhammad, G., 189
Mukherjee, S., 431, 464
Mullis, I., 238
Mulsow, M., 151
Munday, C., 465
Muntaner, C., 164, 388, 432
Murdaugh, C., 418
Murname, R., 237
Muroff, J. R., 470, 472
Murphy, C., 93, 95, 356
Murphy, M., 96
Murphy, P. K., 189
Murphy, S., 406
Murphy, S. L., 352
Murphy, T. K., 357
Murray, A. D., 177
Murray, C., 38, 211, 225
Murray, C. B., 69, 79t, 80, 107, 108, 271
Murray, H. A., 83
Murray, N., 357
Murray, S. O., 324
Murray, V. M., 437
Murry, V., 488
Murry, V. M., 273, 278
Musick, M., 93, 96
Mutua, K., 225
Myers, H. F., 405
Myers, J., 378, 421
Myers, L. J., 9, 10, 20, 37, 39, 42, 44, 47, 49, 51, 76, 78, 79t, 83, 84, 364, 483, 485, 488

Nabors, N. A., 461, 462
Nacoste, R., 288
Nadal, K. L., 165, 166, 228, 229, 258
Nagayama Hall, G. C., 459
Naglieri, J. A., 225
Nakkula, M., 190
NaS, 136
Nash, K. B., 419
Nasim, A., 244, 473, 474
Natriello, G., 178
Neal, A. M., 336, 353, 402, 403, 410
Neal, L. I., 354, 356
Neal-Barnett, A., 451, 464
Neal-Cooper, F., 420
Neblett, E. W., Jr., 259
Neely, D., 289, 475
Neff, J. A., 405
Neidert, L., 470
Neighbors, H., 93, 95, 96, 290, 335, 337, 338, 339, 340, 343, 344, 345, 346, 378, 381, 404, 405, 406, 407, 435, 463, 465
Nell, V., 460
Nels, D., 408
Nelson, A., 340, 342
Nelson, C., 340, 343
Nelson, C. B., 336, 337, 346
Nelson, J. M., 355
Nelson, K., 390
Nelson, T., 95, 96
Nesse, R., 337, 339, 340, 343, 344, 404, 463
Nettles, R., 312, 314, 326
Nettles, S. M., 84, 387, 391
Neufeld, J. E., 377
Nevid, J., 402
Neville, H. A., 159, 160, 161, 163, 301, 364, 365, 369, 486, 487
Nevitt, J., 290
Newacheck, P. W., 109
Newman, B. S., 319
Nghe, L. T., 288
Nichols, J. F., 356
Nichols, T. R., 474
Nickerson, K., 259, 260, 261, 301, 302
Nickerson, K. J., 300, 301, 302, 304, 432
Nickerson, K. L., 303
Niehart, M., 223
Niemann, Y., 193
Nilsson, L. G., 107
Nisbet, P. A., 406
Nixon, S., 151
Nobles, W. W., 6, 7, 8, 9, 11, 14, 38, 43, 47, 48, 49, 50, 51, 52, 61, 62, 63, 76, 78, 83, 104, 109, 293, 365, 366, 375, 378, 381, 483
Nolan, E. E., 354
Nolen-Hoeksema, S., 357
Noll, E., 274

Noll, M., 355
Noll, R. B., 419
Norem-Hebeisen, A. A., 81
Norman, G. S., 420
Norris, E. F., 452, 453
Norris, F. H., 402
Northrup, T., 404, 410
Notorious B.I.G., 129
Nowicki, S., Jr., 203
Nuru-Jeter, A., 343
Nussbaum, K. M., 381
Nyborg, V. M., 167
Nystedt, L., 107

Oakes, J., 187
Oatts, T., 355
Obasi, E., 364
Obasi, E. M., 49, 51, 52
Obenga, T., 8, 39
Obrist, P. A., 337
O'Bryant, R., 152
O'Bryant, S. E., 462
O'Bryant, S. L., 148
Ocampo, C., 462
O'Campo, P. J., 76, 79t, 84, 259, 260, 261, 385, 387, 388, 391
O'Carroll, P., 405
O'Carroll, P. W., 408
O'Connor, R., 419
Oddone, E. Z., 421
Oetting, E. R., 474
Ogamdi, S. O., 417
Ogbonnaya, O., 83
Ogbu, J., 188, 193, 205, 211, 226, 228, 230, 387
Oguejiofor, J. O., 368
O'Jile, J. R., 462
Okundaye, J. N., 118, 121, 123
Olarte, S., 431, 464
Olfson, M., 340
Oliver, W., 121
Oliveri, J., 149
Olney, R. S., 423
Olopade, O. I., 420
Olupona, J. K., 76
O'Malley, P. M., 357
Omari, S. R., 19
Omosupe, K., 325
Onwubiko, O. A., 368
Opoku, K. A., 51, 52
Ordman, V. L., 129, 133
Orfield, D., 356
Ornstein, P. A., 176
Orpinas, P., 357
Orringer, E., 418, 419, 422
Orubch, T. L., 122
Osborne, J. W., 216, 217

Oshodi, J. E., 76, 79t, 82, 83
Ossana, S. M., 109
Ossé, R., 131
O'Sullivan, L. F., 119
Ottens, A. J., 79t, 84
Overly, K., 178
Owen, R., 463
Owens, A. S., 154
Owens, D. L., 355
Owens, M., 95
Oyeku, S. O., 417
Oyserman, D., 259

Padgett, D. K., 431
Pahl, K., 118, 119, 381, 435, 436
Palcic, J., 355
Pallas, A. M., 178
Panayotova, E., 95, 98
Panigrahi, B., 473
Papas, M. A., 389
Paradies, Y., 164, 167, 345
Paradis, A. D., 473
Paradis, C., 402, 403, 410, 464
Pardun, C., 149
Parette, P., 110
Pargament, K. I., 408
Parham, T. A., 4, 5, 6, 7, 8, 9, 10, 13, 14, 15, 22, 26, 44, 45, 48, 51, 76, 84, 110, 228, 230, 263, 284, 287, 288, 292, 367, 378, 433, 436, 439, 440, 441
Parham, W. D., 4, 7
Parker, J. B., Jr., 463
Parker, N., 421
Parker-Dominguez, T., 404
Parks, L., 93, 95
Parra, P., 110
Pastor, M., 152
Pastor, P. N., 354
Patel, P. G., 357
Pathman, D. E., 421
Patrick, P., 207
Patterson, C. J., 276
Paxton, K. C., 353
Payne, Y. A., 128, 131, 132, 133, 134
Peacock, M. J., 69, 79t, 80
Pearson, J. L., 407, 408
Peden, B., 448
Pedersen, P. B., 77, 231
Pegnato, C. W., 224
Peisner-Feinberg, E. S., 179
Pellmar, T., 406
Penberthy, L. T., 420
Penn, D. L., 301
Peplau, L. A., 318
Perencevich, K., 243
Perilla, J. L., 402

Perkins, K., 147
Perkins, W. E., 128, 129, 130, 131, 134, 136
Pernick, Y., 356
Perry, I., 131
Perry, T., 200
Peters, M. F., 109, 260, 261
Peters, R. J., 357
Peters, R. M., 304, 421
Petersen, A., 274
Peterson, C., 376, 378
Peterson, J. L., 409
Peterson, K., 417
Peterson, R. A., 354
Peterson, S., 149
Peterson, S. A., 162
Peterson Bishop, A., 152
Petraitis, J., 472, 478
Pettigrew, T. F., 180, 270, 271
Petty, R. E., 216
Petukhova, M., 337
Pfefferbaum, B., 151
Phelan, J., 369
Phelps, E. A., 377
Phelps, R. E., 301
Philip, C. L., 259
Phillips, C. M., 473
Phillips, F., 15, 276, 277, 489
Phillips, F. B., 422, 439, 453, 489
Phillips, G., 419
Phillips, G., Jr., 419
Phillips, L. D., 121, 259, 260
Phillips, M., 211, 237, 356
Phillips, R. L., 421
Philogene, G., 270
Phinney, J. S., 82, 178, 259, 291, 292
Phyllis-Jones, C., 344
Piaget, J., 271
Pickering, D., 242, 245
Pierce, C., 13
Pierce, C. M., 163, 165
Pierre, M., 69
Pierre, M. R., 80
Pierre-Pierre, G., 343
Piers, E., 188
Pierson, W. D., 405
Pieterse, A. L., 167, 434, 488
Pietromonaco, P., 145
Pike, K. M., 451
Pincus, H., 340
Pinderhughes, E., 109, 120, 121, 122, 123, 124
Pinel, E. C., 216
Pinkett, R., 152
Pinto-Martin, J. A., 356
Piotrowski, H., 152
Pipes-McAdoo, H., 380

Pittinsky, T., 191, 213, 219
Plant, E. A., 167, 405
Ployhart, R. E., 214, 217, 218
Plummer, D. L., 291
Plybon, L. E., 473, 474, 475, 476, 477
Podolski, C. L., 146
Politzer, R., 206
Pollock, J., 242, 245
Pollock, K., 207
Pollydore, C., 150
Poloni-Staudinger, L., 181
Ponicki, W. R., 473
Ponterotto, J. G., 77, 122, 164, 231, 288, 292, 293, 302, 433
Pope, J. T., 129, 133
Pope-Davis, D. B., 290
Popenoe, D., 104
Popenoe, P. B., 38
Poran, M., 148
Porter, C., 149
Porter, L. S., 418, 419, 422
Porter, M. M., 120
Portes, P. R., 176
Postmes, T., 369
Poston, C. W., 432
Poston, W. S. C., 303
Potgieter, C., 324
Potts, R., 92
Potts, R. G., 489
Poussaint, A., 325
Poussaint, A. F., 136, 144, 447
Powe, N., 340, 342, 343
Powell, B., 431
Powell, C. T., 129, 131
Powell, K., 406
Powell, P., 189
Powell-Hammond, W., 93
Power, T. J., 355
Prange, A. J., Jr., 463
Pratt, T., 168
Pratto, D. J., 133
Pratto, F., 446
Prelow, H. M., 379
Prentice, K., 245
Price, A. W., 353, 408
Pridgen, E., 291
Prieto, A. G., 224
Prokhorov, A., 357
Prosser, E. C., 377
Pugh, R., 5
Pungello, E. P., 179
Purcell-Gates, V., 206
Puri, R., 388
Purnell, B., 289, 475
Purselle, D., 404

Pyles, L., 379
Pynoos, R. S., 151

Qian, Z., 122
Quatman, G., 150
Quinn, D., 213, 216
Quintana, S. M., 278

Rabaka, R., 484
Rabian, B., 354
Rabins, P. V., 408
Rackley, R., 69, 70, 71, 83
Raikes, H., 179
Raio, C. M., 377
Ramey, C. T., 179
Ramseur, H. P., 365
Randolph, S. M., 76, 79t, 84, 259, 260, 261, 435, 489
Range, L. M., 408
Rankin, B., 181
Rao, R. P., 419
Rasmussen, H. N., 377
Raudenbush, S. W., 242
Rauh, M. J., 356
Raven, J., 214
Raven, J. C., 214
Ready, J., 418, 419
Recknor, J. C., 419
Redd, T. M., 152
Redding-Lallinger, R., 418, 419
Redmond, L., 226
Reed, E. S., 484
Reed, J., 257, 259, 263
Reed, M. C., 474, 475, 476, 477
Reed, W., 148
Reese, L., 98
Reeve, C. L., 214
Regier, D., 336, 337, 338, 346, 404
Reid, H., 409
Reid, P. T., 445, 446
Reid, R., 354, 355
Reilly, J., 462
Reinherz, H. X., 473
Reis, S. M., 223
Renard, G., 386
Renthal, W., 379
Resnick, H., 151
Reuben, C. A., 354
Reyna, J. W., 110
Reynolds, A. L., 378
Reynolds, C. R., 354
Reynolds, L., 146
Rhee, E., 459
Rhue, S., 312
Riccardi, A. M., 377

Rice, C., 356
Richards, G., 38
Richards, M. H., 381
Richeson, J., 150
Richmond, B. O., 354
Richter, D., 356
Richter, L., 489
Rickels, K., 83
Rickford, J., 200
Rideout, V., 143
Ridley, C. R., 54, 431, 433
Rieppi, R., 167
Riggio, J. M., 418
Riggs, M., 323
Riley, A. W., 385, 388, 389
Rimm, S. B., 224
Rinn, A. N., 355
Risley, T. R., 176
Rist, R. C., 224
Ritter, P. L., 107, 177
Rivas, D., 190
Robbins-Brinson, L., 69, 71
Roberson, J. K., 270
Roberts, A., 104, 106
Roberts, C. R., 353, 354, 357
Roberts, D., 143, 460
Roberts, D. F., 177
Roberts, J. D., 420
Roberts, J. W., 129
Roberts, R. E., 353, 354, 357
Roberts, R. J., 461
Robillard, A., 143, 149
Robins, L., 336, 337, 338, 340, 346, 404
Robinson, A., 223
Robinson, J., 177, 293
Robinson, N. M., 223
Robinson, T., 93
Robinson, T. L., 446
Robinson, T. N., 154
Robinson, W. L., 353
Rock, A., 83
Rockett, R. H., 406
Rodrigue, J. R., 419
Rodriguez, J., 256, 257, 261, 371, 380
Rodriguez, J. R., 272
Rodriguez, M. L., 473
Rodriquez, N., 405
Roe, K. M., 106
Roeder, M. R., 409
Rogan, T. J., 356
Rogers, L., 207
Rogers-Adkinson, D., 355
Rogers-Dulan, J., 97
Rohit, M., 462
Rohrbeck, C. A., 245
Rojecki, A., 144
Rokeach, M., 83
Romero, R., 450, 453
Romero, R. E., 118
Rompf, W. J., 277
Ronsaville, D. S., 179
Rooney, S. C., 106
Root, M. P., 164
Rosario, M., 358, 409
Roscoe, W., 324
Rose, A., 128
Rose, C., 131
Rose, S., 120
Rose, T., 128, 130, 131, 132, 133, 134, 136, 138
Roseff, S. D., 420
Rosell, J., 440
Rosen, A. M., 464
Rosen, B., 188
Rosen, M. A., 431
Rosenthal, R., 224
Rosner, R., 152
Ross, C., 179
Ross, T., 461
Rothenberg, R., 422
Rotheram-Borus, M. J., 409
Rotter, J., 188
Rouse-Arnett, M., 121
Rowan, G. T., 385, 386, 391, 392, 393, 397
Rowan, S. A., 385, 386, 391, 397
Rowe, Z., 345
Rowell, R., 317
Rowley, S., 488
Rowley, S. A., 285, 286, 287, 288
Rowley, S. J., 288
Roy, A., 406
Rozelle, R., 193
Rozin, P., 459
Rubin, H., 276
Rubin, K., 177
Rubin, R., 94
Ruck, M. D., 239
Ruffin, J., 417
Rumbaut, R., 338
Ruscio, A., 336
Rusk, D., 351
Russell, T. M., 288
Russo, S., 379
Rutter, M., 380
Ryan, A., 345
Ryan, A. M., 192, 193, 218, 238
Ryan, E. L., 462
Ryan, E. R., 218
Ryan, K. E., 192, 193, 238
Ryff, C. D., 378

Sabnani, H. B., 302
Sachs, L., 355
Sachs-Ericsson, N., 404, 405, 410
Sackett, P. R., 213, 214, 215, 216
Sadava, S. W., 419
Saint-Jean, G., 473
Salazar, L. F., 120
Salinas, M. F., 213, 216, 217, 289
Salive, M. E., 346
Sambrano, S., 475, 476, 477
Samms-Vaughan, M. E., 392, 397
Samora, J. B., 406
Samuels, D., 421
Sanchez, D., 433, 437, 462
Sanchez-Hucles, J., 434, 435
Sanddal, M. S., 408
Sanders, M. G., 371
Sanders, M. M., 110
Sanders Thompson, V. L., 261, 432, 436, 437
Sandy, J. M., 473
Sano, M., 461, 462
San Vant, S., 230
Sarata, B. P. V., 452, 455
Sargent, R. G., 356
Satel, S., 421
Saunders, J., 189
Sauvageot, J. A., 402
Sawyer, K., 177
Saxton, E., 462
Sbrocco, T., 402, 403, 410
Scales, M. T., 418, 423
Scarborough, H. S., 201, 207
Schaeffer, J. J. W., 418, 419, 422
Schafer, J. L., 389
Schallert, D., 189
Scheinnholtz, J., 433
Schilling-Estes, N., 207
Schinke, G., 476, 477
Schinke, S., 474
Schinke, S. P., 438
Schmader, T., 216
Schmeelk-Cone, K. A., 164, 488
Schmeelk-Cone, K. H., 290, 291, 379
Schmerund, A., 289
Schmitt, N., 213, 214, 216, 391, 392
Schnur, E., 179
Schoeny, M. E., 353
Schooler, D., 147
Schorr, L. B., 273
Schrimshaw, E. W., 358
Schrimsher, G. W., 462
Schuerger, J. M., 227, 229
Schulman, K. A., 421
Schweinhart, L. J., 179
Schwinn, T., 474

Scipio, C., 418, 419
Scott, A. A., 421
Scott, C., 132, 207
Scott, J. W., 109
Scott, K. D., 421
Scott, L. D., 303, 387, 388, 389
Scott, L. D., Jr., 258
Scott, R. B., 417, 420
Scott, Y. M., 306
Scott-Heron, G., 130
Scott-Jones, D., 177
Seaton, E. K., 291
Sedway, J. A., 418, 419, 422
Segal, S. P., 463
Seibt, B., 192
Sekaquaptewa, D., 219
Sekar, P., 470
Sekayi, D., 147
Seligman, C. R., 206
Seligman, M. E. P., 376, 377, 378
Sellers, R. M., 164, 256, 258, 259, 260, 261, 263, 285, 286, 287, 288, 289, 291, 487, 488
Selvin, S., 356
Semaj, M. T., 271
Serjeant, G. R., 420
Serna, G. S., 293
Serpell, Z., 244
Serrano, A., 200
Serrano-Garcia, I., 483, 486, 489
Servon, L., 152
Shade, B. J., 371, 461
Shah, S., 353
Shaka Zulu, N., 321
Shakur, T., 136
Shakur, T. A., 132
Sharma, J., 391
Sharot, T., 377
Shavelson, R., 188
Shaw, C. M., 261
Shaw, P. A., 258
Shear, K., 336
Shegog, R., 357
Shelton, J., 285, 286, 287, 288, 289
Shelton, J. N., 487, 488
Shelton, R. C., 463
Shenoy, U., 440
Sherbourne, C., 340
Sherman, M., 433
Sheu, Y., 166
Shih, M., 191, 213, 219
Shilalukey, K., 420
Shore, D., 462
Shorter-Gooden, K., 42, 168, 405, 449, 450, 451, 452, 454, 486
Shukla, S., 431, 464

Shultz, A. J., 345
Shumow, L., 224
Shyne, 127
Sidanius, J., 446
Siddique, J., 405
Sidney, S., 168
Siegal, J., 146
Siegel, J. M., 451
Sigman, M., 178
Signorielli, N., 145, 148
Sillen, S., 5, 77
Silvera, M., 321
Silverman, M. M., 408
Silverman, W. K., 354
Silverstein, L. B., 109
Simmons, A. B., 181
Simmons, H. D., 228, 230
Simmons, R., 127, 128, 131, 132, 138
Simmons, R. G., 255
Simons, R., 488
Simpson, A. G., 261
Siqueira, L. M., 357
Sirota, P., 420
Siryk, B., 84
Sizemore, O. J., 461
Sjomeling, M., 213, 216
Skiba, R. J., 181
Skipper, J. K., Jr., 133
Slater, M. D., 149
Slaughter-Defoe, D. T., 276
Slavin, R., 242
Small, S. A., 461, 462
Smalls, C., 488
Smedley, B., 340, 342
Smith, A., 314, 462
Smith, B., 319, 406
Smith, B. L., 352
Smith, D. L., 346
Smith, E. J., 378, 379
Smith, E. M. J., 227, 229, 230
Smith, E. P., 256, 257, 261, 272, 273, 371, 380
Smith, J., 464
Smith, J. L., 216, 217, 218
Smith, L. A., 417
Smith, L. C., 402, 403
Smith, M. A., 285, 286, 287, 288, 488
Smith, P., 93, 476
Smith, R., 386
Smitherman, G., 201, 203, 204, 206
Smith Morris, T., 422
Snowden, L., 340, 402
Snowden, L. R., 432, 456
Snyder, C. L., 377
Snyder, T., 105
So, D., 288

Sofola, J., 72
Solomon, P., 193, 194
Solorzano, D., 188
Solórzano, D., 434
Somervell, P. D., 337, 404
Sonn, C. S., 167
Sorey, M., 404
Soto, T., 409
South, S., 120
Spanierman, L. B., 167
Sparling, J., 179
Speight, S. L., 162, 256, 288, 364, 371, 378, 449, 450
Spence, S. A., 19
Spencer, L. E., 355
Spencer, M. B., x, 132, 227, 230, 257, 258, 260,
    261, 270, 271, 274, 275, 276, 354, 379
Spencer, S. J., 213, 216
Spenser, M. B., 13
Spicer, P., 256, 257, 261, 272, 371, 380
Spielberger, C. D., 213, 463
Sprafkin, J., 354
Spratt, E. G., 419
Springer, A. E., 357
Stack, S., 380, 406, 407
Stafford, R. S., 421
Stangor, C., 219
Stansbury, R., 354, 410
Stanton, M., 224
Staples, R., 105, 109, 446
Starost, H., 177
Steele, C. M., 167, 191, 212, 213, 214, 215,
    216, 217, 223
Stein, R. E. K., 109
Steinberg, L., 107, 177
Steketee, G., 403
Stephens, D. P., 121, 259, 260
Stephens, T., 133
Steptoe, A., 419
Stern, Y., 462
Stevens, T., 151
Stevenson, H. C., 13, 84, 93, 98, 152, 255, 256, 257,
    258, 259, 260, 261, 263, 272, 371, 380, 386
Stevenson, H. C., Jr., 272
Stewart, P. E., 368
Stewart, S. M., 357
Stibbe, A., 420
Stipek, D., 191
Stith, A., 340, 342
Stock, M., 95, 98
Stockman, I., 207
Stokes, A., 242
Stokes, J. E., 69, 79t, 80
Stolzfus, J., 274
Stone, J., 213, 216
Stoppelbein, L., 93, 408

Storm, P., 390
Storm, R., 390
Storm, S., 390
Stott, D. H., 354
Stracuzzi, T. L., 433
Strakowski, S., 338, 463, 464
Strayer, R., 324, 325
Streisand, R., 419
Stricker, L. J., 214, 215, 216
Strickland, T. L., 461, 462
Striegel-Moore, R. H., 451
Strom, R., 106
Strom, S., 106
Stroman, C. A., 144, 146
Strube, M., 147
Strychacz, C., 96
Su, M., 336, 337, 339, 340, 402
Suarez-Balcazar, Y., 152
Suchday, S., 403, 410
Sudarkasa, N., 104
Sue, D., 99, 231, 432, 437, 440
Sue, D. W., 165, 166, 228, 229, 231, 258, 432, 437, 440
Sue, S., 5, 431, 455
Sugar Hill Gang, 130
Sugarman, J., 421
Sullivan, E., 193
Sussman, L., 340
Suzuki, L. A., 231, 433
Suzuki, S., 357
Swaim, R. C., 149
Swanson, D. P., 258, 260, 274, 276, 379
Swanson, J. L., 288, 292, 293
Swanson, J. W., 431
Swartz, M., 451
Swartz, M. S., 431
Sweet, J., 103
Sweetman, J., 337, 339, 344, 404, 463
Swick, K. J., 182, 183
Swiecki, E., 419
Swim, J. K., 168
Swords, R., 206

Taboada, A., 243
Tafoya, T., 317
Taheri-Kenari, A., 177
Tait, C., 474
Takeuchi, D., 256, 343, 346, 431
Takeuchi, K., 357
Taliaferro, J., 167
Tan, A., 146
Tan, A. S., 150
Tan, G., 146
Tang, M., 461
Tapper, M., 421
Tata, S. P., 111

Tate, W. F. I. V., 263
Tavegia, B., 224
Taylor, A., 194
Taylor, A. T., 319
Taylor, B. A., 179
Taylor, C. S., 385
Taylor, E., 263
Taylor, J., 92, 121, 166, 167, 301
Taylor, J. D., 301
Taylor, L. C., 176
Taylor, L. K., 403
Taylor, L. M., 419
Taylor, M. J., 446, 450, 451
Taylor, O., 206
Taylor, R., 92, 93, 94, 95, 340, 343, 344, 380
Taylor, R. D., 105
Taylor, R. J., 108, 258, 260, 261, 454
Taylor, S. E., 133
Telfair, J., 421
Tenebaum, H. R., 239
Terhune, P. S., 109, 110
Terman, L. M., 224
Terrell, A. S., 304
Terrell, F., 300, 301, 302, 303, 304, 432
Terrell, S., 432
Terrell, S. L., 300, 301, 302, 303, 304
Terry, K., 259
Terry, N. P., 207
Thakur, A., 420
Tharp, R., 250
Thesiger, C., 178
Thomas, A., 5, 77
Thomas, A. J., 118, 162, 256, 288, 371, 449, 450
Thomas, C., 5, 13, 488
Thomas, C. W., 284, 285, 286
Thomas, D. E., 259, 276, 385, 386, 387, 389, 437
Thomas, D. S. G., 258
Thomas, H., 339
Thomas, V. G., 445, 449, 454
Thomas, V. J., 419
Thompson, B., 402
Thompson, C., 319
Thompson, C. E., 159, 160, 161, 364, 365, 369, 433, 485, 486, 487, 488
Thompson, C. L., 450
Thompson, D., 95
Thompson, E. E., 465
Thompson, G., 151
Thompson, J., 188
Thompson, J. H., 391
Thompson, M., 219
Thompson, M. P., 408
Thompson, R., 408
Thompson, R. J., 418, 419

Thompson, S., 69, 79t, 80, 420
Thompson, S. H., 356
Thompson, S. N., 367
Thompson, V. L., 401
Thompson, V. L. S., 379
Thorn, G. R., 452, 455
Thornburg, K. R., 258
Thornton, M., 94
Thornton, M. C., 258, 260, 261
Tinney, J., 93, 94
Tinsley, S. C., 404, 410
Tiro, J. A., 408
Tivis, R. D., 151
Tix, A. P., 293
Toepke, A., 200
Tokar, D. M., 288, 292, 293
Tolleson, J., 132
Tolliver, G., 131
Toms, F. D., 255, 256, 257, 258, 262
Toney, S. T., 355
Torino, G. C., 165, 166, 228, 229, 258
Torres, M., 343, 344
Touradji, P., 461, 462
Townes, D. L., 303
Towns, D. P., 242
Townsend, T. G., 259, 276, 289, 385, 386, 387, 389, 437, 473
Townsend-Gilkes, C., 94
Tracey, T. J. G., 302, 305
Trawalter, S., 150
Treadwell, K. R. H., 353, 354
Treadwell, M. J., 417, 420
Treed, G., 302, 304
Triandis, H. C., 381
Trierweiler, S. J., 465
Troyer, L., 107
Tryon, R. J., 385, 391
Tubman, J. G., 305
Tucker, B., 120
Tucker, C. M., 432
Tucker, G. R., 206
Tucker, M. B., 108, 120
Tull, E. S., 166, 167
Tung, Y. P., 420
Turkle, S., 278
Turner, L. D., 200
Turner, M. A., 180
Turner, R., 337
Turner, R. J., 167
Turner, S. M., 336, 402, 403, 410
Turner-Musa, J., 489
Tyler, R., 448
Tynes, B., 146, 151
Tyroler, H. A., 337
Tyson, C. A., 224, 232

Urdan, T., 192
Uridin, J., 130
Usinger, P., 190
Utsey, S. O., 51, 76, 77, 80t, 81, 82, 163, 164, 167, 381, 408, 422, 435, 436, 437, 448, 452, 473, 474, 483, 485

Vacek, J., 96
Vaden, N. A., 276
Valdes-Sueiras, M., 462
Valencia, E. Y., 355
Valencia, R., 225, 243
Valenstein, M., 463
Valrie, C., 418, 419
VanBiervliet, A., 110
Vandiver, B. J., 223, 228, 284, 286, 288, 289, 290, 487
Van Horn, L., 404, 410
Van Hulle, C., 204
Vannatta, K., 419
Van Ryn, M., 340, 342
Van Sertima, I., 4
Varon, S. R., 385, 388, 389
Vega, C., 338
Vega, W., 342
Velasquez, R. J., 462
Velli, S. A., 462
Vera, E. M., 288
Veroff, J., 93, 122
Vevaina, T., 95
Viadero, D., 175, 178
Vichinsky, E., 417
Vincent, R., 133
Visnic, S., 463
Viswanathan, R., 403
Vitols, M. M., 463
Vogel, D. L., 289
Voils, C. I., 421
Vu, H., 340, 343
Vygotsky, L. S., 271

Wade, J. C., 261, 446, 447
Wagendnecht, L. E., 470
Wagner, H. R., 431
Wagner, N. S., 111
Wahba, R., 319
Wailoo, K., 417, 421
Waite, R., 451
Wakefield, J. C., 465
Walberg, H. J., 242
Walker, E., 147, 149
Walker, R. L., 404, 407, 408, 410
Walkerdine, V., 278
Wallace, A., 152
Wallace, B. C., 166, 379, 431, 434, 436, 437

Wallace, B. G., 435, 436, 437
Wallace, D. K., 463
Wallace, J., 98
Wallace, J. M., 345, 470, 472, 473
Wallace, J. M., Jr., 357
Wallace, M., 242
Wallace, S. A., 260, 261, 263
Walrath, C., 432
Walsh-Childers, K., 148, 149
Walters, E., 336
Walters, E. E., 401, 402
Walters, K., 315, 326
Walwyn, S., 276, 277
Wang, C. S., 420
Wang, M. C., 242
Wang, P., 340
Wanner, J., 301
Want, V., 433
Ward, E. C., 433
Ward, L. M., 146, 147, 148, 149
Ward, W., 214, 215, 216
Ward Brown, B. J., 353
Ware, J. E., 345
Warheit, G., 338
Washington, J., 207
Washington, N. C., 166
Wasic, B. J., 387
Wasik, B., 245
Wasik, B. H., 177
Wasserman, I., 380
Wasserman, I. M., 406, 407
Wasserman, M. S., 473
Watkins, A. V., 224
Watkins, C. E., 303, 432
Watkins, D. C., 405
Watlington, C., 93, 95
Watson, M. A., 463
Watson, S. E., 118, 119, 121, 123
Watts, R., 168, 488
Watts, R. J., 483, 486, 488, 489
Watts, S. E., 403
Way, N., 118, 119
Weatherford, C. B., 321, 322, 323, 325
Weatherford, R. J., 321, 322, 323, 325
Weaver, S. R., 379
Webb-Johnson, G., 354, 356
Weems, C. F., 403
Weems, L. X., 47, 78, 83
Wei, M., 289
Wei, R., 407, 408
Weikart, D. P., 179
Weinberg, M., 312
Weinfurt, K. P., 421
Weinrich, J., 311
Weinstein, R., 191, 219

Weisner, T. S., 278
Weiss, A. L., 176
Weiss, B., 178
Weissman, M. M., 404
Weisz, J. R., 178
Wekker, G., 323
Wells, E. A., 98
Wells, K., 340, 355
Welte, J. W., 357, 470
Werner, E., 386, 420
Wessel, T. R., 288
West, B. T., 462
West, C., 12, 136, 317, 319, 321, 324, 325
West, C. M., 120, 449, 450, 453
West, S. A., 463, 464
Wester, S. R., 150, 289
Westerling, R., 419
Whaley, A. L., 256, 260, 271, 276, 299, 300, 302, 342,
  346, 410, 432, 433, 452, 463
Wheeler, R., 206
Wheeler, S. C., 216
White, A., 105
White, A. M., 484
White, D. L., 357
White, J., 378, 486
White, J. C., 121, 450
White, J. L., 4, 5, 6, 7, 14, 15, 21, 22, 26,
  43, 48, 51, 370, 452, 453
White, K. S., 354, 473
White, P. H., 217
White, R., 488
Whitehead, B. D., 14, 104
White-Means, S. L., 106
Whitfield, K. E., 462
Whiting, G. W., 224, 225, 226, 227, 229, 230, 231
Whitley, E. B., Jr., 319
Whitted, K. S., 307
Whitten, C. F., 419
Whitten, L., 450
Whitworth, E., 419
Wicherts, J. M., 219
Wiegerink, R., 179
Wieringa, S. E., 323, 324
Wiezmann, F., 446
Wigfield, A., 191, 243
Wilcox, C., 98
Wilcox, R., 61
Wilder, M., 206
Wiley, C., 462
Wilfley, D. E., 451
Wilkinson, G. S., 462
Willett, J., 237
Williams, B., 165, 167, 289, 293
Williams, B. H., 22
Williams, C., 5, 49, 51

Williams, C. B., 446, 452, 453, 454, 455
Williams, D., 92, 93, 95, 96, 98, 336, 337, 338, 340, 343, 402, 463
Williams, D. R., 151, 166, 335, 336, 337, 339, 343, 344, 345, 346, 365, 370, 404, 462, 463
Williams, E., 365
Williams, E. A., 448
Williams, J., 189
Williams, J. E., 270
Williams, K. E., 403
Williams, N. C., 483, 486
Williams, O., 381, 408
Williams, O. D., 470
Williams, O., III, 81, 167, 448, 452
Williams, R., 200
Williams, R. A., 211
Williams, R. L., 5, 21, 26, 30, 62, 63, 64, 65, 67, 211, 376, 387, 460, 462
Williams, T., 189
Williams, V. M., 376
Williams-Morris, R., 166, 344, 345, 364
Willig, A., 190
Willis, L. A., 406, 407
Willoughby, M., 355
Wills, T. A., 473, 474
Wilson, A., 42
Wilson, B. D. M., 358
Wilson, C., 338, 343
Wilson, E., 421
Wilson, L., 256
Wilson, W. J., 130, 181
Windle, M., 472
Wingood, G. M., 120, 143, 149
Wiredu, K., 49
Wise, S. L., 288, 292
Witherspoon, K. M., 162, 288, 449, 450
Withey, S., 338
Wohl, V., 420
Wolf, N., 449
Wolfgang, M. E., 408
Wolfram, W., 201, 207
Wong, L. M., 459
Wood, M., 422
Wood, T., 301
Woodle, J., 431, 464
Woods, D., 420
Woods, L., 98

Woods, L. N., 437
Woodson, C. G., 11, 41, 42, 211
Workman, E., 418, 419
Worrell, F. C., 289, 290, 351, 352, 356
Wright, B. J., 65, 66
Wright, S., 303
Wu, J., 190
Wyatt, G., 324, 325
Wyatt, G. E., 446, 449

Xing, Y., 353, 354, 357

Yaeger, A. M., 473
Yancey, A. K., 451
Yang, O., 423
Yanico, B. J., 288, 292, 293
Yardley-Jones, A., 420
Yasin, Z., 417, 421
Yasui, M., 259
Yeargin-Allsopp, M., 356
Yee, A. H., 446
Yip, T., 291
Yosso, T., 434
Young, A., 340, 364
Young, J., 93, 180
Young, J. L., 346
Young, S. L., 408
Younge, S. N., 107
Yu, Y., 335, 337
Yuen, E., 418

Zady, M., 176
Zamboni, B. D., 409
Zamel, P. C., 259
Zane, N., 431
Zapata, A., 93, 95
Zhang, A. Y., 456
Zhao, S., 336, 337, 346
Ziegert, J. C., 214, 217, 218
Ziegler, E., 179
Zigler, E., 269, 379
Zillman, D., 129, 133, 150
Zima, B. T., 355
Zimmerman, F. J., 151
Zimmerman, M. A., 164, 290, 291, 379, 387, 388, 390, 391, 488
Zucker, S. H., 224
Zuckerman, B., 417

SUBJECT INDEX

Academic achievement motivation:
   academic self-concept, 188–189
   achievement goal theory, 191–193
   attributions, 90–191
   barriers, 193–194
   cultural-ecological theory, 193
   ego goal, 191
   gender research, 189, 191
   grade point average (GPA), 188, 189, 190, 192, 194
   learning goal, 191
   mastery goal, 191
   motivational theory, 189–190
   oppositional identity, 193
   perceived competence, 189–190
   performance approach goal, 191
   performance avoidance goal, 191
   performance goal, 191
   racial disparity, 187–188, 189, 192
   regulatory focus, 192
   research directions, 194–195
   self-beliefs, 188–193
   self-efficacy, 189
   spotlight anxiety, 191
   stereotype threat, 191, 192–193
   task goal, 191
Accent, 201
Acculturation, 403, 461–462
Achieved identity status, 291
Achievement goal theory, 191–193, 218
Adaptive racial socialization, 258
Additive approach, 232–233
Affect sensitivity, 437
African American English (AAE):
   accent, 201
   consonantal variation, 202*t*
   Creolist hypothesis, 200
   defined, 199–200
   Ebonics, 21, 26, 200
   educational assessment, 207
   educational implications, 200–208
   English hypothesis, 200
   gender research, 204
   grammatical variation, 202, 203*t*
   instigating, 204
   lexical variation, 201
   origins, 200
   phonological variation, 201–202
   pragmatic variation, 203–204
   prosodic variation, 202–203
   racial identity, 205–206
   racism, 204–205
   reading, 201–202, 207
   research directions, 207–208
   research literature, 200–201
   Rural English, 200
   socioeconomic status (SES), 199, 200, 204
   speaker variability, 204
   Standard American English (SAE), 199–200, 207
   Urban English, 200
   vowel variation, 201–202
   White English, 199–200
   writing, 207
African American personality:
   African Self-Consciousness Theory, 66–71
   Africentric theories, 62–71
   Extended-Self Model, 62
   research directions, 71–72
   Spiritual Core Model, 62–63
   WEUSI Model, 62, 63–66
African American Psychology:
   hybridity, ix–xi
   research directions, 497–501
African American Psychology (Belgrave & Allison), 7
African American Psychology (Burlew), 378
African American Psychology foundations:
   African roots, 9–10
   Africentric worldview, 10–11, 12–13
   Akan, 9–10
   American social pathology, 11–12
   black strivings, 11–12
   competing worldviews, 12–13
   core constructs, 10
   cultural identity, 5–6
   drapetomania, 5
   ethos, 4, 6

fundamental questions, 10–11
Kemetic civilization, 7–9
Maafa, 4, 5, 16n1
Ma'at, 8
microaggressions, 13
ordered behavior, 8
psychohistory, 4–7
racial identity, 5–6
racism, 4–6
research implications, 14–16
scientific colonialism, 11
within-group variability, 13–14
African American Vernacular English, 26
African-Centered Psychology:
   Akan, 48–49, 50, 51–52, 53
   ancestral/spiritual guides, 55
   astrological charts, 55–56
   axiology, 50
   case study, 56–58
   communal order, 76
   conceptual features, 76–77
   consubstantiation, 76
   cosmology, 49
   cultural functional paranoia, 54
   defined, 47–49
   divination, 55
   dreams, 55
   epistemology, 49–50
   healers, 53–54
   healing process, 54–58
   health and disease, 52–58
   healthy cultural suspicion, 54
   human beingness, 51–52
   humility, 54
   metaphysical interconnectedness, 76
   nature, 76
   ontology, 50
   research directions, 58
   research limitations, 50–51
   sacrificial rites, 55
   Sahku Sheti, 48–49, 51, 53, 56–58
   self-definition, 76
   self-knowledge, 76
   spirit, 76
   Supreme Being, 55
   teleology, 50
   Utamawazo, 48, 49–58
   Western psychology, 50–51, 58
   Yorùbá, 51, 52
African Psychology approaches:
   Africentric worldview, 36–37, 38–39, 44
   assimilation, 37, 41–42
   bicultural reform, 37, 42–43
   critical theory, 40
   cultural congruence, 37, 43–44

   culture, 35–37
   deconstructionism, 40
   disciplinary evolution, 38–39
   drapetomania, 38
   dysaesthesia aethiops, 38
   education, 41–42
   Eurocentrism, 37–38, 40
   fearless studies, 44
   Nigrescence Theory, 42–43
   pre-assimilation, 37, 40–41
   pro-Africentric perspective, 39
   pro-Black perspective, 39
   racial identity, 42–43
   racism, 38
   research directions, 41, 42, 44
   research implications, 44–45
   schools of thought, 39–44
   self-determination, 38, 40
   shifting, 42
   Western psychology, 36, 37–39, 40–41, 43–45
African Psychology conceptualization, ix, xi-xii
African Psychology (Nobles), 375
African Self-Consciousness Scale (ASCS), 65, 69–71, 75, 76, 77, 79*t*, 290
   description/development, 78, 80
   evaluation, 80
   mental health conceptualization, 367
   psychometric properties, 80
African Self-Consciousness Theory:
   African American personality, 66–71
   African personality development, 67–68
   African personality dynamics, 67
   African Self-Consciousness (ASC), 66, 67–71
   African Self-Extension Orientation (ASEO), 66–67
   African Survival Thrust, 67, 69
   Cultural Misorientation (CM), 66, 68–71
   Cultural Misorientation Scale (CMS), 69–71
   empirical research, 69–71
   European Survival Thrust, 68
African Self-Extension Orientation (ASEO), 66–67, 77
African Survival Thrust, 67, 69
African Unconscious, The (Bynum), 44
Africentric developmental space, 64–65
Africentric Home Environment Inventory (AHEI), 76, 79*t*, 85
   description/development, 84
   evaluation, 84
   psychometric properties, 84
Africentric psychological measures:
   African-Centered Psychology, 76–77
   African-centered research, 77–78
   African people, 75, 86n1
   African Personality Theory, 77
   African philosophy, 77

Subject Index

disciplinary subfields, 75–76
instrumentation overview, 79–80t
instrumentation review, 76–84
research directions, 84–85
scale development, 77–78
See also specific instrumentation
Africentric Sentence Completion Test. *See* Oshodi Sentence Completion Index (OSCI)
Africentric worldview:
African American Psychology foundations, 10–11, 12–13
African Psychology approaches, 36–37, 38–39, 44
Black Psychology profession, 28
mental health conceptualization, 365–367, 369–370
mental health services, 435–437
positive psychology, 379–380
Africentrism Scale (AS), 75, 76, 80t, 85
description/development, 82
evaluation, 82
psychometric properties, 82
Africultural Coping Systems Inventory (ASCI), 76, 80t, 85
description/development, 81
evaluation, 82
psychometric properties, 81–82
Afrolantica, 491–492
Afro-typing, 64–65
Age research:
drug use, 471t
mental health services, 435
racial identity theory, 291
Aggression, 145, 149
Akan, 9–10, 19, 77
Alcohol, 357, 470, 471t
Alston, Henry, 6
American Behavioral Scientist, The, 284
American Psychological Association (APA), 6, 19, 22, 23, 26, 39, 41, 376
American Psychologist, 376
Anger, 365, 447–448
Anglocentric developmental space, 64–65
Animal Trickster Tales, 129
Anti-self issues, 365
Anxiety:
characteristics, 402
defined, 401
diagnosis, 402–403
differential symptomatology, 402–403
gay/lesbian population, 409–410
patterns, 402
prevalence, 402
research directions, 410–411
theoretical conceptualization, 403

Anxiety disorders:
adults, 336, 341–342t
children, 353–354
psychological assessment, 464
Assimilation, 37, 41–42
African Psychology approaches, 37, 41–42
gay/lesbian population, 313, 323–327
Nigrescence Theory, 228
Association of Black Psychologists (ABPsi), 5, 6–7, 19, 20, 21, 22, 23, 26, 41, 160–161, 284, 364, 376
Attention-deficit/hyperactivity disorder (ADHD), 151, 354–355
Authentic Happiness (Seligman), 377
Authoritarian parenting, 107, 176–177
Aversive racism, 165
Azibo Nosology, 366

Bad Man Tales, 129
Bakari Project, 15
Before the Mayflower (Bennett), 4
Behavioral Assessment for Children of African Heritage (BACAH), 391–397
form development, 392
international procedures, 396–397
psychometrics, 392–393
sample evaluation, 393–396
Behavioral/emotional strengths:
conceptualization versus theory, 387–388
cultural foundation, 386
defined, 385–386
psychosocial adjustment, 385
racial socialization, 387
research literature, 388–391
research measures, 390–397
resilience, 385, 386
sample evaluation, 393–396
scientific research, 389–390
social capital, 385
social functioning, 385
strengths, 385, 397n2
theoretical models, 386–388
See also Positive psychology
Belief Systems Analysis Scale (BSAS), 76, 79t, 85
description/development, 83
evaluation, 84
psychometric properties, 83–84
Bicultural reform, 37, 42–43
Black agency, 167–168, 169
Black awareness, 65
Black families:
alternative structures, 105–108
authoritarian parenting, 107
Black fathers, 105
cohesive-authoritative family, 108
conflictive-authoritarian family, 108

defensive-neglectful family, 108
demographics, 103–104
disability, 109–111
drug use, 472–473, 474
ecological model, 111
elders, 105–106
extended family, 105
family characteristics, 104
fictive kin, 104
gay/lesbian population, 106–107
gender role socialization, 108–109
grandparent-headed households, 106
matricentric family, 105
mental health services, 110–111
Nigrescence Theory, 108, 109
parenting style, 107–108
racial socialization, 108
research directions, 111–112
research perspectives, 104–105
spiritual kin, 110
systems approach, 111
systems orientation, 110–111
typological methodology, 107–108
Black Identity Development Model, 285–286t
Black Intelligence Test of Cultural
    Homogeneity, 21, 65
Black Liberation Psychology:
    best practices, 487–489
    control of sexuality, 486–487
    coping, 488
    cultural control, 487
    economic exploitation, 486
    key features, 484–485
    oppression patterns, 485–487
    political exclusion, 486
    process therapy research, 490
    public collective self-esteem, 488
    racial identity theory, 487–488
    racial interaction model, 488
    research directions, 489–492
    sociopolitical identity development, 488–489
    violence, 485–486, 490–491
Black Man Emerging (White & Cones), 43
Blackness, 63, 64
Black pastoral/preaching, 129
Black Personality Questionnaire (BPQ), 65–66
Black Power Movement, 22–24, 26
Black Psychology, ix–xi
Black Psychology (Jones), 5, 29, 43, 78, 378
Black Psychology profession:
    advancements, 28–29
    adversity, 23–26
    Africentric worldview, 28
    clinical recommendations, 30–31
    contextual factors, 21–26

deficiency models, 22
disciplinary definitions, 27–28
disciplinary development, 26–28
elder biographies, 20–21
future directions, 29–31
institutional racism, 24
institutional support, 25
research directions, 31
role models, 23–24
Sankofa, 19–20
sexism, 24–25
Traditional School, 26–27
training recommendations, 30
validation, 25–26
Western psychology, 22, 28–29
Black Racial Identity Attitude Scale (BRIAS),
    288–289
Black Rage (Grier & Cobbs), 447
Black Skins, White Masks (Fanon), x, 160
Black strivings, 11–12
Black Studies, 26
Black World, 284
Blessed Assurance (Myers), 20
Book of Knowing (Karenga), 40
Breast cancer, 110
Brown v. Board of Education of Topeka, Kansas
    (1954), 41, 227, 270

Canady, Herman, 6
Caribbean Strength and Difficulties Checklist
    (Lambert et al.), 397
Carolina Abecedarian Project, North Carolina, 179
Children's developmental learning:
    authoritarian parenting, 176–177
    dialogic practices, 176
    ecological theory, 175–176, 178
    neighborhood influence, 180–181
    parenting effects, 177–178
    parenting practices, 178, 180
    parenting recommendations, 182, 183t
    parenting style, 176–177
    research directions, 181–183
    school role, 178–180
    socioeconomic status (SES), 176, 177, 179, 180, 181
    tough love, 177
Children's psychological health:
    anxiety disorders, 353–354
    attention-deficit/hyperactivity disorder (ADHD),
        354–355
    categorical disorders, 352–357
    cognitive-behavioral therapy (CBT), 354
    drug abuse, 357
    eating disorders, 356
    gay/lesbian population, 357–358
    health factors, 351–352

HIV/AIDS, 352
learning disorders, 356
mental health services, 358
mental retardation, 356
mood disorders, 356–357
pervasive developmental disorders, 355–356
physical health, 352
socioeconomic status (SES), 352
Chronosystem, 111
Cigarettes, 357, 470, 471*t*
Civil Rights Movement, 22–24, 26, 376
Cocaine, 357, 470, 472
Cognitive-behavioral therapy (CBT), 354
Cohesive-authoritative family, 108
Collectiveness, 63, 64
Collective racism, 164
Color-blind racial ideology, 163
Coming Together (Williams), 22
Communalism, 244, 436
Communalism Scale (CS), 76, 79*t*
   description/development, 80–81
   evaluation, 81
   psychometric properties, 81
Communal order, 76
Comprehensive Child Development Program, 179
Conflictive-authoritarian family, 108
Consequences of Marriage for African Americans, The (Blackman, Clayton, Glenn, Malone-Colon, & Roberts), 104, 106
Consubstantiation, 76
Contributions approach, 232–233
Cool-pose persona, 448
Coping:
   Black Liberation Psychology, 488
   drug use, 474
   measurement, 76, 80*t*, 81–82, 85
   reactive coping strategies, 274, 275*f*
Correct orientation, 366
Counseling. *See* Mental health services; Psychotherapy
Counseling Persons of African Descent (Parham), 44
Counseling Psychologist, The, 378
Counselor Effectiveness Rating Scale, 303–304
Counterracial scripts, 162–163
Creolist hypothesis, 200
Critical race theory, 40, 263, 365
Crossover effect, 470
Cross Racial Identity Scale (CRIS), x, 293
Cultivation theory, 145
Cultural Blackness, 64
Cultural congruence, 37, 43–44
Cultural-ecological theory, 193
Cultural Experiences in Prevention Project, 438
Cultural identity, 5–6
Cultural Misorientation (CM), 66, 68–71

Cultural Misorientation Scale (CMS), 69–71
Cultural mistrust:
   conceptual models, 301
   controversies, 300–301
   cultural paranoia, 300
   defined, 299–300
   ecological theory, 301
   educational correlates, 304–305
   gender research, 302–303
   historical evolution, 300
   interpersonal relations, 305
   justice system, 306–307
   medical settings, 304
   mental health services, 303–304, 432–433
   mild paranoia, 300
   money management, 306
   research directions, 306–307
   research implications, 305–306
   research measures, 301–302
   socioeconomic status (SES), 303, 306
   youth, 307
Cultural Mistrust Inventory (CMI), 301–305, 307
Cultural paranoia, 300
Cultural racism, 163, 164
Cultural similarity, 368
Cultural socialization, 255–256, 262–264
Cultural uniformity, 368
Culture:
   African Psychology approaches, 35–37
   conceptualization, x–xi
Cyberrace, 146

Dating, 120
Deconstructionism, 40
Defensive-neglectful family, 108
Deficiency models, 22
Deficit thinking, 225
Delusional denial tendencies, 365
Depression:
   diagnosis, 404–405
   gay/lesbian population, 409–410
   life span theory, 405
   measurement, 404–405
   research directions, 410–411
   women, 451
Developmental space, 64–65
Diagnostic and Statistical Manual of Mental Disorders—Fourth Edition, Text Revision (DSM-IV-TR), 351, 352–353, 410, 463–464
Diagnostic and Statistical Manual of Mental Disorders—Third Edition (DSM-III), 336
Dialect, 387
Dialogic practices, 176
Diffused identity status, 291
Disabilities, 109–111

Discriminatory harassment, 165
Disinhibition effects, 146
Diunitalism, ix–xi
Domain identity, 217
Dominant racial scripts, 162
Double consciousness, 283–284
Down low phenomenon, 121, 316
Drapetomania, 5, 38
Drench hypothesis, 145
Drug abuse:
  children's psychological health, 357
  defined, 469–470
  mental health status, 337, 341–342t
Drug use:
  age research, 471t
  consequences, 470, 472
  crossover effect, 470
  cultural factors, 473–474
  culturally appropriate interventions, 475–477, 478
  definitions, 469–470
  ecological theory, 474
  family factors, 472–473
  family theory, 474
  illicit drug use, 469, 470, 471t, 472
  individual factors, 472
  intervention recommendations, 477–478
  interventions, 474–478
  neighborhood influence, 473
  peer cluster theory, 474
  peer influence, 473
  prevalence, 470, 471t
  problem behavior theory, 474
  protective factors, 472–474
  quadratic influence system, 478
  racism, 473, 474
  religion/spirituality, 473–474
  research directions, 478
  risk factors, 472–474
  school factors, 473
  social-cognitive approach, 474–475
  stress coping theory, 474
  triadic influence theory, 478
Dysaesthesia aethiops, 38

Early Childhood Longitudinal Study-Kindergarten Cohort (ECLS-K), 177–178, 179
Early Head Start, 179
Eating disorders, 356
Ebonics, 21, 26, 200
Ebony, 26, 120
Ecological theory:
  Black families, 111
  children's developmental learning, 175–176, 178
  cultural mistrust, 301
  drug use, 474
  racial identity formation, 273–274
Education:
  African Psychology approaches, 41–42
  cultural mistrust, 304–305
  racial identity theory, 289
  See also Academic achievement motivation; African American English (AAE); Children's developmental learning; Gifted students; Stereotype threat; Talent Quest Model for Comprehensive School Reform (TQM)
Educational core, 242, 249–250
Ego goal, 191
Elders, 105–106
Empowerment, 152–153
English hypothesis, 200
Essence, 120
Ethnic socialization, 255–256, 262–264
Ethos, 4, 6, 76–77
Eurocentrism:
  African American Psychology foundations, 3–4, 12–13
  African Psychology approaches, 37–38, 40
  Black Psychology profession, 22, 28–29
  mental health conceptualization, 363–364, 366
  mental health services, 432
  racial identity formation, 270–271, 272, 274
  suicide, 405–406
European Survival Thrust, 68
Even the Rat Was White (Guthrie), 4–5, 43, 375
Evolutionary mechanisms, 370
Exosystem, 111, 175–176
Extended family, 105
Extended-Self Model, 62

Faces at the Bottom of the Well (Bell), 491–492
Familial socialization, 292
Families. *See* Black families
Family theory, 474
Fearless studies, 44
Fictive kin, 104
Flourishing, 339
Foreclosed identity status, 291
Frazier, E. Franklin, 6
Friendships, 118–120
From Slavery to Freedom (Franklin), 4
Funk (Vincent), 133

Gay/lesbian population:
  African American homophobia, 319–323, 324–327
  Black families, 106–107
  children's psychological health, 357–358
  coming-out process, 314–318

cultural assimilation, 313, 323–327
down low phenomenon, 121, 316
ethnosexual stereotypes, 317–318
family of origin, 314
general considerations, 311–314
intimate relationships, 121, 124
mental health services, 435
psychological challenges, 318–319
psychological distress, 409–410
relationship challenges, 316–317
religion/spirituality, 98–99, 100
religiously derived homophobia, 321–323, 325
Gender research:
   academic achievement motivation, 189, 191
   African American English (AAE), 204
   cultural mistrust, 302–303
   gender defined, 445–446, 454–455
   mental health services, 434
   racial identity theory, 290–291
   racial socialization, 259–260
   sickle cell disease (SCD), 420, 423n3
   See also Psychotherapy; Women
Gender roles:
   Black families, 108–109
   intimate relationships, 117–118, 121, 122–123
   media effects, 148–149
   socialization, 108–109, 117–118, 121, 122–123
Gender role strain, 121, 446, 448–449
Genetic Blackness, 64
Gifted students:
   additive approach, 232–233
   contributions approach, 232–233
   deficit thinking, 225
   educational recommendations, 230–233
   education programs, 224, 226–227
   environmental position, 225
   family education, 233
   hereditarian orientation, 225
   mentors, 231–232
   multicultural counseling, 230–231
   multicultural education, 232–233
   Nigrescence Theory, 228–229
   peer pressure, 226–227, 228
   racial identity, 227–229, 231
   racism, 225
   role models, 231–232
   social action approach, 233
   social experiences, 230–231
   student choice, 226–227
   teacher referral, 224–225
   teacher training, 233
   testing, 225
   transformation approach, 233
Global self-concept, 188

Good Kids From Bad Neighborhoods (Elliott et al.), 181
Grade point average (GPA):
   academic achievement motivation, 188, 189, 190, 192, 194
   stereotype threat, 211–212, 214–215
Grandparent-headed households, 106
Grooved Pegboard Test, 462

Harmony, 436
Healers, The (Armah), 53
Healthy People 2010, 112
Helms, Janet, 20
Hereditarian orientation, 225
Hip-hop music:
   Bling-Bling Era, 131
   contemporary relevance, 136–137
   defined, 128
   Disco Era, 130, 131
   economic opportunity, 137–138
   First Golden Era, 131, 133
   jive talk, 129–130
   lyrical analysis, 135–136
   origins, 128–130
   phases, 130, 131–132
   phenomenology, 132
   scholarly documentation, 132–133
   Second Golden Era, 131
   sexism, 133–135, 138
   site of resiliency, 128, 135–136, 137–138
   social structural stage, 130–131
   street-life orientation, 128, 129, 131, 132, 137–138, 138n1
   violence, 133–135, 138
HIV/AIDS, 120–121, 352, 409–410
Homophobia, 319–323, 324–327
Homosexuality. *See* Gay/lesbian population
Hybridity, ix–xi

Index of Race-Related Stress, 164
Individual racism, 159–160, 163, 164, 344
Individuals with Disabilities in Education Improvement Act (IDEIA) (2004), 351, 353
Infant Health and Development Program, 181
Instigating, 204
Institutional racism, 24, 159–160, 163, 164, 345
Intelligence testing, 460
Internalized racism, 162–163, 166, 344–345
Internet, 146, 150–151, 152
Interracial relationships, 122, 123–124
Intersectionality, ix–xi
Intimate relationships:
   clinical implications, 123
   couple resilience, 122
   dating, 120
   friendships, 118–120

gay/lesbian population, 121, 124
gender role socialization, 117–118, 121, 122–123
influencing factors, 117–120
interracial relationships, 122, 123–124
invisibility syndrome, 118
marital satisfaction, 121, 122
marriage, 121, 122
mate availability, 120, 122
media effects, 148–149
racism, 122–123
research directions, 123–124
research implications, 122–124
sexuality, 119–121
Invisibility syndrome, 118, 434, 447, 448
Invisible Man (Ellison), 13

Jet, 120
Jim Crow, 24, 122
Jive talk, 129–130
John Henrik Clarke (Clarke), 7
Journal of African American Psychology, 160–161
Journal of Black Psychology, xi, 6, 78, 160, 289, 378, 441
Journal of Black Studies, 78
Journal of Counseling Psychology, 294
Journal of Personality and Social Psychology, 212
Journal of Positive Psychology, 376
Justice system, 306–307, 486

Kemetic civilization, 7–9, 38, 76

Language. *See* African American English (AAE)
Language You Cry In, The (Toepke & Serrano), 200
Learning disorders, 356
Learning goal, 191
Lesbians. *See* Gay/lesbian population
Life span theory:
    depression, 405
    racial identity formation, 272–273
    suicide, 408

Maafa, 4, 5, 16n1, 22, 485
Ma'at, 8, 50
Macrosystem, 111, 175–176
Major Depressive Disorder (MDD), 404–405
Marijuana, 357
Marriage, 121, 122
Martin Luther King Junior Elementary School Children et al. v. Ann Arbor School District Board (1979), 204–205
Mastery goal, 191
Matricentric family, 105
Media effects:
    African American portrayal, 143–145
    aggression, 145, 149
    Black programming, 146–147, 154
    consumption statistics, 143
    cultivation theory, 145
    disinhibition effects, 146
    drench hypothesis, 145
    empowerment, 152–153
    gender roles, 148–149
    Internet, 146, 150–151, 152
    intimate relationships, 148–149
    media self-knowledge profiles, 153
    mental health, 151
    priming effects, 145–146
    racial attitudes, 146, 149–151, 153–154
    research directions, 153–154
    research literature, 144–145
    risk taking, 149
    self-concept, 146–147
    social learning theory, 145
    theoretical analysis, 145–146
    violence exposure, 144, 145–146, 149, 150
    woman's body image, 147–148
Media self-knowledge profiles, 153
Medical settings:
    care quality, 421
    cultural mistrust, 304
    sickle cell disease (SCD), 421
Mental health:
    media effects, 151
    racial identity theory, 288–289
Mental health conceptualization:
    Africentric models, 365–367, 369–370
    Azibo Nosology, 366
    correct orientation, 366
    critical race theory, 365
    Eurocentrism, 363–364, 366
    evolutionary mechanisms, 370
    mental disorders, 363
    psychological misorientation, 366
    racism models, 364–365, 369–370
    reactionary mechanisms, 370
    research directions, 370–371
    stress models, 364–365, 369–370
    TRIOS model, ix–x, 367–368, 369–370
    within-group variability, 368–369
Mental Health in Black America (Neighbors & Jackson), 378
Mental health services:
    access, 340
    affect sensitivity, 437
    Africentric worldview, 435–437
    age research, 435
    Black families, 110–111
    care quality, 340, 342–343
    children, 358
    communalism, 436
    counseling, 431–434

counseling skills, 439–441
cultural mistrust, 432–433
Eurocentrism, 432
gay/lesbian population, 435
gender research, 434
harmony, 436
intervention recommendations, 438–441
psychotherapy, 432
race issues, 433
racial identity attitudes, 433
racism, 434, 441
religion/spirituality, 435–436
service utilization, 340, 341–342t
socioeconomic status (SES), 435
utilization, 431–432, 437
well-being maintenance, 437
within-group variability, 434–438
See also Psychological assessment; Psychotherapy
Mental health settings, 303–304
Mental health status:
  anxiety disorders, 336, 341–342t
  drug abuse disorders, 337, 341–342t
  flourishing, 339
  mood disorders, 336–337, 341–342t
  perceived discrimination, 345
  population heterogeneity, 343–344
  prejudice, 344
  problem persistence, 339–340
  problem prevalence, 335–339
  psychiatric disorders, 335–339
  psychological distress, 338
  psychological well-being, 338–339
  psychotic disorders, 337–338
  racism, 344–346
  religion/spirituality role, 346
  research directions, 344–346
  schizophrenia, 337–338
  socioeconomic status (SES), 337, 338
  treatment disparity, 340–343
  See also Children's psychological health
Mental retardation, 356
Mentors, 231–232
Mesosystem, 111, 175–176
Metaphysical interconnectedness, 76
Microaggressions, 13, 165–166, 228, 434
Microsystem, 111, 175–176
Mild paranoia, 300
Money management, 306
Mood disorders:
  adults, 336–337, 341–342t
  children, 356–357
  psychological assessment, 463–464
Motivational theory, 189–190

Multiculturalism:
  gifted students, 230–233
  Nigrescence Theory, 229
  positive psychology, 377
Multidimensional Inventory of Black Identity (MIBI), x, 287, 288–291, 293
Multidimensional Model of Racial Identity (MMRI), 285–286t, 287–288, 290, 291
Multigroup Ethnic Identity Measure (MEIM), 291, 292
Myers, Linda James, 20

National Conference of Levels and Patterns of Training in Professional Psychology (Colorado, 1973), 23
National Institute of Child Health and Human Development, 179–180
Naturalness, 63, 64
Nature, 76
Nature of Prejudice, The (Allport), 160
Negro American Family, The (Moynihan), 104
Negromachy Model, 285–286t
Negro-to-Black conversion experience, 284
Nigrescence Theory:
  African Psychology approaches, 42–43
  anti-white, 228
  assimilation, 228
  Black families, 108, 109
  immersion-emersion stage, 228–229, 231
  intense African American involvement, 228–229
  internalization biculturalist, 229
  internalization multiculturalist, 229
  internalization nationalist, 229
  internalization stage, 229
  miseducation, 228
  pre-encounter stage, 228, 229, 231
  racial identity theory, 284, 285–286t, 287, 289
  racial self-hatred, 228
Nihilistic tendencies, 365
No Child Left Behind Act, 180
NTU psychotherapy, 439, 453

Obsessive-compulsive disorder (OCD), 401–402, 403
Online Victimization Scale, 151
Oppositional identity, 193
Optimal Psychology, 28, 44
Ordered behavior, 8
Oshodi Sentence Completion Index (OSCI), 76, 79t, 85
  description/development, 82–83
  evaluation, 83
  psychometric properties, 83

Parent Experiences of Racial Socialization (PERS), 261, 264n2
Parenting style, 107–108, 176–177

Peer cluster theory, 474
Peer groups:
   drug use, 473
   gifted students, 226–227, 228
Perceived competence, 189–190
Perceived discrimination, 345
Perceived racism, 163, 164, 167–168
Performance approach goal, 191, 218
Performance avoidance goal, 191, 218
Perry Preschool, Michigan, 179
Personal Identity-Racial Group Orientation
   (PI-RGO), 271–272
Pervasive developmental disorders, 355–356
Phenomenological Variant of Ecological Systems
      Theory (PVEST), x
   emergent identities, 275f, 276
   net stress engagement, 274, 275f
   net vulnerability level, 274, 275f
   racial identity formation, 274, 275f, 276
   reactive coping strategies, 274, 275f
   self-appraisal process, 275f
Physical health:
   children, 352
   racism effects, 167, 169
   See also Sickle cell disease (SCD)
Piers Harris Self-Concept Scale, 188
Playing the dozens, 129
Positive psychology:
   African American perspective, 377–378
   Africentric worldview, 379–380
   defined, 376–377
   historical overview, 378–379
   multicultural perspective, 377
   racial identity, 379–380
   racial socialization, 379–380
   religion/spirituality, 380–381
   research directions, 381
   resilience, 380
   See also Behavioral/emotional strengths
Post Traumatic Slave Syndrome (Leary), 13
Posttraumatic stress disorder (PTSD), 151, 401–403
Pre-assimilation, 37, 40–41
Prejudice, 344
Prejudice and Your Child (Clark), 160
Priming effects, 145–146
Problem behavior theory, 474
Project Napa, 438
Psych Discourse, 6
Psychiatric disorders, 335–339
Psychological assessment:
   anxiety disorders, 464
   cultural equivalence, 461–462
   cultural relevance, 461–462
   education-corrected norms, 462
   intelligence testing, 460
   mood disorders, 463–464

   neurological assessment, 460–463, 464–465
   psychiatric assessment, 463–465
   race impact, 460–461
   research directions, 464–465
   schizophrenia, 463
Psychological autopsy projects, 410
Psychological Blackness, 64
Psychological distress, 338
   anxiety, 401–403, 409–410, 411t
   depression, 404–405, 409–410, 411t
   gay/lesbian population, 409–410
   psychological autopsy projects, 410
   research directions, 410–411
   suicide, 405–409, 411t
Psychological misorientation, 366
Psychological Nigrescence Model.
   See Nigrescence Theory
Psychological well-being, 338–339
Psychology Caucus of the American Teachers
   Association, 6
Psychology of Blacks, The (White), 21
Psychology of the Afro-American (Jenkins), 5
Psychology of the Black Experience, The (Pugh), 5
Psychosocial adjustment, 385
Psychosocial model of racism (PMR), 160–168
Psychotherapy:
   cool-pose masculinity, 448
   female sexual devaluation, 449
   female symptoms, 451
   female victimization, 449
   gender defined, 445–446, 454–455
   invisibility syndrome, 447, 448
   literature critique, 454–455
   male anger, 447–448
   male gender role strain, 446, 448–449
   men, 446–449, 453
   religion/spirituality, 454
   research directions, 455
   research limitations, 455–456
   Sisterella complex, 451
   strong-black-woman persona, 450–451, 453
   therapeutic orientations, 452–454
   utilization, 432
   women, 449–452, 453–454
   women's self-image, 449–450
   See also Mental health services
Psychotic disorders, 337–338

Quadratic influence system, 478
Queen's English, 387

Race-based traumatic stress, 164–165
Race conceptualization, x–xi
Race Is a Nice Thing to Have, A (Helms), 20
Racial categories, 146
Racial discrimination, 165

Racial harassment, 165
Racial identity:
    African American English (AAE), 205–206
    African American Psychology foundations, 5–6
    African Psychology approaches, 42–43
    anxiety, 403
    gifted students, 227–229, 231
    mental health services, 433
    positive psychology, 379–380
    sickle cell disease (SCD), 421
Racial Identity Attitude Scale-Brief Version
    (RIAS-B), 288–289, 290
Racial Identity Attitude Scale-Long
    Form (RIAS-L), 293
Racial Identity Attitude Scale (RIAS), x, 26, 284, 292–293
Racial identity formation:
    child outcomes, 276–277
    developmental progression, 370–372
    ecological theory, 273–274
    Eurocentrism, 270–271, 272, 274
    life span theory, 272–273
    Phenomenological Variant of Ecological Systems
        Theory (PVEST), 274, 275f, 276
    research directions, 278–279
    research literature, 269–270
    research methodology, 277–278
    theoretical analysis, 272–276
Racial identity theory:
    academic correlates, 289
    achieved identity status, 291
    age research, 291
    attitude correlates, 289–290
    Black Liberation Psychology, 487–488
    diffused identity status, 291
    double consciousness, 283–284
    familial socialization, 292
    foreclosed identity status, 291
    gender research, 290–291
    historical context, 283–284
    mental health correlates, 288–289
    model analysis, 287–288
    moratorium identity status, 291
    research directions, 293–294
    research literature, 283–284, 288–292
    research measures, 284, 287–293
    research methodology, 292–294
    seminal models, 284, 285–286t, 287
    skin tone significance, 291–292
    within-group differences, 290–292
Racial interaction model, 488
Racialism, 258–259
Racial mapping, 146
Racial meanings, 146
Racial residential segregation, 345
Racial socialization:
    adaptive racial socialization, 258
    behavioral/emotional strengths, 387
    Black families, 108
    conceptualization, 255–257
    critical race theory, 263
    cultural socialization, 255–256, 262–264
    ethnic socialization, 255–256, 262–264
    gender research, 259–260
    necessity of, 257–258
    parental transmission, 258
    positive psychology, 379–380
    qualitative measures, 261
    quantitative measures, 260–261
    racialism, 258–259
    research directions, 261–264
    research literature, 256–261
    triple-quandary theory, 255–256, 262–264
    youth acquisition, 258–259
Racial Socialization Measure, 260
Racial stereotypes, 162–163
Racism:
    African American English (AAE), 204–205
    African American Psychology foundations, 4–6
    African Psychology approaches, 38
    aversive racism, 165
    black agency, 167–168, 169
    collective racism, 164
    color-blind racial ideology, 163
    counterracial scripts, 162–163
    cultural racism, 163, 164
    defined, 160
    discriminatory harassment, 165
    dominant racial scripts, 162
    drug use, 473, 474
    gifted students, 225
    individual racism, 159–160, 163, 164, 344
    institutional racism, 24, 159–160, 163, 164, 345
    internalized racism, 162–163, 166, 344–345
    intimate relationships, 122–123
    mental health conceptualization,
        364–365, 369–370
    mental health services, 434, 441
    mental health status, 344–346
    microaggressions, 13, 165–166, 228, 434
    perceived racism, 163, 164, 167–168
    physical outcomes, 167, 169
    psychosocial model of racism (PMR), 160–168
    psychosocial outcomes, 167
    race-based traumatic stress, 164–165
    racial discrimination, 165
    racial harassment, 165
    racial ideology, 161–163, 168–169
    racial stereotypes, 162–163
    racial structure, 161–162, 168–169
    racism-related stress, 163–164
    research directions, 168–169
    research focus, 166–167

research literature, 160–161
research measures, 164
resistance, 167–168
structural racism, 345
tripartite model of racism, 163
White supremacy, 160, 161–163, 165, 167–168
women, 162–163, 169
Racism and Life Experiences Scales, 164
Racism and Psychiatry (Thomas & Sillen), 5
Racism Learned at an Early Age Through Racial Scripting (Williams), 21
Racism-related stress, 163–164
Reactionary mechanisms, 370
Regulatory focus, 192
Religion/spirituality:
   cultural pathways, 93–99
   drug use, 473–474
   emotional/behavioral control, 97–98
   gay/lesbian population, 98–99, 100, 321–323, 325
   homophobia, 321–323, 325
   identity coherence, 98–99
   meaning-making, 96–97
   mental health services, 435–436
   mental health status, 346
   nonorganizational involvement, 92, 96
   organizational involvement, 92, 93–95
   positive psychology, 380–381
   psychological health correlates, 92–99
   psychological health defined, 92, 99–100
   psychotherapy, 454
   religiosity defined, 91–92
   religious institutions, 92, 93–95
   research directions, 99–100
   research limitations, 99–100
   research literature, 92–93
   research measures, 99
   sickle cell disease (SCD), 421–422
   spirituality defined, 91–92
   subjective religiosity, 92
   subjective spirituality, 92
Religious problem-solving styles, 435–436
Resilience:
   behavioral/emotional strengths, 385, 386
   positive psychology, 380
Risk taking, 149
Role models, 231–232
Role of Men, 15
Rural English, 200
Rwanda genocide, x, xi

Sahku Sheti. See African-Centered Psychology
Sankofa. See Black Psychology profession
SBA (Hilliard), 7

Scale of Racial Socialization (SORS), 260–261
Schizophrenia, 337–338, 463
Scientific colonialism, 11
Self-concept, 62
   academic, 188–189
   media effects, 146–147
Self-definition, 76
Self-determination, 38, 40
Self-efficacy, 189
Self Healing Power and Therapy (Fu-Kiau), 9–10
Self-knowledge, 76
Sexism:
   Black Psychology profession, 24–25
   hip-hop music, 133–135, 138
Sexuality:
   Black Liberation Psychology, 486–487
   gay/lesbian population, 317–318
   intimate relationships, 119–121
   women's devaluation, 449
Shifting, 42
Sickle cell disease (SCD):
   characteristics, 418
   crises, 418
   defined, 417, 423n1
   gender research, 420, 423n3
   internal processes, 419–420
   medical settings, 421
   psychological consequences, 418–419
   racial identity role, 421
   religion/spirituality role, 421–422
   research directions, 421, 423
   sociocultural influences, 420–422
   socioeconomic status (SES), 422
   therapeutic implications, 422–423
Signifying, 129
Sisterella complex, 451
Site of resiliency, 128, 135–136, 137–138
Slave Trickster Tales, 129
Social action, 233
Social capital, 385
Social functioning, 385
Socialization. See Gender roles; Racial socialization
Social learning theory, 145
Socioeconomic status (SES):
   African American English (AAE), 199, 200, 204
   anxiety prevalence, 402
   children's developmental learning, 176, 177, 179, 180, 181
   cultural mistrust, 303, 306
   depression prevalence, 405
   mental health services, 435
   mental health status, 337, 338
   sickle cell disease (SCD), 422
Sociopolitical identity development, 488–489
Souls of Black Folk, The (Du Bois), 12, 283

Subject Index

Spirit, 76
Spiritual Blackness, 64
Spiritual Core Model:
    African American personality, 62–63
    African consciousness, 63
    African institutions, 63
    African personality dynamics, 63
    Africentric functioning, 63
Spirituality. *See* Religion/spirituality
Spiritual kin, 110
Spotlight anxiety, 191
Standard American English (SAE), 199–200, 207
State-Trait Anxiety Inventory, 213
Stereotype Task Engagement Process (STEP), 218, 219–220
Stereotype threat:
    academic achievement motivation, 191, 192–193
    achievement goal theory, 218
    defined, 212
    domain identity, 217
    educational implications, 214–216, 218–220
    grade point average (GPA), 211–212, 214–215
    industrial-organizational research, 214
    performance approach goal, 218
    performance avoidant goal, 218
    psychosocial variables, 217–218
    research critique, 213–216
    research directions, 219–220
    research generalizability, 214–216
    research literature, 212–213
    research methodology, 213–214, 218–291
    standardized test scores, 211, 212, 213, 214–215, 216, 217, 219, 220n2
Strengthening Families Program (SFP), 476–477
Stress:
    mental health models, 364–365, 369–370
    posttraumatic stress disorder (PTSD), 151, 401–403
    race-based traumatic stress, 164–165
    racism-related stress, 163–164
Stress coping theory, 474
Strong African American Families Program, 437–438
Strong-black-woman persona, 450–451, 453
Structural racism, 345
Substance abuse. *See* Drug abuse; Drug use
Suicide:
    alternative conceptualization, 408–409
    characteristics, 406–407
    contemporary perspectives, 407
    determinants, 407–408
    Eurocentrism, 405–406
    gay/lesbian population, 409
    life span theory, 408
    patterns, 406–407

    prevalence, 406–407
    research questions, 410–411
Sumner, Francis, 6
Suppressed anger expression, 365
Symbol Digit Modalities Test, 462–463
Systems orientation, 110–111

Talent Quest Model for Comprehensive School Reform (TQM):
    co-construction, 239, 240*t*
    communalism, 244
    constructive social interactions, 244–245
    continuous improvement, 240*t*, 241
    cultural resources, 243–244
    educational core, 242, 249–250
    evidence-based activities, 239, 240*t*, 241
    information management and scrutiny, 245
    intervention results, 247–248, 249*t*
    learning community, 245
    meaningful learning, 243
    model approach, 238–245
    model components, 245, 246*f*, 247
    operating principles, 240*t*
    optimizing classroom transactions, 240*t*, 242–245, 250
    research directions, 248–249
    research implications, 249–250
    success overdetermination, 239, 240*t*, 247
Talent Quest Model for Comprehensive School Reform (TQM), integrity-based strategies, 240*t*, 242–245, 248
    whole-child outcomes, 240*t*, 241–242, 250
Task goal, 191
Teenager Experiences of Racial Socialization (TERS), 260, 264n1
Television and the Socialization of the Minority Child (Berry & Mitchell-Kernan), 144
They Came Before Columbus (Van Sertima), 4
Toasting, 129
Toms, Coons, Mulattoes, Mammies, and Bucks (Bogle), 144
Tough love, 177
Trail Making Test, 462
Transformation approach, 233
Triadic influence theory, 478
TRIOS model, ix–x, 367–368, 369–370
Tripartite model of racism, 163
Triple-quandary theory, ix, 255–256, 262–264
Typological methodology, 107–108

Understanding an Afrocentric World View (Myers), 20
Urban English, 200

Violence:
    Black Liberation Psychology, 485–486, 490–491
    hip-hop music, 133–135, 138
    media effects, 144, 145–146, 149, 150
Virtual Experience Project, 151

WEUSI Model:
    African American personality, 62, 63–66
    Africentric developmental space, 64–65
    Afro-typing, 64–65
    Anglocentric developmental space, 64–65
    Black awareness, 65
    Blackness, 63, 64
    Black personality development, 64–65
    Black personality measures, 65–66
    Collectiveness, 63, 64
    cultural Blackness, 64
    developmental space, 64–65
    genetic Blackness, 64
    Naturalness, 63, 64
    psychological Blackness, 64
    spiritual Blackness, 64
White, Joseph, 20–21
White English, 199–200

White Racism (Kovel), 161
White supremacy, 160, 161–163, 165, 167–168
Williams, Daniel, 21
Williams, Robert L., 21
Womanist identity model, 109
Women:
    body image, 147–148
    breast cancer, 110
    depression, 451
    media effects, 147–148
    psychotherapy, 449–452, 453–454
    racism, 162–163, 169
    self-image, 449–450
    sexism, 133–135, 138
    sexual devaluation, 449
    Sisterella complex, 451
    strong-black-woman persona, 450–451, 453
    victimization, 449
    See also Gender research
Wretched of the Earth, The (Fanon), 160

Young Warriors, 168

ABOUT THE EDITORS

Helen A. Neville is Professor of Educational Psychology (Counseling Psychology Division) and African American Studies at the University of Illinois at Urbana–Champaign. Her research on racial ideology and women's issues has been published in a wide range of psychology and Black Studies outlets. She has served on a number of editorial boards, including as Associate Editor of *The Counseling Psychologist* and the *Journal of Black Psychology*. She has received numerous teaching and mentoring awards, including the Kenneth and Mamie Clark Award for Outstanding Contribution to the Professional Development of Ethnic Minority Graduate Students.

Brendesha M. Tynes is Assistant Professor of Educational Psychology, Psychology, and African American Studies at the University of Illinois at Urbana–Champaign. Her research focuses on the role of the Internet in child and adolescent development with special attention to Internet safety, online victimization, the psychosocial and educational benefits of online interaction, and the construction of race and gender. She is also interested in African American children's psychosocial development in schools and in after-school programs. Tynes teaches African American Psychology, the Psychology of the African American Child, and Adolescent Development, and she is currently developing an online teaching certificate in African American Children's Development and Culture. She received a BA in History from Columbia University in 1997, an MA in Learning Sciences from Northwestern University in 2001, and a PhD in Psychological Studies in Education from the University of California, Los Angeles, in 2005. She is the recipient of a Ford Predoctoral and Postdoctoral Diversity Fellowship for Excellence in Teaching and was awarded a postdoctoral fellowship from the American Educational Researchers Association. Tynes has published articles in the *Journal of Applied Developmental Psychology*, *Developmental Psychology*, *The Black Scholar*, the *Handbook of Children, Culture and Violence*, and other books and journals. One of her recent articles was the number 1 most frequently read in the *Journal of Adolescent Research*. Her work has been cited in the *New York Times* online, *Science Daily*, he (Nashville) *Tennessean*, *MedIndia*, the *Daily Illini*, and other news outlets across the country.

Shawn O. Utsey is Chair of the Department of African American Studies and Associate Professor of Counseling Psychology in the Department of Psychology at Virginia Commonwealth University. In addition, he is currently Editor-in-Chief of the *Journal of Black Psychology*. Dr. Utsey received his BA in Psychology from North Carolina A&T State University, his MA in rehabilitation counseling from New York University, and his PhD in Counseling Psychology from Fordham University. He completed his clinical internship at Pace University in New York City. Prior academic appointments include Assistant Professor of Counseling Psychology at Seton Hall University from 1997 to 2001 and Associate Professor of Counseling Psychology at Howard University from 2001 to 2004. His research interests are primarily related to the psychology of the African American experience. He is interested in understanding how race-related stress impacts the physical, psychological, and social well-being of African Americans. Dr. Utsey has published articles on African American Psychology in a number of journals, including the *Journal of Black Psychology, Journal of African American Men, Journal of Personality Assessment, Journal of Cross-Cultural Psychology, Cultural Diversity and Ethnic Minority Psychology,* and the *Journal of Counseling Psychology*. More recently, however, he has sought to examine how trauma manifests itself in the victims of racial violence. Other areas of interest include examining the influence of African American culture (e.g., collective social orientation, spiritual centeredness, verve) on indicators of health and well-being.

ABOUT THE CONTRIBUTORS

Valerie N. Adams is a doctoral candidate in the Interdisciplinary Studies in Human Development program at the University of Pennsylvania's Graduate School of Education; she spent the early part of her career working with urban African American and Latino adolescents. Her research interests are racial socialization, civic engagement, gender, and media influences on youth. Before returning to school to pursue doctoral studies, Valerie served as a Volunteer Teacher for Africa in Katima Mulilo, Namibia. She believes her experience teaching educational theory and practice in Katima has influenced her research interests and perspectives on racial socialization. She holds a BS from Philadelphia University and an MEd from Temple University.

Dorienna M. Alfred is a licensed psychologist on staff at the University of Missouri–Columbia Student Health Center. She earned a doctorate in counseling psychology from Indiana University. Her clinical interests include college student mental health, with specialties in eating disorders and trauma recovery in women. Her research interests include health disparities affecting African American women, Black liberation psychology and health advocacy, and multicultural counseling and teaching competence. She has spent the last several years involved in research aimed at understanding the role of race- and gender-related stress in African American women's management of hypertension.

Deidre M. Anglin is a licensed clinical psychologist with specialized research training in psychiatric epidemiology from Columbia University. She is Assistant Professor of Psychology at City College, City University of New York. Clinically, she specializes in racially diverse populations of all ages, with a particular focus on neuropsychological testing with school-age children and integrative psychotherapy with adults. Her research focuses on determinants of racial disparities in mental health treatment-seeking patterns and in psychiatric diagnostic patterns. Dr. Anglin also studies the role of childhood risk factors in the development of psychosis. She has published articles on racial biases among clinicians diagnosing schizophrenia, African American racial socialization and identity, and mental health stigma within African American communities.

Oscar Barbarin is the L. Richardson and Emily Preyer Bicentennial Distinguished Professor for Strengthening Families in the School of Social Work, and a Fellow at the Frank Porter Graham Child Development Institute, at the University of North Carolina at Chapel Hill. He earned a PhD in clinical psychology at Rutgers University in 1975 and completed a postdoctoral fellowship in Social Psychology at Stanford University in 1983. Until 2000, he was Professor of Psychology and Social Work at the University of Michigan. His research has focused on the social and familial determinants of ethnic and gender achievement gaps. He is principal investigator of a national study whose focus is the socioemotional and academic development of boys of color. His work on children of African descent extends to a 20-year longitudinal study of the effects of poverty and violence on child development in South Africa.

Ronald K. Barrett received his PhD in Social Psychology in 1977 from the University of Pittsburgh. He is Professor of Psychology and Acting Chair of the African American Studies Department at Loyola Marymount University in Los Angeles. He is a member of the Association of Black Psychologists and a Fellow in the Association of Death Education. Dr. Barrett is interested in cross-cultural differences in death, dying, and funeral rites, with a special interest African American funeral practices. Dr. Barrett was recently honored by the Kellogg Foundation for work in the area of death and dying.

Rabiatu Barrie is a doctoral student in the Counseling Psychology program at Loyola University Chicago. She received her bachelor's degree in Psychology from Florida State University and her master's degree in Clinical Psychology from The Chicago School of Professional Psychology. She is currently employed as a counselor at the Cook County Temporary Juvenile Detention Center. She is also a member of several research teams studying stereotypes of African American adolescent females, coping strategies for inner-city families, and just-world beliefs. Her primary research interests are gendered ethnic identity development of African American adolescent females and attributions of racial microaggressions.

Shawn M. Bediako is Assistant Professor of Psychology at the University of Maryland, Baltimore County. His program of research investigates the influence of sociocultural factors and interpersonal processes on health outcomes among adults with sickle cell disease. Dr. Bediako earned a bachelor's degree in Psychology from the University of Central Arkansas and completed a master's in Community Psychology from Florida A&M University. His doctorate in social/health psychology was earned from Stony Brook University. Prior to joining the faculty at the University of Maryland, Baltimore County, he completed a Carolina Postdoctoral Fellowship for Faculty Diversity at the University of North Carolina at Chapel Hill (2001–2003) and held a joint appointment in Psychology and Hematology at the University of Cincinnati (2003–2005).

Faye Z. Belgrave is Professor of Psychology at Virginia Commonwealth University and founding director of the Center for Cultural Experiences in Prevention. Her programmatic and research interests are in the areas of substance abuse and HIV prevention. Her research also focuses on the role of culture and context in preventive interventions and on gender and female related issues. Dr. Belgrave has been (and currently is) the principal investigator of several research and intervention grants. She has published extensively, including two books and several monographs, and she is an invited speaker on topics of culture and gender issues. She is the recipient of many national and local awards for her work with ethnic minority populations. Dr. Belgrave received her PhD from the University of Maryland; her master's from the University of Nebraska, Lincoln; and her BS from North Carolina A&T State University.

Benita Belvet is a doctoral student in the Counseling Psychology program at Virginia Commonwealth University. She received her BA in Psychology with a minor in African American Studies at the University of North Carolina at Chapel Hill. She is interested in researching the impact of racism-related stress on the quality of life and psychological well-being of African Americans.

Keisha L. Bentley is a doctoral candidate within the Interdisciplinary Studies in Human Development program at the University of Pennsylvania's Graduate School of Education. Her research focuses on the interactions among racial socialization, inter- and intraracial racism, and social mobility and community investment for African Americans. She is particularly interested in bolstering resources or processes that lead to resiliency in urban adolescents. Prior to her doctoral studies, Keisha directed university initiatives targeting Black and first-generation student persistence to graduation, faculty of color retention, and the evaluation of academic diversity objectives. She received her undergraduate and graduate degrees from Howard University and Teachers College, Columbia University, respectively.

Sha'Kema M. Blackmon is a fourth-year doctoral candidate at Loyola University Chicago in the department of Counseling Psychology. She received her MA in Developmental Psychology from Teachers College, Columbia University, in 2001. Her academic work focuses on a variety of multicultural and social justice issues. More specifically, her interests include ethnic–racial socialization and identity development processes as they relate to people of color. She is also interested in the identity processes of individuals who work with people of color. She is currently working on her dissertation, which will explore the diversity attitudes of White physicians in training.

Terra Bowen-Reid is a tenured Associate Professor in the Department of Psychology at Morgan State University, where she also has served as the program director/principal investigator of the Minority Mental Health Research Scholars Program since 1998. She received her BS and MS degrees in Community Psychology from Florida A&M University and her PhD in Personality Psychology from Howard University. Her scholarly interests are in the general area of African/Black Psychology, and her research and publications focus on stress coping and health behaviors among African Americans.

A. Wade Boykin is Professor and Director of the Graduate Program in the Department of Psychology at Howard University. He also serves as executive director of the Capstone Institute for School Reform at Howard University. Between 1994 and 2004, he served as codirector of the Center for Research on the Education of Students Placed At Risk. Dr. Boykin has done extensive work on research methodology and the interface of culture, context, motivation, and cognition, and he has held professional development workshops on topics such as school reform, culturally responsive pedagogy, multicultural education, and minority student achievement. He has published numerous research and theoretical journal articles and book chapters relevant to his research interests. He is currently completing a coauthored book on *Closing the Achievement Gap* and a coedited book titled *Promoting High Achievement for All Children: Evidence-Based Programs, Practices and Procedures.* Most recently, Dr. Boykin served on the President's National Mathematics Advisory Panel, advising the President and the Secretary of Education with respect to the conduct, evaluation, and effective use of the results of research relating to proven, evidence-based mathematics instruction in order to foster greater knowledge of, and improved performance in, mathematics among American students.

A. Toy Caldwell-Colbert passed on March 12, 2008. Dr. Caldwell-Colbert served as Provost and Vice President for Academic Affairs and Professor of Psychology at Central State University. She served as Vice Chair for Psychological Services and Professor of Psychiatry at the College of Medicine at Howard University and as Senior Research Associate, Center for Advancement of Racial and Ethnic Equity, at the American Council on Education. A board-certified licensed clinical psychologist, Dr. Caldwell-Colbert was President of American Psychological Association (APA) Division 45 (Society for the Psychological Study of Ethnic Minority Issues), and chair of the APA Commission for the Recruitment, Retention, & Training of Ethnic Minorities Task Force. Dr. Caldwell-Colbert's 27-year career in higher education includes administrative and faculty appointments; she taught some of the first Psychology of Women courses and conducted research and workshops addressing date rape, sexual harassment, and women's leadership styles. Her research interests also included advancing APA's Multicultural Guidelines, the infusion of racial and ethnic diversity into the curriculum, and clinical assessment/diagnosis of mood disorders. In 2004, she was awarded the Stanley Sue Award of Achievement for Significant Contributions to Advancing the Clinical Psychology of Ethnic Minorities and the 2003 Mentor of the Year award.

Collette Chapman is a first-year doctoral student in the Counseling Psychology program at the University of Texas at Austin. Her research interests are in how theories of ethnic and racial identity may be used to conceptualize and/or explain attitudes toward academic achievement and future orientations of self among minority youth.

Anne Harper Charity Hudley is Assistant Professor of English and Linguistics and Director of the Linguistics Laboratory at The College of William and Mary. She is a Ford Fellow and a National Science Foundation Minority Postdoctoral Fellow in Linguistics and Psychology. Her research concerns regional variation in English and the relationship between language variation and educational practices and policies. Her publications include "Familiarity With School English in African-American Children and Its Relation to Early Reading Achievement" (2004; coauthored with Hollis Scarborough and Darion Griffin), "Regional Differences in Low-SES African-American Children's Speech in the

School Setting" (2007), and "Standardized Assessment of African-American Children: A Sociolinguistic Perspective." She is currently working on a book about language variation for educators with Christine Mallinson.

Trenette Clark is currently a doctoral candidate in the School of Social Work at Virginia Commonwealth University. She received an MSW from the University of North Carolina at Chapel Hill, with a concentration in Management and Community Practice. Ms. Clark's primary research interest is the role of context and culture in adolescent drug use prevention.

Kevin Cokley is Associate Professor in the Department of Educational Psychology, Counseling Psychology Program, at the University of Texas at Austin. His research can be broadly categorized in the area of African American Psychology, and his interests include the construction of racial and ethnic identities, academic self-concept, academic motivation, and understanding the psychological and environmental factors that impact African American student achievement. He is the recipient of the 2008 "10 Rising Stars of the Academy" award by Diverse Issues in Higher Education, the 2007 Association of Black Psychologists' Scholarship Award, and the 2004 corecipient of the Emerging Professional Award given by the Society for the Psychological Study of Ethnic Minority Issues of the American Psychological Association. His recent articles have been published in the Journal of Counseling Psychology, Journal of Black Psychology, and the Harvard Educational Review.

M. Nicole Coleman received her PhD in Counseling Psychology from the University of Missouri–Columbia. She has been a member of the faculty in the Department of Educational Psychology at the University of Houston since 2005. Her primary research interests are in color-blind racial attitudes, racial identity, and multicultural counselor training.

Madonna G. Constantine is a former Professor of Psychology and Education in the Department of Counseling and Clinical Psychology at Teachers College, Columbia University. She received her doctorate in Counseling Psychology from the University of Memphis and completed bachelor's and master's degrees from Xavier University of New Orleans. Dr. Constantine is a researcher in the areas of Black Psychology and multicultural counseling. The scope of her work includes exploring the psychological, educational, and vocational issues of African Americans; developing models of cross-cultural competence in counseling, training, and supervision; and examining the intersections of variables such as race and ethnicity in relation to mental health and educational processes and outcomes.

Michael Cunningham is Associate Professor at Tulane University. He holds a joint appointment in Psychology Department and the university's African and African Diaspora Studies Program. Dr. Cunningham's primary research interests include examining adolescent development in diverse contexts; specifically, he examines how self-perceptions influence the way African American adolescents develop proactive and reactive coping styles. His research also focuses on using an asset's perspective to understand resilience and vulnerability in African American populations. He serves on the editorial boards of *Developmental Psychology* and *Psychological Bulletin* and is the Associate Editor of *Child Development*.

Claytie Davis III is Director of Training in Counseling & Psychological Services at the University of California, Berkeley. He earned his PhD in Counseling Psychology from the University of Texas at Austin. He is an Associate Editor for the journal *Training and Education in Professional Psychology*. His professional interests include supervision, ethics, multicultural competence (development and assessment), and internship and postdoctoral training.

Tara R. Earl was a former National Institute of Mental Health–funded postdoctoral Fellow and Research Associate with the Center for Multicultural Mental Health Research, a division of Harvard Medical School and Cambridge Health Alliance when the chapter was written. She is now an assistant professor at Boston College, where she is working on a Robert Wood Johnson Foundation New Connections initiative award to study ways to improve the quality of mental health care for racial and ethnic minority patients.

Constance M. Ellison is a teacher, scholar, researcher, and educational consultant who earned a Bachelor of Science degree from

Boston University and a Doctorate of Philosophy degree in Development Psychology from Howard University. Her postdoctoral training was conducted at the University of Maryland, College Park, in the Applied Developmental Psychology Program. Dr. Ellison is currently the Director of Graduate Studies and Graduate Associate Professor of Educational Psychology in the School of Education. Her published work focuses on educational issues pertaining to African American children. Dr. Ellison's research examines classroom cultural dynamics that operate in schools that serve African American children with specific emphasis on the association between reflective teacher practice and collective teacher efficacy in enhancing school climate and student achievement outcomes. Dr. Ellison is currently coediting a book titled *Promoting High Achievement for All Children: Evidence-Based Programs, Practices and Procedures*. Her professional affiliations include American Educational Research Association, National Staff Development, and American Association of Colleges for Teacher Education.

Sussie Eshun is a licensed psychologist and Professor of Psychology at East Stroudsburg University. She has lived in and experienced diverse cultural settings. Born and raised in Ghana, she received a BA in Psychology (with a minor in Sociology) at the University of Ghana and an MA and a PhD in Clinical Psychology at the State University of New York at Stony Brook (now Stony Brook University). Dr. Eshun is also a dedicated teacher and researcher who has taught several undergraduate and graduate courses in psychology. She has made several conference presentations and published many times on topics related to depression, suicide, stress, and culture. She is a member of several professional organizations and has been actively involved in issues related to cross-cultural and cross-ethnic influences. She currently serves as Chair for the Commission on Racial and Ethnic Diversity at her campus and has been involved in diversity-related workshops with the Pennsylvania State System of Higher Education.

Nicole Fischer is currently pursuing her PhD in Counseling Psychology at Virginia Commonwealth University. She received her BA in Psychology at the University of Virginia in 2004. Afterward, she served 2 years in the U.S. Peace Corps as a community development volunteer for the Girls' Education and Empowerment Program in Togo, West Africa. Ms. Fischer's primary research interest includes the acculturation experience among West African immigrants living in the United States and the specific factors that influence social stress and subjective well-being. She is also interested in race-related stress among African Americans and how it affects physical and psychological well-being.

Donna Y. Ford is a professor in the Department of Special Education in the Peabody College of Education at Vanderbilt University. She earned her doctoral degree in urban education from Cleveland State University; from this same institution, she earned an MEd in Counseling and a BA with a dual major in Communications and Spanish. Dr. Ford's primary areas of scholarship focus on the underrepresentation of African American students in gifted education, the achievement gap, underachievement among gifted students, and multicultural gifted education. She has published extensively in these areas, with numerous articles and book chapters, as well as five books. She has made hundreds of presentations nationally, and she consults with school districts on the aforementioned topics. Dr. Ford's scholarship has been recognized by several organizations and universities, including the National Association for Gifted Children, the American Educational Research Association, the Association of Black Psychologists, The Ohio State University, and Vanderbilt University.

LaMar Rashad Gibson is a senior undergraduate student at the University of Delaware. He has a double major in English, with a concentration in Ethnic and Cultural Studies, and Black American Studies. He is part of a five-student research team that has spent 2 years using a nontraditional methodological framework titled "Participatory Action Research" for an exploratory study, *The Lived Experiences of Black Students, Faculty and Staff at the University of Delaware*. Mr. Gibson has been invited to present the results of this study at an academic conference titled "The Theorizing Blackness Conference" in spring of 2008, which is hosted at the Graduate Center–City University of New York. Also, Mr. Gibson is third author on a paper currently under review at *Qualitative Inquiry:*

Contextualizing Black Boys' Use of a Street Identity: Why Black Boy Use Street Life as a Site of Resiliency in High School. He has also been invited to present the findings of this study at the American Education Research Association National Conference in March 2008.

Sheila V. Graham is a doctoral candidate in the Department of Counseling and Clinical Psychology at Teachers College, Columbia University. She received a bachelor's degree from Amherst College with a double major in Black Studies and Psychology. Throughout her graduate career, she has made several conference presentations and has coauthored several publications. Ms. Graham's research interests include issues of multicultural counseling competence, the psychological effects of racism, and the impact of immigration-related separation on Latino/a families.

Beverly Greene is Professor of Psychology at St. John's University and a practicing psychologist in New York City. She is a Diplomate in Clinical Psychology from the American Board of Professional Psychology and is a Fellow in seven divisions of the American Psychological Association (APA). She is the recipient of nine national awards for publications deemed outstanding contributions to the psychological literature, and in 2006, she became the first African American in APA's nearly 50-year history to receive the Florence Halpern Award for Distinguished Professional Contributions to Clinical Psychology (APA Division 12). She is also the recipient of the 2007 award for Distinguished Scientific Contributions to Lesbian, Gay and Bisexual Psychology (APA Division 44), the 2007 Distinguished Career Award (Association for Women in Psychology) and numerous other national awards for distinguished professional contributions. A member of the APA Council of Representatives, she has also served on the APA task forces charged with drafting APA policy on same-sex marriage and adoption policy and appropriate therapeutic responses to sexual orientation distress.

Cynthia Hudley is a professor in the Gevirtz Graduate School of Education at the University of California, Santa Barbara, where she has also served as Associate Dean of the Graduate Division. She researches children's social development, with a special interest in peer relationships, achievement motivation, and aggressive behavior. Dr. Hudley has developed an aggression-reduction curriculum, the Brain Power Program http://www.brainpower program .com), to improve peer relations in elementary school. The curriculum, designated a "Promising Program" by the Substance Abuse and Mental Health Administration, is the subject of her recently completed book. Dr. Hudley has also edited a volume on academic achievement motivation in diverse populations and served a coeditor of a volume on the African American experience. Prior to her academic career, Dr. Hudley spent 15 years as a professional educator, working as both a teacher and an administrator.

Lora Rose Hunter graduated from Emory University with a BA in Psychology and a minor in Sociology. She is pursuing a doctorate in Clinical Psychology at Florida State University under the guidance of major professor, Dr. Norman Brad Schmidt. Her research is mainly focused on the impact of culture in the manifestation of anxiety disorders, and she is poised to pursue an academic career in the area of anxiety pathology.

Iheoma U. Iruka is a trained applied developmental psychologist from the University of Miami and a past postdoctoral fellow and current social scientist at FPG Child Development Institute at the University of North Carolina at Chapel Hill. Her interests center on low-income and ethnic minority children's early academic and social success and the role of the family and early childhood environment in this process. At FPG, Dr. Iruka is codirector of a project focused on preschool programs' nutrition and physical activity practices, increasing parents' book-reading activities, and promoting positive parenting behaviors. She is project coordinator for a project evaluating Miami-Dade County's Quality Rating System for child care programs and examining how the system is being implemented and its impact on children, families, and the wider early education system. She has published articles focused on parenting and their role in children's development.

Adanna J. Johnson is a graduate of Marquette University, where she received her PhD in Counseling Psychology. She became a member of the faculty in the Department of Psychology at Loyola College in Baltimore, Maryland, in August 2008. Her areas of research are recruitment and retention of Blacks in the field of psychology and the use of African traditional healing modalities in therapy.

Kobi Kambon (aka Joseph A. Baldwin) is Professor of Psychology in the Department of Psychology at Florida A&M University (FAMU). He holds a PhD in Personality Psychology from the University of Colorado at Boulder and has been a professor at FAMU since 1980. He has authored several books and numerous research articles related to African/Black Psychology and African American personality and mental health. He is also a former chair of the FAMU Psychology Department (1985–1997) and a Past President of the Association of Black Psychologists, and he has been the recipient of numerous awards and recognition for his widely regarded contributions to the field over his 30-plus-year career.

Naa Oyo A. Kwate centers her research on determinants of African American health, with particular attention to individual-level experiences of identity and inequality and the intersection of these variables with more distal structural factors. Dr. Kwate trained as a clinical psychologist specializing in children and adolescents and, during graduate school, she studied the cultural construction of psychiatric disease classification, the cultural context of clinical practice, African-centered Psychology, and the impact of racial/cultural identity on mental health. Dr. Kwate has published articles on the cultural context of mental health practice, African American racial/cultural identity, the role of perceived racism in negative health outcomes, and determinants of African American neighborhood features and food environments.

Michael Canute Lambert, is a senior researcher at 3-C Institute for Child Development (3-C ISD) and a clinical psychologist practicing in 3-C Family Services (3-C FS) in Cary, North Carolina. Prior to joining 3-C ISD and 3-C FS, he held the Millsap Professorship Chair in the Department of Human Development and Family Studies and an Adjunct Professorship in the Department of Psychological Sciences at the University of Missouri–Columbia. Before joining the faculty at the University of Missouri–Columbia, Dr. Lambert was Associate Professor in the Department of Psychology at Michigan State University. Before joining the faculty at Michigan State, he was Assistant Professor of Psychology at the University of Mississippi. A graduate of Hahnemann University, where he received his BS, and Bryn Mawr College, where he received his MSS in Clinical Social Work, he received his MA and PhD in Clinical Psychology from the University of North Carolina at Chapel Hill. Dr. Lambert is a licensed psychologist in the states of Michigan and Missouri. Dr. Lambert's professional interests include measurement of behavioral and emotional functioning in children, adults, and families internationally, with special focus on behavioral and emotional strengths in persons of the African Diaspora.

Jacqueline S. Mattis received her doctorate in Psychology from the University of Michigan. Currently, she is the department chair of Applied Psychology at New York University. Her research on the role of religiosity and spirituality in the lives of African American adults has been published widely. Her research more specifically engages the ways in which religion and spirituality inform prosocial development and positive psychological outcomes (e.g., altruism, volunteerism, civic engagement, optimism, and forgiveness) among African Americans.

Harriette Pipes McAdoo is Distinguished Professor of Sociology at Michigan State University. She received a BA and MA from Michigan State University and a PhD from the University of Michigan, and she has done postdoctoral study at Harvard University. She formerly taught at Howard University in the School of Social Work, where she was Acting Dean for 2 years. She has been a visiting lecturer at the Smith College School of Social Work, the University of Washington, and the University of Minnesota. She has served as Director of the Groves Conference on Marriage and the Family, as National Advisor to the White House Conference on Families, and as President (in 1994) of the National Council on Family Relations. She has been a member of the Governing Council of the Society for the Research in Child Development and is a lifetime member of the National Association of Black Psychologists. Dr. McAdoo was the first person honored by the National Council on Family Relations with the Marie Peters Award for Outstanding Scholarship, Leadership, and Service in the Area of Ethnic Minority families. She was the recipient of the Helms Award from Columbia University Teachers College, and she was a Fellow of the Institute of Children, Youth, and Families at Michigan State University. She has published widely on racial issues and self-esteem in young children, Black mobility patterns, Black middle-class families, coping strategies of single mothers, parental coping strategies of children with learning disabilities, professional Kenyan women, and AIDS and pregnancy in Zimbabwean women. She is an acclaimed public speaker and has spoken on many campuses and professional meetings. She has edited *Family Ethnicity: Strength in Diversity* (2nd ed.) and *Black Families* (4th ed.). She is coeditor of *Services to Young Families: Program Review and Policy Recommendations*, and *Black Children: Social Educational and Parental Environments*. She is coauthor of *Women and Children: Alone and in Poverty*.

Jeffery Menzise received in his PhD in Clinical Psychology in 2006 from Howard University. He is Assistant Director of the Race Relations Institute at Fisk University. Dr. Menzise is a member of the Association for Black Psychologists and the American Psychological Association. Dr. Menzise is interested in the study children and adolescents who engage in risky sexual behavior. He is also studying the relationship between cultural mistrust and the willingness of Blacks to report illegal activities. Dr. Menzise has been recognized by Howard University for the quality of his research.

Linda James Myers is an intellectual and cultural critic whose research and scholarship places African Diaspora Studies at the forefront of the paradigm shift occurring in Western science and converging with Eastern philosophies. Her work has led to the development of theory of divine consciousness grounded in the wisdom tradition of African deep thought and supported by contemporary science and experience. Dr. James Myers is currently Dean of the Graduate School of Psychology at New College of California. She taught for years in the African American and African Studies, Psychology, and Psychiatry Departments at Ohio State University. She also serves as executive director of the Center for Optimal Thought, a private nonprofit education and training organization dedicated to transformative learning, spiritual, and leadership development.

Aashir Nasim is Associate Professor of Psychology at Virginia Commonwealth University, where he occupies a joint position with Psychology and Africana Studies. He received his PhD in Developmental Psychology from Howard University in 2001. He is a Health Disparities Scholar at the National Center on Minority Health and Health Disparities. His research interests are in risk and resilience among African American youth. His most recent publications have examined the promotive and protective influences of culture on the substance use behaviors of urban and rural African American adolescents. He has received grant funding from federal and state agencies and is currently a principal investigator on the Cultural Pathways to Prevention Project (CP3) funded by the Virginia Tobacco Settlement Foundation.

Ezemenari M. Obasi is Assistant Professor in the Department of Counseling and Human Development Services at the University of Georgia. Prior to this appointment, he was an assistant professor in the Department of Psychology at Southern Illinois University–Carbondale. He received a BS in Physics from the University of California, Irvine; a PhD in Psychology from The Ohio State University; and completed his predoctoral internship at Harvard Medical School's McLean Hospital. His research program in substance abuse, social neuroscience, biomarkers, and cross-cultural psychology (with an emphasis on African psychology) examines biopsychosocial risk and protective factors that impact health disparities experienced by people of African descent throughout the Diaspora. Dr. Obasi is currently serving on the editorial boards of *Cultural Diversity Ethnic Minority Psychology*, the *Journal of Black Psychology*, and *Training and Education in Professional Psychology*.

Desmond Odugu is a doctoral candidate in the Cultural and Educational Policy program at Loyola University Chicago with disciplinary focus on Comparative and International Education. His academic background is in Philosophy and

Educational Psychology, with master's degrees from Nigeria and the United States. Mr. Odugu is currently pursuing active research projects in the areas of multilingualism, personal epistemology, and cognition. He is well studied in African Studies and African philosophy, and he orients his scholarly activities toward preserving and advancing positive African values.

Thomas A. Parham is Assistant Vice Chancellor for Counseling and Health Services and an adjunct faculty member at the University of California, Irvine. Dr. Parham is a Past President of the National Association of Black Psychologists. For the past 25-plus years, Dr. Parham has focused his research efforts in the area of psychological Nigrescence and has authored numerous articles in the area. Writing in the areas of identity development and multicultural counseling remains his primary focus. The dozens of honors and awards he has received include election to Fellow status of Division 17 (Counseling Psychology) and 45 (Ethnic Minority Issues) of the American Psychological Association (APA) in 1994; the Samuel H. Johnson Award for Exemplary Service and Scholarship from the Association for Multicultural Counseling and Development in 1995; election to the title of Distinguished Psychologist by the Association of Black Psychologists (the association's highest honor) in 1998; the APA Dalmus Taylor Award for Leadership, Scholarship, and Advising in 1999; the Association of Black Psychologists' Certification and Proficiency in African Centered/Black Psychology–Board Certified Fellow and Board Certified Diplomate, July 2007; and APA's Division 17 (Society of Counseling Psychology) Award for Lifetime Achievement in Mentoring, August 2007.

Fayth M. Parks is Associate Professor of Counselor Education at Georgia Southern University and Program Coordinator. She is a licensed psychologist with special interest in mental health service access to rural and urban communities, poverty, cultural and linguistic competency, and bridging the health disparities gap. In 1997, Dr. Parks earned her doctorate in counseling psychology at the University of Illinois at Urbana and that same year received the graduate research award in psychology from the Interamerican Society of Psychology. Her research focus is psychotherapeutic implications of folk healing practices as culturally endorsed complementary therapies to summon positive human strengths. Dr. Parks is founding director of the Hurston/Gullah Project and editor of Dust Tracks, the project's semi-annual scholarly publication. She serves as co-chair of the National Youth-At-Risk Conference and on the planning committee for the Southeastern Conference on Cross-Cultural Issues in Counseling and Education. Dr. Parks is a former editorial board member of PsycCRITIQUES, Contemporary Psychology: APA Review of Books. She was also appointed to the American Psychological Association Task Force for Multicultural Training, which was charged to advise the organization's long term response to the mental health needs of survivors of Hurricane Katrina.

Yasser Arafat Payne is Assistant Professor in the Black American Studies Program at the University of Delaware. Dr. Payne completed his doctoral work at the Graduate Center–City University of New York, where he was trained as a social–personality psychologist. His specific interests include exploring notions of resiliency with street-life–oriented Black men using an unconventional methodological framework titled "Participatory Action Research." Dr. Payne just completed a postdoctoral fellowship funded by the National Institutes of Health–National Institute of Drug Abuse whereby he worked on a reentry and intervention-based research project in New York City's largest jail, Rikers Island—a project designed to reduce recidivism drug use and other risky behavior leading to HIV/AIDS. Furthermore, he has published in a number of peer-reviewed journals, including the *Journal of Black Psychology*, *Teachers College Record*, *Culture Diversity and Ethnic Minority Psychology*, *Men and Masculinities*, the *Journal of Social Issues*, and the *International Journal of Critical Psychology*. Dr. Payne also has worked on several book chapters that examine notions of resiliency, racial identity, urban education, and participatory action research, and he has coauthored a book titled *Echoes of Brown: Youth Documenting and Performing the Legacy of Brown v. Board of Education*.

Alex L. Pieterse is Assistant Professor in the Graduate School of Education of George Mason

University. He holds a BHSc (Nursing) from the Australian Catholic University, an MA (Counseling) from New York University, and a PhD (Counseling Psychology) from Teachers College, Columbia University. Dr. Pieterse has published and presented in the areas of racial identity, social justice, antiracism training, and racial–cultural awareness.

Rebecca M. Redington is an advanced doctoral student in the Counseling Psychology Program at Teachers College, Columbia University. She received a BA from the College of the Holy Cross and a master's degree in Child Development from Tufts University. Ms. Redington served as the cocoordinator of the Winter Roundtable Conference on Cultural Psychology and Education at Teachers College, Columbia University, from 2005 to 2008. Her research interests include counselors' perceptions of interracial families, including those formed through interracial unions as well as through transracial and international adoptions.

Kumea Shorter-Gooden is a professor at the California School of Professional Psychology, and Systemwide Director, International–Multicultural Initiatives, Alliant International University. She formerly served as Coordinator of the Multicultural Community–Clinical Psychology Emphasis Area of the California School of Professional Psychology, Los Angeles campus. She is the coauthor of *Shifting: The Double Lives of Black Women in America*, which was a winner of the 2004 American Book Awards. A Fellow of the American Psychological Association, Dr. Shorter-Gooden has numerous published articles and chapters on topics such as African American women and identity, psychotherapy with African Americans, and cultural diversity, and she is a Consulting Editor for *Professional Psychology: Research and Practice*. A licensed psychologist based in Pasadena, California, she also has a private psychotherapy and organizational consultation practice, and she is an active speaker and workshop leader around issues related to African American mental health, women's issues, and multiculturalism and diversity.

Crystal Simmons is a doctoral student in the School Psychology Program at the University of California, Berkeley. Her research interests include racial identity measurement and development, psychosocial and biogenetic influences on the achievement gap, culturally relevant pedagogical interventions and practices, and the relationship between racial identity and academic achievement or academic engagement. In the future, she hopes to design and incorporate interventions to help low-income or disengaged minority adolescent students perform at their academic best within the schools and the broader community.

Anthony J. Smith received his PhD in Counseling Psychology from Southern Illinois University–Carbondale in 1996. Currently, he is the Executive Director/Founder of the Alase Center for Enrichment. Dr. Smith has been involved in the mental health field for more than 12 years. He is a licensed psychologist and certified health services provider in North Carolina. He was previously on the faculty at the Duke University Medical School as a professor of Behavioral Science before starting his own practice. In his practice, he provides a host of psychological services, including short-term individual, family and couples therapy, crisis management, fitness for duty evaluations, and psychological testing. He also directs an adolescent Saturday Academy, which teaches youth critical thinking skills. He serves as a consultant to a number of case management agencies and provides presentations and workshops on a variety of mental health topics. Dr. Smith also is involved in several professional organizations, including the Association of Black Psychologists and the American Psychological Association, and he serves on the state board of the North Carolina Psychological Association. He was previously president of the Triangle Chapter of the Association of Black Psychologists.

William K. Smith is currently a graduate student at the University of Missouri–Columbia in the Department of Human Development and Family Studies. His research interests include the strengths in African Americans, low-income families, and the effect public housing has on this group, behavioral disorders, and family policy. William has an MSE from the University of Missouri and a BS in Criminal Justice from Lincoln University. He has 8 years of experience working with at-risk youth in various capacities, including as a social worker and a behavioral specialist conducting behavioral analysis on children with behavioral disorders. Mr. Smith has participated in various research projects, including the Disproportionate Minority Contact Study with Dr. Anne Dannerbeck. He currently works as a graduate teacher's assistant at the university. After completing his degree, William plans to devote his time to teaching at the collegiate level and researching issues he is passionate about. William is originally from southern California and is the son of an immigrant mother and an American father. His mother's unique experiences, and the experience he garnered from growing up with multiple cultures, fostered his desire to study people of African descent from Caribbean and South American countries.

Suzette L. Speight is now at the University of Akron, in the Department of Psychology. She was an Associate Professor of Counseling Psychology in the School of Education at Loyola University Chicago from 1991 through 2008. She received her PhD in Counseling Psychology from The Ohio State University in 1990. Her scholarly interests include multicultural competence and social justice, African American women and mental health, the psychological impact of oppression, African-centered Psychology, suicide in the African American community, and identity development issues.

Margaret Beale Spencer, a developmental psychologist, is the Board of Overseers Professor of Applied Psychology and Human Development in the Graduate School of Education, and Professor of Psychology (School of Arts and Sciences) at the University of Pennsylvania. She directs both the Center for Health Achievement Neighborhood Growth and Ethnic Studies and the W. E. B. Du Bois Collective Research Institute. She earned her doctorate degree from the University of Chicago, Committee on Human Development, in the area of Child Development and Developmental Psychology. Dr. Spencer's scholarly activities focus on youth of color and families who live under varying levels of economic and social hardship. The goal of the work is to understand how policymakers, teachers, and service providers can better assist in helping youth and families to live healthy, successful, and productive lives. Her work is used internationally, nationally, and locally.

J. Corey Steele is a third-year student in the Counseling Psychology PhD program at Loyola University Chicago. He is from Dallas, Texas, and received a master's degree in School Counseling from Texas Christian University. J. Corey is currently participating in research that explores the influence of stress and oppression on the identity development and psychological functioning of African American young men and women.

Howard C. Stevenson is Associate Professor and Chair of the Applied Psychology and Human Development Division of the Graduate School of Education at the University of Pennsylvania. His teaching and research have focused on looking for cultural strengths in youth and families of color and using those strengths to improve their academic and emotional well-being. He has written numerous articles and two books; the most recent is titled *Playing With Anger: Teaching Coping Skills to African American Boys Through Athletics and Culture.* A second research project involved the Success of African American Students in Independent Schools, in which his research team investigated the cross-sectional and longitudinal factors that promote school engagement, stimulate psychological adjustment, and reduce dropout of African American boys and girls in independent schools. In this study, racial identity and socialization were found to be key factors in the student emotional success.

Dena Phillips Swanson is Assistant Professor of Counseling and Human Development in the Warner School at the University of Rochester. Her research with minority youth focuses on identity development and its impact on preventing behavioral problems and enhancing youth-based program implementation. Her consultative work with organizations contributes to program development and staff training. In addition, she provides counseling support for youth experiencing difficult school or family transitions. The goal of her work is to bridge research and practice related to minority youth in providing optimum opportunities for their development. She is a faculty affiliate of several interdisciplinary research centers and is on the advisory board for the Research to Practice Council, which is involved in restructuring mental health practices to meet the developmental and cultural needs of minority youth. She also serves on the editorial board of *Child Development.*

Jerome Taylor received his PhD in Clinical Psychology in 1969 from Indiana University at Bloomington. He is Associate Professor in Psychology and Africana Studies at the University of Pittsburgh and Director of the Center for Family Excellence. His major interests include the role of cultural identity on personal growth and parenting as well as intimate relationships within Black families. Recently, he was a recipient of the Chancellor's Award at the University of Pittsburgh and the Kujichaquilia Award from the Sankofa Institute of Pittsburgh, Pennsylvania.

Francis Terrell received his PhD in Clinical Psychology in 1975 from the University of Pittsburgh. He is Professor of Psychology at the University of North Texas. His major interests include the study of the relationship between cultural mistrust and the behavior of Blacks in therapy, educational, and interpersonal situations. Dr. Terrell is a member of the Association for Black Psychologists and a member of its Editorial Advisory Board. He is also a Charter Fellow Emeritus of the Association for Psychological Science and a former Fellow of the American Psychological Association and Society for Personality Assessment. Recently, Dr. Terrell was recognized by the Office of Substance Abuse and Mental Health Services Administration for his volunteer work during the Hurricane Katrina disaster, recognition for which he wishes there had been no reason to receive.

Anita Jones Thomas is a counseling psychologist with specializations in multicultural counseling and family therapy. Dr. Thomas received her bachelor's degree in Human Development and Social Policy from Northwestern University, a master's degree in Community Counseling from Loyola University Chicago, and a doctorate in Counseling Psychology from Loyola University Chicago. Dr. Thomas is currently Assistant Professor at Loyola University Chicago, where she teaches courses in school counseling, human development, theories, multicultural issues, and family therapy. Her research interests include gendered racial identity of African American girls and women, racial socialization, and parenting issues for African Americans.

Chalmer E. Thompson is Associate Professor in the School of Education at Indiana University–Purdue University Indianapolis. She is the author of several articles and book chapters that relate primarily to race and racial identity as pertaining to psychological practice, educational practices, and grassroots organizing. In 1997, she edited a book with Robert T. Carter titled *Racial Identity Theory: Applications to Individual, Group, and Organizational Interventions*. She and Dr. Carter are currently working on a second edition of this volume. Recently, she has linked with educators and administrators from Kyambogo University in Kampala, Uganda, and is working on a series of projects related to the application of racial identity theory to peace education. She is Fellow of the American Psychological Association's Division 17 (Society for Counseling Psychology) and Division 45 (Society for the Psychological Study of Ethnic Minority Issues). She was honored at the 2008 International Counseling Psychology Conference as 1 of 14 recipients of the Many Faces of Counseling Psychology recognition. This honor is given to individuals and groups who are extending traditional counseling psychology activities into new professional undertakings.

Rheeda L. Walker is Assistant Professor in the Department of Psychology at the University of Georgia and a licensed clinical psychologist. Previously, Dr. Walker has held faculty appointments at Southern Illinois University and the University of South Carolina, in addition to being invited as a Visiting Research Scientist at the Center for the Study and Prevention of Suicide at the University of Rochester Medical Center's Department of Psychiatry. Her primary research foci are in sociocultural determinants of suicide risk and African American mental health processes. Dr. Walker has authored or coauthored numerous peer-reviewed articles in journals such as *Suicide and Life-Threatening Behavior*, *Cultural Diversity and Ethnic Minority Psychology*, and the *Journal of Black Psychology*.

L. Monique Ward is Associate Professor of Psychology at the University of Michigan. Her research examines children's and adolescents' developing conceptions of both gender and sexuality and explores the contributions of these notions to their social and sexual decision making. Dr. Ward also explores associations among gender ideology, race, body image, and sexuality.

She is particularly interested in the role of the media in the process of sexual socialization and has published extensively on this topic in several academic journals, including the *Journal of Research on Adolescence, Developmental Review, Psychology of Women Quarterly*, and the *Journal of Sex Research*. She served as a member of the American Psychological Association's Task Force on the Sexualization of Girls, and she serves on the editorial board of the *Journal of Adolescent Research* and the *Journal of Media Psychology*.

Carolyn R. Watson is a doctoral student in the Department of Applied Psychology in the Steinhardt School of Culture, Education, and Human Development at New York University. Her research focuses on the roles of religiosity and spirituality in the lives of people of African descent. Of particular interest to her are the roles of religiosity and spirituality in the lives of African youth.

Gilman W. Whiting is Assistant Professor and Director of Undergraduate Studies in the African American and Diaspora Studies Program in the College of Arts and Science at Vanderbilt University. He also teaches in the Peabody College of Education in the Department of Human Organizational Development. Dr. Whiting earned his doctoral degree in Curriculum & Instruction from Purdue University's College of Education. His Master of Arts and Teaching degree is in African American Studies and Urban Development from Rhode Island College, and he earned his undergraduate degree in Communication and Psychology from the University of Rhode Island. Whiting is the author of more than 30 scholarly publications relating to minority populations, especially males. He consults with school districts nationally on various issues related to psychosocial behavior and motivation among young students. Whiting is the creator of the Scholar Identity Model and directs the Scholar Identity Institute for young Black males.

David R. Williams is the Norman Professor of Public Health and Professor of African and African American Studies and of Sociology at Harvard University. His prior academic appointments were at Yale University and the University of Michigan. His research has focused on trends and determinants of socioeconomic and racial disparities in health, the effects of racism on health, and the ways in which religious involvement can affect health. He is the author of more than 150 scholarly articles in scientific journals and edited collections, and he has been ranked as one of the Top 10 Most Cited Researchers in the Social Sciences during the last decade. *Black Issues in Higher Education* ranked him as the 2nd Most Cited Black Scholar in the Social Sciences in 2006. He is an elected member of the Institute of Medicine and of the American Academy of Arts and Sciences.

Frank C. Worrell is Director of the School Psychology program and Faculty Director of the Academic Talent Development Program at the University of California, Berkeley. His research interests include academic talent development, African American educational issues, at-risk youth, scale development and validation, and teacher effectiveness. In his work, he examines psychosocial variables related to academic achievement in adolescent populations and the reliability and validity of instruments used to measure psychosocial constructs. Author of more than 60 scholarly articles, he is a member of the editorial boards of *Assessment, Cultural Diversity and Ethnic Minority Psychology; Gifted Child Quarterly;* the *Journal of Advanced Academics; Psychology in the Schools; Roeper Review; School Psychology Quarterly;* and *Training and Education in Professional Psychology*. Dr. Worrell serves as a consultant to the Student Support Service Unit of the Ministry of Education and the School Leadership Center in Trinidad and Tobago.

Joseph Youngblood II is the Associate Vice President for Public Affairs, Dean of the John S. Watson School of Public Service, and Director of the John S. Watson Institute for Public Policy of Thomas Edison State College. Dr. Youngblood spent 17 years working in public education, law, and public policy. He joined the Watson Institute after serving as Special Assistant to the Superintendent for Leadership Development and Director of School Based Youth Services for the Trenton (New Jersey) Public School District. The Watson Institute is an organization that seeks to respond to the needs of public sector and nonprofit decision makers across New Jersey. Dr. Youngblood serves as Policy Adviser to the New Jersey Urban Mayors' Association and the Watson Institute, providing applied research, analysis, and other assistance in response to the public policy needs of its partners, which include 24 urban municipalities, state, and local nonprofit groups and grassroots/community-based organizations.

Sinead N. Younge is Assistant Professor in the Department of Psychology at Morehouse College. Dr. Younge completed her doctorate in Ecological–Community Psychology and Urban Affairs at Michigan State University. She also completed a postdoctoral fellowship with the Fellowships in Research and Science Teaching program at the Rollins School of Public Health at Emory University. Dr. Younge is a Fellow with the American Psychological Association's Minority Fellowship Program. As a community psychologist, she examines the psychosociocultural antecedents of health behaviors, specifically HIV/AIDS and other acute and chronic conditions. Dr. Younge conducts research in the United States and in Tanzania, East Africa. Her research has appeared in the *Journal of African American Studies*, the *Journal of Adolescence*, *Race and Society*, *African American Research Perspectives*, *SAGE Handbook of Child Development*, *Multiculturalism*, and *Media and the Handbook of Child Behavioral Issues: Evidenced-Based Approaches*. Dr. Younge is a member of the center for AIDS research at Emory University; a Fellow of American Psychological Association Division 27 (Society for Community Research and Action); and a member of the Association of Black Psychologists, the American Association of University Women, and the American Public Health Association.